Flash™ MX 2004 ActionScript Bible

Flash™ MX 2004 ActionScript Bible

Robert Reinhardt and Joey Lott

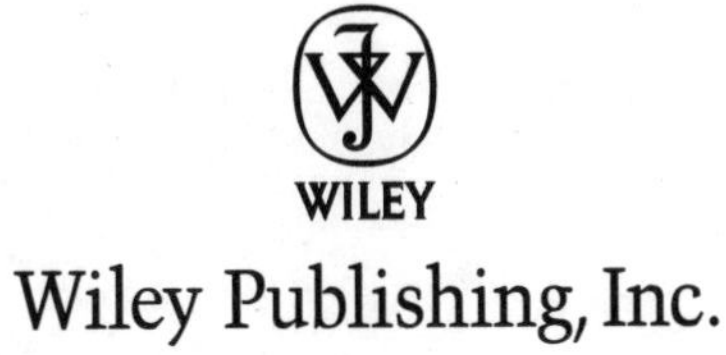

Wiley Publishing, Inc.

Flash™ MX 2004 ActionScript Bible

Published by
Wiley Publishing, Inc.
10475 Crosspoint Boulevard
Indianapolis, IN 46256
www.wiley.com

Published simultaneously in Canada

Library of Congress Control Number: 2004103173

ISBN: 0-7645-4354-7

Manufactured in the United States of America

10 9 8 7 6 5 4 3 2 1

1O/RU/QU/QU/IN

For general information on our other products and services or to obtain technical support, please contact our Customer Care Department within the U.S. at (800) 762-2974, outside the U.S. at (317) 572-3993 or fax (317) 572-4002.

Wiley also publishes its books in a variety of electronic formats. Some content that appears in print may not be available in electronic books.

About the Authors

Robert Reinhardt, Director of Multimedia Applications for The Content Project (`www.contentproject.com`), is internationally regarded as an expert on multimedia application development, particularly in Macromedia Flash. Robert is the lead author of the *Flash Bible* series and *Flash ActionScript Bible* (Wiley), as well as *Macromedia MX: Building Rich Internet Applications* (Macromedia Press). He has developed multimedia courses for educational facilities in Canada and the United States and has been a featured speaker at several Web conferences. Robert also provides multimedia consulting through his company, [theMAKERS].

Joey Lott has written several books on Flash and ActionScript. He lives in Los Angeles.

Credits

Executive Editor
Chris Webb

Development Editor
Kezia Endsley

Technical Editors
Troy Gardner
Steve Nowicki

Production Editor
Eric Newman

Copy Editors
Nancy Rapoport
Luann Rouff

Editorial Manager
Mary Beth Wakefield

Vice President &
Executive Group Publisher
Richard Swadley

Vice President and
Executive Publisher
Bob Ipsen

Vice President and Publisher
Joseph B. Wikert

Executive Editorial Director
Mary Bednarek

Project Coordinator
April Farling

Graphics and Production Specialists
Beth Brooks
Lauren Goddard
Joyce Haughey
Jennifer Heleine
Kristin McMullan
Heather Ryan

Special Help
Joni Burns

Quality Control Technicians
John Greenough
Andy Hollandbeck
Luisa Perez
Carl Pierce
Charles Spencer

Permissions Editor
Laura Moss

Media Development Specialist
Angela Denny

Proofreading and Indexing
TECHBOOKS Production Services

To the future of expression on the Internet and the Web.
We owe it to ourselves to continually share our ideas
and experiences with one another.
—Robert

May there be peace within and among all beings.
May all recognize that which is.
—Joey

Foreword

Flash has become an important and pervasive feature of the Web. Consider the numbers: In June 2003 an NPD Research study showed that 97.4 percent of Web users have Flash installed on their computer. The study was conducted roughly a year after the release of the Flash Player 6 and showed that version 6 of the player was already available on more than 86 percent of Web users' computers. The Flash Player is preinstalled in Internet Explorer and other browsers. But that doesn't explain why more than 86 percent of Web users had version 6 a year after its release. At the time, IDC Research estimated there were 448 million people using the Web. A year after the release of the version 6 player, something like 386 million of those people had version 6. The statistics don't show how many people downloaded the player and how many found that it came with their browser, but it's a safe bet that hundreds of millions of player downloads had to take place to get the player onto so many machines so quickly.

The pervasiveness of the Flash Player has a lot to do with how widely Flash is used. But it is not the only driving force. In 2003, during the course of history-making world events, large media sites made extensive use of Flash to provide multimedia coverage of these events and background information. At the same time, individuals created Flash animations and games that were used to express views across the political spectrum. Flash was then, and is now, an important vehicle for providing an expressive and dynamic Web. It is used for almost everything. Advertisers love Flash advertisements because they are difficult to ignore. Educators use Flash to create compelling online learning objects that enliven courses and provide online simulations. Artists are always finding new uses for Flash, and institutions such as museums rely on it more and more. Cartoonists continue to discover Flash and are constantly pushing the envelope of animation length and quality. Flash front-ends to online applications are popping up everywhere and allow you to do everything from booking a hotel reservation to making banking transactions.

The capacity of Flash to deliver compelling experiences on the Web encourages people to download the latest player. In turn, the near ubiquity of the Flash Player encourages designers and developers to make regular use of Flash. The two trends continue to feed off and reinforce each other.

Internet technologies are constantly appearing, evolving, and in some cases disappearing. Each new technology takes time to learn and apply effectively. As each technology evolves, keeping up with it takes more time and effort, as does learning how to apply it to old problems and how to use it to solve new ones. At some point designers and developers have to make big choices. It just isn't possible to learn every Web technology in depth. After the baseline requirements of learning HTML and style sheets, creating effective Web images, and learning some JavaScript, what comes next? Just keeping up with the abbreviations can be irritating. In no particular order: XML, XML-RPC, XUL, MXML, SQLXML, SVG, EPML, SMIL, WSDL, SOAP, WAP, WMA, EJB, J2EE, SAX, JAX-RPC, LDAP, PHP, CFML, and on and on.

Web designers and developers naturally gravitate to systems that are capable of reaching the greatest number of people, provide the richest set of capabilities, and are still cost effective to use. In other words, designers and developers need systems that provide ubiquity, utility, and usability.

Flash has evolved from a vector-based animation tool to an amazingly rich, flexible, and integrated design and development environment. Today you can seamlessly blend unique vector-based animation with images, components such as the Datagrid and Tree components, progressive download and streaming audio and video, real-time communications, and connectivity to every type of enterprise-class computing system. Flash works with many of the technologies already mentioned and provides some of its own for good measure, such as AMF and RTMP. The power of the Flash authoring system does not lie only in the fact that it does one or two things well. It delivers so many features in one integrated development and delivery system with which both designers and developers can effectively work. As Flash continues to evolve, the need to bring together a complex variety of difficult-to-integrate systems and tools continues to diminish.

At the core of both the Flash development process and delivery system is the ActionScript language and interpreter. Designers often make extensive use of ActionScript to simplify their Flash movies and provide the kind of fine-grained control they need for visual elements. Developers use ActionScript to make increasingly full-featured Web-based applications with rich user interfaces and excellent responsiveness to the user's actions. ActionScript can accommodate the needs of both designers and developers because it is based on JavaScript (also known as ECMAScript).

ECMAScript/JavaScript is first and foremost a scripting language. It was designed from the beginning to provide easy-to-use object scripting capabilities. In Flash, that means it is relatively simple to do things such as attach a behavior to a button that in turns manipulates another object such as an animation running within a Movie Clip. The ActionScript code to add a behavior that manipulates an object is short and simple, and the Flash authoring environment makes it easier still. However, ActionScript is not restricted to scripting objects. It is possible to build large and complex applications using traditional object-oriented design and development methods that are realized in ActionScript. With the release of the 2004 Flash products, ActionScript has evolved further to increase support for advanced object-oriented development without sacrificing the language's utility for designers.

Learning to work with ActionScript is an essential Flash skill. How far you go with ActionScript and how you approach learning the language will vary depending on your background—especially how much computer programming you already know. However you approach learning ActionScript, you will constantly be working with both the language and the objects it allows you to manipulate—especially Movie Clips. *Flash MX 2004 ActionScript Bible* provides an excellent roadmap to the language and the variety of objects it allows you to create and manipulate. The two authors bring a great deal of practical experience to the book and are also accomplished teachers and learners. I first met Robert Reinhardt when he was a first-year student at Ryerson University. Robert was the kind of student professors pray for. He is intelligent, inquisitive, and remarkably energetic. As I have with so many students who have graduated from Ryerson, I completely lost track of Robert after he got his degree. Some years later when I finally decided to learn something about Flash I asked one of my colleagues which book I should read. I was told to buy Reinhardt and Lentz's *Flash 4 Bible*. When I realized that

I knew one of the authors, I was delighted. But I was not surprised by the high quality of Robert's work. Some time later Robert met Joey Lott while teaching a class on Flash. Joey stood out for Robert in much the same way Robert stood out for me. Joey has moved on to write a number of books on different facets of programming in Flash and with Robert has produced a book I'm happy to sneak my name into by writing these few pages. *Flash MX 2004 ActionScript Bible* shows a concern for the needs of designers and developers who want to learn ActionScript through experimentation and exploration. Enjoy.

Brian Lesser
Assistant Director, Teaching and Technology Support
Computing and Communications Services
Ryerson University, Toronto, Canada

Preface

If you've picked up this book, then you are undoubtedly familiar with Flash. Since Macromedia first acquired the program, Flash has become increasingly popular to the point where there are few people who don't know what Flash is. Flash applications, sometimes referred to as Flash movies, can be deployed in many types of environments. But by far the most popular use of Flash is on the Web. The reason is simple: Flash provides a much more robust and interactive experience than HTML can. The opportunities that Flash provides appeal to a wide audience—from artists to corporations. It offers a medium for expressing creativity, ideas, and messages in unique and innovative ways. Whether it is an artist wanting to create interactive art, an organization wanting to provide resources and information, a company wanting to sell products, a group wanting to create a real-time interactive community, or a university wanting to create collaborative learning experiences, Flash is the medium of choice.

But as Flash has evolved, and as the demands of the community have grown, so have the complexities and intricacies of the application. This is true of ActionScript more than any other aspect of Flash. In its early versions ActionScript, the programming language within Flash, consisted of nothing more than a few commands that could be applied via menus only. Flash 5 marked a huge step in the evolution of ActionScript. In Flash MX, ActionScript adapted to the wants of the developers by providing more programmatic control within a Flash application. And Flash MX 2004 represents another big leap in ActionScript.

Using Flash MX 2004, you can do a great many things programmatically. All of the ActionScript-based features from previous versions of Flash are still available. For example, you can still send and load variables and XML and use Flash Remoting. You can still load MP3s at runtime. You can still load SWF and JPEG content, but Flash MX 2004 provides you with an improved way of doing so. Using Flash MX 2004 you can still display HTML, but new is the cascading style sheet (CSS) support that enables you to effectively apply formatting. Flash MX 2004 replaces the older printing functions with the new `PrintJob` class to afford you more control. The list goes on and on. In fact, it took us an entire book to provide you with all the information!

Macromedia Flash MX ActionScript Bible was the first edition, and we've updated it to produce this second edition. But this book is much more than just a basic update to its previous incarnation. Although we made every effort to make the first edition as good as possible, in the time that has passed since its publication, we have learned a lot. We've listened to your feedback. And we think you will find that this new edition is filled with valuable and accurate information that is well organized, readable, and practical. We've done our best to provide in-depth research combined with practical, working knowledge.

Some of the features you'll find in this book are:

- **Comprehensive coverage of ActionScript:** We've included just about everything you could think of, and a few things you probably didn't think of. We've attempted to make sure the information is relevant, practical, and significantly more than just a basic reference. We have included coverage of basic ActionScript syntax; all the built-in commands, functions, and classes; and even some coverage of related technologies such as Flash Remoting.

- **Complete coverage of ActionScript 2.0:** ActionScript 2.0 is new in Flash MX 2004, and we've detailed it in depth. You'll find descriptions of the syntax, best practices, and beginner, intermediate, and advanced topics.
- **Working examples and exercises:** We know that one of the best ways to learn ActionScript is to practice writing it. So throughout the chapters you can find lots of exercises that you can use to practice the concepts as you read them. You'll find the completed files on the CD-ROM that accompanies this book in case you get stuck and want to see the working examples.
- **Practical expertise and advice:** Theory is useful up to a point. But if you want to use Flash and ActionScript to build a working application, you'll need more than that. While we provide all the theory, we also back it up with explanations, tips, and advice based on practical experience building professional applications.
- **Continuing community and support:** The official Web site for the book is `www.flashsupport.com`. There you'll find updates and notes about the book as well as support forums for readers so you can ask any questions you might have.

We encourage your feedback. In fact, we've set up a system so that you can submit feedback on specific chapters. Your comments will help us make the next edition even better. You can find the feedback application at `www.flashsupport.com/feedback`.

How to Get the Most Out of This Book

You can read and utilize this book in many ways. If you are a beginning programmer or even if you're just new to ActionScript, we encourage you to read Parts I and II first. We also recommend that you read Chapter 9. Following that, you can browse the chapters and sections that most interest you. ActionScript is a large subject, and you will likely find that you will master one part at a time.

If you already know ActionScript from previous versions of Flash, but you don't yet know ActionScript 2.0, you will likely find it helpful to follow the same advice that we offer to beginning coders. Part II is probably the most important section for you to start with, however.

Intermediate and advanced ActionScript developers can still benefit from the book. You can turn to any chapter for a reference. For example, even an advanced ActionScript developer might not necessarily know all the details about a particular class. If you want to learn more about a class, or just brush up on it, read the chapter for reference.

Keep the book on your desk. Read sections over and over. Try the exercises. You'll learn more each time. At first, just getting a `MovieClip` object to move across the screen may be difficult. But upon returning to that section months later, you will undoubtedly discover something you didn't notice before.

Conventions Used in the Book

Throughout the book when we refer to application menus, the menu names and nested menu items are separated by arrow icons. For example, to open a new Flash document within Flash MX 2004 you can select the New option from the File menu. We indicate that in the text by suggesting you choose File ⇨ New.

Although the icons are pretty standard and self-explanatory (they have self-explanatory labels), here's a brief explanation of what they are and what they mean.

Tips offer you extra information that further explains a given topic or technique, often suggesting alternatives or workarounds to a listed procedure.

Notes provide supplementary information to the text, shedding light on background processes or miscellaneous options that aren't crucial to the basic understanding of the material.

When you see the Caution icon, make sure you're following along closely to the tips and techniques being discussed. Some external applications might not work exactly the same with Flash on different operating systems.

If you want to find related information to a given topic in another chapter or section, look for the cross-reference icon.

The New Feature icons point out any differences between Flash MX 2004 and ActionScript 2.0 and previous versions.

This icon indicates that the CD-ROM contains a related file in the given folder.

When you see this icon, you will find Web URLs that point to further information about the topic at hand.

Also, many code samples that are printed in this book have lines of code that are too long to fit on one line. These lines of code are broken into two or more lines and end with the line continuation symbol, ⮐. This symbol should not be typed into the actual code of your Flash document. Simply continue to type the following line(s) of code on the same line in the Actions panel. For example, you would type the following line all on the same line in the Actions panel:

```
mcPhoto._accProps.description = "Picture of attendees at the round table ⮐
   discussion";
```

Because Flash MX 2004 is available for both the Windows and Mac OS X operating systems, when applicable we provide keyboard shortcuts for both. In many cases the Ctrl key in a Windows environment is analogous to the Command key on the Macintosh, which we represent using the ⌘ symbol. You'll also notice that many keyboard shortcuts are denoted using a + symbol when Flash requires that you press several keys at the same time. For example, the notation Shift+N indicates that you should press and hold the Shift key while then pressing the N key.

How This Book Is Organized

We've reorganized this edition of the book in ways that we think will make it most approachable and helpful. The ten parts of the book are outlined in the following sections.

Part I: Conceptualizing Flash

When you are first starting to develop ActionScript-rich Flash applications, you'll want to make sure that you are planning the projects appropriately. Part I provides you with the information you need to put Flash into the context of application development, and it helps you to plan your projects appropriately.

Part II: Laying the ActionScript Foundation

When you build a building, the first thing you do is lay the foundation. Doing so helps to ensure a sturdy base from which something can be created. Part II aims to provide you with the basic information and practical exercises that can assist you in getting a fundamental understanding of ActionScript. You'll learn all about how ActionScript works, where to place it, how to write it, syntax, structure, and much more.

Part III: MovieClip, Button, and Drawing API

The `MovieClip` class is one of the primary classes in ActionScript. Part III introduces you to the `MovieClip` class (which includes the Drawing API—which enables you to draw programmatically). And because the `Button` class is so closely related to `MovieClip`, you will also learn all about how to use the `Button` class as well.

Part IV: The Core Classes

The core classes provide important, yet non-visual functionality within your Flash applications. The classes include `Array` for grouping and indexing data, `Math` for performing advanced mathematical operations, `Date` for working with date and time values, `String` for working with textual values, and the wrapper classes `Number` and `Boolean`. Part IV looks at each of these classes (and related functions) in depth.

Part V: The Movie Classes

Part V looks at each of the classes that have some kind of visual representation within an application (minus `MovieClip` and `Button`, which are discussed in Part III) or handles user interaction within the application. This group includes classes such as `Color` for adjusting color and `TextField` for working with visual text. It also includes other assorted classes such as `Mouse` for working with the mouse interaction, `ContextMenu` for controlling the items in the right-click/⌘-click menu, and `PrintJob` for printing Flash content.

Part VI: The Audio and Video Classes

Flash MX 2004 has increased multimedia support. The `Sound` class is supported as previously. In addition, Flash MX 2004 enables you to load FLV video files programmatically without the use of Flash Communication Server. This functionality is provided by means of the `NetStream` and `Video` classes. Part VI provides complete coverage of the `Sound`, `NetStream`, and `Video` classes.

Part VII: The Data Classes

Although Flash was originally an animation medium, it has steadily grown to supported more and more data capabilities. In Part VII you can read about the classes that support sending and loading data, including coverage of the `SharedObject`, `LocalConnection`, `XML`, `LoadVars`, and `XMLSocket` classes.

Part VIII: Using Components

Components are an important part of Flash MX 2004. By encapsulating functionality, components can provide a simple drag and drop solution to what might otherwise require hundreds or even thousands of lines of code. In Part VIII you'll learn about the user interface components that are included with Flash as well as how to create your own components.

Part IX: Working with Flash in Other Environments

Part IX discusses how Flash can interact with the environment in which it is being played back. For example, you'll get a chance to learn how to use Flash within a Web browser as well as how you can issue special commands when publishing a stand-alone player version of your application.

Part X: Creating Flash Applications

Once you've learned the basics, Part X shows you how to put it all together when creating complete applications. You'll get a chance to read about how to optimize and manage the download and presentation of content, special tips for working with data exchange, working with Web services, and creating user input forms with Flash.

CD-ROM Chapter

Be sure to check the CD-ROM for an additional chapter that wasn't added to the printed version of the book. You'll find extra information such as how to perform pattern matching using the `RegExp` class.

Appendix

The appendix contains information regarding the CD-ROM that accompanies this book.

Getting in Touch with Us

The official Web site for this book is:

```
www.flashsupport.com
```

At the site you'll find updates, notes, and more. Additionally, you can find support forums so you can post and answer questions and get to know others in the *Flash Bible* and *ActionScript Bible* community.

We appreciate your feedback. If you have found this book to be helpful, please let us know. And if you have suggestions for ways we might improve subsequent editions, please let us know that as well. You can contact us by e-mail at the following addresses:

- Robert: `fmx2004@flashsupport.com`
- Joey: `joey@person13.com`

Getting in Touch with Macromedia

Macromedia wants to constantly improve Flash in ways that help you. The only way they get to know how you are using Flash (or how you'd like to use Flash) is if you send them feedback. The more feedback you can provide to them, the better equipped they are to adapt Flash to your requests. In order to hear from you, Macromedia has set up a system by which you can submit your feedback at:

`www.macromedia.com/support/email/wishform/?6213=9`

If there are features that work particularly well for you, let them know. If there are features that are not working for you, let them know. And if there are things that Flash does not do that you'd like it to do, then let Macromedia know that as well.

To support the Flash community Macromedia has created a searchable registry that allows clients to find Flash developers by location or by services offered. To create a custom developer profile, register yourself at:

`www.macromedia.com/locator`

Regardless of your geographic location, you always have access to the global Flash community for support and the latest information through the Macromedia Online Forums:

`http://webforums.macromedia.com/flash`

You can also visit Macromedia's new Designer & Developer Center, where you can find the latest news and tutorials for Macromedia MX software:

`www.macromedia.com/devnet`

For inspiration and motivation, check out the site of the day, weekly features, and case studies at:

`www.macromedia.com/showcase`

Acknowledgments

This book represents the collective efforts of many people, all of whom have contributed in some way to make it as good as it can be. We thank everyone at John Wiley & Sons for helping with each step of the process. Thanks go to Chris Webb, the acquisitions editor for this project, for his guidance and assistance, and for acting as a liaison to make sure that the best interests of the book were kept in mind at the publisher. This book is also, in large part, made possible by Kezia Endsley, our development editor, who has gone over every word, coordinated schedules, and ensured that the book is of the highest quality possible. Thank you, Kezia.

We thank our agent, David Fugate, for being there and for assisting when needed.

Of course, this book about Flash wouldn't even exist without the hard work of the people at Macromedia who continue to develop and promote Flash. Many thanks to the developers, engineers, and support staff at Macromedia. Particularly we thank Lucian Beebe, Gary Grossman, Nigel Pegg, Nivesh Rajbhandari, Erica Norton, Mike Shroeder, Barbara Herbert, and Heather Hollaender.

Troy Gardner and Steve Nowicki provided their support throughout the book by editing the chapters for technical content. Thank you, Troy and Steve, for double-checking all the code and all of our claims to make sure that the book is as technically accurate as it can be.

Many thanks are due to the many developers, designers, artists, coders, and other members of the Flash community. You've pushed the limits. You've innovated. You've inspired. In particular we thank those people with whom we have shared dialogues throughout the writing of this book. Thanks go to Peter and Jen deHaan, Chafic Kazoun, Tom Muck, and Shane Elliott.

We especially thank you. It is the readers who make this book what it is. Thank you for your questions, your comments, and your feedback.

Robert's acknowledgments: I couldn't have completed this revised edition without my partner, Snow Dowd. I thank her for her encouragement and support during the long nights and lost weekends I spent updating this book. I extend my deepest gratitude to Joey Lott, whose vast knowledge of Flash programming makes this book the valuable resource that it is. I also thank all of the wonderful people at The Content Project who have enriched my breadth and depth of Flash design and programming. Without their collaboration, I wouldn't have as many exciting opportunities to push the limits of Flash experiences.

Joey's acknowledgments: I thank Robert for having offered me the opportunity to write this book with him. I'd like to thank my parents and sister for their love and support. I'd like to give thanks to that which cannot be put into words — that which is the very essence of all being.

Contents at a Glance

Contents

PART I

Conceptualizing Flash

In This Part

An Introduction to Flash MX 2004

✦ ✦ ✦ ✦

In This Chapter

Contextualizing Flash MX 2004

Expanding the capabilities of Flash MX 2004

Introducing what's new in Flash MX 2004

Understanding the framework for Flash

Applying Flash MX 2004

Planning Flash development

✦ ✦ ✦ ✦

Macromedia Flash MX 2004 is the latest version of one of the world's most popular and widely used Web authoring and animation applications. With every new release, Flash continues to increase in strength, capability, and diversity. Flash MX 2004 is a powerful multimedia tool capable of integrating a wide array of media formats and data formats from server-side applications. Never before has there been more support for developers in what has traditionally been an animation and graphics-centric program. This chapter provides an overview of the many new advancements and structure of Macromedia Flash MX 2004.

Considering Flash MX 2004 in Context

Like its predecessor, Flash MX 2004 has the power to unite many technologies, techniques, and languages while supporting development in several different programs. With added and expanding support for native file formats of third-party software and the ability to directly edit and compress digital video, the program can be considered a multimedia application approaching the breadth and depth of Macromedia's original powerhouse multimedia studio, Director. The Flash Player also integrates more technologies with direct support for Web services and runtime Flash Video file (FLV file) loading, enabling you to tap more data and media formats, respectively. Flash has influenced and penetrated all forms of visual media—it is now often seen in broadcast advertisements, video and special effects, corporate Web sites, and e-commerce.

Flash MX 2004 is an advanced application that can deploy products ranging from streaming animations to interactive and dynamic presentations that work with server-side languages and applications. Published movies can be accessed by a wide range of platforms, from portable devices to desktop computers to broadcast television. Flash movies do not usually have to be significantly altered for a wide and diverse audience to access your content within these different contexts. ActionScript is the object-oriented programming (OOP) language used in Flash MX 2004. ActionScript has experienced significant evolution, from the earlier days of drag-and-drop programming seen in Flash 4 to the robust and standardized OOP language it is today.

ActionScript has officially graduated to a new version, dubbed *ActionScript 2.0*. We explore the implications of this new version throughout this book.

Flash MX 2004 is now a mature and complex environment for development that is increasingly respected by professional programmers. The possibilities are virtually endless when you use Flash MX 2004 as your central authoring tool. This chapter takes a look at what is possible in Flash, the new and improved features found in Flash MX 2004, and the general context of Flash development.

The Flash product line now officially includes two products: Flash MX 2004 and Flash MX Professional 2004. This book assumes you are using Flash MX Professional 2004 for most of its content. If you are using the trial version of Flash MX 2004, make sure you using the Professional version. Note that Macromedia also refers to Flash MX Professional 2004 as Flash MX Pro or Flash MX Pro 2004.

Understanding the Capabilities of Flash MX 2004

Although the Macromedia Flash authoring tool was originally a front-end graphics application, it is very far from this point of origin today. Since the early days when it was known as FutureSplash up to the Flash MX 2004 version today, Flash has always excelled as a vector drawing and animation tool. Even though animation is still a large part of what Flash does, now it is only a fraction of its toolset. Here are the broad categories available in Flash MX 2004 authoring:

- **Vector graphics:** Vector drawings are made up of many lines and curves and fills, each defined by a set of coordinates and the paths along them. These paths — vectors — are described via mathematical functions. Because mathematical formulas are used to store and create the image, they are resolution independent and can be resized arbitrarily smaller or larger with no loss of quality. Also, images based on calculations are generally smaller in file size than bitmap images, which is an advantage for bandwidth-limited Web delivery.
- **Bitmap graphics:** Bitmap (a.k.a. raster) images are made up of a grid of pixels. Every pixel's color and location in the grid must be stored individually, which usually (but not always) means larger file sizes than images made of vector calculations. Although Flash handles bitmap graphics, the program is not built for direct image manipulation on a pixel level; rather, Flash is primarily an image handler. Flash can retain JPEG compression of imported JPEG files, as well as apply lossless or custom lossy compression to imported bitmap images.

Tip

Flash Player 6 or higher can load standard JPEG images at runtime.

- **Animation:** Flash is an excellent tool for vector animation, given that the native file format is vector-based. Color and alpha effects can be applied over time by using Flash's built-in tweening, by using a series of manually modified keyframes or by controlling symbols with ActionScript. Time-based animations can also be streamed so that playback can begin before the entire Flash movie has downloaded into the Flash Player.

- **Multimedia authoring:** Flash MX 2004 can import a wide range of media formats in addition to standard vector and bitmap image formats. For example, Flash MX 2004 is capable of importing video directly into the authoring environment. Flash can also import audio files in most common formats at author-time or dynamically stream MP3 audio at runtime. Both of these can be used to enhance your productions and animations. You can manipulate these assets with ActionScript and add interactive functionality to them.
- **Dynamic content:** Flash can incorporate dynamically loaded information into your productions. Text, images, and MP3s can be loaded into the movie at runtime, and information can also be sent from the movie to a server or database.
- **Rich Internet Applications:** Since the release of Flash MX, Macromedia has coined the term Rich Internet Applications, or RIAs, to refer to a new breed of Web applications that use Flash Player technology to access sophisticated enterprise-level server applications. Several technologies have been developed by Macromedia, including Flash Remoting MX and Flash Communication Server MX (also known as Flash Com or Comm Server), to add enterprise-level features to Flash content. Flash Remoting MX is the fastest means of sending and receiving data from a Flash movie to server-side applications, whereas Flash Communication Server MX can enable simultaneous interaction among several users in real time. Flash Com can also deliver live or prerecorded audio/video to Flash movies as well.

To see some inspiring examples of what Flash can do, check out Macromedia's featured Site of the Day at `www.macromedia.com/showcase`.

What's New in Flash MX 2004 and Flash MX Pro 2004

There are many new advantages to working with Flash MX 2004 to develop dynamic, manageable, and complex Web sites or applications. Some of the new features and support offered in the latest release will undoubtedly benefit your productions with fewer steps or lines of code than before. And of course, Flash MX 2004 is capable of many new functions. This section explores some of the new features in Flash MX 2004 and Flash MX Pro 2004.

Improvements to the User Interface

Several improvements to the user interface speed up development time. Panel layout and the functionality of individual panels have been optimized from Flash MX, and organizational enhancements promote efficient workflow.

Timelines, Forms, and Screens

Although the Flash MX 2004 timeline has not changed from the previous release of Flash MX, Flash MX Pro 2004 adds a new authoring structure known as *forms*. This structure is also called screens or slides. Forms-based authoring allows you to divide your Flash application or presentation into sections, each with its own independent timeline. You can think of forms as an ActionScript upgrade to traditional scenes.

Actions Panel and the Script Editor

There have been a number of improvements to the Actions panel. In addition to the features introduced in Flash MX such as automatic indenting, color-coding, code hints, and auto-completion, the Actions panel in Flash MX 2004 features an improved Script Navigator and multiple script pinning. The Reference panel from Flash MX is now integrated in the Help panel of Flash MX 2004. The Actions panel also includes useful buttons for formatting and checking syntax. This enhanced coding environment benefits advanced and aspiring ActionScripters alike.

Flash MX Pro 2004 also features a Script editor, which allows you to open one or more external ActionScript documents (AS files) in their own document windows, separate from the document window of Flash document (FLA files). If you're using the Windows version of Flash MX Pro 2004, you can tab between Flash documents and ActionScript documents as well. The Script editor has most of the features found in the Actions panel.

Project Panel

In Flash MX Pro 2004, you can organize all of the files associated with a Flash production in the Project panel. Just as you can check in and check out files in Dreamweaver, the Project panel can synchronize local copies of your files with those on a remote server. You can quickly open ActionScript documents (AS files) or Flash documents (FLA files). You can also publish the entire project with the click of one button.

ActionScript

If you're reading this book, chances are you already know that ActionScript is the term that refers to the collective set of actions, functions, events, and event handlers that allow you, as a developer, to author complex interactive Flash movies. ActionScript has continued its evolution toward a standardized programming language, and Macromedia has officially graduated the language to version 2.0. ActionScript 2.0 refers to a new style of coding, closely adhering to ECMAScript 4, the standard upon which JavaScript is based. If you were familiar with Flash MX or Flash 5, you can continue to code using ActionScript 1.0.

Unless you are developing object-oriented programming structures in your Flash movies, chances are that you can continue coding your Flash movies just as you did in previous versions of the Flash authoring environment—publishing your movies as ActionScript 2.0. Most of this book is dedicated to teaching you how to use ActionScript 2.0 with your Flash MX 2004 documents.

If you are an aspiring coder, you will find ActionScript consistent and approachable. Part of what has made Flash so popular is the gentle learning curve that allows you to get started easily and to make progress quickly. Many interactive tasks such as a mouse click on a button that directs the Web browser to a new URL are relatively simple to accomplish. In fact, you can develop large projects without knowing complicated ActionScript code.

Flash MX 2004 introduces the Behaviors panel, which can be used to quickly add scripts to your Flash movie elements. Behaviors are discussed in *Flash MX 2004 Bible*, by Robert Reinhardt and Snow Dowd (Wiley, 2004).

If you read the next few sections in this chapter and it seems like a foreign language, rest assured that these concepts are gradually introduced in the chapters that follow. One person we know who had experience with other scripting languages became addicted to Flash after discovering that he could actually author an interactive game in a weekend. It's called Flash for a reason! If you are an accomplished coder in other languages such as JavaScript, you will appreciate the flexibility and the continually expanding capabilities of ActionScript.

New Classes

Flash MX 2004's ActionScript language includes several new classes that expand the capabilities of your Flash movies. You can create or load external CSS (cascading style sheet) files with the `TextField.StyleSheet` class. Loading external Flash movies (SWF files) or JPEG images at runtime is much simpler with the aid of the `MovieClipLoader` class. Add right mouse-click (or Control-click on the Mac) menu items to hyperlinked text with the `ContextMenu` class. With the new `PrintJob` class, you have precise control over print output generated by your Flash movie. These are just a few of the new additions to the ActionScript language that can be used with Flash Player 7.

You can use these new classes in either ActionScript 1.0 or 2.0. ActionScript 2.0 is a new style of constructing your code—the classes and objects used in either version are essentially the same.

Server-Side Flash

Flash MX Pro 2004 continues to improve data integration with server-side technologies, and now supports Web services as a data source at runtime. You can also still use data technologies introduced in early versions of Flash, such as form-encoded name/value pairs and XML. In addition, you can tap data from Flash Remoting MX-enabled gateways on Macromedia ColdFusion MX or JRun servers. Flash Remoting MX is also available as an add-on product for J2EE and Microsoft .NET application servers. Macromedia Flash Communication Server MX 1.5, another server-side technology, allows a Flash movie to connect to multiple users to share audio and video streams directly from their Webcams and microphones! These server technologies enhance the creation of dynamic and manageable sites, even when working with large projects.

Components

Continuing upon the success of the Flash MX components (now dubbed V1 components), Flash MX 2004 and Flash MX Pro 2004 add several prebuilt components to the authoring environment. Although Flash MX 2004 ships with 13 standard user interface (UI) components such as `ComboBox`, `List`, and `Button`, Flash MX Pro 2004 ships with 30 data, media, and UI components. These components are dubbed V2 components. V2 components use an entirely new architecture (based largely on a new `UIObject` custom class) incorporating a new listener event model. These components are also compiled. Compiled clips, as they are called in the Library panel, can be thought of as self-contained components whose internal architecture is protected. Once a component is compiled, you cannot view or edit the component's code or individual assets in the authoring environment.

You can install or purchase additional components from online resources such as the Macromedia Exchange (www.macromedia.com/exchange) or Macromedia's DevNet site (www.macromedia.com/devnet).

Flash Player 7 Improvements

Flash Player 7 has been significantly modified since the last version of the player. In addition to the many enhancements of Flash Player 6 such as Unicode and accessibility support, this release of the Flash Player has been completely overhauled to enable the fastest performance from Flash movies.

Web Services Support

As mentioned earlier in this chapter, you can write ActionScript or add data components to your Flash Player 7-compatible movies to consume Web services data. Flash Player 7 supports Simple Object Access Protocol (SOAP) based Web services. With SOAP, you can enable Rich Internet Applications to access dynamic data with more ease than previous Flash Players allowed.

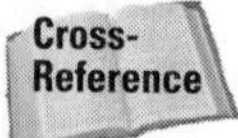

You can find more information about Web services in Chapter 36.

We still highly recommend the use of Flash Remoting MX and AMF data for the best performance and fastest data transfer speeds in Flash Player 6 or 7.

Improved Runtime Performance

Flash Player 7 has been rebuilt from the ground up, enabling Flash movies to perform faster. You will see anywhere from a 2x to 10x performance boost with Flash Player 7.

According to Macromedia, you should recompile Flash MX documents in Flash MX 2004 to achieve the best performance in Flash Player 7. Even Flash Player 6 movies published from Flash MX 2004 will perform better in Flash Player 7 than the same document published from Flash MX.

ECMA-262 Strict Mode Compliance

Flash Player 7 enforces strict case-sensitivity with ActionScript code, instances names, and frame labels. Whether you publish the movie with ActionScript 1.0 or 2.0, Flash Player 7 movies will be governed by this new compliance. Make sure you consistently spell your ActionScript terms, instance names, and frame labels in Flash MX 2004 documents that will be published for Flash Player 7.

Security Model Improvements

Flash Player 7 introduces major changes to the way in which Flash movies can access other content at runtime. These security changes are applied to Flash Player 6 or higher movies. By default, Flash Player 6 or higher movies can load data only from the originating domain of the Flash movie.

For example, if your Flash movie resides on `www.mydomain.com`, you can access only external data from `www.mydomain.com`. If you try to access data from `other.mydomain.com`, Flash Player 7 presents a security dialog box to the user, asking for permission to load the data.

If you load an external Flash movie (SWF files) into another Flash movie, you can access scripts in the loaded movie only if the movie is from the same domain *or* if you use the `System.security.allowDomain()` method in the loaded movie.

If you need to load data from a domain that is not the same as the originating Flash movie, you can add a cross-domain policy file to the Web server. These policy files are simple XML documents that specify which domains can access the data.

Flash Video Runtime Loading

Flash Player 7 can now progressively download external Flash Video (FLV files) at runtime. Flash Video files can be created with the new Flash Video Exporter tool that ships with Flash MX Pro 2004. This tool has a separate installer and enables most QuickTime-enabled video applications to export video in the FLV format. You can also use third-party utilities such as Sorenson Squeeze or Wildform Flix to encode video in this format.

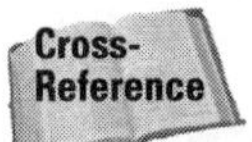

To learn how to load Flash Video files with the `NetStream` class, refer to Chapter 24, "The NetStream and Video Classes."

For the best video playback control and performance, use Macromedia Flash Communication Server MX to stream Flash Video (FLV files) to Flash movies, especially for longer duration movies. FlashCom can seek to any point in the movie with little or no wait time experienced by the end user.

Better Video Playback and Display

Flash Player 7 has made improvements to video playback and display. In Flash Player 6, Flash Video displayed at only 18-bit color depth. Now, Flash Player 7 displays video at its true 24-bit color depth. For many video files, you might not notice any qualitative difference in the video picture. You'll likely see the difference in any video that has subtle gradients or details in shadow (or darker) areas of the video picture.

Video performance has also been improved in Flash Player 7. Video performance is now 15 to 70 percent faster—with most examples falling into the 30 to 60 percent range. Here, performance refers to the ability of the Flash Player to keep up with frame rendering and display. You shouldn't notice as many frames being dropped, especially in video that uses faster frame rates (at or above 24fps). This performance enhancement will be most apparent in computers with slower processors, which could not originally maintain the display refresh rate at the actual speed of the video in the earlier player.

You won't need to make any changes to your Flash Video files (or Flash movies containing embedded video) to take advantage of the new color display feature. The bit depth restriction was player-based. There have been no changes to the actual Sorenson codec used by Flash Video.

Enhanced Hyperlink Support

In Flash Player 7, any Flash movie that uses `<a href>` links in HTML text can open the link in a new browser window or copy the link to the Clipboard. This enhancement moves Flash Player functionality closer to that of a normal Web browser. To access the new feature, simply right-click (or Control-click on Mac) hyperlinked text in a Flash text field and choose the Open in New Window or Copy Link Item in the player's contextual menu.

Improved Small Text Rendering

Flash Player 7 supports small text rendering, a feature that can be enabled in the Flash MX 2004 authoring environment for text fields. Prior to Flash Player 7, only device fonts could be displayed without anti-aliasing (smooth text). Text utilizing embedded fonts would always be smoothed. Usually, font smoothing is a desirable feature, but for small font sizes, such text is illegible. In Flash Player 7, you can specify that text below a specific custom font size be rendered without smoothing.

Mouse Wheel Support (Windows Only)

Flash Player 7 on Windows browsers supports the use of the mouse wheel to scroll text fields or components that use scroll bars. The mouse wheel functionality can be controlled with the new `TextField.mouseWheelEnabled` property. The mouse wheel support works on Flash Player 5 or higher movies in Flash Player 7. You can also capture mouse wheel events with the `onMouseWheel()` event handler for `Mouse` listeners.

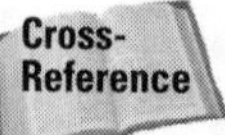

For more information on the `onMouseWheel()` handler, see Chapter 19.

Automatic Updating of Player (Windows Only)

The ActiveX control for Flash Player 7 can be automatically updated. By default, when a user installs the ActiveX control, the Flash Player will check for an updated version every 30 days. A user can change the auto-update settings at:

`www.macromedia.com/support/flashplayer/help/settings/global_notification.html`

This page on the Macromedia site loads a special Flash movie that can change the settings of the Flash Player installed on your computer.

As you may be aware, Macromedia usually releases several minor updates with each Flash Player major version cycle. For example, Flash Player 6 was released with over five minor updates, starting with the first minor release, r29, all the way through r79. Note that the minor release version numbers are not consecutive in public releases. For instance, r30 is not a version of Flash Player 6 that was released publicly. Often, new features are introduced in minor releases. As such, you need to check for specific minor release versions in your ActionScript code to make sure that the user can utilize these new features, if employed by your Flash movie.

Product Integration

The Macromedia product line is ever-expanding, with newly updated software integrating with Flash MX 2004 to offer a more powerful authoring environment. Web developers and designers alike can use these products, which were built to transfer settings and data between each other with ease. Products such as Macromedia Flash Remoting MX and Macromedia Flash Communication Server MX 1.5 specifically tie into Flash development and deployment. Macromedia has also publicly announced *FLEX*, a new server-side authoring and deployment environment. Macromedia Central enables Flash developers to sell unique out-of-the-browser applications that appeal to wireless laptop and normal desktop users.

Not only is the Macromedia family built to support easy integration among the product line, but Flash MX 2004 enables third-party software companies to develop extensions to the authoring environment, as well as to sell prepackaged components.

Templates

Flash MX 2004 continues to ship with templates (prebuilt FLA files) customized for standard ad formats, mobile devices such as the Nokia 9200 and Pocket PC, menus, TV broadcast graphics, slideshows, and simple presentations. These handy files help speed up initial development of standard projects and help maintain design consistency. The option to create and save your own custom templates can greatly reduce repetitive production time on projects that have similar structures or redundant features.

Some templates use Flash forms (or screens). You need to use Flash MX Professional 2004 in order to use these templates.

Shared Libraries

Runtime shared libraries have been improved in Flash MX 2004 and Flash Player 6 r65 and higher. With author-time shared libraries, developers can easily edit and swap symbols used in their documents while working on them, either on their local computers or across a network. Runtime shared libraries make it possible for multiple Flash movies to use assets from a single source file. This reduces file size and makes updates more streamlined. After changes to the original symbol are made, they can be either automatically or manually updated across the various documents sharing them.

Flash Player 6 r65 and higher now allow multi-tiered runtime shared library files. This means that you can link assets from one shared library to another. When a Flash movie using one of the shared library's assets is used, the other linked items will automatically be available as well.

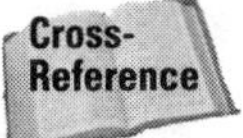

Chapter 34 covers the features associated with shared libraries.

Understanding the Framework

Now that we've introduced most of the features of Flash MX 2004 and Flash MX Professional 2004, it is time to look at how Flash is set up as an authoring environment. Organization along a timeline and various tools for sequencing content in time and in space are at the core of Flash, due to its roots in animation.

- **Frames:** Each layer in a timeline contains a sequence of frames, and these frames are displayed by the playhead of the timeline. Different types of frames can be used to display content in different ways. Static frames repeat the content on a previous frame. Keyframes change the content, either for frame-by-frame animation (each keyframe is changed) or for tweening (two keyframes are placed, and content auto-animates in between). Movie clips contain their own timelines that run independently from the main timeline.
- **Scenes:** Scenes are segments, or partitions, of the Flash movie's main timeline. Each scene can contain a variable number of frames and keyframes, and the Flash Player must load each scene sequentially. These are sometimes (but not always) used by developers to organize content into a playing order. Scenes can be played sequentially or jump from scene to scene nonlinearly via script, perhaps triggered by the user's interaction.

Generally, we recommend against using scenes. It's far better to organize your content across several `MovieClip` objects or separated into individual Flash movies. You can also use the new forms (or screens) authoring mode in Flash MX Pro 2004.

- **Layers:** Layers hold the content of your Flash document and they organize the stacking order of elements within a scene, with the topmost layer located at the front or foreground of the scene and the lowest layer situated at the back. Layers can contain any element placed on the document's stage. A layer's timeline always begins with a keyframe.

You can also use a folder layer to organize or group multiple layers.

- **Elements or Assets:** These are items that you place within each layer. Elements have a stacking order (front to back) within any given layer. These items can be bitmaps, text, grouped items, or symbol instances from the library.

This book assumes you have a basic understanding of the Flash MX 2004 authoring environment. For more information on user interface fundamentals, see *Flash MX 2004 Bible* by Robert Reinhardt and Snow Dowd.

Your ActionScript code enables the interaction between all of these various systems and also between your movie and input from the end user and/or remote servers. ActionScript can manage the sequencing of the movie's content and the information flow to and from specific elements.

Movie Playback

Flash movies can be presented in a few different ways. The most common method of viewing Flash movies is through the Flash Player plug-in or ActiveX control installed in a Web browser. A Flash movie (or movies) can be a presentation entirely built with Flash content or built as individual elements within an HTML framework. You can also develop movies for a stand-alone Flash Player, also known as a *projector*. In a projector, the Flash Player is embedded within the movie, so a plug-in or Web browser is not required. Developers frequently use this method to deploy their presentations on fixed media such as CD-ROMs or DVDs. Flash movies can also be exported into QuickTime (MOV) or Video for Windows (AVI) formats, opening the doors for broadcast productions created in Flash MX 2004. These formats can be incorporated into video editing tools such as Adobe Premiere or Apple Final Cut Pro. Your Flash document (FLA file) can also be published as a series of bitmap or vector images. Many possibilities exist for presenting your movies, both directly out of Flash and with subsequent incorporation with other technologies.

File Types in Flash MX 2004

When you create and edit your multimedia content in Flash MX 2004, you are working with Flash documents (FLA files). When you publish these files for the Web, a Flash movie (SWF file) is created, which can be understood by the Flash Player plug-in or stand-alone player. If you debug a Flash movie (SWF file), Flash MX 2004 creates a Flash Debug file (SWD file). You can also create an external ActionScript file (AS file) to store your code. Refer to Figure 1-1 for a sample folder window showing the various file types that Flash MX 2004 creates.

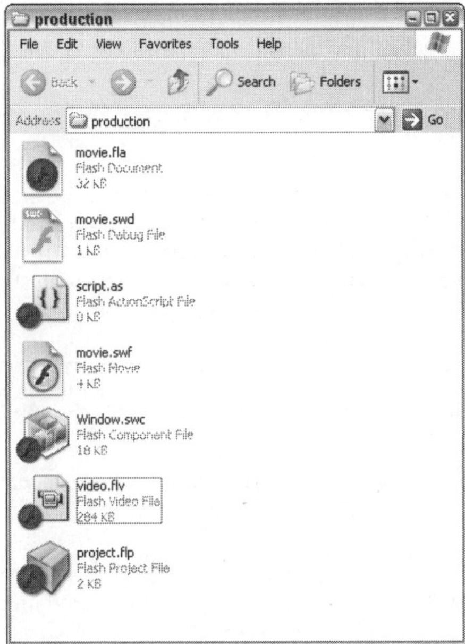

Figure 1-1: Flash MX 2004 file formats

As we discussed, content in a Flash movie exists on a stage and timeline. The items are stored in the Library panel, which can be shared among several movies. The library can contain components, graphics, fonts, movies, sounds, or video. When you are ready to publish your Flash document (FLA file), only the elements used on stage are retained in the Flash movie (SWF file) in order to create the smallest file size possible, which helps to optimize your movie for Web delivery. During this publish process, all of the elements are retained in your movie (SWF file), except the layers are flattened and run on a single timeline. Any unused elements in the library are not exported, and reused assets are saved to the SWF file only once and referenced thereafter. Almost everything in your file will be altered for optimization purposes. This compression is not similar to ZIP or SIT files because bitmaps and audio are compressed independently, depending on your settings in the library. Like Flash MX, Flash MX 2004 has an option for compression in the Flash tab of the Publish Settings dialog box (File ➪ Publish Settings).

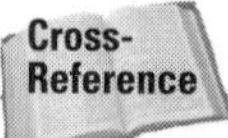

For more information on Flash movie architecture, see Chapter 3.

Moving Data Using Flash

In the past few releases of the Flash authoring tool, there has been an incredible growth of support for dynamic content. Dynamic information (or data) in Flash movies is being used more frequently by Web developers as they realize the effectiveness of Flash movies used as a front-end client for back-end systems. Information can be stored in a database and retrieved at runtime, or even gathered from an end user and inserted into the database. The server-side language used to accomplish this data transfer is up to the developer, although server-side applications such as Flash Remoting MX and ColdFusion have allowed faster and more efficient techniques for transferring data to and from Flash movies. XML is also widely used by the Flash community and in the Flash Player itself, and with the improvement in transfer and parsing speed, XML and Web services data will likely be used more often by developers.

Applying Flash MX 2004

The capabilities of Flash continue to expand with each new version. By allowing the development of third-party importers, more native file formats are beginning to be supported directly in the Flash MX 2004 authoring environment. This simplifies your workflow when you require several technologies in a single project. Flash can be used for many projects, ranging significantly in scope, design, and intention. By integrating the use of server-side scripts, you can even further expand the capabilities of your project. Take a look at just a few of the creations you can produce using Flash MX 2004:

- ✦ A video portfolio using new, built-in video-import capabilities and dynamic loading of content.
- ✦ A form collecting user information and dynamically loading customized information based on this input.
- ✦ An interactive map that can be updated by the client through a database.
- ✦ A stand-alone presentation on a CD-ROM for distribution that loads requested information from a server.

- ✦ A customized user experience when the user returns to a Web site. Store the user's input using local shared objects.
- ✦ Robust chat rooms based on Flash Communication Server MX or XML server-socket technology.
- ✦ An MP3 player dynamically loading requested songs using new features built into Flash Player 6 or higher.
- ✦ Single- or multiplayer online games.
- ✦ A set of customized components for online distribution to other Flash developers.
- ✦ Projectors used for slide show presentations in the style of Microsoft PowerPoint, either on a CD-ROM or on an alternative storage device.
- ✦ The front end of an e-commerce site shopping cart.
- ✦ A movie or interface accessible to screen readers.
- ✦ A single movie that customizes itself at runtime for targeted information delivery on desktops or mobile devices.
- ✦ Flash movies exported for use in digital video editing environments for special effects or layering graphics on top of live action video for broadcast delivery.

This list is far from complete. It's up to you to expand upon the possibilities and pursue the creation of exciting new productions.

Planning Flash Development

After you have your creative ideas in order for a production, it is important to understand how to work efficiently in the Flash environment. There have been many changes in the structure of the program, just between Flash MX and Flash MX 2004. If you are familiar with earlier versions of Flash, you will notice a different organization in the panel structure and modifications to the timeline. Familiarizing yourself with the location of the tools and how they can be used before starting a project will speed up development time and perhaps even give you new ideas inspired by MX 2004 features available for use in your production.

When you have a large project to complete, and you have decided what you want your production to accomplish, you probably want to look at what languages and applications you have access to. Will you need a programmer who is familiar with XML, CFML (ColdFusion Markup Language), or Flash Remoting to create a back-end for your Flash interface? Are you a back-end programmer who needs a professional designer for your front-end interface? Which application servers (or middleware) does your server support? Which language is best for the job?

You will also want to familiarize yourself with some of the new code in ActionScript — new objects, methods, and slight modifications to the language. For example, even though `loadVariables()` is still valid code, the newer `LoadVars` class is generally a much better method for sending and loading URL form-encoded data into Flash. Or perhaps you can even move on to the use of the `WebServices` class. This book helps to familiarize you with the new methods, functions, and best practices for using ActionScript.

When you are planning your Flash movie production, you may want to consider creating a flowchart that depicts the flow of data throughout your movie, to and from your movie, and, of course, to each different area of your production. Refer to Figure 1-2 for a simple flowchart of a small movie incorporating a database into the data flow.

Flowcharts can help you organize your movie and help designers and developers understand what needs to be in place to reach production goals. There are many ways you can handle preproduction for your movie. Most important is that you have an idea of what you want to accomplish and an initial plan of how to reach your goals. Thoroughly planning your production and recording your ideas of how to reach these goals will save you time and money in the long run.

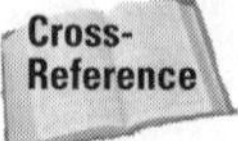

For more information on using flowcharts in preproducion, see Chapter 3.

We'd like to know what you thought about this chapter. Visit `www.flashsupport.com/feedback` to fill out an online form with your comments.

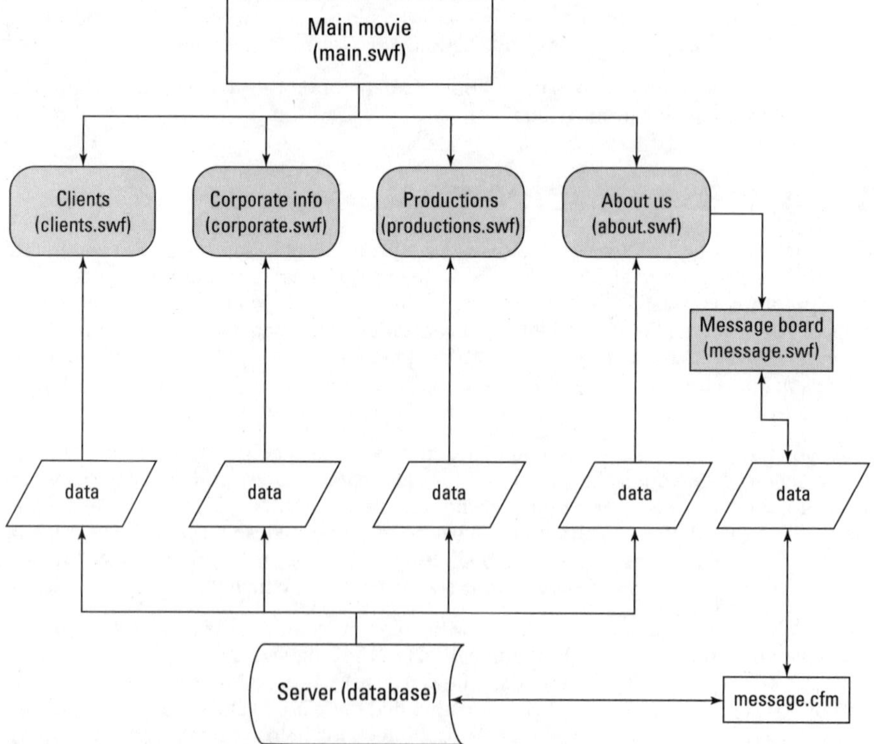

Figure 1-2: A sample flowchart for a Flash movie production

Summary

- Macromedia Flash MX 2004 combines the most useful tools for multimedia authoring into one powerhouse of a program. The integration it facilitates with other programs and languages promotes better Web content.
- Flash content is not only found on the Web. It is used for CD-ROM authoring and business presentations, for example.
- Flash MX 2004 can publish Flash Player 7 movies that consume data from Web services. A growing number of free data services support SOAP, such as weather look-up and language translation services.
- Flash continues to develop its programming language: ActionScript. This release of Flash distinguishes two types of coding: ActionScript 1.0 and ActionScript 2.0. Most of this book focuses on the use of ActionScript 2.0.
- Carefully planning your projects before you start development in Flash will undoubtedly save you time and effort in the long run. Flowcharting is an essential tool to adopt in preproduction.

✦ ✦ ✦

Working with Web Technologies and Interactive Models

In This Chapter

Using Flash on the Web

Knowing the limits of Flash

Evaluating technologies that compete with Flash

Preparing yourself for Flash development

Before you can begin to create powerful Flash movies that incorporate advanced interactivity with ActionScript, you might want to consider what Flash movies can offer in the growing realm of Web plug-in technologies. If you're new to scripting (or programming), we strongly recommend that you read this chapter. This chapter explores Flash's place on the Web and its context among other technologies.

Where Flash Fits into the Ever-Evolving Web

It seems that every week—sometimes every day—there is a new, exciting development for the World Wide Web. Just how wide is the Web, though? Can everyone interact with any Web site in the same way? This section takes a look at what's happening to Flash as people continue to push the limits of the Web environment.

Expecting the Best Experience

Nowadays, business clients and Web visitors expect to be able to get a fantastic, engaging Web site for less money in less time. Not only that, but many believe everyone else on the Web will be able to see (or get) the same thing, regardless of what specialized content they might want to include. And, of course, they want everything to download instantaneously, regardless of what kind of Internet connection is used.

Sound familiar? Each time that Macromedia has released a new Flash version, the ante for Web content is raised. In 1997, Flash 2 gave developers the capability to create vector animations that were significantly smaller than GIF animations. In 1998, Flash 3 started to add more interactive features to Flash, and developers were able to make basic games and rich "sites" in Flash.

In late 1998, Macromedia also released the first version of Generator. Macromedia Generator was a server-side application that could create Flash, GIF, or JPEG graphics on the fly. Generator could also integrate data sources (that is, data from databases) into Flash movies. Very few companies used Generator at first, because Flash was just gaining ground as an accepted plug-in format, and was not yet seen as a standard for Web graphics, let alone Web data. But it was really Flash 4 that opened the doors to data interactivity in 1999. Developers could create Flash sites that interacted with databases, providing dynamic (that is, real-time) data processing without the expense of Generator. News content, product prices, search results, and more could be integrated into Flash movies. Unfortunately, Flash developers had to write ActionScript using a small drag-and-drop interface — code could not be typed in an external editor and brought into Flash (not unless you were using the Windows-only SwiffTools Flash ActionScript Tool — aka FAST! — application).

Note Since the original release of Flash MX, Macromedia has discontinued Generator as a server-side technology. In fact, you can no longer create Generator templates (as Flash documents, or FLA files) in Flash MX or Flash MX 2004. You need to use Flash 5 to create or edit Generator templates.

Macromedia answered developers' woes in 2000 with the release of Flash 5. Flash 5 expanded its data capabilities to incorporate XML data. More importantly, ActionScript finally matured into an object-oriented programming (OOP) language, mimicking the syntax and structure conventions of the widely known JavaScript language.

In 2002, Web designers and developers were given Flash MX. With the new software and player, XML transmissions process remarkably faster, developers can create more accessible movies, and by using Flash MX components and ActionScript, they can utilize functions that were previously provided by Generator. Developers can import digital video files directly into their FLA files, and Flash movies that use the new named anchor feature can be bookmarked by many Web browsers. Even after the remarkable improvements in the release of Flash 5, ActionScript continued to develop into an even more robust "real" programming language, for the benefit of programmers and developers alike.

Perhaps more importantly, Flash MX sparked a new wave of client- and server-side integration. With Macromedia Flash Remoting MX and Macromedia Flash Communication Server MX (and its follow-up release, 1.5), Macromedia introduced a whole new paradigm to create the most efficient and feature-rich Flash applications. These server technologies breathed desperate new life into the Web economy largely abandoned after the dotcom crash in 2001. Flash content suddenly added new value to traditional HTML and Web applications. With Flash Remoting, large transfers of data from remote databases can be loaded and displayed in Flash movies. With Flash Communication Server, you can create an interface that connected several users to one another in real time, sharing data, audio, and video! Truly, the sky was (and still is) the limit.

In late summer of 2003, Macromedia released Flash MX 2004, and introduced two editions of the product: a standard edition featuring core updates to Flash MX, and a Professional edition showcasing additional product tools and enhancements. Both editions shared many of the same upgrades: a Behaviors panel that enables new users to Flash authoring to add interactivity to their movies; Timeline Effects that give designers and developers alike the capability to quickly animate elements on the stage; and new ActionScript classes and methods that expanded the capabilities of the Flash Player. For developers, Flash MX Professional 2004 enables you to author with forms (or screens), instead of keyframes and timelines. Flash Player 7 also provides the capability to tap Web Services and load Flash Video (FLV files) at runtime, among other features. And just when you thought ActionScript had seen it all, Macromedia officially graduated the language to version 2.0, enabling developers to use common object-oriented programming structures to build extensive applications.

So, in just over six years — equivalent to the amount of time you might spend finishing undergraduate and graduate degrees — Flash has made monumental steps, becoming the most prominent plug-in-based technology on the Web. In 2000, the last year of the Great Internet, Flash had become *the* buzzword for hot, multimedia Web branding. Just about every company wanted some sort of Flash on its Web site. Despite several opponents branding Flash "unusable," Flash continued to gain momentum. As designers and developers learned to address usability issues while making beautiful work, even leading critics of Flash such as Jakob Nielsen realized that the technology itself had almost limitless potential. In 2002, Nielsen partnered with Macromedia to design and test sample Flash interfaces to further explore the Flash usability issue.

Even through present day, when dotcoms are closing down and many Web departments are being downsized or shut down, Flash is going strong. Why? Flash was akin to color TV for Web surfers — who wants to go back to black-and-white TV after they have experienced color TV? To push the metaphor further, Flash was like color TV with a remote control, compared with black-and-white TV with a manual channel dial. Never before had so much interactive fun been available, especially over slower connection speeds. The Flash Player's size, which is still under 500KB, has made it one of most affordable technologies for Web users everywhere.

As of this writing, the current release of Flash Player 7 is 466KB for the Windows ActiveX control download. Other plug-in installers might be larger. For a complete list of Flash Player 7 installers, go to `www.macromedia.com/shockwave/download/alternates`.

Flash Player Statistics

As of June 2003, an NPD Research study found that Flash content can be experienced by 97.4 percent of Web users. This, of course, is a statistic for *any* version of the player, including Flash Player 2. So let's now take a look at how the different versions stack up against one another, and how well the Flash Player has penetrated different regions of the world (see Table 2-1). (The lag in numbers is due to the normal delay in users upgrading to the most recent version.)

Table 2-1: Flash Player Penetration (percent)

Player Version	*US*	*Canada*	*Europe*	*Asia*
Flash 2	97.4	97.5	97.7	96.1
Flash 3	97.3	97.3	97.7	95.3
Flash 4	97.0	96.8	97.5	94.2
Flash 5	94.8	95.6	97.1	92.6
Flash 6	86.3	86.9	87.2	82.7

Another important consideration is which version of each player is available for the different platforms you are targeting. The Flash Player is available for handheld computers, WebTV, and now even cell phones. Nokia is among the first of many cell phone manufacturers building Flash Player support into their products. But not all of these platforms support the most recent version of the player. As of October 2003, current players are as follows (see Table 2-2).

Table 2-2: Flash Player Availability

Platform	*Player Version*	*Support*
Windows	Flash Player 7	98, 2000, Me, NT, XP
Mac	Flash Player 7	OS X, OS 9 (Power PC)
Pocket PC	Flash Player 6	Any Pocket PC running Pocket PC 2003
OS/2	Flash Player 5	Created by third party. See `www.innotek.de/flash/` for supported systems and browsers.
Sun Solaris	Flash Player 6	Sparc or Intel version
Linux	Flash Player 6	x86
SGI IRIX	Flash Player 4	For use with Netscape (or Netscape-compatible) browsers.

To see the most current statistics of Flash Player penetration, visit Macromedia's Web site at `www.macromedia.com/software/player_census/`.

To Flash or Not to Flash?

This is the only place in the book that discusses the appropriateness of Flash for Web or multimedia development. However, it *is* important to know why you want to use Flash. We hope your answer isn't just "because I want to" or "because I hear it's the best thing out there." Although these answers are a good starting point, you should be prepared to give your clients strong reasons why a project should be done in Flash instead of some other technology. You'll read about other multimedia technologies later in this section, but for now, take look at what Flash can do for you and your business clients.

What Flash Can Do

If you need a checklist of the things Flash can bring to life, you might want to consider the following features. Flash can do the following:

- **Produce incredibly small file sizes and incorporate high-quality sound for high-end animation.** Many media companies, such as Disney and Warner Bros., use Flash for online film trailers, short cartoons, or banner ads. With small file sizes, Flash movies can also be attached to e-mails without lengthy download (or upload) times.
- **Integrate just about any multimedia file format**. For example, bitmap image formats (such as GIF, JPEG, PNG, PCT, and TIF), vector image formats (including FreeHand files, EPS, Illustrator files, and now PDF files), and sound formats (WAV, AIF, and MP3) can all be imported into a Flash document. No additional "extras" or plug-ins are required to play back these file formats in the Flash Player. Just as important, you can now import Macromedia FreeHand and Fireworks files to access editable objects that retain several settings (such as layer formatting) when they are imported into the Flash authoring environment. With such flexibility, you can easily collect your business client's raw resources for integration with your Flash production workflow.

Flash MX Pro 2004 ships with a FlashLite emulator. FlashLite is the Flash Player used by DoCoMo phones in Japan. With Flash MX Pro 2004, you can import a sound file that is a proxy for a MIDI file. When you test such a movie in Flash MX Pro 2004, the FlashLite emulator plays the MIDI file.

- **Create precise layouts with embedded fonts.** Although most HTML formatting is not 100 percent consistent from browser to browser, you can be assured that Flash content will look the same on every device that supports the Flash Player.
- **Display and manipulate data from remote data sources, such as a database.** As long as your database can be accessed from an application server such as Macromedia ColdFusion MX 6.1, PHP, or some other server-side solution and its data can be formatted properly, you can enable your Flash movies to work with dynamic (that is, ever-changing) data.
- **Send data to remote data sources.** Flash movies can accept input from the user, and send it to your application server. Instead of using HTML to make forms for a Web site, you can encourage more user feedback by including engaging animations and sounds with your Flash forms. Flash is by no means limited to this type of activity—you can send many different types of information, such as environmental data (for example, Flash Player version, tracking information about the user's activity in the movie, and so on), to your databases as well.

The most efficient and optimized way to send and receive data in a Flash movie is to use Flash Remoting MX, which uses AMF, Action Messaging Format, a proprietary data format developed by Macromedia. AMF uses binary compression and is automatically serialized and deserialized by the player and the Flash Remoting gateway. You can use Flash Remoting with Flash Player 6 or higher. Refer to Joey Lott's excellent book *Complete Flash Remoting MX* (Wiley, 2003) for the most comprehensive coverage of this technology.

- **Enable multiuser interactivity with games, chat sessions, and so on, with the appropriate server-side software.** Several people can communicate with each other through a Flash movie (called a *client*), which constantly sends and receives data to and from a socket server. Flash Player 5 allowed movies to use XML sockets for instantaneous transmission between the movie and a socket server. With Flash Player 6 or higher, you can use Macromedia Flash Communication Server MX 1.0 or higher to synchronize live data with multiple participants.
- **Load other Flash movies into one large "presentation" movie.** For example, you can create a Flash movie that loads several other Flash movie "assets." This enables you to distribute a project's workflow to many Flash designers and developers working in a Web department (or as independent contractors). More importantly, this feature allows you to create very large yet manageable Web sites.
- **Dynamically load JPEG, MP3, or FLV files directly into your movie using components and ActionScript.**
- **Enable developers to create templates for design and functionality.** Using components (that is, Movie Clip symbols accepting custom parameters), you can create reusable interface elements. Flash MX 2004 also includes prebuilt templates for dynamic Flash movie production, and offers the option of creating and saving custom templates. Templates increase your productivity by allowing you to change settings and specifications without having to rebuild an entire project from scratch.

- **Play on a wide variety of platforms and devices.** As you saw earlier in this chapter, versions of the Flash Player are available for Windows, Macintosh, Linux, Solaris, OS/2, SGI IRIX, and the Pocket PC. Some mobile telephones are now able to play Flash movies! With such delivery options, you can author once (on either Windows or Macintosh) and distribute Flash content to several audiences.

Because of varying screen sizes between desktop and mobile devices, you'll likely need to retool some aspects of a Flash movie to distribute it across several platforms.

- **Play movies as stand-alone presentations, called projectors.** Projectors are Flash movies with an embedded player—you don't even need a Web browser to play Flash movies! You can burn Flash projectors to CD-ROMs or DVDs, or copy them to a 1.44MB floppy disk.
- **Send content to a printer.** Flash movies can print the contents of an entire frame (or sequence of frames) or dynamic content on the fly. For example, you can create a Flash ad that prints a discount coupon for a product.

New Feature

Flash Player 7 greatly expands the capabilities of Flash printing with the new `PrintJob` class. You can learn more about this new class in Chapter 22, "The PrintJob Class."

- **Create accessible movies.** Flash MX 2004 continues to offer built-in support for assistive technologies by incorporating MSAA into the Flash Player 6 or higher. Movie content is recognizable to screen-readers, and opens the door for developers required to meet the standards of Section 508.
- **Create multilingual movies.** Flash Player 6 or higher supports Unicode formatted text. Flash MX Pro 2004 also features a new Strings panel, which makes it easier to create multi-lingual movies.

Cross-Reference

Refer to Chapter 32, "Making Movies Accessible and Universal," for more about working with assistive technologies.

- **Import digital video directly into your movie.** The Sorenson Spark compressor is built into Flash MX 2004, allowing you to import video while controlling the quality and frame rate of your file. Although other options are still available, it is no longer necessary to use third-party utilities, plug-ins, or tedious workarounds to include video content in your movies.

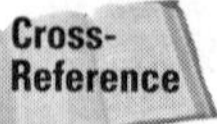

This book explores many aspects of ActionScript-driven video delivery. For more information on the basics of video conversion in Flash MX 2004 (including the new Video Import Wizard), refer to *Flash MX 2004 Bible* by Robert Reinhardt and Snow Dowd (Wiley, 2004).

- **Stream audio and video from one user to another.** Using Macromedia Flash Communication Server MX and Flash Player 6 or higher, you can deploy Flash applications that connect several users together. Flash Player 6 can access each user's Webcam and microphone, allowing you to develop real-time video conferencing applications.

You might already have a list of other features that Flash can provide. Regardless of what you need Flash to do, be ready to justify its use to your business clients or your site's visitors! The next section looks at a few reasons why Flash might not always be the most appropriate multimedia technology for all your projects.

What Flash Can't (or Shouldn't) Do

As much as you might like to think of Flash as the only tool to consider for exciting Web and multimedia development, there are reasons why you might not want to use Flash for every project that comes your way. Reflect on the following list:

- **Flash movies still require a separate plug-in download (or installation) for most browsers.** Many companies and institutions do not allow employees or students to install applications onto computer systems.
- **The type of browser can restrict the functionality of a Flash movie.** Although internal Flash content will likely be unaffected by the Web browser, some scripting and data interactivity might be limited by the browser. For example, Internet Explorer on the Macintosh does not allow Flash movies to communicate with JavaScript via the `fscommand`. Similarly, the named anchors feature (introduced in Flash MX) works only on Internet Explorer 4 or higher on the PC and Netscape 3.*x*–4.*x*/7.*x* or higher on both platforms using Flash Player 6 or higher.
- **Web browsers will not automatically redirect to alternative content if the Flash Player is not installed.** You as a developer are required to create detection mechanisms for the Flash Player. However, Flash MX 2004 offers a new detection feature in the Publish Settings dialog box to help you create a Flash-friendly Web site.
- **You might find that video compression and playback in Flash Player 7 is still not of the same quality as some of the players developed exclusively for this purpose, such as QuickTime or Windows Media.** For example, Flash video does not take advantage of enhanced video drivers for optimized playback at enlarged sizes.
- **Flash movies cannot import or display true 3D file formats.** Currently, you need to mimic 3D effects with frame-by-frame Flash vector animation. Although you can use ActionScript to create some 3D effects, you might want to consider using Macromedia Director MX and Shockwave to design fully featured interactive 3D presentations.
- **Typical Web search engines (or spiders) cannot index the content of Flash movies.** If you create 100 percent Flash-based Web sites, you need to provide some text or HTML on your Web pages if you want your content to be indexed. This is one area where usability experts have criticized the use of Flash.
- **Although the integration of MSAA compatibility into Flash Player 6 and higher is a big step forward and has been heralded by accessibility experts, many kinds of screen-readers do not yet support MSAA or the Flash Player.**
- **Flash should not replace text-based HTML sites.** If the primary content of your project is text-based with simple interface graphics, you might not want to use Flash. Many Web surfers don't feel comfortable selecting and printing text from Flash movies. Printing and selecting text in Flash movies is not as simple (or familiar) as it is in HTML sites in which news, stocks, and entertainment articles are offered.
- **If you are not already an experienced Flash user, Flash might not be the technology of choice when your development time is incredibly short.** Depending on your familiarity with Flash technology, it's usually faster to produce HTML content and GIF/JPEG graphics. There are many more applications that support drag-and-drop HTML production and management.

Pending the result of a lawsuit against Microsoft regarding the use of plug-in content, you might need to build awkward workarounds to use Flash content on Internet Explorer for Windows. As you may know, Internet Explorer for Windows is the most widely used browser. For more information, see Macromedia's site at `www.macromedia.com/devnet/activecontent`.

Of course, there are always exceptions to any "rule," and these suggestions should be considered only guidelines or cautions to be examined before you embark on Flash development. In the next section, you'll look at some alternatives to Flash for multimedia development.

Competing Technologies

This section takes a brief look at what the competition offers over (or in addition to) Flash. This section is not intended to give you a comprehensive background on these technologies. Rather, we seek to give you some context for Flash as it exists in the rest of the multimedia world.

DHTML

DHTML, or Dynamic HTML, is a specialized set of markup tags that taps into an extended document object model (DOM) that version 4.0 browsers or higher can utilize. Using `<layer>` or `<div>` tags, you can create animations and interactive effects with Web-authoring tools ranging from Notepad or SimpleText to Macromedia Dreamweaver. You can actually combine Flash content with DHTML to create Flash layers on top of other HTML content. One problem with DHTML is that Netscape and Internet Explorer do not use it in the same way. Usually, you need to make sure you have a specialized set of code (or minor modifications) for each browser type.

XML with XSL

XML stands for e*X*tensible *M*arkup *L*anguage. XML looks like HTML, but it's really a language that can manage structured or related data such as pricing information, contact information, or anything else that you would store in a database. XSL stands for e*X*tensible *S*tylesheet *L*anguage. XSL documents apply formatting rules to XML documents. Together, XML and XSL documents can create interactive data-driven Web sites. However, older browsers cannot read and display XML and XSL documents. Nearly every graphical Web browser available, regardless of the browser's version, supports some version of the Flash Player. This means that you can install the Flash Player and play Flash movies on Netscape 4.0 or IE 4.0. As you see later in this chapter, XML can also be used to supply data to Flash.

SVG

Backed by several software companies, including Microsoft and Adobe, SVG is the *S*calable *V*ector *G*raphics format. The World Wide Web Consortium (or W3C) has proposed SVG as the vector graphics standard for the Web. However, SVG is more than a graphics format — it is also a Web development language based on XML. Adobe remains the industry's strongest supporter of SVG by enabling its vector applications (mainly Adobe Illustrator and GoLive) to create files in this format. Adobe has also taken it upon itself to make the plug-in for this file format. The W3C tries to establish standards for the Web, and hopes that browsers will one day natively support SVG without the necessity of a plug-in. Currently, however, SVG has had a very slow adoption rate by both Web developers and surfers. As such, it's not likely to be a feasible development solution for most of your business clients.

To keep up with SVG developments, see Adobe's SVG Web site at `www.adobe.com/svg` or the W3C's SVG coverage at `www.w3c.org/Graphics/SVG`.

Macromedia Shockwave Director

Originally Macromedia's flagship product, Director remains *the* powerhouse authoring solution for offline interactive rich-media projects. Since its inception in the 1980s, Director has had the benefit of many years to establish its mature interface and development environment. Director can integrate and control many media types, including video, audio, and entire Flash movies. Director also has an Xtras plug-in architecture, which allows third-party developers to expand or enhance Director's capabilities. More recently, Director 8.5 added true 3D modeling support. Now you can create Shockwave games with textured models and lighting effects! However, there are two major drawbacks to Shockwave Director: It requires a large download for the full player installation, and the player is available only for Windows and Macintosh platforms. Director is the primary authoring tool for CD-ROM and DVD-ROM development.

SMIL, Real Systems RealPlayer, and Apple QuickTime

SMIL is the *S*ynchronized *M*ultimedia *I*ntegration *L*anguage, and it also looks a lot like HTML markup tags. SMIL allows you to layer several media components in SMIL-compatible players such as RealPlayer and QuickTime. You probably have seen SMIL at work when you load RealPlayer and see the snazzy graphics that make up the channel's interface. With SMIL, you can layer interactive buttons and dynamic text on top of streaming video or audio content. You may not even think of SMIL as a competing technology, but rather a complementary one—Flash can be one of the multimedia tracks employed by SMIL! You can even use Flash as a track type in QuickTime alone, without the use of SMIL. With Flash 4, Macromedia and Apple announced QuickTime Flash movies, which allow you to create Flash interfaces that lay on top of audio-video content. RealPlayer will also play "tuned" Flash files directly, without the use of SMIL. A tuned Flash file is weighted evenly from frame to frame to ensure synchronized playback. Note, however, that tuned files usually need to be strict linear animations without any interactive functionality.

Macromedia Authorware

Like Flash, Authorware was a technology developed by another company and purchased by Macromedia. Since this acquisition, Macromedia has significantly developed the features and capabilities of Authorware. It is an authoring application and a companion plug-in technology, with similar audio-video integration capabilities as Macromedia Director. However, Authorware was developed with e-learning in mind. You can structure training solutions and monitor student learning with Authorware. We mention Authorware as a potential competitor to Flash because many Flash developers use Flash to create training modules that interact with server-side databases.

Microsoft PowerPoint

As you frequently see in business meetings, conferences, or even classrooms, many interactive presentations are still developed using PowerPoint. Many people turn to PowerPoint for its ease of use, especially when making slide-show presentations for conferences and meetings. You can even download and set up a PowerPoint Viewer for your browser so these files can be made accessible online. However, your presentations can contain much more complex animation by using Flash, and Flash presentations can be presented from laptops, or even on Pocket PCs, using the Flash Player instead.

An Overview of Companion Technologies

Now that you have a clear understanding of how Flash fits into the current World Wide Web, you can consider the technologies that contribute to Flash's well-being. In today's world, the developer not only needs to know how to script Flash movies, but also how to introduce Flash into existing environments, such as a Web browser or your business client's Web-ready (or not-so-Web-ready) databases.

The Web Saga: HTML Lives!

Just like a "good" horror movie, HTML keeps coming back in your face. Get used to it — you'll be living with HTML for the foreseeable future, so if you haven't embraced it for what it is, now's the time. Even Web sites that are 100 percent Flash content require some rather intricate HTML in order to work. Consider the following uses of HTML for Flash:

✦ **To format and display Flash movies on a Web page:** As simple as it sounds, it can be a little tricky to hand-code the HTML for both the Active X Control for Internet Explorer and the plug-in for Netscape.

✦ **To scale Flash movies within the browser window:** One of Flash's exciting features is to stretch to the size of the browser window, allowing Web surfers with large monitors to view Flash movies at a larger size.

✦ **To provide an alternative HTML version to the Flash content on the site, for users who don't have (or can't use) the Flash Player plug-in:** Despite the addition of support for screen-readers to Flash Player 6 or higher, not all screen-readers are currently compatible with the built-in support. An HTML version of your content is sure to broaden your potential audience.

✦ **To access content that can't be displayed in a Flash movie:** For example, if you want to link to QuickTime movies from a Flash movie, you need to write the proper HTML to embed and play back QuickTime movies. PDF documents are another example of a file format you might need to access from Flash links.

✦ **HTML is also used within Flash itself:** For instance, when you're using Dynamic text fields to display text, you have the option of formatting it using HTML. An understanding of the language, or at least the tags used to format text, will give you better control over this feature for use in your Flash productions.

Flash Player 7 can also load external CSS (cascading style sheet) files. CSS is used by many HTML 4.0 (or DHTML) sites to determine how pages should be rendered in the browser.

Although most people find HTML a little painful to use — partly because of its inconsistencies from browser to browser — it's well worth the time to brush up on your HTML. If you have a particularly strong aversion to HTML, we recommend that you start using a WYSIWYG HTML editor such as Macromedia Dreamweaver to make life a little simpler.

Scripting on the Client Side: JavaScript

If you're new to ActionScript, *and* you haven't learned JavaScript, you're in luck. Much of what you learn from this book can be applied to JavaScript in HTML documents. If you're new to ActionScript, but know some JavaScript, you're also in luck — it'll be easier for you to grasp some of ActionScript's programming principles. Simply put, JavaScript is the interactive language of the HTML world, just as ActionScript is the interactive language of the Flash world. But why do you need to know JavaScript in order to develop Flash projects?

- **JavaScript allows you to pass data into a Flash movie when the Web page containing the Flash movie loads.** For example, maybe you want to pass a search term (from a search engine's text field in a `<form>` element) into a Flash movie. JavaScript allows you to dynamically insert that search term into the Flash movie as a variable. On some browsers, you can continue to pass data back and forth between JavaScript and Flash, as the user navigates your site.
- **With JavaScript, you can create customized browser pop-up windows that open from Flash movies.** By "customized," we mean browser windows that don't have any scroll bars, button bars, or menu items across the top of the browser window.
- **JavaScript can dynamically write Flash movie properties, such as width and height, when the Flash movie loads into the browser.** Using JavaScript, you can detect the size of a user's monitor, and open a new window based on that size.
- **Perhaps most importantly, JavaScript allows you to write (or use) detection mechanisms for the Flash Player.** On most browsers, you can use JavaScript to detect the presence (or absence) of the Flash Player plug-in. Likewise, you can use VBScript on Internet Explorer for Windows to detect the Flash Player Active X Control.
- **As mentioned earlier in this chapter, any plug-in content displayed with Microsoft's Internet Explorer browser might require JavaScript to dynamically write the <object> and <embed> tags to display Flash content.** Pending the results of a court appeal to a lawsuit brought against Microsoft, this change may go into effect sometime in 2004.

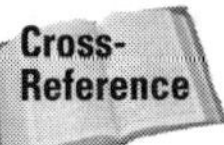

A great companion to this book is *JavaScript Bible, Fifth Edition* by Danny Goodman (Wiley, 2004). If you want to learn the ins and outs of JavaScript, look no further.

Transmitting and Storing Data

Depending on what type of Flash projects you accept, you might not need to develop Flash movies that work with external data. External data, in this section, means any text-encoded information that does not exist within the original Flash movie (SWF file); external data is information that is loaded into the Flash movie while it's playing live in a Web browser or in a standalone projector. Chances are, if you are reading this book, you're more than likely going to need to make a Flash movie that uses interactive forms, retrieves pricing information from an inventory database, or displays text of some kind that needs to be updated on a regular basis.

Dynamic or Static?

Whenever you're working with external data, you have to decide how that data will exist. Will it exist as a real text file (as a TXT file) on your Web server, or will it be generated on the fly from an application server and database? Any external data that is preformatted into an actual text file is called *static* data. You'll read about formatting issues in the next section. On the other hand, any data retrieved at a specific point in time from a database is considered *dynamic* data.

How do you know when you need to use static or dynamic data? How will you build the data versus store the data? Usually, there are three factors to consider:

- **Schedules:** Will you need to update the information within short time intervals (that is, hourly or daily)?
- **Size:** Will you need to store a lot of data? For example, do you need to track pricing for only 10 items, or for 1,000 or more items?
- **Frequency:** Will the data need to be accessed by several users? How many people will be visiting the site and downloading the information?

If you answered a resounding "yes" to any of these questions, you probably need a database that can feed dynamic data to Flash movies on the fly. However, if you answered no or aren't that sure, it's entirely possible that you won't even need a true database to store the data that will be accessed by a Flash movie. For example, if your business client wants to update a greeting message (such as the CEO's welcome message in a Flash movie) on a weekly or monthly basis, you can simply store that message in a single text file on the client's Web server, and load it into the Flash movie when it plays in a Web browser. Generally, you have three options for storing and retrieving data with Flash movies on the Web:

✦ **Dynamic data:** Create a database (for example, Oracle, Microsoft SQL Server, mySQL, postgreSQL, Microsoft Access, FileMaker, and so on) and use a middleware server application such as Macromedia ColdFusion to properly format the data dynamically for use in the Flash movie. Data that changes constantly, for example, might be weather conditions or forecasts, or news events. These scenarios require you to keep your databases online and active 24 hours a day, as shown in Figure 2-1.

✦ **Static data from an offline data source:** Create a database and build a flat file from that database containing the relevant information needed by the Flash movie. This flat file will contain the proper formatting so that Flash can recognize it. For example, if you maintain a database of 100 products and want to download each product's name, description, and price into a Flash movie, you can feasibly export that information to a text file that Flash can load. This solution allows you to keep your real data source (that is, the database) offline on a local network, whereas your "live" data is kept in one (or several) text file on the Web server, as shown in Figure 2-2.

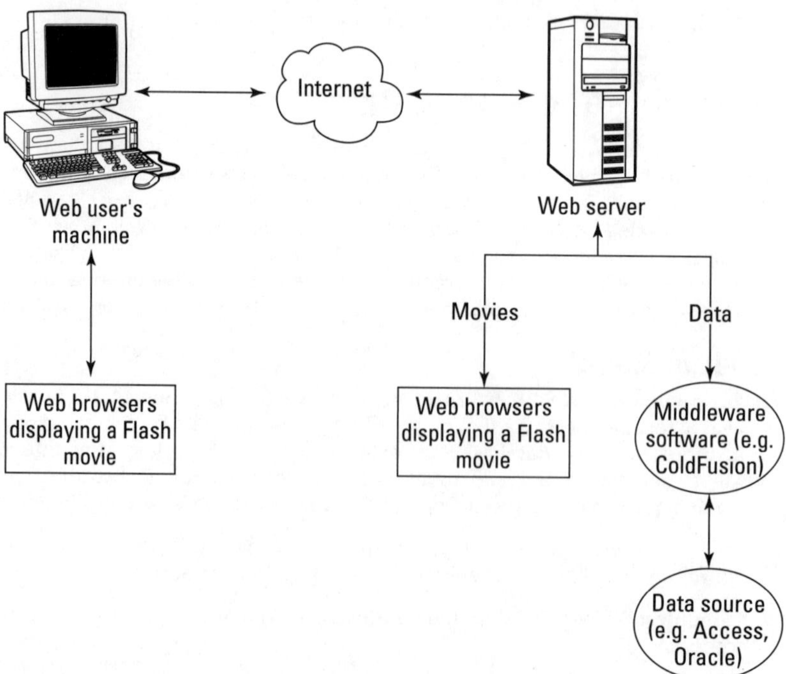

Figure 2-1: A dynamic data workflow

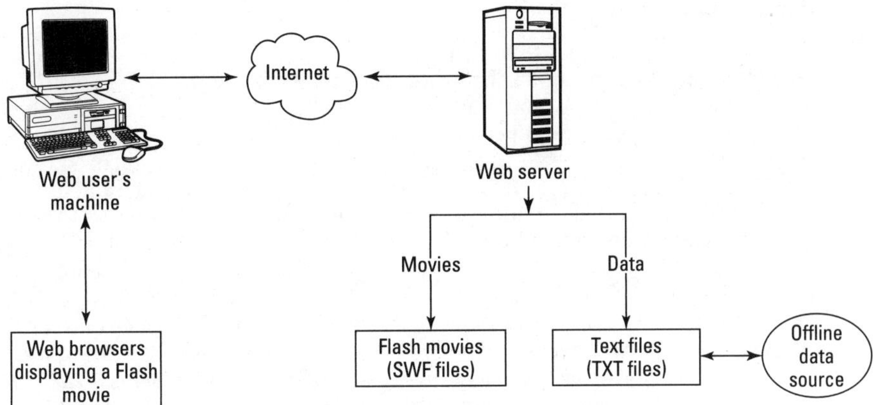

Figure 2-2: A static data workflow with an offline database

✦ **Static data in a nondynamic source:** Create a data file that simply stores the information you need to keep separate from the Flash movie. In the earlier example with the CEO's welcome message, you don't really need a structured database to store such simple information. This solution, as shown in Figure 2-3, requires you to keep your data files on a Web server, just as the previous solution indicated.

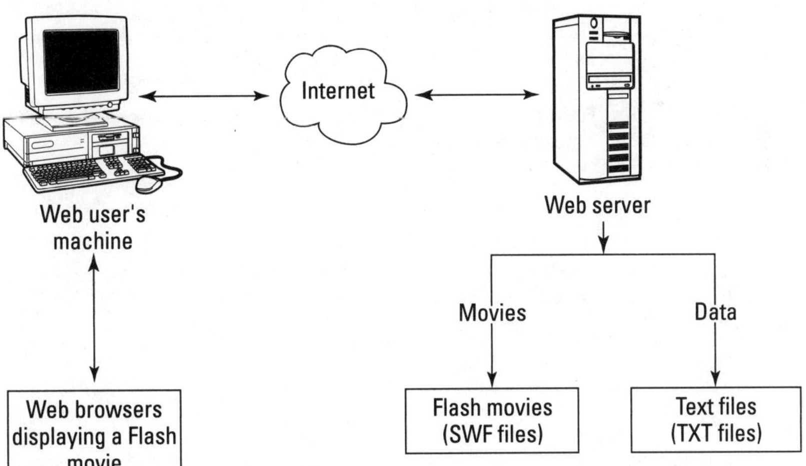

Figure 2-3: A static data workflow with text files

The following material examines a couple of ways you can format external data for use in a Flash movie.

Name/Value Pairs

One of the most basic ways to format external data for Flash use is to apply name/value pair formatting with all names and values URL-encoded. What does all of this mean? Let's start with name/value pairs. Let's say you want to create that CEO's welcome message. She wants it to state, "Welcome to the new millennium." Although we'll discuss this topic more extensively in chapters to come, we dissect this example quickly. In this example, you need to assign a *name* to this data. You can call it `greeting`. (You can name it anything you want, just as long as you consistently call it this name throughout the entire data exchange process.) The *value* of name is "*Welcome to the new millennium.*" or

```
greeting=Welcome to the new millennium.
```

This is the basic structure of a name/value pair, in which the name and value are separated by an equals (=) sign. However, just as you can't use blank spaces in URLs or filenames of documents for the Web, you shouldn't try to use empty spaces in values. This doesn't mean that you have to format the value as `Welcometothenewmillennium`. It simply means that you need to encode the value, including any spaces or special characters, so that it can be properly transmitted and read by the Flash movie. We won't get into the specifics of URL-encoding here, but this is how the value would look encoded:

```
greeting=Welcome%20to%20the%20new%20millennium%2E
```

The value `%20` represents an empty space, and `%2E` represents a period. Although you can perform your own manual encoding for static data (just as you did here), this type of formatting and encoding is usually performed by a middleware server application for true dynamic data that is being supplied by real-time databases. Middleware is software that stands in-between two other pieces of software; in this case, it could be Macromedia ColdFusion fetching data from a Microsoft Access database and sending it to the Flash movie.

We discuss how Flash movies send and receive actual data in several chapters throughout this book, notably those in Part X.

XML

You can also format external data using XML documents. Starting with Flash Player 5, Flash movies can parse (or break apart into separate units) XML data structures. As an example, the greeting name/value pair discussed earlier could also be represented in XML as the following:

```
<site>
     <greeting>Welcome to the new millennium.</greeting>
</site>
```

Looks a lot like HTML, doesn't it? This is by no means a complete XML document, but it's a starting point. Information is grouped by sets of tags, and structure is dictated by the order of the tags. In the previous example, the `<greeting>` tags belong to the parent tags of `<site>`. A set of tags is referred to as a *node*. Using this terminology, the `<greeting>` tag is a child node belonging to its parent node `<site>`. But this XML doesn't really show you the structure of relationships. The following is the rough XML of a list of books:

```
<booklist>
    <book>
        <title>Flash MX 2004 ActionScript Bible</title>
        <author>Robert Reinhardt and Joey Lott</author>
    </book>
    <book>
        <title>Flash MX 2004 Bible</title>
        <author>Robert Reinhardt and Snow Dowd</author>
    </book>
    <book>
        <title>JavaScript Bible</title>
        <author>Danny Goodman</author>
    </book>
</booklist>
```

Can you start to see the structure of this XML document? Here, each book is represented by its own `<book>` node. Within each of these nodes, there are two child nodes: `<title>` and `<author>`. When Flash loads an XML document like this, it recognizes this inherent structure, and orders the data. Of course, you have to know how to manipulate the XML data so that it displays correctly in Flash text fields, or so that you can access the data for other ActionScript calculations such as finding product prices in a shopping cart.

XML is discussed more thoroughly in Chapters 26 and 27. Because the book can't provide an exhaustive resource for XML, try *XML Bible* by Elliotte Rusty Harold (Wiley, 2001) for everything you ever want to know about XML.

SOAP (Web Services)

With Flash Player 6 r79 or higher and Flash MX Pro 2004, a Flash movie can consume data from a Web Service that uses SOAP, or Simple Object Access Protocol. SOAP is fast becoming the standard protocol to transfer data over the Web, especially for B2B (business-to-business) applications. Web Services are usually described in the WSDL format, or Web Services Description Language. SOAP, pronounced *soap*, and WSDL, pronounced "whiz-dull," are based on XML. To see a quick example of a Web Service described in WDSL, type the following address into your Web browser:

```
live.capescience.com/wsdl/GlobalWeather.wsdl
```

In the browser window, you'll see a rather complicated XML-like structure of tags, describing the GlobalWeather service offered by Cape Science.

You can open the Web Services panel in Flash MX Pro 2004 by choosing Window ⇨ Development Panels ⇨ Web Services. Click the Define Web Services button in the panel (the icon of the globe), and add the URL mentioned earlier to the list. The Web Services panel will then make the functions within the service much more readable.

With SOAP, information transferred from the Web Service can retain its data type. For example, if you retrieve a date from a Web Service, the Flash movie will automatically translate the data into a native `Date` object. As discussed in the next section, Flash Remoting offers this advantage as well.

To learn more about how to integrate SOAP data in a Flash movie, read Chapter 36.

AMF (Flash Remoting)

Flash Player 6 or higher movies can exchange data to and from Flash Remoting gateways with AMF data. Of all data formats, AMF is by far the most efficient to use, in just about all aspects of development and production. The AMF data structure uses binary compression, and it automatically serializes and deserializes data. What exactly does this mean? It means that you can script your application server to build a native `Object` (or `struct`) instance, for example, and send it directly to the Flash movie as an object. AMF retains the data type information with each transfer. With XML, you need to reconstruct (or deserialize) the data sent from the server into native Flash data types.

Let's look at a simple example of serialization. Imagine you have a list of product names, and you want to store these items in an array in a Flash movie so that you can build a dynamic menu or catalog. Without Flash Remoting, you would need to come up with a data structure that describes the list.

With URL-encoded name/value pairs, you can create a server-side script that outputs something like:

```
product_1=Coats&product_2=Shoes&product_3=Hats&productCount=3
```

Using a `LoadVars` object in the Flash movie, you can integrate this data:

```
myData.onLoad = function(success){
   if(success){
      var products:Array = new Array();
      for(var i=1; i<=this.productCount; i++){
         products.push(this["product_" + i]);
      }
   }
};
```

That's a lot of work just to get a simple array built in a Flash movie. With XML, the task isn't much simpler. You can create a server-side script that outputs:

```
<list>
   <product name="Coats" />
   <product name="Shoes" />
   <product name="Hats" />
</list>
```

As you might have noticed, with an XML structure, a count variable doesn't need to be established — any XML parser can count the number of nodes described in the document. In a Flash movie, an `XML` object can load this data and create an array:

```
myData.onLoad = function(success){
   if(success){
      var products:Array = new Array();
      var productItems:Array = this.firstChild.childNodes;
      for(var i=0; i < productItems.length; i++){
         products.push(productItems[i].attributes.name);
      }
   }
};
```

Although the XML structure is more easily expanded to incorporate new data, it's still a lot of work just to build a simple array of product names. With Flash Remoting, the server-side script can return the data directly to Flash as an array. Because Flash Remoting's AMF data is binary, you can't use text to show the data as it would be transferred. However, we can show you how simple it is to construct a ColdFusion script that returns the array directly to the Flash movie calling the script:

```
<cfcomponent>
   <cffunction name="getProducts" access="remote" returntype="array" >
      <cfquery name="productQuery" datasource="myDataConnection" >
         SELECT name FROM products
      </cfquery>
      <cfset productList = ArrayNew(1) />
      <cfloop query="productQuery" >
         <cfset temp = ArrayAppend(productList, name) />
      </cfloop>
      <cfreturn productList />
   </cffunction>
<cfcomponent>
```

Although this might seem like a lot of code in the server-side script, you need the same amount of code — if not more — to "write" an XML file for output to the Flash movie. Once the server-side script builds the array, the Flash movie consumes the data as a native `Array` object:

```
myData.onResult = function(arrResult){
   this.products = arrResult;
};
```

In the preceding code, `arrResult` is the data returned by the Flash Remoting call. Flash Remoting greatly reduces the client-side logic that you need to program in the Flash movie.

For all of these examples, we omitted the client-side code that sets up the initial object consuming the data. For now, we just want to distinguish Flash Remoting from other data transfer methods.

If you're still unconvinced, take this point to heart: Flash Remoting transfer packets are one-quarter the size of XML or SOAP packets. This means that it takes much less time for Flash Remoting to be received by a Flash movie.

Flash Remoting MX support is built into ColdFusion MX or higher or JRun 4 or higher. Macromedia also sells Flash Remoting MX software for Microsoft .NET or J2EE application servers.

There are also free Flash Remoting gateways available on `sourceforge.net` for PHP and other open source application servers.

It's not really important which data format a Flash movie uses for external data. What *is* important is knowing what is possible with each of these data formats, and knowing which formats are available as a solution for your specific business client's data. Some middleware applications can serve both types of data formats to Flash movies. Once you determine the data format, you'll know how to structure and format the external data.

Visualizing Multimedia Potential

This final section provides an overview of the types of Flash projects that are possible. This is just a starting point to prime your creative juices and break through any limiting perceptions that you might have garnered about Flash media. The categories devised here are by no means industry standards — they're broad, generalized groups into which most Flash development will fall.

Linear Presentations

Back in the heyday of the Internet revolution, Flash animated cartoons, or "shorts," were all the rage. A linear presentation is any movie that plays from the beginning and continues until it reaches the end. Flash movies in this category simply load into the Flash Player and play. The Web surfer passively sits by and (one hopes) is entertained by the content he or she watches. Linear presentations aren't necessarily just keyframes, tweens, and frame-by-frame animation. Some complex animations utilize ActionScript for randomized content and movement. Dedicated Flash animators believe that we have only seen the beginning of linear Flash presentations and they are proving that there are many exciting options for delivering this content beyond the Web.

Interactive Presentations

One step up from a linear presentation is an interactive presentation. An interactive presentation is any movie that gives the user control of the flow of information or the overall multimedia experience. Most Web sites, either Flash or HTML, fit into this category. If you have fixed content in discrete sections of your Flash movie, you most likely have an interactive presentation. For example, if you have a design portfolio as a Web site with categories of images for your different types of work, the user is allowed to navigate the site to access the content he or she chooses to see. All of the content that the visitor sees is stored within the Flash movie or across several Flash movies.

Data-Driven Presentations

This category of Flash development includes any movies that load external data (either dynamic or static) to drive the content to the user. For example, a weather site that uses Flash might download dynamic Flash graphics of precipitation maps to display to the site's visitors. These graphics can be customized for each user of the site, depending on where he or she lives. *Data-driven* might simply mean that static text information within the Flash movie changes from time to time, without any editing of the original Flash movie itself. Simply put, any time information data is being delivered *through*, rather than *embedded in* the actual Flash movie, it can be considered data-driven.

Data-Driven Applications (or RIAs)

As discussed in Chapter 1, the term Rich Internet Application (RIA) is a classification coined by Macromedia when Flash Remoting, Flash Communication Server, and Flash MX were launched. This category is somewhat loosely defined as those Flash movies that allow the user to accomplish some sort of task or enable a transaction from the Flash movie to an external remote data source. For example, an online Flash ATM (that is, bank machine) could allow a bank customer to log in to the bank's secure server, and transfer funds to another account or pay a bill. All of these tasks would require a transaction from the Flash movie to the bank's server. Another example is an online Flash shopping cart, in which visitors add products to their virtual carts, and check out with their final order. Again, these tasks require that data to be sent from and received by the Flash movie.

We'd like to know what you thought about this chapter. Visit `www.flashsupport.com/feedback` to fill out an online form with your comments.

Summary

- Each new version of Flash has pushed people's expectations of rich interactive Web sites. Web sites that don't evolve with new developments may miss the opportunity to reach a larger potential audience.
- Flash has many unique capabilities that make it a favorable technology for Web development, such as small file sizes, consistent delivery, and precision layout.
- Flash is not necessarily the tool to use for every multimedia project; users are required to download and install a plug-in, and they are not automatically redirected in this circumstance. Flash content is not easily accessible by search engines, or by all available screen-reader technology.
- There are a wide variety of multimedia file formats available on the Web today. Although most users have at least some of the popular plug-ins installed, many users still have restricted bandwidth and computer system environments. Flash has the capability to produce small movie files that can play identically on a range of devices.
- In order to develop advanced Flash projects, one should know the necessary HTML, JavaScript, and data-formatting standards that allow Flash to interact with other environments and data sources.
- Flash movies can be loosely categorized by the type of functionality that they provide to the users. These categories can help you visualize and plan your projects for the benefit of your clients or customers.

✦ ✦ ✦

Architecture for Flash Movies

✦ ✦ ✦ ✦

In This Chapter

Making design documents

Defining a functional spec

Architecting a structure for Flash movies

Organizing your files and folders

✦ ✦ ✦ ✦

As described in the Chapter 2, Flash development can take a number of forms, from linear presentations to data-driven applications. A vital aspect of Flash development concerns the way in which you construct the project files. There's more than one way to organize a Flash experience, and this chapter proposes guidelines that you can use to develop a Flash project of any size.

An Overview of Flash Development

Before you dive into the heart of ActionScript, you'll want to make sure that you have a plan. What do you want to accomplish with your project? How much time do you need to complete it? How will you keep track of your Flash files and other assets, such as images, sounds, and text? This chapter discusses four key areas of Flash project management:

- ✦ Designing the Flash experience
- ✦ Architecting the Flash movies
- ✦ Structuring the data used by the Flash movies
- ✦ Organizing assets for production

Although this chapter was written in a logical progression, feel free to quickly skim over the section headings to get a sense of what this chapter presents. If you already know what a design document is, you might want to skip ahead to "Considering Flash Architecture Solutions" and "Considering Data Architecture Solutions." If you're about to start your first "big" Flash project, we recommend that you read this chapter from start to finish.

Also, this chapter is not meant to be an exhaustive reference for project management and development. More importantly, the tasks associated with project management are relegated to one or more people — these individuals do not usually do any of the actual Flash design or programming work. Therefore, this book provides you with a Flash-centric approach to Web production. We want to make sure you are somewhat familiar with the process, so you know where your work "fits" into the overall scheme of project development. There are several excellent books covering the subject of Web project management in much more detail. Our favorites include the following:

✦ *Interactive Design for New Media and the Web*, by Nicholas V. Iuppa (Focal Press, 2001)

✦ *Software Project Survival Guide*, by Steve McConnell (Microsoft Press, 1997)

✦ *Web Project Management: Delivering Successful Commercial Web Sites*, by Ashley Friedman (Morgan Kaufmann Publishers, 2000)

You can find an up-to-date reference of books we recommend at `www.flashsupport.com/resources`.

Creating a Flash Plan

This section looks at the preliminary requirements for any multimedia project. You learn about the elements of a design document, a functional specification, and flowcharts.

Design Documents

Loosely defined, design documents are a set of ideas, illustrations, concepts, and prototypes that comprise a multimedia project. You can think of design documents as the actual business proposal for your Flash idea. Like any good business proposition or sales pitch, you need to be able to sell your ideas in a convincing manner. The following key questions or points should be answered in the design documents:

✦ Who is the audience for the project (that is, who will use this product or application)?

✦ What does this audience want, need, or desire? Identify the factors that create a need for the product in the marketplace.

✦ How will this product fulfill or serve the audience? What information will the product provide?

✦ What will the product look like? Will there be more than one appearance or interface for the product? Will the product look the same to all users, or will it vary by some other indicator (that is, by geographic location, by language, by age group, customized by the user, and so on)?

✦ What will be required of the audience to be able to use the product? Do they need a powerful computer with a high-speed Internet access or can they use a Flash-enabled smart phone? Do they have to be at a specific location? Can they use it off a CD, offline?

✦ Who will be executing the design and implementation of the product? Why are you and your team best-suited for this task?

✦ What resources will be required to complete the project? Will you need to create original artwork, video, audio, and photography; or will your client make these materials available to you? Will you need to pay a third party for licensing fees in order to use any of the media necessary for the project?

✦ How long will it take to make the product? Will there be several phases required for production? What features will go first and which will be in a given phase? How many prototypes will be created?

✦ How much will it cost to make the product? When will payment be due? Will there be a flat fee for the project? Will the developers receive a royalty or portion of the profits?

As the term indicates, the design and scope of your project should be very clear and also be understood by everyone involved with the project's development. Depending on the goals of your project, the design document can be fewer than three pages long or the size of a book. Although it's beyond the scope of this book, particular attention should be paid to the look and feel of the design document. Establish a strong sense of your design aesthetic and interactive sensibility with the layout, typography, and graphic style of your design documents.

Your client may expect a fully functional prototype or a demo version of the product. In some cases, you may be able to show the client a similar project that you previously created. However, it's usually best to create a mock-up of the actual product. The degree of functionality can vary from project to project, but you will most likely want to showcase all of the primary features. For example, if you want to create a Flash application that can search a company's database and display results of a search, you can create the interface and "fake" the functionality. Obviously, the real data will not be available to display, but you can show the client what the data would look like in the interface. But how do you know how much functionality the project will require? The next section covers the importance of describing in exact detail the actual operability of your project in a functional specification.

Functional Specifications

Although this term might sound a bit complex, the concept behind a functional specification, or functional spec, is quite simple. A functional spec outlines the scope of a project in a step-by-step fashion. The actual design of a functional spec can vary widely, but the following information should be supplied for each screen (or section) of the actual Flash experience:

- What is the name of the project? It's possible to use a code name for the project while it is in development.
- What is the current version of the project? Is this the first version (v1.0), a follow-up, or an update to an existing project?
- What is the name of the section (or screen) in the context of the overall project? For example, is it the first section out of 10 possible sections (or screens)? Is there a name for the section, too (for example, "Home Page")?
- What elements are presented on the screen? Identify every icon, graphic, text block, image, and sound that the user will see or hear. For example, in a search page, you may have a text field with the words "Search for:" to the left of it, and a button with the text "Proceed." Label each element with an ID number, and indicate the format of the asset (for example, Flash button, HTML form, JPEG image, and so on). Also denote which components are supplied with Flash, and which have custom features that will have to be bought or built.
- Why are those elements being used? What is the purpose of the particular interface? Continuing with the previous example, the search field allows users to enter words or phrases that may not be represented in the site's menus.
- Who will be responsible for each element's development? The spec should indicate who can be contacted for further discussion and troubleshooting of specific elements in the design.

Again, this list is meant to be a starting point for your development process. It is well worth the time to thoroughly research the process of creating functional specs outside of the material covered in this book. The functional spec is perhaps the single most important part of the overall design document. Depending on the size of your project, the creation of a comprehensive functional spec could take many weeks. For this reason, many developers include the cost of a functional spec with the price quoted for preproduction on a project.

For an excellent tutorial on design documents and functional specifications, see `www.mojofat.com/tutorial`. This tutorial includes a sample design document as a downloadable PDF file.

Making Flowcharts

Design documents also include flowcharts, visually depicting the structure and experience of the project. Sometimes, flowcharts are created during the process of formulating the initial design document. They can provide an easy form of brainstorming or reworking ideas. There are a variety of flowcharting software applications available, and most of them work with a universal set of symbols, such as rectangles, ovals, and diamonds.

Flowcharts are generally provided in two forms: *organizational* and *process*. An organizational flowchart shows the general structure of the project, grouping material into logical sections (or subsections) of the project. This logical "flow" demonstrates the hierarchy of the material, as shown in Figure 3-1. These flowcharts are also called site maps because they can be used to structure a Web site and to clearly indicate the paths between various areas.

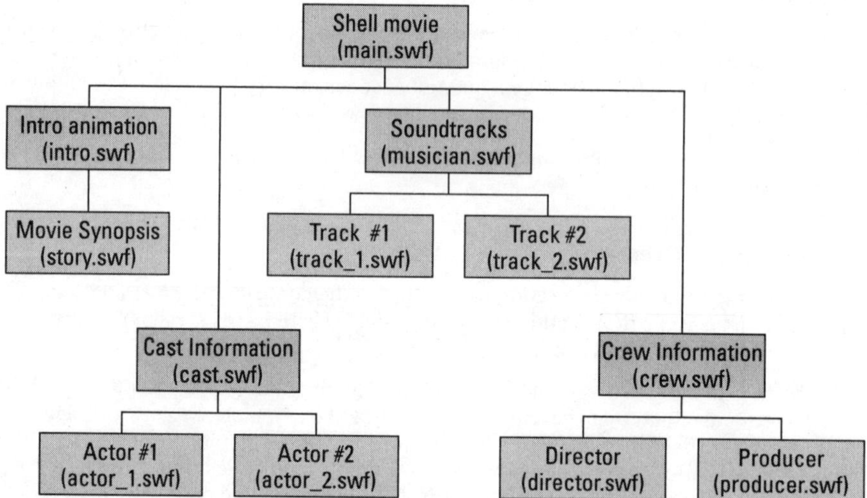

Figure 3-1: A sample organizational flowchart

A process flowchart details the interactive "possibilities" of the project. Using the organizational chart as a starting point, you can map the areas of the project in which the user can choose between various options, and where they are required to follow a linear path. (For example, the user might have to watch a series of screens in order to answer a question in a testing environment.) Figure 3-2 shows a process flowchart for a project that involves user testing.

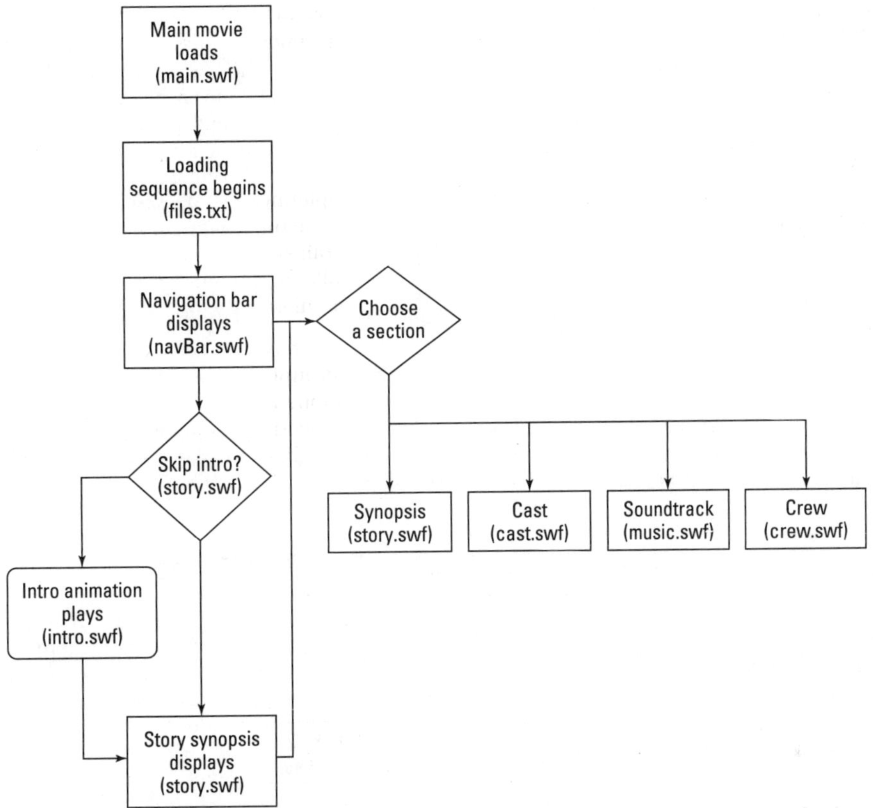

Figure 3-2: A sample process flowchart

Flowcharting applications vary greatly in their capabilities, features, and price. Tools for making charts and diagrams range from popular professional software such as Microsoft Visio to more economical solutions such as SmartDraw. Visio is an intuitive and fully featured program for the charts similar to the ones featured in this chapter; it is also used for floor plans, system diagrams, and so on. The program is designed so it is extremely easy to get started with basic charts right away. The add-ins and automated features are extensive in Visio. There are also charting solutions, which might not contain nearly as many features that are available even as freeware online. Establish what your needs are and the extent of features you require, and research which software solution will be most appropriate.

You can download a trial version of SmartDraw at `www.smartdraw.com`.

Gantt Charts

Most design documents include some type of schedule for the project. The schedule helps you and your production team keep track of what needs to be done within a given timeframe. The schedule also helps your client understand why a given amount of time is needed to complete the project. Each section of the project (as defined by the functional spec and flowcharts) is mapped into the schedule, from start to finish. The most popular format for scheduling charts is the Gantt system, developed by Rodger Gantt. Many popular applications such as Microsoft Project or even Microsoft Excel can be used to create schedules using the Gantt style.

If you've never made a Gantt chart, you can create one on the Web at `www.associate.com/gantt`.

The Gantt system is not only used for scheduling charts; it is a system of notations used to describe functionality in a categorical fashion. You can learn more about this notation in Nicholas Iuppa's book *Designing Interactive Digital Media*, published by Focal Press.

Considering Flash Architecture Solutions

Okay, you finally made it to the section where Flash is actually discussed again. After you have created a complete design document, you'll have a very good idea about where you need to start with your Flash development. The first consideration for Flash project development should be how you intend to create the "shell" for the experience. Will you be using Flash movies for specialty content, such as animations or site introductions? Or will Flash be used as the backbone of the site structure?

Flash as Specialty Content: Multipage HTML

If your Web project is using Flash as just one of many multimedia formats such as Shockwave Director, Apple QuickTime, or Windows Media, you'll probably use HTML pages to form the individual sections (or screens) of the project. In this scenario, you place Flash movies (SWF files) into an HTML layout, probably consisting of tables, layers, or frames. For example, if you produce a series of Flash "shorts" (or animated cartoons), you may have a series of HTML pages, each containing one Flash movie. The navigation for the site isn't necessarily provided in any of the Flash movies — you will likely have an HTML navigation bar created in Macromedia Fireworks and Dreamweaver. An example of this scenario is shown in Figure 3-3.

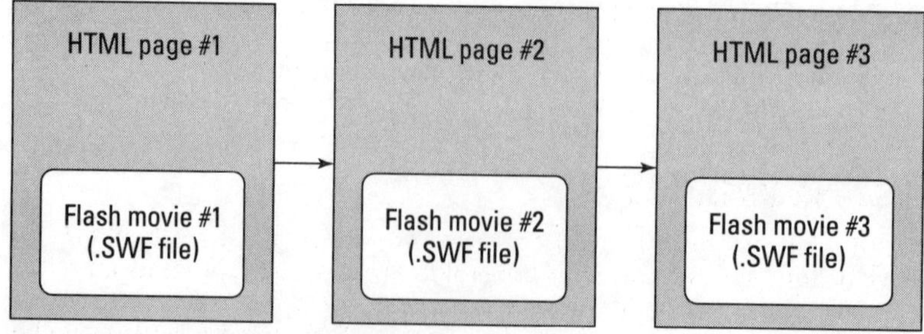

Figure 3-3: Flash movies within an HTML Web site

The primary benefit of restricting Flash technology to specialty content is that you (and your business clients) are free to use existing HTML structures for the project. You don't have to convert everything into a Flash-friendly SWF file in order to use it in the project.

Flash as the Backbone: One-Page HTML

If you plan to develop your project using Flash as the core technology, you are essentially using Flash to do the following:

- ✦ Control the layout of the Web site, instead of relying on HTML layout tags for constructing an interface using tables, layers, and/or framesets.
- ✦ Control the use of fonts, graphics (JPEG, GIF, and PNG files) audio (WAV, AIF, and MP3 files) and video (FLV), instead of using HTML markup.
- ✦ Control the interactive functionality of the site by using ActionScript instead of using HTML (or DHTML) and JavaScript. Note that many "backbone" Flash sites use JavaScript to complement Flash interactivity.
- ✦ Connect to remote data sources to retrieve "raw" data using dynamic server-side scripting languages.

Put simply, if you use Flash to accomplish any of the tasks that were postulated for Flash in the last chapter, you could reasonably be using it as a core technology for your Flash project. When you use Flash as the backbone for a project, everything comes and goes through the Flash Player plug-in. The Web browser is just a tool to display the Flash movies. All images, sounds, and fonts are formatted as SWF files. Figure 3-4 illustrates a site structure using Flash as its core technology.

Loaded Assets

A significant concern for "pure" Flash Web sites existed with older versions of Flash, when all of the material for the Web site had to be formatted as SWF files. Luckily, things have changed since the release of Flash MX and Flash Player 6. Built-in runtime loading features make it possible to bring JPEG images and MP3 audio dynamically into your main Flash interface.

With Flash Player 7, Flash Video (FLV files) can also be loaded at runtime.

Fortunately, if your client has a large number of JPEG files, you do not need convert them into Flash movies or use a server-side solution for graphics conversion.

Pop-up Browser Windows

Many Flash Web sites use additional browser pop-up windows to display content that cannot be used with the Flash Player, such as Apple QuickTime, Windows Media, or RealPlayer content. New browser windows can help augment existing material for a Flash-based Web site. With the help of JavaScript, you can also customize the look and feel of pop-up windows.

Using DHTML with Flash

Of course, not all solutions are black or white. You could have created a solution that's primarily HTML-based, but one specific portion of the project is an entire Flash-based mini-site. You can also use some crafty workarounds to get beyond some of the limitations that were mentioned earlier. You can combine a core Flash Web site with other multimedia technologies such as RealPlayer and QuickTime by layering multimedia content on top of the Flash content.

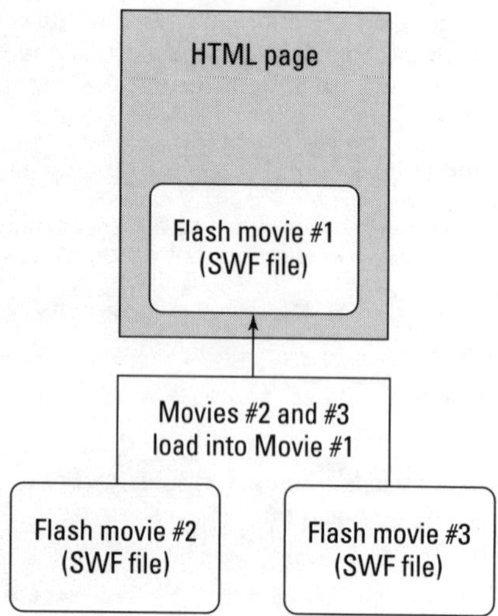

Figure 3-4: Flash movies within a core Flash Web site

Considering Data Architecture Solutions

After you have defined the way (or ways) in which you will integrate Flash into your project, you need to determine how to integrate any external data with your project. The topic of external data was introduced in Chapter 2. Here, the methods you can use to store all data are emphasized, both internally (that is, within the Flash movie, SWF file) and externally (that is, outside of the Flash movie, SWF file).

Internal Data Storage

When you develop a project in Flash, you probably need to store a lot of information within the movie. Following is a short list of common data that you might store in Flash movies:

- **URLs:** You may want to store frequently used URLs as variables, and use these variables in loading actions such as `getURL()`, `loadMovie()`, `loadVariables()`, and the new `LoadVars` object. These URLs can be the domain name, without any specific resource, such as:

```
var serverPath:String = "http://search.mydomain.com";
```

- **Object placement:** The X and Y coordinates of `MovieClip` objects on the stage can be stored in Flash movies. These values can be used to place Movie Clips in specific places at certain points in the Flash movie's playback.
- **File paths and names:** You can store the names of other Flash movie files and their location paths as variables in the Flash movie. For example, you may want to store additional SWF files in a folder named "assets" on your Web server. You can use a variable named `assetPath` to refer to this path. This way, any changes to the actual location can be made directly to the `assetPath` variable.

- **Initialization data:** This is any information that tells your Flash movie how to behave when the movie begins playback, such as setting up navigation bars with default menu choices or telling a tutorial movie to play on a user's very first time to the site.
- **Interactive functionality:** As simple as it sounds, all ActionScript code must be parsed within the SWF file. The Flash Player cannot load or compile ActionScript code from external sources such as text files or server-side scripts.

As you become more familiar with Flash ActionScripting, you will find that other types of data will need to be stored (or calculated) internally.

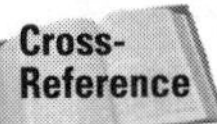

If you don't know what a variable is, don't worry. Variables are discussed at length in Chapter 5.

Since Flash 5, you have the ability to create generic code objects that are appropriately named the `Object` class. Objects are created directly in ActionScript. Objects are most useful for storing data that is descriptive, such as color, sound, and text properties.

To learn more about the `Object` class in ActionScript, read Chapter 7.

External Data Storage

As discussed in the Chapter 2, Flash movies can load data from external sources, as long as the data is formatted correctly. Some types of data that can be stored internally in Flash movies can be stored externally as well.

Data Storage in SWF or Other Asset Files

You can use other SWF files to store data. Using `loadMovie()` actions, you can load this data only when it is required by the user for a particular task. Here, *any* material that is loaded into a Flash movie is considered to be data. Some common uses of SWF files as data containers include the following:

- **Individual media files:** In order to keep file sizes down, you can elect to load graphics and sounds as separate SWF, JPEG, MP3, or FLV files. For example, if you have a soundtrack player, you can dynamically load songs as they are requested. This prevents the user from spending long periods of time waiting for one large download containing all the sounds.
- **Shared libraries:** Since Flash Player 5, the Flash Player can use runtime shared libraries, which are special SWF files that contain reusable elements such as fonts and Movie Clips. You can share one SWF file across several SWF files required for a Flash Web site. Flash MX introduced a distinction between author-time and runtime shared libraries. Author-time libraries allow the elements within libraries to be easily updated and swapped among any Flash document (FLA file) on your network or computer. Runtime shared libraries can be used to store elements that are included in multiple live SWF files. When a change is made to the original, shared symbols among the documents can be automatically or manually updated.

✦ **Preparsed relational data:** The Flash Player is a slow parser, which means that it can't breakdown raw text data very quickly. For this reason, you may want to create separate SWF files with prebuilt arrays, instead of creating arrays on-the-fly from loaded text data. That said, XML is parsed at much faster rates using Flash Player 6 or higher. However, earlier versions of the player are significantly slower in this regard, and workarounds to accommodate this may be necessary.

Don't be confused by this list being under "data storage." These uses fit just as well under the "loaded assets" category for the Flash backbone architecture. You should start thinking more about how items are related to one another in your project, and how you will assign those relationships to different storage formats. In the next section, you'll look at the types of data stored in text files.

The use of shared libraries is discussed in Chapter 34, "Managing and Loading Flash Content."

Data Storage in Text Files

You can use standard text files that are created in ordinary applications such as MS Notepad, WordPad, Word, or BBEdit on the Mac to store data that can be loaded into the Flash Player. As discussed in the last chapter, this data needs to be formatted as URL-encoded name/value pairs or as XML markup. By using text files, you can easily update the information used by a Flash presentation. Instead of having to open the Flash document (FLA file) and re-edit the information, you can simply edit the information in the text file loaded into the SWF file. This also makes it easier for you to hand over maintenance tasks to your client or to another developer who may not be familiar with Flash design and development.

Here is a short list of information that you may want to store in text files:

✦ **URLs:** If you have a long or frequently changing list of URLs that are used in a Flash project, you can maintain the list outside of the Flash movie.

✦ **Filenames:** If you need to load many SWF files into your project, and the names of these SWFs will vary on a regular basis (that is, your client will want to swap different SWF files into the site periodically), you can maintain a list of SWF files in a text file.

✦ **Data for Flash text fields:** Any text that you want to display in Flash text fields (including Flash HTML text fields) can be stored in text files. News articles, product information or pricing, or contact information are examples of such text.

You can actually store ActionScript code in text files with the extension AS. However, this code cannot be loaded directly into the Flash Player—it is included in the SWF file as soon as you publish the Flash movie.

Data Storage in Online Databases

If you need to access evolving information such as stock quotes, account information, and product orders, you need to store your data in an online database. There are several database applications that range in complexity and price, from Oracle to MS Access to FileMaker Pro. Usually, you need to integrate another software application (known as middleware or application servers) to retrieve and format data from the database for use in Flash movies or other Web applications. Examples of languages commonly used to communicate with middleware servers include CFML (ColdFusion Markup Language), ASP (Active Server

Pages), PHP, and Perl. The type of middleware server required depends on the language you are using, and may include ColdFusion Server, IIS (with built-in support for ASP), PHP Application server, and so on.

Organizing Assets for Production

After you have developed your project's design documents and decided on the appropriate architectures for your Flash movies and data, you're ready to dive in to the toughest part: making the Flash movies that will enable your wonderfully powerful Web application. Before you do that, however, make sure you've thought about the simple things, such as how you name your files and organize them on your computer or network.

Naming Conventions

A naming convention is a system of assigning descriptive labels (or names). If you're a designer who uses names such as `Untitled1.fla`, `Untitled2.fla`, `Movie1.fla`, and so on for your Flash movies, this section is just for you. Keep reading!

Naming Flash Movie Files

Using your organizational flowcharts as a guide, get in the habit of naming your Flash movies with names you use throughout the project. Refer to Figure 3-1 for an example of naming Flash movies for a Flash backbone site.

Readers using the Macintosh platform should also be in the habit of keeping the FLA file extension to Flash movie filenames for easier portability to the Windows platform. Now that Flash MX 2004 is available for Mac OS X only, Mac users should automatically see the FLA extension added (unless the default option was changed).

Naming Movie Clip Instances, Labels, and Variables

In all your Flash projects, you need to assign names to elements within the Flash movies. Many developers use prefixes and suffixes to indicate the element type. Develop a distinctive naming convention for each Flash element type. Keywords used in ActionScript should never be used as names for your own items. There are at least eight elements in Flash movies that can be assigned a name (or unique identifier):

✦ Frame labels

✦ Movie Clip instances

✦ Linked Library items

✦ Variables

✦ Function, method, or class names

✦ Property names

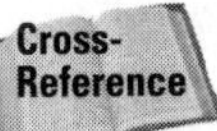

Read Chapter 5, "Constructing ActionScripts," for more information on and recommendations for naming conventions.

File Versions

When you are saving Flash documents (FLA files), you may want to append a version number to the filename. Many developers make a habit of starting all Flash files with a `_100.fla` suffix to signify the first version of the document. If any change is made to the file, the document is saved as a new file with a higher number suffix. For minor changes, simply increase the suffix number by 1, as in `_101`. For major changes, increase the first digit by one, as in `_200`. By saving your files with version numbers, you and the rest of your team know which file has the most recent changes.

If you are working with two or more people in your Flash development, you will most likely want to keep your project files on a networked file server. You don't necessarily need any fancy hardware to run a file server. If you have an older computer that you don't use much because you just upgraded to the next best thing, connect all your computers to a 10/100 Fast Ethernet hub or switch. Keep your project files in a password-protected volume on the older computer.

There are many existing applications that ease the management of versioning and collaboration of your files, such as WebDAV and CVS. The Concurrent Version System (CVS) is a popular open-source program used to keep versioning consistent and under control when many team members are working on the same files. Rather than having a directory full of files with different names for each version, the CVS system enables you to keep a single copy of a file in your local directory, while keeping track of all modifications made to it as well as historical versions in its database. WebDAV (Distributed Authoring and Versioning) is a standard associated with the W3C for remote team collaborative authoring on the Internet, which uses a specialized set of HTTP extensions. Whichever versioning system you decide to adopt, whether it is your own or an established standard, it will undoubtedly be beneficial whether you are working in a team setting or independently.

You can download a free version of CVSNT for Windows servers at `www.cvsnt.org`. You can find other system builds at `www.cvshome.org`. We recommend using WinCVS as a client for CVS servers. You can download WinCVS at `www.wincvs.org`.

File Formats

It's important to discuss how you will import asset files such as graphics and sounds into your Flash movie. Some designers prefer to have Flash do the compression for bitmap images and sound files. Others prefer to precompress bitmaps in Macromedia Fireworks or Adobe Photoshop and retain those compression settings in published Flash movies. Whichever route you choose, be sure to always keep a high-quality uncompressed version of the file available so you will have a source file for use in print, video, or multimedia.

Folder Hierarchies

When you are creating files for your Flash project, you may want to keep your Flash documents (FLA files) and source files for bitmaps and sounds in separate folders from the actual movie (SWF files) and HTML files for the project. In the next section, we offer some suggestions for managing file locations.

Using the Project Panel in Flash MX Pro 2004

In this final section of this chapter, you learn how to use the Project panel in Flash MX Pro 2004 with some sample files provided to you on this book's CD-ROM. You'll jump right into the Project panel, so you may want to review some of the content in the Help panel of Flash MX 2004 before proceeding. The following pages in the Help panel (Help ➪ Help) contain useful information about the Project panel:

✦ Using Flash ➪ Working with Projects overview

✦ Using Flash ➪ Creating and managing projects

You can quickly find these pages in the Help panel by searching with the keyword "project."

Before you start using the Project panel, consider a scenario in which you would *want* to use the feature. The Project panel lets you organize and group all of the files related to a Flash production. You can include any file type you want in the Project panel. All of the asset names and locations are stored in a Flash Project file, which uses a `.flp` file extension. This file is essentially an XML file that describes the files you want to manage.

Once you have a Flash Project file created, you can quickly open any document directly in Flash or another application. You can publish one or more Flash documents in the project. But more importantly, you can use the Project panel to directly upload content to your FTP server or a local network server. The Project panel can check in and check out files so that other members on your team know that you're working on them.

The Project file is linked to a site definition in the Project panel. The site definition is exactly the same site you may have created in Dreamweaver MX 2004. If you have made a site in Dreamweaver, it will automatically be available to Flash MX Pro 2004 as well.

One important factor to keep in mind when you use the Project panel is that you open only a local copy of the project's files on your computer. In this way, everyone working on the project has his/her own copy of the files. One member can be editing, implementing, and testing changes while other members are doing the same with their copies. When a member is done editing a file, she can check the file back into the server.

Unless you're implementing a version control system with your project files, you should *not* edit the same file that another person is using. Currently, Flash MX Pro 2004 ships with support for only Microsoft SourceSafe, a version control product. You can develop your own plug-in, however, for your particular version control product. Version control systems have the ability to merge changes to the same document. For example, if two people edit the same ActionScript document (AS file), the version control system merges the changes into one file and even flags potential conflicts during the process. The Project panel cannot perform this type of merge without the assistance of a separate software product such as SourceSafe. Also, it's important to note that version control software cannot merge changes in two Flash documents (FLA files) because such files are binary, not ASCII (or Unicode). Usually, only text documents can be merged by version control systems.

Let's quickly review the procedure used in the next exercise:

1. Establish a site definition in Flash MX Pro 2004. This definition describes where you'll store your local copy of the project files and where to upload the master copies of the project.
2. Add the files to the Flash Project file in the Project panel of Flash MX Pro 2004.
3. Open, edit, and test one of the sample files.
4. Create a new blank document to add to the project.
5. Publish an entire project.

In order to easily reference each of these procedures in the exercise, look for the procedure number from the previous list in the respective heading of the following sections.

Establishing a Project and a Site

Before you can start making or editing documents in Flash MX 2004 for a project, you need to define a site that the Project panel can use. In this section, you learn how to define a site and establish a local mirror copy of your site's files on your machine.

1. On your computer, choose a location that you can use to store all of the files with a project. For example, if you're on Windows, you can create a folder named Sites at the root of your C drive. If you're on a Mac, you can create a folder named Sites at the root of your startup drive, such as Macintosh HD.
2. Inside of the Sites folder, copy the robertreinhardt.com folder from the ch03/starter_files folder located on this book's CD-ROM. As shown in Figure 3-5, the robertreinhardt.com folder has two subfolders: dev and wwwroot.

   The dev folder, short for *development*, will contain any source files, specifications, planning documents, raw assets (images, video and sound), and so on. The fla folder inside of the dev folder will hold all Flash documents (FLA files) for the project.

You could also make an include folder to store ActionScript files (AS files). Feel free to add as many folders in the dev folder as you need.

The wwwroot folder will contain any and all files that will be part of the final application as a publicly accessible Web site or application. All of the Flash movies (SWF files), runtime assets (JPEGs, MP3s, FLVs, and so on), and HTML documents will be kept here. The copy of wwwroot from the CD-ROM includes several subfolders, to store external assets necessarily for the Flash movie (SWF file) at runtime.

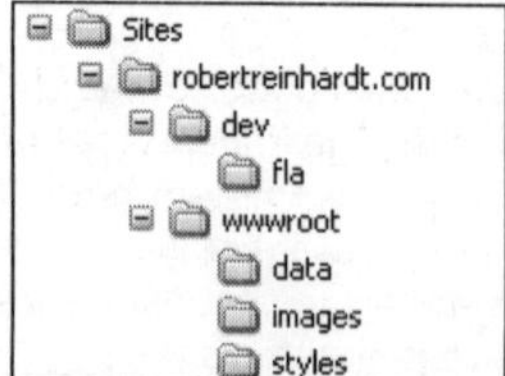

Figure 3-5: The layout of folders for a site named robertreinhardt.com

3. Now you're ready to create a Flash Project file to put into the project folder you created in the last step. Open Flash MX Professional 2004. Choose Window ➪ Project (Shift+F8).

4. Click the Create a New Project link in the Project panel (shown in Figure 3-6).

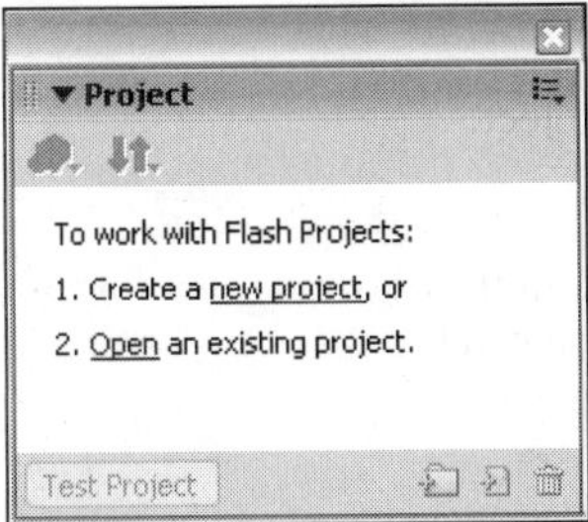

Figure 3-6: The Project panel

5. In the New Project dialog box, browse to the robertreinhardt.com folder on your computer. Save a new project file named `reinhardt_site.flp` in this location, as shown in Figure 3-7.

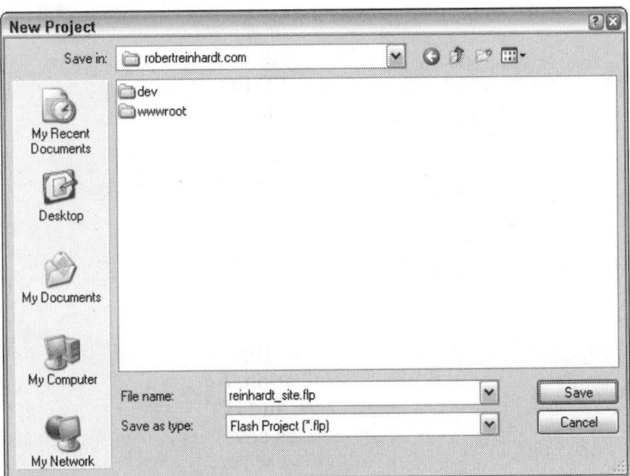

Figure 3-7: The New Project dialog box

6. With a project file created, you're ready to define a site in Flash MX Pro 2004. In the Project panel, click the Version Control button, which features an icon of two arrows pointing in opposite directions. In this menu, choose the Edit Sites option, as shown in Figure 3-8.

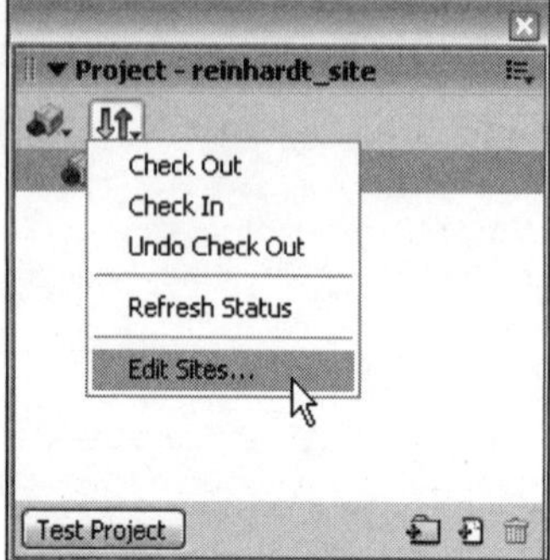

Figure 3-8: The Version Control menu

7. In the Edit Sites dialog box, you may see other sites already defined (as shown in Figure 3-9) if you use Dreamweaver MX or Dreamweaver MX 2004. You can use one of these sites, or create a new site for the project. For this example, create a new site by clicking the New button.

Figure 3-9: The Edit Sites dialog box

8. In the Site Definition dialog box, specify a name for the site such as robertreinhardt.com. Most important, specify the path to the robertreinhardt.com folder in the Local Root field, as shown in Figure 3-10. For the Email and Check Out Name fields, type your own information. In the Connection parameters, you must decide how you will connect to the testing (or live) server that will host the "master" copy of all project documents. You can use a location that's accessible via FTP, the local network, or a SourceSafe database. This location will also store the lock files (LCK files) necessary for members in your team to check in and check out documents. When

you are finished specifying the connection details, you may want to click the Test button to make sure that Flash MX Pro 2004 can connect to the location. Click OK to close the dialog box, and click the Done button in the Edit Sites dialog box.

The Connection parameters shown in Figure 3-10 are for demonstration purposes only. These parameters will not connect to an actual FTP site. If you use an FTP connection, make sure that the FTP Directory field specifies the path to the *parent* folder of your public HTML or Web folder for the site. The public Web folder of your server will vary depending on your server's operating system and Web server software.

It is entirely optional to use the Version Control features of a Flash Project file. If you simply want a way to quickly access all of the documents within a project for yourself, you do not need to create or link a site to your Flash Project file.

9. Now you will link the newly defined site to your `reinhardt_site.flp` project file. Right-click (or Control-click on Mac) the `reinhardt_site` file in the Project panel, and choose Settings. In the Project Settings dialog box, choose robertreinhardt.com in the Site menu. Refer to Figure 3-11. Click OK to close the dialog box.

Figure 3-10: The Site Definition dialog box

Figure 3-11: The Project Settings dialog box

Adding Files to the Project

After you have created a Flash Project file and defined a site for the project, you're ready to start adding files to the project:

1. Begin the process of recreating the folder structure of the local site folders in the `reinhardt_site.flp` project file. In the Project panel, click the Add Folder icon at the lower-right corner of the panel. Name the first folder dev. Repeat this process until you have created all the folder names you had in the robertreinhardt.com folder, including the subfolders. When you are finished, you should have the same folder structure shown in Figure 3-12.

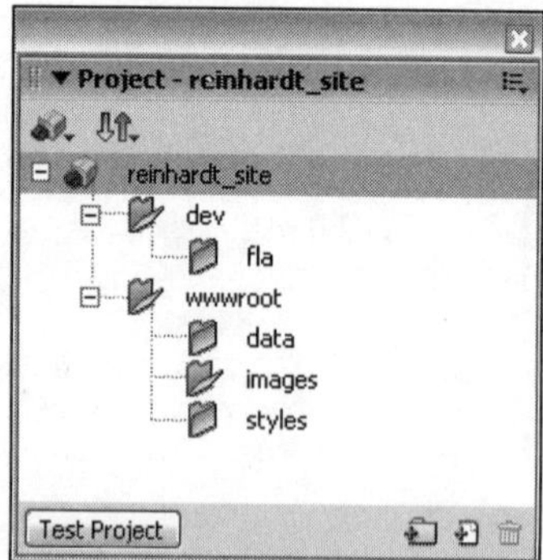

Figure 3-12: The folder structure of the site within the project file

2. Select the fla folder you created in the last step, and click the Add File button in the lower-right corner of the Project panel. Browse to the Sites ➪ robertreinhardt.com ➪ dev ➪ fla folder and select the bio_100.fla file located there. Repeat this process for all of the files contained in the robertreinhardt.com folder. Do not add the reinhardt_site.flp file itself. When you are finished, your Project panel should resemble Figure 3-13.

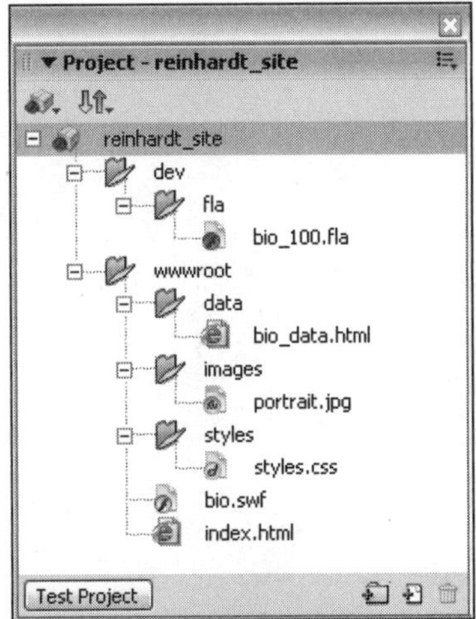

Figure 3-13: The folder and document structure of the site within the project file

3. It is highly likely that you'll have more than one Flash document (FLA file) in a project. As such, you should define the default document for the project. This file should be the master file, the one "most in charge" per se. This could be the Flash document that controls the loading of other runtime assets or the document that contains the most code. In the dev folder of the Project panel, right-click (or Control-click on Mac) the bio_100.fla document and choose Make Default Document in the contextual menu. The icon of the document should change to a downward-pointing green arrow.

Committing and Editing Files in the Project

Once you have added files to your project, you should commit the files to your testing server. In this section, you learn how to commit project files, and how to open and edit documents from the Project panel.

When you are finished creating folders and adding files to your Flash Project file, you should check in the documents to your remote testing server. You can do this procedure only if you have defined a site for the project file.

1. Choose the reinhardt_site file at the top of the Project panel. Right-click (or Control-click on the Mac) the filename, and choose Check In. Flash MX Pro 2004 will then connect to your remote server and check in the file. When the file has been successfully checked in, a lock appears next to the file (see Figure 3-14).

2. Repeat the process in Step 1 for the dev and wwwroot folders in the Project panel. When you check in an entire folder, all of the files within the folder will be checked in. When you are finished, you should see locks next to all of your documents, as shown in Figure 3-14.

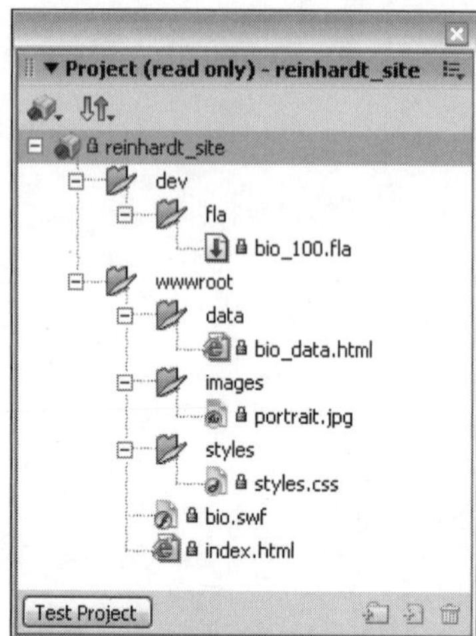

Figure 3-14: A file checked in will display a lock icon.

3. When you're ready to edit a specific file in Flash MX Pro 2004, right-click (or Control-click on Mac) the file in the Project panel and choose Check Out in the contextual menu. Try this step with the `bio_100.fla` document. Once you have checked out this file, double-click the file to edit it in the Flash authoring environment.

When you have checked out a file, you'll see a green check mark next to the file icon. Other members of your team subscribed to the same project will see a lock next to the same file in their Project panels.

4. With the `bio_100.fla` open, let's take a look at how the `bio.swf` file (located in the wwwroot folder) is published. Choose File ⇨ Publish Settings. In the Formats tab, notice that relative paths are declared for the `bio.swf` and `index.html` files (see Figure 3-15) in the Flash and HTML fields, respectively. The ../../wwwroot/ prefix tells Flash MX 2004 to publish these files two folders above the fla folder, inside of the wwwroot folder. Click Cancel to close the dialog box. Leave the `bio_100.fla` file open for the next series of steps in the following section.

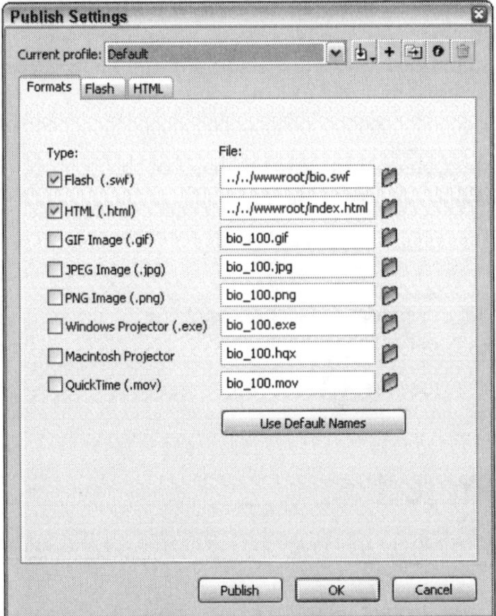

Figure 3-15: You can publish files with relative paths in the Formats tab.

Adding New Files to the Project

In this section, you learn how to create a new ActionScript document (AS file), using code extracted from the `bio_100.fla` document. This ActionScript document will be added to the project file as well.

1. From your desktop, browse to the location of the dev folder (for example, C:\Sites\robertreinhardt.com\dev). At this location, create a new folder named includes. This folder will be used to store ActionScript files.

2. In Flash MX Professional 2004, add the same folder name (includes) as a child of the dev folder in the Project panel.

3. Choose File ➪ New. In the General tab of the New Document dialog box, choose ActionScript File and click OK. When the new document opens, save the empty file as `functions.as` in the includes folder you created in Step 1. Leave the `functions.as` document open.

4. Go back to the `bio_100.fla` document. In the Timeline window, select frame 1 of the actions layer and open the actions panel (F9). Select lines 1–48 and press Ctrl+X or ⌘+X to cut the code from the frame.

5. Switch back to the `functions.as` document, and choose Edit ➪ Paste (Ctrl+V or ⌘+V) to move the code into the document. Save and close the `functions.as` document.

6. Now, add the `functions.as` document to the includes folder of the Project panel. To do this, you'll need to check out the `reinhardt_site` project file. Then, right-click (Control-click on the Mac) the includes folder and choose Add File. Browse to the includes folder on your local drive, and add the `functions.as` file. When you are finished, check in the `functions.as` document and the `reinhardt_site` project file.

7. Go back to the `bio_100.fla` document, and select frame 1 of the actions layer and open the actions panel (F9). Add the following line of code at the top of the Script pane (line 1):

   ```
   #include "../includes/functions.as"
   ```

   This directive tells Flash MX 2004 to insert the contents of the `functions.as` document at the time of publishing or testing.

8. Save and close the `bio_100.fla` document. Leave this document checked out while you proceed to the last section.

Publishing the Entire Project

In this final section, you'll learn how to test an entire project and upload the updated runtime files to your testing server.

1. Before you can publish or test the project, you'll need to unlock the files that will be published by Flash MX 2004: `bio.swf` and `index.html`. Check out these files in the wwwroot folder of the Project panel.

2. Click the Test Project button in the lower-left corner of the Project panel. Flash MX Pro 2004 will publish all of the Flash documents (FLA files) in the project file. In this example, there's only one FLA file, `bio_100.fla`. The newly published `bio.swf` file, located in the wwwroot folder, will then open in the Test Movie environment.

3. If everything is working correctly, check in the `bio.swf`, `index.html`, and `bio_100.fla` documents. If there was an error, double-check the code added in the last section for syntax errors. The Output panel will likely provide clues about any errors associated with improper URLs for runtime assets.

You can find the final site files in the ch03/final_files folder of the book's CD-ROM. If you try to open the `reinhardt_site.flp` document from the CD-ROM (or a copy of it), you'll likely need to relink the documents to the locations of the copies on your system.

We'd like to know what you thought about this chapter. Visit `www.flashsupport.com/feedback` to fill out an online form with your comments.

Summary

✦ A design document contains a business proposal, development schedules, a functional specification, and flowcharts.

✦ A functional spec outlines every step of the user's experience, and provides a detailed account of every element in the interface, screen by screen.

- Flash movies can be used as specialty content within larger HTML-framed Web sites, or they can actually be the backbone or core technology for the site.
- Some data, such as movie configurations or initializations, can be described via ActionScript code, which is stored internally within the Flash movie SWF file. ActionScript cannot be compiled on-the-fly by the Flash Player directly.
- You can store your external data in several formats, ranging from Flash SWF files to simple text files to complex databases.
- You should develop a comprehensive and consistent naming convention for your Flash movies and assets.
- The new Project panel in Flash MX Pro 2004 can help you organize and keep track of all documents associated with your Flash production.

✦ ✦ ✦

P A R T

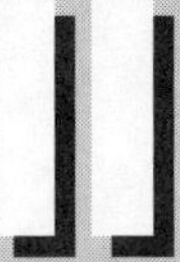

Laying the ActionScript Foundation

✦ ✦ ✦ ✦

In This Part

✦ ✦ ✦ ✦

Learning ActionScript Basics

In This Chapter

Understanding ActionScript as a language and learning what you can do with it

Examining the event-event handler model in Flash and ActionScript

Using the Actions panel to author your code

Customizing the Actions panel

Before you can effectively start working with anything new, you first have to do a few things:

- Gather a general overview of the topic, understanding the scope of what you can hope to accomplish.
- Learn the basic mechanics of the medium. In other words, you want to have a broad understanding of how the pieces fit together to make a whole.
- Familiarize yourself with the tools of the trade, so to speak. You want to be comfortable with the environment within which you are working.

This chapter covers each of these fundamentals so you can begin working with ActionScript. First, you learn about what ActionScript is and what it can do. Then you read about how ActionScript functions at a very high level. And last, you become familiar with the Actions panel, which is the "command center" for ActionScript within Flash.

Introducing ActionScript

ActionScript is the programming language used to send instructions to your Flash movie. It is how you "talk" to your Flash movie, telling it exactly what you want it to do. The more effectively and fluently you are able to communicate in ActionScript, the more effective you will be in creating Flash movies that do what you want.

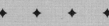

Note This book uses the terms *coding, scripting,* and *programming* interchangeably. Although each is sometimes used in a more specific context, nothing is implied by using one term over the other at any point.

To help you understand what ActionScript is, it is helpful to understand the similarities between ActionScript and something you already know — human languages. Any human language is merely a collection of symbols and sounds to represent ideas. The same is true of any programming or scripting language. ActionScript, for example, is merely a collection of words and symbols with the purpose of communicating instructions to the Flash movie. Additionally, human languages have syntax and vocabulary that are specific to that language, but not wholly dissimilar to those of other languages. You find the same to be true of scripting languages. Not only is ActionScript similar to other scripting languages in many ways, but you may also find that with the right perspective it is quite similar to the English language.

Programming languages are remarkably similar to the languages humans speak to one another in order to communicate. Therefore, although hearing a foreign language might seem like gibberish at first, with a little training, you can begin to share your ideas with people in a language they understand. It is much the same with ActionScript. Think of this book as your language teacher. You'll start in this chapter by understanding the ActionScript culture, the environment, and the tools you can use to begin your ActionScript journey. Then, in Chapter 5 you look at and investigate the parts of speech and the syntax and structure. With these fundamentals under your belt, you'll be well on your way to communicating with Flash.

ActionScript is based on the ECMA-262 specification, although it does not adhere to it fully. If you want to learn more, you can read about it at the ECMA Web site at `www.ecma.ch`.

Learning What You Can Do with ActionScript

Before you dive into the details of ActionScript, let's first briefly discuss what you can do with it. Presumably you already have at least some minimal experience with Flash, and you are familiar with the playback of the timeline. The default behavior in Flash is such that when a SWF is opened in a player, the timeline begins to play automatically. In many cases, this is not, in and of itself, problematic. However, when the playhead reaches the end of the timeline, it loops back to the beginning of the timeline and starts playing it again. Often you want an animation to play only one time and then stop at the end. In order to prevent the Flash movie from looping the playback, you actually have to give it the instruction to stop. You can do this by placing one line of code on the last frame. That one line of code looks like this:

```
stop();
```

With this first command, you can see that ActionScript really can read very much like English. The command (or statement) `stop()` instructs the Flash movie to stop playback. Of course, you can do many more complex things with ActionScript besides a simple stopping of the playback. Using ActionScript, you can load external data into your movie for the purposes of creating dynamic, user-specific customizations or even e-commerce applications. Using ActionScript, you can create nonlinear, interactive presentations and animations. The possibilities with ActionScript are practically limitless, and they allow you to create Flash applications with tremendous potential. In fact, there is very little that you can think up that cannot be accomplished with ActionScript.

Creating Your First ActionScript

All right, so far this all sounds great, right? We've suggested that ActionScript is perhaps not going to be as difficult and baffling as it might seem at first. We've even shown you a sample ActionScript statement that reads pretty much just like plain English. But there's still nothing like a working example to demonstrate a point.

So let's create your first ActionScript. In this example, we introduce a statement that can prove invaluable during Flash development. The `trace()` statement causes Flash to display a message in the Output panel when you are playing the movie in the test player. Although the `trace()` statement is not used during production, it is a great way to perform simple debugging (more complex debugging is covered in Chapter 8) and it is an excellent first statement for learning ActionScript.

When you use the `trace()` statement, you need to tell Flash what message you want to display in the Output panel. To do this, you simply place the quoted message within the opening and closing parentheses. For example:

```
trace("If music be the food of love, play on");
```

Technically, the value between the parentheses of a statement such as `trace()` does not need to be a quoted value, as in the previous example. However, it does need to evaluate to a string. You can find more discussion of this topic in Chapter 5 when variables and datatypes are discussed.

Now that we've looked at the `trace()` statement, you may be wondering where this statement goes so that Flash will do something with it. At this point you have the statement ready to go, but you need to actually "speak" it to Flash to get Flash to do what you want—which is to display the message in the Output panel.

The most fundamental technique for adding ActionScript code to a Flash movie is to use the Actions panel. We'll examine this panel in much more detail later in this chapter (see "Understanding the Actions Panel"). For the purposes of getting up and running with ActionScript in this example, simply complete the following steps. You'll read about the theory in more depth in just a moment.

1. Open a new Flash document.
2. Select the first keyframe of the default layer of the main timeline.
3. Open the Actions panel by choosing Window ➪ Developer Panels ➪ Actions or by pressing F9.
4. The right portion of the Actions panel is the Script pane. Type the following code into the Script pane:

   ```
   trace("If music be the food of love, play on");
   ```

5. Test the movie by choosing Control ➪ Test Movie or by pressing Ctrl+Enter (Windows) or ⌘+Enter (Macintosh).

When you've tested the movie in this way, you should see the Output panel open and display the following:

```
If music be the food of love, play on
```

If the Output panel does not open and display the message, make sure that `trace()` actions have not been omitted. You can do this by choosing File ➪ Publish Settings. In the Publish Settings dialog box, choose the Flash tab, and make sure that Omit trace actions is *not* checked.

Understanding the Event Model: How ActionScript Works

In the simplest form, ActionScript can be viewed as simple commands, called *statements*, given to the Flash player. This is not unlike giving commands to a trained dog. The difference is that (one hopes) Flash responds the same way to the same commands with consistency, whereas Rover might not be so easily persuaded to sit or roll over when he has the idea of chasing the mail carrier.

It is also important to understand the bigger picture within which ActionScript works. One of the most important things to understand in Flash with respect to ActionScript is the concept of events and event handlers.

Events are those things that occur and can trigger another action or actions to happen. An event handler, on the other hand, can catch and process the event. Therefore, an event can occur independently, whether or not an event handler exists. And an event handler can exist independently of the occurrence of an event. However, without an event to trigger the event handler to respond, the event handler merely sits dormant, so to speak. It is much like pushing a button on the outside of a house to ring a bell on the inside. Pushing the button (the event) does nothing as long as there is not a bell (event handler) waiting to ring (action) inside. And the bell inside does not ring until the button is pushed. Here is another analogy to help you better understand this concept. An answering machine sits and waits until someone calls the phone line. The answering machine does nothing but sit there listening until the phone line is called. The answering machine represents the event handler. The call represents the event. And the answering machine recording a message represents the action that occurs when the event handler handles the event.

In Flash, the events can be grouped into several categories. The two most common types of events are what we'll call time-based and user-based. The most common time-based example is that of the playhead entering a new frame. Each time this happens, it is an event. User-based events include mouse and keyboard activity.

The event handlers in Flash are those things equipped to handle specific events. Just like a lock and key, the event handlers accept only the events they are explicitly designed to handle. When you place your desired actions within the context of that event handler, they can execute when that event occurs. For example, if you create code within an event handler that handles mouse clicks, a keystroke entered by the user will never trigger that code. But if the mouse is clicked, the event is handled, and the code is executed.

Assigning Actions

As just discussed, Flash needs all actions to be placed within event handlers. There are two basic types of event handlers — keyframes and event handler methods. When you place ActionScript code on a keyframe, it is executed when the playhead enters the frame. When you place code within an event handler method, the code is executed when the corresponding event occurs. There are many types of event handler methods, as you'll see in the section "Event Handler Methods."

In addition to keyframes and event handler methods, it is also possible to add code to Flash 5–style event handlers directly on `MovieClip` and `Button` instances. However, we do not recommend this practice, as event handler methods allow much more programmatic and runtime control.

Keyframes

If you've worked with Flash at all, you're likely already familiar with keyframes. Keyframes are integral to any type of Flash development, be it simple motion tweens or complex ActionScript-driven applications. Each new layer in a timeline always has a single keyframe on the first frame. You can also insert new keyframes by selecting a frame and choosing Insert ➪ Timeline ➪ Keyframe or by pressing F6. You can recognize a keyframe in a timeline because it is represented by a circle within the frame (see Figure 4-1). When no code has been assigned to the keyframe, and when no content has been placed on the stage for the keyframe, it is represented by an unfilled circle. If you add ActionScript code to the keyframe, an "a" appears above the circle. And if you add content to the stage for a keyframe, the circle is filled.

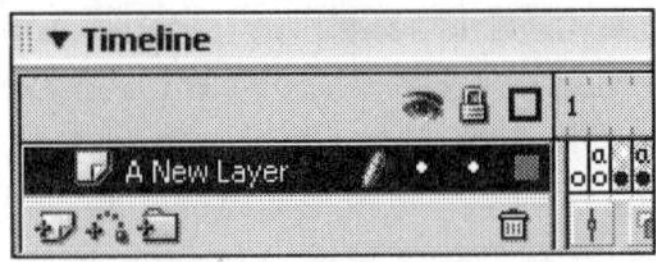

Figure 4-1: A keyframe is indicated by a circle within the frame on the timeline. In this figure there are four keyframes – each showing the different ways a keyframe can be represented depending on the status (code/no code, content/no content).

In order to place code on a keyframe, do the following:

1. Select the keyframe.
2. Open the Actions panel either by choosing Window ➪ Development Panels ➪ Actions or by pressing F9.
3. In the Actions pane (lower-right portion of the Actions panel) type the code (as shown in Figure 4-2).

As a best practice, consider always creating a layer specifically for ActionScript code. Use a consistent name such as Actions for the layer, and keep the layer at the top of the timeline so it is easy to locate.

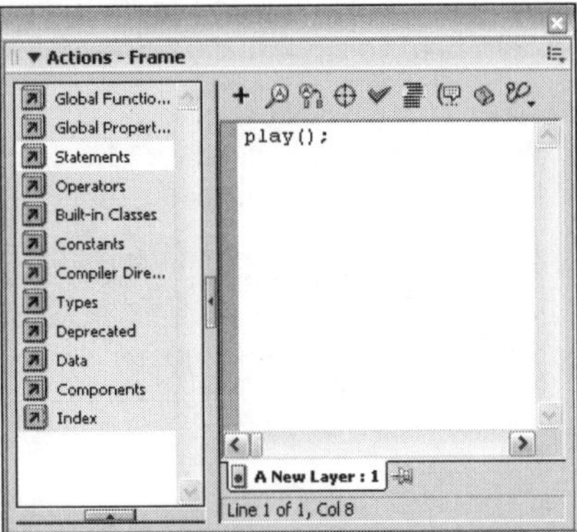

Figure 4-2: Adding code to a keyframe using the Actions panel

Code placed on keyframes will run as soon as the playhead enters the frame during runtime (as the movie is playing). This means that if you place code on a keyframe on the first frame of the main timeline, it will execute as soon as the movie starts playing. On the other hand, if you place code on a keyframe on a later frame such as the hundredth frame of the main timeline, the code on the later keyframe will not execute until the playhead has entered that frame.

All we're trying to do at this point is introduce the basics of where and how to add ActionScript to a Flash movie. If you want more detailed information and examples, you'll find it as you continue reading this chapter and the next.

Event Handler Methods

You can also place your code within an event handler method. Event handler methods are actually quite simple, but a thorough explanation requires slightly more background information than you've yet learned. So, for the time being, we'll cover how to implement basic event handler methods without going into the theory. Don't worry. We will discuss the theory at a later point. When you first start taking a foreign language course, you are generally taught some basic expressions for saying "hello" and "how are you?" without necessarily understanding the theory. You just need to know these basic phrases to get by at first, and you later back them up with a deeper knowledge. Likewise, you should understand how to use event handler methods now, and later you can back them up with a greater understanding.

Event handler methods are always applied to objects such as `Button` and `MovieClip` instances. In order to accomplish this you should complete the following steps:

1. Create an object instance. For example, drag a Movie Clip symbol onto the stage.
2. Make sure the instance has a name. In the case of a `MovieClip` or `Button` instance that you have created on the stage during authoring time, you should select the instance on the stage and enter an instance name via the Property inspector (see Figure 4-3).

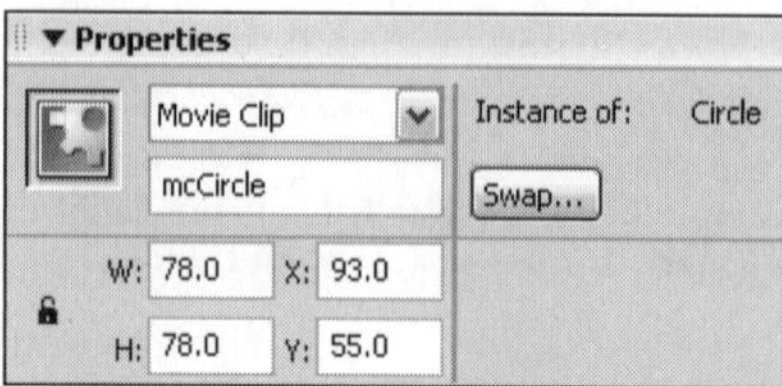

Figure 4-3: Naming a MovieClip instance in the Property inspector

3. If you have not done so already, create a new layer specifically for ActionScript. (We'll refer to this as the Actions layer.)
4. If the object (such as the `MovieClip` object) has been created on a frame other than the first frame, create a keyframe on the Actions layer at the same frame.
5. Select the appropriate keyframe on the Actions layer, and open the Actions panel either by choosing Window ➪ Developer Panels ➪ Actions or by pressing F9.
6. Add the event handler method code to the keyframe. For example:

```
mcCircle.onRelease = function ():Void {
  trace("Alas, poor Yorick! I knew him, Horatio");
};
```

The structure for an event handler method is always the same, although the specific details may change depending on what object, what event, and what actions you are using. The general structure is as follows:

```
objectName.eventHandlerMethodName = function ():Void {
  Actions to occur on event handling go here.
};
```

In the example in Step 6, the object name was `mcCircle`, the event handler method name was `onRelease`, and when the event was handled the code instructed Flash to display a message in the Output panel. The name of the object variable is always the instance name you have assigned to the item on the stage. For example, if you create a button named `btnAnimate`, and you want to assign the same event handler method to it as in the previous example, your code would look like this:

```
btnAnimate.onRelease = function ():Void {
  trace("Alas, poor Yorick! I knew him, Horatio");
};
```

You should choose the event handler method name from the list of predefined method names that are available for the specific type of object. In each of the relevant chapters in this book, you can read about the available event handler methods for a type of object. In the preceding examples we used the name `onRelease` because that is an event handler method that is available for both `Button` and `MovieClip` instances. That event handler method is invoked when the instance is clicked on and then released.

Another key point to understand with event handler methods is that they should be defined within a keyframe. This part might seem a little confusing because earlier we stated that actions should be defined *either* on a keyframe *or* within an event handler method. And now, we're telling you to define the event handler method on a keyframe! This might appear to be a contradiction. In fact, the definition of the event handler method should be defined on a keyframe, but the execution of the code within the event handler method is deferred until the corresponding event takes place. For example, in Step 6 in the preceding example, the `trace()` action does not occur when the playhead enters the keyframe. Instead, the event handler method is defined. Then, at any point after that, if the event (in the example, the event is the click and release of a `MovieClip` object named `mcCircle`) occurs, the `trace()` action is executed.

Understanding the Actions Panel

If you owned the world's most sophisticated and powerful computer, but all you knew how to do was check your e-mail with it, you might feel that the computer was a very limited thing. Similarly, if you are using Flash, but you do not familiarize yourself with all that is available within it, you are limiting your experience and the power that you can wield with it. For this reason, having a thorough understanding of the environment in which you write ActionScript can be extremely important.

Opening the Actions Panel

The Actions panel can be toggled open and closed either through the Flash menus or by keyboard shortcuts. To open and close the Actions panel using the Flash menus, choose Window ➪ Developer Panels ➪ Actions. If the menu item is checked, it means that the panel is already opened, and selecting it will close the panel. Otherwise, if unchecked, selecting the menu option will open the Actions panel. However, it is generally far easier and faster to use the F9 keyboard shortcut to toggle the Actions panel open and closed.

Once the Actions panel has been opened, there are a few things to consider.

✦ The Actions panel defaults to being docked at the bottom of the Flash window, just above the Property inspector. You can undock the Actions panel if you prefer by clicking the panel by the gripper in the upper-left corner (as shown in Figure 4-4) and dragging it so that it displays as being undocked (no dark outline) and releasing it. When clicking the gripper, make sure the cursor changes to the cross-arrows as shown in Figure 4-4. Likewise, if you have undocked the panel, and you want to redock it, you can click on the panel on the gripper in the upper-left corner and drag it over an area of the window until the outline displays as docked. Then release it. Or you can also choose a layout from the Window ➪ Panel Sets menu option. When you do this, however, be aware that the entire panel layout will adjust to the selected panel set.

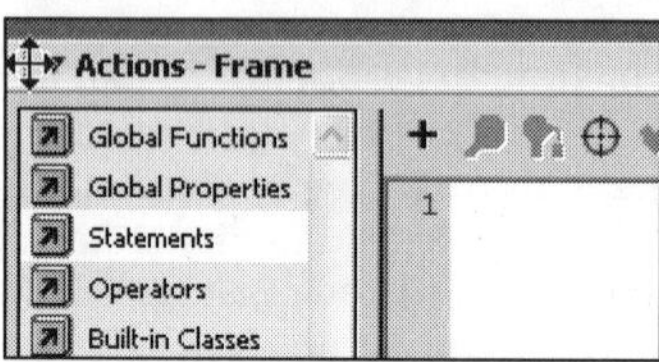

Figure 4-4: Click the gripper on the Actions panel to dock and undock it.

✦ The title of the Actions panel should always read Actions - Frame (see Figure 4-5) before you add any code to it. If it says Actions - Movie Clip or Actions - Button, you should make sure that you have selected the correct frame, not an object instance on the stage. This is a common mistake that people make — beginners and experts alike. If you accidentally place code on a `MovieClip` or `Button` instance instead of a frame, you will get an error when you try to export the movie. The error will read something like this:

```
**Error** Scene=Scene 1, layer=Layer 1, frame=1:Line 1:

Statement must appear within on handler
```

or

```
**Error** Scene=Scene 1, layer=Layer 1, frame=1:Line 1:

Statement must appear within onClipEvent handler
```

We don't promote the use of ActionScript on instances in these ways. So if you get these kinds of messages, it means you have probably accidentally placed the code on an instance rather than on a frame. Simply locate the `MovieClip` or `Button` instance on which the code has been accidentally placed, open the Actions panel, and move the code to the correct frame.

Figure 4-5: The Actions panel displays Actions - Frame when a frame has been selected.

✦ You can use the shader feature of the Actions panel to show and hide the panel while the title bar remains visible. In order to accomplish this, you can click anywhere on the actual title (the Actions - Frame title) in order to toggle the visibility of the panel.

The Actions panel consists of two main parts, as you can see in Figure 4-6. On the left is the Actions toolbox, and on the right is the Script pane. If you have Flash MX Professional 2004, the lower portion of the Actions toolbox contains the Script Navigator. It is intended to allow you to navigate through all the scripts you have added to your movie. If you don't have Flash Professional, you are not lacking any functionality, but rather just the convenience that the Script Navigator may provide. Keep in mind, however, that if you have structured your movie correctly, there should never be a problem locating your code, and the Script Navigator does not offer you too many advantages in that case.

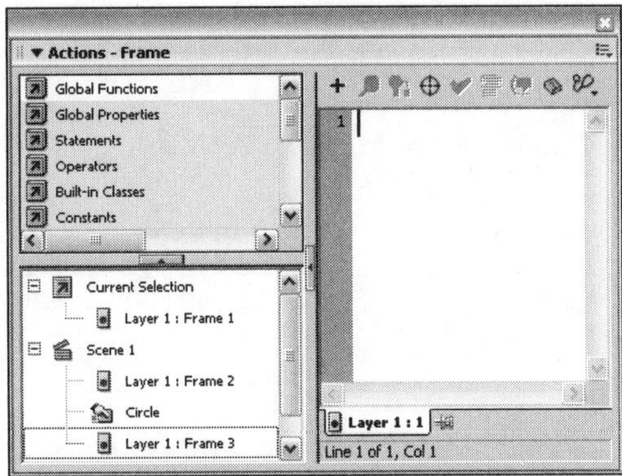

Figure 4-6: The Actions panel: On the left is the Actions toolbox with the Script Navigator, and on the right is the Script pane.

Working with the Actions Toolbox

On the left side of the Actions panel is the Actions toolbox. Within the Actions toolbox, you find all the available ActionScript actions, operators, classes, and so on categorized according to definition and use. You will find that everything is organized into *folders* with names such as Global Functions, Statements, Operators, and so on. Each folder can, in turn, contain subfolders. Clicking a folder expands it to reveal any items and/or subfolders contained within it. For example, if you expand the Global Functions folder, you will see several subfolders revealed within it, and if you expand one of those subfolders, you will see that the subfolder contains items indicated by circular icons, as shown in Figure 4-7.

To learn more about customizing the Actions toolbox, see "Customizing the Actions Panel," later in this chapter.

You can add actions to the Script pane by either double-clicking the item in the Actions toolbox or by dragging it from the Actions toolbox to the Script pane. It is important to understand that the Actions toolbox is a potentially useful feature, but it is not the only way to add actions. If you find that it works well for you, use it. If not, rest assured that it is not a better way than the other methods discussed later in this chapter.

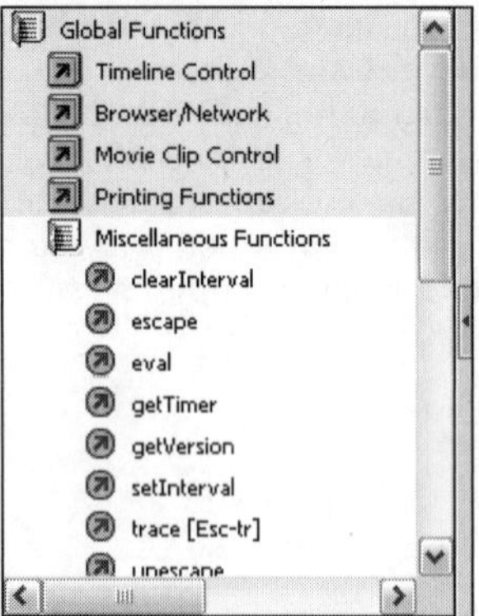

Figure 4-7: Expanding a folder in the Actions toolbox reveals the contents.

The Actions panel pop-up menu (see the heading of the same name in this chapter for details) offers an option to View Esc Shortcut Keys (see Figure 4-8). When this option is toggled to on, the Esc shortcut key combinations appear next to each item in the Actions toolbox where applicable. This useful feature provides a quick reference.

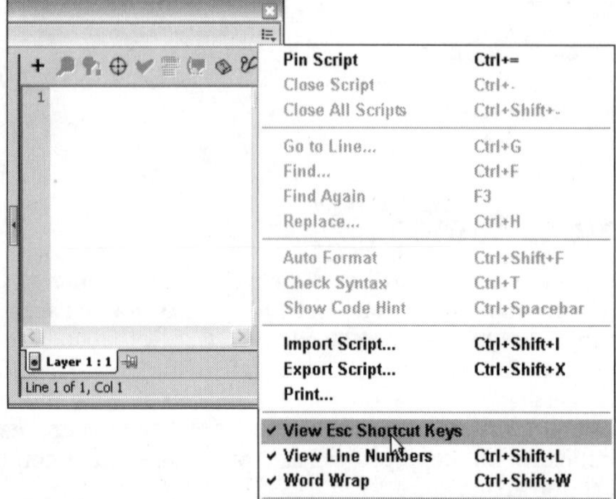

Figure 4-8: Select the View Esc Shortcut Keys option from the Actions panel menu to display the Esc sequences next to items in the Actions toolbox.

Working with the Script Navigator

The Script Navigator is available only in Flash Professional, and it can be found in the lower portion of the Actions toolbox. The Script Navigator (see Figure 4-9) has several top-level items within it. Current Selection is always an option, and when you expand that item, you can choose the current selection, be it a frame or an object. Then there are top-level items for each of the scenes in your movie. If you expand one of the scene items, you can select from all the frames and/or object instances within the scene that currently contain code. And last, if any library symbols contain code internally, and if any instances of those symbols have been placed within your movie, those symbols show up under the top-level item named Symbol Definition(s). When you expand one of those items, you can select from a list of scripts within the symbol.

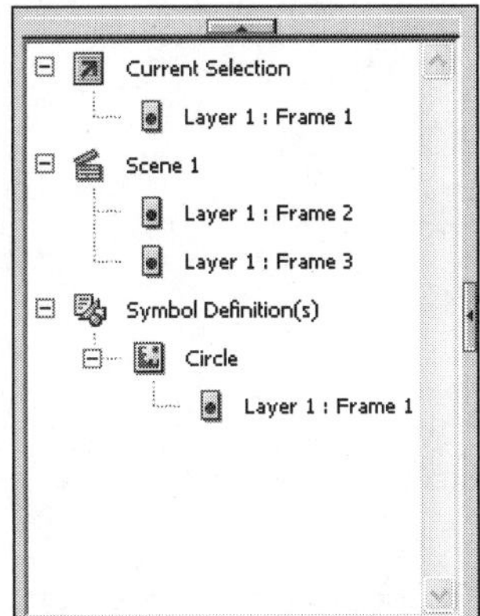

Figure 4-9: The Script Navigator allows you to select from available scripts in your movie.

By selecting a script in the Script Navigator, that script becomes the current script and is displayed in the Script pane.

If you want to adjust the size of the Script Navigator, you can use the mouse, click on the resize bar between the Script Navigator and the rest of the Actions toolbox, and drag the resize bar to where you want it.

Working with the Script Pane

The Script pane is, for most ActionScript developers, the focal point of the Actions panel. It is via the Script pane that you can add ActionScript code to your movies, and hence, it is an indispensable element.

If you used previous versions of Flash, you may notice there is something new to the current version. More accurately, something old has been removed. The Actions panel has only one mode now instead of the normal and expert modes that previously were available. The one mode is essentially what used to be called expert mode, and so for those of you who already used expert mode, this is not much of a change. If you were used to using normal mode, you'll need to learn how to use the Script pane in the new mode.

Figure 4-10 shows the Script pane. At the top of the Script pane is the toolbar that allows you to quickly and easily access some of the functionality built into the Actions panel such as syntax checking and auto-formatting. The main portion of the Script pane consists of a text area in which you can type code. And at the bottom of the Script pane there are a few more options for tabbing and pinning scripts that you'll learn about in just a moment.

Figure 4-10: You can add code to your movies in the Script pane.

In the figure, a `trace()` action has already been added. On your own computer you will notice that before you add any code to the Script pane, the majority of the options on the toolbar are disabled. Once you add some code to the Script pane, the options become available, as shown in the preceding figure. Starting from the left the toolbar options are as follows:

- ✦ **Actions Add Menu:** You can add code to the Script pane not only by typing or by selecting an item from the Actions toolbox; you can choose an item from the Actions Add Menu, and it will appear in the Script pane.
- ✦ **Find:** You can use the Find option to search for text within the current script.
- ✦ **Replace:** Use the Replace option to find instances of particular text, and replace them with some other text.
- ✦ **Insert Target Path:** This option offers you a graphical interface alternative for choosing a target path to a `MovieClip` instance.
- ✦ **Check Syntax:** You can use this option to check the syntax of a script before trying to export the movie. If any errors occur, they will be displayed in the Output panel.
- ✦ **Auto Format:** You can use this option to have Flash format your code for you for optimal readability. See "Working with Formatting" later in this chapter for more details.
- ✦ **Show Code Hint:** This option reveals code hinting for the currently selected code, if available. You can read more about code hinting in the section "Using Code Hinting."
- ✦ **Reference:** Click on this option to open the Help panel.
- ✦ **Debug Options:** Choose from this option's menu items to assist with setting debugging options in your script. See Chapter 8 for more information on debugging.

✦ **View Options:** Choose from the three options in this menu to adjust the view:

  - **View Esc Shortcut Keys:** As previously mentioned, when this option is selected the Esc sequences are displayed next to every applicable item in the Actions toolbox.
  - **View Line Numbers:** When this option is selected, each line in the Script pane is numbered. This makes it easy to communicate with other developers and it also assists in tracking errors when you know what line is problematic.
  - **Word Wrap:** Flash automatically wraps the view of lines in the Script pane if they extend beyond the visible area. This does not place actual line breaks in the code. It affects only the view of the code.

Managing Scripts

When you are creating simple Flash applications, you may have only a single script within the entire document. In such cases, you don't have to concern yourself with how you are going to keep multiple scripts at hand. However, when you start adding scripts to multiple frames, within symbols, and so forth, it can quickly become a hassle to switch back and forth between more than one script. Fortunately, the current version of Flash improves upon the pinning functionality and includes tabbing on the Script pane so that you can have more than one script open at the same time. This functionality allows you to open a script, pin it so that it remains open, and then open an additional script. You can then tab between the two scripts without having to continually open and reopen the same scripts as in previous versions of Flash.

In order to open and pin several scripts, do the following:

1. Open a script in the Script pane. For example, open the script on the first frame of the main timeline by selecting that frame. Figure 4-11 shows how the tab at the bottom of the Script pane will indicate that the script has been opened.

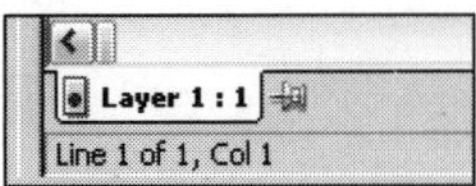

Figure 4-11: The Script pane tab indicating that the open script is from layer 1, frame 1

2. Next, click the pin button next to the tab. This toggles the state of the button and pins the current script. It then opens a second tab to the left of the first. Figure 4-12 shows this. The new tab will open to the pinned script.

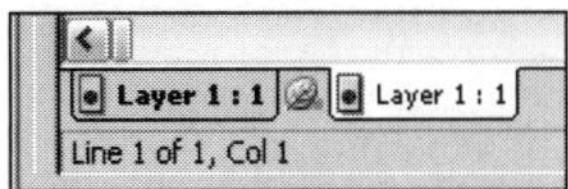

Figure 4-12: Once you have pinned a script, the second tab appears.

3. Now you can select a second script. The second script appears in the original tab while the pinned script remains opened in the new tab. Figure 4-13 shows an example in which a script from frame 2 has been opened in addition to the pinned script.

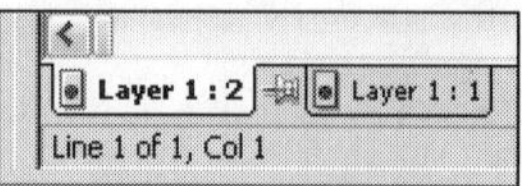

Figure 4-13: The pinned script from frame 1 is opened at the same time as the unpinned script from frame 2.

4. You can pin more than a single script if you want. If we continued this example, we could also pin the script from frame 2 and then open a script from frame 3 as shown in Figure 4-14.

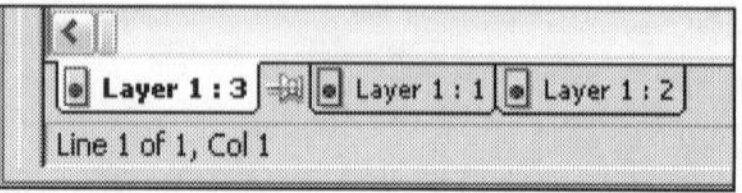

Figure 4-14: You can pin more than one script at a time.

You can also use the keyboard shortcuts to quickly pin and unpin scripts. In order to pin the current script, press Ctrl+= or ⌘+=. To unpin the current script, press Ctrl+- or ⌘+-. You can also unpin all pinned scripts either by selecting the Close All Scripts option from the Actions panel menu or by pressing Ctrl+Shift+- or ⌘+Shift+-.

Setting Actions Panel Preferences

The Actions panel has its own set of preferences that you can adjust to your liking. You can access the preferences either from the Actions panel pop-up menu (the Preferences menu item) or by opening the Preferences dialog box (Edit ➪ Preferences) and selecting the ActionScript preferences tab. Figure 4-15 shows the ActionScript preferences.

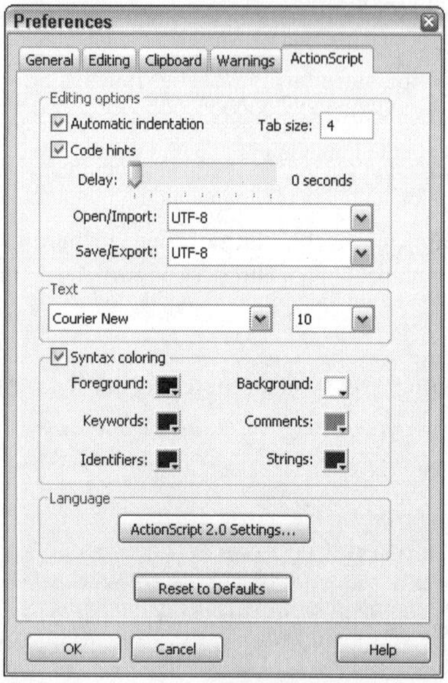

Figure 4-15: The ActionScript Preferences tab

As you can see from the picture, the ActionScript preferences are categorized into four groups: Editing Options, Text, Syntax Coloring, and Language. Let's take a closer look at each of these sections.

Editing Options

Flash is capable of automatically detecting and placing indentation in your code as you write it. For instance, after you type the following and press Enter, Flash can automatically indent the next line:

```
if(true){
```

Then, when you type the next closing brace (}), Flash automatically unindents that line. In the ActionScript Editor preferences, you can turn off Automatic Indentation by unchecking the box, or you can adjust the amount that it indents (Tab size). By default, the Tab size is set to 4, meaning the tab value is equal to the width of four spaces.

Code hinting is on by default. You can turn it off by unchecking the box, and you can adjust the rate at which the code hints appear. By default, code hints appear immediately. You can use the slider to change the number of seconds before code hints appear. For more information regarding code hinting in general, see the section "Using Code Hinting."

Additionally, you can select the format that Flash uses to open/import or save/export a file.

Text

You can adjust the font and font size used in the Script pane by changing the preferences in the Text section of the ActionScript Editor preferences.

Syntax Coloring

The Actions panel has a syntax-highlighting feature that you can modify in the ActionScript Editor preferences. After unchecking the Syntax Coloring box, all text appears in black on white within the Script pane. Leaving the box checked, however, color-codes your script. Six types of syntax are distinguished for the purposes of color coding:

- ✦ Foreground is anything that doesn't fall into any other category.
- ✦ Background
- ✦ Keywords include all the items grouped within the Statements folder in the Actions toolbox as well as items grouped in Compiler Directives.
- ✦ Comments
- ✦ Identifiers include predefined class names, constants, predefined functions, properties, and methods.
- ✦ Strings include all quoted strings.

You can modify the colors used to suit your own preferences.

Language

The Language portion of the ActionScript preferences allows you to adjust the ActionScript 2.0 settings. We discuss this in greater detail in upcoming chapters.

Working with Formatting

ActionScript gives you flexibility in how you format your code. With a few exceptions, you can use spaces, carriage returns, and indentation as you please without affecting the way in which the code works. There are many styles for writing code that programmers choose to adopt. But whatever style they choose, chances are good that each programmer will remain fairly consistent with his or her own style. Doing so ensures that the code remains more readable.

For several reasons, you may find that your code is not consistently formatted. For example, you might be drawing together snippets of code from various sources, or you simply might not have applied consistent formatting along the way. For this reason, Flash offers you an auto-formatting feature that you can access either from the Actions panel toolbar or from the Actions panel pop-up menu. Auto Format follows a set of rules that you can adjust, and formats the selected code uniformly.

The rules that the Auto Format feature follows are set in the Auto Format Options dialog box, which can be opened from the Actions panel pop-up. In the dialog box (shown in Figure 4-16), you have five check boxes from which you can alter the formatting style. Below those options is a preview. If you check and uncheck the boxes, you can see how the formatting style changes.

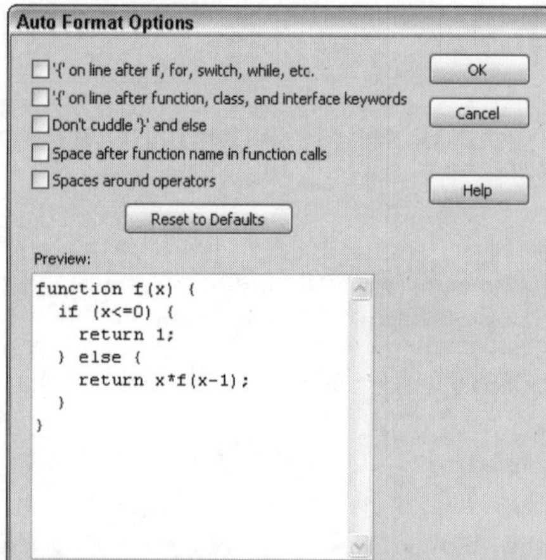

Figure 4-16: The Auto Format Options dialog box

Using Code Hinting

Code hinting was introduced in Flash MX, and in the latest version there are some slight enhancements. Using code hints, Flash can give you a hint for syntax of certain code structures as well as methods and properties for objects. When you type certain code elements in the Script pane, Flash automatically recognizes them and pops up a hint. The addition of strong typing to ActionScript (see Chapter 5 for more details) has enabled even greater flexibility in code hinting.

There are two types of code hints. Tooltip code hints (see Figure 4-17) appear as pale yellow pop-ups, showing the correct syntax for a recognized statement or code snippet. Menu code hints (see Figure 4-18) appear as drop-down menus from which you can choose the appropriate selection.

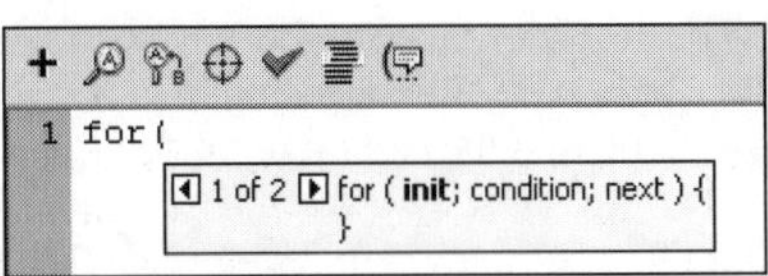

Figure 4-17: A tooltip code hint

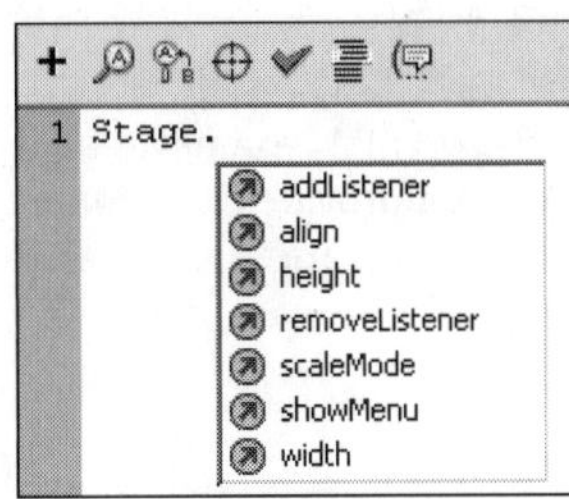

Figure 4-18: A menu code hint

There are two ways to get code hints to display. By default, code hints are invoked automatically as soon as any recognized snippet, object, or variable is entered into the Script pane. However, you can also invoke a code hint manually by one of three methods:

✦ Pressing the code hint button on the Actions panel toolbar

✦ Choosing Show Code Hint from the Actions panel pop-up menu

✦ Pressing Ctrl+Spacebar (Windows) or ⌘+Spacebar (Mac)

When you are invoking code hints manually, the cursor must be located after the opening parenthesis and before the closing parenthesis. Or, if it is an object/variable, the cursor must be after the dot operator (`.`) and before the semicolon (`;`).

You can adjust the speed at which code hints are invoked (from 0 to 4 seconds) or even turn off automatic code hinting altogether in the ActionScript preferences. (See the section "Setting Actions Panel Preferences" for more information.)

Obviously, in order for Flash to be able to open the correct code hints, it needs to recognize the type of code that is being entered. When you enter code snippets such as the following:

```
for (
```

Flash is able to recognize that code snippet because a `for` statement always starts the same way. So as soon as you type in that code, Flash will be able to recognize it for code hinting. Additionally, there are some other keywords that happen to be the names of what we called top-level objects or classes such as `Math` or `Stage` that are capable of invoking code hints because `Math` and `Stage` both happen to be classes that don't need to be instantiated (more on this in Chapter 7). However, when you want Flash to provide code hinting for variables and instantiated objects, you need to provide Flash some assistance in determining what code hints to offer.

See Chapter 5 for more information on variables and Chapter 7 for more information on objects.

To see the problem, let's first examine the following code. Even though you have not yet read about variables (variables are discussed in depth in Chapter 5) the following line of code should not be too perplexing. It's simply assigning a value to a variable named `firstName`.

```
firstName = "Joey";
```

Then, once the variable has been defined, if you try, on another line, to invoke code hinting for the code, you will not get any hints, as you can see in Figure 4-19.

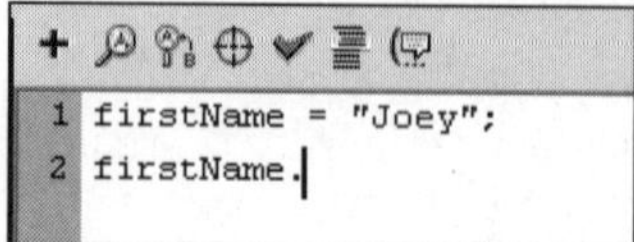

Figure 4-19: Flash doesn't know what type of variable firstName is, and therefore cannot provide any code hints.

You do not get any code hints, because Flash does not recognize the data type of the variable `firstName`. There are several options for how to you can provide this information to Flash.

✦ **Use strong typing.** Strong typing is a new feature introduced in Flash MX 2004, and it is the preferred way to tell Flash what type of code hinting to provide. When you use strong typing, you can declare a variable (more on variables in Chapter 5) to be of a particular type such as String, Date, MovieClip, and so on. Then, when you type the variable name later in the code, Flash already knows the type of the variable, and it is able to provide the proper code hinting. Not only does strong typing provide the means by which Flash can offer code hinting, but it also provides additional benefits such as compile-time error checking. We'll take a closer look at strong typing in Chapter 5, but for now, here is an example of how to declare a strongly typed variable:

```
var firstName:String = "Joey";
```

The `var` keyword tells Flash that you are declaring a variable. The name of the variable is followed by a colon and then the type of data the variable will represent — in this case it will be string data. The rest of the statement looks the same as before.

✦ **Use a code hint suffix in the variable name.** For example, `firstName_str` uses the `_str` suffix, which Flash will recognize as indicating a string variable. This is a technique that was introduced in Flash MX prior to strong typing.

✦ **Declare the data type in a specially formatted comment.** For example:

```
// String firstName;
```

You need to use one of the preceding techniques only if you want to tell Flash which type of code hinting to provide you for each variable. As already mentioned, the strong typing technique is the preferred approach, as it offers additional benefits that you'll read about in Chapter 5.

Using the Help Panel

The Help panel is the primary point of access to Flash and ActionScript reference material and documentation within Flash MX 2004. The Help panel replaces the Reference panel from Flash MX.

You can locate Help documents that concern ActionScript in various ways:

✦ Open the Help panel, choose the Table of Contents option from the Help panel toolbar, and navigate to the document(s) via the contents of the folders that appear in the left pane.

✦ Open the Help panel, choose the Search option from the Help panel toolbar, search for a keyword, and select from the search results.

✦ Open the Help document for a particular item in the Actions toolbox. You can right-click/⌘-click an item in the Actions toolbox and choose the View Help option from the context menu. The Help panel will open and display the relevant Help document.

✦ Open the Help document for a snippet of code in the Script pane. You can right-click/⌘-click a snippet of code in the Script pane and choose the View Help option from the context menu. Flash will open the Help panel, and if it is able to locate documentation on the snippet, it displays that information.

You can also update the Help panel's contents. If you have an Internet connection, you can click the Download Help Contents button in the Help panel toolbar (it is labeled Update).

Customizing the Actions Panel

At this point, you should be familiar with the Actions panel and the general Flash environment you'll be using to create ActionScript code in Flash movies. You will likely find that many of the default settings for the Actions panel provide you with a more than adequate working environment. Therefore, what we are about to discuss is completely optional. However, you may be interested in knowing that you can actually modify the contents of the Actions toolbox as well as some of the words that Flash will recognize for color coding.

In Chapter 7 we discuss how you can use a special `CustomActions` class to programmatically add and remove certain elements from the Actions toolbox. When you want to simply add or remove custom actions, we recommend you use the `CustomActions` technique. However, there are certain things that the `CustomActions` class cannot do. In order to understand this, let's take a look at how Flash configures the Actions panel, including color coding and the contents of the Actions toolbox.

Flash uses several XML documents in order to configure the Actions panel each time Flash is opened. You can find XML documents discussed in this section in the following location:

✦ **Windows 98 and ME:** C:\[Windows Directory]\Application Data\Macromedia\Flash MX\Configuration\ActionsPanel

✦ **Windows NT:** C:\[Windows directory]\profiles*user name*\Application Data\Macromedia\Flash MX\Configuration\ActionsPanel

✦ **Windows 2000 and XP:** C:\Documents and Settings*user name*\Application Data\Macromedia\Flash MX\Configuration\ActionsPanel

✦ **Mac OS Classic (Mac OS 8.*x* and above) Single-User:** Hard Disk:System Folder:Application Support:Macromedia:Flash MX:Configuration:ActionsPanel

✦ **Mac OS Classic (Mac OS 8.*x* and above) Multi-User:** Hard Disk:Users:*user name:*Documents:Macromedia:Flash MX:Configuration:ActionsPanel

✦ **Mac OS X:** Hard Disk/Users/*user name*/Library/Application Support/Macromedia/Flash MX/Configuration/ActionsPanel

Continued

Continued

In the main directory are three XML documents—`ActionsPanel.xml`, `AsColorSyntax.xml`, and `AsCodeHints.xml`. The `ActionsPanel.xml` document contains the data that Flash uses to populate the Actions toolbox. `AsColorSyntax.xml` contains with regards to which keywords Flash recognizes for color coding, and the `AsCodeHints.xml` document contains data that Flash uses to recognize naming patterns for the purposes of code hinting. In addition, you'll see that there is a `CustomActions` directory that likely contains some additional XML documents. Any data added via the `CustomActions` class is placed into an XML document in the `CustomActions` directory. And all the content from those XML documents is appended to the content from the `ActionsPanel.xml` document in memory when Flash is opened. The result is that you don't necessarily have much control over how the data from the CustomActions documents will be ordered within the Actions toolbox. You may find it preferable to make edits to the `ActionsPanel.xml` file directly because you'll have more control over the order in which folders and items appear in the Actions Toolbox.

The next several sections discuss these XML documents, and how you can work with them. If you are unfamiliar with XML, you may still find that you are able to follow along. If, however, you feel you would benefit from a basic XML primer, consult Chapter 26.

ActionsPanel.xml

The `ActionsPanel.xml` file deals with the Actions toolbox configuration rather than the configuration of the entire Actions panel, as the name might suggest. Opening the file in a text editor reveals an XML file that is quite long. At first glance, it may appear overwhelming and confusing. However, when you look more closely, you will see that it follows a very basic pattern that you will be able to follow with just a little practice.

The following table provides you with a quick reference for all the tags and their attributes that are available for use in the `ActionsPanel.xml` file.

Tag	*Attribute*	*Description*
`<actionspanel>`		This tag is required as the root element. This means that it encapsulates the rest of the elements of the XML document.
`<folder>`		This tag is used to create folders within the Actions toolbox.
	`name`	The name of the folder as it should appear in the Actions toolbox.
	`sort`	Indicates whether the contents of the folder should appear in the order in which they are listed in the XML document (false) or should be sorted alphabetically (true). If the attribute is not defined, the contents are listed alphabetically.
	`tiptext`	The value displayed in the tooltip that appears when the item is moused over in the Actions toolbox.
	`helpid`	The ID that corresponds to the reference information for that item.
`<action>`		This tag creates an action item in the Actions toolbox. Although it does not have to be, it is most often nested within a folder tag.
	`name`	The name as it should appear in the Actions toolbox.

Tag	*Attribute*	*Description*
tiptext		The value that is displayed in the tooltip that appears when the item is moused over in the Actions toolbox.
	helpid	The ID that corresponds to the reference information for that item.
	quickey	The escape keyboard sequence for the action. For instance, the sequence esc+sa would be indicated by assigning the value of sa to the `quickey` attribute.

	text (text2, text3, and so on)	The tooltip code hint text that appears in the Script pane, as well as the code that appears in the Script pane when the item is double-clicked in the Actions toolbox or the escape keyboard sequence is typed. The first such attribute is named text. Subsequent attributes are named text2, text3, and so on. In the event of multiple text attributes, the tooltip code hint shows one at a time, with arrow buttons that allow the user to scroll through them. If the action is one that takes parameters, the percentage sign (%) can be placed around the parameters. This instructs Flash to place the cursor in this spot when the escape keyboard sequence is used. The percentage signs do not show up in the tooltip code hints. For example, the following:
		`<action name="someAction" tiptext="a tip" helpid="1" text="someAction(% param1, param2 %);\n" quickey="sa" />`
		results in the following displaying in the Script pane:
		`someAction();`
		but the code hint shows up as follows:
		`someAction( param1, param2 );`

	version	The version of the Flash player with which this action is recognized. A value of 5 indicates that the action is recognized by the Flash 5, 6, and 7 Players, whereas a value of 7 indicates that the action is recognized by the 7 Player only.
<string>		This tag creates an item in the Actions toolbox much as the `<action>` tag does. The difference is that the string tag supports two additional attributes and is used for methods, properties, events, and listeners instead of actions.
	name	The name as it should appear in the Actions toolbox.
	tiptext	The value that displays in the tooltip that appears when the item is moused over in the Actions toolbox.
	helpid	The ID that corresponds to the reference information for that item.
	quickey	See description of `<action>`'s `quickey` attribute.

Continued

Continued

Tag	*Attribute*	*Description*
	`text` (`text2`, `text3`, and so on)	See description of `<action>`'s `text` attribute.
	`version`	See description of `<action>`'s `version` attribute.
	`type`	Can have one of three possible values: `procedure`, `event`, or `listener`.
	`object`	Signifies which object this is – a property, method, event, or listener of. The item is then added to the menu code hint for that object.

Although the `ActionsPanel.xml` file determines most of the contents of the Actions toolbox, some additional XML files in the `CustomActions` subdirectory append content to the Actions toolbox. You learn more about these files in Chapter 7. Also, Flash always creates an Index folder in the Actions toolbox. The Index folder is an alphabetized list of all the code elements in the Actions toolbox.

Writing the ActionsPanel.xml Document

In this exercise, you will create a new `ActionsPanel.xml` document for Flash to use. You will make changes to the existing document. At the end of the exercise you will delete the XML document, and Flash should automatically restore the default document. That said, however, you may want to make a backup of the original "just in case." Even though things *should* work a particular way doesn't mean they always do.

1. Make sure Flash is closed.
2. Open the `ActionsPanel.xml` document from the location specified earlier in this chapter.
3. Select all the text in the file and delete it.
4. Insert the following into the document, and save the document:

```
<?xml version="1.0"?>
<actionspanel>
</actionspanel>
```

5. Open Flash, and open the Actions panel. You should see the following folders in the Actions toolbox: Data, Components (both generated by XML documents in `CustomActions`), and Index.

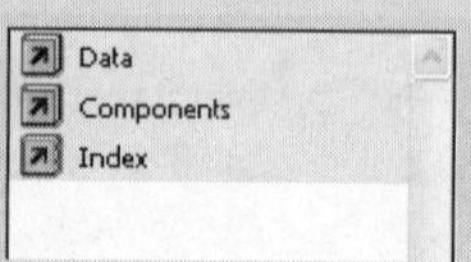

6. Close the Flash application.

7. In the `ActionsPanel.xml` document, add the following element between the opening and closing Actions panel tags, and save the document:

```
<folder name="MyFolder" id="MyFolder" tiptext="this is my new folder">
</folder>
```

8. Open Flash, and open the Actions panel. In addition to the previously available folders, you should now see the `MyFolder` folder at the top of the Actions panel.

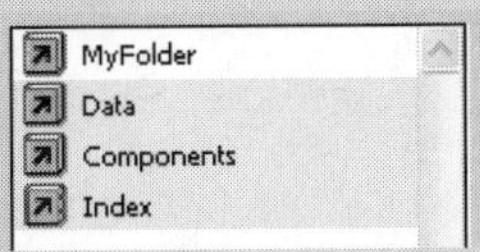

9. Close Flash.

10. In the `ActionsPanel.xml` document, add the following elements between opening and closing folder tags:

```
<action name="MyAction" tiptext="my very first action"
quickey="ma" text="MyAction();" text2="MyAction
(% param1, param2 %);" />
<folder name="MyProperties" id="MyProperties" tiptext=
"my properties folder">
    <string name="myProperty" tiptext="my very first property"
 text=".myProperty" object="MyAction" />
</folder>
<folder name="MyMethods" id="MyMethods" tiptext="my methods folder">
    <string name="myMethod" tiptext="my very first method"
 text=".myMethod(% param1 %)" type="procedure" object="MyAction" />
</folder>
<folder name="MyEvents" id="MyEvents" tiptext="my events folder">
    <string name="myEvent" tiptext="my very first event"
 text=".myEvent" type="event" object="MyAction" />
</folder>
<folder name="MyListeners" id="MyListeners" tiptext=
"my listeners folder">
    <string name="myListener" tiptext=
"my very first listener" text=".myListener"
 type="listener" object="MyAction" />
</folder>
```

11. Open Flash, and open the Actions panel. Within the `MyFolder` folder, you should now have a code item (`MyAction`) as well as four folders (`MyProperties`, `MyMethods`, `MyEvents`, and `MyListeners`), each containing a single code item (`myProperty`, `myMethod`, `myEvent`, and `myListener`, respectively).

Continued

Continued

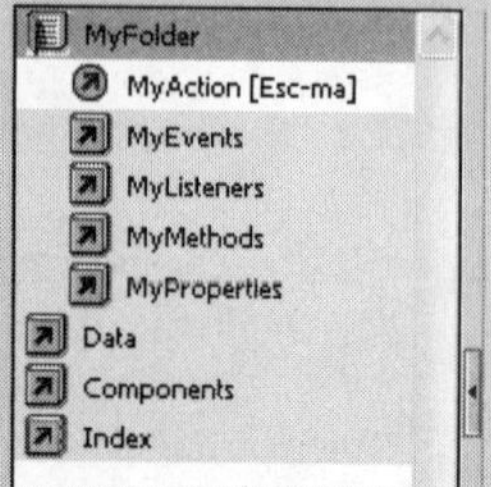

12. In the Script pane, type the following:

```
var anInstance:MyAction;
anInstance.
```

If the code hint doesn't come up automatically, invoke it manually. You should see a menu code hint with four choices: `myProperty`, `myMethod`, `myEvent`, and `myListener`.

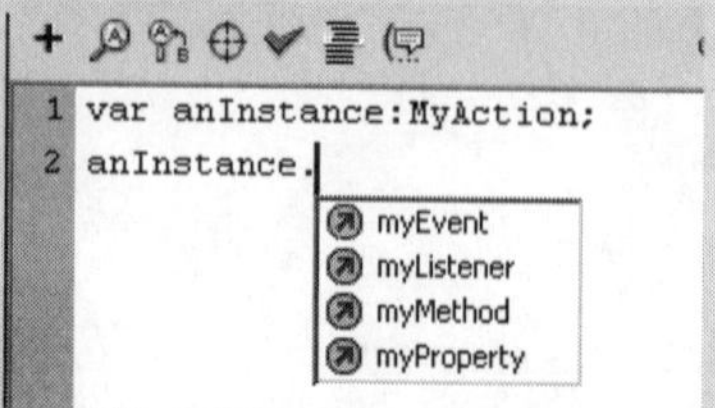

13. Select `myMethod` from the list. It should appear in the Script pane, the cursor should be placed between the parentheses automatically, and the tooltip code hint should appear.

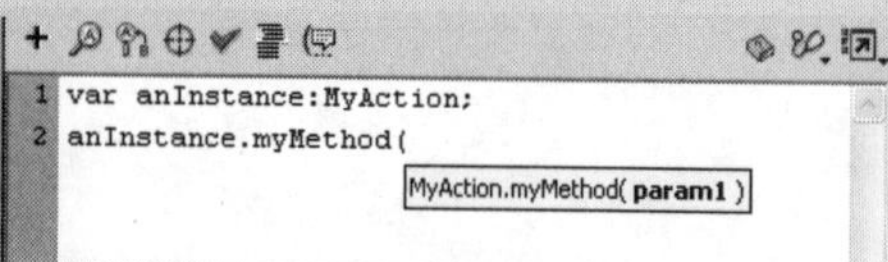

14. Close Flash.

15. Close `ActionsPanel.xml`.

16. To restore the default `ActionsPanel.xml`, delete the file, and restart Flash MX 2004. The default contents should appear in the Actions toolbox. If it does not, for some reason, close Flash, overwrite `ActionsPanel.xml` with your backup copy, and then restart Flash.

AsColorSyntax.xml

Using the `AsColorSyntax.xml` file, you can modify which words are recognized by Flash as identifiers and keywords for syntax color coding in the Script pane. The ActionScript Editor Preferences allow you to modify the color in which six types of elements are coded in the Script pane. Of those six, however, four are nonconfigurable by their very nature. The foreground is always the foreground, the background is always the background, comments are always comments, and quoted string literals are always quoted string literals. But words to be designated as keywords and identifiers need to be flexible so that new words can be added for new objects, functions, and so on.

If you open the default `AsColorSyntax.xml` file, you see that it is really quite simple. Aside from the root element and the conditional elements, there are only three types of elements in the file: `identifier`, `keyword`, and `property`. The type of element determines how the word will be coded in the Script pane.

Tag	*Attribute*	*Description*
`<colorsyntax>`		Required as the root element. This means that it encapsulates the rest of the elements of the XML document.
`<identifier>`		Indicates a keyword that Flash should color code using the identifier color (see "Setting Actions Panel Preferences").
	`text`	Specifies the word that will be color coded when entered into the Script pane.
`<keyword>`		Indicates a keyword that Flash should color code using the keyword color (see "Setting Actions Panel Preferences").
	`text`	Specifies the word that will be color coded when entered into the Script pane.
`<property>`		Indicates a property that Flash should color code using the keyword color (see "Setting Actions Panel Preferences"). Notice that the `<keyword>` and `<property>` tags define keywords that are color coded with the same color.
	`text`	Specifies the word that will be color coded when entered into the Script pane.

AsCodeHints.xml

The `AsCodeHints.xml` file is used by Flash to define the naming patterns that Flash can recognize for the purposes of code hinting. In Flash MX it was potentially useful to edit this file if you wanted to modify the naming patterns. However, starting with Flash MX 2004, we recommend you use strong typing (see the section "Using Code Hinting" in this chapter) instead of relying on the name pattern technique employed by Flash MX. For this reason, it is no longer necessary to modify the `AsCodeHints.xml` file.

We'd like to know what you thought about this chapter. Visit `www.flashsupport.com/feedback` to fill out an online form with your comments.

Summary

- ActionScript enables you to control your Flash movies programmatically.
- Events are those things in Flash that can trigger an action to occur. Event handlers are those things that can detect events.
- All ActionScript code must occur within an event handler.
- ActionScript is added to keyframes, `MovieClip` objects, and `Button` objects by way of the Actions panel.
- The Actions panel has many configurable features (preferences), allowing you to customize your ActionScript authoring environment.
- In addition to the Actions panel preferences, you can modify the `ActionsPanel.xml`, `AsColorSyntax.xml`, and `AsCodeHints.xml` files to make changes to the contents and appearance of the Actions panel.

✦ ✦ ✦

Constructing ActionScript

In This Chapter

Using variables and understanding the data they can represent

Working with data using expressions

Instructing the Flash movie with statements

Controlling the flow of code using control structures

If you decide to become a car mechanic, you learn the names and functionality of all the common parts of cars. Learning ActionScript is very similar because it is a good idea to learn what all the basic terms mean and how they function within the whole. This will aid you, not only in thinking through your own code, but also in communicating it to others.

For the purposes of learning about how ActionScript works, we're going to examine it syntactically in smaller pieces. Of course, as with any language, these pieces are not useful in isolation. For example, to create a complete sentence in English you need to use both a noun and a verb at the minimum. But if you examine each of the pieces, learn how they are structured, and learn how they fit together to create correct syntax, you'll be much better prepared to communicate with Flash. Flash is not nearly as tolerant about syntactical errors in ActionScript — even minor ones — as a human might be when listening to you speak English or any other human language. If you accidentally drop a preposition or conjugate a verb incorrectly, the listener will generally be able to understand the meaning from the context of the conversation. But Flash does not know about the context. Flash does not know what you are trying to accomplish. It knows only how to do each instruction, exactly as you provide it. Therefore, the simple omission of a parenthesis can cause Flash to misunderstand you. For this reason, it is especially important to have a good understanding of the syntax of ActionScript.

Fortunately, ActionScript is composed of only a handful of elements that repeat many of the same structural patterns. So even though Flash demands perfect syntax, the structure of the language is simple enough that you'll be up and running in no time.

In this chapter, we take a look at variables and datatypes, operators and expressions, and statements and control structures.

Understanding Datatypes

When we talk about data, we're talking about information or values. These values can be of many types. For example, even in a very simple movie you might still have a number, some text, and a `MovieClip` instance. All three of these examples are data of different types — what ActionScript calls *datatypes*.

Datatypes were somewhat less important in previous versions than they are in Flash MX 2004 because Flash is actually capable of performing datatype conversions when necessary. However, this can, and did, lead to some sloppy coding practices on the part of ActionScript developers. For this reason, the new ActionScript 2.0 standards request that you pay closer attention to the datatypes you are using.

In ActionScript, you'll work with many different datatypes. However, for the sake of understanding how these datatypes work, you can consider them in two basic categories: primitive types and reference types. The primitive types are called *primitive* because they are the basic foundational datatypes, not because they lack importance. The reference datatypes are called reference types because they *reference* the primitive types.

Primitive datatypes include strings, numbers, Booleans, `undefined`, and `null`. We'll examine each of these primitive datatypes a little more closely here in this chapter. Reference datatypes are all objects, which is the subject of Chapter 7 as well as all of Part III in this book, so we'll defer the majority of the discussion of reference datatypes to those later chapters.

Working with Strings

Strings are characters or words. String values must always be enclosed in either single quotes or double quotes. Here are a few examples of strings:

```
"a"
'b'
"1"
"Joey"
'123'
'abc'
"****"
```

Strings are used whenever you want to work with characters or words. For example, you can use strings to populate text fields in your movie or you can use strings to programmatically create names for new `MovieClip` instances. You've also already seen how strings can be used with actions such as `trace()`. The `trace()` action requires that you provide it with a message to display in the Output panel. That message must evaluate to a string value.

```
trace("I know him; Marley's Ghost!");
```

As already mentioned, you can use either double quotes or single quotes when defining a string value. Which you choose is often purely a matter of personal preference. There are two rules that you must follow, however, if you want your code to work without error. First of all, you must have a matching closing quote for every opening quote. And whichever type of quote you use to open the string literal must be used to close it. In other words, mismatched quotes are not allowed. Here are two examples of correctly matched quotes on string literals:

```
"here is a string"
'here is a string'
```

And here are three examples of incorrect quotes on string literals:

```
"here is a string'
'here is a string"
"here is a string
```

There are times when more than personal preference might dictate which type of quotes you choose to use. Notice what would happen if you tried the following:

```
trace('I know him; Marley's Ghost!');
```

The semicolon at the end of a line denotes the end of an expression or a statement. It is similar to a period in an English sentence.

This line of code would actually cause an error because it would interpret the apostrophe as the closing quote and then fail to know what to do with the remainder of the string. This is easily remedied by using double quotes around the string:

```
trace("I know him; Marley's Ghost!");
```

The inverse is true as well, of course—if you want to use a double quote as a character in a string literal, you can use single quotes around the entire value. The problem arises when you want to use both single and double quotes as characters within a string literal. There is an easy way to accommodate this: by using special characters. To learn more about special characters, see Chapter 15.

Working with Numbers

In Flash, all numbers are treated as the number *datatype*. Positive, negative, floating point, integer, and so forth are all simply considered numbers, with no further differentiation generally required on your part.

In order to define a number, you need only type the number without any quotes. The following are examples of numbers.

```
6
12
-1
3.3
1.8
```

Number datatypes allow you to perform all kinds of mathematical operations, as shown in the following examples:

```
trace(5 + 5);  // Displays: 10
trace(5 - 4);  // Displays: 1
trace(5 / 2);  // Displays: 2.5
```

It is important to understand when to use numbers and when to use strings. If you try to use a string when you really want to use a number, you can end up with unexpected results. For example:

```
trace("5" + "5");  // Displays: 55
```

In the example, the resulting value of `addedAges` is `"55"`, not `10` (as you may expect). This is because ActionScript treats the two values as strings and concatenates them, rather than adding the numeric values!

Concatenation refers to when two string values are appended. You can read more about concatenation operations in Chapter 15.

However, it should also be understood that there are legitimate reasons for numbers to be treated as strings. For example, even though a phone number is composed of numbers, it is usually treated as a string. And if you want to format the phone number with spaces, parentheses, dashes, and so on, it is necessary that the phone number be treated as a string by enclosing the value in quotation marks.

Using Booleans

Boolean data is data that can hold only two values: `true` and `false`. Boolean variables are used to test conditions within your Flash movie. Boolean values are used commonly in *conditional expressions* within statements such as the `if` statement and control structures such as the `for` and `while` statements. For more information about conditional statements and control structures, read the section "Using Statements That Control Flow: Control Structures," later in this chapter.

Understanding undefined and null

ActionScript has two additional primitive datatypes — `undefined` and `null` — with which you'll want to familiarize yourself. In order to have a better understanding of these datatypes, it is useful to first be familiar with variables. Therefore, we'll interweave the discussion of these two datatypes with the discussion of variables later in this chapter.

Casting Data

ActionScript allows you to tell Flash to convert a value to a specific datatype by what is known as *casting*. When you cast a value, you should use the following syntax:

```
Datatype(value)
```

For example, you can cast a string to a number as follows:

```
Number("123")
```

When you are casting data you have to be careful. Some casting will have unexpected results. For example, the numeric value of `0` can be converted to a Boolean `false`, and any non-zero value will be converted to `true`. For example:

```
trace(Boolean(0));  // Displays: false
trace(Boolean(1));  // Displays: true
```

Therefore, if you convert the string values of `true` and `false`, they will both convert to the Boolean `true` value because both string values are nonzero values.

```
trace(Boolean("true"));  // Displays: true
trace(Boolean("false"));  // Displays: true
```

Using Variables

In Flash movies you're going to be using a lot of data. Now, with all that data floating around, you're going to want some way to keep track of it. This is where variables become very useful.

Introducing ActionScript 2.0

Flash 2004 has introduced some rather significant changes to ActionScript—significant enough that Macromedia is distinguishing between the Flash MX–style ActionScript and the new, Flash MX 2004–style ActionScript. The old style is now called ActionScript 1.0, whereas the new style is called ActionScript 2.0.

The changes that have been implemented in ActionScript 2.0 are primarily of two sorts. First, ActionScript 2.0 allows you to use strong typing with your variables. This subject is discussed in more detail in the next section. But briefly, this means that in ActionScript 2.0 you are asked to tell Flash what type of data a variable can hold. The second major change to ActionScript 2.0 is in the way that classes are structured. We examine this in greater detail in Chapter 7.

ActionScript 2.0 is a compile-time-only feature in Flash MX 2004. This means that ActionScript 2.0 is a layer of specification that Flash checks against while exporting the movie. If everything meets the ActionScript 2.0 rules, Flash actually renders the code into the ActionScript 1.0 equivalent. So, in effect, the compiled versions of ActionScript 1.0 and ActionScript 2.0 are the same. That being the case, the question seems to be: Why bother using ActionScript 2.0? If you are already familiar with ActionScript 1.0, why would you want to learn ActionScript 2.0? The primary reason is that ActionScript 2.0 promotes better coding practices. It also formalizes the class structure. (See Chapter 7 for more information on this topic.) What this means to you is that ActionScript 2.0 can assist you in creating Flash applications that are better planned.

This book provides coverage of ActionScript 2.0 only. You still have the option of writing ActionScript 1.0 code if you prefer. You can choose to export the movie using ActionScript 1.0 from the Publish Settings dialog box. However, ActionScript 1.0 is no longer the preferred or suggested way to write your code. There is some likelihood that ActionScript 1.0 will be dropped from future releases of Flash. That, combined with all the benefits that ActionScript 2.0 can provide you, makes it well worth learning.

A *variable* is a named container that you can use to hold or reference some particular data. Once you have created a variable, you can store and retrieve data in the variable. Although a variable can contain only one value at a time, you can use the same variable to contain or reference different data at different times. For example, if you create a variable named `nYear` then it may contain the value of 2003 at one point, but at another point it may contain the value 2004.

Consider a rental storage space as a metaphor for a variable. You can rent a space (declaring the variable), and when you do so, you can begin to place things in that space (assigning data to the variable). At a later time you may want to view the things from the storage space (retrieving the value from the variable), or you may decide to place other contents in the storage space (assigning a new value to the same variable). And when you are done with the storage space, you can stop renting it (deleting the variable.)

Declaring Variables

Before you can meaningfully use a variable, you must first bring it into being by *declaring* it. Flash MX 2004 introduces support for a new way of declaring variables using *strong typing*. Strong typing means that when you create the variable, you also specify the type of data that it can hold. When you export your movie, Flash then makes sure that you consistently tried to store the correct type of data in that variable. If Flash detects that you mismatched the datatype with the variable at any point, an error message is generated, alerting you to the fact. This is helpful for ensuring that your Flash applications are well planned and designed using good coding practices.

Strong typing is a new feature in Flash MX 2004 that you can use when writing ActionScript 2.0 code.

In order to declare a variable using strong typing, you should use the following pattern:

```
var variableName:datatype;
```

The `var` keyword lets Flash know that you are declaring a variable (that is, creating the variable). The variable name is up to your choosing, but it should follow the rules for variable naming (see the next section, "Naming Variables"). A colon separates the name of the variable and the name of the datatype, and there should be no space between the name, colon, or datatype. If you have code hinting turned on, you should get a drop-down list of built-in datatypes from which you can select. Alternatively, if you have defined your own custom datatype (see Chapter 7) you can declare a variable of that type as well. You'll also see that the line ends with a semicolon. Generally, statements in ActionScript should end with a semicolon. That is how Flash is able to determine the end of the statement—just as a period denotes the end of a sentence in English.

Here is an example in which we declare a variable named `nQuantity` as a number.

```
var nQuantity:Number;
```

Now, we've declared a variable with the name `nQuantity`, and we've told Flash that all values we assign to the variable must be numbers. The variable has been created, but we have not defined any value for it yet. If we use `trace()` to display the value of the variable, we can see that this is so:

```
trace(nQuantity);
```

When you test this, you should see the value `undefined` appear in the Output panel. The value `undefined` is a special value that Flash uses for any variable that has not yet been assigned any value.

Once a variable has been declared, you can assign a value to it using a simple assignment statement with an equals sign.

```
var nQuantity:Number;
nQuantity = 6;
```

You can also declare the variable and assign a value, or initialize the variable, all on one line:

```
var nQuantity:Number = 6;
```

We mentioned that when a variable has not yet been assigned a value, the value is `undefined`. There is another special value that you can assign to a variable that indicates that the variable does not contain any other, specific value. The `null` value can seem to be much like `undefined`. However, there is a difference. You should use `null` to distinguish between when a variable has intentionally been left without any other value (`null`) or when the variable has been left as `undefined`. It is often a good practice to initialize your variables to some value other than `undefined`. And because `null` allows you to quickly distinguish between values intentionally or unintentionally left without another value, it is a good practice to initialize your variables to `null` when you don't have any other specific value to assign to them.

```
var nQuantity:Number = null;
```

You can use a variable in any situation in which you could use the value the variable contains. You've already seen an example of this with the `trace()` actions. You can use a variable to tell Flash what message to output:

```
var sMessage:String = "Welcome!";
trace(sMessage);
```

You can also perform other kinds of operations using variables, just as you would on the actual values themselves. For example:

```
var nQuantity:Number = 6;
var nPrice:Number = 9.99;
trace(nQuantity * nPrice);  // Displays: 59.94
```

Naming Variables

Now that you've looked at declaring and defining variables, the next thing you'll want to examine is how to name the variables. There are two main parts to this discussion. First, there is the matter of using valid variable names that Flash will understand. So we'll look at the rules for naming variables. Second, we'll also examine some additional guidelines for naming variables that, while not strictly enforced by Flash, will aid you in creating more readable code.

Let's take a look at the few rules that you should keep in mind when naming your variable in ActionScript. The following are the rules that you must follow for Flash to be able to understand your variable names.

- The first character must be an underscore (_), a dollar sign ($), or a letter. The first character *cannot* be a number. Although underscores and dollar signs are allowable as the first character, in practical application, you will almost always start the variable name with a letter.
- The subsequent characters must be underscores (_), dollar signs ($), letters, *or* numbers.
- Variable names can have no spaces.
- The name cannot be a keyword or other special value recognized by Flash. For example, the names `MovieClip`, `true`, `String`, and `undefined` are not allowable variable names because they already have other meanings in ActionScript.
- The name must be unique (within its scope). If you create two variables with the same name in the same scope (more on scope in Chapters 6 and 7), the latter will overwrite the former.

Next, let's talk about some good naming conventions that you can use. First, because you'll want to be using strong typing with all your variables, it is a good idea to have a convenient way to be reminded of what type of value a variable can hold. A system named Hungarian notation has been devised that can assist in this. For our purposes, we'll use a modification of Hungarian notation specifically designed for ActionScript. With this system, you can prefix each variable name with a character (or, in some cases, several characters) that can help you to remember what type of datatype the variable can hold. You may have already seen this in the previous examples in this chapter. When we define a variable named `nQuantity`, the variable name is prefixed with the character `n`. This tells us that the variable holds a number value. Table 5-1 shows a list of other recommended prefixes.

Hungarian notation is a convention originally credited to Charles Simonyi, a Hungarian who was Chief Software Architect at Microsoft. He suggested naming conventions that later were adopted by many developers for many different languages.

Table 5-1: Modified Hungarian Notation ActionScript Prefixes

Prefix	*Datatype*
a	Array
b	Boolean
bt	Button
c	Color
cam	Camera
cm	ContextMenu
cmi	ContextMenuItem
d	Date
lc	LocalConnection
lv	LoadVars
mc	MovieClip
mcl	MovieClipLoader
mic	Microphone
n	Number
nc	NetConnection
ns	NetStream
o	Object
pj	PrintJob
rs	RecordSet
s	String
snd	Sound
so	SharedObject
t	TextField
tf	TextFormat
vid	Video
xml	XML
xmls	XMLSocket

This modified Hungarian notation convention is completely optional, but it can be very useful. It helps not only you, but also others who may read your code. By adding the appropriate prefix to the variable name, it makes it immediately clear what type of datatype the variable can hold.

It's also important when naming your variables to make the names as descriptive as possible. For example, the variable name `nQuantity` is much more descriptive than `nQ`. Of course, the level of descriptiveness required depends on the context. For example, if your Flash application deals with quantities of widgets as well as cogs, `nQuantity` might not be sufficiently clear. It would be better, in such a case, to have variables named `nQuantityCog` and `nQuantityWidget`, for example. The more descriptive the variable name, the better, in most situations. Just remember, though, that most likely you'll be typing the same variable name multiple times. So it is important also to achieve the correct balance between descriptiveness and name length. You can always use abbreviations in the variable names if appropriate. For example, rather than defining a variable named `nQuantityWidget` you might find it easier to define a variable named `nQntyWidget`.

Remember that you cannot use spaces in your variable names. However, when you want to make your variable names descriptive, the names will often consist of more than one word. There are two conventions that are commonly used when naming variables with multiple words. The first of the two conventions is to use the underscore (_) to separate your words in the variable name. An example of this method follows:

```
var sFirst_name:String = "Joey";
```

The second of these conventions is known as the *interCap* method (also known as studlyCaps or camelCaps). The word "interCap" refers to the capitalization of the first letter of each word subsequent to the first, using no spaces or underscores — internal capitalization. An example of this method is the following:

```
var sFirstName:String = "Joey";
```

It would behoove you to use one of these conventions. Pick one that you like, and if you decide you prefer the other one later on, switch to it. In this book, we tend to prefer the interCap method, so you see a preference for it in the examples. But neither convention is more correct or offers any advantages over the other one.

It is also important to remember that ActionScript is case-sensitive. This means that `sFirstName`, `sFirstname`, `SfirstName`, and so on are all different variables. If you accidentally type the name of a variable with incorrect capitalization, the result will be that Flash will not recognize that the variable is defined. Here is an example:

```
var sFirstName:String = "Joey";
trace(sFirstName);  // Displays: Joey
trace(sfirstName);  // Displays: undefined
```

Flash Player 7 is a case-sensitive environment for ActionScript. This differs from previous player versions that were only partially case-sensitive.

Using Expressions

Anyone who has taken at least very basic mathematics (using addition and subtraction and the like) has worked with expressions. Expressions are simply those parts of statements that evaluate to be equal to something. Here are some very simple examples:

```
1
"abcd"
nQuantity
```

Even though these examples are all either simple values or variables, they all evaluate to a single value, and therefore, are considered expressions. Slightly more complex (although still simple) expressions might look something like this:

```
1 + 1
"a" + "b"
nQuantity * nPrice
```

Expressions are an important part of ActionScript. You use expressions in all kinds of situations. For example, you can use an expression within a `trace()` statement:

```
trace("Welcome!");
```

You can also use expressions in variable assignment statements:

```
var nQuantity:Number = 6;
var nPrice:Number = 9.99;
var nTotal:Number = nQuantity * nPrice;
```

We'll also look at other kinds of expressions that perform comparisons and tests. For example:

```
6 < 10
55 == 56
```

In the preceding examples, we use comparison operators to determine how two values compare. The first expression is determining whether 6 is less than 10. That expression evaluates to `true`. The second expression determines whether 55 is equal to 56. That expression evaluates to `false`.

There are many other examples of expressions, and we'll examine some of them throughout the rest of this chapter.

Working with Operators

As you have seen, expressions can be composed of a single value. But expressions can also be more complex by combining several different values to make one expression. In expressions involving multiple values, two types of ActionScript elements are involved: *operands* and *operators*. The *operands* are the values on which the operation acts. The *operators* determine the action taken. In the expression 4 + 5, for instance, there are two values, or operands —4 and 5—and there is one operator: the plus operator (+).

In the Actions toolbox, you can see that the operators are grouped into six categories: arithmetic, assignment, bitwise, comparison, logical, and miscellaneous. In the following sections let's take a closer look at each of these groups, and the operators of which they are composed. We'll look at each of these groups in the order they are listed in the Actions toolbox with the exception of the bitwise operators. We'll look at the bitwise operators after the rest because except in specialized situations, you are more likely to use the other operators than you are to use bitwise operators.

Working with Arithmetic Operators

The arithmetic operators should be familiar to you because they are, for the most part, the operators you used in math class. They are the operators used on number operands for mathematical computations. The result of an operation using an arithmetic operator is a number value. Table 5-2 lists all the arithmetic operators.

Table 5-2: Arithmetic Operators

Operator	*Name*	*Example*	*Result*
+	Plus	x + y	x + y
-	Minus/Negation	x - y	
-x	x - y		
x * (-1)			
*	Multiply	x * y	x * y
/	Divide	x / y	x / y
%	Modulo	x % y	Remainder of x / y

The addition, subtraction, multiplication, and division operators don't really require any discussion. They work just as you would expect them to.

The modulo operator (%) may be new to you. Even if it is not new, you might need a little refresher on what it does. Quite simply, it returns the value of the remainder after the first operand is divided by the second. In the following example, we use the modulo operator with a variable nYear and the second operand of 4. The result is 0. This means that 2004 is divisible by 4. In practical terms, the implication of this is that the year 2004 is a leap year.

```
var nYear:Number = 2004;
trace(nYear % 4);
```

Also worth pointing out is that the minus and negation operators use the same character but operate differently. The negation operator has the same effect as multiplying a number by -1. For example, this operation:

```
y = -x;
```

is the same as this operation:

```
y = x * (-1);
```

Working with Assignment Operators

Table 5-3 presents a rather daunting list of operators that all fall under the category of *assignment operators*. But don't be scared off just yet. In fact, there is only one fundamental operator in the bunch—the equal sign (=). This one should not be a new operator to you. It does just as you would expect it to do: It assigns the value of the operand on the right to the operand on the left. The remainder of the operators are compound assignment operators that function as shortcuts, as you'll see in a moment.

In the following example, the operand on the left (nQuantity) is assigned the value of the operand on the right (6):

```
nQuantity = 6;
```

Of course, you might want to use expressions that are slightly more complex than simply nQuantity = 6. You might, for instance, want to add several operands together on the right side of the equal sign operator, as in the following:

```
nQuantity = 6 + 36 + 24;
```

In this case, you notice that the addition takes place before the assignment. In other words, x is assigned the value of the sum of 6, 36, and 24, not just the value of 6. This is due to the operator precedence of the plus operator (+) being greater than that of the assignment operator (=). See the section later in this chapter titled "Considering Operator Precedence." Additionally, you can find a complete list of operators and their precedence in the Flash Help system. See the section "Operator Precedence and Associativity."

Table 5-3: Assignment Operators

Operator	*Name*	*Example*	*What It Means*
=	Equals (assignment)	x = y	X = y
+=	Add by value	x += y	X = x + y
-=	Subtract by value	x -= y	X = x - y
*=	Multiply by value	x *= y	X = x * y
/=	Divide by value	x /= y	X = x / y
%=	Modulo by value	x %= y	x = x % y
<<=	Left shift by value	x <<= y	X = x << y
>>=	Right shift by value	x >>= y	X = x >> y
>>>=	Right shift zero fill by value	x >>>= y	X = x >>> y
&=	Bitwise AND by value	x &= y	X = x & y
|=	Bitwise OR by value	x |= y	X = x | y
^=	Bitwise XOR by value	x ^= y	X = x ^ y

As we mentioned, there is really only one fundamental operator in the assignment operator category—the equal sign. Each of the additional operators merely saves you some time typing. For example, the following expression

```
nQuantity += 6;
```

is the shorthand version of this operator:

```
nQuantity = nQuantity + 6;
```

Either of the two preceding expressions means that you want Flash to add 6 to the current value of nQuantity. It just so happens that the former variation is shorter and quicker to type.

The operators compounded with the equals (=) operator are either mathematical operators or bitwise operators (covered in the following sections of this chapter). So if you have any questions about how the compound operators work, simply consult the appropriate section in which the basic operators are discussed. In each case, the compound operator follows the same pattern. For example:

```
nQuantity *= 6;
```

is the same as:

```
nQuantity = nQuantity * 6;
```

Working with Comparison Operators

Comparison operators allow you to compare operands. The result of a comparison is a Boolean value: `true` or `false`. These operators are most often used in expressions called *conditionals* within `if...else` blocks, and *control of flow* expressions within `for` and `while` blocks. (You learn about these types of statements later in this chapter.) But the basic premise is that if the conditional expression evaluates to `true`, then a block of code is executed, and if it evaluates to `false`, the block of code is skipped over.

Using comparison operators (see Table 5-4), you can compare strings, numbers, and Boolean values. These primitive datatypes are equal only if they contain the same value. You can also compare reference data types such as objects, functions, and arrays. But reference data types are equal only if they reference the same object, whether or not they contain the same value.

Table 5-4: Comparison Operators

Operator	*Name*
`==`	Equals
`!=`	Not equals
`>`	Greater than
`<`	Less than
`>=`	Greater than or equal
`<=`	Less than or equal
`===`	Strict equality
`!==`	Strict inequality

Perhaps the most common mistake made in programming is confusing the equality equals operator (==) with the assignment equals operator (=). In fact, even among seasoned professionals, it is not uncommon to make this error on occasion. The difference is so tiny in print, but the result is so drastic. Take, for instance, the following example:

```
var nQuantity:Number = 999;
if (nQuantity = 4){
    trace("if condition true");
}
trace(nQuantity);
```

What would you expect this code to do? Even if you don't know what some of the code structures mean, you can probably figure out that after `nQuantity` is assigned a value of `999`, you want the code to check to see *if* `nQuantity` is equal to `4`. If that condition is true, it should write a message to the Output panel. Finally, it writes the value of `nQuantity` to the Output panel.

You might expect that the final value of `nQuantity` is still `999`. But because the wrong operator was mistakenly used in the `if` condition (`nQuantity = 4`), `nQuantity` has been assigned the value of 4! Can you see the problems that have been caused by one missing character? So the corrected code looks more like this:

```
var nQuantity:Number = 999;
if (nQuantity == 4){
    trace("if condition true");
}
trace(nQuantity);
```

Any datatype can be compared using the equality operators. String characters are first converted to the ASCII values and then compared, character by character. Therefore, "a" is less than "z" and lowercase letters have higher values than their uppercase counterparts. Tables 5-5 and 5-6 show examples of numbers and strings being compared, using the equality operators along with the resulting value of the expression.

Table 5-5: Number Comparison

Expression	*Result*
6 == 6	`true`
6 != 6	`false`
6 > 6	`false`
6 < 6	`false`
6 >= 6	`true`
6 <= 6	`true`

Table 5-6: String Comparison

Expression	*Result*
`"Joey" == "Joey"`	`True`
`"joey" != "Joey"`	`True`
`"joey" > "Joey"`	`True`
`"Joey" < "Joseph"`	`false`

The only two operators in this category that you have not yet looked at are the strict equality (===) and strict inequality (!==) operators. These operators work much like the non-strict counterparts (== and !=) with one difference: They don't perform datatype conversions automatically. What this means is that when using the regular equality equals operator (==), Flash automatically converts the operands to the same datatype before testing for equality. Therefore, the values 5 and "5" are equal when testing using the regular equality operator (==) but not when using the strict equality operator (===). Table 5-7 gives some examples of the difference between using regular and strict equality operators.

Table 5-7: Strict Equality and Inequality Operators

Regular	*Regular Result*	*Strict*	*Strict Result*
`6==6`	`true`	`6===6`	`true`
`6!=6`	`false`	`6!==6`	`false`
`6=="6"`	`true`	`6==="6"`	`false`
`6!="6"`	`false`	`6!=="6"`	`true`

Working with Logical Operators

As you learned with comparison operators, sometimes you want to check for equality in an expression before performing a certain statement or group of statements. But there are times when you want to check multiple conditions before some statement or statements execute. This is when you should use the logical operators to link your conditions. There are also times when you simply want to see whether some expression is not true. Again, you should use a logical operator. Table 5-8 shows the logical operators.

Table 5-8: Logical Operators

Operator	*Name*
`&&`	And
`||`	Or
`!`	Not

The following is an example of creating a script that checks for a user's login and password before admitting them. Without using the logical AND operator (&&), you can write your code as follows:

```
if (sUsername == "Joey"){
  if (sPassword == "isAwesome"){
    trace("That is the correct username and password.");
  }
}
```

This works, but it is inefficient. Just imagine if you want to check for five or ten conditions! You can easily simplify the code like this:

```
if (sUsername == "Joey" && sPassword == "isAwesome"){
  trace("That is the correct username and password.");
}
```

This new condition is checking to make sure that *both* expressions are true in one single line.

Now, imagine a situation in which you have a block of code that you want to execute if either one of two conditions is true. This is a perfect example of when to use the logical `OR` operator (||). The next example shows how you might use this operator:

```
if (sLocation == " California" || sLocation == "Florida"){
  trace("Yay for oranges!");
}
```

In this case, you want to output a message if the location is equal to California *or* Florida.

The third and final logical operator is the `NOT` operator (`!`). You use this operator when you want to test for an expression *not* being true. The simplest example of an expression using the logical `NOT` operator is the following:

```
!true
```

A more real-world example is something like this one:

```
if (!(sLocation == "California") && !(sLocation == "Florida")){
  trace("Your location is not California and not Florida");
}
```

In this example, you combine the logical `NOT` operator with the logical `AND` operator to create a more complex expression. And, of course, you can combine all three of the logical operators to create complex expressions of multiple joined simpler expressions.

Working with String Operators

There is no string operator category in the Actions panel. And you should already recognize the string operators (see Table 5-9) from the mathematical and assignment operator discussions. We're discussing them here because they function slightly differently when used with strings instead of numbers. The join operator (+) is reused in a slightly different way to join, or concatenate, the strings. The result of any use of the plus operator to join two strings is a new string. The join by value operator (+=) is also used to work with string values, not just number values.

Table 5-9: String Operators

Operator	***Name***	***Example***	***Result***
+	Join	"x" + "y"	"xy"
+=	Join by value	x += "y"	x = x + "y"

Working with Miscellaneous Operators

In addition to the other categories for operators you can find in the Actions toolbox, there are six operators categorized as miscellaneous. Table 5-10 lists these operators.

Table 5-10: Miscellaneous Operators

Operator	*Name*	*Example*	*Result*
`++`	Increment	`x++`	`x = x + 1;`
`--`	Decrement	`x--`	`x = x - 1;`
`?:`	Conditional	`(x == y) ? a : b`	If `x` equals `y` then `a`. Otherwise, `b`.
`Instanceof`	Instanceof	`nQuantity instanceof Number`	True if `nQuantity` is a number, false if not.
`Typeof`	Typeof	`typeof nQuantity`	`"number"` (assuming `nQuantity` is a number)
`Void`	Void	n/a	n/a

Using the Increment and Decrement Operators

The increment and decrement operators are shorthand operators. The following examples are equivalent:

```
x++;
++x;
x = x + 1;
```

As are the next three:

```
y--;
--y;
y = y - 1;
```

Notice that it does not matter whether the increment or decrement operator appears before or after the operand. But there are some cases in which this distinction is important. You should note that when using the increment and decrement operators in conjunction with an assignment operator (=), the order matters. For instance, this operator

```
y = x++;
```

and the following operator are not equivalent:

```
y = ++x;
```

In the first example, the `x` is incremented *after* `y` is set equal to its value. The result is that `x` has a value of one greater than `y`. However, in the second example, `x` is incremented *before* `y` is set equal to its value. So in the second example, `x` and `y` are equal. This is due to (you guessed it) operator precedence.

Using the Conditional Operator

All the operators you have learned about so far are what are known as *unary* and *binary operators*, meaning that they operate on one and two operands, respectively. ActionScript has one operator that can operate on three operands. These kinds of operators are known as *ternary operators*. ActionScript's one ternary operator is the conditional operator (`?:`).

The three operands that the conditional operator works on are as follows: the conditional expression, the expression to use if the condition is true, and the expression to use if the condition is false.

```
(conditional expression) ? expression a : expression b
```

Most often, the conditional operator is used in assignment statements when you want a shorthand way of assigning one of two values to a variable depending on the result of a condition. For example, consider the scenario in which you want to display the number of seconds remaining in a countdown. For every value except 1, you'll want to use a label of "seconds" after the number. But when only one second is remaining, you want to use a label of "second" instead. In order to make this decision, you can use the conditional operator. For this example, we'll assume that the number of seconds has already been calculated and assigned to a variable named `nSeconds`, and we'll assume that the variable `sLabel` has already been declared.

```
sLabel = (nSeconds == 1) ? "second" : "seconds";
```

The same result can be achieved using an `if/else` statement (see this chapter's section "Using Statements That Control Flow: Control Structures"), but it takes more lines of code.

```
if(nSeconds == 1) {
  sLabel = "second";
}
else {
  sLabel = "seconds";
}
```

Using the typeof Operator

The `typeof` operator works on a single operand, and it returns the name of datatype of the operand. For example:

```
var nQuantity:Number = 6;
trace(typeof nQuantity); // Displays: number
```

Table 5-11 lists the types of operands and the value that a `typeof` operation will return.

Table 5-11: Return Values for typeof Operations

Operand Type	*Return Value*
String	`string`
Number	`number`
Boolean	`boolean`
Function	`function`
MovieClip	`movieclip`
All other types	`object`

Using the instanceof Operator

The `instanceof` operator returns true or false depending on whether or not the first operand is an instance of the class specified (or an instance of a subclass of that class) as the second operand. (See more about classes in Chapter 7.)

```
trace(mcCircle instanceof MovieClip);
```

Assuming that `mcCircle` is the name of a `MovieClip` instance, the preceding statement would output `true`.

Understanding Bitwise Operators

The bitwise operators are group of operators available within ActionScript that are seldom used and usually only in specific cases. The purpose of this class of operators is to allow you lower-level manipulation of numbers within Flash for faster operations. If you don't want to, or if you don't feel comfortable learning bitwise operations, don't feel obligated to do so. More often than not, you can use other operations in place of bitwise operations (although the bitwise operations will likely be more efficient). However, if you are interested, read on. There are some scenarios in which working with bitwise operations can be convenient. Extracting and synthesizing color values is one such example of the usefulness of bitwise operations.

All the bitwise operators convert any operands to the 32-bit equivalent before performing any operations. Table 5-12 lists all the bitwise operators.

Table 5-12: Bitwise Operators

Operator	*Name*
&	Bitwise AND
|	Bitwise OR
^	Bitwise XOR (exclusive or)
<<	Bitwise Left Shift
>>	Bitwise Right Shift
>>>	Bitwise Unsigned Right Shift
~	Bitwise Not

Using Bitwise AND

The bitwise `AND` operator (`&`) converts both of the operands to 32-bit format and then compares each of the bits of each operand. If the corresponding bits in the two values are 1, that bit in the resulting value is 1. Otherwise, the bit in the resulting value is 0. So the bit in the resulting value is 1 only if the corresponding bits in the first operand *and* the second operand are 1. The following example results in `z` being equal to `210`:

```
var x:Number = 1234;
var y:Number = 4567;
var z:Number = x & y;
```

Why? Here's a closer look:

x	0000 0000 0000 0000 0000 0100 1101 0010
y	0000 0000 0000 0000 0001 0001 1101 0111
z	0000 0000 0000 0000 0000 0000 1101 0010

Using Bitwise OR

The bitwise `OR` operator (|) operates in much the same way as the bitwise `AND` operator, except that the `OR` operator checks to see whether the corresponding bit in either the first operand *or* the second operand is 1. If either bit is 1, the bit in the resulting value is set to 1, as shown in the following example:

```
var x:Number = 1234;
var y:Number = 4567;
var z:Number = x | y;
```

This time, the result is 5591. Don't worry if you can't figure this out in your head! You can use Flash to check the results. Here is a closer look:

x	0000 0000 0000 0000 0000 0100 1101 0010
y	0000 0000 0000 0000 0001 0001 1101 0111
z	0000 0000 0000 0000 0001 0001 1101 0111

Using Bitwise XOR

The bitwise `XOR` (^, exclusive or) operator is the same as the bitwise `OR` operator, except that it sets the bits in the resulting value equal to 1 *exclusively* when the corresponding bit in one of, but not both, the operands is 1. Using the example again, `z` results in 5381 this time:

```
var x:Number = 1234;
var y:Number = 4567;
var z:Number = x ^ y;
```

Here is a closer look:

x	0000 0000 0000 0000 0000 0100 1101 0010
y	0000 0000 0000 0000 0001 0001 1101 0111
z	0000 0000 0000 0000 0001 0001 0000 0101

Using Bitwise Left Shift

The bitwise left shift (<<) operator simply shifts bits 0 to 30 (preserving the sign) of the first operand over to the left by the value of the second operand. The following example results in `y` having a value of `12`:

```
var x:Number = 3;
var y:Number = x << 2;
```

Understanding 32-Bit Integers

Computers speak in binary. Everything that computers do is a matter of 1s and 0s. But because humans are better able to communicate in decimal (base-10) numbers, applications such as Flash convert all the "human" stuff into binary. This conversion can slow down things a bit, so sometimes developers may want to work with the binary values themselves.

Integers are classified in most languages as ranging from approximately negative to positive two billion. This is because this is the range that can be represented by 32 *bits*. Bits are the smallest components of data. They are the fundamental binary unit. They can be on or off, which means they can have a value of 1 or 0. Incidentally, 8 bits are called a byte, and 1,024 bytes are a kilobyte. The accompanying table shows some examples of decimal numbers represented as 32-bit integers.

Number	***32-Bit Representation***
1	0000 0000 0000 0000 0000 0000 0000 0001
2	0000 0000 0000 0000 0000 0000 0000 0010
3	0000 0000 0000 0000 0000 0000 0000 0011
4	0000 0000 0000 0000 0000 0000 0000 0100
5	0000 0000 0000 0000 0000 0000 0000 0101
1978	0000 0000 0000 0000 0000 0111 1011 1010
2147483648	0111 1111 1111 1111 1111 1111 1111 1111
-1	1111 1111 1111 1111 1111 1111 1111 1111
-2	1111 1111 1111 1111 1111 1111 1111 1110
-3	1111 1111 1111 1111 1111 1111 1111 1101
-2147483648	1000 0000 0000 0000 0000 0000 0000 0000

The bits are numbered from right to left, from 0 to 31. If you look at this table, you'll notice that all positive values have a 0 value in the bit 31 position. Likewise, all negative values have a 1 value in the 31-bit position. This is because the 31st bit holds the value of the sign in signed 32-bit integers.

Following is a simple chart that shows this bit shift:

x	0000 0000 0000 0000 0000 0000 0000 0011
y	0000 0000 0000 0000 0000 0000 0000 1100

The result of a bitwise left shift is the equivalent of multiplying the first operand by 2 to the power of the second operand. In other words, the following

```
a << n
```

is a shortcut way to write the following in ActionScript:

$a * 2^n$

Using Bitwise Right Shift

The bitwise right shift (>>) operator shifts bits 0 to 30 (preserving the sign) of the first operand to the right by the value of the second operand. In this example, you can see how the right shift and left shift operators are the inverse of one another because y ends up with a value of 3:

```
var x:Number = 12;
var y:Number = x >> 2;
```

Following is a simple chart that shows this bit shift:

x	0000 0000 0000 0000 0000 0000 0000 1100
y	0000 0000 0000 0000 0000 0000 0000 0011

You can see then that in most cases then, the bitwise right shift operator is the same as dividing the first operand by 2 to the power of the second operand.

The bitwise unsigned right shift operator (>>>) works the same as the signed counterpart (>>) except that it shifts all the bits to the right and therefore does not preserve the sign:

```
var x:Number = -12;
var y:Number = x >>> 2; // y = 1073741821
```

Here is what the shift of the bits looks like:

x	1111 1111 1111 1111 1111 1111 1111 1011
y	0011 1111 1111 1111 1111 1111 1111 1101

Using Bitwise NOT

The bitwise NOT operator (~), also called the *one's complement operator,* works by inverting all the bits in the operand. The following are equivalent:

```
var x:Number = ~6;
var x:Number = -(6+1);
```

Working with Bitwise Operations

You may be wondering why you would want to use bitwise operations. The truth is that in the majority of smaller Flash applications, bitwise operations are not going to have a big impact one way or the other. But in larger applications, it is possible to see performance gains by using bitwise operations in place of Boolean operations whenever possible because bitwise operations save the steps of converting between binary and Boolean data. With enough operations, this can add up.

Even if you are not concerned with faster computing in your application, convenience can still be a factor when determining whether to use bitwise operations. Once you become comfortable with the bitwise operators, you may well find that there are plenty of scenarios in which it is simply more convenient to use the bitwise operators. In contrast to bitwise operations, the Boolean equivalents often take a little more code.

Bitwise operations are often more convenient when working with RGB color values and when working with a series of related Boolean flags. In the case of the RGB color values, bitwise operations can be used to quickly extract the color parts (red, green, and blue) from the single RGB value, or to synthesize a single RGB value based on the red, greed, and blue parts. In the case of related Boolean flags, often it is more convenient to group these values together into a single number—each bit of which can represent one of the Boolean flags. Let's take a closer look at each of these scenarios.

Using Bitwise Operations with Color

As you may or may not know, RGB color values are composed of three values: red, green, and blue—each ranging from 0 to 255. Often, this is represented by a six-digit hexadecimal (base-16) number such as 00FF00 (green). In the hexadecimal representation, the red, green, and blue values are in pairs (for instance, 00, FF, and 00). What you might not realize is that this is easily represented in binary. The red, green, and blue values are represented by 1 byte (8 bits) each. You may notice that the maximum value for a pair in the hexadecimal representation is 255, and the maximum value for a byte is 255. The following chart shows the binary representation of an RGB color value (the same as 00FF00 in hexadecimal):

Red	*Green*	*Blue*
0000	1111	0000
0000	1111	0000

It's important to note that the bytes can be shifted by doing a left bitshift of 8, and the bitshifted bytes can be added using the bitshift or (|) operator. The following example shows how you can assemble a color value from the red, green, and blue parts:

```
var nRed:Number = 123;  // 0111 1011
var nGreen:Number = 45;  // 0010 1101
var nBlue:Number = 78;  // 0100 1110

// 0111 1011 0010 1101 0100 1110
var nRGB:Number = nRed<<16 | nGreen<<8 | nBlue;
```

You can also use bitwise operations to extract the red, green, and blue parts from an RGB value. Simply use the bitshift right operator (>>) in conjunction with the bitwise `AND` (&) operator. Shift the bits of the RGB value to the right by 16 and combine that value with 0xFF using an `AND` operation to extract the red part. Then, perform the same operation, but shift the bits to the right by only 8 to extract the green part. And simply combine the RGB value with 0xFF using bitwise `AND` to extract the blue part.

```
var nRedPart:Number = nRGB >> 16 & 0xFF;
var nGreenPart:Number = nRGB >> 8 & 0xFF;
var nBluePart:Number = nRGB & 0xFF;
```

ActionScript uses 0x*NNNNNN* to indicate hexadecimal representation of a number. Therefore, 0xFF is the equivalent of the decimal representation 255. You can read more about numbers in Chapter 12.

Using Flag Variables

The other useful implementation of bitwise operations is in working with flag variables. A flag variable is a sort of glorified setting-tracking variable conglomerate. It is a way of using a single variable to keep track of multiple settings. Actually, the 3-byte RGB value is a sort of complex flag variable. It allows for a single variable to keep track of three settings in one value.

The more common type of flag variable, however, uses each bit much like a Boolean variable—but more efficiently. In this way, a single variable can be used instead of multiple Boolean variables. The following chart shows how the bits of a flag variable can be thought of as Boolean variables describing the state of an animation within an object:

Bit Position	***3***	***2***	***1***	***0***
Bit position meaning	Is it visible?	Is it playing?	Is it draggable?	Is it right-side-up?
Bit value	1	0	0	1
Bit value meaning	It is visible.	It is not playing.	It is not draggable.	It is right-side-up.

Each bit has a decimal value that works out to be 2 raised to the power of its bit position. In other words, if bit 0 is on (has a value of 1), the decimal value is 1 (or 2^0). If bit 1 is on, then the decimal value is 2 (or 2^1). For this reason, it is good to create some variables where the name describes the function of the bit and the value is the decimal value of that bit when on. For example:

```
RIGHT_SIDE_UP = 1;
DRAGGABLE = 2;
PLAYING = 4;
VISIBLE = 8;
```

You can then use these variables to turn the bits in your flag variable on and off through bitwise operations. You can turn a bit on using the bitwise `OR` operator:

```
myFlag |= VISIBLE; // makes it visible
```

You can turn a bit off (called *clearing a bit*) by using both the bitwise `AND` the bitwise `NOT` operators:

```
myFlag &= ~PLAYING; // makes it stop playing
```

And you can toggle a bit by using the bitwise `XOR` operator:

```
myFlag ^= DRAGGABLE; // toggles draggability on and off
```

Considering Operator Precedence

It is important to remember your basic rules of operator precedence, or order of operations, from high school algebra. (We bet you never thought you would use *that* again!) This means that the operators in your expression perform in order, according to a hierarchy or precedence, and may yield different results from what you want if you are not careful. For example, the following results in the value of `177` instead of `65`, as you might expect:

```
var nAverageScore:Number = 90 + 78 + 27 / 3;
```

This is because the division operator (/) has higher precedence than the addition operator (+). In order to accommodate for this, you can use parentheses to enclose the part of the expression you want to have perform its operations first, as in the following example:

```
var nAverageScore:Number = (90 + 78 + 27) / 3;
```

In the previous example, operators enclosed in parentheses take precedence over other operators. For this reason, the "better safe than sorry" approach to operator precedence is recommended. Use parentheses to encapsulate the operations you want to take precedence over others, which saves a great deal of debugging later on and makes your expressions more reader-friendly when you need to go back to them. It also saves you time by not having to look up precedence each time.

Using Comments Effectively

There are times in every programmer's experience when she or he has to revisit some old code. What you may find is convoluted logic that you swear you could never have written. But the truth is that you did—you just cannot remember what you were thinking when you wrote it. No matter how much you think you will remember what you were thinking, chances are you will not, which is why comments are so helpful.

Comments are exactly what they sound like. They are a way for you to write, in your own words, what the purpose of the code is at any point. Your comments are never interpreted by Flash; they are for your own benefit later on. So feel free to be as verbose as you need to be.

Of course, you need to signify to Flash that what you are typing is a comment, not a part of the code. You do this by using characters to indicate a comment. There are two styles for doing this that are recognized in ActionScript. The first is a multiline comment indicated by `/*` at the beginning, and `*/` at the end. For example:

```
/* This is the first line of my first comment.
   And this is the second line.*/
```

This style is most appropriate when you want to give an in-depth comment about the logic or function of a particular piece of code.

The second style of comment is the single-line comment, which is indicated by `//`, as follows:

```
// This is a single-line comment.
```

These comments are often useful for indicating the meaning of a particular line of code, as shown in the following instance:

```
// Keeps track of how many widgets the user has selected.
var nQuantity:Number = null;
```

In this case, the comment gives an idea of the function of the variable being declared.

Another very important function of comments is what is known as "commenting out" code. As you already know, comments are not interpreted in your Flash movie at runtime. In other words, they are not seen by your program; they serve only as reminders for you. Sometimes, when you are debugging your code, it can be useful to omit certain statements or blocks of statements for the time being. A clever way to do this is to simply make the code into a comment, thus preventing it from being executed. This saves you from having to delete and retype code. Here is an example of code that has been commented out:

```
//for (var i = 0; i < 5; i++){
//var nQuantity:Number *= 2;
//}
```

When you want to comment out more than one line of code, as in the preceding example, it can sometimes be more convenient to use multiline comments as shown here:

```
/*
for (var i = 0; i < 5; i++){
  var nQuantity:Number *= 2;
}
*/
```

Working with Statements

Statements are among the basic building blocks of ActionScript and are the equivalent of sentences in the English language. They are stand-alone commands or instructions given to a Flash movie.

You've already seen a lot of statements up to this point. For example, the following is a statement:

```
trace('"Mr. Sherlock Holmes, I believe?" said she.');
```

The following is also a statement, the likes of which you've also already seen:

```
var sName:String = "Sherlock Holmes";
```

There are additional types of statements that have not yet been formally introduced. The following types of statements in ActionScript are discussed in this chapter:

- **Action/function calls:** These include built-in actions and functions such as `trace()` and `play()`. They also include custom functions and methods, topics covered in Chapters 6 and 7.
- **Variable declaration/assignment**
- **Built-in keyword statements:** These include statements such as `continue` and `return`.
- **Control structures:** These include structures that group together other statements, and either loops the execution of those statements or makes the execution conditional.

Understanding Statement Syntax

Conceptually, you can say that there are two types of statement syntax. These two types can be differentiated by their complexity. The first kind of statement syntax is for simple statements that generally occupy a single line of code. An example of this kind of statement is as follows:

```
var sBookTitle:String = "ActionScript Bible";
```

You may have noticed that most of the statements in this book thus far have ended in a semicolon. The semicolon is what tells Flash that what precedes it is a complete statement. This is just like a period in an English sentence. The punctuation signals the reader that the preceding was a complete sentence.

The second type of statement syntax applies to complex, or compound statements. These types of statements can actually contain statements (substatements). Examples of these types of statements are the `if` and `for` statements that are discussed in the next section. The `if` statement, for example, allows you to set a condition that must be met in order for the substatements to be executed. An example of a simple `if` statement is as follows:

```
if(nQuantity > 0) {
  trace("Thank you for your order.");
}
```

Even though you have not yet read about the `if` statement, you can probably understand what the preceding example says. It simply checks to see whether the condition (`nQuantity > 0`) is true. If so, it executes the `trace()` substatement. The substatement is enclosed in the opening and closing curly braces. It is possible to have more than one substatement within the curly braces. For example:

```
if(nQuantity > 0) {
  trace("Thank you for your order.");
  trace("An email has been sent to you.");
}
```

The syntax for the `if` statement is the same for all of the statements in the same category— statements such as `while` and `for`. The basic syntax is as follows:

```
parentStatement {
  substatement(s)
}
```

The substatements enclosed in the curly braces make up a *statement block*. Notice that the statement block is *not* followed by a semicolon.

Using Statements That Control Flow: Control Structures

Control structures group multiple substatements together and control the flow of code execution. There are six control structures we will examine in this chapter:

- **if:** This statement makes the execution of the substatements conditional.
- **for:** This statement loops the substatements a specific number of times.
- **for...in:** This statement loops through the properties of an object (see Chapter 7 for more information on objects).
- **while:** This statement loops the substatements until a condition is no longer met.
- **do while:** This statement loops the substatements until a condition is no longer met just as a `while` statement. But a `do while` statement always executes the substatements at least once.
- **switch:** This statement selects and executes specific substatements determined by the value of the expression you specify.

Working with the if Statement

There are times in your code when you want certain statements to execute only *if* a condition is met. For instance, you might want a message to be displayed only if a certain user has logged in. To accomplish this, you use the `if` statement. For example:

```
if (sUsername == "Arun"){
  sMessage = "hello, Sir!";
}
```

All `if` statements begin with the keyword `if`. Immediately following the `if` keyword is the condition in parentheses, and after the condition is the statement block (the code encapsulated in curly braces). If the condition is `true`, the statement block is executed. Otherwise, the statement block is skipped, and the code is resumed immediately following the closing curly brace.

There are a couple of variations on the `if` statement: the `if...else` statement and the `if...else if` statement. If you want to display a custom greeting for a particular user, as in the previous example, but display a different greeting for everyone else, you can use the `if...else` statement. It functions the same way as the `if` statement, but if the condition is `false`, the block of code in the `else` portion of the statement is executed as follows:

```
if (sUsername == "Arun"){
  sMessage = "hello, Sir!";
}
else{
  sMessage = "hi";
}
```

If you have a different personalized greeting for several users, you can use the `if...else if` variation, as follows:

```
if (sUsername == "Arun"){
  sMessage = "hello, Sir!";
}
else if (sUsername == "Carolyn"){
  sMessage = "hi, mom! :)";
}
```

Of course, you can combine `if...else` and `if...else if`, as follows:

```
if (sUsername == "Arun"){
  sMessage = "hello, Sir!";
}
else if (sUsername == "Carolyn"){
  sMessage = "hi, mom! :)";
}
else{
  sMessage = "hi";
}
```

Working with the for Statement

A `for` statement uses an index or a counter to loop through the block of code a set number of times. The following is an example of a `for` statement that loops 25 times:

```
for (var i:Number = 0; i < 25; i++){
  trace(i);
}
```

Notice that inside the parentheses are three expressions separated by semicolons (;). The first of these expressions (`var i:Number = 0`) is the *initialization expression* that sets the initial value of the index (`i`). This expression is evaluated only the first time the `for` statement header is encountered. The second expression (`i < 25`) is the *conditional expression* that is tested on each iteration through the `for` statement. As long as the condition is met, the block of code executes. The final expression (`i++`) is the *updating expression*, and it is processed after each iteration. This expression can manipulate the value of the index in any way, although the use of the increment (++) and decrement (`--`) operators is most common.

You may notice that the index variable, `i`, does not use the modified Hungarian notation. Using single-letter variable names in `for` statements is a convention used in programming. Typically, the variable name `i` is used first.

You use `for` loops when you want to loop through a block of code a known number of times. Even though it is a known number of times, that does not mean that the number cannot be dynamic. The number of times can be determined by a hard-coded integer value, as in the previous example, or by a variable or expression that evaluates to an integer value. Often, `for` loops are used with arrays to loop through each element of the array, as in the following example:

```
for (var i:Number = 0; i < aTitles.length; i++){
  trace(aTitles[i]);
}
```

Note that `for` loops do not have to initialize with `0`, nor do they have to use the increment operator as the previous two examples have shown. Additionally, the expressions can be compound by using the logical AND (&&), OR (||), and NOT (`!`) operators as well as the conditional operator (`?:`). Here are some examples of valid `for` loops:

```
for (var i:Number = 25; i > 0; i--){
  trace(i);
}

for (var i:Number = (aTitles.length * 10); i > -50; i -= 5){
  trace(i);
}

for (var i:Number = 50; i > -50; i -= (i > 0 || i < -30) ? 5 : 10){
  trace(i);
}
```

It is even possible to perform more complex initializations and increments by adding expressions separated by commas. For example:

```
for(var i:Number = 0, a:Number = 25; i < 25; i++, a -= 2) {
  trace(i + " " + a);
}
```

In the preceding example, the variable `i` is initialized to 0, and the variable `a` is initialized to 25. Then, at the end of each iteration, `i` is incremented by 1 and `a` is decremented by 2. One important thing to notice with this form is that the `var` keyword is used only once in the compound initialization expression regardless of how many variables you initialize. This is a form that you are not likely to see all too often, but it can be convenient in some scenarios.

You can also work with nested `for` loops — `for` loops inside of `for` loops. This is an extremely useful practice in many situations. Often, when working with multiple arrays, nested `for` loops are invaluable. When you do use nested `for` loops, you need to be very aware of which `for` loop's index you are using within the block of code. It is probably the most common mistake to use the wrong index and end up with unexpected results. Also, be aware that nested `for` loops need to use different names for their index variables. The outermost `for` loop conventionally still uses `i`, whereas the nested `for` loops would use `j`, `k`, `l`, and so on, respectively. The following is an example of nested `for` loops:

```
for (var i:Number = 0; i < 3; i++){
  trace(i);
  for (var j:Number = 100; j > 97; j--){
    trace("\t" + j);
  }
}
/*
```

This example outputs the following:

```
0
  100
  99
  98
1
  100
  99
  98
2
  100
  99
  98
*/
```

Working with the while Statement

A `while` statement helps you to execute a block of statements repeatedly *while* a condition is true. The structure of the `while` statement is the following:

```
while (condition){
  statements
}
```

Many programmers are confused about when to use the `while` statement versus when to use the closely related `for` statement. Essentially, the `for` statement is a more compact form of the `while` statement, and for that reason, you can often use them interchangeably. For example, consider the following `while` statement:

```
var i:Number = 0;
while(i < 25) {
  trace(i);
  x++;
}
```

You may be able to see that this `while` loop could be written as a `for` loop as follows:

```
for(var i:Number = 0; i < 25; i++) {
  trace(i);
}
```

Working with the do while Statement

There is a variation on the `while` statement called the `do while` statement. Notice that in a `while` statement, the condition is tested at the beginning of the statement, so that if it is `false` the first time through, the block of code is never executed. But with the `do while` statement, the condition is placed at the end of the block of code, so the statements in the block are executed *at least* once. Here is an example:

```
do{
  counter++;
} while (!keyPressBoolean)
```

Using break and continue in Statement Blocks

In any looping statement, there are times when you want to break out of the loop in order to prevent an infinite loop, or simply because a condition has been satisfied and there is no longer any point in wasting resources looping through something. To do this, you should use the `break` statement, which is used within the code block of a `while` or `for` statement. When encountered, it stops the loop, and resumes the code immediately following the close of the `while` or `for` statement.

An example of when you might use a `break` statement is as follows: Consider that you have an array (more on arrays in Chapter 11) named `aTitles` that contains the names of the titles of many books. You can use a `for` statement to loop through all the elements of the array in order to try and find the element that matches a particular title. Now, what if the title happens to be the first element of the array? In that case, you will have found the match right away, and there would not be any point in continuing to search through the rest of the elements. You can use the `break` statement to tell Flash to stop looping through the elements once a match has been found.

```
for (var i:Number = 0; i < aTitles.length; i++){
  if(aTitles[i] == "ActionScript Bible") {
    trace("Title found.");
    break;
  }
}
```

The `break` statement is also used within the `switch` statement, as you will see in the next section, "Working with the switch Statement."

Sometimes, you want to skip over a certain iteration in a loop, which is when the `continue` statement is handy. The `continue` statement is very similar to the `break` statement because it stops the current iteration of a loop wherever it is encountered. But rather than breaking out of the loop, it simply returns to the condition and continues the loop.

The use of `continue` can be useful to avoid errors. For instance, dividing by 0 causes an error. Actually, Flash is smart enough to not generate an error, but it returns infinity as a result, which can be undesired. The following example shows how to use `continue` to avoid dividing by 0:

```
for (var i:Number = -10; i < 10; i++){
  if (i == 0){
    continue;
  }
  trace(100/i);
}
```

In this example, the loop iterates from -10 to -1, essentially skips 0, and resumes with 1 to 9. Notice that it is important where you place the `continue` statement in the code block. If it comes at the end of the code block, it is of little value to you because the rest of the block has already executed.

Working with the switch Statement

Using the `switch` statement is very similar to writing a series of `if` statements. It is slightly different, however, and you may find that it suits your needs better on occasion. The basic structure of a `switch` statement is as follows:

```
switch(expression){
  case testExpression:
    statement;
  [case testExpression2:
    statement;
  default:
    statement;]
}
```

It works by testing to see if the expression evaluates to be strictly equal to the test expressions. If it is strictly equal, it executes all the remaining statements in the `switch` block. An example might help to make this clearer:

```
var nQuantity:Number = 6;
switch(nQuantity){
  case 10:
    trace("10");
  case 6:
    trace("6");
  case 1:
    trace("1");
}
```

In this example, the following would be displayed in the Output panel:

```
6
1
```

because `nQuantity` evaluates strictly to be equal to 6. Therefore, it executes the statements from that `case` to the end of the `switch` code block. This might not have been exactly what you expected. You might have expected it to execute only the `trace("6")` statement. You can easily accomplish this by adding a `break` statement:

```
var nQuantity:Number = 6;
switch(nQuantity){
  case 10:
    trace("10");
    break;
  case 6:
    trace("6");
    break;
  case 1:
    trace("1");
}
```

You might also want to have a sort of catchall, an equivalent to the `else` statement, in the event none of the cases are met. You can accomplish this by adding a `default` statement:

```
var nQuantity:Number = 6;
switch(nQuantity){
  case 10:
    trace("10");
    break;
  case 6:
    trace("6");
    break;
  case 1:
    trace("1");
    break;
  default:
    trace("none of the cases were met");
}
```

We'd like to know what you thought about this chapter. Visit `www.flashsupport.com/feedback` to fill out an online form with your comments.

Summary

- ✦ Variables are one of the fundamental pieces of ActionScript. They provide a way to give a name to the value they store.
- ✦ There are three primitive datatypes in ActionScript: string, number, and Boolean. In addition, there are two special values that have no datatype: `null` and `undefined`.
- ✦ Operators allow you to manipulate operands and form expressions. Using operators, you can perform a wide range of tasks — from adding and subtracting to joining strings together.
- ✦ It is important to use comments in your code. Comments are not executed in the program, but they serve as reminders to you about the logic and function of your code.
- ✦ Control structures are statements that enable you to control the flow of your code. You can use `if` statements to execute a block of code *only* if a condition is true. You can use `for` and `while` loops to repeatedly execute a block of code.

✦ ✦ ✦

Working with Functions

✦ ✦ ✦ ✦

In This Chapter

Understanding the purpose of functions

Writing your own custom functions

Passing parameters to functions

Returning values from functions

Understanding the importance of variable scope in functions

Creating reoccurring functions with setInterval()

✦ ✦ ✦ ✦

You've learned a lot so far. You've learned all of the basic building blocks of ActionScript. If you thought all of that was exciting (or even if you didn't) then hold on to your hat because in this chapter you're going to take it to the next level. Using functions, you can create reusable code, readable code, and portable code. With functions, you can write efficient, neatly organized, well-maintained code in place of long, unwieldy routines. Sounds exciting, doesn't it? So let's get to it.

Understanding Programming with Functions

Functions are a revolution. Writing code without functions is like publishing books without a printing press. In the days before the printing press, books were copied by hand. The publishing business was much less productive, to say the least. Then, along came the printing press. Suddenly, a plate could be made one time, and many copies could be made from that one plate. The printing press was a revolution. It enabled more copies of more books to be made more quickly. There was much less redundant effort being put into the process. Likewise, programming without functions means you have to write each line of code over and over if you want to accomplish the same (or similar) tasks within the application. But when you write a function, you can encapsulate the statements, and you can invoke that function (the group of statements) repeatedly, without having to rewrite the same code. That's working smarter.

As we already stated, functions are a way of grouping together a block of code in which execution is deferred until invoked (directly or indirectly) from within the main routine of the code. In other words, a function is a way of packaging up a block of code that performs a particular task when (but not before) it is called.

Functions offer many advantages over unstructured programming. Some of these advantages are the following:

- ✦ Code becomes more readable by eliminating clutter and redundant bits of code.
- ✦ The program becomes more efficient by reusing functions rather than retyping the entire block of code each time.

- A procedure becomes a centralized point for making changes. By making a change to the procedure, that change is affected in each instance the procedure is invoked.
- Well-written procedures can be reused through many programs. In this way, you can develop a library of procedures that can be used to build many kinds of programs without starting from scratch every time.
- Encapsulating code in a function provides the basis for user interaction. Without functions, the application runs as a single routine. With functions, a user-initiated action can invoke a function.

Defining Custom Functions

You have read some of the advantages and reasons to use functions in your ActionScript code. Now you need to learn how to write them. Writing a function is also called defining a function or declaring a function.

A function is actually a statement, and it uses syntax similar to some of the other statements you saw in Chapter 5, such as `if` and `for`. Therefore, the following syntax should be somewhat familiar already:

```
function functionName():datatype {
  statements
}
```

Here are some of the key points to notice in the function syntax:

- The `function` keyword tells Flash that you are defining a function. When you define a function you must always include the `function` keyword as shown.
- The function name is a name that you choose. It should follow the same naming rules as a variable. Also like naming variables, it is a good idea to give your function a name that indicates what it does. A name such as `someFunction` is probably not as good a name as `createNewCircle`.
- All function definitions must include a pair of parentheses following the function name. Although it is not shown in the preceding code block, it is possible to add what are known as parameters within the parentheses. You'll read about parameters in more detail later in the chapter. But regardless of whether a function defines any parameters, the parentheses must be in the definition.
- The parentheses should be followed by a colon and a valid datatype name. The datatype is for the type of data that the function will return. You'll look at returning data later in this chapter. For the time being, use the `Void` name. This means that the function does not return a value.
- The body of the function is defined by an opening and closing curly brace (`{}`).

Now that we've examined the basic syntax, let's look at a very simple example function:

```
function displayGreeting():Void {
  trace("Hello.");
}
```

Calling Functions

The term "function" was defined previously in this chapter as a block of code in which execution is deferred. This means that a function can be defined, but nothing will happen until you invoke it or call it. You can test this for yourself by creating a new Flash movie with the following code on the first frame of the main timeline:

```
function displayGreeting():Void {
  trace("Hello.");
}
```

When you test your movie, you will see that nothing happens, even though there is a `trace` action in the code. So now that you know how to define functions, you need to learn how to use them in your programs by calling them.

In order to call a function, you need to use the name of the function followed by the parentheses, which is called the *function call operator*. When you invoke a function, the call to the function is, itself, a statement. Therefore, you should use a semicolon after the statement. Here is an example that defines a function and then invokes it. If you want to follow along and test this yourself, simply place the code on the first frame of the main timeline.

```
function displayGreeting():Void {
  trace("Hello.");
}
displayGreeting();
```

The result of the preceding code is that when you test the movie, the following should appear in the Output window:

```
Hello.
```

Passing Parameters

Some functions you write do not need any information to be passed to them. For example, the `displayGreeting()` method shown in the preceding section did not require any parameters.

On the other hand, many functions that you write require parameters to be passed to it. For example, you could make the `displayGreeting()` function much more interesting if it was possible to display a personalized greeting using different names. With a parameter, this is quite simple to accomplish. Here is how the modified function might look:

```
function displayGreeting(sFirstName:String):Void {
  trace("Hello, " + sFirstName);
}
```

Once the function has been defined in this way, you can invoke it, and pass it different values for the parameters. Here are some examples:

```
displayGreeting("Joey");   // Displays: Hello, Joey
displayGreeting("Robert");  // Displays: Hello, Robert
```

A parameter is a variable within a function in which the value is assigned when the function is invoked. As you can see by the example with `displayGreeting()`, the parameter is named `sFirstName`, and the value of that variable is set each time the function is invoked. When the function is invoked with the value `Joey`, the variable is assigned that value. Or, if the same function is invoked with the value `Robert`, the variable is then assigned that value.

The parameter (variable) is declared within the parentheses of the function definition. You may notice that the declaration of a parameter is similar, yet slightly different than the declaration of a regular variable. First of all, the declaration is similar in that you are asked to create a name for the parameter and define the datatype. However, when you declare a parameter, you should not use the `var` keyword. Nor should you use a semicolon. And you cannot initialize a parameter within the parentheses. The following are *incorrect* examples and will result in errors.

```
// You cannot use the var keyword.
function displayGreeting(var sFirstName:String):Void {
  trace("Hello, " + sFirstName);
}

// Do not use a semicolon.
function displayGreeting(sFirstName:String;):Void {
  trace("Hello, " + sFirstName);
}

// Do not try to initialize the variable in the parentheses.
function displayGreeting(sFirstName:String = "Arun"):Void {
  trace("Hello, " + sFirstName);
}
```

What if you want to use multiple parameters in your function? That's not a problem; it is very easy to do. When you define your function, you can declare multiple parameters by simply separating them by commas. Likewise, when you invoked the function, you can pass it multiple values by simply delimiting them using commas. Here is an example of the `displayGreeting()` function definition with multiple arguments:

```
function displayGreeting(sFirstName:String, sGreeting:String):Void {
  trace("Hello, " + sFirstName + ". " + sGreeting);
}

// Displays: Hello, Joey. Good morning.
displayGreeting("Joey", "Good morning.");
```

You may notice that when you start adding more and more parameters to the parameters list in a function definition, the code starts to run off the side of the editor. You can opt for turning on word wrap in the Actions panel. Or you can also place each parameter (or groups of parameters) on new lines in the definition. This is a common convention because it makes it easier to read the function's parameter list when it consists of many parameters. The syntax remains the same. The only difference is that you are adding new lines between each parameter in the list to make it easier to read. For example:

```
function displayGreeting(sFirstName:String,
                         sGreeting:String):Void
{
  trace("Hello, " + sFirstName + ". " + sGreeting);
}
```

Passing Parameters by Value or by Reference

When you pass parameters to functions, those parameters get passed in one of two ways: by value and by reference. The difference has to do with datatype. Primitive datatypes such as string, number, and Boolean are passed by value. That means that the literal value is passed to the function, and any connection with the variable from which the value came is severed. In other words, after a value is passed to a function, any variable that was used to pass that value along is left alone. Here is an example:

```
function incrementByOne(a:Number):Number{
  a++;
  return a;
}
var nQuantity:Number = 5;
var nQuantityPlusOne:Number = incrementByOne(nQuantity);
trace(nQuantity);
trace(nQuantityPlusOne);
```

The Output window displays the following:

```
5
6
```

In this example, even though the value of `nQuantity` is passed to the function, and that value is increased by one within the function, `nQuantity` retains its value of `5`. Why? Because the *value* of `nQuantity` was passed to the function, not to the variable itself. That value was then assigned to a parameter named `a` within the function, incremented, and returned. The returned value was then assigned to a new variable named `nQuantityPlusOne`.

On the other hand, when reference datatypes (see Chapter 7 for more information on objects and reference datatypes) are passed as an argument, they are passed by reference. This means that an object passed to a function is a reference to the actual object. The result is that anything you do to the object reference within the function affects the object itself. No copy of the object is made. Here is an example using a `MovieClip` instance named `box`:

```
function move(mcA:MovieClip, x:Number, y:Number):Void{
  mcA._x = x;
  mcA._y = y;
}
```

Working with the arguments Property

All the functions you've looked at thus far either do not use any parameters, or the parameters are declared as a parameters list within the parentheses. However, regardless of whether or not a function declares any parameters, all parameters passed to the function are stored in a special array named `arguments`. Each function has an `arguments` variable (object) that gets created within it when the function is called.

ActionScript does not enforce symmetry between the number of arguments in the function definition and the number of arguments passed to the function when it is called. That means that any values not passed in the call, but defined in the argument string for the function, have an `undefined` value. And any values passed in the function call that are in addition to the arguments defined for the function are discarded.

Using the arguments Object to Reference Other Functions

Every `arguments` object has two special properties that reference functions. These properties, `caller` and `callee`, although not often used, can be useful in some circumstances—especially when developing highly abstract functions.

The `caller` property of the `arguments` object returns a reference to another function, if any, that called the current function. If the current function was not called from another function, the `caller` property has a `null` value.

```
function function1():Void{
  function2();
}

function function2():Void{
  if(arguments.caller == function1)
    trace("function2 called from function1");
  else
    trace("function2 not called from function1");
}

function1();
function2();
```

In this example, the Output window displays the following:

```
function2 called from function1
function2 not called from function1
```

The `callee` property of a function's `arguments` object is a reference to the function itself. It may not be apparent immediately why this is useful. But consider the scenario of an anonymous (see the section "Creating Function Literals") recursive function (see the section "Creating Recursion") for a moment. You can write a function literal that is capable of calling itself recursively as follows:

```
factorial  = function(n:Number):Number{
  if(n > 0){
    return n * arguments.callee(n-1);
  }
  else{
    return 1;
  }
}
```

Therefore, it is entirely possible to define no parameters in the function declaration but rather rely on using the `arguments` object. Here is an example of how you can use the `arguments` object as an array:

```
function traceParams():Void{
  for(i = 0; i < arguments.length; i++){
    trace(arguments[i]);
  }
}
traceParams("one", "two", "three");
```

In this example, the following is displayed in the Output window:

```
one
two
three
```

In the majority of functions, it is far better to declare the parameters. The `arguments` object is mostly useful when you are overloading a function (see the section "Overloading a Function") or other similar situation. The `arguments` object is mentioned here for completeness and also as a reference for when it is mentioned later in this chapter and in other parts of the book.

Overloading a Function

Overloading a function normally involves having multiple functions with the same name but with different numbers of parameters. This can be useful in a lot of situations. For example, you could have a function named `calculateArea()` that calculates the area of a rectangle based on two parameters (the lengths of the sides). But you might also want to have a `calculateArea()` function that calculates the area of a circle based on a single parameter (the radius). The trouble is that, as already mentioned, ActionScript does not require symmetry between the number of parameters defined for a function and the number of parameters passed to it. That means that you cannot have two functions with the same name—even if they expect different numbers of parameters.

You can simulate function overloading if you desire by using `if` statements in the function to check for the number of parameters. The following shows how you can write a function that calculates the area of either a rectangle or a circle depending on the number of parameters it is passed (determined by `arguments.length`):

```
function calculateArea():Number {
  switch(arguments.length) {
    case 1:
      var radius:Number = arguments[0];
      return (Math.PI * (radius * radius));
    case 2:
      var a:Number = arguments[0];
      var b:Number = arguments[1];
      return (a * b);
    default:
      return null;
  }
}
```

Returning a Value from a Function

Up to this point, you've mainly looked at functions that serve as subroutines. That is, the functions can serve to break up the main routine into smaller, more manageable chunks. In the cases where a function operates as a subroutine in that fashion, the function does not need to return a value. On the other hand, sometimes you want to create a function that performs some calculations or operations and then returns a value.

You can use the `return` statement within a function to return a specified value. The syntax for a `return` statement is as follows:

```
return value;
```

When you use the return statement to return a value from a function, you should specify the datatype that is being returned. You do this in the function definition just after the parenthesis. In the examples up to this point, the return type has been Void. But when you return a string, you should set the return type to String, when you return a number you should set the return type to Number, and so on.

Here is an example of a function that calculates the area of a rectangle and returns the value as a number.

```
function calculateArea(a:Number, b:Number):Number {
  var nArea:Number = a * b;
  return nArea;
}
```

As soon as a return statement is encountered, Flash exits the function. So, if any other code remains after the return statement, it is not encountered. For example:

```
function calculateArea(a:Number, b:Number):Number {
  var nArea:Number = a * b;
  return nArea;
  trace("The area is: " + nArea);
}

calculateArea(6, 6);
```

In the preceding example, the trace() statement is never executed. This is because the code in the function stops executing after the return statement.

Here is an example that uses several return statements. Obviously only one of the return statements can be encountered in any given call to the function. But in this case, one return statement occurs if a condition is met, and the other occurs if the condition is not met. The function accepts two parameters—an array (of strings) and a string value. This function searches through the array using a for statement until it finds an element that matches the string. Once it finds the match, it returns the index. If no match is found the function returns null.

```
function findMatchingElement(aTitles:Array,
                             sTitle:String):Number
{
  // Loop through all the elements in the array.
  for(var i:Number = 0; i < aTitles.length; i++) {

    // If one of the elements matches the value of sTitle
    // the return the index. This will cause the function to
    // stop executing.
    if(aTitles[i] == sTitle) {
      return i;
    }
  }

  // If no match was found then (and only then) this
  // statement is encountered.
  return null;
}
```

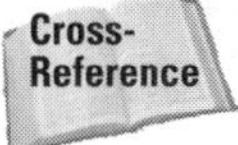

For more information on arrays, see Chapter 11.

Regardless of what a function does, if it returns a value, chances are good that you should invoke the function as part of an expression. For example, the `calculateArea()` function could be used in the following way:

```
var nArea = calculateArea(6, 6);
```

Essentially, the function becomes a value just like a string, number, variable, and so on. Therefore, just as the following is a valid yet not-too-useful ActionScript statement:

```
6;
```

so too is this:

```
calculateArea(6, 6);
```

You want to actually use the returned value in some meaningful way. You can use a function that returns a value in any of the same situations in which you would use a variable. You already saw the `calculateArea()` function used in an assignment statement. Here is another example in which the function is used as part of a conditional expression.

```
if(calculateArea(6, 6) > 18) {
  trace("The area is more than 18.");
}
```

Referencing Functions

You can reference a function by its name. When you use the function name in conjunction with the function call operator (parentheses) the function is invoked. But the name by itself serves as a reference to the function. This means that you can actually use the function name to assign a reference to a variable, for example. Once you have assigned a reference to the function to a variable, you can invoke the function using that variable name in conjunction with the function call operator. Here is an example:

```
function calculateArea(a:Number, b:Number):Number {
  var nArea:Number = a * b;
  return nArea;
}
var fCalcA:Function = calculateArea;
trace(fCalcA(6, 6));
```

The reason for this is not likely immediately apparent. But you'll see how this can be useful shortly. In the next section, you'll see how you can use this fact to assign anonymous functions to variables. And later in the book, you'll see examples in which a reference to a function can be passed into an object to be used as a callback at a later point.

Creating Function Literals

Thus far you have examined how to define functions using the standard, named function syntax. There is, however, another way of defining a function using a function literal. A function literal, also sometimes called an *anonymous function,* allows you to create a function that does not have a name. The function can then be assigned to a variable.

Here is the syntax for a function literal:

```
function():datatype {
  statements
};
```

You might notice that the syntax between a standard function declaration and a function literal is really quite similar. There are really only two differences: First of all, the function literal does not include a function name. And second, the function literal should be followed by a semicolon, whereas a standard function declaration should not.

As mentioned, you typically want to assign the function literal to a variable. Otherwise, the function falls *out of scope* (meaning that it becomes undefined) as soon as it is defined. Here is an example of a function literal assigned to a variable.

```
var fSayHi:Function = function(sName:String):Void {
  trace("Hi, " + sName);
}
fSayHi("Joey"); // Displays: Hi, Joey
```

As you can see, you can invoke a function literal using the variable to which it has been assigned.

Why, then, you might ask, use a function literal instead of a standard function declaration? In ActionScript 1.0 there were many more reasons. In ActionScript 2.0 there are fewer reasons, but they are still important.

In Chapter 7, you take a look at objects and methods. In short, an object is a collection of data, and a method is a function assigned to that object. When you define methods for object instances in ActionScript, it is convenient to use a function literal. You've actually already seen a few examples of this in Chapter 4 when you assigned some event handler method definitions to MovieClip instances.

```
mcCircle.onPress = function():Void {
  trace("Circle has been pressed.");
};
```

Understanding Scope

Scope is the area within which something is defined within ActionScript. Some things are defined only within a timeline. Others are defined within the scope of an entire movie. And yet, others can be defined only within a function. When discussing scope and functions, there are two types of scope that need to be examined: variable scope and function scope. *Variable scope* is the scope of variables within a function; *function scope* is the scope of a function within a movie.

Variable Scope

When you declare a variable inside of a function properly, the variable is what's known as a *local variable*. A local variable means that when you declare a variable within a function, its definition does not persist after the function call. This is a good way to avoid naming conflicts with other variables.

The following is an example of a function that declares and initializes a local variable named sMessage. The local variable is defined within the function. But if you try to use trace() to display the value of the variable outside of the function, the result will be undefined.

```
function testScope():Void {
  var sMessage:String = "hello, world!";
}
testScope();
trace(sMessage); // Displays: undefined
```

In a large program with many functions, using local variables helps to assure that you will have fewer conflicts between variables with the same name. Although you should always attempt to use unique names for your variables, it is possible that you will reuse the same name for a variable in different functions. If each has global scope, one might interfere with the other, leading to undesired values and results. Another possible reason to use local variables is for memory management. Even though it might not be a really significant amount, every variable that is defined in your program takes up memory. If you are not using a variable for anything, but it is still defined, it is a waste of memory. By using local variables, the memory is freed up after the function is finished. Again, the amount of memory is probably not anything to be concerned about, but it is something to keep in mind.

Parameters are treated as local variables — having scope within the function, but not outside it. You can see this with the following example:

```
function testParamScope(sMessage:String):Void {
  trace(sMessage);
}
testParamScope("hello, world!");  // Displays: hello, world!
trace(sMessage); // Displays: undefined
```

In contrast with this, variables declared outside of the function, but on the same timeline in which the function is defined, can be used within the function. For example:

```
function testScopeTimeline():Void {
  trace(sMessage);
}
var sMessage:String = "hello, world!";
testScopeTimeline(); // Displays: hello, world!
```

In the preceding example, the variable sMessage is defined outside of the function, but it is available within the function.

Function Scope

As you've seen thus far, when you declare a function, it is scoped to the timeline on which it has been defined. That means that it can be called from within the same timeline by its name or outside that timeline if a target path is used. If you want to use the function within the same timeline then this is not a problem. If you want to use the function from within another timeline, it is slightly less convenient. And if you want to use the function from within an object that has no timeline, it becomes problematic.

In ActionScript 1.0 it was a common practice to create globally accessible functions using the special _global scope. It was (and is) possible to assign a function to a globally scoped variable. Then the function could be invoked from anywhere in the movie using that variable. For example:

```
_global.calculateArea = function(a:Number, b:Number):Number {
  var nArea:Number = a * b;
  return nArea;
};
```

You could then invoke the function anywhere in the movie as follows:

```
calculateArea(6, 6);
```

However, in ActionScript 2.0 this is no longer a recommended practice. Instead, it is a good idea to create classes containing static methods that accomplish these tasks. This issue is covered in Chapter 7.

Creating Recursion

Recursion is simply when a function calls itself from within the function body. This is a necessary process in some cases. The classic example of recursion is that of calculating the factorial of a number. As a refresher, remember that a factorial of a number n is given by the formula:

```
n * (n-1) * (n-2) ... * 1
```

For example, the factorial of 5 is 120 (5 * 4 * 3 * 2 * 1). In order to create a function that calculates the factorial of a number, you have to use recursion. Listing 6-1 shows a function that does just that.

Listing 6-1: Recursive Function Example

```
function factorial(n:Number):Number{
  if(n > 0){
    return n * factorial(n-1);
  }
  else{
    return 1;
  }
}
```

Recursion is a pretty simple concept, but it is often a new concept to people who have not written a lot of code. For this reason, it can sometimes be a bit confusing. You might get it right away. But if you feel perplexed, the function from Listing 6-1 is discussed in more detail. To see how the recursion in this example works, look at what happens when the function is invoked. In this case, we use a small number to keep it short:

```
trace(factorial(3));
```

When the `factorial()` function is first called, it is called with a value of `3`. It executes the statement within the `if` statement because `n` is greater than `0`. The statement instructs the function to return the value of the expression `n * factorial(n-1)`. In order to evaluate the expression, the function must call itself (`factorial(n-1)`). This time, when `factorial()` is called, it is called with a value of `2`. Again, the value of `n` is greater than `0`, so the first `return` statement is executed. And once again, the function calls itself. This time, it is with a value of `1`. The same process is run again with `factorial()` being called one more time with a value of `0`. On this function call, however, `n` is no longer greater than `0`, so `1` is returned and the function is not called again.

You should be very careful to make sure that your recursive functions have a limit to the number of recursions that can take place. Consider what would happen if the function from Listing 6-1 were written like this:

```
function factorial(n:Number):Number{
  return n * factorial(n-1);
}
```

The function would keep calling itself forever. This infinite loop would most likely lead to a crash. Fortunately, Flash has a safeguard against this, and after a set number of recursions, the ActionScript is disabled in the movie. If you use this sort of function of infinite recursion (meaning that there is no condition that will cause the recursion to stop) in your movie, you get a message like this in the Output window when you test it:

```
256 levels of recursion were exceeded in one action list.
This is probably an infinite loop.
Further execution of actions has been disabled in this movie.
```

Writing for Reusability

When writing functions, keep in mind the importance of portable or reusable code. Ideally, you should strive to make your functions as generalized and as encapsulated as possible A function should typically operate like a black box. This means that the activity of a function is essentially independent of the rest of the program. A well-written function should be able to be plugged into many different programs, like a master key fits many different locks.

When you write your functions, you should write them with the idea of reusability. Here are some points to remember when writing generalized functions:

✦ **In general, do not use variables that have been defined outside the functions.** The variables (and objects) that are used within your functions should be declared within the function or passed to the function as parameters. If you need to assign a value to a variable that will be used outside the scope of the function, consider using a `return` statement instead. Because a function can return only one value at a time, you may find that using a `return` statement seems limiting. If this is the case in your function, then probably one of two things is happening: Either the values you want to return are related values, and you can put them into an array or object and return that, or they are unrelated, and your function should be broken up into multiple functions. There are exceptions to this rule of functions that are completely portable. Sometimes you simply want to use a function to group together some functionality in a movie for the purposes of organizing your code into subroutines. In such cases, it is acceptable to directly access variables and objects declared outside of the function.

✦ **Give your functions names that describe the task they perform.** This helps you to easily identify what a function does when you are looking for it again. If you find this difficult because your function does many things, consider breaking up that function into multiple functions. Even though you want to write generalized functions, they should perform specific tasks.

Sometimes, it simply is not appropriate to write a really generalized function. If the task for which you are writing a function is very specific to a program you are working on, then trying to make it too generalized is not necessarily appropriate. On the other hand, the points mentioned are still very good guidelines, so keep them in mind.

Using Built-in Functions

Thus far, you've learned how you can create custom functions in ActionScript. Typically, these are the types of functions to which people are referring when they talk about functions. However, there are many other built-in functions in ActionScript that you can use in much the same way as you would use a custom function. If you look in the Actions toolbox you'll see a folder named Global Functions. Inside this folder are additional subfolders containing all the built-in functions. Many of these functions have been replaced by classes and methods (see Chapter 7) and therefore it is best to use the newer replacements. For example, all of the timeline control, movie clip control, and printing functions have been replaced by methods. But there are still some global, built-in functions that are useful. Some of these functions include:

✦ **fscommand ():** This function is used only in very specific circumstances. The `fscommand()` function enables your Flash movie to communicate with the player. You can read more about this function in Chapters 31 and 33.

✦ **setInterval()/clearInterval():** These functions enable you to instruct Flash to invoke other functions at specific, timed intervals. See the section "Creating Interval Functions" for more information.

✦ **escape()/unescape():** These functions are used to convert text to and from URL-safe format. See Chapter 15 for more information.

✦ **getTimer():** The `getTimer()` function returns the number of milliseconds since the Flash movie began playing. This can be potentially useful for some timed processes in which great accuracy and precision are not required. For instance, you may want to have certain loops in your movie "time out," and `getTimer()` is an appropriate function to use in these cases. For instance, you may have a movie that waits for a response from a server. But if no response is obtained after 30 seconds or so, you might want to stop waiting and alert the user that the server is not responding.

✦ **trace():** The `trace()` function is one you've already seen throughout this book. It is useful for displaying messages while testing your Flash applications.

✦ **isFinite()/isNaN():** These functions test whether or not a value is finite or even a valid number.

✦ **parseFloat()/parseInt():** These functions parse a number from a string.

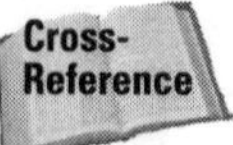

For more information on the `isFinite()`/`isNaN()` and `parseFloat()`/`parseInt()` functions, see Chapter 12.

Creating Interval Functions

One very useful thing that you can do with functions is create interval functions by utilizing the `setInterval()` command. Using `setInterval()`, you can specify a function and an interval (in milliseconds) on which the function should be continually called. The command returns an ID that can be used to stop the interval at a later point. Here is the standard syntax for `setInterval()` when used with a function:

```
setInterval(function, interval [, param1 ... , paramN])
```

The first parameter for `setInterval()` should be a reference to the function. That means you should *not* include the function call operator. In other words, if you are using `setInterval()` with a custom function, `writeMessage()`, then the first parameter for `setInterval()` is simply `writeMessage`.

The `interval` parameter is given in milliseconds. If you pass a value of 1000 for the `interval` parameter, the function is called once approximately every second. Be aware, however, that the interval on which the function is called is not exact. Flash calls the function as close to the interval as possible. But the processor on the computer on which the player is running has an impact on how accurately the interval is maintained.

You can optionally pass parameters to the function by way of the `setInterval()` action. Any parameters passed to `setInterval()` subsequent to the first two (required) parameters, are passed along to the function. For example, Listing 6-2 shows a function, `writeMessage()`, that takes two parameters. Using `setInterval()`, you can tell Flash to call this function every 1000 milliseconds and to also pass two values to the function.

Listing 6-2: Passing Parameters to an Interval Function

```
function writeMessage(sName:String, sMessage:String):Void {
  trace("Hello, " + sName + ". " + sMessage);
}
var nWriteInterval:Number = setInterval(writeMessage, 1000, "Joey",
"Good morning.");
```

One common mistake that Flash developers make with `setInterval()` is thinking that variables passed to the function through `setInterval()` will be evaluated each time the function is invoked. For example, Listing 6-2 could be rewritten as:

```
function writeMessage(sName:String, sMessage:String):Void {
  trace("Hello, " + sName + ". " + sMessage);
}
var sNameParam:String = "Joey";
var sMessageParam:String = "Good morning.";
var nWriteInterval:Number = setInterval(writeMessage, 1000, sNameParam,
sMessageParam);
```

It is tempting to believe that subsequently changing the values of `sNameParam` and/or `sMessageParam` would result in a different value being displayed in the Output window. However, the variables `sNameParam` and `sMessageParam` are not evaluated each time the function writeMessage() is invoked. Instead, they are evaluated one time—when setInterval() is called. Those values are then used for each call to the function. Therefore, even if you change the values of the variables, the same values will be passed to the function.

Listing 6-3 shows an example of a test you can use to check the precision with which Flash is able to invoke the interval function. You can place the code on the first frame of the main timeline of a new Flash document.

Listing 6-3: **Testing setInterval() Precision**

```
function traceTimer():Void {
  trace(getTimer());
}
var nTimerInterval:Number = setInterval(traceTimer, 200);
```

When you test this, you see that the function is called at intervals regularly close to 200 milliseconds apart, but the interval is not precise.

Frame rate can also have an influence on how you use setInterval() if you use setInterval() to affect animation on the stage. The movie updates the stage only visually at a rate equal to the frame rate of the movie. That means that if some process occurs within the movie at a rate higher than that of the frame rate, it is not reflected in the appearance on the stage at a rate higher than the frame rate. So if you were to use setInterval() to move a MovieClip instance across the stage and the frame rate is set at 1fps (frames per second), whereas the interval at which the function is being called is 10 milliseconds, it is likely that the movement seen on the stage would be choppy. You can remedy this easily by using the updateAfterEvent() action in the function being called by setInterval(), as shown in Listing 6-4. The updateAfterEvent() action instructs Flash to update the display regardless of the frame rate.

Listing 6-4: **Using updateAfterEvent() to Refresh Stage**

```
function moveRight(mcA:MovieClip):Void {
  mcA._x++;
  updateAfterEvent();
}
var nMoveRInterval = setInterval(moveRight, 10, mcCircle);
```

You can also define an anonymous function within setInterval() instead of passing the name or a reference to a function. Using this technique, the code in Listing 6-3 could be rewritten as follows:

```
var nTimerInterval:Number = setInterval(function()
{trace(getTimer());}, 200);
```

Now that you know how to set an interval for a function to be called, you probably want to know how to stop the function from being called. In other words, you want to know how to clear the interval. This is done very simply by calling the `clearInterval()` function, which takes a single parameter — the ID for the interval that should be cleared. Remember that `setInterval()` returns an ID that can be used to point to the interval. This ID can then be used as a parameter for `clearInterval()` to clear the desired interval. You can, for example, stop the interval set in Listing 6-3 with the following code:

```
clearInterval(nTimerInterval);
```

We'd like to know what you thought about this chapter. Visit `www.flashsupport.com/feedback` to fill out an online form with your comments.

Summary

- ✦ Functions are a way of grouping blocks of code that you can use again and again by calling them by name or reference.
- ✦ Functions can act as subroutines, or they can perform some algorithm and return a value.
- ✦ Functions can be named or anonymous. Each of these two types has different advantages and disadvantages.
- ✦ Using the `arguments` object created for a function, you can invoke a calling function, invoke an anonymous function recursively, and work with the arguments that have been passed to the function as an array rather than as separate variables.
- ✦ It is desirable to define generalized functions that can be used in many different contexts.

✦ ✦ ✦

Programming with Objects and Classes

In This Chapter

Understanding objects and classes

Using properties and methods

Working with objects as associative arrays

Creating classes

Using packages to organize classes

Using interfaces to define rules for classes

Objects are quite possibly the most powerful structures with which you can work in ActionScript. An object is simply a programming structure that has certain intrinsic qualities and characteristics. In that way, an object in ActionScript is not unlike an object you can hold in your hand. This chapter takes a look at objects, their blueprints (classes), as well as other important object-oriented programming (OOP) concepts. And, along the way, we hope the chapter demystifies OOP in general so that you can begin to harness the power of objects with confidence and authority.

Introducing Objects

Objects. We've been hinting at them since Chapter 4. So let's take a moment and really examine what an object is, what it does, and how you can use objects to assist in programming.

As mentioned in the introduction to this chapter, an object is a programming construct that has intrinsic qualities and characteristics. This is really the same idea as an object you can see in the so-called real world. For example, a book is an object. Books have intrinsic qualities — each book has a title, an author, a publisher, a page count, and so on. In programming terms, these qualities or characteristics are called *properties*.

In addition to having properties that are descriptive, objects can also perform actions. Your computer is an object. It is capable of performing actions such as turning on and off, opening and closing applications, and so on. Cars can accelerate, birds can fly, and so on. These are all examples of actions that objects can perform. When programmers talk about the actions that ActionScript objects can perform, we call them *methods*.

Understanding Object Blueprints

Objects can be categorized according to the blueprint from which they were created. This is true of nonprogramming objects as well. You can categorize all cars as car objects. Clearly not all cars are exactly the same. Even two cars that rolled off the same line one after the other are going to have some differences, and cars of different make, model, and year are going to be quite different. Nonetheless, all cars can be said to have similar characteristics such as having tires, engines, steering wheels, and so on. Likewise, all cars (okay, well, all *running* cars) are capable of the action of accelerating, braking, and the like. It is possible to say, therefore, that cars all derive from the same fundamental blueprint.

In this same way, objects in ActionScript can be categorized based on the type of blueprint from which they have been derived. In programming terms, the blueprint is called a *class*. The class defines all the basic properties and methods for any objects that are derived from it. For example, a class with which you may already be familiar, the `MovieClip` class, defines properties such as `_x` and `_y` as well as methods such as `play()`. These properties and methods are defined in the class and then each `MovieClip` object inherits them.

If you look in the Actions toolbox you should find a folder named Built-In Classes. In that folder are several subfolders organizing all the built-in classes in ActionScript. Using ActionScript you can create objects from the built-in classes as well as from custom classes that you (or someone else) have created. First, let's take a look at the built-in classes. Then, later on in the chapter, you learn how you can create your own custom classes.

Creating an Object

Before you tell Flash to create an object, all you have is the blueprint—the class. You need to specifically tell Flash that you want it to create an instance of that class. An *instance* of a class is synonymous with an object that is derived from the class. In most cases, you create an instance of a class by invoking the class's constructor. The *constructor* is a special function that shares the name of the class and creates a new instance. The constructor should be invoked as part of a `new` statement, and the returned value (the new instance) can be assigned to a variable.

```
var varName:datatype = new ClassName();
```

The datatype you should use to declare the variable should match the name of the class from which you are instantiating the object.

The constructor function, just like any other function, might not accept parameters. This depends entirely on how the constructor has been defined. In Chapters 9 through 27 you'll get a chance to review the constructors for all the built-in classes, and so you'll know what, if any, parameters their constructors expect. Also, when you use code hinting in the Actions panel, you can quickly see what parameters a given constructor may expect.

To begin with, let's take a look at the most basic kind of object there is—an `Object` object. The `Object` class is the most fundamental class in all of ActionScript, so it is a good place to start. Here is how you can create a new `Object` instance using the constructor.

```
var oFirstObj:Object = new Object();
```

That wasn't too difficult now, was it? You can now use the `instanceof` operator (see Chapter 5) to verify that `oFirstObj` is, in fact, an instance of the `Object` class.

```
trace(oFirstObj instanceof Object);  // Displays: true
```

Now that you've seen how to create a basic `Object` object, how about creating a `String` object? When you create a `String` object using the constructor, you typically will want to pass the constructor a string literal (a quoted string) as a parameter.

```
var sTitle:String = new String("ActionScript Bible");
```

Again, you can test to verify that the new object is actually an instance of the `String` class.

```
trace(sTitle instanceof String);
```

Accessing Object Properties

Many classes have properties defined such that instances of the class inherit those properties. For example, the String class defines a length property. You can see this if you look in the Actions toolbox. The length property holds the value of the number of characters in the string. For example, if you define a String object as follows:

```
var sTitle:String = new String("ActionScript Bible");
```

then the length property of that object (sTitle) will have a value of 18 because the value ActionScript Bible has eighteen characters. If you create another String object:

```
var sName:String = new String("Joey Lott");
```

the object (sName) would have a length property with a value of 9.

The preceding examples created two String objects named sTitle and sName. Each of these objects was derived from the same blueprint — the String class. Therefore, both of these objects inherited the same set of properties and methods, including the length property. However, the objects don't have the same *value* for the property. Even though the objects share the same blueprint, they are still able to operate independently of one another.

In order to access a property of an object, you need only use the name of the object, a dot, and the name of the property — in that order and without spaces. This syntax is called *dot syntax* because, rather obviously, it uses a dot. For example, you can access the length property of a String object named sTitle in the following manner:

```
sTitle.length;
```

Now, although the preceding statement is perfectly valid ActionScript, it clearly would not be very useful. The length property yields a value, and you likely want to do something with that value. Therefore, you can use a property in exactly the same ways that you can use a variable. In fact, a property is essentially a variable associated with an object. Here are a few examples of how you can use the length property:

```
trace(sTitle.length);
if(sTitle.length > 12) {
  trace("The title has more than twelve characters.");
}
var nLenDif:Number = sTitle.length - sName.length;
```

Properties can differ from normal variables in one way, however. Typically, you can both read and write to a variable. For example:

```
var nQuantity:Number = 15; // Write
trace(nQuantity);  // Read
nQuantity = 16;  // Write again
trace(nQuantity);  // Read again
```

Many properties work in the same way. For example, you can read and write the _x and _y properties of a MovieClip object. On the other hand, some properties are *read-only properties*. That means that you can read the property value, but you cannot assign a new value to the property directly. The _currentframe property of a MovieClip object is an example of this. Even if you try to assign a new value to the property, it will not take. Here is an example with a MovieClip instance named mcCircle. Assume its timeline is stopped on frame 1.

```
trace(mcCircle._currentframe);  // Displays: 1
mcCircle._currentframe = 6;  // Will not take
trace(mcCircle._currentframe);  // Displays: 1
```

Accessing Object Methods

A method is, as we have already discussed, an action that an object can take. That is a very high-level explanation of a method. In more technical terms, a method is a function that has been associated with an object. Therefore, when accessing the method of an object, you use the same terminology as when accessing a function—you say that the method is called or invoked. Furthermore, you use the same function call operator (`()`) in order to invoke a method, and you can pass parameters to a method in the same way as you pass parameters to a function.

The differences between a method and a function are as follows:

- ✦ When invoking a method you use dot syntax as with a property. That means that you use a dot between the name of the object and the method call.
- ✦ When you invoke a method, Flash automatically knows to perform the action specifically for that one object. This is unlike a function. A function does not inherently perform any action on any particular object.

The following is an example in which a method is invoked on an object. First, a `String` object is created. Next the `substr()` method is invoked. This method returns a portion of the original string starting at the specified index (0), and containing the specified number of characters (12).

```
var sTitle:String = new String("ActionScript Bible");
var sSubject:String = sTitle.substr(0, 12);
trace(sSubject);  // Displays: ActionScript
```

Methods can perform all kinds of actions. In the preceding example, you saw how a method can extract a portion of a string and return it. ActionScript classes have methods that do everything from playing a sound to loading an XML document to creating new text fields. Throughout the upcoming chapters, you will get an opportunity to see almost all of the methods built into ActionScript.

Working with Static Properties and Methods

Thus far you've read about properties and methods invoked from instantiated objects. For example, you can create a new `String` object and then read the value of the `length` property or invoke the `substr()` method. When you do so, the property or method that is accessed is specific to that particular object. In other words, the `substr()` method acts upon the specific `String` object from which it is invoked—not from any other object.

However, there are some properties and methods that are invoked from the class itself, and not from an instantiated object. These kinds of properties are called *static properties* and the methods invoked from a class are called *static methods*. The reason for static properties and methods may not seem clear at first, but when you take a look at the specific static properties and methods available within ActionScript, the purpose should become obvious.

Here are a few examples of the static properties available within ActionScript: From the `Math` class you can read static properties such as `PI` and `SQRT2` and from the `Key` class you can read static properties such as `ENTER`, `SPACE`, and `CAPSLOCK`. If you look at the names of these static properties, even if you don't know anything about ActionScript, you can probably guess what values they represent. The static property `Math.PI`, for example, holds the value of the mathematical pi (~3.142). The `Key.SPACE` static property holds the key code value for the space key on the keyboard. Because these values don't change with each instance of the class there is no need to have to access the values from instances. In fact, you cannot even create an instance of some of these classes such as `Math` and `Key` because there is no need to create instances that would all be exactly the same. There would not be any possible benefit derived from creating an instance of the Math class, for example. Why? Because the Math class serves simply as a container for mathematical static properties and static methods.

A handful of built-in classes have static methods. Some examples of static methods include Mouse.hide(), Math.sqrt(), and Selection.getFocus(). As with the static properties, when you look at the static methods, it becomes apparent why they are invoked from the class. Consider the Mouse.hide() method. There is only one mouse, and so there is no need to create multiple instances of the Mouse class. Likewise, only one selection can be made at a time. Therefore, there is no need to instantiate the Selection class.

As you continue through the rest of the book, we'll point out static properties and static methods as they are relevant.

Adding New Object Properties

The majority of the built-in ActionScript classes are what we refer to as *dynamic* classes. This means that you can add new properties (and methods as discussed in the next section) to instances even if those properties are not defined for the class. In order to define a new property for an object, all you need to do is assign a new value to it as though it already existed for the object. Here's an example:

```
var oDynamicObj:Object = new Object();
oDynamicObj.dynamicProperty = "New property value";

// Displays: New property value
trace(oDynamicObj.dynamicProperty);
```

If you look in the Actions toolbox, you will see that the Object class does not define any property named dynamicProperty. But once the object was instantiated, you can create the new property for that object (and only that object).

That the built-in classes happen to be dynamic is quite useful in many situations. It enables a lot of flexibility in your code. You can define new properties for objects for all kinds of reasons. For example, by assigning a property to an object you can then quickly reference that same value internally within the object. Additionally, it is useful when an object is self-descriptive. For example, you might want to assign custom properties to a MovieClip instance such as defaultX and defaultY. You could then assign to these properties some default coordinates to which the instance should move when, for example, a user resets a puzzle movie application.

Adding New Object Methods

Dynamic classes enable you not only to define custom properties for the instances but also custom methods. Typically, adding custom methods to an object is not a particularly good practice. But for some scenarios you could encounter, it is potentially useful. Therefore, for the sake of completeness, we'll include a brief discussion of this feature here.

You can add a new method to an object in much the same way that you can add a new property—by simply defining the method and assigning it to a custom property of the object. We have already covered all the information you need to accomplish this. Let's revisit it here: First, in Chapter 6, we covered how to assign a function literal to a variable and how to then invoke the function by way of the variable. Then, earlier in this chapter we mentioned that methods are, in fact, functions associated with an object. Therefore, combining these two pieces of information, you can assign a custom method to an object as in the following example:

```
var oDynamicObj:Object = new Object();
oDynamicObj.dynamicMethod = function():Void {
  trace("Method invoked");
};

// Now, call the method.
ODynamicObj.dynamicMethod();
```

Defining Event Handler Methods

We first mentioned event handler methods back in Chapter 4. They are specially named methods that exist for certain types of objects that Flash automatically invokes when a corresponding event occurs. For example, the onPress() event handler method is automatically invoked for a MovieClip object when the user clicks the instance with the mouse. However, by default these event handler methods are not defined. That makes sense because what you want to occur when the event happens is up to you. So you have to define the method.

Once an object that accepts event handler methods has been created, you can define the event handler method(s) using essentially the same technique as outlined in the section, "Adding New Object Methods." The only difference is that in this case, you want to assign the function literal to the specific event handler method name. The following is an example in which the onPress() event handler method is defined for a MovieClip object named mcCircle:

```
mcCircle.onPress = function ():Void {
  trace("You clicked the circle.");
};
```

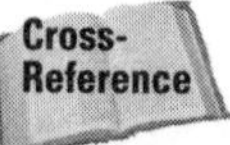

We discuss event handler methods in more detail in Chapter 9, "MovieClip and Button Classes."

Telling Objects to Talk to Themselves

Admit it. You talk to yourself. And that's exactly what you want to help objects to accomplish as well. You see, when you create a custom method for an object, or when you define an event handler method, you need to be able to tell an object to address itself. For example, if you define an onPress() method for a MovieClip object, you might want to be able to reference the object's properties from within that method. As you've already learned, you use dot syntax when accessing properties, and so that will hold true in this scenario as well. The only thing you need to know is what name an object uses to refer to itself. In ActionScript you can use the keyword this to reference an object from within its own methods. Here's an example in which a MovieClip instance named mcCircle references its own _xscale and _yscale properties within an onPress() event handler method. The result is that when the user clicks the instance, the MovieClip object scales up by 50 percent.

```
mcCircle.onPress = function():Void {
  this._xscale = 150;
  this._yscale = 150;
};
```

And, of course, you can reference an object's methods in the same way, using the `this` keyword within a custom method or event handler method definition. In this example, when the user clicks the `MovieClip` instance named `mcCircle`, the object's timeline begins to play back.

```
mcCircle.onPress = function():Void {
  this.play();
};
```

The `this` keyword is always a reference to the current object. In the preceding examples, `this` referred to the `MovieClip` instance `mcCircle`. Internally, the object does not know its name. It knows only how to refer to itself as `this`.

The only exception to the use of the keyword `this` occurs with `Button` instances. Unlike every other kind of object, `Button` objects cannot refer to themselves. Instead, the keyword `this` refers to the parent timeline when used within a `Button` object method. `Button` objects can be useful in some situations. They do provide a quick and convenient way to define button states (up, over, and down). However, because `Button` objects don't work in the same ways as other objects, we tend to give preference to `MovieClip` objects in place of `Button` objects. As you will read in Chapter 9, it is possible to accomplish the same tasks with a `MovieClip` as with a `Button`.

Displaying the Time with an Object

Now that you have learned about variables, functions, and objects, it's about time you created a Flash application that utilizes some of the things you have learned. In this exercise, you'll create a new Flash application that uses a function and a simple `Date` object to write the current time to the Output panel.

1. Open a new Flash document. Save the document as `displayTime001.fla`.

2. Select the first frame of the default layer on the main timeline, and open the Actions panel. You can open the Actions panel either by pressing F9 or by choosing Window ➪ Development Panels ➪ Actions.

3. In the Script pane type the following code:

```
function displayTime():Void {
  var dNow:Date = new Date();
  var nHours:Number = dNow.getHours();
  var nMinutes:Number = dNow.getMinutes();
  var nSeconds:Number = dNow.getSeconds();
  trace("Hours: " + nHours);
  trace("Minutes: " + nMinutes);
  trace("Seconds: " + nSeconds);
}
displayTime();
```

4. Test the movie by pressing Ctrl+Enter on Windows or ⌘+Enter on the Mac. Or, you can choose Control ➪ Test Movie.

If all went according to plan, you should see something that looks similar to what is shown in Figure 7-1. Of course, your number values will be different. They should match up with the current time on your computer. If you test the movie again, you should see a different time displayed.

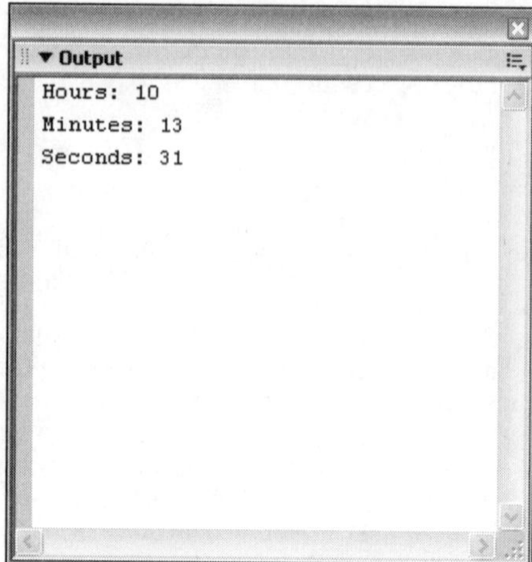

Figure 7-1: Sample output from the Flash application

Let's take a closer look at the code in this application. First of all, you want to create a function named `displayTime()` that returns no value. Therefore, the function should be declared as `Void`.

```
function displayTime():Void {
  // function statements to go here
}
```

Next, within the function you want to create a new `Date` object. We'll discuss the `Date` class in further detail in Chapter 14. For now, simply know that when you call the `Date` constructor with no parameters, Flash automatically creates a new object representing the computer's current time.

```
var dNow:Date = new Date();
```

Next, you want to extract the hours, minutes, and seconds parts from the object. If you look in the Built-in Classes ➪ Core ➪ Date ➪ Methods folder in the Actions toolbox, you will see that, among many others, there are three methods that suggest they might do exactly what you want. The `getHours()`, `getMinutes()`, and `getSeconds()` methods return the hours, minutes, and seconds parts of the `Date` object as numbers. You can assign those values to variables for convenience.

```
var nHours:Number = dNow.getHours();
var nMinutes:Number = dNow.getMinutes();
var nSeconds:Number = dNow.getSeconds();
```

You can then use `trace()` to display the results:

```
trace("Hours: " + nHours);
trace("Minutes: " + nMinutes);
trace("Seconds: " + nSeconds);
```

The function has been successfully defined. The only remaining step is to invoke the function.

```
displayTime();
```

Working with MovieClip Objects

The `MovieClip` class belongs to a small conceptual group of built-in ActionScript classes that are not instantiated in the standard way using a constructor. Instances of the `MovieClip`, `Button`, and `TextField` classes are objects that can be created at authoring time by dragging or drawing an instance on the stage. (You'll also see how to create instances of these programmatically in Chapter 9.) Even if you weren't aware of it, every time you created a `MovieClip` or `Button` on the stage and every time you drew a dynamic or input `TextField` instance, you were creating an object.

Because these types of objects can be created at authoring time, you cannot use a constructor to instantiate them. For example, this code will not create a new `MovieClip` instance on the stage:

```
mcCircle:MovieClip = new MovieClip();
```

Instead, when you create the instance at authoring time, you should make sure to give it an instance name via the Property inspector. Figure 7-2 shows an instance of a circle `MovieClip` placed on the stage and the name `mcCircle` entered into the Property inspector. If you don't see the Property inspector in your version of Flash, choose Window ➪ Properties to show it.

You should also name `Button` and `TextField` instances in the same way when you create them at authoring time. The Property inspector for a `Button` looks almost identical to the Property inspector for a `MovieClip`. The Property inspector for a `TextField` looks slightly different, as shown in Figure 7-3. When you want to create a `TextField` object at authoring time, you can use the text tool to draw the text shape on the stage. Then, from the Property inspector make sure to choose either Dynamic or Input text. Static text is not an object.

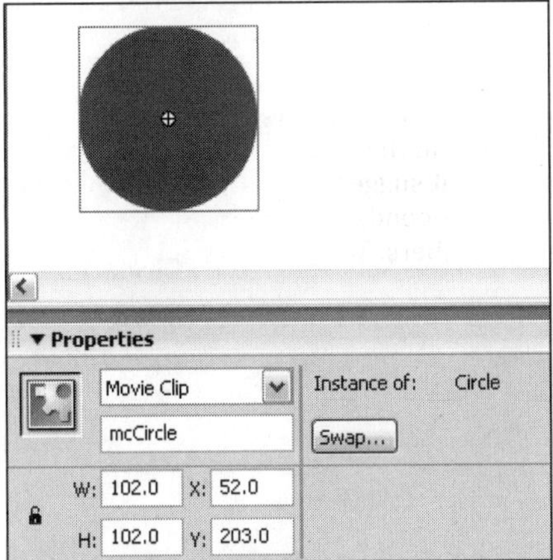

Figure 7-2: Creating an instance of a MovieClip on the stage and naming it with the Property inspector

Once you have created a new MovieClip, Button, or TextField object, you can invoke the properties and methods in the same way as with any other object. For example, if you have created a MovieClip instance named mcCircle, you can access the _x property using standard dot syntax.

```
trace(mcCircle._x);
```

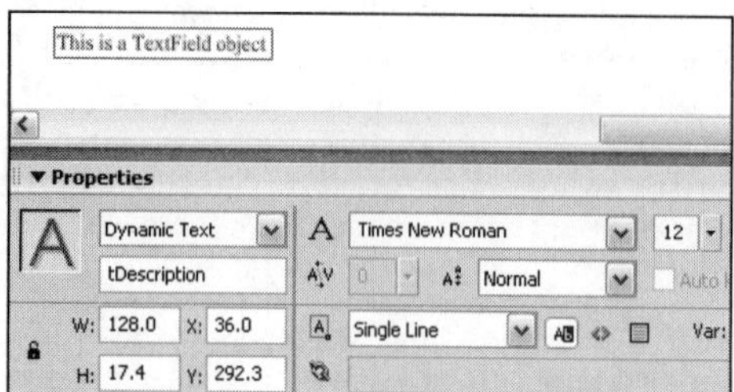

Figure 7-3: Creating a TextField object and naming it with the Property inspector

The only caveat at this point is that the ActionScript that references the object must be on the same timeline on which the object has been created. In other words, the object must exist within the same scope in which you are attempting to reference it. If you create a new MovieClip object on the main timeline, then you can reference it from ActionScript on the main timeline. You'll see how you can use different kinds of targeting techniques in order to reference objects on different timelines when you get to Chapter 9.

Displaying the Time Using a Movie Clip

In the previous section, "Displaying the Time with an Object," you created a Flash application with a function that displays the time in the Output panel when invoked. In this exercise you will modify that idea just slightly such that the time gets displayed when the user clicks a MovieClip instance on the stage.

1. Open a new Flash document and save it as displayTime002.fla.
2. Create a new Movie Clip symbol. You can accomplish this by pressing Ctrl+F8 on Windows or ⌘+F8 on the Mac. Or you can choose Insert ➪ New Symbol.
3. The Create New Symbol dialog box appears. In the Name field, type **Circle**. Make sure the Movie Clip option is selected, and click OK.
4. The new symbol should open in editing mode. Use the Oval tool to draw a filled circle. The exact size and color of the circle is not particularly important. Just make sure that it is visible and large enough that a user can click it.
5. Return to the main timeline.
6. Rename the default layer Circle.
7. Open the library and drag an instance of the Circle symbol onto the stage.
8. With the instance selected on the stage, give it a name via the Property inspector. Name the instance mcCircle.
9. Create a new layer. Name the layer Actions.

10. Select the first (and only) frame of the Actions layer and open the Actions panel.

11. Add the following code to the Script pane:

```
mcCircle.onPress = function():Void {
  var dNow:Date = new Date();
  var nHours:Number = dNow.getHours();
  var nMinutes:Number = dNow.getMinutes();
  var nSeconds:Number = dNow.getSeconds();
  trace("Hours: " + nHours);
  trace("Minutes: " + nMinutes);
  trace("Seconds: " + nSeconds);
};
```

12. Save the document and test the movie. When you click the circle, you should see the current time values displayed in the Output panel. Each time you click on the circle a new, updated set of values should be appended to the list in the Output panel.

Now that you've had an opportunity to complete the steps in this exercise, you're ready to take a closer look at what's going on.

First, you simply created a new Movie Clip symbol containing circle artwork. This is probably already a familiar process to you. Once you created the symbol, the next step was to create a new instance of it on the stage. So you returned to the main timeline, dragged an instance from the library onto the stage, and named the new instance.

It is a good practice to create your ActionScript code on its own layer. This is helpful when you need to locate your code. Therefore, the next thing you did was create a new layer named *Actions* specifically for this purpose. With that layer created, you then added the code to the keyframe on the layer. You may have noticed that the code looked remarkably similar to the code from the previous exercise. In fact, the majority of the code is identical. The only difference is that now the code is encapsulated in an event handler method instead of a regular function, and the code is invoked when the event occurs instead of manually invoking the function as before. The `onPress()` event handler method is used here because it handles the event of the user clicking on the object with the mouse.

Creating Interval Methods

In Chapter 6, you learned how to create interval functions using the `setInterval()` statement. Because methods are special kinds of functions, it is possible to create interval methods in much the same way that you created interval functions. In fact, you still use the same `setInterval()` command. The difference is that you need to provide `setInterval()` with some slightly different parameters because Flash now needs to know not just the function to invoke but the object from which to invoke the function (method).

When you want to use the `setInterval()` command to create an interval method, use the following syntax:

```
setInterval(object, functionName, interval[,
param1 ..., paramN]);
```

Other than a slight difference in the syntax, the `setInterval()` command works the same when invoking a method of an object as when invoking a function. The method is invoked at the specified interval; if any parameters are specified they are passed on to the method with each call, and the `setInterval()` command returns an ID that can be used to stop the interval later using `clearInterval()`.

It is important that the parameters you pass to setInterval() are of the correct type. The first parameter should be a reference to the object whose method you want to invoke. In contrast, the second parameter is not a reference to the method, but rather the name of the method as a string. The third parameter should be a number value specifying the interval in milliseconds. Here is an example that tells Flash to invoke the nextFrame() method of a MovieClip object named mcCircle at an interval of approximately once per second.

```
var nFrameInterval:Number = setInterval(mcCircle, "nextFrame", 1000);
```

If you need any more information on the setInterval() statement and how it operates in general, refer to Chapter 6.

Understanding the Object Class

The Object class is the most fundamental class in ActionScript. In fact, all the other classes in ActionScript are based on this basic class.

Because the Object class is basic, it does not serve a specific purpose like many other classes. For example, the String class deals specifically with strings, and it enables you to perform all kinds of tasks specific to strings. Likewise, the Color class enables you to work with colors programmatically. The Object class does not pertain to any specific tasks. Instead, the most common use of the Object class is to create simple objects that act as containers for related properties. Programmers often refer to this kind of construct as an *associative array* or a *hashtable*. An associative array is simply a basic object with properties that have something in common. For example, you could create an associative array that contains information about a car. The object could have properties such as make, model, and extColor. In ActionScript the code to create such an object would look like this:

```
// First, create the new Object object.
var oCar:Object = new Object();

// Next, define new properties and values.
oCar.make = "Oldsmobile";
oCar.model = "Alero";
oCar.extColor = "blue";
```

Remember that most of the built-in ActionScript classes are dynamic, meaning you can add new properties to an instance, even if they are not defined within the class. In the case of an Object object used as an associative array, you can also refer to the custom properties as *keys*. In the preceding example, the associative array named oCar has three keys — make, model, and extColor.

Associative arrays can be useful for grouping together related data. For example, in the preceding example it makes sense to group together the three pieces of data (the make, model, and exterior color) because they all pertain to the same car. You could, alternatively, create three variables such as the following:

```
var sCarMake:String = "Oldsmobile";
var sCarModel:String = "Alero";
var sCarExtColor:String = "blue";
```

However, grouping these values together as keys of a single associative array has several advantages. First, it makes it easier to see the relatedness between the data if they are all grouped together in a single object. And second, it is much easier to pass that data to a function or method—or to return that data from a function or method—if it is grouped together in a single object.

Creating Object Literals

You can create `Object` objects not only with the constructor as shown previously, but also using object literal syntax. Object literal syntax is as follows:

```
{property1:value1[, ... propertyN:valueN]}
```

For example, you can create the same `oCar` object from the previous section using the following object literal syntax:

```
var oCar:Object = {make:"Oldsmobile", model:"Alero", extColor:"blue"};
```

As you can see, this syntax can sometimes be more concise. This is one of the advantages of object literal syntax. Another advantage is that you can create the object inline within a function call or the like. For example, if a function or method expects an `Object` object as a parameter, you can define the object right within the function or method invocation. For example, the following shows a function named `displayCarInfo()` that expects a single object parameter. Then you can invoke the function and define the parameter value inline.

```
function displayCarInfo(oCarInfo:Object):Void {
  trace("Make: " + oCarInfo.make);
  trace("Model: " + oCarInfo.model);
  trace("Exterior Color: " + oCarInfo.extColor);
}

displayCarInfo({make:"Oldsmobile", model:"Alero", extColor:"blue"});
```

The result of the preceding code is that the following is displayed in the Output panel:

```
Make: Oldsmobile
Model: Alero
Exterior Color: blue
```

It is important to keep in mind that there is a time and place for object literals and a time and place for objects created using the constructor. If you want to simply define an object inline within a function call, use the object literal syntax. On the other hand, if the object is going to have many properties/keys, defining the object with object literal notation might be less readable than defining the object using standard constructor syntax.

Accessing Associative Array Keys and Values

In the preceding sections you've already seen how to create an associative array. You have also seen one of the two ways of accessing keys and values in an associative array. The first way uses dot syntax—which should already be familiar to you. However, there are certain limitations to dot syntax. The two primary issues that arise with dot syntax and associative arrays are:

- ✦ The key names must follow the variable naming rules. For example, the key name `extColor` is valid, but the name `Exterior Color` is not because it contains a space.
- ✦ There is no way to use variables to dynamically access the keys and values of an associative array when using dot syntax.

The solution to all of this is to use what programmers call *array-access notation*. When you use array-access notation, the basic syntax looks like the following:

```
object[key]
```

For example, the following statement uses dot syntax:

```
oCar.make = "Oldsmobile";
```

That same statement can be rewritten in array-access notation as follows:

```
oCar["make"] = "Oldsmobile";
```

Notice that the name of the key is in quotes. In other words, when using array-access notation the key is specified as a string.

You can use array-access notation in the same situations in which you can use dot syntax. For example, you can both assign a value to a key and read the value from the key as shown here.

```
oCar["make"] = "Oldsmobile";
trace(oCar["make"]);
```

Because the key is specified as a string when using array-access notation, you can use key names that you cannot use in dot syntax. For example, you cannot do the following:

```
oCar.Exterior Color = "blue";  // Will cause an error
```

However, you can do this:

```
oCar["Exterior Color"] = "blue";  // Correct
```

Creating keys such as `Exterior Color` can be useful in several scenarios. For example, the key names can be user-generated or can come from another source such as a database. In such a case, you cannot necessarily guarantee that the key names will follow variable naming rules. Another example is that you may want to display the names of the keys and their values to the user. In that case it is probably preferable to display a value such as `Exterior Color` instead of `extColor`.

When you use array-access notation you can also use variables for the keys. For example:

```
var keyName:String = "make";
trace(oCar[keyName]);  // Displays: Oldsmobile
```

Using variables as the key names can be quite useful in many situations. For example, if the names of the keys are unknown (they are retrieved from an outside source or specified by the user), the use of variables enables you to create such an application.

Looping Through Object Properties

If you have created an associative array, often it is useful to be able to loop through all the keys and values even if you don't necessarily know the key names. For this purpose you can use the `for...in` statement. The `for...in` statement syntax is as follows:

```
for(var prop:String in object) {
  statements
}
```

When Flash encounters a `for...in` statement, it automatically loops through all the enumerable (more on enumerable and non-enumerable properties later in this chapter) properties of the specified object. Through each iteration the next property name is assigned to the variable prop. The name of the variable is up to you. You can use the names item, prop, key, or any other valid variable name. Within the body of the for...in statement (inside the curly braces) you can use the variable to access the corresponding value in the associative array. Here is an example that creates an associative array and then uses a for...in statement to iterate through all the keys and values, and finally writes those to the Output panel.

```
var oCar:Object = new Object();
oCar["Make"] = "Oldsmobile";
oCar["Model"] = "Alero";
oCar["Exterior Color"] = "blue";

for(var key:String in oCar) {
  trace(key + ": " + oCar[key]);
}
```

The result in the Output panel is:

```
Exterior Color: blue
Model: Alero
Make: Oldsmobile
```

Notice that the order in which Flash iterates through the keys in the associative array does not match the order in which the keys were assigned to the object. Nor is it in alphabetical order. You cannot control the order in which ActionScript iterates through the keys. If you need to control the order you should use an integer-indexed array—an instance of the Array class.

For more information on Array objects see Chapter 11, "Using the Array Class."

Creating Watched Variables

The Object class adds functionality such that you can have Flash watch certain properties of an object. When a new value is assigned to the property, a specified function or method is automatically invoked. ActionScript passes the function at least three parameters—the name of the property being changed, the previous value, and the new value. This callback function can then perform any number of actions and/or logic, and then return the value that should be assigned to the property—either the previous value, the new value, or an entirely different value.

The watch() method was utilized more often in ActionScript 1.0. In ActionScript 2.0, as you will see shortly, the new syntactical structure of classes enables you to much more easily handle what the watch() method used to do. The watch() method may still be useful for some situations in which you want to watch the properties of an instance of a built-in class.

The following is an example that creates an associative array object named oCar that contains information about a car such as the make, model, and exterior color. Additionally, the example will place a watch on the Exterior Color key. Within the callback function there is an if statement that checks to see if the colors are acceptable. If the newly assigned value is in that list then the new value is returned, thus confirming the assignment of the new value. Otherwise, the previous value is returned, and the new value is discarded.

```
// First, create a function that displays the values of the
// associative array. This way we can invoke this function
```

```
// multiple times instead of rewriting the same for...in
// statement.
function displayKeysValues(oObj:Object):Void {
  for(var key:String in oObj) {
    trace(key + ": " + oObj[key]);
  }
}

// This is the callback function. Notice that we declare
// three parameters - the name of the property/key, the
// previous value, and the new value. Flash will take care
// of passing the appropriate values.
function chooseColor(sProp:String,
                     sPrevVal:String,
                     sNewVal:String):String
{

  // Check to see if the new value is in the list of
  // acceptable colors - blue, orange, or pink. If so,
  // return the new value. Otherwise, return the previous
  // value.
  if(sNewVal == "blue" ||
     sNewVal == "orange" ||
     sNewVal == "pink")
  {
    return sNewVal;
  }
  return sPrevVal;
}

// Create the oCar associative array object, and defined
// the three keys and values.
var oCar:Object = new Object();
oCar["Make"] = "Oldsmobile";
oCar["Model"] = "Alero";
oCar["Exterior Color"] = "blue";

// Tell Flash to watch the Exterior Color key for any
// changes. If there is a change, invoke the chooseColor()
// function.
oCar.watch("Exterior Color", chooseColor);

// Display the original values.
displayKeysValues(oCar);

// Set the Exterior Color to orange.
oCar["Exterior Color"] = "orange";

// Display the values. Since orange is in the list of
// acceptable color values, it shows up here.
displayKeysValues(oCar);

// Set the Exterior Color to green.
```

```
oCar["Exterior Color"] = "green";

// Display the values. Since green is not in the list of
// acceptable color values, the previous color value of
// orange is retained.
displayKeysValues(oCar);
```

Creating Custom Classes

Now that you've had a chance to learn about objects in general, and you've created a few instances of objects based on built-in classes, the natural progression is to next delve into creating custom classes. Note that in many cases creating custom classes is considered to be an advanced topic. Furthermore, the majority of the remaining chapters in this book do not specifically rely on your having an understanding of how to create your own classes. Therefore, if you prefer, you are welcome to momentarily skip this portion and move on to the next. Also, as you read this section, if there are any parts that are not completely clear to you, don't despair. ActionScript is not the kind of thing that you are likely to master in a day . . . or a week . . . or a year. The authors of this book have been working with ActionScript for years, and yet we continue to learn things daily. So keep an open mind, and you'll have some fun with custom classes.

Understanding the Purpose of Custom Classes

You've looked through the Actions toolbox. Perhaps you've flipped through the table of contents of this book. You've seen that ActionScript has a whole slew of built-in classes. They seem to do just about everything. So why would you want to create your own custom class?

Good question. The answer is: To make your programming a little easier, a little more easily understood, and a little easier to share and reuse. Every application involves different types of concepts that can be grouped together. A storefront application would involve concepts such as products, users, shopping basket, and so forth. Each of these concepts can be modeled as a class by grouping together the common characteristics and actions. For example, each user can have a name, a password, and a shipping address. These are the characteristics of a user. Likewise, a user can perform actions such as logging in, checking out, and so on. A storefront application is likely to have many users. So it is convenient to create a single class that helps to describe all users in generic terms. Then, each specific user can be an instance of that class.

Custom classes are not limited to creating something that describes a user in a storefront application. You can create custom classes that describe just about anything. If you are creating a message board application, you might create classes to describe threads, posts, and categories. In a whiteboard application, you might create classes to describe lines, shapes, and so on. Classes can also describe less tangible types of objects. Some classes can be used to create objects for sending and receiving, processing, and otherwise working with data. The possibilities for classes are limitless.

Working with the Classpath

All ActionScript classes should be defined in AS files located in a directory within Flash's classpath. AS files refer to text files saved with the file extension `.as`. The Flash classpath is a list of directories to which Flash will automatically look for these AS files. By default the classpath consists of the following two directories:

✦ The same directory to which the FLA file has been saved. This is convenient for classes that pertain only to one project. But for classes that you are likely to reuse in multiple projects, this is not the recommended location.

✦ The Classes directory in what Macromedia refers to as the user configuration directory. This directory is found in the following locations depending on your operating system.

```
Windows 98 and ME: C:\[Windows Directory]\
Application Data\Macromedia\
Flash 2004\[language]\Configuration\Classes
Windows NT: C:\[Windows directory]\profiles\
[user name]\Application Data\Macromedia\
Flash 2004\[language]\Configuration\Classes
Windows 2000 and XP: C:\Documents and Settings\
[user name]\Application Data\Macromedia\Flash
2004\[language]\Configuration\Classes
Mac OS Classic (Mac OS 8.x and above) Single-User:
Hard Disk:System Folder:Application
Support:Macromedia:Flash 2004:[language]:Configuration:Classes
Mac OS Classic (Mac OS 8.x and above) Multi-User:
Hard Disk:Users:[user name]:
Documents:Macromedia:Flash 2004:[language]:Configuration:Classes
Mac OS X: Hard Disk/Users/[user name]/Library/
Application Support/Macromedia/
Flash 2004\[language]\Configuration\Classes
```

You can also add your own directories to the classpath. Flash actually enables you to set two classpaths. First of all, you can add a directory to the global Flash classpath that is active for all Flash movies. You can also specify a classpath for each FLA file. You just need to add a directory to one or the other. If the directory is intended to hold classes that may well be used in other FLA files, it is wise to include that directory in the global classpath. If you simply want to add another directory to the classpath for a single FLA (meaning that in all likelihood the class files are going to be used by only that one FLA), you should add that directory to the classpath for the FLA.

To edit the global classpath, do the following:

1. Choose Edit ➪ Preferences or press Ctrl+U on Windows or ⌘+U on the Mac.
2. Choose the ActionScript tab in the Preferences dialog box.
3. In the Language section near the bottom of the ActionScript preferences screen, click the ActionScript 2.0 Settings button.

To edit the document-level (FLA-specific) classpath, do the following:

1. Choose File ➪ Publish Settings or press Ctrl+Shift+F12 on Windows or ⌘+Shift+F12 on the Mac.
2. Click the Flash tab in the Publish Settings dialog box. If the Flash tab is not shown, first select the Format tab and make sure Flash (.SWF) is checked.
3. Make sure that ActionScript 2.0 is selected for the ActionScript Version option, and then click the Settings button to the right of the drop-down menu.

Whether working with the document-level or the global classpath, you can add, remove, or reorder directories in the same ways.

You can add a new directory to the classpath by clicking the Add New Path button (the button with the plus sign) and typing the path to the directory in the new entry that is made following the other, existing paths. The path can be either a relative or absolute. The global classpath (assuming you have not already changed it) has two default entries in the classpath. These entries are `$(UserConfig)/Classes` (which points to the `Classes` directory in the user configuration directory) and `.` (which refers to the same directory to which the FLA is saved).

You can remove a path from the classpath by selecting the entry from the list and clicking the Remove Selected Path button (the button with the minus sign).

You can also reorder the directories in the classpath. Flash searches for classes in the directories in the order they are listed. This means that if you have two classes with the same name in two different directories in the classpath, Flash uses the one that it encounters first.

Also, be aware that Flash always searches in the document-level classpath first. That means that if you have two classes with the same name, the one found in the document-level classpath will be used instead of the one in the global classpath.

If you plan to create many classes that you want to make accessible globally to your FLA files, you might consider creating a directory for those files and adding it to the global classpath. You can save your custom classes to the user configuration directory's Classes directory. However, you may find that navigating to that directory may prove tiresome because it is nested within many parent directories. A directory such as C:\ActionScriptClasses may be much easier for the purposes of saving and editing the AS files.

Making AS Files

In order to create your AS files, you need nothing other than a text editor. Although you can use any text editor you want for this purpose, if you are working with Flash Professional, you can use the integrated Script window. The Script window provides you with color coding, code hinting, and syntax checking—things that a regular text editor is not likely to do.

In order to create a new AS file using the Script window in Flash Professional, do the following:

1. Choose File ➪ New or press Ctrl+N on Windows or ⌘+N on the Mac.
2. In the General tab, select ActionScript File from the list.
3. Click OK. A new document will open up in the Script window.

Sapien Technologies has an excellent script editor application called PrimalScript. Version 3.1 provides support for ActionScript 2.0, and in many ways surpasses the Script window that ships with Flash MX Professional 2004. PrimalScript provides project and source control, color coding, excellent code hinting, integrated Flash help, and much more. Even if you have Flash MX Professional 2004, you still may want to check out PrimalScript if you plan to write a lot of ActionScript 2.0 class files. You can find more about PrimalScript at `www.sapien.com`.

If you do not have Flash Professional and don't want to invest in PrimalScript, you may want to opt for a simple text editor that readily saves to plain text format.

Creating a Simple Class

Each class must be defined in its own file. The name of the file must correspond to the name of the class. For example, if you want to create a `Car` class, the name of the file should be `Car.as`.

Within the file, all the code should be enclosed in the following code structure:

```
class ClassName {
  // The rest of the code goes here.
}
```

Every class definition must begin with the keyword `class`. This helps Flash to know that what is being defined is a class. The body of the class is enclosed in curly braces as shown.

The *`ClassName`* in the preceding syntax example should be the name of the class such as `Car`. The names of classes follow the same rules as variables. Your class names cannot contain any spaces or other special characters. Typically, class names contain only letters, and perhaps, in rare occasions, numbers (but the name can never start with a number). By convention, class names begin with capital letters. Capital letters help to distinguish classes for instances. Therefore, following this convention, `Car` is a better choice for a class name than `car`.

Defining Properties for a Class

Once you have told Flash that you are creating a class by using the syntactical structure described in the last section, the next step is to determine what properties you want to define for the class. For example, in a `Car` class you might want to define properties such as `make`, `model`, and `extColor`.

When defining a class's properties, you need to decide whether they should be public or private. A public property is one that can be accessed directly from instances, whereas a private property cannot be accessed from the instances. The difference between declaring a public or private member is simply the difference between using the `public` or `private` keyword in the declaration. The syntax for a public member declaration is as follows:

```
public var memberName:datatype = initialValue;
```

The syntax for a private member declaration is:

```
private var memberName:datatype = initialValue;
```

You probably have noticed that declaring a public or private class member is almost identical to declaring a standard variable. You need to add only the additional `public` or `private` keyword at the beginning of the declaration.

You might sometimes see classes in which public members are declared without the use of the `public` keyword. If you do not specify public or private, Flash defaults to public. However, it is a good practice to always explicitly declare the member to be public when it is public.

You might wonder why you would ever want to define private members—properties that cannot be directly accessed from the instances of the class. After all, isn't the entire purpose of a property that it can be accessed from the instances? It may surprise you to find out that we actually recommend that you make *all* members private. Instead of allowing the members to be directly accessed from the instances of the class, you create special methods called *getter* and *setter* methods that handle the getting and setting of the property values. This practice is called *data hiding*, and it is encouraged in all object-oriented programming. The reasons may not be immediately apparent. But with a little investigation they become obvious:

✦ If you allow the values of members to be directly retrieved and set from the instances, you open up the possibility for data corruption. For example, if you create a `Car` class, you may want to ensure that the value for the `extColor` property is one of the valid options. For example, `red`, `silver`, `green`, and so on would be valid colors. But you don't want the color to be accidentally set to `rabbit`, `dog`, or `cow`. Using a setter method enables you to ensure the quality of the data. Another example: The same `Car` class might have a `mileage` member. Obviously, the mileage on a car cannot be negative. Using a setter method enables you to ensure that the value is always positive.

✦ Another reason for getter and setter methods is that they enable you to perform other tasks when the value is retrieved or set. It might be that two or more members are interrelated, and the value of one affects the values of the others. Using a setter method enables you to perform the appropriate checking and assignments.

✦ Using getter and setter methods allows you to create read-only (or, theoretically write-only) properties in addition to standard read-write properties. By defining only a getter method, and no setter method, for example, the property is a read-only property. This is useful for properties that are dependent on the values of other properties. For example, an `area` property of a `Circle` class could be a read-only property whose value is dependent on the value of a read-write property named `radius`.

Therefore, we suggest that you create only private members in your classes, and that you expose them by way of getter and setter methods only. For reasons that we'll elucidate further in a moment, we also recommend that you begin the names of all private members with an underscore (_). For example, the private member declarations for an example `Car` class might look like this:

```
private var _make:String = null;
private var _model:String = null;
private var _extColor:String = null;
```

Once you have declared the private members for your class, the next step is to define the corresponding getter and setter methods. The syntax for a getter method is as follows:

```
public function get propertyName():datatype {
  // Method code goes here. At some point there should be
  // the following:
  // return correspondingPrivateMember;
}
```

The syntax for a setter method is:

```
public function set propertyName(valueParam:datatype):Void {
  // Method code goes here. At some point there should be
  // the following:
  // correspondingPrivateMember = valueParam;
}
```

As you can see, the syntax for getter and setter methods is quite similar to the syntax for regular functions. The differences are simply that the getter and setter method declarations should include the `public` keyword and that the keyword `get` or `set` should come just before the method name. The method name is the name of the property as it should be accessible from the instances. Typically, the name of the getter/setter methods and the corresponding private member should differ only by the underscore. For example, if the private member is `_make`, the name of the getter and setter methods should be `make`. The reason that we use the underscore to differentiate the private member is that ActionScript will not allow you to successfully define getter/setter methods and private members with the same name. Using the underscore to differentiate private members is a standard programming convention.

Here is an example of simple getter and setter methods that correspond to the `_make` member.

```
public function get make():String {
  return _make;
}

public function set make(sMake:String):Void {
  _make = sMake;
}
```

When you have defined getter and setter methods, you can then access those methods from an instance using the getter and setter method name as though it were a property of the instance. Here is an example. First, create a simple `Car` class. If you want to follow along you'll need to create this class in an AS file named `Car.as`. This file should be saved in your Flash classpath.

```
class Car {
  private var _make:String = null;

  public function get make():String {
    return _make;
  }

  public function set make(sMake:String):Void {
    _make = sMake;
  }
}
```

Then, in a new Flash document, on the first frame of the default layer of the main timeline, you can create an instance of the `Car` class and then get and set the values as shown here:

```
var crTest:Car = new Car();
trace(crTest.make);  // Displays: null
crTest.make = "Oldsmobile";
trace(crTest.make);  // Displays: Oldsmobile
```

Notice that you didn't define any public member named `make` for the `Car` class. Instead, you created a private member named `_make` and defined getter and setter methods named `make`. Flash then knows that any time you access the `make` property from an instance of the class, it should invoke the getter or setter method. You can test to see that you cannot directly access the private member `_make` with the following addition to the FLA code:

```
trace(crTest._make);
```

When you add that code and then try to test the movie, you should get the following error message:

```
The member is private and cannot be accessed.
```

If you are following along, you should delete or comment out the line causing the error. This line just verifies that the private member was, indeed, private.

You can also test to make sure that Flash is actually invoking the getter and setter methods. By adding some simple `trace()` actions, you can clearly see that the methods are, in fact, being invoked.

```
class Car {
  private var _make:String = null;

  public function get make():String {
    trace("Getting the value...");
    return _make;
  }

  public function set make(sMake:String):Void {
    trace("Setting the value...");
    _make = sMake;
  }
}
```

Defining Methods for a Class

Adding properties to a class is the hard part. Now that you've done that much, adding methods will be quite simple.

Like class members, methods can be either public or private. Public methods are accessible from the instances of the class. Private methods are accessible only from other methods within the class. Private methods are useful for encapsulating certain logic or processes that you want to use internally within the class.

The syntax for a public method is as follows:

```
public function methodName([paramList]):datatype {
  // Method code goes here.
}
```

The syntax for a private method is almost identical:

```
private function methodName([paramList]):datatype {
  // Method code goes here.
}
```

Here's an example of a public method for a `Car` class:

```
public function drive(yesNo:Boolean):Void {
  if(yesNo) {
    trace("Car is driving.");
  }
  else {
    trace("Car is stopped.");
  }
}
```

And here is an example of how to invoke the preceding method from an instance of the `Car` class named `crTest`.

```
crTest.drive(true);  // Displays: Car is driving.
crTest.drive(false);  // Displays: Car is stopped.
```

Creating a Constructor

If you don't explicitly define a constructor method for your class, Flash automatically creates an empty constructor for you (in the compiled code, not in the AS file). This means, as you saw in the preceding example with the Car class, you can create an instance of the class using a constructor that does not require any parameters. For example:

```
var crTest:Car = new Car();
```

On the other hand, there are at least two good reasons to explicitly define a constructor for your class.

- ✦ If you define a constructor, even if it doesn't require any parameters, you can perform initialization when the instance is created.
- ✦ You can define a constructor that accepts parameters. For example, a Car constructor might accept parameters that set the values for some of the properties.

The correct syntax for a constructor method is as follows:

```
function ClassName([paramList]) {
  // Constructor code goes here.
}
```

A constructor method should never return a value; therefore, it is unnecessary to declare a return type. Likewise, a constructor must always be public in ActionScript. So there is no need to declare the method as public or private.

Here is an example of a constructor for the Car class:

```
function Car(sMake:String) {
  _make = sMake;
}
```

In ActionScript, you cannot currently have more than one constructor per class. If you want to mimic overloaded constructors, you can create a single constructor that determines the number or parameters and then invokes the correct private method. The following is an example of a Car class that mimics overloaded constructors:

```
class Car {
  private var _make:String = null;
  private var _model:String = null;
  private var _extColor:String = null;

  function Car() {
    switch(arguments.length) {
      case 0:
        Car_0();
        break;
      case 1:
        Car_1(arguments[0]);
        break;
      case 2:
        Car_2(arguments[0], arguments[1]);
        break;
      case 3:
        Car_3(arguments[0], arguments[1], arguments[2]);
        break;
```

```
      }
    }

    private function Car_0():Void {
      trace("Car_0");
    }

    private function Car_1(sMake:String):Void {
      trace("Car_1");
      _make = sMake;
    }

    private function Car_2(sMake:String, sModel:String):Void {
      trace("Car_2");
      _make = sMake;
      _model = sModel;
    }

    private function Car_3(sMake:String,
                           sModel:String,
                           sExtColor:String):Void
    {
      trace("Car_3");
      _make = sMake;
      _model = sModel;
      _extColor = sExtColor;
    }

  }
```

In the preceding example, when the constructor is called with no parameters, the private method `Car_0()` is invoked. When the constructor is called with one parameter, the private method `Car_1()` is invoked, and so on.

Adding Static Properties to a Class

You learned earlier about static properties in some of the built-in ActionScript classes. You can also define static properties in your own, custom classes. In order to create a static property, all you need to do is use the `static` keyword in the declaration. Here is the basic syntax for a constant declaration:

```
static var STATIC_PROPERTY_NAME:Datatype = value;
```

Static properties can be useful when you want to associate a value or some values with a class, but you don't need to create copies of the value in each instance. Here is an example in which an array (see Chapter 11 for more on arrays) is created as a constant in the `Car` class. This constant holds the possible values for the exterior color.

```
static var EXT_COLORS:Array = ["red", "silver", "gold", "white", "blue"];
```

Remember, static properties are always accessed from the class, not from an instance. Therefore, you would always access the `EXT_COLORS` constant as `Car.EXT_COLORS`. This is true even within a regular public or private method of a class. For example, within a method of the `Car` class you would still access the constant as `Car.EXT_COLORS`.

By convention, constant names are always in uppercase.

Adding Static Methods to a Class

You can also add static methods to custom classes. Static methods are accessed directly from the class itself. The syntax for a static method is as follows:

```
static function methodName([paramList]):datatype {
  // Method code goes here.
}
```

Within a static method you cannot access the public or private members of a class, and the keyword `this` is not accessible.

Making Your First Class

In this exercise, you create a `Car` class. You'll build the class in stages so that you can see how each step works.

This exercise uses two files: an AS file named `Car.as` and an FLA file named `car.fla`. These files are often simply called the AS file and the FLA file.

1. Create a new FLA file. Save this file as `car.fla`.
2. Create a new AS file. Save this file as `Car.as`. Make sure to save the file to the same directory as the FLA file. This will ensure that the AS file is in the classpath for the FLA.
3. In the AS file, define a simple `Car` class with three private members, `_make`, `_model`, and `_extColor`. Define the getter and setter methods for them as well.

```
class Car {
  private var _make:String = null;
  private var _model:String = null;
  private var _extColor:String = null;

  public function get make():String {
    return _make;
  }

  public function set make(sMake:String):Void {
    _make = sMake;
  }

  public function get model():String {
    return _model;
  }

  public function set model(sModel:String):Void {
    _model = sModel;
  }

  public function get extColor():String {
    return _extColor;
  }

  public function set extColor(sExtColor:String):Void {
```

```
    _extColor = sExtColor;
  }
}
```

4. In the FLA file, create an instance of the `Car` class, set the properties, and then use the `trace()` action to display the values.

```
var crTest:Car = new Car();
crTest.make = "Oldsmobile";
crTest.model = "Alero";
crTest.extColor = "blue";
trace(crTest.make);
trace(crTest.model);
trace(crTest.extColor);
```

5. Test the movie. You should see the following in the Output panel.

```
Oldsmobile
Alero
blue
```

Once you have tested the movie, close the SWF file and return to the FLA file.

6. In the AS file, add a constructor that allows you to specify the make, model, and exterior color as you create the object. The class definition should look like the following (changes in bold).

```
class Car {
  private var _make:String = null;
  private var _model:String = null;
  private var _extColor:String = null;

  function Car(sMake:String, sModel:String, sExtColor:String) {
    _make = sMake;
    _model = sModel;
    _extColor = sExtColor;
  }

  public function get make():String {
    return _make;
  }

  public function set make(sMake:String):Void {
    _make = sMake;
  }

  public function get model():String {
    return _model;
  }

  public function set model(sModel:String):Void {
    _model = sModel;
  }

  public function get extColor():String {
```

```
    return _extColor;
  }

  public function set extColor(sExtColor:String):Void {
    _extColor = sExtColor;
  }
}
```

7. In the FLA file, change the code to the following:

```
var crTest:Car = new Car("Oldsmobile", "Alero", "blue");
trace(crTest.make);
trace(crTest.model);
trace(crTest.extColor);
```

8. Test the movie. You should get the same results as before. When you have tested the movie, close the SWF file and return to the FLA file.

9. In the AS file, add a getter method named `description`. Notice that you have not defined a private member named `_description`. In this case, `description` is based on the values of the other properties.

```
class Car {
  // Member declarations, Constructor, and other getter
  // and setter methods go here...

  // The description is comprised of the values of the
  // other properties. The description property is a read-
  // only property.
  public function get description():String {
    var sDescription:String = "";
    sDescription += "Model: " + _model + newline;
    sDescription += "Make: " + _make + newline;
    sDescription += "Exterior Color: " + _extColor + newline;
    sDescription += "Mileage: " + _mileage;
    return sDescription;
  }
}
```

10. In the FLA file, change the code to the following:

```
var crTest:Car = new Car("Oldsmobile", "Alero", "blue");
trace(crTest.description);
```

11. In the AS file, add a read-only property named `mileage`:

```
class Car {
  // Other private member declarations here...

  private var _mileage:Number = 0;

  // Constructor and other getter/setter methods here...

  // Define only a getter method for mileage to make it
  // a read-only property.
  public function get mileage():Number {
```

```
    return _mileage;
  }
}
```

12. In the AS file, add a private member named `_driveIntervalID`. Next, add a public method named `drive()` that accepts a Boolean parameter. If the parameter value is `true`, the method sets an interval method. If the parameter value is `false`, then the method clears the interval. You'll also need to define a private method named `incrementMileage()`. This is the method that gets called at an interval when the `drive()` method is invoked with a value of `true`.

```
class Car {
  // Other private member declarations here...

  private var _driveIntervalID:Number = null;

  // Constructor and other getter/setter methods here ...

  // The drive() method should accept a Boolean parameter.
  public function drive(bStartDrive:Boolean):Void {

    // If the parameter value is...
    if(bStartDrive) {

      // ... true, tell Flash to start invoking the
      // incrementMileage() method of this class at a
      // rate of approximately once every second. Assign
      // the interval ID to _driveIntervalID.
      _driveIntervalID = setInterval(this,
                                     "incrementMileage",
                                     1000);
    }
    else {

      // ... otherwise, clear the interval.
      clearInterval(_driveIntervalID);
    }
  }

  // The incrementMileage() method is a private method
  // that simply increments the value of _mileage by 1.
  private function incrementMileage():Void {
    _mileage += 1;
  }
}
```

13. In the FLA file, create a new Movie Clip symbol named `DriveCar`. In the symbol, draw a filled circle.

14. On the main timeline, rename the default layer to Actions, and create a new layer named Artwork.

15. On the Artwork layer, drag an instance of the `DriveCar` Movie Clip symbol. Name the object `mcDriveCar`.

16. Select the Actions layer, and open the Actions panel. Modify the code so that it reads as follows:

```
var crTest:Car = new Car("Oldsmobile", "Alero", "blue");

// Create a custom property for the mcDriveCar instance.
// The property references the Car object, crTest. This
// enables you to reference the Car object within the
// MovieClip object's event handler methods.
mcDriveCar.carObj = crTest;

// Define an onPress() event handler method. When the user
// clicks on the MovieClip, Flash tells the Car object to
// invoke the drive() method, and it passes it a value of
// true.
mcDriveCar.onPress = function():Void {
  this.carObj.drive(true);
};

// Define an onRelease() event handler method. When the
// user releases the click on the MovieClip, Flash tells
// the Car object to stop driving by invoking the drive()
// method with a value of false. Also, use the trace()
// action to output the description property value.
mcDriveCar.onRelease = function():Void {
  this.carObj.drive(false);
  trace(this.carObj.description);
};
```

17. Test the movie. Click and hold the circle for a few seconds. Then, when you release the click, the current description should display in the Output panel. Do this a few times. Notice that the mileage keeps increasing cumulatively.

In this exercise, when the user clicks the circle, the `Car` object's `drive()` method is invoked, telling the object to start driving. Internally, that method sets an interval by which the private method `incrementMileage()` is invoked once per second. This interval continues as long as the user holds down the mouse click. As soon as the click is released, the `drive()` method is again invoked—this time telling the `Car` object to stop driving. This causes the interval to be cleared, so the mileage is no longer incremented. However, the value for the mileage is not reset. Thus, the next time the user clicks the circle, the mileage increases even more.

Working with Advanced Class Topics

Now you have learned all the basics needed to create simple classes. The next step is to examine some of the more advanced topics. These topics include working with packages (organizing your classes), extending classes (creating parent/child relationships between classes), creating and implementing interfaces (rules for how to create a class), and making dynamic classes.

Organizing Your Classes with Packages

It is a good idea to organize your classes. This is true for several reasons. First of all, and likely rather apparently, organizing your classes helps you to locate classes and to remember what their purposes are. In addition, it is likely that you will download and install custom classes that were designed by others. It is possible, therefore, for you to end up with classes with the same name. If all your classes simply go in one directory, you run into a problem trying to have classes with the same name.

You organize your classes the same way that you would organize other files on your computer — using directories. In object-oriented terminology, these organizational directories are called *packages*. These directories (and their subdirectories, if applicable) should be placed somewhere within the classpath.

Consider the following scenario: You have created three classes — `Rabbit`, `Hummingbird`, and `Ladybug`. Now, these classes all happen to be related because they are animals. It makes sense to then package them together into an `animal` package. You can accomplish this by doing two things:

- First, you need to make a slight modification to the code in the AS file. The name of the class should reflect the package. Packages are indicated using dot syntax. For example, the `Rabbit` class should be declared as follows:

```
class animal.Rabbit {
  // Class code goes here.
}
```

- The AS file should be moved within the appropriately named directory. In the case of the `Rabbit` class, the AS file should be placed within a directory named animal.

You can create subpackages as well. For example, if you wanted, you could create subpackages such as `mammal`, `bird`, and `insect` within the `animal` package. The same rules apply. For example, if you want to place the `Rabbit` class in the `mammal` subpackage, you need to first modify the class definition as follows:

```
class animal.mammal.Rabbit {
  // Class code goes here.
}
```

Then you need to create a subdirectory named mammal within the animal directory, and move the AS file into that subdirectory.

Now that you have created the `Rabbit` class within the `animal.mammal` package, you can also have other types of `Rabbit` classes — for example, a `Rabbit` class in the `car.vw` package.

Once you have created a class within a package, you have to be careful how to reference that class. Classes even within the same package cannot reference one another using the simple class name as you've done up to now. If you have a `Rabbit` class and a `RabbitFood` class within the `animal.mammal` package, you cannot create a new `RabbitFood` instance within the `Rabbit` class as follows:

```
var rfVeggies:RabbitFood = new RabbitFood();
```

Instead, you have to tell Flash where it can find the RabbitFood class. You can do this in one of two ways:

✦ Use the fully-qualified name (including package) when declaring the variable. For example:

```
var rfVeggies:animal.mammal.RabbitFood = ⮐
new animal.mammal.RabbitFood();
```

✦ Use an import statement to tell Flash where to look for the classes.

The same holds true for classes in different packages. If you happen to have a PetAdoptions class within a package named pets.group, you cannot simply create a new instance of the Rabbit class as follows:

```
var rBunny:Rabbit = new Rabbit();
```

In most cases, an import statement is the preferred choice. It makes it easier to see what classes are being used and it makes for less code for you to type (at least, assuming you are defining more than one instance of a given class). The syntax for the import statement to import a single class is:

```
import package[.subpackages].ClassName;
```

For example, you can import the Rabbit class as follows:

```
import animal.mammal.Rabbit;
```

Alternatively, you can also import an entire package or subpackage. The * is a wildcard that tells Flash to import all the classes in a class or subclass. The basic syntax is:

```
import package[.subpackages].*;
```

For example, you can import all the classes in the animal.mammal package as follows:

```
import animal.mammal.*;
```

Note

Using the asterisk will only import the classes in the animal.mammal package. If there are classes in a package called animal.mammal.primate, the import statement will not recurse into that package. You would need to add another import statement to import the classes in the primate subpackage.

The import statement or statements should always appear at the top of an AS file if used. An import statement should never appear within a class definition. For example, if you want to import the Rabbit class in the PetAdoptions class, your code will look something like:

```
import animal.mammal.Rabbit;

class pets.group.PetAdoptions {
  // Class code goes here.
}
```

The same issue occurs not only in other AS files but within an FLA file. If you want to use a packaged class within your FLA, you need to tell Flash how to find the class. Again, you can declare the instance using the fully qualified name of the class:

```
var rBunny:Rabbit = new Rabbit();
```

Or you can use an import statement. When you use an import statement in your FLA files, you should place the statement(s) at the top of the rest of the code.

Extending Classes

One of the most powerful things you can do with classes is establish parent-child relationships between them. When you create a class that is a child of another class, that class is said to *extend* the parent class. Programmers often refer to the parent class as the superclass and the child class as a subclass.

The reasons for extending classes might not be readily apparent. The purpose is two-fold: First, it is good for organizational purposes. Second, you can define shared characteristics and functionality in the superclass and then create multiple subclasses that inherit the common, core elements, while also adding their own specific characteristics and functionality. For example, the `Rabbit` class might extend a more generic superclass such as `Mammal`. The `Mammal` class can define the types of things that all subclasses have in common. Then, not only the `Rabbit` class, but also any other subclasses such as `Elephant`, `Rhinoceros`, or `Squirrel` will also be able to inherit the common elements without having to redefine them each time.

In order to create a class that extends another, you can use the keyword `extends` in the class declaration. The basic syntax is as follows:

```
class ClassName extends SuperClassName {
  // Class definition goes here.
}
```

Here is an example of a `Mammal` class. This class defines a single property with getter and setter methods:

```
class animal.mammal.Mammal {

  private var _name:String = null;

  public function get name():String {
    return _name;
  }

  public function set name(sName:String):Void {
    _name = sName;
  }

}
```

The `Mammal` class is the superclass. One of the subclasses of the `Mammal` class might be `Rabbit`. Here is an example of the `Rabbit` class that extends `Mammal`.

```
import animal.mammal.Mammal;

class animal.mammal.Rabbit extends Mammal {

  public var _coloration:String = null;

  function Rabbit(sName:String, sColoration:String) {
    _name = sName;
    _coloration = sColoration;
  }

  public function get coloration():String {
```

```
        return _coloration;
    }

}
```

Notice that Rabbit does not have a name property defined within it. However, within the constructor method, you see that the value of the _name member is assigned. This is possible because the Rabbit class inherits that member, as well as the getters and setters, from the superclass. Therefore, if you use the following code in an FLA file, it will work without a problem:

```
import animal.mammal.Rabbit;

var rBunny:Rabbit = new Rabbit("William", "White and Brown");

trace(rBunny.name);  // Displays: William
trace(rBunny.coloration);  // Dislays: White and Brown
```

A superclass of one class can be the subclass of another. For example, the Mammal class is the superclass of Rabbit. But Mammal could also be the subclass of another superclass — maybe a class named Animal. A class inherits everything from the entire chain of superclasses. So in the example in which Animal is the superclass of Mammal, and Mammal is the superclass of Rabbit, the Rabbit class inherits from both Animal and Mammal. It inherits from Mammal directly and indirectly from Animal (because Mammal inherits directly from Animal). In fact, the Object class is the superclass for any class in which no superclass has been explicitly defined. Therefore, all classes inherit from Object either directly or indirectly.

When you extend a class, you sometimes want to implement particular methods in the subclass slightly differently from in the superclass. For example, all classes inherit the toString() method from the Object class. But you might want to *override* the toString() method for a particular class. In other words, you might want to define a method named toString() in the Rabbit class that is specific to that class. To do so is not complicated. All you need to do is to simply declare a method in the Rabbit class with the same name. If Flash encounters a toString() method in the Rabbit class, for example, it will not look any further up the superclass chain.

There is another scenario that can occur, however. Sometimes you want to use the functionality of the superclass method, but you want to add some additional code to the subclass's implementation of it. For example, the Mammal class might have a method named eat(). You might want to allow Flash to use the functionality of that method, but in addition, you want the Rabbit class implementation to reduce the amount of rabbit food that the rabbit has left. In such a case, you can use the super keyword to refer to the superclass. Here is an example of the Rabbit implementation of the eat() method:

```
public function eat():Void {
  // First, call the eat() method of the superclass.
  super.eat();

  // Code goes here to decrement the amount of rabbit food.
}
```

Before moving on to another topic, we should also mention, for the sake of clarity, that you can extend built-in classes just as you can extend custom classes. This means that you can create classes that extend String, Array, or XML to name a few. You can even extend the MovieClip class, although it requires a few additional steps, which are discussed in Chapter 9.

Creating Interfaces

One of the things that you cannot do is create a class that extends two other classes at the same time. Although you can create a subclass of a subclass (that is, Animal as the superclass of Mammal as the superclass of Rabbit), you cannot create a class that directly inherits from two classes. For example, the Rabbit class can extend the Mammal class only, and not both the Mammal and the FurryCritter classes.

This business of extending two or more classes at the same time is known as *polymorphism*, and it is something you can do in some languages such as C++. But other languages such as ActionScript do not permit it. Instead, what ActionScript offers is interfaces.

An *interface* is different from a class in that it does not actually include any code within its methods. Instead, it serves as a guideline. Any class that *implements* the interface must include the methods that are declared in the interface. This set of rules in the interface helps to ensure that any class that implements the interface does what it is supposed to do (at least in structure).

A class can implement one or more interfaces. It can also extend a class at the same time. In order to implement an interface you use the implements keyword in the class declaration. Here is the basic syntax for a class that implements a single interface.

```
class ClassName implements InterfaceName {
  // Class code goes here.
}
```

In order to implement multiple interfaces, you need only to list the interfaces using comma delimiters:

```
class ClassName implements Interface1Name, Interface2Name, Interface3Name {
  // Class code goes here.
}
```

And if you want to declare a class that both extends a superclass and implements one or more interfaces, you should use the following syntax:

```
class ClassName extends SuperClassName implements InterfaceName {
  // Class code goes here.
}
```

The next thing you will want to know is how to create an interface. Many of the same concepts that you learned about creating classes apply to creating interfaces, so you don't have too much new material to learn.

Each interface should be in its own AS file. The name of the file should correspond to the name of the interface. For example, if the name of the interface is IFurryCritter, the name of the AS file should be IFurryCritter.as.

Within the AS file, you should declare the interface. The syntax is very similar to the syntax for a class declaration. The difference is that the interface declaration uses the interface keyword instead of the class keyword. The interface should be declared using the following syntax:

```
interface InterfaceName {
  // Interface code goes here.
}
```

The interface name should follow the same naming rules as variables and classes. As a best practice, name your interfaces starting with a capital *I* to indicate interface. For example, use interface names such as `IFurryCritter` or `IPolygon`.

The interface definition should consist of nonimplemented methods only. You cannot declare any members within the interface. For example, the following would cause an error:

```
interface IFurryCritter {
  private var _numberOfPaws = null;  // Incorrect.
}
```

A nonimplemented method definition consists of everything within a regular method definition except the curly braces and everything contained within them. Here is an example of a non-implemented method:

```
public function frolic(nFrolicTime:Number):Void;
```

You cannot make nonimplemented getter or setter functions.

As an example, to have a better understanding of how interfaces work, let's create an interface named `IPolygon`. The interface will look like this:

```
interface IPolygon {
  public function calculateArea():Number;
}
```

Now you can define a class named `Rectangle` that implements `IPolygon`. At first, if you try to define the class as follows, you'll get an error:

```
class Rectangle implements IPolygon {
  private var _sideA = null;
  private var _sideB = null;

  function Rectangle(nSideA:Number, nSideB:Number) {
    _sideA = nSideA;
    _sideB = nSideB;
  }
}
```

The reason for the error is that because `Rectangle` implements `IPolygon`, it must follow the guidelines that `IPolygon` has defined. `IPolygon` says that any class that implements it must implement a public method named `calculateArea()`. Therefore, you have to define such a method in the `Rectangle` class. If you define `Rectangle` as follows (changes in bold), you no longer get an error.

```
class Rectangle implements IPolygon {
  private var _sideA = null;
  private var _sideB = null;

  function Rectangle(nSideA:Number, nSideB:Number) {
    _sideA = nSideA;
    _sideB = nSideB;
  }

  public function calculateArea():Number {
    return (_sideA * _sideB);
  }
}
```

Now, if you want, you can also define another interface for Rectangle to implement. This interface, IDrawnObjects, can be defined as follows:

```
interface IDrawnObjects {
  public function countPoints():Number;
}
```

Now, if you want Rectangle to implement IDrawnObjects, this is what the class looks like (changes in bold):

```
class Rectangle implements IPolygon, IDrawnObjects {
  private var _sideA = null;
  private var _sideB = null;

  function Rectangle(nSideA:Number, nSideB:Number) {
    _sideA = nSideA;
    _sideB = nSideB;
  }

  public function calculateArea():Number {
    return (_sideA * _sideB);
  }

  public function countPoints():Number {
    return 4;
  }
}
```

Interfaces can also extend other interfaces. This works almost exactly like when one class extends another. In the interface declaration, use the extends keyword to specify what interface it extends. For example, IPolygon might extend IShape.

```
interface IPolygon extends IShape {
  public function calculateArea():Number;
}
```

This means that whatever methods are declared within IShape are inherited by IPolygon, and any class that implements IPolygon must implement those methods as well.

Also, interfaces can be packaged just like classes. When you package an interface, you place the AS file in the directory and you include the package name in the interface declaration.

Making Dynamic Classes

If you recall from an earlier discussion in this chapter, the built-in ActionScript classes are dynamic. That means that you can create new, custom properties for objects derived from those classes, even if those properties are not defined in the class. This is not so, by default, for custom classes. For example, if you create the following class:

```
class Circle {
  private var _radius:Number = null;

  public function get radius():Number {
    return _radius;
  }

  public function set radius(nRadius:Number):Void {
```

```
      _radius = nRadius;
    }
  }
```

Then when you create an instance of this class, you cannot add new properties to it.

```
var cirTest:Circle = new Circle();
cirTest.customProperty = "test value"; // This will not work!
```

When you try to add custom properties to nondynamic classes, you will get a compile error telling you as much.

Now, before we reveal how to make a class dynamic, consider whether or not you really need to make the class dynamic. Generally, it is not a good practice. You typically want to define your classes so that they work in a very specific way. If you find you are defining all kinds of dynamic properties for instances, you should consider whether or not you are really using the instances of the class properly, whether or not the class needs to be redefined, or whether you should, perhaps, create a new class to handle the specific needs.

Now, if you have decided that you have good reason to make your class dynamic, all you need to do is add the `dynamic` keyword to the beginning of the class declaration.

```
dynamic class ClassName {
  // Class code goes here.
}
```

If you extend any dynamic class, the subclass is automatically dynamic. For example, if you create a subclass of one of the built-in ActionScript classes, the subclass is dynamic.

Using the CustomActions Class

After you have created a custom class, you might want to include folders and items for this class in your Actions toolbox. You can do this through editing the `ActionsPanel.xml` and `AsColorSyntax.xml` files, as shown in Chapter 4. However, using the `CustomActions` class, you can accomplish this without having to actually edit the files at all. This is particularly useful if you want to distribute your custom classes and provide an easy means for other users to add the class and its methods and properties to the Actions toolbox.

For the purposes of the remaining subsections, we'll reference the example `Circle` class shown in Listing 7-1.

Listing 7-1: The Circle Class

```
class Circle {
  private var _radius:Number = null;

  function Circle(nRadius:Number) {
    _radius = nRadius;
  }

  public function get radius():Number {
    return _radius;
  }

  public function set radius(nRadius:Number):Void {
```

```
      _radius = nRadius;
    }

    public function calculateArea():Number {
      return (2 * Math.PI * _radius * _radius);
    }
  }
```

Writing the Custom Action XML File

The CustomActions class uses an XML file to install your custom elements. The XML file combines the three main elements of ActionsPanel.xml, AsColorSyntax.xml, and AsCodeHints.xml into a single file. The main element of the XML file for use with CustomActions is customactions, within which are the actionspanel, colorsyntax, and codehints elements. Reference Chapter 4 for more details on these elements, their attributes, and possible child elements and attributes.

Because the codehints element is essentially deprecated in Flash MX 2004, it is not shown in the following example.

Installing the Actions

After you have an XML document prepared, you can install the custom actions by way of the install() method of the CustomActions class. The install() method is a static method, and it takes two parameters: the name by which Flash will know the group of actions being installed (which is largely arbitrary, and is used for uninstalling at a later date) and the text of the XML document:

```
CustomActions.install(name, xmlText);
```

This means you have essentially two options for getting the XML text into Flash. The first option is to create a string variable, and assign the XML to the variable as a string. This means that you have to add the XML without any newlines or carriage returns. This option is a little clunkier than the second option, but given what you've learned up to this point, it is the simplest to examine. The following is an example of a *very* simplified XML string being installed in this manner:

```
var sXMLText:String = '<customactions><actionspanel>
<folder name="Circle" id="Circle" sort="false" tiptext=
"Circle class"><string name="new Circle" tiptext=
"Human object constructor" text="new Circle(%radius%)"
/></folder></actionspanel></customactions>';
CustomActions.install("Circle", sXMLText);
```

The preceding example, when placed on the first frame of a new FLA file and run, will create a new Circle.xml file in the ActionsPanel\CustomActions directory in the Flash application settings directory. Flash will then automatically load that content and append it to the rest of the content in the Actions toolbox.

The previous example kept the XML relatively simple because it would be tedious to try and type a long XML string within Flash. Fortunately, you don't have to type the XML string in Flash if you don't want. Instead, you can place the XML in an external file, and you can load it into Flash using an XML object.

You have not yet learned about the XML class, and so therefore, if you want to have a better understanding of this option you might want to review Chapter 26 first, or you can come back to this section later after you have read Chapter 26.

You can create an external XML file complete with newlines, carriage returns, tabs, and the like. An example of such a file is shown in Listing 7-2.

Listing 7-2: Custom Actions XML Document

```
<customactions>
  <actionspanel>
    <folder name="Circle" id="Circle" sort="false" tiptext="Circle class">
      <string name="new Circle" tiptext="Human object constructor" text=
"new Circle(%radius%)" />
      <folder name="Properties" id="Properties" tiptext="properties
of Human object">
        <string name="radius" tiptext="circle radius" text=".radius"
 object="Circle" />
      </folder>
      <folder name="Methods" id="Methods" tiptext="methods of Human object">
        <string name="calculateArea" tiptext="calculate the
 area" text=".calculateArea()" object="Circle" />
      </folder>
    </folder>
  </actionspanel>
  <colorsyntax>
    <identifier text="Circle" />
    <identifier text=".radius" />
    <identifier text=".calculateArea" />
  </colorsyntax>
</customactions>
```

Once you have created the external XML file, you can load that content into a Flash movie using an XML object. You should be sure to set the ignoreWhite property to true to remove all whitespace nodes from the loaded content. Load the XML from the file. And then, within the onLoad() method, invoke the CustomActions.install() method. Here is an example that loads an XML file called Circle.xml that contains the XML text from Listing 7-2.

```
var xmlCircle:XML = new XML();
xmlCircle.ignoreWhite = true;
xmlCircle.load("Circle.xml");
xmlCircle.onLoad = function(){
  CustomActions.install("Circle", this.toString());
}
```

If you place the preceding code in a Flash document (where the FLA and the Circle.xml files are saved to the same directory) and run it, the new Circle folder and its subfolders and items are added to the Actions toolbox. That's all there is to it.

Using the CustomActions object to install actions to the Actions toolbox will modify the Actions toolbox every time you open Flash, until which time you opt to uninstall the actions. In other words, this is not a "temporary" thing. Installing the actions updates files in the Flash installation so you don't need to worry about keeping the XML document you used to install the actions once you have successfully completed the installation.

Listing the Custom Actions

Once you have installed custom actions files, you can view a list of them by using the list() method of the CustomActions class. The list() method returns an array of the names of the files (minus the XML extension) installed in the CustomActions directory for Flash. If you had installed the custom actions for the Circle class and nothing else and you ran the following:

```
var aCustomList:Array = CustomActions.list();
for(i = 0; i < aCustomList.length; i++){
  trace(aCustomList[i]);
}
```

you would see the following in the Output panel:

```
Flash Data
FlashJavaScript
UIComponents
Circle
```

The Flash Data, FlashJavaScript, and UIComponents files are installed automatically when Flash is installed on your system.

You can view the contents of the files by using the get() method of the CustomActions class. The get() method takes a single parameter: the name of the custom actions file without the XML extension (the value given for the first parameter of the install() method). Here is an example that gets the contents of the Circle.xml file that have been stored in the CustomActions directory, and displays contents in the Output panel.

```
trace(CustomActions.get("Circle"));
```

Removing Custom Actions

Last, you might decide to remove custom actions that you had previously installed. This can be easily achieved using the uninstall() method of the CustomActions class. The method takes a single parameter: the name of the custom actions file without the .xml extension. You can remove the custom actions installed for the Circle class as follows:

```
CustomActions.uninstall("Circle");
```

We'd like to know what you thought about this chapter. Visit www.flashsupport.com/feedback to fill out an online form with your comments.

Summary

- A *class* is a blueprint that ActionScript uses to know how to define instances. Those instances are called *objects*, and each object defined from the same blueprint shares common traits.
- An object can have properties and methods. The properties are essentially variables associated with the object. The methods are essentially functions associated with the object.
- Objects can be used as associative arrays. An *associative array* is a collection of data that is indexed by name.
- You can create your own custom classes. An ActionScript 2.0 class must be defined in an external AS file stored within the classpath.
- Packages are a good way to organize your classes and avoid naming conflicts.
- Interfaces provide a set of guidelines to which all implementing classes must agree. That can be helpful to ensure that a group of classes use a uniform set of methods.

✦ ✦ ✦

Error Handling and Debugging

In This Chapter

Establishing different kinds of troubleshooting

Catching errors in your movies

Finding help

Preventing errors before they happen

Learning useful tips for locating errors in your code

Using trace() for debugging

Understanding how the List Variables and List Objects features aid you in locating errors

Familiarizing yourself with the Debugger

Performing both local and remote debugging

You've read through the first seven chapters of this book and worked on some of the exercises provided. Now you try to apply the concepts you have learned to create your own project with ActionScript. Everything seems to be going perfectly . . . until you test your movie and discover that nothing is working as planned! First of all, take a deep breath and know that even the very best have this happen quite frequently. Next, read this chapter and learn what techniques are available to help you solve the problems.

Anyone who has development experience in any language and for any platform knows that good debugging skills are absolutely essential to a successful project. Debugging simply means troubleshooting and finding the causes of errors in the program. And debugging skills are as important to ActionScript as they are to any other language.

If you find yourself trying to determine what is not working with your Flash movies in almost every project, don't think you are alone. Having errors and oversights in your code is not necessarily a mark of poor programming skills. Rest assured that you are in good company. The real issue is not in having errors but in how well you are able to troubleshoot them. Consider it like a puzzle. It can even be a lot of fun to track down the culprit. But as with any game, it can be frustrating if you are not equipped with the proper tools and know-how. The purpose of this chapter is to acquaint you with successful debugging techniques in ActionScript so that you are ready to sort out what is going on.

This chapter explores several interrelated topics. First, the chapter looks at where mistakes are commonly made and then describes the steps you can take during production to help avoid them in the future. Next, it looks at how to add special code to your movies that handles errors when they occur. And last, the chapter covers the ways to debug your Flash applications when errors still occur.

Troubleshooting Your Flash Application

Troubleshooting a movie is something all Flash developers have to do frequently while creating their productions. Countless problems can occur during development, but most of them fall into the following categories:

✦ A problem with your computer system

✦ A bug in the Flash authoring application

✦ A movie works incorrectly — or simply doesn't work at all

Probably the most common problem you will encounter is a problem right in your movie. The least common problem is finding a bug in Flash software. When you first find an error, you should determine which one of these types of issues is occurring.

Discovering Computer System Issues

Every once in a while your computer just needs to be rebooted. This just seems to be the way of things. If you are working on your Flash document and encountering unexplainable errors, try restarting the computer. Developers have spent countless hours trying to discern a problem in their code when the problem was merely that the computer needed to be restarted. It sounds simple. But sometimes simple is what works. So keep this in mind — especially when your movie works one moment and then stops working the next with no significant changes to the code.

If Flash crashes while you are authoring a Flash document, it's a good idea to reboot before you resume working on your file.

It is also possible, although less likely, that an error could occur on your computer system that would both affect your Flash document and not be fixed by restarting. One way to determine whether this is the case is to move your Flash document to another computer and test it there. If your Flash document works on another computer, that should indicate that the problem is with your computer. In the unlikely event that you should have this happen, you should try reinstalling the Flash authoring application. If that does not help, try consulting with a professional.

Encountering Bugs in Flash

Encountering a software error in Flash does not happen very often. Every version of Flash has gone through extensive testing to find any problems and correct them before public release. However, it is possible you may encounter an oddity (an undocumented "feature") or find a bug with the software during development.

When you think you have found a bug with the program, there are several steps you should take before assuming that this is the source of your problem and reporting it to Macromedia:

1. Make sure this problem is with Flash MX 2004 itself, and does not have to do with your operating system, movie, browser, or external languages or servers.

2. Check all documentation and errata, and search the tech notes on Macromedia's Web site to see whether the problem has been reported, and whether there are established workarounds for it. A good place to start is at `www.macromedia.com/support/flash`.

3. Ask other people in the Flash community if they can reproduce this problem on different computers. If you don't have a Flash friend handy on your instant messenger client, post your problem to one of Macromedia's Flash newsgroups (listed at `www.macromedia.com/support/forums/`) or a Flash user forum such as UltraShock.com. You can also share problems with other *Flash MX 2004 ActionScript Bible* readers at `www.flashsupport.com`.

You can find these and other resources described in the "Finding Help in the Flash Community" section, later in this chapter.

If you determine that there is an error with the software, you can report bugs or feature requests at `www.macromedia.com/support/email/wishform/`.

Detecting Errors in the Flash Document

If the problem with your movie is not with the operating system, there could be a mistake in the Flash document (`.fla` file). You have published your movie, but it is not functioning the way you intended. Perhaps it is running inconsistently on your system or across several platforms or browsers. Maybe certain elements simply do not work at all. These types of problems are a large part of what will be covered in this chapter. But before you look to your code, there are several troubleshooting steps you can take.

1. Consider the history of building your production and the last point at which it worked correctly. You might want to save a new copy of the movie, and work backward by deleting elements and seeing whether certain older parts of your movie work on their own.
2. Verify that the problem happens in a new Flash document (FLA file). Test individual sections to see if they work by copying and pasting your problematic instances and code into a new Flash document. Your problem may lie in individual sections or perhaps with interactions between these and other parts of the movie. You can narrow down your problems by isolating your error.
3. Consider *where* you are testing your movie. As strange as it sounds, Flash movies can behave differently in the stand-alone player (or Test Movie mode) than they do in a Web browser. You may need to run your tests in the browser, or perhaps even live on a server. If you are working with several scenes, you can cut down on your troubleshooting requirements by testing individual scenes. You may also consider the earlier step at this point of copying a portion of your movie into a new file and testing it.
4. Check the player versions (including revisions) you are using with the Flash movie. It is also possible to have a different version running in the Test Movie environment within Flash than the Flash Player plug-in you have installed with your browser. Stand-alone players are frequently released at a different time than browser players, so you may find that you have to work with different versions. Regularly check Macromedia's Web site for the latest versions of the Flash Player plug-in and stand-alone players.

Of course, many of the errors you will encounter and have to troubleshoot will concern ActionScript. Typos and instance or variable naming are two of the most common errors you will encounter. You will learn about how to find these errors and many more in your code in the next section.

Finding Errors in Your Application

After you have taken some time to review the steps mentioned in the preceding section, your movie *still* may not function properly. This section reviews common problems that occur as you author Flash documents.

It's common that many of your Flash movies will not be perfect in the first version or draft of the Flash document. As you develop a movie, several problems can happen along the way.

This section covers typical problems that occur during development. Walking through these steps may save you a lot of time during the troubleshooting process.

Troubleshooting a movie can often take as long as (or longer than!) the development and production process, particularly if you are working on several integrated Flash movies in a large project or if you are learning the tools or ActionScript features in Flash. However, even seasoned developers run up against common and/or simple errors along the way.

Errors that you will encounter in your Flash application can be categorized as two types:

✦ **Compile-time errors:** These types of errors occur when Flash attempts to compile (export) your movie. Compile-time errors are often the simplest to discover because Flash will actually give you a message with details telling you that an error has occurred.

✦ **Runtime errors:** Detecting these types of errors can sometimes be a subtler art. When a runtime error occurs it means that your ActionScript code is syntactically correct, but somewhere in your code is faulty logic.

Fixing compile-time errors is generally a straight-forward process. For example, if you try to assign a number value to a string variable, you will get a compile-time error message in the Output panel. You can read the error message and locate the problematic code relatively quickly. The main difficultly that developers have with compile-time errors is simply not reading the error messages. As funny as it might seem, it is fairly common for developers to close the Output panel without regarding the message. Then they wonder why their movie doesn't work. So the primary tip for working with compile-time errors is simply to read the error messages.

Because detecting and fixing runtime errors can be seemingly more complicated, let's take a closer look at some of the common issues that might occur.

Detecting Naming Conflicts and Problems

Unintentionally giving two objects or instances the same name is an easy mistake to make, and is quite common during development. Making sure each of your objects has a unique name should be one of the early steps taken when you troubleshoot your movie.

Another common mistake is misspelling the names of objects, function, instances, and frame labels in your movie. It is easy to get confused — particularly if your names are different on labels, layers, symbols, instances, objects, variable names, or linkage identifiers. If a particular object or event is not happening when it should, check — and double-check — the names (and references) to the affected object(s). Verify an object's name in the Property inspector (if applicable) and in any actions referring to the object. It is surprisingly easy to accidentally omit or add an extra letter to a name (such as `dog` to `dogs`) when you type the text into the Property inspector or the Actions panel.

Problems also occur if you duplicate a `MovieClip` instance and then forget to change the instance name. This can create errors when you are trying to manipulate one of the instances using ActionScript. If two `MovieClip` objects have the same name, and that name or object reference is targeted with an action, only one object will respond.

Watch out that you don't accidentally "overwrite" an object. For example, if you create a `Sound` object named `sndOne` in one area of your code and later create another object on the same timeline with the same name of `sndOne`, the former object will be replaced with the new one. You can certainly plan to do this with your code, but many beginners unintentionally replace objects with new ones.

Troubleshooting may become unnecessarily frustrating when a duplicated or forgotten instance is hidden underneath a graphic, is an object on a lower layer, or is an empty text field. Use the Movie Explorer (Window ➪ Other Panels ➪ Movie Explorer or Alt+F3 or Option+F3) to help you track down multiple instances with the same name. This method applies only to physical instances that you may have created on the stage—you can't use the Movie Explorer to find dynamically created instances in ActionScript.

Naming Variables

It is also important to make sure your variable names include *only* letters, numbers, and underscores. Also, the first character of your variable names cannot be a number. For a review of variable naming rules, see Chapter 5.

Additionally, we strongly recommend that you adopt a standard naming convention. This is also discussed in Chapter 5.

Using Reserved Words

Another mistake is to use reserved words as instance names in a Flash movie. There are many words that should never be used as variable or instance names because they result in a conflict. You should always avoid using predefined constructs of the ActionScript language when naming anything in your movie. This will help you avoid conflicts and make your code more readable. For example, object names such as `System`, `Key`, and `Stage` should not be used as variable or instance names. Using the suggested modified Hungarian notation convention (see Chapter 4) should help alleviate this issue.

Watching for Case Sensitivity

Because ActionScript 2.0 is a case-sensitive language, if you are inconsistent with your use of case in your code, you will find that things don't work as you expect. Let's take a look at a few examples.

ActionScript 2.0 is a case-sensitive language. This is new to Flash MX 2004. Previous versions of ActionScript were only partially case-sensitive.

Variable and class names as well as stored values are case-sensitive. If you declare a variable named `sTitle` and you then later have a typo in which you use a variable named `stitle`, the latter will be undefined. And unfortunately, because of legacy support, the ActionScript compiler will not catch that error. So be sure to review your code to make sure you have been consistent with your capitalization for variable names. Also, a consistent naming convention can help you to keep consistent use of case in variable and class names.

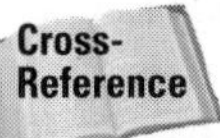

See Chapter 5, "Constructing ActionScript," for more information on variable naming conventions. See Chapter 7, "Programming with Objects and Classes," for more information on class-naming conventions.

ActionScript is also case-sensitive when comparing string values. For example, the string literal values of `ActionScript Bible` and `actionscript bible` are not the same. You can see this for yourself with the following `trace()` actions.

```
trace("ActionScript Bible" == "actionscript bible");
```

Also, keywords and identifiers are case-sensitive in Flash. For example, the following ActionScript will return an error to the Output panel:

```
myButton.onRollOver = Function () {
  _root.box._xscale = 100;
```

```
    _root.box._yscale = 100;
};
```

The keyword `function` should not be capitalized. Likewise, `var`, `this`, `while`, `else`, and `typeof` are a few other examples of code in ActionScript that are case-sensitive. An easy way to tell if you have correct case is if your ActionScript color-codes in the Actions panel. If a piece of code turns blue (or whatever color you have assigned to identifiers and keywords), you know you have the correct case.

Using Expressions and Strings

A common cause of error is the misuse or confusion between expressions and strings when writing ActionScript. When you are referring to a variable, object, or function, you should not have quotes around the name. However, when you are writing a string, you should use quotation marks. If you do not use quotations, the code will be sent as a value (or object reference) as opposed to a string.

Providing an Accurate Scoping Path

If you are having problems with your movie simply not working, make sure you have provided a strict scoping path. All variables in your movies need to be scoped. We recommend that you use relative paths (or object references) instead of absolute paths (or object references) for variable scoping. You should attempt to build your chain from the `_parent` (see Chapter 9 for more information on `_parent`) or `this`, which increases your ability to reuse your code and move it around movie architectures. This may also help reduce future problems or need for modification.

To properly work with scoping, it is important to understand how variables are referenced across timelines and functions. In the following example, you look at an inline function. This code is looping over five button `MovieClip` objects (0–4, inclusive). It sets an `onRelease()` handler, which creates an inline function intended to execute a `gotoAndPlay()` action.

```
for(i=0;i<=4;i++){
  this["mcButton"+i].onRelease = function(){
    this._parent.gotoAndPlay("frame_" + i);
  };
}
```

This code will not work, because the variable scoping is incorrect. Functions (and methods) have their own scope, and the variable `i` does not exist in the `onRelease()` method's scope.

So, to correct this problem with scope, you can add a custom property to each `MovieClip` object. This example defines a custom property named `targetFrame` and sets its value to the appropriate value. Because the variable `i` *is* scoped outside of the `onRelease()` method, this will work. Then, within the `onRelease()` method, you can reference the property using `this.targetFrame`.

```
for(i=0;i<=4;i++){
  this["mcButton"+i].targetFrame = "frame_"+i;
  this["mcButton"+i].onRelease = function(){
    this._parent.gotoAndPlay(this.targetFrame);
  };
}
```

Checking Paths

You take a closer look at target paths in Chapter 9. If you discover that you are having problems with target paths in your movie, you can refer back to this section.

When you write ActionScript, correctly creating a relative path can get confusing. An incorrect path creates major problems — objects won't do what you tell them to do if they don't know they are being addressed. Sometimes it is a good idea to use the Insert Target Path button in the Actions panel to write the path for you, as shown in Figure 8-1. This makes complicated targeting, particularly of nested `MovieClip` instances, much easier as you write your code. If you are having problems with addressing your targets, delete your path and try again using this feature.

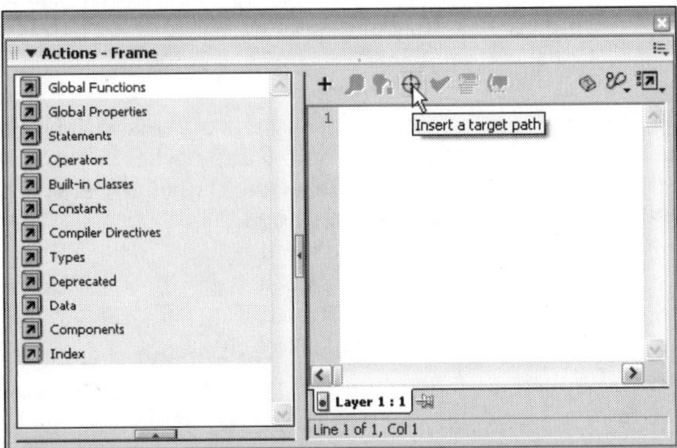

Figure 8-1: Inserting a relative or absolute path is made easier with the Insert Target Path button on the Actions panel.

Finding Conflicts in Frame Actions

Sometimes, you run into problems with conflicting actions on frames. This can occur when conflicting code is placed at the same frame number, but in different layers. On frame 1, for example, you may have a `stop()` action in layer 2 and a `play()` action in layer 3. But what exactly happens in such conflicting circumstances?

The answer is that Flash has a specific order in which it executes the actions on a frame. It starts at the first line of code on the top-most layer, and it continues sequentially through all the code on that layer for that frame. Then, it moves next to the next layer from the top. It continues this until all the actions on the frame have been executed. Therefore, if the top-most layer contains a `stop()` action, but the next layer contains a `play()` action, the movie will play and not stop on that frame.

Importing Images, MP3s, and Video

Flash Player 7 allows developers to dynamically load JPEG and MP3 files into Flash movies at runtime. If you are having trouble dynamically loading JPEG images, check that they are not progressive JPEG files. Flash Player 7 can load only standard JPEG images.

Another problem may arise when you try to import certain MP3 files at author-time. You may get the following error message during an import session:

```
One or more files were not imported because there
were problems reading them.
```

This error message can result because Flash MX 2004 isn't able to import MP3 files with a bit rate higher than 160Kbps. MP3 files with this bit rate or higher need to be imported via QuickTime. If this does not work, and you have QuickTime installed, ensure that you have the latest version of the software installed. Note, however, that the user does not need to have QuickTime installed to load high bit rate MP3 files into Flash Player 7 at runtime. This issue only affects MP3 files that you want to work with in the authoring environment.

You also see the previous error if you are trying to import certain kinds of images. A complete install of QuickTime is necessary to import TGA, TIF, PNG, PCT, PIC, SGI, QTIP, or PSD files. If you have a *minimal* install of QuickTime, you see the same error as previously.

When you are working with video files, you may also run into some problems with QuickTime Flash movies and correct version support. In QuickTime 6, Flash 5 and earlier is supported. Therefore, if you are attempting to publish a SWF track inside a QuickTime movie with a version not supporting the Flash version, you get the following error:

```
The installed version of QuickTime does not have a
handler for this type of Macromedia Flash movie.
```

You therefore need to publish your movie in version 5 or earlier. The version of QuickTime on your computer affects your ability to publish, so make sure you have the latest available version installed.

Publishing Your Movies

When you publish your movie, your content may not appear or sound as you expect it should. It is easy to make mistakes with imported content or forget to adjust your settings within the Flash authoring environment to control your content when it is published.

If you have imported uncompressed bitmap or audio files, you can adjust the compression settings for each media file in the Library panel. It is not advisable to recompress already compressed files because it may have a negative effect on the quality of your Flash movies (SWF files). If your file size is too large after you have published your movie, go back to the Library panel, and adjust export settings for the media files. Remember that the settings in the Library override what is set in the Publish Settings dialog box. However, if the Override sound settings check box is selected in Publish Settings in the sound area of the Flash tab, any compression settings for sound assets in the Library will be ignored.

On the Flash tab of the Publish Settings dialog box, select the Generate Size Report check box in the Options area. When you publish or test your Flash movie, this option creates a text file that outlines the number of bytes used by each element in the Flash movie. You can view this text file directly in the Output panel when you use the Control ⇨ Test Movie command to view your Flash movie in the authoring environment of Flash MX 2004.

Another publish-related problem is the accidental overwriting of HTML files. In any Flash project, you likely create (or modify) a custom HTML document to display your Flash movie. If you are working with a custom HTML page in the same directory (or folder) as your Flash movie and document, it is a good idea to make sure your Publish Settings' Format tab does not have the HTML check box selected. Therefore, you will not accidentally overwrite your custom HTML document when the Flash movie is published.

Including Hidden Layers

A common mistake while coding in Flash is to forget about locked or hidden layers. Collapsed layer folders can hide several layers from your view. It is easy to forget about `MovieClip` objects on hidden layers. Additionally, ActionScript on layers within collapsed layer folder can be easily overlooked as you troubleshoot your code. You should also remember that any content on Guide layers is not published in your Flash movie (SWF file).

Although ActionScript attached to content in a Guide layer is not exported with your final Flash movie (SWF file), actions on keyframes in a Guide layer will be exported. The only way to temporarily omit code from executing is to comment the code in the Actions panel.

Fixing Blurry Text

Blurry text has been a long-standing issue in the Flash community. Text blurring in published movies is caused when your fonts are anti-aliasing when published. The X and Y position of text on the stage and the font size of text are two important things to consider if you want to avoid blurriness.

The top-left X and Y coordinates of any text field should be whole numbers (integers), such as 10, 15, 23, and so on. These values can be adjusted in the Info panel or the Property inspector. If text is placed on integers that have not been rounded, anti-aliasing will be applied. Also, if you are working with text inside a Movie Clip, try to position the Movie Clip at an integer as well.

Make sure that the registration point in the Info panel is set to use the top-left corner of selected items.

When you specify a font face and a font size, it is important to know what the intended sizes of the font should be — fonts are designed to work optimally at specific point sizes. Make sure you use only multiples of this intended size (an 8 pt font should be set at 8, 16, 32 pts and so on). At other points, blurriness occurs because anti-aliasing is applied.

It is advisable to work with fonts made specifically for Flash, because they have been proven to work well in the Flash environment. Fonts that have been well-designed and tested look and work a lot better in your movies, even when placed deeply within many nested layers of Movie Clips. This is when blurring most likely occurs.

A respected source of reliable pixel fonts for use with Flash is `www.miniml.com`. The intended size is 8 pts. Some fonts are free, and others are available for a modest cost.

Even if you have made sure your font is not blurry, ensure that it is actually legible to your audience. Some fonts commonly used in Flash movies are barely legible, even to those with perfect eyesight. Despite the popularity of small fonts, make sure that what you say on your site at the very least can be read by those viewing your movie.

Another solution to the blurry text problem is to use Dynamic (or Input) text fields that don't embed the fonts assigned to them. Any nonembedded (or device) font is aliased in any field type (Static, Dynamic, or Input).

From an ActionScript point of view, any scaling of the Flash movie may cause text to blur as well. If text legibility is a concern, make sure you use the following `scaleMode` of the `Stage` object on frame 1 of your Flash movie:

```
Stage.scaleMode = "noScale";
```

See Chapter 20 for more information on the `scaleMode` property of the `Stage` object.

Considering External Issues

Many problems you encounter are associated with the Web browser or the Flash Player environment. The operating system and version (for example, Windows XP or Mac OS X) can also introduce problems for Flash movies.

Watching for Browser Caching

Most browsers will cache a Web content that is displayed on a Web page. When you click the refresh button in the browser's toolbar, usually the content—even if it's in the cache—will be reloaded from the Web server. However, some browsers, such as Internet Explorer, are known to be stubborn with the refresh of Flash movie (SWF file) content. Even when you upload a new version of the movie to your server, you still see the cached version online. One of the quickest ways to view a new version of a SWF file is to append a variable onto the end of your movie's URL, such as `www.flashmxbible.com/f5b_main.swf?num=2324`. Another way to escape this is by working with meta-refresh tags in your HTML file or by changing your file's name.

Netscape does not seem to suffer from these caching issues. Remember to hold down the Shift key when you click the refresh button. In Netscape, this forces the movie to reload from the URL instead of the cache.

Considering Platform Issues

There are differences in the way a movie is handled on a Mac as opposed to a PC. Published movies play differently in the browsers across these two platforms. Macs have been known to handle frame rates differently, and monitors display colors in a different way, too. We recommend that you test your movies on different platforms and in different browsers when testing and troubleshooting your productions.

Server Issues

Sometimes, errors in your movie don't occur until it has been uploaded to a server. If this is the case, try it on a different server(s) to see if the problem continues to occur. If not, it may be an issue with the MIME settings on the server. MIME types may need to be set up to include those for Flash movies (SWF files).

You can find more information about server issues and MIME types on Macromedia's Web site at `www.macromedia.com/support/flash/ts/documents/tn4151.html`.

As you saw in the beginning of this chapter, your errors can be in many different areas: the server, external scripts or elements, the browser or platform, and, of course, the movie itself. You need to determine where the source of the problem is during the troubleshooting process.

Finding Help in the Flash Community

You may get to the point where you simply cannot find an error in your code, or your movie still doesn't work despite everything you've tried. There are no errors reported in the Output panel when you check your code in the Actions panel or when you test your movie. You have checked your code syntax with references in this book or the Reference panel in the Flash MX 2004 authoring environment, yet your movie still seems to behave unpredictably. What is the next step?

You could be dealing with a bug or errata in documentation, and may need to find a workaround. Macromedia's Flash support area of its Web site (`www.macromedia.com/support/flash`) has an extensive amount of searchable tech notes. These can be very helpful when you are dealing with unexplainable errors and problems. Tech notes include information on the player and authoring, errata, and tutorials.

Another recommendation is to check the archives of the many extensive Flash communities online, and approach other coders about your problem.

After you feel you have exhausted all of the possible solutions, it is a good idea to turn to those around you for assistance. The Flash community is a wonderful resource for inspiration, ideas, code, and even support and troubleshooting. It is very common to find someone who has already experienced your problem and can help you resolve the issue. Flash communities are most easily found online, but if you are lucky, your own city may have an active Flash Users Group where you can discuss Flash in person with fellow developers.

Web Resource

A starting place for finding a local Flash Users Group is on the Macromedia Web site at `www.macromedia.com/v1/usergroups/`.

The following resources are just a few of the online communities of Flash users. Most of these sites also contain tutorials and resources, as well as the forums we will discuss. You may even come across undocumented features useful to your application. Most of these forums have searchable archives, which may be a quick way to resolve your problem instead of waiting for an answer on a message board.

✦ **www.flashsupport.com:** Associated with the *Flash Bible* series, this Web site is centralized around a forum in which you can ask questions about the *Flash Bibles* and Flash authoring. It is a great place to discuss your projects or help fellow readers. You can also find extra tutorials and files to download from this Web site.

✦ **www.ultrashock.com:** Some of the community's giants hang out in the Ultrashock forums. A respected resource by many, Ultrashock is a great place to hang out and ask and learn from the masters.

✦ **www.were-here.com:** A large part of this site is focused on an extensive and busy community forum.

✦ **www.flashkit.com:** Flash Kit is well known for being a great place to find content for your Flash movies and tutorials to help you learn. Flash Kit also has a busy Web forum, in which you can share tricks, ideas, and seek help for your problems.

✦ **chattyfig.figleaf.com:** You can join e-mail-based forums from this location. Be sure to read the etiquette FAQ at this Web site before e-mailing the list. These groups are very high volume e-mail lists, so you had better prepare your inbox before signing up!

✦ **webforums.macromedia.com/flash:** Macromedia forums are a great place to find help from others in the community, and also Team Macromedia volunteers and employees. You can also access these forums as newsgroups using the `forums.macromedia.com` server.

Preventing Errors

Now that you have considered many of the possible errors you can run into when working on a production, you should look at how to prevent these common mistakes before they even happen. Adopting these practices inevitably helps you avoid the previously discussed errors, which means you will save time and headaches during production.

Planning Before Development

Planning your productions is perhaps the most important step in the development process. It is also the primary method you can use to prevent errors in production. If you develop your concept and goals before you begin production in Flash, you will probably encounter fewer problems and errors along the way.

Good Communication Practices

Effective communication between the members on your team also helps you avoid problems in your production. Flowcharts, notes, diagrams, and mockups all reduce redundant work and errors because of misunderstandings. Determine the best ways to streamline the communication process, and spread information among all members in your development team.

You should also remember to establish healthy communication with clients. If you have a firm grasp on what your clients want to see in their product, you will probably save a lot of time and money in the long run. A happy client is a paying client, so it is well worth the effort to keep in close contact with your client and to know what he or she wants to receive.

Simplification of the Production

Before you start your movie, you should try to find a way to reach your goals in the simplest way possible. The act of planning in itself should help you achieve this. However, it is a good idea to consider your ActionScript during the planning stage as well. Either create pseudocode, or sketch out rough ideas as to which objects, functions, or properties you are going to use and where. Create data flowcharts, and note what you will use for facilitating this transfer (for example: `LoadVars`, XML, and Flash Remoting).

During the planning phase, you should also determine the easiest way to structure your movie. You want to take the fewest steps possible, with the simplest data and movie structure to achieve your predetermined goals. Your navigation and its usability should also be considered. The most simple and streamlined projects encounter fewer problems and errors along the way.

Saving Your Documents Incrementally

Saving incrementally greatly helps you when encountering problems with your movie. If you have older versions of the document you can revert back to, you can determine which area of the movie has errors. You also have a version of the movie to "start over" with.

We recommend that you save a new version of your document before each major change in your production.

Saving often during development is a good idea in case your computer crashes or freezes up. Backing up your document in different locations can also help if your file gets corrupted or lost. This is particularly important if you are working with the same file on different platforms.

Testing Your Movie

Frequent testing of your movie is very important for pinpointing errors. It is much easier to troubleshoot and fix your errors if you combine frequent testing with incrementally saving your documents. Usually, you have to fix only one thing (your latest modifications) instead of having to locate all your errors at once. This is much easier than attempting to debug all of your errors all at once.

When testing your movie, it is also important to consider the different kinds of computers that will play your movie to your audience. You may decide to author toward a target audience who will most likely have one certain kind of computer. Or, perhaps you may require your movie to work well across a wide spectrum of capabilities. Whatever the case may be, testing on different kinds of platforms, browsers, processors, and connections helps determine what fixes and optimizations should take place.

There are many useful tools in the test environment (Control ➪ Test movie, or Ctrl+Enter or ⌘+Enter). The Bandwidth Profiler and the ability to list all the objects and variables within a movie help developers optimize and debug their movies.

Testing Your Movie with Server-Side Scripts

When you are working on a large integrated production, it can often be very difficult to determine the source of the error you are encountering. If you are involving server-side scripts, it is a good idea to develop your script with an HTML interface, instead of with Flash. Then you can determine whether your problem is in the server-side script, or in your ActionScript or Flash movie. After your server-side script is in working order, move on to integrating the scripts with Flash. Therefore, you will know that any problems you encounter in your production will be with your Flash movie, and not your server-side scripts.

You may also want to temporarily use the `getURL()` with `POST` action with your Flash movie, instead of `LoadVars` or any other code you are using to interact with server-side scripts. This way, you can see what variables are being returned to help troubleshoot your movie.

Working with the Bandwidth Profiler

The Bandwidth Profiler can help you determine whether you need a preloader for your movie. This feature shows a graphical depiction of how your movie will download on various connections. The profiler lets you see when playback will be halted because not all frames are loaded. From this information, you can either modify your movie to include a preloader or distribute your content differently on the timeline.

A known problem with the Bandwidth Profiler is how the streaming graph uses the uncompressed SWF file size to generate the report. Flash MX 2004 reduces the size of your movies using compression when you publish them. Therefore, when you use the feature to Show Streaming, the download speed and depiction in the Profiler are not entirely accurate.

Correcting Choppy Movie Playback

When a movie is played online, sometimes you may notice that it does not run smoothly. You can generate a size report, which can help you optimize your movie. This option is found in the Publish Settings dialog box. The report generates a numerical report and helps you determine which frames are slowing during playback. You may choose to either restructure or eliminate some content from these frames so your movie plays smoothly.

Testing Platforms and Browsers

It is true that many, if not most, of your end users will be on a PC using Internet Explorer. However, we don't recommend that you create your movies with only this setup in mind. You should be aware of what the other browsers are capable of and the differences that exist between them. Internet Explorer on the Macintosh is entirely a different beast than that on a PC, and a Macintosh has a variety of capabilities that are different from a PC. If you are aware of these differences and test your movies in different situations, you will be able to author your movies with fewer errors along the way.

You can find more information on Internet Explorer for Macintosh and Flash authoring at Macromedia's Web site at `www.macromedia.com/support/flash/ts/documents/mac_ie_issues.htm`.

ActionScript Placement

We strongly recommend that you keep the code within your movie as centralized as possible (meaning that you should try to put all your code in just a few easy-to-find places). When you are debugging your movie, it can be difficult to find all your code if it is scattered on many timelines, frames, and instances. Therefore, you should keep your code in a few centralized areas, so you do not have to search (and perhaps miss) a few places where code has been applied.

If you have been working with ActionScript for some time now, it is possible you may have gotten in the habit of adding ActionScript directly to object instances on the stage. If so, you may find it beneficial to consult Chapters 4 and 9 to see how you can place all your ActionScript code on keyframes. This makes is much simpler to locate your code.

Working with Compatible Actions

When looking at the Flash Player statistics, it is important to consider which version of the Flash player has been installed in your target population. A statistic that shows that 98.3 percent of computers have the Flash player installed does not mean that 98 percent of all browsers have the latest version of the plug-in installed. This number includes *all* versions of the player.

When you develop a movie, you should determine your prospective audience. Will most of your users have Flash Player 7, or will a number of them still be using only Flash Player 6?

Different versions of the Flash Player will display varying content on the audience's computer. You need to author your movie in a specific way to be compatible with different Flash Player versions.

You can find up-to-date information about Flash Player statistics at Macromedia's Web site at `www.macromedia.com/software/player_census/`.

A movie authored entirely with code compatible with earlier players must be published in an earlier version number under the Flash tab in Publish Settings. Refer to Figure 8-2 for where to find this drop-down menu. For example, if all code within your movie uses Flash 5 actions, and you publish your movie as version 7, it will not necessarily be fully compatible with Flash Player 5. You should publish your movie as version 5 for full compatibility.

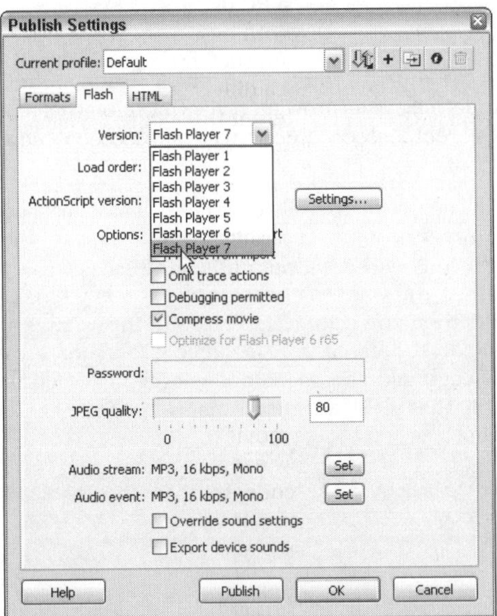

Figure 8-2: You must publish your movie in an earlier version for your actions to be compatible with a particular version of the Flash Player.

The best way to test the compatibility of your movie is by downloading old versions of the plug-in and running your movie through the different players.

You can download old versions of the Flash Player from Macromedia. You can find them at `www.macromedia.com/support/flash/ts/documents/oldplayers.htm`.

Catching Errors Programmatically

New to Flash MX 2004 are the `try`, `catch`, and `finally` statements. You can use these to build programmatic error checking right into your application. This is a useful feature that you are likely to see more of in the future.

Working with Basic try/catch Statements

The `try` and `catch` statements are typically used together. The basic syntax is as follows:

```
try {
  // Code to try.
}
catch (errorObj:Error) {
  // Code to run if the try code throws an error.
}
```

When Flash encounters a `try` block, it first attempts to run the `try` block's substatements. Within the `try` block, it is possible that something can throw an error (more on this in a moment). As soon as an error is thrown, the remainder of the `try` block is skipped, and the `catch` block code is run.

The problem is that you have to tell Flash to throw an error if some condition is or is not met. For example, you may want to tell Flash to process some data, but in order to do so, the condition must be met that the user has successfully entered a username. If the username is not entered then the rest of the code might fail. So you want to check, within the `try` block, to see if the username has been entered. If not, then you want to tell Flash to throw an error. You do this by using a `throw` statement. The `throw` statement takes a single parameter — the object you want to throw. Typically, the object should be an instance of the `Error` class (or a subclass of `Error`). Here is a simple example that illustrates how this works:

```
// Assume that you have an input TextField object named
// tUsername that is on the stage. Here, assign the input
// value to a string variable.
var sUsername:String = tUsername.text;

// Flash will first attempt to run the code in the try block.
try {

  // If the user has not entered a username...
  if(sUsername == "") {

    // ...use a throw statement to throw a new Error object.
    // This tells Flash to stop running the rest of the code
    // in the try block, and jump immediately to the catch
    // block.
    throw new Error();
  }

  // Rest of try block code goes here. For the purposes of
```

```
    // this example, we'll use a trace() statement to see when
    // this code is run.
    trace("The try block ran successfully.");

  }
  catch (errorObj:Error) {

    // If an error is thrown, the catch statement block is
    // invoked. The Error object that was thrown is
    // passed to the catch block (more on this in a moment.)
    // For the purposes of this example, we'll use a trace()
    // statement to see when this code is run.
    trace("An error was thrown.");
  }
```

If you want to place the preceding code on a frame of the same timeline in which an input `TextField` object named `tUsername` is defined, you can test for yourself to see the results. If `tUsername` has no value, an error is thrown and the `catch` block is invoked. Otherwise, if `tUsername` has a value, the `try` block runs successfully, and the `catch` block is never invoked.

At this point, you may be wondering how a `try/catch` combination is any more than a glorified `if` statement. First of all, one of the benefits of a `try/catch` combination is that as soon as an error is thrown in the `try` block, the remainder of the `try` block code is skipped, and the `catch` block is invoked. Accomplishing this task with simple `if` statements would require a lot of nested statements. The `try/catch` combination is much simpler to implement.

Another benefit of `try/catch` that might not be immediately apparent is that errors can be thrown from within functions and methods that are invoked within the `try` block. For example:

```
function checkUsername(sUsernameParam:String) {
  if(sUsernameParam == "") {
    throw new Error();
  }
}

var sUsername:String = tUsername.text;

try {
  checkUsername(sUsername);
}
catch (errorObj:Error) {
  trace("An error was thrown.");
}
```

The preceding code does essentially the same thing as the previous example but uses a function to check whether the username has been entered. Although this is a fairly simplistic example, it illustrates that an error can be thrown from within a function that is invoked within a `try` block.

The finally statement can also be used in conjunction with try and catch. The code within the finally block always runs, regardless of whether there was an error thrown. The finally block can be useful for "cleaning up." You can use try and finally together:

```
try {
  // Code to try.
}
finally {
  // Code to run regardless.
}
```

Or you can use try, catch, and finally:

```
try {
  // Code to try.
}
catch (errorObj:Error) {
  // Code to run if the try code throws an error.
}
finally {
  // Code to run regardless.
}
```

Understanding Error Objects

In the previous examples with try and catch, you saw that in order for Flash to know to break out of a try statement you must throw an error. The catch statement then catches that error. You use the built-in Error class to create your errors. For example:

```
throw new Error();
```

The Error class has two constructor options — the first requires no parameters. The second takes a string parameter specifying a message to assign to the object. The message can then be retrieved within the catch statement using the message property of the caught object.

```
var sUsername:String = tUsername.text;
try {
  if(sUsername == "") {
    throw new Error("Missing Username.");
  }
}
catch (errorObj:Error) {
  trace(errorObj.message);  // Displays: Missing Username.
}
```

Error objects also have another property — name. You are not likely to use the name property.

Typically, you will want to create subclasses of Error. These subclasses can assist you in throwing and catching different types of errors. You can have multiple catch clauses associated with a single try statement. Each catch clause must handle a different datatype. For example:

```
var sUsername:String = tUsername.text;
var errorToThrow:Error = null;
try {
  if(sUsername == "") {
    throw new EmptyStringException();
```

```
    }
    if(sUsername == undefined) {

      throw new UndefinedException();
    }
  }
  catch (errorObj:EmptyStringException) {

        // Code to handle error.


  }
  catch (errorObj:UndefinedException) {
    // Code to handle error.
  }
```

The preceding code assumes that you have defined classes named `EmptyStringException` and `UndefinedException` that subclass `Error`.

Throwing Exceptions

If you are familiar with exception handling in other languages, you might initially find ActionScript exception handling to be somewhat limited because unlike other languages, ActionScript's built-in class methods do not throw errors automatically. This is something that may or may not change in the future. But one thing that you can do is to make sure that all your own custom functions and methods do throw errors when appropriate.

Debugging Your Flash Application

Perhaps you've already reviewed your application using the troubleshooting steps outlined earlier in this chapter, but you are still finding that your application does not work as you want. Flash provides you with several tools you can use to go through your code in order to discover where the errors are occurring. Primarily, you'll look at the following:

- **The Output panel:** The Output panel is really quite simplistic. But don't discount it on account of that simplicity. Often you may find that the Output panel is simpler to use, and can assist you in locating errors relatively effectively.
- **The Debugger panel:** The Debugger panel is more sophisticated than the Output panel. You can do more complicated and intricate tasks such as stepping through your code piece by piece.

Using the Output Panel

The Output panel can be an invaluable resource for simple debugging of ActionScript in your Flash movies. The Output panel is available when you test your movie in the Flash MX 2004 application, and it allows you to view the following:

- `trace()` output
- A list of all variables (and their values) in the movie
- A list of all objects in the movie

trace (the Poor Man's Debugging Utility)

Hey, if it works, it works. And nothing can be more truly said of `trace()`. Despite its simplicity, don't be misled into thinking that `trace()` is not for you. Throughout this book, you have seen `trace()` used time and time again, so you should be familiar with its function by now. It simply takes a single value as a parameter and displays it in the Output panel when testing the Flash movie.

The `trace()` action is a great place to start when debugging ActionScript because of its simplicity and ease of use. The learning curve with `trace()` is very small. All you need to do is know when to apply it.

Tip

When you use `trace()` actions in your Flash document, they are only for the purpose of testing. There is no need to include them in the final published movie. It would be painstaking, however, to go through and manually remove the `trace()` actions that you had put into the document in the first place. So fortunately you can easily omit these actions in the published file by checking the Omit Trace Actions check box in the Flash movie's Publish Settings dialog box. This will simply omit all the `trace()` actions in the published movie without you having to actually remove them from the code.

The first rule of debugging when using `trace()` actions is to drill down to the problem. Sometimes, you will have a pretty good idea of where the problem is. For example, you may have an error that you know is related to a specific `for` loop. But other times, you may not know where the problem is at all. In such cases, it is best to start with the largest scope and then narrow it down to where the specific error is occurring. Listing 8-1 shows an example of when you might want to use such a technique:

Listing 8-1: Using trace() to Locate an Error

```
var nVal:Number = null;
var bIsOne:Boolean = null;
for(var i:Number = 0; i < 4; i++){
  for(var j:Number = 0; j < 3; j++){
    for(var k:Number = 0; k < 5; k++){
      nVal = i + j + k;
      if(nVal = 1){
        bIsOne = true;
      }
    }
  }
}
```

In this example, the `if` statement in the innermost `for` loop evaluates as `true` every time because the assignment operator (=) is used instead of the comparison operator (==). But depending on how the `bIsOne` variable is used in the rest of the code, it could be tricky to spot the problem right away. So it can be really helpful to use `trace()` here to narrow down the problem. Start with the largest scope—the outermost `for` loop—and add a `trace()` action that will output useful debugging information such as the value of `i`:

```
var nVal:Number = null;
var bIsOne:Boolean = null;
for(var i:Number = 0; i < 4; i++){
  trace("i:" + i);
  for(var j:Number = 0; j < 3; j++){
    for(var k:Number = 0; k < 5; k++){
      nVal = i + j + k;
      if(nVal = 1){
        bIsOne = true;
      }
    }
  }
}
```

This outputs the following:

```
i: 0
i: 1
i: 2
i: 3
```

This looks correct, so the problem is probably not in the outermost `for` loop. Next, try placing a `trace()` action in the next `for` loop:

```
var nVal:Number = null;
var bIsOne:Boolean = null;
for(var i:Number = 0; i < 4; i++){
  for(var j:Number = 0; j < 3; j++){
    trace("j:" + j);
    for(var k:Number = 0; k < 5; k++){
      nVal = i + j + k;
      if(nVal = 1){
        bIsOne = true;
      }
    }
  }
}
```

This outputs the following:

```
j: 0
j: 1
j: 2
j: 0
j: 1
j: 2
j: 0
j: 1
j: 2
j: 0
j: 1
j: 2
```

Again, this looks about right. So, move on to the next smaller scope until something looks amiss. In this example, you would keep placing `trace()` actions and testing the movie until you reached the `if` statement. At that point, you would see that it evaluates to `true` every time, and this should indicate to you that there is a problem. Closer examination will show you that you simply used the wrong operator.

Listing the Variables

Another useful selection that the Output panel makes available is the List Variables option. You can choose this option from the Debug menu when testing your movie. This option simply displays all the current variables and their values, and can be very useful for determining whether or not a variable is even being created, as well as what value is being assigned a variable. The code in Listing 8-2 will result in the output from Listing 8-3 when List Variables is selected.

Listing 8-2: Some Sample Code to Use with List Variables Example

```
var sTitle:String = "ActionScript Bible";
var nReaders:Number = 1000000;
var oCar:Object = {make:"Oldsmobile", model:"Alero"};
```

Listing 8-3: List Variables Output

```
Level #0:
Variable _level0.$version = "WIN 7,0,0,221"
Variable _level0.sTitle = "ActionScript Bible"
Variable _level0.nReaders = 1000000
Variable _level0.oCar = [object #1, class 'Object'] {
    model:"Alero",
    make:"Oldsmobile"
  }
```

The output for List Variables does not update automatically when values change. You must choose the List Variables option every time you want updated information. For movies in which you want to see updated data frequently, it might be a good idea to use the Debugger window.

Listing the Objects

You can use the List Objects option (available from the Debug menu when testing your movie) to view the `Button`, `MovieClip`, and `TextField` objects in your movie. This can be a really useful tool—for example, when you are using `duplicateMovieClip()` or `attachMovie()` to dynamically add `MovieClip` objects to a movie. If some of the `MovieClip` objects do not seem to be appearing, you might want to consult the List Objects output to see whether they are being created, or whether they are there, but just not visible. Listing 8-4 shows an example of the List Objects data that might be displayed in the Output panel.

Listing 8-4: Sample List Objects Output

```
Level #0: Frame=1
  Shape:
  Movie Clip: Frame=1 Target="_level0.mcCircle"
    Shape:
  Movie Clip: Frame=1 Target="_level0.mcSquare"
    Shape:
  Edit Text: Target="_level0.tUserInput" Variable= Visible=true Text = "
```

Notice that again the output is grouped by level. In this example, only level 0 exists, but if other levels existed, the objects on those levels would appear grouped by level. Notice, too, that each object lists the object type (`Movie Clip` indicating a `MovieClip` object, `Button` indicating a `Button` object, and `Edit Text` indicating a `TextField` object) and absolute target path to the object. Nested objects are indicated by indention.

Debugging Using the Debugger

The Debugger is a more sophisticated and complex means of debugging appropriate when any of the following conditions are true:

- ✦ Using the Output panel techniques has not helped to solve the problem.
- ✦ You want to see real-time updates of variable and property values.
- ✦ You want to be able to set values of variables while testing the movie.
- ✦ You are using breakpoints in your ActionScript code, and want to be able to step through it while the movie is running.
- ✦ The movie you want to debug is running from a remote location.

There are two ways to run the Debugger, depending on where the movie being debugged is running:

- ✦ Debugging the movie from the Flash authoring application (local debugging)
- ✦ Debugging the movie running in a Web browser or in the stand-alone debug player (remote debugging)

Once the Debugger is running, however, the process is the same for both local and remote debugging.

Local Debugging

Local debugging is done when the movie is running in the test player within the Flash authoring application. You can run the Debugger by choosing Control ➪ Debug Movie instead of the normal Test Movie option. This opens the movie in the debug test player and automatically opens the Debugger window as well.

Remote Debugging

On the other hand, you can also debug movies remotely. This means that you can debug a movie playing in the stand-alone debug player. Macromedia has debug players available for download at the following site:

```
www.macromedia.com/support/flash/downloads.html
```

Exporting the Movie for Debugging

The first step in debugging a movie remotely is to export the movie with debugging enabled. In order to do this, open Publish Settings (File ➪ Publish Settings), choose the Flash tab, and check the box next to Debugging Permitted (see Figure 8-3).

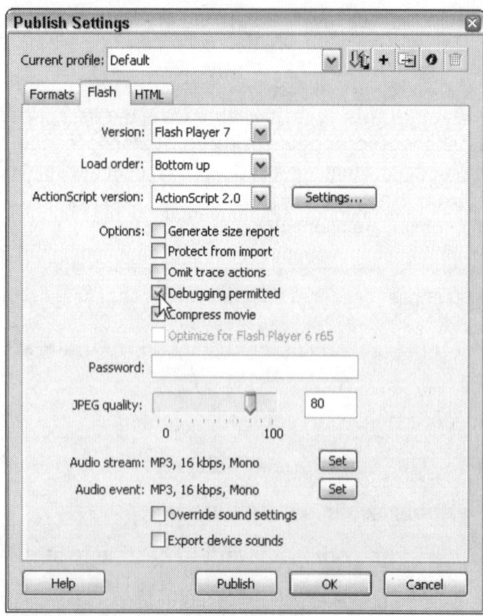

Figure 8-3: Exporting a movie with the debugging option selected

When you enable debugging for a movie, you have the option of adding a password. This ensures that only people with the password can open the movie with the Debugger. You can set the password in the same Publish Settings dialog box.

When a movie is published with debugging enabled, it generates both a SWF and an SWD file. Both files should be kept together when moved. The SWD file contains additional information specifically for the purposes of debugging.

Opening the Debugger Window

When performing remote debugging, you must ensure that Flash MX 2004 is currently running on the machine from which you wish to use the Debugger. You can manually open the Debugger window if you want (Window ➪ Debugger), but otherwise it will be automatically opened when the debug player attempts to make a connection (see the next section). Either way, in order for the Debugger to be able to receive connections from the debug player, you must enable remote debugging. To do this, open the Debugger window, and choose Enable Remote Debugging from the pop-up menu accessible from the icon at the top right.

Opening the Movie for Debugging

Once you have a movie with debugging enabled, you can open that movie in the debug player:

1. Open the debug player.
2. Choose File ➪ Open.
3. Enter the location of the movie (SWF) you want to debug. It may be on the local hard disk (`myMovie.swf`) or on a Web server (*`www.myserver.com/myMovie.swf`*).
4. Click OK.

Once the movie is opened in the debug player, you should be prompted to select the machine on which you want to run the Debugger. You can choose either the localhost, or you can specify an address for another computer. Either one will work as long as Flash MX 2004 is currently running on the specified machine and the remote debugging is enabled for the Debugger.

When you have clicked OK for the selection, the player attempts to connect to the Debugger on the specified computer. If it can make the connection, the Debugger is opened for the movie. When the movie is connected to the Debugger the movie is initially paused to allow for the setting or removal of *breakpoints* (discussed later in this chapter).

If the debug player cannot find the SWD file, you will not be automatically prompted to select a location for the Debugger. If this happens you can still run remote debugging (although perhaps with less functionality) by right-clicking or ⌘-clicking in the movie (that has been opened in the player) and choosing the Debugger menu option.

Understanding the Debugger Window

Regardless of whether you are using local or remote debugging, the functionality within the Debugger window is the same. The Debugger is composed of several sections (see Figure 8-4):

- The status bar indicates whether the Debugger is active. If it is active, the status bar will display the location of the movie being debugged.
- The Display list allows you to choose from the `MovieClip` and `TextField` objects in the movie.
- The Properties, Variables, Locals, and Watch lists allow you to see values, and (in some cases) edit values for properties and variables.
- The Call Stack viewer displays the stack trace, if any.
- The Code View pane (with accompanying jump menu and toolbar) allows you to view the code in the movie (if there is an SWD file).

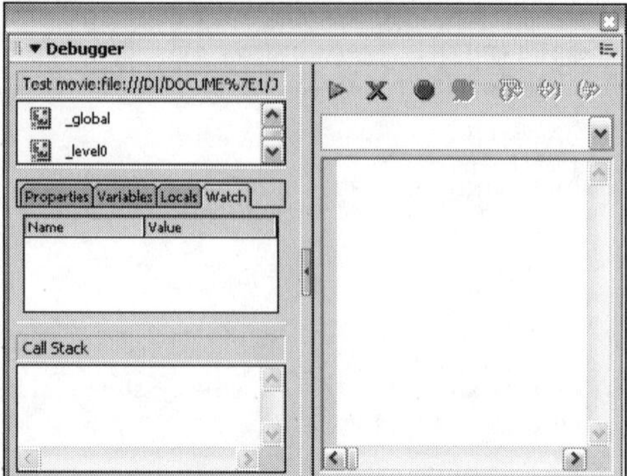

Figure 8-4: The Debugger and its parts

Viewing and Setting Variables and Properties

One of the benefits of the Debugger is that it allows you to see real-time values for properties and variables in your movies. For example, if a `MovieClip` object is moving, you can see the `_x` and `_y` properties being updated in real time in the Properties list. You can even set many properties and variables in your movie as well.

The Properties List

The Properties list allows you to view and set properties of the object selected in the display list. The properties in the Properties list include only the predefined properties that are shared by all graphical objects. Table 8-1 lists the properties.

Table 8-1: Properties List Elements

Property Name	*Is It Editable?*	*Property Name*	*Is It Editable?*
`_alpha`	Yes	`_target`	No
`_currentframe`	No	`_totalframes`	No
`_droptarget`	No	`_url`	No
`_focusrect`	Yes	`_visible`	Yes
`_framesloaded`	No	`_width`	Yes
`_height`	Yes	`_x`	Yes
`_highquality`	Yes	`_xmouse`	No
`_name`	Yes	`_xscale`	Yes
`_quality`	Yes	`_y`	Yes
`_rotation`	Yes	`_ymouse`	No
`_soundbuftime`	Yes	`_yscale`	Yes

If the property is editable, you can change the value, and it will be reflected in the movie being debugged.

The Variables List

The Variables list is very much like the Properties list. It displays any variables in an object except for those listed in the Properties list. For example, the `_level0` object always has at least one variable in it (`$version`), which has a value of the player version. `TextField` objects will always have a whole list of variables that are the properties not included in the Properties list, such as `autoSize` and `text`. Any user-defined properties and variables show up in the Variables list as well.

The Locals List

The Locals list includes only local variables. You can really do only so much with the Locals list when you have set breakpoints (discussed later in this chapter) within a function or have stepped into (also discussed later in this chapter) a function. Otherwise, the Locals list operates just like the Variables list or the Properties list.

The Watch List

The Watch list is a list of variables that you can put together. It is useful for being able to monitor variables from different objects at the same time. You can add only variables from the Variables and Locals lists to the Watch list, not from the Properties list. In order to add a variable to the Watch list, you can do one of the following:

✦ In the Variables or Locals list, right-click or ⌘-click the variable you want to add to the Watch list, and select Watch from the menu.

✦ In the Watch list, right-click or ⌘-click, and choose Add from the menu. In the Name column, type the full path to the variable you want to add.

If you want to remove a variable from the Watch list, you can right-click or ⌘-click the variable and choose Remove from the menu.

Working with Breakpoints

One of the great features of debugging in Flash MX 2004 is the ability to use breakpoints and to step through the code. Breakpoints are points within the code that you can set on which the movie playback will pause during debugging. They are useful for determining where problems are occurring within the code.

Setting and Removing Breakpoints

You can set and remove breakpoints either in the Actions panel, when authoring the movie, or in the Debugger, when debugging the movie. Setting the breakpoints in the Actions panel is advantageous if you want to have the breakpoints remembered from one debugging session to the next. Breakpoints set in the Actions panel are saved as part of the Flash document. On the other hand, setting breakpoints in the Debugger is advantageous for one-time tests that you don't need to have recalled the next time you debug the movie. You can also remove breakpoints in the Debugger that were set in the Actions panel without affecting the breakpoints that are saved to the document.

To set breakpoints in the Actions panel:

1. Place the cursor in the line of code to which you want to add a breakpoint.
2. Then do one of the following:
   - Right-click or ⌘-click, and select Set Breakpoint from the menu.
   - Choose Set Breakpoint from the Debug Options menu in the toolbar.

To remove a single breakpoint in the Actions panel:

1. Place the cursor in the line of code from which you want to remove a breakpoint.
2. Then do one of the following:
   - Right-click or ⌘-click, and select Remove Breakpoint from the menu.
   - Choose Remove Breakpoint from the Debug Options menu in the toolbar.

And you can remove all breakpoints from a document by doing one of the following:

- ✦ Right-click or ⌘-click anywhere in the Actions panel, and choose Remove All Breakpoints from the menu.
- ✦ Choose Remove All Breakpoints from the Debug Options menu in the toolbar.

Setting and removing breakpoints in the Debugger are very similar. When a movie is first opened for debugging, it is paused specifically so that you can add or remove breakpoints within the code. You can use the Jump menu to select the group of code to which you want to add or remove breakpoints.

To set a breakpoint in the Debugger:

1. In the Code View pane, place the cursor in the line of code to which you want to add a breakpoint.
2. Then do one of the following:
   - Right-click or ⌘-click, and select Set Breakpoint from the menu.
   - Click the Toggle Breakpoint button in the toolbar.

To remove a single breakpoint in the Debugger:

1. In the Code View pane, place the cursor in the line of code from which you want to remove a breakpoint.
2. Then do one of the following:
   - Right-click or ⌘-click, and select Remove Breakpoint from the menu.
   - Click the Toggle Breakpoint button in the toolbar.

And you can remove all breakpoints from the movie by doing one of the following:

- ✦ Right-click or ⌘-click anywhere in the Actions panel, and choose Remove All Breakpoints from the menu.
- ✦ Click the Remove All Breakpoints button in the toolbar.

Stepping Through the Code

Once you have set breakpoints, you can begin stepping through the code. When the movie has begun playing (you must first choose Continue), it pauses when a breakpoint is encountered. The current line of code is indicated by a yellow arrow in the margin.

In the Debugger toolbar (see Figure 8-5), you will find the following options for stepping through code:

- **Continue (F10):** A movie is paused when first being debugged, so you must choose to continue when you want the movie to begin playing. Continue can be chosen any time the movie is stopped to resume playback until the next breakpoint is reached.
- **Stop Debugging (F11):** At any point, you may stop debugging the movie. When you choose this option, the movie continues to play normally without any breakpoints, and the Debugger is inactivated.
- **Step Over (F7):** Choosing to step over will move the playback to the next line of code and pause again.
- **Step In (F6):** Choosing to step in will step into a function or method. If the current line does not contain a function or method call, stepping in is the same as stepping over.
- **Step Out (F8):** Stepping out is the reverse of stepping in. If the current line is within a function or method, then choosing Step Out will move the playback to the line after which the function or method was called. It finishes executing the function first.

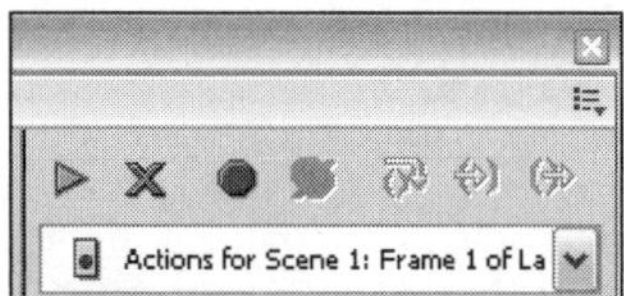

Figure 8-5: The Debugger toolbar

An Exercise in Debugging

In this brief exercise, you will familiarize yourself with debugging using the Debugger. You will edit values for properties and variables, create a Watch list, set and remove breakpoints, continue, step over, step in, step out, and stop debugging.

1. Open a new Flash document and save it to your local hard disk.
2. Rename the default layer to `Objects` and add a new layer named `Actions`.
3. On the Objects layer, draw a square with the rectangle drawing tool.
4. Select the square and convert it to a Movie Clip symbol by choosing Modify ⇨ Convert to Symbol or by pressing F8. Name the symbol `Square` and click OK.
5. Name the instance of the square `mcSquare` using the Property inspector.
6. On the Objects layer use the Text tool to create a Dynamic Text box (a `TextField` object) on the stage. Make sure the color of the text will be visible on the movie's background.
7. Name the `TextField` object `tDebugText` using the Property inspector.

8. On the Actions layer, add the following code:

```
// a function to call later on
function showMessage() {
  tDebugText.text = sMessage + " " + nCounter;
  nCounter++;
}

function rotateMovieClip() {
  showMessage();
  mcSquare._rotation += 15;
}


var sMessage:String = "default message";
var nCounter = 0;

// create an interval for the text to change
var movieClipRotaterInterval:Number = setInterval(rotateMovieClip,
                                                        1000);
```

9. Set a breakpoint on the following line:

```
mcSquare._rotation += 15
```

   You are setting this breakpoint solely for the purpose of removing it in the Debugger. It is just for exercise.

10. Now debug the movie (choose Control ➪ Debug Movie).
11. In the Debugger, choose Actions for Scene 1: Frame 1 of Layer name actions from the jump menu.
12. Choose the line of code with the breakpoint, and remove the breakpoint.
13. Choose the previous line of code:

```
showMessage();
```

   and add a breakpoint.

14. Now choose Continue; the movie will play until it reaches the breakpoint and pauses.
15. Choose Step Over to step over `showMessage()`. Notice that the function is still executed. You are not stepping over the execution of the function. All you are doing is telling Flash you don't want to debug within the function.
16. The application should now be paused on the next line. Even though you have not set a breakpoint there, Flash automatically goes to and pauses on the next line of code after you do a Step Over. Click Step Out to cause Flash to finish with the function. The function will automatically be called again (because of the interval you set) and Flash will pause at the breakpoint again.
17. Choose Step Out. Notice that this time Flash does not pause on the next line of code. Instead, the function call is finished and because of the interval, the function is called again.

18. Choose Step In to step into the function `showMessage()`.
19. Choose Step Out.
20. In the Display list, select `_level0`.
21. Click the Variables list tab, and notice the values of `nCounter` and `sMessage`. What happens if you change these values and then click Step Out?
22. Choose Stop Debugging.

We'd like to know what you thought about this chapter. Visit `www.flashsupport.com/feedback` to fill out an online form with your comments.

Summary

- ✦ Common errors can occur in several areas of your movie. You may have to troubleshoot your computer system, the movie within a player, the movie within browsers, server-side scripts, or the code or instances within the movie itself.
- ✦ Certain types of errors are very easy to make when authoring a movie. Perhaps the most common error is with naming instances and spelling errors.
- ✦ Improper variable scoping and incorrectly defined paths are common mistakes in Flash authoring.
- ✦ Resources for help are easy to find online from the established and helpful Flash community and the Macromedia Web site.
- ✦ You can adopt certain practices to help prevent common mistakes from occurring in the first place, including naming conventions and regular testing and saving.
- ✦ Tracking down errors in your code is called debugging.
- ✦ Flash MX 2004 allows you to use the Output panel and the Debugger for debugging your movies.
- ✦ When using the Output panel for debugging, you can use `trace()` actions as well as the List Variables and List Objects features.
- ✦ The Debugger is a sophisticated tool that allows you to view real-time changes in variables as well as step through each line of code.
- ✦ The Debugger can be run with local or remote movies.
- ✦ Breakpoints allow you to pause on lines of code while the movie is playing.

✦ ✦ ✦

PART

MovieClip, Button, and Drawing API

✦ ✦ ✦ ✦

In This Part

✦ ✦ ✦ ✦

MovieClip and Button Classes

✦ ✦ ✦ ✦

In This Chapter

Creating MovieClip and Button objects during authoring

Targeting MovieClip and Button objects

Handling events

Modifying appearance of objects with appearance properties

Controlling playback of MovieClip objects

Creating new MovieClip objects programmatically

Making draggable content

Loading SWF and JPEG content

✦ ✦ ✦ ✦

Chances are good that if you've worked with Flash for any time at all, you've worked with `MovieClip` and `Button` objects. And you may not even have known you were working with objects! But every time you create an instance of a `MovieClip` or `Button` symbol, you are creating an ActionScript object. If you are new to ActionScript, you might not have actually controlled these objects with code yet. Perhaps you have animated these objects using tweens, and maybe you have added masks at authoring time. But these same things and more can be achieved using ActionScript with `MovieClip` and `Button` objects.

The fact that ActionScript has objects that are represented visually makes it unique as a programming language. In fact, this is largely to your advantage. In the face-to-face world, we think of objects as *things* — things we can see. But in most programming languages an object is difficult to grasp as a concept because you cannot typically see the object. In ActionScript, however, you can actually see `MovieClip` and `Button` objects. This makes ActionScript an ideal language for learning object-oriented concepts.

If you recall for a moment what you've learned about objects so far in this book, you can see that these concepts apply to `MovieClip` and `Button` instances, even if you don't yet know any of the ActionScript behind these types of objects. For example, you just read that objects must be derived from a class that determines shared qualities and actions. You can see that this is true of all `MovieClip` instances, for example. All `MovieClip` instances have qualities such as their x and y coordinates on stage and their dimensions. Likewise, they have shared actions such as playing and stopping the timeline. These are some of the readily visible qualities and actions of all `MovieClip` objects.

Creating MovieClip and Button Objects at Authoring Time

In this chapter, you'll learn about two ways of creating `MovieClip` and `Button` instances — at authoring time and at runtime. You're probably already familiar with the process for creating an authoring time instance, whether you know it or not. All you need to do is to create a `MovieClip` or `Button` symbol and then drag an instance from the library to the stage.

When you create an instance of a `MovieClip` symbol or a `Button` symbol by dragging it on the stage from the Library, you have the opportunity to give a name to that instance—that object. You can do so by selecting the object on stage and typing a value into the <Instance Name> field within the Property inspector (see Figure 9-1).

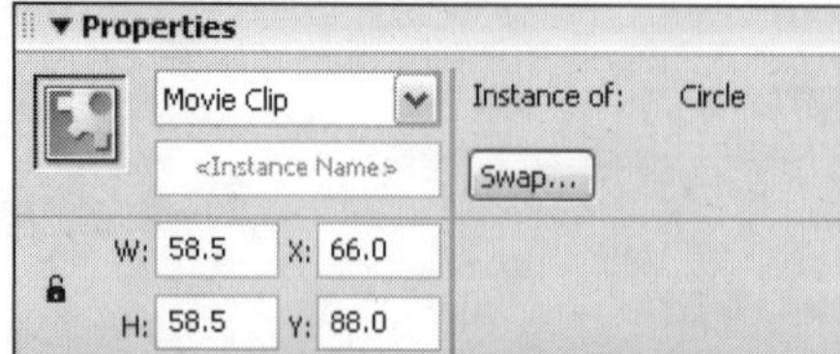

Figure 9-1: The <Instance Name> field in the Property inspector

When you give an instance a name in this way, you are giving a name to the object, enabling you to reference it from within ActionScript. This is important so that you can access the properties and methods of that object to be able to affect it with ActionScript. The variable naming rules (see Chapter 5) apply to naming `MovieClip` and `Button` instances as well. And you should be sure that you give each instance a name that is unique within its scope. For example, if you create two `MovieClip` instances on the same timeline with the same name of `mcCircle` and then try to target one of them, Flash will not know which one you are referencing.

Because every object has to have a name, even if you don't provide a name for an object, it is assigned one by Flash. Every unnamed instance has a name of `instanceN` where `N` is an integer value from 1 upward. The first unnamed object is `instance1`, the second is `instance2`, and so on. If you ever see these instance names showing up (in the Output panel or in the Debugger panel, for example), you will know that you have neglected to name an instance somewhere.

Addressing MovieClip and Button Objects

To begin with, let's look at the simplest example of how to address, or target, a `MovieClip` or `Button` instance. If you have created an instance during authoring time, you can address that instance using ActionScript on the same timeline by simply using the instance name. You can then use dot syntax with the instance just as you would with any other type of object. For example, if you have created a `MovieClip` instance named `mcCircle` on the first frame of the main timeline, you can add the following code to tell the instance to play back its own timeline:

```
mcCircle.play();
```

So if you need to reference only a `MovieClip` or `Button` object from the same timeline on which it has been created, this is all you need to know. However, there are other situations that often arise in which you will want to be able to target a `MovieClip` or `Button` instance from another timeline. Let's take a look at some of those situations and what ActionScript to employ.

Targeting Nested Instances

`MovieClip` and `Button` instances can be nested within other `MovieClip` objects. An example of this kind of nesting of objects would be a `MovieClip` symbol of a car within which are four instances of a wheel MovieClip symbol. Let's say that the wheels are given instance names of mcWheel1, mcWheel2, mcWheel3, and mcWheel4 within the car symbol. You then might create an instance of the car symbol on the main timeline and name the instance mcCar. At this point you would have a single MovieClip object on the main timeline, but within that single instance are four nested objects—the wheels. In order to create the animation effect of the car starting and stopping, you would surely want to also instruct the nested wheel instances to start and stop at the appropriate times. So you then need a way to target the wheel instances from the main timeline. Nested instances are treated by Flash as properties of the parent instance. So in order to access the nested instances you need merely use the following syntax:

```
parentMovieClip.nestedInstance.methodOrProperty
```

Listing 9-1 shows how you could target the wheel instances within the car object and instruct them to play their respective timelines. The play() method is a MovieClip method that tells the targeted object to play its own timeline.

Listing 9-1: Accessing Nested Objects

```
mcCar.mcWheel1.play();
mcCar.mcWheel2.play();
mcCar.mcWheel3.play();
mcCar.mcWheel4.play();
```

You can extend this knowledge to objects nested within nested objects. Take a look at another example to illustrate this. In this example, assume that you've created a MovieClip on the main timeline, and you've named the instance mcStore, and within mcStore there are nested objects, among which is an instance named mcShelf1. Also within mcShelf1 are nested objects, among which is mcProduct1. If you want to then target mcProduct1 from the main timeline, and instruct Flash to move it so that its x coordinate is 100, you could use the following code:

```
mcStore.mcShelf1.mcProduct1._x = 100;
```

For reasons you will read about in a moment, you should not try to nest MovieClip or Button objects within other Button instances. However, you *can* nest Button instances within MovieClip objects just as you would nest MovieClip objects within MovieClip objects. And you can target a nested Button instance in the same way. For example, the following code positions a Button instance named btHorn within its parent MovieClip, mcCar.

```
mcCar.btHorn._x = 25;
```

Working with Absolute Addressing

Every Flash movie has a main MovieClip object whose existence is inherent in the Flash movie; it cannot be added or removed. This is simply because it is the necessary *root* of all the content of a movie. As a result, all other MovieClip objects within a Flash movie are properties of the main MovieClip object. The main MovieClip object is sometimes called the main timeline, and it has a specific identifier by which it can be referenced in ActionScript: _root.

The _root reference is a global property that addresses the main MovieClip object from any timeline, thereby enabling you to reference an absolute target. For this reason, targeting a MovieClip using _root is called *absolute addressing*.

Using absolute addressing, you always target a MovieClip using a top-down approach. For example, if the main timeline contains a MovieClip object named mcA, which in turn contains a MovieClip object named mcB, this means mcB can be addressed from any other timeline in the same movie as:

```
_root.mcA.mcB;
```

Although it may be tempting to do otherwise, it's best to use the _root reference sparingly if at all. When one movie is loaded into another (you'll see how to do this later in the chapter), the _root reference can change. It always has to reference the main timeline—and there can be only one actual main timeline. If a movie is loaded into another, the loaded movie's main timeline can become a nested instance of the loader movie. For this reason, it's best to give preference to relative addressing, the next subject you are going to examine.

Working with Relative Addressing

Although we didn't call it such, the first kind of addressing we examined was relative addressing. No absolute reference was used, but instead the addressing was always relative to the timeline from which the code was being issued. For example, if the main timeline contains a MovieClip object named mcCar, you can issue the following command successfully from the main timeline:

```
mcCar.play();
```

But if you issue that same command from within another timeline, it will not work. Why? Because Flash is looking for a MovieClip instance with that name relative to the timeline in which the code is placed.

Using relative addressing is often a good idea when you want to target a MovieClip object whose location is known relative to the timeline on which the code is given. This is useful for creating modular pieces within your Flash movie. Relative addressing enables you to create, for instance, a MovieClip symbol containing nested MovieClip objects and code to instruct those nested objects. They can then be placed anywhere in the path hierarchy of your Flash movie and still operate as expected. Relative addressing is useful, therefore, for creating a sort of timeline independence of code.

You have seen how to target nested MovieClip objects from within a parent MovieClip object. Listing 9-1 demonstrates how objects nested within another MovieClip can be addressed relatively. But it is also useful for an object to be able to address both itself and its own parent (if any) MovieClip in a relative fashion.

First, let's look at how a MovieClip can address itself. You've actually already seen how to do this back in Chapter 7 when you were learning about objects. Remember that a MovieClip is an object, so all the things that applied to objects in general are going to apply to MovieClip instances as well. Therefore, using the this keyword, you can tell a MovieClip instance to address itself. Why would you want to have a MovieClip address itself, you ask? The most common case for this is within a method definition such as an event handler method. For example, you might want a MovieClip instance to begin playing back its own timeline when the user clicks it. The following is the code that tells an instance mcCar to play its own timeline when the user clicks it:

```
mcCar.onPress = function():Void {
  this.play();
};
```

In the same situation, you can use the this keyword to tell a MovieClip where to start looking for nested instances. For example, if you want to not only tell the mcCar instance to play its own timeline when clicked, but also the timelines of the nested wheel MovieClip objects, you need to use the this keyword to tell Flash that the nested instances are located within the mcCar object.

```
mcCar.onPress = function():Void {
  this.play();
  this.mcWheel1.play();
  this.mcWheel2.play();
  this.mcWheel3.play();
  this.mcWheel4.play();
};
```

If you neglect to include the this keyword in the preceding examples it will not work as expected. Flash does not assume this if you don't include it.

Next, let's look at how a MovieClip can address its parent. Each MovieClip has a built-in property named _parent that is a reference to its parent MovieClip. Because _parent is a property of the object, remember to use the this keyword first to tell Flash which object's _parent property you are referencing. Here is an example in which when a MovieClip instance is clicked, it tells its parent MovieClip object's timeline to play.

```
mcCircle.onPress = function():Void {
  this._parent.play();
};
```

You may notice that we have not yet discussed how to perform relative addressing from within a Button. This is because relative addressing works slightly differently within a Button. When you use the this keyword within a Button instance's method, for example, it does not target the Button, but rather the parent MovieClip. In fact, there is no way for a Button to reference itself. For the same reason, you should not nest MovieClip instances within Button objects if you want to be able to target the nested MovieClip. Because Button instances cannot target themselves, we typically recommend that you use MovieClip instances as buttons in your applications when relevant. We'll discuss this more later in the chapter.

Accessing Nested Instances with Array-Access Notation

As you may recall from the discussion in Chapter 7, objects can be treated like associative arrays in ActionScript. This fact creates some important possibilities when targeting nested MovieClip and Button instances.

Because nested MovieClip and Button instances are treated by Flash as properties of the parent object, that means that in addition to using standard dot syntax, you can also use array-access notation. For example, the following two lines are equivalent:

```
mcCar.mcWheel1.play();
mcCar["mcWheel1"].play();
```

You may be wondering why you would ever want to use array-access notation to address nested instances. Array-access notation is preferable in some scenarios because it enables you to dynamically evaluate the nested instance name. For example, for various reasons you may not want to hardcode the actual nested instance name into the code. Instead you might want to use a variable whose value is determined by user input. The problem is that using dot syntax Flash doesn't have any way of knowing you want it to try and evaluate a variable. Instead it will think you are trying to target an instance with that variable name.

```
var sInstance:String = "mcWheel1";
mcCar.sInstance.play();  // Incorrect!
```

The preceding example tells Flash to try and find a nested instance named `sInstance`, not `mcWheel1`. But if you use array-access notation, Flash first evaluates the expression in the array-access operator (the square brackets).

```
var sInstance:String = "mcWheel1";
mcCar[sInstance].play();
```

Another very good use of array-access notation is when you have a group of sequentially named nested instances that you want to target. In the previous example `mcCar` had four sequentially named nested instances: `mcWheel1` through `mcWheel4`. You can use a `for` statement to target all the nested instances:

```
for(var i:Number = 1; i <= 4; i++) {
  mcCar["mcWheel" + i].play();
}
```

Of course in the preceding example there are only four nested instances, so the benefit might appear minimal. However, there is a substantial benefit when there are many nested instances or when the number of nested instances is dynamic and therefore unknown to you.

Handling Events

Chapter 4 discussed the basic event model that ActionScript uses. Recall that events can occur within Flash movies. These events can be things such as the playhead entering a frame, a user clicking the mouse, or data loading from an external source to name just a few. When these events occur, Flash automatically looks for and invokes special event handler methods. These event handler methods are left undefined by default. Therefore, you can define these event handler methods for `MovieClip` and `Button` instances in order to tell Flash which actions to call when an event occurs. Each event handler method corresponds to a particular event. For example, the `onPress()` event handler method is called only when the press event (when the user clicks the mouse on the instance) occurs for a particular object. Let's take a closer look at the event handler methods for `MovieClip` and `Button` objects.

Handling Button Events

Since the release of Flash MX, both `Button` and `MovieClip` instances have been capable of handling button events. Therefore, all the event handler methods described in the following sections apply both to `MovieClip` and `Button` instances.

onPress, onRelease, and onReleaseOutside

Probably the most commonly used event handler methods are the `onPress()`, `onRelease()`, and possibly `onReleaseOutside()` methods. These methods enable basic button functionality for a `Button` or `MovieClip` instance. The `onPress()` method is invoked when the user clicks the instance. The `onRelease()` method is invoked when the user releases the mouse click while still over the instance. And the `onReleaseOutside()` method is invoked when the user has clicked the instance but then releases the mouse click after having dragged the mouse off the instance.

Often, the `onPress()` or `onRelease()` methods are used on their own. In such cases, which you use depends entirely on whether you want the action to occur as the user first clicks the instance or after he or she releases the click. On the other hand, sometimes both methods are used in conjunction with one another. For example, when creating draggable `MovieClip` instances (discussed later in this chapter) you want the instance to start dragging when the user first clicks it, but you want the instance to stop dragging once the user releases the click.

onRollOver and onRollOut

The `onRollOver()` and `onRollOut()` methods are invoked when the user mouses over and mouses out of an instance, respectively. These methods are, quite obviously, helpful for creating rollover effects.

onSetFocus and onKillFocus

When a `MovieClip` or `Button` instance receives focus within the movie the `onSetFocus()` method is invoked. Likewise, when the instance loses focus, the `onKillFocus()` method is invoked. The focus within an application refers to the active portion. The object that has focus can receive keyboard-initiated events.

onDragOver and onDragOut

The `onDragOver()` method is invoked when the user clicks a `Button` or `MovieClip` instance, drags the mouse off the instance while still holding the click, and then drags the mouse back over the instance. The `onDragOut()` method is invoked when the user clicks an instance and then drags the mouse out of the instance. Be careful with these methods because they will not work if another instance has focus. For example, you cannot detect a drag over if you are simultaneously dragging another `MovieClip`. In such cases, you may find it better to use the `hitTest()` method, described in the section “Checking for Overlapping,” later in this chapter.

Handling MovieClip Events

The former group of event handler methods is applicable to both `MovieClip` and `Button` instances. This second group of methods, however, can be applied only to `MovieClip` instances. Take a look at what these methods are, and what events they handle.

onUnload

The `onUnload()` method is automatically invoked when a `MovieClip` instance is removed from the stage with a `removeMovieClip()` method (see details later in this chapter). This method can be useful for handling any kind of actions you want to occur when a `MovieClip` has been removed. For example, you may want to automatically load another instance, move to another screen, alert the user, and so on.

onEnterFrame

The `onEnterFrame()` method is invoked at the same frequency of the movie's frame rate, regardless of whether the playhead is moving. The `onEnterFrame()` method can be a way to create animation effects and continual monitoring within a movie. However, this technique is somewhat limited by the fact that it works at the frame rate. Therefore, you may find that the `onEnterFrame()` method gets called too frequently or too infrequently for your particular application. Instead, this example gives preference to interval functions and methods as discussed in Chapters 6 and 7. Using interval functions and methods enables you to set the frequency at which they are called — be it once an hour or once every 10 milliseconds.

Additional Event Handler Methods

If you look in the Actions toolbox, you may notice quite a few additional event handler methods that we have not yet discussed. These additional event handler methods are not, by and large, used in Flash MX 2004. For example, the `onLoad()` method works under very specific conditions that are encountered only when you are authoring ActionScript 1.0. The `onData()` method is invoked when using `loadVariables()` and `loadMovie()`. However, we no longer recommend using `loadVariables()` as the `LoadVars` and `XML` classes provide more robust capabilities. And the new `MovieClipLoader` class does away with the need to detect loaded content with `onData()`. The `onMouseUp()`, `onMouseDown()`, and `onMouseMove()` methods are better handled by the `Mouse` class, whereas the `onKeyUp()` and `onKeyDown()` methods are better handled by the `Key` class.

Using MovieClip Objects as Buttons

As you've already seen, `MovieClip` objects are capable of handling all the same events as `Button` objects. And, because `MovieClip` objects provide much more robust functionality coupled with the fact that `MovieClip` objects can contain addressable, nested instances, in many cases `MovieClip` objects are preferable to `Button` objects when working with ActionScript.

Although `MovieClip` objects are often preferable to `Button` objects, this is not to say that you can never use `Button` objects. The key is to understand the limitations of `Button` objects and to learn to discern when to use a `MovieClip` instead. By and large, if you are creating simple applications and if you want to utilize the button states that are inherent to `Button` instances (up, over, down), `Button` objects may be your best choice. The problem occurs when you want to start creating more dynamic, complex applications. When you want to add instances to the stage at runtime, remove instances programmatically, or programmatically change the artwork or label of a button, a `MovieClip` instance is your best choice.

The single drawback to using `MovieClip` objects instead of `Button` objects is that `Button` instances have built-in button states. For example, if you define the up, over, and down states for a `Button` symbol, the instances of that symbol will automatically respond to those states during runtime. However, with just a little extra effort it is possible to create up, over, and down states for a `MovieClip` object as well. You can achieve this by creating keyframes within the `MovieClip` symbol's timeline with frame labels of `_up`, `_over`, and `_down`, respectively. Once the `MovieClip` object is set to handle a button event, Flash automatically looks for these frame labels when the states are triggered. If the labels are found, Flash automatically goes to and stops on those frames. In addition, however, you should also place a `stop()` action on the first frame of the `MovieClip` symbol's timeline. Otherwise, the timeline will continue to play until a button event occurs.

You can also specify a hit area for a MovieClip object that is acting like a Button. All MovieClip objects have a hitArea property. If the hitArea property is undefined, the hit area of the MovieClip object is the object itself. But by assigning a reference to another MovieClip object to the property, the referenced object becomes the hit area instead. For example, you could make a MovieClip object called mcHitArea the hit area of a MovieClip called mcCircle with the following assignment statement:

```
mcCircle.hitArea = mcHitArea;
```

The referenced object can overlap the Button-like MovieClip, but it does not have to. Having the referenced object (the hit area object) in another part of the stage can be really useful for creating complex rollover effects, for instance. And the referenced object does not even need to be visible for the hit area to be active.

Practicing Targeting

In this exercise, you are going to get to practice what you've learned so far in this chapter. You'll create a new Flash application that contains artwork of a cartoon person as well as his coat, hat, glasses, beard, shoes, and cane. You will add ActionScript code that enables the user to click the various accessories and toggle them as either visible or not.

1. For this exercise, there's a starter FLA file on the CD-ROM. This file contains the artwork for the application. Open person_starter.fla from the CD-ROM. Save it to your local disk as person001.fla.

2. On the stage you should see an instance of the Man MovieClip symbol. Select this object and give it an instance name of mcMan.

3. Edit the Man MovieClip symbol. Within this symbol you will find that there are multiple layers, each containing its own MovieClip instance. None of the instances have yet been named. You should give each a name. The objects should be named mcHat, mcGlasses, mcBeard, mcCoat, mcShoes, mcCane, and mcBody.

4. Return to the main timeline, and add the following code to the first frame of the Actions layer:

```
function setHandlers():Void {

  // Loop through all the nested MovieClip objects in
  // mcMan.
  for(var sMcName:String in mcMan) {

    // If the MovieClip is mcBody, skip it.
    if(sMcName == "mcBody") {
      continue;
    }


    // When the user clicks on the accessory, toggle
    // the visibility.
    mcMan[sMcName].onRelease = function():Void {

      this._visible = !this._visible;
```

```
        };
      }
    }

    setHandlers();
```

5. Save and test the movie.

When you test the movie, you should be able to click each of the accessories and have them disappear and reappear. Let's take a closer look at the code to make sure everything is clear.

First, you define a function so that you can encapsulate some of the code. Within the function you use a `for...in` statement to loop through all the nested `MovieClip` objects within the `mcMan` instance. Remember, you named all those nested instances — `mcHat`, `mcGlasses`, and so on. Although you could specify the same code for each nested instance one at a time, a `for...in` statement is more efficient in this case.

```
for(var sMcName:String in mcMan) {
```

Within the `for...in` statement, the first thing you want to do is check to see whether the name of the current nested `MovieClip` is `mcBody`. If so, you use a `continue` statement to skip to the next instance because you don't want to make `mcBody` clickable.

```
if(sMcName == "mcBody") {
  continue;
}
```

Within the `onRelease()` event handler method, you want to toggle the value of `_visible` with each click. If `_visible` is `true`, this statement sets it to `false`. Or, if `_visible` is `false`, this statement sets it to `true`:

```
this._visible = !this._visible;
```

Then, after you've defined the function, all you need to do is call it:

```
setHandlers();
```

Working with Appearance Properties

`Button` and `MovieClip` objects share a common set of properties that afford you the ability to read and programmatically alter the appearance of the instances. Table 9-1 lists these appearance properties.

Table 9-1: Appearance Properties

Property	*Description*
`_x`	X coordinate within parent `MovieClip`
`_y`	Y coordinate within parent `MovieClip`
`_width`	Width of object in pixels
`_height`	Height of object in pixels

Property	Description
_xscale	Scale of the object in the X direction, in percentage
_yscale	Scale of the object in the Y direction, in percentage
_alpha	Transparency of the object
_visible	Can be set to make the object either visible or invisible
_rotation	Rotation of the object in degrees
_xmouse	X coordinate of the mouse within the object's coordinate space
_ymouse	Y coordinate of the mouse within the object's coordinate space

Now that you've seen a list of the appearance properties, the next section takes a closer look at each of them, and explains how you can work with these properties in your own applications.

Working with Coordinates

The stage of a Flash movie is measured in pixels from the upper-left corner, and each MovieClip or Button symbol's internal coordinates are measured from the center point of the symbol's own canvas. Every MovieClip or Button object on any timeline has x and y coordinate values relative to their own timeline. If an object is on the main timeline with coordinates of 0,0, it will appear in the upper-left corner of the stage.

MovieClip and Button objects have two properties that tell about their own location within its parent's timeline. The properties are _x and _y—the x and y coordinates, respectively. You can read or write these properties using dot syntax. Here is an example in which the coordinates of a MovieClip instance, mcCircle, are displayed in the Output panel.

```
trace(mcCircle._x);
trace(mcCircle._y);
```

Not only can you read the values from these properties; you can set the values. This enables you to programmatically place the instances on the stage. Also, when combined with an interval function, for example, it allows you to create animation effects. Here is an example in which an instance named mcCircle is placed at 0,0 within its parent's coordinate space.

```
mcCircle._x = 0;
mcCircle._y = 0;
```

This technique works well for moving graphical objects to absolute positions, and it can be very handy for initializing a movie with objects in set positions. But sometimes, you want to move an object relative to its own position. You can also combine the reading and writing of these properties to move graphical objects in this relative fashion:

```
mcCircle._x = mcCircle._x + 1;
mcCircle._y = mcCircle._y + 1;
```

Or, of course, you can use a compound operator to write the same thing in shorthand:

```
mcCircle._x += 1;
mcCircle._y += 1;
```

Or even the following:

```
mcCircle._x++;
mcCircle._y++;
```

You can also use an interval function or method to continually update the x and y coordinates of an object. Here is an example:

```
function animate():Void {
  mcCircle._x++;
  mcCircle._y++;
  updateAfterEvent();
}

// Next, set an interval at which Flash should call the
// function.
var nAnimInterval:Number = setInterval(animate, 50);
```

You can even read and write the _x and _y properties of the _root object. Although you cannot use this to move the Flash Player around, you can change the _root MovieClip object's position within the player. By default, _root is located with 0,0 at the upper-left corner of the stage. However, you can move _root's position within the player in order to move the entire contents of your movie.

Working with Dimensions

Every graphical object has a height and a width, measured in pixels. And every graphical object has properties, _height and _width, which allow you to read and write these values. Just like _x and _y, you can set the height and width of an object to absolute values:

```
mcCircle._height = 10;
mcCircle._width = 20;
```

And you can also assign these values relative to the current height and width:

```
mcCircle._height *= 2;
mcCircle._width *= 2;
```

Graphical objects can be be scaled in both the x and y directions using the _xscale and _yscale properties. These values are given in percentages. Setting a graphical object's _xscale property to 50, for example, would result in the object appearing to be squished to half its original width:

```
mcCircle._xscale = 50;
```

If you want to scale an object while maintaining the original aspect ratio, you should be sure to set the _xscale and _yscale properties to the same value. Otherwise, the object will appear to be squished. Also, in order to reset an object to the original size after having scaled it, simply set the _xscale and _yscale properties back to 100.

The _root object, like all MovieClip objects, also enables you to work the _height, _width, _xscale, and _yscale properties. You can get and set these properties for _root just as with any other object. But remember, you will be able to set the properties only of the _root object, not the player itself. Setting the properties of _root will change the dimensions of the main MovieClip object within the player, just as with any other MovieClip object. Because _root happens to contain all other objects within a movie, however, setting these properties can be an effective way to scale or alter the dimensions of the entire movie.

Working with Transparency and Visibility

Graphical objects in ActionScript can have different levels of transparency—from 0 (completely transparent) to 100 (completely opaque). Each object has a property called _alpha that contains a value from 0 to 100 to describe the transparency of the object. You can set the property of the object in an absolute fashion:

```
mcCircle._alpha = 50;
```

And you can set the value in a relative fashion:

```
mcCircle._alpha--;
```

Setting the _alpha property in this relative manner allows you to create programmatic fade-ins and fade-outs for your animations:

```
mcCIrcle.fadeOut = function():Void {
  if(this._alpha > 0){
    this._alpha--;
    updateAfterEvent();
  }
};
var nFadeInterval:Number = setInterval(mcCircle, "fadeOut", 100);
```

Note Be careful when working with the _alpha property because its values can range below 0 and beyond 100. But obviously, the display of the property cannot exceed 0 percent (completely transparent) or 100 percent (completely opaque). That means that if you increment or decrement beyond these values, you might not see any visible differences, but the value of the property can still be getting larger or smaller. It is good to impose limits through conditional statements:

```
if (mcCircle._alpha > 0 && mcCircle._alpha < 100)
```

Related to the _alpha property, yet with important differences, is the _visible property of graphical objects. The _visible property has two possible values: false (for not visible) and true (visible).

At first glance, the differences between setting _alpha to 0 and _visible to false might not be clear. (No pun intended.) But the subtle difference is an important one. If a graphical object has event handlers for Button events, the Button events will remain active, even when the _alpha property is set to 0. However, when _visible is set to false, the Button events are no longer active. As you can see, both properties can be very advantageous over the other in different situations.

You can set the _alpha and _visible property values for _root, as well as any other MovieClip object. Doing so to _root has the effect of changing the transparency or visibility of the entire movie.

Working with Rotation

By default, a graphical object is rotated 0 degrees, unless otherwise specified by the author. But by setting the value of the _rotation property of your graphical object, you can spin the object by degrees. Positive values are in the clockwise direction, whereas negative values are in the counterclockwise direction. The _rotation property range of possible values extends beyond -359 to 359. You could, for example, set the _rotation property to a value of 720, and the graphical object would appear just as if the _rotation was set to 0 (because 720 is twice 360, meaning two full rotations). This is useful for continual incrementing or decrementing of the _rotation property of an object because you do not have to concern yourself with remaining within a specific range of values, as you might with the _alpha property.

You can set the _rotation property of a graphical object, just as you did with many other properties — both in an absolute:

```
mcCircle._rotation = 45;
```

or a relative manner:

```
mcCircle._rotation++;
```

You can also set the _rotation property for _root. Remember, doing so simply alters the _root MovieClip object's orientation within the player.

Working with Mouse Coordinates

The _xmouse and _ymouse properties (both read-only) of graphical objects return the x and y coordinates of the mouse cursor within that object's coordinate space. Remember that because every object has its own coordinate space the _xmouse and _ymouse properties of any two objects may not necessarily be equal. In fact, they will be equal only if the two objects happen to have their registration points aligned. As you'll see later on, the _xmouse and _ymouse properties can be very helpful when creating advanced rollover effects.

Working with Self-Describing Properties

MovieClip and Button objects also contain information about their name, location, and origin with the _name, _target, and _url properties.

The _name property returns the instance name for a MovieClip or Button object. This property was far more useful in the days of Flash 5, but it can still be useful in specific situations in Flash MX 2004.

Like the _name property, the _target property is little used in recent versions of Flash. It returns the target path to the object, but in Flash 4 syntax. If you rarely have a practical need to get an object's target path, a better option is to use the targetPath() function. You can pass this function a MovieClip object, and it returns a string indicating the target path in dot syntax.

The _url property returns a string indicating the location from which the object's contents were loaded. If the contents were loaded from a Web server then the value is in the form of an absolute URL such as http://www.flashsupport.com/test.swf. If the contents were loaded locally, the value is an absolute path to the location on the local computer. The _url property can be useful in special situations in which you want to, for example, make sure that your application can be run exclusively from a particular URL. You can achieve this by inserting a single blank keyframe before all the rest of the content in the movie and adding the following code:

```
if(this._url != "http://yourdomain/path/file.swf") {
  this.stop();
}
```

Enabling Button-Like Behavior

The default setting for all MovieClip and Button objects is that they are enabled to handle button events. Therefore, if you define an event handler method for the object, when the corresponding event occurs the method will be invoked. However, there are times when you might want to temporarily disable the object from handling button events. For example, you may want to disable a submit button for a form until all the required fields have been filled.

You can set the enabled property of any MovieClip or Button object to either true or false. The default setting is true. If you set the property to false, the object is temporarily disabled from handling button events.

```
mcCircle.enabled = false;  // Temporarily disable.
```

You can set the enabled property of a graphical object at any time, and you can switch back and forth between true and false. You might opt to do this at specific points in a movie to disable a Button or a MovieClip when you don't want the user to be able to interact. For example, you may have a Button that, when clicked, attempts to load another movie into the player by way of loadMovie() (discussed later in this chapter). However, once the user has clicked the Button, you may want to disable the Button until the movie has been successfully loaded.

Another button-like behavior for MovieClip and Button objects is the automatic changing of the cursor icon when the user mouses over the object. When the user mouses over any enabled object with button event handler methods applied to it, the cursor icon becomes a hand icon. This default behavior is expected in most situations. However, you may want to modify this behavior in some circumstances. You can disable the hand cursor by setting the useHandCuror property to false. If you later want to re-enable the hand cursor, all you need to do is set the useHandCursor property to true again.

```
mcCircle.useHandCursor = false;  // Turn off hand cursor.
```

Tab-Switching, Focus, and Menus

The Tab key allows a user to switch focus between graphical objects of a movie. Button, MovieClip, and TextField objects are all tab-switchable. By default, all Button objects, TextField objects, and MovieClip objects handling Button events are enabled for tab-switching; and the ordering is dependent solely upon the Flash Player's own ordering. However, by taking advantage of the tabEnabled and tabIndex properties of graphical objects, you can determine which objects are tab-switchable, and in what order they should be switched.

The tabEnabled property of graphical objects can be set to either true or false. By default, it is undefined. When the value is either true or undefined, the object is included in the tab-switching for the movie. However, you can set the property to false to remove the object from those between which the user can tab. This is useful when you have objects within the movie that you do not want to be enabled for tab-switching. For example, if you create a form in Flash, you may well want the elements of the form to be enabled for tab-switching. These might include TextField objects, menu MovieClip objects, and Button objects. However, you may also have other MovieClip objects within the movie that are not part of the form. By default, these objects would be included in the tab-switching. But you can disable them by setting their tabEnabled properties to false.

Also, it can often be desirable to set the order in which objects are switched. By default, the order is determined by the objects' coordinates within the movie. But this may not always be the order in which you want them to be switched. You can, therefore, set the `tabIndex` property of each object to determine the order in which it will be switched. The `tabIndex` property can be assigned any positive integer value, but it should be unique from that of any other object in the movie at that point in the timeline. If any object has a `tabIndex` property defined, all other objects are removed from the tab-switching order.

Additionally, when `Button` and `MovieClip` objects are enabled for focus and have been selected, by default a yellow rectangle outlines the object of focus. This is intended so that a user can see where the focus is in a movie. However, you can turn off this focus rectangle with the `_focusrect` property. There is a global `_focusrect` property that allows you to turn off focus rectangles for the entire movie but not for individual objects.

```
_focusrect = false;
```

In addition, you can set this property for each graphical object individually so that some objects have focus rectangles when selected, and others do not:

```
mcCircle._focusrect = false;
```

The global `_focusrect` property is set to `true` by default. Each object's `_focusrect` property has a `null` value by default. Either a `null` or a `true` value turns on the focus rectangle. Setting the property to `false` turns off the focus rectangle.

MovieClip-Specific Tab-Switching and Focus-Related Properties

`MovieClip` objects have two additional properties that deal with focus and tab-switching, which are not needed for `Button` objects. Because `Button` objects can receive focus by default, there is no need to ever specifically instruct them to be able to receive focus. `MovieClip` objects, on the other hand, are not able to receive focus in their default state. As stated in the previous section, `MovieClip` objects can receive focus when they have an attached event handler or event handler method for `Button` events. In other words, when `MovieClip` objects act like `Button` objects, they can receive focus. Additionally, by setting the `tabIndex` property of a `MovieClip` object, it will be included in the tab-switching order, regardless of whether or not it handles `Button` events. But you can also force a `MovieClip` object to be able to receive focus by setting the `focusEnabled` property to `true`. However, just by setting the `focusEnabled` property to `true`, the `MovieClip` object will not be included in the tab-switching order. In this manner, the only way to get the object to receive focus is through the `Selection.setFocus()` method (discussed in more detail in Chapter 17):

```
mcCircle.focusEnabled = true;
Selection.setFocus(mcCircle);
```

When a `MovieClip` object has nested, or child, graphical objects that are tab-switching-enabled, they are automatically included in the automatic tab ordering (if no `tabIndex` properties have been set for any of the graphical objects). It may be the case, however, that you would desire that they *not* be included in the tab order. For example, it might be that the children of a `MovieClip` are menu items for a menu `MovieClip`, and you want for the Tab key to switch between menus, but not the items of the menus. In that case, you would want to set the `tabChildren` property of the parent `MovieClip` object to `false`. The property is `undefined`, by default. If it is either `undefined` or set to `true`, the child objects of the `MovieClip` object are included in the automatic tab ordering.

Tracking Objects as Menus

In their default state, Button objects and MovieClip objects behave in the following manner: When moused over, the object registers an over state. When clicked, the object registers a down state. As long as the mouse click is held, the object registers a down state, even if the mouse is moved off of the object and over another. And because only one object at a time can handle the mouse events, no other objects will register over states, even if the mouse is moved over them, as long as another object is in a down state. Although this is a desirable behavior in many cases, it is not when you work with menus. This sort of behavior is contrary to how people expect menus to behave.

Conventionally, when a menu is clicked and the mouse click is held, the user expects that the menu will drop down to reveal the items that can then be navigated by dragging the still-clicked mouse over the items, each item highlighting as it is moused over. When the mouse click is released, the user expects that the item the mouse was over to then be selected, the resulting operation to be performed, and the menu to close. In order to accommodate this kind of behavior, ActionScript includes the trackAsMenu property for Button and MovieClip objects. By default, the property is false. However, setting it to true for a Button or MovieClip will change that object's behavior, so that even if the mouse click is still held down and the mouse is moved over another object, the new object will receive the mouse event and register the down state instead of the first object.

Affecting Timeline Playback

All MovieClip objects have timelines. In some cases, the timelines consist of only a single frame. But when a MovieClip object's timeline has multiple frames, it can be useful to affect the playback programmatically.

There are a handful of methods that enable you to affect the playback of a timeline. They are as follows:

- **play():** This method simply instructs the MovieClip object's timeline to start playback from the current frame until it is told to stop.
- **stop():** This methods instructs the MovieClip object's timeline to stop playback on the current frame.
- **gotoAndPlay():** This method instructs a MovieClip object's timeline to go to a specific frame and begin playback from that frame. The method requires a parameter that can either be the frame number or a string specifying a frame label within the timeline.
- **gotoAndStop():** This method instructs a MovieClip object's timeline to go to a specific frame and stop on that frame. As with gotoAndPlay(), this method can accept either a frame number or a frame label as the parameter.
- **nextFrame():** This method instructs a MovieClip object's timeline to go to and stop on the frame just following the current frame.
- **prevFrame():** This method instructs a MovieClip object's timeline to go to and stop on the frame just previous to the current frame.

In addition to the methods just described, there are two properties that report information about a MovieClip object's timeline. The _currentframe property returns the frame number of the current frame and the _totalframes property returns the total number of frames in a MovieClip. Although both of these properties are read-only, they can still be useful. By dividing the _totalframes value by the _currentframe value you can obtain a ratio that you can use to create, for example, a slider to control the playback of a MovieClip object's timeline.

Creating MovieClip Objects Programmatically

Not only can you create MovieClip objects at authoring time by dragging instances onto the stage from the library; you can create them programmatically using ActionScript. The following sections explore some of the options for accomplishing this, and discuss the benefits of each.

Understanding Stacking Order Within Flash Movies

Before discussing the MovieClip methods for programmatically creating other MovieClip objects, you need to first consider a key issue to understanding how to work with all of them. Flash uses an internal concept of depths in order to determine stacking order of objects on the stage. Let's take a closer look at this idea.

You are probably already familiar with how layers work within your Flash movies. In the Flash authoring application, you can create, reorder, and delete layers from timelines within the movie. Contents of a layer placed above others will appear above the contents of the layers below. Layers are a means of creating a z-axis within two-dimensional spaces. This is a convention seen in many other applications and should not be unfamiliar to you. What you might not know is that there are several additional possible levels of stacking order that can take place within a Flash movie.

But layers are an authoring time convention only. Once Flash has exported the movie, the SWF doesn't know anything about layers. Instead, everything in the movie is converted into a depth. A depth is a numeric value that Flash uses to determine the z-axis placement of an object. Objects with higher depth values appear in front of objects with lower depths. Each MovieClip object has its own internal depths. Therefore depth 1 within _root does not interfere with depth 1 of a nested MovieClip object. However, within each MovieClip each depth can contain only one object. Therefore, if you attempt to create a new instance at the same depth as another object, the original object will be overwritten.

Flash automatically assigns unique depths to instances created during authoring time. The first instance within each MovieClip is given a depth of -16384. Subsequent objects are given incrementally higher depths (-16383, -16382, and so on). Flash uses these very low numbers so that they are not likely to interfere with instances you create programmatically. It is suggested that you begin creating new programmatically generated instances with a depth of 0.

When you create a lot of MovieClip objects (and TextField objects as well), it can become somewhat of a chore to keep track of what depths have been used. Remember, if you accidentally add a new instance at a depth that is already used, the new object will overwrite the existing instance. As a result of this, Flash MX 2004 introduces the new getNextHighestDepth() method. This method always returns the next highest depth (starting from 0) within the MovieClip from which it is called. For example, to get the next highest depth within an instance named mcCircle, you can use the following code:

```
var nDepth:Number = mcCircle.getNextHighestDepth();
```

However, getNextHighestDepth() does not verify that the MovieClip doesn't already have another instance at that depth. In other words, you can rely on getNextHighestDepth() exclusively as long as you use the method to generate the depths for all instances you create programmatically. However, if you also create instances with hardcoded depths, you'll need to verify that the depth returned by getNextHighestDepth() has not already been taken. For this purpose another new method was introduced in Flash MX 2004 that enables you to check to see if any instances currently occupy a given depth. The method getInstanceAtDepth() checks to see if a MovieClip contains any nested instances at a specified depth. If so, it returns the instance name as a string. Otherwise, it returns undefined.

```
var sInstance:String = mcCircle.getInstanceAtDepth(1);
if(sInstance == undefined) {
  trace("mcCircle does not have any instances at depth 1.");
}
else {
  trace("instance, " + sInstance + " found.");
}
```

Here's an example of how to use both getNextHighestDepth() and getInstanceAtDepth() to ensure that the new depth value is unique.

```
var nDepth:Number = this.getNextHighestDepth();
while(this.getInstanceAtDepth(nDepth) != undefined) {
  nDepth = this.getNextHighestDepth();
}
```

Remember, however, that if you use getNextHighestDepth() exclusively to generate the depths you use, you can dispense with the complexities of having to use getInstanceAtDepth() to check.

Additionally, you can change the depth of any existing MovieClip object using the swapDepths() method. The swapDepths() method accepts one of two types of parameters: either the name of the object (as a string) with which you want to exchange depths or the new depth value you want to assign to the instance. If you pass the method the name of an object, that object must reside within the same timeline as the object from which you are invoking the method. For example, if mcCircle and mcSquare are on the same timeline then you can use the following code:

```
mcCircle.swapDepths("mcSquare");
```

However, if mcCircle and mcSquare are on different timelines then the preceding code will not work.

If you pass swapDepths() a number value then Flash will change the depth of the MovieClip to that value. If any object already resides on that depth, the object on that depth is assigned the depth that had previously been assigned to the object that just took its depth.

The result of swapDepths() is that the two objects (assuming that there are actually two objects involved) change their order along the z-axis. Therefore, the object that previously appeared behind will then appear in front.

You can get a MovieClip object to report its own depth using the getDepth() method. This can be very important in situations when you want to decide if two objects should change their depths or not. For example, if two objects begin to overlap you may want to make sure a specific one appears in front. You already know how to use swapDepths() to change the order of the two objects. But if the object you want in front is *already* in front, calling that method can have the exact opposite effect from what you want. So it is a good idea to compare the depths of the two objects first. You can use the `getDepth()` method to get the depths of the two objects and compare them. The following example first checks to see whether `mcCircle` is in front of `mcSquare`. If so, it changes the order.

```
if(mcCircle.getDepth() > mcSquare.getDepth()) {
  mcCircle.swapDepths(mcSquare);
}
```

Creating Duplicate MovieClip Objects

You can actually tell Flash to create a duplicate of any `MovieClip` object in your movie (excepting `_root`) using the `duplicateMovieClip()` method. If you have created a `MovieClip` instance during authoring time you can create a duplicate of it. You can even create a duplicate of an instance that was created during runtime (such as an instance created using `duplicateMovieClip()`—duplicates of duplicates!).

In its basic format the `duplicateMovieClip()` method takes two parameters—the name and the depth for the new, duplicate instance. For example:

```
mcCircle.duplicateMovieClip("mcNewCircle", this.getNextHighestDepth());
```

The new, duplicate instance is created in the same timeline as the original instance. It is assigned the new instance name and depth. The new instance is a duplicate of the original, and Flash duplicates the values of the majority of its properties. For example, the duplicate instance has the same values for `_x`, `_y`, `_width`, `_height`, `_xscale`, `_yscale`, and `_alpha` as the original at the time of duplication. But some properties' values are not copied. For example, regardless of whether or not the original's `_visible` property was set to `false`, the duplicate's `_visible` property defaults to `true`. In addition, regardless of the `_currentframe` value for the original, the duplicate always begins with the playhead at frame 1. Also, custom properties are not copied to the duplicate instance, and nested instances that were created programmatically are not duplicated either.

You can use the `duplicateMovieClip()` method to create multiple duplicates at once with the aid of a `for` statement. Here is an example that creates `MovieClip` instances named `mcCircle0` through `mcCircle6`.

```
for(var i:Number = 0; i < 7; i++) {
  mcCircle.duplicateMovieClip("mcCircle" + i, this.getNextHighestDepth());
}
```

In some cases, you may be creating a duplicate instance that uses a variable to name the object. The preceding code is an example of this. In such a case it can sometimes be cumbersome to have to write out the target path to the instance after it has been duplicated. For example, if, within the preceding for statement you want to instruct each duplicate instance to play its timeline and to set the `_x` and `_y` properties to random values, you could write the code as follows:

```
for(var i:Number = 0; i < 7; i++) {
  mcCircle.duplicateMovieClip("mcCircle" + i, this.getNextHighestDepth());
  mcCircle["mcCircle" + i].play();
  mcCircle["mcCircle" + i]._x = Math.random() * 300;
  mcCircle["mcCircle" + i]._y = Math.random() * 300;
}
```

However, the duplicateMovieClip() method also returns a reference to the newly created instance. You can utilize the reference to make your job a little easier. Here is an example of how you could rewrite the preceding code:

```
var mcDup:MovieClip = null;
for(var i:Number = 0; i < 7; i++) {
  mcDup = mcCircle.duplicateMovieClip("mcCircle" + i,
 this.getNextHighestDepth());
  mcDup.play();
  mcDup._x = Math.random() * 300;
  mcDup._y = Math.random() * 300;
}
```

When you create duplicate MovieClip instances, remember that the duplicates will have the same x and y coordinates as the original by default. Therefore, unless you set the _x and _y properties it may not seem that any duplicates were created. You can set the _x and _y properties after creating the duplicate as shown in the preceding code. Or, alternatively, you can use an init object when calling the duplicateMovieClip() method. For more information on the init object, see the section "Working with Init Objects."

Adding MovieClip Objects from the Library Programmatically

Duplicating MovieClip instances is great assuming you already have an instance on the stage to duplicate. But if you don't already have any authoring time instances on the stage you're not going to be able to accomplish much with duplicateMovieClip(). Instead, you'll want to use the attachMovie() method. This method enables you to add new MovieClip instances to your movie from MovieClip symbols in the library.

When you want to use the attachMovie() method to programmatically add instances from the library you'll need to do a little pre-planning. Here's why: Flash exports into the SWF only the symbols that are actually used in the movie. This is a feature that makes sure that your SWF files are not filled with unused symbols. But if you want to use some of those symbols programmatically you need to make sure that Flash exports them in the SWF. In order to accomplish this, do the following:

1. Open the library (choose Window ⇨ Library or press F11).
2. Select the Movie Clip symbol in the library that you want to add programmatically.
3. Either from the library menu or from the right-click/⌘-click menu, choose the Linkage option (see Figure 9-2).
4. In the Linkage Properties dialog box, select the Export for ActionScript box. When you select that box the Export in first frame box is also selected by default. Leave that box selected as well for now.
5. Give the symbol a linkage identifier name. In the Linkage Properties dialog box enter the value. By default Flash will fill in the same name as the symbol. As a best practice add "Symbol" to the end of that name. For example, if the symbol is named "Circle," give it a linkage identifier of CircleSymbol.
6. Click OK to close the dialog box.

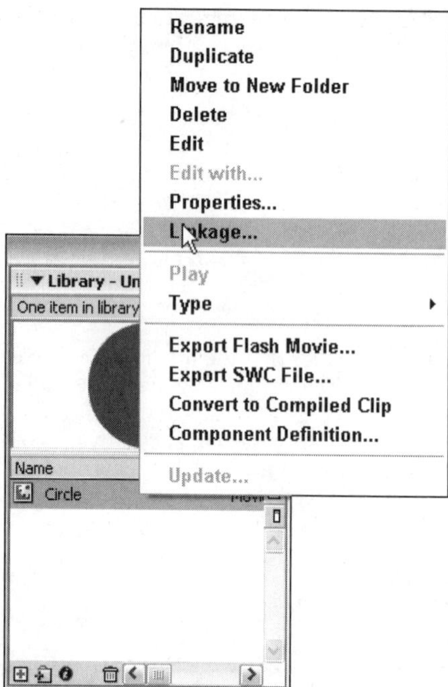

Figure 9-2: Select the Linkage option for a symbol.

Congratulations. You've just told Flash to export the symbol so that you can access it programmatically. And you've assigned it a linkage identifier by which you will be able to specify to Flash which symbol you want to reference. The preceding steps are for assigning linkage settings to a symbol that you already created. You can also assign linkage settings to a symbol as you are creating it. From either the Create New Symbol or Convert to Symbol dialog box you can choose to show the advanced settings by clicking the Advanced button as shown in Figure 9-3. (If your dialog box already shows the advanced settings your button will read *Basic*, and you don't need to click it.) From the advanced settings you can set the linkage settings at the time you create the symbol. You can always change them later if you want by accessing the linkage settings for the symbol.

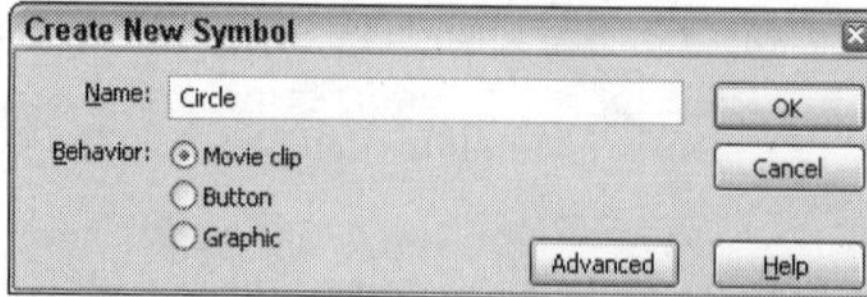

Figure 9-3: Showing the advanced settings

Now that you've accomplished all the preliminary work, the next step is to write the ActionScript code to add an instance of the symbol programmatically. The `attachMovie()` method creates the new instance nested within the `MovieClip` from which it is called. For example, if you call the method from an instance named mcContainer, the new instance will be nested within mcContainer.

The method itself requires at least three parameters — the linkage identifier of the symbol, the name for the new instance, and the depth for the new instance. Here's an example that creates a new instance of a symbol with the linkage identifier CircleSymbol. The new instance is named mcCircle and it is nested within a MovieClip instance named mcHolder:

```
mcHolder.attachMovie("CircleSymbol",
                     "mcCircle",
                     mcHolder.getNextHighestDepth());
```

Notice that in this example, the getNextHighestDepth() method obtains a new depth *within* mcHolder. This is because the new instance is being created within mcHolder. So you want to make sure you are providing a valid depth for within that timeline, not the parent.

When you create a new instance using attachMovie(), the new instance is always placed at 0,0 of the parent object's coordinate space. For example, if you create a new instance within _root, the new object will appear in the upper-left corner of the stage. You can, of course, assign new values to the _x and _y properties immediately after you create the instance. Additionally, you can use an init object to accomplish this. See "Working with Init Objects" for more information.

As with the duplicateMovieClip() method, the attachMovie() method returns a reference to the newly created instance. And, as with duplicateMovieClip(), this can be helpful when you would otherwise have to type long or awkward target paths.

Working with Init Objects

When you are creating new instances using duplicateMovieClip() and/or attachMovie(), often you want to initialize the new object with certain values. For example, you might want to assign each instance x and y coordinate values so that the instances don't overlap (with duplicateMovieClip()) or so that the instance does not appear at 0,0 (with attachMovieClip()). As you've already seen, it is possible to set these values immediately after creating the new instance. But ActionScript also includes an option by which you can assign these property values when creating the new object. In order to accomplish this both the duplicateMovieClip() and the attachMovieClip() methods accept an additional, optional parameter called an *init object*.

An init object is an Object instance to which you have assigned properties and values that correspond to the properties for the new MovieClip instance you want to create. For example, you can create a new init object with _x and _y properties. Flash will then automatically assign the values from the init object to the corresponding properties in the new MovieClip instance. You can create the init object using an Object constructor. However, in many cases you may find it more convenient to use object literal notation to define the init object inline within the attachMovie() or duplicateMovieClip() method. Let's take a look at an example. In the following code, a new MovieClip instance is attached using attachMovie(). The first three parameters remain as before — the linkage identifier, the new instance name, and the depth. Additionally, an init object is defined with _x and _y properties.

```
mcHolder.attachMovie("CircleSymbol",
                     "mcCircle",
                     mcHolder.getNextHighestDepth(),
                     {_x: 50, _y: 60});
```

In the preceding example the new instance is initialized with an x coordinate of 50 and a y coordinate of 60.

Likewise, you can utilize an init object with duplicateMovieClip(). Here's an example:

```
mcCircle.duplicateMovieClip("mcNewCircle",
                              this.getNextHighestDepth(),
                              {_x: 50, _y: 60});
```

If you recall, we said earlier that when you create a duplicate MovieClip using duplicateMovieClip() none of the custom properties of the original are copied to the duplicate. However, with the init object you can conveniently copy all those properties to the duplicate. As mentioned previously, all classes extend, either directly or indirectly, the Object class. Therefore, any type of object, including a MovieClip object, can serve as an init object. With this in mind, if you want a duplicated MovieClip to contain all the same custom properties as the original, you can use the original object as the init object. Here is an example:

```
mcCircle.radius = 100;
mcCircle.duplicateMovieClip("mcNewCircle",
                              this.getNextHighestDepth(),
                              mcCircle);
trace(mcNewCircle.radius);   // Displays: 100
```

Creating Empty MovieClip Objects

Why in the world would you want to create an *empty* MovieClip instance? Simple: Because you can. Okay, and also because it can be extraordinarily beneficial. Although an empty MovieClip object may not immediately appear useful, it is exactly its emptiness that makes it such a powerful object. Here are two of the most common uses of empty MovieClip objects:

✦ **Attaching several MovieClip instances within the empty MovieClip object.** By nesting the objects within the single parent it makes it simple to move, resize, or otherwise alter the entire group.

✦ **Loading content.** As you'll see shortly, you can load other SWF files or JPEG files from external sources into a MovieClip instance. It is very useful to be able to programmatically create an empty MovieClip for this purpose.

You can create a new empty MovieClip instance with the createEmptyMovieClip() method. This method creates a new instance nested within the MovieClip from which it is called. The method requires two parameters — the name and depth for the new instance. Here is an example:

```
this.createEmptyMovieClip("mcExternalSWFHolder", this.getNextHighestDepth());
```

The createEmptyMovieClip() method creates the new instance at 0,0 within the coordinate space of the parent object. Unlike duplicateMovieClip() and attachMovie(), the createEmptyMovieClip() method does not accept an init object. If you want to change the placement of the new object you have to set the _x and _y properties of the new instance after it has been created. Also, like duplicateMovieClip() and attachMovie(), the createEmptyMovieClip() method returns a reference to the new instance.

Removing Programmatically Generated MovieClip Objects

Once you've added `MovieClip` instances programmatically with `duplicateMovieClip()`, `attachMovie()`, or `createEmptyMovieClip()` you can work with those `MovieClip` objects in the same way as any other `MovieClip` objects. You can read and write properties to set placement, visibility, alpha, and so on. You can invoke the methods to affect timeline playback, change depths, and so on. But in addition to all that, you can also do one thing that you cannot do with an authoring time `MovieClip` instance—you can remove them. The `removeMovieClip()` method, when invoked from a programmatically generated `MovieClip` object will remove the object from the stage. This method works only for `MovieClip` objects created using one of the three aforementioned methods. If you invoke `removeMovieClip()` on an authoring time clip there is no effect.

Loading External Content

Not only can you programmatically create `MovieClip` instances; you can load external content programmatically. In both the Flash 6 and Flash 7 players you can load SWF files as well as JPEG files. If you are authoring to earlier versions of the player, you can load only SWF files.

Loading external content can be of great benefit when creating Flash applications. Here are just a few scenarios in which loading external content can be beneficial:

- Your application consists of several parts and you have different teams working on each part. You can have each team create its own SWF, and you can load the multiple SWF files into a single framework.
- Your application consists of some parts that you know will be updated frequently. You can make those parts into their own SWF files and load them into the main SWF. This makes updating the application more manageable.
- Your application consists of dynamically generated catalog or inventory contents. If the images in your application need to be generated dynamically based on database lookups and user input then you can make this possible by loading the JPEG files programmatically.
- Your application is a news application that provides up-to-date articles with images. The article contents are loaded from a database (see Chapters 26 and 35 for more information on loading data) and the images that accompany the article reside on the server.

Let's take a closer look at how to achieve these results. First, you'll look at the simplest way to load SWF and JPEG content. Next, you'll take a look at how to load content so that you can monitor the load progress. Even if you want to always monitor load progress of content, you should first read how to load content without monitoring the load progress.

Loading SWF Content

First let's look at how you can load SWF content into your movie at runtime. The `loadMovie()` method loads the content from an SWF specified by a URL parameter. The content is loaded into the `MovieClip` from which the method is invoked, and it replaces the timeline of the `MovieClip` with the main timeline of the loaded SWF.

The loadMovie() method requires that you provide, at minimum, the URL at which the SWF can be found. The URL can be relative or absolute. Here is an example that uses a relative URL:

```
mcHolder.loadMovie("circleFun.swf");
```

The preceding line of code searches for an SWF file named circleFun.swf that is in the same directory as the loading SWF. Assuming that circleFun.swf can be found at http://www.person13.com/asb/circleFun.swf, you can use an absolute URL as follows:

```
mcHolder.loadMovie("http://www.person13.com/asb/circleFun.swf");
```

When you use loadMovie() to load SWF content into a holder MovieClip, it is a particularly good example of when you might want to use the createEmptyMovieClip() method to actually instantiate the holder object. For example:

```
this.createEmptyMovieClip("mcHolder", this.getNextHighestDepth());
mcHolder.loadMovie("circleFun.swf");
```

When you load an SWF everything within the holder object is replaced. That is, the entire timeline as well as all the custom properties and methods of the instance are replaced. The majority of the appearance properties will retain their values, however. For example, _x, _y, _alpha, and so on, will not remain the same as prior to the loading of the content. The exception to this is that you should not set the _height and _width properties of an empty MovieClip object until after the content has loaded. If you set the _height and _width properties of an empty MovieClip before the content has loaded, the content will not show.

When you load an external SWF into a MovieClip object, the loaded contents will be aligned within the MovieClip object just as they were in the external SWF. But remember, the upper-left corner of the stage for the main timeline is 0,0. Therefore, when you load an external SWF into a MovieClip object, it is not centered within the object. All the content appears to the right and below the center point (which is 0,0).

For more complex scenarios you can also send variables along with the request for the external SWF. You can accomplish this in one of two ways:

✦ Append a query string to the URL parameter.

```
mcHolder.loadMovie("http://www.person13.com/asb/circleFun.swf?nCircle
s=10");
```

✦ Add the variables to the holder MovieClip object as properties, and then specify a second, optional parameter letting Flash know whether to send the variables using HTTP GET or POST.

```
mcHolder.nCircles = 10;
mcHolder.loadMovie("http://www.person13.com/asb/circleFun.swf", "GET");
```

SWF files cannot accept the POST method when you load them with loadMovie(). You need to use the GET method only when directly loading an SWF. You may use the POST method when loading content by proxy by way of a server-side script that accepts POST requests.

Loading JPEG Content

In addition to loading SWF content, you can also load JPEG content into your Flash movies since Flash Player 6. The only catch is that the JPEG must *not* be in progressive JPEG format. If the image is a progressive JPEG, nothing will load.

In order to load JPEG content, you use the `loadMovie()` method just as when you load an SWF. The only difference is that you provide a URL to a JPEG resource instead of an SWF resource. The `loadMovie()` method works the same way with JPEG files as with SWF files. The loaded content replaces the timeline of the `MovieClip` object into which it loads. Here is an example:

```
this.createEmptyMovieClip("mcHolder", this.getNextHighestDepth());
mcHolder.loadMovie("http://www.person13.com/asb/image1.jpg");
```

However, you should be aware of the implications of the `MovieClip` object's timeline being replaced by JPEG data. Once the JPEG data loads, the object can no longer be fully treated as a `MovieClip` object. Instead, it becomes more like an instance of a Graphic symbol. If you want to continue to be able to work with the loaded content as though it is a `MovieClip` object, there is a simple solution. What you can do is create a nested `MovieClip` object into which you load the JPEG content. Then the parent `MovieClip` object will contain the nested JPEG and you can still work with the parent as a `MovieClip` object. Here is an example:

```
// First, create the parent MovieClip.
this.createEmptyMovieClip("mcHolder", this.getNextHighestDepth());

// Next, created the nested object.
mcHolder.createEmptyMovieClip("mcJPEG", this.getNextHighestDepth());

// Then, load the JPEG into the nested object.
mcHolder.mcJPEG.loadMovie("http://www.person13.com/asb/image1.jpg");
```

Monitoring Loading

New to Flash MX 2004 is the `MovieClipLoader` class. This class enables you to effectively monitor the load progress of SWF and JPEG content. This feature was missing in previous versions of Flash. Although it was possible to monitor load progress using `getBytesLoaded()` and `getBytesTotal()`, it was somewhat difficult to implement, and it didn't always work as effectively as one might hope. The `MovieClipLoader` class marks significant progress in being able to monitor load progress.

`MovieClipLoader` objects rely on listener objects to monitor the progress of loading content. The listener object for a `MovieClipLoader` instance is simply an object with the following three methods defined:

- **onLoadStart():** This method is invoked when content begins to load. The method is passed a reference to the `MovieClip` object into which the content is being loaded.
- **onLoadProgress():** This method is invoked continually each time data is loaded. At each interval the method is passed three parameters — a reference to the `MovieClip` object into which the content is being loaded, the number of loaded bytes, and the number of total bytes.
- **onLoadComplete():** This method is invoked when the content has completed loading. It is passed a reference to the `MovieClip` object into which the content is being loaded.

Here is an example of a simple `MovieClipLoader` listener object:

```
var oListener:Object = new Object();
oListener.onLoadStart = function (mcHolderClip:MovieClip):Void {
   trace(mcHolderClip + " started loading.");
}
oListener.onLoadProgress = function(mcHolderClip:MovieClip,
                                    nLoaded:Number,
                                    nTotal:Number):Void
{
   trace(mcHolderClip + " loaded " + nLoaded + " of " + nTotal + "bytes");
}
oListener.onLoadComplete = function(mcHolderClip:MovieClip):Void {
   trace(mcHolderClip + " completed loading");
}
```

In order to use the `MovieClipLoader` class, complete the following steps:

1. Create the `MovieClip` object into which you are going to load the content. For example:

   ```
   this.createEmptyMovieClip("mcHolder",
                             this.getNextHighestDepth());
   ```

2. Instantiate a `MovieClipLoader` object with the constructor. For example:

   ```
   var mclLoader:MovieClipLoader = new MovieClipLoader();
   ```

3. Create a listener object.
4. Use the `addListener()` method to add the listener object to the `MovieClipLoader` instance.

   ```
   mclLoader.addListener(oListener);
   ```

5. Invoke the `loadClip()` method from the `MovieClipLoader` object. Pass the method two parameters—the URL for the content and a reference to the `MovieClip` into which you want to load the content.

   ```
   mclLoader.loadClip("http://www.person13.com/asb/circleFun.swf",
   mcHolder);
   ```

Monitoring the load progress for SWF and JPEG content is important for several reasons:

✦ When you monitor load progress you can report to the user how much of the content has downloaded. This is important when the download might potentially take some time. You want to assure the user that something is happening and that they are not just waiting for nothing.

✦ You cannot do too much with a `MovieClip` until the content has loaded. Although you can adjust some of the appearance properties, the object will not report accurate dimensions until it has loaded completely. Also, you cannot assign any custom properties to the instance until after the content has loaded because if you assign the properties first they will be overwritten. SWFs and JPEGs load asynchronously. That means that after you instruct Flash to try and load the content, the content begins to load in the background while the rest of the actions are run in the movie. Therefore, you need a way to be able to detect when the content has loaded before you try to do anything with it. The `MovieClipLoader` class offers you this kind of functionality—the listener's `onLoadComplete()` method is invoked once the entire content has been loaded.

Unloading Content

You can unload SWF content from a MovieClip object in one of two ways:

✦ You can load new content into the MovieClip object. This will replace the previously loaded content.

✦ You can call the unloadMovie() method.

The unloadMovie() method will unload the content that had previously been loaded into the object. This method cannot remove content from objects if the content was not loaded with loadMovie() or MovieClipLoader in the first place. Also, because a MovieClip into which JPEG data has been loaded cannot be treated as a MovieClip any longer, you cannot unload JPEG data. Instead, if you want to remove a JPEG you should make sure that you have loaded the content into a nested MovieClip as previously recommended. You should also make sure that the parent object was instantiated programmatically. Then you can use the removeMovieClip() method to remove the parent object.

When you use unloadMovie(), the original timeline is not retrieved. Once you have loaded content into a MovieClip object, the original timeline cannot be retrieved. That means that you should be careful not to indiscriminately load content into MovieClip objects if you want to retain the original contents in them.

When you load SWF content into your Flash application using one of the techniques described previously, you might encounter a problem with _root references. If the loaded content contains ActionScript that references _root, the code will likely not work once loaded because _root may no longer target the location that was originally intended.

Flash MX 2004 and Flash Player 7 introduce the _lockroot property for MovieClip objects. The property defaults to false, meaning that _root references within that MovieClip instance reference _root just as in Flash Player 6 and previous versions. But if you set _lockroot to true Flash automatically converts all references to _root within that MovieClip so that they target the MovieClip instance.

Opening Web Pages

The getURL() method allows you to communicate with Internet browser programs. It will communicate with the browser program from which the movie is being played or from the default browser if the movie is being played from a projector or other application. Typically, this method is used to change the URL of the current browser window. However, you can also use it to launch new windows and send JavaScript commands.

You must always specify a URL as a string as a parameter when calling the getURL() method. For example:

```
this.getURL("http://www.person13.com.com");
```

If the Flash movie containing the preceding code is being viewed in a browser window, the window's location will change to the specified URL. Otherwise, if the movie is being viewed as a projector or in the stand-alone Flash Player, it will launch a new browser window of the computer's default browser with the specified URL.

You can also pass a second optional parameter: a window/frame name as a string. This allows you to open URLs in other browser windows or frames without redirecting the current window and losing the Flash movie in the process:

```
this.getURL("http://www.person13.com", "_blank");
```

The JavaScript property `_blank` indicates that a new, blank browser window should be opened. `_blank` is not a keyword, and has no significance, within ActionScript. To learn more about JavaScript, see Danny Goodman's *JavaScript Bible, Fifth Edition* (Wiley, 2004), an excellent resource.

You can pass a third optional parameter: the HTTP method for sending variables. You can specify a string value of either `GET` or `POST`. When you pass this third parameter to the `getURL()` method, you send any custom properties of the `MovieClip` object from which the method is invoked as string values in `URLEncoded` format. There is one exception. Nested `MovieClip` objects are not sent. Custom properties refer to those properties that you, the author, have created. Predefined properties such as `_alpha` and `_totalframes` are not included. It is also important to understand what values are being sent. Primitive data types such as numbers and Booleans are easily converted to string values. But other data types may yield unexpected results. For instance, custom objects will have the value of `"[object Object]"` when converted to strings. Also note that because all the properties of the `MovieClip` object are converted to strings before they are sent, none of the properties of nested objects are sent. This means that you have to be very careful that any values that you need to send using the `getURL()` method are properties of the `MovieClip` object from which you invoke the method. Here is an example of the `getURL()` method invoked from a `MovieClip` object named `mcCircle`:

```
mcCircle.getURL("http://www.person13.com/", "_blank", "GET");
```

If the `mcCircle` `MovieClip` object has two custom properties, radius and velocity, the location in the browser might look something like this:

```
http://www.person13.com/?radius=100&velocity=12
```

You can also use the `getURL()` method to make calls to JavaScript functions in the HTML page within which the Flash movie is embedded. To do this, simply use the following technique:

```
mcObject.getURL("javascript:functionName([parameters])");
```

Creating Draggable MovieClip Objects

Draggable `MovieClip` objects can be utilized in many ways. Here are just a few examples:

✦ Windows containing various content that the user can move around the stage.

✦ Drag and drop functionality. For example, you can enable a user to drag an item from a catalog of your online store, and drop it into their basket.

✦ Games. All kinds of games utilize draggable objects. Puzzles, for example, require that the user be able to move the pieces.

There are essentially two parts to creating a basic draggable MovieClip. First, you need to tell Flash to start dragging the object — this means that the object should follow the movement of the mouse. Then, at some point, you need to tell Flash to stop dragging the object. Typically draggable MovieClip objects do both of these things, although in some unique situations an object will only start dragging — for example, when creating a custom mouse cursor (see Chapter 19). But for the most part you will utilize both the starting and the stopping.

Telling Flash to Start Dragging a MovieClip

To start dragging a MovieClip object all you need to do is call the startDrag() method from the MovieClip instance. In the most basic format it might look like this:

```
mcCircle.startDrag();
```

Typically, you will invoke a startDrag() method within an object's onPress() event handler method. For example:

```
mcCircle.onPress = function():Void {
  this.startDrag();
};
```

In the preceding code example the MovieClip mcCircle starts dragging when the user clicks the object. The object will follow the mouse relative to the point on the object at which the user clicked. For example, if the user clicks the very edge of the object, the user will drag the object from the very edge. In the majority of situations this is exactly what you want. However, you can also tell Flash to snap the object so that the center of the object aligns with the mouse. You can do this by passing the method a single parameter value of true.

```
mcCircle.onPress = function():Void {
  this.startDrag(true);
};
```

Typically, this technique is employed when creating a custom mouse cursor or other similar goal.

There is one more variation on the startDrag() method. You can also tell Flash that you want the object to be draggable only within a particular area. This is particularly useful when creating sliders or any other situation in which you want to make sure the user can move the object only within a particular range. In these cases you need to pass the method five parameters — a Boolean value indicating whether or not to snap to the center of the object, the left-most x value of the area, the top-most y value of the area, the right-most x value of the area, and the bottom-most y value of the area. All the coordinate values should be specified relative to the object's parent's coordinate space. Here is an example in which mcCircle is made draggable only within a rectangle defined by 0, 0, 200, 300.

```
mcCircle.onPress = function():Void {
  this.startDrag(false, 0, 0, 200, 300);
};
```

Note

Only one object can be dragged at a time.

Telling Flash to Stop Dragging a MovieClip

Any time you want to stop the dragging action, simply invoke the stopDrag() method from the draggable object. For example:

```
mcCircle.stopDrag();
```

The stopDrag() method does not require any parameters. It simply drops the object at the current position on the stage.

Just as the startDrag() method is typically invoked within an onPress() event handler method, the stopDrag() method is typically invoked within an onRelease() event handler method. When the user clicks the object it becomes draggable, and when the user releases the click, the object is dropped.

```
mcCircle.onRelease = function():Void {
  this.stopDrag();
};
```

Determining Where an Object Is Dropped

You can determine when two objects are overlapping using the hitTest() method. You'll take a closer look at this method in the next section.

Checking for Overlapping

In some of your Flash movies, it is absolutely essential that you can detect when two MovieClip objects enter the same space in the x and y coordinate space. For example, if you create a game, you might need to detect when a ball hits against a wall or a laser beam hits a spaceship. Other times, you simply need to see if a MovieClip object is within a certain "hotspot" space. You can do all this quite simply with the hitTest() method of any MovieClip object. The hitTest() method allows you to check for overlapping objects in two ways. In either case the method returns a Boolean value — true if there is overlap and false if there is not overlap:

✦ You can pass the method a reference to another MovieClip object. Flash will then check to see if the object from which the method is called overlaps with the object you pass as a parameter. When you use this technique, Flash checks to see if the bounding boxes of the two objects overlap. This means that, for example, even if the two objects are circles, they will report as overlapping at some times even when the actual circles are not overlapping. Here is an example of the first usage of hitTest():

```
var bOverlap:Boolean = mcCircle.hitTest(mcSquare);
```

✦ You can also call the hitTest() method by passing it three parameters — an x coordinate, a y coordinate, and a Boolean value indicating whether you want to test on the actual shape of the object or the bounding box of the object. Here is an example of this second usage in which you check to see if the mouse is currently overlapping the object:

```
var bOverlap:Boolean = mcCircle.hitTest(this._xmouse, this._ymouse,
true);
```

Typically, you don't perform hit tests as a one-time operation. Instead, you normally place your hitTest() calls within an interval function or method so that you can continually poll to check the current status. Here is an example:

```
function checkOverlap():Void {
  if(mcCircle.hitTest(mcSquare)) {
    trace("The objects overlap.");
  }
}

var nOverlapInterval:Number = setInterval(checkOverlap, 100);
```

Working with Coordinate Spaces

As you already know, the coordinate spaces within nested MovieClip objects might not coincide with the coordinates for the parent object. This depends on the placement of the nested object. This can make it somewhat tricky when you want to compare coordinates within different coordinate spaces.

When converting between coordinate spaces, there are essentially two types of coordinate spaces—global and local. The coordinates within the _root object are referred to as the global coordinates. The coordinates within the nested MovieClip objects are referred to as the local coordinates. Using the globalToLocal() and localToGlobal() methods you can convert between these two types of coordinates.

The localToGlobal() method converts local coordinates to the global equivalents. Likewise, the globalToLocal() method converts global coordinates to the local equivalents. In either case, the methods each require a single parameter in the form of a points object. A points object is simply an object with two properties—x and y. The x property should have the value of the x coordinate, and the y property should have the value of the y coordinate. Here is an example of how to create a points object:

```
var oPoints:Object = {x:30, y:60};
```

With a points object created, you can pass it to the respective method. The methods do not return any values. Instead, they convert the points object values to the global or local equivalents. Here is an example that converts the local coordinates 30,60 from the mcCircle instance to the global equivalents:

```
var oPoints:Object = {x:30, y:60};
mcCircle.localToGlobal(oPoints);
trace(oPoints.x + " " + oPoints.y);
```

By combining the localToGlobal() and globalToLocal() methods, you can convert the coordinates from one nested object's coordinate space to that of another nested object. Here is an example that converts the coordinates 30,60 from the mcCircle object's coordinate space to the equivalent coordinates within the mcSquare instance:

```
var oPoints:Object = {x:30, y:60};
mcCircle.localToGlobal(oPoints);
mcSquare.globalToLocal(oPoints);
trace(oPoints.x + " " + oPoints.y);
```

You can also use the getBounds() method to determine the bounding coordinates of one object within the coordinate space of another. From the first MovieClip object, invoke the getBounds() method, and pass it a single parameter — a reference to a MovieClip object in whose coordinate space the results should be given. The method then returns a new object containing four properties — xMin, xMax, yMin, and yMax. Here is an example that gets the boundaries of mcCircle within the coordinate space of the mcSquare instance:

```
var oBoundaries:Object = mcCircle.getBounds(mcSquare);
```

Creating Scriptable Masks

Using setMask(), you can assign another MovieClip to function as a mask for the object from which the method is invoked. Here is an example in which mcMask is set as the mask of mcCircle:

```
mcCircle.setMask(mcMask);
```

The MovieClip that works as the mask can contain animation (that is, shape tweens or motion tweens), and it can be controlled through ActionScript itself to create complex masks. If and when you no longer want the masked object to be masked, you can again call the setMask() method and pass it the null value. For example:

```
mcCircle.setMask(null);
```

A *mask* is a shape that defines the visible area for an object. For example, a MovieClip object containing a rectangular image can be masked so that it displays only a circular portion of that image.

Practicing Attaching and Dragging MovieClip Objects

In this exercise, you'll continue working from where you left off in the last exercise. This time you add all the MovieClip instances programmatically. And, instead of making the accessories show and hide when clicked, you'll make them draggable so that you can place them on the man. You'll need to have person001.fla available. If you didn't complete the previous exercise, you can find person001.fla on the CD-ROM.

1. Open person001.fla and save it as person002.fla.
2. Delete the Man layer. This will delete the layer and its contents — the mcMan instance. Don't worry; you'll add it programmatically now.
3. Open the library. Set each symbol to export for ActionScript. Set the linkage identifiers to HatSymbol, GlassesSymbol, BeardSymbol, CoatSymbol, ShoesSymbol, CaneSymbol, ManSymbol, and BodySymbol.
4. On the Actions layer, remove all previous code, and add the following code:

```
function addArtwork():Void {

  // Create an empty MovieClip into which we will add all
  // the subsequent instances.
```

```
  this.createEmptyMovieClip("mcMan", this.getNextHighestDepth());

  // Use attachMovie() to add instances to the mcMan
  // object.
  this.mcMan.attachMovie("ManSymbol",
                         "mcClothedMan",
                         this.mcMan.getNextHighestDepth());
  this.mcMan.attachMovie("BeardSymbol",
                         "mcBeard",
                         this.mcMan.getNextHighestDepth());
  this.mcMan.attachMovie("CaneSymbol",
                         "mcCane",
                         this.mcMan.getNextHighestDepth());
  this.mcMan.attachMovie("CoatSymbol",
                         "mcCoat",
                         this.mcMan.getNextHighestDepth());
  this.mcMan.attachMovie("GlassesSymbol",
                         "mcGlasses",
                         this.mcMan.getNextHighestDepth());
  this.mcMan.attachMovie("HatSymbol",
                         "mcHat",
                         this.mcMan.getNextHighestDepth());
  this.mcMan.attachMovie("ShoesSymbol",
                         "mcShoes",
                         this.mcMan.getNextHighestDepth());
}

function makeHidden():Void {

  // Loop through all the instances in mcMan.mcClothedMan
  // and except for the mcBody instance, set them all to
  // be invisible.
  for(var sMcName:String in mcMan.mcClothedMan) {
    if(sMcName == "mcBody") {
     continue;
    }
    mcMan.mcClothedMan[sMcName]._visible = false;
  }
}

function setHandlers():Void {

  // Loop through all the instances in mcMan and except
  // for mcClothedMan make them draggable.
  for(var sMcName:String in mcMan) {
    if(sMcName == "mcClothedMan") {
      continue;
    }
    mcMan[sMcName].onPress = function():Void {
      this.startDrag();
    };
    mcMan[sMcName].onRelease = function():Void {
```

```
          this.stopDrag();
        };

        // Set all the instances placement so they appear to
        // the right of the man.
        mcMan[sMcName]._x = 450;
        mcMan[sMcName]._y = 200;
      }
    }

    addArtwork();
    makeHidden();
    setHandlers();
```

5. Save and test the movie.

When you test the movie, you should be able to drag and drop all the accessories. Now you can take a closer look at the code.

The `addArtwork()` function should be fairly self-explanatory. In this function, you create a new empty `MovieClip` object named `mcMan`, and then use `attachMovie()` to create nested instances within it. The nested instances are created from the symbols you set to export previously.

Next is the `makeHidden()` function. You may be wondering why you would have attached an instance of the `Man` symbol instead of an instance of the `Body` symbol. After all, if you attached an instance of the `Body` symbol you wouldn't have to hide all the nested instances within it. This is a good point. You're going to want to have those hidden nested instances in there for the next exercise so in order to hide them (the nested instances within the `mcClothedMan` object), this example uses a `for...in` statement and sets the `_visible` property of each to `false`. The only exception is the `mcBody` instance—you want that instance to remain visible. In order to ensure that instance remains visible, you use an `if` statement to check for the current instance name, and if it is `mcBody`, you use a `continue` statement to skip to the next.

```
function makeHidden():Void {
  for(var sMcName:String in mcMan.mcClothedMan) {
    if(sMcName == "mcBody") {
     continue;
    }
    mcMan.mcClothedMan[sMcName]._visible = false;
  }
}
```

The `setHandlers()` function in this exercise shares its name with the function from the last exercise, but it is different in what it does. Again, you use a `for...in` statement—this time looping through all the nested instances of `mcMan`. With the exception of the `mcClothedMan` instance you assign `onPress()` and `onRelease()` methods to each such that each instance is made draggable. And, additionally, you set each instance's placement so that it appears to the right of the man.

```
function setHandlers():Void {
  for(var sMcName:String in mcMan) {
    if(sMcName == "mcClothedMan") {
      continue;
    }
```

```
      mcMan[sMcName].onPress = function():Void {
        this.startDrag();
      };
      mcMan[sMcName].onRelease = function():Void {
        this.stopDrag();
      };
      mcMan[sMcName]._x = 450;
      mcMan[sMcName]._y = 200;
    }
  }
```

Once you've defined all the functions, you then need only to call them.

```
addArtwork();
makeHidden();
setHandlers();
```

Practicing Checking for Overlaps and Loading Content

In the last exercise, you made an application in which you can drag and drop the accessories onto the cartoon man. In this exercise, you'll add some feature enhancements to that application, including the following:

- **Snap to:** When the user drags and drops an accessory near the correct location, the accessory will automatically snap to.
- **Correct location hinting:** When the accessory is dragged over the correct area, the instance will lower its alpha to 50.
- **Current object on top:** The current object (the object being dragged) always appears on top.
- **A JPEG background image:** You'll load a JPEG at runtime to use as the background.

So let's get started. Follow along with these steps:

1. Open `person002.fla` and save it as `person003.fla`. If you didn't complete the last exercise, you can find `person002.fla` on the CD-ROM.
2. Modify the code on the first frame of the main timeline as shown here (additions in bold):

```
function addArtwork():Void {
  this.createEmptyMovieClip("mcMan", this.getNextHighestDepth());
  this.mcMan.attachMovie("ManSymbol",
                         "mcClothedMan",
                          this.mcMan.getNextHighestDepth());
  this.mcMan.attachMovie("BeardSymbol",
                         "mcBeard",
                         this.mcMan.getNextHighestDepth());
  this.mcMan.attachMovie("CaneSymbol",
                         "mcCane",
                          this.mcMan.getNextHighestDepth());
```

```
  this.mcMan.attachMovie("CoatSymbol",
                          "mcCoat",
                          this.mcMan.getNextHighestDepth());
  this.mcMan.attachMovie("GlassesSymbol",
                         "mcGlasses",
                         this.mcMan.getNextHighestDepth());
  this.mcMan.attachMovie("HatSymbol",
                         "mcHat",
                         this.mcMan.getNextHighestDepth());
  this.mcMan.attachMovie("ShoesSymbol",
                         "mcShoes",
                         this.mcMan.getNextHighestDepth());
}

function makeHidden():Void {
  for(var sMcName:String in mcMan.mcClothedMan) {
    if(sMcName == "mcBody") {
     continue;
    }
    mcMan.mcClothedMan[sMcName]._visible = false;
  }
}

function setHandlers():Void {
  for(var sMcName:String in mcMan) {
    if(sMcName == "mcClothedMan") {
      continue;
    }
    mcMan[sMcName].onPress = function():Void {
      this.startDrag();

      // Set a custom property of the parent MovieClip
      // so that we can detect which object is being
      // dragged.
      this._parent.selected = this;
    };
    mcMan[sMcName].onRelease = function():Void {
      this.stopDrag();

      // Set the custom property to null so we know that
      // the object is no longer being dragged.
      this._parent.selected = null;

      // Set the alpha back to 100 in case it wasn't
      // already.
      this._alpha = 100;

      // If the custom snapTo property is true...
      if(this.snapTo) {

        // Create a points object with the points of the
        // corresponding instance within mcClothedMan.
```

```
        var oPoints = new Object();
        oPoints.x = this._parent.mcClothedMan[this._name]._x;
        oPoints.y = this._parent.mcClothedMan[this._name]._y;

        // Convert the points to the local points within
        // mcMan (this._parent), and then move this object
        // to that location.
        this._parent.mcClothedMan.localToGlobal(oPoints);
        this._parent.globalToLocal(oPoints);
        this._x = oPoints.x;
        this._y = oPoints.y;
      }
    };
    mcMan[sMcName]._x = 450;
    mcMan[sMcName]._y = 200;
  }
}

function setOverlapChecker():Void {
  mcMan.check = function():Void {

    // If the selected object is overlapping with the
    // corresponding object within mcClothedMan...
    if (this.selected.hitTest
(this.mcClothedMan[this.selected._name])) {
      this.selected.snapTo = true;
      this.selected._alpha = 50;
    }
    else {
      this.selected.snapTo = false;
      this.selected._alpha = 100;
    }

    // Loop through every instance in mcMan...
    for(var sMcName:String in this) {
      if(sMcName == this.selected._name ||
         sMcName == "mcClothedMan")
      {
        continue;
      }

      // If the current object overlaps with any of the
      // others, and if the instance has a lower depth,
      // change the depths.
      if(this.selected.hitTest(this[sMcName]) &&
         this.selected.getDepth() < this[sMcName].getDepth())
      {
        this.selected.swapDepths(this[sMcName]);
      }
    }
  };
```

```
  setInterval(mcMan, "check", 100);
}

function loadBackground():Void {

  // Create an empty MovieClip for the background. And
  // because we're loading a JPEG, create a nested
  // MovieClip named mcJPEG into which we'll load the
  // content.
  this.createEmptyMovieClip("mcBackground",
                            this.getNextHighestDepth());
  this.mcBackground.createEmptyMovieClip("mcJPEG",
                  this.mcBackground.getNextHighestDepth());

  // Create a listener object for the MovieClip loader.
  var oListener:Object = new Object();
  oListener.onLoadComplete = function(mcRef:MovieClip):Void {

    // When the JPEG loads, set the depth of mcBackground
    // to 0 so that it appears below the other instances.
    var mcBG:MovieClip = mcRef._parent;
    mcBG.swapDepths(0);
  };
  var mclLoader:MovieClipLoader = new MovieClipLoader();
  mclLoader.addListener(oListener);
  mclLoader.loadClip("http://www.person13.com/asb/image1.jpg",
                  mcBackground.mcJPEG);
}

addArtwork();
makeHidden();
setHandlers();
setOverlapChecker();
loadBackground();
```

3. Save and test the movie.

When you test the movie, you should be able to drag the accessories over the man. If you drag the instances over the correct locations, they should lower in transparency, and if you drop the instance it should snap to its exact location. The object you are dragging should always appear above the others. A background should load behind the rest of the content.

Now you'll take a closer look at some of the new code.

Within the `setHandlers()` function you've added some code. When the user clicks an accessory, you assign a value to a custom property of the `mcMan` object. The custom property, selected, contains a reference to the accessory that is currently being dragged.

```
mcMan[sMcName].onPress = function():Void {
  this.startDrag();
```

```
    this._parent.selected = this;
  };
```

When the object is released, you set the selected property to null so that Flash will know that the object is no longer being dragged. In addition, just in case the object was not already at 100 alpha, you set the `_alpha` property to 100. A little later in the code you assign values to the custom `snapTo` property for the accessories. If the `snapTo` property is `true` then when the accessory is released you want the object to move to its correct location. Now, in order to achieve this you create corresponding `MovieClip` instances. Within the `mcMan` object are nested instances with names such as `mcHat`, `mcCoat`, and so on. Similarly, nested within `mcClothedMan` are instances with the same names. The instances within `mcClothedMan` are invisible, but in the correct locations. Therefore, you can use the fact that these instances have corresponding names in order to snap the accessories to the correct locations. You first create a points object with the coordinates of the correctly placed instance within `mcClothedMan`. Then, using `localToGlobal()` and `globalToLocal()`, you convert the coordinates to the corresponding points within `mcMan`.

```
  mcMan[sMcName].onRelease = function():Void {
    this.stopDrag();
    this._parent.selected = null;
    this._alpha = 100;
    if(this.snapTo) {
      var oPoints = new Object();
      oPoints.x = this._parent.mcClothedMan[this._name]._x;
      oPoints.y = this._parent.mcClothedMan[this._name]._y;
      this._parent.mcClothedMan.localToGlobal(oPoints);
      this._parent.globalToLocal(oPoints);
      this._x = oPoints.x;
      this._y = oPoints.y;
    }
  };
```

Next, you define the `setOverlapChecker()` function. In this function, you define a custom method, `check()`, for the `mcMan` object. Within this method, you first want to check to see if the selected object is overlapping with the corresponding object in `mcClothedMan`. If so, you set the custom `snapTo` property to `true` and lower the transparency to 50. Otherwise, you set `snapTo` to `false` and make sure the transparency is at 100.

```
  if (this.selected.hitTest
(this.mcClothedMan[this.selected._name])) {
    this.selected.snapTo = true;
    this.selected._alpha = 50;
  }
  else {
    this.selected.snapTo = false;
    this.selected._alpha = 100;
  }
```

Then you use a `for...in` statement to loop through all the nested instances. You don't want to check for overlap with `mcClothedMan` and you also don't want to check for overlap of the selected object with itself. You then check to see if the selected instance overlaps with any of the other instances. If so, and if the selected instance's depth is lower than the other instance, you'll want to change their depths so that the selected instance always appears on top.

```
    for(var sMcName:String in this) {
      if(sMcName == this.selected._name ||
          sMcName == "mcClothedMan")
      {
        continue;
      }
      if(this.selected.hitTest(this[sMcName]) &&
          this.selected.getDepth() < this[sMcName].getDepth())
      {
        this.selected.swapDepths(this[sMcName]);
      }
    }
};
```

You then set an interval on which the `check()` method of `mcMan` is called so that the application continually checks for overlaps:

```
setInterval(mcMan, "check", 100);
```

We'd like to know what you thought about this chapter. Visit `www.flashsupport.com/feedback` to fill out an online form with your comments.

Summary

✦ Each time you drag an instance of a `MovieClip` or `Button` symbol onto your movie, you are creating a `MovieClip` or `Button` object. You should always name your instances so that you can address them with ActionScript.

✦ You can address named `MovieClip` and `Button` objects to tell them what you want them to do via ActionScript. Addresses are either absolute or relative, with preference being given to relative addresses.

✦ Handling events with `MovieClip` and `Button` objects is accomplished by defining event handler methods.

✦ The appearance properties for `MovieClip` and `Button` objects enable you to programmatically set an object's location, dimensions, rotation, and so on.

✦ You can create new `MovieClip` objects programmatically with the `duplicateMovieClip()`, `attachMovie()`, and `createEmptyMovieClip()` methods.

✦ You can create draggable `MovieClip` objects with `startDrag()` and `stopDrag()`.

✦ Flash allows you to load SWF and JPEG content into `MovieClip` objects at runtime.

✦ ✦ ✦

The Drawing API

✦ ✦ ✦ ✦

In This Chapter

Learning how the Drawing API enables you to draw lines, fills, and shapes programmatically with ActionScript

Creating and working with a custom DrawingUtils class for more powerful scripted drawing

Working with the Drawing API to create fully scripted masks

Practicing using the Drawing API

✦ ✦ ✦ ✦

Macromedia introduced the ActionScript Drawing API in Flash MX, enabling you to develop Flash applications in which lines, curves, shapes, fills, and so on can be programmatically drawn. This creates a whole slew of possibilities that were not previously available. Scripting simple artwork can be an effective and efficient part of your Flash applications. In this chapter we'll explore how you can programmatically draw everything from simple lines to shapes filled with complex gradient fills. We'll also take a look at some of the many possible uses of scripted graphics.

Introducing the Drawing API

What is referred to as the Drawing API in Flash is simply a subset of methods accessible from `MovieClip` objects. These methods enable you to draw within the object from which they are invoked. Typically, therefore, it is recommended that you create a new `MovieClip` instance for each shape you want to draw. If you recall from our discussion in Chapter 9, the `createEmptyMovieClip()` method allows you to programmatically create empty `MovieClip` objects. This is the perfect technique for creating `MovieClip` objects for use with the Drawing API.

When discussing the Drawing API it is convenient to work with the metaphor of a pen. You can think of Flash as having an invisible pen that you can command. For example, you can tell it to move to a point without drawing a line — similar to lifting a pen off the paper to move to another point. You can also tell the pen to draw a line from its current location to another point. The Drawing API itself does not consist of many methods. In the following sections, we take a look at each of the handful of methods.

Setting a Line Style

Before you can do anything with the pen, you have to first tell it what kind of lines to draw. This is kind of like selecting among a set of different pens before drawing on a piece of paper. You want to choose the right pen for the job. Do you want a thin or thick line? What color should the line be? Each `MovieClip` object has its own pen. So you have to set the line style for each `MovieClip` before you can draw in it. In order to set the line style you can use the `lineStyle()` method. This method requires three parameters:

- **Line thickness:** This numeric value can range from 0 (hairline) to 255. This value indicates how many points across the line should be.

✦ **Line color:** This numeric value should be the color for the line. Typically it is convenient to work with hexadecimal representation for this value, though it is not required. For example, to draw a blue line, you can use the value 0x0000FF.

✦ **Line alpha:** This is a value from 0 to 100 indicating the alpha of the line. Typically, a value of 0 is used only when you want to create a filled shape that displays no outline.

Here is an example in which we create a new `MovieClip` and set the line style. We'll use a hairline, red line with 100 alpha.

```
this.createEmptyMovieClip("mcShape", this.getNextHighestDepth());
mcShape.lineStyle(0, 0xFF0000, 100);
```

You can change the line style at any point as well. For example, you may want to draw one red line and then one green line. You'll take a look at the `lineTo()` method in more detail in a moment, but for right now, here is a simple example that demonstrates how you can change the line style.

```
this.createEmptyMovieClip("mcShape", this.getNextHighestDepth());
mcShape.lineStyle(0, 0xFF0000, 100);
mcShape.lineTo(100, 0);
mcShape.lineStyle(0, 0x00FF00, 100);
mcShape.lineTo(100, 100);
```

Moving the Pen Without Drawing

If you've ever worked with an Etch-a-Sketch, you know how limiting it is to not be able to lift the pen in order to move it without drawing a line. Fortunately, the Flash Drawing API does not have this limitation. You can use the `moveTo()` method to instruct the pen to move to a specific point within the `MovieClip` object's coordinate system without drawing a line. The `moveTo()` method requires two parameters — the x and y coordinate values. Here is an example that creates a `MovieClip` object, sets the line style, and then moves the pen to 100,100 without drawing a line yet.

```
this.createEmptyMovieClip("mcShape", this.getNextHighestDepth());
mcShape.lineStyle(0, 0xFF0000, 100);
mcShape.moveTo(100, 100);
```

Remember, the point to which you are moving is a coordinate within the coordinate space of the `MovieClip` object.

Drawing a Straight Line

The simplest type of drawing in ActionScript is a line. You can create a straight line with the `lineTo()` method. The `lineTo()` method, like the `moveTo()` method, requires that you specify the x and y coordinates to which you want to move the pen. The difference is that unlike `moveTo()`, the `lineTo()` method actually draws a line to that point. The line is always drawn from the current coordinate of the pen. If you have not otherwise moved the pen within a `MovieClip` object, the pen rests at 0,0. Once you have moved the pen using `moveTo()`, `lineTo()`, or the `curveTo()` method (which you'll look at in just a moment), the pen rests at the destination point you specified in the method call. The following example creates a `MovieClip` object, sets the line style, and then draws a line to 100,0:

```
this.createEmptyMovieClip("mcShape", this.getNextHighestDepth());
mcShape.lineStyle(0, 0xFF0000, 100);
mcShape.lineTo(100, 0);
```

Now that you have drawn one line, if you add another `lineTo()` that draws a line to 100,100, the second line will be drawn starting from 100,0—the previous resting place for the pen.

```
mcShape.lineTo(100, 100);
```

Of course, if you don't want to start drawing from 0,0, or if you want to draw a line and then draw another line not immediately adjacent to the first, you can use `lineTo()` in conjunction with `moveTo()`. Here is an example:

```
this.createEmptyMovieClip("mcShape", this.getNextHighestDepth());
mcShape.lineStyle(0, 0xFF0000, 100);
mcShape.moveTo(100, 100);
mcShape.lineTo(150, 100);
mcShape.moveTo(200, 100);
mcShape.lineTo(250, 100);
mcShape.moveTo(125, 200);
mcShape.lineTo(225, 200);
```

Drawing a Curve

Okay. You've mastered drawing straight lines, and you're anxiously awaiting the next exciting drawing method. Your anticipation is not in vain. The next method looks at the `curveTo()` method—it's leaps and bounds more exciting than drawing simple lines. Now you can tell Flash to draw a *curved* line.

In order to draw a curved line, Flash needs several pieces of information—the starting point (which it already knows without your having to tell it), the destination point, and a control point. A control point is a point that is not on the curve. Rather, it is the point at which the tangents to the curve at the starting and ending points of the curve will intersect. Figure 10-1 illustrates this concept.

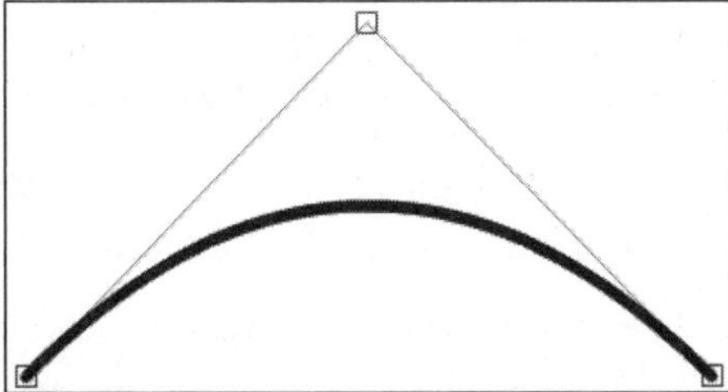

Figure 10-1: A curve and its control point

The `curveTo()` method, therefore, requires four parameters—the x and y coordinates for the control point and the x and y coordinates for the destination point. Here is an example that draws a curve starting at 0,0 to 100,0. The curve has a control point of 50,100.

```
this.createEmptyMovieClip("mcShape", this.getNextHighestDepth());
mcShape.lineStyle(0, 0xFF0000, 100);
mcShape.curveTo(50, 100, 100, 0);
```

Adding a Simple One-Color Fill

When you draw closed shapes, you can have Flash fill the shape with either a solid color or a gradient. The solid color fill is much simpler, so we'll look at that first.

The `beginFill()` and `endFill()` methods should always be used in conjunction with one another. The `beginFill()` method should be called just prior to the `lineTo()` and/or `curveTo()` methods that draw a closed shape. The `endFill()` method should be called just after those methods. The `beginFill()` method requires one parameter — the numeric color value you want to use to fill the shape. The `endFill()` method does not require any parameters. Here is an example that draws a 100 by 100 pixel square with a red outline and a yellow fill.

```
this.createEmptyMovieClip("mcShape", this.getNextHighestDepth());
mcShape.lineStyle(0, 0xFF0000, 100);
mcShape.beginFill(0xFFFF00,100);
mcShape.lineTo(100, 0);
mcShape.lineTo(100, 100);
mcShape.lineTo(0, 100);
mcShape.lineTo(0, 0);
mcShape.endFill();
```

If you call the `beginFill()` method before a sequence of `lineTo()` and/or `curveTo()` methods that do not create a closed shape, Flash will automatically add a line to close the shape if possible. Here is an example:

```
this.createEmptyMovieClip("mcShape", this.getNextHighestDepth());
mcShape.lineStyle(0, 0xFF0000, 100);
mcShape.beginFill(0xFFFF00,100);
mcShape.curveTo(50, 100, 100, 0);
mcShape.endFill();
```

Notice that the code creates only a single curve. However, if you test this code you will discover that Flash automatically adds another line to create a closed shape.

Adding a Simple Gradient Fill

The ActionScript Drawing API also enables you to add gradient fills. The process works the same as with solid fills, but instead of using the `beginFill()` method, you now use the `beginGradientFill()` method. All gradient fills — from simple to complex — require the following information:

- ✦ **Linear or radial:** Should gradient be *linear* (the color changes gradually along a line) or *radial* (the color changes gradually from a central point and moving outward).
- ✦ **Colors:** ActionScript expects you to specify an array of numeric color values. For linear gradients, the colors gradate from left to right. For radial gradients, the colors gradate from the center out.
- ✦ **Alphas:** For each color value you must include an accompanying alpha value. Again, ActionScript expects an array for these values. Each element of the alphas array should correspond to an element of the colors array. The alpha values should be from 0 to 100.
- ✦ **Ratios:** Flash also needs to know what ratios to use for the colors. Where along the spectrum of the gradient should Flash center each color from the colors array? Flash uses values from 0 to 255 to indicate the ratios. A value of 0 means that the corresponding

color's center should be located at the far left (linear) or center (radial) of the gradient. A value of 255 indicates that the corresponding color's center should be located at the far right (linear) or outside (radial) of the gradient.

✦ **Matrix:** The default gradient used by Flash is a 1 pixel by 1 pixel gradient. Obviously that is not going to fill most shapes. Therefore, Flash needs to know how to transform this unit gradient to fill the shape in the way that you want. In order to accomplish this, Flash uses a transformation matrix. This is the part that can be either simple or complex. To begin with you'll look at the simplest matrix type—the box matrix.

The simplest type of gradient fill uses a box matrix. This matrix can be represented in ActionScript using an object with the following properties:

✦ **matrixType:** This property must always have a value of `box`.

✦ **x and y:** These properties tell Flash where to position the gradient relative to the center point of the `MovieClip` object.

✦ **w and h:** These properties tell Flash what width and height to use for the gradient.

✦ **r:** This property tells Flash how to rotate the gradient. The rotation must be specified in radians.

To recap, the `beginGradientFill()` method requires five parameters—a string value of either linear or radial, an array of color values, an array of alphas, an array of ratios, and a matrix object. The matrix object can be of several types. The simplest type is called a box matrix. The box matrix should be represented by an object with the six properties—`matrixType`, `x`, `y`, `w`, `h`, and `r`.

Let's take a look at an example. This example creates a `MovieClip` object into which you can draw a square filled with a gradient fill. The gradient is linear and has three colors—red, light purple, and yellow.

```
var aColors:Array = [0xFF0000, 0xFF00FF, 0xFFFF00];
var aAlphas:Array = [100, 100, 100];
var aRatios:Array = [0, 127.5, 255];
var oMatrix:Object = {matrixType:"box", x: 0, y: 0, w: 100, h: 100,
r:0};
this.createEmptyMovieClip("mcShape", this.getNextHighestDepth());
mcShape.lineStyle(0, 0xFF0000, 100);
mcShape.beginGradientFill("linear", aColors, aAlphas, aRatios,
oMatrix);
mcShape.lineTo(100, 0);
mcShape.lineTo(100, 100);
mcShape.lineTo(0, 100);
mcShape.lineTo(0, 0);
mcShape.endFill();
```

Figure 10-2 shows what this code creates.

Figure 10-2: A linear gradient, unrotated

If you change the value of the `r` property for the matrix object, you can cause the gradient to rotate. A value of `Math.PI/4` is the radian equivalent of 45 degrees. Figure 10-3 illustrates the new fill.

Figure 10-3: The linear gradient, rotated

And if you then change the first parameter of the `beginGradientFill()` method from linear to radial, the result is as shown in Figure 10-4.

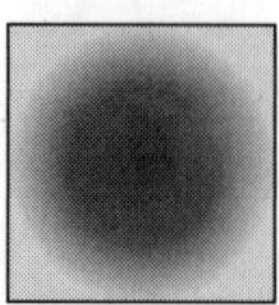

Figure 10-4: A radial gradient

Adding Complex Gradient Fills

We have already alluded to the fact that all gradient fills are added using the `beginGradientFill()` method. The difference between simple gradient fills and complex gradient fills has to do with the type of matrix used. The simple gradient fill uses a box matrix as described in the last section. A complex gradient uses a three by three matrix represented by an object with properties `a`, `b`, `c`, `d`, `e`, `f`, `g`, `h`, and `i`.

It is entirely possible for you to create a matrix object with these properties manually. For example:

```
var oMatrix:Object = {a:1, b:1, c:1, d:1, e:1, f:1, g:1, h:1, i:1};
```

However, working with the matrix in this way requires that you know what each property does. And furthermore, even if you know what each property does, performing transformations on the matrix can be complicated. Instead, you may find it convenient to work with an instance of a custom `DrawingTransformMatrix` class. This custom class includes methods that enable you to perform matrix transformations such as scaling, rotating, and so on.

You can find a copy of the class on the CD-ROM that accompanies this book. Copy `DrawingTransformMatrix.as` from the CD-ROM to a directory in Flash's global classpath.

Once you have copied `DrawingTransformMatrix.as` to your global classpath, you can begin to work with `DrawingTransformMatrix` objects. The first thing you need to do is create a new instance:

```
var dtmMatrix:DrawingTransformMatrix = new DrawingTransformMatrix();
```

This creates a *unit* matrix (a 1 pixel by 1 pixel matrix). Without any transformations, the matrix will not appear to do much, however. So once you have created the matrix you should invoke one or more of the methods to perform translations. Let's look at the methods.

Scale

The `scale()` method is necessary in just about every scenario in which you use a `DrawingTransformMatix` object. Because the default object represents a unit matrix it is necessary to scale it so that it will fill the shape properly. The `scale()` method takes two parameters — the percentage in the x and y directions to which the gradient should be scaled.

Let's take a look at an example that uses a `DrawingTransformMatrix` object to fill a square. In this example you'll use code almost identical to the code used to create a simple gradient. The difference is that instead of using a box matrix, you'll now use a `DrawingTransformMatrix` object.

```
var aColors:Array = [0xFF0000, 0xFF00FF, 0xFFFF00];
var aAlphas:Array = [100, 100, 100];
var aRatios:Array = [0, 127.5, 255];

// Instead of the oMatrix object we used previously, create a new
// DrawingTransformMatrix object.
var dtmMatrix:DrawingTransformMatrix = new DrawingTransformMatrix();

// Scale the matrix so it represents a gradient that is 50 pixels
// by 100 pixels.
dtmMatrix.scale(50, 100);

this.createEmptyMovieClip("mcShape", this.getNextHighestDepth());
mcShape.lineStyle(0, 0xFF0000, 100);

// When calling beginGradientFill(), pass it a reference to the
// DrawingTransformMatrix object.
mcShape.beginGradientFill("radial", aColors, aAlphas, aRatios, dtmMatrix);
mcShape.lineTo(100, 0);
mcShape.lineTo(100, 100);
mcShape.lineTo(0, 100);
mcShape.lineTo(0, 0);
mcShape.endFill();
```

The preceding code results in a gradient like the one in Figure 10-5.

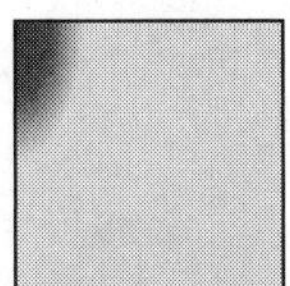

Figure 10-5: A gradient scaled to 100 by 100

As you can see by the figure, the gradient is centered at 0,0 within the `MovieClip` object. In order to move the gradient, you'll need to use another method.

Translate

The translate() method enables you to shift a gradient in the x and y directions. The method takes two parameters—the number of pixels to shift in the x direction and the number of pixels to shift in the y direction. All of the methods of the DrawingTransformMatrix class have a cumulative effect, so you normally use several in conjunction with one another. For example, in almost every scenario you will first scale the object, and then, perhaps, apply other transformations. Here is an example in which you add a translate() method to the code from the previous section.

```
var aColors:Array = [0xFF0000, 0xFF00FF, 0xFFFF00];
var aAlphas:Array = [100, 100, 100];
var aRatios:Array = [0, 127.5, 255];
var dtmMatrix:DrawingTransformMatrix = new DrawingTransformMatrix();
dtmMatrix.scale(50, 100);
dtmMatrix.translate(50, 50);
this.createEmptyMovieClip("mcShape", this.getNextHighestDepth());
mcShape.lineStyle(0, 0xFF0000, 100);
mcShape.beginGradientFill("radial", aColors, aAlphas, aRatios, dtmMatrix);
mcShape.lineTo(100, 0);
mcShape.lineTo(100, 100);
mcShape.lineTo(0, 100);
mcShape.lineTo(0, 0);
mcShape.endFill();
```

The preceding code will result in a gradient, as shown in Figure 10-6. As you can see, the gradient is now centered within the square because the code translated the fill 50 pixels in the x and y directions, placing it at the center of the 100 by 100 square. Note that because all transformations on a DrawingTransformMatrix object are cumulative, if you invoke translate() again, the fill will shift further from the original translation.

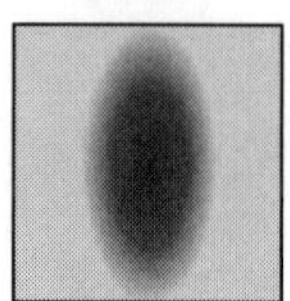

Figure 10-6: A scaled and translated fill

Rotate

The rotate() method allows you to rotate a fill in the clockwise direction. The method expects a value in radian measurements, not degrees.

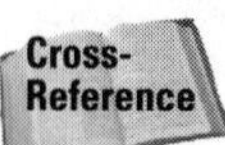

For help converting between degrees and radians, you might find the degToRad() method of the custom MathUtils class helpful. It's discussed in Chapter 13, "The Math Class."

Here's the first example you'll look at that uses rotate(). In this example, you scale, translate, and then rotate the fill 45 degrees (Math.PI/4 is the radians equivalent of 45 degrees).

```
var aColors:Array = [0xFF0000, 0xFF00FF, 0xFFFF00];
var aAlphas:Array = [100, 100, 100];
var aRatios:Array = [0, 127.5, 255];
```

```
var dtmMatrix:DrawingTransformMatrix = new DrawingTransformMatrix();
dtmMatrix.scale(50, 100);
dtmMatrix.translate(50, 50);
dtmMatrix.rotate(Math.PI/4);
this.createEmptyMovieClip("mcShape", this.getNextHighestDepth());
mcShape.lineStyle(0, 0xFF0000, 100);
mcShape.beginGradientFill("radial", aColors, aAlphas, aRatios, dtmMatrix);
mcShape.lineTo(100, 0);
mcShape.lineTo(100, 100);
mcShape.lineTo(0, 100);
mcShape.lineTo(0, 0);
mcShape.endFill();
```

Figure 10-7 shows what the fill created by this code looks like. It may not be exactly as you expected.

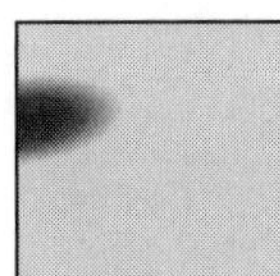

Figure 10-7: A scaled, translated, and rotated fill

The rotation occurs from 0,0 of the `MovieClip`. Therefore, if the fill has already been translated, then when you rotate the fill, it will appear to rotate from the corner of the square in this case. If, instead, you want to rotate from the center of the radial gradient, you should rotate *before* translating. Just change the order in which you call the `translate()` and `rotate()` methods so that you call `rotate()` first. Then the code will generate a fill as shown in Figure 10-8.

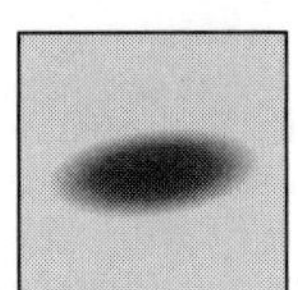

Figure 10-8: A scaled, rotated, and translated fill

Skew

The `skew()` method enables you to cause a gradient to skew—to twist vertically by a specified angle. The angle should be given in radians, as with the `rotate()` method. Also, as with the `rotate()` method, the `skew()` method skews the fill from the 0,0 point of the `MovieClip` object. That means that if you want to skew from the center of the gradient, you should call `skew()` before calling `translate()`. Here is an example that skews a gradient by 45 degrees (again, `Math.PI/4` is the radians equivalent).

```
var aColors:Array = [0xFF0000, 0xFF00FF, 0xFFFF00];
var aAlphas:Array = [100, 100, 100];
var aRatios:Array = [0, 127.5, 255];
var dtmMatrix:DrawingTransformMatrix = new DrawingTransformMatrix();
dtmMatrix.scale(50, 100);
```

```
dtmMatrix.skew(Math.PI/4);
dtmMatrix.translate(50, 50);
this.createEmptyMovieClip("mcShape", this.getNextHighestDepth());
mcShape.lineStyle(0, 0xFF0000, 100);
mcShape.beginGradientFill("radial", aColors, aAlphas, aRatios, dtmMatrix);
mcShape.lineTo(100, 0);
mcShape.lineTo(100, 100);
mcShape.lineTo(0, 100);
mcShape.lineTo(0, 0);
mcShape.endFill();
```

The preceding code creates a fill, as shown in Figure 10-9.

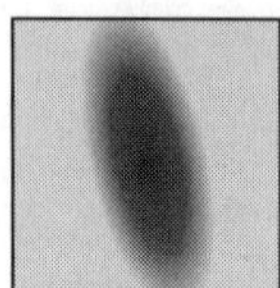

Figure 10-9: A scaled, skewed, and translated fill

Clearing Previously Drawn Graphics

Of course, even the trusty Etch-a-Sketch allows you to clear what you have drawn so that you can draw again. The ActionScript Drawing API, not to be shamed by Etch-a-Sketch, also provides you the means by which you can clear what you have drawn. The `clear()` method removes all lines, curves, and fills that have been drawn within a `MovieClip` object:

```
mcShape.clear();
```

Working with a Drawing Utilities Class

Although the Drawing API is a great foundation, it does not appear particularly robust. For example, it does not provide methods for drawing simple shapes such as rectangles, circles, and assorted, regular polygons (triangles, hexagons, and so on). In order to provide this kind of functionality, you'll need a custom class. On the CD-ROM you will find just such a custom class.

To use the custom class, copy the `DrawingUtils.as` file from the CD-ROM to a directory in your global Flash classpath.

Getting Started with DrawingUtils

The `DrawingUtils` class is a helper class for working with the Drawing API. The class includes all the basic Drawing API functionality (`lineTo()`, `moveTo()`, and so on), but it also includes methods for drawing other kinds of shapes. And, in addition, the class has a default line style so that if you want to use a black hairline as the line style, you don't have to invoke the `lineStyle()` method explicitly.

In order to work with the DrawingUtils class, you must first create an instance. The constructor for DrawingUtils requires that you pass it a reference to the MovieClip into which it should draw. Here is an example in which you create a new MovieClip object and then create a new DrawingUtils object to draw into that MovieClip:

```
this.createEmptyMovieClip("mcShape", this.getNextHighestDepth());
var duDrawer:DrawingUtils = new DrawingUtils(mcShape);
```

Once you've created a new DrawingUtils instance that targets a MovieClip instance, you can invoke all the same Drawing API methods from the DrawingUtils instance. For example:

```
this.createEmptyMovieClip("mcShape", this.getNextHighestDepth());
var duDrawer:DrawingUtils = new DrawingUtils(mcShape);
duDrawer.lineStyle(12, 0xFFFF00, 100);
duDrawer.lineTo(100, 100);
```

Of course, if that was all you intended to do, it would be rather silly to create the DrawingUtils instance in the first place. You might as well invoke the methods directly from the MovieClip instance. The benefits of working with a DrawingUtils object are in being able to work with the built-in methods for creating shapes. Let's take a look at some of those methods now.

Drawing Rectangles

One of the simplest types of shapes is the rectangle. The drawRectangle() method can be invoked from a DrawingUtils object in order to draw a rectangle within the target MovieClip instance. The method requires four parameters — the width and height of the rectangle to be drawn and the x and y coordinates of that rectangle's center within the MovieClip. Here's an example:

```
this.createEmptyMovieClip("mcShape", this.getNextHighestDepth());
var duDrawer:DrawingUtils = new DrawingUtils(mcShape);
duDrawer.drawRectangle(100, 150, 200, 200);
```

The preceding code will draw a rectangle outline as shown in Figure 10-10.

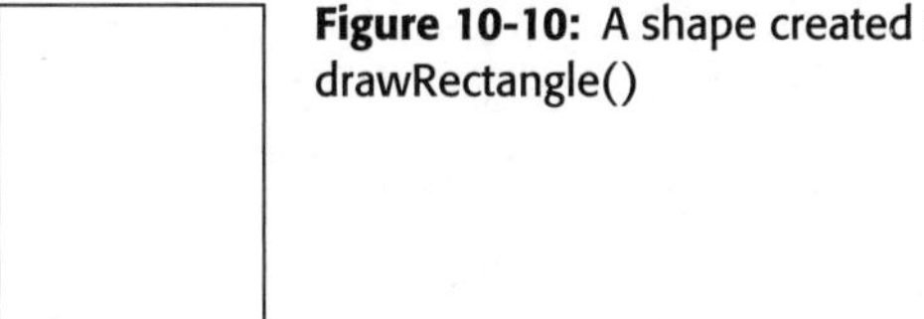

Figure 10-10: A shape created with drawRectangle()

If you want to fill the rectangle, all you need to do is invoke the beginFill() (or beginGradientFill()) method before calling drawRectangle() and invoke the endFill() method after calling drawRectangle():

```
this.createEmptyMovieClip("mcShape", this.getNextHighestDepth());
var duDrawer:DrawingUtils = new DrawingUtils(mcShape);
duDrawer.beginFill(0xFF0000, 100);
duDrawer.drawRectangle(100, 150, 200, 200);
duDrawer.endFill();
```

The preceding code will draw a rectangle, as shown in Figure 10-11.

Figure 10-11: A filled shape drawn with drawRectangle()

Notice that in the preceding code examples, the `lineStyle()` method was not explicitly called. This is because the `DrawingUtils` class uses a default line style. If you want to change the line style you can do so by invoking the `lineStyle()` method from the `DrawingUtils` object with the same parameters as when you invoke the method from a `MovieClip`.

Drawing Circles

Another common shape is the circle. Drawing a good circle on your own with the Drawing API can be a bit of a challenge. But with the `drawCircle()` method of the `DrawingUtils` class it is as simple as a single method call. The method expects three parameters — the radius of the circle and the x and y coordinates of the center of the circle. Here is an example:

```
this.createEmptyMovieClip("mcShape", this.getNextHighestDepth());
var duDrawer:DrawingUtils = new DrawingUtils(mcShape);
duDrawer.beginFill(0xFF0000, 100);
duDrawer.drawCircle(100, 200, 200);
duDrawer.endFill();
```

The preceding code will draw a filled circle with a radius of 100, as illustrated in Figure 10-12.

Figure 10-12: A shape drawn with drawCircle()

Drawing Regular Polygons

Regular polygons are closed shapes in which each of the sides is equal (necessarily, therefore, all the interior angles are equal and all the exterior angles are equal). An equilateral triangle is a three-sided regular polygon, and a square is a four-sided regular polygon. The `drawPolygon()` method allows you to draw a regular polygon with five parameters — the radius from center to vertex, the number of sides, the rotation in radians, and the x and y coordinates of the center of the polygon. Here is an example that draws a triangle rotated by 0 (in other words, not rotated).

```
this.createEmptyMovieClip("mcShape", this.getNextHighestDepth());
var duDrawer:DrawingUtils = new DrawingUtils(mcShape);
duDrawer.drawPolygon(100, 3, 0, 200, 200);
```

Figure 10-13 shows the triangle that the code will draw.

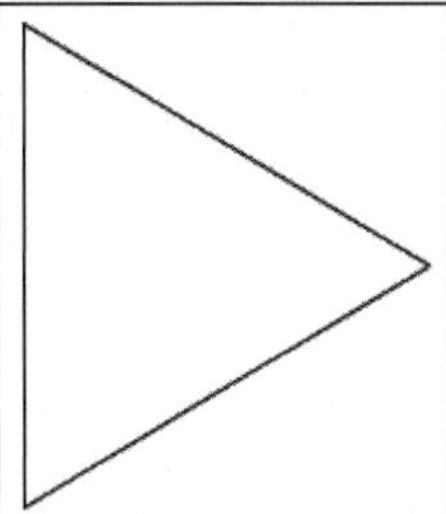

Figure 10-13: A shape drawn with drawPolygon()

Drawing Fills

The `DrawingUtils` class also includes a rather unique method. The `drawPatternFill()` method draws a series of shapes to fill an area. The method takes a single parameters — an object with any of the properties shown in Table 10-1.

Table 10-1: Properties of the drawPatternFill() Parameter Object

Property Name	*Default Value*	*Description*
`width`	`100`	The width in pixels of the fill area.
`height`	`100`	The height of the fill area in pixels.
`cols`	`10`	The number of columns within the fill area.
`x`	`0`	The starting x coordinate of the fill area relative to the `MovieClip` object's coordinate space.
`y`	`0`	The starting y coordinate of the fill area relative to the `MovieClip` object's coordinate space.
`rotation`	`0`	The amount of rotation for the shapes in radians.
`offset`	`1`	A number indicating how much each row should be offset from the adjacent rows. A value of 0 lines up all the columns.
`shape`	`{shape:"circle"}`	An object with a shape property. The shape property can have a value of `circle`, `square`, or `polygon`. If the value is `polygon`, you should also include a `sides` property with a numeric value of 3 or more.
`fill`	`Undefined`	If defined, this numeric value is used as the color to fill the shapes.
`randomizeColor`	`False`	A Boolean value indicating whether to randomize the colors of each of the shapes in the fill.

If you don't pass any parameter to the drawPatternFill() method then it uses all defaults. Otherwise, if you pass it an object it still uses the defaults for any properties you don't define. Here's an example that uses the default values:

```
this.createEmptyMovieClip("mcFill", this.getNextHighestDepth());
var duDrawer:DrawingUtils = new DrawingUtils(mcFill);
duDrawer.drawPatternFill();
```

The preceding code uses all the default values. The fill that it generates looks like what you see in Figure 10-14.

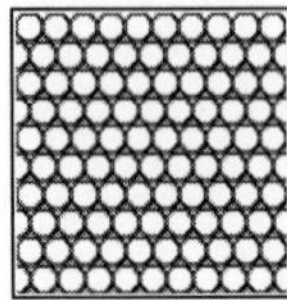

Figure 10-14: The default pattern fill

Notice that the MovieClip is automatically masked. This is a feature built into drawPatternFill(). This feature works as long as you have used getNextHighestDepth() to generate all the depths for programmatically created MovieClip, Button, and TextField objects within the same parent object as the fill MovieClip.

Here's another example that draws a pattern fill with some parameters other than the defaults:

```
this.createEmptyMovieClip("mcFill", this.getNextHighestDepth());
var duDrawer:DrawingUtils = new DrawingUtils(mcFill);
var oParams:Object = new Object();
oParams.shape = {name: "polygon", sides:"6"};
oParams.cols = 6;
oParams.rotation = Math.PI/4;
oParams.width = 300;
oParams.height = 300;
oParams.space = 1;
duDrawer.drawPatternFill(oParams);
```

Figure 10-15 shows what the preceding code creates.

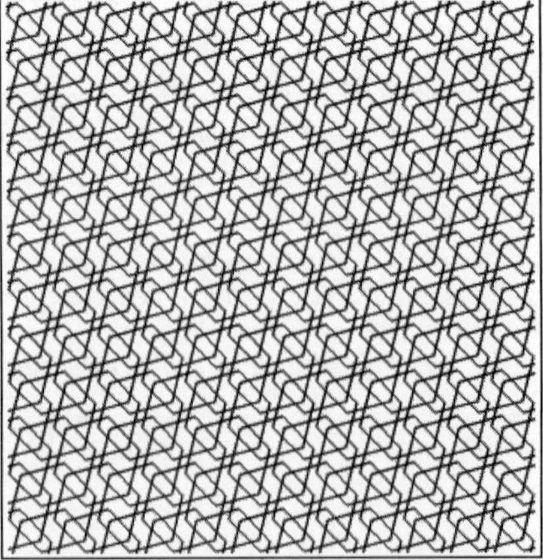

Figure 10-15: A nondefault pattern fill

Here's yet another example that shows how you can use the `fill` parameter to fill each of the shapes in the fill. Also, this example sets the `lineStyle()` for the `DrawingUtils` object in order to specify the color of the lines.

```
this.createEmptyMovieClip("mcFill", this.getNextHighestDepth());
var duDrawer:DrawingUtils = new DrawingUtils(mcFill);
var oParams:Object = new Object();
oParams.shape = {name: "polygon", sides:"3"};
oParams.rotation = Math.PI/4;
oParams.width = 200;
oParams.height = 200;
oParams.fill = 0xFF0000;
duDrawer.lineStyle(2, 0xFF00FF, 100);
duDrawer.drawPatternFill(oParams);
```

The preceding code creates a fill, as shown in Figure 10-16.

Figure 10-16: A filled pattern

Practicing Dynamic Masking

In Chapter 9 you had the opportunity to read about scriptable masking. But scriptable masking is only minimally useful and only if you cannot dynamically create the mask itself. The Drawing API enables you to do just that. In this example, you'll place two `MovieClip` objects containing images on the stage. The objects will be placed such that they overlap and only the topmost image can be seen. Then, you'll use the Drawing API to draw a mask to the dimensions of the top `MovieClip` object, and you'll tell Flash to animate the mask when the stage is clicked. This creates a simple wipe transition effect between the two images. Complete the following steps:

1. Open `dynamicMask_starter.fla` from the CD-ROM and save it to your local disk as `dynamicMask001.fla`.

2. Open the library and view the linkage settings for the two Movie Clip symbols. Notice that each of them has already been set to export and has been assigned a linkage identifier.

3. Add the following code to the first frame of the default layer of the main timeline:

```
this.attachMovie("ImageOneSymbol", "mcOne",
this.getNextHighestDepth());
this.attachMovie("ImageTwoSymbol", "mcTwo",
this.getNextHighestDepth());
```

```
this.createEmptyMovieClip("mcMask", this.getNextHighestDepth());
var duMaskDrawer:DrawingUtils = new DrawingUtils(mcMask);
duMaskDrawer.beginFill(0, 0);
duMaskDrawer.drawRectangle(mcTwo._width, mcTwo._height, ⮐
mcTwo._width/2, mcTwo._height/2);
mcTwo.setMask(mcMask);
mcMask.direction = "off";
mcMask.interval = null;
mcMask.slide = function():Void {
  this._x -= 10;
  if(this.direction == "on") {
    if(this._x <= 0) {
      clearInterval(this.interval);
      this.interval = null;
      this._x = 0;
      this.direction = "off";
    }
  }
  else {
    if(this._x < -this._width) {
      clearInterval(this.interval);
      this.interval = null;
      this._x = this._width;
      this.direction = "on";
    }
  }
  updateAfterEvent();
};
this.createEmptyMovieClip("mcClickNext", this.getNextHighestDepth());
var duClickDrawer:DrawingUtils = new DrawingUtils(mcClickNext);
duClickDrawer.lineStyle(0, 0, 0);
duClickDrawer.beginFill(0, 0);
duClickDrawer.drawRectangle(mcTwo._width, mcTwo._height, ⮐
mcTwo._width/2, mcTwo._height/2);
mcClickNext.mask = mcMask;
mcClickNext.onRelease = function():Void {
  if(this.mask.interval == null) {
    this.mask.interval = setInterval(this.mask, "slide", 10);
  }
};
```

4. Save the document and test the movie.

When you test the movie, you should be able to click the stage and see a simple wipe occur between the two images. Click again and the application will wipe between the images again.

Now that you've had a chance to see the application work, take a closer look at the code.

First, of course, you use the `attachMovie()` method to add the two instances to the stage. You name them `mcOne` and `mcTwo`, where `mcTwo` has the higher depth of the two and thus appears above `mcOne`.

```
this.attachMovie("ImageOneSymbol", "mcOne",
this.getNextHighestDepth());
this.attachMovie("ImageTwoSymbol", "mcTwo",
this.getNextHighestDepth());
```

Next you create an empty `MovieClip` named `mcMask`. This is the object into which you'll draw the mask using a `DrawingUtils` object. Notice that the mask is a filled rectangle with the same dimensions as `mcTwo`.

```
this.createEmptyMovieClip("mcMask", this.getNextHighestDepth());
var duMaskDrawer:DrawingUtils = new DrawingUtils(mcMask);
duMaskDrawer.beginFill(0, 0);
duMaskDrawer.drawRectangle(mcTwo._width, mcTwo._height, ⮐
mcTwo._width/2, mcTwo._height/2);
```

You use the `setMask()` method to assign `mcMask` as the mask for `mcTwo`.

```
mcTwo.setMask(mcMask);
```

The `direction` and `interval` properties are two custom properties you assign to `mcMask`. The `direction` property can have a value of either `off` or `on`. This value determines whether the mask is sliding off or on `mcTwo`. The `interval` property is what you'll use to store the ID for the interval when you set the interval method.

```
mcMask.direction = "off";
mcMask.interval = null;
```

The `slide()` method is a custom method that animates the mask so that it slides on or off of `mcTwo`. First, it moves the mask by 10 pixels to the left. Then it checks to determine the direction in which the mask is moving relative to `mcMask`. Based on the direction, it checks to see if the mask has completed its slide. If so, it moves it to the correct resting location, clears the interval, and sets the direction to the opposite:

```
mcMask.slide = function():Void {
  this._x -= 10;
  if(this.direction == "on") {
    if(this._x <= 0) {
      clearInterval(this.interval);
      this.interval = null;
      this._x = 0;
      this.direction = "off";
    }
  }
  else {
    if(this._x < -this._width) {
      clearInterval(this.interval);
      this.interval = null;
      this._x = this._width;
      this.direction = "on";
    }
  }
  updateAfterEvent();
};
```

In addition to creating the mask and the image MovieClip objects, you want to create another MovieClip object. This object, mcClickNext, serves as a button. You use a DrawingUtils object to draw a rectangle with the same dimensions as mcTwo. The rectangle has an alpha level of 0 so that it appears transparent. You don't want the user to see this object. Instead, it should simply enable the user to click anywhere on the stage.

```
this.createEmptyMovieClip("mcClickNext", this.getNextHighestDepth());
var duClickDrawer:DrawingUtils = new DrawingUtils(mcClickNext);
duClickDrawer.lineStyle(0, 0, 0);
duClickDrawer.beginFill(0, 0);
duClickDrawer.drawRectangle(mcTwo._width, mcTwo._height,
mcTwo._width/2, mcTwo._height/2);
```

The mask property is a custom property to which you assign a reference to mcMask. Then, within the onRelease() method you set an interval at which the slide() method of the mask is called. You make that part conditional because you want the user to be able to set a new interval only if the previous one has completed. Otherwise, each time the user clicked, if the previous interval hadn't completed, the mask would begin to move twice as fast, and if the user clicks enough times successively, it could take its toll on the processor.

```
mcClickNext.mask = mcMask;
mcClickNext.onRelease = function():Void {
  if(this.mask.interval == null) {
    this.mask.interval = setInterval(this.mask, "slide", 10);
  }
};
```

Practicing Responsive Objects

In this exercise, you'll use the Drawing API to create a square that responds to the mouse. When the user moves the mouse near a side of the square, that side will appear to be pressed in, following the movement of the mouse. Complete the following steps:

1. Open a new Flash document.
2. On the first frame of the first layer, add the following code:

```
var aColors:Array = [0xFEEFD6, 0xEDFED6, 0xDED7FD, 0xFED6ED,
0xFFD5D5];
makeColorOptions(aColors);
var nSelectedColor:Number = aColors[0];
var aSides:Array = new Array();
aSides.push({name:"mcRight", y:0, x:110, rotation:90});
aSides.push({name:"mcBottom", y:100, x:0, rotation:0});
aSides.push({name:"mcLeft", y:0, x:0, rotation:90});
aSides.push({name:"mcTop", y:-10, x:0, rotation:0});
makeBoxAndSides(aSides);
addBoxMethod();
mcShape.mcBox.drawSquare();
mcShape._x = Stage.width/2 - mcShape._width/2;
mcShape._y = Stage.height/2 - mcShape._height/2;
```

```
function makeBoxAndSides(aSides:Array) {
  this.createEmptyMovieClip("mcShape", this.getNextHighestDepth());
  mcShape.createEmptyMovieClip("mcBox",
mcShape.getNextHighestDepth());
  var mcSide:MovieClip = null;
  var duDrawer:DrawingUtils = null;
  for(var i:Number = 0; i < aSides.length; i++) {
    mcShape.createEmptyMovieClip(aSides[i].name, ⮐
mcShape.getNextHighestDepth());
    mcSide = mcShape[aSides[i].name];
    duDrawer = new DrawingUtils(mcSide);
    duDrawer.lineStyle(0, 0, 0);
    duDrawer.beginFill(0, 30);
    duDrawer.drawRectangle(100, 10, 50, 5);
    mcSide.useHandCursor = false;
    mcSide.x = aSides[i].x;
    mcSide.y = aSides[i].y;
    mcSide.rotation = aSides[i].rotation;
    mcSide.onRollOver = function():Void {
      if(this._parent.current == this) {
        return;
      }
      this._parent.current.reset();
      this._parent.current = this;
      this.startDrag(true);
      this.interval = setInterval(this._parent.mcBox, "drawSquare",
10);
    };
    mcSide.reset = function():Void {
      this._y = this.y;
      this._x = this.x;
      this._rotation = this.rotation;
      this.stopDrag();
      clearInterval(this.interval);
    };
    mcSide.reset();
  }
  addBoxMethod();
  mcShape.mcBox.drawSquare();
  mcShape._x = Stage.width/2 - mcShape._width/2;
  mcShape._y = Stage.height/2 - mcShape._height/2;
}

function makeColorOptions(aColors:Array):Void {
  for(var i:Number = 0; i < aColors.length; i++) {
    this.createEmptyMovieClip("mcColorSwatch" + i, ⮐
this.getNextHighestDepth());
    mcSwatch = this["mcColorSwatch" + i];
    mcSwatch.colorVal = aColors[i];
    duDrawer = new DrawingUtils(mcSwatch);
    duDrawer.beginFill(aColors[i], 100);
```

```
      duDrawer.drawRectangle(15, 15, 7.5, 7.5);
      duDrawer.endFill();
      mcSwatch._x = 30;
      mcSwatch._y = 20 * i + 30;
      mcSwatch.onRelease = function():Void {
        this._parent.nSelectedColor = this.colorVal;
        this._parent.mcShape.mcBox.drawSquare();
      };
    }
  }

  function addBoxMethod():Void {
    mcShape.mcBox.drawSquare = function():Void {
      var oRight:Object = {x:this._parent.mcRight._x - 10, ⮐
  y:this._parent.mcRight._y};
      var oBottom:Object = {x:this._parent.mcBottom._x, ⮐
  y:this._parent.mcBottom._y};
      var oLeft:Object = {x:this._parent.mcLeft._x, ⮐
  y:this._parent.mcLeft._y};
      var oTop:Object = {x:this._parent.mcTop._x, ⮐
  y:this._parent.mcTop._y + 10};
      var nMx:Number = this._xmouse;
      var nMy:Number = this._ymouse;
      switch (this._parent.current._name) {
        case "mcRight":
          if(nMx > 110) {
            this._parent.current.reset();
            this._parent.current = null;
          }
          if(nMx < 25) {
            nMx = 25;
          }
          else if(nMx > 100) {
            nMx = 100;
          }
          if(nMy < 25) {
            nMy = 25;
          }
          else if(nMy > 75) {
            nMy = 75;
          }
          oRight.x = 2*nMx - 100;
          oRight.y = 2*nMy - 50;
          break;
        case "mcBottom":
          if(nMy > 110) {
            this._parent.current.reset();
            this._parent.current = null;
          }
          if(nMx < 25) {
            nMx = 25;
```

```
    }
    else if(nMx > 75) {
      nMx = 75;
    }
    if(nMy < 25) {
      nMy = 25;
    }
    else if(nMy > 100) {
      nMy = 100;
    }
    oBottom.x = 2*nMx - 50;
    oBottom.y = 2*nMy - 100;
    break;
  case "mcLeft":
    if(this._parent._xmouse < -10) {
      this._parent.current.reset();
      this._parent.current = null;
    }
    if(nMx < 0) {
      nMx = 0;
    }
    else if(nMx > 75) {
      nMx = 75;
    }
    if(nMy < 25) {
      nMy = 25;
    }
    else if(nMy > 75) {
      nMy = 75;
    }
    oLeft.x = 2*nMx;
    oLeft.y = 2*nMy - (.5 * 100);
    break;
  case "mcTop":
    if(this._parent._ymouse < -10) {
      this._parent.current.reset();
      this._parent.current = null;
    }
    if(nMx < 25) {
      nMx = 25;
    }
    else if(nMx > 75) {
      nMx = 75;
    }
    if(nMy < 0) {
      nMy = 0;
    }
    else if(nMy > 75) {
      nMy = 75;
    }
    oTop.x = 2*nMx - (.5 * 100);
```

```
            oTop.y = 2*nMy;
            break;
        }
        this.clear();
        this.lineStyle(0, 0, 100);
        this.beginFill(nSelectedColor, 100);
        this.curveTo(oTop.x, oTop.y, 100, 0);
        this.curveTo(oRight.x, oRight.y, 100, 100);
        this.curveTo(oBottom.x, oBottom.y, 0, 100);
        this.curveTo(oLeft.x, oLeft.y, 0, 0);
        this.endFill();
        updateAfterEvent();
    };
}
```

3. Save the document as `responsiveBox001.fla` and test the movie.

When you test the movie you should initially see a large square in the center, and five smaller squares on the left side, as shown in Figure 10-17. The large square is the responsive object that will reshape according to the mouse movement. The five smaller squares allow you to select a new color for the responsive square.

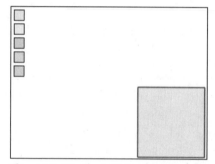

Figure 10-17: The initial appearance of responsiveBox.swf

When you move the mouse so that it touches one of the sides of the square, you'll see that it pushes the side inward as shown in Figure 10-18.

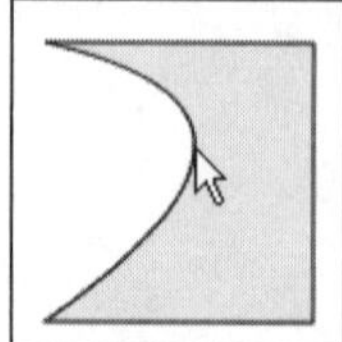

Figure 10-18: The square responds to mouse movement.

So now that you've seen it working, the question is *how* does it work? If you make a temporary change to a single line of code, you'll be able to see the process a little better. On or around approximately line 26 is the following line:

```
duDrawer.beginFill(0, 0);
```

Change that line of code to:

```
duDrawer.beginFill(0, 30);
```

This changes the transparency of the four previously invisible rectangles that border the sides of the box. If you test the movie now, you can see these rectangles move with the mouse when you roll over them (as shown in Figure 10-19).

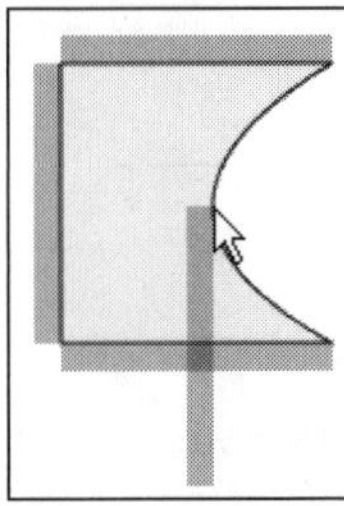

Figure 10-19: Setting the alpha value to 30 displays the four rectangles on the sides.

The four rectangles enable Flash to know when the mouse has moved near one of the sides . . . and it allows Flash to know *which* side. Once the rectangle has been rolled over, it is set as draggable, and the corresponding side of the square is redrawn to match the current mouse location.

You can set the alpha value back to 0. Now let's take a look at the code that makes this all work.

The first thing you want to do is define an array of color values. You pass this array of colors to the makeColorOptions() function — a function you'll examine in just a moment.

```
var aColors:Array = [0xFEEFD6, 0xEDFED6, 0xDED7FD, 0xFED6ED, 0xFFD5D5];
makeColorOptions(aColors);
```

You then assign the first color value to a variable, nSelectedColor. This variable is used throughout to determine which color to assign to the box.

```
var nSelectedColor:Number = aColors[0];
```

Next, you define an array of values for drawing the four rectangles adjacent to the sides of the square. Each element of the array is an associative array with four keys — the name of the rectangle, the MovieClip to create, and the default x and y coordinates and rotation for the rectangle. Once you've populated the array, you call the makeBoxAndSides() function to actually create the objects:

```
var aSides:Array = new Array();
aSides.push({name:"mcRight", y:0, x:110, rotation:90});
aSides.push({name:"mcBottom", y:100, x:0, rotation:0});
aSides.push({name:"mcLeft", y:0, x:0, rotation:90});
aSides.push({name:"mcTop", y:-10, x:0, rotation:0});
makeBoxAndSides(aSides);
```

The makeBoxAndSides() function does several things. First, it generates a parent MovieClip that will contain the square and the side rectangles:

```
this.createEmptyMovieClip("mcShape", this.getNextHighestDepth());
```

Next, the function creates a MovieClip object into which you'll draw the responsive box:

```
mcShape.createEmptyMovieClip("mcBox", mcShape.getNextHighestDepth());
```

Then, it loops through all the elements of the array parameter, and it creates the rectangles defined by each element of the array. The name of each rectangle MovieClip object is defined by the name property of the array element. Then, using a DrawingUtils object, Flash draws a 100 × 10 rectangle:

```
    mcShape.createEmptyMovieClip(aSides[i].name, ⮐
mcShape.getNextHighestDepth());
    mcSide = mcShape[aSides[i].name];
    duDrawer = new DrawingUtils(mcSide);
    duDrawer.lineStyle(0, 0, 0);
    duDrawer.beginFill(0, 30);
    duDrawer.drawRectangle(100, 10, 50, 5);
```

By setting useHandCursor to false, you tell Flash not to change the cursor when the user moves the mouse over the rectangles:

```
mcSide.useHandCursor = false;
```

You then set the custom x, y, and rotation properties of the rectangle MovieClips. These values are determined by the corresponding properties of each element of the array parameter. You'll use these values to reset each rectangle to its default placement adjacent to the sides of the square.

```
mcSide.x = aSides[i].x;
mcSide.y = aSides[i].y;
mcSide.rotation = aSides[i].rotation;
```

The onRollOver() event handler method for each rectangle tells Flash to make the rectangle draggable. In order to ensure that each rectangle snaps back to its original placement, you assign the current rectangle to a custom property named current. When a rectangle is rolled over, the current property holds a reference to the previously current rectangle. Therefore, you first want to call that object's reset() method. Then you assign the current rectangle to the current property. The interval tells Flash to continually call the drawSquare() method of the mcBox object as long as the current MovieClip is being dragged.

```
    mcSide.onRollOver = function():Void {
      if(this._parent.current == this) {
        return;
      }
      this._parent.current.reset();
      this._parent.current = this;
      this.startDrag(true);
      this.interval = setInterval(this._parent.mcBox, "drawSquare",
10);
    };
```

The reset() method resets the placement of the rectangle to its original, default placement alongside the square. Then you also want to make sure the object is no longer being dragged. And you clear the interval so that you don't call the drawSquare() method of mcBox needlessly:

```
      mcSide.reset = function():Void {
        this._y = this.y;
        this._x = this.x;
        this._rotation = this.rotation;
        this.stopDrag();
        clearInterval(this.interval);
      };
      mcSide.reset();
    }
```

You also add a drawSquare() method to the mcBox object by calling the custom function addBoxMethod(). Then you call drawSquare() to draw the initial square and set the entire mcShape object to the center of the stage:

```
    addBoxMethod();
    mcShape.mcBox.drawSquare();
    mcShape._x = Stage.width/2 - mcShape._width/2;
    mcShape._y = Stage.height/2 - mcShape._height/2;
```

The makeColorOptions() function creates each of the color swatch MovieClip objects on the left side. It does this by looping through each of the elements of the array parameter, creating a MovieClip object, and drawing a colored square in that object with a DrawingUtils object. The onRelease() method is assigned to each swatch so that when it is clicked the nSelectedColor variable is assigned the new color value.

```
    for(var i:Number = 0; i < aColors.length; i++) {
      this.createEmptyMovieClip("mcColorSwatch" + i, ⮐
  this.getNextHighestDepth());
      mcSwatch = this["mcColorSwatch" + i];
      mcSwatch.colorVal = aColors[i];
      duDrawer = new DrawingUtils(mcSwatch);
      duDrawer.beginFill(aColors[i], 100);
      duDrawer.drawRectangle(15, 15, 7.5, 7.5);
      duDrawer.endFill();
      mcSwatch._x = 30;
      mcSwatch._y = 20 * i + 30;
      mcSwatch.onRelease = function():Void {
        this._parent.nSelectedColor = this.colorVal;
        this._parent.mcShape.mcBox.drawSquare();
      };
    }
```

The addBoxMethod() function adds the drawSquare() method to mcBox. This method lets Flash knows how to draw the responsive box. First, you set four objects—to correspond to each side of the square. Each one of these objects has x and y properties, the values of which determine the control point for a curve that will form a straight line. These are the default settings that create a square:

```
      var oRight:Object = {x:this._parent.mcRight._x - 10, ⮐
  y:this._parent.mcRight._y};
      var oBottom:Object = {x:this._parent.mcBottom._x, ⮐
  y:this._parent.mcBottom._y};
      var oLeft:Object = {x:this._parent.mcLeft._x, ⮐
```

```
y:this._parent.mcLeft._y};
    var oTop:Object = {x:this._parent.mcTop._x, ⮐
y:this._parent.mcTop._y + 10};
```

Then you want to get the current x and y coordinates of the mouse. You'll use these values to help determine the control point for one of the curved sides if necessary:

```
    var nMx:Number = this._xmouse;
    var nMy:Number = this._ymouse;
```

You want to calculate a new control point if the mouse position will cause one of the sides to be curved. Which side should be curved is determined by the currently selected side rectangle. You use a `switch` statement to figure out which side is being affected (if any).

```
    switch (this._parent.current._name) {
```

If the right side is being affected then you first want to see if the user has moved the mouse off to the right—away from the square. If that is the case, you'll want to reset the `mcRight` rectangle:

```
        if(nMx > 110) {
          this._parent.current.reset();
          this._parent.current = null;
        }
```

Then you want to set some boundaries within which the side can be pushed. If the mouse has moved beyond those boundaries, you want to set some default values:

```
        if(nMx < 25) {
          nMx = 25;
        }
        else if(nMx > 100) {
          nMx = 100;
        }
        if(nMy < 25) {
          nMy = 25;
        }
        else if(nMy > 75) {
          nMy = 75;
        }
```

This next calculation enables you to determine the control point for the curve that corresponds to the mouse location. This uses a standard Bezier formula to determine the x and y coordinates of the control point.

```
        oRight.x = 2*nMx - 100;
        oRight.y = 2*nMy - 50;
```

Each of the other cases is similar but corresponds to a different side of the square.

Then, once all the points have been calculated, you use the Drawing API methods to draw a filled shape determined by four curves. If the mouse has not affected any points, these curves will appear as straight lines.

```
this.clear();
this.lineStyle(0, 0, 100);
this.beginFill(nSelectedColor, 100);
this.curveTo(oTop.x, oTop.y, 100, 0);
this.curveTo(oRight.x, oRight.y, 100, 100);
this.curveTo(oBottom.x, oBottom.y, 0, 100);
this.curveTo(oLeft.x, oLeft.y, 0, 0);
this.endFill();
updateAfterEvent();
```

Practicing Drawing

In this exercise you'll create an application that allows the user to draw using either a line tool or a pencil tool. Follow along with these steps:

1. Open `drawingApp_starter.fla` from the CD-ROM and save it to your local disk as `drawingApp001.fla`.

2. Notice that on the stage there are already three `MovieClip` instances. These objects are named `mcLine`, `mcPencil`, and `mcClear`. These are the buttons that the user can choose in order to use the line tool or pencil tool or to clear the canvas in order to start again.

3. On the first frame of the default layer of the main timeline, add the following code:

```
var sSelectedTool:String = null;
mcPencil.onPress = function():Void {
  this._parent.sSelectedTool = "pencil";
};
mcLine.onPress = function():Void {
  this._parent.sSelectedTool = "line";
};
this.createEmptyMovieClip("mcCanvas", this.getNextHighestDepth());
mcCanvas.onMouseDown = function():Void {
  if(this._parent.mcLine.hitTest(this._parent._xmouse, ⮐
this._parent._ymouse, false) || ⮐
this._parent.mcPencil.hitTest(this._parent._xmouse,
this._parent._ymouse, false) || ⮐
this._parent.mcClear.hitTest(this._parent._xmouse, ⮐
this._parent._ymouse, false)) {
    return;
  }
  this.pressed = true;
  this.selectedTool = this._parent.sSelectedTool;
  var nDepth:Number = this.getNextHighestDepth();
  this.createEmptyMovieClip("mcHolder" + nDepth, nDepth);
  this.mcHolder = this["mcHolder" + nDepth];
  this.mcHolder.startX = this.mcHolder._xmouse;
  this.mcHolder.startY = this.mcHolder._ymouse;
  this.mcHolder.lineStyle(0, 0, 100);
```

```
    this.mcHolder.moveTo(this.mcHolder._xmouse, this.mcHolder._ymouse);
    this.mcHolder.drawLine = function(nColor:Number):Void {
      this.clear();
      this.lineStyle(0, nColor, 100);
      this.moveTo(this.startX, this.startY);
      this.lineTo(this._xmouse, this._ymouse);
      updateAfterEvent();
    };
    this.mcHolder.drawPencil = function():Void {
      this.lineTo(this._xmouse, this._ymouse);
      updateAfterEvent();
    };
    if(this.selectedTool == "line") {
      this.interval = setInterval(this.mcHolder, "drawLine", 10,
  0xFF0000);
    }
    else {
      this.mcHolder.onMouseMove = function():Void {
        this.drawPencil();
      };
    }
  };
  mcCanvas.onMouseUp = function():Void {
    if(!this.pressed) {
      return;
    }
    this.pressed = false;
    if(this.selectedTool == "line") {
      clearInterval(this.interval);
      this.mcHolder.drawLine(0);
    }
    else {
      delete this.mcHolder.onMouseMove;
    }
  };
  mcCanvas.clear = function():Void {
    for(var mcElement in this) {
      if(this[mcElement] instanceof MovieClip) {
        this[mcElement].removeMovieClip();
      }
    }
  };
  mcClear.onRelease = function():Void {
    this._parent.mcCanvas.clear();
  };
```

4. Save the document and test the movie.

When you test the movie you should be able to select either the line tool or pencil tool and draw on the stage (see Figure 10-20). When you want to start over, you can click the clear button to clear the canvas.

Figure 10-20: Drawing in a Flash application

Now take a look at the code that makes this work.

First you declare a variable named `sSelectedTool`. The value of this variable determines whether to draw using the pencil or line tool. Within the `onPress()` event handler methods for `mcPencil` and `mcLine`, you assign the appropriate value to `sSelectedTool`.

```
var sSelectedTool:String = null;
mcPencil.onPress = function():Void {
  this._parent.sSelectedTool = "pencil";
};
mcLine.onPress = function():Void {
  this._parent.sSelectedTool = "line";
};
```

Next you create `mcCanvas`, a `MovieClip` that will hold all the drawings.

```
this.createEmptyMovieClip("mcCanvas", this.getNextHighestDepth());
```

When the user clicks the mouse you want to tell Flash to draw using the selected tool. First, however, you want to make sure that the mouse isn't over the `mcLine`, `mcPencil`, or `mcClear` buttons. You use a `hitTest()` method to check for each of these conditions. If any of them are true, you use a `return` statement so that Flash doesn't run any of the remaining code in the method.

```
if (this._parent.mcLine.hitTest(this._parent._xmouse, ⮐
this._parent._ymouse, false) || ⮐
this._parent.mcPencil.hitTest(this._parent._xmouse, ⮐
this._parent._ymouse, false) || ⮐
this._parent.mcClear.hitTest(this._parent._xmouse, ⮐
this._parent._ymouse, false)) {
   return;
}
```

Otherwise, you want to create a new nested MovieClip object into which to draw the line or pencil movement. This means that each time the user clicks the mouse over the canvas, a new nested MovieClip is created. Each line, for example, is therefore drawn into its own object. To make it simple to access the MovieClip object, you assign a reference to this.mcHolder:

```
this.createEmptyMovieClip("mcHolder" + nDepth, nDepth);
this.mcHolder = this["mcHolder" + nDepth];
```

You want the holder object to know where to begin drawing, and so you let it know the current x and y coordinates of the mouse and move the pen to that starting point:

```
this.mcHolder.startX = this.mcHolder._xmouse;
this.mcHolder.startY = this.mcHolder._ymouse;
this.mcHolder.lineStyle(0, 0, 100);
this.mcHolder.moveTo(this.mcHolder._xmouse, this.mcHolder._ymouse);
```

Next you create the methods for the holder object that enable it to draw using a line tool or pencil tool. First, take a look at the drawLine() method. This method draws a line from the starting x and y coordinates to the current x and y coordinates of the mouse:

```
this.mcHolder.drawLine = function(nColor:Number):Void {
  this.clear();
  this.lineStyle(0, nColor, 100);
  this.moveTo(this.startX, this.startY);
  this.lineTo(this._xmouse, this._ymouse);
  updateAfterEvent();
};
```

The drawPencil() method draws a new line to the x and y coordinates of the mouse. Notice that the drawLine() method always draws a line from the starting x and y coordinates, clearing any previous lines first. The drawPencil() method is cumulative in its effect. It just keeps drawing new (short) lines from the previous mouse location to the new mouse location:

```
this.mcHolder.drawPencil = function():Void {
  this.lineTo(this._xmouse, this._ymouse);
  updateAfterEvent();
};
```

Then, you check for the selected tool. If it is the line tool, you set an interval on which drawLine() is called. Otherwise, you want to tell Flash to call the drawPencil() method every time the mouse is moved.

```
if(this.selectedTool == "line") {
  this.interval = setInterval(this.mcHolder, "drawLine", 10,
0xFF0000);
}
else {
  this.mcHolder.onMouseMove = function():Void {
    this.drawPencil();
  };
}
```

When the user releases the mouse, you want to clear the interval or delete the onMouseMove() method:

```
mcCanvas.onMouseUp = function():Void {
  if(!this.pressed) {
    return;
  }
  this.pressed = false;
  if(this.selectedTool == "line") {
    clearInterval(this.interval);
    this.mcHolder.drawLine(0);
  }
  else {
    delete this.mcHolder.onMouseMove;
  }
};
```

The clear() method of mcCanvas is a custom method. In this method, you loop through all the nested MovieClip objects and delete them:

```
mcCanvas.clear = function():Void {
  for(var mcElement in this) {
    if(this[mcElement] instanceof MovieClip) {
      this[mcElement].removeMovieClip();
    }
  }
};
```

When the user clicks mcClear, you tell Flash to call the clear() method of mcCanvas:

```
mcClear.onRelease = function():Void {
  this._parent.mcCanvas.clear();
};
```

We'd like to know what you thought about this chapter. Visit www.flashsupport.com/feedback to fill out an online form with your comments.

Summary

- The Drawing API is a set of MovieClip class methods that enable you to draw lines, curves, fills, and shapes with ActionScript.
- Scripted drawing enables you to create highly dynamic content.
- By creating and working with a custom DrawingUtils class, you can simplify drawing shapes such as circles, rectangles, and regular polygons.
- You can work with the Drawing API to create fully scripted masks.

✦ ✦ ✦

PART

IV

The Core Classes

✦ ✦ ✦ ✦

In This Part

✦ ✦ ✦ ✦

Using the Array Class

✦ ✦ ✦ ✦

In This Chapter

Using arrays to give structure and order to your data

Creating arrays using several techniques

Adding elements to arrays

Removing elements from arrays

Reading from arrays

Learning different ways to use arrays to best suit your program's needs

Sorting arrays

✦ ✦ ✦ ✦

Arrays (ordered data structures) are among the simplest yet most useful objects in ActionScript. Your programs will benefit many times over from the proper use of arrays. Many tasks that you might try to do using multiple variables, `String` object methods, and `for` and `while` loops can be handled much more efficiently with an array. For example, an array can be much more efficient than storing related values in separate variables with incremental names (for example, `sVar0`, `sVar1`, `sVar2`, and so on) or than storing the values in a list (for example, `"val1, val2, val3, val4"`). By the time you have finished this chapter, you should be armed with some powerful tools for making your ideas come to life with ActionScript.

Creating Ordered Structures

In most any program, there comes a time when you work with groups of related data. Sometimes this data comes in the form of lists, such as the following:

```
var sEmployees:String = "Arun, Peter, Chris,
Heather";
```

If you want to handle the data as a single string, the previous example works just fine. But what happens when you want to work with each piece of data individually? A comma-delimited list is too awkward and difficult to work with. It might require complicated loops and many variables to accomplish even a simple task, such as sorting the list alphabetically. Here is a perfect case for an array.

Arrays are simply ordered data structures. These structures are composed of *elements*—values with indices that correspond to those values. In other words, each value has a unique identifier by which it can be referenced. In the case of arrays created using the `Array` class, these indices are numbers. For instance, in the previous example, you could restructure the `sEmployees` string into an array in which Arun would have an index of 0, Peter an index of 1, Chris an index of 2, and Heather an index of 3.

Notice that the first index we mentioned was a 0. Much like other languages, ActionScript uses zero-indexed arrays, meaning the first element of an array in ActionScript has an index of 0.

Remember that ActionScript arrays are zero-indexed. That means that the first element of an array has an index of 0, not 1.

You can think of a basic array as a table from a spreadsheet program. In its basic form, an array is a single column with as many rows as it has elements. The employee example can be graphically represented as in the following table.

Index	*Value*
0	Arun
1	Peter
2	Chris
3	Heather

There are many examples of arrays in real life. Libraries keep all the books in order according to the unique numbers assigned to the books. If you know the index, you can find it in order. The same is true of driver's license numbers, license plate numbers, social security numbers, and so on. Examples of *arrays*, collections of organized data with unique indices, are all around us.

Creating Arrays

Now that you have a general sense of what an array is, you'll first need to know how to create one. All arrays are instances of the `Array` class, and as such, you can create instances using the `Array` constructor. There are three variations with the constructor:

✦ **No parameters:** This option creates a new array with zero elements. You'll read the different alternatives for adding new elements to such an array in the next section.

```
// Create a new array with zero elements.
var aEmployees:Array = new Array();
```

✦ **A single parameter specifying the number of elements:** This option creates a new array with the specified number of elements. However, each element is left undefined. You then need to assign values to each of the elements. This is discussed in the next section.

```
// Create a new array with four elements.
var aEmployees:Array = new Array(4);
```

✦ **A list of parameters, each of which is a new value to insert into a new element in the array:** For example, a constructor called with three parameters will create a new array with three elements. The parameter values are assigned to the new elements.

```
// Create a new array with zero elements.
var aEmployees:Array = new Array("Arun", "Peter", "Chris",
                                 "Heather");
```

In addition to creating arrays with the constructor, you can create array literals. An *array literal* is still an instance of the Array class just as an array created with the constructor. The only difference is that the array literal notation is slightly more condensed. With array literal notation, you tell Flash to create a new array using square brackets. Within the square brackets, you can provide a list of elements to add to the array. Here is an example:

```
var aEmployees:Array = ["Arun", "Peter", "Chris", "Heather"];
```

You may notice that the array literal notation essentially is no different from the third variation of the Array constructor. Why would you then choose one over the other? Generally, one is not any better than the other. It is largely just a matter of preference. In fact, you can also use array literal notation as an alternative to the first variation of the constructor.

```
var aEmployees:Array = [];
```

The preceding creates a new array with zero elements. It is only the second variation on the constructor that is somewhat awkward to mimic using array literal notation.

Adding Values to an Array

In the preceding section you learned how to create a new array. Often, after you have created an array, the next thing you want to do is add new elements and/or assign values to existing elements. Let's take a look at some of the ways you can do this.

Assigning Values Using Array-Access Notation

Array-access notation allows you to assign values to specific elements in an array if you know the index of the element. The basic syntax for assigning a value to an element using array-access notation is as follows:

```
arrayName[index] = value;
```

Here is a specific example that creates a new array with four undefined elements. Then, using array-access notation, you can assign new values to the array.

```
var aEmployees:Array = mew Array(4);
aEmployees[0] = "Arun";
aEmployees[1] = "Peter";
aEmployees[2] = "Chris";
aEmployees[3] = "Heather";
```

A simple way to see the contents of an array is to use a trace() action to write the contents to the Output panel. You can allow Flash to implicitly convert the array to a string, or you can explicitly invoke the toString() method. In either case, when the array is converted to a string, it is represented as a comma-delimited list.

```
trace(aEmployees.toString());
```

The result of the preceding trace() action is as follows:

```
Arun,Peter,Chris,Heather
```

As you can see, the array contains four elements with the values that you assigned them. Also, in this example, notice that the first element of the array has an index of 0. As mentioned earlier, all ActionScript arrays are zero-indexed.

Another quality of ActionScript arrays is that they size dynamically. This means that if you assign a value to an element that has not yet been created, Flash automatically creates that element and any other elements with indices between. For example, you can assign a value to an element with index 9 of the aEmployees array:

```
aEmployees[9] = "Ruth";
```

If you then use a trace() action to see the contents of the array, you'll see the following in the Output panel:

```
Arun,Peter,Chris,Heather,undefined,undefined,undefined,undefined,undefined,Ruth
```

Notice that the first four elements remain the same. A value of Ruth has been assigned to the tenth element. Because the tenth element did not previously exist, it was automatically created. However, because the fifth through ninth elements didn't exist either, they were also created with undefined values. You cannot create an array with gaps in the indices. The indices must always be contiguous.

Appending Values to the End of an Array

When you are dynamically adding elements to an array, it is sometimes difficult to keep track of the number of elements. Fortunately, ActionScript offers a convenient and simple way to append elements to an array using the push() method.

The push() method accepts one or more parameters and automatically appends those values to the end of the array. Here is an example:

```
var aEmployees:Array = ["Arun", "Peter", "Chris", "Heather"];
aEmployees.push("Ruth");
trace(aEmployees.toString());
```

The result is as follows:

```
Arun,Peter,Chris,Heather,Ruth
```

You are not limited to adding a single element at a time. Here is another example:

```
var aEmployees:Array = ["Arun", "Peter", "Chris", "Heather"];
aEmployees.push("Ruth", "Hao", "Laura");
trace(aEmployees.toString());
```

The result is as follows:

```
Arun,Peter,Chris,Heather,Ruth,Hao,Laura
```

The push() method always appends new elements, even if all the existing elements have undefined values. Therefore, be careful when you want to insert values in an array with undefined elements. For example:

```
var aEmployees:Array = new Array(2);
aEmployees.push("Ruth", "Hao", "Laura");
trace(aEmployees.toString());
```

In this example, the Output panel will display the following:

```
undefined,undefined,Ruth,Hao,Laura
```

The first two elements remain undefined.

Prepending Elements to the Beginning of an Array

Appending elements to an array is enough of a challenge without using the `push()` method. Prepending elements to the beginning of an array without the use of a built-in method would be a struggle. Fortunately, you can rely on the built-in `unshift()` method.

The `unshift()` method works in much the same way as the `push()` method, but it adds the new elements to the beginning of the array instead of to the end. Any existing elements are shifted (or *un*shifted, if you will) to higher indices. For example, if you use `unshift()` to add one new element to an array, the new element is inserted at index 0 and all the existing elements' indices are incremented by one.

The following is an example of the `unshift()` method:

```
var aEmployees:Array = ["Arun", "Peter", "Chris", "Heather"];
aEmployees.unshift("Ruth", "Hao", "Laura");
trace(aEmployees.toString());
```

And this is the resulting output:

```
Ruth,Hao,Laura,Arun,Peter,Chris,Heather
```

Inserting Elements into an Array

You have already seen how to append and prepend elements to an array. How about inserting elements into an array, not necessarily at the beginning or end? Once again, ActionScript provides a method for that very purpose. You can use the `splice()` method to insert new elements into an array starting at a given index. All subsequent elements are shifted to accommodate the new elements.

The basic syntax to use the `splice()` method to insert new elements is as follows:

```
arrayName.splice(startingIndex, numberOfElementsToDelete,
  element1[,...elementN]);
```

As you can see from the syntax, the `splice()` method not only has the capability of inserting new elements into an array but can remove existing elements at the same time. The first parameter of the method is the starting index. For example, if you want to begin inserting and/or removing elements at the second element, you would specify a value of 1. The second parameter is the number of elements to delete. If you don't want to remove any elements, but only insert new elements, you should specify a value of 0. Otherwise, indicate the number of elements to remove, and Flash removes that many elements from the array starting with the specified index. Then, for the remaining parameters in the `splice()` method, you should indicate the values for the element or elements you wish to insert into the array. The following is an example of the `splice()` method being used to insert three new elements into an array:

```
var aEmployees:Array = ["Arun", "Peter", "Chris", "Heather"];
aEmployees.splice(3, 0, "Ruth", "Hao", "Laura");
trace(aEmployees.toString());
```

The preceding code will display the following in the Output panel:

```
Arun,Peter,Chris,Ruth,Hao,Laura,Heather
```

Removing Elements from an Array

Of course, if you have the ability to add elements to an array, you also should have the ability to remove elements from an array. Let's take a look at some of the ways you can achieve this.

Removing the Last Element of an Array

You can use the pop() method to remove the last element from an array. Because the pop() method always removes the last element, it does not require any parameters. The method returns the removed value in the event that you want to do something with it other than simply remove it from the array. The following is an example of how to use the pop() method:

```
var aEmployees:Array = ["Arun", "Peter", "Chris", "Heather"];
var sAnEmployee:String = aEmployees.pop();
trace(aEmployees.toString());
trace(sAnEmployee);
```

The Output panel will display the following:

```
Arun,Peter,Chris
Heather
```

Removing the First Element of an Array

Like the pop() method, the shift() method removes and returns an element from the array, but instead of removing the element from the end of the array, the shift() method removes the element from the beginning of the array. All subsequent elements are shifted such that their indices are decremented by one. The following is an example of the shift() method:

```
var aEmployees:Array = ["Arun", "Peter", "Chris", "Heather"];
var sAnEmployee:String = aEmployees.shift();
trace(aEmployees.toString());
trace(sAnEmployee);
```

The Output panel will display the following:

```
Peter,Chris,Heather
Arun
```

Removing Elements from Within an Array

You've seen how to remove elements from the beginning and end of an array, but how about elements not at the beginning or end? You can use the splice() method to accomplish this. We've already seen how to use this method to insert new elements into an array. You can use the same method with only the first two parameters in order to simply remove elements. The method not only removes the specified elements but returns a new array containing the removed elements. The following is an example:

```
var aEmployees:Array = ["Arun", "Peter", "Chris", "Heather"];
var aRemovedEmployees:Array = aEmployees.splice(2, 2);
trace(aEmployees.toString());
trace(aRemovedEmployees.toString());
```

The preceding code will result in the following display in the Output panel:

```
Arun,Peter
Chris,Heather
```

Reading Data from Arrays

You can read the data from an array using array-access notation to access one element at a time. For example:

```
var aEmployees:Array = ["Arun", "Peter", "Chris", "Heather"];
trace(aEmployees[0]);  // Displays: Arun
trace(aEmployees[1]);  // Displays: Peter
trace(aEmployees[2]);  // Displays: Chris
trace(aEmployees[3]);  // Displays: Heather
```

You can use array-access notation to access any element, and you can use this syntax in any situation in which you can use a variable.

Often you will find that you want to read all the elements of an array. For example, if you have an array of the names of the months of the year, you might want to be able to read all those elements in order to display them to the user. Using a `for` statement and a special property, `length`, or the array, you can loop through all the elements of an array with just a few lines of code.

The `length` property of an array returns the number of elements in the array. Knowing the number of elements in the array and knowing that all arrays are zero-indexed, you can quickly construct a `for` statement to loop through the elements of an array from first to last. Here is an example:

```
var aEmployees:Array = ["Arun", "Peter", "Chris", "Heather"];
for(var i:Number = 0; i < aEmployees.length; i++) {
  trace(aEmployees[i]);
}
```

The preceding example will display the values in the array one at a time in the Output panel as follows:

```
Arun
Peter
Chris
Heather
```

Notice that the `for` statement condition checks to see if `i` is less than the number of elements in the array— not less than or equal to. Because arrays are zero-indexed, the greatest index value will always be exactly one less than the number of elements in the array. For example, an array with six elements will have index values of 0, 1, 2, 3, 4, and 5. The greatest index value of 5 is one less than the number of elements in the array.

Now, how about if you want to loop through the elements of the array starting with the last element and working backward? No problem. Just change the `for` statement expressions slightly. Instead of initializing the loop at 0 and running until less than the number of elements, you should initialize the loop at one less than the number of elements and run until equal to zero, decrementing by one each time:

```
var aEmployees:Array = ["Arun", "Peter", "Chris", "Heather"];
for(var i:Number = aEmployees.length - 1; i = 0; i--) {
  trace(aEmployees[i]);
}
```

The preceding example will display the values in the array one at a time in the Output panel as follows:

```
Heather
Chris
Peter
Arun
```

In fact, you can come up with just about any set of conditions on which to loop through an array. Depending on what you are trying to accomplish, you might want to skip every other element, begin looping in the middle of the array, and so on.

Using Different Types of Arrays

There are many ways to approach arrays. What determines how you will treat an array in your programming is the functionality you require from it. In different scenarios, different approaches to using arrays will be more appropriate than others. This section outlines different ways to use arrays in your programs.

Working with Single-Dimension Arrays

The arrays you have seen in this chapter so far are called single-dimension arrays. That is, they are single columns of indexed data. You create these arrays in many ways — through the use of array literals and different `Array` constructors. Some examples of a single-dimension array are the following:

```
var aLetters:Array = ["a", "b", "c"];
var aNoLetters:Array = new Array();
var aMoreLetters:Array = new Array("d", "e", "f");
```

Working with Parallel Arrays

There are occasions in your programming when you will have two groups of data that are related. For example, you might be working with data such as employee names and their corresponding phone numbers. Each employee has a phone number, and you want a way to connect the two pieces of data together. You could create a single array in which each element is a string containing both pieces of data, separated by a delimiter such as a colon (:):

```
var aEmployees:Array = new Array();
aEmployees.push("Arun:555-1234");
aEmployees.push("Peter:555-4321");
aEmployees.push("Chris:555-5678");
aEmployees.push("Heather:555-8765");
```

Then you could use `String` object methods to extract the names and the birthdays when you want to use them:

```
// The split() method separates string by specified
// delimiter into a new array.
var aEmployees:Array = new Array();
aEmployees.push("Arun:555-1234");
```

```
aEmployees.push("Peter:555-4321");
aEmployees.push("Chris:555-5678");
aEmployees.push("Heather:555-8765");
var aTempEmployeeInfo:Array = null;
for(var i:Number = 0; i < aEmployees.length; i++) {
  aTempEmployeeInfo = aEmployees[i].split(":");
  trace("Employee:" + aTempEmployeeInfo[0]);
  trace("Phone Number:" + aTempEmployeeInfo[1]);
}
```

The preceding will result in the following display in the Output panel:

```
Employee:Arun
Phone Number:555-1234
Employee:Peter
Phone Number:555-4321
Employee:Chris
Phone Number:555-5678
Employee:Heather
Phone Number:555-8765
```

Although that works, it is somewhat overly complex when all you want to do is something as simple as store and retrieve a name and corresponding phone number. A much easier way to solve this problem is to use what are known as *parallel arrays*.

The idea behind parallel arrays is simply to create two (or more) arrays in which the elements with the same indices are related. So using the employee scenario, you could create two parallel arrays as follows:

```
var aEmployeeNames:Array = ["Arun", "Peter", "Chris", "Heather"];
var aEmployeePhone:Array = ["555-1234", "555-4321", "555-5678", "555-8765"];
```

Then it is much easier to retrieve the corresponding elements from each array than to try and parse through a string as you did earlier. All you need to do is to access the elements with the same index from each array:

```
var aEmployeeNames:Array = ["Arun", "Peter", "Chris", "Heather"];
var aEmployeePhone:Array = ["555-1234", "555-4321", "555-5678", "555-8765"];
for(var i:Number = 0; i < aEmployeeNames.length; i++) {
  trace("Employee:" + aEmployeeNames[i]);
  trace("Phone Number:" + aEmployeePhone[i]);
}
```

This displays the following in the Output panel:

```
Employee:Arun
Phone Number:555-1234
Employee:Peter
Phone Number:555-4321
Employee:Chris
Phone Number:555-5678
Employee:Heather
Phone Number:555-8765
```

Notice that this is the same output as before, but the code is simplified.

You are not limited to using just two arrays with corresponding data. You can use as many as you need and can manage. Let's continue on with the same employee example and imagine that you want to add one more piece of information about each employee. Perhaps you want to add the number of years employed. You could then easily add a third parallel array:

```
var aEmployeeYears:Array = [5, 7, 3, 1];
```

Working with Multidimensional Arrays

You can think of the standard, single-dimension array as a single column of data. Many other languages support what are known as multidimensional arrays. You can think of a two-dimensional array, for example, as a grid where each element is determined by two indices—a row and a column index. A three-dimensional array can be thought of as representing three-dimensional space, and each element is determined by three indices—the row, column, and depth. In ActionScript, you can represent this construct using an array of arrays. Here is an example:

```
var aEmployees:Array = new Array();
aEmployees.push(["Arun", "555-1234"]);
aEmployees.push(["Peter", "555-4321"]);
aEmployees.push(["Chris", "555-5678"]);
aEmployees.push(["Heather", "555-8765"]);
for(var i:Number = 0; i < aEmployees.length; i++) {
  trace("Employee:" + aEmployees[i][0]);
  trace("Phone Number:" + aEmployees[i][1]);
}
```

The preceding code creates a new array, `aEmployees`, and appends to it four elements that are, themselves, arrays. Then, notice that each value is accessed using two indices. The first index specifies the row (the element of the outermost array), whereas the second index specifies the column (the element of the innermost arrays). The result is very similar to what you achieved using parallel arrays in the earlier section. In fact, parallel arrays and two-dimensional arrays can be used almost interchangeably.

Of course, you can create arrays as elements of arrays that are, themselves, elements of an array. Such a scenario would mimic a three-dimensional array. You can even create arrays of greater dimensions, although once you get beyond three or four dimensions, it can become confusing.

Working with Arrays of Objects

Another type of array that can be useful is an array of associative arrays. We discussed associative arrays in Chapter 7. As a quick refresher, however, an associative array is an object with named indices called *keys*. Arrays of associative arrays can be useful when you have a list of data in which each element is composed of various, named subelements. For example, this same employee/phone number example is a good candidate for this type of construct. Here is an example:

```
var aEmployees:Array = new Array();
aEmployees.push({Employee:"Arun", Phone:"555-1234"});
aEmployees.push({Employee:"Peter", Phone:"555-4321"});
```

```
aEmployees.push({Employee:"Chris", Phone:"555-5678"});
aEmployees.push({Employee:"Heather", Phone:"555-8765"});
for(var i:Number = 0; i < aEmployees.length; i++) {
  trace("Employee:" + aEmployees[i].Employee);
  trace("Phone Number:" + aEmployees[i].Phone);
}
```

Converting Arrays to Lists

A single string that represents a group of related data is often called a *list*. Here's a simple example of a list:

```
var sEmployees:String = "Arun,Peter,Chris,Heather";
```

The character used between each element in the list is generally called a *delimiter*. Although any character can be used as a delimiter, one of the most common is the comma.

When you have an array of elements, there are various reasons why you might want to convert it to a list. One of the most common uses of lists is in sending values to a server-side script, but that is certainly not the only possible use. In any case, when you want to convert an array to a list you can use the `join()` method. The `join()` method returns a new list (a string) containing all the elements of the array delimited by the character you specify. You specify the delimiter as a parameter of the `join()` method. Here is an example:

```
var aEmployees:Array = ["Arun", "Peter", "Chris", "Heather"];
var sEmployees:String = aEmployees.join(",");
trace(sEmployees);
```

The Output panel will display the following:

```
Arun,Peter,Chris,Heather
```

You may notice that in this case the `join()` method results in the same value as the `toString()` method. However, the `toString()` method does not allow you to specify a delimiter other than the comma. With `join()` you can use any delimiter you want. For example:

```
var aEmployees:Array = ["Arun", "Peter", "Chris", "Heather"];
var sEmployees:String = aEmployees.join(";");
trace(sEmployees);
```

The Output panel will display the following:

```
Arun;Peter;Chris;Heather
```

On the other hand, sometimes you have a list that you want to convert to an array. You can convert any list into an array using the `String` class `split()` method. The `split()` method asks that you specify the delimiter it should use to determine the elements of the list. Here is an example:

```
var sEmployees:String = "Arun,Peter,Chris,Heather";
var aEmployees:Array = sEmployees.split(",");
```

The result of the preceding code is a new array with four elements.

Creating New Arrays from Existing Arrays

The Array class provides you with several ways to create new arrays based on an existing array. There are two basic scenarios in which you will create a new array from existing elements:

- ✦ You want to add together the elements of several arrays to create a new array.
- ✦ You want to create a new array that contains a subset of the elements of the original.

Concatenating Arrays

You can create a new array that contains the elements of several other arrays using the concat() method. You invoke the method from an array and pass it parameters specifying the other arrays whose elements you want to add to the new array. Flash then creates a new array and adds all the elements of the original arrays to the new one. Here is an example:

```
var aEmployeesExec:Array = ["Arun", "Peter", "Chris", "Heather"];
var aEmployeesNew:Array = ["Gilberto", "Mary"];
var aEmployeesStaff:Array = ["Ayla", "Riad"];
var aEmployeesAll:Array = aEmployeesExec.concat(aEmployeesNew, aEmployeesStaff);
trace(aEmployeesAll.toString());
```

In the example, the Output panel will display the following:

```
Arun,Peter,Chris,Heather,Gilberto,Mary,Ayla,Riad
```

The newly created array, aEmployeesAll, contains copies of all the elements of the other arrays.

You can also use the concat() method without any parameters as a shortcut to creating a copy of an array. Here is an example:

```
var aEmployees:Array = ["Arun", "Peter", "Chris", "Heather"];
var aEmployeesCopy:Array = aEmployees.concat();
```

Extracting Subsets of Array Elements

The slice() method (not to be confused with splice()) returns a new array containing a subset of elements from the original. When you invoke the slice() method, you specify the starting and ending indices of the array. Flash then returns a new array containing all the elements between those indices, including the first, but not the last. Here is an example:

```
var aEmployeesAll:Array = ["Arun", "Peter", "Chris", "Heather",
                           "Gilberto", "Mary", "Ayla", "Riad"];
var aEmployeesExec:Array = aEmployeesAll.slice(0, 4);
var aEmployeesNew:Array = aEmployeesAll.slice(4, 6);
var aEmployeesStaff:Array = aEmployeesAll.slice(6);
trace(aEmployeesExe.toString());
trace(aEmployeesNew.toString());
trace(aEmployeesStaff.toString());
```

In this example, the Output panel will display the following:

```
Arun,Peter,Chris,Heather
Gilberto,Mary
Ayla,Riad
```

Sorting Arrays

An important feature of arrays is that you can sort them. There are different sorting algorithms that developers use, but fortunately you don't have to concern yourself with them because ActionScript provides methods that take care of all of that for you. We examine three sorting methods more closely in the following sections:

- **sort():** This method sorts regular, single dimension arrays.
- **sortOn():** This method sorts arrays of associative arrays based on one of the keys of the associative arrays.
- **reverse():** This method reverses the order of the elements.

Sorting Simply

The most basic type of sort you can perform on an ActionScript array is an alphabetical sort. In order to achieve an alphabetical sort, simply create your array and invoke the `sort()` method with no parameters. This is a very useful type of sort to perform. For example, in the sample array used throughout this chapter, you can quickly sort the elements in alphabetical order as follows:

```
var aEmployees:Array = ["Arun", "Peter", "Chris", "Heather"];
aEmployees.sort();
trace(aEmployees.toString());
```

The Output panel displays the elements in alphabetical order:

```
Arun,Chris,Heather,Peter
```

It is important to keep in mind that any sort is going to necessarily reorder the elements—meaning new indices for some elements. Be sure that before you perform a sort on an array you are not relying on any particular indices for any particular elements. For example, if you are using parallel arrays, and you sort one of them, the array elements will no longer correspond.

A simple sort works wonderfully when you want to sort an array of strings in ascending alphabetical order. However, ActionScript also provides you with some ways of performing more complex sorting.

Sorting More Complexly

You can choose from six types of complex sorts when you use the `sort()` method. Five of these complex sorts rely on the new `Array` sorting flag constants. The following sections take a look at each of them.

Sorting Numerically

When the `sort()` method sorts the elements, it generally compares all the elements as though they were string values. This is true, even if the values are numeric. And this can lead to some unexpected sort orders when you want to sort an array of numbers. You can test this for yourself with the following code:

```
var aNumbers:Array = [10, 1, 2, 15, 21, 13, 33, 3];
aNumbers.sort();
trace(aNumbers.toString());
```

What you'll see in the Output panel, should you try this, is the following:

```
1,10,13,15,2,21,3,33
```

Clearly, these values are not sorted in numerical order. But they are sorted in the correct order if they are treated as strings. The only problem is that you don't want to compare them as strings. You want to compare them as numbers. Fortunately, the `Array` class has a constant, `Array.NUMERIC`, that allows you to sort the values numerically. All you need to do is pass this constant to the `sort()` method.

```
var aNumbers:Array = [10, 1, 2, 15, 21, 13, 33, 3];
aNumbers.sort(Array.NUMERIC);
trace(aNumbers.toString());
```

In the Output panel, the correctly ordered numbers will appear:

```
1,2,3,10,13,15,21,33
```

Sorting in Descending Order

Thus far, you've seen how to sort arrays in ascending order. That is the default setting. But with the `Array.DESCENDING` constant you can tell Flash to sort your array in descending order instead. Here is an example:

```
var aEmployees:Array = ["Arun", "Peter", "Chris", "Heather"];
aEmployees.sort(Array.DESCENDING);
trace(aEmployees.toString());
```

This causes the array to sort in reverse alphabetical order. The following will display in the Output panel:

```
Peter,Heather,Chris,Arun
```

Sorting Regardless of Case

When Flash compares two strings, the cases of the values are a factor. Uppercase characters sort before lowercase characters. Therefore, if you perform a simple sort on an array in which the initial case of the words is not consistent, you should be aware that the sorted array may be other than you expect. Here is an example:

```
var aWords:Array = ["orange", "Sedona", "apple", "Caracas"];
aWords.sort();
trace(aWords.toString());
```

In this case, the array will be sorted as follows:

```
Caracas,Sedona,apple,orange
```

Although that is the default behavior, you can explicitly tell Flash to perform a case-insensitive sort using the `Array.CASEINSENSITIVE` constant. Here is an example:

```
var aWords:Array = ["orange", "Sedona", "apple", "Caracas"];
aWords.sort(Array.CASEINSENSITIVE);
trace(aWords.toString());
```

With the simple addition of the constant as a parameter to the `sort()` method, the array will now be sorted as follows:

```
apple,Caracas,orange,Sedona
```

Sorting and Testing for Unique Values

You can also use the `sort()` method to test and ensure that the values of the array are unique. If you pass the `sort()` method the `Array.UNIQUESORT` constant then it has the following behavior:

- ✦ If the elements of the array are all unique, the array is sorted alphabetically in ascending order.
- ✦ If there are one or more duplicate elements, the `sort()` method returns 0 and the array is not sorted.

Here is an example of the `sort()` method with the `Array.UNIQUESORT` constant:

```
var aEmployees:Array = ["Arun", "Peter", "Chris", "Heather"];
if(aEmployees.sort(Array.UNIQUESORT) != 0) {
  trace(aEmployees.toString());
}
else {
  trace("Array has duplicate elements, and has not been sorted. ");
  trace(aEmployees.toString());
}
```

The preceding code will display the sorted array because `aEmployees` has no duplicate entries. If you modify the first line of code as follows:

```
var aEmployees:Array = ["Arun", "Peter", "Chris", "Heather", "Arun"];
```

you can see that the `sort()` method catches the duplicate element, and the array is not sorted.

Getting Sorted Indices

Another option available to you is to use the `sort()` method to return an array of indices that represent the sorted elements. This option does not sort the original array, but gives you a way to access the element in a sorted order. When you invoke the `sort()` method and pass it the `Array.RETURNINDEXEDARRAY` constant, Flash does not modify the original array, but rather returns a new array containing elements representing the indices from the original. The order of the elements in the new array can be used to access the elements from the original array in sorted order. Here is an example:

```
var aEmployees:Array = ["Arun", "Peter", "Chris", "Heather"];
var aSortedIndices:Array = aEmployees.sort(Array.RETURNINDEXEDARRAY);
trace(aEmployees.toString());
```

```
trace(aSortedIndices.toString());
for(var i:Number = 0; i < aSortedIndices.length; i++) {
  trace(aEmployees[aSortedIndices[i]]);
}
```

This example will display the following in the Output panel:

```
Arun,Peter,Chris,Heather
0,2,3,1
Arun
Chris
Heather
Peter
```

You can see that the original array is not modified. The new array contains number elements that represent the indices of the original array. If you loop through the elements of the new array and use those values as the indices to access the values from the original array, you can access the values from the original array in ascending alphabetical order.

Sorting with Multiple Flags

So great, you say, you can perform a case-insensitive search. You can even perform a descending order search. But what if you want Flash to sort using both criteria at the same time? No problem, says Flash. Simply use the bitwise `OR` operator (`|`) to join together each of the constants you want Flash to use for the sort. Here is an example:

```
var aWords:Array = ["orange", "Sedona", "apple", "Caracas"];
aWords.sort(Array.DESCENDING | Array.CASEINSENSITIVE);
trace(aWords.toString());
```

The Output panel will display the following:

```
Sedona,orange,Caracas,apple
```

Sorting with Custom Algorithms

If none of the built-in sorting options is what you are looking for, you can use a custom sorting algorithm instead. For the most part, the sorting options discussed previously should work for just about any scenario you might have with a single-dimensional array containing strings or numbers. In the next section, we also discuss how to use the `sortOn()` method to sort arrays of associative arrays. Therefore, custom algorithms are less and less likely to be essential.

Should you need to use a custom sorting algorithm, here's how it works:

1. Create a function that Flash will use to sort the elements. The function should accept two parameters. Flash will automatically pass it two elements at a time (called a and b). Within the function, you need to put in place the logic to determine which element should be sorted before the other. Once you have determined the order, you can return one of three values:

   a. 1—a should be sorted after b.

   b. -1—b should be sorted after a.

   c. 0—leave the original order of a and b.

2. When you call the `sort()` method, pass it a reference to the custom sorting function. Flash handles the rest.

Here's a basic example that uses a custom sorting algorithm to perform a case-insensitive sort that sorts in descending alphabetical order. You can also achieve the same results by first performing a sort with the `Array.CASEINSENSITIVE` and `Array.DESCENDING` flags.

```
function sorter(a:String, b:String):Number {
  if(a.toUpperCase() > b.toUpperCase()) {
    return -1;
  }
  else if(a.toUpperCase() < b.toUpperCase()) {
    return 1;
  }
  else {
    return 0;
  }
}
var aWords:Array = ["orange", "Sedona", "apple", "Caracas"];
aWords.sort(sorter);
trace(aWords.toString());
```

The output is as follows:

```
Sedona,orange,Caracas,apple
```

The following is another example that is more complex. In this example, the function sorts the array's values first according to the type of value (name of city or name of country) and then alphabetically:

```
function isInArray(sElement:String, aArray:Array) {
  for(var i:Number = 0; i < aArray.length; i++) {
    if(sElement == aArray[i]) {
      return true;
    }
  }
  return false;
}
function sorter(a:String, b:String):Number {
  var aCountries:Array = ["Mexico", "Vietnam", "Japan"];
  var aCities:Array = ["Caracas", "Paris", "Berlin"];
  if(isInArray(a, aCountries) && isInArray(b, aCities)) {
    return 1;
  }
  if(a.toUpperCase() > b.toUpperCase()) {
    return 1;
  }
  else if(a.toUpperCase() < b.toUpperCase()) {
    return -1;
  }
  else {
    return 0;
  }
}
```

```
var aPlaces:Array = ["Berlin", "Vietnam", "Japan", "Caracas",
                     "Mexico", "Paris"];
aPlaces.sort(sorter);
trace(aPlaces.toString());
```

The output is as follows:

```
Berlin,Caracas,Paris,Japan,Mexico,Vietnam
```

Sorting Arrays of Associative Arrays

You can use the sortOn() method to sort an array's elements by key name if the elements of the array are all associative arrays. For example, consider the following array:

```
var aCars:Array = new Array();
aCars.push({make: "Oldsmobile", model: "Alero", extColor: "blue"});
aCars.push({make: "Honda", model: "Accord", extColor: "red"});
aCars.push({make: "Volvo", model: "242", extColor: "red"});
```

With this array, you may want to sort its elements by make, model, or exterior color. With the sortOn() method, this is as simple as a single method call. But sortOn() can do more. Let's take a look at a few of the options available with the sortOn() method.

Sorting by a Single Key

The simplest type of sort with sortOn() is to sort an array based on a single key. In these cases you need only to pass the name of the key to the sortOn() method as a single, string parameter. Here is an example:

```
function displayArray(aArray:Array) {
  var sElement:String = null;
  for(var i:Number = 0; i < aArray.length; i++) {
    sElement = "";
    for(var key in aArray[i]) {
      sElement += aArray[i][key] + " ";
    }
    trace(sElement);
  }
}

var aCars:Array = new Array();
aCars.push({make: "Oldsmobile", model: "Alero", extColor: "blue"});
aCars.push({make: "Honda", model: "Accord", extColor: "red"});
aCars.push({make: "Volvo", model: "242", extColor: "red"});
aCars.sortOn("make");
displayArray(aCars);
```

In this example, you first define a function that displays the contents of the array. Because the array's elements are not simple string or number values, a toString() call will not yield a value for displaying the contents of the array. So the displayArray() function simply loops through the contents of the array and displays each element's values. Next, you define the array. The array consists of three associative arrays, all with the same keys, but different values. Then, you invoke the sortOn() method, telling it which key to sort on. The display in the Output panel looks like this:

```
Honda Accord red
Oldsmobile Alero blue
Volvo 242 red
```

Notice that the elements have been sorted alphabetically by the value of the make. If you want to sort on the model instead, you can simply invoke `sortOn()` with the value of `model` instead of `make`. In that case, the output will be as follows:

```
Volvo 242 red
Honda Accord red
Oldsmobile Alero blue
```

And, of course, you can also sort on the exterior color if you want. In order to do that, you simply invoke the `sortOn()` method with the value of `extColor`.

Sorting on Multiple Keys

When you are sorting arrays of associative arrays, it can be useful to be able to sort not only on a single key, but also on multiple keys. For example, if you have an array of associative arrays that describe cars, as in this example, you might want to tell Flash to sort it by make, by model, and finally by exterior color. The `sortOn()` method has a built-in option for this kind of sorting. All you need to do is pass the `sortOn()` method an array of the key names on which you want to sort, in the order you want Flash to sort them. Here is an example:

```
function displayArray(aArray:Array) {
  var sElement:String = null;
  for(var i:Number = 0; i < aArray.length; i++) {
    sElement = "";
    for(var key in aArray[i]) {
      sElement += aArray[i][key] + " ";
    }
    trace(sElement);
  }
}

var aCars:Array = new Array();
aCars.push({make: "Oldsmobile", model: "Alero", extColor: "blue"});
aCars.push({make: "Honda", model: "Accord", extColor: "red"});
aCars.push({make: "Volvo", model: "242 DL", extColor: "red"});
aCars.push({make: "Oldsmobile", model: "Alero", extColor: "red"});
aCars.push({make: "Honda", model: "Accord", extColor: "gold"});
aCars.push({make: "Volvo", model: "242", extColor: "white"});
aCars.push({make: "Oldsmobile", model: "Aurora", extColor: "silver"});
aCars.push({make: "Honda", model: "Prelude", extColor: "silver"});
aCars.push({make: "Volvo", model: "242", extColor: "red"});

aCars.sortOn(["make","mode","extColor"]);
displayArray(aCars);
```

In this example, the Output panel will display the following:

```
Honda Accord gold
Honda Accord red
Honda Prelude silver
```

```
Oldsmobile Alero blue
Oldsmobile Alero red
Oldsmobile Aurora silver
Volvo 242 DL red
Volvo 242 red
Volvo 242 white
```

Notice that the array has been sorted first by make. Therefore all the elements with the same make are grouped together. Then, within each make group, the elements are sorted by model. Therefore the Accords are sorted before the Prelude, for example. And then, within each model group, the elements are sorted by exterior color. For example, the gold Accord is sorted before the red Accord.

It is very important that when you want to sort on multiple keys you pass the `sortOn()` method a *single* parameter. The single parameter is an array. If you try and pass the `sortOn()` method multiple key name parameters the sort will not be correct.

Sorting with Sort Flags

You can also use all the same sorting flags with `sortOn()` that you can use with `sort()`. If you are sorting on a single key then the first parameter for the `sortOn()` method is still the key name. Then, you can pass the method a sorting flag constant as the second parameter. Here is an example:

```
function displayArray(aArray:Array) {
  var sElement:String = null;
  for(var i:Number = 0; i < aArray.length; i++) {
    sElement = "";
    for(var key in aArray[i]) {
      sElement += aArray[i][key] + " ";
    }
    trace(sElement);
  }
}

var aCars:Array = new Array();
aCars.push({make: "Oldsmobile", model: "Alero", extColor: "blue"});
aCars.push({make: "Honda", model: "Accord", extColor: "red"});
aCars.push({make: "Volvo", model: "242", extColor: "red"});
aCars.sortOn("make", Array.DESCENDING);
displayArray(aCars);
```

The result of this sort is as follows:

```
Volvo 242 red
Oldsmobile Alero blue
Honda Accord red
```

You can also use sorting flags when sorting with multiple keys. The first parameter should still be an array of the keys on which you want to sort. The second parameter should be the sorting flag constant. Here is an example:

```
function displayArray(aArray:Array) {
  var sElement:String = null;
  for(var i:Number = 0; i < aArray.length; i++) {
    sElement = "";
    for(var key in aArray[i]) {
      sElement += aArray[i][key] + " ";
    }
    trace(sElement);
  }
}
var aCars:Array = new Array();
aCars.push({make: "Oldsmobile", model: "Alero", extColor: "blue"});
aCars.push({make: "Honda", model: "Accord", extColor: "red"});
aCars.push({make: "Volvo", model: "242 DL", extColor: "red"});
aCars.push({make: "Oldsmobile", model: "Alero", extColor: "red"});
aCars.push({make: "Honda", model: "Accord", extColor: "gold"});
aCars.push({make: "Volvo", model: "242", extColor: "white"});
aCars.push({make: "Oldsmobile", model: "Aurora", extColor: "silver"});
aCars.push({make: "Honda", model: "Prelude", extColor: "silver"});
aCars.push({make: "Volvo", model: "242", extColor: "red"});
aCars.sortOn(["make","mode","extColor"], Array.DESCENDING);
displayArray(aCars);
```

The Output panel for this example will display the following:

```
Volvo 242 white
Volvo 242 red
Volvo 242 DL red
Oldsmobile Aurora silver
Oldsmobile Alero red
Oldsmobile Alero blue
Honda Prelude silver
Honda Accord red
Honda Accord gold
```

And, of course, whether sorting on single or multiple keys, you can combine multiple sorting flags using the bitwise `OR` operator.

Reversing an Array

With the sorting flags that are now available there is little need for the `reverse()` method anymore. But should you want to quickly and simply reverse the order of an array's elements, you can still use this method.

```
aEmployees.reverse();
```

We'd like to know what you thought about this chapter. Visit `www.flashsupport.com/feedback` to fill out an online form with your comments.

Summary

- Arrays are indexed data structures in which each piece of data, called an *element*, has a unique index by which it can be referenced.
- Arrays can be created as array literals using the constructor methods, or as a returned value from a method such as `slice()` or `concat()`.
- You can use the array access operator (`[]`) to read and write to the elements of an array. You place the index of the element you want to read or write to between the square brackets of the operator. Numbered indices start with 0.
- There are many ways to work with arrays. The basic array is the single-dimensional, numbered indices array. You can work with multiple arrays with corresponding elements in what are known as parallel arrays. And you can even create arrays of arrays to provide support for more complex collections of data.
- You can sort your arrays using many of ActionScript's built-in sorting options.

✦ ✦ ✦

CHAPTER 12

The Number Class

In This Chapter

Examining the differences between integers and floating-point values in ActionScript

Using base-10, base-2, base-8, and base-16 numbers

Converting string values to numbers

Working with Number objects and creating a NumberPlus class

Chances are good that in the majority of Flash applications, you'll be using numbers. Numbers show up when you're using ActionScript to animate objects, calculate prices, quantities, and so on, and in a whole lot of scenarios in which you might not even have thought of numbers. In this chapter, you'll get a chance to learn more about different types of numbers and how to work with them.

Understanding Number Types

Although all numbers in ActionScript are classified as the number datatype, there are different types of numbers with which you can work. The following sections examine some of these types.

Integers and Floating-Point Numbers

The first category of numbers is base-10. These numbers should be familiar to you. They are the numbers that you use to count in everyday life. But within this category, you can have two classifications of precision: integers and floating-point numbers.

Integers are whole numbers, including 0 and negative values. The following are examples of integers:

```
1, 25, 0, -36, -3, 2932
```

Integers are the numbers you use to count whole things. For instance, you count frames in integer values — you cannot have anything between two frames. You use integers as indices for arrays, and you use integers to count most items (for example, people, paper clips, and pens).

There are, however, times when you require more precision in your numbers (for instance, when you are working with monetary values). Imagine the chaos that would ensue if banks worked only in integer values! In other words, $3.50 is not the same as $3. In these cases, you need more precision in your numbers. That is what floating-point numbers are for.

Floating-point numbers are also called *fractional numbers* because they can include fractions of integer values. Examples of floating-point numbers are as follows:

```
2.1, -32.012, 3.14, 3833.222223
```

Because both integers and floating-point numbers fall under the same datatype (and same class as well) in ActionScript, you don't need to do anything fancy to perform operations with both types of values together. For instance, you can use any of the mathematical operators using both types of numbers as operands:

```
5.1 + 3;         // results in 8.1
22 - 98.2223;    // results in -76.2223
5 % 2.1;         // results in 0.8
```

However, you should be aware that ActionScript automatically adjusts the precision of the number value to whatever is necessary. In other words, you might have noticed that adding a floating-point number to an integer results in a floating-point value. But when you add two (or more) floating-point values together that add up to a whole number, the precision of the resulting value is less than the precision of the operands. For example:

```
3.2 + 4.1 + 0.7;  // results in 8, not 8.0
```

In the previous example, even though all the operands have a precision to one decimal place, the result lost that precision. In most cases, this is not a problem.

Decimal Numbers

The type of numbers you work with most often are numbers in base-10, also known as decimal numbers. The term "decimal" simply means that multiplying a number by 10 to the power of *n* moves the decimal point *n* places without affecting the value of the digits of the number. In fact, decimal numbers can be represented in this fashion:

$$1.23 * 10^2 == 123$$

In ActionScript, the letter *e* with a plus sign (+) or minus sign (-) is used to create this kind of notation:

```
var nDecimalOne:Number = 1.23e+2;  // results in 123
var nDecimalTwo:Number = 1.23e-2;  // results in 0.0123
```

Notice that for numbers in which the exponent is positive and is less than 15, ActionScript writes the values (to the Output panel, for instance) in full form. But any number that has an integer part greater than or equal to 1000000000000000 is automatically converted to this exponential format. Likewise, with negative exponents, the cutoff is -5.

Other Bases for Numbers

As we alluded to earlier, base-10 (also known as decimal—*deci* means 10) is not the only base for numbers. Among the more commonly used are binary (base-2), octal (base-8), and hexadecimal (base-16). ActionScript supports numeric bases from 2 to 36.

If you have no clue about what any of this means, don't worry. You are not alone. But the idea is really quite simple. To start with, take a closer look at the world of base-10 numbers. When you count, you start with 0 and go up to 9, increment the value of the next column (tens, hundreds, thousands, and so on), and start over with 0 again. In other words, you have only 10 digits to cycle through in each column: 0 through 9.

You could just as easily work with fewer or more digits, however. Take, for instance, binary numbers—the kind of numbers that your computer can understand. Binary has the root *bini*, which means two. Therefore, the base for binary numbers is 2. Table 12-1 shows some binary numbers with their decimal equivalents.

Table 12-1: Binary Numbers

Binary	*Decimal*
0	0
1	1
10	2
11	3
100	4
101	5
110	6

Likewise, you can work with bases that are greater than 10 (in which case, letters are used to represent values greater than 9). For example, the hexadecimal value is the equivalent of the decimal value of 10. (Hexadecimal refers to numbers in base-16.) Therefore, the letters *a* through *f* are used in addition to 0 through 9. Table 12-2 shows some hexadecimal values with their corresponding decimal values.

Table 12-2: Hexadecimal Numbers

Hexadecimal	*Decimal*
a	10
b	11
c	12
2c	44
2d	45
5b	91
7b	123

Converting Strings to Numbers

If you work with any external data, be it from XML, CGI script, PHP, ColdFusion, or any other source, chances are good that you will need to convert a primitive string datatype to a number datatype. Although ActionScript tries to handle the conversion for you in many cases, it is still good form to make sure these conversions are done properly. Otherwise, you might end up with unexpected results.

Let's take a look at several of the ways you can convert strings to numbers.

Casting to a Number

You can convert any string to a number by *casting* it. In order to cast from a string to a number, you use the following syntax:

```
Number(stringValue)
```

Here are a few examples:

```
var nOne:Number = Number("468");     // 468
var nTwo:Number = Number("23.45");  // 23.45
var nThree:Number = Number("abc");    // NaN (Not a Number)
var nFour:Number = Number("0101");   // 101
```

Casting a string to a number will work just fine in many situations. However, when you cast from a string to a number, you don't get to control the precision of the number value it parses. That is to say, if you are interested only in the integer part of a string value, you have to go through several steps to strip the fractional part:

```
var nOne:Number = = Number("13.3");  // 13.3
nOne = Math.floor(num); // 13
```

The `floor()` method is a method of the `Math` class. It returns the integer part of the value passed to it. For rounding values you would use the `Math` class's `round()` method. All the methods of the `Math` class are discussed in Chapter 13, "The Math Class."

Alternatively, you can use the `parseInt()` and `parseFloat()` methods to afford more control over precision when converting from a string to a number.

Converting to a Number with Precision

ActionScript offers two additional functions for parsing number values from strings: `parseInt()` and `parseFloat()`.

The `parseInt()` function always tries to convert the string value to an integer, even if the string represents a floating point number. The `parseFloat()` function, on the other hand, always attempts to convert the string to a number with the greatest precision possible. If the string represents a floating point number, `parseFloat()` converts it to a floating-point value. If the string represents an integer, `parseFloat()` converts it to an integer.

Here are some examples:

```
var nOne:Number = parseInt("13.3");  // 13
var nTwo:Number = parseFloat("13.3");  // 13.3
var nThree:Number = parseInt("54");  // 54
var nFour:Number = parseFloat("54");  // 54
```

You can also parse number values from strings with bases other than 10 using the `parseInt()` function. The function takes a second optional parameter, allowing you to specify the numeric base:

```
var nOne:Number = parseInt("11", 10);    // 11
var nTwo:Number = parseInt("11", 2);     // 3
var nThree:Number = parseInt("gg", 17);   // 288
```

Furthermore, if you omit the second parameter, ActionScript attempts to parse the number value using the most appropriate base. As you have seen, often this is base-10, but it is not always the case. For instance, octal (base-8) numbers are represented in ActionScript by a leading 0. So any string (representing an integer) that begins with 0 is converted as an octal number. To see how this works, let's first look at how the string `0101` is cast using `Number()`:

```
var nOne:Number = Number("0101");  // 101
```

When you try parsing the same value with `parseInt()`, however, you get very different results:

```
var nOne:Number = parseInt("0101");  // returns 65
```

For this reason, it is usually a good idea to always specify the base of the number you are parsing from a string. Typically, you parse number values from strings returned from a server, so the values and formats are unknown. It is much simpler to just specify the base (probably base-10, in most cases) than to worry about invalid return values.

Tip

You can also convert hexadecimal string representations to numbers using `parseInt()` and `Number()`. For example:

```
var nColorValue:Number = parseInt("0xFF0000");
```

This technique can be particularly useful for converting user-entered hexadecimal strings to their correct numeric equivalents.

Detecting When a Number Is Not a Number

There are times when numbers are not numbers at all. You saw in the previous section that sometimes when a string cannot be parsed to return a number value, the functions simply return the special `NaN` value. Also, in cases of division by 0, the returned value is `NaN`. It is a good idea to check for this unexpected result whenever you are parsing numbers from strings. If it goes unnoticed, it can result in a whole set of errors.

The way to check for `NaN` values is to use the `isNaN()` function. The function takes a single parameter (the value in question) and returns a Boolean value — `true` if the value is not a number or `false` if the value is a number. Here is an example of how to use the `isNaN()` function to verify the values parsed from a string:

```
var sValue:String = "abc";
if (isNaN(sValue)){
    trace("not a number!");
}
else{
    trace("number!");
}
```

Dealing with Infinite Values

There are times when values are recognized by ActionScript as numbers, but the values are out of the range that ActionScript can understand. This can result in undesirable results if not caught.

Flash uses the constants `Number.POSITIVE_INFINITY` and `Number.NEGATIVE_INFINITY` to represent the positive and negative numbers that are out of the range of acceptable values. You can use these constants in your code if you want to represent infinite numbers. But more often than not, you want to detect and catch infinite values rather than intentionally work with them. ActionScript provides a built-in function that enables you to determine whether a value is within the valid range of numbers. The `isFinite()` function takes a parameter (the value to be tested) and returns a Boolean value. It returns `false` if the number is out of range (not finite, or infinite) or `true` if the value is within the valid range.

```
trace(isFinite(10));  // Displays: true
isFinite(Number.POSITIVE_INFINITY);   // Displays: false
```

Handling Minimum and Maximum Values

There are limits to how large and how small the number values that ActionScript works with can be. The largest number value is 1.79769313486231e+308, and the smallest value is 4.94065645841247e-324. If you are like most people, you probably are not going to remember those values off the top of your head. Therefore, ActionScript has two built-in constants with those values. They are `Number.MAX_VALUE` for the largest number value and `Number.MIN_VALUE` for the smallest value.

It is a good idea to use these properties to make sure that the numbers you are working with in your scripts are all within the acceptable range.

The `MAX_VALUE` and `MIN_VALUE` properties hold the largest and smallest possible *positive* values for numbers in ActionScript. The largest and smallest *negative* values for numbers are the negative counterparts:

```
-Number.MAX_VALUE;
-Number.MIN_VALUE;
```

Working with Number Instances

For the most part, when you work with numbers in ActionScript, you work with primitive numbers instead of instances of the `Number` class. However, you *can* create instances of the `Number` class using the constructor as follows:

```
var nInstance:Number = new Number(primitiveVal);
```

In most situations, there are no advantages to creating an instance of the `Number` class versus just simply working with a number primitive. The primary situation in which it is advantageous to create a `Number` instance is when you want to create a string that represents the number in a nondecimal base . . . for example, if you want to display a numeric value in hexa-decimal format.

The `toString()` method of the `Number` class is overloaded so that you can specify a radix. The default value, if none is specified, is 10. But if you specify 16, for example, Flash generates a hexadecimal string representation of the number. Here is an example:

```
var nVal:Number = new Number(123);
trace(nVal.toString(16));  // Displays: 7b
```

Creating a NumberPlus Class

The built-in Number class does not, as you have just seen, provide much additional functionality. You may find it useful to create a custom NumberPlus class that extends the Number class and adds some additional functionality such as a method to create a currency formatted string or a zero fill string. In order to accomplish this, complete the following steps:

1. Create a new AS document.

2. Add the following code to the document:

```
class NumberPlus extends Number {


  function NumberPlus() {
    if(arguments.length == 0) {
      super();
    }
    else {
      super(arguments[0]);
    }
  }

  public function toCurrencyFormat(sSymbol:String):String {
    sSymbol = (sSymbol == undefined) ? "$" : sSymbol;
    var nVal:Number = this.valueOf();
    nVal = nVal * 100;
    nVal = Math.round(nVal);
    nVal = nVal / 100;
    var sVal:String = String(nVal);
    var aValParts:Array = sVal.split(".");
    if(aValParts.length == 1) {
      return (sSymbol + aValParts[0] + ".00");
    }
    var npCoins:NumberPlus = new NumberPlus(aValParts[1]);
    return (sSymbol + aValParts[0] + "." + npCoins.toZeroFill());
  }

  public function toZeroFill(nDigits:Number):String {
    nDigits = (nDigits == undefined) ? 2 : nDigits;
    var sVal:String = this.toString();
    if(sVal.length >= nDigits) {
      return sVal;
    }
    for(var i:Number = sVal.length; i < nDigits; i++) {
      sVal = "0" + sVal;
    }
    return sVal;
  }
}
```

3. Save the document to your Flash global classpath as NumberPlus.as.

Once you have created the NumberPlus class, you can test its functionality with the following code in a new Flash document (FLA file):

```
var npCurrency:NumberPlus = new NumberPlus(1.23456);
trace(npCurrency.toCurrencyFormat()); // Displays: $1.23

var npForZeroFill:NumberPlus = new NumberPlus(123);
trace(npForZeroFill.toZeroFill(6));  // Displays: 000123
```

We'd like to know what you thought about this chapter. Visit www.flashsupport.com/feedback to fill out an online form with your comments.

Summary

- ✦ Numbers can be integers (whole numbers) or floating-point values (fractional numbers).
- ✦ ActionScript can understand number values in bases other than 10—from base-2 to base-36.
- ✦ You can convert a string value to a number value by casting or with the parseInt() and parseFloat() functions. Only parseInt() allows you to specify a base (for non-base-10 values) for the conversion.
- ✦ When ActionScript attempts to work with a value that it cannot recognize as a number, it assigns it a NaN value (not a number). You can test for NaN using the isNaN() function.

CHAPTER 13

The Math Class

✦ ✦ ✦ ✦

In This Chapter

Discovering when to use math in your Flash applications

Making code more readable using with statements

Generating random numbers

Working with trigonometric functions

Working with additional constants and methods of the Math class

✦ ✦ ✦ ✦

If you tend to shy away from anything with the word "math" in it, you're not alone. It brings up painful memories of high school algebra classes, perhaps. But by not delving deeper into the `Math` class and the use of math in your animations, you are cheating yourself out of some powerful techniques. This chapter gently guides you through using math in your Flash applications.

As you have already seen, ActionScript operators take care of all the fundamental mathematical operations such as addition, subtraction, multiplication, and division. The `Math` class, therefore, does not concern itself with such things. As you will learn in this chapter, you can use the `Math` class to generate random numbers, perform trigonometric or exponential functions, and much more.

Performing ActionScript Math

You might be asking yourself, "What in the world could I ever use math for in Flash?" Well, as you will see in this chapter, you can do some pretty amazing stuff using math to power your Flash movies. Of course, it is not appropriate in every scenario. But if you want to create a project that can calculate areas of objects or even a simple interest-bearing account, you need the `Math` class. But what is even more important is how you can use Flash in your movies to create visual effects. Animations can occur on mathematically determined paths. And the `Math` class is key when you want to create artwork with the Drawing API (see Chapter 10).

Physics studies how things move, among other things. And at the heart of physics (at least Newtonian physics) is mathematics. There is no way around it. So, if you want to move things in your Flash movie—controlling them with ActionScript—and you want to bring more life into them, you need to master how to use mathematics in your code.

In this chapter, you will see how to use the properties and methods of the `Math` class in your Flash movies. It is not enough just to know which method to use to take one number to the power of another. You need to know how to apply it in the context of your Flash movie.

Learning About ActionScript Math

As with several other classes in ActionScript, `Math` is a static class. This means that you never instantiate `Math` objects. You never create a `Math` object using `new` and a `Math` constructor method. Instead, you access the properties and methods directly from the class:

```
Math.propertyOrMethod;
```

This makes sense when you look at the functionality that the `Math` class makes available. The `Math` class essentially does little more than group together a bunch of related mathematical functions and constants. There would not be a need to create multiple instances of `Math` objects simply to find the cosine of an angle, for instance.

Utilizing the with Statement to Make Code More Readable

When you work with the `Math` class, it is not uncommon to use it many consecutive times, accessing various properties and methods. For instance:

```
var hyp = 10;
var angle = 60;
var radians = (Math.PI * angle)/180;
var yCoor = hyp * Math.sin(radians);
var xCoor = hyp * Math.cos(radians);
```

In just that short example, the `Math` class was used three times. You can save yourself a lot of typing and make your code more readable simply by using the `with` statement around the whole block of statements. In doing so, ActionScript assumes the `Math` part of any operand:

```
with(Math){
  var hyp = 10;
  var angle = 60;
  var radians = (PI * angle)/180;
  var yCoor = hyp * sin(radians);
  var xCoor = hyp * cos(radians);
}
```

This example yields the same result as the previous, but it is a bit easier to read. Using the `with` statement is entirely optional, however. It provides no additional functionality. The idea is that it simply saves you from having to type and read `Math` over and over again for a block of code.

Working with the Math Constants

There are a handful of mathematical constants you can access directly from the `Math` class. Table 13-1 shows a list of the properties and their values.

Table 13-1: Math Constants

Property	*Value*	*Description*
`E`	~2.718	Base of natural logarithm
`LN10`	~2.302	Natural logarithm of 10

Property	*Value*	*Description*
`LN2`	~0.693	Natural logarithm of 2
`LOG10E`	~0.434	Base-10 logarithm of E
`LOG2E`	~1.442	Base-2 logarithm of E
`PI`	~3.142	π
`SQRT1_2`	~0.707	Square root of ½
`SQRT2`	~1.414	Square root of 2

The `Math` class constants are the values of frequently used numbers in mathematics. However, with the exception of `PI`, it would be entirely possible to obtain the rest of the values by means of the methods of the `Math` class. That fact, along with the fact that the value π happens to be central to a great many operations, makes `PI` perhaps the most important of the properties of the `Math` class.

Finding Absolute Values

The absolute value method `abs()` takes a single parameter—a number. It returns the distance of that number from 0. In other words, any positive value returns itself. Any negative value returns itself negated (made positive).

It can be useful to use `abs()`for determining whether a value is between a positive and negative counterpart. For example, the following `if` statement

```
if(nVal < 10 && nVal > -10) {
  // Code goes here.
}
```

can be rewritten in the following way using the abs() method:

```
if(Math.abs(nVal) < 10) {
  // Code goes here.
}
```

Rounding and Truncating Numbers

The three methods, `round()`, `ceiling()`, and `floor()`, are quick and easy ways to ensure that you are always working with an integer value. There are plenty of times when this is important. For instance, when instructing a timeline to go to a frame number, you must specify an integer value. After all, there is not a 23.232 frame!

Each of these three methods takes one parameter—a number value to be converted to an integer. The `round()` method is the function that should seem most familiar to you. If you think back to grade school math, you can probably recall having to round numbers. The idea is that the initial value (the parameter) is converted into the integer value nearest to it. In other words, if the starting value is `n.5` or greater, where `n` is the integer part of the value, the `round()` method returns `n+1`. If the starting value is less than `n.5`, the method returns `n`. For example:

```
trace(Math.round(5.75));  // Displays: 6
trace(Math.round(93.3));  // Displays: 93
```

On the other hand, there are times when you will want to find the next-nearest higher or next-nearest lower integer value for a number. In these cases, you will want to use the `ceil()` or `floor()` methods of the `Math` class.

The `ceil()` method returns the next-highest integer value of the number passed it as an argument. If the initial value is an integer already, the method returns the same number. Otherwise, it returns the integer part of the number plus one:

```
trace(Math.ceil(5.75));  // Displays: 6
trace(Math.ceil(93.3));  // Displays: 94
trace(Math.ceil(93));  // Displays: 93
```

The `floor()` method is the counterpart to `ceil()`. But rather than return the next highest integer, it returns the next-lowest integer. Just like `ceil()`, if the value passed to the method is already an integer, it returns the same number. Otherwise, it returns the integer part of the value:

```
trace(Math.floor(5.75));  // Displays: 5
trace(Math.floor(93.3));  // Displays: 93
trace(Math.floor(93));  // Displays: 93
```

The methods `round()`, `ceil()`, and `floor()` all have a great many applications within your ActionScript code. You should use these methods any time you want to ensure that you are working with a whole number value. For example, if you are performing math operations on values representing people, you likely want to make sure that you end up with a whole number value. If you created a contest that allowed 8.3 people to win, it could prove problematic.

You can also use these methods to round or truncate to decimal place values. The basic idea is to first multiply the value you want to round, or truncate by 10 to the power of the number of desired decimal places. For example, if you want to end up with two decimal places you should multiply the number by 100. Then, use the `round()`, `ceil()`, or `floor()` method (depending on what kind of operation you want to perform). Last, divide the value by the same number you initially used to multiply. Here is an example:

```
var nValue:Number = 6.39639;
nValue *= 100;
nValue = Math.floor(nValue);
nValue /= 100;
trace(nValue);  // Displays: 6.39
```

Generating Random Numbers

Creating random numbers in an application is an important feature. It allows for games to vary with each playing. It is an essential part of any card game or casino-style game. You might even come up with applications for randomness in controlling animations. Whatever your application of randomness, you need to learn how to work with the `random()` method of the `Math` class.

The random() method is the only method of the Math class that does not take any parameters. The method always returns a floating-point value between 0 and 0.999999, inclusive. Although this may not immediately seem useful, consider that you can simply multiply the returned value by any other number you want to yield a value between 0 and that number. A general formula for this is:

```
var randomFloat:Number = Math.random() * n;
```

where n is the highest possible value you want to work with. So, if you want to work with a random number between 0 and 45, you can use the following statement:

```
var randomFloat:Number = Math.random() * 45;
```

But what if you want to generate a random number within a range that does not start with 0? The answer: Just add the starting value to the end of the equation. So if you want to work with a range of numbers between 20 and 30, first figure what the size of the range is (10) and then the starting point (20), and put it together:

```
var randomFloat:Number = (Math.random() * 10) + 20;
```

But in many cases, you will want to work with integer values. As you can see, none of the examples so far can guarantee an integer value. For instance, the previous line of code can generate a value of 20, 25, or 30; but it can also generate a value of 23.345, 26.102, or 29.0004. This is no good if you want to use the random number to control something that requires an integer value. But if you combine this random() method with the floor() method, you can achieve exactly that goal.

The technique is very similar to creating a random floating point number. Now, you'll use the floor() method to truncate the random number, thus ensuring an integer. Here is an example:

```
var randomInt:Number = Math.floor(Math.random()*10);
```

In this example, the right side of the expression returns a random integer value between 0 and 9. Remember that a range from 0 to 9 is a range of 10 possible values. If you want to generate a range of 10 values starting with 1, you can use the following code:

```
var randomInt:Number = Math.floor(Math.random()*10) + 1;
```

At this point, you might be asking, "Why use floor()? Why not use round()?" Those are good questions. By using the floor() method you can ensure that the randomness is equally distributed. If you use round(), the likelihood of the minimum or maximum values in the range being generated is only half the chance of any other number in the range.

To give you an idea of how you might use random numbers in your movies, consider the scenario of a game program that uses dice. If you are working with one six-sided die, you want to generate a random number between 1 and 6 each time a button is pressed:

```
mcRollDice.onRelease = function():Void {
  var nValue:Number = Math.floor(Math.random() * 6) + 1;
}
```

Finding the Greater or Lesser of Two Numbers

In some cases, you want to compare two values and work with either the greater or the lesser of the two. An example is a comparison between two test scores, in which you want a simple and fast way to choose the higher of the two. For these cases, there are the max() and min()

methods, respectively. Each method simply takes the two values to be compared and then returns one of those values. In the case of `max()`, the maximum of the two values is returned. In the case of `min()`, the minimum value is returned.

```
trace(Math.min(25, 2));  // Displays: 2
trace(Math.max(25, 2));  // Displays: 25
```

Working with Exponents and Square Roots

Arguably one of the most important theorems in mathematics is the Pythagorean Theorem, named for the Greek mathematician who discovered it. Basically, it states that for any right triangle (a triangle with a 90-degree angle, as you can see in Figure 13-1), the sum of the square of the two adjacent sides between which the right angle is formed is equal to the square of the hypotenuse (the side opposite the right angle). In other words:

$a^2 + b^2 = c^2$

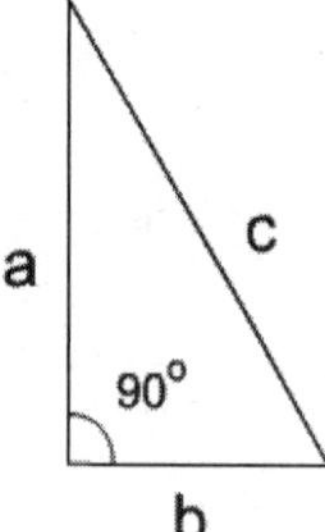

Figure 13-1: The sides of a right triangle

This is enormously powerful when you are working in a coordinate system such as Flash. It means that given any two of the sides of a right triangle, you can find the value of the other (and the angles between, as you will learn later). "But why would this possibly be of any importance?" you ask.

Simple. Imagine that you want to move something a fixed distance in a diagonal direction. You are not given any methods for the `MovieClip` object that allow you to move objects in diagonals. In fact, you can move objects only in the x and y directions. But do not lose hope. Given that you know the hypotenuse and one other side of the right triangle formed by the diagonal along which you want to move your object, you can solve for the missing side.

One way to work with exponents (such as squaring a number) and square roots in ActionScript is with the `pow()`and `sqrt()` methods of the `Math class`. The `pow()` method takes two parameters—the value to be raised to a power and the power to which to raise the first number (the exponent):

```
Math.pow(val, exponent);
```

The `sqrt()` method takes one parameter—the value whose square root you want:

```
Math.sqrt(val);
```

You can use both of these methods together to work with the Pythagorean Theorem, as in the following example:

```
/*
We know the hypotenuse and the one side of the triangle,
and want to find the value of the third side.
*/
var nHyp:Number = 5;
var nA:Number = 3;
var nB:Number = undefined;  // unknown

// Given that a^2 + b^2 = hyp^2
nB = Math.sqrt(Math.pow(nHyp, 2) - Math.pow(nA, 2));
```

You might notice that this code was a bit unreadable. One way to make it much easier to read is to use the `with` statement trick. The last line of the previous example can be cleaned up as follows:

```
with(Math){
   nB = sqrt(pow(nHyp, 2) - pow(nA, 2));
}
```

Of course, solving for an unknown side of a triangle is not the only application of the `pow()` and `sqrt()` methods. But when working with a Cartesian coordinate system (a simple x and y grid as in Flash), this can turn out to be a really useful tool for plotting coordinates of `MovieClip` objects.

You might also want to use the `pow()` method when working with any kind of interest-bearing account or value. It is entirely possible that you might want to do such calculations for real-life scenarios or maybe even as part of a role-playing or strategy game you design. The calculation for finding compound interest is the following:

$$newValue = originalValue * (1 + rate/cp)^{(cp*t)}$$

In this equation, `cp` is the number of compounding periods per year (12 if it is compounded every month), and `t` is the number of years. This sort of equation can be represented in ActionScript in the following way:

```
var nNew = nOrig * Math.pow((1 + nRate/nCp), (nCp*nT));
```

Using Trigonometric Functions in ActionScript

Chances are that you never thought you would actually want to apply anything you learned in trigonometry. We hope this section will make you rethink that. You can do some powerful things with basic trigonometric functions.

Let's start out with a simple example. You know how to move `MovieClip` objects along a motion guide using Flash's authoring tools. But what about using ActionScript to do it? Of course, moving a `MovieClip` object along a straight line is no big challenge. But how do you attempt to move it along a path in the shape of a circle, for example?

This is exactly where the `Math` class's trigonometric methods become really useful. But first, you have to know some of the basics of trigonometry and circles. There are a few fundamental properties of any circle. First, you must have an origin for the circle: a point directly in the center. And second, you must have a *radius:* the length from the center to the edge of the circle. If you take two axes, one for y and one for x, that run perpendicular to one another and intersect at the center of your circle, you see that the axes always form a right triangle, as shown in Figure 13-2. The lengths of the sides (a and b) are the same as the length of the radius of the circle.

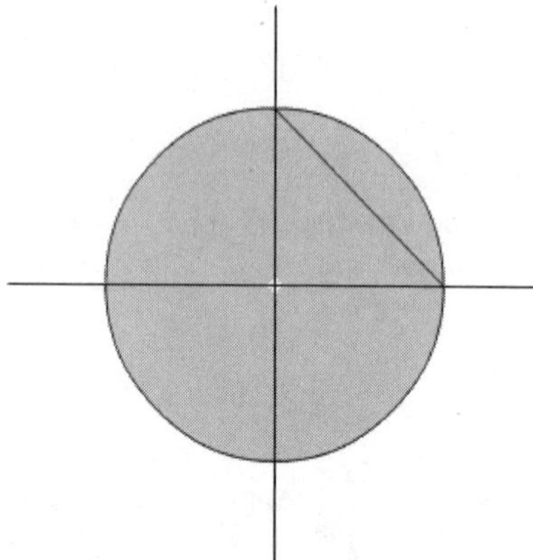

Figure 13-2: The axes intersect at a circle's center to form a right triangle.

When you have a triangle, especially a right triangle, some really interesting formulas surface that enable you to derive almost any unknown value when given at least two of the others. When you are working with a circle, one value remains constant: the radius, or the hypotenuse of the triangle. The thing that varies is the angle (θ) between the radius and the x axis that runs through the center of the circle. But if you know these two values for a right triangle, you can derive the x and y coordinates using the following formulas:

```
sin(θ) = y/hypotenuse
cos(θ) = x/hypotenuse
```

Or in more useable format:

```
y = sin(θ) * hypotenuse
x = cos(θ) * hypotenuse
```

Therefore, if you know the radius of a circular path, and you continually increment the angle value, you can form right triangles over and over, and derive the corresponding x and y coordinates, thus moving an object around in a circular path.

There is only one little catch when doing this in ActionScript—the `Math` class trigonometric methods work with *radians*, not degrees. A radian is the measure of an angle in terms of π. But don't worry; there is an easy conversion between degrees and radians:

```
radians = (π * degrees)/180
```

After you have a radian measurement for the angle, you can then use the trigonometric methods of the `Math` class. Here is the basic syntax for `sin()`, `cos()`, and `tan()`:

```
Math.sin(radians)
Math.cos(radians)
Math.tan(radians)
```

This next example (Listing 13-1) shows how to revolve a `MovieClip` object (on the main timeline) around a circular path.

First, to make it easier, you want to adjust the `_x` and `_y` properties of the `_root` object, as well as set up a few properties of the revolving object `mcBall`.

Listing 13-1: Using Trigonometric Functions to Move MovieClip Objects

```
// Place 0,0 of the _root object at the center of the stage
this._x = 275;
this._y = 200;

// Create revolving object and its properties. We'll use the
// attachMovie() method to add a MovieClip to the
// stage from a library symbol with a linkage id of
// "CircleSymbol". For more information on attachMovie()
// see Chapter 9.
this.attachMovie("CircleSymbol", "mcBall", 0);

// Add two custom properties to the MovieClip instance.
// The pathRadius determines the radius of the circle path
// along which the MovieClip should move. The degrees
// should be initialized to 0.
mcBall.pathRadius = 100;
mcBall.degrees = 0;

// Define a custom method that we'll call repeatedly using
// setInterval().
mcBall.moveInCircle = function():Void{

  // Use a with statement to make the code simpler to
  // read.
  with(Math){
    // Get radian value for degree measurement.
    var nRadians:Number = this.degrees*(PI/180);

    // Derive x and y coordinates.
    var nX = this.pathRadius * sin(nRadians);
    var nY = this.pathRadius * cos(nRadians);
  }

  // Move the object.
  this._x = nX;
```

Continued

Listing 13-1 *(continued)*

```
    this._y = nY;

    // Increment degrees.
    this.degrees++;

    // Update the view on stage.
    updateAfterEvent();
  };

  // Use setInterval() to call the moveInCircle() method of the
  // MovieClip object repeatedly.
  setInterval(mcBall, "moveInCircle", 10);
```

This is just one example of how to use trigonometric functions in your animations.

For the sake of thoroughness, you should also be familiar with the inverse trigonometric functions also available as methods of the `Math` class. ActionScript provides four methods for inverse trigonometric functions: `asin()`, `acos()`, `atan()`, and `atan2()`. The first three take a parameter (a sine value, a cosine value, and a tangent value, respectively) and return a value of the corresponding angle as measured radians:

```
Math.asin(sineValue)
Math.acos(cosineValue)
Math.atan(tangentValue)
```

And the fourth inverse trigonometric function, `atan2()`, takes two parameters (an x and y coordinate) and returns the angle formed by the right triangle measured in radians:

```
Math.atan2(x, y)
```

Using inverse trigonometric functions is really useful if, for example, you know an angle's sine, cosine, or tangent; or you know the x and y values of the sides of a triangle, and want to know the angle measurement. You can use this in real situations if you know, for example, a `MovieClip` object's position and you want to rotate another `MovieClip` relative to the first.

Calculating Natural Logarithms and Exponentials

The `exp()` and `log()` methods of the `Math` class are probably most suited for things other than animation. Natural logarithms (logarithms with base e) and their counterpart exponential functions are often used for plotting graphs. Don't let that discourage you from using them in creative ways to control your animations, but also be aware that they can serve other purposes.

First of all, you need to know what the two methods are. The `exp()` method requires one parameter: a number. It then raises e (`Math.E`) to the power of that number. In other words:

```
Math.exp(5) == Math.pow(Math.E, 5)
```

The `log()` method takes one parameter as well: a number. It then returns the natural logarithm of that number:

```
Math.log(number);
```

These two methods are related in the following way:

```
Math.log(x) = y
```

and:

```
Math.exp(y) = x
```

You can use these types of methods to plot graphs of stock market trends. It is common practice to plot the natural log of the indices versus time. Therefore, if you receive stock market data from, let's say, an XML document, you can use the `log()` method of the `Math class` to plot the values on a graph.

There are some more powerful techniques for which both the `exp()` and the `log()` methods are useful. Although probably not something you will need in all your Flash movies, you can use the `log()` method to approximate integrals and derivatives. And you can use the `exp()` method to approximate hyperbolic trigonometric functions. These sorts of approximations can be useful for finding areas under curves or for finding values in physics equations (such as the velocity at a point in time given a constant acceleration).

Creating MathUtils

Because are likely to want to convert between radian and degrees relatively frequently (that is, if you plan to animate using ActionScript), you might find it helpful to create a custom `MathUtils` class containing `degToRad()`, `radToDeg()`, and `randomInt()` methods. In order to accomplish such a class, complete the following steps:

1. Create a new AS file.
2. In the AS file, add the following code:

```
class MathUtils {
  public static function degToRad(nDeg:Number):Number {
    var nRad:Number = (Math.PI * nDeg)/180;
    return nRad;
  }

  public static function radToDeg(nRad:Number):Number {
    var nDeg = (nRad * 180)/Math.PI;
    return nDeg;
  }

  public static function randomInt(nMinVal:Number,
                                   nMaxVal:Number):Number
  {
    var nRange:Number = nMaxVal - nMinVal + 1;
    var nRandomFloat:Number = (Math.random() * nRange) + nMinVal;
    return Math.floor(nRandomFloat);
  }

}
```

3. Save the file as MathUtils.as in your global Flash classpath.

Once you have created the MathUtils class, you can use the two static methods to convert between radians and degrees. Here are some examples:

```
trace(MathUtils.degToRad(90));
trace(MathUtils.radToDeg(Math.PI));
trace(MathUtils.randomInt(5, 10));
```

Using Math to Draw and Animate

In this simple example, you'll use ActionScript to generate some random circles that animate by moving across the stage. This exercise relies on the custom DrawingUtils class that you created in Chapter 10. If you have not yet created the DrawingUtils class you have at least two options:

- ✦ Complete the instructions in Chapter 10 for creating the DrawingUtils class.
- ✦ Copy the DrawingUtils.as file from the CD-ROM to a directory in your global Flash classpath. (For more information on classpaths, see Chapter 7.)

Once you have the DrawingUtils class installed, complete the following steps:

1. Open a new Flash document (FLA) and save it as animatingCircles001.fla.
2. Add the following code to the first frame of the default layer on the main timeline:

```
// Define a function that creates the circles. The
// function takes a parameter specifying how many circles
// to create.
function createCircles(nHowMany):Void {

  // Get the width and height of the stage (see Chapter
  // 20 for more information on the Stage class) and
  // assign them to variables.
  var nStageWidth:Number = Stage.width;
  var nStageHeight:Number = Stage.height;

  // Declare some variables.
  var duDrawer:DrawingUtils = null;
  var mcCircle:MovieClip = null;
  var nRandomRadius:Number = null;

  // Utilize a for statement to loop the code for
  // making the circles as many times as nHowMany.
  for(var i:Number = 0; i < nHowMany; i++) {

    // Create a new MovieClip instance, and then assign
    // a reference to that MovieClip to the mcCircle
    // variable for convenience.
    this.createEmptyMovieClip("mcCircle" + i, i);
    mcCircle = this["mcCircle" + i];

    // Create a new DrawingUtils instance that targets the
```

```
    // MovieClip instance you just created.
    duDrawer = new DrawingUtils(mcCircle);

    // Set the line style, create a random radius value,
    // and draw the circle.
    duDrawer.setLineStyle(1, 0, 100);
    nRandomRadius = Math.random() * 50 + 10;
    duDrawer.drawCircle(nRandomRadius);

    // In addition to drawing the circle, also draw a
    // radial line so that you can see that the circle
    // is rotating.
    duDrawer.moveTo(0, 0);
    duDrawer.lineTo(0, nRandomRadius);

    // Move the circle to a random location on the stage.
    mcCircle._x = Math.random() * (nStageWidth - 2 *
nRandomRadius) + nRandomRadius;
    mcCircle._y = Math.random() * (nStageHeight - 2 *
nRandomRadius) + nRandomRadius;

    // Assign some properties to the circle MovieClip
    // that it can use internally when the roll() method
    // is invoked.
    mcCircle.radius = nRandomRadius;
    mcCircle.velocity = (Math.random() * 5 + 5)/10;
    mcCircle.stageWidth = nStageWidth;

    // The roll() method is a custom method that will
    // get called on an interval.
    mcCircle.roll = function():Void {

      // Increment the rotation by the velocity/
      this._rotation += this.velocity;

      // Set the x coordinate of the circle to
      // correspond to the amount of rotation.
      this._x += (this.radius * 2 * Math.PI) * ((this.velocity)/360);

      // If the x coordinate is off the stage, then move
      // the circle to the left side of the stage.
      if(this._x - this.radius > this.stageWidth) {
        this._x = -2 * this.radius;
      }

      // Update the view.
      updateAfterEvent();
    };

    // Set the interval.
    setInterval(mcCircle, "roll", 10);
```

```
        }
    }

    // Create a random number and call createCircles().
    var nRandom:Number = Math.floor(Math.random() * 7 + 3);
    createCircles(nRandom);
```

3. Save the document and test the movie.

You should see a random number of circles moving across the stage from left to right. The radii and velocities of the circles are randomized as well. When the circles reach the right side of the stage, they should automatically jump to the left side and start moving across the stage again.

Now you can take a closer look at some of the code from this example:

Within the function, the first thing you want to do is get the current width and height of the stage. You can achieve this with the `Stage.width` and `Stage.height` properties. You assign those values to variables so you can then create the circles within the stage.

```
var nStageWidth:Number = Stage.width;
var nStageHeight:Number = Stage.height;
```

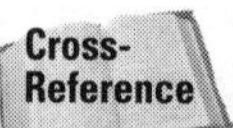

For more information about the `Stage` class, see Chapter 20, "The Stage and ContextMenu Classes."

Next, you declare some variables that are initialized to `null`. These are variables that you will use within the `for` statement. Each variable will be reused, so rather than declaring the variables each time they are used, you can declare them once, outside the `for` statement, and then assign new values repeatedly within the `for` statement.

```
var duDrawer:DrawingUtils = null;
var mcCircle:MovieClip = null;
var nRandomRadius:Number = null;
```

Now, you declare the `for` statement. You want to create as many circles as was specified by the `nHowMany` parameter. So the `for` statement should loop from 0 to less than `nHowMany`.

```
for(var i:Number = 0; i < nHowMany; i++) {
```

Create the new `MovieClip` using the `createEmptyMovieClip()` method. Then, to make it simple to reference the `MovieClip`, you assign it to the `mcCircle` variable. This is not necessary, but it allows you to use `mcCircle` to reference the `MovieClip` rather than `this["mcCircle" + i]`.

```
this.createEmptyMovieClip("mcCircle" + i, i);
mcCircle = this["mcCircle" + i];
```

Once the `MovieClip` is defined, you create a `DrawingUtils` instance that targets the `MovieClip`. Set the line style, create a random radius, and draw the circle:

```
duDrawer = new DrawingUtils(mcCircle);
duDrawer.setLineStyle(1, 0, 100);
nRandomRadius = Math.random() * 50 + 10;
duDrawer.drawCircle(nRandomRadius);
```

You want to be able to see that the circle is rotating as it moves across the stage. A perfect circle rotating does not really look any different from a nonrotating perfect circle. So, in order to be able to see the rotation, you can add a radial line:

```
duDrawer.moveTo(0, 0);
duDrawer.lineTo(0, nRandomRadius);
```

Now, you randomly place the circle on the stage. Here, you want to generate a random number that will place the circle completely on the stage. Because the x and y coordinates of a circle are determined by its center, you need to create a range of possible values that make sure the entire circle is on stage, not just half.

```
    mcCircle._x = Math.random() * (nStageWidth - 2 * nRandomRadius) +
nRandomRadius;
    mcCircle._y = Math.random() * (nStageHeight - 2 * nRandomRadius) +
nRandomRadius;
```

In order to be able to access some values internally to the `MovieClip` object, you need to assign those values to custom properties.

```
mcCircle.radius = nRandomRadius;
mcCircle.velocity = (Math.random() * 5 + 5)/10;
mcCircle.stageWidth = nStageWidth;
```

The `roll()` method is a custom method that's defined here so that each time it is called, it does two things: First it should rotate the circle. Then, it should also move the circle in the x direction. There is a correspondence between the amount that the circle rotates and the amount that it moves in the x direction. This can be determined simply if you keep in mind that the ratio of the amount rotated to the total rotation in a circle (360 degrees) is equal to the ratio of the amount of movement in the x direction to the circumference of the circle:

```
mcCircle.roll = function():Void {
  this._rotation += this.velocity;
  this._x += (this.radius * 2 * Math.PI) * ((this.velocity)/360);
  if(this._x - this.radius > this.stageWidth) {
    this._x = -2 * this.radius;
  }
  updateAfterEvent();
};
```

Next, you want to tell Flash to invoke the `roll()` method at an interval. For this, you call the `setInterval()` action:

```
setInterval(mcCircle, "roll", 10);
```

Once the function has been defined, all that remains is to generate a random number of circles to create, and to call the `createCircles()` function:

```
var nRandom:Number = Math.floor(Math.random() * 7 + 3);
createCircles(nRandom);
```

We'd like to know what you thought about this chapter. Visit `www.flashsupport.com/feedback` to fill out an online form with your comments.

Summary

✦ Math is an essential tool for creating advanced animations and Flash applications. The ActionScript `Math` class provides the advanced mathematical functionality to accommodate these mathematical needs.

✦ `Math` is a static class. Therefore, you never create an instance of the class, but always access the properties (constants) and methods directly from the `Math` class itself.

✦ Because it is common to use many properties and methods of the `Math` class in a single expression, the code can become difficult to read. For this reason, it can be useful to place such expressions within a `with` statement that specifies `Math` as the object being used in all statements.

✦ ✦ ✦

CHAPTER 14

Working with Dates and Times

In This Chapter

Learning about time zones and how your computer keeps track of time

Creating a Date object to work with current, past, and future dates and time

Complete coverage of all the Date methods and constructors

Learning to work with ActionScript's dates and times can benefit you many times over. ActionScript's `Date` class allows you a great deal of control over creating objects that store date and time information. `Date` objects store date information including year, month, date, day, hour, minute, second, and millisecond. You can create a `Date` object for just about any date. Although you could create variables and arrays to accomplish much the same thing, a `Date` object has built-in functionality to make working with dates a bit easier.

Working with Computer Dates

In order to understand `Date` objects, you must first understand three points:

- What time zones are and how they work
- Where Flash retrieves the time and date information
- How Flash calculates time and date information

In the days before computers, telephones, and even trains, time was kept locally, and there was no standardization on a global scale. Each town would keep its own time by setting the clockmaker's clock to 12:00 noon, when the sun was at the center of the sky. This meant that times would vary from town to town. But with the advent of global travel and communications, it became necessary to have some kind of standardization of time internationally. So in the late nineteenth century, the idea of time zones was proposed and quickly adopted. Although not every country and region adheres perfectly to the time zones, the world is divided up into roughly 24 parts—one for each hour in a day. Each zone is one hour ahead of the zone directly to the west. The contiguous states of the United States are divided into four zones. Thus, when it is 12:00 noon in Los Angeles, it is 2:00 in the afternoon in St. Louis or Chicago, and it is 3:00 in the afternoon in New York. Understanding time zones is key to truly understanding `Date` objects.

The description of how time zones work is very simplified. Some areas of the world don't use time as most of the world knows it at all and thus have no need for time zones. Additionally, some areas use time zones that are half an hour apart from other time zones instead of an hour. And lastly, to confuse matters even more, the practice of Daylight Savings Time has been adopted in many places in the world. In those areas, clocks are offset by an hour for approximately half the year. This practice is used in some places and not in others, which means that the difference between some time zones is not always uniform. If a deeper understanding of time zones is important to your movie, you might want to deepen your understanding beyond the extremely simplified explanation given in this chapter.

What Is UTC?

In order to make time zones work, there has to be a standard and center from which all time is based. The center for the Earth's time zones is in Greenwich (pronounced GREN-ich), England. It is known as Greenwich Mean Time, or GMT. However, as time went on, global efforts produced more accurate ways of measuring time — to one-billionth of a second. This new time, though essentially the same as GMT, is called Coordinated Universal Time and is abbreviated UTC.

Coordinated Universal Time is abbreviated UTC, not CUT, because of the way the name originated. At first, the name was Universal Time, abbreviated UT. Variations on Universal Time were abbreviated with numbers to indicate version such as UT0, UT1, UT2, and so on. When the name Coordinated Universal Time was chosen, the abbreviation UTC was agreed upon to adhere to the format of the earlier abbreviations.

UTC is always the reference point for all other time zones. Computers measure time in UTC and then offset the value to account for time zones. For instance, Los Angeles is eight hours behind UTC, so it has an offset of -8.

Computer Time

If you ask yourself where time and date information comes from in your programs, including Flash, it might appear to be a mystery. The answer is that it comes from the computer itself, which keeps track of time in very small fractions of a second in the computer's hardware clock. The computer then has a software clock as part of the operating system (Windows XP, Mac OS X, and so on) that offsets the value from the hardware clock to produce a UTC time and date. Then the software clock also allows you to modify settings such as time zone and daylight savings time. In this way, your computer can display local times and dates, which are more meaningful than UTC times and dates.

This means that Flash has access to both the UTC and the local time of the computer on which the Flash movie is playing. This is a very important point that can cause confusion for beginning programmers. Even though many Flash movies are served from a remote location, the movie itself is played within the Flash Player on a user's local machine. This means that the current dates and times reported by your `Date` objects are based entirely on the user's local settings, hardware, and software. If the user's clock is off, your calculations may not work.

If you intend to use the `Date` object as a timer in your Flash movie, it is best to perform a simple check to make sure that the user's clock is even running! You can do this by querying for the time and then querying again and seeing if there is a difference between the times.

If having accurate current dates is important to the functionality of the Flash movie you are authoring, you can use a slightly advanced technique to compare the value of the user's time to the time on a remote server. If you want to do this, you need to use some kind of server-side scripting together with an XML object, a LoadVars object (both discussed in Chapter 26), or Flash Remoting, discussed in Chapter 35.

ActionScript Time

ActionScript works with all dates in milliseconds. Just as time zones have a point of reference from which they are all derived, so do dates in ActionScript. The point of reference for all dates in ActionScript is January 1, 1970, also called the Epoch, and all dates are measured in milliseconds from that starting date. If you create a Date object that uses the current date of the local computer, it queries the local computer for the date and then converts it to milliseconds from January 1, 1970. The next section discusses in more detail the formatting issues with ActionScript Date objects.

Creating a Date Object

The first thing you need to know when creating a Date object is how to instantiate an object using the Date constructor method. There are several variations on the Date constructor, and your usage depends on what you want to accomplish. Let's look at the options.

Getting the Current Date and Time

If you want to create a Date object that contains the current local date and time, simply use the Date constructor method with no parameters. Here is an example:

```
var dNow:Date = new Date();
```

This constructor captures the time of the local computer to the precision of a millisecond.

Even though the precision of the time returned by a Date object is milliseconds, it does not mean that it is necessarily accurate to the same degree. Precision merely refers to how small of a unit is used in the measurement. Hence, milliseconds are more precise than seconds. However, the clock interrupt of a computer often varies the value returned by up to 55 milliseconds or so. For this reason, it is best to not depend on a reading from the Date object for accuracy beyond seconds.

You can verify that the preceding code did, in fact, create an object that represents the current date and time by using trace():

```
var dNow:Date = new Date();
trace(dNow.toString());
```

You should see a string representation of the current date and time in the Output panel if you test the preceding code. The string will look something like the following, but, of course, your exact values will be different:

```
Sun Jul 20 20:07:48 GMT-0700 2003
```

This is the default manner in which Flash converts a Date object to a string. Later in this chapter you'll see how you can format your Date object output differently.

In many situations, it can be useful to create an object that contains the current local date and time. The following are a few such circumstances:

- ✦ Creating a value to insert into a database when the user registers, makes a purchase, posts a message, and so on.
- ✦ Creating a value to display to the user, showing the current date and/or time.
- ✦ Getting the current date and time to compare with another value. For example, if you want to make sure that a user's account has not yet expired.

Making a Date Based on Epoch Milliseconds

You can also create `Date` objects that represent specific times other than the current time. There are two basic ways to accomplish this with the `Date` constructor. Let's first look at how you can create a new `Date` object based on Epoch milliseconds. If you recall from the earlier discussion, the Epoch milliseconds are the number of milliseconds from midnight of January 1, 1970 to the time and date you are referencing. Now, of course, it is not common for humans to think in terms of Epoch milliseconds, and if we asked you the Epoch millisecond value for your birthday it is doubtful that you will know. But computers do tend to think in terms of Epoch time—be it milliseconds or, in some cases, seconds. For this reason, it is a convenient way for your Flash application to communicate with other applications. This is especially true if you are using server-side scripts and databases with your Flash application, and you are using either a `LoadVars` or an `XML` object to load and send your data.

In order to create a `Date` object based on Epoch milliseconds, use the following syntax:

```
var dDateObj:Date = new Date(epochMilliseconds);
```

Typically, when you instantiate a `Date` object using Epoch milliseconds, you'll be retrieving the milliseconds value from another source. For the purposes of this example, you can just hard-code a value:

```
var dSometime:Date = new Date(1058756698625);
trace(dSometime.toString());
```

Depending on your local time zone offset value, the Output panel will display something very close to the following:

```
Sun Jul 20 20:04:58 GMT-0700 2003
```

Making a Date Based on Year or Month

Another option for the constructor is to pass it numeric values indicating the year, month, and so on, for the date and time you want to represent. The basic syntax for this option is as follows:

```
var dDateObj:Date = new Date(year, month, date, hour,
 minute, second, millisecond);
```

Each of the parameters expects a number—an integer, to be exact—value, as shown in Table 14-1.

✦ The year parameter can be any full four-digit year, such as 1875 or 2675. You can also pass the Date constructor any integer value from 0 to 99, and ActionScript will interpret it to mean a date from 1900 to 1999. This means that a value of 100 will produce a Date object for the year 100, not 2000; but a value of 99 will result in a Date object for the year 1999, not 99. If you want to work with dates before the year 99, you need to actually pass the constructor function a negative value for the year parameter. The value you pass will be subtracted from 1900, the reference point for ActionScript dates with two-digit year values. Passing a value of -1850 creates a Date object for the year 50.

✦ Perhaps the most likely place for an error when creating a Date object is in passing the correct month value. Most cultures represent the months numerically, starting with 1 and ending with 12. Thus, it is natural enough to think of January as the month with the index of 1. But remember from the discussion of arrays that ActionScript is a 0-indexing language. Therefore, when creating a Date object, January is represented by the number value 0; the last month, December, is represented by the number value 11.

✦ The date parameter is the parameter that refers to the day of the month. If for no other reason but to make it confusing, date is the only property of the Date object that has a 1-index. Therefore, the first day of the month is represented by the number value of 1. The last possible day in any month is 31, although some months obviously do not have 31 days. For example, the last day in February will have a value of 28 on non–leap years and 29 on leap years.

✦ The hour, minute, second, and millisecond values are integer values used for the time of day component of the Date object. Each of these value ranges starts with 0, not 1. Therefore, with 24 hours in a day, the first hour, midnight, is represented by the number value 0, and the last hour, 11 p.m., is represented by the number value 23. The values for minute and second range from 0 to 59, and millisecond values range from 0 to 999.

Table 14-1: Date Constructor Parameters

Parameter	*Meaning*	*Value Range*
year	Calendar year	0–99, 99 and up, -1801 and down
month	Integer index of month	0 to 11
date	Integer index of day of month	1 to 31
hour	Integer index of hour in day	0 to 23
minute	Integer index of minute in hour	0 to 59
second	Integer index of second in minute	0 to 59
millisecond	Integer index of millisecond in second	0 to 999

You must always specify at least the year and month when creating a Date object in this way. Any of the subsequent values that you leave undefined will default to 0 (or 1 in the case of the date parameter). Here are a few examples:

```
var dSometime1:Date = new Date(2003, 6);
trace(dSometime1.toString());
var dSometime2:Date = new Date(2003, 6, 21);
trace(dSometime2.toString());
var dSometime3:Date = new Date(2003, 6, 21, 6);
trace(dSometime3.toString());
var dSometime4:Date = new Date(2003, 6, 21, 6, 55);
trace(dSometime4.toString());
var dSometime5:Date = new Date(2003, 6, 21, 6, 55, 33);
trace(dSometime5.toString());
var dSometime6:Date = new Date(2003, 6, 21, 6, 55, 33, 24);
trace(dSometime6.toString());
```

The Output panel will display the following:

```
Tue Jul 1 00:00:00 GMT-0700 2003
Mon Jul 21 00:00:00 GMT-0700 2003
Mon Jul 21 06:00:00 GMT-0700 2003
Mon Jul 21 06:55:00 GMT-0700 2003
Mon Jul 21 06:55:33 GMT-0700 2003
Mon Jul 21 06:55:33 GMT-0700 2003
```

As with all examples in this chapter, if you test this code, you might get slightly different values due to time zone offsets.

You might notice that the last two strings are the same, even though one specified the milliseconds and the other did not. The actual values are different by 24 milliseconds. The string that Flash generates with the `toString()` method does not display to the precision of milliseconds.

When you create a new `Date` object in this way, make sure that you always include at least both the year and month parameters. If you specify only one parameter, Flash interprets that to mean the Epoch milliseconds. For example:

```
var dSometime:Date = new Date(2003);
trace(dSometime.toString());
```

You might expect this to create a date and time representing the year 2003. But, instead, because Flash interprets the parameter to mean Epoch milliseconds, the Output panel displays something like the following (depending on your time zone offset):

```
Wed Dec 31 16:00:02 GMT-0800 1969
```

Working with Date Objects

The ActionScript `Date` class has a rather daunting number of methods available to it, as shown in Table 14-2. Although at first glance, the methods can appear a bit overwhelming, don't worry. At a closer look, you notice that these methods can be easily grouped into only four categories. The first group of methods is called `get` because the method names all start with the word "get," and these methods are responsible for *getting* the values of the properties of the `Date` object from which they are invoked. The second group of methods is called `set` because the method names all start with the word "set," and these methods are responsible for *setting* the values of the properties of the `Date` object from which they are invoked. The third group of methods is called inherited because they are the methods inherited from the `Object` object. And finally, there is the one static method that is invoked directly from the `Date` class.

Table 14-2: Date Object Methods

Category	*Method*	*Description*
`get`	`getFullYear()`	Returns four-digit value of year
	`getYear()`	Returns integer value of year relative to 1900
	`getMonth()`	Returns integer value of month of year
	`getDate()`	Returns integer value of day of month
	`getDay()`	Returns integer value of day of week
	`getHours()`	Returns integer value of hour of day
	`getMinutes()`	Returns integer value of minutes of hour
	`getSeconds()`	Returns integer value of seconds of minute
	`getMilliseconds()`	Returns integer value of milliseconds of second
	`getTime()`	Returns integer value of milliseconds from 1/1/70
	`getTimezoneOffset()`	Returns integer value of minutes offset from UTC
	`getUTCFullYear()`	Returns four-digit value of year
	`getUTCMonth()`	Returns integer value of month of year
	`getUTCDate()`	Returns integer value of day of month
	`getUTCDay()`	Returns integer value of day of week
	`getUTCHours()`	Returns integer value of hour of day
	`getUTCMinutes()`	Returns integer value of minutes of hour
	`getUTCSeconds()`	Returns integer value of seconds of minute
	`getUTCMilliseconds()`	Returns integer value of milliseconds of second
`set`	`setFullYear()`	Sets four-digit value of year
	`setYear()`	Sets integer value of year relative to 1900
	`setMonth()`	Sets integer value of month of year
	`setDate()`	Sets integer value of day of month
	`setHours()`	Sets integer value of hour of day
	`setMinutes()`	Sets integer value of minutes of hour
	`setSeconds()`	Sets integer value of seconds of minute
	`setMilliseconds()`	Sets integer value of milliseconds of second

Continued

Table 14-2 *(continued)*

Category	*Method*	*Description*
	`setTime()`	Sets integer value of milliseconds from 1/1/70
	`setUTCFullYear()`	Sets four-digit value of year
	`setUTCMonth()`	Sets integer value of month of year
	`setUTCDate()`	Sets integer value of day of month
	`setUTCHours()`	Sets integer value of hour of day
	`setUTCMinutes()`	Sets integer value of minutes of hour
	`setUTCSeconds()`	Sets integer value of seconds of minute
	`setUTCMilliseconds()`	Sets integer value of milliseconds of second
`inherited`	`toString()`	Returns the string value of the `Date` object
`static`	`UTC()`	Returns the milliseconds since 1/1/70 for a specified date

For the purposes of most calculations, whether you use UTC or local time is of little importance, as long as you stick with one or the other. But when you need to take into consideration time zone differences, pay attention to which you are using.

get Methods

The `get` methods allow you to retrieve the properties of your `Date` objects. You may notice that the `get` methods include several methods for getting the day of the week. However, notice that there are not any analogous methods in the `set` methods. This is because the day of the week is not an independent variable, so to speak. Its value is determined by the value of the year, month, and date.

Getting the Year

Several methods are available to return the value of your `Date` object's year. If you are working with local time, you can use either `getYear()` or `getFullYear()`. If you need to work with UTC, you can opt for the `getUTCFullYear()` method.

The difference between `getYear()` and `getFullYear()` is that `getYear()` returns an integer representing the difference between the `Date` object's year and the year 1900, whereas `getFullYear()` returns the value of the actual year. For example:

```
var dWhen:Date = new Date(1978, 9, 13);
trace(dWhen.getYear());  // Displays: 78
trace(dWhen.getFullYear());  // Displays: 1978
```

The difference becomes much more apparent when working with dates before 1900. For example:

```
var dThen:Date = new Date(1779, 6, 4);
trace(dThen.getYear());  // Displays: -121
trace(dThen.getFullYear());  // Displays: 1779
```

You can also use getUTCFullYear() to determine the UTC year that corresponds to a given local date. If you want to know what the year in England was when your local time was December 31, 1964 at 8 p.m., you could do the following:

```
var dThen:Date = new Date(1964,11,31, 20, 0, 0, 0);
trace(dThen.getUTCFullYear());
```

Getting the Month

You can return the month value of your Date object with the getMonth() and getUTCMonth() methods. Both methods return an integer from 0 to 11, representing January through December. The getMonth() methods returns the integer value of the local month, whereas the getUTCMonth() method returns the integer value of the corresponding month in UTC.

Getting the Date

You can use the getDate() and getUTCDate() methods to return the values of the local day of the month and the corresponding day of the month UTC, respectively. These values can be integers from 1 to 31. For example:

```
var dThen:Date = new Date(1523, 3, 13);
trace(dThen.getDate());  // Displays: 13
```

Getting the Day

As we mentioned earlier, ActionScript Date objects actually calculate the value of the day of the week based on the year, month, and date values. You cannot set the day value for a Date object, but you can retrieve it using getDay() or getUTCDay(). Both methods return the day of the week as an integer from 0 to 6. A value of 0 corresponds to Sunday, and a value of 6 corresponds to Saturday. Here is an example:

```
var dWhen:Date = new Date(1978, 9, 13, 20);
trace(dWhen.getDay());
trace(dWhen.getUTCDay());
```

The first value that this example will display is a 5 because the day of the week was a Friday. The second value depends on the time zone offset. If my local time zone is on Pacific Standard Time, it will return 6, or Saturday, because the time in Greenwich, England, is eight hours ahead.

Getting the Hours, Minutes, Seconds, and Milliseconds

You can retrieve the hour value of your Date objects using the getHours() and getUTCHours() methods. These methods return integers from 0 to 23 for the local date and the UTC corresponding date, respectively. For example:

```
var dThen:Date = new Date (2727, 9, 27, 5);
trace(dThen.getHours());  // Displays: 5;
trace(dThen.getUTCHours());  // Displays: 5 + offset
```

In much the same way, you can use getMinutes(), getUTCMinutes(), getSeconds(), getUTCSeconds(), getMilliseconds(), and getUTCMilliseconds(). The minutes and seconds are given in integer values from 0 to 59. The milliseconds are given in integer values from 0 to 999.

Getting the Time

There are occasions when you want to work with dates in terms of millisecond values. The getTime() method returns an integer value of milliseconds elapsed since midnight of January 1, 1970 UTC. The usefulness of this method might not be apparent at first. But imagine if you wanted to create a new Date object and give it the value of another Date object, essentially creating a copy. You *could* do the following:

```
var dOriginal:Date = new Date();
var yyyy:Number = dOriginal.getFullYear();
var mm:Number = dOriginal.getMonth();
var dd:Number = dOriginal.getDate();
var hh:Number = dOriginal.getHours();
var min:Number = dOriginal.getMinutes();
var ss:Number = dOriginal.getSeconds();
var ms:Number = dOriginal.getMilliseconds();
var dCopy:Date = new Date(yyyy, mm, dd,hh, min, ss, ms);
```

But the preceding is quite laborious, especially when compared with the following code that accomplishes the same thing.

```
var dOriginal:Date = new Date();
var dCopy:Date = new Date(dOriginal.getTime());
```

Getting the Time Zone Offset

So far, you have seen that you can work with either local dates *or* UTC dates. However, as long as you know the offset between the two, you can work with both together. The getTimezoneOffset() method returns an integer value of the difference between the local time and the UTC in minutes. Here is an example of the getTimezoneOffset() method in use:

```
var dNow:Date = new Date();
trace("Your time zone offset: " + dNow.getTimezoneOffset() + " minutes");
```

set Methods

The set methods of Date objects allow you to set the individual attributes of the object you are working with. Once you have created a Date object, you can modify the year, month, date, hours, minutes, seconds, milliseconds, and time since midnight of January 1, 1970.

Setting the Year

You can set the year value of a Date object by using the setYear(), setFullYear(), and setUTCFullYear() methods. These methods are very similar to their get method counterparts. Each takes a parameter. The setYear() method can take any integer value between 0 and 99 to set the object's year to 1900 through 1999. If you pass it a value outside the 0 to 99 range, it interprets the value literally. For instance:

```
var dSometime:Date = new Date();
dSometime.setYear(5);  // Set the year to 1905
```

But:

```
dSometime.setYear(105);  // sets the year to 105
```

The setFullYear() method takes an integer parameter that is interpreted literally in all ranges, even 0 to 99. Thus:

```
dSometime.setFullYear(5);  // Set the year to 5
```

And as you might expect, setUTCFullYear() takes an integer value interpreted literally in all ranges. It then sets the UTC year value to that year. When the local date value is displayed, it reflects the UTC change plus the time zone offset.

Setting the Month

You can set the local and UTC month values using the setMonth() and setUTCMonth() methods, respectively. Both methods require an integer value from 0 to 11. For example:

```
dSometime.setMonth(0);  // Set the month to 0, January
```

If you set the value of the month greater than 11, the year value of the object will increment. In other words, a value of 12 results in the year value increasing by 1, and the month value set to 0. For example:

```
var dSometime:Date = new Date(2003, 5, 23);  // June 23, 2003
dSometime.setMonth(12);  // January 23, 2004
```

You can also pass negative values to these methods. When you do this, it starts with 0, January, and subtracts. Thus, a value of -1 is the same as saying December of the previous year. For example:

```
var dSometime:Date = new Date(2003, 5, 23); // June 23, 2003
myDate.setMonth(-1);  // December 23, 2002
```

Setting the Date

You can use the setDate() and setUTCDate() methods to set the day of the month for a Date object. Both methods require a single parameter of an integer value from 1 to 31. For example:

```
dSometime.setDate(23);  // Set the day of the month to 23
```

Just like the methods for setting the month value, if you pass these methods values greater than the number of days in the month, the month will increment. For example:

```
var dSometime:Date = new Date(3433, 1, 8);  // February 8, 3433
dSometime.setDate(29);  // March 1, 3433
```

And just as with the methods for setting the month value, you can also pass negative values to the methods. For example:

```
var dSometime:Date = new Date(3433, 1, 8);   // February 8, 3433
dSometime.setDate(-1);  // January 30, 3433
dSometime.setMonth(-1);  // December 30, 3432
```

Note that because the date portion of a Date object is 1-indexed, setting the date to -1 sets the date value to two days prior to the beginning of the month value. A value of 0 passed to the setDate() method would set the date value to one day prior to the beginning of the month.

Setting the Hours, Minutes, Seconds, and Milliseconds

As you might expect, you can also set the hour, minutes, seconds, and milliseconds of your Date objects for both local time and UTC. The methods for doing this are setHours(), setUTCHours(), setMinutes(), setUTCMinutes(), setSeconds(), setUTCSeconds(), setMilliseconds(), and setUTCMilliseconds().

Each method takes integer values as parameters. Hours range from 0 to 23. Minutes and seconds range from 0 to 59. And milliseconds range from 0 to 999. Here is an example:

```
var dSometime:Date = new Date(2020, 0, 1);
dSometime.setHours(5);
dSometime.setMinutes(30);
dSometime.setSeconds(5);
dSometime.setMilliseconds(900);
trace(dSometime.toString());
```

The Output panel will display something like the following (depending on time zone offset):

```
Wed Jan 1 05:30:05 GMT-0800 2020
```

And like the other set methods, you can also increment the other values by setting an attribute higher than its uppermost value. For instance, if you added the following line to the previous example, the resulting date would have a seconds value of 6 and a milliseconds value of 0.

```
dSometime.setMilliseconds(1000);
```

Likewise, you can also pass any of these methods negative values. Let's use the same example again to illustrate this:

```
dSometime.setSeconds(5);  // Set the seconds value back to 5
dSometime.setMilliseconds(-1);  // 05:30:04:999
```

Setting the Time

You learned about the getTime() method earlier. The setTime() method is the counterpart in the set methods category. It allows you to set the value of your Date object with an integer of the number of milliseconds since midnight on January 1, 1970. (For an example, refer to the explanation of getTime()).

```
var dOriginal:Date = new Date();
var dCopy:Date = new Date(dOriginal.getTime());
```

You can just as easily write this in the following way using the setTime() method of the dCopy object:

```
var dOriginal:Date = new Date();
var dCopy:Date = new Date();
dCopy.setTime();
```

Inherited Methods

The toString() method is inherited from the Object class, and, as you've already seen, it returns a string representing the value in the following format:

```
Day Mon dd hh:mm:ss GMT+/-Time Zone Offset yyyy
```

The toString() method is implicitly invoked in any situation in which you try to use a Date object as a string. The examples in this book generally call the method explicitly to be clear.

Static Methods

All the methods you have looked at so far are invoked from Date objects that have been instantiated using the Date constructor. However, one method is invoked directly from the Date class.

UTC() is a method that returns the time value in milliseconds UTC from midnight on January 1, 1970 UTC of the date specified in the arguments. The UTC() method takes the same arguments as the Date constructor: year, month, date, hour, minutes, seconds, milliseconds. The following is an example of the UTC() method:

```
myUTCDate = Date.UTC(1970, 0, 1, 0, 0, 0);
```

In this example, myUTCDate would have a value of 0 because the UTC date created is the same as the starting date, January 1, 1970, and thus 0 milliseconds have elapsed for this date. Parameters that are omitted are set to 0, so the preceding example could be written as follows:

```
myUTCDate = Date.UTC(1970, 0, 1);
```

The UTC() static method could be useful as a shortcut to creating a local date if you know the UTC date. For instance, the following code is the longhand way of doing just this:

```
var dLocal:Date = new Date();
dLocal.setUTCFullYear(1970);
dLocal.setUTCMonth(0);
dLocal.setUTCDate(1);
dLocal.setUTCHours(0);
dLocal.setUTCMinutes(0);
dLocal.setUTCSeconds(0);
dLocal.setUTCMilliseconds(0);
```

Or, using the UTC() method, you could write the same thing in this way:

```
var nUTCMillis:Number = Date.UTC(1970, 0, 1);
var dLocal:Date = new Date(nUTCMillis);
```

Working with Advanced Date and Time Issues

If you plan to work with dates and times extensively, especially for the purposes of displaying values to the user, you may find it useful to create a new custom DateTime class that extends the Date class. In order to do this, complete the following steps:

1. Open a new AS file.
2. In the AS file add the following code:

```
class DateTime extends Date {
  static var SEC:Number = 1000;
  static var MIN:Number = DateTime.SEC * 60;
  static var HOUR:Number = DateTime.MIN * 60;
  static var DAY:Number = DateTime.HOUR * 24;
  static var YEAR:Number = DateTime.DAY * 365;
  static var LEAPYEAR:Number = DateTime.DAY * 366;
```

```
static var DAYS:Array = new Array("Sunday",
                                  "Monday",
                                  "Tuesday",
                                  "Wednesday",
                                  "Thursday",
                                  "Friday",
                                  "Saturday");
static var MONTHS:Array = new Array("January",
                                    "February",
                                    "March",
                                    "April",
                                    "May",
                                    "June",
                                    "July",
                                    "August",
                                    "September",
                                    "October",
                                    "November",
                                    "December");

function DateTime() {
  var nArgs:Number = arguments.length;
  switch (nArgs) {
    case 0:
      super();
      break;
    case 1:
      super(arguments[0]);
      break;
    case 2:
      super(arguments[0], arguments[1]);
      break;
    case 3:
      super(arguments[0], arguments[1], arguments[2]);
      break;
    case 4:
      super(arguments[0], arguments[1], arguments[2],
            arguments[3]);
      break;
    case 5:
      super(arguments[0], arguments[1], arguments[2],
            arguments[3], arguments[4]);
      break;
    case 6:
      super(arguments[0], arguments[1], arguments[2],
            arguments[3], arguments[4], arguments[5]);
      break;
    case 7:
      super(arguments[0], arguments[1], arguments[2],
            arguments[3], arguments[4], arguments[5],
            arguments[6]);
      break;
  }
}
```

```
public function toFullDisplay():String {
  var sDay:String = DateTime.DAYS[this.getDay()];
  var sMonth:String = DateTime.MONTHS[this.getMonth()];
  var sDisplay:String = sDay + " ";
  sDisplay += sMonth + " ";
  sDisplay += String(this.getDate()) + ", ";
  sDisplay += String(this.getFullYear());
  return sDisplay;
}

public function toUSDisplay(sSpacer:String):String {
  if(sSpacer == undefined) {
    sSpacer = "/";
  }
  var sDisplay:String = "";
  sDisplay += zeroFill(this.getMonth() + 1) + sSpacer;
  sDisplay += zeroFill(this.getDate()) + sSpacer;
  sDisplay += String(this.getFullYear());
  return sDisplay;
}

public function toEuroDisplay(sSpacer:String):String {
  if(sSpacer == undefined) {
    sSpacer = "/";
  }
  var sDisplay:String = "";
  sDisplay += zeroFill(this.getDate()) + sSpacer;
  sDisplay += zeroFill(this.getMonth() + 1) + sSpacer;
  sDisplay += String(this.getFullYear());
  return sDisplay;
}

private function zeroFill(nVal:Number):String {
  if(nVal < 10) {
    return ("0" + String(nVal));
  }
  else {
    return String(nVal);
  }
}

static function toDateTime(dDateObj:Date):DateTime {
  return new DateTime(dDateObj.getTime());
}

public function parseDateTime(sDateTimeStr:String):Void {
  var bTimeZonePlus = false;
  var aDateTime:Array = sDateTimeStr.split("T");
  var aDateParts:Array = aDateTime[0].split("-");
  var aTimeOffset:Array = aDateTime[1].split("-");
  if(aTimeOffset.length == 1) {
    bTimeZonePlus = true;
    aTimeOffset = aDateTime[1].split("+");
  }
```

```
        var aTimeParts:Array = aTimeOffset[0].split(":");
        var aOffset:Array = aTimeOffset[1].split(":");
        var nYear:Number = parseInt(aDateParts[0], 10);
        var nMonth:Number = parseInt(aDateParts[1], 10) - 1;
        var nDay:Number = parseInt(aDateParts[2], 10);
        var nHour:Number = parseInt(aTimeParts[0], 10);
        var nMinutes:Number = parseInt(aTimeParts[1], 10);
        var nSeconds:Number = parseInt(aTimeParts[2], 10);
        var nOffset:Number = parseInt(aTimeOffset[1], 10);
        if(bTimeZonePlus) {
          nHour -= nOffset;
        }
        else {
          nHour += nOffset;
        }
        var nEpochMillis:Number = Date.UTC(nYear, nMonth, nDay,
                                  nHour, nMinutes, nSeconds,
                                  0);
        this.setTime(nEpochMillis);
      }

      public function isLeapYear():Boolean {
        var nYear:Number = this.getFullYear();
        if (nYear % 4 != 0) {
          return false;
        }
        else if (nYear % 400 == 0) {
          return true;
        }
        else if (nYear % 100 == 0) {
          return false;
        }
        else {
          return true;
        }
      }

    }
```

3. Save the file as `DateTime.as`. Save the file to a directory in your global Flash classpath.

The preceding code is just an example to get you started. You may want to modify the code to suit your own application development needs. However, the example code is a good starting point. Now let's take a closer look at the example code.

First, you declare the class to extend `Date`. No matter what modifications you might make to the class, you should make sure that `DateTime` always extends `Date`. By extending the `Date` class, you ensure that you can use all the same functionality of the built-in `Date` class by way of a `DateTime` object.

```
class DateTime extends Date {
```

Next, you define some constants that may be useful. The first set of constants is helpful for performing date math (see the section "Performing Date Math"). The second set of constants contains arrays of string values that correspond to the numeric day of week and month values:

```
static var SEC:Number = 1000;
static var MIN:Number = DateTime.SEC * 60;
static var HOUR:Number = DateTime.MIN * 60;
static var DAY:Number = DateTime.HOUR * 24;
static var YEAR:Number = DateTime.DAY * 365;
static var LEAPYEAR:Number = DateTime.DAY * 366;

static var DAYS:Array = new Array("Sunday",
                                  "Monday",
                                  "Tuesday",
                                  "Wednesday",
                                  "Thursday",
                                  "Friday",
                                  "Saturday");
static var MONTHS:Array = new Array("January",
                                    "February",
                                    "March",
                                    "April",
                                    "May",
                                    "June",
                                    "July",
                                    "August",
                                    "September",
                                    "October",
                                    "November",
                                    "December");
```

Then you define the constructor for the `DateTime` class. You need to define only the constructor because the `Date` class has overloaded constructors, so you need to tell `DateTime` how to call the correct superclass constructor depending on the number of parameters:

```
function DateTime() {
  var nArgs:Number = arguments.length;
  switch (nArgs) {
    case 0:
      super();
      break;
    case 1:
      super(arguments[0]);
      break;
    case 2:
      super(arguments[0], arguments[1]);
      break;
    case 3:
      super(arguments[0], arguments[1], arguments[2]);
      break;
    case 4:
      super(arguments[0], arguments[1], arguments[2],
            arguments[3]);
      break;
    case 5:
      super(arguments[0], arguments[1], arguments[2],
            arguments[3], arguments[4]);
      break;
```

```
      case 6:
        super(arguments[0], arguments[1], arguments[2],
              arguments[3], arguments[4], arguments[5]);
        break;
      case 7:
        super(arguments[0], arguments[1], arguments[2],
              arguments[3], arguments[4], arguments[5],
              arguments[6]);
        break;
    }
  }
```

The first method displays the full date including the name of the day and the name of the month:

```
public function toFullDisplay():String {
  var sDay:String = DateTime.DAYS[this.getDay()];
  var sMonth:String = DateTime.MONTHS[this.getMonth()];
  var sDisplay:String = sDay + " "
  sDisplay += sMonth + " "
  sDisplay += String(this.getDate()) + ", "
  sDisplay += String(this.getFullYear());
  return sDisplay;
}
```

The `toUSDisplay()` and `toEuroDisplay()` methods return the date in U.S. or European format. In both cases, you can specify the character you want to use between the month, day, and year. The default is a forward slash.

```
public function toUSDisplay(sSpacer:String):String {
  if(sSpacer == undefined) {
    sSpacer = "/";
  }
  var sDisplay:String = "";
  sDisplay += zeroFill(this.getMonth() + 1) + sSpacer;
  sDisplay += zeroFill(this.getDate()) + sSpacer;
  sDisplay += String(this.getFullYear());
  return sDisplay;
}

public function toEuroDisplay(sSpacer:String):String {
  if(sSpacer == undefined) {
    sSpacer = "/";
  }
  var sDisplay:String = "";
  sDisplay += zeroFill(this.getDate()) + sSpacer;
  sDisplay += zeroFill(this.getMonth() + 1) + sSpacer;
  sDisplay += String(this.getFullYear());
  return sDisplay;
}
```

The `zeroFill()` method is private and is used by the preceding methods in order to make sure the month and date are always two digits. For example, if the month is 9, you display 09.

```
private function zeroFill(nVal:Number):String {
  if(nVal < 10) {
    return ("0" + String(nVal));
  }
  else {
    return String(nVal);
  }
}
```

The static `toDateTime()` method can be invoked from the `DateTime` class. You can pass it a `Date` object, and it returns a new `DateTime` object representing the same value:

```
static function toDateTime(dDateObj:Date):DateTime {
  return new DateTime(dDateObj.getTime());
}
```

The `parseDateTime()` method accepts a string and parses the string into a `DateTime` object. The example method accepts and parses a string in the following format: yyyy-mm-ddThh:nn:ss+/-hh:mm. For example, 2003-07-17T00:19:05-05:00 indicates July 17, 2003, at 12:19:05 a.m. with a time zone offset of -5 hours.

```
public function parseDateTime(sDateTimeStr:String):Void {
  var bTimeZonePlus = false;
  var aDateTime:Array = sDateTimeStr.split("T");
  var aDateParts:Array = aDateTime[0].split("-");
  var aTimeOffset:Array = aDateTime[1].split("-");
  if(aTimeOffset.length == 1) {
    bTimeZonePlus = true;
    aTimeOffset = aDateTime[1].split("+");
  }
  var aTimeParts:Array = aTimeOffset[0].split(":");
  var aOffset:Array = aTimeOffset[1].split(":");
  var nYear:Number = parseInt(aDateParts[0], 10);
  var nMonth:Number = parseInt(aDateParts[1], 10) - 1;
  var nDay:Number = parseInt(aDateParts[2], 10);
  var nHour:Number = parseInt(aTimeParts[0], 10);
  var nMinutes:Number = parseInt(aTimeParts[1], 10);
  var nSeconds:Number = parseInt(aTimeParts[2], 10);
  var nOffset:Number = parseInt(aTimeOffset[1], 10);
  if(bTimeZonePlus) {
    nHour -= nOffset;
  }
  else {
    nHour += nOffset;
  }
  var nEpochMillis:Number = Date.UTC(nYear, nMonth, nDay,
                                     nHour, nMinutes,
                                     nSeconds, 0);
  this.setTime(nEpochMillis);
}
```

The isLeapYear() method returns true if the year is a leap year and false otherwise:

```
public function isLeapYear():Boolean {
  var nYear:Number = this.getFullYear();
  if (nYear % 4 != 0) {
    return false;
  }
  else if (nYear % 400 == 0) {
    return true;
  }
  else if (nYear % 100 == 0) {
    return false;
  }
  else {
    return true;
  }
}
```

The toDateTime() method allows you to set a DateTime object based on a Date object:

```
static function toDateTime(dDateObj:Date):DateTime {
  return new DateTime(dDateObj.getTime());
}
```

Creating a DateTime Object

Once you have defined the DateTime class, you can create a DateTime object in essentially the same ways as you can create a Date object. Here are a few examples:

```
var dtNow:DateTime = new DateTime();
var dtWhen:DateTime = new DateTime(2003, 6, 21);
var dtThen:DateTime = new DateTime(123456789);
```

Working with Date Methods

You can work with all the same Date methods for a DateTime object. This includes all the get and set methods as well as the toString() method and the static UTC() method.

Performing Date Math

When working with dates, you will undoubtedly find that you want to do calculations from time to time—calculations about differences between two dates or forming a new date by adding or subtracting from an existing one. When this happens, you should convert all your values to milliseconds. Remember, this is the format ActionScript is storing all your date information in, anyway.

If you work with the DateTime class, you already have constants for seconds, minutes, hours, days, weeks, and even years in terms of milliseconds. This should make it simpler to perform date and time math. For instance, you can now calculate the date three days and one minute from now with the following code:

```
var dtNow:DateTime = new DateTime();
var nSoon:Number = dtNow.getTime() + (3 * DateTime.DAY) + DateTime.MIN;
var dtSoon = new DateTime(nSoon);
```

Displaying the Date

When you work with the example DateTime class, you have three options for displaying the date: full date display, U.S. format, and European format. Here are a few examples:

```
var dtWhen:DateTime = new DateTime(2003, 6, 21);
trace(dtWhen.toFullDisplay());
trace(dtWhen.toUSDisplay());
trace(dtWhen.toEuroDisplay());
trace(dtWhen.toUSDisplay("-"));
trace(dtWhen.toEuroDisplay("-"));
```

The Output panel will display the following:

```
Monday July 21, 2003
07/21/2003
21/07/2003
07-21-2003
21-07-2003
```

Creating a DateTime Object from a Date Object

There are plenty of scenarios in which you might have a Date object that you want to convert to a DateTime object. For example, if you retrieve a date from the server using Flash Remoting, you might retrieve a Date object. If you then want to display that value to the user or utilize any of the other DateTime methods, you should first convert the Date object to a DateTime object. You can accomplish this with the static toDateTime() method:

```
var dtServerDate:DateTime = DateTime.toDateTime(dFromServer);
```

Parsing a Date String into a DateTime Object

In many scenarios, you can retrieve a string that represents a date. You can use the parseDateTime() method to parse the string into a DateTime object. The example method parses strings such as 2003-07-17T00:19:05-05:00. Here is an example:

```
var dtBlogDateTime:DateTime = new DateTime();
dtBlogDateTime.parseDateTime("2003-07-17T00:19:05-05:00");
```

Detecting Leap Years

The isLeapYear() method simply returns true or false. You can see if a given DateTime object represents a leap year or not with this method:

```
var dtNow:DateTime = new DateTime();
trace(dtNow.isLeapYear());
```

Displaying the Time and Date

In this exercise, you utilize some of the things you have learned in this chapter in order to create an analog clock face that displays the current time. This exercise relies in part on the custom DateTime class from earlier in this chapter as well as the custom DrawingUtils class from Chapter 10. If you have not yet done so, you should either create the classes following the steps provided, or you should copy the class files from the CD-ROM that accompanies this book to your global Flash classpath.

Now let's create the application. Complete the following steps:

1. Create a new Flash document and save it as `clock001.fla`.
2. Add the following code to the first frame of the default layer of the main timeline:

```
function drawClock():Void {
  var nStageWidth:Number = Stage.width;
  var nStageHeight:Number = Stage.height;

  // Create the MovieClip objects into which you will draw
  // the clock parts. All the parts go into a single
  // MovieClip, mcClock, making it easy to move the entire
  // clock around.
  this.createEmptyMovieClip("mcClock", ⮐
 this.getNextHighestDepth());
  this.mcClock.createEmptyMovieClip("mcFace", ⮐
this.mcClock.getNextHighestDepth());
  this.mcClock.createEmptyMovieClip("mcHourHand", ⮐
this.mcClock.getNextHighestDepth());
  this.mcClock.createEmptyMovieClip("mcMinuteHand", ⮐
this.mcClock.getNextHighestDepth());
  this.mcClock.createEmptyMovieClip("mcSecondHand", ⮐
this.mcClock.getNextHighestDepth());

  // Create the DrawingUtils instances for each of the
  // parts.
  var duFace:DrawingUtils = ⮐
new DrawingUtils(this.mcClock.mcFace);
  var duHourHand:DrawingUtils = ⮐
new DrawingUtils(this.mcClock.mcHourHand);
  var duMinuteHand:DrawingUtils = ⮐
new DrawingUtils(this.mcClock.mcMinuteHand);
  var duSecondHand:DrawingUtils = ⮐
new DrawingUtils(this.mcClock.mcSecondHand);

  // Draw the clock face and hands.
  duFace.drawCircle(100);
  duHourHand.setLineStyle(6, 0xFF0000, 100);
  duHourHand.lineTo(70);
  duMinuteHand.setLineStyle(6, 0xFF0000, 100);
  duMinuteHand.lineTo(90);
  duSecondHand.lineTo(90);

  // Move the clock to the center of the stage.
  this.mcClock._x = nStageWidth/2;
  this.mcClock._y = nStageHeight/2;
}
```

```
function moveHands(mcClockHolder:MovieClip):Void {

  // Get the current time.
  var dNow:Date = new Date();

  // Set the rotation of the hands based on the current
  // time.
  mcClockHolder.mcHourHand._rotation = dNow.getHours() * 30 - 90;
  mcClockHolder.mcMinuteHand._rotation = dNow.getMinutes() ⮐
* 6 - 90;
  mcClockHolder.mcSecondHand._rotation = dNow.getSeconds() ⮐
* 6 - 90;

  // If it is just after midnight, call the
  // updateDateDisplay() function to update the display
  // of the date.
  if(dNow.getHours() == 0 && dNow.getMinutes() == 1 && ⮐
dNow.getSeconds() < 6) {
    updateDateDisplay();
  }

  // Update the view.
  updateAfterEvent();
}

function makeDateDisplay():Void {

  // Create a new TextField to display the current date.
  // For more information on TextField objects, see
  // Chapter 17.
  this.createTextField("tDateDisplay", ⮐
this.getNextHighestDepth(), 0, 0, 0, 0);
  this.tDateDisplay.autoSize = true;

  // Call the updateDateDisplay() function to display
  // the current date.
  updateDateDisplay();

  // Move the TextField to just below the clock.
  this.tDateDisplay._x = this.mcClock._x - ⮐
this.tDateDisplay._width/2;
  this.tDateDisplay._y = this.mcClock._y + ⮐
this.mcClock._height/2;
}

function updateDateDisplay():Void {

  // Create a DateTime object representing the current
  // date and time. Then set the display to the value
  // returned by toFullDisplay().
  var dtToday:DateTime = new DateTime();
```

```
    this.tDateDisplay.text = dtToday.toFullDisplay();
  }

  // Call the drawClock() and makeDateDisplay() functions.
  drawClock();
  makeDateDisplay();

  // Set the interval on which the moveHands() function is
  // called.
  setInterval(moveHands, 100, mcClock);
```

3. Save the document and test the movie.

Let's take a closer look at the code.

You define the `drawClock()` function in order to create the `MovieClip` objects and draw the artwork in them with `DrawingUtils` instances. First, create the `MovieClip` objects:

```
this.createEmptyMovieClip("mcClock",
          this.getNextHighestDepth());
this.mcClock.createEmptyMovieClip("mcFace",
          this.mcClock.getNextHighestDepth());
this.mcClock.createEmptyMovieClip("mcHourHand",
          this.mcClock.getNextHighestDepth());
this.mcClock.createEmptyMovieClip("mcMinuteHand",
          this.mcClock.getNextHighestDepth());
this.mcClock.createEmptyMovieClip("mcSecondHand",
          this.mcClock.getNextHighestDepth());
```

Then create the `DrawingUtils` instances to target each of the `MovieClip` instances:

```
var duFace:DrawingUtils = new DrawingUtils(this.mcClock.mcFace);
var duHourHand:DrawingUtils = new DrawingUtils(this.mcClock.mcHourHand);
var duMinuteHand:DrawingUtils = new DrawingUtils(this.mcClock.mcMinuteHand);
var duSecondHand:DrawingUtils = new DrawingUtils(this.mcClock.mcSecondHand);
```

Then draw the artwork. The face of the clock is a circle with a radius of 100. The hour and minute hands are red lines 70 and 90 pixels in length. And the second hand is a black line 90 pixels in length.

```
duFace.drawCircle(100);
duHourHand.setLineStyle(6, 0xFF0000, 100);
duHourHand.lineTo(70);
duMinuteHand.setLineStyle(6, 0xFF0000, 100);
duMinuteHand.lineTo(90);
duSecondHand.lineTo(90);
```

Once the clock has been drawn, move the clock to the center of the stage:

```
this.mcClock._x = nStageWidth/2;
this.mcClock._y = nStageHeight/2;
```

The `moveHands()` function is an interval function that continually updates the clock hands to indicate the current local time. The first thing you want to do in this function is get the current date:

```
var dNow:Date = new Date();
```

Next, you set the rotation of the hand MovieClip objects based on the current time. There are 360 degrees in a circle, and so the number of degrees between each hour on the clock is 30 (360 divided by 12) and the number of degrees between each minute and second on the clock is 6 (360 divided by 60). In each case, you subtract 90 degrees because the default rotation of the hands is at 90 degrees from the twelve o'clock position.

```
mcClockHolder.mcHourHand._rotation = dNow.getHours() * 30 - 90;
mcClockHolder.mcMinuteHand._rotation = dNow.getMinutes() * 6 - 90;
mcClockHolder.mcSecondHand._rotation = dNow.getSeconds() * 6 - 90;
```

You don't need to update the date display every time the interval function is called. Instead, the code checks to see if the current time is somewhere between midnight and six seconds after midnight (just to give a safe interval). If it is, you tell Flash to call the updateDateDisplay() function:

```
if(dNow.getHours() == 0 && dNow.getMinutes() == 1 && dNow.getSeconds() < 6) {
  updateDateDisplay();
}
```

The makeDateDisplay() and updateDateDisplay() functions are fairly self-explanatory. For more information on TextField objects, see Chapter 17.

We'd like to know what you thought about this chapter. Visit www.flashsupport.com/feedback to fill out an online form with your comments.

Summary

- ✦ ActionScript Date objects enable you to work with past, present, and future dates and time. You can construct Date objects with specific times, or allow the constructor function to query the local computer for the current time and date information.
- ✦ The Date object works with all date information in terms of milliseconds from midnight on January 1, 1970. You can use the methods of the Date object to work with user-friendly values such as year, month, date, day, hour, minutes, seconds, and milliseconds. You can also use some methods to work directly with the milliseconds value.

✦ ✦ ✦

Working with Strings

✦ ✦ ✦ ✦

In This Chapter

Distinguishing between primitive strings and String objects

Joining together multiple string values to create a single value

Using special characters within strings

Catching common mistakes when working with strings

Searching for substrings

Escaping and unescaping strings for interacting with other applications

✦ ✦ ✦ ✦

Thus far in the book, you've had the opportunity to see a lot of string values. You've primarily seen string literals, which are *primitive string data*. The `String` class is a wrapper class in that it provides some additional functionality around a primitive datatype—in this case, the primitive string type. As a primitive type, a string cannot do much. For example, if you want a string to report the number of characters it contains, it cannot. Instead, you need to first create a `String` object. This chapter looks at the `String` class and discusses how it applies to your applications.

Understanding Primitives and Objects

The primitive string type is a value. Although useful, it cannot be more than a value. The `String` class allows you to instantiate a `String` object that can do much more. For example, a `String` object can report the number of characters in the value and it can convert the value to all uppercase or all lowercase. If all you want to do is have a simple value then you should work with a primitive type. Most of the time this will suffice and there is no need to use the extra resources to create a `String` object. However, if you want to work with the additional functionality of the `String` class, you should create a `String` object. There are two ways you can accomplish this. The preferred way is to use a constructor. The `String` constructor requires that you pass it the primitive string value you want it to wrap. Here is an example:

```
var sTitle:String = new String("ActionScript
Bible");
```

The new `String` object, `sTitle`, wraps the primitive value of `ActionScript Bible`. Once you have created the object, you can utilize the properties and methods. For example:

```
trace(sTitle.length);  // Displays: 18
```

Technically, you can also pass a `String` object to a `String` constructor. Flash automatically calls the `toString()` method of the `String` object to convert it to a string primitive value. However, the same does not work for other datatypes. For example, you

cannot simply pass a Date object to a String constructor. You would need to explicitly call the toString() method:

```
// This code causes an error because Flash will not
// automatically convert the Date object to a string.
var dToday:Date = new Date();
var sDate:String = new String(dToday);

// This code will work because it calls the toString()
// method explicitly.
var dToday:Date = new Date();
var sDate:String = new String(dToday.toString());
```

The second way you can create a String object is to allow Flash to implicitly create a String object by simply invoking a property of method of the String class from a primitive string value. For example:

```
trace("ActionScript Bible".length);  // Displays 18
```

With this second technique, Flash actually creates a new String object on the fly. However, this is sloppy coding, and it is not recommended. Although it will work, there are at least two downsides:

- ✦ There is no way to manage the object, because it is created and then essentially lost in memory. It is better to create the object explicitly so that you can manage it.
- ✦ If you are going to invoke properties and/or methods from the same string value several times Flash will create several String objects. This is wasteful. If you explicitly create a String object, only one object needs to be created.

Getting and Setting Primitive Values

The String class is treated as a wrapper class because it wraps a primitive value and provides additional functionality. In the previous section, you saw how to set the primitive value for a String object. You set the value when you instantiate it with the constructor. For example:

```
var sTitle:String = new String("ActionScript Bible");
```

In order to get the primitive value from the object, you can use one of three techniques:

- ✦ **Call the valueOf() method.** The valueOf() method of any class returns the primitive value if one exists:

  ```
  trace(sTitle.valueOf()); // Displays: ActionScript Bible
  ```

- ✦ **Call the toString() method.** This method returns the string representation of any type of object if available. In the case of a String object, the string representation is a string primitive:

  ```
  trace(sTitle.toString()); // Displays: ActionScript Bible
  ```

- ✦ **Simply use the object as is.** By default, the toString() method of an object is called if you attempt to use it where Flash is expecting a string. This is not necessarily the recommended technique, but it works:

  ```
  trace(sTitle); // Displays: ActionScript Bible
  ```

Joining Strings

The concat() method of a String object allows you to concatenate one or more primitive string values with the primitive string value of the object. The concatenated value (which is a primitive string) is returned and the String object's value is unaffected. Here is an example:

```
var sTitle:String = new String("ActionScript Bible");
trace(sTitle.concat(" rocks!"));  // Displays: ActionScript Bible rocks!
trace(sTitle.valueOf());  // Displays: ActionScript Bible
```

Notice that the value of sTitle remained unchanged in the preceding example. If you want to concatenate values and then reassign the new value to the String object, you need to do the following:

1. Call the concat() method to return the new primitive string.
2. Pass the primitive string to a new String constructor.
3. Assign that new String object to the same variable as the original String object.

Here's an example:

```
var sTitle:String = new String("ActionScript Bible");
sTitle = new String(sTitle.concat(" rocks!"));
trace(sTitle.valueOf());  // Displays: ActionScript Bible rocks!
```

Of course, the concat() method is not the only option for concatenating strings. In Chapter 5 you learned how to work with the string concatenation operator (+) for this purpose. There is no reason why you should abandon this practice now. In fact, most of the time you'll still see the string concatenation operator used instead of the concat() method. For one thing, it is more convenient. And for another, it is more flexible because it allows you to both prepend and append values. Here's an example:

```
var sTitle:String = new String("ActionScript Bible");
trace("the" + sTitle.valueOf() + " rocks!");
// Displays: the ActionScript Bible rocks!
```

Regardless of which technique you use, however, there are some special considerations when working with strings in general. Some of these things were mentioned briefly in Chapter 5, but the following sections elaborate a bit more.

Escaping Characters

When you are forming string values, you should be careful to escape characters when necessary. If you recall from the discussion in Chapter 5, there are several situations in which you need to escape characters. One of the most common is when you are working with quotation marks within a string. It is important that you watch that the starting and ending quotes for the string literal match up and that there are no rogue matches inline. Here's an example of a string literal that would yield an error.

```
var sPhrase:String = 'Ain't ain't a word.'; // error
```

The problem is that the apostrophes inline will be interpreted by Flash as single quotes, and the first of the two will match up with the starting single quote. The simplest solution in this case is to use double quotes around the string literal instead of single quotes. The following change makes the code valid.

```
var sPhrase:String = "Ain't ain't a word."; // correct
```

The same goes for inline double quotes. Typically, if you are going to use inline double quotes, you should use single quotes around the string literal. Here's an example:

```
var sQuote:String = '"hello"';
```

But the problem occurs when you want to use both double and single (apostrophes) quotes inline. For example:

```
var sPhrase:String = '"Ain't" ain't a word.';
```

In the preceding example, even if you use double quotes instead of single quotes around the string literal, there will be an error. In such cases you can use the backslash to escape the problematic characters. The backslash tells Flash to interpret the following character in a special way. In the case of a quote, it tells Flash to interpret the quote literally rather than thinking that it should try and match it to a starting or ending quote around the string. Here is the corrected example:

```
var sPhrase:String = '"Ain\'t" ain\'t a word.';
```

The backslash can be used to escape any other special characters, as you'll see in the next section.

Nonvisible Characters

There are some special characters with which you should familiarize yourself. To begin with, let's take a look at the backslash. Obviously, the backslash character has a special function when used in a string literal, so it is not displayed. So, in the event that you wish to display a backslash in a string, you must place another backslash in front of it:

```
trace("\");  // Displays:
trace("\\");  // displays: \
```

There are some additional special character combinations to note. Table 15-1 shows a list of some of the special characters.

Table 15-1: Non-Visible Characters

Character Sequence	*Meaning*
`\b`	Backspace
`\t`	Tab
`\n`	Newline
`\r`	Carriage return
`\f`	Form feed

Here's an example of the newline character used in a string:

```
trace("line one\nline two");
```

The preceding code will display the following in the Output panel:

```
line one
line two
```

If you want to display one of the values literally rather than as the interpreted value, you need to escape it with a backslash. For example, if you want to display \n literally, instead of a newline, you can add a backslash just before it. For example:

```
trace("\\n");  // Displays: \\n
```

Avoiding Common Mistakes

There are a handful of mistakes that developers seem to make. Even with experience, it is possible to make mistakes. However, the difference is that with some education you can more easily troubleshoot when you do make a mistake. The first point for consideration is that it is always a good idea to consult the Output panel when there is an error. All too often, when a developer tests the movie and the Output panel pops up, he or she immediately dismisses and closes it rather than learning what is wrong. This might seem obvious, but it is the first common mistake. After you have successfully located the line or lines causing the problem, it is likely that it is one of the following common mistakes:

- ✦ There is a mismatched quote somewhere in the string.
- ✦ Because the backslash character is not frequently used in displays, it is fairly common to forget how to use it. This mistake is essentially the same mistake as the previous bullet point. The difference is, however, that the first mistake will cause errors, whereas this mistake will not. The rather frustrating result of this mistake is simply a failure to display the string as desired.
- ✦ Another really common mistake is to omit the concatenation operator (+) when joining multiple strings. For instance, it is easy enough to forget an operator in a line such as the following:

  ```
  var sGreeting:String = "hello, " + username + ⮐
  ". today is " todaysDate;
  ```

  But unfortunately, this results in an error because of the missing operator just before todaysDate. So the correct line reads as follows:

  ```
  var sGreeting:String = "hello, " + username + ⮐
  ". today is " + todaysDate;
  ```

- ✦ It is also common to accidentally omit quotes when joining multiple string literals, or even sometimes at the beginning or end of a single string literal. For instance:

  ```
  var sVal:String = "this is string one." + " " + this is string two";
  ```

  This code clearly does not work. But sometimes it can be hard to see the missing quotes. The correct line reads as follows:

  ```
  var sVal:String = "this is string one." + " " + ⮐
  "this is string two";
  ```

- ✦ It is a common mistake to use the = operator instead of the += operator when appending strings such as the following:

  ```
  var sVal:String = "string one.";
  sVal += "string two.";
  sVal = "string three.";
  ```

This results in a string with the value of `string three`. The problem is that the last line uses just the assignment operator instead of the += operator. The correct code reads as follows:

```
var sVal:String = "string one.";
sVal += "string two.";
sVal += "string three.";
```

✦ When you are retrieving string values from a database or other server-side datasource, you sometimes find that extra whitespace characters have been added to the beginning and/or end of the string value. Depending on your usage of the string, that extra whitespace might not have much effect. If you are finding that you are having some kind of issue with your code that could potentially be caused by such extra whitespace, you can add a simple debugging test by outputting the string value with a character such as a ' or a | at the beginning and end so you can see if there are any extra nonvisible characters. For example, if you have a variable named `sValue`, you would use the following:

```
trace("|" + sValue + "|");
```

Then, when you test the application you will be able to quickly see if there is extra whitespace. If the value of `sValue` is `some text` and there is no extra whitespace, it will appear as:

```
|some text|
```

On the other hand, if there is an extra space at the end of the text, you can see it:

```
|some text |
```

Working with Character Codes

When you are working with strings, there are many characters that you can display beyond the standard characters on the keyboard. Doing so requires the use of the character codes. Each character has a numeric value associated with it. For instance, the letter "a" has the character code of 97. There is a separate character code for upper- and lowercase letters. In the discussion of the `charCodeAt()` and `fromCharCode()` methods later in this chapter, you learn how to generate a list of the character codes.

Determining the Number of Characters

Every `String` object has a length property that reports the number of characters in a `String` object. You've already seen this used in several of the previous examples.

```
var sTitle:String = new String("ActionScript Bible");
trace(sTitle.length);  // Displays: 18
```

All characters in a `String` object's value are counted. This includes spaces, punctuation, and special character sequences. Even the backspace sequence counts as a character. This might seem counterintuitive, but it is true nonetheless.

Working with Substring Values

A substring is made up of a portion of another string. For example, "accord" is a substring of "accordion". A substring can be a single character or the entire original string. The `slice()`, `substring()`, and `substr()` methods of the `String` class are all used for selecting a substring value. Each works in a slightly different way, but all return a new string value without changing the String object. In addition, the charAt() method returns a single-character substring.

substr

The substr() method allows you to select a substring by specifying a starting point and a length. Each character in a String object's value is assigned an index. The first character has an index of 0, the second has an index of 1, and so on. Figure 15-1 helps to illustrate this.

0	1	2	3	4	5	6	7	8	9	10	11	12	13	14	15	16	17
A	c	t	i	o	n	S	c	r	i	p	t		B	i	b	l	e

Figure 15-1: The characters of a String object are indexed with numbers. The first character has an index of 0.

The following is an example of how to use the substr() method:

```
var sTitle:String = new String("ActionScript Bible");
trace(sTitle.substr(6, 6));  // Displays: Script
trace(sTitle.substr(0, 6));  // Displays: Action
trace(sTitle.substr(0, 12)); // Displays: ActionScript
```

In this example, the value assigned to the String object is ActionScript Bible. Then, you can display various substrings such as Script, Action, and ActionScript.

You may optionally omit the second parameter. When you do this, it returns a substring starting at the specified index and going to the end of the original string. For example:

```
var sTitle:String = new String("ActionScript Bible");
trace(sTitle.substr(6));  // Displays: Script Bible
```

It is also worth noting that you can specify negative values for a starting index. Specifying a negative value simply counts backward from the end of the string where -1 is the last character. So, the previous example can also be written as follows:

```
var sTitle:String = new String("ActionScript Bible");
trace(sTitle.substr(-12, 6));  // Displays: Script
```

However, it does not work to specify negative values for the length parameter.

substring

There are other times when it is more convenient to specify a starting and ending index for the substring value you are selecting. You can do this by using the substring() method of the String class. This method returns a substring starting with the starting index specified and containing all the characters up to, but not including, the ending index. Here's an example:

```
var sTitle:String = new String("ActionScript Bible");
trace(sTitle.substring(6, 12));  // Displays: Script
```

Notice that the value passed for the ending index, 12, is one greater than the index of the last character returned. Also, with the substring() method, you cannot use negative numbers for the indices.

slice

You can use the slice method to extract a substring as well. This method works similarly to both substr() and substring(). The method takes two parameters, a starting and ending index, just as substring() does. And just like substring(), the returned value contains the characters from the starting index up to but not including the ending index. However, unlike substring(), the second parameter is optional. If omitted, the last index of the string is used. Additionally, using slice(), you can specify the indices with negative numbers where -1 is the last character in the string. Here's an example:

```
var sTitle:String = new String("ActionScript Bible");
trace(sTitle.slice(6, 12));  // Displays: Script
trace(sTitle.slice(6));  // Displays: Script Bible
trace(sTitle.slice(-12, 0));  // Displays: Script Bible
```

charAt

When you want to parse through a string, one character at a time, you can take advantage of the charAt() method. The method takes one parameter, a value for an index within the string. This method returns a new one-character string that contains the value of the character at the specified index.

```
var sTitle:String = new String("ActionScript Bible");
var sChar:String = sTitle.charAt(0);
```

The preceding will return a value of A. You can employ the use of a for loop to loop through the characters of a string, one at a time:

```
var sTitle:String = new String("ActionScript Bible");
for (var i:Number = 0; i < sTitle.length; i++){
   trace(sTitle.charAt(i));
}
```

Notice that the charAt() method is really a simplified version of the substr(), substring(), or splice() methods.

Finding Substrings

There is often a need to search a string for the occurrence of a substring. You can use the indexOf() and lastIndexOf() methods to do this. The methods each take the same parameters and operate in much the same way. They both require one parameter—the substring for which to perform the search. And for each, there is a second optional parameter, the starting point for the search within the string. In each case, if the substring is not found, a value of -1 is returned. Otherwise, the value of the index of the first character of the found substring is returned. For example:

```
var sTitle:String = new String("ActionScript Bible");
trace(sTitle.indexOf("ActionScript")); // Displays: 0
trace(sTitle.indexOf("i"));  // Displays: 3
trace(sTitle.lastIndexOf("i"));  // Displays: 14
trace(sTitle.indexOf("i", 4));  // Displays: 9
trace(sTitle.lastIndexOf("i", 12));  // Displays: 9
trace(sTitle.indexOf("q"));  // Displays: -1
trace(sTitle.lastIndexOf("g"));  // Displays: -1
```

You can use either of these methods in a while statement to find all the occurrences of a substring. Here's an example:

```
var sTitle:String = new String("ActionScript Bible");
var nMatch:Number = sTitle.indexOf("i");
while(nMatch != -1) {
  trace(nMatch);
  nMatch = sTitle.indexOf("i", nMatch + 1);
}
```

The preceding code will result in the following output:

```
3
9
14
```

Notice that within the while statement each call to indexOf() is passed not only the substring to match, but also the starting index from which to search. The starting index for each search should be one more than the previous match to ensure that you don't keep getting the same match (and, therefore an infinite loop!).

The indexOf() and lastIndexOf() methods can be particularly useful for form validation—for example, when you want to make sure that a particular type of value has been entered into a field. For instance, you might want to ensure that a valid e-mail address has been entered into a field. A really simple check for a valid e-mail address is to make sure that it contains both an @ and a . within it:

```
var nCheckOne:Number = sEmail.indexOf("@");
var nCheckTwo:Number = sEmail.lastIndexOf(".");
if (nCheckOne!= -1 && nCheckTwo!= -1 && nCheckOne < nCheckTwo){
   trace("good email address");
}
```

Although the basic indexOf() and lastIndexOf() methods can be useful for simple pattern matching as shown in the example, regular expressions are much better suited to matching complex patterns.

Getting a Character Code

Sometimes you may want to work with numeric values instead of characters in your strings. There are several reasons why you might want to do this. For example, in order to compare some special characters you might find you need to compare the character codes rather than the characters themselves. You can easily do this by using the charCodeAt() method of the String object. The method takes a single parameter—an index within the string. It then returns the character code for the character at that index. For example:

```
var sTitle:String = new String("ActionScript Bible");
trace(sTitle.charCodeAt(12));  // Displays: 32
```

Using Character Codes to Get Characters

The fromCharCode() method is a static method of the String class. This method returns a new string primitive value with the character that corresponds to the character code you specify. This can be useful when you want to work with characters that are not part of the standard keyboard. For example, you might want to display the copyright symbol in your Flash movie. You can do this quite simply if you know that the character code for the copyright symbol is 169. You can try it out by using the following code:

```
trace(String.fromCharCode(169));
```

You can easily generate a list of characters and their codes by using the `trace()` function in a `for` loop to write them to the Output panel. The following code outputs the first 150 characters and codes:

```
for(var i:Number = 0; i < 150; i++){
   trace(i + ": " + String.fromCharCode(i));
}
```

Converting a String into an Array

There are occasions when you have strings of delimited values that you want to split apart into an array of values. The `split()` method does just that. This is particularly useful when you have passed values to your Flash movie from another application, and some values were from an array. As you'll read in later chapters, when you utilize the `LoadVars` class to load data, you can pass name-value pairs only, not complex data structures such as arrays. However, you can convert the array to a delimited string on the server before passing it to Flash. And when it is in Flash, you can parse it into an array again. The `split()` method requires one parameter—the delimiter (this was optional in previous versions of Flash). The method then returns a new array populated by the values from the string. The following is an example:

```
var sValue:String = "a,b,c,d,e,f";
var aValues = sValue.split(",");
for (i = 0; i < aValues.length; i++){
   trace(aValues[i]);
}
```

This example outputs the following:

```
a
b
c
d
e
f
```

If you use another delimiter in the string, you need to specify it as the argument for the `split()` method appropriately. For example:

```
var sValue:String = "a b c d e f";
var aValues = sValue.split(" ");
for (i = 0; i < aValues.length; i++){
   trace(aValues[i]);
}
```

This example outputs the following:

```
a
b
c
d
e
f
```

Make sure you specify the correct delimiter when you call the `split()` method. Otherwise, Flash will not know how to correctly split the string.

Using an empty string ("") as the delimiter for the `split()` method will create an array containing each of the characters of the string.

Changing the Case of a String

The `toLowerCase()` and `toUpperCase()` methods are both fairly intuitive. The `toLowerCase()` method returns a new string with all the uppercase letters converted to lowercase. And the `toUpperCase()` method returns a new string with all the lowercase letters converted to uppercase. In other words, calling either method returns a string with all letters either uppercase or lowercase. Here are some examples:

```
var sTitle:String = new String("ActionScript Bible");
trace(sTitle.toLowerCase());  // Displays: actionscript bible
trace(sTitle.toUpperCase());  // Displays: ACTIONSCRIPT BIBLE
trace(sTitle.valueOf());  // Displays: ActionScript Bible
```

Notice that the value of the original `String` object is unaffected.

The `toLowerCase()` and `toUpperCase()` methods are particularly useful for comparing strings in a case-insensitive manner. For example:

```
var sTitleOne:String = new String("ActionScript Bible");
var sTitleTwo:String = new String("ActionScript bible");
trace(sTitleOne.valueOf() == sTitleTwo.valueOf());
trace(sTitleOne.toUpperCase() == sTitleTwo.toUpperCase());
```

In the preceding example, the first `trace()` outputs `false`, whereas the second outputs `true` because upper- and lowercase letters are not equal. Therefore a `B` and a `b` are not going to match. However, if you convert the string values to all uppercase (as in this example) or all lowercase prior to comparing them, you can get a case-insensitive comparison.

Passing String Values to and from Applications

Earlier in this chapter, we used the word "escape" to mean placing a backslash character before a character within a string literal so that Flash interprets it literally instead of with any special meaning. The term "escape" is also used to signify something else in ActionScript and in general Web development. When passing values to and from applications, particularly in

URLEncoded format, it is important that special characters be converted to another standard format when being passed back and forth. Consider, for instance, that the & and = characters have special meanings in name-value pairs being passed to and from applications. Therefore, it is important that these characters be converted to another form while being exchanged between applications. This encoding process is called *escaping* the string.

Because of the importance of encoding these special characters, there is a function within ActionScript that specifically takes care of this process. The escape() function can be called at any time to convert a string to the encoded equivalent. This saves you a great deal of time and energy when the need arises. It is important to notice that the escape() function does not make changes to the existing string, but returns a new string. Here is an example:

```
var sTitle:String = new String("ActionScript Bible");
trace(escape(sTitle));  // Displays: ActionScript%20Bible
```

The %20 is a hexadecimal escape sequence that represents a space. Because spaces are not permitted in values passed via the HTTP protocol, it is important that it be encoded. These hexadecimal escape sequences are standard, and just about every programming language has a library or built-in function to encode and decode them.

Likewise, there is a function, unescape(), that decodes any string that is URL-encoded. So, for instance, if you were loading a variable from another application, you might need to call the unescape() function to display it properly. Like the escape() function, the unescape() function does not modify the existing string, but returns a new string. The following is an example of the unescape() function:

```
var sTitle:String = new String("ActionScript%20Bible");
trace(unescape(sTitle));  // Displays: ActionScript Bible
```

Most of the time, Flash automatically unescapes all string values without requiring that you explicitly call the unescape() function.

We'd like to know what you thought about this chapter. Visit www.flashsupport.com/feedback to fill out an online form with your comments.

Summary

- ✦ Strings are primitive datatypes for which the String class is a wrapper class. This simply means that a String object contains the string value and provides additional functionality.
- ✦ There are character sequences or combinations used in place of special characters with other meanings within a string.
- ✦ The String class includes methods for finding substrings and matching substrings.
- ✦ When passing values to and from other applications, it can be important to make sure that the name-value pairs are properly URL-encoded, with all characters escaped. This means that characters such as spaces are substituted with other characters or sequences of characters. You can do this easily with the escape() function (the opposite of which is the unescape() function).

✦ ✦ ✦

PART

V

The Movie Classes

✦ ✦ ✦ ✦

In This Part

✦ ✦ ✦ ✦

The Color Class

Although the MovieClip class can do a lot with its own methods and properties, some interactive functions require other classes, such as the Color and Sound classes. These classes can add new characteristics to Movie Clips (such as scripted audio) or change properties that aren't prescribed in the MovieClip class (such as color). This chapter explores the construction of these classes and shows you how to implement them in your Flash movies.

In This Chapter

Filling a Movie Clip with an entire color

Applying advanced color changes to interfaces

Using Movie Clips as buttons

An Introduction to the Color Class

As you will see in the following sections, the Color class works with targeted MovieClip objects. The Color class enables you to take the same settings you use in the Property inspector panel (for Tint and Advanced modes) and apply them to MovieClip objects at runtime with ActionScript. The syntax for Color class usage is almost identical to the Sound class, which is discussed in Chapter 23, and the manner in which they control assets in Flash is similar as well. See Figure 16-1 for an illustration of its usage.

As Figure 16-1 shows, an instance of a Color class is referenced to control its assets. Color objects control MovieClip objects. What this figure does not show you is the syntax to create a new Color object. In the next section, you explore just that.

Creating a New Object

As with many predefined ActionScript classes, Color objects require a constructor to create a new instance of the class.

For the Color class, you need to specify an instance name and a new constructor with a MovieClip instance as its argument:

```
var cMenu:Color = new Color(mcMenu);
```

where cMenu is the name of this specific Color object, and mcMenu is the name of the MovieClip object you want to control.

For example, if you had a MovieClip object named mcCircle on the main timeline, and you wanted to create a Color object to control its color, you would use the following ActionScript:

```
var cCircle:Color = new Color(mcCircle);
```

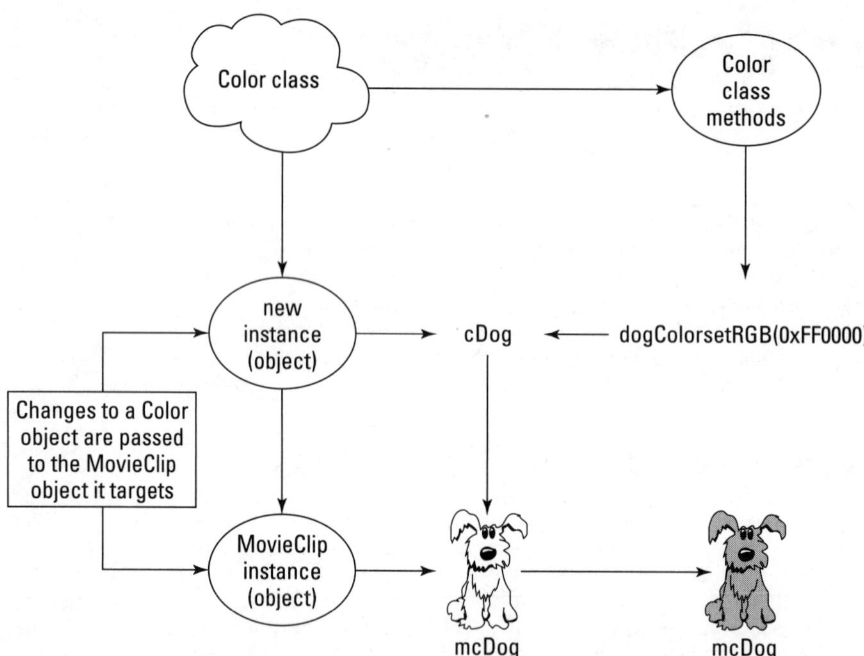

Figure 16-1: A Color object is a bridge between a MovieClip object and its color attributes.

It's important to note that what you decide to call your `Color` object names (that is, `cCircle` in the previous line of code) is completely arbitrary. You can use any name you want, as long as you consistently refer to that name in subsequent ActionScript.

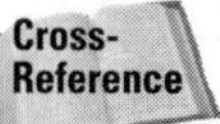

For details about proper naming procedures, refer to Chapter 5, "Constructing ActionScript."

Once a new instance of the `Color` class is created, you can then control the color of the targeted `MovieClip` object through the new `Color` object.

Always assign a unique name to any object. For example, you don't want to create a `MovieClip` object and a `Color` object both named `circle` on the same timeline because the names will conflict.

An instance of the `Color` class can exist in a separate timeline from the actual `MovieClip` object that is being controlled. In Figure 16-2, you can see the prior example plotted on a timeline chart.

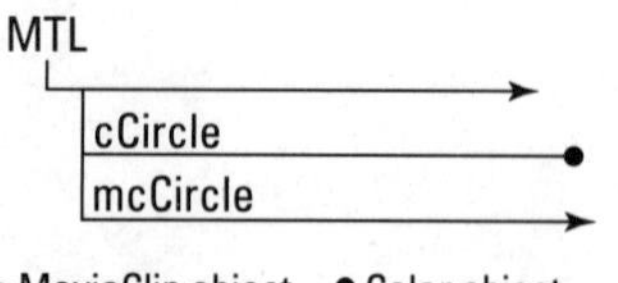

Figure 16-2: Color objects are separate from the MovieClip object that they control.

Referring to the Color Class Methods

Once a `Color` object is created, you can use any of the methods of that object's class. Unlike static classes such as `Mouse` and `Key` discussed in later chapters, `Color` objects have specific instances. For example, you can't do the following in ActionScript:

```
Color.setRGB(0xFF0000);  // This code won't even compile.
```

Although you haven't looked at the `setRGB()` method yet, this code shows that method being invoked from a generic `Color` object. It's the same principle as simple `gotoAndPlay()` actions with `MovieClip` objects. You wouldn't use the following syntax:

```
MovieClip.gotoAndPlay(10); // This code doesn't target an instance.
```

More appropriately, you need to specify the `MovieClip` instance you want to control:

```
mcCircle.gotoAndPlay(10); // Correct syntax.
```

Likewise, with `Color` objects, you invoke their methods through their specific instances, such as:

```
cCircle.setRGB(0xFF0000); // Correct syntax.
```

You explore the syntax and use of `Color` objects in the next sections.

Understanding the Color Class

The `Color` class brings an exciting realm of design control and interactivity to Flash movies. Have you ever wanted to create skins for your Flash movies, or create a product showcase that shows each product in a variety of colors? Prior to the addition of the `Color` class to ActionScript, a Flash developer needed to create several instances of the same symbol, each with a different effect setting, as you now have in the Property inspector, to achieve these effects. Alternatively, you can take control of a `MovieClip` object's color attributes with ActionScript.

There are four methods for the `Color` class. These methods can be broken into two sets: `setRGB()` and `getRGB()` work just like the Tint setting in the Property inspector, whereas `setTransform()` and `getTransform()` function identically to the Advanced setting in the Property inspector. When you're trying to achieve scripted effects with the `Color` class, it's best to predetermine what actual color settings you want to apply by doing the following steps:

1. Create a Movie Clip symbol on to the stage. You can make a simple shape with the Oval or Rectangle tool and convert it into a Movie Clip symbol.

2. With the instance selected, open the Property inspector.

3. To make whole color changes to the entire `MovieClip` instance, choose Tint from the Property inspector drop-down menu. To make additive or subtractive color changes to the MovieClip instance, choose Advanced from the Property inspector drop-down menu, and click the Settings button for a Settings dialog box.

4. For Tint, choose a color chip that matches the color you want to use for the MovieClip object. Record the R, G, and B values for this color on a piece of paper. Alternatively, record the hexadecimal values that appear in the color chip pop-up menu, as shown in Figure 16-3. Do not apply any percentage changes in Tint mode (in the % field); this value cannot be translated into ActionScript.

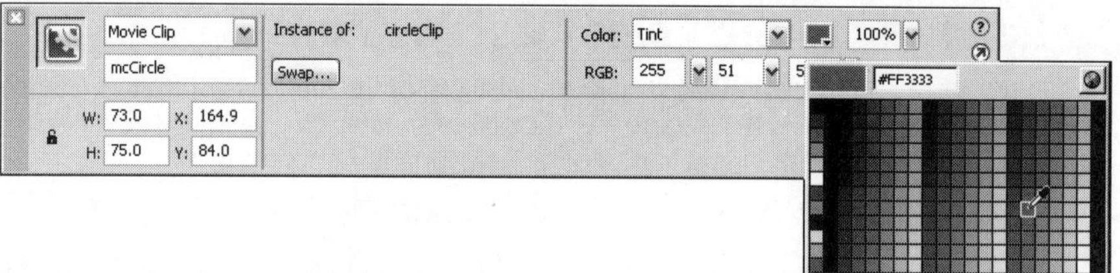

Figure 16-3: The color chip pop-up menu in Tint mode displays the Web-safe hexadecimal value for the selected color.

5. For the Advanced mode in the Property inspector drop-down menu, choose a combination of percentage and/or offset settings for each color channel and the alpha channel (if desired). The percentage settings are those in the first column (a) of fields, whereas the offset settings are those in the second column (b) of fields. Record any changed values, using the property names shown in Figure 16-4, where `ra` = red percentage, `rb` = red offset, `ga` = green percentage, `gb` = green percentage, `ba` = blue percentage, `bb` = blue offset, `aa` = alpha percentage, and `ab` = alpha offset.

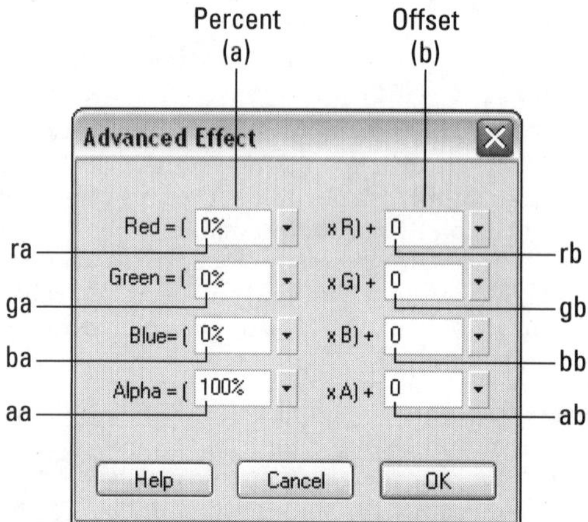

Figure 16-4: Advanced mode allows you to control the additive and subtractive properties of a Movie Clip's color.

6. After you record the appropriate values, you should reset the `MovieClip` instance to its original appearance by choosing None in the Property inspector's drop-down menu.

Once you have determined the color effect that you want to perform on the fly with ActionScript, you can learn how to use the following methods of the `Color` object.

Setting a Solid Color

The `setRGB()` method of the `Color` class controls the tint of a `MovieClip` object. The single argument of this method can be a decimal number or a hexadecimal number. Hex values are written as `0xRRGGBB`, where *RR* is the Red channel, *GG* is the Green channel, and *BB* is the

Blue channel. The setRGB() method performs identically to the Tint mode of the Property inspector's effect settings. It changes the MovieClip object's entire color, including strokes and fills, to the specified value. The following example changes a MovieClip object named mcHero to a solid black color, as shown in Figure 16-5:

```
var cHero:Color = new Color(mcHero);
cHero.setRGB(0x000000);
```

Figure 16-5: The original hero artwork is on the left, and the color change to the hero is on the right.

You can also use numeric values with the setRGB() method. For example, if you want to have a text field input for the hex value, you need to convert the hex value to a numeric value. If your Input text field's instance name was tHexInput, you could put the following code on a Button instance to change a MovieClip object named mcHero:

```
on(release){
  var nVal:Number = parseInt(tHexInput.text, 16);
  var cHero:Color = new Color(mcHero);
  cHero.setRGB(nVal);
}
```

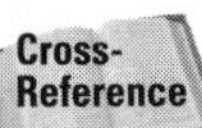

The parseInt() function is discussed in more detail in Chapter 12, "The Number Class."

In ActionScript, you can't assign a variable within a 0x expression, such as:

```
cHero.setRGB(0xtHexInput.text);
```

or

```
var hexNum:String = "0x" + tHexInput.text;
cHero.setRGB(hexNum);
```

Neither of the preceding code examples work because the argument for setRGB() must be typed as a number.

You can refer to the heroColor_demo_setRGB.fla and heroColor_demo_hexInput.fla files, located in the ch16 folder of the book's CD-ROM.

Retrieving Solid Color Information

The getRGB() method of the Color class can retrieve the RGB value of any MovieClip instance of the stage. This method works only on instances that have been changed with the setRGB() method or have been physically altered with the Tint mode in the Property inspector. The getRGB() method returns the numeric value of the solid color. Because setRGB() can accept numeric values, it is usually not necessary to perform any additional changes to the getRGB() return value. Following is a sample of ActionScript code that uses the color value of a MovieClip object named mcDog for a new color change to a MovieClip object named mcHero:

```
var cDog:Color = new Color(mcDog);
var cHero:Color = new Color(mcHero);
var nColor:Number = cDog.getRGB();
cHero.setRGB(nColor);
```

This technique works only with tint values, not with brightness and alpha values.

where nColor is a variable that stores mcDog's current color attributes. This variable is then used to set the color of the mcHero instance.

If you need to retrieve the hexadecimal color of a MovieClip object, you can convert the numeric value returned by getRGB() into a hexadecimal string by using the following code:

```
var sHexColor:String = colorObj.getRGB().toString(16);
```

In the preceding code, colorObj refers to a previously created Color object, and sHexColor is the name of a new variable to store the getRGB() value.

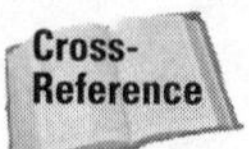

The toString() method of the Number object is discussed in Chapter 12, "The Number Class." In the previous example, hexadecimal numbers are base-16, which is used in the toString() method.

The getRGB() method can be used in situations in which you want to pass one MovieClip object's solid color to another (or series of) MovieClip objects. You'll use the getRGB() method in the "Controlling the Absolute Color of a Movie Clip" section of this chapter.

If you use the percentage field (or scale) in the Tint mode, getRGB() will apply only the percent to the actual RGB values and return that solid color reference. You can see this effect in getRGB_error.fla, located in the ch16 folder of the book's CD-ROM.

Setting Advanced Color Effects

The setTransform() method of the Color class is much more complex than the setRGB() method. Although setRGB() works much like the Tint mode of the Property inspector, setTransform() mirrors the Advanced mode of the Property inspector exactly. If you recall from the step-by-step exercise earlier in this section, the Advanced mode has a total of eight settings. In order to pass all eight values to the setTransform() method, you need to create a transformObject, a generic Object object containing the color settings you want to apply to a MovieClip object. In Figure 16-6, you see a MovieClip object with specific Advanced mode settings in the Property inspector.

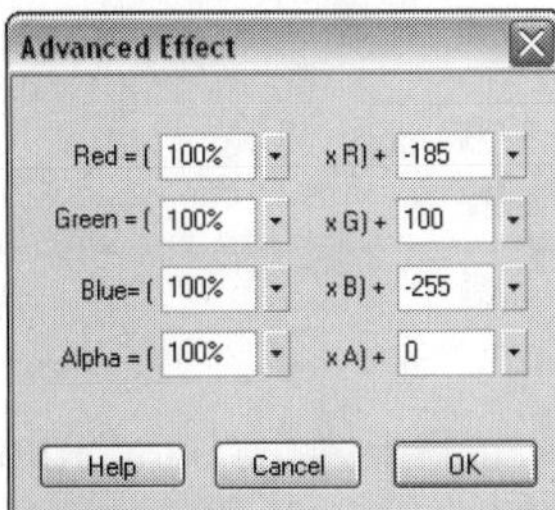

Figure 16-6: The mcHero object has three applied values in the Advanced mode of the Property inspector.

To translate these values into ActionScript, you create an `Object` instance (referred to as the `transformObject` for `Color` objects) as follows:

```
var oGreenColor:Object = new Object();
oGreenColor.rb = -185;
oGreenColor.gb = 100;
oGreenColor.bb = -255;
```

Once you have a `transformObject` created with the color code properties (as shown in Figure 16-6), you can then use the object in the `setTransform()` method:

```
var cHero:Color = new Color(hero);
cHero.setTransform(oGreenColor);
```

You can also create a `transformObject` with the following syntax:

```
var transformObject:Object = {
   ra: value,
   rb: value,
   ga: value,
   gb: value,
   ba: value,
   bb: value,
   aa: value,
   ab: value
};
```

In this syntax, the `= { };` notation is a shortcut to creating an `Object` instance with `ra`, `rb`, `ga`, `gb`, `ba`, `bb`, `aa`, and `ab` as the properties of that object. With this notation, you omit the initial `new Object()` line used previously. This syntax performs identically to the previous notation.

Caution Do not insert a comma after the last property/value pair in the shortcut syntax. For example, the following code will produce an error: `var transformObject:Object = { ra: 100, rb:0, };`. The last value, `rb`, should not end with a comma.

It is important to note that you do not need to specify all of the eight properties (and values for them) in the `transformObject`. You need to list only the properties that have a new value. For example, if you want to change only the red offset for a `MovieClip` object, you need to specify only `rb` in the `transformObject`.

Tip

You can create a transformObject named oResetColor, which sets a MovieClip object's color effects back to its default: var oResetColor:Object = { ra:100, rb:0, ga:100, gb: 0, ba:100, bb:0, aa:100, ab:0};. In this example, all eight values need to be specified in order to be assured that any and all previous changes to the MovieClip object are reset.

Retrieving Advanced Color Information

The getTransform() method of the Color object allows you to retrieve the color attributes of MovieClip objects that have Advanced mode effects applied to them or MovieClip objects that have been changed with the setTransform() method of the Color class. Much like using the getRGB() method, you can use this method to duplicate color effects across multiple MovieClip objects. For example, the following code transfers the color properties of the MovieClip object named mcDog to the MovieClip object named mcHero:

```
var cDog:Color = new Color(mcDog);
var cHero:Color = new Color(mcHero);
cHero.setTransform(cDog.getTransform());
```

Here, we simply refer to the getTransform() method directly within the setTransform() method of another Color object. In the getRGB() method, we created a transition variable to pass along the attributes, which could have been done here as well. However, there is a difference between getTransform() and getRGB() beyond their applied color effects. The getTransform() method will return a fully built transformObject, with all color properties and values.

Controlling the Absolute Color of a Movie Clip

In this section, you learn how to apply the setRGB() and getRGB() methods to a Flash movie. You'll start with a prebuilt Flash document (FLA file) containing the following:

- ✦ A MovieClip object named mcHero. This is artwork of a cartoon character provided by Sandro Corsaro (www.sandrocorsaro.com). Inside of mcHero, there are two MovieClip objects: mcBodyFill (the hero's body suit) and mcGloveEmblem (the hero's gloves and chest emblem).
- ✦ A Movie Clip symbol named chipClip. This symbol is used to apply color changes to the mcHero object.

This exercise shows you how to enable instances of the chipClip symbol to pass its color property (as a solid RGB color) to the mcBodyFill instance, contained within the mcHero instance. To change MovieClip objects to solid colors, you use the setRGB() method of the Color class. Remember, setRGB() and getRGB() work in a fashion similar to the Tint mode of the Property inspector. Once the ActionScript is added to the movie, you can pass the Flash document along to a Flash designer, who can then easily change the colors that are applied to the mcHero instance.

In order to complete this exercise, make a copy of the heroColorMenu_starter.fla file, located in the ch16 folder of the book's CD-ROM.

Before you edit the starter file, let's review the process of the movie's interactive functionality. You will change the color of the first instance of the `chipClip` symbol using the Property inspector. Then, you'll create two `Color` objects: one that targets the `mcHero.mcBodyFill` instance, and one that targets the first instance of the `chipClip` symbol. Then, you'll add a button event handler to the `chipClip` symbol. This handler will pass the color of the `chipClip` instance along to the `mcBodyFill` object. Once you've done this, you can create several `chipClip` instances to form a color menu for the hero artwork. Ready? Let's get started.

1. When you open the starter Flash document (FLA file) from the CD-ROM, you should see two layers: buttons and hero. On the stage, you will see one instance of the `heroClip` symbol, with an instance name of `mcHero` in the Property inspector; and one instance of the `colorChip` symbol, which is not named. Refer to the stage shown in Figure 16-7.

2. Double-click the `mcHero` instance on the stage or the `heroClip` symbol in the library. On its timeline, you'll see a layer holding an instance of the `heroSuit_body` Movie Clip, named `mcBodyFill`, in the Property inspector. You need to create a `Color` object targeting this `mcBodyFill` instance. Go back to Scene 1 (that is, the main timeline), and create a new layer named `actions`. On the first frame of this layer, create a `Color` object named `cBody` that targets `mcBodyFill`:

   ```
   var cBody:Color = new Color(mcHero.mcBodyFill);
   ```

   Here, you need to make sure that the entire path to `mcBodyFill` is specified. Because `mcBodyFill` is inside of the `mcHero` object, this action needs to know where it can find `mcBodyFill`. Later, keep in mind that any change to `cBody` will be passed along to `mcBodyFill`.

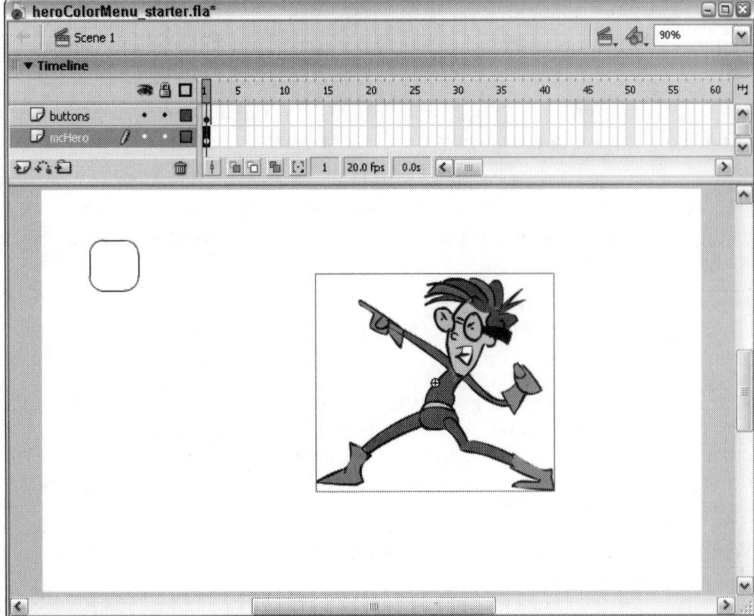

Figure 16-7: The heroClip and colorChip symbols on the main timeline

3. You need to change the color properties of the `chipClip` symbol instance located on the main timeline. Select the instance (on the buttons layer), and open the Property inspector. Name the instance `mcBlueChip`. In the Color menu, choose Tint mode, and specify the Web-safe color, `#3333CC`. This is also the same as Red 51, Green 51, Blue 204. Refer to Figure 16-8.

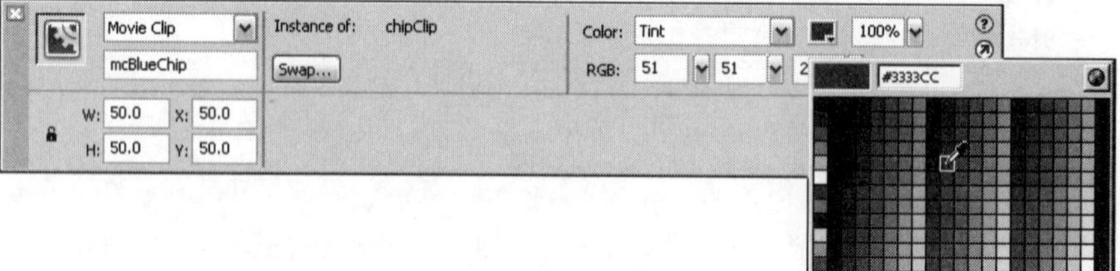

Figure 16-8: This color will be passed from the mcBlueChip instance to the hero.

4. You need to create a `Color` object that identifies each `chipClip` instance. To do this, double-click the `mcBlueChip` instance on the stage. In Edit mode on the `chipClip` timeline, create a new layer named `actions`. Select frame 1 of this layer and open the Actions panel (F9). Add the following code:

```
var cTarget:Color = this._parent.cBody;
var cChip:Color = new Color(this);
```

   Here, you want to make a reference to the `cBody` object you created in Step 2. You'll make this a variable named `cTarget`. Because `cBody` is not within the instance of the `chipClip` symbol, you need to make sure this code will properly reference it. By using `this._parent.cBody`, you tell ActionScript to look at the parent timeline of this instance. Remember, `cBody` is linked to the `mcBodyFill` object inside of the `mcHero` object (from Step 2).

   You also want to create a new `Color` object that targets the current object, `this`, which represents this instance of the `chipClip` symbol.

5. You need to reference the `cTarget` variable in a `setRGB()` method to actually change the color of `mcBodyFill`. This action will occur within an `onRelease()` handler assigned to each instance of the `chipClip` symbol. After the code you added in Step 4, insert the following code:

```
this.onRelease = function() {
   cTarget.setRGB(cChip.getRGB());
};
```

   This code changes the color of `mcBodyFill`, referenced through the `cTarget` variable you created in Step 4. More importantly, you need to make sure you use the color of the current instance of `chipClip` to pass along to `mcBodyFill`. In the previous step, you created a `Color` object named `cChip` that referred to the current instance, as `this`.

6. Save your Flash document as `heroColorMenu.fla`, and test it (Ctrl+Enter or ⌘+Enter). When you click the `mcBlueChip` instance, the `mcBodyFill` color will match the color of the `mcBlueChip` instance.

7. Go back to the main timeline, and duplicate the mcBlueChip instance (Edit ⇨ Duplicate or Ctrl+D or ⌘+D). For each new instance, assign a new name in the Property inspector and change its Tint value. When you test your movie again, each instance will pass its color along to the mcBodyFill object.

If you are wondering why you can have so many cTarget variables in the same movie, don't worry. Because each cTarget variable is declared on a separate MovieClip object, ActionScript will not overwrite the values of other cTarget variables. Remember that all objects and variables belong to a specific timeline.

You can see a finished version of this exercise on the book's CD-ROM. In the ch16 folder, you will find a file named heroColorMenu.fla.

Applying Advanced Color Effects to Movie Clips

In the last section, you learned how to use the setRGB() and getRGB() methods in order to apply solid color changes to MovieClip objects. In this section, you learn how to apply Advanced mode changes to MovieClip objects using setTransform() and getTransform(). The technique is very similar as well:

1. Apply an Advanced color setting to a MovieClip object using the Property inspector.
2. Create a Color object for that MovieClip object.
3. Using getTransform(), retrieve the color properties of the MovieClip object, and pass those properties to another MovieClip object using setTransform().

Again, you'll start with a prebuilt Flash document (FLA file) that has all of the elements already made — the artwork and initial MovieClip objects. Before you add the ActionScript for the setTransform() and getTransform() methods, however, examine the heroChipClip Movie Clip symbol in the movie.

In order to proceed, you'll need to make a copy of the heroColorMenu_adv_starter.fla file, located in the ch16 folder of the book's CD-ROM.

Open the starter file, and double-click the heroChipClip symbol in the document's Library panel. Inside of this symbol, you will see two layers: mcHero and mcHitArea. An instance of the heroClip symbol is on the mcHero layer (the instance name is mcHero as well). This is the same symbol that is presented at 100 percent on the main timeline (_root). Here, however, the mcHero object will be used as an icon. Later, you'll apply color changes to instances of the outer heroChipClip symbol (using the Advanced color mode of the Property inspector), which will affect the appearance of the nested mcHero icon.

The mcHitArea layer holds a MovieClip instance named mcHitArea. This object contains a nested Graphic instance of the invisibleButton symbol. The mcHitArea object will be used as the hit area of the heroChipClip symbol. In this exercise, you learn how to build MovieClip objects that behave as buttons. The heroChipClip symbol needs to be given ActionScript that will change the color of the larger mcHero object on the main timeline.

The rest of the document structure is exactly the same as the example from the previous section. This movie also contains a set of five chipClip symbol instances already using the setRGB() and getRGB() methods. The only thing left for you to do is add the functionality to the heroChipClip symbol.

1. First, create a Color object that targets the mcHero object on the main timeline. If you select frame 1 of the actions layer and open the Actions panel, you will see the Color object from the previous exercise. The cBody variable sets up a Color object that targets the mcBodyFill object within the mcHero object. For this exercise, you want to create a Color object that will change the entire mcHero object—not just the mcBodyFill object. After the existing code on frame 1, add the following code:

```
var cHero:Color = new Color(mcHero);
```

2. Select the instance of heroChipClip symbol on the stage, and open the Property inspector. Name the instance mcHeroChip_1.

3. Next, you set up all instances of the heroChipClip symbol to work with the cHero object. You also need to create a specific Color object for each mcHeroChip_ object that you add, in order to pass its color information to the cHero object (which is linked to mcHero). Double-click the mcHeroChip_1 instance to edit the heroChipClip symbol. Create a new layer named actions, and place this layer at the top of the layer stack in the heroChipClip timeline. Open the Actions panel (F9), and add the following code into the Script pane:

```
var cTarget:Color = this._parent.cHero;
var cChip:Color = new Color(this);
```

   Here, cChip is the name of the Color object that targets the current instance of the heroChipClip symbol, referred to as this, and cTarget is a variable that references the cHero object created in Step 1.

4. Because you have two Color objects in the timeline (cHero and cChip), you can pass color attributes between them. In this exercise, you pass Advanced mode color effects using the setTransform() and getTransform() methods. You'll use both of these methods in one line of ActionScript, in the same frame. After the last line of code you typed in Step 3, add the following code:

```
this.hitArea = mcHitArea;

this.onRelease = function(){
   cTarget.setTransform(cChip.getTransform());
};
```

   This code uses the new button behaviors that can be directly applied to MovieClip objects. The first line of code uses the hitArea property to specify which MovieClip instance will be designated as the hit area of the "button" MovieClip object. The next block of code assigns an onRelease() event handler to the current instance of the heroChipClip symbol. This function will change the color attributes of cTarget (which references the cHero object) to those of the current instance, cChip. Both of these objects were created in the last step.

5. Go back to the main timeline (that is, Scene 1). With the ActionScript now in place, you can change the appearance of the mcHeroChip_1 instance in the Property inspector. Select the mcHeroChip_1 instance, and open the Property inspector. Choose the Advanced mode in the Color menu, and apply a new color effect. In this example, you

can use the settings shown in Figure 16-9. This color effect will be passed to the mcHero object when the mcHeroChip_1 instance is clicked.

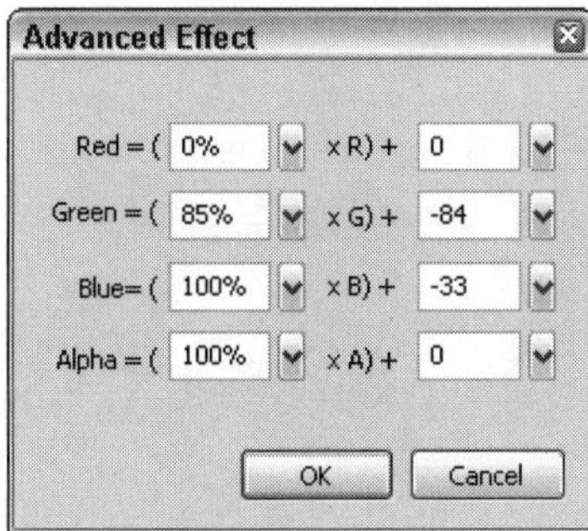

Figure 16-9: These settings give the instance a shaded blue color effect.

6. Save your Flash document as heroColorMenu_adv.fla, and test it (Ctrl+Enter or ⌘+Enter). When you click the mcHeroChip_1 instance, the color of the mcHero object will change.
7. Go back to the stage and duplicate the mcHeroChip_1 instance. In the Property inspector, rename the new instance to mcHeroChip_2. Change the Advanced color mode settings for this chip so that they're different from the previous one. Test your movie again, and notice that each chip's color is passed to the mcHero object when the chip is clicked.

You can now implement the same strategy with other aspects of Flash interface design. For example, you can use the same methodology to create "skins" for your Flash movie. Skins are color schemes and motifs for user interface elements, such as windows, menus, and background color.

You can see the completed movie, heroColorMenu_adv.fla, in the ch16 folder of this book's CD-ROM. In this document, you will see a reset button that uses a separate object named oResetColor (in frame 1 of the actions layer) to reset the mcHero and mcBodySuit objects to their original colors.

We'd like to know what you thought about this chapter. Visit www.flashsupport.com/feedback to fill out an online form with your comments.

Summary

- ✦ The constructor for Color objects uses the new operator. Each instance of a Color object should be constructed in the following syntax: var objectName:Color = new Color(movieClipTarget);.
- ✦ All methods of the Color object are used with a specific instance, as in cHero.getRGB();. You cannot invoke methods through the class name itself, as in Color.getRGB();.

- The `setRGB()` and `getRGB()` methods of the `Color` class work with color values just like the Tint mode in the Property inspector.
- The `setTransform()` and `getTransform()` methods of the `Color` class work with color values, just like the Advanced mode of the Property inspector.

✦ ✦ ✦

CHAPTER 17

The TextField and Selection Classes

✦ ✦ ✦ ✦

In This Chapter

Learning about types of text

Creating text at authoring time and creating programmatic text at runtime

Working with TextField objects via ActionScript

Using HTML with TextField objects

Scrolling text

Getting and setting focus

Using the Selection class with TextField objects

✦ ✦ ✦ ✦

Text is an indispensable part of most any Flash application. In this chapter, you get a chance to look at the many facets of working with text within Flash. You'll read about how to create text that can be controlled with ActionScript and how to actually use the ActionScript to effect changes. You can render HTML, scroll text, embed fonts, and much more.

Closely related to text is the `Selection` class. You can use the `Selection` class to get and set *focus*. The active object on the stage, the one receiving the user's mouse and keystroke interaction, has focus. And you can also use the `Selection` class to get and set the selection within a `TextField`. That means that you can set an insert point for input text and you can retrieve the text that the user highlights. Read on in this chapter to learn about these things and more.

Understanding Types of Text

In Flash you can work with three types of text: static, dynamic, and input. Prior to learning ActionScript you have likely used static text almost exclusively. However, although static text has its place, it is not something that you will work with when managing text in ActionScript. Static text is not scriptable or controllable in the same ways as dynamic or input text. So let's take a closer look at the two types of text that you will be working with via ActionScript.

Dynamic Text

Dynamic text is the basic type of text that you can manage with ActionScript. With dynamic text you can display, scroll, format, resize, and even create text completely with code. That is something that you'll be sure to want to do as you start developing more Flash applications that contain greater amounts of dynamic content. For example, if you want to display updated news or features, you'll want to use dynamic text. Any text that you want to update while the application is running, whether that update occurs based on loaded data, user interaction, or any other reason, should be dynamic text.

Input Text

Input text enables a user to provide textual interaction. Input text actually includes all the same functionality as dynamic text, but it also provides the additional functionality of allowing the user to enter text values. Input text fields allow users the opportunity to do everything from entering their username and password to inputting shipping information for an e-commerce application.

Creating TextField Objects

When you create a dynamic or input text field you are actually creating a `TextField` object. This is important because dynamic and input text fields are instances of the `TextField` class, which means that you can utilize all the built-in properties and methods of the `TextField` class in order to control the instances with ActionScript code.

Obviously, before you can do anything with a `TextField` instance you first need to create it. In the following sections you'll get a chance to see the various ways that you can create `TextField` objects. Essentially, you can categorize these ways as either authoring-time creation or runtime creation. Whether you create a `TextField` object at authoring time or at runtime, the object is still a `TextField` object that can be managed in the same way as any other `TextField` object. So the main consideration should be simply which technique is most appropriate given the scenario. Let's take a closer look.

Making Text at Authoring Time

Creating text at authoring time means that you are creating the text using the Text tool and drawing the `TextField` object on the stage. Creating text at authoring time has some advantages (over creating text at runtime) in certain situations:

- ✦ For a visually oriented person it might be much more convenient to layout text created during authoring time than text created at runtime.
- ✦ When you create text at authoring time you can use the Property inspector to set many properties of the `TextField` object, and thus you don't have to necessarily write all the ActionScript code to initialize the object with those values.

If you've created static text before, you already know the basics of how to create a dynamic or input `TextField` object during authoring time because in order to create dynamic or input text, just as with static text, you should choose the Text tool and draw the shape of the new `TextField` object. The primary difference between creating static text or dynamic or input text is that you should select the correct type from the Text type menu before drawing the text on the stage. Therefore, after selecting the Text tool, but before drawing the `TextField` object, you should select the appropriate type—Dynamic Text for a dynamic `TextField` object or Input Text for an input text field—from the Text type menu in the Property inspector, as shown in Figure 17-1.

Note You can modify the text type for a `TextField` object after you've drawn it. We recommend setting the type before drawing it only as a general workflow tip. It works much in the same way as drawing a shape on the stage: You can select the fill color beforehand, or you can select the shape after it's been drawn and change the fill color.

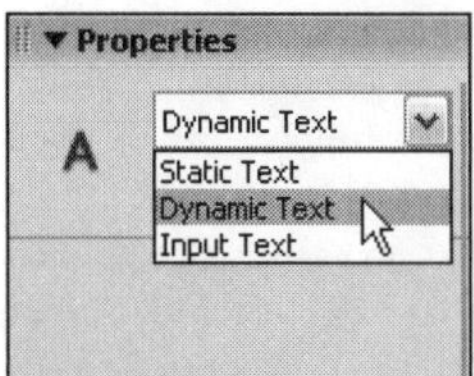

Figure 17-1: Select Dynamic Text or Input Text from the Text type menu.

Although you can change the type of a `TextField` object after you've drawn it, in many cases it is important that you make sure that either Dynamic Text or Input Text is selected *before* you draw the object. Often when you create dynamic and/or input text, you don't want to add any value to it during authoring time. Instead, you'll want to add the value at runtime (in the case of dynamic text) or allow the user to enter a value (in the case of input text). However, if you don't enter a value for static text, Flash will remove it from the stage. Dynamic and input text, on the other hand, will allow you to draw the object and not provide a value.

Once you've drawn the `TextField` object on the stage, the next step is to give the object an instance name. This is a crucial step because the instance name is the way in which you can manage the object with ActionScript. You can add the instance name by way of the Property inspector. With the `TextField` object selected on the stage, open the Property inspector and enter the value in the Instance name field just as you would do with a `Button` or `MovieClip` object. The instance name should follow the same naming rules as any other object. If you need a refresher for those naming rules, you can refer back to Chapter 5; the naming rules are the same for variables and objects.

If you've been using Flash for a while, it is possible that you have used the Flash 5 technique of assigning a variable name to text. Although Flash MX 2004 still allows you to do so for the purposes of authoring backward-compatible applications, under no circumstances should you give text a variable name instead of an instance name if you are authoring Flash 6 or Flash 7 content. If you try to work with text with a variable name instead of an instance name, you will not be able to access the properties and methods that it inherits from the `TextField` class. Figure 17-2 shows the Property inspector for an example `TextField` object. Notice that on the left is the `<Instance Name>` field. That is the correct place to assign an instance name to the object. On the right you'll see a field labeled `Var:` and in the box to the right of it you can assign a variable name to the text but only when authoring content for older player versions. Otherwise, you should not assign a value to the field labeled `Var`.

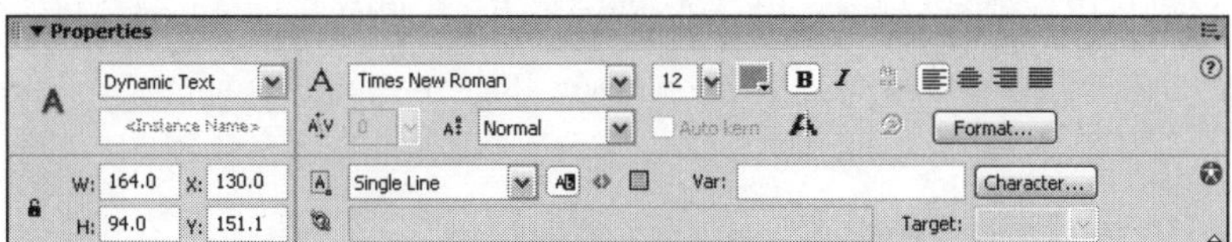

Figure 17-2: The Property inspector for a TextField object

When you create a `TextField` object during authoring time, you can set the many of the properties with the Property inspector as well. Many of the options should be fairly self-evident and familiar to you. For example, you will likely have no difficulties understanding how to select the font face, size, color, or alignment. Some of the other options may be somewhat unfamiliar to you, and therefore this section examines them in more detail. Namely, we'll look at the line type, selectable, HTML-enabled, border, and maximum character settings. In this section you'll get a chance to see how to modify those settings in the Property inspector. The corresponding ActionScript properties are discussed later in the chapter.

The Line type menu allows you to select from the following options:

✦ **Single line:** This default setting allows only one line of text to be typed into the input text. However, in the unlikely event that you need to assign text to this field using ActionScript expressions, you can use the `newline` operator (or `\n` backslash, discussed later) to force a carriage return in the field.

✦ **Multiline:** This setting allows several lines of text to be typed into the field, and automatically wraps each line of text.

✦ **Multiline no wrap:** This setting allows several lines of text to be entered into the field by the user, but only pressing the Enter or Return key starts a new line of text. Text does not automatically wrap if the user types beyond the length of the text field.

✦ **Password:** You can hide the user's input from displaying by using this option. Each typed character is seen as an asterisk (*), just like most password fields in other common user interfaces. However, if you access the field's value in ActionScript expressions, the actual typed characters are available.

Immediately to the right of the Line type menu, you find other options that control the formatting of the editable text field. The first option, Selectable, if enabled, allows users to highlight text within a `TextField` object in order to copy it and paste it into another field (or external document). To the right of the Selectable option is the Enable HTML option, which allows you to use HTML formatting tags within your editable `TextField` object when you assign the value via ActionScript. Just to the right of the HTML option is the Show border option. When enabled, this option automatically formats an input text field with a white background and black hairline border. If you do not enable the Show border option, the Flash Player displays the `TextField` object with a dashed outline during authoring time. This outline is not visible when you publish your movie and view it in the Flash Player.

Make sure that the text color is one that will stand out. A common mistake is to have white text on a white background. When that occurs, obviously the text will not seem to be visible, even though it is. Should you notice that your text does not seem to appear, make sure that the color is set correctly.

On the far right of the Property inspector, you find a field labeled Maximum Characters. This option allows you specify a limit to the number of characters that can be typed into the input text field. By default, it is set to zero (0), which means that an unlimited number of characters can be typed into the field.

Making Runtime Text

Runtime text refers to a `TextField` object that you create using ActionScript code instead of using the Text tool during authoring time. Although authoring time text has its benefits, it does not allow you the same programmatic control that runtime text can provide. Runtime text provides such benefits as the following:

✦ Runtime text can be created based on content that is loaded from external sources such as XML files and databases.

✦ Runtime text can be created based on user interaction.

✦ When you have sequences of text you want to create, runtime text can provide a more efficient way of adding it rather than trying to add it at authoring time.

There is just one technique for creating runtime text — regardless of whether you want it to be used for input or as dynamic text. The `createTextField()` method can be called from any `MovieClip` object in order to create a new `TextField` object nested within it. The `createTextField()` method requires six parameters: instance name, depth, x, y, width, and height. So, for example, to create a new `TextField` object named `tLabel` within the current `MovieClip` object you could use the following code:

```
this.createTextField("tLabel", this.getNextHighestDepth(), 0, 0, 100, 20);
```

The preceding code creates the new `TextField` object with the next highest depth, places it at 0,0, and sizes it to 100 by 20 pixels.

The `createTextField()` method does *not* return a reference to the newly created `TextFIeld` instance—something that you might expect given how methods such as `attachMovie()` and `duplicateMovieClip()` work.

By default, when you create a new runtime `TextField` object its properties are as follows:

```
autoSize = "none"
background = false
BackgroundColor = 0xFFFFFF
border = false
borderColor = 0x000000
condenseWhite = false
embedFonts = false
html = false
maxChars = null
multiline = false
password = false
restrict = null
selectable = true
textColor = 0x000000
type = "dynamic"
variable = null
wordWrap = false
```

You'll take a look at these properties in more detail throughout this chapter.

Working with TextField Object Basics

Creating a `TextField` object is only the first step. After you've done that you'll surely want to work with the object by assigning new values to properties and calling methods. The following sections will detail many of the types of things you can do programmatically with a `TextField` object.

Understanding Basic TextField Properties and Methods

The `TextField` class shares some common properties and methods with the `Button` and `MovieClip` classes. As such, they aren't discussed in detail in this chapter. Instead, if you have questions about any of the properties and methods, you can refer back to Chapter 9 for a more in-depth description.

The shared properties and methods are as follows: `_accProps`, `_alpha`, `_focusrect`, `_height`, `_name`, `_parent`, `_rotation`, `_target`, `_url`, `_visible`, `_x`, `_xmouse`, `_xscale`, `_y`, `_ymouse`, `_yscale`, `tabEnabled`, `tabIndex`, and `getDepth()`.

Many of these properties can be used to change the way in which the instance appears visibly. You can use many of those properties in the same way that you would use them for a `MovieClip` or `Button` instance. For example, if you want to move a `TextField` object named `tLabel` to 100,100, the ActionScript would look like the following:

```
tLabel._x = 100;
tLabel._y = 100;
```

There are a few of the properties, however, that will not work in the same way with the default settings for a `TextField` object. The properties `_alpha` and `_rotation` cannot be utilized on a `TextField` object unless the font has been embedded. If you attempt to set one of those properties for a `TextField` object that does not have an embedded font, the instance will simply no longer be visible. See the section "Embedding Fonts" later in this chapter for more information on how to address such a situation.

Adding Text

Once you've created a `TextField` object, either at authoring time or at runtime, one of the things you're most likely to want to do is to give it a new text value so that it displays in the application. In order to do this you need to assign a new string value to its `text` property. For example, if you have created a `TextField` object named `tLabel`, you can add text to be displayed in the following manner:

```
tLabel.text = "This is a label.";
```

You can then later replace the text shown in a `TextField` object by assigning a new value to the `text` property. For example:

```
tLabel.text = "This is another label.";
```

Using Unicode with TextField Objects

You can specify UTF-8, UTF-16LE, or UTF-16BE encodings with text data sources that are loaded into the Flash movie at author-time or runtime. You can also use `\u` escape sequences in the values of `TextField` object properties, such as the `text` and `restrict` properties. If you want to see a specific character's escape sequence, open the Character Map application in Microsoft Windows (for Windows XP, you can choose Start ➪ Programs ➪ Accessories ➪ System Tools ➪ Character Map).

In ActionScript, you can specify the character for a copyright symbol (`U+00A9`) in the text property of a text field, as shown in the following code.

```
tArticle.text = "\u00A9";
```

If you don't want to use escape sequences, you can specify UTF-8 text in a separate AS file that is referenced in an ActionScript `#include` directive. The following text can be found in the `title_multilanguage.as` file located in the ch18 folder of this book's CD-ROM. This AS file was saved from Notepad in Windows XP. Notepad, like many text editors (including TextEdit on Mac OS 9), can save UTF-8 encoded text.

```
//!-- UTF8

title_english = "Welcome to our site.";
title_japanese = "私達の場所への歓迎。";
title_chinese = "欢迎到我们的站点。";
title_arabic = "مرحباً إلى موقعنا";
```

You need to specify the `//!--UTF8` description on the first line of an included AS file in order for Flash MX to properly interpret the encoded characters. In the Flash document, the following actions will attach the `title_multilanguage.as` file, and set the text field named `output` to the `title_english` value.

```
#include "title_multilanguage.as"
this.createTextField("tOutput", this.getNextHighestDepth(), 25, 25, 150, 18);
tUutput.text = title_english;
```

You can also use UTF-8, UTF-16LE, and UTF-16BE encoding with dynamic data sources that are loaded into a Flash movie at runtime by using the `LoadVars` or the `XML` class.

You may also find the following language translation sites helpful in your experimentation with Unicode text:

- ✦ `babelfish.altavista.com`
- ✦ `tarjim.ajeeb.com/ajeeb/default.asp?lang=1`

For more information, Macromedia has prepared very detailed tutorials on Unicode for Flash MX at the following URL:

`www.macromedia.com/support/flash/languages/unicode_in_flmx/`

In order for multiple languages to display on your operating system, you need to make sure that you have installed the required language packs. For example, Japanese characters will not display within a Flash movie unless you have the Japanese language pack installed on your system.

Managing Multiline Text

`TextField` objects can display single-line or multiline content. When you are working with dynamic text then you can display single-line or multiline content regardless of the setting of the object's `multiline` property. However, when using input text, it makes a difference. By default a `TextField` object is single-line, and if you want to allow the user to enter multiple lines of text, you need to set the object's `multiline` property to `true` (it's `false` by default).

```
tLabel.multiline = true;
```

Word wrapping is another consideration. When you are working with multiline text you may want to have the text wrap to the next line when it reaches the extent of the bounding box width. In order to achieve that with ActionScript, you need only set the `wordWrap` property to `true`.

```
tLabel.wordWrap = true;
```

Otherwise, as long as `wordWrap` is `false` the text will continue to extend past the width of the bounding box until a line break is encountered.

Resizing a TextField Object

Because the text in a `TextField` object is subject to change dynamically, it is not necessarily going to be the case that you'll know the dimensions of the text during authoring time. Instead, you may want to change the dimensions based on the content.

When we discuss resizing a `TextField` object, we are distinguishing between resizing and scaling. If you set the `_xscale` and/or `_yscale` property for a `TextField` object, the text that it displays will also scale. If you want to resize a `TextField` object, that means you want to change the dimensions of the bounding box while maintaining the font size of the text.

The simplest type of resizing involves telling Flash to automatically resize the `TextField` to accommodate any text that is assigned to it. You can do that by assigning the corresponding value to the object's `autoSize` property. The following is a list of the possible values:

- **none:** This is the default setting, and it means that the `TextField` object does not resize automatically.
- **left:** This means that the object automatically resizes to the content using the upper-left corner of the `TextField` instance as the fixed point.
- **right:** This means that the object automatically resizes as with the setting of left, but it uses the upper-right corner as the fixed point instead of the left corner.
- **center:** This means that the object automatically resizes as with a setting of left or right, but it uses the upper center as the fixed point.

If you assign a Boolean value to the `autoSize` property it will work. A value of `true` is synonymous with `left` and a value of `false` is synonymous with `none`. However, we encourage you to use the correct string values, especially considering ActionScript's move toward stronger typing.

In order to understand how the `autoSize` property affects resizing, it is helpful to see an actual example. The following code creates three `TextField` objects, adds text to them, and tells them to resize in different ways:

```
this.createTextField("tLabel1", this.getNextHighestDepth(), 0, 0, 0, 0);
tLabel1.text = "Label one";
tLabel1.autoSize = "left";
this.createTextField("tLabel2", this.getNextHighestDepth(), 0, 25, 0, 0);
tLabel2.text = "Label two";
tLabel2.autoSize = "right";
this.createTextField("tLabel3", this.getNextHighestDepth(), 0, 50, 0, 0);
tLabel3.text = "Label three";
tLabel3.autoSize = "center";
```

Figure 17-3 shows what the preceding code displays when tested. The vertical line is added where *x* is 0 to give you a reference point.

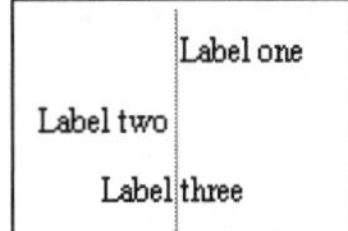

Figure 17-3: An example of three TextField objects with different autoSize values

You can also, of course, simply assign new values to the `_width` and `_height` properties. That will cause the bounding box to resize to specific pixels widths. The `textWidth` and `textHeight` properties return the pixel width and height of the text contained within a `TextField` object and, as such, can be used for some simple resizing effects. Flash places a two-pixel margin around the text within a `TextField` object, and so when you use the `textWidth` and/or `textHeight` properties, be aware that you'll probably want to add four pixels to those values. The following code creates a `TextField` object sized to match the width of the text, but is set to a fixed 20 pixels in height:

```
this.createTextField("tSample", this.getNextHighestDepth(), 0, 0, 0, 0);
tSample.text = "This is\nsome\nsample\ntext.";
tSample._height = 20;
tSample._width = tSample.textWidth + 4;
```

The preceding example would be useful if, for example, you wanted to create a `TextField` that is a specific number of pixels in one dimension but that fits the text exactly in the other dimension. You can then use the scrolling properties to scroll the text as shown in the section "Scrolling Text" later in this chapter.

The `textWidth` and `textHeight` properties provide very simplistic information about the text dimensions within a `TextField` object. For more complex information, you can use the `getTextExtent()` method of a `TextFormat` object as described in Chapter 18.

Making Text Non-Selectable

The default setting for text is that it is selectable. That means that the user can use the mouse to highlight and copy the text as well as place the cursor within the instance for input (in the case of input text). In some situations that is preferable. For example, input text must be selectable, and if you want the user to be able to copy and paste something you should make sure it is selectable. However, you might well want other text to be nonselectable. Labels, titles, and so on, should probably be made nonselectable. And when text is used within a button it should definitely be made nonselectable so that it doesn't interfere with the state detection of the button.

You can change the selectable state of a `TextField` object with the `selectable` property. The default value is `true`, which means that the user can select the text. Setting the value to `false` makes the instance nonselectable.

```
tLabel.selectable = false;
```

Setting Border and Background

`TextField` objects display without borders and backgrounds by default. However, you can programmatically control whether or not these things are displayed.

The border property defaults to false. If you set the value to true, Flash displays a hairline border around the TextField instance:

```
tLabel.border = true;
```

Likewise, the background property defaults to false, but if you set the property to true, a background fill is displayed behind the text within the TextField object:

```
tLabel.background = true;
```

By default the border is black and the background is white. You can programmatically change the colors with the borderColor and backgroundColor properties. The properties expect a numeric value representing the color you want to assign to the border and/or background. The following assigns a red border color and a yellow background color to an instance named tLabel:

```
tLabel.borderColor = 0xFF0000;
tLabel.backgroundColor = 0xFFFF00;
```

Creating Input Text

As we already mentioned earlier in this chapter, both dynamic text and input text are TextField objects. Flash distinguishes between the two with a single property: type. The type property can have two values: dynamic or input. The default value is dynamic. Setting the value to input makes the object an input TextField object that allows the user to type or paste text into it. For example, the following creates a new object named tUsername, and it assigns the value input to the type property, thus allowing for user input:

```
this.createTextField("tUsername", this.getNextHighestDepth(), 0, 0, 100, 20);
tUsername.type = "input";
```

Typically, when you create input text you'll want to make sure that the border is displayed so that the user knows where to enter the text:

```
tUsername.border = true;
```

Managing Input

When working with input text, you may want to control the text that can be input into a field. There are two ways that ActionScript enables you to exercise this control. You can assign a maximum number of characters that can be input and you can specify which specific characters might not be input.

The maxChars property controls the maximum number of characters that a user can input. By default, this property has a value of null, which allows an unlimited number of characters to be typed into the field. Regardless of the value for this property, ActionScript code has unrestricted access to add content. This value is strictly for the amount of text allowed by the user. The following example limits the number of characters that can be input to 10 for an instance named tUsername:

```
tUsername.maxChars = 10;
```

The restrict property controls the allowable characters for a particular object. As the name implies, you can use this property to restrict the range of characters that the user can type into the field. The value for this property is a string value specifying the acceptable and/or unacceptable characters (or character ranges).

Even if a field is restricted, you can still insert whatever text you want via ActionScript. The `restrict` property can prohibit users from entering undesired characters into a field.

To specify enabled characters, simply type the characters in the string value. These values are case-sensitive. The following code tells the `tArticle` field to accept only characters `A`, `B`, `C`, or `D`.

```
tArticle.restrict = "ABCD";
```

You can also use a dash (-) to indicate a range of characters. The following code is another way of establishing characters `A` through `D`:

```
tArticle.restrict = "A-D";
```

You can specify several ranges in one string. The following code enables `A` through `D`, a space character, and 1 through 4:

```
tArticle.restrict = "A-D 1-4";
```

To omit or specify unacceptable characters, precede the character (or character range) with the ^ character. The following code enables all characters except 0–9 for a text field named article:

```
tArticle.restrict = "^0-9";
```

You can use all of these syntax elements together to specify both enabled and disabled character sets. The following code enables all uppercase letters, but disables all lowercase letters:

```
tArticle.restrict = "A-Z^a-z";
```

Note that the previous line of code does not enable a space character. You must specify a space directly in the restricted value.

To specify one of the syntax operators used to denote ranges (`-`) or omissions (`^`), precede the operator with a backslash. The following code prevents the user from typing a minus character (`-`) in the `tArticle` text field. You can also use a backslash pair to denote the backslash character (`\`) itself as `\\`.

```
tArticle.restrict = "^\-";
```

You can also enable or disable Unicode characters from text fields using `\u` escape sequences. See the "Using Unicode with TextField Objects" sidebar earlier in this chapter.

Creating Password Text

When you are creating input fields for potentially sensitive data such as passwords, you may want to make the input field a password field. That means that rather than displaying the text that the user enters, Flash will display asterisk characters. This prevents other people who can see the screen from being able to read the data. You can make any input text field a password field simply by setting the value of its `password` property to `true`.

```
tPassword.password = true;
```

It is important to understand that a password field does nothing more than alter how the content is displayed in the application. The data that the user enters is still accessible via ActionScript as usual. This also means that using a password field does not provide any additional security or encryption functionality to your application. You should be very careful to not send sensitive data from a Flash application without encryption. That typically means using SSL, another technology supported by Flash.

You can read more about SSL at `www.netscape.com/eng/security/`.

Changing Text Color

There are several ways in which you can change text color:

- ✦ Assign a new value to the `TextField` object's `textColor` property.
- ✦ Use HTML and `<font>` tags.
- ✦ Use a `TextFormat` object.
- ✦ Use CSS.

The `textColor` property can be used to apply a single color to all the text in a `TextField` object. All you need to do is assign a numeric value to the property. For example, the following makes all the text red in a `TextField` object named `tLabel`:

```
tLabel.textColor = 0xFF0000;
```

Using String Hexadecimal Values in Color Properties

Many Flash developers and students learning ActionScript often ask if it's possible to convert a string value containing a hexadecimal value into a number that's recognized by ActionScript object methods and properties that require number data types, not strings. Such methods include the `setRGB()` method of the `Color` object and the numerous color properties of the `TextField` class. For example, the following code will not function correctly in ActionScript:

```
tArticle.textColor = "0xFFFFFF";
```

The `textColor` property requires a number data type. Luckily, the answer is pretty simple. You can convert a string value specifying a hexadecimal value into a numeric data type by using the `parseInt()` function. The following code converts a string variable named `nHexColor` to a numeric data type for the `textColor` property of the `TextField` object:

```
nHexColor = "FF0000";
article.textColor = parseInt("0x" + nHexColor);
```

The significance of this approach may not be immediately apparent. However, what if you wanted to provide an input text field to your user so that he or she could enter a hexadecimal value for a custom interface element? His or her input in the text field would be typed as string data, and you would need a way of converting this string into a number. Again, `parseInt()` can do the work for you. Another use for this process is the conversion of any loaded text values from an external data source. For example, you may have a database of custom colors for a Flash movie. When the Flash movie loads that data, it will be typed as a string. Using the `parseInt()` function, you can convert the loaded variable's variable into a number.

The HTML, TextFormat, and CSS options provide you with much more control over the color (as in you can apply different colors to different text) within a TextField object. The HTML solution is discussed in more detail in the next part of this chapter. The TextFormat and CSS options are discussed in Chapter 18.

Removing Text

You can remove TextField objects programmatically only if they were created programmatically. The removeTextField() method can be called from a TextField object, and if the object was created using createTextField(), it will remove the object from the stage:

```
tLabel.removeTextField();
```

Creating a Simple Notes Application

In this exercise you'll get the opportunity to put into practice many of the things you've learned thus far in the chapter. You'll create a very simple notes application in which the user can log in and view and store notes. The notes are stored in a local shared object. For more information on local shared objects, you might want to consult Chapter 25.

This application provides a simple login process before the user can read and/or update the notes. The primary purpose is to illustrate the various basic TextField properties in context. You should therefore be made aware that the login process in this example is not secure. The username and password in this example are stored within the SWF file, and can quite simply be read by most any user. Username and password combinations, in secure applications, should be stored externally in a repository such as a database.

1. Open the notes_starter.fla on the CD-ROM, and save it to your local disk as notes001.fla.
2. Open the library so you can see that there are two Movie Clip symbols that have already been added to the FLA file. If you open the linkage settings for the two symbols you can see that they have been set to export for ActionScript.
3. Add to the first frame of the main timeline the ActionScript code shown in Listing 17-1.

Listing 17-1: The createLoginScreen() function

```
function createLoginScreen():Void {

  // Create the TextField and MovieClip objects.
  this.createTextField("tUsername", this.getNextHighestDepth(), 100, 100, ⮐
     200, 20);
  this.createTextField("tPassword", this.getNextHighestDepth(), 100, 140, ⮐
     200, 20);
  this.createTextField("tMessage", this.getNextHighestDepth(), 100, 60, ⮐
     200, 20);
  this.attachMovie("LoginButtonSymbol", "mcLoginButton", ⮐
     this.getNextHighestDepth());
```

Continued

Listing 17-1 *(continued)*

```
  // Set the properties of the TextField objects.
  tUsername.border = true;
  tPassword.border = true;
  tUsername.type = "input";
  tPassword.type = "input";
  tPassword.password = true;
  tMessage.textColor = 0xFF0000;

  // Place the button.
  mcLoginButton._x = 100;
  mcLoginButton._y = 180;

  mcLoginButton.onRelease = function():Void {

    // Check to see if the user has entered the correct username
    // and password. If so, call the login() function.
    // Otherwise, display
    // a message to the user and clear the values from the login
    // TextField objects.
    if(tUsername.text == "admin" && tPassword.text == "admin") {
      login();
    }
    else {
      tMessage.text = "Try again.";
      tUsername.text = "";
      tPassword.text = "";
    }
  };
}

function login():Void {

  // Remove the TextField and MovieClip objects that made up the
  // login screen.
  tUsername.removeTextField();
  tPassword.removeTextField();
  mcLoginButton.removeMovieClip();

  // Create the TextField and MovieClip for the notes screen.
  this.createTextField("tNotes", this.getNextHighestDepth(), 100, 100, ⮐
     350, 200);
  this.attachMovie("SaveButtonSymbol", "mcSaveButton", ⮐
     this.getNextHighestDepth());

  // Set the properties of the TextField object.
  tNotes.border = true;
  tNotes.type = "input";
```

```
    // Place the button.
    mcSaveButton._x = 100;
    mcSaveButton._y = 320;

    // Open a local shared object.
    var lsoNotes:SharedObject = SharedObject.getLocal("notes");

    // Assign the stored text, if any.
    tNotes.text = (lsoNotes.data.notes == undefined) ? "" : lsoNotes.data.notes;

    // When the user clicks and releases the button, store the
    // current notes.
    // in the shared object.
    mcSaveButton.onRelease = function():Void {
      lsoNotes.data.notes = tNotes.text;
      lsoNotes.flush();
    }
}

createLoginScreen();
```

4. Test the movie.

If you attempt to log in with the incorrect username and password combination, you will see the message appear in red text. Otherwise, if you log in with the admin/admin username/password combination, you will get access to the notes screen.

Using HTML with TextField Objects

Not only can `TextField` objects display regular text, but they can also display HTML. Flash supports only a subset of HTML tags, including the following:

- **<a>:** Flash supports only the `href` and `target` attributes of the `anchor` tag. That means you can use `<a>` to create hyperlinks in your text.
- **
:** The `<br>` tag creates a line break in the text.
- **<font>:** The color, face, and size attributes are supported for this tag. You can use `<font>` to apply simple formatting to parts of the text.
- **<p>:** The align and class attributes are supported for this tag. The align attribute aligns the text to left, right, or center. The class attribute is used with cascading style sheets, a new feature in Flash that is discussed in more detail in Chapter 18.
- **<span>:** The class attribute is supported for this tag, and the tag is therefore used only in conjunction with cascading style sheets as discussed in Chapter 18.
- **<b>, <u>, and <i>:** These tags make text appear bolded, underlined, and italicized, respectively.
- **<li>:** This tag creates a list element. List elements appear indented and with bullet points to their left.

Flash also provides support for the `<img>` tag and a tag called `<textformat>`. The `<img>` tag support is discussed in more detail in the section "Embedding Content in Text." The `<textformat>` tag is unique to Flash, and it is more commonly utilized with of a TextFormat object. You can read more about TextFormat objects in Chapter 18.

Rendering HTML in Text

By default, Flash TextField objects render all text literally. That means that if you ask the TextField to display the following:

```
<font color="#FF0000">Red Text</font>
```

Flash displays that text literally instead of rendering the HTML and displaying only Red Text with a red color applied to it. If you want Flash to render the text in a TextField object as HTML, you need to tell it to do so. You can do that by setting the object's html property to true. For example, the following tells Flash to allow a TextField object named tTitle to render HTML:

```
tTitle.html = true;
```

Once an object is set to render HTML you should assign all HTML content to the object's htmlText property. Even though a TextField object may be set to render HTML, if you assign the value to the text property it will still render literally. The following shows an example of some HTML content assigned to the htmlText property of tTitle.

```
tTitle.htmlText = "<b>ActionScript Bible</b>";
```

Even though you may set the html property to true for a TextField object, it will still render newline, multiple sequential spaces, and tab characters normally. As you may know, that is not how HTML is typically rendered. In HTML, for example, typically newline characters are not rendered. Line breaks are rendered only with the `<br>` tag. Sometimes one way is advantageous, and sometimes the other way is advantageous. Flash provides you with the option to render whitespace characters (spaces, newline characters, and so on) or not when you have enabled a TextField to display HTML. The default setting is that it does render such characters. By setting the value of the condenseWhite property to false, however, you can tell Flash to disregard whitespace characters (other than single spaces) just as HTML is typically rendered in a Web browser.

Inserting Special Characters into HTML Fields

Often, you may want to use text characters in HTML text fields that aren't included in the regular alphanumeric set (that is, alphabet and numbers). Although most characters outside of this set can be found as Shift key combinations on keyboards (for example, Shift+2 produces an @ symbol), you need to encode certain characters — on or off the keyboard — in order to properly use them within HTML text fields. For example, if you want to display a greater-than (>) or less-than (<) sign in an HTML text field, you won't see it if you simply type that character in an ActionScript expression. ActionScript interprets less-than and greater-than signs as the opening and closing characters (respectively) for HTML tags. Therefore, if you type a < or > character into a string value used for an HTML field, ActionScript treats the text around it as part of an HTML tag and does not display it. You can try this for yourself with the following code:

```
this.createTextField("tInfo", this.getNextHighestDepth(), 0, 0, 0, 0);
tInfo.autoSize = true;
tInfo.html = true;
tInfo.htmlText = "< is a less than sign";
```

When you place the preceding code on the first frame of a new Flash document and test the movie, you'll see that no text displays.

So, in order to tell ActionScript that you want to display special characters literally, you need to encode the character as an *entity name* or a *decimal character reference*. You've probably seen entity names in regular HTML. The entity name for a less-than sign is <. If you insert this name in the ActionScript expression, the Flash Player properly displays the < character:

```
tInfo.htmlText = "&lt; is a less than sign";
```

When you test your movie with the entity name instead of the literal <, you see < is the less than sign display in the movie. Many HTML entity names, such as © for the © symbol, do *not* work in Flash ActionScript. For these symbols, use the decimal character reference instead, as in:

```
tInfo.htmlText = "&#169; is the copyright sign.";
```

For a list of common character entity names (or decimal character references), refer to Table 17-1.

Table 17-1: Special Characters for HTML Text Fields

Character	*Name*	*ActionScript Value*	*Unicode Value*
<	Less-than sign	<	\u003C
>	Greater-than sign	>	\u003E
"	Double quote	"	\u0022
&	Ampersand	&	\u0026
•	Bullet	•	\u2022
¶	Pilcrow sign	¶	\u00B6
©	Copyright sign	©	\u00A9
®	Registered sign	®	\u00AE
™	Trademark sign	™	\u2122
£	Pound sign	£	\u00A3
¢	Cent sign	¢	\u00A2
°	Degree sign	°	\u00B0
÷	Division sign	÷	\u00F7

Some of these upper ASCII characters will not display correctly in Flash Player 6 or later if you do not set the new System.codePage property to the correct value. See Chapter 21 for more information. If you do not want to use a different codePage value, you can also use a Unicode value (as shown in Table 17-1) for consistent display in Flash Player 6 or later.

Troubleshooting the htmlText Property

You may experience problems if you successively invoke the `htmlText` property for a given `TextField` object. If you add HTML-formatted text to existing HTML text in a text field, a line break occurs at the new addition because a `<P>` tag is automatically inserted around the new additions. For example, the following code creates two separate lines of text in a multiline text field—even though no `<BR>`, `<P>`, or `\r` is indicated:

```
this.createTextField("tArticle", this.getNextHighestDepth(), 25, 35, 300,
100);
tArticle.html = true;
tArticle.multiline = true;
tArticle.wordWrap = true;
tArticle.htmlText = "<B>Bold text</B>";
tArticle.htmlText += "<I>Italic text</I>";
```

To avoid unwanted line breaks, you can set the `htmlText` property once, or store the current content into a new `String` variable and set the `htmlText` to that new variable. This latter solution is shown in the following code.

```
this.createTextField("tArticle", this.getNextHighestDepth(), 25, 35, 300,
100);
tArticle.html = true;
tArticle.multiline = true;
tArticle.wordWrap = true;
var sTempHTML:String = "<B>Bold text</B>";
sTempHTML += "<I>Italic text</I>";
tArticle.htmlText = sTempHTML;
```

Another problem with `htmlText` can occur if you use the `htmlText` property in looping code, such as a `for` or `while` loop. If you need to process multiple items for insertion into a text field, the Flash Player can more efficiently render text as HTML if there is only one execution of the `htmlText` property. Here's an example of code that could potentially slow down the Flash Player. A text field is inserted into a `for` loop that cycles 50 times, adding HTML-formatted text with each pass:

```
this.createTextField("tArticle", this.getNextHighestDepth(), 25, 35, 300,
100);
tArticle.html = true;
tArticle.multiline = true;
tArticle.wordWrap = true;
trace(getTimer());
for(var i:Number = 0; i < 100; i++) {
  tArticle.htmlText += "<b>item</b><br>";
}
trace(getTimer());
```

If you insert this code into an empty Flash document, the second `trace()` action will take quite some time to display in the Output panel. Although the actual difference between the value reported before and the value reported after the for statement will vary; our tests have shown values ranging from three seconds to seven seconds. Next take a look at how you can make a slight change to the code that dramatically changes the execution time:

```
this.createTextField("tArticle", this.getNextHighestDepth(), 25, 35, 300,
100);
tArticle.html = true;
tArticle.multiline = true;
tArticle.wordWrap = true;
trace(getTimer());
var sTempHTML:String = "";
for(var i:Number = 0; i < 100; i++) {
  sTempHTML += "<b>item</b><br>";
}
tArticle.htmlText = sTempHTML;
trace(getTimer());
```

The preceding code will likely take less than 150 milliseconds to run. That's quite a difference!

Adding Hyperlinks to Text

You can use the <a> tag to add hyperlinks to your text. For example, the following will create a hyperlink within a TextField named tContent:

```
tContent.html = true;
tContent.htmlText = "<a href='http://www.person13.com'>www.person13.com</a>";
```

Caution: Be sure that you are careful with your use of quotation marks. Notice that in the preceding example the inner quotation marks are single quotes so that they don't conflict with the outer quotation marks. If you prefer to use all double quotes or all single quotes then make sure to escape the inner quotes with the backslash character. You can read more about this topic in Chapter 15.

Hyperlinks in Flash text don't necessary behave like standard HTML hyperlinks. Pay particular attention to the target that you use for opening the new links. The default target for opening a hyperlink is the current browser frame. That means that if the Flash application is being played in a browser window, the current browser frame will be replaced by the new content. If you want to specify another target, you can use a target attribute in the <a> tag. For example, the following will open the link in a new browser window:

```
tContent.htmlText = "<a href='http://www.person13.com' ⮐
target='_blank'>www.person13.com</a>";
```

You'll also notice that unlike most Web browsers, Flash does not render hyperlinks in such a way that they stand apart from the rest of the text. If you are accustomed to using Web browsers to view HTML then you are probably familiar with how hyperlinks are typically underlined and blue (or purple if they've been visited). Because Flash doesn't distinguish hyperlink text in any visual way you may want to add some simple formatting to help the user know that the text is a link. For example, the addition of a <font> and <u> tag can format the linked text just as it might show up in a Web browser:

```
tContent.htmlText = "<font color='#0000FF'><u> ⮐
<a href='http://www.person13.com' ⮐
target='_blank'>www.person13.com</a></u></font>";
```

Adding Mail Links

Flash supports several other href directives, including the mailto directive. The mailto directive allows you to open a new e-mail message to an e-mail address.

A mailto directive in Flash text behaves just like a mailto directive in a regular HTML Web page. When the user clicks the link, a new e-mail message opens in the user's default e-mail application, such as Microsoft Outlook (or Outlook Express). The user needs to actually send the e-mail though; the mailto directive simply opens the new e-mail window with a predefined "to" field (and, optionally, the subject and body fields).

In order to do that, simply use an <a> tag as shown in the preceding section, but use a mailto directive followed by a colon and the e-mail address to which you want to have the new message sent. For example:

```
tContent.htmlText = "<a href="mailto:joey@person13.com">send email</a>";
```

Calling JavaScript Functions

If your Flash application is playing within a Web browser that supports JavaScript, you can call JavaScript functions using the javascript directive within an <a> tag. We recommend that you also enclose all the JavaScript calls within the void() operator so that no other windows are opened. The following shows how you can add a simple link that pops open a JavaScript alert:

```
tContent.htmlText = "<a href=\"javascript:void(alert( ⮐
'This is a message from Flash'));\">click this text</a>";
```

Of course you can also use the javascript directive to call custom JavaScript functions you have defined within the hosting HTML page.

You can find more details about which browsers support which functionality by viewing the page at www.macromedia.com/support/flash/ts/documents/browser_support_matrix.htm.

Calling ActionScript Functions from Text

One feature not well-known but often quite useful is the ability to call ActionScript functions from text. The asfunction directive can be used within an <a> tag to call an ActionScript function. This functionality allows to you add much more interactivity to your text.

The asfunction syntax is as follows:

```
asfunction:functionName[,param1...,paramN]
```

There should be no spaces between the directive, colon, function name, commas, or parameters. The only permissible spaces in the syntax are spaces within the parameter values.

Here's an example that calls the trace() statement and passes it a value of a message:

```
tContent.htmlText = "<a href='asfunction:trace,a message'>click this text</a>";
```

You can also use the asfunction directive to call custom functions. For example:

```
tContent.htmlText = "<a href='asfunction:changeTextColor'> ⮐
   click to change color</a>";
function changeTextColor():Void {
  tContent.textColor = Math.random() * 255 * 255 * 255;
}
```

It is also worth mentioning that you can use the asfunction directive with static text. You can enter the asfunction directive in the URL link field in the Property inspector for static text. For example:

```
asfunction:trace,a message from static text
```

Embedding Content in Text

One of the new features supported in Flash MX 2004 is embedding content within HTML-enabled TextField objects. The content can be an external JPG (non-progressive) or SWF, or a Movie Clip symbol with a linkage identifier. Before discussing this feature, we should mention that at the time of this writing it is inconsistent at best. Although you are, of course, welcome to try using the feature, be forewarned that our tests have shown that there are a great many factors that seem to affect how it works—if it even works at all under some circumstances. If you try to embed multiple content items in the text, they may overlap such that one or more might not seem to be there. And when creating TextField objects programmatically and attempting to add embedded content prior to any text, we've noticed it simply doesn't work. You should check the Macromedia Web site for any player updates that may fix these issues.

Although the feature appears rather buggy at this time, Flash Player 7 supports JPEG, SWF, and Movie Clip content embedded within TextField objects.

With all that said, let's take a look at how the feature is at least supposed to work. The HTML <img> tag allows you to embed an image within a standard HTML document. Flash extends upon that functionality slightly by allowing you to use an <img> tag within an HTML-enabled TextField object to display not only images, but also SWF content and Movie Clip symbol content. For example, you can use the following code to display an image in a TextField object:

```
this.createTextField("tContent", this.getNextHighestDepth(), 0, 0, 200, 200);
tContent.border = true;
tContent.html = true;
tContent.htmlText = "A picture of a lake: <img width='180' ⮐
   height='120' src='http://www.person13.com/asb/image2.jpg'>";
```

You'll notice from the preceding example that the Flash support for the <img> tag includes the width and height attributes. The complete list of supported attributes is as follows:

- ✦ **width:** The width, in pixels, at which to display the content.
- ✦ **height:** The height, in pixels, at which to display the content.
- ✦ **src:** The URL or linkage identifier for the content. If you are specifying a URL it can be an absolute or relative URL. Alternatively, you can also display MovieClip content added from a symbol in the library with a linkage identifier.

✦ **align:** The horizontal alignment of the content within the TextField object. You can align left (default), right, or center.

✦ **hspace:** The number of pixels that space the content in the vertical direction. The default value is 8.

✦ **vspace:** The number of pixels that space the content in the horizontal direction. The default value is 8.

✦ **id:** An identifier for the content that you can use to target the embedded content with ActionScript.

Note that when you load graphical content into a TextField object it loads asynchronously. That means that the TextField initializes based on textual content. Therefore, once the graphical content loads the TextField might not reinitialize. For example, when you load an image into a TextField object with autoSize set to true, the object will not properly resize to accommodate the loaded image (although our tests show that it will resize in the vertical direction). Additionally, we have noticed that you cannot have an <img> tag as the first content within a TextField object created at runtime. In such cases the <img> tag is seemingly ignored. That issue does not seem to be the case for authoring time objects.

All of the preceding statements are true at the time of this writing. We encourage you to check for player updates, which may potentially correct some of the issues with embedded graphical content in TextField objects.

In the list of supported <img> tag attributes you will notice that Flash supports an attribute named id. The attribute can be used to target the graphical content that is nested within the TextField. The content is loaded into a nested MovieClip object with the instance name specified by the id attribute. That means that you can use any of the properties and methods of the MovieClip class with the embedded content. For example, you might want to instruct a loaded SWF to stop or play. For example, you can check the load progress of an image and tell the TextField to resize once the content has loaded and initialized. For example:

```
this.createTextField("tContent", this.getNextHighestDepth(), 0, 0, 200, 200);
tContent.html = true;
tContent.htmlText = "A picture of a lake: <img id='mcImage' ⮐
   width='180' height='120' align='center' vspace='0' hspace='0' ⮐
   src='http://www.person13.com/asb/image2.jpg'>";

// Define a function that checks for the load progress of the image.
function checkLoad():Void {
  var nLoaded:Number = tContent.mcImage.getBytesLoaded();
  var nTotal:Number = tContent.mcImage.getBytesTotal();

  // If the content has loaded and initialized, tell the TextField
  // to resize and clear the interval.
  if(nLoaded/nTotal >= 1 && tContent.mcImage._width > 0) {
    tContent.autoSize = "left";
    clearInterval(nInterval);
  }
}

// Set an interval that calls the checkLoad() function at approximately 100
// millisecond intervals.
var nInterval:Number = setInterval(checkLoad, 100);
```

When you implement the preceding code, you should be aware of two things:

✦ If you display the border in the `TextField` object, the border will not resize correctly.

✦ You must create the `TextField` object such that its initial dimensions are large enough to accommodate the loaded content. Otherwise it will crop the loaded content.

Creating an HTML-Based Information Viewer

In this section you use some of the HTML concepts you learned in the previous sections to create an application that allows the user to select a topic from an index and view more information about that topic in an HTML-enabled `TextField` object.

1. Open a new Flash document and save it as `informationViewer001.fla`.

2. Add the code shown in Listing 17-2 to the first frame of the main timeline.

Listing 17-2: The createTextFields() and viewSection() functions

```
function createTextFields():Void {

  // Create the two TextField objects.
  this.createTextField("tIndex", this.getNextHighestDepth(),50,100,100,200);
  this.createTextField("tContent", this.getNextHighestDepth(),200,100,200,200);

  // Set the properties of tIndex.
  tIndex.selectable = false;
  tIndex.border = true;
  tIndex.html = true;
  tIndex.multiline = true;
  tIndex.wordWrap = true;

  // Create the HTML text for the index, and then assign it to
  // the object's htmlText property.
  var sIndex:String = "Click on one of the following links:<br>";
  sIndex += "<li><a href='asfunction:viewSection,text'>text</a></li>";
  sIndex += "<li><a href='asfunction:viewSection,html'>html</a></li>";
  sIndex += "<li><a href='asfunction:viewSection,scrolling'>scrolling</a></li>";
  tIndex.htmlText = sIndex;

  // Set the properties for tContent.
  tContent.selectable = false;
  tContent.border = true;
  tContent.html = true;
  tContent.multiline = true;
  tContent.wordWrap = true;
}

function viewSection(sSection:String):Void {

  // Determine which content to display based on which selection
```

Continued

Listing 17-2 *(continued)*

```
    // was clicked.
    switch (sSection) {
      case "text":
        tContent.htmlText = "This is the section about text.";
        break;
      case "html":
        tContent.htmlText = "HTML allows you to <font ⮐
           color='#FF0000'>colorize</font> text";
        break;
      case "scrolling":
        tContent.htmlText = "Read more about scrolling in the next part ⮐
           of the chapter.";
    }
}

createTextFields();
```

3. Test the movie.

Scrolling Text

The text within a text field can be scrolled both horizontally and vertically with ActionScript. The TextField scrolling properties come into play whenever the amount of text that you assign to a text field exceeds the actual space available in the viewable portion of the field. For example, if you have ten lines of text, but have a text field with a height of only five lines, you'll need to adjust the scroll property in order to view the remaining five lines of text. Each line of text in a text field has an index number. This index number is 1-based, meaning the first line is index 1. Figure 17-4 illustrates how programmatic scrolling works with `TextField` objects.

Scrolling Text Vertically

The `scroll` property of a text field controls which line index of a text field's content is currently at the top of the actual viewable portion of the field. This property is a read-write property, which means you can assign a new value to it to cause the text to scroll vertically. When you assign a text value to a `TextField` object with ActionScript, the text context is automatically indexed as it "fills" the text field. The example shown in Figure 17-4 has 31 lines of text content, but the field displaying the content has only 18 viewable lines. However, the number of content lines is *not* equivalent to the number of `scroll` values — you'll see why in the `maxscroll` property description.

To scroll the content of a field upward, add to the `scroll` property. The following code will advance the text within a text field named `tArticle` by one line with each click of `mcScrollUp`.

```
mcScrollUp.onRelease = function():Void {
  tArticle.scroll++;
}
```

		Line index	
scroll		1	Amendment I
		2	
		3	Congress shall make no law respecting an establishment of
		4	religion, or prohibiting the free exercise thereof; or abridging
		5	the freedom of speech, or of the press; or the right of the
		6	people peaceably to assemble, and to petition the
		7	Government for a redress of grievances.
		8	
		9	
		10	Amendment II
		11	
		12	A well regulated Militia, being necessary to the security of a
		13	free State, the right of the people to keep and bear Arms,
maxscroll	1	14	shall not be infringed.
	2	15	
	3	16	
	4	17	Amendment III
bottomScroll	5	18	
	6	19	No Soldier shall, in time of peace be quartered in any house,
	7	20	without the consent of the Owner, nor in time of war, but in
	8	21	a manner to be prescribed by law.
	9	22	
	10	23	
	11	24	Amendment IV
	12	25	
	13	26	The right of the people to be secure in their persons,
	14	27	houses, papers, and effects, against unreasonable searches
	15	28	and seizures, shall not be violated, and no Warrants shall
	16	29	issue, but upon probable cause, supported by Oath or
	17	30	affirmation, and particularly describing the place to be
	18	31	searched, and the persons or things to be seized.

Figure 17-4: This text field has been assigned content that has 31 lines, yet the viewable portion of the field has only 18 lines.

To scroll the content of a field downward (the text moves from top to bottom), subtract from the `scroll` property. The following code will retreat the text back by one line with each click of the button:

```
mcScrollDown.onRelease = function():Void {
   tArticle.scroll--;
}
```

As the text advances or retreats within the field, the `scroll` property will update to reflect the index value currently visible at the top of the field.

Note You can use the `scroll` property with Flash 4 and 5 text fields. Target the `Var` name of an editable text field to use the `scroll` property.

The bottomScroll property returns the index number for the text currently displayed in the last viewable line of the TextField object. Unlike the scroll property, the bottomScroll is read-only; you cannot change the position of the text content with bottomScroll. For the example shown in Figure 17-4, the range of possible values for bottomScroll is 18 through 31.

The maxscroll property, as the name implies, is the maximum scroll value that a TextField object can return. This property is read-only, and unless you dynamically add or subtract actual text from a TextField object, the maxscroll value is fixed. You cannot scroll beyond the maxscroll value, nor can you scroll to negative values within text fields.

As you add to the scroll property, the text field will stop advancing as soon as the last line of the text content is displayed at the very bottom of the text field. In the example shown in Figure 17-4, the last line of text is line 31, and the text field is 18 lines high. Eighteen lines up from line 31 is line 14. Line 14 is the maximum scroll value for this content in this particular text field. This value is the same value that the maxscroll property will return for this text field. The maxscroll property can be calculated manually in the following way:

```
maxscroll = total number of lines - viewable number of lines in text field + 1
```

The maxscroll property is available via the Var name of editable text fields in Flash 4 and 5 movies.

Scrolling Text Horizontally

ActionScript also offers the capability to scroll text field content horizontally. Unlike the previous scrolling methods, hscroll and maxhscroll use pixel units — not line index numbers.

The hscroll property is a read-write property that retrieves or sets the current horizontal scroll position (in pixels) of the TextField object. When a TextField object is initialized with default values, the value of hscroll is 0. If you increase the value of hscroll, the text within the TextField object moves from right to left. If you decrease the value of hscroll, the text moves from left to right. The value of hscroll cannot be set below 0. The following code placed on the main timeline creates a TextField object containing text that scrolls from right to left by 10 pixels whenever the stage of the Flash movie is clicked.

```
_this.createTextField("tDisplay", 1, 25, 25, 30, 300);
tDisplay.text = "Hello, how are you? This text scrolls with each mouse click.";


this.onMouseDown = function(){
   tDisplay.hscroll += 10;
};
```

The read-only property maxhscroll returns the maximum hscroll value of the text field. Like maxscroll, this property returns the maximum offset of the text within the text field. The value of hscroll cannot be set beyond the value of maxhscroll. The value of maxhscroll depends on the amount of text that cannot be displayed within the visible area of the text field. As you add text to an individual line within a field, the value of maxhscroll increases.

Using Events for Text Fields

Flash ActionScript has some exciting event handlers for editable text fields. These event handlers can execute code whenever the user interacts with a text field in the movie. You can specify an anonymous or named function for each of these handlers.

Detecting Text Changes

The `onChanged()` event handler method detects any text changes initiated by the user within the object. If the user is adding text to a field via the keyboard, this handler is invoked when the user presses the key, not when it is released.

The `onChanged()` handler method does not detect changes to a text field made via ActionScript. In other words, if you change the contents of a `TextField` object using the `text` or `htmlText` property, the `onChanged()` handler method is not called.

The following code sends a `trace()` message to the Output panel whenever text is added to a `TextField` object named `tComments` in Test Movie mode:

```
this.createTextField("tComments", 1, 25, 25, 100, 20);
tComments.border = true;
tComments.type = "input";
tComments.onChanged = function(){
  trace("Text within comments field = " + tComments.text);
};
```

If you need to define several functions to be executed with a specific `TextField` object's `onChanged()` handler method, you can create several listener objects for the `TextField` object. Each listener object can have its own `onChanged()` handler. You learn about listeners for the `TextField` object in the "Adding Listeners to TextField Objects" section of this chapter.

Detecting Focus Changes

When focus is moved to a `TextField` object by means of user interaction (that is, the user clicks on the `TextField` object or moves focus to it by way of the Tab key), Flash calls that object's `onSetFocus()` event handler method. The method is passed a parameter indicating the previous object that held focus (if any existed). The following code displays a `trace()` action in the Output panel when the movie is in Test Movie mode. If the user clicks in either of the two fields, the `trace()` action indicates which field received focus. If a previous field was focused, the `onSetFocus()` method also reports that object's name.

```
this.createTextField("tMessageOne", this.getNextHighestDepth(), 25,25,200,20);
this.createTextField("tMessageTwo", this.getNextHighestDepth(), 250,25,200,20);
tMessageOne.border = true;
tMessageTwo.border = true;
tMessageOne.text = "message one";
tMessageTwo.text = "message two";

tMessageOne.onSetFocus = function(oPrevFocus:Object):Void {
```

```
  trace(this._name + " is now focused.");
  if(tPrevFocus._name != null){
    trace(tPrevFocus._name + " no longer has focus.");
  }
};

tMessageTwo.onSetFocus = function(oPrevFocus:Object):Void {
  trace(this._name + " is now focused.");
  if(tPrevFocus._name != null){
    trace(tPrevFocus._name + " no longer has focus.");
  }
};
```

On the other hand, when the focus shifts away from a `TextField` due to user interaction, Flash calls the `onKillFocus()` method of the object. This handler is passed a reference to the object that receives the new focus. If focus leaves the field and is not directed to a new object, the parameter is equal to `null`. The following code sends a `trace()` action to the Output panel in Test Movie mode when the `onKillFocus()` handler method is invoked. If you click inside the `tMessage` text field and then click outside of it, the handler is invoked. The `obj` argument represents the object (if any) that receives the new focus.

```
this.createTextField("tMessage", this.getNextHighestDepth(), 25, 25, 200, 20);
tMessage.text = "You have a message waiting.";
tMessage.border = true;
tMessage.onKillFocus = function(oPrevFocus:Object):Void {
  trace(this._name + " is no longer focused.");
  trace(oPrevFocus._name + " is now focused.");
};
```

Detecting Scrolling

The `onScroller()` handler method detects when the `TextField` object's scroll properties change. Among other uses, this handler can advance the `scroll` property of a `TextField` to always make sure the last line of text is displayed at the bottom of the field. The following code creates a mouse listener that adds text to the message field when the user clicks and then releases the mouse. When the text in the message field exceeds the number of lines visible in the field, the `onScroller()` handler method is invoked, setting the `scroll` property equal to the value of the `maxscroll` property:

```
this.createTextField("tMessage", this.getNextHighestDepth(), 25, 25, 200, 100);
tMessage.border = true;
tMessage.multiline = true;
tMessage.wordWrap = true;

var nCount:Number = 0;

tMessage.text = "You have " + nCount + " message(s) waiting.\n";

tMessage.onScroller = function(){
   this.scroll = this.maxscroll;
};

oAddTextListener = new Object();
```

```
oAddTextListener.onMouseUp = function(){
   nCount++;
   tMessage.text += "You have " + nCount + " message(s) waiting.\n";;
};
Mouse.addListener(oAddTextListener);
```

Creating a Scrolling Text Viewer

In this exercise, you will create a simple application that implements many of the scrolling concepts you read about in the preceding sections. The application creates several programmatically generated `TextField` objects — one for displaying the text of a story and two nested within `MovieClip` objects used as buttons to scroll the story text. In order to get enough text into the text field for the purposes of scrolling, you'll use the `LoadVars` class. If you are not yet familiar with `LoadVars`, you might want to refer to Chapters 26 and 35 for more information.

1. On the CD-ROM, you'll find a text file called `story.txt`. The file contains the text that you'll load into the SWF so you need it to be in the same directory as the SWF file. Therefore, copy the file from the CD-ROM to your local disk.
2. Open a new Flash document and save it as `storyViewer001.fla`. Make sure to save the file in the same directory as `story.txt`.
3. Add the code shown in Listing 17-3 to the first frame of the main timeline.

Listing 17-3: The scrolling text viewer code

```
function createContentField():Void {

  // Create the TextField object you'll use to display the
  // story text.
  this.createTextField("tContent", this.getNextHighestDepth(), 100,100,300,300);

  // Set the properties of the TextField so that it can correctly
  // display the content.
  tContent.border = true;
  tContent.selectable = false;
  tContent.multiline = true;
  tContent.wordWrap = true;
}

function createScrollButtons():Void {

  // Create the MovieClip objects that you'll use as buttons to
  // scroll the story text.
  this.createEmptyMovieClip("mcScrollDown", this.getNextHighestDepth());
  this.createEmptyMovieClip("mcScrollUp", this.getNextHighestDepth());

  // Add TextField objects nested within the MovieClip objects.
```

Continued

Listing 17-3 *(continued)*

```
  mcScrollUp.createTextField("tLabel", mcScrollDown.getNextHighestDepth(), ⮐
     410, 100, 75, 20);
  mcScrollDown.createTextField("tLabel", mcScrollUp.getNextHighestDepth(), ⮐
     410, 380, 75, 20);

  // Set the properties of the TextField objects.
  mcScrollUp.tLabel.border = true;
  mcScrollUp.tLabel.selectable = false;
  mcScrollDown.tLabel.border = true;
  mcScrollDown.tLabel.selectable = false;

  // Set the display text in the TextField objects.
  mcScrollUp.tLabel.text = "Scroll Up";
  mcScrollDown.tLabel.text = "Scroll Down";

  // When the user clicks on the MovieClip instance scroll the
  // story text down by one page.
  mcScrollDown.onPress = function():Void {
    tContent.scroll = tContent.bottomScroll + 1;
  };

  // When the user clicks on the MovieClip instance scroll the
  //  story text up by one page.
  mcScrollUp.onPress = function():Void {
    tContent.scroll -= (tContent.bottomScroll - tContent.scroll) + 1;
  };
}

function loadText():Void {

  // Create a new LoadVars object.
  var lvText:LoadVars = new LoadVars();

  // When the content loads, assign it to the display text for
  // the ytContent TextField object.
  lvText.onData = function(sData:String):Void {
    tContent.text = sData;
  };

  // Tell Flash to load the data from story.txt.
  lvText.load("story.txt");
}

createContentField();
createScrollButtons();
loadText();
```

4. Test the movie.

When you test the movie, the story should show up in the `tContent` field; clicking up and down scroll buttons should scroll the content a page at a time.

Adding Listeners to TextField Objects

`TextField` objects can use listeners that detect changes to the text content or scroll properties. The methods that you define for the listeners behave identically to the methods by the same names discussed in the previous section. The primary difference between `onChanged()` and `onScroller()` as listener object methods and `TextField` methods is that you can create several listener objects for the same text field — each listener can have its own `onChanged()` and `onScroller()` handlers.

Detecting Text Changes

The `onChanged()` method of a listener object works identically to the `onChanged()` method for a `TextField` object. In order to use the `onChanged()` method with a listener object, first define the listener object. The listener can be of many types, the simplest of which is an `Object` object. Then, register the listener with the `TextField` object via the `addListener()` method.

The following code creates two `TextField` objects. The first is an input field that allows the user to enter text. A listener object's `onChanged()` method is called each time the user modifies the value in the first field, and it updates the second in order to display the reverse text:

```
this.createTextField("tInput", this.getNextHighestDepth(), 25, 25, 200, 200);
this.createTextField("tCopy", this.getNextHighestDepth(), 250, 25, 200, 200);
tInput.border = true;
tCopy.border = true;
tInput.type = "input";
var oListener:Object = new Object();
oListener.onChanged = function():Void {
  var sText:String = tInput.text;
  var aText:Array = sText.split("");
  aText.reverse();
  sText = aText.join("");
  tCopy.text = sText;
};
tInput.addListener(oListener);
```

Detecting Scrolling

The `onScrolled()` method for a listener object detects changes to the scroll properties of a `TextField` object. Just as with the `onChanged()` method, you should defined the method for a listener object and then register the listener with the `TextField` using the `addListener()` method.

Working with Fonts

The following sections look at some of the ways you can work with fonts in Flash.

Embedding Fonts

One nice feature of Flash movies on the Web is the fact that you can consistently view artwork and fonts with any version of the Flash Player. Font embedding is usually the most overlooked optimization step in Flash deployment. If you're not careful, you can add a substantial file size to your Flash movies (SWF files) by embedding entire fonts.

Aside from just allowing text to look the way you want it to look, embedded fonts actually enable your `TextField` objects to do some things that they wouldn't otherwise do. For example, as mentioned, a `TextField` object that uses device fonts (non-embedded fonts) cannot be rotated nor can you change the alpha. But once you embed the font, you can do both of these things.

Static Text

Whenever you create static text in a movie, Flash MX automatically embeds the specific characters that you typed into the field. Because static text cannot change dynamically Flash embeds only the characters you actually type into the field on the stage. However, if you want to disable font embedding for static text, you can choose the Use Device Fonts option in the Property inspector when you have selected the static text on the stage. This prevents the font characters from embedding in the Flash movie (SWF file), and displays the font selected in the Property inspector *only* if the user has that exact font installed on his or her system. Otherwise, a generic system font is substituted in its place.

Authoring Time Dynamic and Input Text

By default Flash does not embed fonts for dynamic and input text. Therefore, if you want to ensure that the proper font is used you need to explicitly tell Flash to embed the font. You can do that by selecting the `TextField` object and clicking the Character button in the Property inspector. Figure 17-5 shows the Character Options dialog box.

The default setting, as you can see, is to embed no characters. However, if you choose the Specify Ranges option you can select any combination of the preset ranges. Or, you can opt to specify a custom set of characters in the Include These Characters field. The more characters you include, the larger the file size. The following list details some of the more common ranges:

✦ **Uppercase (A–Z):** This option embeds only the uppercase alphabetical characters of the chosen font face. The following characters listed are added with this option. For Times New Roman, these characters add about 3KB.

```
ABCDEFGHIJKLMNOPQRSTUVWXYZ
```

✦ **Lowercase (a–z):** This option embeds only the lowercase alphabetical characters of the chosen font face. With Verdana, these characters add about 3KB to the size of the Flash movie. The following characters are added to the SWF file:

```
abcdefghijklmnopqrstuvwxyz
```

✦ **Numerals (0–9):** This option embeds the numeric characters of the chosen font face. The characters shown following are added to the Flash movie. Using Times New Roman as the selected font face, this option increases the file size by about 1KB.

```
0123456789
```

✦ **Punctuation (!@#$%...):** This option includes all the punctuation for the English language. If Times New Roman is used for the text field, the file size of the Flash movie increases just over 2KB. The following characters are added with this option:

```
!"#$%&'()*+,-./:;<=>?@[\]^_`{|}~
```

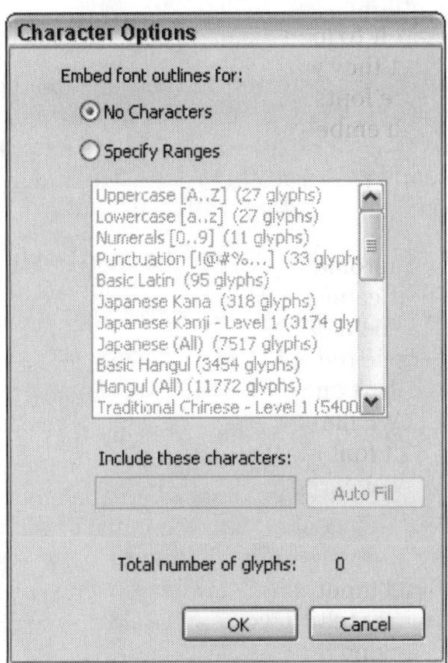

Figure 17-5: The Character Options dialog box has specific font-embedding features for editable text fields.

If you need to embed only a limited set of characters, type the desired character(s) into the Include These Characters field. Note that for some fonts you actually need to embed a space character (that is, insert an empty space by pressing the spacebar in this field).

Many Flash developers like to include Internet URLs in dynamic and input text fields. Make sure you enable the @ (for e-mail) and the &, =, +, and - (for script queries) characters in the character option described previously if you intend to display such URLs to the user in your Flash movie.

Following is a list of common behaviors for some of the font embedding options:

✦ If you enable only one case (lowercase or uppercase) the non-embedded case is displayed as the embedded case. For example, if you embed lowercase characters and the user types an uppercase `A`, a lowercase `a` is displayed in the field.

✦ If you try to assign non-embedded characters to an editable text field via an ActionScript expression (either through a `Var` name or the `text` property of the `TextField` object), the character does not display in the text field. However, the variable or text property still retains the value prescribed in the expression until the user focuses the text or until the variable is given a new value with a new ActionScript expression.

✦ The Property inspector's font style buttons, Bold and Italic, also influence the file size and visual appearance of the text field in the Flash movie (SWF file). The first character of any editable field determines the color, style, and point size of the entire field. If you want to control specific formatting within individual sections of the same text field, we recommend that you use the HTML option of editable text fields. This issue (working with HTML and TextField objects) is discussed later in the chapter.

✦ If you enable several different fields to embed different subsets of the same font face, all the fields can use each other's embedded characters. For example, if one editable text field has lowercase letters of Verdana, and another field has uppercase letters of Verdana enabled, both fields can use upper- and lowercase characters. These fields do *not* need to coexist on the same frame (or timeline) in order for this effect to work.

✦ You must use embedding options for any editable text field that will be masked by a Mask Layer or nested within a `MovieClip` instance that is transformed with settings in the Transform panel or the Color menu of the Property inspector for symbol instances. The Flash Player rendering engine needs to have the outlines of any characters embedded in the Flash movie (SWF file) to perform these visual effects.

✦ You cannot access embedded fonts in one Flash movie (SWF file) from another Flash movie (SWF file). For example, if you enable lowercase Verdana characters in a `TextField` object of your initial Flash movie and embed uppercase Verdana characters in a `TextField` object of another Flash movie that is loaded into the initial Flash movie, you cannot interchangeably use the lowercase and uppercase characters between the two movies. In order to share an embedded font across several Flash movies, you need to create font symbols in shared libraries and link them to your text fields.

You can read about shared libraries and font symbols in Chapter 34.

Runtime Text

When you create a `TextField` object at runtime the only way to embed fonts is programmatically. There are two ways you can do this. The first way is to create an authoring time `TextField` instance (that is, create an input or dynamic text field with the Text tool) that embeds the font, and then tell your runtime instances to use that same font. The second way is to use a font symbol. We'll take a look at each way.

Using an Authoring Time TextField's Font

Perhaps the simplest way to programmatically use an embedded font is to embed the font first with an authoring time `TextField`. You can create a single dynamic `TextField` object off the stage, and embed the characters you want to use as discussed in the section "Authoring Time Dynamic and Input Text." The advantage of embedding fonts with an authoring time `TextField` is not only that it is somewhat simpler to implement, but it also enables you to have more control over what characters are embedded. Use the following steps to programmatically use fonts embedded in an authoring time TextField:

1. Create an authoring time TextField off the stage. You can give the instance and name or not, and you can add text to it or not. Because you will not necessarily be using the TextField for any other purposes, those things are not particularly pertinent.
2. Embed the characters of the font you want to use in the authoring time TextField by following the instructions in the section "Authoring Time Dynamic and Input Text."
3. Create the runtime text using the createTextField() method.
4. Set the embedFonts property of the TextField to true.
5. Create a TextFormat object.
6. Assign the embedded font name to the TextFormat object's font property.
7. Assign the TextFormat object to the TextField using the setTextFormat() method.

We haven't yet discussed font symbols or the TextFormat class. You can read more about each of those topics in detail in Chapters 34 and 18, respectively. However, you'll get the basic information you need to know in this section.

You've just read the generalized instructions. Let's take a look at a specific example:

1. Create a new dynamic TextField object at authoring time. Place the object offstage; you don't need to give it an instance name.
2. Open the Character Options dialog box for the TextField, and embed the Uppercase Letters. Then click OK.
3. Add the following code to the first frame of the main timeline:

```
this.createTextField("tLabel", this.getNextHighestDepth(), ⮐
   100, 100, 100, 20);
tLabel.text = "abcdefg";
```

4. Test the movie. You should see the text appear in the default serif font. You're testing the movie just to confirm that the text does, in fact, display before you set it to embed the font.
5. Append the following code after the code you added in Step 3:

```
this.createTextField("tLabel", this.getNextHighestDepth(), ⮐
   100, 100, 100, 20);
tLabel.text = "abcdefg";
tLabel.embedFonts = true;

var tfFormatter:TextFormat = new TextFormat();
tfFormatter.font = "Verdana";

tLabel.setTextFormat(tfFormatter);
```

6. Test the movie again. You should not see any text this time, because you have embedded the uppercase characters only for the Verdana font.

7. Open the Character Options dialog box for the authoring time `TextField` once again. Set it to embed the lowercase letters instead.

8. Test the movie again. This time you should see the text display in the Verdana font.

Using a Font Symbol

You can also embed a font using a Font symbol. A font symbol allows you to use shared libraries, and may be preferable in some situations. On the other hand, a font symbol requires that you embed the entire font. So if you are using only a few characters, you may want to use an authoring time `TextField` to embed just those specific characters.

The following are the basic steps for using a Font symbol:

1. Create a font symbol in the library, and set the symbol to export for ActionScript.

2. Set the `embedFonts` property for the `TextField` object to `true`.

3. Create a `TextFormat` object and assign the linkage identifier for the font symbol to the `TextFormat` object's `font` property.

4. Assign the `TextFormat` object to the `TextField`.

Let's take a closer look at some of the preceding steps.

To create a font symbol complete the following:

1. Open the library and select the New Font from the library's menu.

2. In the Font Symbol Properties dialog box, give the symbol a name and select the font you want to embed.

3. After you've created the symbol, open the symbol's linkage settings, check the Export for ActionScript option, and give the symbol a linkage identifier.

The `embedFonts` property for a `TextField` object defaults to `false`. By setting the property to `true` you tell Flash to use only the specified embedded font (which you specify in the next step with a `TextFormat` object). If Flash is unable to find the specified embedded font then no text will display in that field.

```
tLabel.embedFonts = true;
```

To create a `TextFormat` object that uses the embedded font and assign the object to the `TextField`, complete the following steps:

1. Create a new `TextFormat` object with the constructor:

   ```
   var tfFormatter:TextFormat = new TextFormat();
   ```

2. Assign the linkage identifier name to the `TextFormat` object's `font` property. For example, if you created a font symbol with linkage identifier `ArialEmbeddedFont`:

   ```
   tfFormatter.font = "ArialEmbeddedFont";
   ```

3. Assign the `TextFormat` object to the `TextField` object with the `setTextFormat()` method:

   ```
   tLabel.setTextFormat(tfFormatter);
   ```

Using Faux Bold and Italic Styles with Embedded Fonts

If you would like to use faux bold or italic style with an embedded font, you can select either option (or both options) in the Font Symbol Properties dialog box. However, each of these options creates specific font outlines to be generated and exported with your Flash movie (SWF file). For example, if you select the Bold check box for the Verdana font you used in the last exercise, you can use only the following `TextFormat` object properties with your text fields. (Note that you can name your `TextFormat` object differently—you don't have to use the name `siteStyle`.)

```
var siteStyle:TextFormat = new TextFormat();
siteStyle.font = "Verdana";
siteStyle.bold = true;
siteStyle.size = 12;
comments.setTextFormat(siteStyle);
```

If you omit the `bold` property, the text does not display in the `TextField` object. Likewise, if you select both the Bold and Italic check boxes in the Font Properties dialog box, you can use that font only if you have the `bold` and `italic` properties set to `true`.

```
var siteStyle:TextFormat = new TextFormat();
siteStyle.font = "Verdana";
siteStyle.bold = true;
siteStyle.italic = true;
siteStyle.size = 12;
comments.setTextFormat(siteStyle);
```

If you want the option to use normal, faux bold, or faux italic styles, you need to create three separate font symbols in the Library panel—one for each style. If you want to use faux bold and faux italic together, you need to add a fourth font symbol that has both the Bold and Italic options selected. Remember, each font symbol must be set to export with the Flash movie (SWF file) in order to be used with ActionScript. Embedding so many fonts may be impractical for the file size requirements for your Flash movie. Make sure you need to use these styles before you decide to include them.

Remember, as well, that these styles are *faux* bold and *faux* italic, meaning Flash MX makes a "best guess" at what a font should look like as bold or italic as it creates the outlines to be exported with the Flash movie. Most professional font faces have individual font files for these styles, such as Futura Oblique (oblique is another term used for italic) or Futura Bold. Instead of using faux bold or faux italic, you may want to embed an original font face designed for bold or italic formatting.

To minimize the added file size (in bytes) of font outlines in the final Flash movies, you may want to explore the use of Macromedia Fontographer to create custom font files that have only the characters you need to use with text fields in your specific project. Flash MX does not offer any font subset options for font symbols as it does for regular dynamic or input text fields in the Character Options dialog box (accessible from the Property inspector).

Using Flash Device Fonts

You can also opt to use three different font faces with unique Flash names. These fonts are listed at the very top (Windows) or very bottom (Macintosh) of the Font menu in the

Property inspector. Alternatively, you can find them listed at the top of the Text ➪ Font menu in both Windows and Macintosh versions of Flash MX:

✦ **_sans:** This font choice uses the system's default sans serif font for displaying text in the specified field. A sans serif (meaning "without serif") typeface consists of rounded corners of all characters—you usually don't find ornamental edges on sans serif typefaces. On Windows, the default sans serif font is Arial. On Macintosh, it's Helvetica. Sans serif typefaces are often called Gothic typefaces.

✦ **_serif:** This font choice uses the system's default serif font for displaying text in the specified field. A serif is a fine line used to complete the edges of characters in a typeface. The typeface used for this book is a serif font—notice the edges of characters such as *F* and *D* compared to the same letters as they appear in this section's title, which is a sans serif typeface. The default system serif font on Windows is Times New Roman. On the Macintosh, it is Times.

✦ **_typewriter:** This font choice uses the system's default monospaced typeface for displaying text in the specified field. A monospaced typeface uses the same width for every character in the typeface. Most fonts are not monospaced—for example, the width required for a *W* is much greater than that required for *I*. On Windows, the default monospaced typeface is Courier New. On Macintosh, it is Courier.

When you use these device fonts, you do not want to use any of the font embedding controls in the Property inspector for the Text tool. Device fonts are commonly used to reduce the file size of Flash movies (SWF files) when an exact typeface is unnecessary for text within the movie. For example, although you may want to make sure your company's logo uses the same typeface that you use in printed materials and signage, you may not need to use that font for a Flash form in which users type their contact information.

Device fonts do not display text in editable text fields that are governed by Mask layers or that are transformed. For example, if you rotate a `TextField` object using a device font, you do not see any text display. Any changes in the Transform panel or the Color menu of the Property inspector for that instance render the text invisible.

Inserting Special Characters into Editable Text Fields

Some characters require special syntax in order to be displayed within an ActionScript-defined editable text field. For example, if you want to use ActionScript to set the value of a `TextField` object, you need to know how to insert carriage returns, quotes, and tabs into the string expression. Following is a list of special formatting characters you can use within ActionScript-assigned text. Most of them are *backslash pairs,* a term used by several scripting languages for special characters. Backslash pairs are always written *inline*, meaning they are specified within the string itself. Backslash pairs are also called escape sequences.

✦ **newline, \n, \r:** `newline` is a Flash-specific operator that forces a carriage return within an editable text field. The `newline` operator is not used within the string expression. However, the backslash pair `\n` or `\r`, which always insert a carriage return, are written as part of the string expression.

✦ **\\:** If you need to insert a backslash character (\) into an editable text field via ActionScript, this backslash pair does it for you.

✦ **\t:** This backslash pair inserts a Tab character into the field. This is actually something you *can't* do manually within an editable text field.

✦ \": This pair inserts a double-quote character within a string.

✦ \': This pair inserts a single quote into the string used for the editable text field.

Although their use may be isolated and rare, you can use other escape sequences, such as \b for a backspace character or \f for a form-feed character. Also, you can specify bytes in octal (\000–\377), hexadecimal (\x00–\xFF), or a 16-bit Unicode character in hexadecimal (\u0000–\uFFFF).

To use these special formatting sequences, simply use them in the string expression that you write for the editable text field. For example, if you created a TextField instance named tArticle and created an action on frame 1 of the current timeline as follows:

```
tArticle.text = "Part I" + newline + "This is how it began.";
```

this code displays the text in the field like this:

```
Part I
This is how it began.
```

You could also write this code with the following syntax:

```
article.text = "Part I\rThis is how it began.";
```

Even though this syntax appears to create one term, I\rThis, ActionScript interprets the backslash pair correctly and displays the text in the field as follows:

```
Part I
This is how it began.
```

These sequences should not be typed into the actual editable text field on the Flash stage. You use these sequences only in ActionScript.

Creating a Random Letter Displayer

In this exercise, you'll create an interesting effect that fades letters in and out randomly across the stage. Because the effect relies on modifying the _alpha property value of the TextField objects, you'll need to embed the font.

1. Open a new Flash document and save it as randomLetters001.fla.
2. Rename the default layer as Embedded Font, and add a new layer named actions.
3. Using the Text tool, add an authoring time dynamic TextField object off the stage on the Embedded Font layer.
4. With the TextField object selected, use the drop-down to change the font to Verdana and then click the Character button in the Property inspector to open the Character Options dialog box.
5. Choose the Specify Ranges option and enter the value abcdef in the Include These Characters field.
6. Click OK to exit the Character Options dialog box.
7. Add the code shown in Listing 17-4 to the first frame of the actions layer.

Listing 17-4: The random letter displayer code

```
function displayLetter():Void {

  // Create a random integer to yield one of the indices from the
  // aLetters array.
  var nRandomIndex:Number = Math.ceil(Math.random() * aLetters.length) - 1;

  // Create random numbers to use for the x and y coordinates of
  // the letter TextField.
  var nRandomX:Number = Math.random() * 550;
  var nRandomY:Number = Math.random() * 400;

  // Get the next available depth;
  var nDepth:Number = this.getNextHighestDepth();

  // Create a new TextField object at the random x and y
  // coordinates.
  this.createTextField("tLetter" + nDepth, nDepth, nRandomX, nRandomY, 0, 0);

  // Assign a reference to a variable to make it more convenient
  // to work with the TextField.
  var tLetter:TextField = this["tLetter" + nDepth];

  // Set the autoSize and text properties so the random letter
  // displays.
  tLetter.autoSize = "left";
  tLetter.text = aLetters[nRandomIndex];

  // Set a custom property called fadeDirection that determines
  // the increment by which the alpha will change. And set the
  // alpha to 0 initially.
  tLetter.fadeDirection = 5;
  tLetter._alpha = 0;

  // Tell Flash to embed the font for the TextField.
  tLetter.embedFonts = true;

  // Create a TextFormat object that tells Flash to use the
  // Verdana font and set the size to 15.
  var tfFormatter:TextFormat = new TextFormat();
  tfFormatter.font = "Verdana";
  tfFormatter.size = 15;

  // Assign the TextFormat to the TextField.
  tLetter.setTextFormat(tfFormatter);

  // Set an interval at which the letter will fade in and out.
  tLetter.nInterval = setInterval(this, "alphaFade", 10, tLetter);
```

```
}

function alphaFade(tLetter:TextField):Void {

  // Increment the letter TextField's alpha.
  tLetter._alpha += tLetter.fadeDirection;

  // Check to see if the letter has faded in completely. If so
  // set the fadeDirection property to -5 so that the TextField
  // starts to fade out. Otherwise, if the letter has faded out
  // completely...
  if(tLetter.fadeDirection > 0 && tLetter._alpha >= 100) {
    tLetter.fadeDirection = -5;
  }
  else if(tLetter.fadeDirection < 0 && tLetter._alpha <= 0) {
    // ... clear the interval and remove the TextField.
    clearInterval(tLetter.nInterval);
    tLetter.removeTextField();
  }

  // Make sure to update the screen.
  updateAfterEvent();
}

// Create the array of letters.
var aLetters:Array = ["a", "b", "c", "d", "e", "f"];

// Set the interval at which a new letter should be displayed.
var nDisplayInterval:Number = setInterval(this, "displayLetter", 1);
```

8. Test the movie.

Understanding the Selection Class

The `Selection` class can help you control focus and selection within your Flash application. `TextField`, `MovieClip`, and `Button` objects can receive focus, but selection only applies to `TextField` objects. You take a closer look at focus and selection in the following sections.

The methods of the `Selection` class are static. That means that you do not need to instantiate the class. Instead, you should call all methods directly from the class itself.

Working with Focus

Focus is a term used in many scripting languages to describe which part of the application is active. For example, with Web browser windows, the foreground window is usually the focused one, meaning that actions such as keyboard input are received by that window, and not another. The same thing applies to Flash applications. A `Button`, `MovieClip`, or `TextField` object can receive focus within Flash. For example, when a user uses the mouse to click within a `TextField` instance, she brings focus to that instance. Once the object has focus, the user can enter text.

Determining Focus

The getFocus() method returns the full path (as a string) to the currently focused TextField, Button, or MovieClip object. If there isn't any object with focus, a null value is returned. For example, if a text field named tUsername on the main timeline is active, Selection.getFocus() returns _level0.tUsername as a string. Usually, this method is used to assign a value to a variable that stores the path information. You'll see this usage in later examples.

If a TextField object has both a variable and an instance name assigned, getFocus() returns the path with the instance name. If only a variable name is specified, getFocus() returns the path with the variable name.

Setting Focus

The setFocus() method brings the focus to the object specified as the parameter. The parameter should be the path (relative or absolute) as a string to a MovieClip, Button, or TextField object. If the object to which you are bringing focus is a TextField object then Flash will also display the I-beam cursor within that instance.

The following example creates a new TextField object and brings focus to it:

```
this.createTextField("tUsername", this.getNextHighestDepth(), 25, 25, 150, 20);
tUsername.border = true;
tUsername.type = "input";
Selection.setFocus("tUsername");
```

Listening for Focus Changes

You can add listener objects to the Selection class to be notified when focus changes occur. To add a listener object, use the Selection.addListener() method. For example, the following registers a new listener named oListener:

```
Selection.addListener(oListener);
```

And to remove a listener, use the Selection.removeListener() method:

```
Selection.removeListener(oListener);
```

When focus changes occur, the Selection class notifies all registered listeners and calls their onSetFocus() method. The onSetFocus() method is automatically passed two parameters—a reference to the object that previously had focus and the object that has just received focus. The following is an example:

```
var oFocusListener:Object = new Object();
oFocusListener.onSetFocus = function(oPrevFocus:Object, oNewFocus:Object):Void {
  trace("Current focus = " + oNewFocus);
  trace("Previous focus = " + oPrevFocus);
};
Selection.addListener(oFocusListener);
```

Working with Selection

A *selection* is the range of characters within a TextField object that is highlighted. Any time you click and highlight characters within text, you make a selection. You can also make a selection programmatically, as you'll see in just a moment. In input text, you can also insert the I-beam cursor at any position within the field. This position is known as the *caret.* With ActionScript and the Selection class, you can retrieve the current value of the caret's position, the current position value of the beginning of a selection, and the position value of the end of a selection. You can also use ActionScript to enable automated selections (or highlights) within a text field.

All methods of the Selection class work with zero-based indices.

Note that all of the Selection class's methods for working with the selection and caret do not require you to specify the TextField object for which you wish to set or retrieve the selection. Because there can be only one selection made at a time, the TextField object that currently has focus is automatically used. As you have already learned, a TextField object can receive focus by user interaction or by programmatic means.

Getting the Current Selection

A selection has a beginning and an ending point that are given by the respective indices within the focused TextField. In order to retrieve the indices you can use the Selection.getBeginIndex() and Selection.getEndIndex() methods.

The Selection.getBeginIndex() method returns the starting index of a selection. If there is no selection, the method returns -1. The Selection.getEndIndex() method returns the index of the position immediately after the last character of the selection. If there is no selection when this method is called, the method returns -1.

You can test these methods with the following code:

```
this.createTextField("tOutput", this.getNextHighestDepth(), 100, 100, 200, 200);
tOutput.border = true;
tOutput.multiline = true;
tOutput.wordWrap = true;
tOutput.text = "The Selection class enables you to retrieve the selected ↩
   text programmatically.";
this.onMouseUp = function():Void {
  trace(Selection.getBeginIndex() + " " + Selection.getEndIndex());
};
```

When you test the preceding code, highlight some of the text, and release the mouse click, the beginning and ending indices of the selection are displayed in the Output panel.

Often you are likely to use the selection indices in conjunction with the substring() and/or substr() methods of the String class. For example, the following code is a slight variation (changes shown in bold) on the previous code in which the current selection is displayed in the Output panel instead of just the indices:

```
this.createTextField("tOutput", this.getNextHighestDepth(), 100, 100, 200, 200);
tOutput.border = true;
```

```
tOutput.multiline = true;
tOutput.wordWrap = true;
tOutput.text = "The Selection class enables you to retrieve the selected ⮐
  text programmatically.";
this.onMouseUp = function():Void {
  trace(tOutput.text.substring(Selection.getBeginIndex(), ⮐
  Selection.getEndIndex()));
};
```

Setting the Selection

In addition to retrieving the selection, you can also programmatically set the selection by calling the `Selection.setSelection()` method. The method requires two parameters—integers specifying the beginning and ending indices. The beginning index is the index of the first character in the selection, and the ending index is the index just following the last character.

Often the `Selection.setSelection()` method is used in conjunction with the `Selection.setFocus()` method. Remember that the `Selection.setSelection()` is applied to the `TextField` that currently has focus so it is generally the case that you will want to programmatically bring focus to the `TextField` first. The following code creates a `TextField` object; when you click and release the mouse, the word "set" is highlighted.

```
this.createTextField("tOutput", this.getNextHighestDepth(), 100, 100, 200, 200);
tOutput.border = true;
tOutput.multiline = true;
tOutput.wordWrap = true;
tOutput.selectable = false;
tOutput.text = "The Selection class also enables you to set the selected ⮐
  text programmatically.";
this.onMouseUp = function():Void {
  Selection.setFocus("tOutput");
  Selection.setSelection(40, 43);
};
```

Working with the Caret

You can get and set the caret within a `TextField` object programmatically as well. The `getCaretIndex()` method returns the current index of the I-beam cursor. If there is no active I-beam cursor, this method returns `-1`.

You can set the caret with the `setSelection()` method. Just set the beginning and ending indices to the same value.

Replacing Selected Text

This `replaceSel()` method of the `TextField` class replaces the active selection with the value specified as the method's parameter. Because a selection must be the current focus in order for this method to work, you will likely use this method in combination with listeners attached to either the `Mouse` or `Selection` object.

Remember that you cannot have focus in two places at once. In other words, you can't use the `replaceSel()` method to enable a user to select some text and then click a button or other user interface element to change the text—as soon as the user clicks the button, the selection (and focus) on the text field is lost.

The following code replaces the selected text (or index) within a TextField object named tArticle with the contents of a field named tWord. The replacement occurs whenever the user clicks and releases the mouse and focus is on the tArticle field.

```
this.createTextField("tArticle", this.getNextHighestDepth(), 100, 25, 200, 100);
this.createTextField("tWord", this.getNextHighestDepth(), 25, 25, 50, 20);
tArticle.border = true;
tWord.border = true;
tWord.type = "input";
tArticle.text = "This is some text in a text field.";
var oListener:Object = new Object();
oListener.onMouseUp = function(){
  if(Selection.getFocus().indexOf("tArticle") != -1){
    tArticle.replaceSel(tWord.text);
  }
};
Mouse.addListener(oListener);
```

Working with Tab Order

When working with TextField objects you may want to consider how focus is brought to them via the Tab key. Standard computing practices allow the user to change focus using the Tab key, and by default TextField objects are enabled to accept focus in that way. You can, however, enable and disable that functionality as well as specify the order in which TextField objects should receive focus when the Tab key is pressed.

Enabling and Disabling Tab-Initiated Focus

You can use the tabEnabled property to determine whether pressing the Tab key can bring focus to the text. By default the property is true, meaning that the instance can receive focus initiated by pressing the Tab key. Typically, input text should be Tab-enabled. But dynamic text likely should not be Tab-enabled.

Changing Tab Order

The tabIndex property allows you to determine the order in which objects are accessed with the Tab key. Any positive integer can be used for the value of the tabIndex property. Lower numbers are accessed in ascending order — an object with a tabIndex value of 1 is the first object that will be focused before an object with a tabIndex value of 2. As soon as you've assigned a tabIndex value to any object current visible on the stage, the Tab order is determined solely by the tabIndex values for the visible objects. If an object does not have a tabIndex property value, it is not included in the sequence.

The following code creates three input TextField objects. The tEmail and tPostalCode objects are assigned tabIndex property values, whereas the tComments object is not. If you test the code, you'll see that you can use the Tab key to change focus between tEmail and tPostalCode. However, in order to bring focus to the tComments field you have to click in the field.

```
this.createTextField("tEmail", 1, 25, 35, 100, 20);
tEmail.border = true;
```

```
tEmail.type = "input";
tEmail.tabIndex = 1;

this.createTextField("tPostalCode", 2, 150, 35, 200, 20);
tPostalCode.border = true;
tPostalCode.type = "input";
tPostalCode.tabIndex = 2;

this.createTextField("tComments", 3, 25, 75, 325, 200);
tComments.border = true;
tComments.type = "input";
```

If you append the following line of code to the preceding, you can see that by setting the `tabIndex` property for `tComments`, `tComments` is included in the sequence:

```
tComments.tabIndex = 3;
```

`TextField`, `MovieClip`, and `Button` objects have the `tabIndex` property. For more information, read the coverage of `tabIndex` in Chapter 9.

We'd like to know what you thought about this chapter. Visit `www.flashsupport.com/feedback` to fill out an online form with your comments.

Summary

- ✦ Text in Flash is classified as static, dynamic, or input. Dynamic and input text are the types of text you'll work with when using ActionScript.
- ✦ You can create `TextField` objects at authoring time using the Text tool or at runtime using the `createTextField()` method.
- ✦ Using the basic properties of the `TextField` class, you can control aspects of object such as the text that is displayed, word wrapping, text color, and more.
- ✦ Flash text can render some HTML tags, enabling you to add formatting and hyperlinks and even to embed content.
- ✦ You can scroll text vertically and horizontally using the built-in scrolling properties.
- ✦ Focus refers to the active portion of an application. You can get and set focus within a Flash application using the `Selection.getFocus()` and `Selection.setFocus()` methods.
- ✦ The `Selection` class also enables you to get and set the selected text within the focused `TextField` object.
- ✦ Using the `tabEnabled` and `tabIndex` properties you can determine how the Tab key affects focus within the application.

✦ ✦ ✦

CHAPTER 18

Using the TextFormat Object and Style Sheets

✦ ✦ ✦ ✦

In This Chapter

Applying formatting to text using a TextFormat object

Understanding the formatting properties for the TextFormat class

Working with cascading style sheets (CSS) in ActionScript

Creating CSS with ActionScript

Loading external CSS files

✦ ✦ ✦ ✦

In the Chapter 17, you learned all about working with text with ActionScript. In this chapter, you'll look at how you can use ActionScript to then format that text. Although you did see how you could use HTML to apply some basic formatting to your text in Chapter 17, this chapter discusses how you can apply more detailed formatting using the `TextFormat` and `StyleSheet` classes.

Working with TextFormat

The `TextFormat` class was introduced in Flash MX, so it is not new to Flash MX 2004. You can use the `TextFormat` class to apply formatting to `TextField` objects' contents for Flash 6 and Flash 7 applications. The `TextFormat` class enables you to specify the following formatting options:

- Alignment
- Margins
- Indentation
- Block indentation
- Tab stops
- Line spacing (called "leading")
- Bolded text
- Italicized text
- Underlined text
- Bullet points
- Text color
- Font face
- Font size
- Hyperlinks and target windows

You can adjust the formatting options for part or all of the content of a `TextField` object.

Creating a TextFormat Object

One of the obvious things that you need to do before you can apply any formatting is create the `TextFormat` object that you'll use. You can create a `TextFormat` object with the constructor. The most common way is to call the constructor with no parameters. For example:

```
var tfFormatter:TextFormat = new TextFormat();
```

Once you've defined a `TextFormat` object in the preceding manner, you can define the values for its properties as discussed in subsequent sections.

The `TextFormat` constructor also enables you to define some of the object's properties as you create the object. Frankly, this option is rarely used because it is difficult to remember the parameter order and because you must specify all 13 parameters to use it. However, if you find it useful, you can create a `TextFormat` object in the following way:

```
var tfFormatter:TextFormat = new TextFormat(font, size, color,
 bold, italic, underline, url, target, align, leftMargin,
 rightMargin, indent, leading);
```

If you prefer not to assign a specific value, you can use `null`. The following code creates a `tfTitle` object that uses BlurMedium font face at 10 point in blue, with a URL pointing to the `http://flashsupport.com` Web site:

```
var tfTitle:TextFormat = new TextFormat("BlurMedium", 10,
 0x0000FF, null, null, null, "http://flashsupport.com", "_blank",
 null, null, null, null, null);
```

As you can see, that syntax can be somewhat cumbersome. You might prefer the following syntax in order to accomplish the same thing:

```
var tfTitle:TextFormat = new TextFormat();
tfTitle.font = "BlurMedium";
tfTitle.size = 10;
tfTitle.color = 0x0000FF;
tfTitle.url = "http://flashsupport.com";
tfTitle.target = "_blank";
```

Also notice that you cannot specify block indentation and tab stops in the constructor. You must specify those values as properties. You can modify the properties of a `TextFormat` object subsequent to instantiating it regardless of which constructor you use.

Assigning Formatting to a TextField Object

Once you have created a `TextFormat` object, the next step is to apply that formatting to a `TextField` object's contents. You can accomplish that with the `setTextFormat()` method of the `TextField` object to which you want to add the formatting. Using the `setTextFormat()` method you can add formatting to the entire contents, a single character, or a range of characters. Let's take a look at these three options:

✦ **setTextFormat(*TextFormat object*)**: This usage applies the properties of the specified `TextFormat` object to the entire contents of the `TextField` object from which the methods are called.

- **setTextFormat(*index*, *TextFormat object*):** This syntax applies the TextFormat object properties to a specific character within the field. Each character is numerically indexed starting at 0. So to apply the formatting to the first character, you use the value of 0 for the first parameter.
- **setTextFormat(*beginIndex*, *endIndex*, *TextFormat object*):** This syntax applies the TextFormat object properties to a specific range of characters within the field.

Now that you've had a chance to see the theory, let's take a look at a few practical examples that use the setTextFormat() method in various ways.

First, the following code creates a TextField object, displays some text within it, and applies bold formatting to the entire text:

```
this.createTextField("tOutput", this.getNextHighestDepth(), 100, 100, 100, 20);
tOutput.text = "Formatted text";
var tfFormatter:TextFormat = new TextFormat();
tfFormatter.bold = true;
tOutput.setTextFormat(tfFormatter);
```

If you change the last line of code as follows, the bold formatting is applied only to the first letter:

```
tOutput.setTextFormat(0, tfFormatter);
```

And if you change the last line again to the following code, the bold formatting is applied only to the second word:

```
tOutput.setTextFormat(10, 14, tfFormatter);
```

The formatting that you apply to the TextField object is removed if and when you change the value of the object's text property. That means you need to reapply the formatting when you change the text content programmatically. For example:

```
this.createTextField("tOutput", this.getNextHighestDepth(), 100, 100, 100, 20);
tOutput.text = "Formatted text";
var tfFormatter:TextFormat = new TextFormat();
tfFormatter.bold = true;
tOutput.setTextFormat(tfFormatter);
tOutput.text = "Different text";
tOutput.setTextFormat(tfFormatter);
```

It is also very important to note that changes you make to the TextFormat object are not applied to the TextField object until you reapply the TextFormat to the TextField. For example, the following code causes the text to appear bolded but not underlined:

```
this.createTextField("tOutput", this.getNextHighestDepth(), 100, 100, 100, 20);
tOutput.text = "Formatted text";
var tfFormatter:TextFormat = new TextFormat();
tfFormatter.bold = true;
tOutput.setTextFormat(tfFormatter);
tfFormatter.underline = true;
```

In order to get the underline setting to take effect, you need to call the setTextFormat() method again to reapply the formatting:

```
this.createTextField("tOutput", this.getNextHighestDepth(), 100, 100, 100, 20);
tOutput.text = "Formatted text";
```

```
var tfFormatter:TextFormat = new TextFormat();
tfFormatter.bold = true;
tOutput.setTextFormat(tfFormatter);
tfFormatter.underline = true;
tOutput.setTextFormat(tfFormatter);
```

Obviously, the preceding example, as is, is not something you would encounter in an actual application. Instead, you simply set the bold and underline properties prior to calling the `setTextFormat()` method the first time. However, consider the scenario in which the bold and underline properties are updated via user interaction. Each time the user changes the setting, you need to reapply the formatting.

The `setTextFormat()` method works only for text that is assigned programmatically. However, it will not apply formatting to new text as the user is entering it. Instead, you use the `setNewTextFormat()` method to tell Flash what formatting to apply to any new text that the user enters. Unlike `setTextFormat()`, the `setNewTextFormat()` method has only one usage syntax. You need only pass it the reference to the `TextFormat` object. You don't need to specify any indices because the formatting with `setNewTextFormat()` is applied only to new text entered by the user at the end of any existing text.

The following shows an example that creates an input `TextField` object and applies formatting so that any user-input text is bolded:

```
this.createTextField("tInput", this.getNextHighestDepth(), 100, 100, 100, 20);
tInput.type = "input";
tInput.border = true;
var tfFormatter:TextFormat = new TextFormat();
tfFormatter.bold = true;
tInput.setNewTextFormat(tfFormatter);
```

Understanding Formatting Properties

The `TextFormat` class has 16 properties that you can use to apply various formatting to `TextField` object content. The following sections detail each of these properties.

Additionally, on the CD-ROM is `TextFormattingExample.fla`, a Flash document that allows you to change many of the formatting properties of some text to see the effects.

align

You can use the `align` property to place the text relative to the right and left edges of the `TextField` object's bounding box. The property can have the following values:

- **left:** This value places the text such that the left side of the text is against the left side of bounding box.
- **right:** This value places the text such that the right side of the text is against the right side of the bounding box.
- **center:** This value places the text such that the center of the text is aligned with the center of the bounding box.
- **null:** The null value is the default value and it resolves to the same thing as a value of `left`.

The following code creates text aligned to the center.

```
this.createTextField("tContent", this.getNextHighestDepth(),
                     100, 100, 200, 200);
tContent.multiline = true;
tContent.border = true;
tContent.wordWrap = true;
tContent.text = "center-aligned text";
var tfFormatter:TextFormat = new TextFormat();
tfFormatter.align = "center";
tContent.setTextFormat(tfFormatter);
```

blockIndent

The `blockIndent` property has an effect on text only when the text is aligned left. In that case, the `blockIndent` property indents the entire block of text inward relative to the left margin. The value should be a number indicating the points value by which you want to indent the text.

The `blockIndent` property indents the entire block of text. To indent just the first line of text in a paragraph, use the `indent` property instead.

The following code creates text that is indented as a block:

```
this.createTextField("tContent", this.getNextHighestDepth(),100, 100, 200, 200);
tContent.multiline = true;
tContent.border = true;
tContent.wordWrap = true;
tContent.text = "a few lines\nof text\nthat are indented\nas a block";
var tfFormatter:TextFormat = new TextFormat();
tfFormatter.blockIndent = 10;
tContent.setTextFormat(tfFormatter);
```

bold

The `bold` property applies faux bold formatting to the targeted text. To turn bold formatting on, use a Boolean value of `true`. To turn bold off, use a Boolean value of `false`. By default, this property is defined with a `null` value, which produces the same effect as `false`.

bullet

The `bullet` property adds a bullet character (•) in front of the text if the property's value is set to `true`. You can turn off bullet formatting by assigning a `false` value to the property. By default, this property has a value of `null`. The font face used for the bullet character is the same as that defined for other text in the `TextFormat` object (via the `font` property, discussed later). The bullet points are placed 19 pixels from the left margin of the field, affected only by the left margin settings. (Properties such as `blockIndent` don't have an effect when bullet points are used.) The bulleted text is spaced 15 pixels to the right of the bullet point.

The built-in spacing provided for bullets remains the same, regardless of font size. Be careful if you are using bullets with large sizes, such as 72 pt. The bullet can appear too close to the actual text. In this case, you might want to avoid the `bullet` property and simply specify a bullet character in the expression used for the `text` or `htmlText` property of the `TextField` object.

The following code displays a list of bulleted text:

```
this.createTextField("tContent", this.getNextHighestDepth(),100, 100, 200, 200);
tContent.multiline = true;
tContent.border = true;
tContent.wordWrap = true;
tContent.text = "a\nb\nc\nd";
var tfFormatter:TextFormat = new TextFormat();
tfFormatter.bullet = true;
tContent.setTextFormat(tfFormatter);
```

color

As the name implies, the `color` property controls the font color of the targeted text. The value for this property should be numeric. The following code displays red text:

```
this.createTextField("tContent", this.getNextHighestDepth(),100, 100, 200, 200);
tContent.multiline = true;
tContent.border = true;
tContent.wordWrap = true;
tContent.text = "red text";
var tfFormatter:TextFormat = new TextFormat();
tfFormatter.color = 0xFF0000;
tContent.setTextFormat(tfFormatter);
```

Do not attempt to use string values (such as `"0xFF0000"`) with the `color` property. If you have a string representation of a hexadecimal value that you want to use with the `color` property, convert the string expression into a number value using the `parseInt()` function.

font

The `font` property controls the font face used for the text. This property uses a string value, indicating the name of the font. The name that you use can depend on how you are working with the font in Flash. If you are not embedding the font or if you have embedded the font using an authoring time `TextField` object, use the name of the font as it displayed in the Font menu of the Property inspector. If you have embedded the font, but you did so using a Font symbol, use the Font symbol's linkage identifier.

By default, the `font` property has a value of `null`, which results in the default font being used. The font face can be applied only if the user has the font installed on his/her system, or if the font has been embedded or shared with the Flash movie.

The following code displays the text formatted with the Verdana font face:

```
this.createTextField("tContent", this.getNextHighestDepth(),100, 100, 200, 200);
tContent.multiline = true;
tContent.border = true;
tContent.wordWrap = true;
tContent.text = "Verdana text";
var tfFormatter:TextFormat = new TextFormat();
tfFormatter.font = "Verdana";
tContent.setTextFormat(tfFormatter);
```

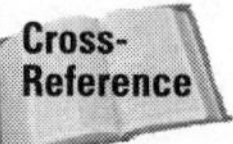

For more information on the use of embedded fonts with TextField and TextFormat objects, refer to Chapter 17.

You might want to use the TextField.getFontList() method in conjunction with the font property of a TextFormat object. The TextField.getFontList() method is a static method that returns an array of the fonts available on the client computer.

For an example of how to use the TextField.getFontList() method to allow the user to select a font, see the example file called TextFormattingExample.fla on the CD-ROM.

indent

The indent property controls the spacing applied from the left margin to the first line of text within a paragraph. A *paragraph* is defined as any text that precedes a carriage return (such as \r). This property uses pixel units. The default value is null. The following code indents the text by 10 pixels:

```
this.createTextField("tContent", this.getNextHighestDepth(),100, 100, 200, 200);
tContent.multiline = true;
tContent.border = true;
tContent.wordWrap = true;
tContent.text = "When you have several lines of text, ";
tContent.text += "and you have set the indent value to a positive ";
tContent.text += "integer, the first line will appear indented."
var tfFormatter:TextFormat = new TextFormat();
tfFormatter.indent = 10;
tContent.setTextFormat(tfFormatter);
```

italic

The italic property controls whether the targeted text uses faux italic formatting. If the property is set to true, the text appears in italic. If the property is set to false, the text appears normal. By default, this property has a value of null, which achieves the same effect as a value of false.

leading

The leading property controls the spacing inserted between each line of text. The values for this property are pixel-based. By default, the value of this property is null. You cannot programmatically set the leading value to be a negative number.

The following code inserts 10 pixels of space between each line of text:

```
this.createTextField("tContent", this.getNextHighestDepth(),100, 100, 200, 200);
tContent.multiline = true;
tContent.border = true;
tContent.wordWrap = true;
tContent.text = "When you have several lines of text, ";
tContent.text += "and you have set the leading value to a positive ";
tContent.text += "integer, the spacing between the lines changes."
var tfFormatter:TextFormat = new TextFormat();
tfFormatter.leading = 10;
tContent.setTextFormat(tfFormatter);
```

leftMargin

The `leftMargin` property determines the spacing (in pixels) inserted between the text and the left border of the `TextField` object. By default, the value of this property is `null`, which achieves the same effect as a value of 0. The following code creates a left margin of 10 pixels:

```
this.createTextField("tContent", this.getNextHighestDepth(),100, 100, 200, 200);
tContent.multiline = true;
tContent.border = true;
tContent.wordWrap = true;
tContent.text = "Left margin";
var tfFormatter:TextFormat = new TextFormat();
tfFormatter.leftMargin = 10;
tContent.setTextFormat(tfFormatter);
```

The `blockIndent` and `leftMargin` properties affect the text offset on the left side in a cumulative manner.

rightMargin

The `rightMargin` property controls the spacing (in pixels) inserted between the text and the right border of the `TextField` object. By default, the value of this property is `null`.

The following code illustrates the effect of the `rightMargin` property:

```
this.createTextField("tContent", this.getNextHighestDepth(),100, 100, 200, 200);
tContent.multiline = true;
tContent.border = true;
tContent.wordWrap = true;
tContent.text = "Right margin text that wraps to the next line";
var tfFormatter:TextFormat = new TextFormat();
tfFormatter.rightMargin = 10;
tContent.setTextFormat(tfFormatter);
```

size

The `size` property determines the size (in points) of the text. Remember that when a value is given in points it will display differently depending on the font face used. Therefore, the actual pixel size for two font faces can differ even if the point size is the same.

The following code creates text that displays with a point size of 20:

```
this.createTextField("tContent", this.getNextHighestDepth(),100, 100, 200, 200);
tContent.multiline = true;
tContent.border = true;
tContent.wordWrap = true;
tContent.text = "Some text";
var tfFormatter:TextFormat = new TextFormat();
tfFormatter.size = 20;
tContent.setTextFormat(tfFormatter);
```

tabStops

The `tabStops` property defines a custom array specifying the values used by tabs within the text. The first element of the array specifies the spacing (in points) to use for the first tab character in succession. The second element specifies the spacing to use for the second tab character in succession, and so on. The value of the last element in the array is used for all subsequent tab characters. For example, if the tabStops array has three elements — 10, 20, 50 — and four tab characters are used in succession, a value of 50 is used.

The default value for tabStops is null. When the property has a value of null, the default value of four points is used between each successive tab character. However, using the tabStops property you can specify how ordered tabs are spaced within text.

For example, you can create a TextFormat object that uses a tab spacing of 10 pixels for the first tab, a tab spacing of 50 pixels for the second tab (in succession), and a tab spacing of 150 pixels for the third tab. The following code does just that:

```
this.createTextField("tContent", this.getNextHighestDepth(),100, 100, 200, 200);
tContent.multiline = true;
tContent.border = true;
tContent.wordWrap = true;
tContent.text = "\ta\n";
tContent.text += "\t\tb\n";
tContent.text += "\t\t\tc";
var tfFormatter:TextFormat = new TextFormat();
tfFormatter.tabStops = [10, 50, 150];
tfFormatter.align = "left";
tContent.setTextFormat(tfFormatter);
```

It is important to understand that the values in the tabStop array determine the pixels from the edge of the TextField, not between each tab. That means that the values in the array are not cumulative but are absolute values. In other words, in the preceding code, the third tab is 150 pixels from the left edge of the TextField, not 210 (which would be the sum of 10, 50, and 150).

target

The target property works in conjunction with the url property (discussed later in this section). You can specify a string value for the target property that indicates the name of the browser window (or frame) where the URL specified in the url property should appear. You can use the predefined target values of "_blank" (new empty browser window), "_self" (the current frame or window), "_parent" (the parent frame or window), or "_top" (the outermost frame or window), or you can use a custom browser window or frame name (as assigned in the HTML document or JavaScript). If you use the url property without specifying a value for the target property, the URL loads into the current frame or window ("_self").

underline

The underline property can add an underline to text. When this property is set to true, an underline appears with the text. When it is set to false, any underlines are removed. By default, the value of this property is null, which has the same effect as a value of false.

Tip You might want to use the underline property to indicate text that is linked to URLs (see the url property, discussed next).

url

The url property allows you to add a hyperlink to text. The Flash Player does not provide any immediate indication that the url property is in use for a given range of text — you may want to change the color and add an underline to the affected text to make the link more apparent to the user. However, the mouse pointer automatically changes to the hand icon when the mouse rolls over the linked text.

In order to use the `url` property, you must make sure the `html` property is set to `true` for the `TextField`. Otherwise, the hyperlink is not applied properly.

The following code applies a hyperlink to a portion of the text:

```
this.createTextField("tContent", this.getNextHighestDepth(),100, 100, 200, 200);
tContent.multiline = true;
tContent.border = true;
tContent.wordWrap = true;
tContent.text = "Visit the Web site";
tContent.html = true;
var tfFormatter:TextFormat = new TextFormat();
tfFormatter.url = "http://www.flashsupport.com";
tfFormatter.target = "_blank";
tfFormatter.underline = true;
tContent.setTextFormat(10, 18, tfFormatter);
```

You can specify `asfunction` code as the value of the `url` property. The `asfunction` directive invokes ActionScript functions when the linked text is clicked. You can read more about `asfunction` in Chapter 17.

Determining Text Metrics

In many cases, you can allow for Flash to handle the text metrics issues automatically. For example, you might want to just allow Flash to automatically resize the `TextField` to match the text, or you can employ various other techniques. However, when you want to have exacting control that allows you to better determine the dimensions of the text, you can use the `TextFormat` class's `getTextExtent()` method. The method returns the text metrics for a string of text as it would appear given the formatting options.

The text metric information that `getTextExtent()` returns is in the form of an object with the following properties:

- **ascent:** The number of pixels above the baseline for the line of text.
- **descent:** The number of pixels below the baseline for the line of text.
- **width:** The width of the text.
- **height:** The height of the text.
- **textFieldWidth:** The width required for a `TextField` to display the text.
- **textFieldHeight:** The height required for a `TextField` to display the text.

The `textFieldWidth` and `textFieldHeight` properties differ from the `width` and `height` properties by four pixels. The reason is that `TextField` objects have a two-pixels margin between the border and the text.

When you call the `getTextExtent()` method, you have two options. First, you can pass it a single parameter — the string of text for which you want to get the metrics. For example:

```
var oMetrics:Object = tfFormatter.getTextExtent("Some text");
```

Flash then calculates the metrics for the text, assuming that the text will not wrap in the text field. Therefore the number of lines of text is based on newline characters only.

If you are authoring to Flash Player 7, you can also pass the `getTextExtent()` method a second parameter indicating the pixel count at which you want to wrap the text. For example:

```
var oMetrics:Object = tfFormatter.getTextExtent("Some text", 10);
```

With the second parameter, Flash calculates the metrics based on the assumption that the text should wrap at the specified width.

The following example uses the returned text metrics to size the `TextField` object:

```
var sCopy:String = "This is the copy to fit in the TextField.";
var tfFormatter:TextFormat = new TextFormat();
tfFormatter.bold = true;
tfFormatter.font = "Verdana";
var oTextMetrics:Object = tfFormatter.getTextExtent(sCopy);
this.createTextField("tContent", this.getNextHighestDepth(), 100, 100, ⮐
   oTextMetrics.textFieldWidth, oTextMetrics.textFieldHeight);
tContent.multiline = true;
tContent.border = true;
tContent.wordWrap = true;
tContent.text = sCopy;
tContent.setTextFormat(tfFormatter);
```

Getting the TextFormat

You can retrieve the `TextFormat` object for a `TextField` or selection within the text. This enables you to make modifications to the current formatting without having to keep track of the formatting in another way.

The `getTextFormat()` method of the `TextField` object returns a `TextFormat` object containing the formatting properties of the text within the field. You can use this method with three syntaxes, similarly to how there are three syntaxes for the `setTextFormat()` method:

✦ **getTextFormat():** If you omit an argument for this method, the returned `TextFormat` object contains the formatting properties for all of the text in the field. If there are mixed formats in the field, the returned property value for the mixed format will be `null`. For example, if the first line uses Times New Roman and the second line uses Courier New as the font face, the `font` property of the returned `TextFormat` object will be `null`.

✦ **getTextFormat(*index*):** You can retrieve the formatting characteristics of a specific character within a text field by using an index argument with the method. This index is 0-based, which means that the first character in the field has an index of 0, the second character has an index of 1, and so on.

✦ **getTextFormat(*beginIndex*, *endIndex*):** This version of the method allows you to retrieve the formatting properties for a specific range of text within the field. The `beginIndex` value is the starting position in the content, whereas the `endIndex` value is the index of the last position in the range. If there are mixed values for any given property in the range of text, that property's value will be `null`.

For an example of how to use getTextFormat(), look at the TextFormattingExample.fla file on the CD-ROM.

The getNewTextFormat() method returns a TextFormat object describing the properties of text that will be added to an input field by the user. It does not require any parameters because it does not target existing text within a field. You can test the properties of the object returned by the getNewTextFormat() method to make sure new text receives the proper formatting.

Working with Cascading Style Sheets

Flash MX 2004 and Flash Player 7 support cascading style sheets (CSS) for HTML or XML formatted text. First, this section discusses some of the basics of what CSS is, how it works, and what properties are supported in Flash. Then, it takes a look at how to create a TextField.StyleSheet object in ActionScript so that you can start working with CSS. Once you have created a StyleSheet object, you have the choice of either creating the style sheet using ActionScript or loading the CSS from an external file—both methods are covered here.

If you're not already familiar with CSS, you might want to consult a good resource such as the W3Schools online tutorial at www.w3schools.com/css. Even if you're not familiar with CSS, you can still benefit from the general overview in the following sections.

Understanding CSS

CSS allows you to define a set of rules that Flash will use to format text. CSS was originally created for the purposes of formatting HTML in Web browsers. The original HTML specification was fairly simple, and had to do with creating academic papers. As such, it was not designed to support complex formatting. To accommodate the formatting needs, new tags such as <font> were introduced. However, these tags managed to make coding HTML more complicated, and they made it very difficult to change formatting. CSS was developed primarily to separate the essential content from the rules that determine how that content is displayed.

You can define essentially two types of styles—those that are automatically applied to a tag and special classes that can be explicitly applied to a tag. Because CSS defines a specification for formatting, you can save a lot of time when trying to format your text. By defining a style for the <p> tag, for example, all content within <p> tags are styled in that fashion. If you later want to change the style, you need change it in only one place. CSS also saves you time in another way. It is called *cascading* style sheets because the rules that you define can be inherited. Nested tags automatically inherit the rules applied to a parent tag, unless they are overridden. That means that if you apply a style to the <p> tag, any nested <a> tag contents also automatically inherit that style. You'll see some examples of that in a bit.

You can apply CSS to both HTML and XML in Flash MX 2004/Flash Player 7. That means that you can even apply styles to unrecognized HTML tags. For example, Flash does not recognize the <html>, <title>, or <body> tags, to name but a few standard HTML elements. If you load an HTML document for display within Flash, you can potentially end up with some unwanted results because the contents of, for example, the <title> tag might display in a way other than what you intended. Using CSS, you can define a style for the <title> tag that either formats the content in a way you want or hides the contents from display.

Flash currently supports only a subset of the standard CSS properties. Table 18-1 shows the supported properties.

Table 18-1: Supported CSS Properties

Standard CSS Property	*ActionScript CSS Property*	*Description*
`color`	`color`	The color of the text. The value should be a hexadecimal representation of the color given as a string. And the first character should be a pound sign (#) as the color values are specified in HTML. For example: `#FF0000`.
`display`	`display`	This property determines how the text should display. The value should be a string. The default value of `block` means that a line break is placed before and after the text. A value of `inline` means that no line breaks are inserted. A value of `none` causes the text to be invisible.
`font-family`	`fontFamily`	This property can be used to specify the font face used. You can use any of the same values you can use with the `TextFormat` class's `font` property.
`font-size`	`fontSize`	The font size can be specified numerically. To support standard CSS values, the value can also be a string such as 12pt. Only the numeric portion is interpreted, and Flash supports only points, so even if the value is specified in pixels Flash will use points.
`font-style`	`fontStyle`	This property can be set to `normal` or `italic`. If it is set to `italic`, the faux italic is applied to the text.
`font-weight`	`fontWeight`	This property can be set to `normal` or `bold`. If it is set to `bold`, the faux bold is applied to the text.
`margin-left`	`marginLeft`	This property can be a numeric value indicating the number of pixels on the left margin. As with the `fontSize` property, the value can be a string such as 20px. Flash uses only pixel values for margins, so even if the value is specified in points the margin is calculated in pixels.
`margin-right`	`marginRight`	This property operates in the same way as the `marginLeft` property, but the value is used to determine the right margin, not the left.
`text-align`	`textAlign`	This property determines how the text aligns in the field. You can specify values of `left`, `right`, or `center`.
`text-decoration`	`textDecoration`	This property can be set to `normal` or `underline`. If you set the property to `underline`, the text is underlined.
`text-indent`	`textIndent`	This property determines how the text is indented. The value can be numeric or a string as with the font size and margin properties. Regardless of the units specified, Flash calculates the indentation in pixels.

Creating a StyleSheet Object

Regardless of whether you are going to create the style sheet information with ActionScript or by loading an external file, you first need to create a StyleSheet object. To create a StyleSheet object, use the constructor as follows:

```
var cssStyles:TextField.StyleSheet = new TextField.StyleSheet();
```

Adding Styles with ActionScript

You can add new styles to a style sheet using several techniques. The first one we discuss is the setStyle() method; it allows you to programmatically add one new style at a time. The method takes two parameters — the name of the style as a string and an object representing the style. The following adds a new style for <p> tags to a StyleSheet object named cssStyles. The style tells Flash to make the text within <p> tags display using the _sans font face.

```
cssStyles.setStyle("p", {fontFamily: "_sans"});
```

The preceding example causes all text within <p> tags to display using the _sans font face when the StyleSheet object is applied to a TextField object. Because the name of the style matches the name of a tag, it is used automatically to format the tag's contents. You can also create style classes that have to be explicitly applied to a tag instance. In order to do so, the style name should start with a dot. The following defines a style class named emphasized:

```
cssStyles.setStyle(".emphasized", {fontWeight: "bold", ⮐
textDecoration: "underline"});
```

The preceding style class is applied to the contents of a tag only when the tag explicitly specifies that it should be by way of the class attribute. When you apply the class in this way, make sure that you do not include the dot at the beginning of the name. The dot is used only to distinguish the style classes from the intrinsic tag styles in the style sheet. The following HTML text example shows how the emphasized class can be applied to some text:

```
<p class="emphasized">This text is emphasized</p>
```

In the preceding case, the text would be rendered with both the _sans font face and the bolded and underlined formatting.

You can also define styles in ActionScript by using the parseCSS() method to parse a CSS string. The parseCSS() method accepts a CSS definition as a string, and it parses it and applies it to the style sheet. The following is an example:

```
cssStyles.parseCSS("html{font-family: _typewriter;}");
```

Applying Styles to Text

Once you've defined a StyleSheet object, you can apply it to a TextField object by assigning it to the object's styleSheet property. For example, the following assigns cssStyles to the styleSheet property of a TextField named tContent:

```
tContent.styleSheet = cssStyles;
```

The styles defined in the StyleSheet object are then applied to any HTML text that is assigned to the TextField object. The only catch is that you must assign the value of the styleSheet property *before* you assign the HTML text. The following example defines a simple StyleSheet object and applies those styles to a TextField object:

```
var cssStyles:TextField.StyleSheet = new TextField.StyleSheet();
cssStyles.setStyle("a", {textDecoration: "underline", color: "#0000FF"});
this.createTextField("tOutput", this.getNextHighestDepth(), 0, 0, 100, 100);
tOutput.border = true;
tOutput.html = true;
tOutput.styleSheet = cssStyles;
tOutput.htmlText = "<a href='http://www.wiley.com'>Wiley Web site</a>";
```

Notice that the styleSheet assignment is before the htmlText assignment in the preceding example code. If you were to reverse those two lines, the style would not be applied.

Formatting an HTML Article with CSS

In this exercise, you load HTML text from an external file using the LoadVars class, display the content in a TextField object, and use CSS to format it. Complete the following steps:

1. On the CD-ROM, find css.html. The document contains a simple HTML-formatted article. Copy the file from the CD-ROM to your local disk.
2. Open a new Flash document and save it as css001.fla to the same directory as you saved the css.html file.
3. Add the code shown in Listing 18-1 to the first frame of the default layer of the main timeline.

Listing 18-1: Applying CSS to loaded HTML text

```
// Create the new StyleSheet object.
var cssStyles:TextField.StyleSheet = new TextField.StyleSheet();

// Define the styles.
cssStyles.setStyle("html", {fontFamily: "_sans"});
cssStyles.setStyle("title", {fontWeight: "bold", ⮐
textDecoration: "underline", textAlign: "center", fontSize: 10});
cssStyles.setStyle(".code", {marginLeft: 15, fontFamily: "_typewriter"});
cssStyles.setStyle("h1", {fontWeight: "bold"});
cssStyles.setStyle("a", {textDecoration: "underline", color: "#0000FF"});

// Create the TextField object.
this.createTextField("tOutput", this.getNextHighestDepth(), 0, 0, 550, 400);

// Set the properties of the TextField object such that it
// has a border, renders as HTML, handles multiple lines
// of text with word wrap, and condenses whitespace.
tOutput.border = true;
tOutput.html = true;
```

Continued

Listing 18-1 *(continued)*

```
tOutput.multiline = true;
tOutput.wordWrap = true;
tOutput.condenseWhite = true;

// Apply the style sheet to the TextField object.
tOutput.styleSheet = cssStyles;

// Define a LoadVars object for loading the HTML.
var lvHTML:LoadVars = new LoadVars();

// When the data loads, assign the value to the htmlText
// property of the TextField object.
lvHTML.onData = function(sData:String):Void {
  tOutput.htmlText = sData;
};

// Tell Flash to load the HTML.
lvHTML.load("css.html");
```

4. Test the movie. You should see the HTML rendered with the formatting you defined using CSS.

Loading External CSS

One of the really nice features of the Flash support for CSS is that you can load an external CSS file. That means that you can define a single CSS file shared between your HTML *and* Flash documents.

To load an external CSS file, use the `load()` method of the `StyleSheet` object into which you want the styles to be parsed. Then, as when loading any other kind of external content (using `XML`, `LoadVars`, and so on) you should define an `onLoad()` method that will automatically be called when Flash has loaded and parsed the CSS. Within the `onLoad()` method, you should assign the `StyleSheet` to the `styleSheet` property of the `TextField` object, and you should assign the HTML text to the `TextField` object. And just as with the `onLoad()` method of other ActionScript classes such as `XML` and `LoadVars`, the `onLoad()` method for a `StyleSheet` object is passed a Boolean parameter indicating whether the CSS loaded successfully.

The following example loads CSS from a file named `styles.css` into a `StyleSheet` object named `cssStyles`. When the CSS is loaded and parsed, it is applied to a `TextField` object named `tContent`.

```
cssStyles.onLoad = function(bLoaded:Boolean):Void {
  if(bLoaded) {
    tOutput.styleSheet = this;
    tOutput.htmlText = "<p>Some text</p>";
  }
};
```

Formatting HTML with CSS Loaded from an External File

In the last exercise, you applied formatting to HTML using CSS that you defined within ActionScript. In this exercise, you apply the same formatting but using CSS that you load from an external file.

1. On the CD-ROM, you'll find a file called `styles.css`. Copy the file from the CD-ROM to your local disk in the same directory to which you have previously saved `css.html` and `css001.fla`. You might want to open `styles.css` to see how the styles are defined and compare that with how you previously had defined the styles within the FLA file.
2. Open a new Flash document and save it as `css002.fla`. Save it to the same directory as you saved `css.html` and `styles.css`.
3. Add the code shown in Listing 18-2 to the first frame of the default layer of the main timeline.

Listing 18-2: Loading an external CSS file

```
// Create the StyleSheet object.
var cssStyles:TextField.StyleSheet = new TextField.StyleSheet();

// Create the TextField object.
this.createTextField("tOutput", this.getNextHighestDepth(), 0, 0, 550, 400);

// Set the properties of the TextField object as before.
tOutput.border = true;
tOutput.html = true;
tOutput.multiline = true;
tOutput.wordWrap = true;
tOutput.condenseWhite = true;

// Define a LoadVars object to load the HTML.
var lvHTML:LoadVars = new LoadVars();

// When the HTML loads, assign it to the htmlText
// property of the TextField object.
lvHTML.onData = function(sData:String):Void {
  tOutput.htmlText = sData;
};

// Define an onLoad() method for the StyleSheet. When
// the CSS loads, assign the StyleSheet object to the
// styleSheet property of the TextField object and then
// tell Flash to load the HTML.
cssStyles.onLoad = function(bLoaded:Boolean):Void {
  if(bLoaded) {
    tOutput.styleSheet = this;
    lvHTML.load("css.html");
```

Continued

Listing 18-2 *(continued)*

```
    }
};

// Tell Flash to load the CSS from the external file.
cssStyles.load("styles.css");
```

4. Test the movie. The formatting should be the same as in the previous exercise.

We'd like to know what you thought about this chapter. Visit `www.flashsupport.com/feedback` to fill out an online form with your comments.

Summary

- ✦ ActionScript provides you with several ways to format text, including the `TextFormat` class and the `TextField.StyleSheet` class.
- ✦ The `TextFormat` class enables you to apply styles to text within a `TextField` object. You can apply the styles to the entire contents, a single character, or a range of characters.
- ✦ The `TextFormat` class includes properties for affecting everything from text color, indentation, and font face to hyperlinks.
- ✦ Cascading style sheets (CSS) is a technology that was developed to efficiently apply formatting to HTML text in a Web browser. Flash MX 2004 and Flash Player 7 support a subset of the standard CSS properties, allowing you to apply CSS to HTML and XML text in Flash.
- ✦ You can define CSS styles in Flash using the `setStyle()` or `parseCSS()` methods. Or you can load CSS styles from an external file.
- ✦ When you apply CSS to a `TextField`, you must do so *before* you assign the text to which you want the styles applied.

✦ ✦ ✦

CHAPTER 19

The Mouse and Key Classes

✦ ✦ ✦ ✦

In This Chapter

Controlling the mouse cursor's appearance

Creating custom cursor icons

Detecting keypresses

Using listeners with the Mouse and Key classes

✦ ✦ ✦ ✦

Previous chapters explored many prebuilt classes in the ActionScript language. You have used the `Date` class to create Flash movies that work with the current date and time of the user's machine. The `Array` class introduced you to techniques for organizing your data. Most of the prebuilt classes that have been discussed use the `new` constructor. However, many prebuilt classes cannot have more than one active instantiation, such as the `Mouse` and `Key` objects. You do not need to use the `new` constructor with these classes, because they are preinstantiated.

The `Stage`, `System`, and `Capabilities` classes (among others) do not use the new constructor. See Chapters 20 and 21 for more information.

More Prebuilt Classes

As you already know, several prebuilt classes are already defined in the ActionScript language. For example, you do not need to tell your Flash movies what a `MovieClip` object is — the Flash Player knows how to create and enable `MovieClip` objects that you place on the stage. Similarly, when you make a new `Date` object, you do not have to explain what the `Date` object can do; it already has its own methods for you to use. With both the `MovieClip` and `Date` objects, it's necessary to create and name new instances of the objects when you use them in a Flash movie. You cannot generically address the `MovieClip` class with a `gotoAndPlay()` action, such as the following:

```
MovieClip.gotoAndPlay(5);
```

The correct way to address a `MovieClip` object is to use the object's instance name in the code, as shown in the following code:

```
mcBallAnim.gotoAndPlay(5);
```

Likewise, you cannot refer to a `Date` object without a new instance of it:

```
Date.getYear();
```

Although `getYear()` is a valid method of the `Date` class, you need to first create a new instance of the `Date` class to use its prebuilt methods. The following example creates a new instance of the `Date` class, named `dCurrentDate`:

```
var dCurrent:Date = new Date();
var nYear:Number = dCurrent.getFullYear();
```

You can use the following syntax that combines the `new Date()` constructor with a method:

```
var nYear:Number = new Date().getFullYear();
```

or you can directly assign this code within an expression, such as the following:

```
tOutput.text = "The year is " + new Date().getFullYear();
```

Finally, the `Date` class does have one static method that is used *without* the `new` constructor: `UTC()`. For more information on this method's usage, see Chapter 14.

Some prebuilt classes, however, do not require the creation of a new instance, and can be used directly. Such classes are classified as *static* classes. Among these classes are `Mouse` and `Key`. With these classes, you simply call the class by its name and invoke one of its methods:

```
Mouse.hide();
```

The preceding line hides the user's mouse cursor icon. Why don't you need to first create a variable that refers to a new instance (or instantiation) of the `Mouse` class? The answer is straightforward: Only one mouse cursor icon is present on the average computer screen at any given time. If you could ever have more than one mouse cursor showing on the screen, you would need to be able to refer to each separately. But rest assured, the objects discussed in this chapter can refer to only one active event generator. In the following sections, you learn more about the following classes:

✦ `Mouse` class: This class controls the display of the mouse cursor icon. Together with the `MovieClip` class and methods, you can create custom mouse cursors with the `Mouse` class.

✦ `Key` class: You can determine which key(s) a user types using this class. Among other uses, the `Key` class can enable your scripts to nudge graphics on the stage using the arrow keys, to create keyboard shortcuts to other sections of the Flash movie, or to guide the user with Flash forms and data entry using the Tab key.

Using the Mouse Class to Control the Cursor

Have you ever wanted to get rid of the regular white or black mouse cursor icon or use a different cursor icon for `Button` instances? The `Mouse` class has the power to not only turn off the default cursor icon, but to also affix a new graphic to the mouse cursor. Figures 19-1, 19-2, and 19-3 show the default cursor icons in a Flash movie.

Figure 19-1: The standard cursor icon in a Flash movie

Figure 19-2: The rollOver cursor icon for a button

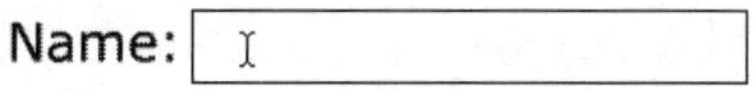

Name:

Figure 19-3: The I-beam cursor for Input text fields and selectable Dynamic text fields

Using the `Mouse` class, you can control the visibility of the standard and rollOver cursor icons. However, Input text fields and selectable Dynamic text fields always display the I-beam cursor when the mouse enters the area of the text field, regardless of the `Mouse` class's settings. In the next section, you learn the methods of the `Mouse` class that control the cursor's appearance.

For those readers familiar with Macromedia Director and Lingo programming, there are no cursor codes in ActionScript.

Method Overview of the Mouse Class

Unlike most prebuilt classes, the `Mouse` class does not have any properties — it has two methods to control the cursor's appearance within the Flash movie.

Properties related to the mouse's position fall within the scope of the `MovieClip` class. Read Chapter 9 to learn more about the `_xmouse` and `_ymouse` properties, which track the coordinates of the mouse pointer. Refer to Chapter 20 for more information about controlling custom context menu items that appear with a right mouse button click (or Control-click on the Mac).

Later in this chapter, you complete exercises that demonstrate how to use the methods discussed in the following sections.

Hiding the Mouse Cursor

The `Mouse.hide()` method does exactly that — it hides the mouse cursor icon, globally throughout the entire Flash movie. When this method is invoked, the mouse cursor continues to be invisible until the `show()` method of the `Mouse` class is invoked.

The I-beam cursor that appears over selectable text is not hidden when the `Mouse.hide()` method is invoked. You cannot hide this cursor type in a Flash movie.

Revealing the Mouse Cursor

The `Mouse.show()` method makes the mouse cursor icon reappear for all default mouse icon states (that is, standard and rollOver mouse icons). The mouse cursor remains visible until a `hide()` method is invoked.

If you scale your Flash movies to fill the browser window, the `hide()` and `show()` methods do not control the appearance of the mouse cursor when the cursor moves outside of the area allocated to the Flash Player and the movie.

Method Overview of Mouse Listeners

In ActionScript, you can assign a listener object to the Mouse class. A listener object contains custom methods that work specifically with a class that can use listeners.

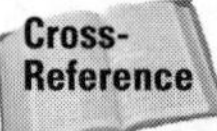

For a detailed discussion of the listener/event model, see Chapter 9.

A listener of the Mouse class can use any of the following four approaches to receive notification of mouse events. After the coverage of these methods, you learn how to apply or delete the listener with the addListener() or removeListener() method, respectively.

Before each method is explained, you should keep in mind that these listener methods perform in the same manner as the event handlers — onMouseDown(), onMouseUp(), and onMouseMove() — for the MovieClip class. The primary difference between using Mouse listeners and these MovieClip event handlers is that MovieClip handlers are created (and exist) with a specific instance of a MovieClip object. As such, if the instance with the handler is removed from the Flash movie, the associated handlers are deleted as well. Using Mouse listeners, you can create universal event handlers for a Flash movie that persist beyond any MovieClip instance's deletion. For example, if you want a specific action or task to occur whenever a mouse event occurs throughout playback of the movie, a Mouse listener can detect the mouse event and perform the task.

Unlike the Mouse class, a listener is not a static class. You must create a new instance of the Object class or assign the listener method to an instance of another class.

Detecting a Press Event

The onMouseDown() method can define a function to occur whenever the mouse button is clicked *anywhere* within the space of the Flash movie. Specifically, this method detects a press of the mouse button — the first downward stroke on the mouse button. The following code creates a listener object named oMouseListener and assigns a trace() action to display a message in the Output panel:

```
var oMouseListener:Object = new Object();
oMouseListener.onMouseDown = function():Void {
   trace("The mouse button has been pressed.");
};
Mouse.addListener(oMouseListener);
```

The act of defining a listener and an onMouseDown() method, however, does not actually enable the code within the method. The listener needs to be enabled with the addListener() method, described in a moment.

For two (or more) button mouse devices, only left-button mouse clicks can be detected with this handler. Some middle-button mouse clicks might also be detected. If you have a specific mouse device, be sure to test your Flash movie with it.

Detecting a Release Event

The onMouseUp() method defines a function that occurs whenever the mouse button is released within the space of the Flash movie. The return motion of the mouse button after a click is considered the release. The following code creates a listener named oMouseListener and displays a message to the Output panel:

```
var oMouseListener:Object = new Object();
oMouseListener.onMouseUp = function():Void {
   trace("The mouse button has been released.");
};
Mouse.addListener(oMouseListener);
```

As stated for the previous method's description, the listener is not enabled until it is initiated with the addListener() method.

Detecting Rolling (or Mouse Movement)

The onMouseMove() method defines a function that occurs when any vertical or horizontal movement, or roll, of the mouse is detected within the space of the Flash movie. The following code creates a listener named oMouseListener and displays a message to the Output panel:

```
var oMouseListener:Object = new Object();
oMouseListener.onMouseMove = function():Void {
   trace("The mouse pointer is moving.");
};
```

This listener is not enabled until it is initiated with the addListener() method.

So far, all the Mouse listener methods perform nearly the same as the MovieClip event handler methods. However, onMouseMove() has one major disadvantage when used as a Mouse listener: the updateAfterEvent() function will not execute. Refer to the sidebar "onMouseMove() and updateAfterEvent()," later in this chapter.

Monitoring the Scroll Wheel Activity (Windows Only)

Flash Player 7 for Windows adds the exciting capability to capture events sent by the scroll wheel of a user's mouse. The new onMouseWheel() method of a listener can be used for this event.

The onMouseWheel() method is available in Flash Player 7 for Windows only. Older and non-Windows versions do not support this method.

The method receives two parameters: delta and scrollTarget. A listener using this method can be constructed in the following way:

```
var oWheel:Object = new Object();
oWheel.onMouseWheel = function(delta:Number, scrollTarget:MovieClip):Void {
   trace(">> onMouseWheel >>");
   trace("\t       delta:\t" + delta);
   trace("\tscrollTarget:\t" + scrollTarget);
};
```

In this code, trace() actions can be built to display more meaningful and visually structured information in the Output panel. The \t backslash pairs indicate a tab insertion. Therefore, when the onMouseWheel() method is invoked, the Output panel displays the following:

```
>> onMouseWheel >>
           delta:  3
    scrollTarget:  mcTarget
```

The `delta` value specifies how many lines each scroll "click" should scroll. This value is usually between 1 and 3 lines and is a hardware setting in the user's system Control Panel for the mouse device. You can use this value to adjust the scroll property of a `TextField` object, increase values displayed in a text field, or move an object on the stage (just to name a few examples).

A downward wheel stroke returns a negative `delta` value, whereas an upward stroke returns a positive `delta` value.

The `scrollTarget` returns the object reference to the topmost `MovieClip` object that is underneath the current position of the mouse cursor when the wheel movement occurs.

Later in this chapter, you build an example that uses this new event handler.

Tip

Several Flash MX 2004 components already use the `onMouseWheel()` handler, such as the `TextArea`, `ComboBox`, and `List` components.

Assigning a Listener to the Mouse Class

After you have created a listener with methods for the `Mouse` class, you can enable the listener by using the `addListener()` method of the `Mouse` class. You can enable the listener immediately after the definition of the listener (as the following code demonstrates) or enable it later in the Flash movie (for example, on a `Button` or `MovieClip` handler):

```
var oMouseListener:Object = {};
oMouseListener.onMouseMove = function(){
   trace("The mouse pointer is moving.");
};
Mouse.addListener(oMouseListener);
```

The preceding code uses a less verbose syntax for the object creation (line 1), using an empty pair of curly braces (`{}`) instead of `new Object()`. You can also define multiple methods per listener, as the following code demonstrates:

```
var oMouseListener:Object = {};
oMouseListener.onMouseMove = function():Void {
   trace("The mouse pointer is moving.");
};
oMouseListener.onMouseUp = function():Void {
   trace("The mouse button has been released.");
};
oMouseListener.onMouseDown = function():Void {
   trace("The mouse button has been pressed.");
};
Mouse.addListener(oMouseListener);
```

In this code sample, the same listener, `oMouseListener`, has three separate methods defined. All of them are passed to the `Mouse` class with one `addListener()` method.

You can also define separate listeners (for example, `oMouseListener_1`, `oMouseListener_2`, and so on) and add (or remove) each one at different times to the `Mouse` class. This is true for all classes that use listeners.

Deleting an Active Listener from the Mouse Class

With the `Mouse.removeListener()` method, you can remove an active listener from the `Mouse` class. Note that this method does not actually delete the listener object from the Flash movie — it simply deletes the listener from the callback list of the `Mouse` class. When a listener is removed, the methods assigned to the listener will no longer be invoked when the event occurs. In the following code, a listener named `oMouseListener` is removed from the `Mouse` class:

```
Mouse.removeListener(oMouseListener);
```

If you would like to reinitiate the listener, specify the listener in a subsequent `addListener()` method of the `Mouse` class.

Showing and Hiding the Mouse Cursor

In this section, you learn how to implement the `hide()` and `show()` methods of the `Mouse` class, using a `MovieClip` instance and the `hitTest()` method of the `MovieClip` object. When the mouse enters the area of the `MovieClip` instance, you execute the `hide()` method of the `Mouse` class. When the mouse leaves the area of the `MovieClip` instance, the `show()` method is invoked.

In order to capture the user's act of moving his or her mouse icon within the Flash movie, you use the `MovieClip` event handler `onMouseMove()` to process the `show()` or `hide()` methods. Now you're ready to get started.

You need to open the `Mouse_showHide_starter.fla` file for the following exercise. This file is located in the ch19 folder of the book's CD-ROM.

1. Open the `Mouse_showHide_starter.fla` file on the CD-ROM. Save it as a local file on your hard drive.
2. Open the document's Library panel (Ctrl+L or ⌘+L). Notice that there are two Movie Clip symbols: earth and moon. Both are set to export as linked assets as well, with the linkage identifiers of `earthClip` and `moonClip`, respectively. The Library panel in Flash MX 2004 shows the linked names, as shown in Figure 19-4.

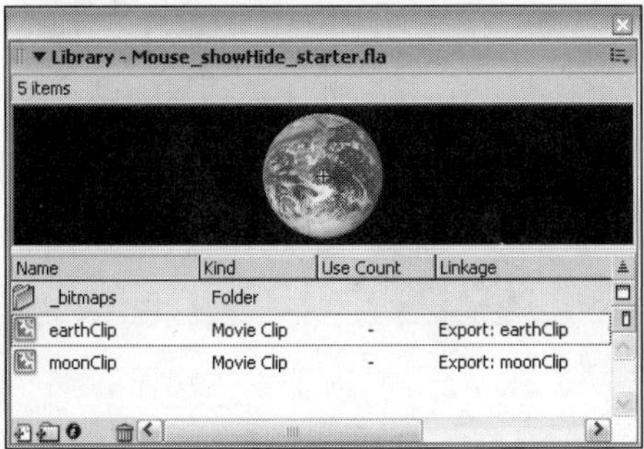

Figure 19-4: The expanded Library panel showing the Linkage column

3. An instance of the `earthClip` symbol is already on the main timeline (that is, Scene 1). In the Property inspector, the instance has the name `mcEarth` (see Figure 19-5).

4. Create a new layer named `actions`, and place it at the top of the layer stack.

5. Select frame 1 of the actions layer, and open the Actions panel (F9). Add the following code to the Script pane:

```
mcEarth.onMouseMove = function():Void {
   if(this.hitTest(_root._xmouse, _root._ymouse, true)){
      Mouse.hide();
   }
};
```

   Here, you use the `onMouseMove()` handler for the `MovieClip` object named `mcEarth` to detect when the user moves the mouse cursor. When that happens, this handler executes the code within the function's curly braces. The next line of code contains an `if` statement with a `hitTest()` condition. `hitTest()` is a method of the `MovieClip` class that is used to detect collisions between `MovieClip` objects or with specific X and Y coordinates. In this condition, when the X and Y coordinates of the mouse cursor occur within the occupied space of the `mcEarth` instance, the nested code within the curly braces of the `if` statement executes. In this example, the `Mouse.hide()` method executes when the `hitTest()` condition returns a `true` value.

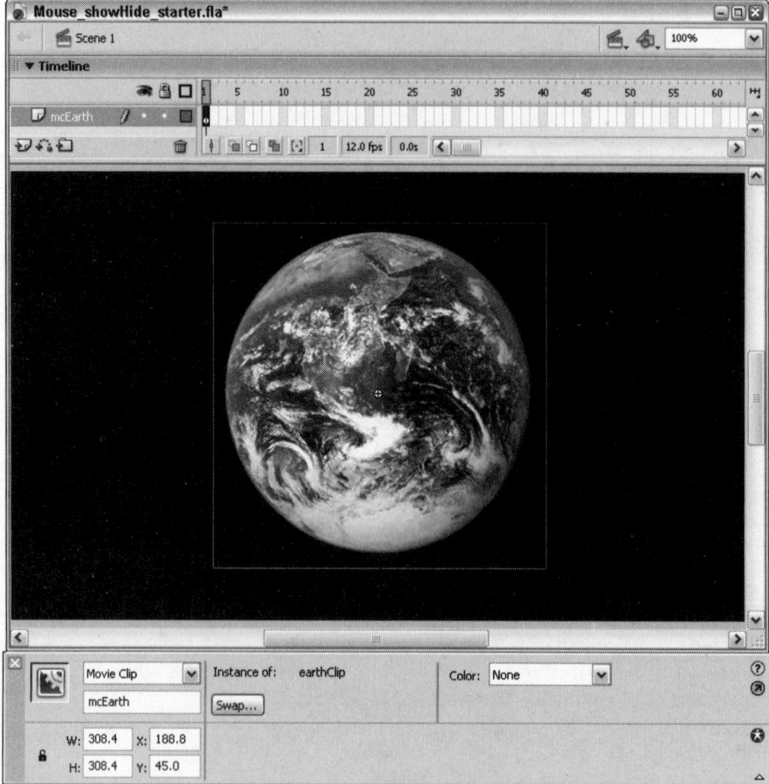

Figure 19-5: The main timeline contains one instance of the earthClip symbol.

6. Save your Flash document as Mouse_showHide_100.fla, and test it using the Test Movie command (Ctrl+Enter or ⌘+Enter). Notice that your mouse cursor disappears when you move the mouse cursor on to the mcEarth instance. Unfortunately, you can't get your mouse cursor back! In the next step, you add an else statement to the previous if statement.

7. Reselect frame 1 of the actions layer, and open the Actions panel. Add an else statement within the onMouseMove() method to display the mouse cursor. The new code is shown in bold:

```
mcEarth.onMouseMove = function():Void {
   if(this.hitTest(_root._xmouse, _root._ymouse, true)){
      Mouse.hide();
   } else {
      Mouse.show();
   }
};
```

   Now, when the hitTest() method returns a false value, the else statement executes. The else statement contains the Mouse.show() method, which makes the mouse cursor visible.

8. Save your Flash document and test it. Move the mouse cursor over the mcEarth instance. Now, when you move the mouse cursor out of the mcEarth instance, the mouse cursor reappears.

In the next section, you learn how to attach a custom graphic to the mouse cursor, so the user has some visual indication of the mouse's position on the screen.

Note

If you execute more than one show() (or hide()) method in succession, the mouse icon's appearance does not reflect any changes. Unlike alpha effects, the process of showing or hiding a mouse produces no cumulative effects. Although the _alpha property of MovieClip instances can exceed 100% (or fall below 0%), the visibility of the mouse cursor is not affected by multiple hide() or show() executions. Therefore, if you execute the hide() method twice, you do not need to execute the show() method twice to "undo" the effect.

For Flash Player 5 compatibility, you can use the onClipEvent(mouseMove) event handler on the mcEarth instance instead of using the onMouseMove() method, which is supported by Flash Player 6 or later.

Attaching a Custom Graphic to the Cursor

Now that you've learned how to show and hide the mouse cursor, you can take your mouse moves to the next step. In this section, you use the attachMovie() method of the MovieClip class to affix an instance of the moonClip symbol to the mouse cursor. Actually, you can't attach anything to the mouse cursor itself. Rather, you attach the instance to another MovieClip object, and set the instance's X and Y coordinates (as _x and _y properties, respectively) to match those of the mouse cursor. Even if the mouse cursor is not visible, it still has readable properties, such as _xmouse and _ymouse.

Working Out the Pseudo-Code

Before you start to hammer out the real ActionScript code into the Actions panel, sit down and plan your strategy. You need to define your problem and then come up with a solution. As an overview statement, you want to make the moon symbol appear if the mouse is moving outside of the earth instance, and you want it to disappear if the mouse is moving within the earth instance.

You can break this down further to clarify it more definitively:

✦ If the mouse cursor is outside of the space occupied by the `mcEarth` instance, bring in a copy of the `moonClip` symbol from the Library, hide the mouse cursor, and make the new `moonClip` instance follow the mouse cursor.

✦ If the mouse cursor is within the space occupied by the `mcEarth` instance, remove any copy of the `moonClip` symbol (if one exists), and show the mouse cursor.

✦ In order to eliminate redundant executions of ActionScript code, you need to ensure that after the `moonClip` instance is attached, it is not reattached with each execution of the `mouseMove` event.

Now that you've done that, start to add a logical structure to your goals:

```
when a mouse movement occurs
  if the mouse is within the space of the earth instance
    then test to see if a moon instance exists
    if one does exist, then:
      show the mouse cursor
      remove the moon instance
    end this if statement
  otherwise, the mouse is not within the earth instance
    then test to see if a moon instance exists
    if one does not exist, then:
      hide the mouse cursor
      attach the moon instance
    end this if statement
    (after the moon is attached:)
    set the moon's X position to the mouse's X position
    set the moon's Y position to the mouse's Y position
  end this if statement
end the mouse movement handler
```

Although most of these concepts should be familiar to you from the previous section, you learn how you can use a condition to detect the existence of a `moonClip` symbol instance.

Translating the Pseudo-Code into Real ActionScript

After you outline the steps that you need to accomplish in order to create the desired effect, you're ready to hit the Flash proving grounds.

Open the `customCursor_starter.fla` file on the book's CD-ROM. You can find it in the ch19 folder. Alternatively, you can use the file you created in the last section. Feel free to view the `customCursor_100.swf` file on the CD-ROM to see the effect you create in the following steps.

1. Open the `customCursor_starter.fla` file in Flash MX 2004. Save it as a local file on your hard drive.

2. Open the document's Library panel (Ctrl+L or ⌘+L), and right-click (Control-click on the Mac) the `moonClip` symbol. Choose Linkage from the contextual menu. In the Linkage Properties dialog box (shown in Figure 19-6), notice that this symbol has been linked as `moonClip`, and exports with the SWF file for use at runtime in ActionScript. Linked assets enable you to use elements in your Flash movie, even if you don't physically place them on a timeline.

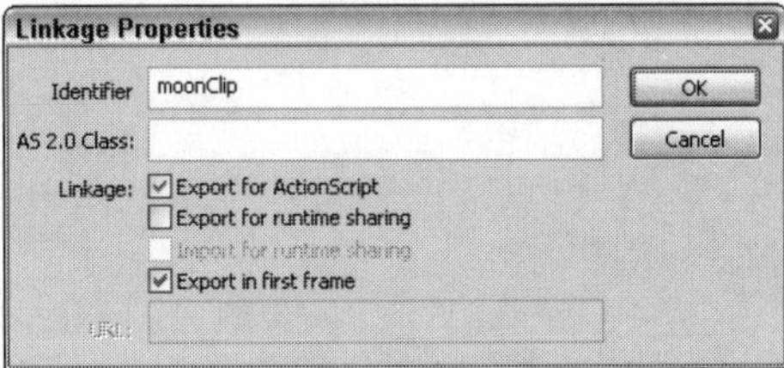

Figure 19-6: The Linkage Properties dialog box for the moon symbol

Because the `moonClip` symbol is set to export, you can dynamically create new instances of it in the Flash movie using the `attachMovie()` method of the `MovieClip` class.

3. Create a new layer named `actions`, and place it at the top of the layer stack. (If you already have an actions layer from the last exercise, skip this step.)

4. Select frame 1 of the actions layer, and open the Actions panel (F9). Add (or change) the ActionScript code to match the code shown in Listing 19-1.

Listing 19-1: **Attaching the moonClip Symbol**

```
mcEarth.onMouseMove = function():Void {
   var xPos:Number = this._parent._xmouse;
   var yPos:Number = this._parent._ymouse;
   if(this.hitTest(xPos, yPos, true)){
      if(mcMoon != null){
         Mouse.show();
         mcMoon.removeMovieClip();
      }
   } else {
      if(mcMoon == null){
          Mouse.hide();
          this._parent.attachMovie("moonClip", "mcMoon", 1);
      }
       with(mcMoon){
          _x = xPos;
          _y = yPos;
       }
   }
};
```

The existence of the moonClip instance (named mcMoon) is tested in line 5 to see whether the mcMoon instance has been attached from the if statement in line 12 using the attachMovie() method. If it has been attached and the mouse cursor is within the mcEarth instance space (lines 4 and 5), the mouse cursor is shown (line 6). Then, the mcMoon instance is removed (line 7).

However, if the mouse cursor is outside of the space occupied by the mcEarth instance (tested in line 4), the else statement starting at line 9 executes. The first step in this else statement is to determine whether the mcMoon instance has already been attached to the main timeline (this._parent). If it hasn't been attached (as tested in line 10), lines 11 and 12 execute: The mouse cursor is hidden (line 11), and the mcMoon instance is attached to the main timeline (line 12).

Finally, after you know that the mcMoon instance exists, you set its X and Y position properties to match those of the mouse's X and Y position (relative to the coordinates of the main timeline, or this._parent) in lines 14–17. Remember that all of this code continuously executes as you move the mouse.

5. After you have added the code in Step 3, save your Flash document as customCursor_100.fla and test it. When you move the mouse outside of the mcEarth instance, the mcMoon instance follows your mouse. When the mouse moves inside of the mcEarth instance, the mcMoon instance disappears and shows the default mouse cursor.

You can find the completed document, customCursor_100.fla, in the ch19 folder of the book's CD-ROM.

Using updateAfterEvent() for Mouse Moves

You might have noticed that the moon's movement in the last section wasn't quite fluid. If you moved the mouse fast enough, you would have noticed that the position of the mcMoon instance didn't update at the same speed you were moving the mouse. Why? Unless told to do otherwise, Flash movies update the screen only at the rate prescribed by the Document Properties dialog box (Modify ➪ Document). In the example, the frame rate was already set to 12fps. Try setting your Flash movie's frame rate to 1fps, and test the movement of the mcMoon instance. Pretty choppy, eh? To improve this situation, you could use an incredibly fast frame rate, such as 20 or 30fps, but many older computers can't keep up with this frame rate.

In Flash 5, Macromedia introduced the updateAfterEvent() function, which enables you to forcibly refresh or update the screen display as soon as an event has finished executing. updateAfterEvent() can be used in the following situations:

- ✦ Within functions defined for the MovieClip class's onMouseMove(), onMouseUp(), onMouseDown(), onKeyDown(), or onKeyUp() methods
- ✦ Within onClipEvent() handlers for the MovieClip class, for the following events: mouseMove, mouseDown, mouseUp, keyDown, or keyUp
- ✦ Within functions invoked by the setInterval() function

The updateAfterEvent() function does not work with the onMouseMove() method of a Mouse listener. See the "onMouseMove() and updateAfterEvent()" sidebar following this section.

Add an `updateAfterEvent()` function to the Flash movie you created in the last section:

1. If you changed the frame rate from its original value of 12fps, set it back to 12fps in the Document Properties dialog box (Modify ⇨ Document).
2. Select frame 1 of the actions layer, and open the Actions panel. Just before the close of the last curly brace for the `onMouseMove()` handler, type the following code:

   ```
   updateAfterEvent();
   ```

3. Save your Flash document as `customCursor_101.fla` and test it. Notice how much smoother the moon's movement is? The `updateAfterEvent()` allows the screen to refresh independently of the movie's frame rate. To test this effect, change the movie's frame rate to 1fps in the Document Properties dialog box (Modify ⇨ Document) and retest the Flash movie. The moon's movement is just as smooth as it was at 12fps.

You'll look at other uses of `updateAfterEvent()` in the following section on the `Key` class.

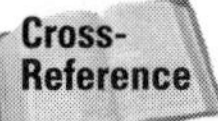

For more information on `updateAfterEvent()`, read the coverage of the `setInterval()` function in Chapter 6.

onMouseMove() and updateAfterEvent()

As discussed in the coverage of the `Mouse` class, the `onMouseMove()` method of a listener cannot use the `updateAfterEvent()` function. Therefore, if you need to control the movement of graphics in tandem with the movement of the mouse, you should use the `onMouseMove()` method of the `MovieClip` class. To illustrate this difference, you can create the following example:

1. In a new Flash document, rename Layer 1 `mcCircle`.
2. On frame 1 of the circle layer, draw a small circle with the Oval tool.
3. Convert the artwork to a Movie Clip symbol named `circleClip`.
4. In the Property inspector, name the instance `mcCircle` in the *<Instance Name>* field.
5. Create a new layer named `Actions`. On frame 1 of this layer, insert the following code:

   ```
   var oMouseListener:Object = {};
   oMouseListener.onMouseMove = function():Void {
      mcCircle._x = _root._xmouse;
      mcCircle._y = _root._ymouse;
      updateAfterEvent();
   };
   Mouse.addListener(oMouseListener);
   ```

   This code uses the `onMouseMove()` method of the `Mouse` listener.

6. Save the Flash document as `updateAfterEvent_problem.fla` and test it. As you move the mouse pointer, notice the sluggish movement of the circle instance.

Continued

Continued

7. Go back to frame 1 of the actions layer, and comment all the code you inserted in Step 5. Your code should resemble the following code:

```
/*
var oMouseListener:Object = {};
oMouseListener.onMouseMove = function():Void {
   mcCircle._x = _root._xmouse;
   mcCircle._y = _root._ymouse;
   updateAfterEvent();
};
Mouse.addListener(oMouseListener);
*/
```

8. After the closing comment code (*/), insert the following code:

```
mcCircle.onMouseMove = function():Void {
   this._x = _root._xmouse;
   this._y = _root._ymouse;
   updateAfterEvent();
};
```

   This code uses the same actions as the listener, except that the actions are applied to the `mcCircle` instance with the `onMouseMove()` method of the `MovieClip` class.

9. Save the document and test the movie. As you move the mouse pointer, the `mcCircle` instance will fluidly follow the mouse pointer.

As this example demonstrates, you cannot accomplish smooth movement with the `onMouseMove()` method of a `Mouse` listener. Use the `onMouseMove()` method of the `Mouse` listener only for tasks that do not require smooth graphic display or movement.

You can find the `updateAfterEvent_problem.fla` document in the ch19 folder of the book's CD-ROM.

Using the Mouse Wheel to Control an Object's Position

In this section, you learn how to use the `onMouseWheel()` listener method to control the X position of a panoramic image of clouds below a dynamic mask.

As discussed earlier in this chapter, the `onMouseWheel()` handler works only in Flash Player 7 on the Windows platform.

When you scroll downward with the mouse wheel, the image will scroll to the left using the `delta` value passed to `onMouseWheel()`. If you scroll upward with the wheel, the image will scroll to the right. You also apply restrictions to the scrolling movement, so that the edges of the image will not scroll beyond the edges of the mask.

Make a copy of the `Mouse_onMouseWheel_starter.fla` and `clouds.jpg` files from the ch19 folder of this book's CD-ROM. You can also run the `Mouse_onMouseWheel_100.swf` movie to see the effect you build in the following steps. You need a mouse with a scroll wheel to enable the effect.

1. Open the Mouse_onMouseWheel_starter.fla document. Select frame 1 of the actions layer and open the Actions panel (F9). The Script pane will display the code necessary to load the clouds.jpg image and add a mask to it. This code is shown in Listing 19-2 and discussed briefly here.

   Line 1 establishes a variable named bApplyMask, which controls the mask mode of the movie. If set to true, the clouds.jpg image loaded into the movie will be masked. If set to false, the mask appears as a white overlay.

   Line 2 establishes a variable named nStartX, which controls the initial X position of the clouds.jpg image and the mask applied to it.

   Lines 3–8 create two MovieClip objects. The outer clip, named mcHolder, contains a nested clip, mcImg, which is used to store the actual clouds.jpg. In lines 5–7, the position of the mcHolder instance is set to 25, 25. In line 9, the clouds.jpg image is loaded into the mcImg instance.

   Lines 10–23 create a MovieClip object named mcMask. Using the drawing API of the MovieClip class, a 500 × 300 shape within the instance is created. The mcMask instance is positioned at the same X and Y coordinates as the mcHolder instance.

   In line 24, if the bApplyMask variable is set to true, the mcMask instance is used as a mask for the mcHolder instance. Otherwise, the mcMask instance appears as a semi-transparent white fill above the clouds.jpg image.

   If you test the movie, you will see the clouds.jpg load into the movie, masked by the mcMask instance. If you go back to the code and set bApplyMask to false (in line 1) and retest the movie, you'll see the entire clouds.jpg image with the mask floating above it.

Listing 19-2: The Starter Code to Load and Mask the Image

```
1.  var bApplyMask:Boolean = true;
2.  var nStartX:Number = 25;
3.  var mcHolder:MovieClip = this.createEmptyMovieClip("mcHolder", 1);
4.  var mcImg:MovieClip = mcHolder.createEmptyMovieClip("mcImg", 1);
5.  with(mcHolder){
6.     _x = nStartX;
7.     _y = 25;
8.  }
9.  mcImg.loadMovie("clouds.jpg");
10. var mcMask:MovieClip = this.createEmptyMovieClip("mcMask", 2);
11. var nWidth:Number = 500;
12. var nHeight:Number = 300;
13. with(mcMask){
14.    beginFill(0xFFFFFF, 50);
15.    moveTo(0,0);
16.    lineTo(nWidth, 0);
17.    lineTo(nWidth, nHeight);
18.    lineTo(0, nHeight);
19.    lineTo(0, 0);
```

Continued

Listing 19-2 *(continued)*

```
20.     endFill();
21.     _x = nStartX;
22.     _y = 25;
23. }
24. if(bApplyMask) mcHolder.setMask(mcMask);
```

2. Now that you have an understanding of what the starter file's code does, you're ready to add an `onMouseWheel()` method to the `mcHolder` object. Not only can you create an instance of the `Object` class as a listener, but you can also use an existing object (such as a `MovieClip` or `TextField` instance) with listener event handlers. After line 24 of the code in the starter file, add the code shown in Listing 19-3.

   When the user activates the scroll wheel of the mouse, the delta value is passed to the `onMouseWheel()` method of the `mcHolder` instance 25. In lines 26 and 27, the range of X values for the image and the mask are calculated, respectively. In line 28, an `if` statement checks two conditions, one for each edge of the mask. The first condition ensures that the right edge of the `clouds.jpg` image has reached the right edge of the mask. The second condition does the same with the left edges of the image and the mask. If neither edge has been reached, the delta value is added to the current X position of the `mcHolder` object (line 29). In line 30, the `mcHolder` instance is passed to the `Mouse` class as a listener.

Listing 19-3: The onMouseWheel() Handler

```
25. mcHolder.onMouseWheel = function(delta:Number):Void {
26.     var nImage:Number = this._x + this._width;
27.     var nMask:Number = mcMask._x + mcMask._width;
28.     if(nImage + delta > nMask && this._x + delta < mcMask._x){
29.         this._x += delta;
30.     }
31. };
32. Mouse.addListener(mcHolder);
```

3. Save the document as `Mouse_onMouseWheel_100.fla` and test it. Click once anywhere with the Flash movie (to give it focus), and begin moving the scroll wheel of your mouse. As you move the scroll wheel down (toward you), the image pans to the left. As you scroll upward (away from you), the image pans to the right.

You can find the finished document, `Mouse_onMouseWheel_100.fla`, in the ch19 folder of this book's CD-ROM.

Processing Keypresses with the Key Class

Prior to Flash 5, you could enable the user's keyboard input in two ways: when gathering text data in Input text fields or when detecting basic keypresses on Button symbol instances. With the `Key` class, you can create powerful functionality for `Button` or `MovieClip` objects, for components, or within custom functions. The `Key` class informs Flash about any data associated with the current key that the user is typing on his or her keyboard.

You can also use listeners with the `Key` class. You learn about this feature in this section.

Using the `Key` class, you can detect when a certain key is pressed, and do something in your Flash movie as a result. For example, you can enable the user to use the left and right arrow keys to go to different keyframe labels. You can create virtual keyboards in a Flash movie that show a graphic of the key being pressed as the user presses the physical key on the keyboard. In this section, you create several examples of the `Key` class in action.

The Flash MX 2004 Buttons Library (Window ⇨ Other Panels ⇨ Common Libraries ⇨ Buttons) now has a Key Buttons folder featuring common keyboard graphics. Also, in the Component Buttons folder of that Library, you will find a keyboard button component that will display a custom character assigned in the Property inspector.

Property and Method Overview of the Key Class

The `Key` class has 18 properties (or constants), all of which are key names to commonly used keys for interactivity. Usually, you need to know the key code value for the key you want to detect, but Macromedia's engineers provided easy access to keys used for games (such as the arrow, Page Up, and Page Down keys). Every key on the keyboard has a unique value, as does any modified keypress, such as a Shift key combination (for example, holding down the Shift key to produce an uppercase A).

What are key codes? Actually, there are many ways to refer to keys on the keyboard: ASCII, EBCDIC (Extended Binary-Coded Decimal Interchange Code), and Unicode are only a few. With ActionScript, you can use Macromedia's virtual key codes, which are distilled values derived from the ASCII character codes, or the traditional and more comprehensive ASCII character codes themselves.

All ASCII codes in ActionScript are decimal-based.

The 18 `Key` constants shown in Table 19-1 are all based on Macromedia's virtual key code. Although each character on the keyboard has a unique ASCII value, the virtual key set uses one numeric value to refer to both the uppercase and lowercase equivalents of a given character. As a general rule, the virtual key code is the uppercase ASCII value for most characters. For example, the ASCII code for a lowercase *a* is 97, but the virtual key code is 65. However, the ASCII code and virtual key code for an uppercase A is the same value: 65.

Table 19-1: Key Class Constants

Grouping	*Constant*	*Uses/Notes*

Direction	`Key.LEFT`
	`Key.RIGHT`
	`Key.UP`
	`Key.DOWN`
		The arrow keys are commonly used to move objects in a Flash movie.

Modifiers	`Key.CONTROL`
	`Key.SHIFT`
	`Key.CAPSLOCK`
	`Key.ESCAPE`
		`Key.CONTROL` represents either the Control or ⌘ key in the Macintosh version of Flash Player 6 or later.

Document keys	`Key.INSERT`
	`Key.DELETEKEY`
	`Key.HOME`
	`Key.END`
	`Key.PGUP` (Page Up)
	`Key.PGDN` (Page Down)
		These keys navigate pages of text, as several lines in one editable text field.

White space	`Key.SPACE` (Spacebar)
	`Key.BACKSPACE`
	`Key.TAB`
	`Key.ENTER`
		The Enter key is commonly used to enable a Send, Submit, or Search button.

The `Key` class also has six methods and two event handlers to enable enhanced keyboard functionality within your Flash movies:

✦ `getAscii()`: This method returns the decimal ASCII value of the current key pressed. For example, if you press the R key, `Key.getAscii()` returns 82. This method does not accept any arguments.

✦ `getCode()`: To retrieve the virtual key code value of the current key pressed, you can invoke the `getCode()` method. Remember that the virtual key code is usually the same for both uppercase and lowercase values. Therefore, if you press the r key, `Key.getCode()` returns the same value as the previous example: 82.

✦ `isDown(keycode)`: If you want to determine whether a specific key is being pressed, you can use the `isDown()` method of the `Key` class. The `isDown()` method returns a Boolean value (that is, `true` or `false`). You should specify a virtual key code as the argument for the `isDown()` method. For example, you can determine whether the user is holding down the P key by using `Key.isDown(80)`.

✦ `isToggled(keycode)`: You can determine whether either the Num Lock or Caps Lock key is enabled with the `isToggled()` method. You can specify the values as either key code values or as `Key` constants — `Key.isToggled(Key.CAPSLOCK)` or `Key.isToggled(20)` return `true` if the Caps Lock key is enabled (that is, toggled).

✦ `addListener(listener)`: You can create a `Key` listener that has an `onKeyDown()` and/or `onKeyUp()` method defined. The process for assigning the listener to the `Key` class is the same as that for the `Mouse` class, as discussed prior to this section:

```
var oKeyListener:Object = new Object();
oKeyListener.onKeyDown = function():Void {
   if(Key.isDown(Key.LEFT)){
```

```
        trace("The left arrow key has been pressed.");
    }
};
Key.addListener(oKeyListener);
```

You'll look at examples of Key listeners later in this chapter.

- Listener.onKeyDown(): This method of a listener enables you to detect when any key is pressed. More specifically, this method detects the downward stroke on any key.
- Listener.onKeyUp(): This method of a listener enables you to detect when a key has been released. The release action is the upward stroke of any key.

✦ removeListener(listener): As with other static classes such as Stage and Mouse, any listener that has been added to the class can be removed with the removeListener() method. You need to specify the object name of the listener to be removed.

The key code values for the Caps Lock and Num Lock keys are identical on the Macintosh platform. You can view the keyTest_mac.fla file in the ch19 folder of the book's CD-ROM.

Capturing Keypresses

Now that you have some familiarity with the syntax for the Key class and its associated properties and methods, in this section you learn how you can use the Key class with Flash events and event handlers. Like all things Flash, you need to know where and when to use the appropriate ActionScript code to fulfill your requirements for interactivity.

The following discussion of key events is not necessarily tied to the Key class—you can use key events without using any reference to the Key class and its properties or methods. However, the Key class is most commonly used in conjunction with key events, as you'll see shortly.

What Is a Keypress?

A *keypress* is actually an event. Whenever a user types a key on the keyboard, three events occur:

✦ keyPress

✦ keyDown

✦ keyUp

keyPress and keyDown are essentially the same events—as the user pushes down on a key, the keyPress and keyDown events are initiated simultaneously. The difference between these two events lies with the event handlers that can use them:

✦ Only Button symbol instances can specify the keyPress event in the on() handler, as in on(keyPress "<Left>") for the Left arrow key.

✦ MovieClip objects can utilize the keyDown event within the onClipEvent() handler, as in onClipEvent(keyDown).

✦ Key listener objects can detect the keyDown event within the onKeyDown() method.

`MovieClip` objects can use the `onKeyDown()` and `onKeyUp()` methods in ActionScript. However, this functionality has extremely limited use. Refer to Chapter 9 for more information.

The `keyUp` event occurs when a key is released — as the user lifts his or her finger from the key. You can use `keyUp` events only with the following objects:

- ✦ `MovieClip` objects can detect `keyUp` events with the `onClipEvent(keyUp)` handler.
- ✦ `Key` listener objects can detect `keyUp` events with the `onKeyUp()` method.

Using Button Symbol Instances

To add `keyPress` events to Button symbol instances, you need to have an `on()` handler for the specific instance.

References to Button instances in this section refer to the Button symbol type, not the new `Button` component that was released with Flash MX 2004.

Use the following syntax to detect a `keyPress` with a Button instance:

```
on (keyPress key as string){
   // insert ActionScript to execute for this keyPress
}
```

For example, the following code sends the main timeline to frame 10 when the right arrow key is pressed:

```
on (keyPress "<Right>"){
   _root.gotoAndPlay(10);
}
```

The key value is specified in quotation marks (as a string) with less-than (<) and greater-than (>) keys surrounding the key's name. Only special keys need the < and > enclosure tags; regular keys such as the letter *a* or the number 1 do not need these tags. The key value for `keyPress` is not the same as the `Key` class constants that were discussed earlier. However, many values look very similar to those constants.

If you want to compare your work in the following steps to the final Flash movie, or need a point of reference during this exercise, open the `keyPress_button.fla` file, located in the ch19 folder of the book's CD-ROM.

To assign `keyPress` events for Button instances:

1. Open the Actions panel with a Button instance selected. The Actions panel should be titled Actions — Buttons, and code hints should be enabled.
2. Click the Script pane to make it active, and type **Esc+o+n** successively (not simultaneously). This code shortcut adds the following code:

   ```
   on (){
   }
   ```

   The I-beam cursor should be automatically positioned within the parentheses of the `on()` handler as well.

3. Within the parentheses of the on() handler, type the following code:

```
release, keyPress
```

As soon as you type the keyPress event, the code hints menu should jump to the keyPress "<Left>" entry, as shown in Figure 19-7. Feel free to scroll the menu to see the other code hints that Flash MX 2004 provides. Choose the keyPress "<Left>" entry. Your Script pane should show the following code:

```
on (release, keyPress "<Left>") {
}
```

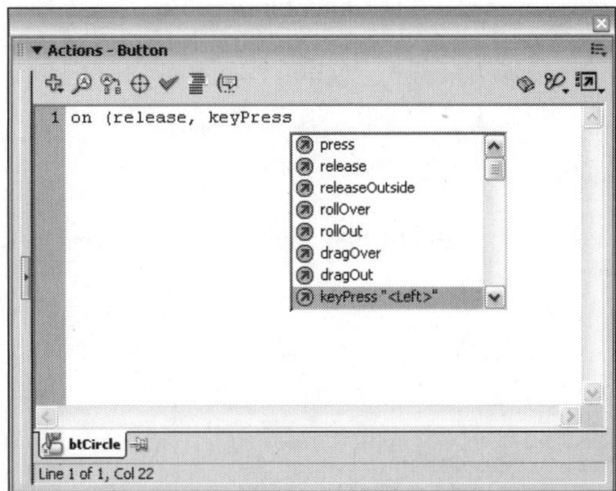

Figure 19-7: Code hints can remind you of the parameters used by various ActionScript objects and methods.

4. Type the following ActionScript between the on() handler's curly braces ({ }):

```
trace("The Left arrow key has been pressed.");
```

5. Save your Flash document and test it (Ctrl+Enter or ⌘+Enter). When you press the left arrow key, the Output panel opens and displays the following text:

```
The Left arrow key has been pressed.
```

As you might have noticed, you can enable a keyPress event with other standard mouse events, such as release and press. Or you can simply specify the keyPress alone for invisible or off-stage buttons that respond only to keypresses.

Tip

If you need to make your Flash movies compatible with Flash Player 4, you can use the keyPress event with the on() handler. The onClipEvent() handler discussed in the next section requires Flash Player 5 or later, and the Key listener and MovieClip methods for key strokes require Flash Player 6 or later.

With Button instances, the keyPress value must be specified as a string. You cannot use a variable in its place. For example, on(keyPress myKey) does not function properly, even if the value of myKey is a string. However, you can dynamically change an active key using methods or handlers of the MovieClip object or Key listeners. You'll learn more about this functionality in the next section.

Caution

While you are developing a Flash movie, be careful to note any keypress that is already mapped to the Flash Player in the Test Movie environment. For example, the Enter key initiates a Play command in Test Movie mode. Therefore, if you enable the Enter key for a `keyPress` event, you might notice unpredictable results. Refer to the Control menu of the Test Movie environment for other mapped keys. If you have used any of these mapped keys, be sure to use the Control ⇨ Disable Keyboard Shortcuts while you are testing the Flash movie.

Using MovieClip Objects

You can also enable keys using `MovieClip` objects and the `onClipEvent()` handler. Earlier, you learned that `MovieClip` objects can use the `keyUp` and `keyDown` events. Unlike the Button instance's `on()` handler, the `onClipEvent()` handler does not specify the enabled key. Rather, it detects *any* keypress that occurs and executes the enclosed ActionScript code. For example, the following code executes a `trace()` action when the user presses any key:

```
onClipEvent(keyDown){
   trace("A key has been pressed.");
}
```

Likewise, the `onClipEvent()` handler can detect when any key has been released, as in the following:

```
onClipEvent(keyUp){
   trace("A key has been released.");
}
```

You can add both handlers to the same `MovieClip` instance. To try this code, do the following:

1. Open a new Flash document, create an empty Movie Clip symbol (Ctrl+F8 or ⌘+F8), and name it `emptyClip`. Flash automatically switches to Edit mode. Exit this mode by going back to Scene 1. You can also use Edit ⇨ Edit Document (Ctrl+E or ⌘+E) to return to the previous scene.

2. Open the Library (Ctrl+L or ⌘+L), and drag an instance of the `emptyClip` symbol onto the stage. Name the instance `mcKeyDetect` in the *`<Instance Name>`* field of the Property inspector.

3. With the `mcKeyDetect` instance selected, open the Actions panel and make sure it is entitled Actions — Movie Clip.

4. In this step, you use the Esc key shortcuts to set up your ActionScript code. With the cursor active in the Script pane of the Actions panel, sequentially press **Esc+o+c**. This creates the `onClipEvent(){}` handler code automatically, and inserts the I-beam cursor between the opening and closing parentheses of the handler.

5. Type the term **keyDown**. When you are finished, position the cursor between the opening and closing curly braces. Then, sequentially type **Esc+t+r**. This shortcut creates a `trace()` action. The highlighted word message appears between its parentheses. Type the following message in the `trace` action:

   ```
   "A key has been pressed."
   ```

   When you are finished, the entire code block should contain the following ActionScript:

   ```
   onClipEvent (keyDown) {
      trace("A key has been pressed.");
   }
   ```

6. If you need to format your code more neatly, click the Auto Format icon in the Actions panel toolbar. Alternatively, you can choose Auto Format (Ctrl+Shift+F or Shift+⌘+F) in the panel's options menu. After doing this, Flash MX 2004 inserts the appropriate line breaks and tabs to make your code more readable. Pin the current script by clicking the pin button in the lower left corner of the panel. The pin button will keep the current actions list active regardless of what other elements are selected in the authoring environment.
7. Save your Flash document as `keyEvent_MovieClip.fla` and test the movie. The Output panel displays the message within the `trace()` action whenever you press a key.
8. Add a `keyUp` event to a separate `onClipEvent()` handler. Close the Test Movie window, and reselect the `mcKeyDetect` object on the stage. In the Actions panel, after the actions you typed from Steps 4 and 5, add the following code using the Esc key shortcuts you have already learned:

```
onClipEvent(keyUp){
   trace("A key has been released.");
}
```

9. Save the document once again and test it. You should see two `trace()` messages in the Output panel every time you press and release a key.

You can find the completed document, `keyEvent_MovieClip.fla`, in the `ch19` folder of the book's CD-ROM.

You might have noticed that `keyDown` events continuously execute if you hold down any key because most keyboards repeatedly type a character if its key is held down. You've probably noticed this effect in a word processing application. Likewise, Flash movies continuously receive `keyDown` (and `keyPress`) events with a "stuck" key.

The rest of the examples in this chapter use `Key` listeners. Some of these examples can be adapted for use in Flash Player 4 by using Button instances and the `on()` handler with `keyPress` events.

Flash movies that use `onClipEvent()` code require Flash Player 5 or later. In order to use the `Key` listener examples, Flash Player 6 or later must be used.

Using a Key Listener

The previous release of Flash MX introduced the capability to detect keypresses directly with the `Key` class, working in tandem with a `Key` listener. Listeners were described earlier in this chapter, so you might want to review the discussion in the section titled "Assigning a Listener to the Mouse Class." Just as the `keyDown` and `keyUp` events for the `onClipEvent()` handler detect any keypress, a `Key` listener will execute with any keypress. One of the primary benefits, though, of using `Key` listeners instead of `onClipEvent()` is that you can script and control `Key` listeners on the fly, whereas `onClipEvent()` handlers need to be assigned to actual `MovieClip` objects that are present on the stage or nested within an attached `MovieClip` object. To remove an `onClipEvent()` in order to prevent it from executing, you have to remove the `MovieClip` object from the stage. `Key` listeners, on the other hand, can be added and removed with straight ActionScript code — no `MovieClip` objects are necessary.

As you will see in later sections of this chapter, ActionScript logic (in the form of `if` and `else` statements) is necessary to detect *specific* keypresses. For now, you will focus on understanding the basic operation of a `Key` listener. The following code executes a `trace()` action when the user presses any key:

```
var oUserKey:Object = new Object();
oUserKey.onKeyDown = function():Void {
   trace("A key has been pressed.");
};
Key.addListener(oUserKey);
```

Likewise, the `onKeyUp()` method can detect when any key has been released, as in the following:

```
var oUserKey:Object = new Object();
oUserKey.onKeyUp = function():Void {
   trace("A key has been released.");
};
Key.addlistener(oUserKey);
```

You can add both methods to the same `Key` listener. To try this code, do the following:

1. Create a new Flash document, and save the document as `keyEvent_listener.fla`.
2. Rename Layer 1 `actions`.
3. Select frame 1 of the actions layer, and open the Actions panel (F9). Create a `Key` listener by typing the following code:

   ```
   var oUserKey:Object = new Object();
   oUserKey.onKeyDown = function():Void {
      trace("A key has been pressed.");
   };
   oUserKey.onKeyUp = function():Void{
      trace("A key has been released.");
   };
   Key.addListener(oUserKey);
   ```

   This code creates one `Key` listener object named `oUserKey`. Two methods, `onKeyDown()` and `onKeyUp()`, are defined for this object. The `oUserKey` object is passed to the `Key` class and made an active listener in the last line of code, using the `addListener()` method.
4. Save your Flash document again, and test the movie (Ctrl+Enter or ⌘+Enter). When you press and release a key on the keyboard, the two `trace()` messages will appear in the Output panel.

You can find the complete document, `keyEvent_listener.fla`, in the ch19 folder of this book's CD-ROM.

In the next section, you continue to explore the dynamics of keypresses with `Key` listeners.

Determining the Key Code

After you know how to enable Flash movies to receive key events, you can start to add more interactive navigation and usability options to your Flash movies. In the following sections, you learn how to navigate Flash movies, scroll text fields, and move graphics using the keyboard.

Because you will be using Key listener objects to detect key events, you need to know how to write ActionScript that can actually *do* something after the key event occurs. Indeed, trace() actions really don't show off the power of key events. The primary construction for key events on Key listener objects works like this:

```
when a key event occurs (either a keypress or release)
  if the key is the key you want to use
    then execute this action
  otherwise
    do nothing (or something else)
  end if
end key event detection
```

So far, you should be able to translate the previous pseudo-code to the following ActionScript:

```
var oUserKey:Object = new Object();
oUserKey.onKeyDown = function():Void {
  if( the key is the key we want to use){
    // do this action
  } else {
    // do something else
  }
};
Key.addListener(oUserKey);
```

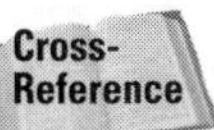

If you need to review logical comparisons using if statements, see Chapter 5.

Using getCode() and Key Constants

The difficulty lies in understanding how to determine whether the key that was pressed is actually the key you want to enable with interactivity. In the examples in previous sections, you detected any keypress. Now you want to narrow the scope of your onKeyDown() (or onKeyUp()) event handler using the Key class. Using the getCode() method and properties of the Key class, you can specifically enable the right arrow key:

```
var oUserKey:Object = new Object();
oUserKey.onKeyDown = function():Void {
  if(Key.getCode() == Key.RIGHT){
    // do this action
  } else {
    // otherwise, do this action
  }
};
Key.addListener(oUserKey);
```

Remember that `Key.getCode()` returns the current virtual key code value for the key(s) being detected by the key event. In this example, you want to compare the current key's value to a reference (or absolute) value — the right arrow key. Because ActionScript has a `Key` constant called `Key.RIGHT` for the right arrow key, you can refer to that value in your comparison. You can also write the code as follows:

```
var oUserKey:Object = new Object();
oUserKey.onKeyDown = function():Void {
  if(Key.getCode() == 39){
    // do this action
  } else {
    // otherwise, do this action
  }
};
Key.addListener(oUserKey);
```

Here, you refer to the actual key code for the desired key. The right arrow key has a virtual key code of 39. Of course, it's much simpler to remember or read a key's shortcut (if it has one, such as `Key.RIGHT`) instead of the numeric assignment for each key.

Calculating Key Code Values the "Easy" Way

Obviously, "easy" is a relative term. However, by the end of this section, you'll know how to assign most keys without ever needing to look up a virtual key code or an ASCII code. Suppose you want to enable the p key to start playback of the Flash movie. Because there is no `Key.P` constant automatically available, you can do one of two things: (1) look up the virtual key code value for the letter P and use it in your `getCode()` comparison; or (2) let ActionScript look up the ASCII key code value and then use that in a `getAscii()` comparison.

Because we advocate the creation of reusable and practical code, you will learn how to let ActionScript do all the work. The basic structure of your Flash movie and ActionScript is as follows:

1. Decide which individual letter or character you want to enable with a key event.
2. Assign that character as the value of a string variable.
3. Retrieve the ASCII code for the variable's value (it must be only one character long) using the `String` class's `charCodeAt()` static method.
4. Compare the value of the currently pressed key using `Key.getAscii()` to the ASCII code value of your variable.
5. If the values are the same, execute the ActionScript for that key's functionality. Otherwise, do something else.

Now you will create a Flash movie that follows these steps. However, you will add one more feature: the capability to enter the desired key into an Input text field. By using an Input text field, you can enable your ActionScript to check the text field's value and convert it to a decimal ASCII code value. Therefore, if you type the letter b in the text field, your ActionScript executes whenever a lowercase b is pressed on the keyboard.

1. Create a new Flash document, and rename Layer 1 `text field`.
2. On frame 1 of the text field layer, create an Input text field with the Text tool. In the Property inspector, make sure that the field has the values and settings shown in Figure 19-8. In addition, use a nonwhite text color for the text field. Most important, make sure you name the text field `tActiveKey` in the *<Instance Name>* field, and assign a maximum character limit of 1.

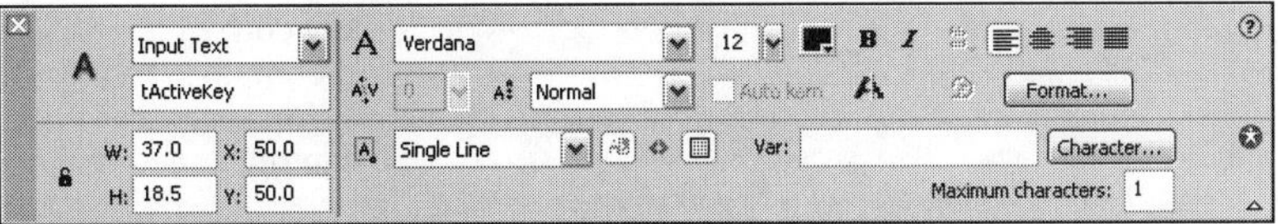

Figure 19-8: This Input text field has an instance name of tActiveKey. You'll compare the value of tActiveKey in your Key listener's ActionScript.

3. Create a new layer named `actions`, and place it at the top of the layer stack.

4. With frame 1 of the actions layer selected, open the Actions panel (F9). Before you add the code to the Script pane, consider the task that you want to accomplish.

   You need to compare the current value of the `tActiveKey` field to the currently pressed key. However, you can't just compare the values directly—you can't say `if(Key.getCode() == tActiveKey.text`—because `Key.getCode()` returns a unique number for each character, whereas `tActiveKey.text` is returning the actual character of the key, not the virtual key code. Therefore, you need to write your code so that you compare one key code to another key code. Luckily, you have access to a `String` static method that enables you to convert ASCII characters into ASCII codes: `String.charCodeAt()`. Because `charCodeAt()` returns decimal-based ASCII code values, you need to use the `Key` class's `getAscii()` method instead of the `getCode()` method. Break this down into pseudo-code:

   ```
   When a keyDown event occurs
     if the key's ASCII value equals the ASCII value of activeKey
       then show me the character of the current key
     otherwise
       do nothing
     end if
   end keyDown event
   ```

   Go back to your Flash document, and get ready to add the appropriate ActionScript to frame 1 of the actions layer.

5. Add the following translation of the pseudo-code to a `Key` listener:

   ```
   var oUserKey:Object = new Object();
   oUserKey.onKeyDown = function():Void {
     if(Key.getAscii() == tActiveKey.text.charCodeAt(0)){
       trace("The " + tActiveKey.text +  " key has been pressed.");
     }
   };
   Key.addListener(oUserKey);
   ```

6. Save your Flash document as `keyDown_getAscii.fla` and test it. Type any single character into the movie's text field and then press that same key again. The Output panel displays the `trace()` message, indicating the currently active keypress. For example, if you type the letter p in the text field, and then press the p key again, you should receive the output `"The p key has been pressed."`, as shown in Figure 19-9.

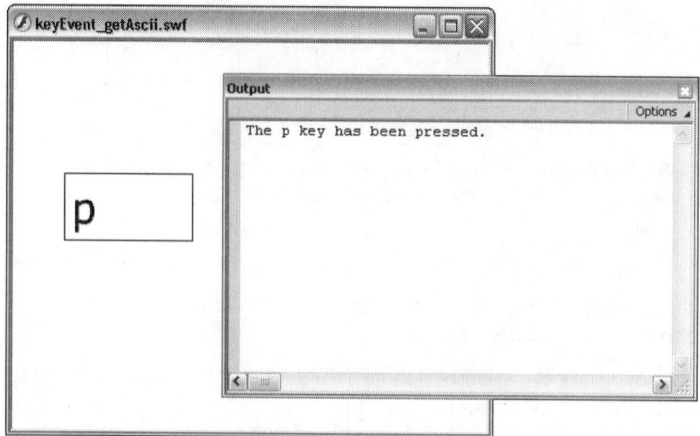

Figure 19-9: You can change the active keypress by replacing the first character of activeKey with a new character.

Admittedly, you still haven't actually done much with your Flash movie after you've detected the keypress and compared it to a specific key code value. But don't worry — now that you have a solid understanding of the basic methods and properties of the `Key` class, you can proceed to create some real-life examples.

To review your work in this section, you can compare your Flash document to the finished example, `keyDown_getAscii.fla`, located in the ch19 folder of the book's CD-ROM.

Nudging a MovieClip Object with the Arrow Key

In this section, you create a movie that enables the user to move an image of the moon by using all four arrow keys. As with any multimedia project, you should map your goals and procedures before you start developing your application in your authoring tool. For this example, you want to accomplish the following tasks:

- ✦ Enable the left arrow key to move the moon to the left of the stage.
- ✦ Enable the right arrow key to move the moon to the right of the stage.
- ✦ Enable the up arrow key to move the moon to the top of the stage.
- ✦ Enable the down arrow key to move the moon to the bottom of the stage.

Translate your arrow keys into actual ActionScript. The `Key` class has each arrow key assigned to a specific constant:

- ✦ `Key.LEFT` is the left arrow key.
- ✦ `Key.RIGHT` is the right arrow key.
- ✦ `Key.UP` is the up arrow key.
- ✦ `Key.DOWN` is the down arrow key.

Next, you need to translate the physical movement of the moon. As already implied, the moon itself is a `MovieClip` object, named `mcMoon`. Therefore, it has all the properties of the `MovieClip` object:

✦ `mcMoon._x` is the moon's X coordinate (and movement) on the stage.

✦ `mcMoon._y` is the moon's Y coordinate (and movement) on the stage.

Finally, you need to have an event handler (and an event) to capture the activity of the arrow keys. To gain the most flexibility and control over keypress detection, you can use a `Key` listener object. Furthermore, you want to use the `onKeyDown()` method for this listener because you need to capture each keypress of the arrow keys. The syntax of the basic listener object is as follows:

```
var oUserKey:Object = new Object();
oUserKey.onKeyDown = function():Void {
   // insert key detection and movement actions here
};
```

Now that you have all the individual elements of your application in place, create the pseudo-code for your interactivity:

```
when the user presses any key
  check the current key that is pressed
  if that key is the Left arrow key
    then move the moon object to the left of the stage
  if that key is the Right arrow key
    then move the moon object to the right of the stage
  if that key is the Up arrow key
    then move the moon object to the top of the stage
  if that key is the Down arrow key
    then move the moon object to the bottom of the stage
end key capture
```

Now translate your pseudo-code into the final ActionScript you'll put into the `oUserKey` listener object. You need to decide just how much the moon object moves with each keypress. For this example, the moon should move 10 pixels in the specified direction for each keypress. See the pseudo-code translated in Listing 19-4.

Listing 19-4: The oUserKey Listener

```
var oUserKey:Object = new Object();
oUserKey.onKeyDown = function():Void {
  var nKey:Number = Key.getCode();
  var mcTarget:MovieClip = mcMoon;
  if (nKey == Key.LEFT){
    mcTarget._x -= 10;
  }
  if (nKey == Key.RIGHT){
    mcTarget._x += 10;
  }
  if (nKey == Key.UP){
```

Continued

Listing 19-4 *(continued)*

```
        mcTarget._y -= 10;
    }
    if (nKey == Key.DOWN){
        mcTarget._y += 10;
    }
};
Key.addListener(oUserKey);
```

Here, you employ the addition assignment operator (+=) to serve as a shortcut to the following code:

```
mcTarget._x += 10 is the same as mcTarget._x = mcTarget._x + 10
```

where mcTarget is a variable representing the mcMoon object. Likewise, you use the negation assignment operator (-=) to simplify the subtraction of 10 pixels from the mcMoon's X (or Y) coordinate:

```
mcTarget._y -= 10 is the same as mcTarget._y = mcTarget._y - 10
```

For more information on ActionScript operators, refer to Chapter 5.

The importance of planning your movie's functionality before starting your work in Flash can't be emphasized enough. Now that you have a grasp of what needs to happen in the Flash movie, go to Flash MX 2004, and start building the project.

Open the key_nudge_starter.fla file located in the ch19 folder of this book's companion CD-ROM. You begin your example with this file, which contains prebuilt Movie Clip symbols.

The key_nudge_starter.fla file contains two MovieClip objects on the stage: mcEarth and mcMoon. For this exercise, you work exclusively with the mcMoon object. You add the key detection code to a listener object named oUserKey, just as you planned in your pseudo-code.

1. After you have opened the key_nudge_starter.fla file, create a new layer named Actions on the main timeline (that is, Scene 1).

2. Select frame 1 of the actions layer, and open the Actions panel. In the Script pane, add the following code:

```
var oUserKey:Object = new Object();
oUserKey.onKeyDown = function():Void {
    var nKey:Number = Key.getCode();
    var mcTarget:MovieClip = mcMoon;
    if (nKey == Key.LEFT){
        mcTarget._x -= 10;
    }
};
Key.addListener(oUserKey);
```

3. Save your Flash document as key_nudge_100.fla and test it. Press the left arrow key. The mcMoon object should move to the left of the stage. If you continue to hold the key down, the mcMoon object animates to the left. When you release the key, the mcMoon object stops moving.

4. Close the test SWF file and return to the Actions panel, with frame 1 of the actions layer selected. Continue to add the ActionScript code that was shown before you started the exercise. When you're finished, your ActionScript code should match that of Listing 19-4.

5. Save your Flash document again and test it. All four keys should be able to move the moon object in the four directions of the arrow keys.

Now you know how to enable arrow keys in order to move MovieClip objects. If you want to pursue this example further, please read the following section. Otherwise, continue to later sections for other Key class examples.

You can find the completed file, key_nudge_100.fla, in the ch19 folder of the book's CD-ROM.

Using setInterval() and onKeyDown for Keypresses

In the key_nudge_100.fla file you created in the previous section, you may have noticed some problems with the changes in movement and direction. If you try to press two arrow keys simultaneously, and release one but not the other, an undesirable effect results. The moon hesitates for a moment before proceeding to move in the new direction. Confused? Go ahead and try this. Test your key_nudge_100.fla document (Ctrl+Enter or ⌘+Enter), and proceed to move the moon in one direction and then quickly switch to another key. In order to fix this bug, you need to change your procedure for moving the mcMoon object.

In its current stage, the mcMoon object moves repeatedly due to a feature of your operating system and the keyboard: the key repeat rate. To see the effect of the key repeat rate on your Flash movie, do one of the following (depending on your operating system):

✦ **Windows:** Open the Control Panel (Start ➪ Settings ➪ Control Panel), and double-click the Keyboard icon. In the Keyboard Properties dialog box (shown in Figure 19-10), change the Repeat rate setting to a new value (that is, if it's currently set to Fast, change it to Slow, or vice versa).

✦ **Macintosh OS X:** Open the System Preferences (Apple Menu ➪ System Preferences), and click the Keyboard icon. In the Keyboard dialog box (shown in Figure 19-11), change the Key Repeat Rate setting to a new value.

Now return to Flash MX 2004 and retest the key_nudge_100.fla movie. You should notice a change in the speed at which the moon object animates across the screen.

As explained for the Mouse listener earlier in this chapter, the updateAfterEvent() function does not work with onMouseMove() methods of a Mouse listener. Sadly, updateAfterEvent() does not work within the onKeyDown() or onKeyUp() methods of the Key class. Simply put, updateAfterEvent() works only with onClipEvent() handlers, setInterval() functions, and the onMouseMove() method of the MovieClip class.

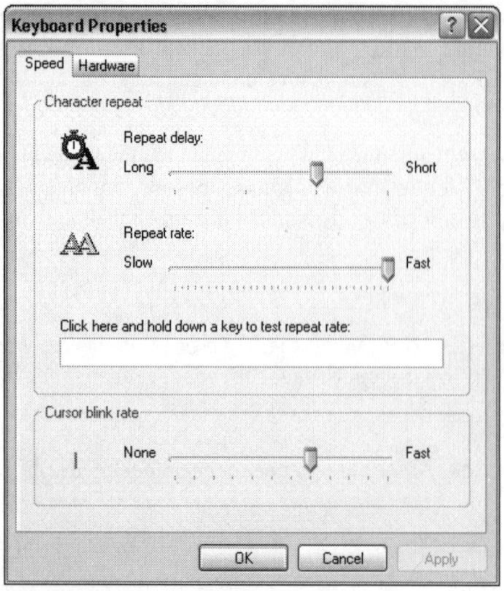

Figure 19-10: Windows XP Keyboard Properties Control Panel

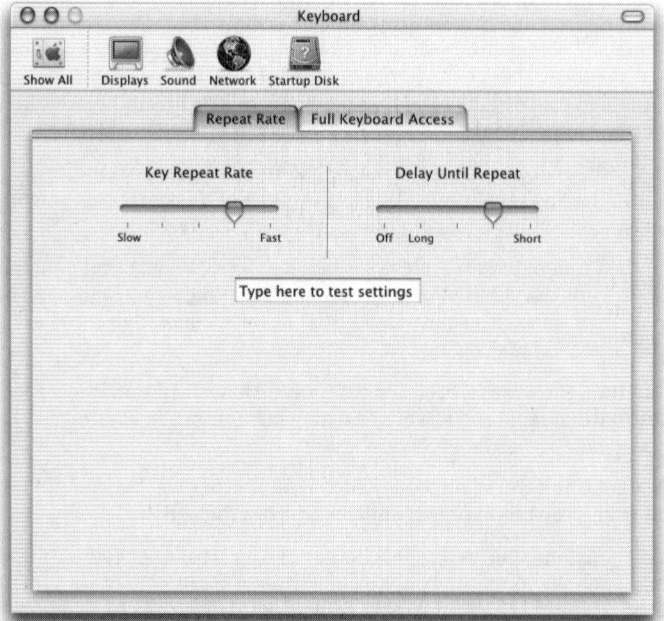

Figure 19-11: Macintosh OS X Keyboard Control Panel

To see this effect, open the `key_nudge_oce.fla` file in the ch19 folder of the book's CD-ROM.

The `key_nudge_oce.fla` file uses the same code structure as `key_nudge_100.fla`, except that the code from the `Key` listener object has been transplanted to an `onClipEvent(keyDown)` handler on the `mcMoon` instance. To see this code, select the `mcMoon` instance on the stage, and open the Actions panel.

You will notice the following line of code in the `onClipEvent()` handler, just before its closing curly brace:

```
updateAfterEvent();
```

The `updateAfterEvent()` function forces a refresh of elements on the stage, independently of frame rate. Now, combined with a fast key repeat rate, test the `key_nudge_oce.fla` document. The `mcMoon` object should move more smoothly across the screen.

You can also change the key repeat delay in your Keyboard Control Panel, which affects the amount of time required to wait before the OS actually starts to repeat the keypress. Because the key repeat rate (and delay) are user settings and not controlled by the Flash movie, you might not want to rely on the `keyDown` event to control the movement rate of the `mcMoon` object. One alternative procedure is to use the `enterFrame` event or a `setInterval()` function to both detect which key is being pressed *and* control the execution of the `MovieClip` property changes. To do this, you need to re-architect your Flash document. The problem can be defined as follows:

✦ You want an arrow key to set the direction, but not control the speed, of the `mcMoon` object.

✦ You need to continuously monitor whether an arrow key is pressed. If one is pressed, proceed to move the `mcMoon` object in that key's direction.

See if you can make some pseudo-code from your problem. Instead of using the `keyDown` event to add or subtract pixels from the X or Y coordinate of the moon object, use the `setInterval()` function to continuously monitor the status of your arrow keys. `updateAfterEvent()` can be used with functions called by `setInterval()`, so you should see smoother movement of the `mcMoon` object. Remember the `isDown()` method of the `Key` class? You can use `Key.isDown(Key.LEFT)` to determine whether the left arrow key is being pressed. If it is, subtract units from the `mcMoon` object's current X coordinate. If other arrow keys are pressed, perform the same actions you used with the `keyDown` event. Here's the pseudo-code:

```
during playback of the Flash movie
if a key is pressed then continuously check which key is active
  if the Left key is being pressed
    then move the moon to the left
  if the Right key is being pressed
    then move the moon to the right
  if the Up key is being pressed
    then move the moon up
  if the Down key is being pressed
    then move the moon down
end the process of monitoring the keys when all keys are released
```

Admittedly, it will be difficult to perform a simple or direct translation of the pseudo-code. `setInterval()` requires at least two arguments: the function to execute repeatedly, and the time interval (or wait time) between executions of that function. Here is the pseudo-code laid out in a procedural order:

```
when a keyDown event is detected
  start a setInterval() function (if one has not already been executed)
  (the setInterval() function will execute a function that checks to see
  if any arrow keys are pressed)
if an arrow key is pressed, then move the mcMoon object appropriately
when a keyUp event is detected
  stop the setInterval() from executing by using clearInterval()
```

Translated into ActionScript, Listing 19-5 shows the new code for your project.

Listing 19-5: **Using setInterval() with a Key Listener**

```
function moveTarget(){
   var mcTarget:MovieClip = mcMoon;
   if (Key.isDown(Key.LEFT)) {
      mcTarget._x -= 10;
   }
   if (Key.isDown(Key.RIGHT)) {
      mcTarget._x += 10;
   }
   if (Key.isDown(Key.UP)) {
      mcTarget._y -= 10;
   }
   if (Key.isDown(Key.DOWN)) {
      mcTarget._y += 10;
   }
   updateAfterEvent();
}

var oUserKey:Object = new Object();
oUserKey.onKeyDown = function():Void {
   if(nKeyID == null) nKeyID = setInterval(moveTarget, 10);
};
userKey.onKeyUp = function():Void {
   if(nKeyID != null){
      clearInterval(nKeyID);
      delete nKeyID;
   }
};
Key.addListener(oUserKey);
```

To see this code in action, do the following:

1. Open the key_nudge_100.fla document that you created in the last section.
2. Select frame 1 of the actions layer, and open the Actions panel. Delete the existing code, and type the code shown in Listing 19-5.
3. Save your Flash document as key_nudge_200.fla and test the movie (Ctrl+Enter or ⌘+Enter).

Not only can you move the mcMoon object without worrying about key releases; you can also move the mcMoon object diagonally by pressing two keys at the same time!

To control the speed of the movement, you can change two settings:

- The number added to or subtracted from the _x and _y properties
- The time interval established within the setInterval() function

That's it! At this point, you can continue to modify the movie for further interactivity. In the next section, you learn how to use setInterval() and the onKeyDown() method to detect keypress combinations.

Detecting Keypress Combinations

The previous section described how to make two keys active at the same time. If you want to detect a simultaneous keypress combination, you need to modify the structure of the setInterval() function and the Key listener. For example, you can write ActionScript code that will detect when the Ctrl or ⌘ key is pressed while the F key is pressed. If you've had experience with writing compound logic statements such as the following code, it's easy to believe that your task will be relatively simple:

```
if(Key.isDown(Key.CONTROL) && Key.isDown(70))
```

The virtual key code for the F key is 70, and the constant for the Ctrl (or ⌘) key is Key.CONTROL.

Caution: Some keypress combinations might not function correctly in all Flash Player environments, especially if the key combo is assigned to the host environment. For example, Ctrl+F or ⌘+F is the View ⇨ Full Screen command in the stand-alone player (or projector). Be sure to check for the existence of sensitive keypress combinations in the host environment before you try to test them.

Unfortunately, this code will not work if it's executed directly from the Key listener. When some keys are pressed in combination with modifier keys such as the Ctrl (or ⌘) key, the key code of the second key may be altered — momentarily. In truth, it's difficult to say with any certainty why the key code is eventually detected correctly. Luckily, you can create this functionality with a little effort. The workaround involves the use of setInterval() to continuously execute a function that checks for the keypress combo. After the key combo is detected (or when all keys are released), the setInterval() function will be removed with a clearInterval() function. Here's an overview of the process:

```
when a key event is detected
  initiate setInterval() with a function that detects a specific keypress combo
when the keypress combo is detected
```

```
  initiate the task assigned to the keypress combo (open a window, and so on)
  remove the setInterval()
when all keys are released
  remove the setInterval()
```

Again, the translation of this pseudo-code is not simple or direct. Three functions are created:

- ✦ `keyDetect()`: This function will check the current key(s) that are pressed. If both the Ctrl (or ⌘) key and the S key are pressed, a linked symbol in the movie's Library will appear on the stage. This symbol displays a search dialog box. When the combo keys are detected, the `disableKeyDetect()` function will be invoked (discussed last in this list).
- ✦ `enableKeyDetect()`: This function is called by the `Key` listener object when any key is pressed. The function creates a variable named `nKeyID` that executes a `setInterval()` function specifying the `keyDetect()` function.
- ✦ `disableKeyDetect()`: This function is invoked by the `Key` listener object when any key is released. The function removes any `setInterval()` calls using the `clearInterval()` function, and deletes the `setInterval()` variable, `nKeyID`.

The `keyDetect`, `enableKeyDetect()`, and `disableKeyDetect()` functions are enabled with a `Key` listener object named `oComboKey`. Listing 19-6 shows the complete code to enable the keypress combination detection.

Listing 19-6: **Detecting Combo Keypresses**

```
function keyDetect():Void {
   var sLetter:String = "S";
   var nActiveKey:Number = new String(sLetter).charCodeAt(0);
   if (Key.isDown(Key.CONTROL) && (Key.isDown(nActiveKey))) {
      var mcWin:MovieClip = this.owner.attachMovie("findWindowClip", ⮐
        "mcWin", 1, {_x:275, _y:200});
      this.onKeyUp();
   }
}
function enableKeyDetect():Void {
   if (nKeyID == null) {
      nKeyID = setInterval(this, "keyDetect", 50);
   }
}
function disableKeyDetect():Void {
   if (nKeyID != null) {
      clearInterval(nKeyID);
   }
   delete nKeyID;
}
var oComboKey:Object = {owner:this};
oComboKey.keyDetect = keyDetect;
oComboKey.onKeyDown = enableKeyDetect;
oComboKey.onKeyUp = disableKeyDetect;
Key.addListener(oComboKey);
```

Before you add this code to a Flash movie, open the starter file, keyEvent_combo_starter.fla, in the ch19 folder of the book's CD-ROM. This document contains the artwork for the Find dialog box. This artwork will be attached with the code you're about to add. Note that the findWindowClip symbol has a Button instance that uses a on(release, keyPress "<Enter>") handler as well.

To see this code in action, do the following:

1. Open the keyEvent_combo_starter.fla document from the CD-ROM.
2. Create a new layer named actions, and place it at the top of the layer stack.
3. Select frame 1 of the actions layer, and open the Actions panel. Type the code shown in Listing 19-6.
4. Save your Flash document as keyEvent_combo_100.fla and test the movie (Ctrl+Enter or ⌘+Enter). With focus on the Test Movie window (that is, click the Flash movie stage to make sure it is active), press Ctrl+S or ⌘+S. The Find dialog box appears, as shown in Figure 19-12. Type a search term into the dialog box, and press the Search button. A Web page will appear in a separate browser window with the search results.

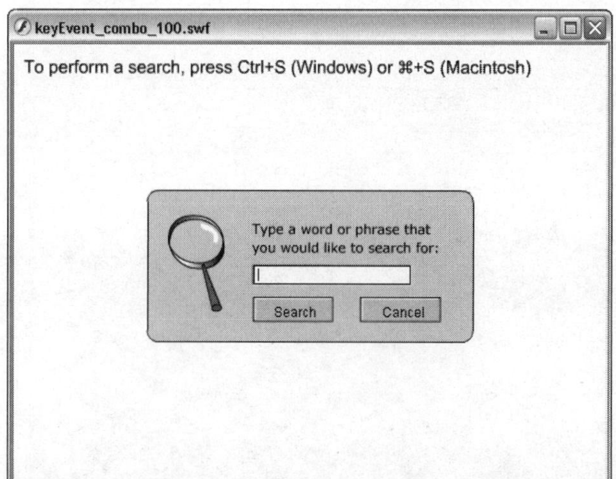

Figure 19-12: The Find dialog box appears when the key combo is pressed.

You can modify the keyDetect() function to work with different keys or even add more keys to the if() statement. For example, you can add another Key.isDown(), specifying the Key.ALT constant.

You can find the completed file, keyEvent_combo_100.fla, in the ch19 folder of the book's CD-ROM. We also created a keyEvent_combo_focus.html document that uses a JavaScript focus() function to automatically focus the Flash movie in the browser window. The JavaScript focus() method works only for Flash movies viewed in Internet Explorer for Windows.

Playing a Flash Animation with a Keypress

In this next example, you use the right arrow key to control the playback of a Flash movie. Specifically, you use the right keys to play the animation forward. Once more, the moon and earth instances are your central elements. With each right arrow keypress, your ActionScript instructs the main timeline to play until the next frame label. At this point, acquaint yourself with the prebuilt starter file.

On the CD-ROM

You can find this section's starter file, `key_playback_starter.fla`, in the ch19 folder of the book's CD-ROM.

After you have located the starter file on the CD-ROM, copy it to your hard drive, and open the local copy in Flash MX 2004. The starter Flash document has a motion-guided Graphic symbol of the moon nested within a mask layer on the main timeline. As you can see in Figure 19-13, there are four stages (each with a separate `stop()` action), representing different positions of the moon as it orbits the earth.

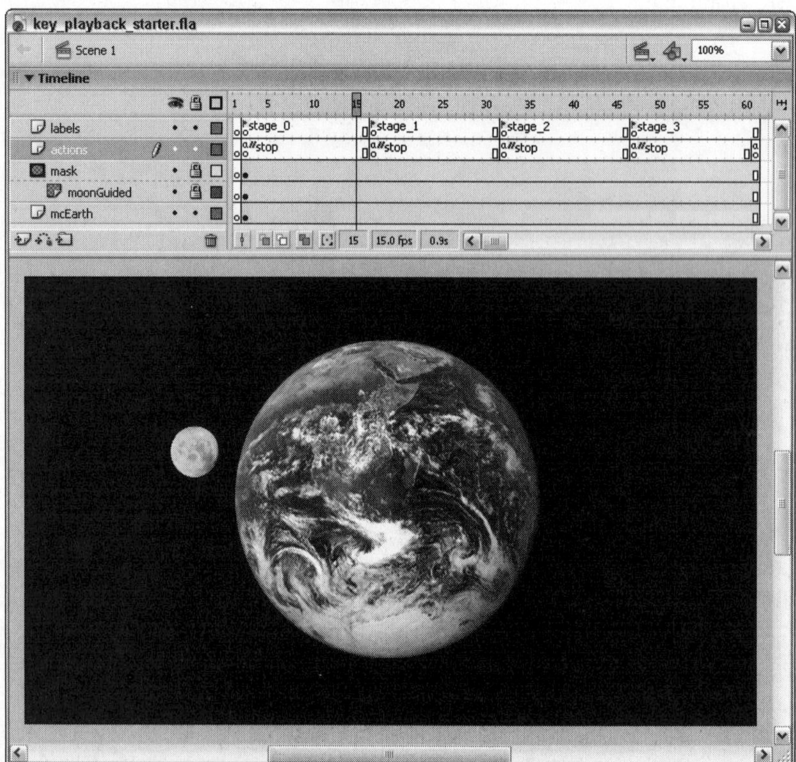

Figure 19-13: The composition of the starter file's main timeline

The frame labels start the numbering scheme with 0, so that they correspond with array values that are introduced in a later example. Basically, you want to enable the right arrow key to issue a simple `play()` command to the main timeline. The timeline automatically stops at the next frame label because there are `stop()` actions at each frame label. After `stage_3`, a `this.gotoAndStop("stage_0");` action resets the timeline.

The first frame of the main timeline is reserved for actions that should be played (or invoked) only once in the Flash movie. With this specific example, you add a `Key` listener that should not be specified with the `addListener()` method more than once. If you add the same listener object to a listener-enabled class more than once, the methods of the listener object will be executed in multiples when the event(s) associated with the listener class are detected.

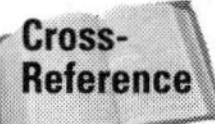

For more information on arrays and indexes, refer to Chapter 11.

Following is your pseudo-code for this example:

```
when a key is pressed
  if the key is the Right arrow key
    then advance to the next frame label
  end if
end key capture
```

Translate this pseudo-code into the proper ActionScript syntax.

1. Create a new layer and name it `listener actions`.
2. With frame 1 of the listener actions layer selected, open the Actions panel (F9). Your translated actions are as follows:

```
var oKeyDetect:Object = { owner: this };
oKeyDetect.onKeyDown = function():Void {
  if (Key.getCode() == Key.RIGHT){
    this.owner.play();
  }
};
Key.addListener(oKeyDetect);
```

3. Save your Flash document as `key_playback_100.fla` and test it. When you press the right arrow key, the moon should come out from behind the earth and stop at the `stage_1` position. Each subsequent press should advance the moon to the next stage.

You can find the completed document, `key_playback_100.fla`, in the ch19 folder of the book's CD-ROM.

That wasn't too difficult, was it? If you want to learn how to make the movie play backward with a left arrow keypress, you can continue this exercise by following along with the next sidebar.

Playing a Movie Backward with a Keypress

To make your playback control more complete, you can enable your key_playback_100.fla document with a rewind feature. You can redefine your project with the following aspects:

- ✦ Enable the left arrow key to play backward until it reaches the preceding stage.
- ✦ If the current stage is stage_0, a left arrow keypress should go to the end of the timeline and play backward until it reaches stage_3.

Before you go any further, you need to look at these issues and see if there are greater problems within them. First of all, how do you play the movie backward? There is no built-in playBackward() method, but you do have a MovieClip method that enables you to go to the previous frame: prevFrame(). If you continuously execute prevFrame(), the targeted timeline begins to play backward. To continuously execute an action (or series of actions), you can use the new onEnterFrame() event handler. If you add the following actions to a MovieClip object such as _root, its timeline begins to play backward:

```
_root.onEnterFrame = function(){
   this.prevFrame();

};
```

Of course, you won't notice anything if the main timeline (_root) is stopped on frame 1, but if you start to execute this code while _root is at frame 100, the movie will start to play backward until it reaches frame 1.

How do you stop the movie after it begins to play backward? You need to know when it reaches the previous frame label (for example, stage_0 from stage_1), and make it stop rewinding when it reaches that label. Unfortunately, ActionScript doesn't have a _currentFrameLabel property. You do, however, have a _currentframe property of the MovieClip class, and you can access this property to determine the currently played frame number. Therefore, you need to create a list of all of the frame numbers associated with your stage frame labels.

Open the key_playback_100.fla movie, add another layer to the main timeline, and rename the layer stage actions. Write the following action on frame 1 of this new layer:

```
var aLabelNum:Array = new Array(2, 17, 32, 47);
```

The values 2, 17, 32, and 47 correspond to the frame numbers associated with stage_0, stage_1, stage_2, and stage_3, respectively. Because the first element of an array has an index value of 0, you also create a reference to this index on the first frame.

Insert an empty keyframe on frame 2 of the stage actions layer, and add the following action to this keyframe:

```
var nCurrentStage:Number = 0;
```

Why 0? Because your first stage is labeled stage_0, and the first index of the aLabelNum array is 0, you can access the array through the nCurrentStage variable, as shown in the following:

```
aLabelNum[nCurrentStage]
```

Your code will increase the value of nCurrentStage by one (+1) each time the right arrow key is pressed, and subtract one (-1) from nCurrentStage each time the left arrow key is pressed. If nCurrentStage is equal to 0, aLabelNum[nCurrentStage] returns the number 2. If nCurrentStage is equal to 1, aLabelNum[nCurrentStage] returns the number 17, and so on. You can use the aLabelNum array to specify when your ActionScript should stop rewinding.

With these basic constructs taken care of, you can begin to map the pseudo-code. Remember that you still need to use the onKeyUp() listener method to capture the keypress. Now you need to enable two keypresses and a rewind feature:

```
when a key is released
  if the key is the right arrow key
    tell the Main Timeline to play
    increase nCurrentStage by 1 (proceeding to the next stage)
  otherwise, if the key is the left arrow key
    if the movie is not at the first stage (stage_0)
      decrease nCurrentStage by 1 (going back one stage)
    otherwise, jump to the end of the timeline
      set nCurrentStage to the last index of the aLabelNum array
      tell the Main Timeline to go to the second to last frame
    end if
    pass aLabelNum to a function that enables an onEnterFrame()
      method
  end if
end key handler

create a function that will enable an onEnterFrame() method
  create an onEnterFrame() method for the Main Timeline
    if the Main Timeline isn't at the next stage's frame
      then tell the Main Timeline to go to the previous frame
    otherwise
      disable onEnterFrame() method
    end if
  end onEnterFrame() method
end function
```

Now translate this to ActionScript syntax. Select frame 1 of the listener actions layer, and change the ActionScript in the Actions panel to read as follows:

```
var oKeyDetect:Object = { owner: this };
oKeyDetect.onKeyUp = function():Void  {
  if (Key.getCode() == Key.RIGHT) {
    this.owner.play();
    nCurrentStage++;
  } else if (Key.getCode() == Key.LEFT) {
    if (nCurrentStage > 0) {
      nCurrentStage--;
    } else {
      nCurrentStage = aLabelNum.length-1;
      this.owner.gotoAndStop(this.owner._totalframes-1);
    }
    playBackward(aLabelNum[nCurrentStage]);
  }
};
Key.addListener(oKeyDetect);

function playBackward(stopFrame:Number):Void {
```

Continued

Continued

```
      this.stopFrame = stopFrame;
      this.onEnterFrame = function():Void {
         if (this._currentframe != this.stopFrame) {
            this.prevFrame();
         } else {
            this.gotoAndStop(this.stopFrame);
            this.onEnterFrame = null;
         }
      };
   }
```

After you have added this code to frame 1 of the listener actions layer, save your Flash document as key_playback_200.fla and test it. Now you can play the animation forward with the right arrow key, or rewind it with the left arrow key.

We'd like to know what you thought about this chapter. Visit www.flashsupport.com/feedback to fill out an online form with your comments.

Summary

- The Mouse class enables you to hide and show the default mouse cursor icons used by the operating system.
- You can create custom mouse cursors by using the MovieClip.attachMovie() method with exported MovieClip symbols in the Library.
- The Mouse class can use listener objects that detect mouse clicks, mouse movement, and mouse scroll wheel activity.
- The updateAfterEvent() function enables the stage of a Flash movie to refresh independently of the movie's frame rate. When used with mouse and key events, you can achieve smoother animation across the stage.
- The Key class can be used to gather information about keypresses initiated by the user.
- The Key class is commonly used with key events, such as keyPress (for Button instances), keyUp and keyDown (for MovieClip objects and the onClipEvent() handler), and onKeyDown() and onKeyUp() for Key listener objects.
- The Key object has 18 prebuilt constants (or properties) for keys that are commonly used in games, such as the arrow keys, the Enter key, and the spacebar.
- The getCode() method of the Key class returns the virtual key code of the pressed key. The virtual key code values used by ActionScript are a subset of the standard, decimal-based ASCII code system.

- The `getAscii()` method of the `Key` object returns the decimal ASCII code of the pressed key.
- `Key` listener objects can work in tandem with `setInterval()` functions to monitor keypress activity.

✦ ✦ ✦

The Stage and ContextMenu Classes

In This Chapter

Controlling how a movie scales and aligns

Detecting the width and height of a Flash movie

Dynamically placing movie elements in the Flash Player space

Adding context menus to Flash movie elements

Have you ever wanted to know the dimensions of a browser window displaying a Flash movie? Prior to Flash MX, a Web developer had to employ JavaScript in the HTML document displaying the Flash movie to determine the size of the browser window. Have you ever wanted to add custom options to the right-click context menu for items in a Flash movie? With ActionScript, you can determine the size of a Flash movie's stage very easily and even reconfigure a movie based on how much room is within the Web browser window. You can also use ActionScript to build custom menu items in the Flash Player's context menu. In this chapter, you learn how to script the properties and methods of the `Stage` and `ContextMenu` classes.

Controlling the Movie's Stage

When Flash Player 6 was released, ActionScript added a new `Stage` class to the language. The `Stage` class represents the physical space occupied by the Flash movie's stage or the area occupied by the Flash Player. This difference is discussed later in the chapter. This class has only one instance at any time in the Flash movie and is therefore called a *static* class. Unlike most ActionScript classes, the `Stage` class is always controlled directly through the `Stage` class name. You do *not* need to define new instances of the `Stage` class with a constructor such as the following:

```
var myStage = new Stage();
```

This syntax is incorrect. Like the `Mouse`, `Selection`, and `Key` classes, the `Stage` class is referenced through the class name:

```
Stage.scaleMode = "noScale";
```

In this code example, the `scaleMode` property of the `Stage` class is set to `"noScale"`. Of course, you need to understand just what `scaleMode` and the other properties of the `Stage` class are. Take a look.

Property Overview of the Stage Class

The Stage class has four properties that can be read or set. The first two properties, scaleMode and align, work exactly like the HTML options in the Publish Settings dialog box of Flash MX 2004. The second set of properties, width and height, describe the dimensions of the Flash movie or the area occupied by Flash Player 6 or later. Before the properties of the Stage class can be defined, however, you must understand how the viewing area of a Flash movie works. To do this, you'll create a few simple Flash movies.

Create a new Flash document and open the Document Properties dialog box (Ctrl+J or ⌘+J). Specify a document width of 400 pixels, a height of 300 pixels, and a green background color. Rename Layer 1 movie area, draw a 400 × 300 black stroked box with a white fill, and center it on the stage.

Now, create a new layer named static text. On this layer, use the Text tool to add the words movie area to the top-left corner of the stage, as shown in Figure 20-1.

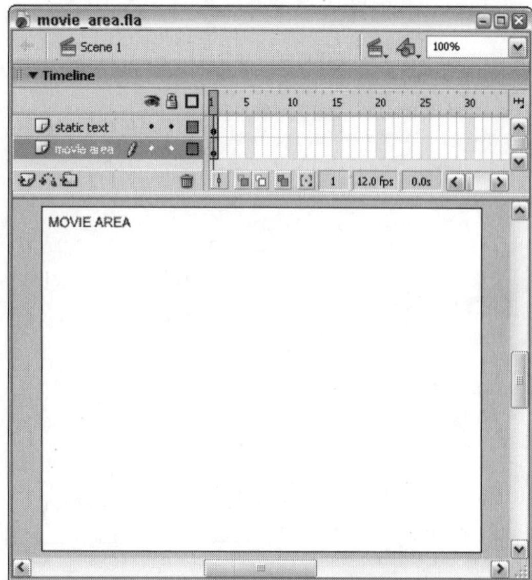

Figure 20-1: This rectangle and text represent the movie's area.

Open the Publish Settings dialog box (File ➪ Publish Settings) and click the HTML tab. For this test, use the Flash Only template, and leave the Dimensions set to Match Movie. In the Scale menu, leave the Default (Show all) option selected. Save the Flash document as showAll_match.fla. Choose File ➪ Publish Preview ➪ Default – (HTML) to view the Flash movie in a Web browser. Try resizing the browser window. Notice that the Flash movie does not scale, nor does it center on the page.

Go back to the Flash document and open the Publish Settings dialog box again. In the HTML tab, change the Dimensions to Percent, and leave the Width and Height fields set to the new

100 percent values. Save your Flash document as `showAll_percent.fla`, and publish preview the HTML document. This time, when you resize the Web browser window, notice that the Flash movie scales to fill the browser window. However, the movie area is never cropped—the green background fills either the left and right or top and bottom sides of the browser window.

Go back to the Flash document and change the Scale option to No Border. Save your Flash document as `noBorder_percent.fla` and publish preview the HTML document. Now, as you resize the document, the Flash movie scales to fill the entire window at the expense of cropping either the horizontal or vertical dimensions of the movie area.

Return to the Flash document and change the Scale option to Exact fit. Save your Flash document as `exactFit_percent.fla` and publish preview the HTML document. The Flash movie will scale to fill the browser window, and the artwork will be stretched or distorted to fill the entire window.

Now, change the Scale option to No scale. Save the Flash document as `noScale_percent.fla` and publish preview the HTML document. The Flash movie does not scale as you resize the browser window. However, the Flash movie stays centered in the window at 100 percent scale. If you size the window smaller than the original dimensions of the Flash movie, the movie area will be cropped.

Finally, test the Flash Alignment options in the HTML tab. So far, each of the previous examples aligned the movie area to the vertical and horizontal center of the window. Go back to the HTML tab, choose Left in the Horizontal menu, and select Top in the Vertical menu—leaving the Scale menu set to No scale. Save your Flash document as `noScale_percent_lt.fla`, and publish preview the HTML document. As you size the browser window, the Flash movie remains at 100 percent and stays fixed in the top-left corner of the window. Although you cannot visibly detect it, the Flash Player area is still expanding to the full area of the browser window.

The important point to remember with these examples is that the Flash Player, when set to use a dimension such as 100 percent for width and height, expands the area of the movie area or the stage. Scale all, No border, and Exact fit scale the movie area to fill the area prescribed by the dimensions. No scale, however, expands the viewing area of the Flash Player to fill the browser window, even though the scale of the Flash movie remains 100 percent. Keep this in mind as you explore the properties and methods of the `Stage` class in the following sections.

If the Flash movie is assigned to a viewing area (in the Dimensions settings) that's the same size as the movie itself, you will not notice any difference with the scale option.

All of the scale options you just used are available in the `Stage` class's `scaleMode` property. The following sections define the properties of the `Stage` class.

You can find each of the files described here in the `ch20` folder of this book's CD-ROM.

Changing the Scale Behavior with Stage.scaleMode

This property of the `Stage` class controls how the Flash movie will fill the area prescribed by the dimension attributes in the `<object>` and `<embed>` tags of the HTML document for the Flash movie (SWF file).

Four string values are recognized by the `scaleMode` property. You will apply each of these values into a working Flash document later in this chapter.

- "showAll": This is the default value of the `scaleMode` property. This option fits the entire Flash movie into the area defined by the dimension attributes in the HTML document. The original aspect ratio of the Flash movie will not be distorted. However, borders can appear on two sides of the Flash movie.
- "noBorder": This value forces the Flash movie to fill the area defined by the dimension attributes without leaving borders. In order to accomplish this borderless effect, the Flash movie's aspect ratio is not distorted or stretched. However, this value may crop two sides of the Flash movie.
- "exactFit": This value stretches the Flash movie to fill the entire area defined by the dimension attributes. Severe distortion or stretching of the Flash movie occurs if the dimensions do not match those defined in the Document Properties dialog box.
- "noScale": When `scaleMode` uses this value, the size of the Flash movie's stage stays fixed at the dimensions prescribed by the Document Properties dialog box. As such, elements within the movie always stay at 100 percent of their original size as you placed or created them in the Flash document.

Controlling the Movie's Alignment with Stage.align

The `align` property controls how the Flash movie is positioned within the area assigned to the Flash Player. In the tests at the beginning of this chapter, you saw how the left and top alignment settings in the Publish Settings dialog box positioned a `noScale` Flash movie in the top-left corner of the browser window. The `align` property works with the same values as Publish Settings, using the string values shown in Table 20-1. The following code sets the Flash movie to display in the top-left corner of the dimensions allocated to the Flash Player:

```
Stage.align = "LT";
```

Any string value other than the values shown in Table 20-1 resets the alignment to the center of the Flash Player area. For example, `Stage.align = "ZZ";` aligns the movie to the default center position. However, we recommend that you use "CC" as a value to align along the center of the horizontal and vertical axes.

Table 20-1: Values for the align Property of the Stage Class

Alignment	*Value*	*Alignment*	*Value*
Left center	"L"	Left top	"LT"
Right center	"R"	Left bottom	"LB"
Top center	"T"	Right top	"RT"
Bottom center	"B"	Right bottom	"RB"

Reporting the Movie's Width with Stage.width

This property of the `Stage` class enables you to access the pixel value currently used for the width of the Flash movie or the Flash Player area. As you will see later, the `width` property can return the width value entered in the Document Properties dialog box, or it can return the width of the current area allocated to the Flash Player. This property is read-only. You cannot set the width of the movie or Flash Player area with this property. In the following code, the value of the `width` property is displayed in a `TextField` object named `tMovieWidth`:

```
tMovieWidth.text = Stage.width;
```

In the section "Working with the Width and Height of a Flash Movie," you learn how to apply the `width` property in a Flash document of your own.

Reporting the Movie's Height with Stage.height

This property retrieves the current height (in pixels) currently used by the Flash movie or the Flash Player area. Like the `width` property, the `height` property returns the height value entered in the Document Properties dialog box or the height of the current area allocated to the Flash Player. In the next section, you learn how to use this property with a Flash document. In the following code, the value of the `height` property is displayed in a `TextField` object named `tMovieHeight`:

```
tMovieHeight.text = Stage.height;
```

Controlling the Standard Flash Player Context Menu Display

With the `Stage.showMenu` property, you can control the user's access to the right-click (or Control-click on Mac) menu options of the Flash Player plug-in or stand-alone projector. `Stage.showMenu` is a Boolean property: a value of `true` enables the right-click menu, and a value of `false` disables the right-click menu.

By default, this property has a value of `true`. With this setting, the user will see the menu shown in Figure 20-2 upon right-clicking the Flash Player movie area in the browser plug-in or stand-alone projector. The following code enables the built-in menu:

```
Stage.showMenu = true;
```

Zoom In
Zoom Out
✔ Show All
Quality ▸
Settings...
Print...
About Macromedia Flash Player 7...

Figure 20-2: The Flash Player 7 standard context menu

Benefits of the Stage Class in Flash 6 Movies

Perhaps one of the best reasons to use the `Stage` class is that it offers control over the scaling and alignment of your Flash movies without relying on plug-in parameters set in HTML documents. In previous releases of the Flash Player, all Flash movies loaded directly into the Flash Player plug-in or ActiveX control would scale to the size of the browser window. For example, if you directly accessed an SWF file in the URL field of a browser, such as the following, the Flash movie would always scale to the current size of the browser window:

```
http://www.theMakers.com/main.swf
```

Now, with Flash Player 6 or later movies, you can have absolute control over the scale and alignment of Flash movies. Note that the `Stage` class works exactly the same in the Flash Player 6 or later plug-in as it does in the stand-alone player or projector.

If the value is set to `false`, the user cannot access the playback control items in the context menu. The restricted player menu is shown in Figure 20-3. The following code disables the standard options in the built-in menu:

```
Stage.showMenu = false;
```

Figure 20-3: The Flash Player 7 estricted context menu

Working with the Width and Height of a Flash Movie

Now that you've had a general overview of the `Stage` class's properties, it's time to apply these properties in a Flash document. In this section, you learn how to control the `scaleMode` of a Flash movie, which in turn influences how the `width` and `height` properties work.

Controlling scaleMode

This first exercise shows you how to control the `scaleMode` of a Flash movie. You will add a `TextField` object that displays the current width and height of the Flash Player area. Using an `onEnterFrame()` event handler, you will update the `TextField` object to continuously retrieve and display the width and height properties of the `Stage` class. Then, you will add several `Button` components to the document. Each `Button` component instance alters the `scaleMode` of the `Stage` class. The `TextField` object displays the new values of the width and height properties based on the current `scaleMode`.

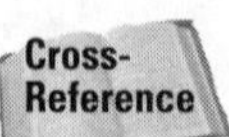

For more information on the use of components, refer to Part VIII of this book.

1. Open a new Flash document. Choose Modify ⇨ Document (Ctrl+J or ⌘+J), and specify 300 pixels for the width and 200 pixels for the height.

2. Save the document as `stageWH_100.fla`.

3. Rename Layer 1 `textfield`. Using the Text tool, create a Dynamic text field. In the Property inspector, assign the instance name of `tOutput` to the text field. Make sure the color of the font for the text field is non-white. Place the text field in the top-left corner of the stage.

4. Create a new layer named `buttons`. On this layer, drag an instance of the `Button` component from the Component panel to the stage. With this instance selected, open the Property inspector. Name the instance `cbtNoScale`. In the Parameters tab of the Property inspector, click the `label` field and type the text `noScale`. When this component button is clicked, a method named `changeScale()` is executed, and the `scaleMode` is changed to `"noScale"`. You will create this function in the next step. Place the instance underneath the text field, as shown in Figure 20-4.

5. Create a new layer named `actions`. Select frame 1 of this layer, and open the Actions panel (F9). Type the code shown in Listing 20-1 into the Script pane.

   In this code, lines 1–4 create a `changeScale()` method. This method is passed an event object whenever the `Button` component is clicked. Using the `label` property for the `Button` component, the `"noScale"` text on the button is retrieved and used for the `scaleMode` property.

   More important, though, you need to add the `changeScale()` method as a listener for the `cbtNoScale` component (line 5). Now, when the user clicks the button, the `changeScale()` method is notified.

   In lines 6–8, you create an `onEnterFrame()` handler for the main timeline (`this`). The function assigned to this handler continuously updates the `tOutput` text field with the width and height properties of the `Stage` class.

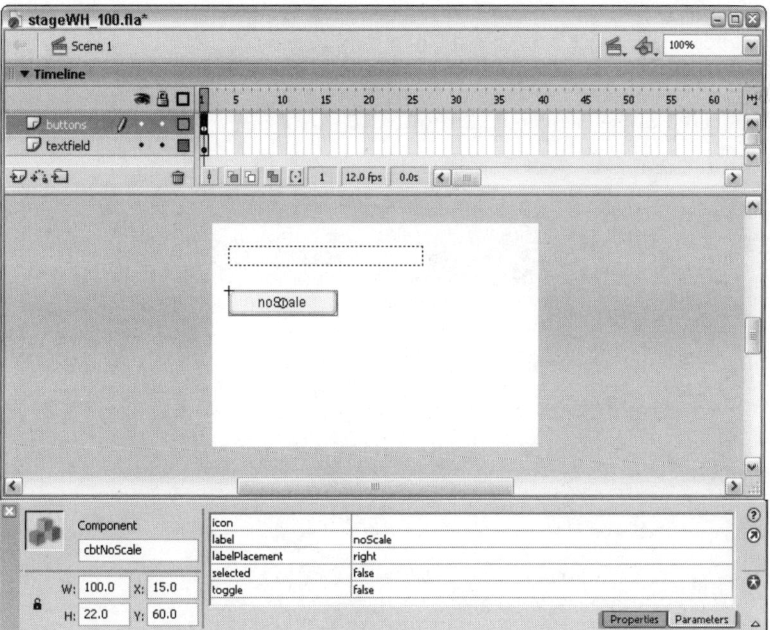

Figure 20-4: The first component button changes the scaleMode to "noScale."

Listing 20-1: Monitoring the Width and Height of the Movie

```
this.changeScale = function(oEvent:Object):Void {
   var sLabel:String = oEvent.target.label;
   Stage.scaleMode = sLabel;
};
cbtNoScale.addEventListener("click", this.changeScale);
this.onEnterFrame = function():Void {
  tOutput.text = "W = " + Stage.width + ", H = " + Stage.height;
};
```

6. Save the Flash document. Open the Publish Settings dialog box (File ➪ Publish Settings). In the HTML tab, choose Percent in the Dimensions menu, and leave the 100 percent values in the width and height fields. Close the Publish Settings dialog box, and choose File ➪ Publish Preview ➪ Default - (HTML), or press the F12 key. In the Web browser, resize the browser window displaying the Flash movie. Notice that the width and height values in the `tOutput` text field remain 300 × 200, despite the fact that the Flash movie is scaling to the size of the window.

   Now, click the `cbtNoScale` button. What happens? The `width` and `height` properties of the `Stage` class report the pixel width and height of the Flash Player area in the browser window. Remember, you set the dimensions to use 100 percent of the width and height of the browser window. In `"noScale"` mode, the Flash movie does not scale to the size of the window, but width and height report the size of the Flash Player area.

7. Go back to the Flash document. Select the `cbtNoScale` instance on the stage, and duplicate it three times (Edit ➪ Duplicate). In the Property inspector, assign each of the following instance names to the new duplicates: `cbtShowAll`, `cbtNoBorder`, and `cbtExactFit`. For each instance, change the label field value to its respective `scaleMode` value: `showAll`, `noBorder`, or `exactFit`. Position these instances along the left edge of the document, as shown in Figure 20-5.

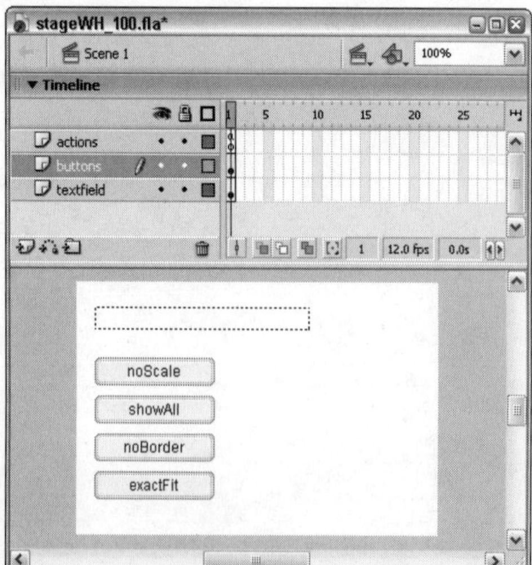

Figure 20-5: When each component instance is clicked, the label value will be set appropriately in the changeScale() function.

8. In order for the new component instances to work with the `changeScale()` method, the method must be registered as a listener of the `click` event for each instance. Select frame 1 of the actions layer, remove line 5, and add the new bold code shown in Listing 20-2.

   Here, an array named `aComponents` is created, containing references to each `Button` component instance (line 5). In lines 6–8, a `for` loop cycles through each element of the array, and adds the `changeScale()` method as a listener for the `click` event.

Listing 20-2: **Adding the changeScale() Method as a Listener**

```
1.  this.changeScale = function(oEvent:Object):Void {
2.     var sLabel:String = oEvent.target.label;
3.     Stage.scaleMode = sLabel;
4.  };
5.  var aComponents:Array = [cbtNoScale, cbtShowAll, cbtNoBorder, cbtExactFit];
6.  for(var i in aComponents){
7.     aComponents[i].addEventListener("click", this.changeScale);
8.  }
9.  this.onEnterFrame = function():Void {
10.   tOutput.text = "W = " + Stage.width + ", H = " + Stage.height;
11. };
```

9. Save the Flash document again, and publish preview the HTML document. Test the effect of each button, and resize the browser window. Notice that only the `"noScale"` mode reports the inner size of the browser window — all other modes simply report the width and height of the Flash movie as set in the Document Properties dialog box.

You can find the completed `stageWH_100.fla` document in the `ch20` folder of this book's CD-ROM.

Controlling the Movie's Alignment

In this section, you learn how to control the alignment of the Flash movie area by setting the value of the `align` property of the `Stage` class. You will add a `ComboBox` component instance to the movie, and use ActionScript to fill the combo box with the `align` property values shown in Table 20-1. Whenever the combo box is accessed, it will execute a function that sets the `align` property to the selected value.

Use the completed file from the previous lesson for this section. If you didn't complete the last section, make a copy of the `stageWH_100.fla` document located in the ch20 folder of this book's CD-ROM.

1. Create a new layer, and name it `combo box`. On this layer, drag an instance of the `ComboBox` component from the Component panel to the stage.

2. With the `ComboBox` instance selected, open the Property inspector. For this instance, you do not specify any information other than an instance name. You assign data to display in this combo box using ActionScript code. In the <***Instance Name***> field, type `ccbAlign`.

3. Now you add code to frame 1 of the actions layer. This code populates the ccbAlign instance with the values for the align property of the Stage class, and it sets up a function that the ccbAlign instance executes when one of these values is selected in the combo box. Select frame 1 of the actions layer. In the Actions panel, add the following code after the existing code:

```
this.changeAlign = function(oEvent:Object):Void {
   var sLabel = oEvent.target.text;
   Stage.align = sLabel;
};
var aAlign:Array = ["L","R","T","B","LT","LB","RT","RB","CC"];
ccbAlign.dataProvider = aAlign;
ccbAlign.addEventListener("change", this.changeAlign);
```

4. Save your Flash document as stageWH_101.fla, and publish preview the HTML document (File ➪ Publish Preview ➪ Default - (HTML)). When the movie loads in the Web browser, click the noScale button. Then, choose an align value in the combo box to change the alignment of the Flash movie within the area allocated to the Flash Player. You can choose CC to reset the movie to the center.

You can find the completed file, stageWH_101.fla, in the ch20 folder of this book's CD-ROM.

Method Overview of the Stage Class

The Stage class has two methods that are shared with many static classes, such as the Key, Mouse, Selection, and TextField classes: addListener() and removeListener(). Listener objects, as discussed throughout this book, enable specific objects to respond to events that are unique to an ActionScript class. For example, the Key class has an onKeyDown() listener method that can define what happens when a key is pressed. The Stage class can use a listener method, too: onResize(). You can use this listener method to detect when the window containing the Flash movie is resized.

Detecting a New Stage Size with the onResize() Method

The onResize() method can be assigned to a listener object that tells the Flash movie what to do when the movie is resized by the user. In order to make this listener object for the Stage class, you can create a new instance of the Object class:

```
var oStageListener:Object = new Object();
```

You can assign any name to this object, but it must then be assigned an onResize() method. For example, if you want to trace the new Stage.width and Stage.height values of a noScale Flash movie, you can define the following method for the oStageListener created previously:

```
oStageListener.onResize = function():Void {
  trace("W = " + Stage.width);
  trace("W = " + Stage.height);
};
```

After the object and method are defined, you can enable the listener by using the addListener() method of the Stage class, which is described next.

Applying a Listener with Stage.addListener()

This method takes a predefined listener object and adds it to the callback list for the `Stage` class. Essentially, this means that any time the event handler(s) defined in the listener object are detected, the `Stage` class responds by executing the function defined for the event handler. Because there is only one listener method, `onResize()`, for the `Stage` class, the only event that can be detected and assigned to the Stage class via `addListener()` is the act of resizing the window containing the Flash movie. To detect the act of resizing the window, you need to add the listener object:

```
Stage.addListener(oStageListener);
```

This code takes the `oStageListener` (and the `onResize()` method defined within it) and adds it to the `Stage` class. When the window containing the Flash movie is resized, the functions within the `onResize()` handler execute.

You can add multiple listener objects to a given class. For example, you can create two objects that have unique `onResize()` methods. You can then selectively add or remove these objects to the `Stage` class.

Disengaging a Listener with Stage.removeListener()

This method removes a listener object from the `Stage` class. The only argument necessary for this method is the name of the object with the `onResize()` callback method assigned to it—you do not need to delete the actual object itself. After a listener is removed, the listener method(s) stop responding to future events. The following code removes an object named `oStageListener` that has an `onResize()` handler defined:

```
Stage.removeListener(oStageListener);
```

In the next section, you learn how to apply a listener object to the `Stage` class.

Controlling Placement of Elements According to Stage Size

In this lesson, you learn how to dynamically change the position of a `MovieClip` object based on properties of the `Stage` class. Regardless of the browser window's size, the elements within the Flash movie dynamically move to the left edge of the browser window. As you learned earlier in this chapter, the same effect can essentially be accomplished by using the `align` property. However, the independent alignment of elements is demonstrated—one element moves, and another stays in a fixed position.

One of the benefits of using the `onResize()` method with a listener object is that it updates and executes ActionScript much more quickly than an `MovieClip.onEnterFrame()` method. The `onEnterFrame()` method was used in earlier examples.

You can view the completed example, `stageWH_200.swf`, in the `ch20` folder of the book's CD-ROM. If you did not complete the previous lesson in this chapter (`stageWH_101.fla`), make a copy of this Flash document to use in this lesson.

Complete the following steps using the `stageWH_101.fla` document created earlier in this chapter:

1. Nest the `Button` component instances and the `tOutput` text field on the stage into a new Movie Clip symbol named `menuClip`. Do not include the `ComboBox` instance. To do this, select the `Button` instances and the text field with the Selection tool (Shift-clicking to select multiple items at once). Press the F8 key to convert the items to a symbol. In the Convert to Symbol dialog box, name the symbol menu, choose the Movie Clip behavior, and click the top-left corner in the Registration icon (see Figure 20-6).

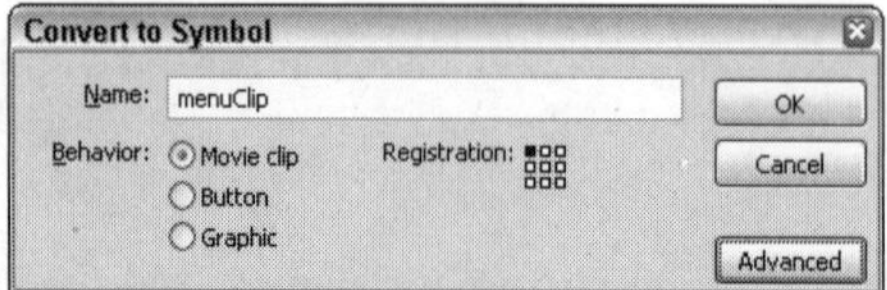

Figure 20-6: The Convert to Symbol dialog box

2. Select the new instance of the `menuClip` symbol on the stage, and assign the instance name of `mcMenu` in the Property inspector. Rename the buttons layer `mcMenu`, and delete the now empty text field layer.

3. Select frame 1 of the actions layer, and open the Actions panel. Select all of the code in the Script pane and copy it (Ctrl+C or ⌘+C). Then remove all of the code from the Script pane *except* for the following lines:

```
this.changeAlign = function(oEvent:Object):Void {
   var sLabel:String = oEvent.target.text;
   Stage.align = sLabel;
}
var aAlign:Array = ["L","R","T","B","LT","LB","RT","RB","CC"];
ccbAlign.dataProvider = aAlign;
ccbAlign.addEventListener("change", this.changeAlign);
```

4. Double-click the `mcMenu` instance on the stage. In this symbol's timeline, rename Layer 1 `objects`.

5. While within the timeline of the `menuClip` (`mcMenu`) symbol, create a new layer named `actions`. Select frame 1 of this layer and open the Actions panel (F9). In the Script pane, paste the code you copied in Step 3. Modify the code to reflect the bold code changes shown in Listing 20-3.

   In the section of code commented as Code Block #1, most of the changes to the existing `changeScale()` method are minor. The primary change is that the method resets the position of the `mcMenu` instance back to its original position. The original X and Y positions are stored in the variables `nStartX` and `nStartY`, respectively. These variables are declared and set in Code Block #4.

   Code Block #2 creates an `onResize()` method for the current instance, `this`. This method updates the `tOutput` text field with the current `width` and `height` of the `Stage` class. This value changes, depending on the `scaleMode` of the `Stage` class. The X and Y position of the `mcMenu` instance is then updated to align the instance with the top-left corner of the area allocated to the Flash Player. If the window containing the

Flash movie is larger than the original dimensions of the movie, these values are always negative—thus, placing them to the left of the actual movie area defined by the Document Properties.

Code Block #3, as shown in previous exercises of this chapter, assigns the `changeScale()` method as the callback handler for the `click` event of the `Button` component instances.

In Code Block #4, the code calculates the initial position of the `mcMenu` instance. Remember that in this lesson, you are moving an element, the `mcMenu` instance, to the left edge of the browser window, regardless of the window's size. If you want to reset the `mcMenu` instance back to its original position, you can refer to `nStartX` and `nStartY`.

Code Block #5 sets the `scaleMode` to `"showAll"` to get an accurate measure of the true width and height of the Flash movie. The `width` and `height` values of the `Stage` class (in `"showAll"` mode) are then stored in `nMovieWidth` and `nMovieHeight`, respectively.

Code Block #6 invokes the `onResize()` method as soon as the `mcMenu` instance loads.

Code Block #7 adds this current instance of `menuClip`, `mcMenu`, as a listener to the `Stage` class. Now, whenever the window containing the Flash movie is resized, the function defined for the `onResize()` method is executed. The `mcMenu` instance is dynamically placed in the top-left corner of the current window size.

Listing 20-3: Applying the onResize() Method

```
// Code Block #1: Callback handler for all Button component instances
this.changeScale = function(oEvent:Object):Void {
   var sLabel:String = oEvent.target.label;
   var mcOwner:MovieClip = oEvent.target._parent;
   Stage.scaleMode = sLabel;
   tOutput.text = "W="+Stage.width+", H="+Stage.height;
     mcOwner._x = nStartX;
     mcOwner._y = nStartY;
};

// Code Block #2: Callback handler for Stage resizing
this.onResize = function():Void {
   tOutput.text = "W=" + Stage.width + ", H=" + Stage.height;
   this._x = (nMovieWidth - Stage.width)/2;
   this._y = (nMovieHeight - Stage.height)/2;
};

// Code Block #3: Array of Button component instances
var aComponents:Array = [cbtNoScale, cbtShowAll, cbtNoBorder, cbtExactFit];
for(var i in aComponents){
   aComponents[i].addEventListener("click", this.changeScale);
```

Continued

Listing 20-3 *(continued)*

```
}

// Code Block #4: Store the initial position of this instance
var nStartX:Number = this._x;
var nStartY:Number = this._y;

// Code Block #5: Store the true size of the Flash movie
var sRemScale:String = Stage.scaleMode;
Stage.scaleMode = "showAll";
var nMovieWidth:Number = Stage.width;
var nMovieHeight:Number = Stage.height;
Stage.scaleMode = sRemScale;

// Code Block #6: Initiate onResize when the instance loads
this.onResize();

// Code Block #7: Add this instance to the Stage class
Stage.addListener(this);
```

6. Save your Flash document as `stageWH_200.fla`. Publish preview the HTML document by choosing File ⇨ Publish Preview ⇨ Default – (HTML). Click the noScale button to enable the corresponding `scaleMode`, and resize the browser window. The `mcMenu` instance snaps to the top-left corner of the window. The `ccbAlign` combo box, however, stays in its original position. (Use it as a gauge of the original movie stage area.)

You can find the completed Flash document, `stageWH_200.fla`, in the ch20 folder of this book's CD-ROM.

Removing a Listener Object from the Stage Class

In this section, you learn how to remove the listener from the Flash movie created in the previous section. You will add another Button component and create a function to remove the listener from the `Stage` class.

If you didn't complete the last section, make a copy of the `stageWH_200.fla` file located in the ch20 folder of this book's CD-ROM.

1. Double-click the `mcMenu` instance on the stage. Inside of this symbol, duplicate one of the existing `Button` component instances.

2. With the new instance selected, open the Property inspector. Rename the instance `cbtRemoveResize`. Change the label value to `Remove Resize`.

3. Select frame 1 of the actions layer. Open the Actions panel (F9) and add the following function to the existing code in the Script pane:

```
this.removeResize = function(oEvent:Object):Void {
  var mcOwner:MovieClip = oEvent.target._parent;
  Stage.removeListener(mcOwner);
};
cbtRemoveResize.addEventListener("click", this.removeResize);
```

The `removeResize()` method executes when the new `Button` instance is clicked. The `removeListener()` method is called for the `Stage` class, removing the current instance from the callback list.

4. Save the Flash document as `stageWH_201.fla` and publish preview the HTML document. Click the noScale button and then resize the window. When you click the Remove Resize button, the movie stops responding to any further resizing of the window.

You can find the completed file, `stageWH_201.fla`, in the ch20 folder of this book's CD-ROM.

Using the ContextMenu Class

ActionScript now gives you the power to control the menu items that are displayed in Flash Player 7's contextual menu. If you refer to Figures 20-2 and 20-3, you can see the menu control that the `Stage` class offers. Remember, you access this menu by right-clicking (or Control-clicking on Mac) the stage area of the Flash Player. With the `ContextMenu` class, not only can you control the built-in menu items such as Zoom, Play, and Rewind, but you can also add your own custom menu items, complete with caption names and custom ActionScript callback handlers. In this section, you learn how to precisely enable (or disable) built-in and custom menu items.

The `ContextMenu` and `ContextMenuItem` classes discussed in this section are new to Flash MX 2004 ActionScript. You can use these classes only with Flash Player 7–compatible movies.

The `ContextMenu` class can be used to attach specific context menus to various elements in your Flash movie, including `MovieClip`, `Button`, and `TextField` objects. Based on the previous paragraph, you might be wondering what the `ContextMenu` class offers over the `Stage.showMenu` property. If you can turn off the player's menu with `Stage.showMenu`, why do you need the `ContextMenu` class? The answer is twofold:

✦ With the `ContextMenu` class, you can *selectively* disable built-in player menu items with various items in your Flash movie. For example, if you want the built-in player menu items (Play, Zoom, Rewind, and so on) available in most areas of the movie but want those same items disabled on a specific piece of artwork (such a `MovieClip` object) in the movie, you can create a `ContextMenu` instance and assign it to that artwork.

✦ You can control your own custom menu items for the player's menu with the `ContextMenu` class. The `Stage` class does not enable you to control, add, or remove specific items in the menu.

As you learn in the following sections, the general process for using the ContextMenu class is as follows:

1. Create an instance of the ContextMenu class using the new constructor of the class.
2. Define the properties of the ContextMenu instance's built-in items using the ContextMenu.builtInItems property (optional).
3. Add your own menu items to the ContextMenu instance using one or more instances of the ContextMenuItem class (optional).
4. Define the callback handlers for the ContextMenu instance and/or ContextMenuItem instances (optional).
5. Assign the ContextMenu instance to a MovieClip, Button, or TextField instance, using the new menu property of those classes.

Controlling Flash Player's Built-in Menu

The builtInItems property of the ContextMenu class controls the display of the Flash Player's default context menu items, as shown in Figure 20-2 earlier in this chapter. The builtInItems property contains the subproperties described in Table 20-2. These subproperties can be set to true (display) or false (hide). By default, all properties have a value of true.

Table 20-2: Properties of the ContextMenu.builtInItems Property

Property	Displayed Name	Description
Save	Save	This menu item is available only in the Macromedia Shockmachine application and a special AOL-only version of the Flash Player. In these environments, the Save item enables you to save a copy of the Flash movie (a SWF file).
Zoom	Zoom In Zoom Out 100% Show All	These menu items enable the user to change the scale of the entire Flash movie. The zoom property controls all of the menu items related to the view.
Quality	Quality	This menu item enables the user to control the anti-aliasing of artwork within the movie. The quality property controls the Quality menu item and the Low, Medium, and High submenu items.
Play	Play	This menu item enables the user to initiate a play() command on the main timeline (_level0) of the Flash movie. This menu item is available only if there is more than one frame on the main timeline.
Loop	Loop	This menu item determines if playback of the Flash movie's main timeline (_level0) will repeat when the last frame is reached. This menu item is available only if there is more than one frame on the main timeline.

Property	Displayed Name	Description
`Rewind`	Rewind	This menu item enables the user to go back to the first frame of the Flash movie's main timeline (`_level0`). This menu item is available only if there is more than one frame on the main timeline.
`Forward_back`	Forward Back	These menu items are equivalent to issuing `nextFrame()` and `prevFrame()` actions, respectively, on the Flash movie's main timeline (`_level0`). These menu items are available only if there is more than one frame on the main timeline.
Print	Print	This menu item enables the user to print the current frame of the Flash movie.

If you want to disable all of these properties (thus hiding all of these menu items), you can use the `hideBuiltInItems()` method of the `ContextMenu` class.

In the following steps, you practice various uses of the `builtInItems` property.

1. Open a new Flash document and save it as `ContextMenu_builtInItems.fla`.
2. Rename Layer 1 `actions`.
3. Select frame 1 of the actions layer and open the Actions panel. Add the following code:

```
var cmMovie:ContextMenu = new ContextMenu();
cmMovie.builtInItems.zoom = false;
cmMovie.builtInItems.print = false;
this.menu = cmMovie;
```

This code adds a new `ContextMenu` instance named `cmMovie` (line 1). In lines 2 and 3, the `zoom` and `print` properties of the `builtInItems` property are set to `false`. In line 4, the `cmMovie` menu is then assigned to the main timeline (`this`), using the `MovieClip` class's `menu` property.

You can apply the same `ContextMenu` instance to multiple objects in your Flash movie.

4. Save your Flash document and test it. When you right-click (or Control-click on the Mac) the movie's stage area, only the Quality and Settings items should be enabled. The Zoom controls and the Print item will not be displayed (or enabled).

The Settings and About Flash Player 7 menu items are always displayed in any context menu. You cannot disable these menu items. If you are using the Debug version of the Flash Player, you will also always see the Debugger menu item.

5. Go back to frame 1 of the actions layer and change your code to the following:

```
var cmMovie:ContextMenu = new ContextMenu();
// cmMovie.builtInItems.zoom = false;
// cmMovie.builtInItems.print = false;
cmMovie.hideBuiltInItems();
this.menu = cmMovie;
```

Here, you use the `hideBuiltItItems()` method to disable and hide all of the default context menu items shown in Table 20-2.

6. Save your document as `ContextMenu_hideBuiltInItems.fla` and test it. When you right-click (or Control-click on the Mac) the stage, you should see only the Settings (and Debugger) menu items. If you test the movie in a Web browser, you should also see the About Flash Player 7 menu item.

You can find the `ContextMenu_builtInItems.fla` and `ContextMenu_hideBuiltInItems.fla` documents in the ch20 folder of this book's CD-ROM.

Building Custom Menu Items with the ContextMenuItem Class

If you want to add a new customized menu item to the Flash Player's context menu, you can use the `ContextMenuItem` class to define the item's name and functionality. When you decide that you need a custom menu item, you need to do the following:

1. Create a `ContextMenu` instance, as described in the earlier exercise.
2. Create a new `ContextMenuItem` instance.
3. Define the name of the menu item (the `caption` property) and the callback handler for the item. The callback handler is invoked when the user chooses the item from the menu.
4. Add the `ContextMenuItem` instance to the `ContextMenu` instance's `customItems` array. The `customItems` property is a built-in array of the `ContextMenu` class. Anytime you create a new `ContexMenu` instance, the `customItems` array is initially empty.
5. Assign the `ContextMenu` instance to the menu property of a `MovieClip`, `Button`, or `TextField` instance in your Flash movie.

In the last two sections, you learn how to build custom menu items using the `ContextMenuItem` and `ContextMenu` classes.

Adding a Reload Feature to a Flash Movie

In the following steps, you learn how to add a Reload item to the Flash Player's context menu. This menu item enables the user to reload the entire Flash movie, in order to reinitialize the movie. This functionality is different from the built-in Rewind control, which simply takes the Flash movie back to frame 1. If you have built dynamic elements with ActionScript, going to frame 1 does not necessarily remove such elements. For this exercise, you use an example file created in a previous chapter as a starting point.

Make a copy of the `Mouse_onMouseWheel_100.fla` and `clouds.jpg` files, located in the ch19 folder of this book's CD-ROM. This movie loads the `clouds.jpg` image into a `MovieClip` object and masks it. When you scroll the mouse wheel, the image pans underneath the mask.

To add a Reload item to the Flash movie:

1. Open the Mouse_onMouseWheel_100.fla document and resave it as ContextMenu_reload_100.fla.

2. Create a new layer and rename it context menu.

3. Select frame 1 of the context menu layer and open the Actions panel (F9). Add the code shown in Listing 20-4.

   In this code, you define an instance of the ContextMenu class and one instance of the ContextMenuItem class. In line 1, a variable named cmMain stores a reference to a new ContextMenu instance. In line 2, you hide the built-in items of the Flash Player's context menu.

   In lines 3–11, you define a custom menu item. Line 3 creates a variable named cmiReload, which is a new instance of the ContextMenuItem class. In line 4, you set the caption property to the name you want to appear in the context menu.

   In lines 5–11, you define the onSelect() handler for the cmiReload instance. The onSelect() handler is invoked whenever the user chooses this menu item in the context menu. The onSelect() handler is passed two arguments: a reference of the object to which the menu was attached (that is, the MovieClip, TextField, or Button instance that's assigned the menu, as shown in line 13), and a reference to the ContextMenuItem instance that defined the menu item. In this example, you use only the first argument, defined as mcObj. In line 6, the URL of the Flash movie is retrieved, using the _url property of the MovieClip object passed as a parameter to the onSelect() handler. In lines 7–9, you remove any existing _global variables in the Flash movie. In line 10, you reload the current Flash movie into Level 0.

   In line 12, you add the cmiReload instance to the customItems array of the cmMain instance. Remember, every ContextMenu instance has a customItems array. By using the push() method of the Array class, you add a reference to the cmiReload instance to this customItems array.

   In line 13, you assign the cmMain menu to the root of the movie (this), using the menu property of the MovieClip class.

Listing 20-4: **Adding a Reload Menu Item**

```
1.  var cmMain:ContextMenu = new ContextMenu();
2.  cmMain.hideBuiltInItems();
3.  var cmiReload:ContextMenuItem = new ContextMenuItem();
4.  cmiReload.caption = "Reload movie";
5.  cmiReload.onSelect = function(mcObj:MovieClip, cmiObj:ContextMenuItem):Void{
6.     var sMovieURL:String = mcObj._url;
7.     for(var i in _global){
8.        _global[i] = null;
9.     }
10.    loadMovieNum(sMovieURL, 0);
11. };
12. cmMain.customItems.push(cmiReload);
13. this.menu = cmMain;
```

4. Save your Flash document and test it. When you right-click the Flash movie's stage, you should see the Reload movie menu item, as shown in Figure 20-7. If you select this item, the movie will reload into the Flash Player.

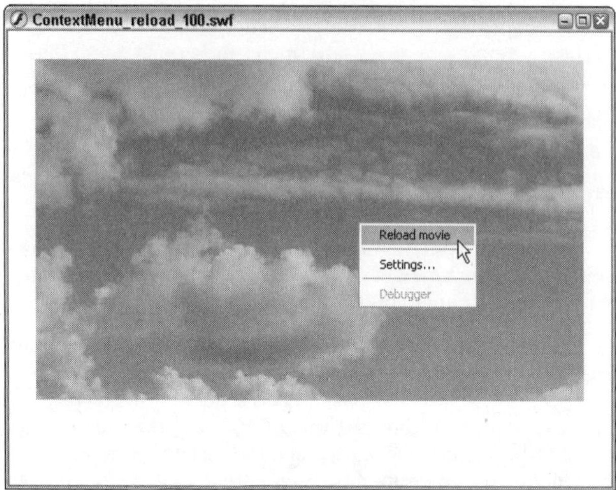

Figure 20-7: The Reload movie menu item

You can find the finished file, `ContextMenu_reload_100.fla`, in the `ch20` folder of this book's CD-ROM.

Manipulating Movie Elements with a Context Menu

In this section, you learn how to use more advanced features of the `ContextMenu` and `ContextMenuItem` classes. Using a Flash document from an earlier chapter, you add Duplicate and Remove menu items to `MovieClip` objects on the stage. Using the Flash Player's context menu, the user can make copies of the artwork, and reposition the copies to a different area on the stage. The user can also delete the copies with a context menu item selection.

Make a copy of the `heroColorMenu_starter.fla` file from the ch16 folder of this book's CD-ROM. This movie contains artwork of a cartoon character. You will enable this artwork with a customized context menu.

To add dynamic menu items to a Flash movie element, review and complete the following steps:

1. Open the `heroColorMenu_starter.fla` file and resave it as `ContextMenu_hero_100.fla`.

2. Delete the `buttons` layer. You do not need the button for this example.

3. Enable the heroClip symbol in the Library for export, so that you can attach the clip with ActionScript when the user chooses the Duplicate menu item from the context menu. Open the Library panel and right-click (or Control-click on the Mac) the heroClip symbol. Choose Linkage. In the Linkage Properties dialog box (see Figure 20-8), select the Export for ActionScript check box. The Identifier field will autofill with the term heroClip. Accept this default value by clicking OK.

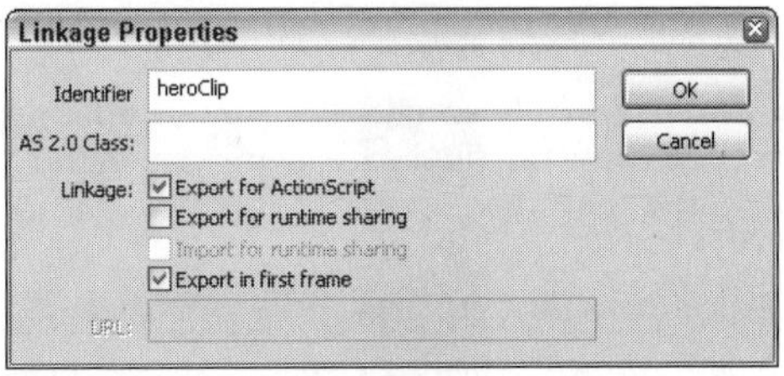

Figure 20-8: The Linkage Properties dialog box

Now you're ready to add the ActionScript code that creates the customized menu items. You'll take this one step at a time, so that you can see how each menu item is built.

4. Create a new layer and rename it actions.

5. Select frame 1 of the actions layer and open the Actions panel (F9). Add the code shown in Listing 20-5.

   In line 1, you create a new ContextMenu instance, named cmHero. In line 2, you hide the built-in menu items.

   In lines 3–6, you define a method named heroChange(). This method is used as the callback handler for all of the custom menu items. For now, you only create a couple of trace() actions to let you know that the handler is being invoked.

   In line 7, you create a new ContextMenuItem instance named cmiDuplicate. Here, you specify the item's caption and callback handler directly in the new constructor.

   In line 8, you add the cmiDuplicate instance to the customItems array of the cmHero instance.

   In line 9, you assign the cmHero instance to the mcHero instance (the MovieClip object on the stage), using the menu property.

Listing 20-5: **Defining the Duplicate Menu Item**

```
1.  var cmHero:ContextMenu = new ContextMenu();
2.  cmHero.hideBuiltInItems();
3.  this.heroChange = function(mcObj:MovieClip, cmiObj:ContextMenuItem){
4.     trace(">>> BEGIN heroChange(" + mcObj + ", " + cmiObj + ") >>>");
5.     trace("<<< END heroChange <<<");
6.  };
```

Continued

Listing 20-5 *(continued)*

```
var cmiDuplicate:ContextMenuItem = new ContextMenuItem("Duplicate", this.heroChange);
cmHero.customItems.push(cmiDuplicate);
mcHero.menu = cmHero;
```

6. Save your Flash document and test it. When you right-click (or Control-click on the Mac) the `mcHero` instance, you should see the Duplicate menu item in the context menu. If you choose this option, the `trace()` actions of the `heroChange()` method should appear in the Output panel.

7. Now you're ready to have the `heroChange()` method do something besides show `trace()` actions. Add the bold code shown in Listing 20-6.

   Lines 5 and 6 enable the movie to attach a new instance of the `heroClip` symbol to the stage. In line 5, an empty depth slot is retrieved. In line 6, a new instance of the symbol is named `mcHero_##`, where *##* indicates the current depth slot used. On the first copy, the name will be `mcHero_1`. On the second copy, the name will be `mcHero_2`, and so on.

   Lines 7–16 define `onPress()` and `onRelease()` handlers for the new instance. These handlers enable the new `MovieClip` object to be draggable.

Listing 20-6: Refining the heroChange() Method

```
1.  var cmHero:ContextMenu = new ContextMenu();
2.  cmHero.hideBuiltInItems();
3.  this.heroChange = function(mcObj:MovieClip, cmiObj:ContextMenuItem){
4.     trace(">>> BEGIN heroChange(" + mcObj + ", " + cmiObj + ") >>>");
5.     var nDepth:Number = mcObj._parent.getNextHighestDepth();
6.     var mcDupe:MovieClip = mcObj._parent.attachMovie("heroClip", "mcHero_" + nDepth.toString(), nDepth, {_x: mcObj._x + 20, _y: mcObj._y + 20});
7.     mcDupe.onPress = function():Void {
8.        this.startDrag();
9.        this.onMouseMove = function():Void {
10.          updateAfterEvent();
11.       };
12.    };
13.    mcDupe.onRelease = mcDupe.onReleaseOutside = function():Void {
14.       this.stopDrag();
15.       this.onMouseMove = null;
16.    };
17.    trace("<<< END heroChange <<<");
18. };
19. var cmiDuplicate:ContextMenuItem = new ContextMenuItem("Duplicate", this.heroChange);
20. cmHero.customItems.push(cmiDuplicate);
21. mcHero.menu = cmHero;
```

8. Save your Flash document and test it. Now, when you right-click the `mcHero` instance and choose Duplicate, a new instance of the hero artwork will appear on the stage, positioned 20 pixels down and to the right of the original instance. You can click and drag the new instance to a different position on the stage.

9. Now, let's add another feature: copying the existing context menu to the newly created `MovieClip` instance of the `heroClip` symbol. Add the bold code shown in Listing 20-7 to the code in frame 1 of the actions layer.

   Lines 17 and 18 use the `ContextMenu.copy()` method to make a duplicate of the `cmHero` instance for the new `MovieClip` object. In line 17, the `copy()` method is used to create an instance named `cmCopy`. In line 18, the new menu copy is assigned to the new `MovieClip` object's `menu` property.

You can truncate this code to one line, such as the following:

```
mcDupe.menu = mcObj.menu.copy();
```

Two lines of code are used in this example to more clearly illustrate the process, and, as you'll see in the next step, the process requires the extra line for additional control.

Listing 20-7: **Copying the ContextMenu Instance**

```
1.  var cmHero:ContextMenu = new ContextMenu();
2.  cmHero.hideBuiltInItems();
3.  this.heroChange = function(mcObj:MovieClip, cmiObj:ContextMenuItem){
4.     trace(">>> BEGIN heroChange(" + mcObj + ", " + cmiObj + ") >>>");
5.     var nDepth:Number = mcObj._parent.getNextHighestDepth();
6.     var mcDupe:MovieClip = mcObj._parent.attachMovie("heroClip",
         "mcHero_" + nDepth.toString(), nDepth, {_x: mcObj._x + 20,
         _y: mcObj._y + 20});
7.     mcDupe.onPress = function():Void {
8.        this.startDrag();
9.        this.onMouseMove = function():Void {
10.          updateAfterEvent();
11.       };
12.    };
13.    mcDupe.onRelease = mcDupe.onReleaseOutside = function():Void {
14.       this.stopDrag();
15.       this.onMouseMove = null;
16.    };
17.    var cmCopy:ContextMenu = mcObj.menu.copy();
18.    mcDupe.menu = cmCopy;
19.    trace("<<< END heroChange <<<");
20. };
21. var cmiDuplicate:ContextMenuItem = new ContextMenuItem("Duplicate",
      this.heroChange);
22. cmHero.customItems.push(cmiDuplicate);
23. mcHero.menu = cmHero;
```

10. The last feature you need to add to this context menu is a Remove menu item. The Remove item will delete the selected `MovieClip` object from the stage. Moreover, the Remove item should be available only on duplicates — it should not be an option enabled on the original `mcHero` instance. Add the bold code shown in Listing 20-8.

Jump down to lines 28–30 first. In line 28, you define a new `ContextMenuItem` instance for the Remove item. Its callback handler is also set to use the `heroChange()` method, so you need to add some logic to the `heroChange()` method to appropriately change the movie's stage.

In line 29, you set the `enabled` property of the `cmiRemove` instance to `false`. The `enabled` property of the `ContextMenuItem` class determines whether the user can select the item in the context menu. Do not confuse the `enabled` property with the visibility of the item itself. If `enabled` is set to `false`, the item is visible, but it is dimmed — the user cannot choose the item from the context menu. For the `mcHero` instance, you do not want the user to be able to delete the instance. Therefore, you set `enabled` to `false`. Later, you will see how `enabled` is set to `true` for *duplicates* of the `heroClip` symbol.

In line 30, instead of using the `push()` method of the `Array` class for the `customItems` array of the `cmHero` instance, you simply overwrite the array with your own array. The `[cmiDuplicate, cmiRemove]` syntax creates an array with the two `ContextMenuItem` instances.

Once you have added the new items to the `customItems` array, you're ready to add some logic to the `heroChange()` method. In line 5, you retrieve the `caption` property of the chosen menu item and use it as the value of the `sCaption` variable. In lines 6 and 22, this value is compared to the strings `"Duplicate"` and `"Remove"`, respectively. If the Duplicate item is chosen by the user, the code nested below the `if()` statement in line 6 will execute. If the Remove item is chosen, the code nested below the `else if()` statement in line 22 will execute.

In line 20, you set the `enabled` property of the second menu item (that is, the Remove item) to `true`. Remember, duplicates should have the Remove item enabled in the context menu. Because the Remove item was the second array element listed in line 29, you use the array index of 1 to address this menu item in the new duplicate.

In lines 22–24, you define the condition for the Remove item. If the `caption` property of the selected item is equal to `"Remove"`, line 23 will execute. This line uses the `removeMovieClip()` method of the `MovieClip` class to delete the selected instance from the stage.

Listing 20-8: **Adding the Remove Item to the Menu**

```
1.  var cmHero:ContextMenu = new ContextMenu();
2.  cmHero.hideBuiltInItems();
3.  this.heroChange = function(mcObj:MovieClip, cmiObj:ContextMenuItem){
4.     trace(">>> BEGIN heroChange(" + mcObj + ", " + cmiObj + ") >>>");
5.     var sCaption:String = cmiObj.caption;
6.     if(sCaption == "Duplicate"){
7.       var nDepth:Number = mcObj._parent.getNextHighestDepth();
```

```
    var mcDupe:MovieClip = mcObj._parent.attachMovie("heroClip",
      "mcHero_" + nDepth.toString(), nDepth, {_x: mcObj._x + 20,
      _y: mcObj._y + 20});
    mcDupe.onPress = function():Void {
      this.startDrag();
      this.onMouseMove = function():Void {
        updateAfterEvent();
      };
    };
    mcDupe.onRelease = mcDupe.onReleaseOutside = function():Void {
      this.stopDrag();
      this.onMouseMove = null;
    };
    var cmCopy:ContextMenu = mcObj.menu.copy();
    cmCopy.customItems[1].enabled = true;
    mcDupe.menu = cmCopy;
  } else if(sCaption == "Remove"){
    mcObj.removeMovieClip();
  }
  trace("<<< END heroChange <<<");
};
var cmiDuplicate:ContextMenuItem = new ContextMenuItem("Duplicate",
  this.heroChange);
var cmiRemove:ContextMenuItem = new ContextMenuItem("Remove",
  this.heroChange);
cmiRemove.enabled = false;
cmHero.customItems = [cmiDuplicate, cmiRemove];
mcHero.menu = cmHero;
```

11. Save your Flash document and test it. Right-click the `mcHero` instance on the stage and choose Duplicate. Notice that on the original `mcHero` instance, the Remove item is dimmed — you cannot choose it. Right-click the new duplicate, and you will see that the Remove item is now enabled. If you choose it, the new instance will be removed from the movie.

You can find the complete Flash document, `ContextMenu_hero_100.fla`, in the ch20 folder of this book's CD-ROM.

Some properties of the `ContextMenuItem` class are not covered by the examples in this chapter. To learn how to use additional and more advanced features of the `ContextMenu` and `ContextMenuItem` classes, go to `www.flashsupport.com/articles`. We'd also like to know what you thought about this chapter. Visit `www.flashsupport.com/feedback` to fill out an online form with your comments.

Summary

✦ Use the HTML options in the Publish Settings dialog box to understand the principles of dimensions, scale, and alignment before you attempt to use the `Stage` class and its properties and methods.

✦ The `Stage` class has five properties: `scaleMode`, `align`, `width`, `height`, and `showMenu`.

✦ The `Stage` class can utilize listener objects that have an `onResize()` handler defined.

✦ Using the `ContextMenu` and `ContextMenuItem` classes, you can control and customize the Flash Player's context menu. This feature enables you to add shortcuts and enhanced features to your movie's elements.

✦ ✦ ✦

CHAPTER 21

The System Class and the Capabilities and Security Objects

✦ ✦ ✦ ✦

In This Chapter

Working with top-level System class properties, methods, and events

Determining client system and player capabilities

Using the System.security object to allow cross-domain access to SWF content

✦ ✦ ✦ ✦

The `System` class is a static class that aggregates many types of functionality and information. The `System` class itself provides you with some rather disparate methods and properties, as well as an event-handler method. In addition, it provides you with access to a `capabilities` and a `security` object. The `capabilities` object returns information about the system on which the player is running. The `security` object provides you with the capability to allow cross-domain access to the SWF. This chapter looks at each of these topics in more detail.

The `System` class is a rather strange assortment of things. This chapter categorizes the discussion of the class as follows:

- Properties, methods, and event-handler methods accessed directly from the `System` class
- The `System.capabilities` object
- The System.security object

Using the Top-Level System Functionality

The `System` class provides you with a motley crew of two methods, two properties (not including the `capabilities` and `security` object references), and one event-handler method. Without further ado, let's look at each of these items.

Setting the Clipboard Contents

If you are authoring to Flash Player 7, you can use the `System.setClipboard()` method to assign a string value to the user's system Clipboard. The Clipboard is where content is normally placed when the user selects and copies some text. When the user chooses to paste text, the contents of the Clipboard are pasted into the focused area of the current application. However, using the `System.setClipboard()` method, you can programmatically replace the contents of the Clipboard without the user having to copy any text. The following example replaces the current Clipboard contents with a string: `Flash MX 2004`.

```
System.setClipboard("Flash MX 2004");
```

Showing the Flash Player Settings

The Flash Player has a Flash Player Settings panel, which you might not be familiar with. The panel opens in three ways:

- ✦ You can open the panel by right-clicking/⌘-clicking in the Player, as shown in Figure 21-1.
- ✦ The panel automatically opens in certain circumstances. For example, if the application is attempting to access the user's camera and/or microphone, the panel opens to ask the user to approve or decline the request.
- ✦ You can programmatically open the panel using the `System.showSettings()` method.

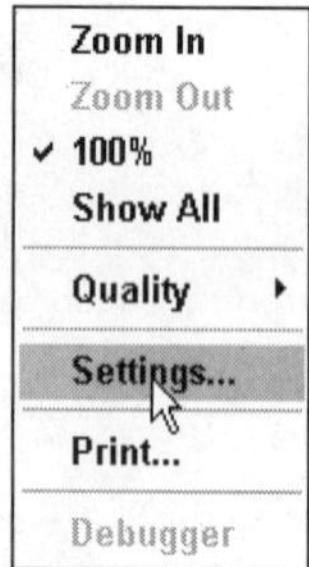

Figure 21-1: You can open the Settings panel from the context menu in the Flash Player.

The Flash Player Settings panel has four tabbed sections. Figure 21-2 shows the panel opened to the Local Storage section. In addition, there are the Privacy, Microphone, and Camera sections.

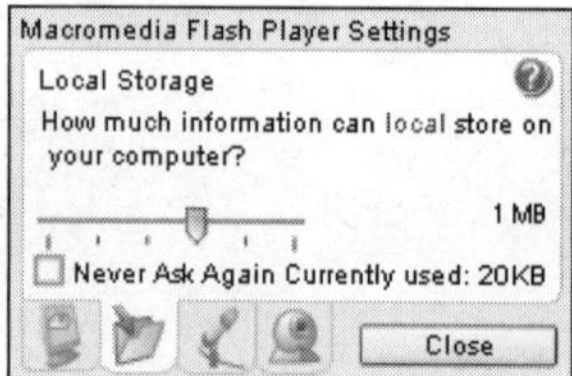

Figure 21-2: The Flash Player Settings panel has four sections; this is one.

The `System.showSettings()` method can be called with or without a parameter. If you call the method without a parameter, the panel opens to the section to which it had last been opened. However, you can also specify the section to which you want it to open by passing the method a numeric parameter. Here are the valid values:

✦ 0: Privacy

✦ 1: Local Storage

✦ 2: Microphone

✦ 3: Camera

For example, the following code tells Flash to open the panel to the Local Storage section.

```
System.showSettings(1);
```

Determining How Local Settings and Data Are Saved

The Flash Player saves some data locally to the client computer. For example, it can save information about whether or not the user has granted access to a microphone and/or camera. Local shared object data is stored to the client computer as well. These types of information are stored by domain. That means that the local settings and the local shared object data can be set for each domain without having to worry about conflicts.

However, in Flash Player 7, the changes to the sandbox security model spilled over into how local data is stored. By default, Flash Player 7 stores Flash 7 local content by exact domain. That means that, for example, `www.somedomain.com` and `staging.domsdomain.com` are treated as two different domains by which local data can be stored. You can use the `System.exactSettings` property to specify whether you want Flash to use the default Flash 7 behavior and save the data by the full, exact domain or save by *superdomain* (for example, `www.flashsupport.com` and `beta.flashsupport.com` share the superdomain of `flashsupport.com`), as Flash 6 content was saved. The default value for `System.exactSettings` is `true`. If you set the value to `false`, content is saved by superdomain. That means that Flash will save local data from `www.somedomain.com` and `staging.somedomain.com` both under the same superdomain, called simply `somedomain.com`.

Flash Player 7 uses a slightly different security model from earlier versions of the player. It requires exact domain-name matching by default, whereas the older security model matched only the superdomain.

If you do want to set `System.exactSettings` to `false`, you must do so before any local settings are accessed within the application. Therefore, you should typically set `System.exactSettings` on the first line of the first frame of the application if you want to set it to `false`. If you want to allow the default behavior, you don't need to do anything with the property.

Using Code Pages

Since Flash Player 6, Flash has supported Unicode. That means that it is much easier to display international and specialized text content to users than in previous versions. Earlier player versions did not support Unicode and instead rendered text using the code page of the user's operating system. That meant that the user had to have the same code page as the one used to author the text. Therefore, if the authoring system used a code page for the Japanese character set, the content would not correctly display on a system using the code page for English. Unicode text, on the other hand, can be correctly rendered without having to rely on the operating system's code page.

Because Flash Player 6 and Flash Player 7 support Unicode, you likely don't need to worry about the System.useCodePage property. As long as you are authoring content for these most recent players, just make sure that any text you load is saved as Unicode and it will display properly. However, if you want to have the text rendered based on the user's code page, you can set the System.userCodePage property to true (it is false by default).

Creating a Catch-All Status Handler

The Camera, Microphone, NetStream, LocalConnection, and SharedObject classes all have onStatus() event-handler methods to handle status messages. Each of the aforementioned status handlers works in the same way. When a status message is returned, the onStatus() method of the relevant class is called and passed a parameter that contains information about the status. Typically, you define the onStatus() method for a specific object. For example, you might attempt to create a local shared object named lsoData, and define an onStatus() method for that object in the following manner:

```
var lsoData:SharedObject = SharedObject.getLocal("settings");
lsoData.onStatus = function(oInfo:Object):Void {
  if(oInfo.code = "SharedObject.Flush.Failed") {
    // Display a message to the user.
    tOutput.text = "Failed to save data to local shared object.";
  }
};
```

However, if the onStatus() method is not defined for an object, and a status event is received, Flash will next look for a System.onStatus() method. The System.onStatus() method can be used as a catch-all for handling status events. You must define the System.onStatus() method. For example:

```
System.onStatus = function(oInfo:Object):Void {
  trace("status event received");
};
```

Determining the Client Computer's Capabilities

The System.capabilities object provides you with information about the computer running the Flash Player on the client. This type of information is particularly useful when you are authoring content that is to be played back on a variety of devices. You can use the information from the capabilities object to determine what content to load and how to display it. The following sections look at some of the information that the System.capabilities object can provide.

The System.capabilities object has a property named serverString. The serverString property contains URL-encoded name-value pairs such as the following:

```
A=t&SA=t&SV=t&EV=t&MP3=t&AE=t&VE=t&ACC=f&PR=t&SP=t&SB=f&DEB=
t&V=WIN%207%2C0%2C14%2C0&M=Macromedia%20Windows&R=1024x768&DP=
72&COL=color&AR=1.0&OS=Windows%20XP&L=en&PT=External&AVD=f&LFD=
f&WD=f
```

The serverString value is parsed by Flash and used to automatically populate the other properties that you'll see in the following sections. For example, in the preceding serverString example value, you can see that there is a parameter named V with a value of WIN%207%2C0%2C14%2C0. That value is used to populate the version property with a value of

WIN 7,0,14,0. Although you can work directly with the serverString value, you'll likely find the values that have been parsed into the other properties to be much more convenient.

Getting Audio and Video Capabilities

The System.capabilities object can return a lot of information about the audio and video capabilities on the client computer. Table 21-1 lists the audio and video-related properties of the System.capabilities object.

Table 21-1: Audio and Video Capabilities

Property	*Description*	*Example*	*Player Version*
avHardwareDisable	A Boolean value indicating whether the client computer's microphone and camera are enabled or disabled.	true	7
hasAudio	A Boolean value indicating whether the client computer has the hardware to play back audio. Does not detect whether the speakers are connected or turned on. Simply indicates hardware capabilities.	true	6
hasAudioEncoder	A Boolean value indicating whether the client computer has the capability to encode an audio stream. An audio stream is most frequently the sound from a microphone.	true	6
hasEmbeddedVideo	A Boolean value indicating whether the client computer can display embedded video.	true	6
hasMP3	A Boolean value indicating whether the client computer has the capability to decode MP3 sounds.	true	6
hasScreenBroadcast	A Boolean value indicating whether the client computer has the capability to broadcast the user's screen. Broadcasting the screen is a live video feature that requires Flash Communication Server.	true	6
hasScreenPlayback	A Boolean value indicating whether the client computer has the capability to play back a live screen broadcast.	true	6
hasStreamingAudio	A Boolean value indicating whether the client computer has the capability to play streaming audio.	true	6
hasStreamingVideo	A Boolean value indicating whether the client computer has the capability to play streaming video.	true	6
hasVideoEncoder	A Boolean value indicating whether the client computer has the capability to encode a video stream. Most often, the video stream is from a Web camera.	true	6

The audio and video capabilities properties can be useful to you when building applications that run on various environments. For example, if the client computer does not have audio capabilities, you likely will not want to have the user load audio content. Audio content can often be some of the most bandwidth-intensive content in an application, and you don't want to have users download that content if they cannot even play it. Therefore, using the `hasAudio` property, you can download the audio only if the users can play it. For example:

```
if(System.capabilities.hasAudio) {
  this.createEmptyMovieClip("mcSoundHolder", this.getNextHighestDepth());
  var sndAudio:Sound = new Sound(mcSoundHolder);
  sndAudio.onLoad = function():Void {
    this.start();
  };
  sndAudio.load("audio.mp3");
}
```

The other audio and video capabilities properties can be used similarly to optimize your application.

Determining Versions

The `System.capabilities` object provides information about player and operating system versions. Table 21-2 shows these properties.

Table 21-2: Version Properties

Property	*Description*	*Example*	*Player Version*
`os`	A string indicating the operating system on the client computer.	`Windows XP`	6
`version`	A string indicating the player version, including revision number.	`WIN 7,0,14,0`	6
`manufacturer`	A string indicating the manufacturer of the player.	`Macromedia Windows`	6
`language`	A string indicating the language used by the client computer. The value is composed of a lowercase two-character language code from ISO 639-1. Optionally, the value can be further specified using an uppercase two-character country code from ISO 3166.	`true`	6
`isDebugger`	A Boolean value indicating whether the player is the debugger version.	`true`	6
`hasAccessibility`	A Boolean value indicating whether the player can communicate with accessibility software.	`true`	6r65 (Player 6, revision 65)

Property	*Description*	*Example*	*Player Version*
`hasPrinting`	A Boolean value indicating whether the player supports printing.	`true`	6
`playerType`	A string indicating the player type. The value is one of the following: `StandAlone`, `External`, `ActiveX`, or `PlugIn`.	`StandAlone`	7
`localFile ReadDisable`	A Boolean value indicating whether the player has access to read content from the local file system.	`true`	7

Determining versions can be potentially useful in a variety of situations. Some features are known to work incorrectly or unpredictably on some operating systems, for example. By detecting the operating system, you can help ensure that you can properly handle such occurrences.

Determining the language used by the client computer can assist you in providing multilingual content. For example, you might have text stored in external files—perhaps one file per language. You can then use the language property to determine which text to load and ultimately display to the users. The following code demonstrates how that might work:

```
var lvText:LoadVars = new LoadVars();
lvText.onData = function(sText):Void {
  tContent.text = sText;
};
switch (System.capabilities.language) {
  case "es":
    lvText.load("copy_spanish.txt");
    break;
  case "ja":
    lvText.load("copy_japanese.txt");
    break;
  default:
    lvText.load("copy_english.txt");
}
```

For more information on ISO 639-1 codes, see `www.loc.gov/standards/iso639-2/englangn.html`.

Getting Screen and Resolution Information

The screen and resolution information properties provided by the `System.capabilities` object are listed in Table 21-3. You can use these properties to ensure that you are displaying the proper content in an optimized format for the viewer's display.

Table 21-3: Screen and Resolution Properties

Property	*Description*	*Example*	*Player Version*
`pixelAspectRatio`	A number indicating the pixel aspect ratio. Most desktop systems report `1`. Other devices can have different aspect ratios.	`1`	6
`screenColor`	A Boolean value indicating whether the screen supports color.	`true`	6
`screenDPI`	A number indicating the dots per inch of the screen.	`72`	6
`screenResolutionX`	A number indicating the horizontal resolution of the screen.	`1024`	6
`screenResolutionY`	A number indicating the vertical resolution of the screen.	`768`	6

To give you an example of how you might use some of these properties, consider a scenario in which you have published several versions of your application to the same URL. Each version is intended for a different device (because these various devices have very different resolutions). The following code shows an example of how you can use the `screenResolutionX` and `screenResolutionY` properties to detect the type of device and display the correct version.

```
var nScreenWidth:Number = System.capabilities.screenResolutionX;
var nScreenHeight:Number = System.capabilities.screenResolutionY;

if (nScreenWidth >= 640 && nScreenHeight >= 480) {
  // Direct probable desktop users to the main movie.
  this.gotoAndStop("mainmovie");
} else if (nScreenWidth == 640 && nScreenHeight == 200) {
  // Load fullscreen Nokia movie which is 640x200.
  this.getURL("nokia_full.swf", "_blank");
} else if (nScreenWidth == 463 && nScreenHeight == 200) {
  // Load regular Nokia movie which is 463x200.
  this.getURL("nokia_reg.swf", "_blank");
} else {
  // Catch-all for all other possible resolutions. Just
  // direct them to the desktop user content.
  this.gotoAndStop("mainmovie");
}
```

Working with Player Security When Loading SWF Content

The Flash Player has sandbox security that prevents an SWF on one domain from loading and then having access to the data within or the properties and methods of the loaded SWF. The security model changed somewhat between Flash Player 6 and Flash Player 7. Previously,

Flash disallowed access only between two completely different superdomains, but allowed access between two different subdomains and/or protocols within the same superdomain. For example, Flash Player 6 would allow a Flash application at `https://secure.somedomain.com` to load and have access to an SWF at `http://www.somedomain.com`. In Flash Player 7, the domains must match exactly—including subdomain and protocol.

Although the default security restrictions prevent you from being able to fully load SWF content across domains, subdomains, and protocols, the `System.security` object enables you to modify some settings that will allow you to grant access to an SWF. The `allowDomain()` and `allowInsecureDomain()` methods provide you with the necessary functionality.

If you want to specify that another domain and/or subdomain (using the same protocol) should be able to load and use the data from an SWF file, you should use the `allowDomain()` method. The method should be placed within the first frame of the SWF that you want to load. It allows you to specify a list of parameters indicating locations from which you want the SWF to be accessible. The parameters should be string values, and they can be in the following formats:

✦ *domainName* (for example, `www.flashsupport.com`)

✦ *protocol://domainName* (for example, `http://www.flashsupport.com`)

✦ *protocol://IPAddress* (for example, `http://123.456.78.9`)

Because the Flash Player 7 model differs slightly from the Flash Player 6 model, the use of the `allowDomain()` method is slightly different. For example, previously the following code would allow any SWF in the `flashsupport.com` domain to load the SWF and have access to its data:

```
System.security.allowDomain("flashsupport.com");
```

However, with the Flash Player 7 model, the preceding code allows access from SWF files being served from `flashsupport.com`, but not from `www.flashsupport.com`, `beta.flashsupport.com`, and so on. With Flash Player 7, you must supply the complete domain name, including subdomain. Therefore, if you want to allow access from both `flashsupport.com` and `www.flashsupport.com`, your code needs to look like the following:

```
System.security.allowDomain("flashsupport.com", "www.flashsupport.com");
```

You can choose to use the `System.exactSettings` property as discussed earlier in this chapter to allow non-exact domain matching.

Although it presents a security risk, you might want to sometimes grant access for an application running over regular HTTP to load and have access to an SWF being served from HTTPS. In order to accomplish that, you cannot simply use the `allowDomain()` method. Instead, you need to use the `allowInsecureDomain()` method. Otherwise, the two methods operate similarly. You can specify one or more domains to which you want to grant access as parameters for the `allowInsecureDomain()` method:

```
System.security.allowInsecureDomain("flashsupport.com", "www.flashsupport.com");
```

We'd like to know what you thought about this chapter. Visit `www.flashsupport.com/feedback` to fill out an online form with your comments.

Summary

- The `System` class is a static class that aggregates many properties and methods, including the `capabilities` and `security` objects.
- The top-level properties, methods, and events of the `System` class include properties for determining code page use and domain-name matching, methods for setting the Clipboard contents and opening the Flash Player Settings panel, and an event-handler method for handling status messages issued by various other classes.
- The `capabilities` object reports information about the client computer system and player, including information about the operating system, player version, and various player capabilities ranging from accessibility to audio, to language.
- The `security` object provides you with the capability to have one SWF grant access so that other SWFs on other domains, subdomains, and protocols can load the SWF and have access to its data.

✦ ✦ ✦

CHAPTER 22

The PrintJob Class

In This Chapter

Controlling print output

Avoiding problems with print functionality

Optimizing artwork for grayscale printers

Printing multiple pages of text

Although the majority of this book focuses on getting your code to control objects and variables that affect the on-screen representation of your Flash movie, this chapter shows you what ActionScript can do with your printer — or the printers of those people who view your Flash movies over the Web. With ActionScript, you can control what portions of your movie are printable, and you can even specify the way those portions print.

Flash MX 2004 introduces an entirely new class, called `PrintJob`, designed exclusively to enhance the printing capabilities of Flash Player 7.

This chapter does not cover the now deprecated `print()` and `printAsBitmap()` functions. These functions are compatible with Flash Player 4, 5, and 6. For more information on these functions, see the archived chapter "Printing with the Flash Player," from the previous edition of this book, at `www.flashsupport.com/archive`.

Why Print from Flash?

You're probably wondering why you would want, let alone need, to print from a Flash movie. Besides, aren't the Internet and digital data all about a paperless society? Well, some things are still better printed, such as driving maps (until everyone has Pocket PCs with GPS units), coupons, and purchase receipts. In this section, you explore some printing features that work with Flash movies.

Problems with Web Browser Printing

Most Web browsers simply can't print *any* plug-in content. Some browsers print a gray area where the plug-in content should be, or they leave it empty. Therefore, if you do want to print from the Flash Player plug-in, you should use ActionScript's `PrintJob` class to do the work. You'll learn the specifics of the `PrintJob` class later in this chapter.

It can be difficult to predict how regular HTML Web pages print, even with traditional layouts without plug-in content. Each browser defines page margins differently, and prints unique header and footer information. Have you ever gone to a Web site that offers driving directions, and printed a map that just barely bled off the edge of the printed version? You can avoid frustrating situations such as this by using the print capabilities of Flash Player 7, which gives you a greater degree of control of the printable area of your movie's content. You can define what area of the stage prints for each frame, if necessary. More importantly, though, you can control the relationship of the Flash movie's stage size to the printed size.

Of course, you also have the normal benefits of using Flash for any type of output, whether it is for the computer screen or the printed page:

✦ **Embedded fonts:** Although many Web pages use the same Web fonts, such as Verdana or Georgia, you can design Flash movies that use whatever fonts you want your visitors to see. These fonts can be used on printed output from Flash movies as well.

✦ **Easy and precise layout tools:** You can create Flash artwork and elements very easily; and place the content without using frames, tables, and DHTML layers.

✦ **Incredibly small file sizes:** Compared to equivalent Acrobat PDF files or HTML pages, Flash movies with graphics and text intended for print can download very quickly. The native vector format of Flash movies makes them ideal for printing anything with logo and branding elements.

With these exceptional features in mind, you explore some potential uses of Flash's printing capabilities in the remainder of this section.

Providing Proof with Printing

Perhaps the best and most practical reason to enable printing from the Flash Player is to provide some form of a receipt to visitors who purchase goods or services from your Flash-enabled Web site. Maybe you want to be able to print the results of an online test so they can be handed over to a department manager or instructor. We still live in a society in which the need for hard copy proof exists — databases can crash, network connections may be unavailable or slow, and e-mails are lost or deleted. In most situations, it's usually a good idea to have a hard copy "backup," just in case everything else fails.

Creating Art with Output

Just as our society likes to have lots of paper documents to store in filing cabinets, we also like material possessions. Getting an e-mail message with a gift certificate is not quite the same as receiving a printed card in the mail with the same information. Still pervasive is the perception that something printed on "real" paper — instead of an ephemeral display on the computer monitor — is inherently worth more than its virtual equivalents.

One of the best uses for Flash printing is outputting drawings or artwork made within Flash movies. Maybe you made a drawing application with a Flash movie. Wouldn't it be nice to print a hard copy of your drawings? Maybe you have a mini-portfolio of company logos that you designed. Using the `PrintJob` class, you can print each of your portfolio samples to a separate page. Another fun example of Flash printing is to create a Flash animation flipbook. You can print each frame of a tweened or frame-by-frame animation to a piece of paper. After all the frames are printed, you can bind the pages to create a flipbook to thumb through.

Expanding the Potential of Small Documents

A final consideration can be given to the radical notion that Flash movies can be a reasonable substitute for Adobe Acrobat PDF documents. Seem far-fetched? Well, with embedded fonts and precision layout, Flash movies can offer many of the same features that PDF documents do. Here are some differences between Flash movies and PDF documents:

✦ PDF files are an industry standard for printable documents on the Web. Just about every major company on the Web, from Macromedia to Sony, provides downloadable and printable information in the PDF format.

✦ PDF files have a more standardized structure than Flash movies. For example, PDF files can have a table of contents (Bookmarks) that does not require the content developer to invent his or her own system of indexing. Creating an index of a printable Flash movie involves much more time and planning.

✦ Some search engines such as Google.com can index (and therefore search) the content of PDF files on the Web. As of this writing, such services for Flash movies are not as developed.

✦ Several Web sites (including this book's publisher) use server-side technology that can convert PDF documents to HTML pages on the fly. Because PDF files have a standard structure, these server-side applications to render HTML layouts are very similar to the PDF original. The Adobe Document Server is just one of several applications that create such HTML documents from PDF files.

✦ The Adobe Reader application and plug-in are much larger downloads (in excess of 8MB!) than the Flash Player plug-in.

✦ The full version of Adobe Acrobat installs the Acrobat PDFWriter or Distiller printer driver, which enables you to print just about any document (for example, Microsoft Word documents) to a PDF file. No printer driver exists yet to create SWF files from applications with File ⇨ Print capabilities.

For a Flash printing driver to exist, there needs to be a standardized method of formatting Flash movies intended to be used in this fashion. For example, does each page create a new frame on the main timeline of the SWF file? Does it make a custom Movie Clip with specific parameters? There also needs to be a standard approach to utilizing such SWF files in your own Flash movies. That means there would be predefined ActionScript custom functions and interface widgets to load, view, and print these documents. This would be akin to a Flash Reader (instead of an Acrobat Reader). It's quite possible that *you* could develop a Flash projector that opens and prints these Flash-printable documents.

In 2003, Macromedia released a new feature in its product, Contribute 2. Contribute provides Web site creators (or people responsible for maintaining Web pages) with the capability to make FlashPaper documents. Contribute 2, currently available only for Windows 2000 and XP, installs a printer driver that can output documents to the Flash SWF format. These documents can be viewed and printed with Flash Player 6. For more information, see `www.macromedia.com/software/contribute/productinfo/flashpaper`.

What kind of content might you want to make available as Flash-printable documents? Maybe a camera manufacturer such as Nikon wants you to develop a Flash ad that features its newest camera, complete with exciting animations of the product and its capabilities. You could also propose to create a technical datasheet that prints a multipage document of all of the camera's specifications, complete with diagrams and accessories. This scenario is something you can create using the `PrintJob` class and a hidden `MovieClip` instance.

If any of these examples sound exciting to you or you have your own unique vision of Flash printing, the next section explains the specifics of ActionScript's `PrintJob` class.

Caution

Many of the examples in this chapter, when tested, attempt to send output to your printer. If you don't want to waste paper, ink, or toner, you might want to enable a print driver such as the Adobe Acrobat PDFWriter or Acrobat Distiller to create virtual documents that enable you to preview the printed output without actually sending output to a physical printer.

Controlling Printer Output from Flash

Flash MX 2004 ActionScript adds a new class, `PrintJob`, to the language. With `PrintJob`, you can define how pages are constructed and sent to the printer. This section describes each of the methods and properties of the `PrintJob` class, collectively known as the `PrintJob` API (*a*pplication *p*rogramming *i*nterface), and explains how each works. If you want to see the `PrintJob` API in action, continue to the next section, "Adding Print Functionality to Movies," as well.

Overview of the PrintJob Class

On the surface, there isn't too much to the `PrintJob` class. In fact, there are only three methods for the class. To create a new instance of the `PrintJob` class, you use the `new` constructor:

```
var pjOutput:PrintJob = new PrintJob();
```

You do not specify any arguments with the `new` constructor. Once you have a `PrintJob` object, you initiate the three methods of the object, in the following order:

✦ **start():** This method opens the Print dialog box on the user's operating system. If the user clicks the Print (or OK) button in the Print dialog box, the method returns a `true` value. If the user cancels the dialog box, the method returns a `false` value. You should use the other two methods only if the `start()` method returns a `true` value.

✦ **addPage():** This method tells the `PrintJob` object which `MovieClip` object to print from your Flash movie. You can invoke several `addPage()` methods. Each method call will add one page to the printer's output. This method uses several complex arguments, which are discussed in the following sections.

✦ **send():** This method finalizes the output and sends the data to the printer's spooler.

Once you have sent the output to the printer with the `send()` method, it's usually a good idea to delete the `PrintJob` object that was created with the `new` constructor. Let's take a closer look at the `start()` and `addPage()` methods.

Retrieving the User's Page Settings with PrintJob.start()

When you initiate a `PrintJob` instance with the `start()` method, you can determine the page settings that the user has prescribed in the Print dialog box. If the user clicks OK in the Print dialog box, the Flash movie will receive information about the page size and orientation that the user has chosen.

The following properties are set on the `PrintJob` object if the user clicks OK to a Print dialog box initiated from a Flash movie. Some of the properties use a unit of measurement called a *point,* abbreviated as *pt*. There are 72 points to one inch.

✦ **paperHeight:** This property returns the height (in points) of the paper size that the user has selected. For example, if the user has selected a paper size of 8.5" × 11", `paperHeight` returns a value of 792 points (11" × 72 pt/inch = 792 pt).

✦ **paperWidth:** This property returns the width (in points) of the paper size that the user has selected. Using the previous example, an 8.5" × 11" paper size returns a `paperWidth` value of 612 points.

✦ **pageHeight:** Perhaps the more useful of the height-based properties, the `pageHeight` property returns the height (in points) of actual printable area. Most printers can print to only a certain portion of the paper size, leaving a margin around the edges of the paper. For example, on an 8.5" × 11" piece of paper, most printers can print only an area sized 8.17" × 10.67". If you are trying to size output to the page, you should use this property over `paperHeight`.

✦ **pageWidth:** As mentioned with the `pageHeight` property, this property is likely to be more useful to you than the `paperWidth` property. This property returns the width (in points) of the actual printable area on the paper.

The datatype of all width and height properties is `Number`.

✦ **orientation:** This property returns a string value of either `"portrait"` or `"landscape"`, based on the user's setting in the Print dialog box. The width and height properties will simply flip-flop from one orientation to the next.

In the following steps, you test the values of these properties with your printer. Note that you need to have at least one printer driver installed on your system in order to complete this example.

Make a copy of the `PrintJob_props_starter.fla` document from the `ch22` folder of this book's CD-ROM. You'll need this file to begin the exercise. The starter document contains a `Button` component instance named `cbtPrint`.

1. Open the starter document and save it as `PrintJob_props_100.fla`.
2. Create a new layer and rename it `actions`.
3. Select frame 1 of this layer and open the Actions panel (F9). Add the code shown in Listing 22-1 to the Script pane.

   In lines 1–12, you define a `startPrint()` method, which is used as a listener method for the `click` event generated by the `cbtPrint` instance (line 13). The `startPrint()` method's purpose is to show you the properties and values set on a `PrintJob` object based on the outcome of the `PrintJob.start()` method.

   In line 2, an initial `trace()` action is invoked, letting you know that the following output is generated by the `startPrint()` handler. In line 3, a `PrintJob` object named `pjOutput` is created.

   In line 4, a variable named `bPrintInit` stores the value of the `start()` method after it is invoked. As soon as the Flash Player executes the `start()` method, the movie is disabled while the Print dialog box opens for the user. If the user clicks the Print (or OK) button in the Print dialog box, the value of `bPrintInit` is set to `true`, and the `PrintJob` page properties are set. If the user cancels the dialog box, the value of `bPrintInit` is set to `false`. The value of the `bPrintInit` variable is sent to the Output panel in line 5.

In lines 6–10, a `for in` loop iterates over the `pjOutput` instance. Remember, if the user clicks OK in the Print dialog box, all of the page properties will be set. In lines 7 and 8, backslash pairs for tab characters are determined, to more cleanly format the text sent to the Output panel (you'll see what this does in just a moment). In line 9, each property of the `pjOutput` instance is read and sent to the Output panel.

Listing 22-1: Defining a Listener for the cbtPrint Instance

```
1.  this.startPrint = function(oEvent:Object):Void {
2.     trace(">>> BEGIN startPrint() >>>");
3.     var pjOutput:PrintJob = new PrintJob();
4.     var bPrintInit:Boolean = pjOutput.start();
5.     trace("\tbPrintInit:\t\t" + bPrintInit);
6.     for(var i:String in pjOutput){
7.        var nPropLen:Number = i.length;
8.        var sTabSuffix:String = nPropLen <= 10 ? ":\t\t" : ":\t";
9.        trace("\t" + i + sTabSuffix + pjOutput[i]);
10.    }
11.    trace("<<< END startPrint() <<<");
12. };
13. cbtPrint.addEventListener("click", this.startPrint);
```

4. Save your document and test the movie (Ctrl+Enter or ⌘+Enter). Click the Print button in the Flash movie. The first `trace()` action (line 2 in Listing 22-1) is sent to the Output panel, and the Print dialog box opens, as shown in Figure 22-1. If you click the Print (or OK) button in the dialog box, the Flash movie resumes playback and outputs the properties of the printer's page size in the Output panel. For example, with a Hewlett-Packard LaserJet 8100 DN using a standard 8.5" × 11" paper size, the Output panel will display the following:

   ```
   >>> BEGIN startPrint() >>>
      bPrintInit:     true
      orientation:    portrait
      pageWidth:      588
      pageHeight:     768
      paperWidth:     612
      paperHeight:    792
   <<< END startPrint() <<<
   ```

   If you retest the movie and click the Cancel button in the Print dialog box, you will see the following text in the Output panel:

   ```
   >>> BEGIN startPrint() >>>
      bPrintInit:     false
   ```

```
   orientation:   undefined
   pageWidth:     undefined
   pageHeight:    undefined
   paperWidth:    undefined
   paperHeight:   undefined
<<< END startPrint() <<<
```

Because the request to print was cancelled, the `bPrintInit` variable was set to `false`. All of the properties in the `PrintJob` object remain `undefined` as a result.

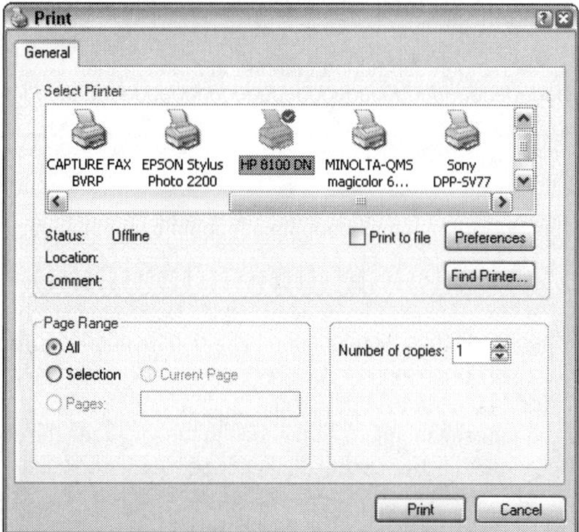

Figure 22-1: A sample Print dialog box from Windows XP

You can find the completed document, `PrintJob_props_100.fla`, in the `ch22` folder of this book's CD-ROM.

Try testing other paper sizes (or printers) with this Flash movie, to see how the values will change in the Output panel. Now that you understand how the `start()` method and `PrintJob`'s properties work, you're ready to learn how to tell ActionScript how to send Flash artwork to the printer.

Determining the Print Target and Its Formatting Options

Perhaps the more difficult aspect of Flash printing involves using the `PrintJob.addPage()` method. The `addPage()` method uses the following syntax, where `pjOutput` represents a `PrintJob` instance:

```
pjOutput.addPage(mcTarget, oPrintArea, oPrintOptions, nFrame);
```

The parameters are as follows:

✦ **mcTarget:** The `MovieClip` object that you want to print. You can also pass a Level number to print. For example, passing the number 0 prints the main timeline (`_root`) of Level 0. This parameter is *required.*

✦ **oPrintArea:** An `Object` instance whose properties determine the margins of the printable target. This parameter is optional; if it is omitted or incorrectly specified, the entire stage of the target clip (or Level) is printed. The `Object` instance, if specified, must contain all four of the following properties:

- **xMin:** The top-left coordinate of the left margin
- **xMax:** The top-right coordinate of the right margin
- **yMin:** The bottom-left coordinate of the left margin
- **yMax:** The bottom-right coordinate of the right margin

The print area's coordinates are determined from the registration point of the target timeline you are printing.

✦ **oPrintOptions:** An `Object` instance that determines how the target's contents are sent to the printer. By default, all contents are sent as vector artwork. This parameter is optional. The `Object` instance has only one property, `printAsBitmap`. This property uses a `Boolean` value. If the property is set to `true`, the artwork is rendered as a bitmap and then sent to the printer. If the property is set to `false`, the artwork is rendered in vectors and then sent to the printer. See the sections titled "Printing Targets as Vectors" and "Printing Targets as Bitmaps" for more information.

✦ **nFrame:** The frame number of the target clip (or Level) to print. If you want to print a specific frame of the target, you can use this optional parameter. If you omit this parameter, the current frame of the target is printed. Note that any ActionScript code on the specified frame will not be executed. As such, if you have any code that you want to affect the look of your printed target, you should make sure that code is invoked before using the `addPage()` method.

You apply these parameters in later examples of this chapter. In the next sections, you learn more specifics of the `addPage()` parameters and how they affect the printed output from the Flash movie.

Printing Targets as Vectors

The `printAsBitmap` property of the `oPrintOptions` parameter should be set to `false` strictly when you are printing the following vector artwork elements in a `MovieClip` object or Level, including the main timeline (`_root`):

✦ Text contained within Static, Dynamic, or Input text fields

✦ Artwork created with Flash tools, or imported from an illustration application such as Macromedia FreeHand or Adobe Illustrator

✦ Symbol instances *without* any alpha, brightness, tint, or advanced color effects. If you've used the Color menu options in the Property inspector for an instance, you've automatically ruled out using `printAsBitmap` set to `false`. (This rule also applies to instances that have been manipulated with the `Color` object in ActionScript code.)

If your Flash content is limited to these considerations, you can safely set printAsBitmap to false to print high-quality output. If the output is directed to a high-quality printer, all lines and artwork print "clean," with very smooth edges.

Any alpha or color settings for symbol instances or artwork are ignored when the printAsBitmap property is set to false. Bitmap images also print with more aliasing (that is, rough, pixelated edges) if printAsBitmap is set to false. When set to false, printAsBitmap also fills alpha channels of any bitmap images with solid white.

Printing Targets as Bitmaps

The printAsBitmap property should be set to true when you are using a variety of sources for your artwork and content. If you have a Flash movie with a mixture of the elements listed in the previous section *and* the following items, you should set printAsBitmap to true in the addPage() method:

- ✦ Symbol instances using alpha, brightness, tint, or advanced color effects. If you have used the Property inspector or a Color object in ActionScript to modify the appearance of a symbol instance, you should set printAsBitmap to true.
- ✦ Artwork or symbol instances containing imported bitmap images. Although bitmap images can be printed with printAsBitmap set to false, they appear sharper when printed with the printAsBitmap set to true. More important, bitmap images with alpha channels print correctly if the transparent areas of the alpha channel overlap other artwork.

What happens to vector artwork (including text) that is printed with the printAsBitmap property set to true? The true setting still prints vector artwork, but it won't be as crisp as artwork outputted with the false setting. However, you might find the differences between true and false settings with vector artwork negligible—if you're ever in doubt, test your specific artwork with both settings and compare the output. The true setting is usually the safest bet if you are using bitmap images and any alpha or color effects.

Colors with alpha settings in the Color Mixer panel used as fills or strokes print perfectly fine with the true setting but not with the false setting.

Controlling the Printable Area of the Target

Perhaps the most difficult concept to grasp with the addPage() method is how the mcTarget is sized to the printed page. Unlike the deprecated print() and printAsBitmap() functions from previous releases of Flash, Flash Player 7 now outputs absolute print sizes. Using a conversion formula, you can determine how large your target will print on the printer's paper:

```
1 pixel = 1 point = 1/72 inch
```

Therefore, if you have a MovieClip object containing a 400 × 400 pixel square, that artwork will print at roughly 5.5" × 5.5" on the printed page. You can keep this formula in mind if you're planning to print on standard page sizes such as 8.5" × 11"—as long as your target's size uses the same aspect ratio (roughly 1:1.3), your target can be resized to fill the page.

Make a copy of the PrintJob_props_100.fla file from the ch22 folder of this book's CD-ROM. Use this document as the starter file for the following exercise.

Try printing some artwork at an absolute size:

1. Open the starter file and save it as `PrintJob_absolute_100.fla`.
2. Create a new layer and rename it `mcSquare`. Place this layer at the bottom of the layer stack.
3. On frame 1 of the `mcSquare` layer, draw a basic square with the Rectangle tool. In the Property inspector, set the width and height to 500 pixels. With these dimensions, the artwork will print at roughly 5.5" × 5.5".
4. Select the square and convert the artwork to a Movie Clip symbol by pressing the F8 key. In the Convert to Symbol dialog box, name the symbol `squareClip`, as shown in Figure 22-2. Make sure the registration point is set to the top-left corner.

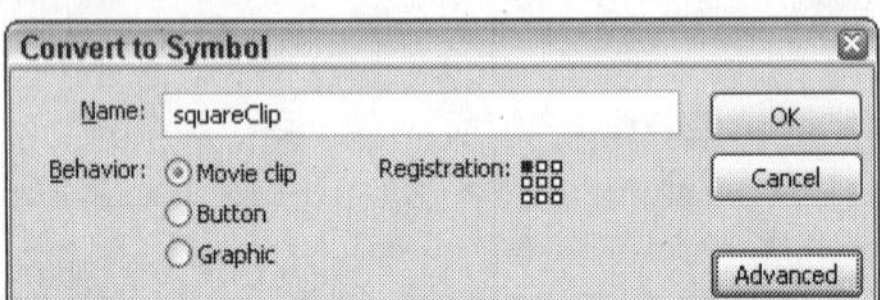

Figure 22-2: The Convert to Symbol dialog box

5. Select the `squareClip` instance on the stage, and in the Property inspector, name the instance `mcSquare`.
6. Select frame 1 of the actions layer and open the Actions panel (F9). Add the bold code shown in Listing 22-2.

   Here, you add an `if()` statement that checks the result of the `bPrintInit` variable. If the user clicked the Print (or OK) button in the Print dialog box, this block of code will execute. After the `trace()` action, the `addPage()` method of the `pjOutput` instance specifies the `mcSquare` instance. Note that all other parameters of the `addPage()` method are omitted—as such, the default values for those parameters will be used. Finally, the output is sent to the printer with the `send()` method of the `PrintJob` class.

Listing 22-2: **Printing the mcSquare Instance**

```
this.startPrint = function(oEvent:Object):Void {
   trace(">>> BEGIN startPrint() >>>");
   var pjOutput:PrintJob = new PrintJob();
   var bPrintInit:Boolean = pjOutput.start();
   trace("\tbPrintInit:\t\t" + bPrintInit);
   for(var i:String in pjOutput){
      var nPropLen:Number = i.length;
      var sTabSuffix:String = nPropLen <= 10 ? ":\t\t" : ":\t";
      trace("\t" + i + sTabSuffix + pjOutput[i]);
   }
   if(bPrintInit){
```

```
        trace("\tprinting mcSquare...");
        pjOutput.addPage(mcSquare);
        pjOutput.send();
    }
    trace("<<< END startPrint() <<<");
};
cbtPrint.addEventListener("click", this.startPrint);
```

7. Save your document and test it. When you click the Print button in the Flash movie, the Print dialog box for your operating system appears. If you click the Print button in this dialog box, the mcSquare instance will be printed at 5.5" × 5.5" on your selected paper size.

You can find the completed document, PrintJob_absolute_100.fla, in the ch22 folder of this book's CD-ROM.

Now you will practice how to scale a target to fill the entire page. With a starter file, you will size a target to fit the stage of the Flash movie, and you will see how the absolute size prints on a piece of paper. Then you will change the scale of the target in ActionScript to fill the entire page.

Make a copy of the PrintJob_scale_starter.fla file from the ch22 folder of this book's CD-ROM.

To see the effects of scaling a target with printed output, complete the following steps:

1. Open the starter file and save it as PrintJob_scale_100.fla.
2. Create a new layer named mcContent. Place this layer at the bottom of the layer stack.
3. On frame 1 of this new layer, drag an instance of the contentClip symbol from the Library to the stage. Using the Property inspector, name this instance mcContent and set the width to 282 pixels and the height to 365 pixels (see Figure 22-3). If you whip out your calculator, you can see that these dimensions use the same aspect ratio as an 8.5" × 11" piece of paper (365 × 282 = 1.29). Using the conversion formula, this artwork, at 282 × 265, will print at 3.9" × 5" on the page.
4. Select frame 1 of the actions layer and open the Actions panel (F9). Add the bold code shown in Listing 22-3.

   This code works exactly the same as the last example, except that the target is changed in the addPage() method.

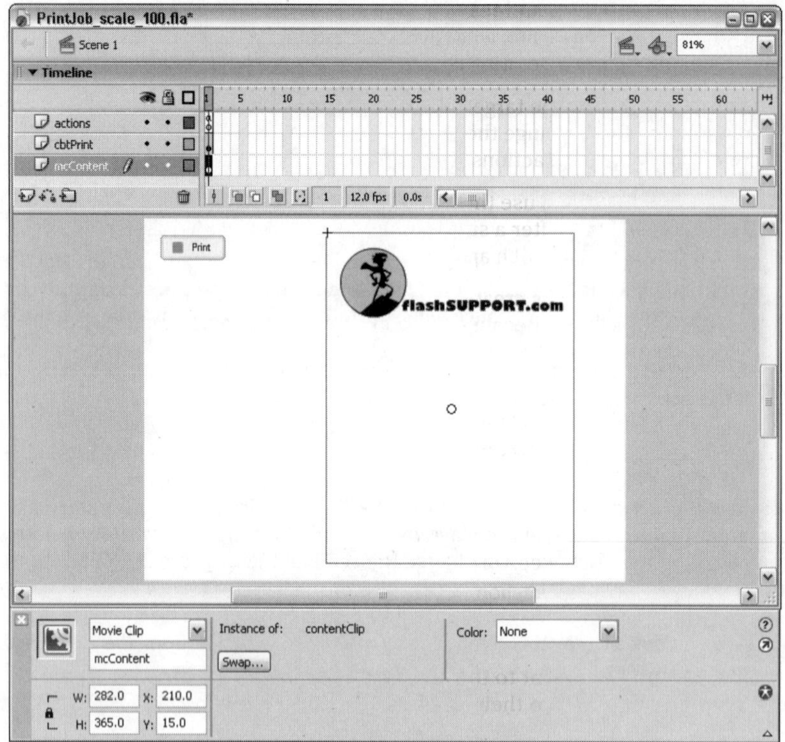

Figure 22-3: The settings for the mcContent instance

Listing 22-3: **Printing the mcContent Instance at Its Fixed Size**

```
this.startPrint = function(oEvent:Object):Void {
   trace(">>> BEGIN startPrint() >>>");
   var pjOutput:PrintJob = new PrintJob();
   var bPrintInit:Boolean = pjOutput.start();
   trace("\tbPrintInit:\t\t" + bPrintInit);
   for(var i:String in pjOutput){
      var nPropLen:Number = i.length;
      var sTabSuffix:String = nPropLen <= 10 ? ":\t\t" : ":\t";
      trace("\t" + i + sTabSuffix + pjOutput[i]);
   }
   if(bPrintInit){
      trace("\tprinting mcContent...");
      pjOutput.addPage(mcContent);
      pjOutput.send();
   }
   trace("<<< END startPrint() <<<");
};
cbtPrint.addEventListener("click", this.startPrint);
```

5. Save your document and test it. When you click the Print button in the Flash movie, the system's Print dialog box will open. If you click the Print (or OK) button, the `mcContent` clip will be printed at the size indicated in Step 3.

6. Now you will scale the target to fit the paper size selected by the user. This operation requires that you change the target's `_width` and `_height` properties to fill the page. Select frame 1 of the actions layer and add the bold code shown in Listing 22-4.

   In this new code, you use the `pageWidth` and `pageHeight` values returned to the `pjOutput` instance after a successful `start()` method has initiated. These values are stored in the `nPageWidth` and `nPageHeight` variables, respectively.

   The `mcProps` object is created to store the original width and height values of the `mcContent` instance. Because you will be changing the width and height for the print output only, you want to reset the instance to these original values after printing is finished.

   The `nPageWidth` and `nPageHeight` values are then applied to the `mcContent`'s `_width` and `_height` properties, respectively. At these new dimensions, the output will fill the entire printed page.

This example assumes that you are using 8.5" × 11" paper with a portrait orientation. Look at `www.flashsupport.com/articles` for a more detailed example that shows you how to adjust the size and rotation of the target clip based on the user's selected paper size and orientation.

After the output is sent to the printer, another `with()` statement resets the `_width` and `_height` properties to their original values, as stored in the `mcProps` object.

Listing 22-4: Printing the mcContent Instance to Fill the Page

```
this.startPrint = function(oEvent:Object) {
   trace(">>> BEGIN startPrint() >>>");
   var pjOutput:PrintJob = new PrintJob();
   var bPrintInit:Boolean = pjOutput.start();
   trace("\tbPrintInit:\t\t" + bPrintInit);
   for (var i in pjOutput) {
      var nPropLen:Number = i.length;
      var sTabSuffix:String = nPropLen <= 10 ? ":\t\t" : ":\t";
      trace("\t" + i + sTabSuffix + pjOutput[i]);
   }
   if (bPrintInit) {
      trace("\tprinting mcContent...");
      var nPageWidth:Number = pjOutput.pageWidth;
      var nPageHeight:Number = pjOutput.pageHeight;
      var mcProps:Object = {
         width: mcContent._width,
         height: mcContent._height
      };
```

Continued

Listing 22-4 *(continued)*

```
      with(mcContent){
         _width = nPageWidth;
         _height = nPageHeight;
      }
      pjOutput.addPage(mcContent);
      pjOutput.send();
      with(mcContent){
         _width = mcProps.width;
         _height = mcProps.height;
      }
   }
   trace("<<< END startPrint() <<<");
};
cbtPrint.addEventListener("click", this.startPrint);
```

7. Save your document as `PrintJob_scale_101.fla` and test the movie. When you click the Print button in the Flash movie and the Print button in the Print dialog box, the `mcContent` instance will print to the full size of an 8.5" × 11" piece of paper.

8. Now you examine how the `oPrintArea` parameter of the `addPage()` method can affect the printed output from a Flash movie. For this example, you will use the `oPrintArea` parameter to selectively print the flashsupport.com logo from the `mcContent` instance. Select frame 1 of the actions layer and open the Actions panel (F9). Add the bold code shown in Listing 22-5.

   This new code creates an Object instance named `oPrintArea` with four properties: `xMin`, `xMax`, `yMin`, and `yMax`, as discussed earlier in this chapter. The values of these properties were determined by going inside of the `contentClip` symbol and selecting the logo graphic to see calculate its X and Y position. The width and height of the graphic were added to these values, respectively, to determine the `xMax` and `ySMax` properties. Note that a buffer area was also factored into the values to avoid cropping the edges of the logo graphic.

   The `oPrintArea` instance is then inserted into the `addPage()` method's parameters.

Listing 22-5: Cropping the Output with the oPrintArea Parameter

```
this.startPrint = function(oEvent:Object) {
   trace(">>> BEGIN startPrint() >>>");
   var pjOutput:PrintJob = new PrintJob();
   var bPrintInit:Boolean = pjOutput.start();
   trace("\tbPrintInit:\t\t" + bPrintInit);
   for (var i in pjOutput) {
      var nPropLen:Number = i.length;
      var sTabSuffix:String = nPropLen <= 10 ? ":\t\t" : ":\t";
      trace("\t" + i + sTabSuffix + pjOutput[i]);
   }
```

```
    if (bPrintInit) {
        trace("\tprinting mcContent...");
        var nPageWidth:Number = pjOutput.pageWidth;
        var nPageHeight:Number = pjOutput.pageHeight;
        var mcProps:Object = {
            width: mcContent._width,
            height: mcContent._height
        };
        with(mcContent){
            _width = nPageWidth;
            _height = nPageHeight;
        }
        var oPrintArea:Object = { xMin: 17, xMax: 306, yMin: 19, yMax: 106 };
        pjOutput.addPage(mcContent, oPrintArea);
        pjOutput.send();
        with(mcContent){
            _width = mcProps.width;
            _height = mcProps.height;
        }
    }
    trace("<<< END startPrint() <<<");
};
cbtPrint.addEventListener("click", this.startPrint);
```

9. Save the document as PrintJob_scale_102.fla and test it. When you click the Print buttons in the Flash movie and Print dialog box, the printed page will show only the flashsupport.com logo graphic. The rectangular border will not be printed.

You can find the PrintJob_scale_100, _101, and _102.fla files in the ch22 folder of this book's CD-ROM.

Potential Problems with the Flash Printed Output

Watch out for the two following pitfalls with the addPage() method parameters, which can cause unpredictable or undesirable output from a printer:

✦ **Device fonts:** If at all possible, avoid using device fonts with the printed output. Make sure all text is embedded for each text field used for printable content. Text that uses device fonts will print — however, if you have several elements in addition to device font text, the device text may not properly align with other elements on the page.

✦ **Background colors:** If you are using a dark background color in the Document Properties dialog box (Modify ➪ Document) for your Flash document, make sure you add a white, filled rectangle behind your printable content within the targeted MovieClip instance.

Be sure to check your movies for these problems before you test your printed output from a Flash movie.

Printing Issues with Flash: Color, Grayscale, and PostScript

Although this book focuses on the development side of Flash movies, you want to make sure that your artwork prints reasonably well on a wide range of printers. Not everyone has a high-quality color inkjet or laser printer connected to her or his computer. As such, you want to test your Flash movie output to a couple of different printers or ask another associate to test the output on his or her printer. The artwork might not have the same contrast ratios when converted to grayscale. Because this book is printed in grayscale, we can't illustrate these differences here, but you can see a side-by-side comparison of colored artwork next to a grayscale equivalent at `www.flashsupport.com/articles/printingflash.html`.

How can you help correct the problem of not-so-great-looking black-and-white print output from a color original? You can try two things to help alleviate poor grayscale translations of colored artwork: Choose colors that have greater tint variation, or make "hidden" grayscale equivalents of artwork directly in Flash. For the former method, use the hero artwork shown later in this chapter as an example; don't use red and green colors that are close in lightness or brightness values. Rather, choose a darkly tinted red and a lightly tinted green. For the latter method, create a separate Movie Clip symbol of a grayscale version of the hero artwork. Just duplicate its symbol in the Library, and use the Paint Bucket and Ink Bottle tools to quickly fill with grayscale colors.

Finally, make sure you test your printed output on both PostScript and non-PostScript printers. According to Macromedia, the Flash Player's print functionality supports both types of printers, but non-PostScript printers convert vectors to bitmaps. Not all non-PostScript printers do an excellent job of converting vector graphics to bitmap graphics (known as *ripping*, from the term RIP, which stands for *r*aster *i*mage *p*rocessing). Therefore, you might decide to let Flash do such image conversions by setting the `printAsBitmap` property to `true` (in the `oPrintOptions` parameter of the `PrintJob.addPage()` method). Again, you should test your content with both types of printers. Most laser printers have PostScript language interpreters, whereas most inkjet printers need additional software such as iProof Systems' PowerRIP software (available as demo software at `www.iproofsystems.com`) to properly render PostScript graphics.

Adding Print Functionality to Movies

Now that you know how to use the parameters of the `PrintJob.addPage()` method, you'll deconstruct a few Flash movies that use these functions to enhance the interactive capabilities of a user interface.

Creating a Dialog Box for Print Notification

One of the problems with the `PrintJob` API is that the `PrintJob.start()` method invokes the operating system's Print dialog boxes rather suddenly. As soon as you click a Flash button invoking the `PrintJob` API, you see a Print dialog box that asks you to choose a printer to use for output. Among other problems with this operation, the user has no idea how many pages will be sent to the printer. In this section, you construct a Flash movie that presents a Flash print message displaying the page count before actually invoking the operating system's Print dialog box.

Make a copy of the `PrintJob_dialog.fla`, `PrintJob_dialog.swf`, and `StageUtils.as` files from the ch22 folder of this book's CD-ROM.

Open the `PrintJob_dialog.swf` file in the Flash authoring application or the Flash Player stand-alone. Click the Print button in the top-left corner of the stage, and you see a Flash print message confirming your choice to print the contents of the movie. If you click the OK button, a handler that creates a `PrintJob` object executes, sending the contents of the `mcChars` instance to the printer. If you click Cancel, the print message disappears, and the movie resumes normal functionality.

To see how the ActionScript code in this example is working, open the `PrintJob_dialog.fla` file in the Flash MX 2004 authoring application. Three primary components enable the print message in this movie:

- ✦ The `cbtPrint` instance in the top-left corner of the stage. This `Button` component instance executes a custom function that displays the print message.
- ✦ The `dialogClip` symbol in the Library. Within this symbol are the graphics for the print message. This symbol is set to export in the Linkage Properties dialog box and has a linkage identifier of `dialogClip`.
- ✦ The `showDialog()` and `printProceed()` methods in the actions layer of the main timeline. The `cbtPrint` instance on the main timeline and the `Button` component instances (that is, the OK and Cancel buttons) within the `dialogClip` instance invoke these methods, respectively.

The `printProceed()` method is nested within the `showDialog()` method.

The showPrintDialog() and printProceed() Methods

You'll start with the custom methods because they are the "brains" of the entire operation. Select frame 1 of the actions layer. Open the Actions panel (F9) and you'll see the code shown in Listing 22-6.

Listing 22-6: The showPrintDialog() and printProceed() Methods

```
import StageUtils;

this.showDialog = function(oEvent:Object):Void {
   var mcOwner:MovieClip = oEvent.target._parent;
   var initObj:Object = { printTarget: mcChars };
   var mcDialog:MovieClip = mcOwner.attachMovie("dialogClip", "mcDialog", ⮐
      1, initObj);
   var oMovieSize:Object = StageUtils.getMovieSize();
   mcDialog._x = (oMovieSize.width/2) - (mcDialog._width/2);
   mcDialog._y = (oMovieSize.height/2) - (mcDialog._height/2);
   mcDialog.printProceed = function():Void {
```

Continued

Listing 22-6 (continued)

```
      var nFrames:Number = this.printTarget._totalframes;
      var pjOutput:PrintJob = new PrintJob();
      var bPrintInit:Boolean = pjOutput.start();
      if(bPrintInit){
         for(var i = 1; i <= nFrames; i++){
            pjOutput.addPage(this.printTarget, {},{printAsBitmap: false}, i);
         }
         pjOutput.send();
      }
   };
};
cbtPrint.addEventListener("click", this.showDialog);
```

The first line of code in this frame uses the `import` directive to use the ActionScript code from the `StageUtils.as` file. This code declares a class named `StageUtils`, which contains a method named `getMovieSize()`. This method returns an object with `width` and `height` properties of the `Stage` object (with a specific `scaleMode` value of `"showAll"`).

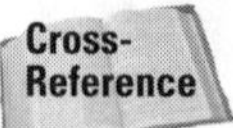

For more information on the `Stage` class (which is used in the `StageUtils.as` file), refer to Chapter 20.

The `showDialog()` method is invoked by the `cbtPrint` instance when the button is clicked. (The event handler is assigned in the last line of code in Listing 22-6.) A reference to the main timeline is made with the variable `mcOwner` by using the `target` property of the event object passed from the `cbtPrint` instance to the `showDialog()` handler. An `initObj` instance is created, with a property named `printTarget`. The `dialogClip` symbol expects to see this property, in order to know which target to print. The `initObj` instance is passed as a parameter of the `attachMovie()` method, which also specifies the `dialogClip` symbol's linkage identifier. Once the `mcDialog` instance is created, it is positioned to the center of the stage, using the `StageUtils` class's `getMovieSize()` method.

The second method, `printProceed()`, is assigned directly to the `mcDialog` instance. This method retrieves the total number of frames in the `printTarget` clip (in this case, the `mcChars` instance) and creates a `PrintJob` object. If the user clicks the Print (or OK) button in the Print dialog box, the `if()` condition will be invoked. Here, a `for` loop adds each frame of the `printTarget`'s timeline to the `PrintJob` object. After all of the frames have been added, the output is sent to the printer.

mcDialog Instance

The other primary element in this example is the `mcDialog` `MovieClip` object that appears on the stage via the `attachMovie()` method in the `showDialog()` method, which is invoked by the `cbtPrint` instance. Take a look inside the `dialogClip` symbol, located in the Library panel. Double-click the `dialogClip` symbol there, and examine the layers within its timeline. Four elements enable the functionality of this timeline: the `tMessage` Dynamic text field, the OK button (`cbtOK` instance), the Cancel button (`cbtCancel` instance), and the first frame of the actions layer.

The content of the tMessage Dynamic text field is scripted by the actions on frame 1. The most important aspect of this text field is that it is named tMessage in the *<Instance Name>* field of the Property inspector. Select the first frame of the actions layer and look at the last line of code in the Actions panel:

```
tMessage.text = "Do you want to print " + this.printTarget._totalframes + ⮐
   " pages  from this Flash movie?";
```

Here, you concatenate string values to be displayed in the tMessage field. The dynamic element of this message is the printTarget variable. Remember the showDialog() method: A printTarget property (or variable) is created on the mcDialog timeline. When the method is executed by the cbtPrint instance, this.printTarget._totalframes has a value of 2 because two frames in the mcChars instance are printed.

Take a look at the two components on the dialogClip timeline: the OK and Cancel Button component instances. Select the OK button and open the Property inspector. This cbtOK instance has a label value of OK. To see how this value is used, go back to frame 1 of the actions layer and open the Actions panel. The following code is used by both Button component instances:

```
this.printControl = function(oEvent:Object):Void {
   var sLabel:String;
   var mcOwner:MovieClip = oEvent.target._parent;
   var sLabel = oEvent.target.label;
   if(sLabel == "OK") mcOwner.printProceed();
   Key.removeListener(oPrintKey);
   mcOwner.removeMovieClip();
};
cbtOK.addEventListener("click", this.printControl);
cbtCancel.addEventListener("click", this.printControl);
```

When the user clicks the OK button, the code within the printControl() method executes. Whenever a component instance executes one of its listener's event handlers (which is defined after the function), an event object is passed to the click handler. The oEvent argument, therefore, will represent this event object. If one of the component buttons executes the function, a local variable named sLabel will be set to the label value of the component button—either "OK" or "Cancel" in the case of this example. If the sLabel variable equals "OK", the printProceed() method on the instance will be executed. Remember that the printProceed() method contains all of the PrintJob object actions, which send output to the printer. If the Cancel button is pressed, the printProceed() function is not processed. Regardless of which button is pressed, the dialog instance is removed from the stage (mcOwner.removeMovieClip();). After the printControl() method is defined, the method is set as an event listener for both the OK button (represented as cbtOK) and the Cancel button (represented as cbtCancel).

After the addEventListener() methods establish the printControl() method for the component buttons, a Key listener object is created to detect if the user presses the Enter key:

```
var oPrintKey:Object = {};
oPrintKey.onKeyDown = function():Void {
   if(Key.isDown(Key.ENTER)){
      printControl({target: cbtOK});
   }
};
Key.addListener(oPrintKey);
```

When an instance of the dialogClip symbol loads onto the stage, the oPrintKey listener object is initiated and added as a listener to the Key class. If the Enter key is pressed while an instance of dialogClip is on the stage, the printControl() method executes with an oEvent object mimicking the cbtOK instance, enabling the same printProceed() method that the OK button does.

In summary, you can reuse these custom methods and the dialogClip symbol in your Flash movies to create a more user-friendly interface that lets users know how many pages are sent to the printer — before they accidentally print 10 pages of paper!

Working with Hidden Content

You can use the PrintJob API to output content not seen in the Flash movie by your Web visitors. By setting the _visible property of printable MovieClip objects to false, you can hide them on the movie's stage, yet still print the frames within. For this example, you learn not only how to print hidden content but how to offer your visitors the choice of printing color or grayscale artwork. Keep in mind that the file contains a grayscale duplicate symbol of a colored Movie Clip symbol. If you're wondering why a grayscale version is offered here, read the sidebar "Printing Issues with Flash: Color, Grayscale, and PostScript," earlier in this chapter.

Make a copy of the PrintJob_dialog_choice.fla and PrintJob_dialog_choice.swf files, located in the ch22 folder of this book's CD-ROM.

Before you look at the Flash document (FLA file), open the PrintJob_dialog_choice.swf file in the Flash MX 2004 authoring environment or in the stand-alone player. When you click the cbtPrint instance in the top-left corner, notice a modified version of the print message window you created in the last section. You can now choose to print a color or black-and-white (B/W) version of the artwork. How is this possible? Can Flash convert graphics to grayscale on the fly? All printers can print grayscale versions of color content, but sometimes this color conversion is not ideal. Therefore, the file contains a manually created grayscale version of the artwork in Flash. Check out the Flash movie to see how this was done.

If you have a black-and-white printer connected to your computer or network, examine the visual differences of the output between the Color option versus the B/W option. The B/W version prints with much better contrast than the color version on a black-and-white laser printer.

Open the Flash document (FLA file) in Flash MX 2004 and open the document's Library panel. Double-click the charsBWClip symbol. Inside the symbol, you'll see a grayscale version of the heroClip symbol. To create this artwork, the artwork of the original heroClip was exported as a PCT image using File ⇨ Export Image. Then, in Adobe Photoshop, we viewed the Green color channel (because it offered the best grayscale contrast), and recorded the grayscale values contained therein. We went back to Flash, duplicated the original hero symbol, and named it heroBWClip. Using the Paint Bucket tool, we filled each colored area of the artwork with the recorded value from Photoshop. Next, we made a duplicate symbol of the characters symbol, and named it charsBWClip. Inside this new symbol, we used the Swap Symbol button in the Property inspector to change the colored version of the heroClip instance to the grayscale version of it, heroBWClip. Finally, and most importantly, we set the charsBWClip symbol to export with the Flash movie (SWF file) by giving it an identifier name of charsBWClip in the Linkage Properties dialog box.

We didn't make a new version of the dog symbol artwork because it already translated well to grayscale values when printed on a grayscale printer. The hero artwork, however, lost much of its contrast when it was printed on a grayscale printer.

Now that you understand how you have two versions of the artwork, you can see how you actually enable the grayscale artwork with the `PrintJob` API. Because you already have custom methods in the last section's example, it's not difficult to modify the `dialogClip` symbol to add the Color and B/W button options. Double-click the `dialogClip` symbol now. Because the `dialogClip` symbol uses components, all of the code for this object can be viewed in one frame. Select the first frame of the actions layer and open the Actions panel. You can see the code shown in Listing 22-7 in the Script pane.

Listing 22-7: The Modified dialogClip Actions

```
this.printControl = function(oEvent:Object):Void {
   var sLabel:String;
   var mcOwner:MovieClip = oEvent.target._parent;
   var sLabel = oEvent.target.label;
   if(sLabel == "Color"){
      mcOwner.printProceed();
   } else if(sLabel == "B/W"){
      var mcCharsBW:MovieClip = mcOwner._parent.attachMovie("charsBWClip", ⮐
         "mcCharsBW", 2);
      mcCharsBW._visible = false;
      mcOwner.printTarget = mcCharsBW;
      mcOwner.printProceed();
   }
   Key.removeListener(oPrintKey);
   mcOwner.removeMovieClip();
};
cbtColor.addEventListener("click", this.printControl);
cbtColor.setStyle("fontWeight", "bold");
cbtBW.addEventListener("click", this.printControl);
cbtCancel.addEventListener("click", this.printControl);
var oPrintKey:Object = {};
oPrintKey.onKeyDown = function():Void {
   if(Key.isDown(Key.ENTER)){
      printControl({target: cbtOK});
   }
};
Key.addListener(oPrintKey);
tMessage.text = "Do you want to print " + this.printTarget._totalframes + ⮐
   " pages from this Flash movie?";
```

The `printControl()` method has been modified to enable the grayscale artwork in the Library. The `if` action has been expanded to include an `else if` expression, checking for a component label value of `"B/W"`. If the `cbtBW` instance on the stage is clicked, this portion of the `if/else if` structure executes. Here, a new `MovieClip` object named `mcCharsBW` is created with the `attachMovie()` method of the `MovieClip` class. This instance is attached to the main timeline, which is the parent timeline of the current instance of the `dialogClip` symbol.

To hide the new `mcCharsBW` instance, set the `_visible` property to `false`. Although it's not visible on the stage, the `PrintJob` actions can still print its frames.

Perhaps most importantly, the `printTarget` value of the `dialogClip` instance is overwritten with a reference to the new `mcCharsBW` clip. The `printProceed()` method is then invoked, to send the output to the printer.

The `addEventListener()` actions were also changed to indicate the new `Button` component instance names, `cbtColor` and `cbtBW`. The text label of the `cbtColor` instance was also emphasized by using the `setStyle()` method of the `UIObject` class.

That's it! The rest of the movie is exactly the same as the previous section's example. When you test the movie and click the `cbtPrint` instance, the Flash dialog box opens with the scripted print message, enabling the user to choose either a color or black-and-white version of the characters artwork for optimized printing purposes.

You can improve the functionality of this example by removing any hidden grayscale artwork after it has been printed. Try adding a `removeMovieClip()` method in the `printProceed()` function to delete the artwork from the stage.

We'd like to know what you thought about this chapter. Visit `www.flashsupport.com/feedback` to fill out an online form with your comments.

Summary

- ✦ You can print many useful items from Flash movies, such as purchase receipts, artwork, and product catalogs or datasheets.
- ✦ The `PrintJob` class (new to Flash MX 2004) has all of the methods and properties necessary to print Flash content.
- ✦ The `addPage()` method of the `PrintJob` class enables you to control which `MovieClip` object (or Level) is printed and how it should be printed.
- ✦ Avoid the use of device fonts or dark background colors for Flash content that you intend to print.
- ✦ You might want to give your users the option of confirming an interaction that will send output to the printer. This confirmation dialog box can contain information about how many pages will be printed.
- ✦ You can print content that is temporarily added to the movie's stage with the `MovieClip.attachMovie()` method. This technique can be useful to print alternatively formatted material from that which the user sees on the stage, such as printing a black-and-white version of a color graphic.

✦ ✦ ✦

PART

VI

The Audio and Video Classes

✦ ✦ ✦ ✦

In This Part

✦ ✦ ✦ ✦

CHAPTER 23

The Sound Class

✦ ✦ ✦ ✦

In This Chapter

Understanding Sound objects and MovieClip object targets

Controlling sound properties

Loading MP3 files at runtime

Adding a volume slider

Using the mouse position with the setTransform() method

✦ ✦ ✦ ✦

Since Flash 5, developers have had the capability to dynamically create and control sound resources. These resources are not placed on keyframes in the Flash timeline. Rather, ActionScript attaches the sound resource to the Flash movie at runtime. In this chapter, you learn how to access the `Sound` class's properties and methods in order to create efficient sound loading and playback in a Flash movie.

In Flash Player 6 or later, external MP3 files can be loaded into Flash movies at runtime. You no longer need to embed a sound file into a Flash movie (SWF file) in order to play it. You learn about this and other features of the `Sound` class throughout this chapter.

An Introduction to the Sound Class

The `Sound` class adheres very closely to the same order of operations as the `Color` class, which was discussed in Chapter 16. A `Sound` object is actually comprised of three elements that work together to initiate and control a sound resource in the Flash movie:

- ✦ A sound file imported into the movie's Library or a sound file downloaded separately as an MP3 file at runtime
- ✦ A `Sound` instance created with the `new Sound()` constructor
- ✦ A `MovieClip` object (or timeline) that stores the attached or loaded sound file. This `MovieClip` object is never targeted with `Sound` object properties or methods — it is specified only in the `new Sound()` constructor. Think of this `MovieClip` object as the sound resource linked to the `Sound` instance.

The syntax and structure for `Color` and `Sound` objects are nearly identical, and the manner in which they control assets in Flash is similar as well. See Figure 23-1 for an illustration of the elements that compose a `Sound` object.

Figure 23-1 shows how an instance of the `Sound` class references its assets. An instance of the `Sound` class controls a sound file placed in a `MovieClip` object. In Figure 23-1, the `Sound` object and the `MovieClip` object are on the same timeline — the main timeline (`_root`). You can declare a `Sound` object in any timeline, and the `MovieClip` object can exist in a completely different location as well. Just as `Color` objects can control the color of nested `MovieClip` objects, `Sound` objects can store sound resources in any `MovieClip` object. In a moment, you learn why `MovieClip` objects are used to store a sound resource.

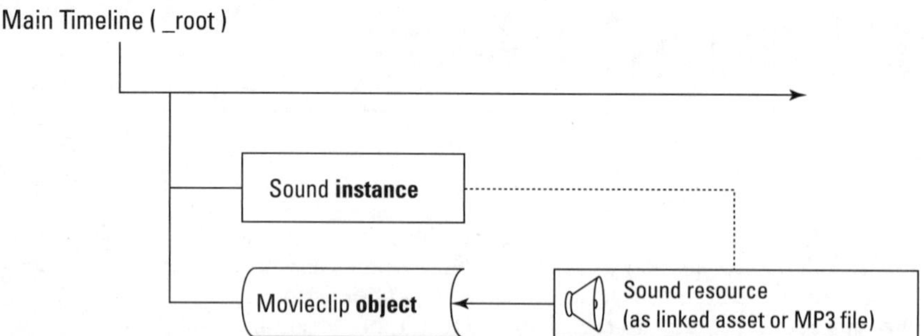

Figure 23-1: Sound objects link a sound resource to a specific timeline (a MovieClip object).

Creating a New Sound Object

As with most predefined ActionScript classes, `Sound` objects require a constructor to create a new instance of the class. The `Sound` class uses a notation similar to the `Color` class's constructor. The outcome, though, is a bit different. To create a new `Sound` object, you need the following constructor:

```
var sndInstance:Sound = new Sound(mcInstance);
```

where `sndInstance` is the name for the specific `Sound` object you're creating, and `mcInstance` is the timeline on which you want the sound resource stored. The new `Sound` object (referred to by its new name) is not the actual sound—it's simply a reference to the sound resource you will be using. You can think of it as a translator between the `Sound` object properties and methods and the actual sound that is being controlled.

The following ActionScript represents a new `Sound` object named `sndBgTrack` that creates a holder for an actual sound (from the Library or an external MP3 file) on a `MovieClip` named `mcSound_1`, within a larger `MovieClip` object named `mcSoundLib`:

```
var sndBgTrack:Sound = new Sound(mcSoundLib.mcSound_1);
```

At this point, the code has not specified an actual sound to be used from the Library (or an MP3 file). If this action were placed on the first frame of the main timeline (`_root`), `sndBgTrack`, as a `Sound` object, exists at `_root.sndBgTrack`, and the holder for its sound resource is located on the `mcSound_1` timeline, as shown in Figure 23-2.

Understanding Sound Resources and Timelines

Before you dive into the complexities of the `Sound` class's properties and methods, you need to know why sound resources should be stored in separate `MovieClip` objects. Technically, the `MovieClip` object reference is an optional argument for the `new Sound()` constructor. If you omit the argument, the `Sound` object stores the sound resource on the `_level0` timeline (that is, Level 0). The following code creates a sound resource on the same timeline as the Sound object (see Figure 23-3):

```
var sndBgTrack:Sound = new Sound();
```

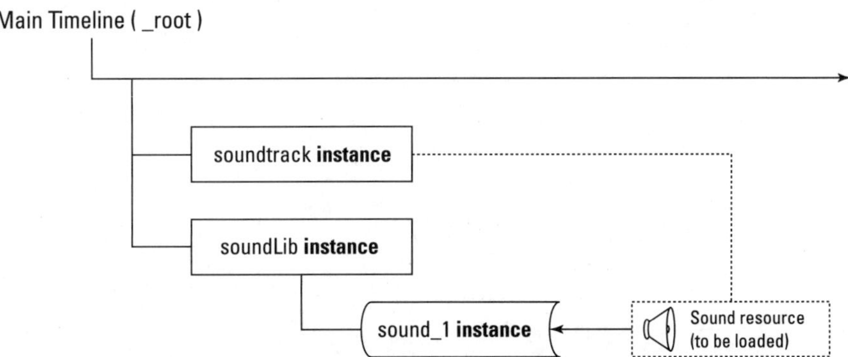

Figure 23-2: A Sound object, such as sndBgTrack, does not actually contain a sound. It provides a link between a sound file and a MovieClip object.

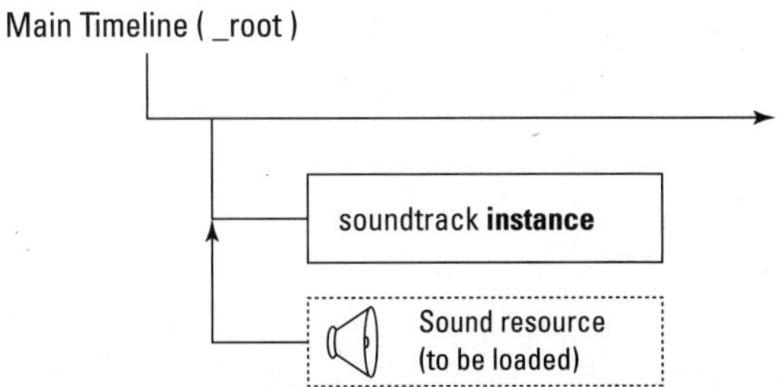

Figure 23-3: When a Sound object is created without a MovieClip object reference, the sound resource is stored on the _level0 timeline.

If you are controlling only one sound with ActionScript in your movie (or if you're *not* using the action in a loaded SWF file), omitting the `MovieClip` object reference might not cause any problems. However, if you start to create multiple `Sound` objects *without* separate `MovieClip` objects to contain the sound resources, you will run into problems. Here is an example of several `Sound` objects (and sound resources) created on the same timeline:

```
var snd_1:Sound = new Sound();
var snd_2:Sound = new Sound();
var snd_3:Sound = new Sound();
```

If this code is declared on frame 1 of the main timeline, any subsequent sound resources loaded into the Sound objects are stored in the same timeline, as shown in Figure 23-4.

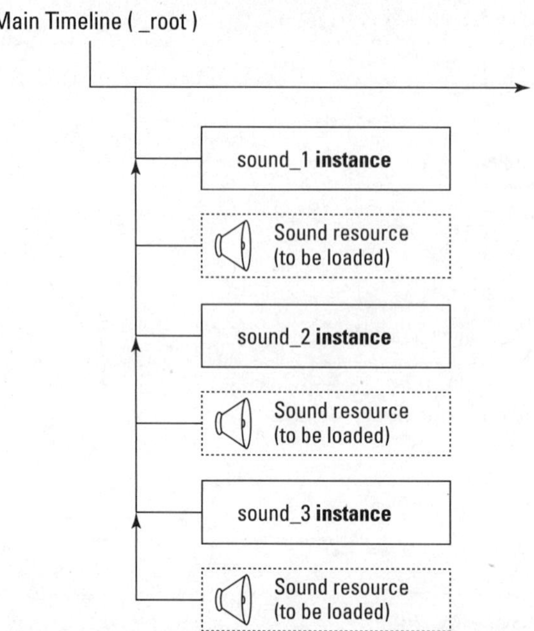

Figure 23-4: Several Sound objects and sound resources on the same timeline

Although the scenario shown in Figure 23-4 might not appear problematic, the structure does not allow each sound resource to be stored in its own container. As a result, if you try to control one `Sound` object, the other sound resources will respond as well. Think of `Sound` instances, `MovieClip` objects, and sound resources as highway traffic lanes, cars, and people, respectively. If several people are in one car, all of the people in the car will respond to changes brought about by a specific lane's condition. However, if each person occupies his or her own car, each car can respond independently to variations in the highway lane. (In the real world, carpooling is highly recommended and encouraged by this book's authors.) In the world of ActionScript, allocating the proper resources to each code element can ensure independence of the associated objects. In order to maintain complete control over each sound resource that is used by each `Sound` object, make sure you create a unique `MovieClip` object to hold each sound resource. The following code examples create three `Sound` objects and three `MovieClip` objects (plus one `MovieClip` object to store the other `MovieClip` objects). Listing 23-1 shows a longer method of specifying `Sound` and `MovieClip` objects, whereas Listing 23-2 shows the same functionality encapsulated within a `for` loop. You can see both of this examples illustrated in Figure 23-5.

Listing 23-1: Creating Sound and MovieClip Objects Without a Loop

```
var mcSoundLib:MovieClip = this.createEmptyMovieClip("mcSoundLib", 1);
var mcSnd_1:MovieClip = mcSoundLib.createEmptyMovieClip("mcHolder_1", 1);
var snd_1:Sound = new Sound(mcSnd_1);
```

```
var mcSnd_2:MovieClip = mcSoundLib.createEmptyMovieClip("mcHolder_2", 2);
var snd_1:Sound = new Sound(mcSnd_2);
var mcSnd_3:MovieClip = mcSoundLib.createEmptyMovieClip("mcHolder_3", 3);
var snd_3:Sound = new Sound(mcSnd_3);
```

Listing 23-2: **Creating Sound and MovieClip Objects with a for Loop**

```
var mcSoundLib:MovieClip = this.createEmptyMovieClip("mcSoundLib", 1);
var aSounds:Array;
for(var i:Number = 1; i <= 3; i++){
  var mcSnd:MovieClip = mcSoundLib.createEmptyMovieClip("mcHolder_" + i, i);
  var sndRef:Sound = new Sound(mcSnd);
  aSounds.push(sndRef);
}
```

When each sound resource has its own storage MovieClip object, any changes to one Sound object responsible for the sound resource will not be passed to other Sound objects. In summary, it is recommended that you store only one sound resource per timeline. You can have several Sound objects on the same timeline, but you should not target the same MovieClip object in more than one new Sound() constructor. Now that you understand how Sound objects store and reference loaded sound assets, you will learn how to use ActionScript to control a Sound object after it has been initialized.

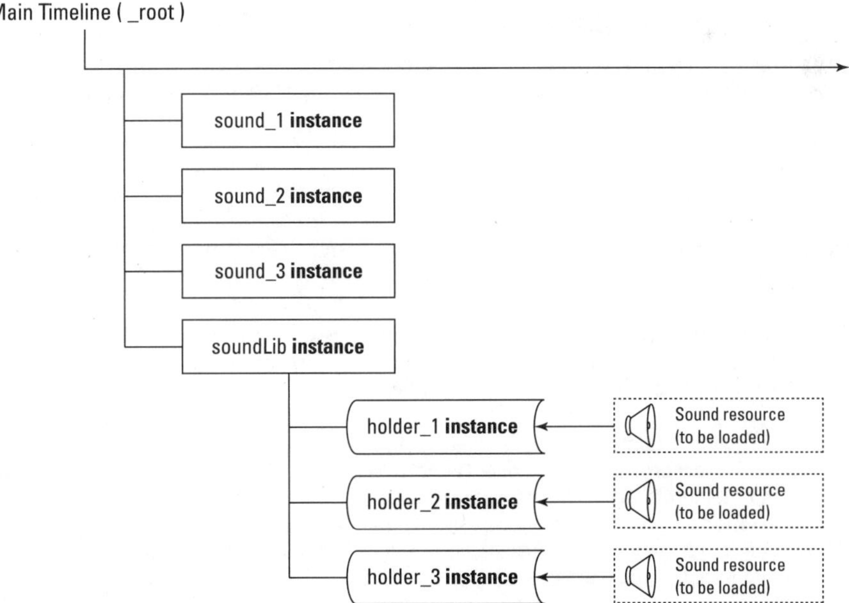

Figure 23-5: Each sound resource has its own MovieClip object.

Scripting Audio with the Sound Class

The Sound class enables you to play audio from the movie's Library or from an external MP3 file. Prior to the Sound class's introduction to ActionScript, all audio had to be manually inserted into a Flash timeline on a specific keyframe. Now, you can control the volume, pan, looping, and playback of a sound in a Flash movie using ActionScript. With these controls, you can add volume knobs or sliders or make a sound "follow" an object on the stage (that is, pan from left to right, or vice versa).

There are four basic steps to use a Sound object in a Flash movie:

1. Set an audio file to export from the Library, or create a separate MP3 file.
2. Create a new Sound object.
3. Attach (or load) the audio file to the Sound object.
4. Play the Sound object, and continue to control the sound (if desired) with other methods of the Sound class.

In the following sections, you learn the properties and methods of the Sound class and create some Flash movies that use it.

Property and Method Overview of the Sound Class

There are three properties, twelve methods, and three event handlers for the Sound class. The methods and event handlers roughly fall into three categories: loading, playback, and transformation. Before you examine these properties, methods, and event handlers, let's review the Sound class's constructor:

```
var sndInstance:Sound = new Sound(mcTarget);
```

where sndInstance is the name of the specific Sound object that you are creating, and mcTarget is the MovieClip object timeline in which the sound resource is stored.

The mcTarget argument for the Sound object constructor is optional. You can use the following syntax:

```
var sndInstance:Sound = new Sound();
```

which stores the sound reference at _level0. Note that the following syntax is not the same:

```
var sndInstance:Sound = new Sound(this);
```

By specifying this, you are putting the sound resource on the current timeline, which isn't necessarily _level0. You must always create a Sound object in order to use any of the following properties, methods, or event handlers.

Caution

You should link only one Sound object to any given MovieClip object. As discussed in the previous sections, changes to one Sound object on a MovieClip object will be passed to other Sound objects on the same timeline. In addition, make sure you never use the name sound for a new Sound object, as in var sound:Sound = new Sound();. Because the word sound stands for an actual class of objects in ActionScript, your movies will behave unpredictably if you use this syntax.

Properties of the Sound Class

Flash Player 6 and later support two properties of the `Sound` class: `duration` and `position`. With these properties, you can monitor the progress of a sound's playback.

Flash Player 6 r40 and later support a property named `id3`. This property enables you to access ID3 tag information stored within an MP3 file. ID3 tags usually contain values for the file's song title, artist, writer, and so on.

`Sound` objects in Flash Player 5 movies cannot use any of these properties.

The original online documentation of the Help panel in Flash MX 2004 (Help ⇨ Help) incorrectly reports the existence of an `ID3` property. This property is not available in Flash Player 7. Macromedia included the `ID3` property in original specifications for Flash Player 7, but later removed it.

Retrieving the Sound's Length with Sound.duration

The `duration` property of the `Sound` class enables you to determine the length of a sound resource loaded into the Flash Player. The value is returned in milliseconds (1 second = 1,000 milliseconds). The `duration` property is a read-only property, meaning that you cannot set it to a new value—every sound resource has a definite length. The only way you can change the duration of a sound resource is to alter the actual sound file in a sound editing application.

You can, however, loop a sound resource, which enables the sound to play for indefinite periods of time. See the description of the `start()` method later in this chapter.

The following code displays the length of a sound resource in the Output panel. This code uses methods described later in this chapter:

```
var snd_1:Sound = new Sound();
snd_1.attachSound("carHorn");
trace("carHorn is " + snd_1.duration + " milliseconds in length.");
trace("carHorn is " + (snd_1.duration/1000) + " seconds in length.");
```

Retrieving the Sound's Current Time with Sound.position

The `position` property of the `Sound` class returns the current playback time (in milliseconds). For example, if a 10-second sound has played back from three seconds, the `position` property returns 3,000. The following code creates and plays a `Sound` object, and creates a `Mouse` listener that enables a mouse click anywhere in the movie to display the current position value (in seconds) in the Output panel:

```
var snd_1:Sound = new Sound();
snd_1.attachSound("soundtrack");
snd_1.start();
this.onMouseDown = function():Void {
  trace("Current position:\t" + (snd_1.position/1000) + " seconds");
};
Mouse.addListener(this);
```

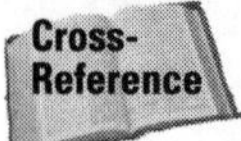

For more information on the `Mouse` listeners, refer to Chapter 19.

Looped sounds return a value relative to the native length of the sound resource. For example, if you loop a 10-second sound three times, the `position` property always returns values between 0 and 10,000.

Reading an MP3 File's ID3 Tags with Sound.id3

You can use the `id3` property of a `Sound` object to retrieve information about an MP3 file loaded into the `Sound` object. ID3 tags contain information about the MP3 file. You can read these tags after the ID3 information has loaded (see the `Sound.onID3` coverage later in this chapter) or after the MP3 file has loaded (see the `Sound.onLoad` coverage).

ID3 information can be stored as ID3 1.0 or ID3 2.0 (or later). If your MP3 file uses ID3 1.0 tags, you can use the following properties in ActionScript:

- `Sound.id3.comment`
- `Sound.id3.album`
- `Sound.id3.genre`
- `Sound.id3.songname`
- `Sound.id3.artist`
- `Sound.id3.track`
- `Sound.id3.year`

For example, the following code shows the MP3's song name, as stored in an ID3 v1.0 tag, in a `TextField` instance named `tDisplay`:

```
var sndInstance:Sound = new Sound(this);
sndInstance.onID3 = function(){
   createTextField("tDisplay", 1, 20, 20, 300, 30);
   tDisplay.text = "Title: " + this.id3.songname;
};
sndInstance.loadSound("atmospheres_1.mp3", true);
```

If your MP3 file uses ID3 v2.0 (or later) tags, several ID3 tags are available, too numerous to list here. Some common ones are the following:

- `Sound.id3.COMM` (comment)
- `Sound.id3.TALB` (album)
- `Sound.id3.TCON` (genre)
- `Sound.id3.TIT2` (songname)
- `Sound.id3.TPE1` (artist)
- `Sound.id3.TRCK` (track number)
- `Sound.id3.TYER` (year)

You can find the complete specification for all ID3 v2.0 tag names at www.id3.org/id3v2.3.0.html#sec4. Using the previous example of reading ID3 v1.0 tags, you simply need to modify the name of the id3 property you want to use for ID3 v2.0 (or later) tags. Note that your MP3 file must contain these tags in order for the Flash Player to read them:

```
var sndInstance:Sound = new Sound(this);
sndInstance.onID3 = function(){
   createTextField("tDisplay", 1, 20, 20, 300, 30);
   tDisplay.text = "Title: " + this.id3.TIT2;
};
sndInstance.loadSound("atmospheres_1.mp3", true);
```

Flash Player 7 automatically copies the values of ID3 v1.0 tags to their ID3 v2.0 equivalents. As such, you should be able to consistently use ID3 v2.0 references in your ActionScript code, provided that an equivalent ID3 v1.0 tag exists in your loaded MP3 file.

Loading Methods of the Sound Class

The following methods can be used to load or monitor the loading of a sound resource into a Sound object. These methods are presented in the order in which they are commonly used:

1. Attach or load a sound into a Sound object.
2. Monitor the download of the sound resource (optional—applies only to loaded sounds, not attached sounds).
3. Execute a function when the sound resource is done loading (optional—applies only to loaded sounds, not attached sounds).

Using an Exported Sound from the Library

The Sound.attachSound() method enables you to link a sound in the movie's Library to a Sound object in the movie. The only argument for the method is a string value that refers to the sound asset's linkage identifier. To set a sound's linkage identifier, right-click (or Control-click on the Mac) the sound in the Library panel, and choose Linkage. In the Linkage Properties dialog box (shown in Figure 23-6), select Export for ActionScript and assign a name in the Identifier field.

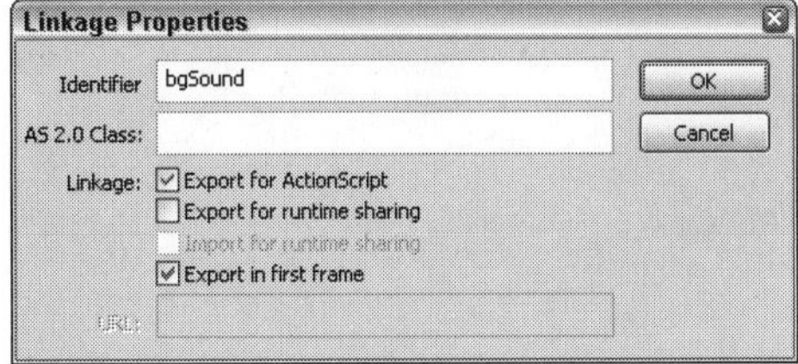

Figure 23-6: The Identifier name is used as the argument of the attachSound() method.

When you select the Export for ActionScript check box, the Linkage Properties dialog box automatically fills the Identifier field with the asset's Library name. Flash also allows you to specify a separate frame in which the sound asset is "stored" in the Flash movie. By default, the Export in First Frame check box is selected, meaning that the entire sound resource must download into the Flash Player before the movie can play frame 1. If you clear this check box, you must manually insert the sound somewhere else in your Flash movie, on a keyframe as an Event sound. You can also view Linkage identifier names in the Library panel—extend the panel's width to reveal the Linkage column information.

The following code creates a `Sound` object named `snd_1` and attaches a sound with the identifier name of `bgSound` to the object:

```
var snd_1:Sound = new Sound();
snd_1.attachSound("bgSound");
```

Note that the `Sound` constructor did not specify a target timeline. Therefore, `snd_1` attaches the sound `bgSound` to the `_level0` timeline.

You can use any string variable as the linkage identifier argument of `attachSound()`. The following code uses the `sCurrentTrack` variable as the identifier name:

```
var sCurrentTrack:String = "bgSound";
var snd_1:Sound = new Sound();
snd_1.attachSound(sCurrentTrack);
```

If you need to create `Sound` objects that are compatible with Flash Player 5, use the `attachSound()` method with linked symbols in the movie's Library. Flash Player 5 cannot use the `loadSound()` method discussed in the next section.

Loading an MP3 File with Sound.loadSound()

Flash Player 6 or later can use the `Sound.loadSound()` method to load MP3 files into Flash movies at runtime. Although the `attachSound()` method works with sound files that have been imported into the Flash document (FLA file) and exported with the Flash movie, the `loadSound()` method loads an external MP3 file directly into Flash Player 6 or later, into virtual memory and the browser's cache.

This method has two arguments: the URL of the MP3 file, and an `isStreaming` Boolean value. The URL for the MP3 file can be a valid `http://` or `ftp://` address, or a relative path to the MP3 file. The following code loads an MP3 file from the FlashSupport.com Web server:

```
var snd_1:Sound = new Sound();
snd_1.loadSound("http://www.flashsupport.com/mp3/atmospheres_1_short.mp3", ⮐
true);
```

You can also use a relative URL. The following code loads an MP3 file located in the same directory as the SWF file:

```
var snd_1:Sound = new Sound();
snd_1.loadSound("atmospheres_1_short.mp3", true);
```

The `ftp://` URL addresses work only when the Flash movie is played in a Web browser. The stand-alone player (or the Test Movie mode) cannot load MP3 files that use FTP.

The second argument of the `loadSound()` method, `isStreaming`, specifies whether the sound resource is a streaming or Event sound. A streaming sound will play as it downloads into the Flash Player. An Event sound, conversely, must fully download into the Flash Player before playback can begin. To treat the sound resource as a streaming sound, use an `isStreaming` value of `true`. For an Event sound, use a value of `false`. The following code establishes a streaming sound that will play the `atmospheres_1_short.mp3` file as soon as enough bytes from the file have loaded into the Flash Player:

```
var snd_1:Sound = new Sound();
snd_1.loadSound("atmospheres_1_short.mp3", true);
```

Streaming sounds are not the same as *Stream* sounds in Flash movies. Stream sounds (which can be set in the Property inspector for a given keyframe) can force the Flash Player to drop frames in order to synchronize playback of a sound with animation on the timeline. Streaming sounds do not control the frame rate of the Flash movie in this manner. Most important, once a streaming sound begins playback, you can only stop the sound—you *cannot* use the `start()` method of the `Sound` object on streaming sounds. Nor can you pause streaming sounds with a controller interface. This is simply an unfortunate limitation of the Flash Player's treatment of streaming sounds.

To make an Event sound, change the `true` value to `false`:

```
var snd_1:Sound = new Sound();
snd_1.loadSound("atmospheres_1_short.mp3", false);
```

Event sounds will not play until the entire MP3 file has downloaded and a `start()` method is executed with the `Sound` object. The `start()` method is discussed later in this chapter.

The `onLoad()` event handler for `Sound` objects can detect if the URL for an MP3 file is invalid. `onLoad()` can also be used to start playback of an Event sound loaded into a `Sound` object. This event handler is discussed in the "Determining When an MP3 Has Fully Loaded" section of this chapter.

Determining How Many Bytes of an MP3 File Have Loaded

The `Sound.getBytesLoaded()` method returns the number of bytes from an MP3 file that are being downloaded via the `loadSound()` method. You can use this method to check the loading progress of an MP3 file. The following code puts the current bytes loaded into a `TextField` object named `tProgress`.

```
var snd_1:Sound = new Sound();
snd_1.loadSound("http://www.flashsupport.com/mp3/atmospheres_1_short.mp3",
true);
this.createTextField("tProgress", 1, 10, 10, 100, 20);
tProgress.border = true;
var nProgressID:Number = setInterval(function(){ tProgress.text = ↩
   snd_1.getBytesLoaded(); }, 100);
```

Here, the `setInterval()` function invokes an anonymous function once every 100 milliseconds, updating the `text` property of the `tProgress` text field with the current bytes loaded of the `snd_1` object.

Getting the Total File Size of the MP3 File

The `Sound.getBytesTotal()` method returns the file size (in bytes) of an MP3 file that is being downloaded into a `Sound` object with the `loadSound()` method. Combined with the `getBytesLoaded()` method, you can determine the percent loaded of the MP3 file, as shown in the following code:

```
function checkLoad():Void {
  var nPercent:Number = (snd_1.getBytesLoaded()/snd_1.getBytesTotal())*100;
  tProgress.text = Math.round(nPercent) + "%";
}
var snd_1:Sound = new Sound();
snd_1.loadSound("http://www.flashsupport.com/mp3/atmospheres_1_short.mp3",
true);
this.createTextField("tProgress", 1, 10, 10, 100, 20);
tProgress.border = true;
var nProgressID:Number = setInterval(checkLoad, 100);
```

This code calculates a `nPercent` variable within a `checkLoad()` function, and inserts the value into the `tProgress` text field.

The `loadSound()`, `onLoad()`, `getBytesLoaded()`, and `getBytesTotal()` methods are *not* available for `Sound` objects in Flash Player 5 or earlier movies.

Determining When an MP3 Has Fully Loaded

The `Sound.onLoad()` event handler can be defined for a `Sound` object to indicate when an MP3 file has finished downloading into Flash Player 6 or later. This handler executes a callback function that tells the movie what to do when either a load operation has completed or a load operation has failed. The method uses a Boolean `success` argument, indicating the status of the load operation. If the load was successful, a `true` value is passed to the callback function. If the load failed (due to an invalid URL or incompatible sound file), the callback function is passed a `false` value. The following code executes a `trace()` action when an Event sound has finished loading, and starts playback of the sound:

```
var snd_1:Sound = new Sound();
snd_1.onLoad = function(success):Void {
  if(success){
    trace("sound has finished loading");
    this.start();
  } else {
    trace("error occurred with loading");
  }
};
snd_1.loadSound("http://www.flashsupport.com/mp3/atmospheres_1_short.mp3", ⮐
   false);
```

Here, an anonymous function is defined for the `onLoad()` event handler. You can also define a named function, as the following code demonstrates:

```
function loadFinished(success):Void {
  if(success){
    trace("sound has finished loading");
```

```
    this.start();
  } else {
    trace("error occurred with loading");
  }
}
var snd_1:Sound = new Sound();
snd_1.onLoad = loadFinished;
snd_1.loadSound("http://www.flashsupport.com/mp3/atmospheres_1_short.mp3", ⮐
   false);
```

Cross-Reference

In the "Loading an External MP3 File" section of this chapter, you create an interface that displays the status of a load operation in a text field.

Playback Methods of the Sound Class

Once a sound resource has been attached or loaded into a `Sound` object, you can control playback of the sound with the methods described in this section.

Note

All of the methods in this grouping, except the `onSoundComplete()` event handler, are compatible with Flash Player 5 or later movies. `onSoundComplete()` requires Flash Player 6 or later, and `onID3()` requires Flash Player 7 or later.

Playing a Sound with Sound.start()

The `Sound.start()` method plays a specific `Sound` object. There are two optional arguments for this method: `offset` and `loopFactor`.

The `offset` argument determines the "in" point of the sound in seconds. For example, if you have a 10-second sound and you want to skip the first three seconds of the sound, you supply the number 3 as the `offset` argument.

The `loopFactor` argument sets the number of times you want to play the sound file. If you decide to use the `loopFactor` argument, you must supply a value for the `offset` argument (use 0 if you want to start the sound at its beginning). A `loopFactor` of 0 or 1 produces the same result: The sound plays once. If you specify a `loopFactor` of 2, the sound plays twice in a row. The following syntax would create a new `Sound` object, attach a sound named `bgSound`, and play it three times—skipping the first two seconds of the sound:

```
var snd_1:Sound = new Sound();
snd_1.attachSound("bgSound");
snd_1.start(2,3);
```

You cannot specify an "out" point for a `Sound` object with the `start()` method. The out point is the place within the sound where playback stops (or loops back to the in point, where playback begins). Unless you are repurposing the same sound file for several uses, we recommend that you trim your sound files in a sound editor application (such as Sony's Sound Forge or Bias Peak) before you import the sound into Flash MX 2004. That way, when you set a sound to export (or download an MP3 file), the entire sound will be included (or downloaded) in your Flash movie (SWF file), regardless of where you specify it to start playing in your ActionScript code. You can, however, use the `position` property of the `Sound` class and the `setInterval()` function to detect when a sound reaches a specific time in playback.

Stopping a Sound with Sound.stop()

The Sound.stop() method halts the sound's playback. There are no arguments for this method, just like the stop() method of the MovieClip object. The following example code placed on a Button instance stops a snd_1 Sound object from playing when the instance is clicked:

```
on (release){
  snd_1.stop();
}
```

This is *not* a pause feature. If you use the stop() method and later issue a start() method for the same Sound object, the sound will start from the beginning (or from its offset value, if one is supplied). However, using the position property of the Sound object, you can pause an attached sound or a loaded Event sound.

Detecting When a Sound Finishes with Sound.onSoundComplete()

The Sound.onSoundComplete() event handler defines a callback function to be executed when a Sound object has finished playing. onSoundComplete() can be used to automatically start a new song in an MP3 playlist. The following code updates a message text field when a sound has finished playing:

```
var snd_1:Sound = new Sound();
snd_1.onSoundComplete = function():Void {
  tMessage.text = "Sound has finished playing.";
};
this.createTextField("tMessage", 1, 10, 10, 200, 20);
tMessage.border = true;
var sUrl:String = "http://www.flashsupport.com/mp3/dog.mp3";
snd_1.loadSound(sUrl, true);
```

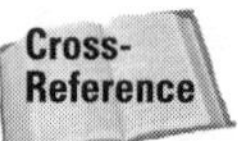

See the section "Making a Looping Playlist" later in this chapter to learn how to automatically play a new sound file using the onSoundComplete() event handler.

Retrieving ID3 Tag Information from an MP3 File

You can use the onID3() handler of the Sound class to determine when the ID3 header information of an MP3 file has loaded. ID3 tags are stored at the very beginning of an MP3 file. As such, you can access the ID3 tag information before the sound is ready for playback. The following code creates a text field named tMessage, displaying all of the ID3 tags available in the loaded MP3 file:

```
var snd_1:Sound = new Sound();
snd_1.onID3 = function():Void {
   tMessage.htmlText += "---- ID3 tags ----\n";
   for (var i:String in this.id3) {
      tMessage.htmlText += "<b>" + i + "</b> : " + this.id3[i] + "\n";
   }
};
this.createTextField("tMessage", 1, 10, 10, 500, 300);
tMessage.border = true;
tMessage.html = true;
```

```
tMessage.multiline = true;
tMessage.wordWrap = true;
var sUrl:String = "http://www.flashsupport.com/mp3/dog.mp3";
snd_1.loadSound(sUrl, true);
```

Note

The `onID3()` handler is actually called twice if both ID3 v1.0 and v2.0 (or later) tags are stored in the MP3 file, once for each set of tags.

Transformation Methods of the Sound Class

Once you understand the basic loading and playback methods and event handlers of the `Sound` class, you're ready to learn the methods that enable control over the volume and balance of the sound output.

Note

All of the methods in this grouping are compatible with Flash Player 5 or later movies.

Controlling the Loudness with Sound.setVolume()

In order to control the volume of your sound, you can invoke the `setVolume()` method of the `Sound` class. The percentage argument is a value in the 0–100 range, where 0 represents no volume (silence), and 100 represents full volume (the default volume of the sound). However, you can specify values higher than 100. Note that increasing the volume beyond 100 percent creates cutouts in your sound quality—any sound levels that are beyond 150 percent already will start to crackle. The following syntax sets a `Sound` object named `snd_1` to a volume of 50 percent:

```
snd_1.setVolume(50);
```

Note

Be aware that the `setVolume()` method does not control the actual volume setting on the computer's speakers, or the system volume. This method simply controls the sound output of the specific Flash sound you are controlling.

Retrieving the Volume with Sound.getVolume()

The `Sound.getVolume()` method retrieves the current volume level of a specified `Sound` object. No argument is required for this method. You can create sound fades using the `getVolume()` method. The following `onEnterFrame()` event handler code tells the `snd_1` object to fade up:

```
var snd_1:Sound = new Sound();
snd_1.attachSound("bgSound");
snd_1.start();
snd_1.setVolume(0);

this.onEnterFrame = function():Void {
  if(snd_1.getVolume() < 100){
    snd_1.setVolume(snd_1.getVolume() +10);
  } else {
    this.onEnterFrame = null;
  }
};
```

Controlling the Balance with Sound.setPan()

The `Sound.setPan()` method works like a balance knob on your stereo system. The method uses a `pan` argument, which is a number in the range of –100 to 100, where negative values favor the left channel (or speaker), and positive values favor the right channel (or speaker). A value of 0 distributes the current volume equally to both channels. For example, –50 cuts 50 percent of the right channel and leaves the left channel at 100 percent, as the following syntax demonstrates:

```
snd_1.setPan(-50);
```

Retrieving the Current Balance with Sound.getPan()

The `Sound.getPan()` method retrieves the current pan value of the specified `Sound` object. You can use this method to create panning sounds that fade from left to right, or vice versa. You will explore such an example later in this chapter.

Controlling Sound with Sound.setTransform()

The `Sound.setTransform()` method is the most advanced method of the `Sound` class. Just as the `Color` class's `setTransform()` method enables you to control subtleties of color variation of `MovieClip` objects, the `setTransform()` method of the `Sound` class provides precision volume distribution over the left and right channels. As with the `Color` class, a `transformObject` is necessary to pass the volume properties to the `Sound` object. The `transformObject` has four properties, each using a value in the range of 0 to 100:

- ✦ **ll:** This value designates what portion of the original left channel should actually be heard in the left channel. A value of 100 retains the original output of the left channel, whereas 0 silences the original output of the left channel.
- ✦ **lr:** This value controls what portion of the original right channel will be heard in the left channel. A value of 100 plays the full output of the right channel in the left channel, whereas 0 silences any applied output of the right channel in the left channel.
- ✦ **rr:** This value specifies how much of the original right channel should actually be heard in the right channel. A value of 100 plays the full output of the right channel, whereas 0 silences the original output of the right channel.
- ✦ **rl:** This value controls what portion of the original left channel will be played in the right channel. A value of 100 plays the full output of the left channel in the right channel, whereas 0 silences any applied output of the left channel in the right channel.

You can use values higher than 100, just as you can with the `setVolume()` method of the `Sound` class. However, levels above 100 will likely distort the quality of the sound.

Any time you create a new `Sound` object, it has the following properties: `ll` = 100, `lr` = 0, `rr` = 100, and `rl` = 0. However, if you want to play both channels in the left speaker, see the code in Listing 23-3.

Listing 23-3: A transformObject Applied to a Sound Instance

```
// Create a new Sound object
var snd_1:Sound = new Sound();

// Attach a sound from the library
```

```
snd_1.attachSound("bgSound");

// Play the sound
snd_1.start();

// Make a new transformObject
var oSoundLeft:Object = new Object();

// Let the left channel to play 100% in the left speaker
oSoundLeft.ll = 100;

// Assign 100% of the right channel to play in the left speaker
oSoundLeft.lr = 100;

// Silence the right channel in the right speaker
oSoundLeft.rr = 0;

// Silence the left channel in the right speaker
oSoundLeft.rl = 0;

// Apply the transformObject to the Sound object
snd_1.setTransform(oSoundLeft);
```

You can also create a `transformObject` and assign its properties within a condensed syntax, as you did with the `Color` class's `transformObject` in the previous chapter:

```
var oSoundLeft:Object = { ll: 100, lr: 100, rr: 0, rl: 0};
```

This produces exactly the same `transformObject` as the code in Listing 23-3 did.

Why would you want so much control over your `Sound` objects? For the most part, `setTransform()` is most useful for Flash movies that incorporate stereo sounds. Later in this chapter, you learn how to play two separate sounds, one in each speaker. As the user moves the mouse to the left of the screen, the sound in the left speaker will start to take over the right channel as well. When the mouse moves to the right of the screen, the sound in the right speaker will start to take over the left speaker.

Retrieving Advanced Sound Properties with Sound.getTransform()

The `Sound.getTransform()` method retrieves the properties of a `Sound` object that was previously altered with `setTransform()`. There is no argument for this method. The method returns properties that can be applied to a new object. For example, the following code returns the current properties for a `Sound` object named `snd_1` and stores those properties in an `Object` instance named `oCurrentProps`:

```
var oCurrentProps:Object = snd_1.getTransform();
```

You can then use `oCurrentProps` in a future use of `setTransform()`. If you had an interface that enabled the user to control sound settings, you could store them temporarily in an object such as `oCurrentProps`. The user could then continue to experiment with different sound properties. Later, if the user wanted to revert to the previously saved sound properties, you could add the following code to a Button instance (labeled "Revert" or something similar):

```
on (release){
  snd_1.setTransform(oCurrentProps);
}
```

Another use of `getTransform()` is to apply one sound's properties to another `Sound` object:

```
// Retrieve the values of one sound
var oCurrentProps:Object = snd_1.getTransform();

// Apply the values to another sound
snd_2.setTransform(oCurrentProps);
```

In the following sections, you will apply your knowledge of the `Sound` class to some practical examples.

Creating and Playing a Linked Sound File

As mentioned earlier in this chapter, there are four basic steps to follow in order to play a sound with the `Sound` class:

1. Set an audio file to export from the Library, or prepare an MP3 file for download.
2. Create a new `Sound` object.
3. Attach the audio file (as an asset in the Library), or load an MP3 file into the `Sound` object.
4. Play the `Sound` object, and continue to control the sound (if desired) with other methods of the `Sound` object.

In this section, you learn the steps required for playing a linked sound file with the `Sound` class. Before you begin, you might want to find an audio file of your own to use with this exercise.

You can use the `atmospheres_1.mp3`, `atmospheres_1_short.mp3`, or `atmospheres_2.mp3` files from the book's CD-ROM, located in the `ch23` folder.

1. Create a new Flash document (Ctrl+N or ⌘+N) and save it as `Sound_100.fla`.
2. Import an audio file into the Flash document. Use File ⇨ Import (Ctrl+R or ⌘+R) to locate your audio file and import it into your document. For this example, feel free to import the `atmospheres_1_short.mp3` audio file from the book's CD-ROM.
3. Open the Library panel (Ctrl+L or ⌘+L) and right-click (Control-click on the Mac) the sound file. In the contextual menu, choose Linkage, as shown in Figure 23-7.
4. In the Linkage Properties dialog box, select the Export for ActionScript check box in the Linkage area. The name `atmospheres_1_short.mp3` appears in the Identifier field. Remove the `.mp3` from this name (as shown in Figure 23-8), and click OK.
5. To see that your sound file is set to export, expand the size of the Library panel. Drag the lower-right corner of the window to expand the right margin, as shown in Figure 23-9. Note the Linkage column that shows the Identifier name for your sound file.

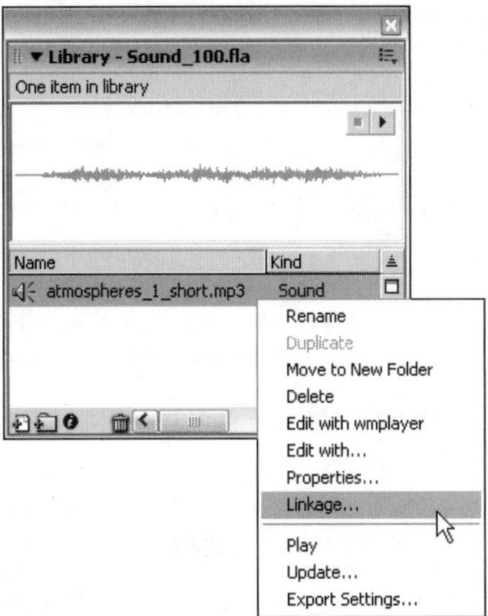

Figure 23-7: The Linkage option in the Library panel

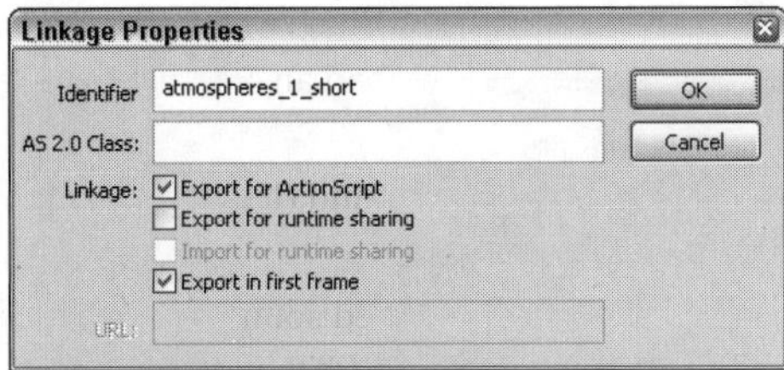

Figure 23-8: You must assign a unique ID name for each exported asset.

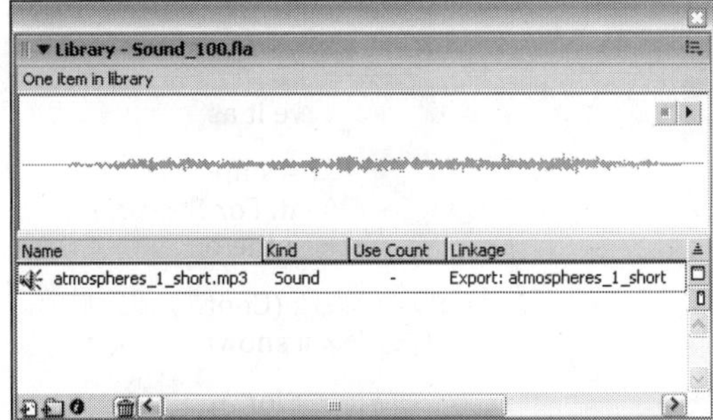

Figure 23-9: The Linkage column of the expanded Library panel

6. Now you're ready to utilize this sound file in your ActionScript. Once the asset is set to export, you can refer to the ID name in the `attachSound()` method of the `Sound` object. Rename Layer 1 to `actions`. Select frame 1 of this layer and open the Actions panel (F9). Type the following ActionScript into the Script pane:

```
var mcHolder:MovieClip = this.createEmptyMovieClip( ⮐
   "mcHolder_1", 1);
var snd_1:Sound = new Sound(mcHolder);
snd_1.attachSound("atmospheres_1_short");
```

   The first line creates a `MovieClip` object (`mcHolder_1`) to store the sound resource. Line 2 establishes the new `Sound` object, named `snd_1`. The third line marries an instance of the `atmospheres_1_short` sound in the Library to this object.

Tip

Remember to press Ctrl+T or ⌘+T (while focus is in the Actions panel) to test your code for syntax errors.

7. Once the sound asset is tied to a specific `Sound` instance, you can then use the `start()` and `stop()` methods of the `Sound` class to either play or halt the sound, respectively. In this example, use some buttons from the built-in Button Library (Window ➪ Other Panels ➪ Common Libraries ➪ Buttons) to activate these methods. Before you bring in some buttons, though, make a new layer and name it `buttons`. In the Playback folder, drag a copy of the gel Right and gel Stop buttons onto your document's stage, as shown in Figure 23-10. You can close the Buttons Library when you are finished copying the buttons.

Figure 23-10: Place an instance of each button anywhere on your movie's stage. Note that this view is magnified.

8. Select the gel Right instance (the one with the right arrow). In the Property inspector, name this instance `btPlay`.

9. Select the gel Stop instance and, in the Property inspector, name the instance `btStop`.

10. Select frame 1 of the actions layer, and add the following code after the existing code:

```
btPlay.onRelease = function():Void {
   snd_1.start();
};
```

This code tells the `snd_1` object to begin playing when the `btPlay` instance is clicked. Note that you can use the optional `offset` and `loopFactor` arguments to start the sound at a specific "in" point and/or loop the sound. For example, `snd_1.start(0, 2);` makes the entire sound play twice.

11. In the actions list for frame 1 of the actions layer, continue to add the following code:

```
btStop.onRelease = function():Void {
   snd_1.stop();
};
```

When this button instance is clicked, the `stop()` method tells the `snd_1` object to halt playback.

12. Now you're ready to test your Flash movie. Save your Flash document. Then test the movie using Control ➪ Test Movie (Ctrl+Enter or ⌘+Enter). When you click the `btPlay` button (gel Right), you should hear the `atmospheres_1_short` sound begin to play. When you click the `btStop` button (gel Stop), the sound should cease to play.

You can examine the completed file, `Sound_100.fla`, located in the `ch23` folder of the book's CD-ROM.

That wasn't too hard, was it? Now that you know how to link a sound asset and control it, it's time to learn how to load an MP3 file into a Flash movie at runtime.

Loading an External MP3 File

In this section, you learn how to load an MP3 file into a `Sound` object, monitoring its download progress. You will apply the percent loaded to a progress bar that grows as bytes download into the movie. You will also create an Input text field that specifies the URL of the MP3 file to download.

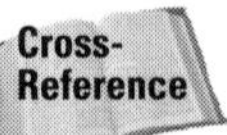

For more information on loaders and assets, read Chapter 34.

1. Create a new Flash document (Ctrl+N or ⌘+N). In the Document Properties dialog box (Modify ➪ Document), change the width of the document to 500 and the height to 200. Save the document as `Sound_200.fla`.

2. Rename Layer 1 `text fields`.

3. Select the Text tool and create an Input text field in the upper-left corner of the stage, as shown in Figure 23-11. In the Property inspector, assign the name `tURL` in the *<Instance Name>* field of the Property inspector. Use any font face and size you want, and enable the Show Border option for the field.

4. Using the Text tool, create a Static text block above the `tURL` text field, indicating the words **File URL**.

5. Create a Dynamic text field named `tStatus`, and place it underneath the `tURL` text field. Place some Static text to the right of the field, indicating **Status:**, as shown in Figure 23-12.

6. On the text field layer, create a Static text block with the word **Progress:**. Place this text underneath the Status: text block.

7. Create a new layer and name it `mcProgressBar`. On frame 1 of this layer, draw a skinny rectangle with a blue fill and a black stroke. The general shape and size is shown in Figure 23-13.

8. Select the stroke of the rectangle and cut it (Edit ➪ Cut). Create a new layer and name it `frame`. Place this layer just above the `mcProgressBar` layer. With frame 1 of this layer selected, choose Edit ➪ Paste in Place. Once the stroke is pasted, lock the frame layer.

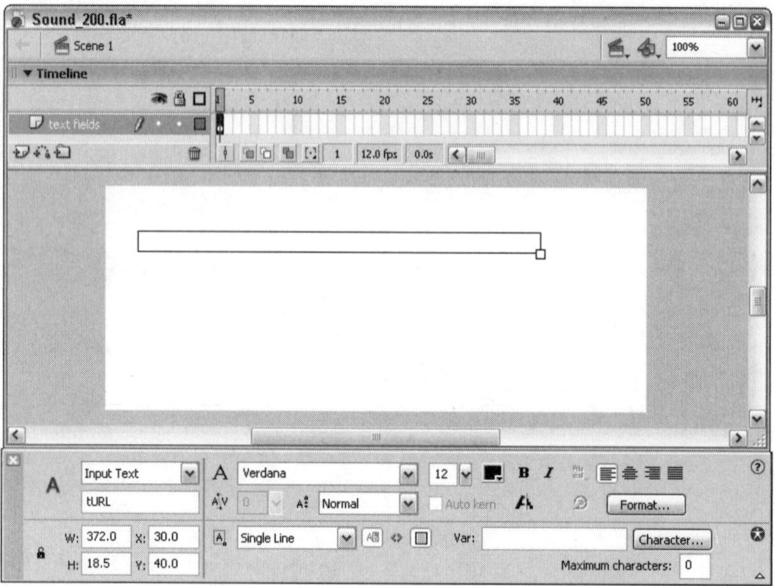

Figure 23-11: The tURL text field accepts the URL to the MP3 file.

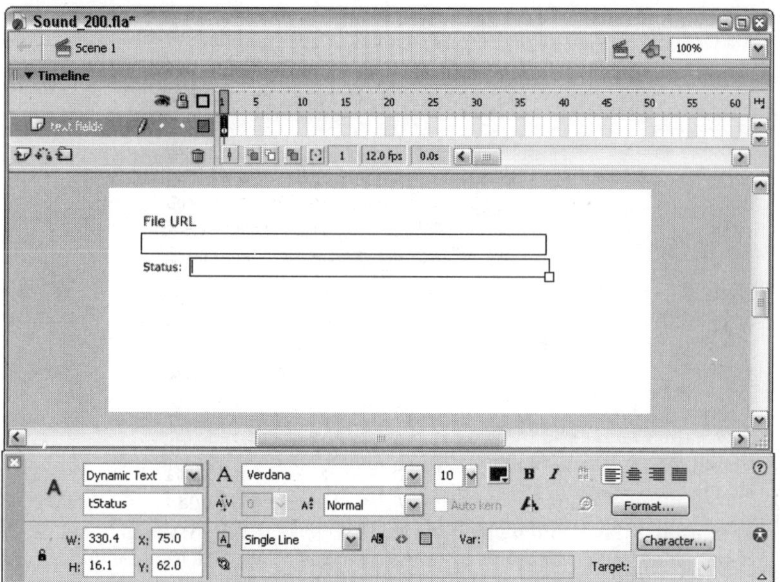

Figure 23-12: The tStatus field displays the result of the MP3 loading.

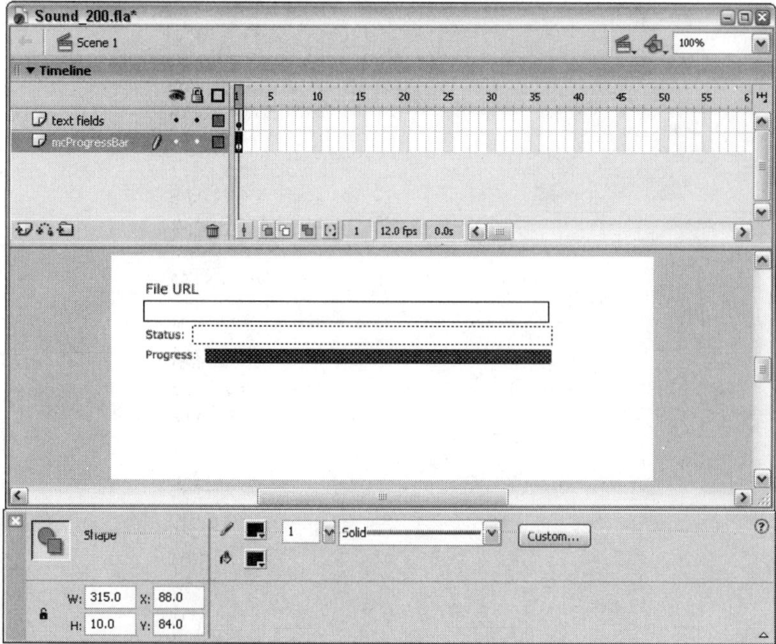

Figure 23-13: This graphic will indicate the progress as the MP3 file loads into the movie.

9. Select the rectangle fill on frame 1 of the `mcProgressBar` layer and press the F8 key. In the Convert to Symbol dialog box, name the symbol `progressBarClip`, choose the Movie Clip behavior, and click the left center registration point, as shown in Figure 23-14.

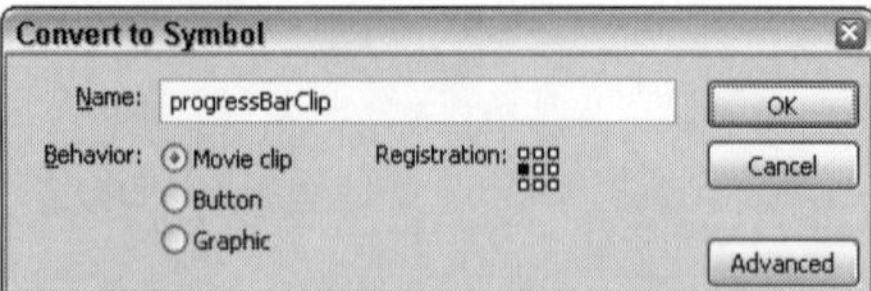

Figure 23-14: Because the progress bar will grow from left to right, the registration point needs to be on the left central edge of the symbol.

10. Select the `progressBarClip` instance on the stage and open the Property inspector. In the <*Instance Name*> field, type the name `mcProgressBar`. Set the width of the instance to one pixel as well.

11. Create a new layer and name it `buttons`. Open the Components panel (Ctrl+F7 or ⌘+F7) and drag the `Button` component to the stage. Place the instance underneath the other elements, at the left edge. In the Property inspector, name the instance `cbtLoad`. In the Parameters tab, assign a label value of Load MP3 (see Figure 23-15).

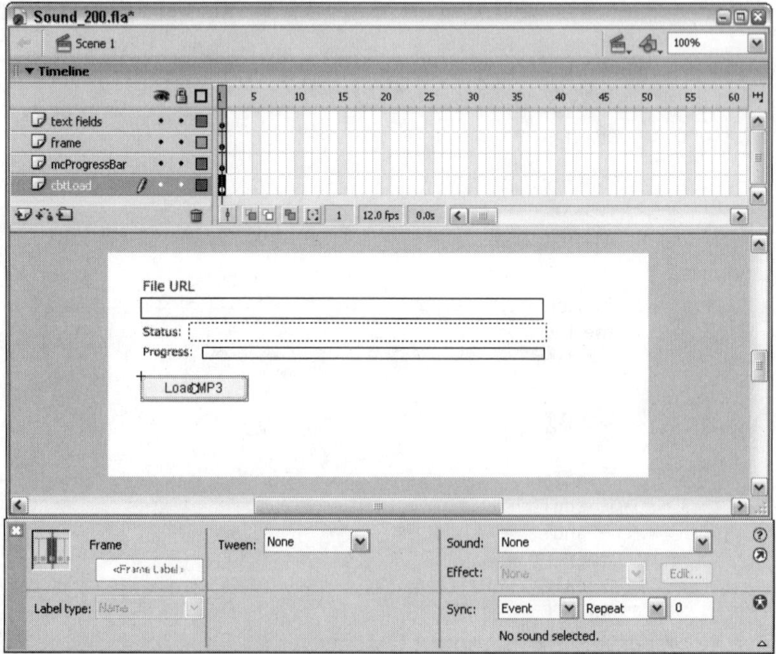

Figure 23-15: The cbtLoad instance invokes a listener method named loadFile(), which is defined in Step 12.

12. Create a new layer and name it `actions`. Place this layer at the top of the layer stack. Select frame 1 of this layer and open the Actions panel. In the Script pane, type the code shown in Listing 23-4.

Listing 23-4: **The Setup of MovieClip and Sound Objects**

```
var mcHolder:MovieClip = this.createEmptyMovieClip("mcHolder", 1);
var snd_1:Sound = new Sound(mcHolder);
snd_1.onLoad = function(bSuccess:Boolean):Void {
   if (bSuccess) {
      tStatus.text = "The MP3 file has loaded.";
   } else {
      tStatus.text = "Invalid URL. Try again.";
   }
};
snd_1.onSoundComplete = function():Void {
   tStatus.text = "The MP3 file has finished playing.";
};
this.loadFile = function(oEvent:Object):Void {
   snd_1.loadSound(tURL.text, true);
   tStatus.text = "The MP3 file is loading.";
};
cbtLoad.addEventListener("click", this.loadFile);
```

13. Save your Flash document and test the movie (Ctrl+Enter or ⌘+Enter). Type the following URL into the `tURL` text field:

    `http://www.flashsupport.com/mp3/dog.mp3`

    Click the Load MP3 button (that is, the `cbtLoad` instance). The `tStatus` text field indicates the progress of the MP3 file loading. As soon as enough of the file has downloaded into the movie, the sound begins to play.

14. Close the Test Movie window and return to the main timeline of your Flash document. Now you add the ActionScript code to check the progress of the MP3 download. Modify the code in frame 1 with the bold code shown in Listing 23-5.

Listing 23-5: **Adding a checkLoad() Function**

```
function checkLoad(sndTarget:Sound):Void {
   var nLB:Number = sndTarget.getBytesLoaded();
   var nTB:Number = sndTarget.getBytesTotal();
   var nPercent:Number = (nLB/nTB)*100;
   mcProgressBar._xscale = nPercent;
   if (nLB >= nTB && nTB > 0) {
      clearInterval(checkProgress);
   }
}
```

Continued

Listing 23-5 *(continued)*

```
var mcHolder:MovieClip = this.createEmptyMovieClip("mcHolder", 1);
var snd_1:Sound = new Sound(mcHolder);
var nProgress:Number;
snd_1.onLoad = function(bSuccess:Boolean):Void {
   if (bSuccess) {
      tStatus.text = "The MP3 file has loaded.";
   } else {
      tStatus.text = "Invalid URL. Try again.";
      clearInterval(progressID);
   }
};
snd_1.onSoundComplete = function():Void {
   tStatus.text = "The MP3 file has finished playing.";
};
this.loadFile = function(oEvent:Object):Void {
   snd_1.loadSound(tURL.text, true);
   tStatus.text = "The MP3 file is loading.";
   nProgress = setInterval(checkLoad, 50, snd_1);
};
cbtLoad.addEventListener("click", this.loadFile);
```

15. Save your Flash document again and test it (Ctrl+Enter or ⌘+Enter). Enter the following URL into the `tURL` text field:

    `http://www.flashsupport.com.com/mp3/atmospheres_1_short.mp3`

    Click the Load MP3 button. The `mcProgressBar` instance will start to indicate the loading progress of the MP3 file.

You can find the completed Flash document, `Sound_200.fla`, in the `ch23` folder of this book's CD-ROM.

Controlling the Volume of a Sound Object

In this section, you make use of the `setVolume()` method of the `Sound` class. If you remember from the earlier coverage, `setVolume()` controls the loudness of a sound. For this example, you will start with a prebuilt slider `MovieClip` object. This `MovieClip` object already has a self-contained `MovieClip` instance (named `mcPos`) and the ActionScript enabling it to be dragged across the rule of the slider.

In this exercise, you need to create the proper event handlers and functionality to apply the slider bar's position to the appropriate volume level. Here is an overview of what you do with the `sliderClip`'s functionality:

1. When the `sliderClip` instance loads, create a function to update a sound target (which is a `Sound` object). This function uses the X position of the slider's bar (that is, the `mcPos` instance) to calculate the volume level. You then apply this volume level to the desired `Sound` object.

2. When the Sound instance has loaded (or attached) the sound resource, decide the volume level that the sound should have when it begins playing.

3. After the slider instance loads, monitor the movement of the slider. When the slider bar moves, execute the function created in Step 1, which updates the sound volume level using the position value of the slider bar.

For this exercise, open (or make a copy of) the `Sound_300_starter.fla` file, located in the `ch23` folder of the book's CD-ROM.

Now you will apply the overview notes to the starter document file. This starter file contains the same code you used in previous sections. There is already a `loadFile()` method that loads and plays an MP3 file.

1. Open the starter file from the book's CD-ROM. The document's stage contains all of the elements from the `Sound_200.fla` document. Save the document as `Sound_300.fla`.

2. Create a new layer on the main timeline and name it `mcVolumeSlider`. Place the layer at the bottom of the layer stack. Select frame 1 of this layer before you proceed to the next step.

3. Open the Library panel and drag an instance of the `sliderClip` symbol onto the stage. Place the instance in the right portion of the stage. In the Transform panel, rotate the instance -90 degrees (you can also use the Free Transform tool to do this). In the Property inspector, name the instance `mcVolumeSlider`. Resize the instance so that it fits within the height of the stage, as shown in Figure 23-16.

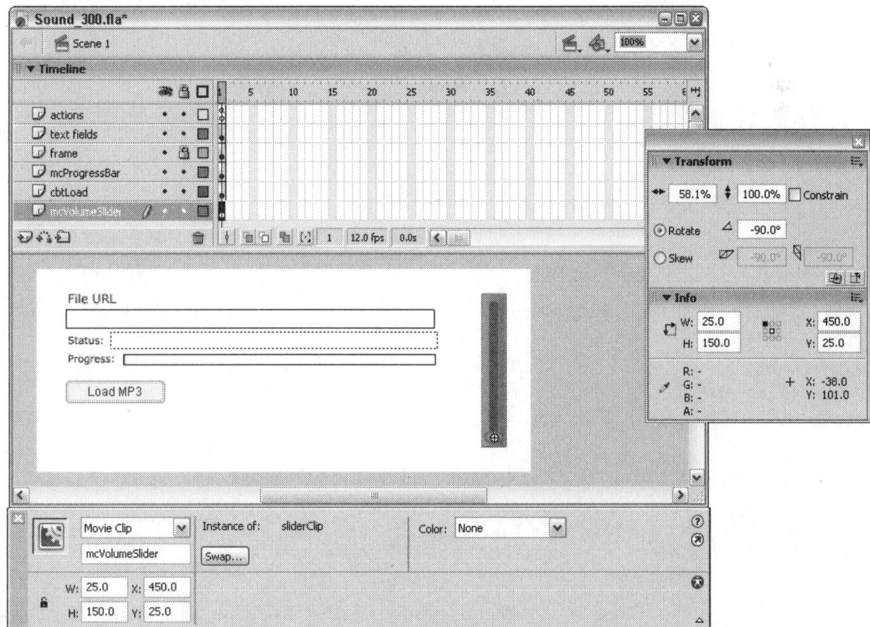

Figure 23-16: The mcVolumeSlider instance placed on the right edge of the stage

4. Double-click the sliderClip symbol in the Library panel. In this symbol, the small circle to the left is a MovieClip instance named mcPos. Test the movie (Ctrl+Enter or ⌘+Enter) and you'll see that you can click and drag the circle graphic on the slider's rule. However, if you try to load an MP3 file into the movie, the slider does not do anything to the sound's volume. In the next steps, you will modify the slider's function to control the volume.

5. Go back to the Flash document and in the sliderClip timeline, select frame 1 of the actions layer. Open the Actions panel (F9) and review the code, which is also shown in Listing 23-6.

Listing 23-6: **The sliderClip ActionScript Code**

```
function setProp(nPos:Number, sProp:String, sndTarget:Sound):Void {
   var a:Number = nPos;
   var b:Number = 225;
   var c:Number = 100;
   var nPropVal:Number = (a/b)*c;
   sndTarget[sProp](nPropVal);
}
function startSlider(bActive:Boolean):Void {
   if(bActive){
      this.onMouseMove = function(){
         setProp(mcPos._x, sProp, sndTarget);
         updateAfterEvent();
      };
   }else{
      this.onMouseMove = null;
   }
}
mcPos._x = 112.5;
mcPos.onPress = function():Void {
   this._parent.startSlider(true);
   this.startDrag(false,0,0,225,0);
};
mcPos.onRelease = mcPos.onReleaseOutside = function():Void{
   this._parent.startSlider(false);
   this.stopDrag();
};
var sProp:String = "setVolume";
setProp(mcPos._x, sProp, sndTarget);
```

The setProp() function is executed by the onMouseMove() event handler created whenever the mcPos instance on the slider moves, as invoked by the onPress() handler and startSlider() function. The following line of code is a translation of the setVolume() method of the Sound object:

```
sndTarget[sProp](nPropVal);
```

Here, sndTarget, an argument of the setProp() function, represents the snd_1 object created on the main timeline. sProp represents the current method of the snd_1 object that you want to invoke. In this example, you want to use the `setVolume()` method. This method is declared as a `String` value in the following line of code:

```
var sProp:String = "setVolume";
```

The `sProp` value is passed to the `setProp()` function from the `onMouseMove()` handler defined in the `startSlider()` function. Finally, the `nPropVal` argument represents the volume level that you want to apply to the `snd_1` object. With these actions in place, you can set the `sndTarget` variable for the `mcVolumeSlider` instance (needed for the proper operation of the `setProp()` function) from the actions on frame 1 of the main timeline, where the `snd_1` object is created.

6. Go back to the main timeline and select frame 1 of the actions layer. In this frame's actions, add the lines of bold code shown in Listing 23-7.

   When the Flash movie starts, you want to tell the `mcVolumeSlider` instance which `Sound` object to monitor. The following line of code does just that:

   ```
   mcVolumeSlider.sndTarget = snd_1;
   ```

   The second new line of code executes the `setProp()` function within the `mcVolumeSlider` instance, passing the starting value of the `mcPos` instance, the method name to be enabled (`"setVolume"`), and the current sound target (`snd_1`).

   ```
   mcVolumeSlider.setProp(mcVolumeSlider.mcPos._x, "setVolume", ⮐
      snd_1);
   ```

Listing 23-7: **The Modified Frame 1 Actions**

```
function checkLoad(sndTarget:Sound):Void {
   var nLB:Number = sndTarget.getBytesLoaded();
   var nTB:Number = sndTarget.getBytesTotal();
   var nPercent:Number = (nLB/nTB)*100;
   mcProgressBar._xscale = nPercent;
   if (nLB >= nTB && nTB > 0) {
      clearInterval(nProgress);
   }
}
var mcHolder:MovieClip = this.createEmptyMovieClip("mcHolder", 1);
var snd_1:Sound = new Sound(mcHolder);
mcVolumeSlider.sndTarget = snd_1;
mcVolumeSlider.setProp(mcVolumeSlider.mcPos._x, "setVolume", snd_1);
var nProgress:Number;
snd_1.onLoad = function(bSuccess:Boolean):Void {
   if (bSuccess) {
      tStatus.text = "The MP3 file has loaded.";
   } else {
      tStatus.text = "Invalid URL. Try again.";
      clearInterval(nProgress);
   }
};
snd_1.onSoundComplete = function():Void {
   tStatus.text = "The MP3 file has finished playing.";
};
```

Continued

Listing 23-7 *(continued)*

```
this.loadFile = function(oEvent:Object):Void {
   snd_1.loadSound(tURL.text, true);
   tStatus.text = "The MP3 file is loading.";
   nProgress = setInterval(checkLoad, 50, snd_1);
};
cbtLoad.addEventListener("click", this.loadFile);
```

7. When you are finished adding the code from Steps 5 and 6, you're ready to try it out. Save your document and choose Control ⇨ Test Movie (Ctrl+Enter or ⌘+Enter). Enter the URL to an MP3 file in the tURL text field and press the Load MP3 button. Once you hear the sound playing, click and drag the slider's bar (that is, the mcPos instance). As you drag the bar down, the sound's volume should lower. As you drag it up, it should become louder.

If you would like to view a completed version of this exercise, open the Sound_300.fla file, located in the ch23 folder of the book's CD-ROM. Look for more sound examples featuring the slider bar at www.flashsupport.com/articles.

You can create other interactive controls that control volume as well. For example, you can create plus (+) and minus (-) buttons to either add or subtract predefined units to the sound's volume. In the next section, you learn how to take the same slider from this example and use it as a balance control (that is, left-right volume control).

Applying Advanced Effects to Sound Objects

For this example, you create Sound objects that respond to mouse movements. Unlike in the previous examples, though, you have two Sound objects: one sound to represent the left side of the stage, and one sound for the right side. When the mouse moves into the left area of the stage, the left sound (which you name sndLeft) will play in both the left and right speakers. If the mouse enters the right area of the stage, the right sound, named sndRight, will play in both speakers. As one sound plays, the other will diminish. If the mouse is right in the middle of the stage, you hear both sounds equally in each speaker.

In order to accomplish these effects, you need to use the setTransform() method of the Sound class, and create custom transformObjects for each sound. You use the ll and rr properties of the transformObject to control the left and right channel output, respectively. The mouse cursor's X position is used to determine the "strength" of this output.

For this exercise, make a copy of the Sound_400_starter.fla file located in the ch23 folder of the book's CD-ROM.

1. Open the starter file. This file contains one layer on the main timeline, as shown in Figure 23-17. The frame layer simply holds artwork that shows the boundaries of the movie's stage, with a division line halfway across the stage.

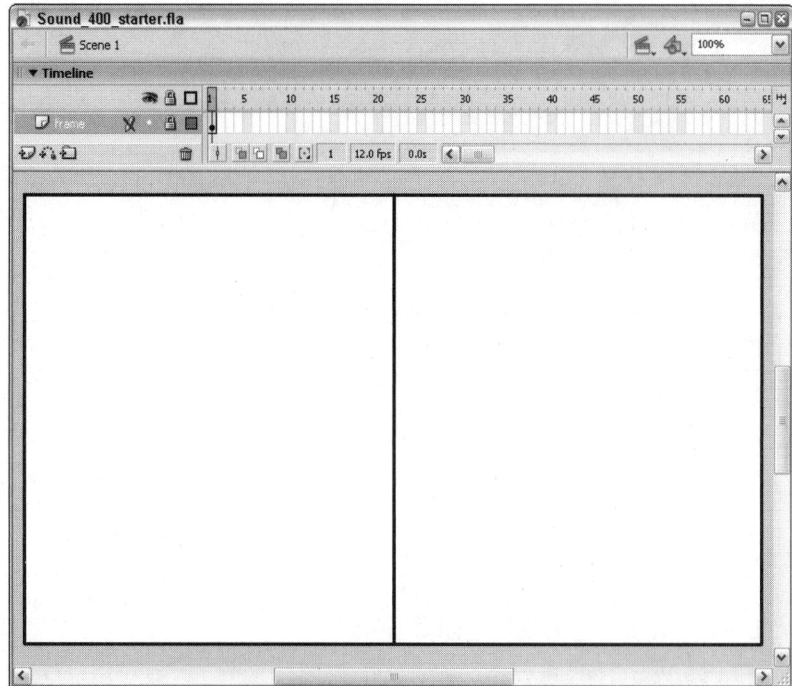

Figure 23-17: The stage of this movie is divided in half by the artwork in the frame layer, to serve as a reference point.

2. Create a new layer and name it `actions`. Place this layer above the frame layer.

3. Select frame 1 of the actions layer and open the Actions panel. Type the code shown in Listing 23-8 into the Script pane.

   This code should be easy for you to decipher because you have seen these methods in previous exercises. The first two lines create two empty `MovieClip` objects, `mcHolder_1` and `mcHolder_2`. These objects store the sound resources specified later in this code block. The remainder of the code creates two `Sound` objects, `sndLeft` and `sndRight`, and binds them to the `mcHolder_1` and `mcHolder_2` `MovieClip` objects, respectively. Next, you attach the atmosphere sounds from the Library to the `sndLeft` and `sndRight` objects, and begin playing the sounds. Finally, you create `transformObjects` named `oLeftProps` and `oRightProps` to be used later (in the next step) with `sndLeft` and `sndRight`, respectively.

Listing 23-8: **Setting Up the sndLeft and sndRight Objects**

```
var mcHolder_1:MovieClip = this.createEmptyMovieClip("mcHolder_1", 1);
var mcHolder_2:MovieClip = this.createEmptyMovieClip("mcHolder_2", 2);

var sndLeft:Sound = new Sound(mcHolder_1);
var sndRight:Sound = new Sound(mcHolder_2);
```

Continued

Listing 23-8 *(continued)*

```
sndLeft.attachSound("atmospheres_1");
sndRight.attachSound("atmospheres_2");
sndLeft.start(0, 999);
sndRight.start(0, 999);
var oLeftProps:Object = new Object();
var oRightProps:Object = new Object();
```

4. Now you add to frame 1 the ActionScript that enables the mouse's interaction with the sounds. Beneath the last line of code entered from Step 3, add the ActionScript code shown in Listing 23-9.

The first and last lines of code establish the `onMouseMove()` handler. This handler detects any mouse movement, and executes the nested code upon such movement.

The second line of code checks the current X position of the mouse cursor, using the `_xmouse` property of the `MovieClip` object. For this example, you want the coordinates of the mouse on the main timeline. Therefore, you refer to the current timeline: `this`.

The third line of code creates a `nPercent` variable. Its value represents how far the mouse cursor has crossed the stage, from left to right. At the left edge, `nPercent` equals 0. At the right edge, it equals 100.

The fourth and fifth lines of code set the `ll` and `rr` properties of the `oLeftProps` `transformObject` to `100 - nPercent`. Because the `oLeftProps` object relates to the `sndLeft` object, you want to make sure it equals 100 (full volume) when the mouse is at the left edge of the stage. When the mouse is at the right edge of the stage, you want to silence the `sndLeft` object.

The sixth and seventh lines of code set the `ll` and `rr` properties of the `oRightProps` `transformObject`. Here, you simply set it equal to `nPercent` because it correlates directly to the 0 to 100 values required for `ll` and `rr`. As the mouse moves to the left edge, the values of `oRightProps` decrease. As the mouse moves to the right edge, the values of `oRightProps` increase.

Lines 8 and 9 apply the `transformObjects` to the appropriate `Sound` objects.

Line 10 forces a faster update of the sound transformations, using the `updateAfterEvent()` function.

When you are finished typing the code, press Ctrl+T or ⌘+T to check for any syntax errors.

Listing 23-9: **Defining the onMouseMove() Handler for the Movie**

```
1.  this.onMouseMove = function() {
2.    var nMouseX:Number = this._xmouse;
3.    var nPercent:Number = (nMouseX/Stage.width)*100;
4.    oLeftProps.ll = 100 - nPercent;
5.    oLeftProps.rr = 100 - nPercent;
6.    oRightProps.ll = nPercent;
```

```
    oRightProps.rr = nPercent;
    sndLeft.setTransform(oLeftProps);
    sndRight.setTransform(oRightProps);
    updateAfterEvent();
};
```

5. Now you're ready to test your code. Save your Flash document as Sound_400.fla and test the movie using Control ⇨ Test Movie (Ctrl+Enter or ⌘+Enter). Move the mouse to the left; you should hear the atmospheres_1.mp3 file playing in both speakers. As you move it away from the left edge, the sound should fade out, replaced with the sound of atmospheres_2.mp3.

You can view the completed Flash document, Sound_400.fla, on the book's CD-ROM. This file, located in the ch23 folder, includes ActionScript that manipulates the rl and lr properties of the transformObjects, so that both channels of one sound will play in either the left or right speaker, adding to the depth perception of the sounds!

Making a Looping Playlist

One of the more practical uses of the onSoundComplete() event handler for Sound objects is the capability to cycle MP3 playlists. In this section, you learn how to add this type of functionality to one of the exercise files you completed earlier in this section. Here's the overview of the steps you need to do.

1. Create a list of MP3 file URLs. Store these values in an array. The array is created by a function named initSongList().
2. Modify the loadFile() method to play the first sound URL in the array if the tURL text field is empty. This URL is also removed from the array, so the next time the loadFile() method is called, a new URL will be used.
3. Modify the loadFile() method to trigger itself when a sound in the playlist has finished playing.

Now that you have a general idea about the process, you're ready to build the Flash document.

Before you begin this exercise, make a copy of the Sound_500_starter.fla, dog.mp3, cat.mp3, duck.mp3, and bird.mp3 files from the ch23 folder of this book's CD-ROM.

1. Open the starter file. This document contains a fully functional interface to load and play MP3 files. Save this document as Sound_500.fla.
2. Select frame 1 of the actions layer and open the Actions panel (F9). At the end of the existing actions list, add the following function and action. This function defines the array containing the URLs to the MP3 files. You can list http:// URLs of your own, or copy other MP3 files into the folder in which you saved your Flash document in Step 1.

Once the initSongList() function is defined, it is invoked when the movie starts. You will also use the initSongList() later, in the loadFile() function modifications.

```
function initSongList():Void {
  aSongs = ["dog.mp3", "cat.mp3", "duck.mp3", "bird.mp3"];
}
var aSongs:Array;
initSongList();
```

3. Now you define a function to check the content of the tURL field. If it is empty (that is, the user did not type any text into it), the function returns the URL of the first file in the array, and also removes that URL from the array using the shift() method. After the initSongList(); action from Step 2, add the following code:

```
function checkField():String {
  if(tURL.text != ""){
    return tURL.text;
  } else {
    if (aSongs.length == 0) {
      initSongList();
    }
    return aSongs.shift().toString();
  }
}
```

4. The last step is to change the loadFile() and onSoundComplete() methods to make use of the two functions you created in Steps 2 and 3. Add (or modify) the following lines of code displayed in bold type. The loadFile() method is called in the onSoundComplete() event handler to initiate the next file in the playlist when the current sound has finished playing. Another modification is the use of the local variable named sLoadURL. This variable retrieves its value from the checkField() function you created in Step 3. The value is then used in the loadSound() method of the snd_1 object.

```
snd_1.onSoundComplete = function():Void {
   tStatus.text = "The MP3 file has finished playing.";
   loadFile();
};
this.loadFile = function(oEvent:Object):Void {
   var sLoadURL:String = checkField();
   snd_1.loadSound(sLoadURL, true);
   tStatus.text = "The MP3 file is loading.";
   nProgress = setInterval(checkLoad, 50, snd_1);
};
```

5. You're ready to test the movie. Save your document and choose Control ➪ Test Movie (Ctrl+Enter or ⌘+Enter). Click the Load MP3 button and the first file in the playlist starts to play. As soon as it is finished, the second file will play, and so on.

You can find the completed file, Sound_500.fla, in the ch23 folder of this book's CD-ROM.

When you have the movie working properly, change the files (or use `http://` locations) in the `aSongs` array defined in the `initSongList()` function. You can make this list of files as long as you want, or load the filenames from an external text data source.

We'd like to know what you thought about this chapter. Visit `www.flashsupport.com/feedback` to fill out an online form with your comments.

Summary

- The constructor for the `Sound` class uses the `new` operator. Each instance of the `Sound` class should be constructed in the following syntax: `var sndName:Sound = new Sound(mcTarget);`.
- `Sound` objects marry sounds from the movie's Library or an external MP3 file to a specific timeline in the movie by using the `attachSound()` or `loadSound()` method, respectively, of the `Sound` class.
- The `start()` and `stop()` methods are used to play or halt `Sound` objects, respectively.
- The `setVolume()` and `getVolume()` methods control or retrieve the loudness of a specific `Sound` object, respectively.
- The `setPan()` and `getPan()` methods work with the balance (that is, the volume distribution between the left and right speakers) of a specific `Sound` object.
- The `setTransform()` and `getTransform()` methods of the `Sound` class enable you to precisely control left and right channel output in the actual left and right speakers of the computer system.
- There are three properties of the `Sound` class: `duration`, `position`, and `id3`. The `loadSound()` method is used to download MP3 files into the Flash Player at runtime, and the `onLoad()`, `onSoundComplete()`, and `onID3()` event handlers enhance the playback control of Sound objects.

✦ ✦ ✦

The NetStream and Video Classes

✦ ✦ ✦ ✦

In This Chapter

Understanding FLV files

Displaying video with the NetStream class

Controlling video

✦ ✦ ✦ ✦

One of the most exciting features of Flash Player 7 is the power to load and display Flash Video files (FLV files) directly into a Flash movie at runtime. When Flash Player 6 first introduced video playback, you had to use either embedded video within a Flash movie (SWF file) or use Flash Communication Server to deliver the FLV file to the Flash movie. In this chapter, you learn how to load FLV files into a Flash movie using the `NetStream` class. You learn how to use a `Video` object to display the visual portion of the `NetStream` output as well.

Working with Flash Video Files

When the original release of Flash MX was announced, Macromedia gave Web designers and developers the capability to compress digital video files with a codec designed exclusively for the Flash Player: Sorenson Spark. With the Sorenson Spark codec, the Flash Player could display video without the aid of any other video plug-in or driver. Flash MX and Flash MX 2004 can automatically import digital video formats such as Windows AVI or QuickTime MOV and compress them with the Spark codec.

If you want to learn how to use the Video Import Wizard of Flash MX 2004, the Flash Video Exporter tool of Flash MX Pro 2004, or Sorenson Squeeze (a third-party tool that compresses digital video into the Spark format) to create FLV files, refer to *Macromedia Flash MX 2004 Bible* by Robert Reinhardt and Snow Dowd (Wiley, 2004). Our coverage in the present book focuses primarily on the ActionScript aspects of the `NetStream` and `Video` objects.

In this section, you learn how to make a Flash Video file (FLV file) from an existing digital video file. You also learn the different ways in which you can access a Flash Video file in a Flash movie. Later in this chapter, you learn how to load the FLV file into a movie using ActionScript.

Making an FLV File in Flash MX 2004

Before you can learn how to work with an FLV file, you have to have access to one. In the following steps, you learn a quick and dirty way to make an FLV file in Flash MX 2004. As mentioned earlier in this chapter, you can create FLV files with other tools that produce better quality video files that are smaller (in byte size) as well.

1. In Flash MX 2004, create a new Flash document. Save this document as `sample_flv.fla`.
2. Choose File ➪ Import ➪ Import to Library. Browse to the ch24 folder on this book's CD-ROM, and select the `sample_high.mov` file. This video file is a QuickTime movie encoded with the Sorenson Video 3 codec.
3. In the Video Import Wizard dialog box, choose Embed Video in Macromedia Flash Document, as shown in Figure 24-1. Click the Next button to proceed to the next screen of the wizard.
4. On the Editing screen, choose Import the Entire Video, as shown in Figure 24-2. Click the Next button.
5. On the Encoding screen, make sure the default compression profile, DSL/Cable 256Kbps, is selected (see Figure 24-3). Click the Finish button to finalize the import process.

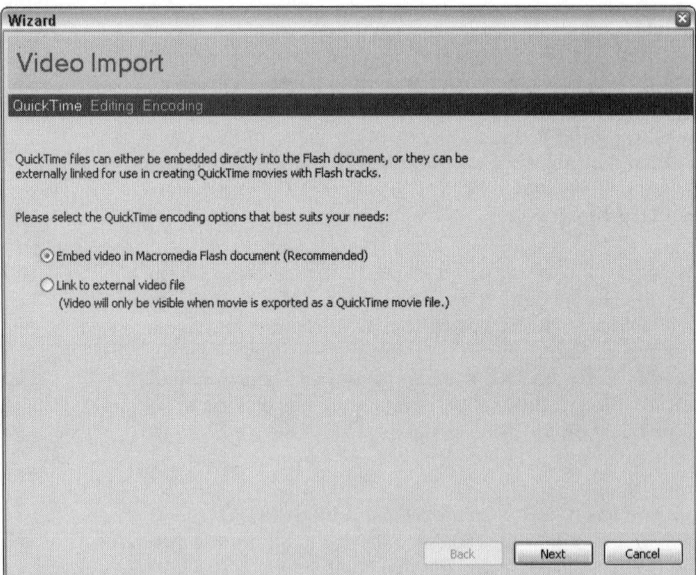

Figure 24-1: The first stage of the Video Import Wizard for QuickTime files

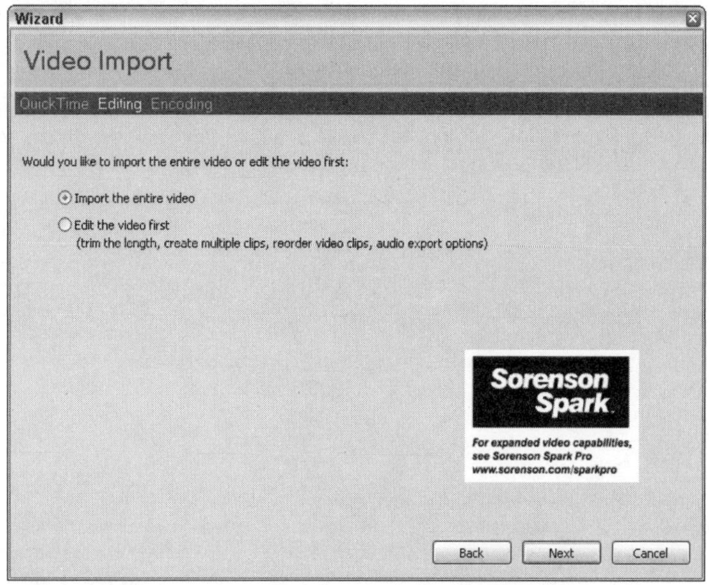

Figure 24-2: The Editing stage of the Video Import Wizard

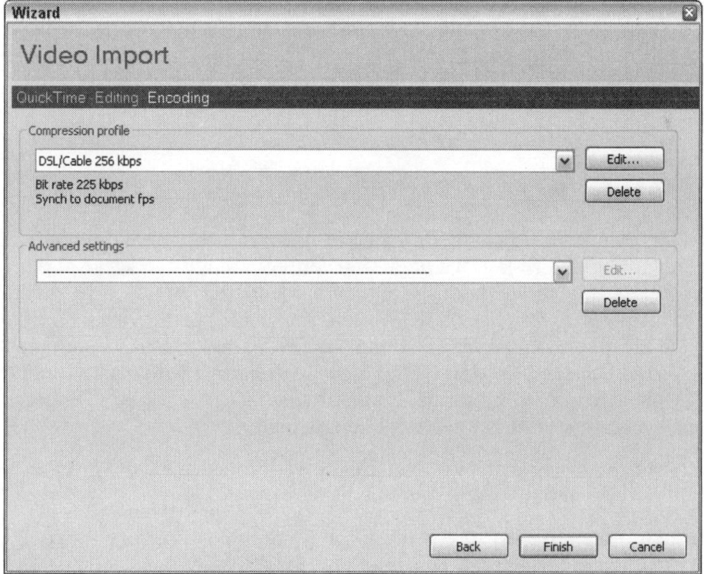

Figure 24-3: The final stage of the Video Import Wizard process

6. You now have an Embedded Video symbol in the document's Library panel. Open the Library panel (Ctrl+L or ⌘+L), and right-click (or Control-click on the Mac) the `sample_high.mov` symbol. In the context menu, choose Properties.

7. In the Embedded Video Properties dialog box (shown in Figure 24-4), click the Export button. In the Export FLV dialog box, browse to a location on your system where you want to save the FLV file, and name the file `sample_high.flv`. Click Save to finish the export process.

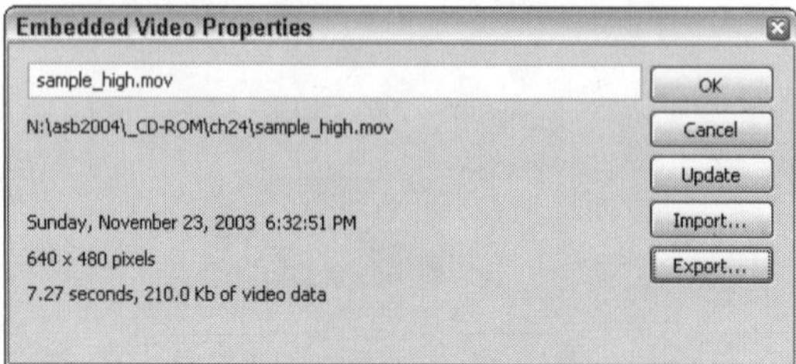

Figure 24-4: The Embedded Video Properties dialog box

Once you have made an FLV file, you can load it into a Flash movie (SWF file) at runtime using ActionScript or a Media component.

You can find the `sample_flv.fla`, `sample_high.mov`, and `sample_high.flv` files in the ch24 folder of this book's CD-ROM. You will also find a version of the video file exported from Sorenson Squeeze, named `sample_high_300k.flv`. In the examples later in this chapter, you can compare the quality of this FLV file to that of the basic export you made from Flash MX 2004.

Using RTMP to Access FLV Files

Flash Video (FLV) files were originally designed to be streamed in real time from Macromedia Flash Communication Server MX. This media server technology can serve audio/video streams to multiple users simultaneously, and even record audio/video streams from a user's Webcam! Flash Communication Server MX uses a proprietary protocol called RTMP, or Real Time Messaging Protocol, to connect Flash movies (SWF files) to Flash Communication Server applications. When Flash Video (FLV) files are streamed with Flash Communication Server, the FLV file is never stored locally in the browser's cache folder — only the current frames being played are stored in the Flash Player's buffer.

The following list provides reasons why you might want to use a Flash Communication Server to deliver audio/video streams (from your FLV files):

✦ **Flash Player compatibility:** If you use Flash Communication Server to deliver FLV files, you can reach a wider market. You need only Flash Player 6 or later to view audio/video streams from Flash Communication Server, rather than using Flash Player 7 for HTTP-loaded FLV files.

✦ **Digital Rights Management (DRM):** If you have a business client that is protective of its content, the use of Flash Communication Server can make it harder for users to copy audio/video content. FLV files are stored in a protected area of the server and can be delivered by the Flash Communication Server only. When viewed by a user, the FLV file is never downloaded in its entirety, nor is it stored as a local file in the browser's cache.

✦ **Immediate playback and seek abilities:** With Flash Communication Server, the user will be able to begin watching the video stream sooner, and the video can begin playback at any point within the FLV file. The user does not have to wait until the entire stream has downloaded up to the point that is desired to be played.

✦ **Minimize bandwidth consumption:** Regardless of a Flash Video file's length (or duration), Flash Communication Server serves only what the user is currently watching. Therefore, if you have a 45-minute video file but the user wants to watch only five minutes, your server's connection will not be burdened with sending the entire video file to the user.

✦ **Extended options:** With Flash Communication Server, you can record ActionScript data to a stream (FLV file), retrieve a stream's length (in seconds), and make new copies of the stream (with different in/out points) on the server.

However, there's always a cost for such things. The following list covers some of these drawbacks:

✦ **Licensing:** You have to purchase a license for Flash Communication Server. Licensing costs vary depending on your connection and user needs.

✦ **Learning curve:** You have to learn how to build and script Flash movies and Flash Communication Server applications to work with real-time streams.

✦ **Port and protocol restrictions:** If your target audience is using a computer that's behind a tight firewall or proxy server, Flash movies (SWF files) might be unable to connect to a Flash Communication Server to view audio/video streams.

✦ **Server installation:** You need to install and maintain Flash Communication Server independently of your Web server. Although you can have a Web server and the Flash Communication Server software running on the same computer, you'll likely want to purchase a dedicated machine for serving and connecting clients with Flash Communication Server.

For more production information on Flash Communication Server, refer to Macromedia's site at `www.macromedia.com/software/flashcom`.

Using HTTP to Access FLV Files

If you don't want to use Flash Communication Server to deliver FLV files to your audience, you're in luck. Flash Player 7 enables Flash movies (SWF files) to directly load FLV files at runtime, over a standard HTTP (Hypertext Transfer Protocol) connection. HTTP is the same protocol used to view regular Web pages and content. You simply upload your FLV file to your Web server, point your Flash movie to the FLV file's location, and you're ready to go. The following list provides some reasons why you might want to deliver FLV files over HTTP:

✦ **Cost effective:** If you're making Flash content for the Web, you already have a Web server that you can use to deliver FLV files.

✦ **Easy to implement:** Once you learn how to load an FLV file into a Flash movie with ActionScript (as discussed in the next section), you do not need to learn a new server-side language to serve the video file (as Flash Communication may require, depending on the complexity of your application).

However, there are some drawbacks, including the following:

✦ **Potential bandwidth overhead:** When you load an FLV file from a Web server, the entire file is downloaded to the user's machine. It doesn't matter if the user watches only a portion of it — once a Web server receives a request for a resource, it can deliver only the whole resource, not just a portion of it.

When you serve an FLV file over HTTP, you are not technically streaming the content into the Flash movie. Media assets served over HTTP are progressive downloads – although it's possible to begin playback before the entire file has downloaded, you can't prematurely pause the downloading process. Once it's started, the only way to stop it is to exit your Web browser and/or Flash movie.

✦ **Digital Rights Management (DRM):** Because the FLV is delivered over HTTP, it must be a public location. Users can potentially load and save the FLV separately from your Flash movie (SWF file), or they can search the browser cache for the FLV file.

✦ **Lack of extended options:** Some simple properties of an FLV file, such as duration (or length), cannot be automatically determined by loading the FLV file from a standard Web server. As such, you'll need to implement a secondary solution to provide the file's length to the Flash movie. Such information is needed for enhanced playback controls such as a playhead indicating the current position in the total duration.

In December 2003, Macromedia released an updater for the Flash Video Exporter tool and the Media components, both of which ship with Flash MX Professional 2004. One of the new features added by this updater is the capability to encode FLV files with embedded length (or duration) information. You can find the Video Update for Flash MX Professional 2004 at `www.macromedia.com/support/flash/downloads.html`.

Regardless of which protocol or server technology you use to deliver FLV files, keep the following points in mind:

✦ Audio/video content is rarely a small download for the user. Serving audio/video content can rack up bandwidth charges on your server hosting account.

✦ Make sure you have the rights to showcase the audio/video content. If you didn't shoot or record the content yourself, chances are that you'll need to obtain written consent to use the material on your own site.

✦ Don't use HTTP solely because it's perceived to be less of a financial hit. Thoroughly analyze the requirements for the audio/video content usage, and provide an overview of HTTP versus RTMP concerns to your business client.

This chapter covers how to load FLV files over HTTP connections, not over RMTP (Flash Communication Server) connections. For more information on Flash Communication Server, see `www.flashsupport.com/ria`.

Loading FLV Files into a Flash Movie

After you make an FLV file, you're ready to load it into a Flash movie (SWF file). Unlike SWF or JPEG loading, however, you have to jump through a few hoops to get an FLV file displayed and playing in the Flash movie.

Building an HTTP Connection to an FLV File

In this section, you learn how to use a NetConnection instance with an FLV file served over HTTP. Usually, the NetConnection class enables you to connect to a Flash Communication Server application or a Flash Remoting–enabled server. However, with HTTP-loaded FLV files, you create a "fake" connection for the NetStream instance used by your FLV file.

1. In Flash MX 2004, create a new Flash document. Save this document as NetStream_100.fla.

2. Rename Layer 1 to actions. Select frame 1 of this layer, and open the Actions panel. Add the following code to the Script pane:

   ```
   var ncDefault:NetConnection = new NetConnection();
   ncDefault.connect(null);
   var nsSample:NetStream = new NetStream(ncDefault);
   ```

   You must always perform these three steps to set up a NetStream instance. In the first line, you create a NetConnection instance named ncDefault. This instance is used by the NetStream instance in the third line. In the second line, a null parameter is passed to the connect() method of the ncDefault instance. This parameter tells the Flash Player that the FLV content will be streamed over HTTP, not RTMP. In the third line, a NetStream instance named nsSample is created, using the ncDefault instance in the new constructor.

3. Save your document. At this point, there is no need to test your movie. Proceed to the next section.

You can find the completed document, NetStream_100.fla, in the ch24 folder of this book's CD-ROM.

Displaying the NetStream Output in a Video Object

Once you have created a new NetStream instance, you need to create a new instance of the Video class in which to display the video content from the FLV file. Unfortunately, you cannot dynamically create a new Video instance with the Video class in ActionScript. You need to manually add an empty Embedded Video symbol in the Library panel and place an instance on the stage.

You can nest an instance of the Embedded Video symbol into a Movie Clip symbol. Set the Movie Clip symbol to export (with a linkage identifier), and attach the symbol to the stage with the MovieClip.attachMovie() method.

In the following steps, you learn how to create a Video object and assign the NetStream instance to it:

1. Open the NetStream_100.fla document you created in the last section and save it as NetStream_101.fla.

2. Create a new layer and rename it vidWin. Place this layer below the actions layer.

3. Open the document's Library panel (Ctrl+L or ⌘+L). In the options menu located at the top-right corner of the panel, choose New Video (see Figure 24-5). After you have selected the option, you should see a new Embedded Video symbol in the Library.

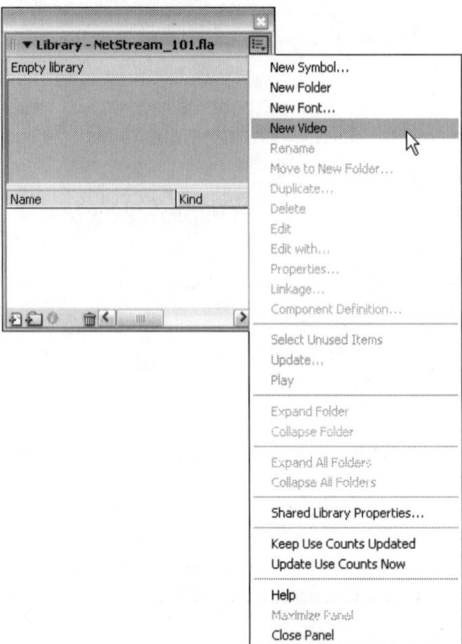

Figure 24-5: The New Video menu item in the options menu of the Library panel

4. Select frame 1 of the `vidWin` layer. Drag an instance of the Embedded Video symbol from the Library to the stage. Position the instance near the top-left corner of the stage. In the Property inspector, name the instance `vidWin` (see Figure 24-6). Notice that the default size of an Embedded Video instance (or `Video` object) is 160 × 120. You can resize this instance to match your preferred video frame size.

You can also resize a `Video` object using the `_width` and `_height` properties of the `Video` class. However, due to a bug in the class files for Flash MX 2004, if you type a `Video` instance as a `Video` object in ActionScript 2.0 style code, the ActionScript compiler will report an error if you attempt to access the `_height` or `_width` properties. Refer to `www.flashsupport.com/articles` for an updated tech note that addresses this issue.

5. Now that you have a named instance of a `Video` object on the stage, you're ready to attach the `NetStream` instance to it. Select frame 1 of the actions layer, and open the Actions panel (F9). Add the following code (shown in bold) to the Script pane.

```
var ncDefault:NetConnection = new NetConnection();
ncDefault.connect(null);
var nsSample:NetStream = new NetStream(ncDefault);
var vidWin:Video;
vidWin.attachVideo(nsSample);
nsSample.play("sample_high.flv");
```

The `Video` class has an `attachVideo()` method that enables you to specify a `NetStream` instance (or `Camera` instance) to be displayed in the video window.

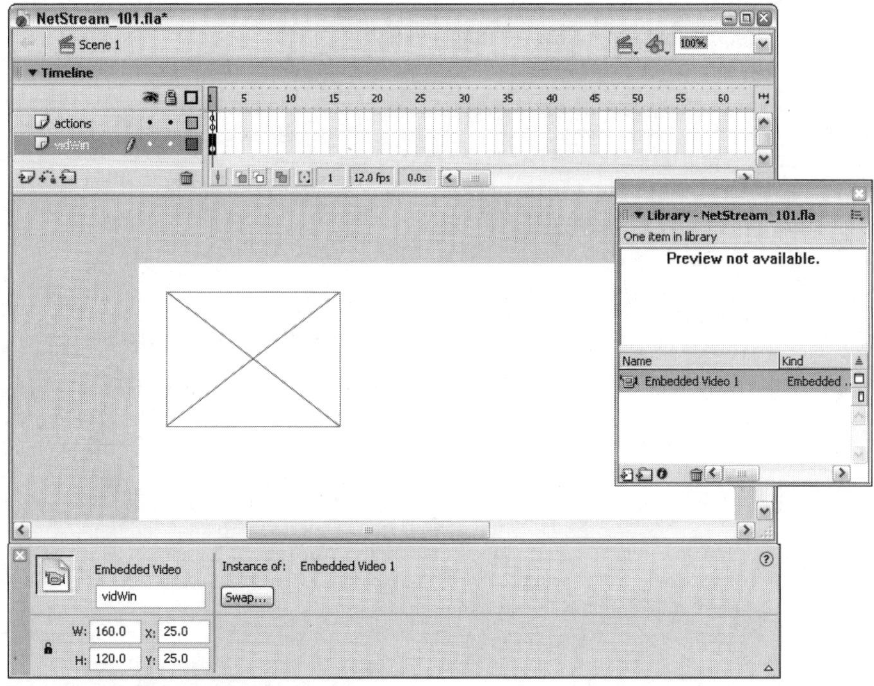

Figure 24-6: The vidWin instance

After you have attached the NetStream instance to the Video object, you can issue a play() method on the nsSample instance, specifying the URL to the FLV file you want to play. You can use a relative URL (such as the one used here), or a fully qualified URL, such as the following resource, http://www.flashsupport.com/flv/sample_high.flv.

6. Save your document and test the movie (Ctrl+Enter or ⌘+Enter). When the movie loads, you should see the sample_high.flv video play in the vidWin instance.

You can find the completed document, NetStream_101.fla, in the ch24 folder of this book's CD-ROM.

Checking Status Messages from the NetStream Class

The NetStream class also has an onStatus() event handler, which can be used to monitor the activity occurring on the NetStream instance. In the following steps, you learn how to add an onStatus() handler to a NetStream instance and view the status messages in the Output panel.

1. Open the NetStream_101.fla document from the previous section. Resave this document as NetStream_102.fla.

2. Select frame 1 of the actions layer, and open the Actions panel. Add the following code (shown in bold) to the existing actions:

```
var ncDefault:NetConnection = new NetConnection();
ncDefault.connect(null);
var nsSample:NetStream = new NetStream(ncDefault);
nsSample.onStatus = function(oInfo:Object):Void {
   trace(">>> BEGIN nsSample.onStatus >>>");
   trace("\tcode:\t" + oInfo.code);
   trace("<<< END nsSample.onStatus <<<\n");
};
var vidWin:Video;
vidWin.attachVideo(nsSample);
nsSample.play("sample_high.flv");
```

As you can see with this `onStatus()` handler, the method is passed an information object, named here as `oInfo`. The `oInfo` object has a `code` property, indicating a specific activity occurring on the `NetStream` instance. In the next step, you see what these messages contain.

Tip Always make sure to define (or assign) the `onStatus()` handler for a `NetStream` instance before you invoke any methods that control playback of the stream, such as `play()`. You risk the chance of missing a message if you define the `onStatus()` handler after you invoke a method that affects the stream.

3. Save your document and test the movie (Ctrl+Enter or ⌘+Enter). As the FLV file plays, you will see the following `trace()` messages in the Output panel:

```
>>> BEGIN nsSample.onStatus >>>
   code:   NetStream.Play.Start
<<< END nsSample.onStatus <<<

>>> BEGIN nsSample.onStatus >>>
   code:   NetStream.Buffer.Full
<<< END nsSample.onStatus <<<

>>> BEGIN nsSample.onStatus >>>
   code:   NetStream.Play.Stop
<<< END nsSample.onStatus <<<

>>> BEGIN nsSample.onStatus >>>
   code:   NetStream.Buffer.Empty
<<< END nsSample.onStatus <<<
```

When a stream begins to play, the `onStatus()` handler receives a `code` property of `NetStream.Play.Start`.

When enough of the FLV file has downloaded into the Flash Player's buffer, the `NetStream.Buffer.Full` message is sent to the `onStatus()` handler.

When the stream playback reaches the end of the FLV file, the `code` property `NetStream.Play.Stop` is sent to the `onStatus()` handler.

When all of the stream data has emptied from the Flash Player's buffer, the code property of NetStream.Buffer.Empty is sent to the onStatus() handler.

For FLV files served over HTTP, there is also a code property of NetStream.Play.StreamNotFound. This value is returned to the onStatus() handler if the URL is invalid. This message can also occur if the Flash Player does not have a working Internet connection. There are other code values for FLV files served over an RTMP connection to a Flash Communication Server application, such as NetStream.Pause.Notify.

All code values are a String datatype. For a full listing of code values, see the Client-Side Communication ActionScript Dictionary PDF on Macromedia's site at www.macromedia.com/support/flashcom/documentation.html.

You can create a System.onStatus() handler to catch NetStream events. If you do not assign an onStatus() handler to a NetStream instance, the Flash Player will pass the message along to a System.onStatus() handler.

Now that you know how to create a NetStream instance and play it, you're ready to work with an example that demonstrates how to control playback.

You can find the completed file, NetStream_102.fla, in the ch24 folder of this book's CD-ROM.

Scripting Basic Controls for a NetStream Object

In this last section, you learn how to add play, stop (pause), and rewind buttons to a Flash movie to control the playback of a NetStream instance. You also learn how to report the current time of a NetStream instance in a TextField object.

1. Open the NetStream_102.fla document that you created in the previous section and resave the document as NetStream_200.fla.
2. Create a new layer and name it buttons. Place this layer above the vidWin layer.
3. Choose Window ➪ Other Panels ➪ Common Libraries ➪ Buttons, to open the Buttons library. In this Library panel, open the Circle Buttons folder. Drag instances of the play, stop, and rewind buttons to the stage, on frame 1 of the buttons layer. Position these instances below the vidWin instance, as shown in Figure 24-7.
4. Using the Property inspector, name the play, stop, and rewind instances btPlay, btStop, and btRew, respectively.
5. Create a new layer and rename it tTime. Place this layer above the buttons layer.
6. On frame 1 of the tTime layer, use the Text tool to create a Dynamic text field. Name the instance tTime in the Property inspector. Place this field to the right of the btPlay instance. See Figure 24-8.

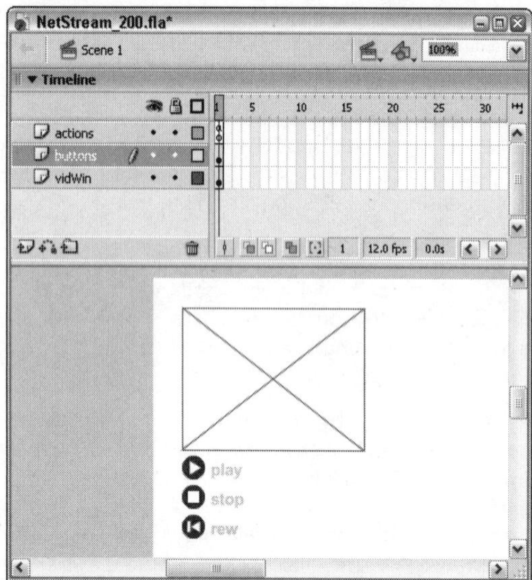

Figure 24-7: The playback control buttons

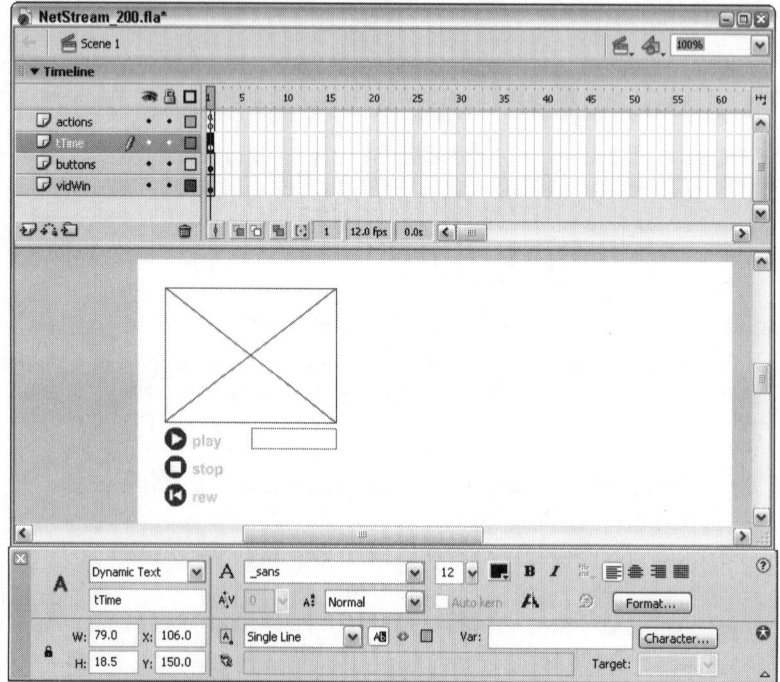

Figure 24-8: The tTime instance

7. Now you're ready to script the buttons to control the NetStream instance. Select frame 1 of the actions layer, and open the Actions panel. Add the bold code shown in Listing 24-1.

   Notice that the `nsSample.play();` code is no longer initiated as soon as the movie loads. Rather, this action is nested with the `onRelease()` handler of the `btPlay` instance.

   The `pause()` method of the `NetStream` class is used by the `btStop` instance. Its `onRelease()` handler will pause the `nsSample` instance's playback. The `pause()` method is a toggle—clicking the stop button once halts playback, and clicking it again resumes playback from the same point.

   The `onRelease()` handler of the `btRew` instance uses the `NetStream.seek()` method to rewind the stream back to a time of 0 seconds. The `seek()` method automatically begins playback once the new point is reached.

   Finally, an `onEnterFrame()` handler is created for the main timeline (`this`). In this handler, the `NetStream.time` property is used to report the time, in seconds, that the stream has played. This time is reported in the `tTime` field.

Listing 24-1: **Scripting the Playback Controls**

```
var ncDefault:NetConnection = new NetConnection();
ncDefault.connect(null);
var nsSample:NetStream = new NetStream(ncDefault);
nsSample.onStatus = function(oInfo:Object):Void {
   trace(">>> BEGIN nsSample.onStatus >>>");
   trace("\tcode:\t" + oInfo.code);
   trace("<<< END nsSample.onStatus <<<");
};
var vidWin:Video;
vidWin.attachVideo(nsSample);
btPlay.onRelease = function():Void {
   nsSample.play("sample_high.flv");
};
btStop.onRelease = function():Void {
   // pause the stream at
   nsSample.pause();
};
btRew.onRelease = function():Void {
   nsSample.seek(0);
};
this.onEnterFrame = function():Void {
   tTime.text = nsSample.time.toString() + " sec";
};
```

8. Save the document and test the movie (Ctrl+Enter or ⌘+Enter). Click the play button to start the `sample_high.flv` video. If you click the stop button, the stream pauses at the current point. If you click it again, playback resumes. If you click the rewind button, the stream goes back to the starting point and plays. During playback, the stream's current time is displayed in the `tField` instance, as shown in Figure 24-9.

Figure 24-9: The playback controls viewed at runtime

You can find the completed file, `NetStream_200.fla`, in the ch24 folder of this book's CD-ROM.

You can find more resources related to the `NetStream` class and the V2 Media Components at `www.flashsupport.com/articles`.

We'd like to know what you thought about this chapter. Visit `www.flashsupport.com/feedback` to fill out an online form with your comments.

Summary

- Flash Video (FLV) files can be played in Flash Players 6 or 7. If you're using Flash Communication Server, FLV files can be streamed to Flash Player 6 or later. If you're loading FLV files over HTTP, the Flash movie must be a Flash Player 7 SWF file viewed in Flash Player 7.
- The `NetStream` class works in conjunction with the `NetConnection` and `Video` classes. A `Video` object displays the visual portion of a `NetStream` instance playing an FLV file.
- The `onStatus()` handler of a `NetStream` instance receives an information object with a code property. The `code` property specifies which particular event is occurring on a `NetStream` instance.
- You can use the `play()`, `pause()`, and `seek()` methods of the `NetStream` class to control the playback of an FLV file. You can also use the `time` property of the `NetStream` class to report the current playback time of the FLV file.

✦ ✦ ✦

The Data Classes

PART

VII

✦ ✦ ✦ ✦

In This Part

✦ ✦ ✦ ✦

The SharedObject and LocalConnection Classes

CHAPTER 25

✦ ✦ ✦ ✦

In This Chapter

Creating cookie-like shared objects

Retrieving and modifying shared objects

Creating local domain communication between Flash movies

Creating communication between Flash movies across domains

✦ ✦ ✦ ✦

The `SharedObject` and `LocalConnection` classes provide you with a way to communicate with Flash movies running on the same computer. The `SharedObject` class allows you to store and retrieve persistent data on a client computer between sessions. The `LocalConnection` class, on the other hand, enables real-time communication between Flash movies running on the same computer.

Saving Data with Shared Objects

One essential feature to applications of all kinds is the capability to save settings to the client machine. Almost every application on your computer has settings and preferences that you can modify to suit your needs. Flash itself has many preferences that allow you to customize your application in the way that you like it best. And when you modify an application's preferences, they are generally saved so that those settings are remembered the next time you open the program. A feature such as being able to modify preferences would not do much good if the data could not be saved. For many applications, these preferences are saved in text files within the application's installation on your computer. For Web applications, such settings are saved in *cookies*.

ActionScript includes a class of objects called `SharedObject`. The `SharedObject` class actually provides two types of functionality—local shared objects and remote shared objects. A local shared object is similar to a cookie in that it allows you to store and retrieve data on a client computer. This chapter covers local shared objects. Unless otherwise specified, each reference to a shared object or `SharedObject` instance in this chapter refers to a local shared object. Remote shared objects are one way in which your Flash application can interact with a FlashCom server.

A Little Bit of Cookie History

Although local shared objects and cookies are different in *how* they work, technically speaking, the concept is very similar. For this reason, having a general understanding of what cookies are and what they can do can be beneficial in understanding local shared objects.

Most programs you run on your computer need only a single set of preferences (per user, that is) because the programs run only one application each, for the most part. But with Web browsers, the story is a little different. The Web browsers can have their own preferences for the browser itself. But because the browser can run many Web applications (Web sites), there is a need to be able to save persistent data for each of those applications. For example, if a Web site asks a user whether she wants to view a Flash version or an HTML version of the site, it is extremely useful to be able to save that choice so the user doesn't have to select again next time she visits the site. Traditionally, this is accomplished with cookies, which are small bits of data saved to the client computer that can be retrieved at a later date to be read and/or modified by the same application. Each cookie is given a name by which it can be retrieved.

Local shared objects fill the same need as cookies do. Because the Flash Player can play many different Flash movies, it is useful to be able to store many different bits of data. For example, a Flash Player could play a movie that is a long presentation. If the user closes the player and then opens the movie again, it would be useful for the movie to be able to resume where it left off. But the same player could play many other movies with different kinds of needs. Another movie might allow a user to save some preferences. Through the use of local shared objects, movies can create many different named pieces of persistent data saved to the client machine.

Understanding Local Shared Object Anatomy

A local shared object can refer to any one of several parts or can refer to the whole of those parts. The data for a local shared object is stored to a file on the client computer. For security purposes, the Flash movie's interface to this file is exclusively by way of the `SharedObject` class in ActionScript. This ensures that local shared objects are safe for the user and cannot be used maliciously.

In addition to the local file, a shared object also consists of a `SharedObject` instance in ActionScript. The instance provides the programmatic interface to the file. So a local shared object can refer to the file, the ActionScript instance, or both. Typically, it should be clear by the context.

Creating a Local Shared Object

The processes for creating a new local shared object and for opening a previously created local shared object are the same. The static method `getLocal()` opens a local shared object with the specified name if it can find one. Otherwise it creates a new local shared object on the client. The method requires at least one parameter—the name of the local shared object file. And the method returns a new `SharedObject` instance that provides the programmatic interface to the local shared object file. Here is an example:

```
var lsoPrefs:SharedObject = SharedObject.getLocal("userPrefs");
```

The preceding example tells Flash to look for a local shared object file named `userPrefs` (the file extension for these files is `.lso`, but you don't include that as part of the parameter). If Flash finds this file, it opens it. Otherwise, Flash creates a new file with this name. In either case Flash then creates a new `SharedObject` instance that interfaces with the file, and assigns that instance to a variable named `lsoPrefs`. You need to know the name of the file on the client computer only when creating or opening the file with the `getLocal()` method. From that point forward you need only to reference the `SharedObject` instance (in this example, `lsoPrefs`) in order to have an interface to that file.

Setting Values within the Shared Object

After you have successfully created a `SharedObject` instance, you can start to assign values to it that you want saved for later use. Each `SharedObject` instance has a `data` property. The `data` property is itself an object to which you can define properties that will be saved to the local shared object file. Properties assigned to the `SharedObject` object itself will not be saved to the client computer, only properties assigned to the object's `data` property. Here's an example that sets some values that will be stored to the file:

```
var lsoPrefs:SharedObject = SharedObject.getLocal("userPrefs");
lsoPrefs.data.bgColor = "red";
lsoPrefs.data.name = "A Reader";
lsoPrefs.data.title = "Yippee!";
```

You can add as many properties to data as you want. Furthermore, you can assign not only primitive datatypes but many types of objects to the data property so that they can be saved to the client computer for later retrieval. For example, the following is valid:

```
lsoPrefs.data.companyInfo = {name: "Widget Factory", location: "New York"};
lsoPrefs.data.lastLogin = new Date();
```

Although you can save many types of objects to a local shared object, you cannot save all types. For example, you cannot save `MovieClip`, `Button`, `TextField`, `SharedObject`, or `Function` types, to name just a few.

Saving the Shared Object to the Client

After you have created a `SharedObject` and added values to it, the next step is to save the shared object to the client computer. This can be the easiest step in the whole process. You don't need to do anything, as a matter of fact. The Flash movie automatically attempts to save the shared object to the client computer when the `SharedObject` instance is deleted. This occurs under four conditions: when the player closes, when the movie is closed or replaced in the player, when the object is deleted using a `delete` statement, or when the object is garbage-collected after it falls out of scope. In any case, after you have created a `SharedObject` object, there will be an attempt to save the local shared object automatically. It is not, however, typically a best practice to rely on the automatic saving feature. Instead, you should explicitly tell Flash to save the data.

The `flush()` method allows you to save the shared object without the `SharedObject` object being deleted. Using the `flush()` method offers some serious advantages over the other, more passive approaches to saving the shared object. One advantage is that you can be assured that Flash attempts to save the data. There are some circumstances in which Flash might not actually save the data if you rely on the automatic saving features. When you call `flush()` you avoid that problem.

Another of the advantages of the `flush()` method has to do with file size considerations. Every shared object occupies a certain amount of disk space. By default, the Flash Player is set to accept all shared objects for a domain (more about domains later in this chapter), up to a total of 100KB. Users can configure their own players to accept shared objects for each domain totaling greater or less disk space. By right-clicking or ⌘-clicking the Flash Player, you can choose settings to bring up the Macromedia Flash Player Settings dialog box (see Figure 25-1). The second tab in the dialog box, Local Storage, allows you to move a slider to choose from None, 10KB, 100KB, 1MB, 10MB, or Unlimited. Choosing 10KB through 10MB allows Flash movies to save all shared objects, up to a total of the selected disk space. Selecting Unlimited allows for shared objects to be saved as long as disk space is available. As soon as the total disk space allotted has been exceeded, the player prompts you (see Figure 25-2) for any shared objects that are being saved by a `flush()` call. Therefore, if the settings are configured with the slider set to None, you will be prompted for every attempted shared object saved with a `flush()` call.

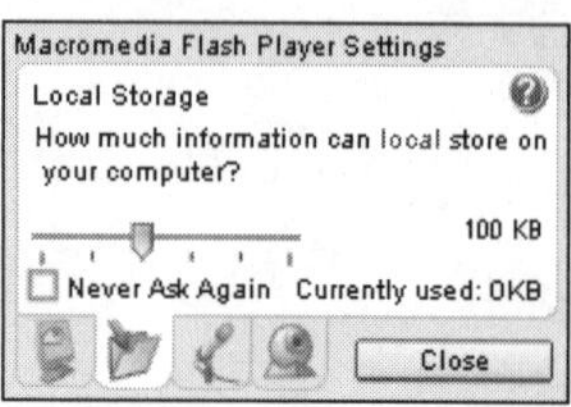

Figure 25-1: The Macromedia Flash Player Settings dialog box allows you to specify how much disk space shared objects can use.

Figure 25-2: The dialog box prompts the user to allow or deny saving a shared object that will exceed the allotted disk space.

If you rely on a means other than `flush()` to save a shared object, the object will be saved only if it does not exceed the limit imposed by the user's player settings. Therefore, if saving the shared object is critical, you should use `flush()`. Here's an example:

```
var lsoPrefs:SharedObject = SharedObject.getLocal("userPrefs");
lsoPrefs.data.bgColor = "red";
lsoPrefs.data.name = "A Reader";
lsoPrefs.data.title = "Yippee!";
lsoPrefs.flush();
```

Even though you add the properties to the data object, you should still call the `flush()` method directly from the `SharedObject` instance.

But there are two more considerations you might take into account when saving the shared object. First of all, you should ask yourself whether the shared object is likely to grow in size over time. If the answer is yes, you might want to try to foresee how large the object is likely to get. For example, a local shared object file might start out at under 1KB. But if that shared object might grow to 1MB in the future, you might want to allot that much space to it from the beginning. Otherwise, the users could be prompted to accept the increase each time the object increases. You can specify a parameter in the `flush()` method that will set aside a certain amount of disk space for the object, whether it uses it all or not. The parameter is given in bytes. So, to set aside 1MB of space for the `lsoPrefs` shared object, you could use the following line of code (1,024 bytes in a KB and 1,024KB in a MB):

```
lsoPrefs.flush(1024 * 1024);
```

You can use the getSize() method to determine the size of the shared object at any point. It returns the size of the shared object in bytes:

```
trace(lsoPrefs.getSize());
```

The second consideration when saving a shared object is to test whether the object was actually saved. There are three ways that a shared object will not be saved. The first way is when the user has checked the Never check box in the player settings. If this is checked, no shared objects are ever saved and the user is never prompted. The second is if the user has selected Unlimited from the player settings, but there is not enough available disk space. This is an unlikely but possible occurrence. And the third way in which an object might not be saved is if the user is prompted but chooses to deny access to save the local shared object.

The flush() method actually returns a value to help you determine the status of the attempted save. It can return true, false, or "pending". If the value is true, the user has enough disk space allotted already, and the object was saved without prompting. If it is false, one of the first two conditions under which an object is not saved occurred. And if it is "pending", the user has been prompted about whether to allow the shared object to be saved. If the result is true, there is no problem. If the result is false, on the other hand, you might want to alert the user that the movie attempted to save some data, but failed. For example:

```
flushStatus = choices.flush();
if(flushStatus == false){
  tAlertMessage.text = "Please check your player settings to make sure you";
  tAlertMessage.text += "allow data to be saved to your computer.";
}
```

The strong typing in ActionScript is a new feature to Flash MX 2004, and it is optional. Because the flush() method can return either a Boolean or a string value, it is better not to strongly type the variable.

If the user has checked Never in the player settings, you might want to suggest that the user change these settings and offer a button that opens the settings dialog box:

```
mcSettings.onRelease = function(){
  System.showSettings(1);  // Open settings dialogue box.
}
```

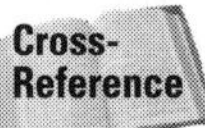

You can learn more about the System object, including the showSettings() method, in Chapter 21, "The System Class and the Capabilities and Security Objects."

If the flush() method returns "pending", it means that the user has been prompted to accept or deny the shared object. You might want to determine what the user selects. To do this, you need to set up an onStatus() event handler method for the SharedObject instance. The onStatus() method, if defined, is invoked for a SharedObject object after the user has selected either to accept or deny the shared object. Flash automatically passes the method a parameter. The parameter is an object with a code property having a value of either SharedObject.Flush.Failed (if the user chose to deny the shared object) or SharedObject.Flush.Success (if the user chose to accept the shared object). Here's an example of an onStatus() method definition for a SharedObject instance named lsoPrefs:

```
lsoPrefs.onStatus = function(oStatus:Object):Void {
  if(oStatus.code == "SharedObject.Flush.Failed")
    trace("denied");
```

```
    if(oStatus.code == "SharedObject.Flush.Success")
      trace("saved it");
  };
```

Retrieving the Data

After you have created a shared object on the client computer, you will, of course, want to be able to retrieve it for use later. And actually, you already know how to do this because retrieving and creating are done with the same method: `getLocal()`. If the `getLocal()` method finds an existing shared object with the name specified, it loads that shared object data into the `SharedObject` instance. Otherwise, the new shared object file is created and the `SharedObject` instance interfaces with it. Earlier in this chapter, you saw an example in which you created a new local shared object file named `userPrefs`. If that file already exists on the client's computer, the same code will open the file.

```
var lsoPrefs:SharedObject = SharedObject.getLocal("userPrefs");
```

It is a good idea to check to see whether the object already existed. If it existed, there will be at least one property in the data object. One way to test is as follows:

```
var bExists:Boolean = false;
for(item in lsoPrefs.data){
  bExists = true;
  break;
}
if(bExists) {
  trace("loaded shared object");
}
```

Conflicts, Domains, and Paths

As you have been learning about shared objects, you may have wondered about possible name conflicts between shared objects. For instance, what would happen if you made a Flash movie that used a shared object file named `userPrefs`, and someone else made a movie using a shared object filed named `userPrefs`, and both were run on the same computer? Will there be a conflict? Will one overwrite the other? These are good questions. The answer is that if the Flash movies run on different domains (`themakers.com` and `person13.com`, for example), there would be no conflict. This is because all shared objects are saved under the domain from which the movie was run. Additionally, there is a local domain under which all shared objects that run locally on your computer are saved.

Additionally, all shared objects are stored according to the path to the movie on the domain. For example, the movies

```
http://www.mydomain.com/myMovie.swf
```

and

```
http://www.mydomain.com/flash/myOtherMovie.swf
```

will save the shared objects to different paths by default, and so each can create a shared object with the same name without a conflict between them.

This brings up an interesting discussion, however, about whether shared objects created by one movie can be accessible to another (see Table 25-1). Shared objects created by movies with the same domain and path are always accessible to one another. Shared objects created by movies with different domains are never accessible to one another. And shared objects created by movies with the same domain but different paths are accessible to one another if the path to the shared object is specified in the `getLocal()` method and is accessible to both movies. The `getLocal()` method accepts a second optional parameter after the shared object name that gives the path to the object.

Table 25-1: Accessibility of Shared Objects

	Same Domain	***Different Domain***
Same Path	Always	Never
Different Path	Sometimes	Never

For instance, if the two movies are on the same domain but with different paths such as

```
http://www.mydomain.com/myMovie.swf
```

and

```
http://www.mydomain.com/flash/myOtherMovie.swf
```

shared objects created or opened in `myMovie.swf` are opened with a default path of / and shared objects created or opened in `myOtherMovie.swf` are opened with a default path of `/flash/`. The `myMovie.swf` can access shared objects only with a path of / but `myOtherMovie.swf` can access shared objects with either the / or `/flash/` path. Likewise, if there was another movie at:

```
http://www.mydomain.com/flash/moreflash/yetAnotherMovie.swf
```

it would be able to access shared objects with paths of /, `/flash/`, or `/flash/moreflash/`. Therefore, if you want to have shared objects accessible to multiple movies on the same domain you must make sure that the path of the shared object is accessible to all the movies. In this case, if you want the shared object to be accessible to all the movies you should make sure to create the shared object with a path of /. Then you also need to make sure that you specify this path each time you access the shared object as well. This would look something like:

```
so = SharedObject.getLocal("mySharedObject", "/");
```

Remembering States with Shared Objects

In this exercise, you will create a Flash application with randomly colored squares. The user can move the squares around on the stage by dragging them with the mouse. By way of a local shared object, Flash will remember the colors and coordinates of the squares so that when the application is run again it will have the same look as when it was last closed. Additionally, the application will have a reset button that allows the user to reset the squares to the original coordinates and assign new, random colors.

1. Open a new Flash document and save it as `blocks001.fla`.
2. On the first frame of the default layer of the main timeline, add the following code:

```
function makeBlocks(nBlocks:Number, lsoBlocksParam):Void {
  var mcBlock:MovieClip = null;
  var duDrawer:DrawingUtils = null;
  var nColumn:Number = 0;
  var nRow:Number = 0;
  var nColor:Number = null;
  this.createEmptyMovieClip("mcHolder",
                          this.getNextHighestDepth());
  for(var i:Number = 0; i < nBlocks; i++) {
    if(lsoBlocksParam.data.colors[i] != undefined) {
      nColor = lsoBlocksParam.data.colors[i];
    }
    else {
      nColor = Math.random() * 255 * 255 * 255;
      lsoBlocksParam.data.colors[i] = nColor;
    }
    mcHolder.createEmptyMovieClip("mcBlock" + i,
              mcHolder.getNextHighestDepth());
    mcBlock = mcHolder["mcBlock" + i];
    duDrawer = new DrawingUtils(mcBlock);
    duDrawer.beginFill(nColor, 100);
    duDrawer.drawRectangle(30, 30, 15, 15);
    mcBlock._x = nColumn * 33 + 50;
    mcBlock._y = nRow * 33 + 50;
    mcBlock.id = i;
    mcBlock.lso = lsoBlocksParam;
    nRow++;
    if(nRow > 6) {
      nRow = 0;
      nColumn++;
    }
    mcBlock.onPress = function():Void {
      this.swapDepths(this._parent.getNextHighestDepth());
      this.startDrag();
    };
    mcBlock.onRelease = function():Void {
      this.stopDrag();
      this.lso.data.coordinates[this.id] = {mc: this._name, ⮐
x: this._x, y: this._y};
      this.lso.flush();
    };
  }
  lsoBlocksParam.flush();
}
function placeBlocks(lsoBlocksParam):Void {
  var oItem:Object = null;
  for(var i:Number = 0; ⮐
i < lsoBlocksParam.data.coordinates.length; i++) {
    oItem = lsoBlocksParam.data.coordinates[i];
```

```
      if(oItem != undefined) {
        mcHolder[oItem.mc]._x = oItem.x;
        mcHolder[oItem.mc]._y = oItem.y;
      }
    }
  }
  function makeResetButton(lsoBlocksParam):Void {
    this.createEmptyMovieClip("mcReset",
                this.getNextHighestDepth());
    mcReset.createEmptyMovieClip("mcButtonBg",
                mcReset.getNextHighestDepth());
    var duDrawer:DrawingUtils = new DrawingUtils(mcReset.mcButtonBg);
    duDrawer.beginFill(0xFFFFFF, 100);
    duDrawer.drawRectangle(50, 20, 25, 10);
    duDrawer.endFill();
    mcReset.createTextField("tLabel",
                          mcReset.getNextHighestDepth(),
                          0, 0, 50, 20);
    mcReset.tLabel.text = "reset";
    mcReset.tLabel.selectable = false;
    var tfFormatter:TextFormat = new TextFormat();
    tfFormatter.align = "center";
    mcReset.tLabel.setTextFormat(tfFormatter);
    mcReset.lso = lsoBlocksParam;
    mcReset.onRelease = function():Void {
      this.lso.data.coordinates = new Array();
      this.lso.data.colors = new Array();
      this._parent.mcHolder.removeMovieClip();
      this._parent.makeBlocks(49, this.lso);
    };
  }
  var lsoBlocks = SharedObject.getLocal("blocks");
  var bExist:Boolean = (lsoBlocks.data.coordinates != undefined);
  makeBlocks(49, lsoBlocks);
  if(bExist) {
    placeBlocks(lsoBlocks);
  }
  else {
    lsoBlocks.data.coordinates = new Array();
    lsoBlocks.data.colors = new Array();
  }
  makeResetButton(lsoBlocks);
```

3. Save the document and test the movie.

4. Move some of the blocks to various locations on the stage.

5. Close the movie (the SWF file) and test the movie again. You should see the blocks in the same locations where you had previously moved them.

Now you can take a closer look at some of the code that makes this work.

First, the example defines the makeBlocks() function. Within this function, you create all the MovieClip objects for the blocks. The first MovieClip object holds all the actual blocks. This instance is called mcHolder:

```
this.createEmptyMovieClip("mcHolder", this.getNextHighestDepth());
```

Then you use a for statement to create each of the nested blocks. If the block's color value was recorded previously in the local shared object, you want to retrieve it. Otherwise, you assign a new, random color, and record that into the local shared object.

```
if(lsoBlocksParam.data.colors[i] != undefined) {
  nColor = lsoBlocksParam.data.colors[i];
}
else {
  nColor = Math.random() * 255 * 255 * 255;
  lsoBlocksParam.data.colors[i] = nColor;
}
```

You create the nested MovieClip to contain the block, and to make it easier to reference the MovieClip, you assign it to a variable, mcBlock:

```
mcHolder.createEmptyMovieClip("mcBlock" + i,
                  mcHolder.getNextHighestDepth());
mcBlock = mcHolder["mcBlock" + i];
```

In order to draw the square, you utilize a DrawingUtils instance. You draw a square and place the instance such that all the blocks are in rows and columns:

```
duDrawer = new DrawingUtils(mcBlock);
duDrawer.beginFill(nColor, 100);
duDrawer.drawRectangle(30, 30, 15, 15);
mcBlock._x = nColumn * 33 + 50;
mcBlock._y = nRow * 33 + 50;
```

The id property is a custom property that you use in order to populate the coordinates array in the local shared object. Also, so that you can reference the local shared object from within a method of mcBlock, you want to assign a reference to that object to a custom property, lso:

```
mcBlock.id = i;
mcBlock.lso = lsoBlocksParam;
```

The next step is to set the onPress() and onRelease() handlers for the block. When the user clicks the instance, you want it to be made draggable and also to set its depth so that it will appear above all the other instances. When the user releases the click on the instance, you want it to stop dragging and to assign the new value to the corresponding element in the coordinates array within the local shared object. The value is an object consisting of three properties—the name of the block MovieClip and the current x and y coordinates:

```
mcBlock.onPress = function():Void {
  this.swapDepths(this._parent.getNextHighestDepth());
  this.startDrag();
};
mcBlock.onRelease = function():Void {
  this.stopDrag();
  this.lso.data.coordinates[this.id] = {mc: this._name, ⮐
```

```
x: this._x, y: this._y};
      this.lso.flush();
    };
  }
```

The next function is placeBlocks(). This function simply uses a for statement to loop through all the elements of the coordinates array within the local shared object. For each element defined, it moves the block MovieClip instance to the saved x and y coordinates:

```
  for(var i:Number = 0; ⮐
i < lsoBlocksParam.data.coordinates.length; i++) {
    oItem = lsoBlocksParam.data.coordinates[i];
    if(oItem != undefined) {
      mcHolder[oItem.mc]._x = oItem.x;
      mcHolder[oItem.mc]._y = oItem.y;
    }
  }
```

The makeResetButton() function creates the MovieClip that serves as the reset button. First, of course, you create the instance, mcReset. Then you create a nested instance, mcButtonBg, into which you draw a rectangle with a DrawingUtils object:

```
this.createEmptyMovieClip("mcReset", this.getNextHighestDepth());
mcReset.createEmptyMovieClip("mcButtonBg", mcReset.getNextHighestDepth());
var duDrawer:DrawingUtils = new DrawingUtils(mcReset.mcButtonBg);
duDrawer.beginFill(0xFFFFFF, 100);
duDrawer.drawRectangle(50, 20, 25, 10);
duDrawer.endFill();
```

Then, you create a TextField object within the reset button, set the label text, and apply some formatting to it:

```
mcReset.createTextField("tLabel",
                        mcReset.getNextHighestDepth(),
                        0, 0, 50, 20);
mcReset.tLabel.text = "reset";
mcReset.tLabel.selectable = false;
var tfFormatter:TextFormat = new TextFormat();
tfFormatter.align = "center";
mcReset.tLabel.setTextFormat(tfFormatter);
```

When the user clicks the button, you need it to reset the application. This means that it should move all the blocks back into columns and rows and assign new colors. By assigning a new array value to both coordinates and colors within the local shared object, the local shared object is essentially reset. Then you want to remove the mcHolder MovieClip and call the makeBlocks() function to redraw everything:

```
mcReset.lso = lsoBlocksParam;
mcReset.onRelease = function():Void {
  this.lso.data.coordinates = new Array();
  this.lso.data.colors = new Array();
  this._parent.mcHolder.removeMovieClip();
  this._parent.makeBlocks(49, this.lso);
};
```

The remaining code creates or opens the local shared object and then calls the makeBlocks(), placeBlocks(), and makeResetButton() functions. The placeBlocks() function is called only if the local shared object was previously defined. Otherwise there is no need to call it; no values exist for which to place the blocks.

```
var lsoBlocks = SharedObject.getLocal("blocks");
var bExist:Boolean = (lsoBlocks.data.coordinates != undefined);
makeBlocks(49, lsoBlocks);
if(bExist) {
  placeBlocks(lsoBlocks);
}
else {
  lsoBlocks.data.coordinates = new Array();
  lsoBlocks.data.colors = new Array();
}
makeResetButton(lsoBlocks);
```

Communicating with the LocalConnection Class

The LocalConnection class allows for any movie in any player to communicate with any other movie in any other player on the same computer without needing any complicated JavaScript or other workaround solutions. The LocalConnection class doesn't care whether the movies are being run from the same domain. It doesn't care if they are being run from the same browser. All that is required is that the movies are running on the same computer and that one is set up to broadcast messages and the other is set up to listen for messages.

Creating a Sending Movie

There are essentially two types of movies related to LocalConnection communication. The first of these is the sending movie. Sending can be accomplished in as few as two steps. The first step is obviously to create a LocalConnection object. The LocalConnection constructor requires no parameters, so you can create an object like this:

```
var lcSender:LocalConnection = new LocalConnection();
```

After you have created the object, you need only to call the send() method in order to send to a receiving movie. At a minimum the send() method requires two parameters — the name of the connection over which you wish to send and the name of the method you want to invoke in the receiving movie. The name of the connection is a name you get to make up, but it must match the name of the connection over which the receiving movie is listening. Here is an example in which a LocalConnection object broadcasts a message over a connection named aConnection. The method invoked is named someMethod:

```
var lcSender:LocalConnection = new LocalConnection();
lcSender.send("aConnection", "someMethod");
```

Sending Parameters

You can send parameters to the receiving movie's method in addition to just calling the method. Any parameters added to the send() method after the required two (connection name and method name) are sent to the receiving movie's method as parameters. For example, this example shows how three parameters can be sent to the remove method:

```
var lcSender:LocalConnection = new LocalConnection();
lcSender.send("aConnection", "myMethod", true, "two", 3);
```

In addition to primitive datatypes, objects and arrays can be sent as parameters:

```
var lcSender:LocalConnection = new LocalConnection();
var oVals:Object = {a: "one", b: "two", c: "three"};
var aVals:Array = [1,2,3,4,5];
lcSender.send("aConnection", "myMethod", oVals, aVals);
```

Checking the Status of a Send

Every time a `send()` method is invoked, the object's `onStatus()` method is invoked if it has been defined. Flash automatically passes an object parameter to the `onStatus()` method. The parameter has a `level` property with one of two values: `"status"` or `"error"`. If the value is `"status"`, the send was successful. It does not necessarily mean that the method on the receiving end was successfully invoked. It merely means that the send was successful. If the value is `"error"`, the send failed.

```
lcSender.onStatus = function(oInfo):Void {
  trace(oInfo.level);
};
```

Creating a Receiving Movie

The receiving movie is slightly more complex than the sending movie, but not by much. It is still quite simple. There are only three steps in the simplest receiving movie:

1. Create a new `LocalConnection` object.
2. Define the method that will get called by the sending movie.
3. Instruct the movie to listen for messages on a particular connection.

The first step is the same as the first step in the sending movie:

```
var lcReceiver:LocalConnection = new LocalConnection();
```

The second step merely defines the method for that `LocalConnection` object that will be called by the sending movie:

```
lcReceiver.methodName = function():Void {
  // Method body goes here.
};
```

And the last step is accomplished by the `connect()` method, which is invoked from the `LocalConnection` object you have created with a parameter of the name of the connection on which the movie should listen:

```
lcReceiver.connect(connectionName);
```

Here's an example that puts all three steps together:

```
var lcReceiver:LocalConnection = new LocalConnection();
lcReceiver.someMethod = function(){
  trace("method called");
}
lcReceiver.connect("aConnection");
```

Notice that the method name must match the method name passed as the second parameter of the send() method in the sending movie. And the connection name for the connect() method must match the connection name passed as the first parameter of the send() method of the sending movie.

Here's another example of a receiving LocalConnection object in which the method accepts three parameters.

```
var lcReceiver:LocalConnection = new LocalConnection();
lcReceiver.myMethod = function(a:Boolean, b:String, c:Number){
  trace(a);
  trace(b);
  trace(c);
}
lcReceiver.connect("aConnection");
```

The receiving movie continues to listen on a connection after the connect() method has been called, unless you instruct it not to. You can close a connection simply by calling the close() method from the LocalConnection object. For example:

```
lcReceiver.close();
```

Confirming Receipt

The onStatus() method can be used to determine whether a send() method call failed to connect to another movie. This can be useful. But it does not offer a way to know whether the method was successfully invoked on the receiving end. You can accomplish this by having the receiving movie communicate back to the sending movie. In this scenario, both movies must be set up for sending *and* receiving.

Here is an example. First, the code in the sending movie:

```
var lcSender:LocalConnection = new LocalConnection();
lcSender.send("aConnection", "someMethod", "confirmMethod");
lcSender.confirmMethod = function():Void {
  trace("the send was received");
};
lcSender.connect("aConnection");
```

And then, the code in the receiving movie:

```
var lcReceiver:LocalConnection = new LocalConnection();
lcReceiver.someMethod = function(confirmer:String){
  trace("method called");
  this.send("aConnection", confirmer);
}
lcReceiver.connect("aConnection");
```

Sending and Receiving Across Domains

By default, LocalConnection objects attempt to communicate to the same domain. That is, if a sending movie is being run from www.person13.com then it defaults to broadcasting to other movies on www.person13.com. With just a few changes, however, you can configure movies to send and receive messages across domains so that, for example, a movie on `www.person13.com` can send to `www.themakers.com`.

The Sending Movie

The sending movie requires only one modification to send to another domain. The first parameter of the `send()` method (the connection name) can be modified to include the domain to which the command is to be sent. When no domain is specified, the local domain is assumed. But another domain can be specified by preceding the connection name by the domain (not including the machine name) and a semicolon:

```
lcObj.send("domain.com:connection", methodName);
```

The domain should never include the machine name. That means that if you want to send to a movie running on `www.yourdomain.com`, you would *not* include the `www` portion of the domain. Instead, the domain you use would simply be `yourdomain.com`. Here's an example of how to send to a movie on the `person13.com` domain with a connection name of `"aConnection"` and a method called `someMethod()`:

```
var lcSender:LocalConnection = new LocalConnection();
lcSender.send("person13.com:aConnection", "someMethod");
```

The Receiving Movie

The receiving movie requires a few more modifications than the sending movie. But, again, it is still quite simple. For security reasons, you want to make sure that `LocalConnection` objects receive only from the domains you specify. By default, the movie will receive only from the local domain. But you can also allow other domains using the `allowDomain()` method.

When a receiving movie receives a communication from a sending movie the `allowDomain()` method, if defined, is automatically invoked. The method is automatically passed a parameter naming the domain of the sending movie. You can then determine whether the sending domain is in a list of allowed domains and return `true` or `false`. If `allowDomain()` returns `true`, the method specified by the sending movie is called. If `allowDomain()` returns `false`, the method is not called. Here is a simple way to allow all domains:

[illegible]

be a bad idea because it allows for anyone to send to your movie [illegible] to make sure the sending [illegible] This example shows an `allowDomain()` method that allows connections only from `themakers.com`.

```
lcReceiver.allowDomain = function(senderDomain:String):Void {
  return (senderDomain == "themakers.com");
}
```

You can easily allow connections from multiple domains. For example:

```
lcReceiver.allowDomain = function(senderDomain:String):Void {
  return (senderDomain == "person13.com" || senderDomain == "themakers.com");
}
```

Additionally, `LocalConnection` objects have a method that returns the domain of the current movie. This can be useful for allowing the local domain to send in addition to others. The `domain()` method requires no parameters and returns a string of the current movie's domain:

```
lcReceiver.allowDomain = function(senderDomain:String):Void {
  return (senderDomain == "person13.com" || ⮐
senderDomain == "themakers.com" || ⮐
senderDomain == this.domain());
}
```

We'd like to know what you thought about this chapter. Visit `www.flashsupport.com/feedback` to fill out an online form with your comments.

Summary

- ✦ Local shared objects allow for the creation of locally persistent data on the client computer. This is useful for saving Flash movie data that can be used the next time the movie is played.
- ✦ Shared objects are saved when the `SharedObject` object is deleted or when the `flush()` method is called. Calling `flush()` allows for the user to be prompted if the file cannot be saved automatically.
- ✦ Flash movies can communicate with other Flash movies with the `LocalConnection` class of objects. `LocalConnection` allows a sending movie to call a method in a receiving movie.
- ✦ By default, the `LocalConnection` object allows connections only between movies on the same domain. However, with some changes in the sending and receiving movies, communication can occur between movies on different domains.

✦ ✦ ✦

The XML and LoadVars Classes

✦ ✦ ✦ ✦

In This Chapter

XML basics, including history, uses, and syntax

Creating XML objects

Loading XML data

Sending XML data

Understanding LoadVars objects

Loading data with LoadVars

Sending data with LoadVars

Sharing data across domains

In this chapter, you learn about transferring data in and out of Flash movies using `XML` objects and `LoadVars` objects. You learn how to create the objects, load data, and send data.

If you don't know what XML is, this chapter also covers the basics from technical specifications to uses. By the end of this chapter, you should have a firm understanding of what XML is and how to work with XML data in Flash.

Working with XML

XML, which stands for Extensible Markup Language, is one of the standards for sharing and exchanging data. If you plan to do any work in which your Flash movie interacts with a Web server, chances are good that sooner or later you are going to want to be able to parse and work with XML data. In fact, XML is an integral part of many of the emerging technologies in the Internet industry. For example, the Web services trend utilizes XML. Flash itself uses XML for many aspects — from custom tools and behaviors to the contents of the Action toolbox.

define a new XML document within your Flash movie.

There are a great many things for which you can use XML in your Flash applications — everything from using news feeds, user management, content listings, and even chat rooms. But first you need to understand what XML is — how it is structured and what the rules are. There are plenty of other books out there on XML. Books with more pages than this one are dedicated entirely to the subject. So it is not our intention to cover all there is to know about XML. But in the next few sections, you learn the basics you need to get up and running.

XML's Origins

If you are familiar with HTML, XML will look very familiar to you. That's because HTML and XML are actually a lot like cousins. HTML, which stands for Hypertext Markup Language, was developed using a very large and complex metalanguage named SGML, or Standard Generalized Markup Language. Metalanguages are used for creating other languages. The SGML specification is a massive document that includes syntaxes for handling a wide variety of data types and formats, and involves some fairly esoteric rules. For the kind of basic markup required to render the simple text content of Web pages, the SGML standard presents an unnecessarily steep learning curve. So HTML was developed as a simpler subset of SGML.

However, HTML served a very specific purpose. It was originally intended for formatting academic physics articles. But, as you well know, HTML quickly became the vehicle for much more than just physics documents. HTML became the way to display all kinds of content on the Web. The difficulty is that HTML is a poor way of organizing and sharing data. So in 1996, a team was formed to bring SGML to the Web.

The initial efforts of the team resulted in an awareness that SGML was far too huge for use on the Web. So the next step was to create a new language that satisfied the requirements that had been set forth. The product was XML, a scaled-down version of SGML that met the need for simplicity while still retaining the necessary features of SGML—namely, extensibility and the capability to give meaningful context to data.

One of the primary differences between HTML and XML is that HTML is not extensible. This means that HTML is limited to a set of predefined tags. On the other hand, XML has infinite possibilities for tags. In fact, the tags are invented entirely by the author of the document.

The other big distinction between HTML and XML is that the purpose of XML tags is to give meaningful context to the data they contain, whereas HTML is largely about presentation of that data. For instance, the following code in HTML will display the data in a particular way but does not lend any particular meaning or significance to that data:

```
<h1>This is an example of HTML</h1>
```

On the other hand, tags in XML are used to provide semantic markup—to indicate the meaning of content. In fact, XML has nothing to do with the presentation of data. XML is only about organizing data and giving context to that data. The following example of XML code uses an arbitrarily named tag to give meaning to the data it contains:

```
<author>Joey Lott</author>
```

As XML emerged in 1998, it began to attract a lot of attention. And although it was initially intended as a way to bring SGML to the Web, it was clear that the applications of this data format were far-reaching. You will see XML being used all over the place, not just on the Web.

Uses of XML

Now that you know a little about the origins and the structure of XML, it is time to take a look at what XML is really designed for. As we already explained, the purpose of XML is simply to present data in a meaningful and structured way. XML has nothing to do with the presentation of that data in contrast with its cousin HTML. The idea is simply to have a universal format for storing and sharing data.

Exchanging Data

In the world today, there is an ever-increasing number of gadgets, gizmos, and devices that send and receive data. Computers, cell phones, PDAs, and many more are all demanding data. But that data needs to be shared by many platforms. Just imagine that a news service must be able to provide current headlines to dozens or maybe even hundreds of platforms. There are a dizzying number of protocols and languages and architectures out there. Despite the fears of some that a technology giant will successfully create a monopoly in the market, there are still many thriving, competing options out there. So what is a company such as the news service to do? There is no way to force everyone to use the same platform. So the idea is to instead create a format that is platform-independent. That is what XML is.

XML has quickly become the standard by which data is shared among platforms. All that is required is that an XML *parser* (the part of a program that can interpret XML data) be written for the platform that is receiving that data. And now, even Flash has an XML parser. That means that in no time, you too can be sending and receiving XML data.

Storing Data

Another great use of XML is simply to store data. Application, environment, and user preferences can be stored in this format for easy processing each time the parameters need to be used. For instance, you might want to store a user's data in XML format for easy retrieval. You could always store it in some other format; there is certainly nothing wrong with that. But then you might well have to write your own parser. If you use XML, the parsing is already handled for you.

Writing Well-Formed XML

Now that you have an idea of what XML is, you need to know what it looks like. XML leaves a lot of control to the author, but it still must conform to some basic rules. XML that conforms to these rules is called "well-formed." Making sure that your XML documents are well-formed

[illegible]

for writing well-formed XML. Not all of these are necessarily important to Flash's implementation, and so they are outside of the scope of this book. But there are several points that you should consider when working with well-formed XML with ActionScript:

- ✦ **An XML declaration:** A tag that gives some basic information about the XML version being used.
- ✦ **Tags:** The basic elements of an XML document must be correctly authored and matched.
- ✦ **Attributes:** Tags can contain attributes that provide additional information.
- ✦ **DTD:** The Document Type Definition defines a set of rules for the XML document.

XML Declaration

The very first thing that must appear in a well-formed XML document is the declaration. The declaration should look like this:

```
<?xml version="1.0"?>
```

This tag describes the version of the document. This will become much more important as newer versions are released.

The ActionScript `XML` class actually doesn't have problems dealing with documents without this declaration. However, you should always include this declaration in your documents because it might be needed by another application trying to use the document.

Tags

As was mentioned previously, the tags in XML are completely arbitrary and up to the author of the document. Although tags in HTML are limited to a predefined set such as the following, tags in XML can be anything you want:

```
<td></td>
<b></b>
```

For example, the following are perfectly valid tags in XML:

```
<fish></fish>
<car></car>
<books></books>
```

The purpose of tags in XML is to describe the data they contain. But although you have a lot of leeway in determining the names of your tags, you have to follow some very specific (but simple) rules for formatting them.

First of all, all tags must be closed. This is in contrast to HTML, in which closing tags is often optional. For example, the following is perfectly legal in HTML:

```
<head>
this is the heading
<body>
this is the body
```

But XML is not so easygoing about it. You must close the tags. To convert the tags from the HTML example into legal tags in XML, it would look like this:

```
<head>this is the heading</head>
<body>this is the body</body>
```

XML allows you to use a shortcut to open and close a tag in one go if there is no data for that tag. This is useful for tags that contain no nested tags or data, but rather contain only attributes (see the next section for more information on attributes) or exist just to satisfy the DTD (see the section on DTD for more information on this subject). You can write the following opening and closing tag pair:

```
<car></car>
```

like this:

```
<car />
```

The next important rule when it comes to tags in XML is that they must be properly nested. In HTML, you can improperly nest tags and get away with it:

```
<b><font color="red">this is some text</b></font>
```

But this simply doesn't work in XML. You must make sure that nested tags are closed first. The HTML example is written in well-formed XML like this:

```
<b><font color="red">this is some text</font></b>
```

Also, it is important to note that all well-formed XML documents have only one main tag, known as the root element or root node. All other tags (elements, nodes) must be nested within the root element.

```
<?xml version="1.0"?>
<people>
  <person>
    <name>Jerry</name>
  </person>
</people>
```

In this example, the root element is `people`.

The ActionScript XML parser treats both tags and text as nodes. In order to distinguish between the types of nodes, there is a property for each node: 1 for an element (a tag) and 3 for a text node.

Attributes

In the previous examples borrowed from HTML, there was a tag that looked like this:

```
<font color="red">Some Text Here</font>
```

The name of the tag in this example is `font`. But the tag has something else besides just a name. It also has what is called an *attribute*. The attribute in this example is `color`. Often, using attributes versus using nested tags is simply a matter of preference. For example, the following XML tags:

```
<book>
  <author>Mark Twain</author>
  <title>Huckleberry Finn</title>
</book>
```

can be written in one tag using attributes:

```
<book author="Mark Twain" title="Huckleberry Finn">
```

And both attributes and nested tags can be used together. For example:

```
<article publication="Daily News">
  <title>How to Use ActionScript to Better Your Life</title>
  <body>
    This is the body of the article. Blah Blah Blah.
  </body>
</article>
```

The decision to use attributes or nested tags, or both, is often just a matter of personal choice. You might find that one way works best for you in a particular situation.

DTD

ActionScript's XML parser is known as a *nonvalidating parser*. That means it does not make sure the XML document it is parsing adheres to its own rules. But any good XML document has a set of rules known as a DTD, or Document Type Definition. Because ActionScript's XML parser is non-validating, it will be completely forgiving if your XML document does not adhere to its own DTD. This is good in the sense that it is very flexible. It can be a downside, however, if you are not careful that your XML document is correctly authored according to its DTD.

Because ActionScript does not pay attention to the DTD when parsing the document, this chapter does not spend much time on it. However, it is still a good idea to know what the DTD is and what it looks like. You will want to know how to create a DTD for the XML documents you create and export from Flash to other applications.

There are two types of DTDs. One is stored in a file separate from the XML document. This chapter does not discuss that kind because it is not relevant to the discussion of XML with regards to Flash and ActionScript. The second kind of DTD is part of the XML document itself.

All internal DTDs typically follow the document declaration. The DTD is enclosed within a single tag:

```
<!DOCTYPE rootNodeName[
   ...DTD tags...
]>
```

So if the root node were named `library`, the DTD would look something like this:

```
<!DOCTYPE library[
   ...DTD tags...
]>
```

Within this tag are the rest of the tags that define the structure of the XML document. These tags can get very involved, so this section covers only the basics.

Listing 26-1 shows an example of an XML document with an internal DTD.

Listing 26-1: XML Document with Internal DTD

```
<?xml version="1.0"?>
<!DOCTYPE library
   <!ELEMENT library   (book)>
   <!ELEMENT book   (author, title)>
   <!ELEMENT author   (#PCDATA)>
   <!ELEMENT title   (#PCDATA)>
]>
<library>
<book>
<author>Mark Twain</author>
<title>Huckleberry Finn</title>
</book>
</library>
```

As you can see, the `<!ELEMENT>` tag defines an element within the XML document. In this example, the first element, `library`, has a nested element, `book`. The next tag defines that nested `book` element as having two nested elements: `author` and `title`. Each of the next two `<!ELEMENT>` tags define the tags as containing `PCDATA`, which stands for parsed character data. In other words, these tags contain important data that the parser should read.

Using XML Objects

Any time you want to work with XML data in ActionScript, you must first instantiate an `XML` object. To do so, you need only to call the `XML` constructor function in a `new` statement:

```
var xmlData:XML = new XML();
```

This creates an empty `XML` object, which you can use to load data from an external source or which you can use to create and export your own XML document within Flash. However, if you are planning to create your own XML document, most of the time it is easier to first create a string containing the value of the XML document and then pass that parameter to the `XML` constructor like this:

```
var sXml:String = "<?xml version=\"1.0\"?><test>great</test>";
var xmlData:XML = new XML(sXml);
```

An alternative to this technique of populating an `XML` object is to use the `parseXML()` method. This method takes a single argument: an XML string to be parsed into the object. Any existing tree in the object is lost and replaced with the XML tree resulting from the parsing of the specified string:

```
var sXml:String = "<blah></blah>";
var xmlData:XML = new XML();
xmlData.parseXML(sXml);
```

As you look at this example, the use of the `parseXML()` method might not be immediately clear. In fact, if it does the same thing as simply passing the string to the constructor, why use the method at all? There are a few good reasons why you might want to use the method.

First of all, if you have an existing `XML` object, and you want to replace the existing XML tree in the object with the result of a parsed string, using `parseXML()` is a good idea. Otherwise, you have to delete the object and create a new one.

The second good reason for using `parseXML()` is when you want to set the `ignoreWhite` property to `true`. (The `ignoreWhite` property is covered later in this chapter.) Setting the property to `true` after the string has been parsed does no good. But in order to have an object for which to set the property, you must first call the constructor. In this case, you would definitely want to use the `parseXML()` method:

```
var sXml:String = "\n\n<blah>\n\n</blah>"; // contains newlines
var xmlData:XML = new XML();
xmlData.ignoreWhite = true;
xmlData.parseXML(sXml);
```

If there is an error parsing a string (or parsing a loaded document), the object's `status` property is automatically set to indicate what kind of error occurred. Table 26-1 shows the possible values for the `status` property.

Table 26-1: Values for the status Property

Value	*Meaning*
0	Successfully parsed
-2	Error in CDATA section
-3	Error with XML declaration
-4	Error with DTD
-5	Error with comment
-6	Error with element (tag)
-7	Out of memory (file is probably too big)
-8	Error with attribute
-9	Starting tag with no ending tag
-10	Ending tag with no starting tag

The following code demonstrates how the `status` property can help indicate what kind of error occurred in parsing:

```
var sXml:String = "<aTag>some value";
var xmlVal:XML = new XML();
xmlVal.parseXML(sXml);
trace(xmlVal.status);
```

In this example, the Output panel displays the following:

```
-9
```

This indicates that there is a missing ending tag somewhere in the string being parsed. And, indeed, there is. If you fix the following string, the `status` property is set to `0` to indicate that the parse was successful:

```
var sXml:String = "<aTag>some value</a>";
var xmlVal:XML = new XML();
xmlVal.parseXML(sXml);
trace(xmlVal.status);
```

Traversing the XML Tree

Once an `XML` object has been created, you will want to be able to extract the data from it. Using the properties of the `XML` object, you can read the data in the object's hierarchy by traversing the data tree and then reading the values of elements and attributes.

Reading the XML Declaration and the DTD

The `xmlDecl` and `docTypeDecl` properties allow you access to the XML declaration and the DTD, respectively. You can read these properties as in the following example:

```
var sXml:String = "<?xml version=\"1.0\"?> ⮐
<!DOCTYPE library[<!ELEMENT book (#PCDATA)>]>";
```

```
var xmlVal:XML = new XML(sXml);
trace(xmlVal.xmlDecl);
trace(xmlVal.docTypeDecl);
```

This example outputs the following to the Output panel:

```
<?xml version="1.0"?>
<!DOCTYPE library[<!ELEMENT book(#PCDATA)>]>
```

Understanding the XMLnode Class

The `XMLnode` class is the superclass to the `XML` class, but more importantly, it is the class definition for all elements of an `XML` object. In the next section, you learn about reading the child nodes of an `XML` object. Each child node is an `XMLnode` instance. The `XMLnode` class and the `XML` class have the same methods and properties, with a few exceptions.

The `XMLnode` class does not include the `loaded`, `status`, `contentType`, or `ignoreWhite` properties. Nor does it include the `load()`, `send()`, or `sendAndLoad()` methods. The reason for this is that `XMLnode` objects never send or load data, but `XML` objects do.

In almost every case, it is not important to know that a child node of an `XML` object is an `XMLnode` object instead of an `XML` object. After all, you probably never will try to load data into a child node. It *does* make a difference, however, when you want to work with an `XML` object recursively.

Reading Child Nodes

You have seen that there exists a hierarchy in an XML document, in which elements are nested within other elements. This hierarchy is often called the document tree. Nested elements are called the *children* or *child elements* of a *parent element.*

The `firstChild`, `lastChild`, `nextSibling`, `previousSibling`, and `childNodes` properties are all read-only properties. This means that you can use them to read the existing data in an `XML` object, but you cannot use them to set values and establish new relationships within the object. Methods later in this chapter are used for doing that.

When you are stepping through the hierarchy of your XML object or traversing the document tree, it is most useful to be able to retrieve the child nodes of a parent element. For instance, given the XML snippet in Listing 26-1, if the current element you are working with is the `book` element, you would likely want to read the names and values of its child nodes. One way to do this is to use the `firstChild` or `lastChild` properties, and then step through all the child nodes by accessing the `nextSibling` or `previousSibling` properties of the child elements. (Sibling elements are simply other elements within the same hierarchy in the tree and that are nested within the same parent element.)

In the example in Listing 26-2, the `firstChild` property of the `book` element is a reference to the `author` node. Likewise, the `lastChild` property of the `book` element is a reference to the `Huckleberry Finn` text node. Remember, both tags and text elements are nodes in the ActionScript XML parser.

The `firstChild` property of an `XML` object that has been parsed from a string or document without any additional spaces or a DTD is the root node. When there are spaces in the string or a document before the root node, or if the string or document contains a DTD, the `firstChild` of the object might not always be the root node. Later in this chapter, you see how to outline a way to handle this uncertainty.

Listing 26-2: Reading Child Nodes of an XML Object

```
var sXml:String = "<book><author>Mark Twain</author> ⮐
<title>Huckleberry Finn</title></book>";
var xmlVal:XML = new XML(sXml);
var xnRootNode:XMLNode = xmlVal.firstChild;  // <book />
var xnAuthorTag:XMLNode = xnRootNode.firstChild;  // <author />
var xnAuthor:XMLNode = xnAuthorTag.firstChild;  // Mark Twain
var xnTitleTag:XMLNode = xnAuthorTag.nextSibling;  // <title />
var xnTitle:XMLNode = xnTitleTag.firstChild;  // Huckleberry Finn
```

You can also access the `title` tag directly from its parent node, `book`, as the `lastChild` property of the parent object:

```
xnTitleTag = xnRootNode.lastChild;
```

In that case, you can reference the `author` node relative to the `xnTitleTag` object as the `previousSibling` property of the `xnTitleTag` object:

```
xnAuthorTag = xnTitleTag.previousSibling;
```

Also, notice that, as was mentioned previously, text nodes are treated as children of the elements that give them context. In this case, the text nodes with the values of `Mark Twain` and `Huckleberry Finn` are the `firstChild` (and, as it turns out also the `lastChild`) properties of the `xnAuthorTag` and `xnTitleTag` objects, respectively.

The `childNodes` property is a collection, or an array, of references to all the child nodes of an `XML` object. This is an alternative to using the `firstChild` and `nextSibling` approach for traversing an XML tree. Listing 26-3 shows how to use the `childNodes` property to create an array of `XMLnode` objects, each being a child of a parent node.

Listing 26-3: Using the childNodes Property

```
var sXml:String = "<?xml version=\"1.0\"?> ⮐
<cars><car><make>Honda</make><model>Accord</model> ⮐
<year>1985</year></car></cars>"
var xmlVal:XML = new XML(sXml);
var xnRootNode:XMLNode = xmlVal.firstChild;  // <cars>
var xnCar:XMLNode = rootNode.firstChild;   // <car>
var aChildren:Array = car.childNodes;  // child nodes of <car>
for(var i:Number = 0; i < aChildren.length; i++){
 trace(aChildren[i].toString());
}
```

This example writes the following to the Output panel:

```
<make>Honda</make>
<model>Accord</model>
<year>1985</year>
```

Each element of the array created by the childNodes property is an XMLNode object, and you can therefore access the methods and properties of those objects as well. You can also access the firstChild properties to display the text node values. The for loop is rewritten like this:

```
for(var i:Number = 0; i < aChildren.length; i++){
 trace(aChildren[i].firstChild.toString());
}
```

And the result in the Output panel is as follows:

```
Honda
Accord
1985
```

When you are working with an element, you might simply want to check to see whether it has child elements before doing anything else with it. You can test to see whether an element has child nodes by invoking the hasChildNodes() method from the element. It returns true if child nodes exist and false if there are no child nodes:

```
if(xmlVal.firstChild.hasChildNodes()){
   trace("the root element has children!");
}
```

This section demonstrates very simplified examples of working with an XML object by using the firstChild, lastChild, nextSibling, and previousSibling properties. These examples assume that you are already certain of the formatting of the string or document that is being parsed into the XML object. On many occasions, you will want to perform additional checks to verify the data you are working with. This includes removing whitespace nodes and the like to eliminate the possibility of offsetting your results. These issues are examined more closely later in this chapter.

Reading Parent Nodes

Every element has exactly one parent node with the exception of the main element, or root element (which has no parent node). This is different from child nodes. A single node can have many child nodes, and therefore there are a handful of different properties for XML objects to access these child nodes. But with only one parent node per element, there is need for only one property to access that parent node. The parentNode property is a reference to an element's parent. If the node has no parent (that is, it is the root element), the property is null.

```
<book>
  <author>Mark Twain</author>
  <title>Huckleberry Finn</title>
</book>
```

For example, in the previous XML snippet, the author and title elements have the same parentNode property value of book.

This property is not immediately as useful in traversing the XML tree as the child and sibling properties. But it is a useful method for determining the relationship between two nodes:

```
if(xnOne.parentNode == xnTwo.parentNode){
  trace("the nodes are siblings!");
}
```

Reading Element Attributes

In many XML documents, you will have elements with attributes. Remember, an attribute is a parameter within the tag. For instance, `color` is an attribute of the `crayon` element in this XML tag:

```
<crayon color="blue"/>
```

In the example used to demonstrate the `childNodes` property (Listing 26-3), we used an `XML` object made from a string with lots of nested tags. A more nicely formatted version of that XML text looks like this:

```
<?xml version=\"1.0\"?>
<cars>
  <car>
    <make>Honda</make>
    <model>Accord</model>
    <year>1985</year>
  </car>
</cars>
```

However, you can easily enough rewrite this so that the `car` tag uses attributes to define the same data:

```
<car make="Honda" model="Accord" year="1985"/>
```

Just as you can create a collection of child nodes using the `childNodes` property, you can create a collection of attributes for a given element with the `attributes` property. The difference is that the collection that `childNodes` creates is an indexed array. The `attributes` collection is an associative array. Listing 26-4 is the example from the previous section that was rewritten to use attributes and the `attributes` property to create a collection.

Listing 26-4: **Reading Attributes from an Element**

```
var sXml:String = "<?xml version=\"1.0\"?><cars>⮐
<car make=\"Honda\" model=\"Accord\" year=\"1985\"/></cars>"
var xmlVal:XML = new XML(sXml);
var xnRoot:XMLNode = xmlVal.firstChild;  // <cars>
var xnCarTag:XMLNode = xnRoot.firstChild;  // <car>
var oAttribs:Object = xnCarTag.attributes;  // attribs of <car>
for(var sAttrib:String in oAttribs){
 trace(sAttrib + ":" + oAttribs[sAttrib]);
}
```

This example writes the following to the Output panel:

```
make:Honda
model:Accord
year:1985
```

Notice that, because the `attributes` property is an associative array, a `for in` loop is used instead of a regular `for` loop.

Reading Element Information

All tags and text are considered to be nodes in XML. Thus, two *types* of nodes can be parsed into an XML object: tags (or tag elements) and text. Each of these different types has an ID. Tag elements have an ID of 1, whereas text nodes have an ID of 3. Every XMLNode object has a nodeType property that reveals what type of node you are dealing with. Listing 26-5 shows a few examples of reading the nodeType property for different elements.

Listing 26-5: Reading the nodeType Property

```
var sXml:String = "<book><author>Mark Twain</author>⮐
<title>Huckleberry Finn</title></book>";
var xmlVal:XML = new XML(sXml);
var xnRoot:XMLNode = xmlVal.firstChild;
trace(xnRoot.nodeType);
var xnAuthorTag:XMLNode = xnRoot.firstChild;
trace(xnAuthorTag.nodeType);
var xnAuthorName:XMLNode = xnAuthorTag.firstChild;
trace(xnAuthorName.nodeType);
```

It writes the following to the Output panel:

```
1
1
3
```

Whitespace nodes such as carriage returns and other special characters are treated as text nodes (nodeType of 3).

When a node has a nodeType value of 1, the nodeName has the value of the tag name. For instance, the following code appended to the code from Listing 26-5:

```
trace(xnRoot.nodeName);
trace(xnAuthorTag.nodeName);
```

writes the following to the Output panel:

```
book
author
```

However, when a node has a nodeType value of 3, the nodeName has a null value:

```
trace(xnAuthorName.nodeName);
```

and results in the following in the Output panel:

```
null
```

So, how do you retrieve the value of a text node? There is yet another property of XMLnode objects that contains the value of the text node. Therefore, this property is null for all objects with a nodeType of 1. For objects with a nodeType of 3, the nodeValue contains the text value of the following node:

```
trace(xnAuthorName.nodeValue);
```

which results in the following in the Output panel:

```
Mark Twain
```

Building a Document Tree

You can construct your own XML objects and build their document trees within ActionScript based on environment and user data. You have seen how to use the constructor function and the parseXML() method to parse a string into the object's document tree. But it can also be convenient to be able to build the document tree node by node. The methods of the XML object enable you to do exactly this.

Writing the XML Declaration and DTD

The xmlDecl and docTypeDecl properties are read-write properties, and you can therefore use these properties to set the values of either the XML declaration or the DTD:

```
var xmlVal:XML = new XML();
xmlVal.xmlDecl = "<?xml version=\"1.0\"?>";
xmlVal.docTypeDecl = "\"<!DOCTYPE library[<!ELEMENT book (#PCDATA)>]>";
```

Creating Nodes

Once you've created a new XML object you next want to create one or more new nodes to add to its document tree. You'll recall that all nodes are instances of the XMLNode class. Therefore, in order to create these nodes, you can use the XMLNode constructor. The XMLNode constructor allows you to create either tag nodes or text nodes by specifying the type ID of 1 or 3, respectively. Listing 26-6 shows an example of each.

Listing 26-6: Making New XMLNode Objects

```
var xnNewElement:XMLNode = new XMLNode(1, "author");
var xnNewTextNode:XMLNode = new XMLNode(3, "Mark Twain");
```

That's all there is to it. You now have a new element, <author>, assigned to the variable xnNewElement. And you have a new text node, Mark Twain, assigned to the variable xnNewTextNode. The only catch is that the nodes don't have any parent, children, or siblings. In other words, the nodes do not have a location in the data tree within the XML object. In order to accomplish this, you need to use either the appendChild() or the insertBefore() methods.

The appendChild() and insertBefore() methods do pretty much just what their names suggest. The appendChild() method adds the specified XMLNode instance to the end of the current child nodes of the object from which it is called. The appendChild() method is essential because you need it in order to create the root node within an XML object. Listing 26-7 shows an example of this.

Listing 26-7: Adding a Root Node with appendChild()

```
var xmlBook:XML = new XML();
var xnRoot:XMLNode = new XMLNode(1, "book");
xmlBook.appendChild(xnRoot);
trace(xmlBook.toString());  // Displays: <book />
```

The `insertBefore()` method also inserts an `XMLNode` object as a child node of the object from which it is called. But instead of appending it to the end of the child node list, the node is inserted just before the node that is referenced as the second parameter of the method. Listing 26-8 shows an example that uses both `appendChild` and `insertBefore()` to populate an XML object.

Listing 26-8: Populating an XML Document Tree

```
var xmlBook:XML = new XML();
var xnRoot:XMLNode = new XMLNode(1, "book");
var xnAuthorTag:XMLNode = new XMLNode(1, "author");
var xnAuthorName:XMLNode = new XMLNode(3, "Mark Twain");
var xnTitleTag:XMLNode = new XMLNode(1, "title");
var xnTitle:XMLNode = new XMLNode(3, "Huckleberry Finn");
xmlBook.appendChild(xnRoot);
xnRoot.appendChild(xnAuthorTag);
xnRoot.insertBefore(xnTitleTag, xnAuthorTag);
xnAuthorTag.appendChild(xnAuthorName);
xnTitleTag.appendChild(xnTitle);
trace(xmlBook.toString());
```

This example constructs the `XML` object and then writes the following to the Output panel:

```
<book><title>Huckleberry Finn</title><author>Mark Twain</author></book>
```

Creating Attributes

Every `XMLNode` object has an `attributes` property that is an associative array of the object's attributes. The property is read-write, meaning that you can use the property to add attributes and update values for a node. In this section, you learn how to add attributes to an element.

Listing 26-6 demonstrated how to create a new element. Once the element is created, you can add attributes by adding array elements to the `attributes` property. The following code demonstrates how to add three attributes (`a`, `b`, and `c`) to the element created in Listing 26-6:

```
xnNewElement.attributes.a = "attribute a";
xnNewElement.attributes.b = "attribute b";
xnNewElement.attributes.c = "attribute c";
```

You can also choose to write the same thing as the following:

```
xnNewElement.attributes["a"] = "attribute a";
xnNewElement.attributes["b"] = "attribute b";
xnNewElement.attributes["c"] = "attribute c";
```

If you were to then view the string value of the following element:

```
trace(xnNewElement.toString());
```

you would see that it looks like this:

```
<firstElement c="attribute c" b="attribute b" a="attribute a" />
```

Cloning Nodes

There are occasions when you want to make copies of an `XML` or `XMLNode` object or parts of the data from the object. You can use the `cloneNode()` method to do exactly this. Using the example from Listing 26-7 as a starting point, you can create a copy of the `xmlBook` object's data, as follows:

```
var xmlCopy:XML = new XML();
var xnRootCopy:XMLNode = xmlBook.firstChild.cloneNode();
xmlCopy.appendChild(xnRootCopy);
trace(xmlCopy.toString());
```

This results in the following being written to the Output panel:

```
<book />
```

You might have expected it to have copied all the child nodes of the root element from `xmlVal`. But the method does not clone all the child nodes recursively by default. You must specify in a parameter passed to the `cloneNode()` method. The parameter can be `false` for no recursive cloning or `true` for recursive cloning:

```
var xmlCopy:XML = new XML();
var xnRootCopy:XMLNode = xmlBook.firstChild.cloneNode(true);
xmlCopy.appendChild(xnRootCopy);
trace(xmlCopy.toString());
```

Now the Output panel will display the following:

```
<book><title>Huckleberry Finn</title><author>Mark Twain</author></book>
```

Removing Nodes

Opposite the methods for creating nodes is `removeNode()`. This method's name pretty much says it all. Invoke the method from the node you want to remove. It takes no parameters:

```
// removes root element and all children
xmlVal.firstChild.removeNode();
```

Loading and Sending XML

One of the powerful characteristics of XML is that it is a platform-independent means of sharing data. Although you can use XML effectively strictly within the confines of your Flash movie, an intended use of the `XML` object is to be able to load XML data in from external sources, as well as send XML data to external sources. Doing so enables you to create sophisticated applications that can call upon external applications to perform specific tasks. For example, many e-commerce Web applications rely on shipping-and-handling calculations being performed by the servers of the shipping company they use. Often, this data is transmitted between the servers by means of XML. Using an XML object and sending and loading that data allow you to incorporate systems that draw upon the databases and resources of other applications.

Loading XML

Using parseXML() works well for parsing XML strings existing within ActionScript already. But if you want to use this same method for XML documents outside of your Flash movie, you have to go through a slightly more involved process to first load the string into your movie. But the load() method takes care of everything for you. The load() method loads an XML document from an external source into your Flash movie and parses it to create the XML tree for your XML object.

The load() method takes a single parameter: the URL (as a string) to the XML document you want to load. Listing 26-9 shows an XML object that loads a document called data.xml from the same directory as the movie that is playing.

Listing 26-9: Loading an XML Document

```
var xmlVal:XML = new XML();
xmlVal.load("data.xml");
```

The reference can also be a full URL. Remember that the Flash movie runs on the client computer and has no access to the server's local file system. For example, if the movie is playing at www.person13.com, the load() method call might look like this:

```
xmlVal.load("http://www.person13.com/data.xml");
```

This raises an important point when working with loading XML documents into Flash. By default, ActionScript allows you to load XML documents only from the same domain as the movie that is playing. This is for security reasons. Obviously, this has implications in Flash movies. How can you then share data with external sources that are on remote servers? There is a solution, however. The crossdomain.xml policy file enables domains to allow access to select other domains. For more information on this file, see the section "Sharing Data Across Domains," later in this chapter.

External XML data does not necessarily have to come from a static XML file with an XML extension. In fact, you can call a CGI, JSP, or other kind of script or program that generates dynamic XML data.

Receiving Loaded Data

XML loads asynchronously. This means that the load() method initiates the loading, but it does not wait until the entire XML document has loaded before going to the next line of code. Otherwise a Flash application could hang on an XML load() command for seconds or even minutes depending on the amount of data and the connection. Instead, the XML data loads in the background as the rest of the application continues. Therefore, you need a way to be able to handle the data once it has been loaded. Fortunately the `onLoad()` method of the XML object is invoked when the data has been loaded and the data has been parsed into the XML tree. All you need to do is define the method with the actions that you want it to complete once the data has loaded, and Flash takes care of calling it at the appropriate time.

When Flash calls the `onLoad()` method of an XML object, it passes it a Boolean parameter indicating whether the data was successfully loaded and parsed. Also, of course, within the method definition, you can refer to the XML object with the `this` keyword. Listing 26-10 shows an example of a very simple `onLoad()` method.

Listing 26-10: Creating an onLoad() Method

```
xmlVal.onLoad = function(bSuccess:Boolean):Void {
 if (bSuccess){
  trace(this.toString());
 }
 else{
  trace("document failed to load or parse.");
 }
};
```

In this example, the function checks to see whether `bSuccess` is `true`. If it is, that means the document was loaded and parsed, and the function uses the `trace()` function to write the XML to the Output panel. If the document failed to load, the function writes an error message to the Output panel.

Monitoring Load Progress

In some cases you might want to monitor the progress of loading XML. The `getBytesLoaded()` and `getBytesTotal()` methods return the loaded and total bytes for the loading XML data. You can use `setInterval()` to set up a polling system that continually checks to see what the progress is. For example:

```
function checkXMLProgess(xmlObj:XML):Void {
  var nLoaded:Number = xmlObj.getBytesLoaded();
  var nTotal:Number = xmlObj.getBytesTotal();
  var nPercentage:Number = 0;
  if(nTotal > 0) {
    nPercentage = nLoaded/nTotal * 100;
  }
  tProgress.text = nPercentage + "% has loaded";
  if(nPercentage == 100) {
    clearInterval(nProgInterval);
  }
}

var nProgInterval:Number = setInterval(checkXMLProgress, 100, xmlVal);
```

Sending XML Data

Sending XML data can be, of course, just as important as loading XML data. And, often sending and loading are using in combination. There are two methods for sending XML data. The `send()` method will convert the `XML` object's data to an XML string and send it to the specified URL. The `sendAndLoad()` method, as the name suggests, will do the same thing as the `send()` method, but it also waits for a response from the server and loads that data back into Flash.

The `send()` method requires at least one parameter—a string specifying the URL to which you wish to send the XML data. For example:

```
xmlData.send("xmlSubmitter.cgi");
```

The `send()` method also allows you to specify a browser window into which you'd like to load the server response. For example, the following sends the XML data to the server and then displays the response in a new browser window:

```
xmlData.send("xmlSubmitter.cgi", "_blank");
```

The `sendAndLoad()` method requires two parameters. The first parameter is the URL to which you want to send the data. The second parameter is the `XML` object you want to have handle the response. The response `XML` object should have an `onLoad()` event handler method defined.

```
xmlData.sendAndLoad("xmlSubmitter.cgi", xmlLoader);
```

Setting Request Headers

By default, when your invoke the `send()` or `sendAndLoad()` methods, the data is sent with a set of default request headers. For example, the default Content-Type header is `"application/x-www-form-urlform-encoded"`. Even though the header would suggest that the content being sent is URL-encoded, the fact is that it is not. The default value is set in this manner to make the data compatible with common application servers (Cold Fusion, ASP, and so on). However, you may find that the Content-Type header needs to be changed for it to be compatible (depending on which application server you are sending your data to). You might also want to add your own request headers.

You can set the request headers with the `addRequestHeader()` method. You should call this method *before* sending the data. If you want to set one header, you can call the method in the following format:

```
xmlObj.addRequestHeader(headerName, headerValue);
```

For example, you can set the Content-Type request header to `text/xml` as follows:

```
xmlVal.addRequestHeader("Content-Type", "text/xml");
```

If you want to set multiple headers at the same time, you can pass the method a single parameter. The parameter should be in the form of an array in which the elements alternate between header name and header value.

```
xmlObj.addRequestHeader([headerName, headerValue,
   headerName, headerValue, ...]);
```

You can also use the `contentType` property to set the Content-Type header. For example:

```
xmlVal.contentType = "text/xml";
```

Dealing with Whitespace

You have learned how the ActionScript XML parser parses whitespace nodes (including tabs, carriage returns, and newlines) in an XML document as text nodes. This can be problematic when you are trying to work with the data because it can produce all kinds of unexpected nodes. Fortunately, you can use the `ignoreWhite` property to remedy this problem.

All `XML` objects default to `ignoreWhite` being `false`. This means that all `XML` objects parse whitespace nodes into the `XML` object by default. However, if you set the property to `true`, whitespace nodes are discarded during parsing. This does not mean that any text node with whitespace in it is discarded; it means that any text node that is *only* whitespace is discarded. Because the whitespace nodes are discarded during the parsing of the document or string into the object's data tree, the `ignoreWhite` property must be set to `true` *before* any parsing takes place in which you want whitespace nodes to be discarded.

Loading and Sending Data with LoadVars

The `LoadVars` class enables you to send and load variables in your Flash applications. The API for sending and loading with the `LoadVars` class is very similar to the API for sending and loading with the XML class. The difference between `LoadVars` and `XML` objects is simply that an `XML` object works with XML data and the `LoadVars` class works with name-value pairs.

Creating a LoadVars Object

You must create a `LoadVars` object before you can do anything with the class. The way to create an object is simply to call the constructor function in a `new` statement. The function requires no parameters:

```
var lvData:LoadVars = new LoadVars();
```

Loading Data

Loading data using `LoadVars` objects works very similarly to loading data using `XML` objects. The first step is to create the object. Next you call the `load()` method from the object, passing it a parameter specifying the URL where the loaded data can be found. As with `XML` objects, the loading process is asynchronous, so you can define an `onLoad()` method that's called when the data has been loaded (or failed to load).

The data that can be processed by the `LoadVars` object must be in `URLEncoded`, name-value pair format. In other words, each name and value should be separated by an equals sign (=), each name-value pair should be separated by an ampersand (&), and non-alphanumeric characters should be escaped. For example, perhaps you want to load data into Flash concerning the book *Huckleberry Finn* by Mark Twain. The data should appear in the format shown in Listing 26-11.

Listing 26-11: URLEncoded Name-Value Pair Format

```
title=Huckleberry%20Finn&author=Mark%20Twain
```

The data can be stored in a text file or can be generated by a server-side script. But either way, the data must be returned in this same format.

Listing 26-12 shows an example of using a LoadVars object to load data from a text file and then display the results in the Output panel.

Listing 26-12: Loading Data with LoadVars

```
var lvData:LoadVars = new LoadVars();
lvData.load("bookResult.txt");
lvData.onLoad = function(bSuccess:Boolean):Void {
  if(bSuccess){
    trace(this.title);
    trace(this.author);
  }
};
```

Assuming the content of bookResult.txt is that shown in Listing 26-11, the Output panel then displays the following:

```
Huckleberry Finn
Mark Twain
```

There are two important things to point out in this example about how LoadVars objects work. First of all, each name-value pair in the loaded data is automatically converted into a property of the LoadVars object from which the load() method was called. In this example, therefore, once the data is loaded, the lvData LoadVars object has two new properties: title and author. The second important thing to notice is that escaped characters are automatically unescaped. In this example, the spaces in the values were escaped and replaced with %20 in the loaded data. However, without having to directly invoke the unescape() function, the values are automatically unescaped.

Like XML objects, LoadVars objects have the getBytesLoaded() and getBytesTotal() methods to provide you with a means of determining how much data has been received by the movie so far.

Sending Data

Again, like XML objects, data can be sent using a LoadVars object with either the send() or sendAndLoad() method. Each method works by sending all the custom properties (variables) of the object to a URL specified as a parameter. In both methods, the variables are sent via POST unless otherwise specified.

The send() method requires only one parameter: the URL to which the variables should be sent. For example, you could use a LoadVars object to send a user's responses to a survey to the server (see Listing 26-13).

Listing 26-13: Sending Data with LoadVars

```
var lvData:LoadVars = new LoadVars();
lvData.favoriteColor = "red";
lvData.favoriteSong = "Row, Row, Row Your Boat";
lvData.favoriteCar = "Ford Model T";
lvData.send("http://www.myserver.com/cgi-bin/surveyResults.cgi");
```

You can also choose to specify two other optional parameters when using the `send()` method: the target browser window for the results of the send and the HTTP `send` method. If the target parameter is omitted or set to `null`, no results are displayed. You might want to specify a target if you are sending to a CGI script, for instance, that generates some HTML that you want to display. (See the `XML` object `send()` method description for more specifics on using a target.) And, as we already mentioned, the `send()` method uses the `POST` method to send the variables, unless otherwise specified. If the server-side script expects the data to be sent using `GET`, you can specify that as the third parameter. Here is an example of the `send()` method call from the previous example (Listing 26-13), modified so that the variables are sent using `GET`, and the results are displayed in a new browser window:

```
lvData.send("http://www.myserver.com/cgi-bin/surveyResults.cgi",
            "_blank", "GET");
```

The `sendAndLoad()` method works very similarly to the `XML` object `sendAndLoad()` method. It requires two parameters: the URL to which to send the variables and the `LoadVars` object to which the results should be loaded. As with the `send()` method, you can also specify a third, optional parameter for the HTTP method used to send the variables. Listing 26-14 shows the same example as in Listing 26-13, but the results are loaded into another `LoadVars` object and processed by that object's `onLoad()` method.

Listing 26-14: Sending and Loading with sendAndLoad()

```
var lvData:LoadVars = new LoadVars();
var lvReceived:LoadVars = new LoadVars();
lvData.favoriteColor = "red";
lvData.favoriteSong = "Red Roses for a Blue Lady";
lvData.favoriteCar = "Ford Model T";
lvData.sendAndLoad("http://www.myserver.com/cgi-bin/surveyResults.cgi",
                   lvReceived);
lvReceived.onLoad = function(bSuccess:Boolean):Void {
  if(success){
    trace(this.responseMessage);
    trace(this.processTime);
  }
};
```

Also like XML objects, LoadVars objects have a addRequestHeader() method. The method allows you to set request headers before sending data. For example, by default, the Content-Type header has a value of application/x-www-urlform-encoded, but if the script to which the data is being sent requires a different content type, you can set the header to that value with addRequestHeader(). See the discussion of the XML class's addRequestHeader() method for more details.

Sharing Data Across Domains

Flash movies have built-in security that restricts access to send or load content from any source that is on a different domain from where the Flash movie is playing. With Flash Player 7, the domains must match exactly, including protocol and port. In other words, a movie playing at http://www.themakers.com can load any data from the same domain, but it cannot load data from http://www.person13.com, and it cannot even load data from http://data.themakers.com. This can be problematic. You might want an SWF file running on one domain to be able to send and load data on another domain. You have three options available:

- **Create a crossdomain.xml policy file.** This requires that you have access to the domain from which you want to load data or to which you want to send data. If you do have access to that domain, this is the suggested technique.
- **Set up DNS aliasing.** This is not a likely candidate for most. It involves a certain level of expertise and access that many folks do not have. The idea is that on the DNS servers that your server uses, you can set up an alias to a remote server so that it appears to be in the same domain.
- **Use a proxy script.** This is probably the option that will be available to most users. You can use a proxy script that will reside on the same domain as your Flash movie and simply relay the data between the Flash movie and the remote domain.

Setting Up a Policy File

The crossdomain.xml policy file is a new feature to Flash Player 7. By default, each domain restricts access to its content such that only Flash movies on the same exact domain can send and load it. However, you can create a crossdomain.xml file for the domain that specifies what domains and IP addresses can have access.

The new sandbox security model in Flash Player 7 requires stricter domain-name matching, but it also allows for greater flexibility in cross-domain data loading using a crossdomain.xml policy file to tell Flash which requests it should accept.

The crossdomain.xml file must be placed in the root directory for the domain. That is, crossdomain.xml must exist such that it is accessible at, for example, http://www.yourdomain.com/crossdomain.xml. The file itself is an XML file in which the root element is a <cross-domain-policy> tag. Nested within the root element can be zero or more <allow-access-from> tags. The <allow-access-from> tag has a domain attribute specifying the allowed domain or IP address. If you are specifying a domain name, you can use the * as a wildcard. Here is an example policy file:

```
<?xml version="1.0"?>
<cross-domain-policy>
  <allow-access-from domain="*.themakers.com" />
  <allow-access-from domain="*.person13.com" />
</cross-domain-policy>
```

The preceding example file allows any requesting SWF served from `themaker.com` or `person13.com` to access the resources on the domain on which the file is located. The requesting movie can be served from `www.person13.com`, `testing.person13.com`, `www2.themakers.com`, or `www.themakers.com`, to give just a few examples. However, if a movie served from `www.anotherdomain.com` makes a request for a resource on the server, the request is denied.

The wildcard character does not work with IP addresses.

Working with a Proxy Script

You can either write your own proxy scripts if you have the knowledge and the desire, or you can use the ones on the CD-ROM. You can write a script using any language that you want. If you want to write a proxy script using PHP, take a look at `www.flash-db.com` for a tutorial on this very subject.

You will find two proxy scripts on the CD-ROM that accompanies this book. One is written in ColdFusion (`proxy.cfm`) and the other is written in Perl (`proxy.cgi`, written by Arun Bhalla). Both of these scripts are provided to you as-is. You are free to use them and modify them as you desire.

The basic idea with the proxy script is that your ActionScript code remains pretty much the same (just a few minor changes), except that your `sendAndLoad()` method calls the proxy script instead of the script or content on the remote domain. The proxy scripts included on the CD-ROM require that you specify the location of the remote resource as a parameter to the script. The parameter name should be `location`. Also, you can optionally pass the script a parameter named `httpmethod` that specifies either `GET` or `POST` for how the rest of the parameters should be passed to the remote resource.

If you use the proxy script to send or load with an `XML` object, you should append the `location` and optionally the `httpmethod` parameters to the proxy script URL as a query string as shown here:

```
var xmlVal:XML = new XML();
xmlVal.load("http://www.localserver.com/proxy.cfm?location=↩
http://www.remoteserver.com/somedoc.xml");
```

When you use the proxy script to request a remote resource with a `LoadVars` object, you should always use the `sendAndLoad()` method whether simply sending or also loading. You should then add `location` and optionally `httpmethod` properties to the `LoadVars` object. Here is an example:

```
var lvData = new LoadVars();
var lvReceiver = new LoadVars();
lvData.a = 1;
```

```
lvData.b = 2;
lvData.c = 3;
lvData.location = "http://www.remoteserver.com/testProxy.cfm";
lvData.httpmethod = "GET";
lvData.sendAndLoad("http://www.localserver.com/proxy.cfm", lvReceiver);
lvReceiver.onLoad = function():Void {
  for(var item:String in this) {
    trace(item + ": " + this[item]);
  }
};
```

Take a look at `www.flash-db.com` for a tutorial on how to write proxy scripts using PHP.

You can still specify an HTTP method parameter when calling the `sendAndLoad()` method. However, the value you specify for the `sendAndLoad()` parameter affects only how the parameters are sent to the proxy script, not how the proxy script sends the parameters to the remote resource.

We'd like to know what you thought about this chapter. Visit `www.flashsupport.com/feedback` to fill out an online form with your comments.

Summary

- XML (Extensible Markup Language) is a language with user-defined tags that give context to data. You can use XML to store and transfer data in a platform-independent format while still retaining both the values as well as the significance of those values in a universally understood structure.
- XML looks similar to HTML in structure, but more strictly enforces rules by which the language must be structured. XML that adheres to the rules is known as well-formed XML.
- Using the `XML` object, you can use ActionScript to create, send, load, and parse XML documents.
- `LoadVars` offers an alternative to the `MovieClip` object `loadVariables()` method. `LoadVars` is advantageous because, among other things, it allows for an `onLoad()` method that gets called when data is loaded.
- `LoadVars` and `XML` objects send and load data in the same ways. Each allows you to define an `onLoad()` method that gets called automatically when the data is loaded. The difference between `LoadVars` and `XML` objects is in the format of the data that they handle. `XML` objects handle XML data, and `LoadVars` objects handle data in name-value pairs.

✦ ✦ ✦

27

CHAPTER

The XMLSocket Class

✦ ✦ ✦ ✦

In This Chapter

Learning the difference between HTTP and TCP communications and what that means to you as a Flash developer

Defining sockets and socket connections

Understanding the methods of the XMLSocket class for establishing connections and transmitting data over socket connections

Creating your own chat application using an XMLSocket object

✦ ✦ ✦ ✦

In Chapter 26, you saw what you can do with XML data in your Flash movies using XML objects. In this chapter, you learn how to use the `XMLSocket` class to create persistent channels of communication by which you can transfer your XML data (as well as non-XML data) to and from a server. You can use it to create applications that require constant, low-latency communication between client and server, such as chat programs and multiplayer games.

The `XMLSocket` class allows you to create persistent connections with a server. These connections are called *sockets*. You can then send and receive XML data across this communication channel. To understand why this is advantageous, you first need to understand the alternative model.

Ways of Transmitting Data

In order to understand the `XMLSocket` class, it is important to understand where it fits into the context of data transfer with Flash. There are two protocols by which data is transmitted using Flash: Data can be sent by using HTTP or by using sockets. In this section, you learn about both and how they operate differently.

Transmitting Data via HTTP

HTTP (Hypertext Transport Protocol) is used to transfer much of Web data. The model is a simple one — a client such as a Web browser connects to a remote server, and makes a request. The server then returns the requested data, if found, and the connection is closed. This model works great for most Web applications such as HTML pages. It is quite efficient to open only a channel and send data when necessary, such as when a user clicks a link. But this model is not very good for creating low-latency applications such as a multiplayer game.

The difficulty with using HTTP for an application such as a multiplayer game is that such an application requires that the client make very frequent requests to always have updated information about player positions and scores. This is not only inefficient, but it simply doesn't work well. A lag of only a few seconds can throw off important calculations. Perhaps this model would work for a game of online chess. But when creating an action game, a few seconds can make a big difference.

Every technique for creating client-server interactivity that you have learned so far in this book uses HTTP. This includes sending and loading data using `XML` objects as well as `LoadVars` objects. And, in fact, even Flash Remoting, a technology you learn about in Chapter 35, uses HTTP. So if Flash is to be able to create low-latency client-server applications, there has to be another solution.

Transmitting Data via Sockets

The answer to the problem of using HTTP for communication is simply to avoid it altogether. Instead, you can use TCP (Transmission Control Protocol) directly to send data as a stream across an open channel between the client and server. HTTP is an application-layer protocol that is actually built on top of TCP. Most Internet protocols are developed on top of TCP, as a matter of fact. For example, FTP (File Transfer Protocol) is an application-layer protocol built on top of TCP for file transmission. Bypassing the higher-level protocols such as HTTP enables lower-level (more) access to the functionality of TCP.

This type of communication (TCP) is implemented today in many computer (Internet) applications (such as instant messenger programs) in order to keep a persistent connection between a client and server. You can think of it in much the same the way that the telephone works. One end initiates the call. After the other end has received the call, the connection remains until the conversation is over.

The fundamental component of this type of communication is called a *socket*. A socket is a basic software representation of a point for network communication. That means that there is a physical point on the computer through which data is sent and received, and the socket provides a way to control that point through code. You can create a connection between two sockets over which data can be sent. This is the general idea behind the use of the `XMLSocket` class in ActionScript. You can create a connection between a socket on the client computer and the server computer that will persist. Thus, anytime data is sent from the client, it is received on the server and vice versa because each is listening for any data being transmitted across the socket connection.

There are several different interface types when it comes to sockets. But the only kind you will be working with when it comes to ActionScript is the *stream socket*, which means that a connection must first be established; then data can be sent and received in the order it was sent. The connection remains alive until it is instructed to close.

The Socket Endpoints

Every socket connection has two endpoints: the server and the client. Again, this is similar to the telephone model whereby a client telephone must connect to a switchboard. Each of the two points performs slightly different tasks. The client socket can connect only to a server socket and send and receive data over that connection. The server, however, can (and most often should) accept multiple client connections, and it serves as a hub through which data is relayed appropriately.

It is important to understand that two Flash movies running on two different machines have no native ability to communicate with one another. Sometimes people will naturally assume this is a possibility. But in order for this to be able to happen there must be additional infrastructure. This chapter describes how to do this using `XMLSocket` objects with a socket server.

The Server

The trick to working with sockets with ActionScript is not on the ActionScript side of things at all. In fact, the `XMLSocket` class is relatively simple and straightforward. The most difficult part of working with sockets with ActionScript is setting up the server side of things.

When we refer to a client and a server in this discussion on sockets, we are referring to that which instantiates the connection and the sending of data as the client, and that which receives and processes the data as the server. In reality, they are simply two ends of a communication channel. And in fact, because computers have thousands of sockets, the client and the server applications can even reside on the same machine.

Discussions in this book always refer to the Flash component as the client. Multiple Flash movies are thought of as multiple clients, and as you will see, working to develop clients is easy in ActionScript. Most of the work is taken care of already by the `XMLSocket` class. However, when it comes to developing the server application, your job is not quite so easy. You have many choices available to you for creating a server application. You can write the application in any number of languages, from C to Perl to Java. If you know about socket programming (or you want to learn), you can develop your own socket server. For most developers, however, there is little reason to reinvent the wheel, so to speak. A number of socket servers have already been developed. Table 27-1 shows a partial list of some of the available socket servers. Some of the listed servers are available for enterprise level applications, and some are intended for fewer users.

Table 27-1: Example Socket Servers

Server Name	*Language*	*URL*
Unity Socket Server	Java	`www.moock.org/unity/`
FlashSock	Java	`http://sourceforge.net/projects/flashsock/`
AquaServer	Java	`www.figleaf.com/development/flash5/`
MultiServer	Java	`www.shovemedia.com/multiserver/`
Fortress	Java	`www.xadra.com/`
Swocket	Python	`swocket.sourceforge.net/`
FlashNow	C	`www.nowcentral.com/`

If you develop your own socket server, you need to know that all data sent to the server is terminated by the zero-byte (`"\u0000"`).

On the CD-ROM accompanying this book you'll find a socket server that you can use for the exercise in this chapter. You are also welcome to use the server for your own personal projects. This server has been provided as-is by Steve Nowicki. You can find out more about the specifications for the server at `http://sourceforge.net/projects/flashsock/`. Instructions for installing the server are provided in the exercise later in this chapter.

Socket Security

Most computers place restrictions on port numbers below 1024 because most of these ports are commonly used for serving Web content (HTTP on port 80), FTP (21), Telnet (23), Mail (25), and other typical services that might run on a computer. To prevent hackers from tampering with these services, most server machines already prevent socket connections to these ports. However, regardless of the computer configuration, the `XMLSocket` object attempts to make a socket connection only to ports 1024 and up.

Another restriction that ActionScript places on the `XMLSocket` object is that it can only connect to computers within its own domain. Therefore, if you are serving your SWF file from `yourserver.com`, and you try to connect to a socket on `myserver.com`, it should fail. This restriction exists only for movies that are being played in the Web browser versions of the player. For stand-alone Flash movies, you can connect to any server on which an application is running to allow for a socket connection.

The Client

For your purposes in this book, the client is always the Flash movie or movies you create that use the `XMLSocket` class to connect to a server. But clients can be developed using all kinds of technologies other than Flash as well. A client sends out a request for a connection, and if available, the server creates the link. The server is identified by an address such as an IP address or a domain name. The client's connection request is sent to the address, and if there is a server listening for socket connection requests on the specified port, a connection is made (see Figure 27-1).

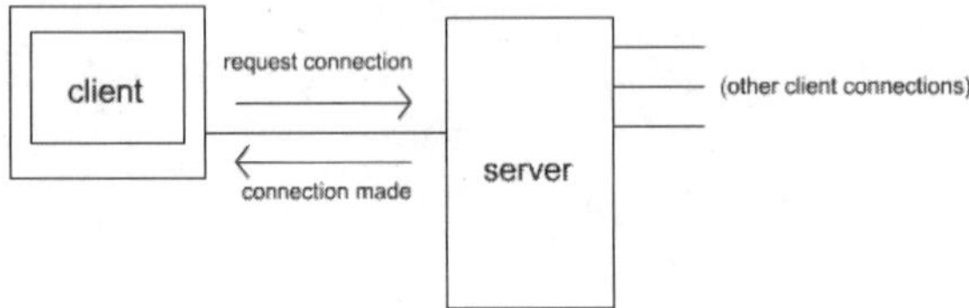

Figure 27-1: Client-server interaction

Working with XMLSocket Objects in Flash Clients

If you use a socket server that has been developed by another party, or if you have already developed your own, the majority of your work in working with socket connections and Flash will be with `XMLSocket` objects in your Flash movies. Fortunately, `XMLSocket` objects are really very simple. Because the functionality of `XMLSocket` objects is very specific — creating a channel between two sockets and then sending and receiving data across that channel — there is very little to learn when it comes to working with sockets in Flash.

Creating an XMLSocket Object

You can create multiple socket connections in a single Flash movie. For instance, you might want to create a socket connection to a server that handles data for a chat application, and you might want to connect to another server that handles data for a news ticker application all within the same movie. For each connection that you want to make, you need first to create the instance of the XMLSocket class.

An XMLSocket object must be instantiated using the constructor method in a new statement:

```
var xsConnection:XMLSocket = new XMLSocket();
```

The constructor takes no parameters. After the object is created, you can attempt to make a connection, and send and receive data over that socket connection. However, if you don't first invoke the appropriate methods, the object does not create any default socket connection.

Creating a Socket Connection to the Server

The first thing you want to do after you have created an XMLSocket object is attempt to create a socket connection to a server. The method to do this is connect(), which takes two parameters (the server name or address as a string, and the port number as a number), and returns a Boolean value indicating whether Flash was able to connect to the server (this does not indicate that a socket connection was yet made). If null is provided as the value for the first parameter, the connection attempt is made to localhost.

```
var bConnected:Boolean = xsConnection.connect("myserver.com", 1234);
```

Although the null value *should* cause the connection to be made to the local computer, some people have reported problems getting this to work. In the event that this happens to you simply change the value to 127.0.0.1 or localhost (unless you have modified these values on your computer) and it should work. If it does not, perhaps you should check to make sure that there is not another problem with your ActionScript code.

The connect() method is asynchronous. That means that it does not wait for the actual socket connection before moving on to the next line of ActionScript code. Therefore, there is a handler method that handles the connect events. The onConnect() method of an XMLSocket object is called once a socket connection is either made successfully or fails. The method is passed a Boolean value indicating whether the socket connection was made.

```
var xsConnection:XMLSocket = new XMLSocket();
var bConnected:Boolean = xsConnection.connect("myserver.com", 1234);
xsConnection.onConnect = function(bSuccess:Boolean):Void {
  if(bSuccess){
    trace("connected");
  }
  else{
    trace("no connection");
  }
}
```

Sending and Receiving Data

XMLSocket objects create bidirectional (or full-duplex) connections. This means that data can be both sent and received. Therefore, there are methods for handling both tasks.

First of all, if you want to send data across your socket connection, you can use the send() method. This method takes a single parameter: the data you want to send. Typically you'll want to send XML data.

```
myXMLSocket.send(new XML("<test />"));
```

Calling the `send()` method from an `XMLSocket` object is all that you need to do to send data across a socket connection after it has been established for that object.

On the other hand, if you want to receive data from the server, you need to create a function to process that data. Any `XMLSocket` object with an established socket connection automatically listens for any incoming data from the server at all times. When your Flash client receives data, you have two choices of methods to handle the receipt: `onXML()` and `onData()`. In previous versions of Flash there were some ActionScript techniques that were considered perfectly okay that are no longer really proper. And due to some of those changes, the `onXML()` method is not as useful as it was in previous versions of Flash. Therefore, we recommend you always use the `onData()` method.

When data is received by the `XMLSocket` object, the `onData()` method is automatically invoked and passed the data as a parameter. The data is always a string. If you want to convert it to XML, you should create a new `XML` object, set the object's `ignoreWhite` property to `true`, and then use the `parseXML()` method to parse the string into the `XML` object. For example:

```
xsConnection.onData = function(sData:String):Void {
  var xmlData:XML = new XML();
  xmlData.ignoreWhite = true;
  xmlData.parseXML(sData);
  // Rest of method definition...
};
```

Closing a Socket Connection

Finally, there needs to be a way to close a socket connection between the client and server with a command from the client. To do this, you simply need to call the `close()` method of your `XMLSocket` object. After the method is called, it attempts to close the connection to the server. When the connection is successfully closed, the `onClose()` method is automatically called. As you may have guessed, if you want something to actually happen when the connection is closed, you need to overload the function. Here is a sample of code that closes the connection and then tells the timeline to play:

```
xsConnection.onClose = function():Void {
  play();
}
xsConnection.close();
```

Creating a Chat Client

In this exercise, you will create a simple chat application that allows multiple users to connect and chat with one another in real time just like many instant messaging programs. The instructions are in three parts: "Installing the Java Runtime Environment," "Installing the Socket Server," and "Setting Up the Client."

Installing the Java Runtime Environment

In order to run the socket server on your machine, you'll need to have the Sun Java Runtime Environment (JRE) installed. If you are working on Macintosh OS X then you already have the JRE installed on your system. If you plan to run the socket server on another platform, such as Linux or Solaris, you can find instructions for installing on these operating systems on the `java.sun.com` Web site. If you're using Windows, follow these instructions:

1. Go to the Sun JRE 1.4.2 download page at `http://java.sun.com/j2se/1.4.2/download.html`.
2. Click the download link in the JRE column for the Windows installation of J2SE v 1.4.2 (there may be an additional revision number) and save the installation file.
3. Once the installation file is downloaded, run it and follow the instructions.
4. You'll need to add the `lib` directory that was just installed to your Windows classpath. To do that, follow these steps:
   a. Open the System Properties dialog box. You can open it by right-clicking My Computer and choosing Properties.
   b. Choose the Advanced tab.
   c. Click the Environment Variables button.
   d. In the Environment Variables dialog box that opens, look for a `CLASSPATH` variable in the System variables list in the lower portion of the box.
   e. If you find that a `CLASSPATH` variable already exists, select it and click the Edit button. Otherwise, click the New button.
   f. If you are creating a new variable, give it a name of `CLASSPATH`; otherwise, the field will be grayed out if you are editing.
   g. If there is a previous value, add a semicolon to the end and then append the new value to the existing value. Otherwise just add the new value. The new value is the path to the `lib` directory in the JRE installation. You'll have to check on your computer to verify the correct path, but it will be something like C:\jre1.4.2\lib.
   h. Click OK in both the Environment Variables and System Properties dialog boxes.

Installing the Socket Server

In order to set up the socket server on your computer, complete the following steps:

1. Copy the entire `socketServer` directory and all its contents from the CD-ROM to a location on your computer. Because Java does not always handle spaces in paths well, it is often best to copy the directory to a location that will not contain any spaces in the path. For example, C:\socketServer is probably better than C:\Program Files\socketServer.
2. Open the `socketServer` directory, and if you are using Windows, run the `runServer.bat` file. If you are in OS X, run the `runServer.sh` file. This will start the server.

Setting Up the Client

The Flash client consists of two ActionScript 2.0 classes and one FLA file. The FLA file includes several of the v2 UI components. Therefore, if you are not yet familiar with the components, and if you find any of the usage of the components confusing, you might want to consult Chapter 28.

For the purposes of this application, the socket server accepts XML packets in the following formats:

```
<msg><type>signon</type>⮐
<to container="user">SYS</to><content>Username</content></msg>

<msg><type>chat</type>⮐
<to container="user">all</to><content>⮐
<from>Username</from><chat>message</chat></content></msg>
```

And the server sends packets such as the following:

```
<msg><type>userlistupdate</type>⮐
<to container="group">all</to><content><users>⮐
<user>Username1</user><user>Username2</user></users>⮐
</content></msg>

<msg><type>signonsuccess</type>⮐
<to container="user">Username</to><content /></msg>

<msg><type>chat</type>⮐
<to container="user">chat</to><content>⮐
<from>Username</from><chat>message</chat></content></msg>
```

In order to create the Flash client, complete the following steps.

1. Open a new ActionScript file.
2. In the ActionScript file, add the following code to define the class for incoming messages from the server:

```
class IncomingMessage {

  var _xmlData:XMLNode = null;
  var _sMessageType:String;
  var _sFromUser:String;
  var _sChatText:String;
  var _aUsers:Array;

  function IncomingMessage(xmlData:XML) {

    // Extract the values from the XML packet.
    _xmlData = xmlData.firstChild;
    _sMessageType = _xmlData.firstChild.firstChild.nodeValue;

    // Depending on the message type, extract the
    // appropriate values.
    switch(_sMessageType) {
      case "chat":
        var aContentNodes:Array = ⮐
xmlData.childNodes[2].childNodes;
        _sFromUser = aContentNodes[0].firstChild.nodeValue;
        _sChatText = ⮐
unescape(aContentNodes[1].firstChild.nodeValue);
        break;
```

```
      case "userlistupdate":
        var aUserNodes:Array = ⮐
xmlData.childNodes[2].firstChild.childNodes;
        _aUsers = new Array();
        for(var i:Number = 0; i < aUserNodes.length; i++) {
          _aUsers.push(aUserNodes[i].firstChild.nodeValue);
        }
        break;
    }
  }

  // Define the getter methods for the properties.
  function get messageType():String {
    return _sMessageType;
  }
  function get users():Array {
    return _aUsers;
  }
  function get fromUser():String {
    return _sFromUser;
  }
  function get chatText():String {
    return _sChatText;
  }
}
```

3. Save the file as `IncomingMessage.as`.
4. Open a new ActionScript file.
5. Add the following code to the new ActionScript file to define the class for outgoing messages:

```
class OutgoingMessage {
  private var _xmlData:XML;

  // Construct the message based on the type, username, and
  // message.
  function OutgoingMessage(sType, sUsername, sMessage) {
    if(sType == "chat") {
      _xmlData = new XML(makeChatXML(sUsername, sMessage));
    }
    if(sType == "login") {
      _xmlData = new XML(makeLoginXML(sUsername));
    }
  }

  private function makeChatXML(sUsername, sChatText) {
     var sXMLStr:String = "<msg><type>chat</type>⮐
<to container=\"user\">all</to><content><from>" + ⮐
sUsername + "</from><chat>" + escape(sChatText) + ⮐
"</chat></content></msg>";
    return sXMLStr;
```

```
  }

  private function makeLoginXML(sUsername) {
    return "<msg><type>signon</type>
<to container=\"user\">SYS</to><content>" + 
sUsername + "</content></msg>";
  }

  public function get message():XML {
    return _xmlData;
  }
}
```

6. Save the ActionScript file as `OutgoingMessage.as` to the same directory where you saved `IncomingMessage.as`.

7. Open a new Flash document and save it as `chatClient001.fla` to the same directory where you saved the two class files.

8. Rename the default layer to Logged In Form. Create two new layers named Log In Form and Actions.

9. On the Log In Form layer, add the following:

   a. A `TextInput` instance named `ctiMessage`. Resize the instance to 200 pixels or so.

   b. A second `TextInput` instance named `ctiUsername`. Place this instance so that it is lower than the `ctiMessage` instance.

   c. A `Button` component instance named `cbtLogin`. Place the `Button` instance to the right of `ctiUsername`. The layout should appear similar to what you see in Figure 27-2.

Figure 27-2: The layout of the sample Log In form

10. Hide the Log In Form layer by clicking the Show/Hide column in the layer so that the red "X" appears.

11. In the Logged In Form, add the following:

   - A `TextArea` component instance named `ctaChatDisplay`. Resize the instance to 300 by 300.
   - A second `TextArea` component instance named `ctaInput`. Resize the instance to 300 by 60, and place it just lower than `ctaChatDisplay`.
   - A `List` instance named `clUserList`. Resize the instance to 150 by 300, and place it to the right of `ctaChatDisplay`.
   - A `Button` instance named `cbtSend`. Place the instance to the right of `ctaInput`. The layout should appear as shown in Figure 27-3.

Figure 27-3: The layout of the Logged In Form layer

12. Add the following ActionScript code to the Actions layer:

```
// The showLoginScreen() and showChatScreen() methods show
// and hide the component instances appropriately so as to
// give the effect of switching between two screens.
function showLoginScreen():Void {
  ctiMessage.visible = true;
  ctiUsername.visible = true;
  cbtLogin.visible = true;
  ctaChatDisplay.visible = false;
  ctaInput.visible = false;
  clUserList.visible = false;
  cbtSend.visible = false;
  sCurrentScreen = "login";
}
function showChatScreen():Void {
  ctiMessage.visible = false;
  ctiUsername.visible = false;
  cbtLogin.visible = false;
  ctaChatDisplay.visible = true;
  ctaInput.visible = true;
  clUserList.visible = true;
  cbtSend.visible = true;
  sCurrentScreen = "chat";
}

// The showConnectedMessage() method shows the appropriate
// message indicating whether or not the client was able to
// make a socket connection.
function showConnectedMessage(bDidConnect:Boolean):Void {
  if(bDidConnect) {
    ctiMessage.text = "connected...please enter a username";
  }
  else {
    ctiMessage.text = "error connecting to server";
  }
```

```
}

// If the connection is lost, then return to the login
// screen and try to reconnect.
function showDisconnectedMessage():Void {
  showLoginScreen();
  ctiMessage.text = "...trying to reconnect...";
  ctiUsername.text = "";
  xsTransferrer.connect("localhost", 2001);
}

function initSocketConnection(xsSocket:XMLSocket):Void {

  // Define the onData() method for the XMLSocket object.
  xsSocket.onData = function(sData:String):Void {

    // Parse the string data into an XML object, then pass
    // that XML to the IncomingMessage constructor.
    var xmlData:XML = new XML();
    xmlData.ignoreWhite = true;
    xmlData.parseXML(sData);
    var imData:IncomingMessage = new IncomingMessage(xmlData);

    // Depending on the message type, perform the
    // appropriate actions.
    switch(imData.messageType) {
      case "signonsuccess":
        showChatScreen();
        break;
      case "userlistupdate":
        clUserList.dataProvider = imData.users;
        break;
      case "chat":
        ctaChatDisplay.text += imData.fromUser + ⮐
": " + imData.chatText + newline;
        ctaChatDisplay.vPosition = ctaChatDisplay.maxVPosition;
      default:
    }
  };

  // When the connection is made (or not), call the
  // function to show the appropriate message.
  xsSocket.onConnect = function(bDidConnect:Boolean):Void {
    showConnectedMessage(bDidConnect);
  };

  // When the connection is closed, show the disconnected
  // message.
  xsSocket.onClose = function():Void {
    showDisconnectedMessage();
  };

  // Connect to the server.
  xsSocket.connect("localhost", 2001);
```

```
}

function initScreens():Void {
  ctaChatDisplay.html = true;
  cbtLogin.label = "Log In";
  cbtSend.label = "Send";

  // Create a listener object to listen for when the
  // user logs in.
  var oLoginListener:Object = new Object();
  oLoginListener.form = this;
  oLoginListener.socket = xsTransferrer;
  oLoginListener.click = function(oEvent:Object):Void {

    // If the user has typed in a user name, create an
    // outgoing message and then send that to the server.
    if(this.form.ctiUsername.text != "") {
      var omLogin:OutgoingMessage = new OutgoingMessage("login",
                                    this.form.ctiUsername.text);
      this.socket.send(omLogin.message);
    }
  };

  // If the user presses Enter, also trigger the click
  // event.
  oLoginListener.onKeyDown = function():Void {
    if(Key.getCode() == Key.ENTER && ⮐
this.form.sCurrentScreen == "login") {
      this.click();
    }
  };
  cbtLogin.addEventListener("click", oLoginListener);
  Key.addListener(oLoginListener);

  // Create a listener object for the chat screen's Button.
  var oChatListener:Object = new Object();
  oChatListener.form = this;
  oChatListener.socket = xsTransferrer;
  oChatListener.click = function(oEvent:Object):Void {

    // If the user has typed something into the input then
    // create an outgoing message and send it to the
    // server.
    if(this.form.ctaInput.text != "") {
      var omChat:OutgoingMessage = new OutgoingMessage("chat",
                                   this.form.ctiUsername.text,
                                   this.form.ctaInput.text);
      this.socket.send(omChat.message);
      this.form.ctaInput.text = "";
    }
  };

  // Like on the login screen, if the user presses the
  // Enter key, trigger the click event.
```

```
  oChatListener.onKeyDown = function():Void {
    if(Key.getCode() == Key.ENTER && ⮐
this.form.sCurrentScreen == "chat") {
      this.click();
    }
  };
  cbtSend.addEventListener("click", oChatListener);
  Key.addListener(oChatListener);
}
var xsTransferrer:XMLSocket = new XMLSocket();
var sCurrentScreen = "login";
initSocketConnection(xsTransferrer);
showLoginScreen();
initScreens();
```

13. Export the SWF file.
14. Test the application by opening the SWF file in several players, logging in, and sending messages.

We'd like to know what you thought about this chapter. Visit `www.flashsupport.com/feedback` to fill out an online form with your comments.

Summary

✦ Much of Web data is transferred via HTTP. Although this works just fine in most situations, it has large drawbacks in situations that require low latency. For these scenarios, such as multiplayer games and chat applications, timing is important, and a lower-level protocol can be used — TCP.

✦ TCP enables you to create socket connections between clients and servers. Socket connections are persistent connections that exist between numbered software interfaces on the client and server application hosts. Because a single machine can have many sockets, a client and host can reside on the same machine.

✦ ActionScript enables you, as a developer, to create socket connections from a Flash client to a server application, such as the socket server provided on the CD-ROM that accompanies this book. You can create these connections using an `XMLSocket` object.

✦ You must create a connection before you can transmit or receive any data over sockets. Use the `connect()` method to create this connection. You are restricted for security reasons to connections to ports greater than 1023 and to computers in the same subdomain. The `onConnect()` method is called when a connection is made or is rejected.

✦ You can send any type of data that can be converted to a string across a socket connection from within Flash to a server application. You use the `send()` method to send the data and the `onData()` and/or `onXML()` methods to receive data across the socket.

✦ You can close a connection with the `close()` method, and after a connection has been closed (whether on the client end or on the server end), the `onClose()` method is called.

✦ ✦ ✦

P A R T

VIII

Using Components

✦ ✦ ✦ ✦

In This Part

✦ ✦ ✦ ✦

CHAPTER 28

Using V2 UI Components

✦ ✦ ✦ ✦

In This Chapter

Introducing v2 UI components

Working with the Components panel

Understanding Listener objects

Utilizing the programmatic interfaces for the components

✦ ✦ ✦ ✦

Components are, in simplistic terms, particular types of Movie Clip symbols that can perform a large array of specialized tasks in your Flash applications. Once you have created an instance of a component, you can set various parameters via the Component Inspector panel and you can even perform complex operations via the component's programmatic interface of properties, methods, and events (also called the API). By allowing for interaction both by a graphical user interface and a programmatic interface, components are designed to appeal to both programmers and non-programmers alike.

The possibilities for components are really limitless. As you'll see in Chapter 30, "Creating Your Own Components," you have the option to build your own components (or, of course, download and install others' components). But for the purposes of this chapter, you're going to look specifically at the built-in user interface components that are included with Flash MX 2004 and Flash MX Professional 2004.

Getting Started with V2 Components

If you worked with components in Flash MX, you'll quickly notice some differences in the components in Flash MX 2004. The Flash MX components were built on what Macromedia calls the v1 architecture. The components in Flash MX 2004 have been completely redesigned, and they are all built on a new architecture that Macromedia calls the v2 component architecture. We therefore refer to Flash MX components as v1 components, and Flash MX 2004 components as v2 components.

The v1 components include any components created for Flash MX, including the components in the DRKs (Developer Resource Kits) that Macromedia released subsequent to the release of Flash MX. Although the v1 components should continue to work in Flash 6 applications authored in Flash MX 2004, they will not work reliably in a Flash 7 application (though the updated versions should — see note). The v2 components are designed to work in Flash 7 applications created in Flash MX 2004. Many of the v2 components will also work in later revisions of Flash Player 6 (revision 65 and revision 79 depending on which components), but they will not work in earlier revisions of Flash 6 nor in Flash 5 and prior. It is recommended that you avoid using v1 and v2 components in the same application.

Macromedia has updated many of the Flash MX components so that they are compatible with Flash 7 applications. You can find them at the Macromedia Flash Exchange Web site at `www.macromedia.com/software/flash/exchange`.

Introducing the Components Panel

When you want to work with components, you will almost inevitably need to open the Components panel. In the default panel layout the Components panel can be found to the right side of the stage along with the Color Mixer and assorted other panels. The panel might be collapsed, and so you might need to click the panel's title bar to expand it. If you don't see the Components panel, you can open it by pressing Ctrl+F7 or ⌘+F7 or by choosing Window ➪ Development Panels ➪ Components. Figure 28-1 shows what the Components panel looks like in Flash MX Professional 2004 (with the Data and Media Components menus collapsed). Flash MX 2004 contains a subset of the components shown in Figure 28-1.

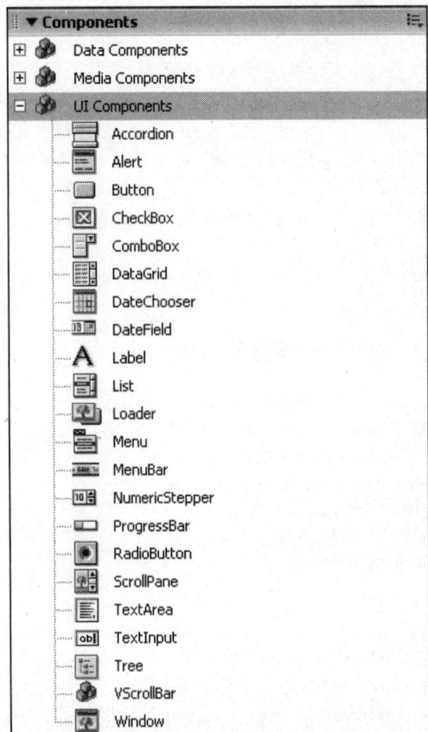

Figure 28-1: The Flash MX Professional 2004 Components panel

Adding New Component Instances

There are a few ways you can add new component instances to your Flash document:

- ✦ Add instances by dragging and dropping at authoring time.
- ✦ Add instances dynamically at runtime with ActionScript.

Adding instances at authoring time means you can drag an instance from the Components panel onto the stage. This copies the component symbol into the Flash document's library and also creates an instance on the stage.

In order to add instances at runtime, you first need to add the symbol to the library. To do this, you need to drag an instance from the Components panel onto the stage as though creating an authoring time instance. Then, you should delete the instance from the stage. The symbol will remain in the library. Once the symbol is in the library, you can add new instances programmatically using one of two methods:

- ✦ Using `createObject()`
- ✦ Using createClassObject()

The `createObject()` method is identical to the `attachMovie()` method (see Chapter 9 for more information on `attachMovie()`). The linkage identifier for each component matches the symbol name (that is, the linkage identifier for the Button component is `Button`). Here's an example that adds a `Button` component instance with ActionScript:

```
this.createObject("Button", "cbtSubmit", this.getNextHighestDepth());
```

The `createClassObject()` method is very similar to the `createObject()` method except that instead of the first parameter indicating the symbol's linkage identifier, it should be a reference to the component's class. All the component classes are in the `mx.contols` package. Here is an example that adds a `Button` component instance with the `createClassObject()` method.

```
this.createClassObject(mx.controls.Button, "cbtSubmit", ⮐
this.getNextHighestDepth());
```

Both the `createObject()` and `createClassObject()` methods allow you to specify a fourth, optional parameter in the form of an `init` object. The `init` object for these methods works just as the `init` object for `duplicateMovieClip()` and `attachMovie()` (see Chapter 9 for more information on `init` objects).

Naming Component Instances

When naming component instances, we suggest that you use the prefixes shown in Table 28-1. These prefixes all begin with the letter *c* to indicate a component. (These suggestions are made only for the purposes of helping you to adopt good coding practices. The prefixes do not offer special functionality or features not otherwise available. But using the prefixes helps you to organize your code and make your code more readable.)

Table 28-1: Component Instance Name Prefixes

Component	*Prefix*
Accordian	cac
Alert	ca
Button	cbt
CheckBox	cch
ComboBox	ccb
DataGrid	cdg
DateChooser	cdc
DateField	cdf
Label	clbl
List	cl
Loader	cld
Menu	cm
MenuBar	cmb
NumericStepper	cns
ProgressBar	cpb
RadioButton	crb
ScrollPane	csp
TextArea	cta
TextInput	cti
Tree	ctr
Window	cw

Setting Component Parameters

There are basically two ways you can set a component's parameters. Which way you set the parameters, depends, in part, on how you have created the instance. If you create the instance at authoring time, you can set the parameters either with the Component Inspector panel or with the API. If, however, you create the instance programmatically, you can set the parameters only via the API.

Working with the Component Inspector Panel

The Component Inspector panel allows you to change the properties for a component instance that was instantiated during authoring time. Figure 28-2 shows what the Component

Inspector panel looks like for a `Button` component instance in Flash MX Professional 2004. The Bindings and Schema tabs are available only in the Professional version.

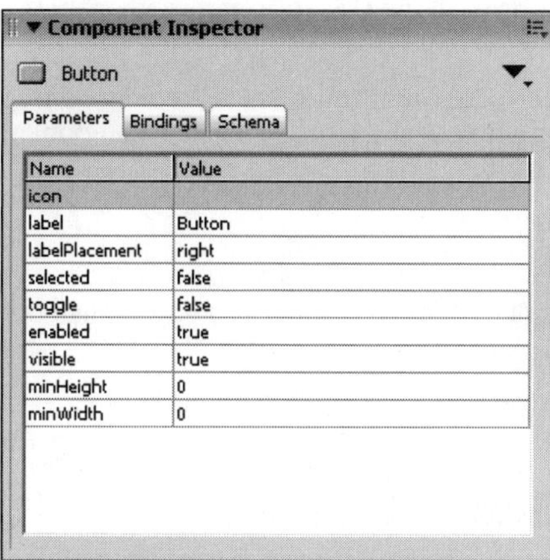

Figure 28-2: The Component Inspector panel for a Button instance (in Flash MX Professional 2004)

In the Parameters tab, you have options for all the available parameters for the selected component instance. In the case of a `Button` component instance there are parameters such as `icon`, `label`, and `labelPlacement`. (You'll look at the parameters for each component type in subsequent sections.) Changing the values of the parameters in the Component Inspector panel can affect the view of the component on the stage if live preview is on. You can turn on live preview by selecting Control ➪ Enable Live Preview.

You can also set some component parameters via the Property inspector. However, the Component Inspector panel allows you to set all the available parameters, not just a subset.

Working with the Component APIs

Each component has its own API (Application Programming Interface — in this case, the *application* being the component you are working with), or programming interface, composed of methods, properties, and events. In the preceding section, you saw how to modify the parameters of a component using the Component Inspector panel. However, you can use that technique to configure component instances only during authoring time. That means that you can use it only to affect components created during authoring time and that you can use it to initialize the settings only of an authoring time component instance.

Working with the API has several advantages:

- ✦ You can set the parameters for component instances that have been created during runtime.
- ✦ The API allows you to control much more than you can control with the Component Inspector panel. For example, you can use the API to set listeners for an instance.

✦ You can set parameters in response to events that take place during runtime. For example, you can load some data via an XML object (or LoadVars, WebServiceConnector, or Flash Remoting) and when the data loads, you can assign that data to the component (perhaps a database query that returns all the U.S. state names in order to populate a ComboBox component).

All the parameters in the Component Inspector panel are properties of a component instance. Therefore, as a simple example, you can programmatically create a Button component instance and set the label with the following code:

```
this.createObject("Button", "cbtSubmit", 1);
cbtSubmit.label = "test";
```

Or you can even use an init object in your call to createObject() to accomplish the preceding in one line of code:

```
this.createObject("Button", "cbtSubmit", 1, {label: "Submit"});
```

Understanding the Fundamental UI Component APIs

All v2 components are based on the same set of parent classes, one of which is UIObject. The UIObject class provides some common functionality for all components. Additionally, each component class has been initialized by the UIEventDispatcher class in order to dispatch events to listener objects. The following sections look at listener objects, the common component functionality, and then each of the component APIs.

Working with Listener Objects

Each component dispatches events. For example, when the user clicks a Button component instance, that instance dispatches a click event. It's up to you to set up something to handle that event. There are several options for how to handle these events, but we advocate the listener object technique.

A listener object can be any instance of any dynamic class. For example, a listener object can be an instance of the Object class or the MovieClip class. You must do two things so that the listener object can handle component instance events:

✦ Define a method for the object that corresponds to the event for which you want it to listen. For example, if you want the object to be able to listen for a Button component's click event, you should define a click() method for the listener object. All events are dispatched with an event object, so the method can/should accept a parameter. The event objects are instances of the Object class that have a target property that is a reference to the component instance that dispatched the event and a type property that specifies the type of event that was dispatched (some event objects might contain other properties as well).

```
var oListener:Object = new Object();
oListener.click = function(oEvent:Object):Void {
  // Displays the path to the component that
  // dispatched the event.
  trace(oEvent.target);
};
```

✦ Add the object to the component instances list of listeners by calling the addEventListener() method. The addEventListener() method requires two parameters — the name of the event as a string and a reference to the listener object.

```
cbtSubmit.addEventListener("click", oListener);
```

A single listener object can listen for more than one event. And the same listener object can listen for events from multiple component instances. For example, if cbtSubmit and cbtReset are both Button component instances, the following code allows the same listener to handle both click and unload events for both component instances:

```
var oListener:Object = new Object();
oListener.click = function(oEvent:Object):Void {
  if(oEvent.target._name == "cbtSubmit") {
    trace("submit clicked");
  }
  else {
    trace("reset clicked");
  }
};
oListener.unload = function(oEvent:Object):Void {
  if(oEvent.target._name == "cbtSubmit") {
    trace("submit unloaded");
  }
  else {
    trace("reset unloaded");
  }
};
cbtSubmit.addEventListener("click", oListener);
cbtSubmit.addEventListener("unload", oListener);
cbtReset.addEventListener("click", oListener);
cbtReset.addEventListener("unload", oListener);
```

Working with Common Component Functionality

Each type of component inherits some common functionality from the superclass UIObject. Rather than discuss each of the common pieces of functionality again for each component, let's take a look at the common functionality first.

Creating and Removing Component Instances

You can use the createObject() and createClassObject() methods (see discussion of these methods earlier in this chapter) to create new instances of a component at runtime. These methods can be called from any MovieClip instance as well as component instances, and they create the new instance nested within the object from which they are called. For example, the following code, called from the main timeline, creates a new Button instance nested within the main timeline:

```
this.createObject("Button", "cbtSubmit", this.getNextHighestDepth());
```

To remove a component instance, use the destroyObject() method. This method should be invoked from the parent object, and it requires that you specify the name of the instance to remove as a string parameter. For example, to remove an instance named cbtSubmit from the current timeline, use the following code:

```
this.destroyObject("cbtSubmit");
```

When you create a new instance, the component dispatches both a load and a draw event. When you remove the instance, an unload event is dispatched.

Moving Component Instances

You can move a component instance in several ways. Because components are subclasses of `MovieClip`, they inherit the standard `MovieClip` properties and methods, including `_x` and `_y`. Therefore, you can move a component instance with the `_x` and `_y` properties. However, it is advantageous to utilize the `UIObject` `move()` method instead. The `move()` method takes two parameters — the x and y coordinates to which to move the instance. But not only does the method move the instance, it also dispatches a move event.

```
cbtSubmit.move(25, 70);
```

Components also have read-only `x` and `y` parameters that report the same values as the `_x` and `_y` properties. Although in their current form reading the values of `x` and `y` offers no real advantages over reading the values of `_x` and `_y`, it is possible that future versions may leverage the component architecture in some way such that `x` and `y` might provide some benefit over `_x` and `_y`. For that reason we recommend that you use `x` and `y`.

Resizing Component Instances

You can resize a component instance in several ways. You can resize either by setting pixels or percentages.

In order to resize a component instance by setting exact pixel dimensions, you can use the `setSize()` method. The `setSize()` method requires two parameters — the width and the height for the component in pixels.

```
cbtSubmit.setSize(200, 22);
```

The height and width properties are read-only properties that report the current dimensions of a component instance. If, in the preceding example, you wanted to set the width of the component to 200 pixels, but you wanted to keep the current height, you could use the following code instead:

```
cbtSubmit.setSize(200, cbtSubmit.height);
```

You should not use the `_width` and `_height` properties inherited from `MovieClip` unless you want the component instance to appear distorted. They will not resize the instances as you want.

When you call the `setSize()` method, the component dispatches a resize event.

You can also resize a component instance by percentages using the `scaleX` and `scaleY` properties. These properties determine the scale factors in the x and y directions by which the component instance should be scaled. A value of 100 means that the instance should be scaled to 100 percent of the width and/or height. In other words, setting the `scaleX` and `scaleY` properties to 100 will cause the component to appear at either the default dimensions or at whatever dimensions you set with `setSize()`. Or, for example, a value of 200 will cause the instance to be scaled to twice the dimension in the given direction.

When an instance is scaled, it does not dispatch any events.

Looking at the Standard Form UI Components

The first group of components you'll look at is the form UI components included in both the standard and professional versions of Flash MX 2004. These components include all the basic controls you need to create standard user input forms.

Working with Button Components

Button components are likely to be one of the most commonly used components in your application. When you use the majority of the other components you will use them in combination with a `Button` component instance. Fortunately, the `Button` component is one of the simplest components as well. `Button` instances can be used for many purposes including as submit buttons, reset buttons, buttons that toggle states, and so on. Figure 28-3 shows a `Button` instance with a label of Submit.

Figure 28-3: A Button component instance

Handling Button Clicks

When the user clicks a `Button` component instance, a click event is dispatched. You can set a listener object to handle the click event with a `click()` method.

```
this.createObject("Button", "cbtSubmit", this.getNextHighestDepth());
var oListener:Object = new Object();
oListener.click = function(oEvent:Object):Void {
  trace(oEvent.target._name + " was just clicked");
};
cbtSubmit.addEventListener("click", oListener);
```

Caution Do not use button event handler methods with `Button` component instances. If you attempt to assign an `onPress()` or `onRelease()` event handler method, for example, to a `Button` component instance, you will get unexpected behavior.

Setting Label and Icon

You can customize the label for a `Button` component instance by setting the `label` property. For example:

```
cbtSubmit.label = "Submit";
```

You can also, optionally, display a graphic in the component instance by assigning a value to the instance's `icon` property. The value of the `icon` property should be the linkage identifier of a symbol in the library. For example, if you have a symbol in the library with a linkage identifier of `SmileySymbol`, you can display that artwork on the `Button` component instance as follows:

```
cbtSubmit.icon = "SmileySymbol";
```

If you add a graphic to the instance, you can also determine the relative placement of the graphic and the label text. By default, the label appears to the left of the graphic. You can explicitly tell Flash to place the text to the left, right, top, or bottom of the graphic by assigning that value, as a string, to the labelPlacement property of the component instance.

```
cbtSubmit.labelPlacement = "right";
```

Changing Button Type

Button component instances can act like standard push buttons that click and release with each press. That is the default behavior. However, you can also choose to have the instance act as a toggle. That means that when the Button instance is pressed, the state changes from deselected to selected or from selected to deselected. In order to achieve this, all you need to do is set the instance's toggle property to true:

```
cbtSubmit.toggle = true;
```

And, of course, if you want to explicitly tell Flash that the instance should act like a standard push button again, you can set the toggle property to false:

```
cbtSubmit.toggle = false;
```

Only if the toggle property is true can you also tell Flash whether or not the instance should be selected (pressed in). Setting the selected property to true sets the instance to the selected state, and setting the selected property to false sets the instance to the deselected state:

```
cbtSubmit.selected = true;
```

Working with Label Components

The Label component enables you to quickly and simply add labels to your applications. Labels can be used for many purposes, but two of the most common uses of the Label component is to add labels to instances of components or groups of components. The Label component is quite simple. It doesn't have any methods or events. It has only a handful of configurable properties.

You can set the value that displays in the Label instance by setting its text property:

```
clblDescription.text = "Description";
```

You can set a Label instance such that it can display HTML by setting its html property to true. When you set the instance to display HTML, the CSS formatting will no longer apply.

```
clblDescription.html = true;
clblDescription.text = "<font color='#FF0000'>Description</font>";
```

The autoSize property of a Label component instance can have the following string values:

- ✦ **none:** This is the default value, and it means that the instance does not resize to fit the text.
- ✦ **right:** This means that the instance will resize to automatically fit the text, and the right and top sides of the instance stay fixed and the left and bottom adjust as necessary.
- ✦ **left:** This means that the instance will resize and that the left and top sides are fixed and the right and bottom sides will adjust as necessary.
- ✦ **center:** This means the instance will resize and that the top-center point will stay fixed while the label will adjust as necessary downward and to the right and left.

Working with TextInput Components

The `TextInput` component is very similar to an input `TextField`. The differences are that it provides a look that is consistent with the rest of the components and that it is built on the component architecture so it provides the same basic functionality as other components. Figure 28-4 shows an example of a basic `TextInput` instance.

Figure 28-4: A TextInput component instance

Setting and Getting the Text Value

The default state for a `TextInput` instance is that it is editable. That means that the user can edit the text using the keyboard. You can explicitly make a `TextInput` instance either editable or not by setting the `editable` property to `true` or `false`.

You can get and set the value of a `TextInput` instance by using the `text` property:

```
ctiPostalCode.text = "12345";
```

The `length` property returns the number of characters in the input text:

```
trace(ctiPostalCode.length);
```

Restricting Input Characters

You can allow or disallow specific characters for a `TextInput` instance. For example, for a `TextInput` field that asks the user for a telephone number, you might want to allow only numbers and spaces. You can use the restrict property to define an allowable and/or disallowable character set. For example:

```
ctiPhone.restrict = "0123456789 ";
```

The preceding code tells Flash to allow the user to enter only numbers and the space character. You can also use ranges of characters by specifying the starting character in the range, a dash, and then the ending character in the range. For example, the preceding code can be simplified as follows:

```
ctiPhone.restrict = "0-9 ";
```

If you want to allow the user to enter a dash, you need to remember to escape the character in the string. For example, it might seem, at first, that you should be able to add the dash to the string as with any other character:

```
ctiPhone.restrict = "0-9 -";  // Will not work
```

However, when you look at the string as Flash will try to interpret it, you may notice that Flash will think that the dash is indicating a range of characters. Instead, you have to escape the dash character so that Flash interprets it literally instead of with its special meaning to indicate a range of characters. If you recall from the discussion in Chapter 15, you can use the backslash character to escape as part of an escape sequence. Therefore, the next guess is usually to try the following:

```
ctiPhone.restrict = "0-9 \-";  // Still will not work
```

Although that is a good guess, it is still not quite correct. The backslash character *will* escape the dash within the string. However, you want the slash itself to be escaped as well so that the correct string value (including a literal backslash) is interpreted by the TextInput instance. If all of that is too confusing, just suffice it to say that when you want to escape a dash in a restrict string you need to place two backslashes before it. The following is the corrected example:

```
ctiPhone.restrict = "0-9 \\-";
```

The following table gives you a few more examples of escape sequences you can use with the restrict property value.

Value to Allow the User to Enter	Normal String Escape Sequence	Value to Use for the restrict Property	Example
^	\^	\\^	To allow emc^2 ctiInput.restrict = "emc\\^2";
-	\-	\\-	To allow 1-800- ctiInput.restrict = "\\-018";
\	\\	\\\\	To allow C:\ ctiInput.restrict = "C:\\\\";

You can also tell Flash what characters to *disallow* by using the ^ character at the beginning of the restrict string. All the characters and ranges that follow are disallowed. For example, the following disallows all upper- and lowercase alphabetic characters:

```
ctiSampleInput.restrict = "^a-zA-Z";
```

As with the dash, if you want to have the ^ character interpreted literally, you need to escape it by preceding it with two backslashes:

```
ctiSampleInput.restrict = "\\^";  // Allows only the ^
```

If you want to allow or disallow a literal backslash, you need to escape that character as well. In order to escape a backslash you need to enter four backslashes:

```
ctiSampleInput.restrict = "\\\\";  // Allows only the \
```

By default, the restrict property has an undefined value. A value of undefined, null, or an empty string allows all characters.

Setting the Maximum Number of Characters

You can set a TextInput field to allow only a certain number of characters. For example, if you have a TextInput instance that asks the user for a U.S. ZIP code, you might want to set the maximum number of characters to five. You can set the maximum number of characters with the maxChars property:

```
ctiZip.maxChars = 5;
```

The default value is null, and if you set the value back to null then the maximum limit is removed.

Making a Password TextInput

The default setting for a TextInput instance displays the text as the user enters it. In some cases you want to hide the entered text from view. For example, when the user types in a password you don't want to display that so that any person passing by can see the value. In such a case you want to set the instance to password mode. In password mode only the * (asterisk) character is displayed, but the actual value is stored programmatically in the text property. You can set a TextInput instance to password mode by setting the password property to true.

```
ctiPassword.password = true;
```

Figure 28-5 shows an example of a TextInput instance in password mode.

Figure 28-5: A TextInput instance in password mode displays only asterisks.

Handling TextInput Events

TextInput components dispatch the following events:

✦ **change:** When the value of the instance changes through user action (not when changed programmatically).

✦ **enter:** When the instance has focus and the user presses the Enter key.

Working with TextArea Components

The TextArea component is similar to an HTML textarea control. It is an area for text input that has built-in vertical and horizontal scroll bars. Figure 28-6 shows an example of a TextArea instance.

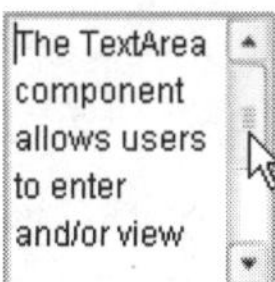

Figure 28-6: A TextArea component instance

Getting and Setting the Text Value

You can get and set the text value of a TextArea instance with the text property in the same way as with a TextInput instance. You can also make a TextArea instance editable or not by using the editable property. See the discussion of the TextInput component for more details.

Restricting Input Characters

You can set the allowable and disallowable characters for a TextArea using the restrict property. This property works the same as the restrict property for the TextInput component. See the discussion of the TextInput component for more details.

Making a Password TextArea

You can set a TextArea instance to password mode with the password property just as with a TextInput instance. See the discussion of the TextInput component for more details.

Wrapping Text

By default, word wrapping is activated in TextArea instances. This means that if a word runs over the width of the instance, the word is moved to the next line of displayed text. You can control whether or not an instance wraps text by setting the value of the wordWrap property. The default value is true. You can turn off wrapping by setting the value to false.

Controlling Scroll Bars

The default setting for a TextArea is such that the scroll bars appear only when necessary. If no text runs off the viewable area, the scroll bars are not visible. When the text runs off the viewable area in the vertical direction, a vertical scroll bar appears. Likewise, when the text runs off the viewable area in the horizontal direction, a horizontal scroll bar appears. You can change these settings with the vScrollPolicy and hScrollPolicy properties. Each accepts the following string values:

- **on:** This means the scroll bar is always visible, regardless of whether it is needed.
- **off:** This means the scroll bar never appears, even when the text runs off the viewable area.
- **auto:** This is the default value that displays the scroll bar when appropriate.

If wordWrap is set to true (the default setting), the horizontal scroll bar will never be visible. This is so even if the hScrollPolicy is set to on.

Handling TextArea Events

TextArea component instances dispatch a change event when the text is changed by user action. This event is not dispatched when the value is changed programmatically.

Working with CheckBox Components

CheckBox component instances are most often used in forms to allow users to select yes/no or true/false for a particular option. Sometimes a single CheckBox instance is used such as when prompting a user to accept licensing conditions for an application or whether or not to opt into a mailing list. In other cases a group of CheckBox instances is used to allow a user to select from a list of related options. For example, a form might prompt a user to select their favorite music genres from a list. Each genre might be represented by a CheckBox instance. The user can then select to check or uncheck each one. Figure 28-7 shows such an example.

Figure 28-7: A group of CheckBox component instances

Setting Label and Label Placement

You can programmatically assign a new label to a `CheckBox` instance using the `label` property:

```
cchOptIn.label = "Opt In";
```

The label will be cut off if you attempt to add more text beyond the bounding box of the component instance.

The default placement for a label is to the right of the actual check box. You can tell Flash to move the label to the left, right, top, or bottom by assigning the corresponding value, as a string, to the `labelPlacement` property:

```
cchOptIn.labelPlacement = "left";
```

Getting and Setting the Checked State

The default state for a `CheckBox` instance is to be unchecked. You can get or set the state with the `selected` property. A value of `true` means the instance is checked. A value of `false` means the instance is unchecked.

```
cchOptIn.selected = true;
```

Handling CheckBox Clicks

When a user clicks a `CheckBox` instance, either to check or uncheck it, the instance dispatches a click event. You can handle that event with a `click()` method on the listener object:

```
var oListener:Object = new Object();
oListener.click = function(oEvent:Object):Void {
  trace(oEvent.target._name + " was just clicked");
};
cchOptIn.addEventListener("click", oListener);
```

Working with RadioButton Components

`RadioButton` component instances and `CheckBox` component instances can be used for very similar purposes. However, whereas a group of `CheckBox` component instances can allow a user to select multiple options, a group of `RadioButton` instances is formally grouped as a `RadioButtonGroup` instance, and the user can select only one value from the group. Figure 28-8 shows an example of a group of `RadioButton` instances.

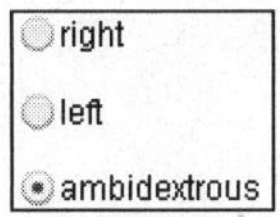

Figure 28-8: A group of RadioButton component instances

Setting Label and Label Placement

You can set the label and label placement for a RadioButton instance in the same way that you set the label and label placement for a CheckBox instance. See the CheckBox discussion for more details.

Setting RadioButton Data

Each RadioButton instance must have both a label and a data value. The data value is hidden from the user, but it is what is used programmatically. You can set the data value by assigning a value to the data property.

```
crbAmidetrous.data = "ambi";
```

Setting the Selected State

You can set the selected state of a RadioButton instance with the selected property. If you set the property to true, the instance is selected. If any other instance in the group was previously selected, that instance is deselected.

```
crbAmbidextrous.selected = true;
```

Grouping RadioButton Instances

Very rarely is a single RadioButton instance used in isolation. Instead, RadioButton instances are generally used in groups, whereby only one value at a time can be selected. Flash needs a way of knowing which instances are grouped together. This is especially true when there is more than one set of radio button groups on the form (for example, male and female) The groupName property determines how instances are grouped. All instances with the same groupName value belong to the same group. The value of groupName must be a string. When you assign a value to an instance's groupName property, Flash checks to see if the group has already been created. If so, it adds the instance to the group. If not, Flash first creates a new RadioButtonGroup object. The RadioButtonGroup object is created within the same scope as the RadioButton instance, and its name is the name assigned to the groupName property. For example, the following code creates a new RadioButtonGroup object named crbgHandedness, and adds the crbAmbidextrous instance to that group:

```
crbAmbidetrous.groupName = "crbgHandedness";
```

Getting Selected Values

You can retrieve the selected value from a RadioButtonGroup with the selectedData property. This property returns the value of the data property for the selected RadioButton instance in the given RadioButtonGroup:

```
trace(crbgHandedness.selectedData);
```

The selection property, on the other hand, returns a reference to the selected RadioButton instance from the group.

Handling Click Events

Both RadioButton instances and RadioButtonGroup objects dispatch click events when the user makes a selection. You can, therefore, assign a listener either to the group or to each instance. In most cases, if you need to handle the click events it would be most appropriate to assign the listener to the group.

```
var oListener:Object = new Object();
oListener.click = function(oEvent:Object):Void {
```

```
    trace(oEvent.target.selectedData);
  };
  crbgHandedness.addEventListener("click", oListener);
```

Working with ComboBox Components

The ComboBox is also often referred to as a drop-down menu. Like RadioButtonGroups, ComboBox instances are useful for presenting users with a set of options from which they can select only one. However, a ComboBox can contain a large range of values (incorporating a scroll bar if necessary), which means it takes up less space on stage compared to RadioButtonGroups and can sometimes be preferable for that reason. Figure 28-9 shows an example of a ComboBox instance that has been opened and from which a value is being selected.

Figure 28-9: A ComboBox instance

Adding Items to a ComboBox Instance

When you first create a ComboBox instance, it contains no values:

```
this.createObject("ComboBox", "ccbCities", this.getNextHighestDepth());
```

Therefore, it is up to you to add new items to the list. There are several ways you can go about this.

Adding Items One at a Time

You can add new items one at a time using the addItem() method. The addItem() method appends a new items to the list. There are three basic variations on how to can call the addItem() method. First, you can call the method with a single parameter:

```
  ccbCities.addItem("Chicago");
```

Generally, this first approach is not recommended, however. Each item in a ComboBox has both a label and a data value. The label is displayed to the user. But the data can be different from the label. For example, if the values were retrieved from a database, the data may be an ID from the database that corresponds to the label. In such cases it is preferable to work with the ID programmatically while displaying the label to the user. When you pass only one parameter to the addItem() method, the item has only a label value, and the data value is left undefined. It is better, typically, to assign both a label and data value, even if they are the same value. You can assign a data value by passing a second parameter to the addItem() method:

```
  ccbCities.addItem("Chicago", 54);
```

You can also call the addItem() method by passing it a single object parameter in which the object has a label and a data property:

```
  ccbCities.addItem({label: "Chicago", data: 54});
```

The addItem() method always appends the item to the end of the current list. If you want to insert a new item into the list at a specific index, you can use the addItemAt() method instead. The addItemAt() method requires that you tell it at what index you want it to insert the new value. The items in a ComboBox are indexed starting with 0, so if you specify a value of 0 then the new item will be added to the beginning of the list. All subsequent items are shifted by one. When you call the addItemAt() method you have two options. First, as with the addItem() method, you can specify the label value.

```
ccbCities.addItemAt(1, "St. Louis");
```

Or, the preferred way is to specify both the label and data values:

```
ccbCities.addItemAt(1, "St. Louis", 33);
```

Whereas the addItemAt() method inserts a new item, shifting all subsequent items by one index, the replaceItemAt() method adds a new item in place of the current item at the same index. As with addItem() and addItemAt(), when you call the replaceItemAt() method you can specify either just the label value or both the label and data values.

```
ccbCities.replaceItemAt(0, "Los Angeles", 81);
```

Adding Items as a Group

You can also add items to a ComboBox instance as a group. The dataProvider property allows you to assign it a value of either an array or any object that implements the DataProvider interface.

You can use an array of strings to assign a group of labels to a ComboBox instance. For example:

```
ccbCities.dataProvider = ["Chicago", "Los Angeles", "New York", "St. Louis];
```

However, that approach is akin to setting only the label value when calling addItem(). Instead, you can set both the label and data values by using an array of objects in which each object has both a label and a data property.

```
ccbCities.dataProvider = [{label: "Chicago", data: 54}, ⮐
{label: "Los Angeles", data: 81}, {label: "New York", ⮐
data: 27}, {label: "St. Louis", data: 33}];
```

Additionally, if your data provider array contains objects that do not contain a label property, you can still use the array to populate the ComboBox. If you set the instance's labelField property to the corresponding property name, it will use that property instead of looking for a label property. For example:

```
ccbCities.labelField = "cityName";
ccbCities.dataProvider = [{cityName: "Chicago", data: 54}, ⮐
{cityName: "Los Angeles", data: 81}, ⮐
{cityName: "New York", data: 27}, ⮐
{cityName: "St. Louis", data: 33}];
```

In some cases, you might want to combine multiple properties from each object in the array in order to make the label. For example, if each object in the data provider array has cityName, estYear, and data properties, you might want to display both the city name and the year the city was established in the label. You can achieve this by assigning a function to the labelFunction property of the ComboBox instance. Flash automatically passes the function each object element from the data provider array, and it should return the label to use. For example:

```
ccbCities.labelFunction = function(oElement:Object):String {
  var sLabel:String = oElement.cityName + " (" + ⮐
oElement.estYear + ")";
  return sLabel;
};
```

Typically, working with the dataProvider property is most useful when you are working with datasets and recordsets returned by various types of service calls via, for example, Flash Remoting.

Getting the Number of Items

The length property returns the number of items in a ComboBox instance:

```
trace(ccbCities.length);
```

Removing Items from ComboBox Instances

You can remove items from a ComboBox instance one at a time with the removeItemAt() method. The method takes a parameter indicating the index of the item to remove:

```
ccbCities.removeItemAt(0);
```

If you want to remove all the items from a ComboBox instance, you can use the removeAll() method:

```
ccbCities.removeAll();
```

Making Editable ComboBox Instances

The default behavior of a ComboBox instance is that the user must select from one of the predefined values. You can, however, make the instance editable so that the user can enter a value by typing it with the keyboard. When you set the editable property to true, the selected value is editable. The user can still select from the list of values. But in addition, if she wants, she can type a value in place of that.

Getting Items and Values from ComboBox Instances

There are several approaches to getting items from a ComboBox instance. First, you can use the getItemAt() method to return an item given an index. For example, if you want to get the first item from a ComboBox instance:

```
var oItem:Object = ccbCities.getItemAt(0);
```

The getItemAt() method returns an object that corresponds to the value that was originally assigned to the item in the list. If you assigned the value with addItem(), addItemAt(), replaceItemAt(), or with a data provider in which the label field property was named label, the object returned by getItemAt() has a label and data property.

If you want to get the selected item then you can use the selectedItem property. Like getItemAt(), the selectedItem property returns an object with label and data properties (unless the labelField property was set to another value than label).

```
trace(ccbCities.selectedItem.label);
```

You can also retrieve the index of the selected item with the selectedIndex property:

```
trace(ccbCities.selectedIndex);
```

More often than not, you want to simply retrieve the selected value. The `value` property returns the selected value for a `ComboBox` instance. The value that it returns depends on the behavior and qualities of the instance:

- ✦ If the instance is a standard, non-editable instance and the selected item has both a label and a data property, `value` returns the data for the selected item.
- ✦ If the instance is a standard, noneditable instance and the selected item has only a label property, `value` returns the label for the selected item.
- ✦ If the instance is editable, `value` returns the value that the user has typed or the label of the selected item.

Opening and Closing ComboBox Instances

The `open()` and `close()` methods allow you to programmatically open and close `ComboBox` instances. These methods are not frequently used because the opening and closing of an instance is normally triggered by user interaction.

You can also set the maximum number of rows that should be displayed in a `ComboBox` when open. The default value is 5. You can assign any reasonable numeric value of one or more to the instance's `rowCount` property to affect this change. If the instance contains more items than the `rowCount` value, the list becomes scrollable.

```
ccbCities.rowCount = 2;
```

Figure 28-10 shows an example of a `ComboBox` instance in which the `rowCount` is set to 2 and the list is scrollable.

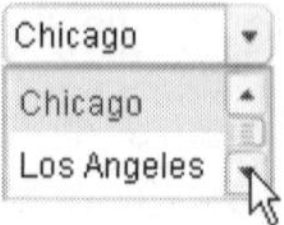

Figure 28-10: A ComboBox instance in which the list is scrollable

Working with the Drop Down List

The portion of a `ComboBox` instance that drops down is actually a `List` component instance. You can access the `List` instance with the `ComboBox` instance's `dropdown` property. You don't need to worry about working with the nested `List` instance directly in most cases because the `ComboBox` API provides all the basic interfaces you need. For example, the `ComboBox` methods and properties for adding items indirectly add items to the nested `List` instance. You can, however, work with the nested `List` instance in order to produce advanced effects. For example, you can add icons next to the `List` items if you work with the `List` instance directly via the `dropdown` reference. Or you can use the sorting methods built into the `List` class. See the `List` component discussion for more details on some of the advanced options available to `List` instances.

Handling ComboBox Events

`ComboBox` instances dispatch the following events:

- ✦ **change:** When a value is selected or entered by the user. If the user enters a value into an editable instance, the event is dispatched with each keystroke.
- ✦ **open:** The instance begins to open.

- **close:** The instance begins to close.
- **enter:** The instance has focus and the user presses the Enter key.
- **itemRollOver:** When the user rolls over an item in the list.
- **itemRollOut:** When the user rolls out of an item in the list.
- **scroll:** When the user scrolls the item list.

Working with List Components

The `List` component is similar to the `ComboBox` in that it allows the user to select from a menu. Unlike the `ComboBox`, however, the `List` component allows the user to view multiple items at a time, and if it is set to accept multiple selections, the user can even select more than one item from the list. `List` instances can be used in place of `ComboBox` instances in situations in which you want to display more than one value to the user at a time. Alternatively, if you set a `List` to allow multiple selections, a `List` can be used in place of a group of `CheckBox` instances because it allows for the same basic type of selection. Figure 28-11 shows a `List` instance.

Figure 28-11: A List instance

Adding Items to a List Instance

You can add items to a `List` instance in the same ways that you can add items to a `ComboBox` instance. See the discussion for `ComboBox` for more details.

Sorting Items in a List Instance

You can sort the items in a `List` instance using the `sortItems()` or `sortItemsBy()` method. The `sortItems()` method works just like the `sort()` method of the `Array` class. You must pass it a reference to a sorter function. A sorter function is a function that is passed two items from the list. Within the function, you should return -1 if the first item should be sorted first, 0 if the order should not be changed, or 1 if the second item should be sorted first. For example:

```
this.createObject("List", "clVehicles", ↩
this.getNextHighestDepth());
clVehicles.dataProvider = [{label: "Cart", data: 0}, ↩
{label: "Boat", data: 1}, {label: "Airplane", data: 2}, ↩
{label: "Automobile", data: 3}, {label: "Bicycle", data: 4}];
var fSorter:Function = function(a, b):Object {
  if(a.label < b.label) {
    return -1;
  }
  else if(a.label > b.label) {
    return 1;
  }
  else {
```

```
        return 0;
    }
};
clVehicles.sortItems(fSorter);
```

The `sortItems()` method is really more applicable in more complex sorting scenarios. In a simple sorting scenario in which you want to alphabetically sort on a single property of each item, you will likely find the `sortItemsBy()` method a simpler option. The `sortItemsBy()` method takes two parameters — the name of the property/field on which to sort and a value of either `ASC` or `DESC` indicating whether to sort in ascending or descending order.

```
clVehicles.sortItemsBy("label", "ASC");
```

Removing Items from a List Instance

You can remove items from a `List` in the same ways that you can remove items from a `ComboBox` instance. See the discussion for `ComboBox` for more details.

Allowing Multiple Selections

The default behavior for a `List` is that it allows the user to select only one item at a time. However, you can allow the user to select multiple values by setting the `multipleSelection` property to `true`. When the `multipleSelection` property is set to `true` the user can select more than one item by holding the Ctrl key or the ⌘ key and clicking multiple values. Or the user can select a range by selecting the first item in the range, holding Shift, and selecting the last item in the range. Figure 28-12 shows an example of a `List` instance that allows multiple selections.

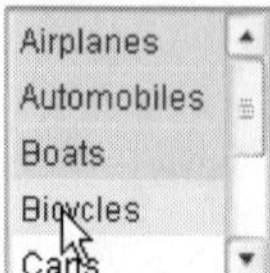

Figure 28-12: A multiple selection list

Getting Items and Values from a List Instance

You can retrieve an item from a `List` instance given the index with the `getItemAt()` method just as with a `ComboBox`. Additionally, when a list is set to allow the user to select only one item at a time, you can retrieve the selected item and selected index in the same way as with a `ComboBox` — with the `selectedItem` and `selectedIndex` properties. If the `List` is set to allow for multiple selections, you should retrieve the selected items with the `selectedItems` property. This property returns an array of the selected items. Likewise, the `selectedIndices` property returns an array of the selected indices.

Adding Icons to List Items

You can add icons next to items in a list. The icon must exist as a `MovieClip` symbol set to export with a linkage identifier. You can then specify a property for each object corresponding to each item of the list such that the property value is the linkage identifier of the icon `MovieClip` symbol. You then need to set the value of the `List` instance's `iconField` property so that it indicates the name of the property/field that specifies the icon symbol. For example, let's say that you have three `MovieClip` symbols in the library with linkage identifiers of SmileyOneSymbol, SmileyTwoSymbol, and SmileyThreeSymbol. You can then define the data provider for a List instance as follows:

```
clUsers.dataProvider = [{label: "luv2Code", data: 8721, ⮐
icon: "SmileyOneSymbol"}, {label: "eyeAS", data: 231, ⮐
icon: "SmileyTwoSymbol"}, {label: "as2master", data: 987, ⮐
icon: "SmileyOneSymbol"}, {label: "scrtcdr", data: 567, ⮐
icon: "SmileyThreeSymbol"}, {label: "varguy", data: 3456, ⮐
icon: "SmileyTwoSymbol"}];
```

You then need to tell Flash to use the icon property/field to obtain the value for each item's icon.

```
clUsers.iconField = "icon";
```

The name of the icon field/property need not be icon.

Figure 28-13 shows how the List instance would appear.

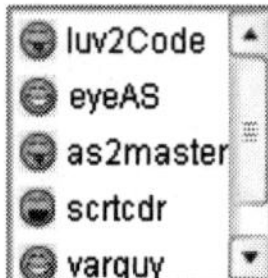

Figure 28-13: A list with icons

You also have the option to use a function to determine which icon to use. For example, you might want to display an icon next to each user that you looked up in your database. Within the database table you might have a field named userType in which you differentiate between 30 types of users. However, for the purposes of displaying the users with icons, you want to group some of those variations together. Perhaps, for example, ten of the different user types between which you differentiate in the database can be considered, for the purposes of display, middle management. Using a function to determine the icon to use allows you to put in place some logic instead of relying on a one-to-one relationship between some field in the data provider and the icon symbols. In such a case you should assign a function to the List instance's iconFunction property. The function is automatically passed an object representing each item, and it should return a string indicating the linkage identifier of the icon symbol to use for that item.

```
clEmployees.iconFunction = function(oItem:Object):String {
  if(oItem.userType >= 0 && oItem.userType < 10) {
    return "StaffIconSymbol";
  }
  else if(oItem.userType >= 10 && oItem.userType < 20) {
    return "MdlMngIconSymbol";
  }
  else {
    return "UpperMngIconSymbol";
  }
};
```

Handling List Events

List component instances dispatch the following events. See the descriptions under the discussion of ComboBox.

- change
- itemRollOver
- itemRollOut
- scroll

Working with NumericStepper Components

The NumericStepper component allows the user to select from a range of numbers by either scrolling through the list of values or by entering the value using the keyboard. NumericStepper instances are commonly used when you want to allow the user to select a numeric value, but you want to exercise some control over the options. For example, you might want to prompt a user for a whole number from 0 to 10, a multiple of 5 from -100 to 100, or a value with one decimal place from 0 to 1. The NumericStepper makes this process simple. Figure 28-14 shows an example of a NumericStepper.

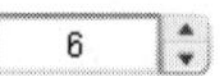

Figure 28-14: A NumericStepper component instance

Setting the Range of Optional Values

The default range for a NumericStepper instance is from 0 to 10 in increments of 1. You can modify these settings, however. The minimum and maximum properties allow you access to the minimum and maximum values in the range, inclusive. So, for example, to adjust the range from 50 to 100 you could use the following code:

```
cnsVolume.minimum = 50;
cnsVolume.maximum = 100;
```

You can access the increment between steps with the stepSize property. For example, if you want to set the instance to increment by 5 instead of 1, you could use the following code:

```
cnsVolume.stepSize = 5;
```

The stepSize property seems to work such that the possible values will be increments of the stepSize starting from 0. You cannot use the technique to get the NumericStepper to count only odd numbers, for example. If you set the stepSize to 2 and initialize the value of the NumericStepper to 1, the next highest value that will display is 2 (followed by 4, 6, 8, and so on).

Working with NumericStepper Values

You can read or write the current value of a NumericStepper by using the value property. For example, to set the value to 75 use the following code:

```
cnsVolume.value = 75;
```

Each NumericStepper instance also provides two read-only properties that return the previous and next values. These properties are named previousValue and nextValue, respectively. They return the same value as if you were to subtract or add the stepSize to the current value, but they save you the extra work.

The previousValue and nextValue properties will report undefined if the next or previous value is out of range.

Handling Change Events

NumericStepper instances dispatch change events when the user changes the value. You can handle the event by defining a change() method for a listener object.

Looking at the Standard Content Display Management Components

The next group of components you'll look at involve content display management. This group includes components for scrolling content, placing content in windows, loading content, and monitoring loading progress.

Working with ScrollPane Components

The ScrollPane component allows you to scroll the display of content. This is particularly useful when you want to manage a lot of content in a not-so-big space. For example, you might want to display a long form on a single screen. In order to show the entire form at once you'd have to set the dimensions of the Flash movie to very large. Instead, however, you can place the form within a ScrollPane instance. Figure 28-15 shows an example of this.

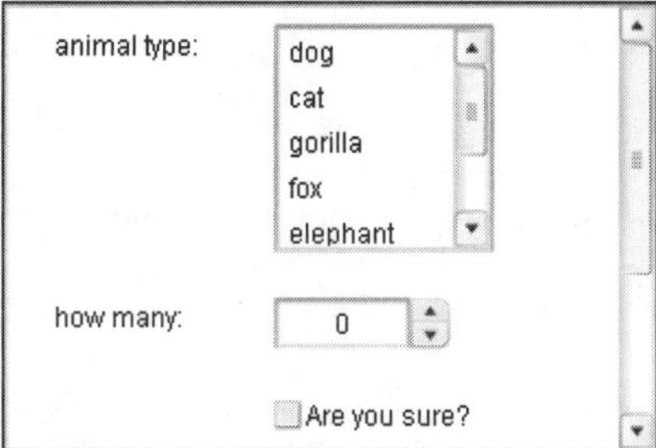

Figure 28-15: A form in a ScrollPane component instance

Adding Content to a ScrollPane

You can add two types of content to a ScrollPane instances: content from a MovieClip symbol or content from an external SWF or JPEG. In either case you tell Flash where to find the content by assigning a value to the ScrollPane instance's contentPath property. The value should be a string, and it can be one of the three following types:

✦ **A linkage identifier:** Use this type when you want to add a `MovieClip` symbol's content to a `ScrollPane` instance. The `MovieClip` symbol must be set to export and must have a linkage identifier.

```
cspFormPane.contentPath = "FormSymbol";
```

✦ **A relative URL:** Use this type when you want to add content to a `ScrollPane` that resides in an external file accessible from a relative location to the loading movie.

```
cspImagePane.contentPath = "image.jpg";
```

✦ **An absolute URL:** Use this type when you want to add content from an external file accessible from another server or domain.

```
cspMoviePane.contentPath = ⮐
"http://www.person13.com/asb/movie.swf";
```

Flash will first look for a symbol in the library with the linkage identifier matching the value of the `ScrollPane`'s `contentPath` property. If it does not find such a symbol it will next look for the content as though the `contentPath` value is a URL.

The content aligns within the `ScrollPane` as follows:

✦ Content from `MovieClip` symbols aligns so that 0,0 within the `MovieClip` coordinate space aligns to the upper-left corner of the `ScrollPane`.

✦ Loaded SWF content aligns so that the upper-left corner of the SWF (the upper-left corner of the stage of the loaded SWF) is aligned to the upper-left corner of the `ScrollPane`.

✦ Loaded JPEG content aligns the upper-left corner to the upper-left corner of the `ScrollPane`.

Once you have added content to a `ScrollPane` instance you can reference the actual content of the `ScrollPane` instance by using the `content` property. This property returns a reference to the nested `MovieClip` instance into which all content is placed. This is very useful if you need to programmatically interface with the content. For example, you might want to change the content somehow by modifying some text values or by retrieving form control values.

The content property will not return a reference to the content Movie Clip properly until the content has completely loaded.

Scrolling Content Programmatically

Typically, the default settings for a `ScrollPane` will suffice when it comes to scrolling. The scroll bars appear and disappear as needed, and the user can scroll the content by clicking and dragging the scroll bar thumb bars. In some cases, however, you might need more control over the scrolling.

As with the `TextArea` component, the `ScrollPane` component manages the scroll bars by hiding and showing them as needed. You can tell Flash how to hide and show the scroll bars with the `vScrollPolicy` (for the vertical scroll bar) and the `hScrollPolicy` (for the horizontal scroll bar) properties. These properties both have a default value of `auto`, which means that the scroll bars automatically hide and show. You can also tell Flash to always show the scroll bars by setting the properties to `on`, or you can tell Flash to always hide the scroll bars by setting the properties to `off`.

The vLineScrollSize and hLineScrollSize properties control the number of pixels that the ScrollPane scrolls when the user clicks the scroll bar arrows. The default setting is 5. You can adjust the settings if you want by simply assigning a new numeric value to one or both of the properties. Likewise, the vPageScrollSize and hPageScrollSize properties determine the number of pixels that the ScrollPane scrolls when the user pages the scroll bars by clicking on the tracks. The default setting is 20.

The vPosition and hPosition determine the scroll position in the vertical and horizontal directions. The value of 0 for each of the properties sets the content so that it is in the original, default position within the ScrollPane. You can set the values by assigning new numeric values indicating how many pixels to scroll.

You can also tell Flash to allow the user to scroll the content by clicking on the content and dragging. By default this functionality is disabled, but you can enable it by setting the scrollDrag property to true. This functionality should be used when the content does not detect any mouse activity (such as Button controls, and so on).

Refreshing the ScrollPane

Sometimes the content within a ScrollPane changes dynamically. For example, a form might add or remove particular controls based on the value that a user selects in another control. Such changes can sometimes affect the dimensions of the content, which in turn can affect how the content fits within the ScrollPane. You can call the refreshPane() method to tell Flash to automatically refresh the ScrollPane to fit the contents.

Handling ScrollPane Events

ScrollPane instances dispatch the following events:

- **scroll:** When the content is scrolled by the user.
- **progress:** When there is load progress for external content.
- **complete:** When the external content has loaded.

When you handle the progress event, you might also find the following methods useful:

- **getBytesLoaded():** Returns the number of bytes loaded.
- **getBytesTotal():** Returns the number of total bytes for the loading content.

Working with Window Components

The Window component allows you to add content to a rectangular window with a title bar. Window instances are draggable, and you can optionally add a close button to them. Window instances do not resize when the borders are dragged. They also do not have shader functionality (meaning the Window instance will not collapse its display when you double-click the title bar). Figure 28-16 shows an example of a Window instance.

Adding Content to Window Instances

You can add content to Window instances in exactly the same way as you add content to ScrollPane instances. And you can add the same types of content as well. Set the contentPath property to the MovieClip symbol linkage identifier or the URL to the SWF or JPEG you want to load. For further discussion of this issue, see the ScrollPane section.

Also, as with the ScrollPane component, you can access the content of a Window with the content property.

Figure 28-16: A Window component instance

Setting the Title of a Window

You can set a `Window` instance's title with the `title` property. Simply assign a new string value to the property as shown here:

```
cwImageWindow.title = "Lake";
```

Adding a Close Button

By default `Window` instances do not have close buttons. You can add a close button by setting the `closeButton` property to `true` (and you can remove a close button by setting the property to `false`).

```
cwImageWindow.closeButton = true;
```

The close button does not automatically close the Window instance when clicked, however. Instead, it dispatches a click event. You then need to set up a listener to handle the click event and close the `Window` instance from which the click event was dispatched. For example:

```
var oListener:Object = new Object();
oListener.click = function(oEvent:Object):Void {
  oEvent.target.visible = false;
};
cwImageWindow.addEventListener("click", oListener);
```

The preceding code simply sets the `Window` instance's visibility to `false`. If you want to remove the Window, use the following code instead:

```
var oListener:Object = new Object();
oListener.click = function(oEvent:Object):Void {
  oEvent.target._parent.destroyObject(oEvent.target._name);
};
cwImageWindow.addEventListener("click", oListener);
```

Creating Pop-Up Window Instances

You can use the `PopUpManager` class to create and remove pop-up `Window` instances. One of the nice features of the `PopUpManager` class is that it allows you to create modal `Window` instances. A modal instance automatically disables all other instances on the screen until it has been closed. This is good for displaying important messages to the user or for prompting the user for essential information.

The PopUpManager class is in the mx.managers package, so when you work with it in your Flash application you might want to first import the class. Otherwise you will have to specify the entire path to the class each time you reference it in your code. To import the class, use the following import statement:

```
import mx.managers.PopUpManager;
```

The PopUpManager methods also require that you specify the class name for the type of component you want to pop-up. In this case, it is the Window class. Again, rather than having to specify the fully qualified class name each time, you may find it more convenient to import the Window class (which is in the mx.controls package). You can import the Window class with the following import statement:

```
import mx.controls.Window;
```

In order to create a new pop-up, you can call the static method createPopUp(). The createPopUp() method requires at least three parameters — a reference to the MovieClip (or component) instance into which you want to add the pop-up, a reference to the class (in this case, Window) for the pop-up, and a Boolean indicating whether the pop-up should be modal. You can also pass the createPopUp() method an init object (see Chapter 9 for more information on init objects). There is also a fifth, optional parameter that allows you to specify whether or not events occur when the user clicks outside the pop-up, but it is seldom used, and so we will not discuss it here. The createPopUp() method returns a reference to the new Window that is created. Here's an example that creates a new pop-up with content from a MovieClip symbol with linkage identifier MessageSymbol.

```
import mx.containers.Window;
import mx.managers.PopUpManager;
var cwMessage:MovieClip = PopUpManager.createPopUp(this, ⮐
mx.containers.Window, true, {contentPath: "MessageSymbol", ⮐
closeButton: true});
```

Note

For the preceding example to work, you need to make sure you have copied the Window component to your library. Additionally, the PopUpManager.createPopUp() method returns a reference to the newly created component instance, but as a MovieClip datatype. If you want to declare the variable as the correct datatype, you need to cast the return value from the method, as shown here:

```
var cwMessage:Window = Window(PopUpManager.createPopUp(this, ⮐
mx.containers.Window, true, {contentPath: ⮐
"MessageSymbol", closeButton: true}));
```

When you want to remove a modal pop-up, it is important that you use the deletePopUp() method instead of destroyObject(). If you use destroyObject() then the modal state is not removed. The deletePopUp() method can be called directly from the pop-up instance, and it removes both the instance and the modal state (re-enabling all the other instances).

```
var oListener:Object = new Object();
oListener.click = function(oEvent:Object):Void {
  oEvent.target.deletePopUp();
};
cwMessage.addEventListener("click", oListener);
```

Working with Loader Components

The `Loader` component is useful when you want to load external SWF or JPEG content, but you don't want it to be framed as with the `ScrollPane` and `Window` components. For example, if you are creating a photo gallery or a product catalog in which you need to dynamically load images, the `Loader` component is a perfect choice.

Loading Content

Once you have created a `Loader` instance, you can load content by assigning the relative or absolute URL to the instance's `contentPath` property.

```
cldImage.contentPath = "http://www.person13.com/asb/image2.jpg";
```

By default, the content begins loading as soon as the value is assigned to the `contentPath` property. However, you can also tell the `Loader` instance to defer the loading by first setting the `autoLoad` property to `false` (the default value is `true`). Then, you can explicitly initialize the loading by calling the `load()` method.

Once the content has loaded, you can get a reference to it by using the `Loader` instance's `content` property.

Sizing the Content

The `scaleContent` property determines whether the content should scale to fit within the `Loader` component instance. The default value is `true`, meaning the content will scale. By setting the `scaleContent` property to `false` you can tell Flash to keep the original dimensions of the content. Keeping `scaleContent` set to `true` is a convenient way to ensure a consistent dimension among loaded content.

Handling Loader Events

`Loader` component instances dispatch two events:

- ✦ **progress:** When there is load progress
- ✦ **complete:** When the content has completely loaded

When handling progress events, the following parameters are passed to the listener's `progress()` method:

- ✦ **bytesLoaded:** The number of bytes that have loaded
- ✦ **bytesTotal:** The total number of bytes
- ✦ **percentLoaded:** The percentage that has loaded

Working with ProgressBar Components

The `ProgressBar` component can monitor the download progress of external content into the following:

- ✦ `MovieClip` instances
- ✦ `Window` instances

✦ `ScrollPane` instances

✦ `Loader` instances

The progress bar displays the progress, as shown in Figure 28-17.

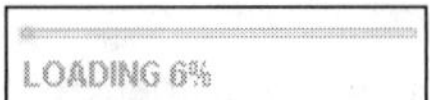

Figure 28-17: A ProgressBar component instance

Assigning Content to Monitor

You need to tell `ProgressBar` components what loading content to monitor. You can achieve this by setting the source property. The source property value should be a string indicating the name of the `MovieClip` or component instance for which you want to monitor the load progress. For example, the following code tells a `ProgressBar` instance named `cpbMonitorImage` to monitor the load progress of the content from a `Loader` instance named `cldImage`:

```
cpbMonitorImage.source = "cldImage";
```

You can also use a path as part of the source string. For example:

```
cpbMonitorImage.source = "this.cldImage";
```

The `ProgressBar` instance can monitor the load progress in several ways. We call these different ways it can monitor "modes." You can set the mode for a `ProgressBar` by assigning a value to the `mode` property. The default value for `mode` is `event`. The `event` mode works with `Loader` instances. Otherwise, set the `mode` to `polled`.

```
cpbMonitorWindomContent.mode = "polled";
```

Setting the ProgressBar Label

The `ProgressBar` label is the text that accompanies the actual progress bar. The default placement of the label is underneath the progress bar. You can set the label to the right, left, top, or bottom (default) by assigning those values (as strings) to the instance's `labelPlacement` property.

```
cpbMonitorImage.labelPlacement = "top";
```

The default label displays the following text:

`LOADING` *`percent loaded%`*

You can assign a new value to the label property of a `ProgressBar` component instance if you want to display a different value. There are three placeholders that you can use in the label string:

✦ **%1:** The amount loaded

✦ **%2:** The total amount

✦ **%3:** The percent loaded

If you want to display a literal percent sign (%), you need to escape it with another percent sign. For example, the following is the default label string:

```
LOADING %3%%
```

Notice that the `%3` is replaced by the percent loaded, and the double percent sign shows appears a single percent sign in the actual label.

Here's an example of how you can assign a label string that displays the bytes loaded, the total bytes, and the percent loaded:

```
cpbMonitorImage.label = "%1 of %2 bytes (%3%%) loaded";
```

By default, the `%1` and `%2` placeholders display the values in bytes. You can also set a conversion value by which the values are divided. To accomplish this, assign a numeric value to the conversion property. For example, if you want `%1` and `%2` to display kilobytes instead of bytes, set conversion to 1,024 (there are 1,024 bytes in a kilobyte).

```
cpbMonitorImage.conversion = 1024;
cpbMonitorImage.label = "%1 of %2 KB (%3%%) loaded";
```

Setting the Fill Direction

The default value for the `direction` property is `right`. This causes the progress bar to fill from left to right. If you set the value to `left`, then the progress bar will fill from right to left.

```
cpbMonitorImage.direction = "left";
```

Handling ProgressBar Events

`ProgressBar` instances dispatch the following events:

- ✦ **progress:** When there is load progress
- ✦ **complete:** When the content has completely loaded

When handling progress events, you might find it useful to work with the `percentComplete` property of the `ProgressBar`. The `percentComplete` property returns the percentage that has loaded.

Looking at the Professional UI Components

In addition to the standard components, Flash MX Professional 2004 includes a handful of additional components. The following sections take a look at each of these components.

Working with Accordion Components

The `Accordion` component allows you to manage multiple pieces of content on the stage by placing them into sliding segments. Each segment has a title bar, and when a user clicks on a segment's title bar, that segment opens and the others collapse. Figure 28-18 shows an example of an `Accordion` component instance.

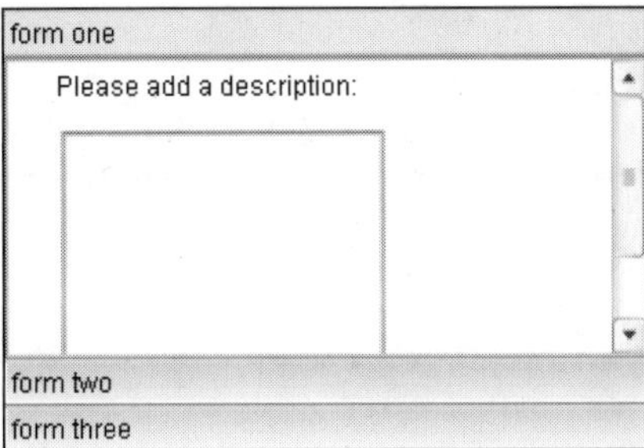

Figure 28-18: An Accordion component instance

Adding Segments to an Accordion

By default, an `Accordion` instance has no segments. You can add segments with the `createSegment()` method. The `createSegment()` method requires at least three parameters. The first parameter can be either a reference to a component class or a string specifying the linkage identifier for the content of the segment. The second parameter is the name to give to the new instance (the content instance is accessible as a property of the Accordion instance). The third parameter is a string specifying the label for the segment title bar. You can also, optionally, specify a fourth parameter indicating the linkage identifier for a symbol to use as an icon in the segment's title bar.

```
cacForms.createSegment("FormOneSymbol", "formOne", "form one");
```

In the preceding example the new segment has an instance name of `formOne`. You can reference the segment as `cacForms.formOne`.

In Figure 28-18, the first segment contains a `ScrollPane` instance. You can achieve this by adding a `ScrollPane` instance as the segment and then adding the content to the `ScrollPane`.

```
cacForms.createSegment(mx.controls.ScrollPane, "formOne", "form one");
cacForms.formOne.contentPath = "FormOneSymbol";
```

When you add a `ScrollPane` to a segment, normally you will want to size the `ScrollPane` so that it fits exactly within the segment. You can calculate the dimensions as follows:

- ✦ `ScrollPane` width should be the width of the `Accordion`.
- ✦ `ScrollPane` height should be the total height of the `Accordion` minus the number of segments in the Accordion times 21.5. The value 21.5 is the height of a title bar.

Here's an example of how you can resize the `ScrollPane` nested as `formOne`:

```
cacForms.formOne.setSize(cacForms.width, ⮐
cacForms.height - (21.5 * cacForms.numChildren));
```

The `numChildren` property returns the number of segments in an `Accordion`.

Getting Selected Segments

You can get a reference to the selected `Accordion` segment with the `selectedChild` property. Alternatively, you can also retrieve the index of the selected segment with the `selectedIndex` property. You can also get a reference to a segment based on the index with the `getChildAt()` method.

Handling Change Events

`Accordion` instances dispatch change events when a segment is opened.

Working with the Alert Component

The `Alert` component is static. You should not create instances of the `Alert` component. Instead, you copy the component to the library, import the class, and then use static properties and methods to open alert windows. Figure 28-19 shows an example of an alert window.

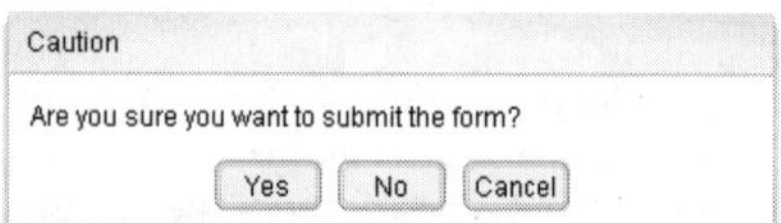

Figure 28-19: An alert window

Opening an Alert Window

In order to work with alert windows, you need to make sure you have first added the component to the library. You can do this by dragging the component from the Components panel onto the stage, and then deleting it from the stage. The symbol remains in the library.

When you are working with alert windows, you access constants and static methods from the `Alert` class, which is in the `mx.controls` package. Therefore, you will find it convenient to import the class rather than having to type the fully qualified class name each time. You can import the class with the following `import` statement:

```
import mx.controls.Alert;
```

In order to open an alert window, you can then call the static method `show()`. The `show()` method allows you to specify from one to seven parameters. In the simplest form you need only specify the message to display. When you specify only the message, the alert window has no title and displays an OK button.

```
Alert.show("Welcome");
```

Figure 28-20 shows the alert window that corresponds to the preceding code.

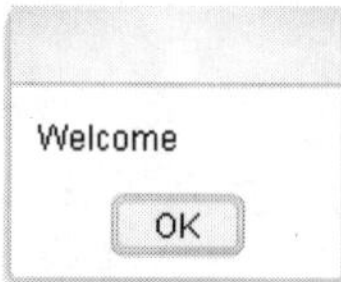

Figure 28-20: A simple alert window

You can optionally specify a title for the alert window with a second parameter. For example:

```
Alert.show("Welcome", "Greeting");
```

The `Alert` class has several constants that you can use as flags for the third parameter. The constants are:

- ✦ **Alert.YES:** Displays the YES button
- ✦ **Alert.NO:** Displays the NO button
- ✦ **Alert.CANCEL:** Displays the CANCEL button
- ✦ **Alert.OK:** Displays the OK button
- ✦ **Alert.NONMODAL:** Makes the window nonmodal (it is modal by default)

You can use any combination of these constants with the bitwise `OR` operator (|). Here is an example that displays both an OK and a CANCEL button.

```
Alert.show("Welcome", "Greeting", Alert.YES|Alert.NO);
```

And if you want to make that same window nonmodal, you can use the following code:

```
Alert.show("Welcome", "Greeting", Alert.YES|Alert.NO|Alert.NONMODAL);
```

Listening for Alert Events

When the user clicks one of the `Alert` buttons, the alert window dispatches a click event. Unlike other, nonstatic components, you do not add a listener to an alert window with the `addEventListener()` method because there is no instance from which to call the method. Instead, you can set an alert window's listener object when you call the `show()` method by passing a reference to the listener object as the fifth parameter. Here is an example:

```
import mx.controls.Alert;
var oListener:Object = new Object();
oListener.click = function(oEvent:Object):Void {
  trace(oEvent.target._name);
};
mx.controls.Alert.show("Welcome", "Greeting", Alert.YES|Alert.NO, this,
oListener);
```

Typically, when you handle `Alert` click events you'll want to know which button the user clicked. The `Event` object passed to the `click()` method contains a `detail` property that holds the value of the button that was clicked. For example:

```
oListener.click = function(oEvent:Object):Void {
  switch (oEvent.detail) {
    case Alert.YES:
      trace("User clicked YES");
      break;
    case Alert.NO:
      trace("User clicked NO");
      break;
    case Alert.CANCEL:
      trace("User clicked CANCEL");
      break;
    case Alert.OK:
      trace("User clicked OK");
  }
};
```

Adding Icons to Alert Windows

You can add an icon to the left of the alert message text by specifying a sixth parameter that indicates the linkage identifier for the symbol that contains the artwork for the icon. For example, if you have a symbol that is set to export with a linkage identifier of `Icon`, the following code will display that symbol's artwork to the left of the text `Welcome`:

```
import mx.controls.Alert;
mx.controls.Alert.show("Welcome", "Greeting", 
Alert.YES|Alert.NO, this, null, "Icon");
```

Setting the Default Button

You can specify which of the Alert buttons should be activated when the user presses the Enter key. You can do so with the seventh parameter you can pass to the `show()` method. The value should be one of the Alert constants that you used to tell Flash which buttons should be displayed. The following example sets the Yes button as the default in an alert with both a YES and NO button.

```
import mx.controls.Alert;
mx.controls.Alert.show("Welcome", "Greeting", 
Alert.YES|Alert.NO, null, null, Alert.YES);
```

Setting the Button Properties

In most cases, the default button settings will suffice. However, you have the option to change the properties of the buttons by assigning new values to the following static properties:

✦ **Alert.buttonHeight and Alert.buttonWidth:** These properties determine the height and width of the alert window buttons. The values are in pixels.

✦ **Alert.cancelLabel, Alert.okLabel, Alert.noLabel, and Alert.yesLabel:** These properties determine the labels on the various button types. They simply give you the option of applying different labels.

Working with DataGrid Components

The DataGrid component enables you to present data in a table/grid-like format as shown in Figure 28-21. Most often DataGrid component instances are used to display data retrieved from a Web service, by way of one of the other data components, or by Flash Remoting.

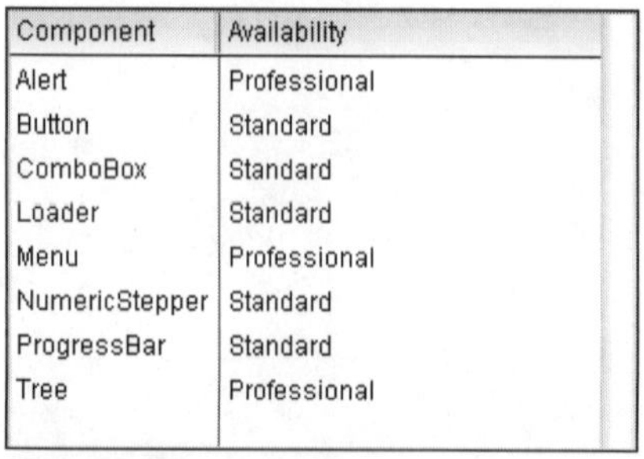

Component	Availability
Alert	Professional
Button	Standard
ComboBox	Standard
Loader	Standard
Menu	Professional
NumericStepper	Standard
ProgressBar	Standard
Tree	Professional

Figure 28-21: A DataGrid component instance

Adding New Columns to a DataGrid Instance

Once you've defined a new `DataGrid` instance, the first step is to tell Flash what columns you want it to display in the grid. There are two basic ways you can accomplish this. The first way is the simpler of the two. You can assign an array of column names to the instance's `columnNames` property.

```
cdgComponents.columnNames = ["Component", "Availability"];
```

In simple cases the preceding will work just fine. But when you want to afford more control over the columns and the data they display, you need to first create `DataGridColumn` objects, and then add those objects to the `DataGrid` instance. The `DataGridColumn` is in the `mx.controls.gridclasses` package, so you will probably find it helpful to first import the class with the following `import` statement:

```
import mx.controls.gridclasses.DataGridColumn;
```

Then, you can create a new `DataGridColumn` instance using the constructor. The constructor requires that you pass it a string specifying the column name.

```
var dgcAvailability:DataGridColumn = new DataGridColumn("Availability");
```

Once you have defined a `DataGridColumn` object you can add it to the `DataGrid` instance with the `addColumn()` or `addColumnAt()` methods. The `addColumn()` method requires you pass it the `DataGridColumn` object, and it appends the column to the `DataGrid` instance.

```
cdgComponents.addColumn(dgcAvailability);
```

The `addColumnAt()` method requires you pass it an index and a reference to the `DataGridColumn` object. Instead of merely appending the column, the `addColumnAt()` method inserts the column at the specified index, shifting any other columns over by one. The first column index is 0.

```
var dgcComponent:DataGridColumn = new DataGridColumn("Component");
cdgComponents.addColumnAt(0, dgcComponent);
```

As an alternative to instantiating the `DataGridColumn` objects via the `DataGridColumn` constructor, you can also simply set the `columnNames` property and then retrieve the `DataGridColumn` objects with the `DataGrid` `getColumnAt()` method. The `getColumnAt()` method returns a reference to the `DataGridColumn` at a specified index.

```
cdgComponents.columnNames = ["Component", "Availability"];
var dgcComponent:DataGridColumn = cdgComponents.getColumnAt(0);
```

Adding Data to a DataGrid Instance

A `DataGrid` without data would be, well, a `DataGrid` without data. So typically the next step after adding columns to your `DataGrid` instance is to add data. There are several ways you can add data. You can add rows to a grid one at a time with the `addItem()` and `addItemAt()` methods. The `addItem()` method appends the new row to the end of the current data. You should pass the method an object containing the data you want to display. In the most basic approach this means that the object should have properties whose names match the column names. For example, if a `DataGrid` named `cdgComponents` has columns named `Component` and `Availability`, the object you pass to `addItem()` should also have properties with those same names. For example:

```
cdgComponents.addItem({Component: "DataGrid", Availability: "Professional"});
```

The addItemAt() method works in basically the same way, but you need also specify the index at which you want Flash to insert the new row. The first index is 0.

```
cdgComponents.addItemAt(0, {Component: "Alert", Availability: "Professional"});
```

You can also use data providers with a DataGrid very similarly to how you can use data providers with a List or ComboBox. In the simplest case, the data provider should have field names that correspond to the column names of the DataGrid. Or, if the data provider is an array of objects, each object should have properties corresponding to the column names of the DataGrid. For example:

```
var aDataProvider:Array = [{Component: "Alert", ⮐
Availability: "Professional"}, {Component: "Button", ⮐
Availability: "Standard"}, {Component: "ComboBox", ⮐
Availability: "Standard"}];
```

You can assign a data provider to a DataGrid using the dataProvider property:

```
cdgComponents.dataProvider = aDataProvider;
```

In some cases the data provider might not have field names that correspond to the column names in the DataGrid. For example, a recordset might contain fields including firstName and lastName. The DataGrid, on the other hand, might have a column named Full Name. In such a case you must make sure you created the Full Name column using the DataGridColumn constructor. You can then assign a function to the DataGridColumn object's labelFunction property. This function will be used by Flash to determine what value to display in the column. The function is automatically passed each item/record from the data provider, and it should return the value that should be displayed. For example:

```
var cdgFullName:DataGridColumn = new DataGridColumn("Full Name");
dgcFullName.labelFunction = new function(oItem:Object):String {
  return (oItem.firstName + " " + oItem.lastName);
};
```

Removing Data from a DataGrid Instance

You can remove data from a DataGrid instance either one item at a time or by removing all the data at once. To remove a single row from the DataGrid use the removeItemAt() method and pass it the index of the row to remove. To remove all rows you can use the removeAll() method.

You can also remove columns either one at a time or all at once. The removeColumnAt() method removes a column given the index. The removeAllColumns() method removes all columns.

Managing Sorting

DataGrid data can be user-sortable. The default is that the data is sortable. This means that when the user clicks the column header, that column sorts the data. The first time the user sorts by a column the data is sorted in ascending order. Subsequent sorts alternate between descending and ascending.

You can disable sorting on the entire DataGrid by setting sortableColumns to false. You can re-enable sorting by setting sortableColumns to true. By default, all the columns are sortable. Therefore, by default, the value of the DataGrid instance's sortableColumns property determines whether the columns are sortable. However, you can also set each column to be sortable or not by setting the sortable property on the DataGridColumn to true or false.

Affecting Column Spacing

There are two ways you can affect the spacing of the columns in a DataGrid instance. If you simply want to have the columns evenly spaced, you can call the spaceColumnsEqually() method from the DataGrid instance.

```
cdgComponents.spaceColumnsEqually();
```

Alternatively, if you want to afford more control over the width of each column, you can set the width property of the columns. For example:

```
cdgComponents.getColumnAt(0).width = 100;
```

Additionally, by default each of the columns can be resized by the user. The user can click the mouse between each of the headers and drag the columns to resize them. You can choose to disable this resizing feature either for the entire DataGrid instance or for individual columns. You can disable or re-enable resizing for the entire instance by setting the resizableColumns property. The default value is true. Setting the value to false disables resizing for the entire instance. You can also set resizing options on each of the columns by setting the column resizable property to true or false.

Making a DataGrid Editable

By default, the data in a DataGrid is read-only. However, you can allow the user to edit the data by setting the DataGrid instance's editable property to true (and you can reset the instance so that it is non-editable by setting the editable property to false). You can also set particular columns so that they are editable or not. By default, if you enable editing for the DataGrid instance, all of the columns are editable. You can explicitly enable or disable editing for each column by setting the column's editable property.

When a DataGrid is editable, you can bring focus to a particular cell by setting the focusedCell property. The focusedCell property value should be an object with two integer properties—columnIndex and itemIndex. These values indicate which cell should receive focus. For example, you can make an instance named cdgComponents editable and bring focus to the first cell of the first item as follows:

```
cdgComponents.editable = true;
cdfComponents.focusedCell = {columnIndex:0, rowIndex:0};
```

Setting Scroll Properties of a DataGrid

The DataGrid has all the same scroll properties of the List component. See the discussion of how to set the scroll properties of a List for more details.

Allowing Multiple Selections

The default setting for a DataGrid is that it allows for a single selection. You can also enable multiple selections for a DataGrid instance by setting the multipleSelection property to true. This property is inherited from the List component. See the discussion of List for more information.

Getting Selected Items

You can get the selected item or items (for a multiple selection-enabled DataGrid) with the selectedItem and selectedItems properties, respectively. You can also get the indices for selected items with the selectedIndex (single selection) or selectedIndices (multiple selection) properties. See the List discussion for more details.

Handling DataGrid Events

DataGrid component instances dispatch the following events:

- **cellPress:** When the user clicks a cell in the DataGrid (mouse down)
- **cellEdit:** When the user edits a cell and then presses Enter or Tab
- **cellFocusIn:** When the user brings focus to an editable cell
- **cellFocusOut:** When the user moves focus from an editable cell
- **change:** When the user selects a new item
- **columnStretch:** When the user resizes the columns
- **headerPress:** When the user clicks one of the column headers

In all but the `columnStretch` and `headerPress` events, the `Event` object passed to the handler method contains `columnIndex` and `rowIndex` properties that contain information about the cell related to the event. The `columnStretch` and `headerPress Event` objects contain `columnIndex` properties.

Working with DateChooser Components

The `DateChooser` component allows the users to select a date from a calendar interface, as shown in Figure 28-22.

◀			October 2004			▶
S	M	T	W	T	F	S
					1	2
3	4	5	6	7	8	9
10	11	12	13	14	15	16
17	18	19	20	21	22	23
24	25	26	27	28	29	30
31						

Figure 28-22: A DateChooser component instance

Configuring the Appearance of the DataChooser

There are several configurable properties of a `DateChooser` component instance that allow you to affect the appearance. These include properties that set both the labels for the days of the week and the months as well as the order in which the days appear within the calendar. By default, the labels for the days of the week are S, M, T, W, T, F, and S. As you can see in Figure 28-22, the labels were slightly altered in that the label for Thursday is *Th* rather than the standard *T*. You can assign new values to the `dayNames` property as an array of strings. The order of the labels should always be from Sunday to Saturday. For example:

```
cdcCalendar.dayNames = ["S", "M", "T", "W", "Th", "F", "S"];
```

Also, by default, the first day of the week displayed in the calendar is Sunday. However, as you see in Figure 28-22, you can alter which day of the week displays first. The `firstDayOfWeek` property determines which days should display first. The possible values are from 0 (Sunday) to 6 (Saturday). To set the `DateChooser` instance to display Monday first as in Figure 28-22, use the following code:

```
cdcCalendar.firstDayOfWeek = 1;
```

You can also adjust the labels that display for the months. The `monthNames` property contains an array of month labels starting with January. You can change the values by assigning a new array of labels to the `monthNames` property.

Setting Current Display

By default, a `DateChooser` instance displays the current month and year. You can tell the instance to display any month and year with the `displayedMonth` and `displayedYear` properties. The `displayedMonth` property can be any integer from 0 (January) to 11 (December), and the `displayedYear` property can be any integer indicating the full year you want to display. The following code displays February of 2004.

```
cdcCalendar.displayedMonth = 1;
cdcCalendar.displayedYear = 2004;
```

Additionally, the default setting for a `DateChooser` instance is such that when the current month and year are displayed, the current date is highlighted. The `showToday` property determines this behavior. The default setting is `true`. If you set the property to `false`, the current date is not highlighted.

Setting Selectable and Nonselectable Ranges and Days

You can enable and disable particular days and ranges within a `DateChooser` instance. You can disable particular days of the week by assigning a value to the `disabledDays` property. The `disabledDays` property value should be an array with up to seven integer values in which the valid values are from 0 to 7. For example, the following disables all Sundays and Saturdays.

```
cdcCalendar.disabledDays = [0, 6];
```

You can also disable specific dates and date ranges by assigning a value to the `disabledRanges` property. The `disabledRanges` property value should be an array containing one or both of the following types of elements:

- ✦ `Date` objects indicating the specific dates to disable
- ✦ Associative arrays (`Object` objects) with a `rangeStart` and/or `rangeEnd` property—both of which should be `Date` objects:
  - If an associative array specifies only the `rangeStart` property, all dates after (and including) that value are disabled.
  - If an associative array specifies only the `rangeEnd` property, all dates before (and including) that value are disabled.
  - If an associative array specifies both the `rangeStart` and `rangeEnd` properties, the entire range from (including) the starting value up through (and including) the ending value is disabled.

Here's an example that displays February of 2004 and disables the 5th of the month, the 10th through the 15th, and then everything from the 23rd and after.

```
cdcCalendar.displayedMonth = 1;
cdcCalendar.displayedYear = 2004;
cdcCalendar.disabledRanges = [new Date(2004, 1, 5), ⮐
{rangeStart: new Date(2004, 1, 10), rangeEnd: ⮐
new Date(2004, 1, 15)}, {rangeStart: new Date(2004, 1, 23)}];
```

You can also specify dates and ranges that you want to enable rather than disable. Telling Flash to enable a range and/or dates has the opposite effect of disabling ranges. Any non-enabled dates and ranges are then automatically disabled. The `selectableRanges` property accepts the same type of value as the `disabledRanges` property, but it enables those dates and ranges rather than disabling them.

Getting and Setting the Selected Date

You can get and/or set the selected date within a `DateChooser` instance using the `selectedDate` property. The value of the `selectedDate` property is a `Date` object. You can programmatically select a date by assigning a `Date` object to the property. For example, if you want to select February 1, 2004, you can use the following code:

```
cdcCalendar.selectedDate = new Date(2004, 1, 1);
```

Handling DateChooser Events

`DateChooser` component instances dispatch the following events:

- **change:** When the user selects a date
- **scroll:** When the user scrolls the months

Working with DateField Components

The `DateField` component combines the functionality of a `DateChooser` and a `TextInput`. It allows users to select a date and have that date displayed in an efficient manner. Figure 28-23 shows a `DateField` instance in which a date has been selected.

Figure 28-23: A DateField component instance with selected date value

Figure 28-24 shows a `DateField` component with the opened `DateChooser` that allows the users to select the date.

Configuring a DateField Instance

The `DateField` component has all the same properties as the `DateChooser` component. That means you can set the day names, month names, first day of week, displayed month and year, and so on. See the `DateChooser` discussion for more details.

You can also access the nested `DateChooser` instance with the `pullDown` property. However, because the `DateChooser` properties affect the nested `DateChooser` indirectly, there really is no reason for you to access the `pullDown` property in most scenarios.

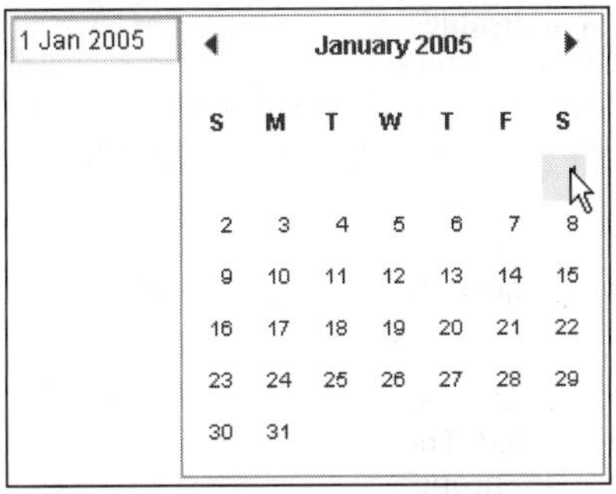

Figure 28-24: A DateField component instance with the nested DateChooser opened

Displaying the Selected Value

By default, the selected value displays in the `TextInput` portion of the instance in the following format: d MM YYYY. You can tell Flash how to display the value differently if you want by assigning a formatting function to the instance's `dateFormatter` property. The function is passed the selected date (a `Date` object) as a parameter, and it should return a string that formats the date as you want it to display. For example:

```
cdfPurchaseDate.dateFormatter = function(dSelected:Date):String {
  var sFormatted:String = "";
  sFormatted += String(dSelected.getDate());
  sFormatted += "/" + String(dSelected.getMonth() + 1);
  sFormatted += "/" + String(dSelected.getFullYear());
  return sFormatted;
};
```

Getting and Setting the Selected Value

Just as with the `DateChooser`, you can get and set the value of a `DateField` with the `selectedDate` property. See the `DateChooser` discussion for more details.

Opening and Closing a DateField Instance

Typically, there is little reason to programmatically control the open and close state of a `DateField` instance. This is because the instance is typically opened when the user clicks it and it is closed when the user selects a date from the nested `DateChooser`. However, you can programmatically open and closer the instance with the `open()` and `close()` methods.

Handling DateField Events

`DateField` components dispatch the same events as `DateChooser`. In addition, they also dispatch open events when the instances are opened and close events when the instances are closed.

Working with Menu Components

The Menu component allows you to add menu systems to your Flash applications. Typically these Menu instances are associated with Button component instances, as shown in Figure 28-25.

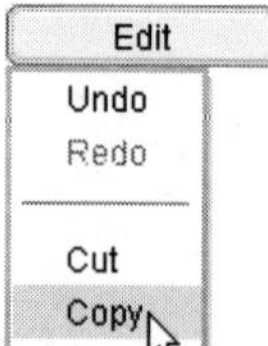

Figure 28-25: A Menu component instance associated with a Button component instance

Creating Menu Instances

You *can* create Menu instances by dragging them onto the stage and naming them via the Property inspector. However, as a result of the way in which Menu component instances work, it is generally much more practical to create the instances programmatically. Unlike other types of UI components, you don't need to create the instances with createObject() or createClassObject(). Instead, the Menu class has a static method called createMenu() that creates a new Menu instance and returns a reference to that new instance.

There are two things you should consider prior to trying to instantiate a Menu component, however. First, like all other components, you need to make sure that it has been added to the library. The only way to accomplish this is to first drag an instance from the Components panel onto the stage, and then to delete the instance from the stage. The component symbol is copied to the library, and it remains there even after the instance is deleted from the stage. Secondly, as with all the other UI components, the Menu class is within the mx.controls package. Therefore, you will likely find it helpful to first import the class. That allows you to reference the class without having to type in the fully qualified name each time. You can import the Menu class as follows:

```
import mx.controls.Menu;
```

You can then create a new Menu instance by calling Menu.createMenu(). If you pass the method no parameters, it creates a new, empty Menu instance on _root:

```
var cmEdit:Menu = Menu.createMenu();
```

If you want to create the Menu instance nested within another MovieClip, you can specify the path to the parent MovieClip as the first parameter to the createMenu() method.

```
var cmEdit:Menu = Menu.createMenu(mcMenuHolder);
```

Populating Menu Instances

There are several ways you can populate Menu instances. Although there are variations, these ways can be categorized into two groups:

- ✦ Populating Menu instances with init objects
- ✦ Populating Menu instances with XMLNode objects (menu data providers)

Working with init Objects

The Menu init objects are Object objects with the following possible properties:

- **label:** The item's label that should appear in the menu.
- **type:** The type of item. Possible values include:
  - normal (default value if none specified)
  - separator
  - check
  - radio
- **icon:** The linkage identifier for a symbol to use as an icon. This is available only for normal items.
- **instanceName:** A name that you can use to reference the item as a property of the Menu instance.
- **groupName:** The name of a radio group. This applies only when the type is set to radio.
- **selected:** Whether to display the item as selected. This applies to radio and check items only.
- **enabled:** Whether the item should be selectable. If set to true, the value is selectable. If set to false, the item is grayed out and non-selectable.

You can add items using init objects with the addMenuItem() and addMenuItemAt() methods. The addMenuItem() method appends the new item to the end of the current items.

```
cmEdit.addMenuItem({label: "cut", instanceName: "cut"});
```

The addMenuItemAt() method adds a new item at a specific index. The first item in the menu has an index of 0.

```
cmEdit.addMenuItemAt(0, {label: "copy", instanceName: "copy"});
```

If you want to add submenus, you need to first create the main Menu item that will open the submenu. The addMenuItem() and addMenuItemAt() methods both return a reference to the newly created item. You haven't needed to work with that reference thus far, but when adding submenu items it is convenient. You can simply set the type of the return value as Object:

```
var oMenuItem:Object = cmEdit.addMenuItem({label: "edit ⮐
options", instanceName: "editOptions"});
```

You can then use the same addMenuItem() and addMenuItemAt() methods to add nested items to the submenu:

```
oMenuItem.addMenuItem({label: "copy", instanceName: "copy"});
oMenuItem.addMenuItem({label: "paste", instanceName: "paste"});
```

Working with Menu Data Providers

A menu data provider is an XMLNode object containing the data to populate the Menu or a Menu item. The actual element names within the XML data are not important. The structure and the attributes of the elements, however, are important. Each item element can have any of the same attributes as the init object properties. For example, the following is an element that represents a normal Menu item:

```
<menuitem label="paste" instanceName="paste" enabled="false" />
```

If you nest elements within another element, the nested elements appear in a submenu:

```
<submenu>
  <menuitem label="open" instanceName="open" />
  <menuitem label="close" instanceName="close" />
</submenu>
```

You can work with menu data providers in several ways. You can use menu data providers as parameters for the addMenuItem() and addMenuItemAt() methods instead of init objects. For example:

```
import mx.controls.Menu;
var sMenuData:String = "<menuitem label='copy' instanceName='copy' />";
var cmEdit:Menu = Menu.createMenu();
cmEdit.addMenuItem(new XML(sMenuData));
```

In the preceding example it might seem like a lot of extra work just to add a single item to the Menu. And, in fact, it is. You can accomplish the same task with an init object with less code. But for adding submenus you might find the menu data provider/addMenuItem() (or addMenuItemAt()) technique a little simpler. For example:

```
import mx.controls.Menu;
var sMenuData:String = "<submenu label='edit options'>↩
<menuitem label='copy' instanceName='copy' />↩
<menuitem label='paste' instanceName='paste' /></submenu>";
var cmEdit:Menu = Menu.createMenu();
cmEdit.addMenuItem(new XML(sMenuData));
```

The preceding code adds a submenu with two elements. For those who are comfortable with XML, the preceding syntax might be simpler than working with multiple addMenuItem() calls, as in the previous section.

The addMenuItem() and addMenuItemAt() method variations for working with menu data providers are moderately useful for initially populating a menu (we'll see how they can be used to modify values). However, the menu data provider is most powerful when used to populate the entire menu at once. There are two ways you can populate an entire menu with a menu data provider. The first is to pass the menu data provider as the second parameter to the createMenu() method when first creating the menu. For example:

```
mx.controls.Menu;
var sMenuData:String = "<menuitem label='undo' ↩
instanceName='undo /><menuitem label='redo' ↩
instanceName='redo' enabled='false' /><menuitem ↩
type='separator' /><submenu label='edit options' ↩
instanceName='editOptions'><menuitem label='copy' ↩
instanceName='copy' /><menuitem label='paste' ↩
instanceName='paste' /></submenu>";
var cmEdit:Menu = Menu.createMenu(this, new XML(sMenuData));
```

You can also assign a menu data provider to the menu instance's `dataProvider` property. So the preceding code can be rewritten as:

```
import mx.controls.Menu;
var sMenuData:String = "<menuitem label='undo' ⮐
instanceName='undo />< menuitem label='redo' ⮐
instanceName='redo' enabled='false' /><menuitem ⮐
type='separator' /><submenu label='edit options' ⮐
instanceName='editOptions'><menuitem label='copy' ⮐
instanceName='copy' /><menuitem label='paste' ⮐
instanceName='paste' /></submenu>";
var cmEdit:Menu = Menu.createMenu();
cmEdit.dataProvider = new XML(sMenuData);
```

Of course, one of the main benefits of working with a menu data provider is that you can define the menus in external XML documents or from XML generated from database data, and so on. For example, you can define an external XML document with the code shown in Listing 28-1.

Listing 28-1: **menu.xml**

```
<menu>
  <menuitem label='undo' instanceName='undo' />
  <menuitem label='redo' instanceName='redo' enabled='false' />
  <menuitem type='separator' />
  <submenu label='edit options' instanceName='editOptions'>
    <menuitem label='copy' instanceName='copy' />
    <menuitem label='paste' instanceName='paste' enabled='false' />
  </submenu>
</menu>
```

Then, you can load the XML data into your Flash movie, and use it to populate a menu as follows:

```
import mx.controls.Menu;
var cmEdit:Menu = Menu.createMenu();
var xmlMenuData:XML = new XML();
xmlMenuData.onLoad = function():Void {
  cmEdit.dataProvider = this.firstChild;
};
xmlMenuData.ignoreWhite = true;
xmlMenuData.load("menu.xml");
```

Notice that the data in the XML file has a root element of `<menu>` to ensure that it is well formed (well-formed XML data has a single root element per document). When the data is loaded, the `firstChild` of the `XML` object is assigned to the `dataProvider` instead of the `XML` object itself.

Removing Items

You can remove menu items with the following three methods:

- **removeMenuItem():** This method requires you pass it a reference to one of the items. You can get references to menu items in several ways, as you'll see in subsequent sections. Alternatively, if this method is invoked directly from a menu item, it requires no parameters, and it removes the item from which it is called.
- **removeMenuItemAt():** This method removes an item given the index.
- **removeAll():** This methods removes all items in a menu or menu item.

Showing and Hiding Menu Instances

Up this point you've seen how to create `Menu` instances, but not how to actually show them. The default setting for a menu is that it is hidden. You can show a menu by calling the `show()` method. The `show()` method requires two parameters — the x and y coordinates at which to display the menu. For example, the following code will show a menu at 100,100.

```
cmEdit.show(100, 100);
```

Most often, `Menu` instances are associated with `Button` component instances such that they display when the button has been clicked. Therefore, you typically call the `show()` method to display the menu just above or below the `Button` instance. For example:

```
var oListener:Object = new Object();
oListener.menu = cmEdit;
oListener.click = function(oEvent:Object):Void {
  var nX:Number = oEvent.target.x;
  var nY:Number = oEvent.target.y + oEvent.target.height;
  this.menu.show(nX, nY);
};
cbtEdit.addEventListener("click", oListener);
```

By default, `Menu` instances disappear once a selection has been made. Therefore you don't often need to programmatically hide the instance. However, should you want to, you can hide the menu with the `hide()` method.

```
cmEdit.hide();
```

Handling Menu Events

`Menu` component instances dispatch the following events:

- **show:** Dispatched when the instance is shown
- **hide:** Dispatched when the instance is hidden
- **rollOver:** Dispatched when the user rolls over an item
- **rollOut:** Dispatched when the user rolls out of an item
- **change:** Dispatched when the user selects an item

The `rollOver`, `rollOut`, and `change` `Event` objects include an additional property not included in the show and hide `Event` objects. The property, called `menuItem`, is a reference to the menu item that initiated the event.

Changing Items

You can alter menu items in two ways — setting the enabled state or selected state. Regardless of what kind of changes you want to make to a menu item, however, you first need to get a reference to the menu item. If you are making the changes within an event handler method such as `rollOver()`, `rollOut()`, or `change()`, the Event object's `menuItem` property is a reference to the menu item that initialized the event. If, within an event handler method, you want to get a reference to a menu item other than the item that initialized the event, you can obtain the reference as one of the nested items of the `Menu` instance that is references by the `Event` object's target property.

There are essentially two ways to get a reference to a menu item from a `Menu` instance (or from a nested menu item). You can use the `getMenuItemAt()` method to get an item by index. Or you can get a reference by name if you gave the menu item an instance name when you created it. (You can give an item an instance name via the `instanceName` property/attribute.)

Each menu item is an instance of the `MenuDataProvider` class. The `MenuDataProvider` class looks very much like the `XMLNode` class. In fact, it has the same properties such as `attributes` and `childNodes`.

If you want to set the enabled or selected state of a menu item, the best way to do that is to use the `setMenuItemEnabled()` or `setMenuItemSelected()` methods. These methods set the state and then also automatically update the view. Both methods require you pass them a reference to the menu item, and then a Boolean value indicating the state to which you want to set the item. For example, the following disables a `Menu` item with an instance name of `undo`:

```
cmEdit.setMenuItemEnabled(cmEdit.undo, false);
```

The following example shows how you can create a `Button` and `Menu` item such that the paste option of the `Menu` item is enabled following the copy option being selected. Then, once paste is selected, it becomes disabled again.

```
import mx.controls.Menu;
var cmEdit = Menu.createMenu();
var xmlMenuData:XML = new XML();
xmlMenuData.onLoad = function():Void {
  cmEdit.dataProvider = this.firstChild;
};
xmlMenuData.ignoreWhite = true;
xmlMenuData.load("menu.xml");

// Create the listener object.
var oListener:Object = new Object();

// Assign a reference to the Menu so that the handler methods
// can address the Menu.
oListener.menu = cmEdit;

// Handle change events from the Menu.
oListener.change = function(oEvent:Object):Void {

  // If the selected item's label is copy, enable the paste
```

```
    // Menu item.
    if(oEvent.menuItem.attributes.label == "copy") {
      oEvent.target.setMenuItemEnabled(oEvent.target.paste, true);
    }

    // If the selected item's label is paste, disable the paste
    // Menu item.
    if(oEvent.menuItem.attributes.label == "paste") {
      oEvent.target.setMenuItemEnabled( oEvent.target.paste, ⮐
false);
    }
};

// Handle click events from the Button to show the menu
// when the user clicks on the Button.
oListener.click = function(oEvent:Object):Void {
  var nX:Number = oEvent.target.x;
  var nY:Number = oEvent.target.y + oEvent.target.height;
  this.menu.show(nX, nY);
};

// Add the listener to the Menu.
cmEdit.addEventListener("change", oListener);

// Create the Button instance and add the listener to it.
this.createObject("Button", "cbtEdit", ⮐
this.getNextHighestDepth(), {label: "Edit"});
cbtEdit.addEventListener("click", oListener);
```

Working with MenuBar Components

The `MenuBar` component allows you to conveniently create a group of nested `Menu` instances. The `MenuBar` component is similar to the menu bar of a standard desktop application. Figure 28-26 shows an example.

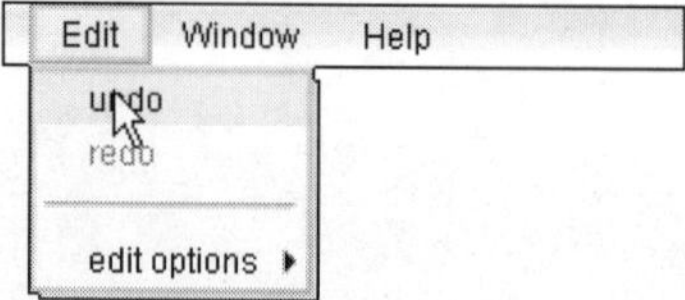

Figure 28-26: A MenuBar component instance

Adding Menus to a MenuBar

You can add menus to a `MenuBar` component in several ways. You can add menus without any items with the `addMenu()` method by passing it a single parameter — the label for the menu. For example:

```
cmbMenus.addMenu("Edit");
```

You can then add items to the menu at a later point. The menu is a Menu component instance, and you can retrieve a reference to it with the getMenuAt() method if you know the index. You can then modify the items of the Menu instance as with any Menu instance.

```
var cmEdit:mx.contols.Menu = cmbMenus.getMenuAt(0);
cmEdit.dataProvider = xnEditData;
```

Optionally, you can add a menu and populate the menu at the same time by passing the addMenu() method a menu data provider as the second parameter. For example:

```
cmbMenus.addMenu("Edit", xnEditData);
```

The addMenuAt() method also allows you to insert new menus at specific indices. You can create a new menu without items at a specific index as follows:

```
cmbMenus.addMenuAt(0, "Help");
```

And you can add a new menu at a specific index and populate that menu as shown in this example:

```
cmbMenus.addMenu(0, "Help", xnHelpData);
```

You can also set a MenuBar instance's data provider to populate the entire MenuBar at once by assigning an XMLNode object to the instance's dataProvider property. The data provider structure for a MenuBar is similar to the data provider structure for a Menu data provider. Each menu should be its own element in the top level of the data provider. The menu elements should have label attributes that define the label as it will appear in the MenuBar. Then, nested within each menu element should be the menu's contents. Listing 28-2 shows an example of the XML document that can be used to create the MenuBar shown in Figure 28-26.

Listing 28-2: **menubar.xml**

```
<menus>
  <menu label='Edit'>
    <menuitem label='undo' instanceName='undo' />
    <menuitem label='redo' instanceName='redo' enabled='false' />
    <menuitem type='separator' />
    <submenu label='edit options' instanceName='editOptions'>
      <menuitem label='copy' instanceName='copy' />
      <menuitem label='paste' instanceName='paste' />
    </submenu>
  </menu>
  <menu label='Window'>
    <menuitem label='control panel' instanceName='control panel' />
    <menuitem label='color panel' instanceName='color panel'/>
  </menu>
  <menu label='Help'>
    <menuitem label='about' instanceName='about' />
  </menu>
</menus>
```

The following code can be used to load the XML from Listing 28-2 and populate a MenuBar instance.

```
var xmlMenuData:XML = new XML();
xmlMenuData.onLoad = function(){
  cmbMenus.dataProvider = this.firstChild;
};
xmlMenuData.ignoreWhite = true;
xmlMenuData.load("menubar.xml");
```

Removing Menus

You can remove menus from a MenuBar instance with the removeMenuAt() method if you know the index:

```
cmbMenus.removeMenuAt(0);
```

Enabling and Disabling Menus

By default all menus in a MenuBar are enabled. You can explicitly enable or disable the menus at specific indices with the setMenuEnabledAt() method. The method requires you pass it the index of the menu and a Boolean indicating whether to enable (true) or disable (false) the menu.

You can also retrieve the enabled state of a menu with the getMenuEnabledAt() method. The getMenuEnabledAt() method requires only the index of the menu.

Handling MenuBar Events

Although the documentation says that the MenuBar component dispatches events, it does not seem to work as described. Instead, it appears you need to add an event listener to each of the nested Menu instances. The following code shows an example:

```
function setListeners():Void {

  // Initialize the variable to 0 because the index of
  // the first menu is 0.
  var nIndex:Number = 0;

  // Retrieve a reference to the first menu.
  var cmMenu:mx.controls.Menu = cmbMenus.getMenuAt(nIndex);

  // As long as Flash finds additional menus, continue to
  // loop with a while statement.
  while(cmMenu != undefined) {

    // Add an event listener to the menu.
    cmMenu.addEventListener("change", oListener);

    // Get the next menu. This will be undefined if there
    // are no more menus.
    cmMenu = cmbMenus.getMenuAt(++nIndex);
  }
}

// This is the same code as in a previous example. It loads
// the XML data from an external file and uses that XML as
```

```
// the data provider for the MenuBar instance. The only
// difference is that with this code you should also call the
// setListeners() function after setting the data provider.
var xmlMenuData:XML = new XML();
xmlMenuData.onLoad = function(){
  cmbMenus.dataProvider = this.firstChild;
  setListeners();
};
xmlMenuData.ignoreWhite = true;
xmlMenuData.load("menubar.xml");

// Create a listener that you can assign to each of the nested
// menu instances.
var oListener:Object = new Object();
oListener.change = function(oEvent:Object):Void {
  trace(oEvent.menuItem);
};
```

Working with Tree Components

The `Tree` component enables you to add controls to your applications that display contents as folders and nested items. The folders and subfolders are expandable and collapsible. The effect is something similar to the interface by which many people navigate through their own computer's directory system. Figure 28-27 shows an example of a `Tree` component instance.

Figure 28-27: A Tree component instance

Adding Items to a Tree

All items within a `Tree` instance are either branching (folders) or non-branching. For the most part Flash takes care of making the items the appropriate type. Generally all you need to do is add a new item by providing the label and data values. The label value is what is displayed in the tree, and the data value is hidden from view, but used programmatically. You can add new items in several ways. The `addTreeNode()` and `addTreeNodeAt()` methods enable you to append or insert a new item by providing the label and data values as parameters. For example, the following code appends a new item named *Photos* and then inserts an item named *Documents* just before it.

```
ctr.addTreeNode("Photos", "photos");
ctr.addTreeNodeAt(0, "Documents", "docs");
```

Both methods return a reference to the newly created node. This is convenient for when you want to add nested items. You can call the `addTreeNode()` and `addTreeNodeAt()` methods on tree nodes as well to add nested items. For example:

```
var oDocsNode:Object = ctr.addTreeNodeAt(0, "Documents", "docs");
oDocsNode.addTreeNode("resume.doc", "resume.doc");
```

```
oDocsNode.addTreeNode("addresses.doc", "addresses.doc");
oDocsNode.addTreeNode("report.doc", "report.doc");
```

You can also add items to a tree by passing tree data providers to the addTreeNode() and addTreeNodeAt() methods. A tree data provider is similar to a menu data provider in that it can be any XMLNode object. The names of the XML elements are not relevant, but the structure and attributes of the elements are. Each element in the XML represents a node in the Tree. The XML element should have a label attribute and a data attribute. If an XML element contains nested elements, that element represents a folder in the Tree. Here's an example that adds a folder node to the tree in which are two nested items.

```
var sTreeData:String = "<node label='Photos' data='photos'> ⮐
<node label='sun.jpg' data='sun.jpg' /><node ⮐
label='moon.jpg' data='moon.jpg' /></node>";
var xmlTreeData:XML = new XML(sTreeData);
ctrDirectory.addTreeNode(xmlTreeData.firstChild);
```

You can also, of course, set the data provider for the entire Tree instance. Simply assign the XMLNode data to the instance's dataProvider property. Typically, when assigning the data provider for the entire Tree the data is loaded from an external source. Listing 28-3 shows a sample XML document's data that can be loaded and used to populate a Tree instance.

Listing 28-3: tree.xml

```
<tree>
  <node label='Documents' data='docs'>
    <node label='resume.doc' data='resume.doc' />
    <node label='addresses.doc' data='addresses.doc' />
    <node label='report.doc' data='report.doc' />
  </node>
  <node label='Photos' data='photos'>
    <node label='sun.jpg' data='sun.jpg' />
    <node label='moon.jpg' data='moon.jpg' />
  </node>
</tree>
```

The XML data from Listing 28-3 can be loaded into a Flash application and used to populate a tree, as shown with the following code:

```
var xmlTreeData:XML = new XML();
xmlTreeData.onLoad = function(){
  ctrDirectory.dataProvider = this.firstChild;
};
xmlTreeData.ignoreWhite = true;
xmlTreeData.load("tree.xml");
```

Notice that the XML data from Listing 28-3 is placed within a root element <tree>. This is just so that the XML is well formed. Because of the extra node, when the data has been loaded into Flash, you must assign the firstChild value to the Tree instance's dataProvider.

Setting Selection Mode

The default setting for a Tree instance is a single selection. That means a user can select only one item at a time. You can set the Tree instance to allow the user to make multiple selections by setting the multipleSelection property to true. Or, to explicitly reset a Tree instance to single selection mode, set the multipleSelection property to false.

Getting Items

You can retrieve references to items (nodes) in several ways. You can retrieve nodes by using the order in which they appear within the Tree instance's data provider. This way returns nodes regardless of whether they are visible or the order in which they are displayed (remember, the visible display order can vary depending on which nodes are expanded or collapsed). The getTreeNodeAt() method returns a reference to a node based on its index within the data provider. In Figure 28-27 the Tree instance's second node is always the *Photos* node regardless of whether any of the nodes are expanded or collapsed. You can retrieve that node as follows:

```
var oPhotosNode:Object = ctrDirectory.getTreeNodeAt(1);
```

You can retrieve nested items in the same way by calling the getTreeNodeat() method from any node object. For example, the following code first retrieves the Documents node, and then retrieves the resume.doc item.

```
var oDocsNode:Object = ctrDirectory.getTreeNodeAt(0);
var oResumeDoc:Object = oDocsNode.getTreeNodeAt(0);
```

You can also retrieve nodes by display index. A node's display index can change based on which nodes are expanded and/or collapsed. You can retrieve a node's display index with the getDisplayIndex() method. For example:

```
var nPhotosDispInd:Number = ctrDirectory.getDisplayIndex(oPhotosNode);
```

Remember, however, that the display index will change. So if you retrieve a node's display index, you cannot rely on the node still having the same display index later on.

If, on the other hand, you want to get the node currently displayed at a given index, you can use the getNodeDisplayedAt() method.

```
var oNode:Object = ctrDirectory.getNodeDisplayedAt(3);
```

You can retrieve the selected node or nodes (if set to multiple select) with the selectedNode and selectedNodes properties, respectively.

Setting Item Type

For the most part, Flash takes care of setting the Tree node types — either branching or non-branching. If a node contains any items then it is automatically made branching (meaning it displays a folder icon and can be expanded and collapsed). The only case in which you are likely to need to explicitly set the type of a node is when you want to display an empty branching node. If a node contains no items, of course, Flash assumes it is non-branching, but you can set the branching status with the setIsBranch() method. The setIsBranch() method requires you pass it the node object and a Boolean indicating whether the node should branch (true) or not (false).

```
var oNode:Object = ctrDirectory.addTreeNode("System", "sys");
ctrDirectory.setIsBranch(oNode, true);
```

You can also retrieve the current branching type of a node with the `getIsBranch()` method. The `getIsBranch()` method requires you pass it the node for which you want to get the value.

```
trace(ctrDirectory.getIsBranch(oNode));
```

Opening and Closing Nodes

Typically there are few reasons to programmatically open and close nodes. This is because nodes are opened and closed through user interaction. However, there are a few reasons you might want to programmatically control whether nodes are opened or closed. For example, you might want to store the state of a `Tree` instance's nodes and then when the user runs the Flash application again you can initialize the states of the nodes to how they were when the user last ran the application. You can set the opened or closed state of a node using the `setIsOpen()` method. The method requires that you provide a reference to the node to open or close it and a Boolean indicating whether to open (`true`) or close (`false`) the node.

```
ctrDirectory.setIsOpen(oPhotos, true);
```

Optionally, you can also specify a third parameter indicating whether to animate the opening or closing of the node. A value of `true` will cause the node to animate open or closed whereas a value of `false` or `undefined` (specifying no value) will cause the node to immediately jump to the opened or closed state:

```
ctrDirectory.setIsOpen(oPhotos, true, true);
```

You can also get the current opened or closed status of a node with the `getIsOpen()` method:

```
trace(ctrDirectory.getIsOpen(oPhotos));
```

Using Custom Icons

You can assign a custom icon for each tree node if you don't want to use the default icons. Use the `setIcon()` method to set the icon for a node. The method requires at least two parameters—the node and the symbol linkage identifier for the icon to use.

```
ctrDirectory.setIcon(oNode, "TreeNodeIconSymbol");
```

If the node is a branching node, you can also specify a second symbol linkage identifier to use when the node is in the opened state.

```
ctrDirectory.setIcon(oNode, "ClosedIconSymbol", "OpenIconSymbol");
```

Removing Items

You can remove items from a `Tree` instance with one of three methods. The `removeTreeNode()` method removes a node given a node reference as the parameters:

```
ctrDirectory.removeTreeNode(oNode);
```

The `removeTreeNodeAt()` method removes a node at a given index:

```
ctrDirectory.removeTreeNodeAt(2);
```

The `removeAll()` method removes all nodes:

```
ctrDirectory.removeAll();
```

As with adding nodes, you can remove nodes from other nodes as well. For example:

```
ctrDirectory.getTreeNodeAt(0).removeTreeNodeAt(0);
```

Scrolling Tree Instances

You can programmatically control the scrolling of a `Tree` instance in several ways. First, as with `List` component instances, you can set the horizontal and vertical scrolling policies using the `hScrollPolicy` and `vScrollPolicy` properties.

You can horizontally scroll a `Tree` instance with the `hPosition` property. See the discussion of the `hPosition` for `List` for more details.

In order to vertically scroll a `Tree` instance, use the `firstVisibleNode` property. The node value assigned to the `firstVisibleNode` property is the first node visible at the top of the `Tree` instance.

Handling Tree Events

`Tree` components dispatch the `change`, `scroll`, `itemRollOver`, and `itemRollOut` events just as with `List` components. In addition, `Tree` components dispatch the following events:

- ✦ **nodeOpen:** Dispatched when a user opens a node
- ✦ **nodeClose:** Dispatched when a user closes a node

The `change`, `nodeOpen`, and `nodeClose` `Event` objects contain a `node` property that references the node that caused the event to dispatch.

We'd like to know what you thought about this chapter. Visit `www.flashsupport.com/feedback` to fill out an online form with your comments.

Summary

The Flash MX 2004 v2 UI components provide many prebuilt controls. You can control the component instances extensively with the APIs, enabling you to provide a rich user interface to your Flash applications.

- ✦ You can find the UI components in the Components panel. Create instances at authoring time by dragging them from the Components panel onto the stage. Or add the components to your library, and create the instances programmatically.
- ✦ The v2 components (which includes all the components discussed in this chapter) are all built on the same architecture. This means that they share many of the same properties, methods, and events.
- ✦ Listener objects are objects that can handle events dispatched by components.
- ✦ In addition to the shared API, each component type includes its own collection of properties, methods, and events that allows you to programmatically control instances.

✦ ✦ ✦

CHAPTER 29

UI Component Style and Focus Management

✦ ✦ ✦ ✦

In This Chapter

Understanding component styles

Applying styles globally

Applying styles to classes of components

Applying styles to instances directly or with style objects

Controlling the tab order of components

Setting and getting focus with FocusManager

✦ ✦ ✦ ✦

In Chapter 28, you learned about the basics of working with the v2 UI components — from creating instances to programmatically configuring and controlling those instances. This chapter looks at two additional related themes. First, you'll look at setting styles for components in your application. Then you'll examine how to manage focus with components.

Working with Component Styles

Similar to nested Movie Clips, the v2 component instance's style exists in a tree-like structure, whereby child styles can override the parent or group styles that they belong to. You can set v2 component styles in the following ways:

- ✦ Set a style for the component instance.
- ✦ Create a style object and apply it to one or more component instances.
- ✦ Create a style object that applies to an entire component class and all its instances.
- ✦ Set a global style that applies to all component instances.

Because you can apply styles in so many places simultaneously, but have only one style applied at a time to any given instance, Flash uses the following rules to determine which style to apply:

1. Flash looks for a style applied to the component instance. If the particular style type is defined explicitly for the component instance, Flash uses that value and doesn't continue looking for that particular style anywhere else. For example, if the `color` style is defined for a `Button` instance, Flash uses the color value defined for that instance.
2. Flash next looks for styles defined by a style object that has been applied to the instance. If a style is found in the style object, that value is used. For example, if the same `Button` instance from Step 1 does not have the `fontFamily` style defined for the

instance, it will next look to the style object for the instance, if one is defined. If that style object has a `fontFamily` style defined, that value is used for the component instance.

3. If a particular style is not defined for the component instance or the style object assigned to the instance, Flash next looks to see whether a style object has been defined for the component instance's class. If so, and if the style is defined for the class's style object, that value is used by the component instance. For example, if the `Button` class style object has been defined, and `fontSize` style has not been set for either the instance or the instance's style object for a `Button` component instance, Flash uses the value defined in the `Button` class style object.

4. The last place that Flash looks for style values is in the global style object. If a style is not defined anywhere else, Flash uses the global style value.

Introducing UI Component Styles

Each of the UI components accepts a different grouping of styles. Tables 29-1 and 29-2 list the components and the styles they accept. Table 29-3 explains the supported styles in detail.

Table 29-1: Supported Styles for Standard UI Components

Style	cbt	cch	ccb	clbl	cl	cns	cpb	crb	csp	cta	cti	cw
alternatingRowColors			✓		✓							
backgroundColor			✓		✓							
borderColor			✓		✓							
borderStyle			✓		✓							✓
color	✓	✓	✓	✓	✓	✓	✓	✓		✓	✓	
defaultIcon			✓		✓							
disabledColor	✓	✓	✓			✓	✓	✓				
embedFonts										✓	✓	
fontFamily	✓	✓	✓	✓	✓	✓	✓	✓		✓	✓	
fontSize	✓	✓	✓	✓	✓	✓	✓	✓		✓	✓	
fontStyle	✓	✓	✓	✓	✓	✓	✓	✓		✓	✓	
fontWeight	✓	✓	✓	✓	✓	✓	✓			✓	✓	
openDuration			✓									
openEasing			✓									
rollOverColor			✓		✓							
selectionColor			✓		✓							
selectionDisabledColor			✓		✓							
selectionDuration			✓		✓							
selectionEasing			✓		✓							
textAlign			✓	✓	✓	✓				✓	✓	

Style	cbt	cch	ccb	clbl	cl	cns	cpb	crb	csp	cta	cti	cw
textDecoration		✓	✓	✓	✓	✓	✓			✓	✓	
textRollOverColor			✓		✓							
textSelectedColor			✓		✓							
ThemeColor	✓	✓	✓		✓	✓	✓	✓	✓			✓
UseRollOver			✓		✓							

Here's the key to the column headers in Table 29-1:

Abbreviation	*Component*
cbt	Button
cch	CheckBox
ccb	ComboBox
clbl	Label
cl	List
cns	NumericStepper
cpb	ProgressBar
crb	RadioButton
csp	ScrollPane
cta	TextArea
cti	TextInput
cw	Window

Table 29-2: Supported Styles for Professional UI Components

Style	cdc	cdf	cm	cmb	ctr	cdg	ca	cac
alternatingRowColors			✓	✓	✓	✓		
backgroundColor	✓	✓						✓
BorderColor		✓						✓
BorderStyle		✓						✓
buttonStyleDeclaration							✓	
Color	✓	✓	✓	✓	✓	✓	✓	✓
DisabledColor	✓	✓	✓	✓	✓	✓	✓	✓
EmbedFonts								

Continued

Table 29-2 *(continued)*

Style	cdc	cdf	cm	cmb	ctr	cdg	ca	cac
FontFamily	✓	✓	✓	✓	✓	✓	✓	✓
FontSize		✓	✓	✓	✓	✓	✓	✓
FontStyle	✓	✓	✓	✓	✓	✓	✓	✓
FontWeight		✓	✓	✓	✓	✓	✓	✓
HeaderHeight								✓
messageStyleDeclaration							✓	
OpenDuration					✓			✓
OpenEasing								✓
RollOverColor	✓	✓	✓	✓	✓	✓		
selectionColor			✓	✓	✓	✓		
selectionDisabledColor					✓	✓		
selectionDuration					✓	✓		
selectionEasing					✓	✓		
TextAlign		✓	✓	✓	✓	✓		
textDecoration	✓	✓	✓	✓	✓	✓	✓	✓
textRollOverColor					✓	✓		
textSelectedColor					✓	✓		
ThemeColor	✓	✓	✓	✓	✓	✓	✓	✓
titleStyleDeclaration							✓	
UseRollOver					✓	✓		

Here's the key to the column headers for Table 29-2:

Abbreviation	*Component*
cdc	DateChooser
cdf	DateField
cm	Menu
cmb	MenuBar
ctr	Tree
cdg	DataGrid
ca	Alert
cac	Accordion

Table 29-3: Descriptions of Supported Styles

Style	*Description*
alternatingRowColors	An array of two or more numeric or predefined string values indicating the colors for the rows in a List instance or other components that have a nested list (such as ComboBox and Tree).
backgroundColor	The color used for the background of the component.
BorderColor	The color of the component's border. If the border is 3D, this value is used to color the portion that defaults to black. If the border is 2D, this value is used for the colored portion of the border (as opposed to the shaded portion).
BorderStyle	Can be inset (component appears to be recessed), outset (component appears embossed), solid (single, solid line), or none.
Color	The color of the text.
DefaultIcon	The linkage identifier to use as the default icon in a list or another component that uses a nested list.
DisabledColor	The color for text when it is within a disabled selection or when the component is disabled.
EmbedFonts	The name of the font symbol linkage identifier to embed.
FontFamily	The name of the font family to use (for example, _serif, Arial, Courier, Courier New, and so on).
FontSize	The point size for the font.
FontStyle	Can be normal or italic.
FontWeight	Can be normal or bold.
OpenDuration	The number of milliseconds for an item with subelements to open.
OpenEasing	A reference to one of the easing methods defined within the mx.transitions.easing package of classes. The classes include Back, Bounce, Elastic, Regular, and Strong. Each class has the following methods: easeIn, easeOut, and easeInOut. There is also a None class with an easeNone method. A complete example of a possible openEasing style values is mx.transitions.easing.Bounce.easeInOut.
RollOverColor	The color of a row's highlight when the mouse rolls over it.
selectionColor	The color of a selected row.
selectionDisabledColor	The color of an item that is disabled.
selectionDuration	The number of milliseconds for a selection's highlight to appear or disappear.
selectionEasing	A reference to one of the easing methods. The options are the same as those for openEasing.
TextAlign	Can be right, left, or center.
textDecoration	Can be normal or underline.

Continued

Table 29-3 *(continued)*

Style	*Description*
textRollOverColor	The color of text when the mouse is over it.
textSelectedColor	The color of text when it is selected.
ThemeColor	The color of the theme applied to the entire component. Some aspects of a themeColor setting can be overwritten by other styles.
UseRollOver	Can be true or false. If it's true, mousing over a selection highlights it. If it's false, no highlighting appears when a selection is moused over.
buttonStyleDeclaration	A style object for the nested button within an Alert instance.
titleStyleDeclaration	A style object for the title within an Alert instance.
messageStyleDeclaration	A style object for the message within an Alert instance.

Working with Colors

Several styles assign color values to particular parts of component instances. Some examples are color, borderColor, backgroundColor, themeColor, disabledColor, rollOverColor, selectionColor, and selectionDisabledColor. When you assign values to these styles, you have several options:

✦ **Use a numeric value.** Typically for colors, you use hexadecimal representation, although it is not required. For example, to assign a red color to one of the styles you can use the value 0xFF0000.

✦ **Use one of the predefined color strings.** These color strings are shown in Table 29-4, and they work only with component styles (meaning you cannot use these values for Color objects, for example).

✦ **Use other options.** For the themeColor style you can also use one of these three additional string values: haloGreen, haloBlue, and haloOrange.

Table 29-4: Style Color String Values

Color String	*Numeric Value*
Black	0x000000
Blue	0x0000FF
Cyan	0x00FFFF
Green	0x00FF00
Magenta	0xFF00FF
Red	0xFF0000
White	0xFFFFFF
Yellow	0xFFFF00

Setting Instance Styles

You can set the styles for a component instance using the setStyle() method directly from the instance. This is most appropriate when you want to make changes to the styles for a single instance when the styles for that instance should appear differently from other component instances in the application. For example, if you want to set the textDecoration style for just one List instance, you can accomplish that by calling setStyle() from that instance.

The setStyle() method requires two parameters — the name of the style as a string and the value for that style. For example, the following code sets the value for the color style of a component instance named clData:

```
clData.setStyle("color", "red");
```

Although you can call the setStyle() method on an instance multiple times in order to set multiple styles, typically you will find it is a better approach to use a style object, as discussed in the next section.

Setting Instance Styles with a Style Object

A style object is an instance of the mx.styles.CSSStyleDeclaration class. You can use a style object to create a set of styles that can be applied to multiple instances. In addition to the benefit of being able to apply a style object to multiple component instances, there is the additional benefit of being able to assign the style values as properties of the style object rather than having to repeatedly use setStyle().

The first step when working with a style object it to instantiate it. The object must be assigned as a new property of the _global.styles object. Here's an example that creates a new style object named customStyle:

```
_global.styles.customStyle = new mx.styles.CSSStyleDecalaration();
```

The name used for the custom style object in the preceding example (customStyle) is not a reserved word with special meaning in Flash. You could just as well call the object styleForComponents, formOneStyle, and so on.

If you are going to create multiple style objects in your application, you might also find it convenient to first import the CSSStyleDeclaration class. Then you don't have to use the fully qualified class name (that is, mx.styles.CSSStyleDeclaration) each time you create a new style object. For example:

```
import mx.styles.CSSStyleDeclaration;
_global.styles.customStyle = new CSSStyleDeclaration();
```

Once you've defined the style object, you can assign styles as properties. For example:

```
_global.styles.customStyle.color = "red";
_global.styles.customStyle.fontFamily = "_serif";
_global.styles.customStyle.textDecoration = "italic";
```

The remaining step is to then apply that style object to one or more component instances. You can achieve this by calling setStyle() from the instances and setting a style named styleName so that its value matches the name of the new style object.

```
clData.setStyle("styleName", "customStyle");
```

Setting Class Styles

You can create a style object on the `_global.styles` object such that the style object's name matches the class name for one of the UI components, and all instances of that class will automatically apply the style object settings. For example, if you create a `_global.styles.Button` style object, all `Button` component instances automatically apply those style settings. Here's an example:

```
import mx.styles.CSSStyleDeclaration;
_global.styles.Button = new CSSStyleDeclaration();
_global.styles.Button.setStyle("color", "red");
```

With the preceding example, all `Button` instances automatically have red text (unless instance styles or styles applied to the instance with a style object override that setting). You'll notice that the `setStyle()` method is used to assign the style value. You can also use the property syntax such as:

```
_global.styles.Button.color = 0xFF0000;
```

However, nested items within the component instance will not inherit the styles this way, unless you use `setStyle()`. This won't show up in a `Button` component, necessarily, but you'll see it with other types of components such as, for example, `ComboBox` instances. The `ComboBox` drop-down is a nested `List` component. If you assign the color style value for a `ComboBox` style class using property syntax, you'll see that the items in the drop-down do not inherit the value. But if you use `setStyle()`, the items are colored appropriately.

The technique of creating a class style object will work with almost all of the component classes. However, the following classes will not allow you to set a class style object: `List`, `DataGrid`, `Tree`, and `Menu`. With some of those classes, setting a class style object simply has no effect. With others, setting a class style object actually breaks all instances of the component. Instead, you can set a class style for all the aforementioned classes (as a group) by assigning style values to the `_global.styles.ScrollSelectList` style object. The `ScrollSelectList` style object already exists, and so you should not reinstantiate it. Instead, just assign the new values to the appropriate styles. For example:

```
_global.styles.ScrollSelectList.setStyle("color", "red");
```

The preceding code causes the text color to change to red for all `List`, `DataGrid`, `Tree`, and `Menu` instances.

Setting Global Styles

You can apply styles globally such that all component instances will apply the same styles (unless overridden by class style objects, style objects applied to the instances, or styles applied to the instances directly). The global style object is already instantiated for you, and it is accessible as `_global.style`.

Notice that the global style object is named in the singular form, style, and not the plural form, styles. The `_global.styles` object is a container for class and custom style objects as detailed in the preceding sections. The global style object, `_global.style`, is different, so be careful to make sure you are using the correct object references because the difference of a single "s" will cause unexpected results.

The `_global.style` object is a `CSSStyleDeclaration` instance on which you can set the style properties just like any other style object with which you've worked thus far. For example:

```
_global.style.setStyle("color", "red");
```

Setting the global color style to red causes all components to display with red text. Applying style settings to the global style object is a good way to create a uniform, styled appearance in your application.

Practicing Applying Styles

In this exercise, you create a simple form using a few of the standard UI components. You then use ActionScript to apply style changes to the components — some global, some as a class style object, some as a custom style object applied to a component instance, and one directly on a component instance.

1. Open a new Flash document and save it as `applyingStyles001.fla`.
2. Open the Components panel, and drag one instance each of the following components onto the stage: `ComboBox`, `List`, and `Button`. Name these instances `ccbRegion`, `clProducts`, and `cbtSubmit`, respectively.
3. Drag two instances of the `Label` component onto the stage, naming them `clblRegion` and `clblProducts`.
4. Arrange the instances on the stage as shown in Figure 29-1, with `clblRegion` matching up with `ccbRegion`, and `clblProducts` matching up with `clProducts`.

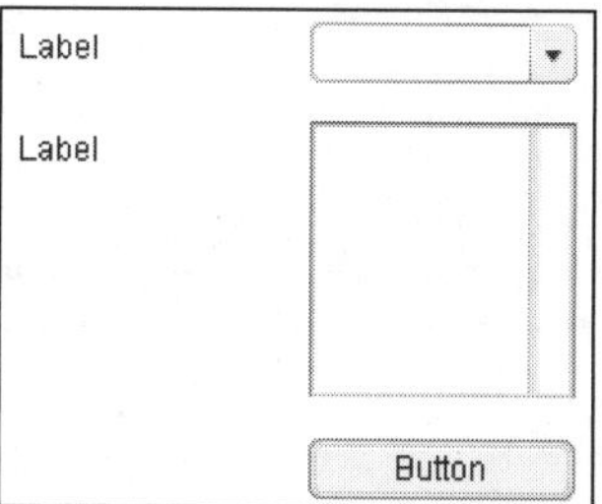

Figure 29-1: The arrangement of the component instances on the stage

5. Rename the default layer to Form, and add a new layer named Actions.
6. Add the following ActionScript code to the first frame of the Actions layer:

```
import mx.styles.CSSStyleDeclaration;
import mx.transitions.easing.Back;
_global.style.setStyle("color", 0xED5A0C);
_global.style.setStyle("themeColor", "haloOrange");
_global.style.setStyle("textSelectedColor", 0x9C3C07);
_global.style.setStyle("textRollOverColor", 0xC54A0A);
_global.styles.Label = new CSSStyleDeclaration();
_global.styles.Label.setStyle("color", "red");
_global.styles.openStyle = new CSSStyleDeclaration();
```

```
_global.styles.openStyle.setStyle("openEasing", Back.easeInOut);
_global.styles.openStyle.setStyle("openDuration", 2000);
ccbRegion.setStyle("styleName", "openStyle");
cbtSubmit.setStyle("themeColor", 0xFDFCCA);
ccbRegion.dataProvider = [{label: "North", data:1}, ↵
{label:"South", data: 2}, {label:"East", data: 3}, ↵
{label:"West", data: 4}];v
clProducts.dataProvider = [{label: "Flash", data: "f"}, ↵
{label: "Dreamweaver", data: "dw"}, {label: "Fireworks", ↵
data: "fw"}, {label: "ColdFusion", data: "cf"}];
clblRegion.text = "Region:";
clblProducts.text = "Products:";
cbtSubmit.label = "Submit";
```

7. Test the movie. The form should look something like Figure 29-2. When you open and close the `ComboBox`, you should notice that it takes two seconds and that it does a slight bounce.

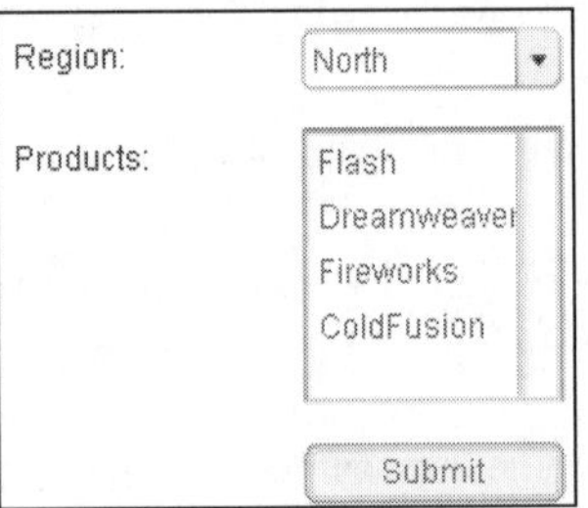

Figure 29-2: The form when testing the movie

Let's take a closer look at the code.

First, you import some of the classes you are going to use so you don't have to use the fully qualified names within the rest of the code. This just makes the code easier to read and can save some typing in the long run.

```
import mx.styles.CSSStyleDeclaration;
import mx.transitions.easing.Back;
```

Next, you set some global styles. You set the global color to a light orange, the theme color to `haloOrange`, the selected color to a dark orange, and the rollover color to a medium orange.

```
_global.style.setStyle("color", 0xED5A0C);
_global.style.setStyle("themeColor", "haloOrange");
_global.style.setStyle("textSelectedColor", 0x9C3C07);
_global.style.setStyle("textRollOverColor", 0xC54A0A);
```

Then you create a class style object for the `Label` class. You set the color style to red for all `Label` instances. Because the class styles override global styles, all the `Label` instances have red text instead of orange text.

```
_global.styles.Label = new CSSStyleDeclaration();
_global.styles.Label.setStyle("color", "red");
```

Next, you create a custom style object named openStyle, and define the open easing and open duration values for it. Then you apply that custom style object to the ccbRegion ComboBox instance:

```
_global.styles.openStyle = new CSSStyleDeclaration();
_global.styles.openStyle.setStyle("openEasing", Back.easeInOut);
_global.styles.openStyle.setStyle("openDuration", 2000);
ccbRegion.setStyle("styleName", "openStyle");
```

You then set the theme color for the Button instance to be yellow instead of using the haloOrange theme color. Because this style is applied directly to the instance, it will override the global setting:

```
cbtSubmit.setStyle("themeColor", 0xFDFCCA);
```

Subsequently, you simply populate the form with values.

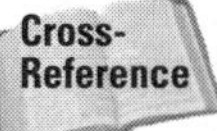

If you have questions about this part of the code, you might want to refer to Chapter 28, which discusses each of the components in detail, including how to set their properties.

```
ccbRegion.dataProvider = [{label: "North", data:1}, ⮐
{label:"South", data: 2}, {label:"East", data: 3}, ⮐
{label:"West", data: 4}];
clProducts.dataProvider = [{label: "Flash", data: "f"}, ⮐
{label: "Dreamweaver", data: "dw"}, {label: "Fireworks", ⮐
data: "fw"}, {label: "ColdFusion", data: "cf"}];
clblRegion.text = "Region:";
clblProducts.text = "Products:";
cbtSubmit.label = "Submit";
```

Managing Focus

When you use the UI components to create forms in your application, one of the things you'll want to be able to do is manage the focus using ActionScript. There are two basic things you want to be able to accomplish:

- ✦ Controlling the order in which focus changes between component instances when the users press the Tab key
- ✦ Setting the focus programmatically

The FocusManager class helps you to accomplish both of these tasks. The FocusManager class also assists you in handling keyboard events for the entire form. For example, you can define a Button instance that serves as the default button for the form. Therefore, if the users press the Enter key at any point, the Button instance will dispatch a click event.

Creating a FocusManager Instance

As long as you have added at least one UI component to your Flash application either at authoring time or at runtime, Flash automatically creates an instance of the FocusManager class for you on _root. That means that you should not need to instantiate your own FocusManager object. The name of the auto-generated object is focusManager, the same name as the class, but with a lowercase "f" at the beginning.

Assigning Tab Order

Standard desktop and HTML Web applications enable users to shift focus between form controls by pressing the Tab key. The same functionality is available in applications developed using Flash MX 2004. It is remarkably simple to achieve as well. Each component instance has a `tabIndex` property. You can set the numeric index value for each component instance that determines the order in which they will receive focus when the users press the Tab key. If you don't want a particular instance to be able to receive focus, simply don't set a `tabIndex` property value for that instance. Here's an example in which the `tabIndex` properties for several component instances are assigned:

```
clProducts.tabIndex = 1;
ccbRegion.tabIndex = 2;
cbtSubmit.tabIndex = 3;
```

In the preceding example, if focus is brought to the `clProducts` instance and the user presses the Tab key, the focus will next move to the `ccbRegion` instance. If the user presses the Tab key again, the focus shifts to the `cbtSubmit` instances. Subsequent Tab key presses will cycle through the three component instances again. You should also note that the indices need not necessarily be contiguous. The following example achieves the same effect as the preceding code, assuming no other components have been assigned `tabIndex` values between the values assigned as follows:

```
clProducts.tabIndex = 6;
ccbRegion.tabIndex = 20;
cbtSubmit.tabIndex = 37;
```

Tip Whereas the Tab key moves focus to the next component instance, pressing Shift+Tab moves focus to the previous instance.

The `FocusManager` class will automatically take care of managing the changes in focus as long as you have set the `tabIndex` for the component instances. The `FocusManager` class is fairly responsive to changes that occur within the application. For example, the user might use the Tab key to shift focus between component instances and then decide to use the mouse to bring focus to another component instance. The `FocusManager` class knows to then use that new component instance's `tabIndex` value as the current value. That ensures that when the user next presses the Tab key, the focus will shift to the component that is next in sequence, and that it will not jump out of order. Additionally, if a component instance's `visible` property is set to `false`, the `FocusManager` class will skip over that instance.

If you want to get the value of the next index to which focus will be given, you can access it with the `nextTabIndex` property of the `FocusManager` instance:

```
trace(focusManager.nextTabIndex);
```

Setting Focus Programmatically

You can also set the focus programmatically by calling the `setFocus()` method from any component instance. Doing so will automatically bring focus to the instance from which the method is called. It will also tell the `FocusManager` instance to update its current index to the `tabIndex` for the component instance from which `setFocus()` was called. One important point to note is that `setFocus()` does *not* bring a focus indicator around the component to which focus is given. The focus indicator appears around a component instance only when focus is shifted to it by the Tab key.

```
cbtSubmit.setFocus();
```

You can also get a reference to the instance with focus by calling the `getFocus()` method from any component instance:

```
trace(cbtSubmit.getFocus());
```

The `FocusManager` class also has `setFocus()` and `getFocus()` methods, and at times you might find that working with these methods is more appropriate than calling the `setFocus()` and `getFocus()` methods from the component instances directly. The `getFocus()` method doesn't require any parameters whether invoked from a component instance or from a `FocusManager` instance. The `setFocus()` method, however, requires a parameter when invoked from a `FocusManager` instance (although not when invoked from a component instance). The reason is that obviously the `setFocus()` method, when invoked from a `FocusManager` instance, needs to know to which component instance you want to bring focus. Therefore, when you call `setFocus()` from the `focusManager` object, pass it a reference to the component to which you want to shift focus.

```
focusManager.setFocus(cbtSubmit);
```

Setting Default Buttons

Another nice feature of the `FocusManager` class is that it enables you to define a `Button` instance that will handle any Enter key presses while the user is filling out a form. This allows the user to fill out some or all of the form and then submit the form without having to actually click the button or bring focus to the button by tabbing to it. This is a feature of standard HTML forms that `FocusManager` enables within your Flash forms as well. In order to define a default button, you need only to assign a reference to that button to the `defaultPushButton` property of the `FocusManager` instance. For example:

```
focusManager.defaultPushButton = cbtSubmit;
```

Once you've assigned the default `Button` instance, that `Button` instance dispatches a click event to all of its listener objects when the user presses the Enter key. The effect is the same as if the user had clicked the button.

You can disable a default button by setting the `defaultPushButtonEnabled` property of the `FocusManager` instance to `false`. This is useful when you want to enable the button only after the user has, for example, filled out required information. You can re-enable the default button by then setting `defaultPushButtonEnabled` to `true`.

You can programmatically send a command from the `FocusManager` instance to the default button, telling the button to dispatch a click event. In order to achieve that you can call the `sendDefaultPushButtonEvent()` method from the `FocusManager` instance.

We'd like to know what you thought about this chapter. Visit `www.flashsupport.com/feedback` to fill out an online form with your comments.

Summary

In this chapter, you learned about working with components styles as well as managing focus with components. Some of the details from this chapter include:

- The components come with a set of predefined styles that allow you to programmatically change the appearance of the instances on the stage.
- You can assign component styles in four ways: globally, to the component class, with a style object, or directly to the instance.
- You can manage focus of component instances using the FocusManager class. An instance named `focusManager` is automatically created for you when you use a component.
- With FocusManager, you can set a default `Button` instance for the application.

✦ ✦ ✦

Creating Your Own Components

✦ ✦ ✦ ✦

In This Chapter

Learning about the benefits of components

Understanding the anatomy of a basic component

Creating components that utilize the v2 architecture

Dispatching events and handling styles

Making your own Slider control component

✦ ✦ ✦ ✦

Components are a powerful part of Flash MX 2004, providing many benefits, including:

✦ **Simplicity:** Simple interfaces make them accessible to programmers and nonprogrammers alike.

✦ **Extensibility:** This means you can build upon existing components to create new and more complex/specified types.

✦ **Reusability:** Rather than reinventing the proverbial wheel with each application, you can simply drag and drop components.

✦ **Encapsulation:** All the code is hidden from view, saving you from having to hassle with the how's and wherefores of a component.

In this chapter, you learn how to create your own custom components, both from scratch and by building upon the existing v2 component architecture.

Understanding Component Anatomy

Components are, simply put, fancy Movie Clips. That is, of course, somewhat of an oversimplification, but it is accurate in its essence and should help you to understand that components need not be overwhelming. With this in mind, let's take a look at the parts that make up a very basic component:

✦ **An ActionScript 2.0 class:** The class must extend `MovieClip` either directly or indirectly.

✦ **A MovieClip symbol:** Each component must have a Movie Clip symbol with which to associate the class:

- The `MovieClip` symbol must be set to `Export` for ActionScript, have a linkage identifier, and must have the fully qualified class named specified within the AS 2.0 Class field of the Linkage settings.
- The `MovieClip` symbol must have a component definition. The class must be specified in the component definition as well as in the linkage settings.

In order to create a very basic component, follow these steps:

1. Create the component's `MovieClip` symbol as well as any additional `MovieClip` symbols that contain elements used within the component. For example, in this chapter, you create a `Slider` control component. That component has one main `MovieClip` symbol as well as two additional `MovieClip` symbols that contain the artwork for the thumb bar and the slider track.

2. Add the instances of the additional `MovieClip` symbols within the main Movie Clip. For example, the main `Slider` symbol contains an instance of the `Slider_thumbbar` symbol and an instance of the `SliderTrack` symbol.

3. Create a new ActionScript 2.0 class for the component. The class should define all the functionality for the component. You'll take a closer look at this step in the exercises in this chapter.

4. Set all of the necessary `MovieClip` symbols to export for ActionScript. This should always include the main component `MovieClip` symbol. Other symbols might not need to be set to export depending on whether you add them to the component during runtime or authoring time.

5. Within the linkage settings for the main component `MovieClip` symbol, assign it the corresponding ActionScript 2.0 class in the AS2.0 Class field. The name should be the fully qualified name of the class.

6. Set the ActionScript 2.0 class in the Component Definition settings as well. The value in the Component Definition settings' AS 2.0 Class field should match the value in the Linkage settings AS2.0 Class field.

7. Export the SWC file. The SWC file is a compiled and distributable version of your component. It provides several benefits when you are working with components. First, it zips up all the necessary component elements into a single file. Second, because it is precompiled, it makes the movie export faster when the component is used within another Flash document.

Don't worry if any of those steps sound unfamiliar to you. The next section clarifies all these steps with an exercise in which you create a custom component.

Making Your First Component

In this section, you create a new UI component from scratch. You'll notice that in the basic set of components there is no component that provides the slider control functionality. So now is your chance to create such a component. Throughout the rest of the chapter, you build upon this foundation as you learn how to create more and more sophisticated components.

1. Create a new directory on your computer called SliderComponents. Because there will be several versions of the component, save them in several nested directories within SliderComponents.

2. Create a new directory within SliderComponents. Name the directory SliderV1.

3. Within SliderV1, create a directory called com. This directory is used as part of the ActionScript 2.0 class package.

4. Within the com directory, create a new directory named asb. Again, this directory is used as part of the package for the ActionScript 2.0 class.
5. Open `Slider_starter.fla` from the CD-ROM. The file contains the basic artwork to get you started. Save the file to the SliderV1 directory as `Slider.fla`.
6. Create a new `MovieClip` symbol named `Slider`. This will be the main component `MovieClip` symbol.
7. Open the `Slider` `MovieClip` symbol in editing mode.
8. Rename the default layer Track and create a new layer named `Thumbbar`.
9. Drag an instance of `SliderTrack` onto the stage on the `Track` layer. Name the instance `mcTrack`.
10. Using the Property inspector, move `mcTrack` to 8,8.
11. Drag an instance of `SliderThumbbar` onto the stage on the `Thumbbar` layer. Name the instance `mcThumbbar`.
12. Using the Property inspector, move `mcThumbbar` to 0,0.
13. Open a new ActionScript file in order to write the ActionScript 2.0 class. If you are using Flash MX Professional 2004, you can open a new ActionScript file in the Flash application. Otherwise, you will need to open a new (plain) text document in your favorite editor.
14. Add the following code to the new ActionScript file:

```
// Declare the class with the name Slider. The class is in
// the com.asb package. The class should extend MovieClip.
class com.asb.Slider extends MovieClip {

  // Declare private members for the two MovieClip objects
  // in the Slider Movie Clip symbol. This is so that the
  // ActionScript interpreter will know about these
  // variables when you reference them within the class.
  private var mcThumbbar:MovieClip;
  private var mcTrack:MovieClip;

  // Define a private member to store the current value of
  // the slider. The range is from 0 to 100. Initialize it
  // to 0.
  private var _nValue:Number = 0;

  // Define a private member in which to store an interval
  // ID.
  private var _nInterval:Number;

  // Define a constructor. The constructor is
  // automatically called when a new instance of the
  // component is created.
  function Slider() {
```

```
    // Have the constructor call the init() method.
    init();
  }

  public function init():Void {

    // Define some custom properties for the mcThumbbar
    // MovieClip object that define the range over which
    // the thumb bar can be dragged. The range should be
    // a straight line that aligns to the line in mcTrack.
    mcThumbbar.minX = mcTrack._x;
    mcThumbbar.minY = mcTrack._y;
    mcThumbbar.maxX = mcTrack._x + mcTrack._width;
    mcThumbbar.maxY = mcTrack._y;

    // Define onPress() and onRelease() methods for the
    // mcThumbbar MovieClip object.
    mcThumbbar.onPress = function() {

      // When the user presses on the object make it
      // draggable within the specified range.
      this.startDrag(false, this.minX, this.minY, ⮐
this.maxX, this.maxY);

      // Set an interval by which the updateValue() method
      // is called.
      this._parent._nInterval = setInterval(this._parent, ⮐
"updateValue", 100);
    };
    mcThumbbar.onRelease = function() {

      // When the user releases the thumb bar, tell Flash
      // to stop dragging it.
      this.stopDrag();

      // Clear the interval so that the updateValue()
      // method is not called needlessly. And then call
      // the updateValue() method one more time just in
      // case the value changed just as the thumb bar was
      // released and the value hadn't yet updated.
      clearInterval(this._parent._nInterval);
      updateValue();
    };

    // In case the thumb bar is released while the mouse is
    // not over it, make sure it performs the same actions
    // as if it is released while the mouse is over it.
    mcThumbbar.onReleaseOutside = mcThumbbar.onRelease;
  }
```

```
    // Define a getter method so that _nValue is publicly
    // accessible as a property named value.
    public function get value():Number {
      return _nValue;
    }


    // The updateValue() method is called on an interval as
    // long as the thumb bar is pressed. It simply updates
    // _nValue to reflect the current x coordinate of the
    // thumb bar.
    private function updateValue():Void {
      _nValue = mcThumbbar._x - mcTrack._x;
    }
  }
```

15. Save the ActionScript file as `Slider.as`. You should save the file to the com/asb directory that you created in Steps 3 and 4.
16. Return to `Slider.fla` and open the library.
17. Select the `Slider MovieClip` symbol and open the Linkage properties (see Figure 30-1).
18. Select the Export for ActionScript box.
19. For the linkage identifier enter the name `Slider`.
20. In the AS 2.0 Class field, enter the fully qualified name of the `Slider` class: `com.asb.Slider`.
21. Click the OK button in the Linkage Properties dialog box.

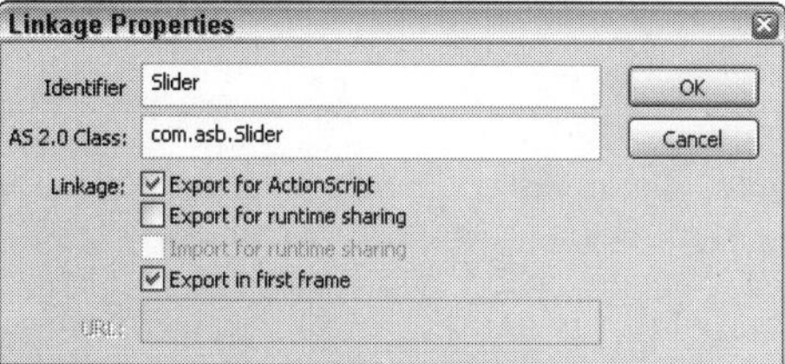

Figure 30-1: Setting the linkage properties for the Slider Movie Clip symbol

22. Open the Component Definition dialog box for the `Slider MovieClip` symbol. You can access the dialog box from the symbol's shortcut menu (right-click/⌘-click) or by choosing that option from the library menu.
23. Within the Component Definition dialog box, enter the fully qualified class name in the AS 2.0 Class field. The value is `com.asb.Slider`.
24. Click the OK button in the Component Definition dialog box.

25. Right-click/⌘-click the `Slider MovieClip` symbol in the library, and then choose Export SWC File from the menu options that appear.

26. Save the SWC file as `Slider.swc` within the Components/UI Components directory of Flash's local settings (on Windows, that is a directory such as C:\Documents and Settings*user name*\Local Settings\Application Data\Macromedia\Flash MX 2004\en\Configuration\Components\UI Components).

27. Open a new Flash document.

28. Open the Components panel and choose the reload option from the Components panel menu.

29. The `Slider` component should appear in the UI Components listing. Select the component and drag an instance onto the stage. Name the instance `cslVolume`.

30. Add a new layer named `Actions`.

31. Add the following code to the first frame of the `Actions` layer.

```
cslVolume.onEnterFrame = function():Void {
  trace(this.value);
};
```

    The preceding code simply demonstrates that the value property of the `Slider` instance reports an updated value repeatedly.

32. Test the movie. You should see the value from the `Slider` instance displayed in the Output panel. As you drag the thumb bar, you will see the value change.

Congratulations are definitely in order. You have just created your first component! Obviously, there are still some ways in which you can build upon the `Slider` component from this section. In subsequent exercises throughout this chapter, you'll be doing just that.

Dispatching Events

One of the things you'll likely want to be able to do with components is have them dispatch events. For example, with the `Slider` component, it would be particularly useful if it would dispatch an event each time the value changes. That way you don't have to continually poll it to get the value, but you can add a listener that is alerted when the value changes. That is just one of a plethora of scenarios in which you are likely to want to have a component dispatch events.

You can configure a component class to dispatch events fairly simply using the `EventDispatcher` class. The `EventDispatcher` class is in the `mx.events` package, and it has a static method called `initialize()` that configures a class to dispatch events. All you need to do is to call the `initialize()` method from within the component class's `init()` method and pass it a value of `this`. For example:

```
private function init():Void {
  super.init();
  mx.events.EventDispatcher.initialize(this);
}
```

With that one piece of code, the class automatically inherits all the necessary properties and methods to be able to accept listeners and dispatch events to those listeners.

Once the class is configured for dispatching events, you can dispatch an event from any other method using the `dispatchEvent()` method that it automatically inherits. The `dispatchEvent()` method takes a single parameter — an object with the necessary event properties such as `type` and `target`. When called, the method then dispatches that object to all listeners:

```
dispatchEvent({type: "change", target: this});
```

Working with Component Metadata

Flash MX 2004 allows you to specify some special component metadata tags in your external ActionScript 2.0 component classes. The metadata is used by Flash during authoring time to allow for different types of interaction between the component instance and the Flash authoring environment. There are seven metadata keywords: `Inspectable`, `InspectableList`, `Event`, `Bindable`, `ChangeEvent`, `ComponentTask`, and `IconFile`. Of those seven, this chapter takes a closer look at three of them — `Inspectable`, `InspectableList`, and `Event`. The remaining tags are outside the scope of this book.

Metadata tags allow you to specify special information about your ActionScript class files. That information can then be interpreted by Flash to provide some additional functionality within the authoring environment.

Understanding Metadata Tag Use

The metadata tags are always enclosed in square brackets, and they should never be followed by a semicolon. For example:

```
[Inspectable]
```

In some cases the metadata tags can accept some additional parameterized data called *attributes*. In those cases, the extra data should be enclosed in parentheses following the metadata tag name. For example:

```
[Inspectable(defaultValue="red")]
```

Metadata tags are bound to the next line of ActionScript code. Different tags should be bound to different class elements. For example, as you'll see, `InspectableList` metadata tags should be bound to the class itself. Other metadata tags should be bound to class members. You look at some specific examples in the next few sections.

Using Inspectable

The `Inspectable` metadata tag tells Flash that a particular class member should be included in the parameters list within the Component Inspector panel. This is very important if you want users to be able to configure the component instances without having to use the ActionScript API.

You can associate an `Inspectable` tag with a public property or a public getter or setter method by placing the tag on the line just preceding the member declaration. Here is a very simple example:

```
[Inspectable]
public var value:Number;
```

In the preceding example, the parameter named `value` will show up in the Component Inspector parameters list.

More often than not, you want to specify some attributes for an `Inspectable` tag. The following list explains the more commonly used attributes for the `Inspectable` tag:

✦ **name:** By default, Flash displays the property name in the parameters list. If you want to specify a custom display name, you can do so with the `name` attribute.

✦ **type:** Specifies the data type for the parameter. By default, Flash assumes the data type of the property that is being made inspectable.

✦ **defaultValue:** The default value to use.

✦ **enumeration:** A list of possible values for the parameter.

Using InspectableList

The `InspectableList` tag allows you to list a subset of all the possible inspectable properties that you want to actually display to the user in the Component Inspector panel. The use of this tag might not be readily obvious. After all, why would you mark some properties as inspectable only to then remove them from the list of displayed parameters? The key to remember is that some component classes extend other components. In such a case, you might not necessarily want to display all the inspectable properties from the superclass for instances of the subclass. Therefore, you can use `InspectableList` to indicate which parameters to display so that not all the inherited inspectable properties are included. The `InspectableList` tag requires that you specify a list of the property names that should be included. For example:

```
[InspectableList("value","velocity")]
```

The `InspectableList` tag should be associated with the class itself, so you should place it on the line preceding the class declaration:

```
[InspectableList("wingspan","velocity")]
class Bird {
```

Using IconFile

The `IconFile` tag tells Flash what image file it should use to display next to the component in the Component panel and in the library as well. Without the `IconFile` tag, Flash uses the default component icon.

The image must follow these specifications:

✦ Must be saved in PNG format.

✦ Must be 18 by 18 pixels.

✦ Must be saved in the same directory as the FLA in which the component symbol is saved. When you export the SWC file, Flash will look for the image in that directory.

The IconFile tag should be associated with the class. Here is an example:

```
[IconFile("bird.png")]
class Bird {
```

Practicing Making an Event Dispatching Component

In this exercise, you'll build upon the Slider component you created in the previous exercise. You will add event dispatching functionality to the component. And additionally, you can add a custom icon to the component.

1. Make a copy of the SliderV1 directory and all its contents. Name the new directory SliderV2.
2. Open Slider.as (make sure to open the SliderV2./com/asb version).
3. Modify the code in Slider.as as follows (changes appear in bold):

```
[IconFile("slider.png")]
class com.asb.Slider extends MovieClip {

  private var mcThumbbar:MovieClip;
  private var mcTrack:MovieClip;
  private var _nValue:Number = 0;
  private var _nInterval:Number;

  // Declare the dispatchEvent() method as a member of the
  // class.
  private var dispatchEvent:Function;

  function Slider() {
    init();
  }

  public function init():Void {

    // Initialize the class so it can dispatch events.
    mx.events.EventDispatcher.initialize(this);

    mcThumbbar.minX = mcTrack._x;
    mcThumbbar.minY = mcTrack._y;
    mcThumbbar.maxX = mcTrack._x + mcTrack._width;
    mcThumbbar.maxY = mcTrack._y;
    mcThumbbar.onPress = function() {
      this.startDrag(false, this.minX, this.minY, this.maxX,
this.maxY);
      this._parent._nInterval = setInterval(this._parent,
"updateValue", 100);
    };
```

```
    mcThumbbar.onRelease = function() {
      this.stopDrag();
      clearInterval(this._parent._nInterval);
      updateValue();
    };
    mcThumbbar.onReleaseOutside = mcThumbbar.onRelease;
  }

  public function get value():Number {
    return _nValue;
  }

  private function updateValue():Void {

    // Assign the new value based on the position of
    // the thumb bar.
    var newValue:Number = mcThumbbar._x - mcTrack._x;

    // Check to make sure the new value is different from
    // the previous value. If so then assign the new value
    // to the _nValue property and then dispatch an event
    // to all listeners.
    if(newValue != _nValue) {
      _nValue = newValue;
      dispatchEvent({type:"change", target:this});
    }
  }

}
```

4. Save `Slider.as`.
5. Open `Slider.fla` from within the SliderV2 directory.
6. Open the `SliderThumbbar` `MovieClip` symbol in editing mode.
7. Choose File ➪ Export ➪ Export Image.
8. In the Export Movie dialog box, browse to the directory in which you have saved the FLA file, and save the image as `Slider.png` (make sure you have selected PNG as the Save as type).
9. Next, the Export PNG dialog box appears. Make sure that the settings are as follows (also shown in Figure 30-2):
   - **Dimensions:** 18 pixels by 18 pixels
   - **Resolution:** 72 dpi
   - **Include:** Minimum Image Area
   - **Colors:** 24 bit with alpha channel
   - **Filter:** None
   - **Interlaced:** Unchecked

- **Smooth:** Checked
- **Dither solid colors:** Unchecked

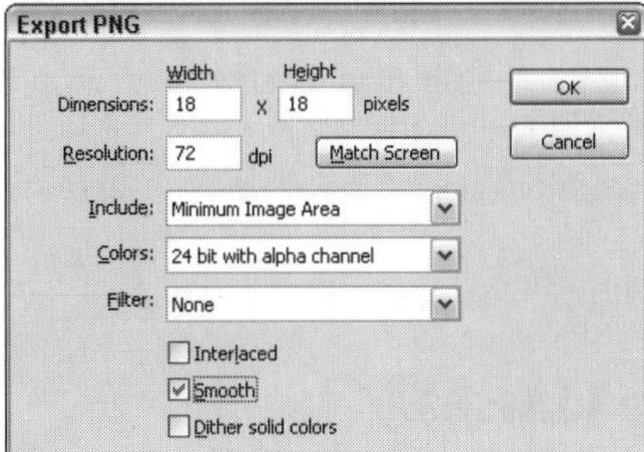

Figure 30-2: The settings for exporting the PNG file

10. Click the OK button.
11. From the `Slider.fla` library, export the SWC file from the `Slider` `MovieClip` symbol. Save the SWC file so that it overwrites the version of `Slider.swc` you exported in the last exercise.
12. Open a new Flash document.
13. Reload the Components panel.
14. Drag an instance of `Slider` from the Components panel onto the stage of the new Flash document. Name the new instance `cslVolume`.
15. With the instance selected on the stage, open the Component Inspector panel.
16. Rename the default layer `Slider`, and add a new layer named `Actions`.
17. Add the following code to the first frame of the `Actions` layer in order to add a `listener` object to the component instance.

```
var oListener:Object = new Object();
oListener.change = function(oEvent:Object):Void {
  trace(oEvent.target.value);
};
cslVolume.addEventListener("change", oListener);
```

18. Test the movie.

Building Components Based on the v2 UI Architecture

One of the features in Flash MX 2004 is the v2 UI component architecture. The architecture consists of a set of classes that ship with the product, enabling some extra functionality such as style management and focus management.

In order to utilize some or all of the features of the v2 UI component architecture, you need to do several things:

- ✦ Write your ActionScript 2.0 class so that it extends one of the core UI component classes—namely `UIObject` or `UIComponent`. The `UIObject` class is the base class for all of the built-in UI components. The `UIComponent` class extends `UIObject`, providing some additional functionality. Descriptions of the functionality included in these classes are provided in Chapter 28, "Using V2 Components."
- ✦ Define the component's `MovieClip` symbol in such a way that it adheres to the v2 UI component specification.

The next sections take a closer look at both of these points.

Extending v2 Architecture Classes

This book, for simplicity, describes only the scenario in which you create a component that extends `UIComponent`, rather than differentiating between extending `UIObject` or `UIComponent`. When you create a class that extends `UIComponent`, there are several considerations:

- ✦ **The class must, rather obviously, be declared to extend the UIComponent class.** `UIComponent` is in the `mx.core` package.
- ✦ **The constructor for the class should be empty.**
- ✦ **All initialization code should be placed within a method named init().** The `init()` method will be invoked automatically when the component instance is created.
- ✦ **The class can have its own implementations of any of the UIComponent methods (which includes init()).** However, in almost every case, the method should also call the same method in the superclass (on the first line of code within the method). Table 30-1 lists some of the most important and common methods defined in `UIComponent` (some of which are inherited from `UIObject`) and what they do/when they are called.

Table 30-1: Some Standard UI Component Methods

Method Name	*Description*
`createChildren`	This method is automatically called when the component is created, and this is where you should place any code that creates nested components or `MovieClip` or `TextField` objects.
`Draw`	This method is automatically called each time the component is drawn or redrawn. This is where you should place any code that has to do with drawing or layout.
`Init`	The `init()` method is called when the component is first created, and it is where you should initialize any properties.
`Move`	This method is called when the component is moved.
`Size`	This method is called when the component is resized.

Creating v2 Component Movie Clip Symbols

The other important step in creating components that extend the v2 UI component architecture is properly constructing the main component `MovieClip` symbol. All such `MovieClip` symbols should have the following characteristics:

- The timeline should have two frames. Everything in frame 1 is automatically displayed in the component when it is used in an application. Frame 2 is for placing instances of any additional `MovieClip` symbols that you want to have included in the SWC. It is important that you add these instances to the main component symbol or else Flash will not know to export them as part of the SWC.
- The first frame of the timeline should have a stop() action.
- The first frame of the timeline should have only one graphical element. You should place an instance of a rectangular Movie Clip on frame 1 and give it a name such as `mcBoundingBox`. This instance serves two purposes. First, if the SWC for the component is used while live preview is turned off, the instance will be what displays on the stage during authoring time. Second, the shape of the instance is what determines the visible area of the automatically generated live preview. In other words, it is used as a mask.
- All artwork and nested elements must be added at runtime within the code of the ActionScript class that corresponds to the component.
- As with any component symbols, the symbol should be set to export and the AS 2.0 Class field in both the Linkage settings and the Component Definition settings should be assigned the value of the fully qualified class name for the corresponding ActionScript class.

Practicing Making a v2 Architecture Component

In this exercise, you'll modify the `Slider` component from the previous exercise so that it uses the v2 framework. You'll modify it in the following ways:

- Define the class so that it extends `UIComponent`. This will also require restructuring the `MovieClip` symbol so that it can generate the live preview.
- Dispatch events when the value changes.
- Add a component icon.
- Define an `inspectable` parameter so that you can modify the way in which the slider is aligned (vertically or horizontally) via the Component Inspector panel.

With those objectives in mind, you can go ahead and get started:

1. Make a copy of the SliderV2 directory and all its contents. Name the new directory SliderV3.
2. Open `Slider.fla` from within the SliderV3 directory.
3. Edit the `Slider MovieClip` symbol.
4. Add two new layers to the Slider timeline. Name the layers `Actions` and `Bounding Box`.

5. On the first frame of the Actions layer, add the following line of code:

```
stop();
```

6. Select the Rectangle tool. Choose black for the outline color and white for the fill color.

7. On the first frame of the Bounding Box layer, draw a square that is 108 pixels by 108 pixels.

8. Select the square (including both the outline and the fill) and convert it into a MovieClip symbol. Name the symbol BoundingBox.

9. When you created the symbol from the artwork on the stage, the original artwork instance was converted into an instance of the new MovieClip symbol. Give that instance the name mcBoundingBox in the Property inspector.

10. The SliderThumbbar and SliderTrack instances already placed on the stage should be moved to frame 2. To do this, highlight frame 1 on the Thumbbar and Track layers. Then, drag the frames over to frame 2. Your timeline should now look like Figure 30-3. Additionally, the instances of SliderThumbbar and SliderTrack no longer need to be named. You are including them in the timeline of the Slider symbol only in order to make sure that they export in the SWC. Therefore, although it won't hurt to keep the instances named, to avoid confusion later, remove the instance names from the SliderThumbbar and SliderTrack instances.

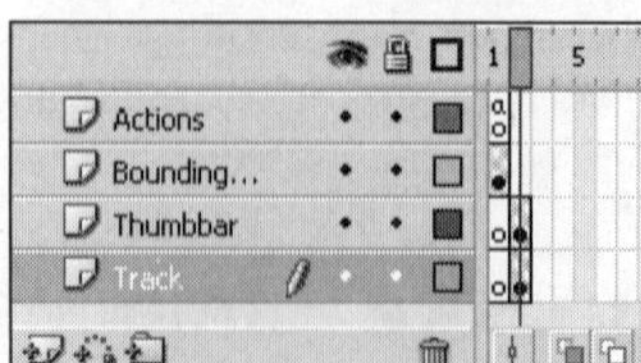

Figure 30-3: The Slider MovieClip timeline

11. Set the SliderThumbbar and SliderTrack symbols to export for ActionScript. Define their linkage identifiers as SliderThumbbar and SliderTrack, respectively.

12. Open Slider.as (make sure to open the SliderV3/com/asb version).

13. Modify the code in Slider.as as follows (changes appear in bold):

```
import mx.core.UIComponent;

[IconFile("slider.png")]
class com.asb.Slider extends UIComponent {

  private var mcThumbbar:MovieClip;
  private var mcTrack:MovieClip;
  private var _nValue:Number = 0;
  private var _nInterval:Number;
  private var dispatchEvent:Function;

  // Declare the mcBoundingBox instance as a member of the
  // class so that you can reference it.
  private var mcBoundingBox:MovieClip;
```

```
function Slider() {
  init();
}

public function init():Void {

  // Call the UIComponent class's init() method.
  super.init();

  mx.events.EventDispatcher.initialize(this);

  // The remaining code has been moved to the createChildren()
  // method.

}

// The createChildren() method is automatically called
// when the component is instantiated. You should place
// all the code that creates new nested MovieClip and
// component instances within the component.
private function createChildren():Void {

  // Add the instances of the track and thumb bar asset
  // Movie Clip symbols to the component. In the first
  // version you had added these instances during
  // authoring time. However, when you use the v2
  // architecture, you must add all instances with code.
  attachMovie("SliderTrack", "mcTrack", getNextHighestDepth(),
          {_x: 8, _y: 8});
  attachMovie("SliderThumbbar", "mcThumbbar",
       getNextHighestDepth(), {_x: 8, _y: 8});

  // This code was previously in init().
  mcThumbbar.minX = mcTrack._x;
  mcThumbbar.minY = mcTrack._y;
  mcThumbbar.maxX = mcTrack._x + mcTrack._width;
  mcThumbbar.maxY = mcTrack._y;

  // Set the _x property of the thumb bar to reflect the value
  // of the slider.
  mcThumbbar._x = _nValue + mcTrack._x;

  // This code was previously in init();
  mcThumbbar.onPress = function() {
    this.startDrag(false, this.minX, this.minY, this.maxX,
        this.maxY);
    this._parent._nInterval = setInterval(this._parent,
        "updateValue", 100);
  };
```

```
    mcThumbbar.onRelease = function() {
      this.stopDrag();
      clearInterval(this._parent._nInterval);
      updateValue();
    };
    mcThumbbar.onReleaseOutside = mcThumbbar.onRelease;
  }

  // The draw() method is automatically called each time
  // the component draws itself. That occurs when the
  // component is first instantiated as well as when the
  // invalidate() or redraw() methods have been called for
  // the component. The draw() method should call the
  // draw() method of the superclass, set the bounding
  // box to be invisible, and then rotate the track as
  // appropriate depending on the alignment setting.
  private function draw():Void {
    super.draw();
    mcBoundingBox._visible = false;
  }



  [Inspectable(defaultValue=0)]
  public function get value():Number {
    return _nValue;
  }

  // The setter method for value assigns the new value to
  // the _nValue property and also moves the thumb bar instance
  // accordingly for the live preview.
  public function set value(nValue:Number):Void {
    mcThumbbar._x = nValue + mcTrack._x;
    _nValue = nValue;
  }

  private function updateValue():Void {
    var newValue:Number = mcThumbbar._x - mcTrack._x;
    if(newValue != _nValue) {
      _nValue = newValue;
      dispatchEvent({type:"change", target:this});
    }
  }

}
```

14. Save `Slider.as` and return to `Slider.fla`.

15. From the `Slider.fla` library, export the SWC file from the `Slider MovieClip` symbol. Save the SWC file so that it overwrites the version of `Slider.swc` you exported in the last exercise. You might want to test the movie before exporting the SWC file just to make sure it is working.

16. Open a new Flash document.

17. Reload the Components panel.

18. Drag an instance of `Slider` from the Components panel onto the stage of the new Flash document. Name the new instance `cslVolume`.

19. With the instance selected on the stage, open the Component Inspector panel.

20. Set the value parameter to 50 via the Component Inspector panel. You should see the thumb bar update to reflect the new value.

21. Rename the default layer `Slider`, and add a new layer named `Actions`.

22. Add the following code to the first frame of the `Actions` layer in order to add a `listener` object to the component instance.

```
var oListener:Object = new Object();
oListener.change = function(oEvent:Object):Void {
  trace(oEvent.target.value);
};
cslVolume.addEventListener("change", oListener);
```

23. Test the movie.

When you drag the slider thumb bar now, you should see the current value appear in the Output panel each time it changes.

Working with Styles

You can allow your components to utilize styles as do the built-in v2 components. In order to initialize your component class to be able to retrieve styles, you need to add the following line of code to the `init()` method:

```
mx.core.ext.UIComponentExtensions.Extensions()
```

The preceding line of code configures the class so that it will recognize the `setStyle()` and `getStyle()` methods. It also enables instances of the class to inherit styles from the global or class style object.

Once you've initialized the class to be able to work with styles, you then have to apply the styles when and where appropriate. If you use any nested components, those components will automatically inherit the styles for which they are configured. For example, if you use a `Button` component instance as an element of your custom component, the `Button` instance will automatically inherit the styles that are applied globally, to the custom component class, or directly to the component instance. On the other hand, if you want to apply styles to other noncomponent elements of your component, you'll need to use the `getStyle()` method to retrieve the style value and apply it appropriately. For example, if you have a nested `MovieClip` object that you want to change color to correspond to the value of the color style, you need to do the following:

1. Create a `Color` object that targets the `MovieClip` instance.

2. Get the color style value using `getColor()`.

3. Use that value as the parameter to `setRGB()` in order to apply the color to the `MovieClip` instance.

Practicing Working with Styles

You've already created a fairly robust `Slider` component by this point. In order to configure the component so that it can easily match the styles of the other component instances in an application, however, you can enable style handling in the `Slider` component with some additional steps outlined as follows.

1. Make a copy of the SliderV3 directory and name it SliderV4.
2. Open the `Slider.fla` document in the SliderV4 directory.
3. Delete the `SliderThumbbar` symbol from the library.
4. Open the `Slider` component symbol in edit mode.
5. Click the second frame of the `Thumbbar` layer where the `SliderThumbbar` instance used to be. Drag an instance of the `Button` component from the Components panel onto the stage. You don't need to worry about placement or resizing or any of that. Remember, you'll be attaching the instance using ActionScript. You are placing the `Button` instance on the second frame only so that the button component will export in the SWC file.
6. Open the `Slider.as` file in SliderV4/com/asb.
7. Modify the code as shown. Changes are in bold.

```
import mx.core.UIComponent;

import mx.core.ext.UIComponentExtensions;
import mx.controls.Button;

[IconFile("slider.png")]
class com.asb.Slider extends UIComponent {

  private var cbtThumbbar:Button;
  private var mcTrack:MovieClip;
  private var _nValue:Number = 0;
  private var _nInterval:Number;

  private var dispatchEvent:Function;

  private var mcBoundingBox:MovieClip;

  function Slider() {
    init();
  }

  public function init():Void {

    super.init();

    mx.events.EventDispatcher.initialize(this);
```

```
  // Call the Extensions() method to set up style
  // handling.
  UIComponentExtensions.Extensions();

}

private function createChildren():Void {

  attachMovie("SliderTrack", "mcTrack", getNextHighestDepth(),
        {_x: 8, _y: 8});

  // Create a new mx.controls.Button instance named
  // cbtThumbbar. Size it to 16 by 16. You'll also
  // notice that we've gotten rid of the assignment of
  // the onPress() and onRelease() methods because you
  // cannot (should not) assign those methods to Button
  // component instances.
  createObject("Button", "cbtThumbbar", getNextHighestDepth());
  cbtThumbbar.setSize(16, 16);
}

// The onMouseDown() and onMouseUp() methods replace the
// onPress() and onRelease() methods that had been
// previously assigned to the nested MovieClip object.
private function onMouseDown() {

  // Check to make sure the mouse is over cbtThumbbar,
  // and not over another part of the component.
  if(cbtThumbbar.hitTest(this._parent._xmouse,
         this._parent._ymouse, false)) {
    _nInterval = setInterval(this, "moveThumbbar", 75);
  }
}

private function onMouseUp() {
  clearInterval(_nInterval);
}

// The moveThumbbar() method is called on an interval as
// long as the mouse is pressed over the thumb bar.
private function moveThumbbar():Void {

  // Move the thumb bar to follow the mouse. Make sure
  // that it doesn't move past 0 or 100.
  cbtThumbbar._x = _xmouse - cbtThumbbar.width/2;
  if(cbtThumbbar._x > 100) {
    cbtThumbbar._x = 100;
  }
  else if(cbtThumbbar._x < 0) {
    cbtThumbbar._x = 0;
  }
```

```
    // Call updateValue() to update the value and call
    // updateAfterEvent() to update the display.
    updateValue();
    updateAfterEvent();
  }


  // The draw() method is automatically called each time
  // the component draws itself. That occurs when the
  // component is first instantiated as well as when the
  // invalidate() or redraw() methods have been called for
  // the component. The draw() method should call the
  // draw() method of the superclass, set the bounding
  // box to be invisible, and then rotate the track as
  // appropriate depending on the alignment setting.
  private function draw():Void {
    super.draw();
    mcBoundingBox._visible = false;
    var cTrack:Color = new Color(mcTrack);
    cTrack.setRGB(getStyle("color"));
  }



  [Inspectable(defaultValue=0)]
  public function get value():Number {
    return _nValue;
  }

  public function set value(nValue:Number):Void {
    cbtThumbbar._x = nValue + mcTrack._x;
    _nValue = nValue;
  }

  private function updateValue():Void {
    var newValue:Number = cbtThumbbar._x - mcTrack._x +
        cbtThumbbar._width/2;
    if(newValue != _nValue) {
      _nValue = newValue;
      dispatchEvent({type:"change", target:this});
    }
  }
```

8. Save `Slider.as` and return to `Slider.fla`.

9. Export the SWC file from the `Slider` component symbol, and save over the SWC file you exported previously. As in previous exercises, you might want to test the movie before exporting the SWC file just to ensure that your file is working.

10. Reload the Components panel.

11. Create a new FLA file.

12. Drag an instance of the `Slider` component from the Components panel onto the stage.

13. Rename the default layer `Slider` and create a new layer named `Actions`.

14. Add the following code to the first frame of the `Actions` layer:

```
_global.style.setStyle("themeColor", "haloOrange");
_global.style.setStyle("color", 0xDB9F17);
```

15. Test the movie. The slider's track and the rollover colors should be orange.

We'd like to know what you thought about this chapter. Visit `www.flashsupport.com/feedback` to fill out an online form with your comments.

Summary

In this chapter, you learned about writing custom components. You learned not only about component basics but about creating components that extend the v2 UI component architecture. Some of the key points include:

✦ Components are subclasses of the `MovieClip` class, either directly or indirectly.

✦ Component classes must be defined in external AS files and then associated with a `MovieClip` symbol.

✦ To build a component that utilizes the v2 UI component architecture, the class should extend `UIObject` or `UIComponent`, either directly or indirectly.

✦ You can dispatch events from your custom components by first initializing the class to do so.

✦ Component metadata can tell the Flash application about the component. Metadata can provide information about parameters to display, component icons, and more.

✦ You can configure your component to accept and inherit styles.

✦ ✦ ✦

P A R T

Working with Flash in Other Environments

✦ ✦ ✦ ✦

In This Part

✦ ✦ ✦ ✦

Working with Flash in the Web Browser

In This Chapter

Examining the HTML used to add Flash movies to pages

Communicating to JavaScript using the getURL() method

Detecting Flash Player versions

This chapter looks at Flash movies embedded in HTML pages. There are several things you'll look at in detail. First of all, it is important to familiarize yourself with the HTML required to add a Flash movie to an HTML page. Once you understand that, you'll next take a look at how you can communicate from Flash to JavaScript in the browser, and vice versa. And then you'll look at how to detect the Flash Player.

Caution JavaScript has been at the center of much controversy for some time because of the lack of standardization. Although the EMCA stepped in and created a specification for the language, the two major competitors – Netscape and Microsoft (Internet Explorer) – have yet to reconcile their differences. The result is inconsistent support for JavaScript across platforms and browsers. Most notably, Internet Explorer for Macintosh and Netscape 6 on both platforms raise a lot of problems for different reasons. That said, this chapter presents as much information about the possibilities and limitations as possible so you can design your projects with confidence.

Understanding Flash and HTML

When you publish your Flash applications you have the option to publish the HTML pages as well. In order to do this, open the Publish Settings dialog box by choosing File ➪ Publish Settings. Then, make sure that you check the HTML option on the Formats tab. Figure 31-1 shows the Publish Settings dialog box with the HTML tag selected. (The HTML tag shows up after you have checked the HTML option in the Formats tab.) Notice the Detect Flash Version check box under the Template box, too. This option is discussed later in the chapter.

Using one of the templates to publish an HTML file can be a time-saver when you're getting started, or it might be all you need. In the majority of Flash targeted for the Web, publishing with the standard Flash Only template works well as is. Sometimes, you might need to communicate with the Flash Player, so you'll read about this process later in this chapter when you read about the `FSCommand` template. In other cases, you might need to customize or extend the template's output — for example, changing the generated HTML code to match the look and feel of your site. Or perhaps the page in which the Flash movie is going to play needs to be dynamically generated by a ColdFusion page or a PHP page. No matter what your reasons for wanting to modify or copy and paste from the generated HTML, it is a good idea to familiarize yourself with the HTML necessary to add a Flash movie to a Web page.

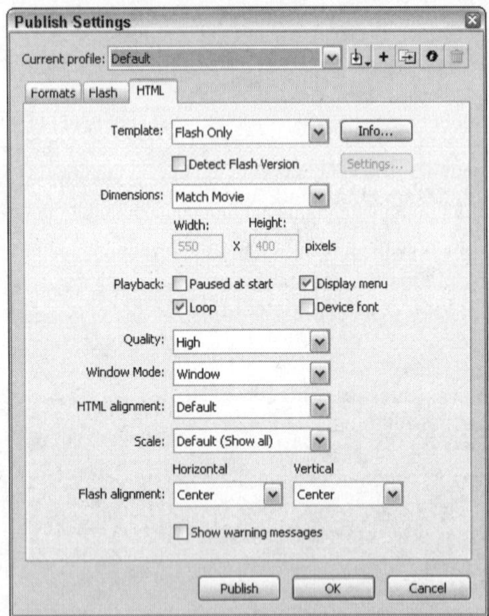

Figure 31-1: The HTML settings in the Publish Settings dialog box

If you use the Flash Only template to publish an HTML page and open the HTML code in a text editor, you will see something that looks like the following:

```
<!DOCTYPE html PUBLIC "-//W3C//DTD XHTML 1.0 Transitional//EN" ⮐
"http://www.w3.org/TR/xhtml1/DTD/xhtml1-transitional.dtd">
<html xmlns="http://www.w3.org/1999/xhtml" xml:lang="en" lang="en">
<head>
<meta http-equiv="Content-Type" content="text/html; charset=iso-8859-1" />
<title>publishTest</title>
</head>
<body bgcolor="#ffffff">
<!--url's used in the movie-->
<!--text used in the movie-->
<object classid="clsid:d27cdb6e-ae6d-11cf-96b8-444553540000" ⮐
codebase="http://download.macromedia.com/pub/shockwave/cabs/flash/swflash.⮐
cab#version=7,0,0,0" width="550" height="400" id="movieName" align="middle">
<param name="allowScriptAccess" value="sameDomain" />
<param name="movie" value="movieName.swf" />
<param name="quality" value="high" />
<param name="bgcolor" value="#ffffff" />
<embed src="movieName.swf" quality="high" bgcolor="#ffffff" width="550" ⮐
height="400" name="movieName" align="middle" allowScriptAccess="sameDomain" ⮐
```

```
type="application/x-shockwave-flash" ⮐
pluginspage="http://www.macromedia.com/go/getflashplayer" />
</object>
</body>
</html>
```

Of that code, the part responsible for actually adding the Flash movie to the page is the following:

```
<object classid="clsid:d27cdb6e-ae6d-11cf-96b8-444553540000" ⮐
codebase="http://download.macromedia.com/pub/shockwave/cabs/flash/swflash.⮐
cab#version=7,0,0,0" width="550" height="400" id="movieName" align="middle">
<param name="allowScriptAccess" value="sameDomain" />
<param name="movie" value="movieName.swf" />
<param name="quality" value="high" />
<param name="bgcolor" value="#ffffff" />
<embed src="movieName.swf" quality="high" bgcolor="#ffffff" width="550" ⮐
height="400" name="movieName" align="middle" allowScriptAccess="sameDomain" ⮐
type="application/x-shockwave-flash" ⮐
pluginspage="http://www.macromedia.com/go/getflashplayer" />
</object>
```

The `<object>` tag is the tag that works with the ActiveX control that plays Flash movies in browsers such as Internet Explorer for Windows. The `<embed>` tag works for the plug-in that plays Flash movies in browsers such as Netscape. Therefore, for any changes that you make to the `<param>` tags or the attributes of the `<object>` tag, you'll need to also change the corresponding attributes of the `<embed>` tag.

Both the `<object>` and `<embed>` tags enable you to specify the width and height of the SWF file that is be scaled to fit within those dimensions. The ID is important for specific JavaScript controls that you can employ so you should generally make sure to assign an ID. And the `align` attribute specifies how the movie is aligned within the browser. The `movie` parameter/attribute is essential because it tells the browser where to find the SWF. The `quality` and `bgcolor` parameters/attributes allow you to override the settings within the SWF. If those parameters/attributes are left out, the values within the SWF are used.

The `allowScriptAccess` parameter/attribute determines the outgoing scripting access from a SWF (outgoing scripting typically meaning calls to JavaScript functions with `getURL()`). A value of `never` prevents all outgoing scripting calls. A value of `always` allows all outgoing scripting calls through. And a value of `sameDomain` allows all outgoing scripting calls to the same domain (that is, if the SWF is on the same domain as the HTML page to which the scripting calls are being made) but it disallows any cross-domain scripting calls.

If you want to add a Flash movie to a page other than the default, published HTML page, you can approach the situation in several ways:

- Memorize the HTML code and type it each time you want to add a Flash movie to a page.
- Use an HTML editor such as Dreamweaver that has a built-in function for adding the necessary code to a page.
- Save the basic code in a text file, copy and paste it into each new page, and modify it as necessary.
- Publish the HTML from Flash and then copy and paste or modify the exported code.

Passing Initialization Values to Flash from HTML

You can pass values to a Flash movie from the HTML as Flash loads using the `FlashVars` parameter/attribute of the `<object>` and `<embed>` tags. The value or values you pass to the Flash movie using `FlashVars` are only passed when the Flash movie loads. That means that even if you update the values for `FlashVars` using JavaScript or VBScript, the new, updated values are not sent to the Flash movie. `FlashVars` is basically used for initializing a Flash movie with certain values. This is a very useful technique that is helpful in many scenarios, including the following:

✦ **Specifying the values for variables within the Flash movie that may update relatively frequently.** By using `FlashVars` instead of coding the values into the movie itself, you can change the values in the HTML rather than having to change the values in the Flash file and then re-export the movie.

✦ **Setting the values that may vary from environment to environment.** For example, the `FlashVars` technique is employed with Flash Remoting (see Chapter 35) to specify the Flash Remoting gateway URL—a value that will likely change from server to server. This way you don't have to maintain different versions of the Flash movie for each environment.

✦ **Initializing a movie with values retrieved from a database recordset or other server-side resource.** If you use, for example, a ColdFusion or PHP page in which you add the Flash movie, you can do a database query and pass some of the results to a Flash movie as it loads. This technique is not intended for passing entire recordsets or large amounts of complex data to a Flash movie. Flash Remoting is a more appropriate choice for that kind of functionality. But if you want to pass certain initialization values to a Flash movie, you can do so through `FlashVars`. For example, you might pass a Flash movie a session ID.

In order to use `FlashVars` you should add a `FlashVars` `<param>` object nested within the `<object>` tag, and you should add a `FlashVars` attribute to the `<embed>` tag. The value for `FlashVars` should be in the URL encoded format. That is to say, it should contain name-value pairs in which each variable name is linked with the value by an equal sign, each name-value pair is separated by an ampersand, and all spaces or other nonalphanumeric (or underscore) characters should be escaped with their hexadecimal equivalents. For example:

```
<object classid="clsid:d27cdb6e-ae6d-11cf-96b8-444553540000" ⮐
codebase="http://download.macromedia.com/pub/shockwave/cabs/flash/swflash. ⮐
cab#version=7,0,0,0" width="550" height="400" id="usingFlashVars" ⮐
align="middle">
<param name="allowScriptAccess" value="sameDomain" />
<param name="movie" value="usingFlashVars.swf" />
<param name="quality" value="high" />
<param name="bgcolor" value="#ffffff" />
<param name="FlashVars" value="sLabel=circle&sDescription=a%20circle" />
<embed src="usingFlashVars.swf" quality="high" bgcolor="#ffffff" ⮐
width="550" height="400" name="usingFlashVars" align="middle" ⮐
allowScriptAccess="sameDomain" type="application/x-shockwave-flash" ⮐
pluginspage="http://www.macromedia.com/go/getflashplayer" ⮐
FlashVars="sLabel=circle&sDescription=a%20circle" />
</object>
```

The preceding code passes two values to the Flash movie: `sLabel` with a value of `circle` and `sDescription` with a value of `a circle`. This creates two variables on the main timeline of the Flash movie named `sLabel` and `sDescription`, and assigns them the associated values. If you want to pass Flash number or Boolean values you should, within Flash, use ActionScript to convert the values from strings to the appropriate types. For example, if you use `FlashVars` to pass a movie a variable named `nQuantity` with a number value then you should use the following code on the main timeline of your Flash movie:

```
nQuantity = parseInt(nQuantity);
```

If you want to pass your Flash movie a variable named `bIsVisible` (a Boolean value), use the following code in your Flash movie to convert the value to a Boolean:

```
bIsVisible = (bIsVisible == "true") ? true : false;
```

Calling JavaScript Functions from Flash

There are two ways you can call JavaScript functions from Flash — using `getURL()` or `fscommand()`. Typically the `getURL()` method is the preferred technique for several reasons. The primary reason is that `getURL()` has greater compatibility with browsers. The secondary reason is that it is much simpler to use the `getURL()` technique than to use the `fscommand()` technique. The following should give you an idea of compatibility of each of these techniques:

- `getURL()` works for all 5+ browsers. It works for all 3.*x* browsers except in IE3 on Windows. And it works in all 4.*x* browsers except IE 4.5 on Macintosh.
- `fscommand()` does not work with the following:
  - IE on the Macintosh
  - Netscape 6 until version 6.2 (does work in all 6.2+ versions of Netscape)
  - 68KB Macintosh (yikes!) or Windows 3.1 (double-yikes!) computers

Sending JavaScript Calls with getURL

As already mentioned, `getURL()` is compatible with more browsers and is simpler to use than `fscommand()`. In order to make a JavaScript call from Flash, all you need to do is to use the `javascript:` directive followed by the JavaScript to execute in the browser. For example:

```
this.getURL("javascript: alert('hello');");
```

When you place the preceding code on the first frame of the main timeline of your Flash file and then do a publish preview (F12), you will see a JavaScript alert window with the message `hello`.

If you have custom JavaScript functions defined within the HTML page, you can call those functions in the same manner. For example, if you have a JavaScript function named `setStatusBar()` defined within the parent HTML page, you could call it from Flash as follows:

```
this.getURL("javascript: setStatusBar('message from Flash');");
```

Ensuring Complete Browser Compatibility

Even though the `getURL()` technique using the `JavaScript:`*`functionName`*`(args)` syntax works for most browsers, it still is not supported by Internet Explorer version 4.*x* (including 4.5) on the Macintosh. However, if you must make sure that your Flash movie can communicate with the JavaScript, there is a clever workaround available.

Even though `getURL()` cannot be used to call a JavaScript function directly on version 4.*x* of IE on the Macintosh, it can still be used to open an HTML page. That includes opening an HTML page within a frame. Therefore, you can use this to create a simple workaround for the whole problem posed by IE 4.*x* on the Macintosh.

The strategy is quite simple. You will create a hidden HTML frame into which you can load various HTML pages containing the desired JavaScript that gets called when the page is loaded. This works for any platform that supports `getURL()` to open an HTML page into a frame.

In this exercise, you use this approach to create a Flash movie and the accompanying HTML pages so that when a button in the Flash movie is clicked, a new browser window with size constraints pops up.

Note In this exercise, save all the files to the same directory.

1. Open a new Flash document and save it as `launchWindow.fla` to a directory on your computer.
2. Rename the original layer `Button`, and add a new layer named Actions.
3. Open the Components panel and drag an instance of the `Button` component onto the stage on the `Button` layer. Name the new instance `cbtLauncher`.
4. On the Actions layer, add the following code to the first frame:

```
var oListener:Object = new Object();
oListener.click = function(oEvent:Object):Void {
  getURL("js_openWindow.html", "jsFrame", "post");
};
cbtLauncher.addEventListener("click", oListener);
cbtLauncher.label = "launch new window";
cbtLauncher.setSize(150, cbtLauncher.height);
```

   This causes an HTML page called `js_openWindow.html` to be loaded into an HTML frame named `jsFrame` when the `Button` component is clicked. It also, of course, sets the label for the `Button`, and resizes it to accommodate the label.

5. Next, simply make sure the publish settings are set to the default (publish an SWF and an HTML page with the Flash Only template), and publish your movie. This creates `launchWindow.swf` and `launchWindow.html`.
6. Now you need to create the additional HTML pages. First, create the frameset page. Use your favorite text/HTML editor, and create a page named `index.html`. In this document, add the code that follows in Listing 31-1.

Listing 31-1: index.html

```
<html>
  <head>
    <title>JavaScript in Frames</title>
  </head>
  <frameset rows="100%, *">
    <frame name="main" src="launchWindow.html">
    <frame name="jsFrame" src="js_blank.html">
  </frameset>
</html>
```

Notice that this creates two frame rows. The first one is 100 percent of the height of the window, so the second frame is hidden. In the first frame, you load the launchWindow.html page, which is the page you published along with your Flash movie. In the second frame named jsFrame, you load an HTML page called js_blank.html.

7. The next step is to create the js_blank.html page. This is an easy one because it really does not contain much code. The page serves only as a placeholder until another page is loaded into the frame. So create a new HTML document called js_blank.html, and place the following code into it:

   ```
   <html></html>
   ```

8. You now need to create js_openWindow.html, which gets loaded into the hidden frame when the Flash button is clicked. Create a new HTML document, and save it as js_openWindow.html. In the document, place the code from Listing 31-2.

Listing 31-2: js_openWindow.html

```
<html>
  <head>
    <SCRIPT language="javascript">
    <!--
      function openWindow(){
        window.open("message.html", "_blank", "height=100, ⮐
width=100");
      }
    -->
    </SCRIPT>
  </head>
  <body onLoad="openWindow();"></body>
</html>
```

This HTML page uses the <SCRIPT> tag to define a JavaScript function called openWindow() and then calls the function from within the <body> tag so that the function is called as the page loads into the frame.

9. Finally, you want to create the `message.html` page that gets opened in the new browser window when the `openWindow()` function is called. Create a new HTML document, and place the code from Listing 31-3 in it.

Listing 31-3: message.html

```
<html>
  <head>
    <title>message</title>
  </head>
  <body>
    welcome!
  </body>
</html>
```

10. Now test your work by opening `index.html` in a Web browser program that supports JavaScript (and Flash) and by clicking the button in the Flash movie.

Detecting the Flash Player in Web Browsers

Time and time again, one of the biggest problems that Flash developers face is making sure that viewers can actually see the content they are supposed to see. Many of the most frequently asked questions among new and veteran Flash developers is how to make sure that people will be able to see the Flash content across platforms, browsers, and versions. In the following two sections, you'll take a look at the two most sensible approaches to player detection.

Manual Player Detection

Often, it seems that companies and individuals want to make their Web sites as fully automated as possible. However, one of the original methods for detecting the Flash Player is still one of the most foolproof. A splash screen can be used to alert users as to what player version is required and to allow them to enter the site/application once they have confirmed that they do have the requested player.

Automated Player Detection

Automated player detection used to be a somewhat complicated task. However, in Flash MX 2004, Macromedia has built automated player detection into the publish settings so that you can have Flash publish all the necessary code and files. When you open the Publish Settings dialog box and choose the HTML tab, you can see a Detect Flash Version check box just underneath the Template combo box (see Figure 31-1). By default, the check box is unselected. If you select this option, you also have the option to change the settings by clicking the Settings button just to the right.

Within the Version Detection Settings dialog box, shown in Figure 31-2, notice that the required Flash version is set to the version to which you are publishing the SWF. If you are publishing to Flash Player 7, for example, then it will automatically set the required version to 7. If you want to require a major and minor revision, you have the option to enter the revision numbers up to the revision you have installed on your system.

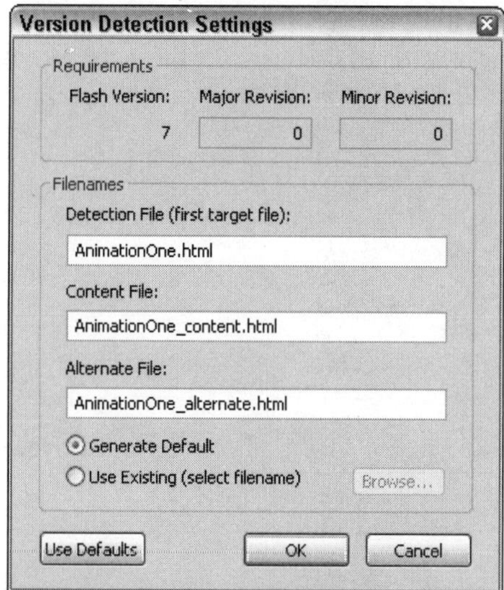

Figure 31-2: The Version Detection Settings dialog box

The detection file is the first page that a user should open. This is not the page with the actual content. Instead, it contains the detection mechanism. The content file is the page that contains the published SWF. If the necessary player is detected, the detection page automatically redirects to the content page. The alternate file is the file to which the user is automatically redirected if the required player is not detected. You can have Flash generate a default alternate page, or you can use an existing page if you want to use your own design.

When you publish, Flash creates several files. It creates the SWF (assuming you are publishing the SWF) as well as the specified HTML files. In addition, Flash exports an extra SWF file named `flash_detection.swf`. When you place your files on the Web server or otherwise distribute them, you must make sure to include all of these files, including the `flash_detection.swf` file. You should point all links to the detection file.

We'd like to know what you thought about this chapter. Visit `www.flashsupport.com/feedback` to fill out an online form with your comments.

Summary

- Flash movies are added to Web pages with the HTML `<object>` and `<embed>` tags.
- You can call JavaScript functions in the parent Web page by using the `getURL()` method in your Flash movie. When using `getURL()` to call a JavaScript function, you pass it a parameter containing the `javascript:` directive followed by the function call.
- An important but often overlooked step in working with Flash on the Web is detecting the Flash Player. Using the version detection system built into Flash MX 2004, you can easily create player-detection systems.

✦ ✦ ✦

CHAPTER 32

Making Movies Accessible and Universal

✦ ✦ ✦ ✦

In This Chapter

Understanding accessibility standards

Utilizing assistive technologies

Knowing the Accessibility panel

Using the Accessibility class

Detecting and controlling accessibility options

Making the most of your accessible movies

✦ ✦ ✦ ✦

Flash Players 6 and later offer features to make your Flash movies more accessible. There is a need to create content that people with special requirements can utilize, as the population of those with Internet access steadily increases. The Internet can be especially important for those with additional needs because it can be much easier to access information online than by other means. Getting into a car, taking public transportation, getting into a building, and so on can be challenging for people with special needs. Macromedia has incorporated accessibility into Flash movies by enabling various parts of a movie to be recognizable to screen-readers. Screen-readers generate certain text, objects, and descriptions of graphic content into spoken word, thereby enabling visually challenged users to access the content. This chapter explains how to make Flash presentations that function successfully when played in conjunction with assistive technologies.

Standardizing Accessibility Concerns

Making computers and the Internet increasingly accessible to all users has been a long-time effort by many government and industry regulatory organizations, as well as software developers. These organizations have acknowledged the challenges that face individuals with physical and cognitive disabilities, looked at what challenges exist for Web users, and then, developed guidelines and standards for the development of technologies to aid them. For example, programs integrating voice commands and text-to-speech have assisted visually challenged individuals in dealing with the navigation of their computers and the Internet.

Why is there such a need when it comes to electronic and online information? The Web, for instance, is full of content not suitably built for assistive technologies, such as images without `alt` tags, video without corresponding descriptions, improperly constructed image maps, and the like. Another problem, now of the past, was completely inaccessible Flash-driven content. Macromedia claimed Flash Player 6 to be the first "rich-media" player to be accessible to screen-readers. Given that Macromedia says that about 25 percent of Web sites include Flash content, many see this development as a giant step in the right direction.

Let's quickly look at why the development of accessible content is important and necessary in Web development.

Section 508

Section 508 is the 1998 amendment to the Workforce Rehabilitation Act of 1973 (a U.S. Federal Act). One of the requirements within it is that all electronic information produced for the U.S. federal government and agencies is to be made accessible to all individuals to the fullest extent possible. If Web sites of a federal agency are not accessible, fines, penalties, or even legal action can be taken against the agency in question. However, this does *not* apply to the private sector or private agencies that receive federal funding. Section 508 follows the guidelines of the World Wide Web Consortium (W3C) in its Web Accessibility Initiative (see the following section). The initiative was implemented for several reasons, one of which was to encourage technologies to develop Web content with Section 508 standards and guidelines in mind.

Details on Section 508 requirements are available at `www.section508.gov`.

The U.S. is not the only nation to require federal Web sites to be accessible these days. Canada and the European Union, as well as other nations, have also implemented regulations similar to Section 508 in the U.S. Therefore, companies and developers worldwide working with these sectors routinely face the issue of creating accessible Web sites. Thankfully, Flash content can be seen as a viable accessibility-minded option for Web developers.

W3C Standards

The W3C, also known as the World Wide Web Consortium, is an organization devoted to creating universal protocols for Internet development. The W3C primarily focuses on the direction of the development of the Internet, present and future technologies involved in it, and the attempt to standardize the technologies and languages within this realm.

Not only does the W3C standardize the use of HTML, CSS, XML, and other languages; it sets standards and provides guidelines for accessibility on the Internet. The W3C is involved in making sure that Web technologies (HTML, XML, CSS, and so on) are supportive of accessibility. The W3C is also involved in outreach, education, and even the development of tools to facilitate accessibility. The program involved with accessibility is called the Web Accessibility Initiative, and it includes a set of guidelines aimed at helping Web developers achieve accessible design.

You can review the current W3C Web Accessibility Initiative and its guidelines at `www.w3.org/WAI`.

Web sites can achieve accessibility in a number of ways. As a result of the varied nature of assistive technology software and/or hardware found on the computers of a user, a Web developer can expect difficulty in creating a Web site that is accessible by everyone.

Depending on how you look at it, in one way we're "fortunate" that there are strict requirements for a Flash movie to utilize accessibility. The user must have a specific combination of Web browser, screen reader software, and a compatible version of the Flash Player to view the accessible part(s) of a Flash movie. Despite this, it is still possible to note some differences among only slight variations in software. When more assistive technologies are developed to work with the Flash Player, we will have to cover many more variables and handle the unpredictable nature of this technology.

Microsoft Active Accessibility (MSAA)

Microsoft developed Microsoft Active Accessibility (MSAA) to improve the connection between assistive technology, such as software and Braille readers, and the Windows-based operating systems. MSAA standards help software developers create products for those with vision, motion, or sight disabilities. MSAA also improves the communication between accessibility software and other Windows applications.

Macromedia built MSAA technologies into Flash Players 6 and 7 to enable screen-readers that also support this technology. As such, these screen-readers can access the Flash content in Web sites. MSAA is considered a basic requisite when working with screen-readers in the Windows environment. Macromedia's adoption of MSAA signals a new era of Flash development where software developers can adhere to an already-established standard in assistive software technology.

At this time, neither Flash Player 6 nor 7 can "talk" to equivalent system-level accessibility layers of Mac OS X.

Reviewing Current Assistive Technologies

Assistive technologies are special programs that help individuals with a disability to use their computers. These programs are varied and support individuals who face various challenges. One of the most prominent challenges for some computer users is an inability to see the monitor. Some examples of software to help these users in this category are JAWS for Windows, IBM Home Page Reader, HAL, and Window-Eyes. Currently, the only screen-readers to work with Flash Player 7 are Window-Eyes and JAWS.

For the most up-to-date information on Flash Player 7's compatibility with screen-reader software, see `www.macromedia.com/macromedia/accessibility/features/flash/player.html`.

In the past, several methods were used to make a Flash movie more accessible. Some of these methods include allowing users to zoom into the movie, navigating by key-press controls, having a narrative in sync with the movie's content, navigating through pages by using Next and Back buttons as opposed to automated progression, and so on. However, this chapter focuses on the accessibility features available to ActionScript. The scope of the `Accessibility` class makes basic-to-advanced support in a movie possible for those with visual challenges. In order for a user to be able to hear your Flash movie content, at this time he or she must have screen-reader software installed.

Screen-readers are programs primarily used by the visually impaired. Individuals who can see, but still have difficulty reading text as a result of conditions such as dyslexia or aphasia, also use this technology. Screen-readers generally work in conjunction with a speech synthesizer. They provide spoken vocal output of content on the monitor, and also when input devices are used (such as when a person is typing). Screen-readers have been around for quite some time but were simply used to read text (for example, when DOS was used). Nowadays, with GUIs and multimedia Web sites, more sophisticated solutions are required.

Screen-readers are sometimes very complicated pieces of software. They are largely based on keyboard input, naturally to benefit the users. Understanding how they work, including the tabbing and key-press actions that are central to using them, can sometimes help your development in Flash. Therefore, it is a good idea to try out the software before or while you are developing your work. As mentioned earlier, there are only two products currently on the market that work with Flash Players 6 and 7. Because Macromedia is using MSAA technology, it is easier for third-party integration with the software. In time, you will probably see other MSAA-compliant screen-readers support the Player. For now, take a look at what is already available.

Window-Eyes

GW Micro makes and distributes Window-Eyes, and the company recently released the newest version of its well-known and widely used software. The current release, which includes support for Flash Players 6 and 7, is called Window-Eyes Standard or Professional 4.5. It is compatible with Windows 95, 98, 2000, 2003, Me, and XP platforms.

You can purchase a copy of Window-Eyes at `www.gwmicro.com`. A demo of Window-Eyes, which runs for 30 minutes at a time, is also available at this site. After that time period, you must reboot your computer to continue using the product.

Window-Eyes is a fairly easy program to get up and running, and to configure based on your requirements or preferences. It should begin "talking" as soon as the program is up and running. If you are installing the program to test your Flash documents exclusively, you might want to make sure that you perform a custom installation and set it up so that the program does not load on startup.

JAWS

No, it's not the action-packed thriller movie with the infamous shark, but it is a popular screen-reader for the Windows operating system. (Consequently, the splash screen for the product does feature a rather menacing-looking shark.) JAWS 5 is the latest version of the application, developed by Freedom Scientific.

You can find more information about JAWS at `www.freedomscientific.com`. A free demo version is available for download.

For both JAWS and Window-Eyes, we recommend that you use the automatic or default installation option. There are many customized options that will likely be unfamiliar. If at all possible, you should install the screen-reader on a separate computer — something other than your primary work computer. Screen-readers tie up many system resources and increase your production time.

Setting Accessibility Options

One of the main differences between the accessibility options you see in Flash compared to other options such as QuickTime and RealPlayer is that Flash enables users to navigate around your movie. Previously, with QuickTime and RealPlayer, the only option was to add captions that could be read by screen-readers. Flash Players 6 and 7 offer many options beyond captioning, as you learn throughout the rest of this chapter.

It is important to understand that only the Flash Player 6 or higher, in conjunction with ActiveX technology, supports Microsoft Active Accessibility. Therefore, the only movies readable by Window-Eyes are in an Internet Explorer browser with Flash Player 6 or higher on the Windows platform. It's also important to remember that in order to support screen-readers and MSAA, the Flash movie cannot be in the opaque or transparent windowless modes. You can control this setting in your Publish Settings and/or HTML attributes for the `<object>` tag.

Flash Players 6 and 7 can "see inside" your Flash movie and send information to the screen-reader about what is contained inside — such as buttons, Movie Clips, and text. The player also automatically sends a "load" message for the screen-reader to announce when new accessible elements are loading into the movie. When scripting the accessibility of your movie, the first and foremost task is to ensure that every possible element of your movie has an instance name. Some of the most critical elements are your buttons and input text fields within your movie because they aid in the navigation of the movie. Static text fields create their own hidden names and therefore are not of the same critical nature. However, if you want to provide a description for static text or have the text read when the cursor is over it, you must convert it to dynamic text. Screen-readers also automatically recognize dynamic text you can load into your movie. A screen-reader will also read text when a mouse cursor is hovering over it. This works the same way when you have text loaded into a `TextArea` component. So, after you take care of naming your objects with instance names, let's look at the Accessibility panel in the Flash MX 2004 authoring environment.

Exploring the Accessibility Panel

The Accessibility panel enables you to control whether your movie and the objects within it are accessible to a screen-reader. It also provides you the opportunity to assign names, descriptions, and shortcuts to these elements. Upon assigning your own names within this panel, you override the automatic labeling assigned to each object. You can also provide descriptions and shortcuts to these elements in this panel, or even turn accessibility off to objects or child objects within your movie or clips. You can find the Accessibility panel by using several methods:

✦ **The menu:** Window ➪ Other Panels ➪ Accessibility

✦ **Shortcut key:** Alt+F2 or Opt+F2

✦ **Accessibility button on the Property inspector**

The Property inspector shown in Figure 32-1 includes a shortcut button for opening the Accessibility panel. The button is a small, circular graphic in the lower-right corner.

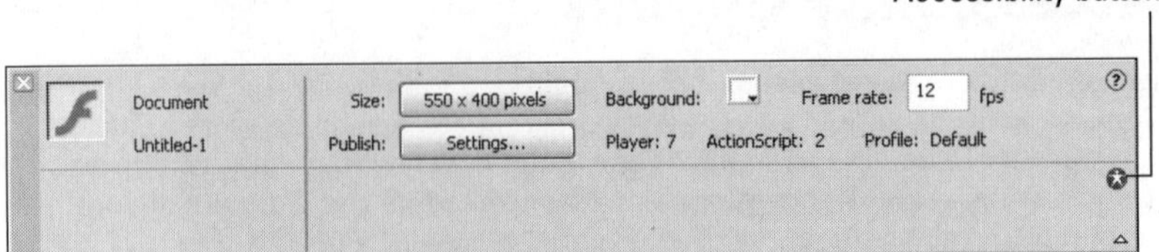

Figure 32-1: The Accessibility button is located on the Property inspector in the lower-right corner.

The following movie elements can be made accessible in Flash MX 2004. The Accessibility panel options might differ, depending on which object you are currently working on. Note that these are the options that you set on elements that you manually add to the movie's stage during authoring time.

If you are using ActionScript to dynamically create `TextField` and `MovieClip` objects, the Accessibility panel's usefulness is limited to the global options of the movie, discussed first in the following list. All of other options must be assigned to the dynamic elements in ActionScript. You learn how to access these properties later in the chapter.

✦ **Entire movie:** Global attributes of the Flash movie can be made accessible in this panel. All of these attributes are applied to the entire movie. To view and change these settings, make sure you have deselected any elements on the stage. You can press the Esc key to do this quickly. The Make Movies Accessible check box tells the screen-reader to read the description and title of the movie. The Make Child Objects Accessible option tells the screen-reader to read the object's attributes within your movie. Auto Label tells the screen-reader to take any text fields next to an object and associate them with each other. Refer to Figure 32-2 for a depiction of the Accessibility panel with these options.

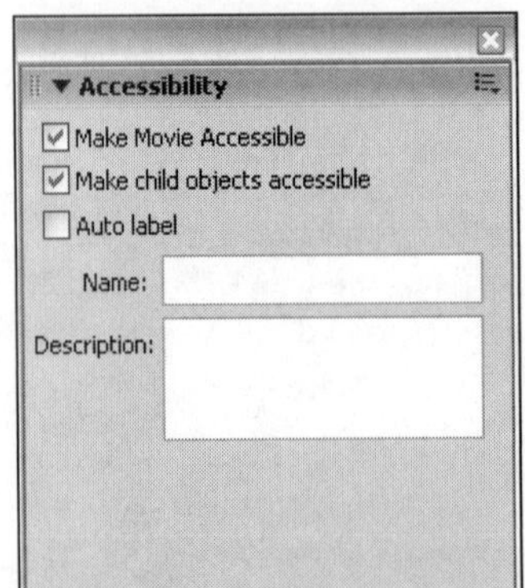

Figure 32-2: You can control global settings for the movie from the Accessibility panel.

✦ **Buttons and Input text fields:** Both of these objects are vital to properly name and describe your movie's functionality to a screen-reader user. You can make buttons accessible, and it reads the name and description. However, embedded objects are ignored in buttons. The shortcut option only announces the keystrokes you want to associate with the button. You must write ActionScript to actually capture these keystrokes within your movie. The tab index option (available only in Flash MX Professional 2004) enables you to specify the element's position in the tab order sequence for the given frame. With Input text fields, names and descriptions are critical. Figure 32-3 shows the options available in the Accessibility panel for text fields and buttons.

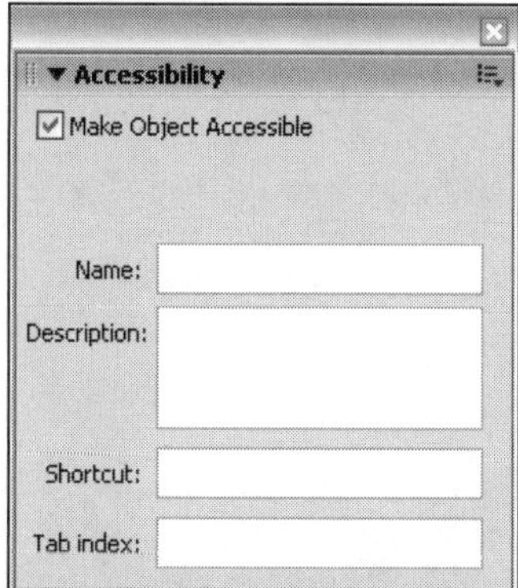

Figure 32-3: The Accessibility panel has the same options for both Button and Input text fields.

A `MovieClip` object that behaves as a button (that is, you have assigned button handlers such as `onRelease()` and `onPress()` to the instance) falls into the button category described previously.

✦ **Dynamic text fields:** These text fields can have a description added to them. This option can be useful when you want to describe static text. As you can see in Figure 32-4, only a description field and tab index field are available in the Accessibility panel for Dynamic text fields.

✦ **Movie Clip instances (or `MovieClip` objects):** Movie Clips have an extra option, and this is a check box to Make Child Objects Accessible. This option tells the screen-reader to recognize and read the objects contained within the Movie Clip as well. The other parts of this panel function the same way as the options for Button instances. Figure 32-5 shows an example of the Accessibility panel options for Movie Clip instances.

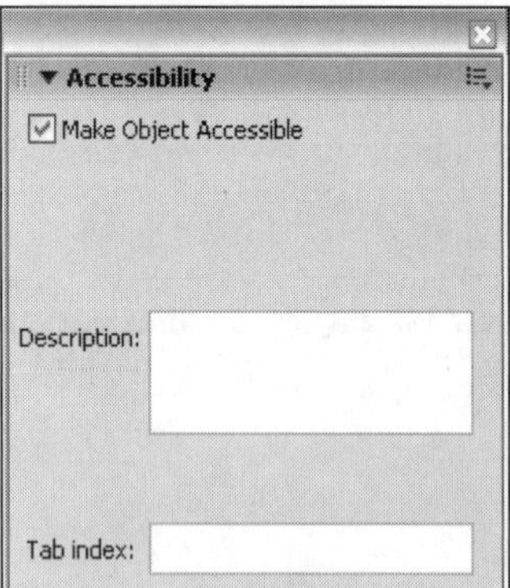

Figure 32-4: Options for Dynamic text fields in the Accessibility panel

Figure 32-5: Movie Clip instances have an additional option to Make Child Objects Accessible.

All other media, including the following items, cannot be made directly accessible in the Flash MX 2004 authoring environment:

- ✦ Graphics
- ✦ Line art
- ✦ Imported bitmaps

In order to work around this limitation, you can always convert your graphics into Movie Clip symbols, which support accessibility, and then assign names and descriptions of the container instance.

Some basic elements of Flash Player 5 content, such as static text and Button symbol instances, will be recognized when played in Flash Player 6 or higher.

Let's look at how to use some of the options in the Accessibility panel, and other considerations when developing your accessible movie.

Naming

We recommend that you keep any names you assign to your objects exact, succinct, and simple. Also, for the benefit and support of screen-reader technology, you should keep these names under 256 characters.

Auto Label

In the main movie options of the Accessibility panel, you can choose to "Auto Label" parts of your movie. With Auto Label active, the movie associates any text close to buttons or input text fields as names for these objects. This is great if you are not providing custom names or descriptions to your objects. However, automatic labeling might not be the best option to enable because it leaves the task of assigning associations between text and buttons to Flash MX 2004.

Shortcut

The Shortcut input field can be a little confusing. Adding a shortcut to this field does not automatically create one assigned to the object. What you enter into this field will simply cause the screen-reader to read the text out loud. You have to manually add a shortcut using ActionScript.

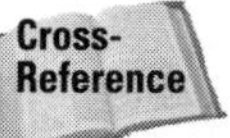

For more information on using the `Key` class to detect keypresses, see Chapter 19.

Hiding Content

There are several reasons why you might want to hide some of the content in your movie from a screen-reader. It can range from a simple reason (such as the object has no content or benefit in being heard), or you might have a very complex movie or series of objects that are best summed up in a single sentence. Hiding some of your content from screen-readers might be useful to you if you find that it will potentially confuse the screen-reader or conflict with other elements in your movie. For instance, you might have a group of objects within a Movie Clip, perhaps not containing any descriptive content. Or perhaps a group of items contained within the Movie Clip are best described as a whole. In this case, it is best to *uncheck* the Make Child Objects Accessible option, and the screen-reader will not list off an illogical and repetitive series of names of the many objects. Instead, you can provide an overall description on the Movie Clip container, thereby avoiding the repetition of similar elements or causing confusion.

Changing Attributes During Playback

You can change the properties of your accessible instance while your movie is in progress. You can let the screen-reader know you are changing attributes at a certain point during your movie, such as at a keyframe. All you need to do is change the properties of that instance, and the screen-reader *should* notice the changes you have made because the reader will treat this as a new instance. Actual results are unpredictable because sometimes only the new instance is read. In some cases, all instances within the entire movie might be read again by the screen-reader.

Accessible Components

Some of the new components provided with Flash MX 2004 support accessibility. In order for the component to work with screen-readers, special ActionScript must be written into the component.

The components built with accessibility options include:

- `Button` (or `SimpleButton`)
- `CheckBox`
- `RadioButton`
- `Label`
- `TextInput`
- `TextArea`
- `ComboBox`
- `ListBox`
- `Window`
- `Alert`
- `DataGrid`

These components have specialized ActionScript that enables screen-readers to recognize and read out the content of the components.

Tabbing

Allowing your users to use the Tab and Enter buttons for navigation is very important when constructing an accessible Web site. They are common tools used for navigation by for those who use screen-readers. You might also find it a very efficient method of navigation, regardless of your abilities. As in the past, Flash Players 6 and 7 automatically enable tabbing through text input boxes, buttons, and Movie Clips. The order is random, or "automatic," by default, although you can control the order of tabbing through the movie, thus increasing the logical progression through the objects or pages. Tabbing through a movie produces a yellow rectangle around each object as it progresses through, which is called the *focusrect*, short for "focus rectangle." It is possible to disable tabbing, the focusrect, and even certain objects from being "tab-able" if you do not want this functionality or if you want to alter it.

Setting the tab order benefits the accessibility of your movie and flow in data entry immensely. You cannot tab static text or graphics — unless, of course, you nest the items with Movie Clips. It is possible for your users to also use the arrow keys to move among the tab-able objects after they have pressed the Tab button once. The users must have the browser window and Flash movie in focus in order to be able to tab.

Using Keypress Actions

It is very important to understand the dependency that many screen-reader users place on the use of navigation based on keyboard commands. A button's `onRelease()` handler executes when the Enter key is pressed while the tab focus is on the button. To make a movie easily accessible to screen-reader users, you might want to design navigation using the Key class instead of mouse clicks or the Tab/Enter keys. Relying on tabbing and the Enter key might be enough functionality for you, although you might want some elements to execute on a certain combination of keys being pressed.

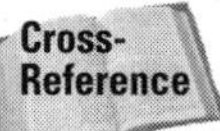

For a detailed description on how to use keypress actions in your movie, see Chapter 19.

The first thing you should do is make sure that each of your buttons or Movie Clips in your movie specifies the keypress you want to associate with it. You can put the shortcut in the Shortcut box of the associated Accessibility panel, making sure it is written with names spelled out (no symbols), using uppercase letters for letters, and joined by a + sign, such as Ctrl+N.

To apply keypress actions to your movies, you can place Key listeners that the movie will process when it loads. A sample of the code using the Key class is as follows:

```
var oNavKey:Object = new Object();
oNavKey.onKeyDown = function():Void {
  if (Key.getCode() == Key.UP) {
      root.gotoAndStop("newpage");
  }
};
Key.addListener(oNavKey);
stop();
```

As you can see, when the up arrow key is pressed, you are taken to the frame labeled newpage.

Detecting and Controlling Accessibility Options with ActionScript

The Accessibility class is available in Flash Player 6 or higher, and it's relatively simple to use — primarily because only two methods are associated with it: Accessibility .isActive() and Accessibility.updateProperties(). Like the Stage, Mouse, and Key classes, the Accessibility class is static. You don't use any new constructor to create new instances. Rather, you simply address the class's functionality directly through its class name.

The Accessibility.updateProperties() method is available only in Flash Player 6 r65 or later. Early releases of Flash Player 6 do not support this method.

Checking the State and Presence of a Screen-Reader

The Accessibility.isActive() method makes the player check to see whether the user is actively using a screen-reader on the computer and returns a Boolean value of true or false. This code enables you to enable or disable certain elements within the content of your Flash document based on the information returned. For instance, you might want to disable background music in your movie, thus leaving the focus on the speech generated by the screen-reader. You might also want keypress actions available only to the users who are using a screen-reader.

The Flash Player requires time to initiate a connection to the screen-reader at the start of a Flash movie. Therefore, you have to build a slight delay into your movies if you use this method to check for a reader. If you can, set up any other movie attributes first, check for the screen-reader at the last possible moment, and then perform any other actions you require to customize your movie. You can use the `setInterval()` function to delay the use of `Accessibility.isActive()` as well.

Let's have a practice run of using the `Accessibility.isActive()` method. Open Flash MX 2004, and create a new Flash document. Rename Layer 1 to actions. Select the first frame of the actions layer, and open the Actions panel. Add the code shown in Listing 32-1.

Listing 32-1: Detecting a Screen-Reader

```
function checkScreenReader():Void {
   var bActive:Boolean = Accessibility.isActive();
   tDisplay.text = "Accessibility.isActive:" + bActive.toString();
   clearInterval(nCheckID);
}
this.createTextField("tDisplay", 1, 25, 25, 300, 30);
var nCheckID:Number = setInterval(checkScreenReader, 2000);
```

Publish your movie. When you test your movie in a Web browser with the Flash Player 6 or 7 plug-in, your text box should report `true` if a screen-reader is active or `false` if one is not currently active. If you do have a screen-reader enabled, try setting the `setInterval()` time period to a lesser value. If you check the `isActive()` method too quickly, the Flash Player reports `false` even if you have a screen-reader present.

You will use the returned Boolean value to control which version of the presentation in Flash the user sees. For instance, you might want to control the music in your movie. Essentially, your movie customizes itself, depending on whether a screen-reader is present. If you want, you can also load a specialized movie for those using a screen-reader program.

Checking the User's Browser for Accessibility Compliance

The `System.capabilities` class helps determine the attributes of a user's system, and part of this functionality includes determining whether the device meets accessibility standards. This class is available only in Flash Player 6 or higher. Specifically, the property related to accessibility is `System.capabilities.hasAccessibility`. This property is different from the `Accessibility.isActive()` method in that it returns information about the presence of MSAA compliance, not whether there is a screen-reader actively running. For instance, if your user is running Netscape, which does not have the ActiveX control this technology requires, the property returns `false`. If your user is running Internet Explorer for Windows, the returned value is `true`.

Let's look at how you can use this object in a Flash movie. To see what is returned, you can run a test much like the previous example. With the same sample document you created in the previous section, add (or modify) the bold code shown in Listing 32-2.

Listing 32-2: Using System.capabilities.hasAccessibility

```
function checkScreenReader():Void {
   var bActive:Boolean = Accessibility.isActive();
   tDisplay.text = "Accessibility.isActive:" + bActive.toString();
   clearInterval(nCheckID);
}
this.createTextField("tDisplay", 1, 25, 25, 300, 30);
var bIsAccessible:Boolean = System.capabilities.hasAccessibility;
if(bIsAccessible){
   var nCheckID:Number = setInterval(checkScreenReader, 2000);
} else {
   tDisplay.text = "You do not have an MSAA compliant browser.";
}
```

Publish your movie. When you test your movie in a browser, you should get different results displayed in the `tDisplay` field, depending on which system and which browser or plug-in the system has.

Scripting Accessibility Properties Dynamically

You can also dynamically assign values to accessibility settings of ActionScript objects, such as `TextField`, `MovieClip`, and `Button` objects. Using the `_accProps` property, you can adjust the following accessible attributes of an instance:

✦ **silent:** This attribute accepts a Boolean value of `true` or `false` and controls whether the instance should be seen by the screen-reader. If it's set to `true`, the instance is ignored by the screen-reader. If it's set to `false`, the screen-reader will see the instance.

✦ **forceSimple:** This attribute accepts a Boolean value and is the inverse of the Make Child Objects Accessible option in the Accessibility panel. If you set this attribute to `true`, any elements within the instance are ignored by the screen-reader. If it's set to `false`, the screen-reader can see internal elements of the instance.

✦ **name:** This attribute specifies a `String` value for the instance's name, as read by the screen-reader. It is equivalent to the Name field in the Accessibility panel.

✦ **description:** This attribute specifies a String value for the instance's description, equivalent to the Description field in the Accessibility panel.

✦ **shortcut:** This attribute requires a String value to describe the keyboard shortcut that is read aloud by the screen-reader for the instance. It is equivalent to the Shortcut field in the Accessibility panel.

Once you have changed an accessible attribute of an instance, you must let the screen-reader know that the value(s) have changed by using the `Accessibility.updateProperties()` method. For example, the following code assigns a name and description to a `MovieClip` object named `mcPhoto`.

```
mcPhoto._accProps.silent = false;
mcPhoto._accProps.name = "Conference Photo";
mcPhoto._accProps.description = "Picture of attendees at the round table ⮐
   discussion";
Accessibility.updateProperties();
```

You can also use the _accProps property to assign the same global movie settings that you do in the Accessibility panel. Simply use the _accProps property without an object reference, and apply the update. The following code names the Flash movie and assigns a description:

```
_accProps.silent = false;
_accProps.name = ""Conference Slideshow";
_accProps.description = "This movie provides the lecture notes and diagrams ⮐
   from the session";
Accessibility.updateProperties();
```

Note that both of these code examples set the silent property to false. If you do not use the Accessibility panel to define initial options for your movie, all properties default to a value of undefined. Be sure to set the silent (and forceSimple, if applicable) property of dynamic instances in your movie.

Go to www.flashsupport.com/articles to see an example of how a sample Flash presentation can use the _accProps property.

Making the Most of Your Accessible Movie

Before moving on to building your own accessible Flash movie, take a look at some of the main things to remember about using screen-readers to make a successful movie:

✦ **Avoid looping animation or movies:** The screen-reader receives a command to return to the top of the page. It also says "Loading page, load done" after loading movies. This is something to keep in mind for your design because looping movies, animated buttons, and the like can cause unnecessary verbiage on the part of the screen-reader.

It is possible to stop the "Loading page, load done . . ." verbiage by pasting the animation into a Movie Clip and then turning off Make Object Accessible in the Accessibility panel.

✦ **Hide objects:** Make sure you combine elements that might be considered redundant if read individually. Also, hide any objects that do not add any overall content to the movie, or hide graphics in accessibility-disabled Movie Clips if they interfere with screen-reader technology.

✦ **Keep graphics/dynamic content to a minimum:** If you are developing your site with screen-readers in mind, do not rely on graphics and dynamic content to display informational content. If you must use graphics and dynamic content, remember to add a detailed description to compensate for those who cannot digest this information.

✦ **Consider your audio:** If you have strong audio elements, you might want to disable them if your user has a screen-reader. Limited audio does not usually interfere with the screen-reader, and can still enhance the experience if used wisely and with due caution.

✦ **Consider navigation:** Your movie will be more accessible if you enable users to navigate by using only the keyboard (keypress actions and tabbing).

✦ **Consider scene (or state) progression:** A logical, user-controlled scene progression is best for screen-reader users. Also, remember that screen-readers might have a difficult time keeping up with rapid changes. Test your movie to ensure that all elements can be read in time if your movie cannot be made user-controlled.

- **Use simple language:** Remember that simple and concise language use is most effective when it comes to screen-readers.
- **Consider text issues:** Be sure to include a description if you *rasterize* (break apart) any text. Remember that if you break text apart into separate objects, you should disable the screen-reader action because otherwise it will read each letter individually. Remember that you can easily convert static text to dynamic text if you want to add a description.
- **Keep buttons simple:** Buttons are generally more effective with screen-readers when they are kept very simple. Do not put any vital information you want the screen-reader to see in the button's Down state. Try to avoid any invisible buttons in your movie; they will almost certainly not be noticed by a screen-reader.

To see an example of an accessible Flash movie (and its deconstruction), visit `www.flash-support.com/articles`.

We'd like to know what you thought about this chapter. Visit `www.flashsupport.com/feedback` to fill out an online form with your comments.

Summary

- Assistive technology includes screen-reader software, which reads aloud certain elements on a user's monitor. MSAA technology has been built into Flash Players 6 and 7 and now enables users with a compatible screen-reader to navigate through Flash movies using Internet Explorer.
- Flash movies can be made accessible with little effort by simply making sure the main movie Accessibility panel has Make Movie Accessible selected. It can be made highly effective by taking more time and care during production and by ensuring a logical order to events such as tabbing and movie progression.
- By using the `Accessibility.isActive()` method and additional ActionScript, you can tailor your movie to users with a screen-reader active. There are many things to keep in mind when building a site for the visually impaired and screen-reader technology, including concise language, logical tabbing progression, keyboard reliance, and brevity.

✦ ✦ ✦

Scripting for the Flash Stand-Alone Player

In This Chapter

Defining a projector

Controlling the size of a projector

Trapping keys in a projector

Although Flash is used primarily to develop multimedia for the Internet, you can publish self-running versions of your Flash movies without the use of a browser or a plug-in. This chapter explores how you can take control of your Flash movies in this unique environment.

Using the Stand-Alone Player

The stand-alone player refers to the Flash Player application that comes preinstalled in the Players folder of your Flash MX 2004 program folder. You can find the stand-alone player in the following default installation folders:

- ✦ **Windows:** C:\Program Files\Macromedia\Flash MX 2004\Players. In this folder, you will find an EXE file named `SAFlashPlayer.exe`.
- ✦ **Mac OS X:** *Startup disk*\Applications\Macromedia Flash MX 2004\Players. In this folder, you will find an application file named `SAFlashPlayer`.

Even though the Flash MX 2004 authoring application is no longer available for Mac OS 9, Flash projectors published from Flash MX 2004 can still be played on a Mac OS 9 machine.

There are two ways you can use SWF movie files outside of the browser and plug-in environment:

- ✦ Open your SWF file with the Flash Player application.
- ✦ Publish your Flash movie as a projector.

For the purpose of this chapter, these applications (Player or projector) are referred to as stand-alone. You'll see this term used in other Flash tutorials and books as well.

Most Flash developers rarely use the Projector options in the Publish Settings dialog box. Go ahead and open this dialog box now (File ➪ Publish Settings). Whether you author on Windows or Mac, you can create Flash movie projectors for either platform. When you publish a projector, Flash MX 2004 bundles the movie's SWF file with the Flash Player engine. If you publish a Windows projector from either the Windows or Mac version of Flash MX 2004, you get an EXE file. If you publish a Macintosh projector from a Windows version of Flash, you get an HQX file. HQX files can be decompressed on a Macintosh with a free utility such as Aladdin Systems' StuffIt Expander. If you publish a Macintosh projector from a Mac OS X version of Flash MX 2004, the projector is an Application file type.

You can also create a projector from the Flash Player application. After you open a SWF file in the Flash Player, you can choose File ➪ Create Projector. However, this method allows you to create a projector only for your specific platform. In other words, if you open a SWF file with the Macintosh Flash Player, you can create projectors for the Macintosh only. One advantage of using this method is that it enables you to make a projector without recompiling the Flash document (FLA file). For example, if you were given a SWF file but not the FLA file from a business client, you could make a projector by opening the SWF in the stand-alone projector. This technique can also come in handy if you have a FLA file that uses embedded fonts that you do not have—if you have the SWF file already compiled with the embedded fonts, you can use the stand-alone to make a projector from the SWF file.

The file overhead of a projector varies between the platform versions. A Windows projector file is about 973KB alone, without the movie. However, an equivalent Macintosh projector file created with the Mac version of Flash MX 2004 is about 1.3MB. You can see this breakdown in Table 33-1.

Table 33-1: Projector File Sizes from Flash MX 2004

Output Type	*Windows*	*Macintosh*
Windows EXE file	973KB	973KB
Mac HQX file	1.7MB	N/A
Mac Application file	N/A	1.3MB

In the following sections, you'll look at the pros and cons of using Flash projectors.

The file of an empty projector was calculated by publishing an empty Flash movie. An empty SWF file is 30 bytes. The Compress movie option in the Publish Settings dialog box has no effect on the size of an empty movie.

Benefits of the Stand-Alone Environment

Some of the potential benefits of the stand-alone are immediately apparent. Following is a short list of reasons why you might want to use a Flash movie in a stand-alone:

✦ No Web browser or plug-in is required for Flash movies in a projector. If you give a projector file to a client or friend, you can be sure that they can view the Flash movie on a Mac or PC.

✦ On Macintosh projectors that run in Classic mode, OS 9 or earlier, you can enable higher memory capacities for larger, complex movies. Windows operating systems dynamically allocate memory as needed. To allocate more memory to Macintosh projectors, select the projector application file, and choose File ➪ Get Info (OS 9 or earlier) or File ➪ Show Info (OS X) from the Finder to change memory settings.

✦ You can build hybrid CD-ROM presentations. Any larger media files and assets can be stored on the CD, whereas dynamic or routinely updated information can be downloaded from the Internet.

✦ You can run Flash presentations in places where Internet connections are unavailable.

✦ You can build presentations for kiosks in museums and other public places. Stand-alones enable you to play Flash movies full-screen and lock out the user's control of the keyboard.

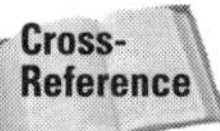

At the end of this chapter, you can find information about other third-party tools that enhance the capabilities of a Flash projector.

Although projectors can provide these features, there are some reasons why you would not want to use stand-alones. They are discussed next.

Limitations of the Stand-Alone Environment

As usual, you can't be a superhero without a weakness. Some of the benefits of a stand-alone can also be seen as drawbacks. Consider the following before you plan a project in the stand-alone format:

✦ Most Internet users are extremely wary of executables (EXE or application files). Why? Many viruses are spread from computer to computer via EXE files that are attached to e-mails and run by unknowing e-mail recipients. It's best not to offer site visitors stand-alones as a download on your site, or as an attachment in your e-mails.

✦ Stand-alones are also unwieldy in file size. As we mentioned, the projector by itself is almost a megabyte. As such, it's not suitable for slower dial-up modem connections to the Internet.

✦ Stand-alones are available only for Windows and the Macintosh. Although the Flash Player is available as a plug-in for Linux, you cannot run projectors on this fast-growing desktop platform. As of this writing, Flash Player 6 is the most current plug-in version available for the Linux platform.

You can use the `POST` and `GET` methods with server-side scripts with Flash movies in a stand-alone.

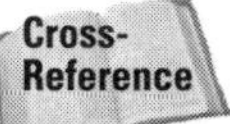

The use of `GET` and `POST` methods with actions such as `MovieClip.loadVariables()` is discussed in Chapter 9.

Now that you've been able to think about the implications of stand-alone use, you're ready to see the interactive commands that you can use specifically to control the stand-alone environment.

Applying fscommand() Actions with Stand-Alones

The primary function for stand-alone interactivity is the `fscommand()` function, also known as the `FSCommand`. The `fscommand()` function enables you to control the viewable area and size of the Flash movie stage, prevent users from using the keyboard to access the system (such as using Ctrl+Q to quit the projector), and more. The next section provides a brief overview of the commands and arguments for the `fscommand()` function. You also explore some examples of their use.

The `fscommand()` is also used to communicate with client-side scripts (such as JavaScript and VBScript) in a Web browser. Refer to Chapter 31 for more information on this use of the function.

Overview of Commands and Arguments

The `fscommand()` function technically uses two arguments. The first argument is referred to as the *command*, whereas the second argument is the command's *argument*. Both arguments of the `fscommand()` are string data types, as the following example illustrates:

```
fscommand("allowscale", "true");
```

In this example, `"allowscale"` is the command, and `"true"` is the argument for the `allowscale` command. From our experiments, we have found that you can also use Boolean data types for those commands that accept `"true"` or `"false"` as the command's argument. Table 33-2 lists the commands and arguments available to the `fscommand()` for stand-alone use. This table has four categories into which the commands fall: those that control the viewing area (View), playback, key capture, and external application use.

Table 33-2: Summary of fscommands for Stand-Alones

Category	*Command*	*Argument*	*Description*
View	`"allowscale"`	`"true"` `"false"`	This command controls whether the size of a movie's stage can be changed from that specified in the Movie Properties (Modify ➪ Document) dialog box in Flash MX 2004. If this command is used with a `"true"` argument, the user can resize the dimensions of the movie by expanding the projector window. The `"false"` argument disallows any change to the movie's size.
	`"fullscreen"`	`"true"` `"false"`	This command tells the stand-alone whether the movie should play in a window (`"false"`) or matted against a blank background that takes over the desktop (`"true"`). The color of the background matches the movie's background color, as set in the Movie Properties dialog box. Note that unless the `allowscale` command is used with a `false` argument prior to this command being executed, the movie's size will match that of the screen resolution.

Category	Command	Argument	Description
Playback	"showmenu"	"true" "false"	This command, when set to "true", allows the user to right-click (or Control-click on the Mac) the movie's stage to access the contextual menu for player control (see Figure 33-5). If this command is set to "false", the only options available in this menu are About Macromedia Flash Player 7 and Settings.
	"quit"	No arguments	As the name implies, this command tells the stand-alone to exit or quit its application from running. This is equivalent to using File ➪ Quit from the stand-alone application bar.
Key Capture	"trapallkeys"	"true" "false"	This feature, when set to "true", enables you to prevent the user from using Ctrl-key combinations to exit or manipulate the stand-alone when the fscommand("fullscreen", "true") command is in use. Note that you must use ActionScript to capture all keypresses to enable keyboard features to the user. When set to "false", normal operation of the keyboard returns to the user.
External	"exec"	path to application	This command enables you to execute local applications on the user's system. You can execute only applications or files that are located in a folder named fscommand, in the same location as the projector file. You can also specify BAT files (Windows) or AppleScript applets (Macintosh) as files. Note that paths use forward slashes (/) on Windows, and colon characters (:) on the Mac.

The fscommand() is a function, not a method of the MovieClip class. The fscommand() controls global properties of the entire movie. Therefore, you do *not* need to specify an object prefix for the fscommand(), as in _root.fscommand(). This is incorrect syntax. Instead, you call the function directly, specifying the arguments, such as fscommand ("allowscale", "false");.

Adding Controls to Projector Movies

Try some of these commands and arguments in actual Flash movies. In this section, you look at the allowscale and fullscreen commands to see how they affect the viewable area of a Flash movie.

Considering the Aspect Ratio for Full-Screen Movies

If you plan to create Flash stand-alones that will expand to the full size of the user's monitor, you should keep in mind the aspect ratio of standard computer screens, which is 4:3, or 1.33:1. Keep in mind that 4:3 is the aspect ratio of television screens and most computer monitors. Flash's default frame size, 550 × 400, is not a 4:3 aspect ratio—it's more like 1.37:1. This original size was determined by Macromedia by the "best fit" for Flash movies that play in a Web browser window. It is recommended that you set your movie size to 640 × 480 or 800 × 600. Both of these computer resolutions are 4:3 aspect ratios. To calculate an aspect ratio, either divide the largest dimension by the smallest dimension, or divide each number by a common factor. For example, 640 and 480 have a common factor of 160, giving you the same fraction: 4 × 3. By using a 4:3 aspect ratio, you can be sure that scaled Flash movies will fit the size of the screen exactly.

Wide-screen computer monitors and HDTV sets use 16:9 aspect ratios. If you plan on presenting Flash projectors on an Apple Cinema display, for example, make sure you size your Flash movies appropriately. You can utilize the `Stage` class (discussed in Chapter 20) to reposition movie elements on a variety of screen sizes.

However, you do not want to make overly large frame sizes, such as 1600 × 1200, unless you are running the Flash projector on an incredibly fast computer. As you might have noticed, as Flash movies scale larger, playback suffers. Vector graphics, albeit small in file size, are mathematically intensive, especially when they are animated. If you want to design a smooth-running presentation that's likely to play back well on most computers, we recommend that you use a 640 × 480 frame size for your Flash movies, and set the system's screen resolution to 640 × 480. Even scaling a 640 × 480 movie to 800 × 600 can slow down the playback of a Flash movie.

Making a Resizable Projector Window

In this section, you see how to add the proper ActionScript in order to control the size of the projector window. You start with a template Flash movie that has prebuilt graphics ready to go.

Make a copy of the `projector_template.fla` document, located in the ch33 folder of this book's CD-ROM.

Now, take a look at the project file. Open the starter Flash document (FLA file), and look at the current objects on the stage. On the window control layer, you find a `MovieClip` instance named `mcWinControl` in the upper-right corner of the stage. The `mcWinControl` instance uses symbols from the `OS_UI_Elements.fla` library, which can be downloaded for free from the Macromedia Exchange Web site at `www.macromedia.com/exchange`. The `mcWinControl` instance contains three elements from this library, and will be the primary focus of this exercise. Here's an outline of the functionality that you want to achieve:

- When clicked, the minimize button (on the far left of the bar) should change the movie's size back to its original settings.
- When clicked, the maximize button (in the middle) should enlarge the movie's size to match that of the computer screen's.
- The close button should quit the Flash projector. However, it should present the user with a warning box to make sure that he or she wants to leave the projector. We have already created this warning box as a Movie Clip symbol named `winQuitClip`, which is set to export from the movie's library.

Now, in order to code your movie efficiently, you create two custom methods that handle your project needs. The first method is named `resize()`, and it is used by both the minimize and maximize buttons. This method uses the `allowscale` and `fullscreen` commands to appropriately size the Flash projector.

Tip When you want to declare a function in the Actions panel, press Esc+f+n (in sequence, not simultaneously). This key combination inserts the function handler, complete with curly braces and argument parentheses. Keep this in mind for Steps 3 and 4 that follow.

The second method is called `closeMovie()`. This method, which is used by the close button, enables the attachment of the warning dialog box. The `quit` command is actually put on the Yes button inside of the warning box. Take a quick look at the warning box now. Double-click the `winQuitClip` symbol in the Library panel. You notice that there are two `Button` instances on the buttons layer. The Yes button executes the `"quit"` command for the projector. Stay inside of the `winQuitClip` symbol while you begin the steps to script the movie.

1. Select the `Button` instance beneath the Yes text. Open the Actions panel (F9), and type the following ActionScript into the Script pane:

   ```
   on (release){
     fscommand("quit");
   }
   ```

   The `"quit"` argument of the `fscommand()` function tells the Flash projector to exit. This function executes when the user clicks the Yes button.

2. Select the `Button` instance beneath the No text. In the Actions panel, you add some ActionScript that will delete the instance of `winQuitClip` from the stage. You will see why you're doing this later, when building the `closeMovie()` function.

   ```
   on (release){
     this.removeMovieClip();
   }
   ```

3. Leave the `winQuitClip` Movie Clip, and go back to the main timeline (Scene 1). Create a new layer and rename it `actions`. Place this layer at the top of the layer stack.

4. Select frame 1 of the actions layer and open the Actions panel (F9). Now you will build the two custom methods mentioned earlier. You can start with the `resize()` method. You want this method to be easily available to the `mcWinControl` instance, so you declare the method on the instance. Type the following code into the Script pane:

   ```
   mcWinControl.resize = function(sType:String):Void {
      fscommand("allowscale", sType);
      fscommand("fullscreen", sType);
   };
   ```

   Using the `function` constructor, you create `resize()` with one argument, `sType`, which will be `"true"` or `"false"`. When the minimize button executes the `resize()` method, the `resize()` method is passed the argument of `"false"`, as in `resize("false")`. Therefore, `sType` is set to `"false"` in each of your `fscommand()` functions: `allowscale` and `fullscreen`. When the maximize button executes the `resize()` function, the `resize()` function is passed the argument of `"true"`, enabling the same `fscommands()` to enlarge the movie to the size of the computer screen.

5. Stay within the actions for frame 1 for this step. Beneath the last curly brace and semicolon of the `resize()` method, add your second method: `closeMovie()`. This function places an instance of the `winQuitClip` in the middle of the projector's stage when the close button is clicked.

```
mcWinControl.closeMovie = function():Void {
   var oInit:Object = {
      _x: Stage.width/2,
      _y: Stage.height/2
   };
   var mcWinQuit:MovieClip = this._parent.attachMovie( ⮐
      "winQuitClip", "mcWinQuit", 500, oInit);
};
```

This method does not require any arguments, as your previous function did. In order to place the `winQuitClip` symbol on the stage, you create an instance with the `attachMovie()` method of the `MovieClip` class. You also create an `Object` instance (named `oInit`) with _x and _y properties to pass to the `attachMovie()` method, positioning the instance's X and Y position to the exact middle of the stage.

Note The registration point of the `winQuitClip` was purposely kept in the middle of the symbol's workspace so that the center of the clip could easily be positioned at the center of the stage.

6. With your `resize()` and `closeMovie()` methods ready for action, invoke these methods from the `Button` instances within the `winControlClip` instance. Double-click the `mcWinControl` instance on the stage, and select the minimize button on the left. This button needs to execute the `resize()` method with a `"false"` argument, so that `allowscale` and `fullscreen` are set to `"false"`. This shrinks the Flash projector back to its original size within a window. Select the `Button` instance, and type the following code in the Actions panel:

```
on (release){
   this.resize("false");
}
```

7. Likewise, you need to add the `resize()` method to the maximize button. However, it uses the `"true"` argument, which causes the projector to expand to the full screen of the computer monitor. Select the maximize button, and type the following code in the Actions panel:

```
on (release){
   this.resize("true");
}
```

8. Finally, add the `closeMovie()` method to the close button. Remember, this function attaches the `winQuitClip` symbol to the main timeline. The `winQuitClip` contains a Yes button with the `fscommand("quit")` function. Select the close button, and type the following code in the Actions panel:

```
on (release){
  closeMovie();
}
```

9. You're ready to test the Flash movie as a projector. But first, save the Flash document as `projector_100.fla`. Then go to the File ➪ Publish Settings dialog box, and make sure that you check either the Windows or Macintosh Projector options in the Formats tab. Click the Publish button in the dialog box, or close the box and choose File ➪ Publish. Go to the folder where you saved the FLA file to see the projector file. Double-click the projector file, and test your buttons. You should be able to switch the view of the projector (as shown in Figures 33-1 and 33-2) or access the warning box when you click the quit button (as shown in Figure 33-3).

You can further modify the `resize()` and `closeMovie()` methods to do other things to your Flash movie as you add content to the presentation. Methods allow you to assign simple statements to interactive controls (such as your control buttons) and continually add more ActionScript without having to access the original controls — simply add the code to the functions.

Some third-party projector utilities (mentioned later in this chapter) enable you to strip the outer default window and title bar from projectors.

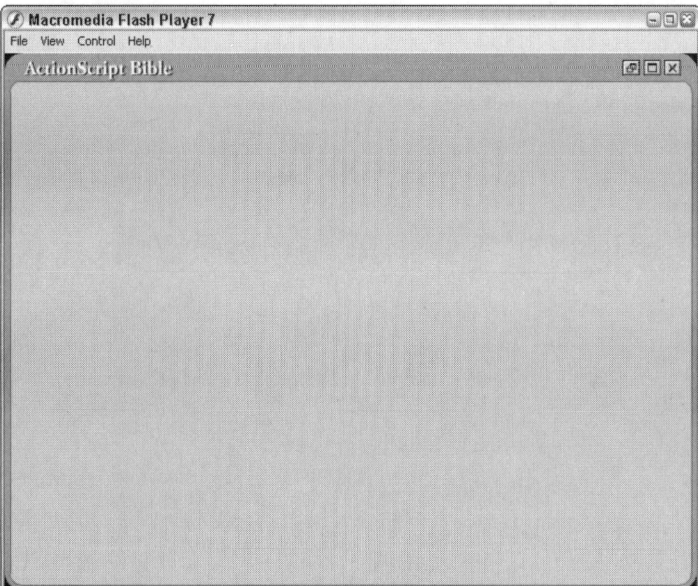

Figure 33-1: The projector in minimize (standard) view

Figure 33-2: The projector in maximize (full-screen) view

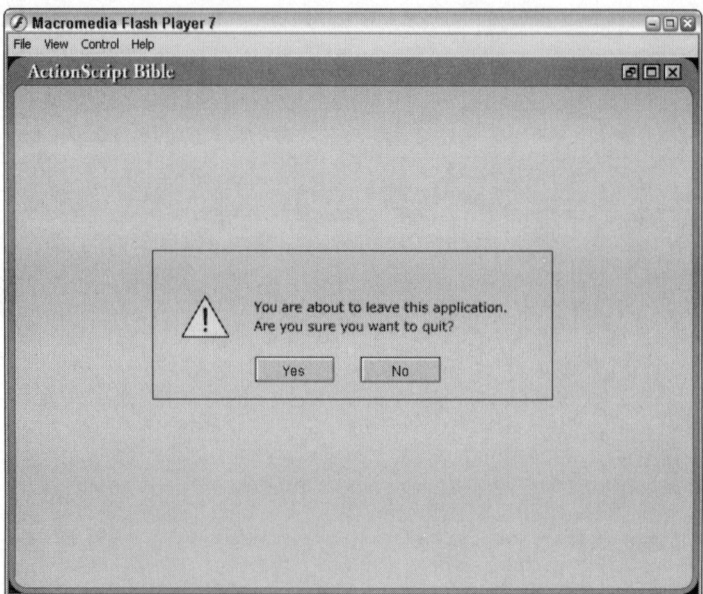

Figure 33-3: The warning dialog box

Using fullscreen and allowscale to Matte a Movie

In this section, you slightly modify the ActionScript created in the previous example. For this incarnation, you simply set `allowscale` to `"false"` directly in the `resize()` method. This prevents the movie from expanding in size, but it enables the projector to take over the desktop.

1. Open the `projector_100.fla` file that you saved from the previous exercise, or open the same titled file from the ch33 folder of this book's CD-ROM.

2. Select frame 1 of the actions layer and open the Actions panel. Adjust the `resize()` method with the bold line of code :

```
mcWinControl.resize = function(sType:String):Void {
   fscommand("allowscale", "false");
   fscommand("fullscreen", sType);
};
```

3. Save your Flash document as `projector_200.fla` and publish a projector file. When you press the maximize button, your computer screen should resemble Figure 33-4.

Figure 33-4: A matted, full-screen Flash projector

As mentioned earlier, you might not want to use the `allowscale` command with your Flash movies, especially if the movies contain intensive vector-graphic animations such as alpha tweens with several symbol instances. As you scale your Flash movies larger, you're likely to notice performance issues such as choppy or slow playback.

You can press the Esc key to force the projector back to the original window and size.

Preventing Access to the Desktop

The `trapallkeys` command enables a projector to prevent the keyboard from being used to access any default system or application options, such as Ctrl+Q or ⌘+Q to quit, Esc to resize, and so on. If you want to create Flash projectors for kiosk displays in public spaces, you can make sure that the user of the kiosk can't access anything except that what you allow in the Flash movie.

You can modify `projector_200.fla` so that the projector will auto-open to full screen. You can also prevent the user from accessing Ctrl+Q or ⌘+Q to exit the movie. The only way the projector exits is when users press the close button.

You also need to turn off the right-click (Control-click on the Mac) menu for the Flash Player in order to prevent the user from controlling any other features in the Flash movie. If you aren't aware of this menu, open the projector file from the last section. When you right-click (or Control-click on the Mac) the Flash movie stage, you should see the context menu shown in Figure 33-5.

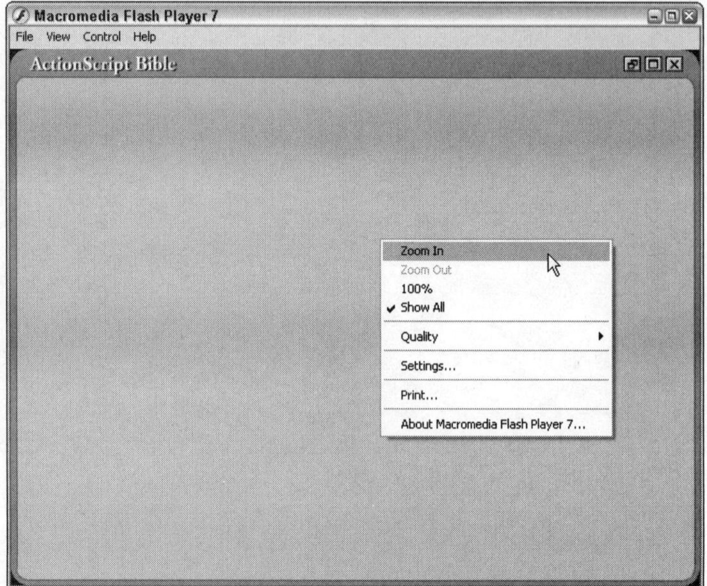

Figure 33-5: By default, the Flash Player allows you to access view and playback commands by right-clicking (or Control-clicking on the Mac) the movie's stage.

You disable all of this menu's features using the `showmenu` command in this exercise. Enough chatter; let's get started!

Tip

With Flash Player 6 or higher projectors, you can use the `Stage.showMenu` property to control the context menu as well (see Chapter 20 for more information). In Flash Player 7 projectors, you can use the new `ContextMenu` class to create custom context menus and/or hide built-in context menu items as well (see Chapter 20). These classes enable you to control the context menu in or out of the stand-alone environment.

1. Open the `projector_200.fla` file that you made in the last section, or open the same file from the book's CD-ROM.

2. Select frame 1 of the actions layer and open the Actions panel. Adjust the `resize()` method with the following bold code:

   ```
   mcWinControl.resize = function(sType:String) {
      fscommand("allowscale", "true");
      fscommand("fullscreen", "true");
   };
   ```

   With this modification, you set `resize()` to always expand the projector to full screen. This effectively disables the minimize and maximize buttons.

3. With this `resize()` modification, you will execute the `resize()` function as soon as frame 1 loads. Just after the last curly brace and semicolon of the `closeMovie()` method, type the following code:

   ```
   mcWinControl.resize();
   ```

4. Now add the `fscommand()` to disable the projector's contextual menu. After the `mcWinControl resize();` line from the last step, type:

   ```
   fscommand("showmenu", "false");
   ```

The `"showmenu"` command works only in the projector environment. It will not restrict the context menu in the plug-in (or Web browser) environment.

5. Finally, you tell the projector to capture all keypresses on the keyboard. After the line of code from Step 4, type:

   ```
   fscommand("trapallkeys", "true");
   ```

6. Save your Flash document as `projector_300.fla` and publish a projector. Double-click the projector file. The movie should open in full-screen mode automatically. Try pressing Ctrl/⌘+Q to exit the projector. It doesn't work, does it? Click the close button in the upper-right corner. By clicking the Yes button in the warning dialog box, you can quit the movie.

Although the `trapallkeys` command does capture most keypresses, it cannot prevent the user from pressing Ctrl+Alt+Del or Alt+F4 (Windows) or Option+⌘+Esc (Mac) to forcibly quit the application on a system level. Some third-party tools, such as Flash Jester's Jugglor, can trap other keys. Refer to the listing at the end of this chapter for the URLs to such tools.

You can find the projector_300.fla document in the ch33 folder of this book's CD-ROM.

Executing Other Applications

Another feature of the Flash stand-alone is the capability to execute programs outside of the projector file. Using the exec command, you can specify another application file to be run concurrently with the Flash projector. In this way, you can use Flash projectors as front-ends to software installers. For this scenario, you include the software installer EXE (or application on the Mac) file on the same CD-ROM or floppy containing the projector. For security reasons, any and all files that you want to run must be located within a folder named fscommand. This folder must be in the same parent folder as the Flash projector file. For example, if you had a software installer named setup.exe in the fscommand folder, you could add the following ActionScript to an install button in the Flash projector:

```
on (release){
  fscommand("exec", "setup.exe");
}
```

The filename and path is relative to the fscommand folder. As such, you can use a forward-slash separator (/) to target files in sub-folders of the fscommand folder.

You can also create applets or scripts with your favorite programming language. You can create Visual Basic EXE files that can perform operations with other installed applications.

It's beyond the scope of this book to delve into other scripting languages such as Visual Basic, but you can find an excellent tutorial on the Web at www.flashgeek.com/tutorials/06_launchapp_01.htm.

On the Mac, you can write AppleScript applets that can be executed from the Flash projector. However, the Flash Player (as a stand-alone) cannot be accessed via AppleScript. There are no AppleScript-defined objects within the Flash Player.

You cannot specify document filenames with the exec command. For example, fscommand("exec", "readme.doc"); does not launch WordPad or Microsoft Word on Windows.

Expanding the Potential of the Stand-Alone Projector

Several third-party software applications allow you to enhance the functionality of a Flash projector. Unfortunately for Mac users, these products are usually available only for Windows. These add-ons allow you to embed files such as video and PDF documents into Flash projectors. Following is a list of Web sites that offer Flash projector utilities:

- www.flashjester.com
- www.northcode.com
- www.screentime.com
- www.alienzone.com/screensaver_features.htm

- `www.screenweaver.com`
- `www.goldshell.com`

Most of these sites offer free downloadable trial versions of their software products.

We'd like to know what you thought about this chapter. Visit `www.flashsupport.com/feedback` to fill out an online form with your comments.

Summary

- You can publish self-running versions of Flash movies. These files are called projectors or stand-alones. You can also play SWF files in the Flash Player application that ships with the application.
- Projectors can be used to distribute your Flash content on floppy disks, CD-ROMs, or DVD-ROMs.
- Data functions, such as the `POST` method of the `loadVariables()` function, work in Flash projectors.
- Using the `fscommand()` function, you can control how a Flash projector behaves and communicates with resources outside the player. The function uses two arguments: a command and an argument for the command.
- The `"allowscale"` and `"fullscreen"` commands control the viewable area of the projector's stage.
- The `"trapallkeys"` command can prevent the user from quitting the projector or using system shortcuts to access other functions.

✦ ✦ ✦

Creating Flash Applications

PART

✦ ✦ ✦ ✦

In This Part

✦ ✦ ✦ ✦

Managing and Loading Flash Content

✦ ✦ ✦ ✦

In This Chapter

Considering Flash content structures

Charting Flash load order

Preloading a Flash movie

Loading JPEG, MP3, SWF, and FLV files

Using Shared Libraries for font management

Preloading a Shared Library

✦ ✦ ✦ ✦

As you develop larger Flash presentations or applications, you will undoubtedly need to develop, produce, and update more than one Flash document (FLA file) and movie (SWF file). You *can* create enormous movie file sizes — the Flash Player can handle file sizes that are several megabytes. However, the users of your Flash content can avoid unnecessarily long downloading times if you think ahead and learn basic project management skills. In this chapter, you learn how to efficiently divide Flash projects into several smaller movies and assets.

Planning the Scope of Your Project

Every Flash project is different. Although this might sound like common sense, you may often find yourself overcomplicating any given production task. Indeed, as you learn new tools in any trade, it's natural for you to let your eagerness get the better part of you and put your newfound knowledge into use. We'll do our best to avoid cliché adages that involve the words "half the battle." Before you begin production on any Flash project, you should evaluate the short-term and long-term goals required for the project. This section serves as a checklist to help you prepare and plan a large Flash project.

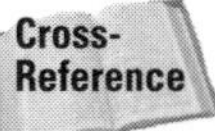

Be sure to read Chapter 3 for a review of Flash production planning.

Conceptualizing the Master Movie and Flash Content

By now, you know that a Flash movie is greater than the sum of its parts. Every team needs a leader (or a coordinated group of leaders), and you can think of Flash movies and assets as the team members working together in a Flash project — coordinated by the guiding hand of a master Flash movie. A master movie controls the direction and flow of content within the Flash presentation or application. As Figure 34-1 illustrates, a master Flash movie is the command center. All the assets and data for the Flash movie work in conjunction with the structure defined within the master movie.

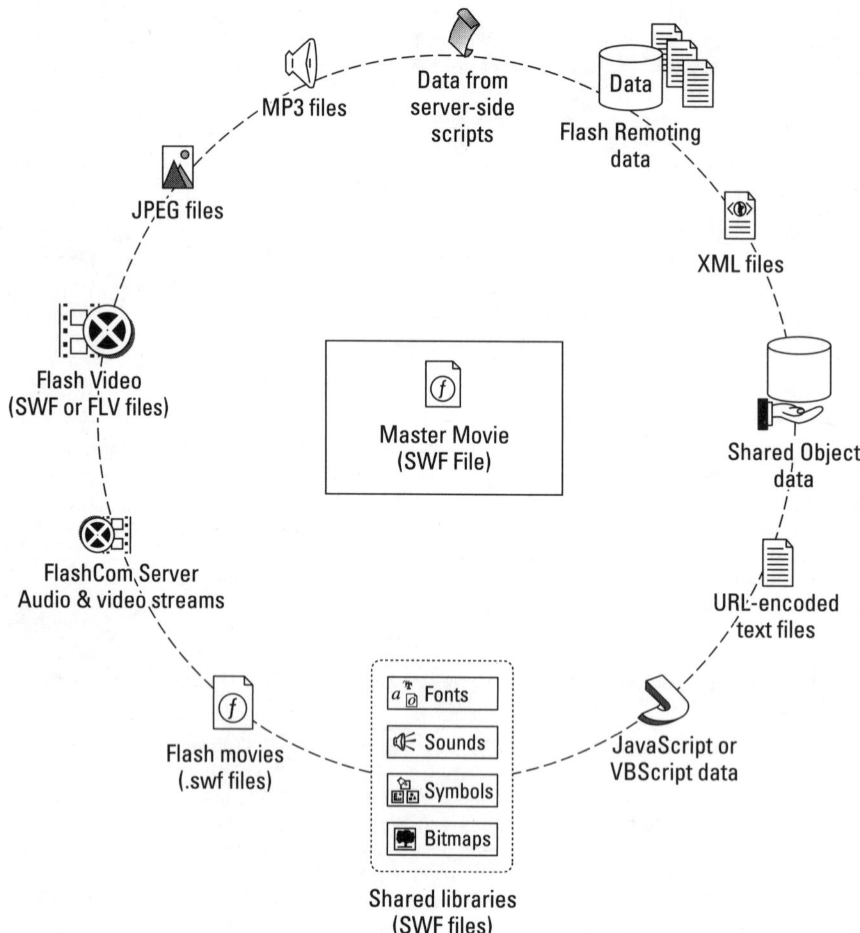

Figure 34-1: A master movie manages the assets and data that load into the presentation.

With Flash MX 2004, you can import and utilize a wide range of media content, from bitmaps to sounds to video. The following list enumerates the media assets that can be extracted and loaded as separate elements into a master Flash movie:

✦ **Bitmaps:** With Flash Player 6 and later, you can load standard JPEG images directly into Flash movies at runtime. More important, though, bitmap images are usually large files, whether they're in or outside of a Flash movie. As such, you might not want to include the images in the exported Flash movie (SWF file). By loading an external image on demand, the user is spared the (often) unnecessary download wait time at the beginning of the presentation.

✦ **Sounds:** MP3 files can also be loaded into Flash Player 6 and later movies at runtime. Sound files are usually several hundred KB (or several MB) in file size. As such, sound files are excellent candidates for external assets that should be kept outside of the master movie.

- **Video:** You can import digital video into Flash MX 2004 documents. The video is converted to the Sorenson Spark codec, which is built into Flash Player 6 and later. You then load a Flash movie (SWF file) containing embedded video into a master movie. In Flash Player 7, Flash movies can load FLV files directly at runtime.
- **Streams:** Macromedia has developed a rich media server technology named Flash Communication Server MX (currently at version 1.5) that enables video, audio, and text data to stream into Flash Player 6 or later movies in real time.
- **Flash movies:** You can load other Flash movies (SWF files) into the master movie. In this way, you can categorize or compartmentalize sections of your Flash application or presentation. Each Flash movie that is loaded into the master movie can act as a sub-master or coordinator for its own assets. We'll examine this process momentarily.
- **Shared library elements:** Since Flash 5, you have had the option of creating shared libraries (SWF files) that contain fonts, graphics, sounds, and symbols. You can then share each of these elements across several movies in a Flash presentation.
- **Text data:** URL-encoded text and XML data can be loaded into Flash movies. Flash Player 4 and later movies can use `loadVariables()` to integrate URL-encoded text, whereas Flash Player 5 and later movies can load XML data with the XML object. Flash Player 6 and later movies can also load URL-encoded text with the `LoadVars` object. Flash Player 7 movies can now consume SOAP-based Web services as well.
- **SharedObject data:** Flash Player 6 movies can load and store data in Local `SharedObject` objects (which are saved on the user's machine) or in Remote `SharedObject` objects (which are saved on servers running Macromedia Flash Communication Server MX). LSOs and RSOs can function as mini-databases that can store information as native Flash datatypes, such as objects in the `Array` or `Object` classes.
- **Flash Remoting data:** By using a Flash Remoting–enabled gateway on a Web server, you can load AMF (Action Messaging Format) binary data directly into a Flash movie. AMF data retains native datatyping, eliminating the need for a Flash developer to serialize and deserialize data packets between a client and server application.
- **Client-side scripts:** JavaScript and VBScript code can be written to initialize Flash movies with data. Using the `document.write()` method in JavaScript, you can assign dynamic data to the new `flashvars` attribute in the `<object>` or `<embed>` tags of HTML documents hosting Flash movies.
- **Server-side scripts:** Flash movies can receive dynamic data (as text, Flash movies, MP3 files, JPEG images — just about any of the assets mentioned in this list) from applications that run on your Web server. Using scripting languages such as CFML (ColdFusion Markup Language), ASP (Active Server Pages), Perl, or PHP, queries can be made to databases that return up-to-date information.

During the planning phase of your Flash project, map the potential use you have for these types of content. Whether you're making rough storyboards or detailed functional specifications (see Chapter 3 for more information), define the use of every asset wherever possible.

Constructing a Flash Asset Architecture

As you develop the functional specifications, flowcharts, and schedule for your Flash project, consider the goals of the project, and decide upon the optimal Flash document structure that will support these goals. The following two sections provide a series of checklists and maps to help you organize your project's goals.

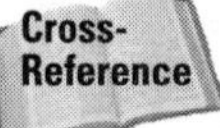

See Chapter 3 for more information on planning Flash projects.

Considering Preliminary Logistics

Have you had ideas — especially ideas for Web presentations and applications — that no one else has had? As you plan to build a Flash presentation that will redefine the experience of the Web, you will provide the necessary ingredients for the project's floor plan. You can't create a blueprint for a structure until you know the pre-existing conditions of the project.

- **What Flash Player version does the target audience need to have installed?** The Flash Player version will affect the range of asset options that you can employ. Flash Player 4 can only load Flash movies (SWF files) using `loadMovie()` or URL-encoded text data using `loadVariables()`. Flash Player 5 adds the capability to load XML data using the `XML` class. Only Flash Players 6 and 7 can load Flash movies (SWF files) containing embedded video. Make sure you decide which version of the Flash Player your presentation will require.
- **What connection speed does the target audience have?** Many developers assume that the people in their target audience have high-speed Internet connections such as DSL, cable, T1, or faster. If you know that most people viewing your Flash presentation or using your Flash application have dial-up connection speeds of 56Kbps or slower, your choice and size of assets should take the user's wait time into consideration. Regardless of connection speed, you should always optimize your Flash movie assets and loading structures.
- **Does the target audience include people with special needs?** If visually impaired people are included in your target audience, you should consider using the Accessibility panel options for assets in your Flash movie — including loaded Flash movies. Flash movies with Accessibility options require Flash Player 6 (and later) and a Flash-supported MSAA (Microsoft Active Accessibility) screen reader such as Window-Eyes.

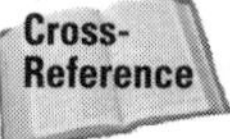

Chapter 32 has more information on the `Accessibility` class in ActionScript.

- **How many assets will the presentation or application require?** The Flash architecture that you plan to use is affected by the number of assets loading into the presentation. You can build simple structures that work with a small number of assets, or you might need to set aside time and testing for larger, more scalable solutions that can work with an unlimited (or ever-changing) number of assets. For example, if you design a town newsletter that has five news articles per week, you can realistically create five placeholders (such as keyframes or Movie Clips) that load images and text into the proper positions within the Flash movie. However, if you need to create a Flash search engine that can display anything from one to 100 "pages" of information in the Flash movie, you need to build an architecture that creates an internal data structure in ActionScript on the fly.
- **Will the presentation or application use static files or dynamic data?** Your Flash project architecture should also take into consideration how assets and data will be created. Will you manually create and upload static text, JPEG, and MP3 files to your Web server, and load them into your master Flash movie? Or, will you develop a database and server-side script that delivers these assets on the fly to the Flash movie? If you think you'll eventually need to "upgrade" a Flash project to use dynamic data, you can simulate complex data structures in static text files during development. When the database and server-side script are ready to be integrated with the Flash movie, you can then switch the URL you are using for the static text file to the live server URL.

Tip

If you need to develop a dynamic data structure for a Flash project while a server-side solution is being developed (and perhaps unavailable to you for testing), you can use a string variable to store the URL of the data source and refer to the variable name in the `loadVariables()`, `LoadVars.load()`, or `XML.load()` methods that require the data source. In this way, you can simply update the variable's value to point to the live server when the data and server-side script are ready.

✦ **How often will the files or data need to be updated, and who will maintain them?** The frequency of asset "turnover" in your Flash project can influence the structure of your Flash movies. If you need to update several bitmaps on a regular basis, you might want to require Flash Player 6 (or later) from your target audience. More importantly, if you are handing off your work to the client, and someone other than you is responsible for updating the content, plan to make the update process as smooth as possible for the client or the responsible party. Although you might be comfortable converting images and sounds into the SWF format (as a Flash movie), most clients do not know how to create assets in Flash. Therefore, you might want to create a structure that can load MP3, JPEG, and FLV files instead of SWF files.

✦ **Will the master Flash movie use Player Levels or `MovieClip` objects (or both) as the primary holder for loaded assets?** You can load Flash movies (SWF files) into either Levels (such as `_level1`, `_level2`, and so on) or `MovieClip` objects. Although the decision to load movies into Levels or `MovieClip` objects may seem trivial, the targets and paths used within your ActionScript code will be greatly affected by the decision. From an organizational standpoint, both Levels and `MovieClip` objects have their own unique advantages and disadvantages, as discussed in the next section. We simply mention the issue here because you should determine your loading strategies before you begin to author any Flash documents in Flash MX 2004.

Charting the Loading Structure

After you have created a functional specification for your Flash project and have considered the Flash asset requirements, you should map the architecture of your Flash project into an organizational chart. Several applications on the market today can help you create organizational charts (also known as *orgcharts*) and process flowcharts. Any multimedia or interactive presentation planning can benefit from a visual representation in an orgchart and a process chart. For Flash-specific projects, though, you might also want to create a *Levels* chart—if you're planning to load assets into Flash Player Levels as well as `MovieClip` objects. A Levels chart illustrates which Levels will be occupied by loaded SWF assets. Figure 34-2 shows an example of an orgchart for a Flash project.

In Figure 34-2, a framework for a Flash site is defined. In this example, the Splash and Detect page checks for the installation of the Flash Player. It also tests the connection speed of the user by timing the download of an image within the sniffer Flash movie (used to detect the Flash Player). The sniffer movie also detects the size of the user's computer screen, using the `Capabilities` object. If the user has the Flash Player installed, one of three scenarios is possible:

✦ The user has a slow Internet connection (below 128Kbps), and is presented with a JavaScript pop-up window sized 510 × 300, and a Flash master movie (SWF file) loads into the custom browser window. JavaScript passes configuration data to the Flash master movie: a variable named `sImgQual` equal to `"low"` and a variable named `sSndQual` set to `"low"`. Throughout the presentation, the master movie then proceeds to load further low-quality (small file size) image assets as well as low-quality audio assets.

✦ The user has a fast Internet connection (above 128Kbps) and a screen size of 1,024 × 768 or larger, and is presented with a JavaScript pop-up window sized 680 × 400, and a Flash master movie (SWF file) loads into the custom browser window. JavaScript passes two variables to the Flash master movie: `sImgQual = "high"` and `sSndQual = "high"`. Throughout the presentation, the master movie proceeds to load high-quality (large file size) image assets as well as high-quality audio assets.

✦ The user has a fast Internet connection (above 128 Kbps) and a screen size of 800 × 600 or smaller, and is presented with a JavaScript pop-up windows sized 510 × 300. The Flash master movie (SWF file) loads into the custom browser window, and JavaScript passes `sImgQual = "low"` and `sSndQual = "high"`. Because the user has a high-speed Internet connection, he or she will be able to listen to high-quality audio. However, because the window is small, there's no need to download high-quality assets into the master movie.

It's important to understand that this example's master movie is sized at 510 × 300 in the Document Properties dialog box in the Flash document (FLA file). The master movie scales to the size of the JavaScript pop-up window: 510 × 300 or 680 × 400. Although all of the Flash assets will be sized to the 510 × 00 window size, high-quality assets will be images with larger dimensions that have been scaled down to "fit" the 510 × 300 size. When the Flash master movie scales larger, the high-quality assets will display their full image quality.

In this example, the `sImgQual` and `sSndQual` values are simply inserted into the file URLs used for `loadMovie()` and `loadSound()` actions. All variables and values initialized through the `flashvars` attribute of the `<embed>` and `<object>` tags appear on the main timeline (`_root` or `_level0`) of the master movie (SWF file). Therefore, the variables are used within the file URL, such as the following:

```
var sImgURL:String = "image_" + _root.sImgQual + ".swf";
mcHolder.loadMovie(sImgURL);
```

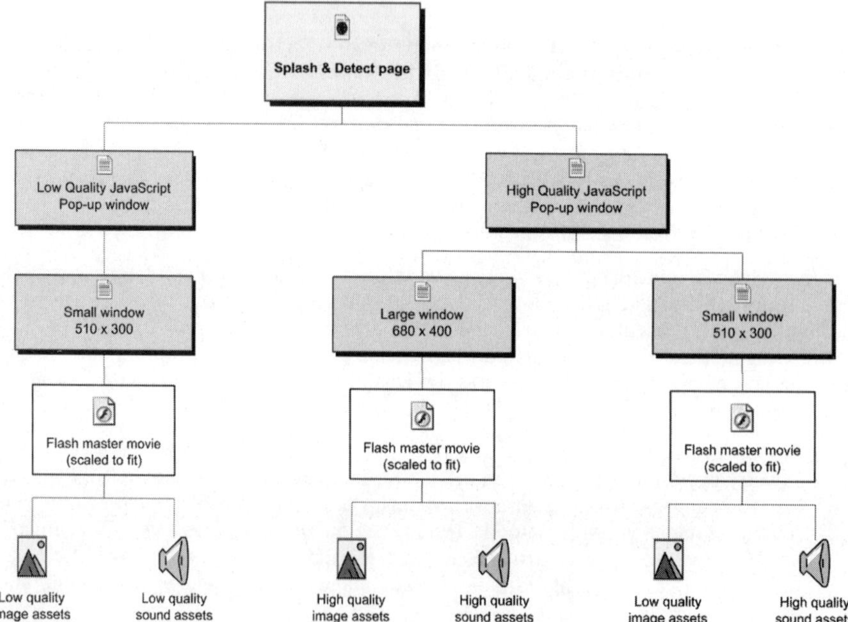

Figure 34-2: An overview orgchart for a feature film Web site

In this code, the sImgQual variable determines whether either the image_high.swf or image_low.swf movie is loaded into the mcHolder MovieClip object.

Now, this code should remind you of another issue mentioned previously: Levels versus MovieClip objects. Levels are stacks in the Flash Player that can be loaded with Flash movies (SWF files). The first movie to load into the Flash Player occupies Level 0, which can be targeted in ActionScript with _level0. As Figure 34-3 shows, Levels stack on top of one another. Therefore, if you load another Flash movie into Level 1 (_level1), that movie will display on top of the movie loaded into _level0. You can use virtually any Level number that you want.

In our tests, we found that the Flash Player can behave unpredictably if you use extremely high Level numbers – any number above 1,000,000 should be avoided. The capacity of Levels is linked to the amount of memory available to the Flash Player. In addition, do not confuse Level numbers with depth numbers – depth is a value associated with MovieClip objects created with the attachMovie(), createEmptyMovieClip(), and duplicateMovieClip() methods. Refer to Chapter 9 for more information on depths.

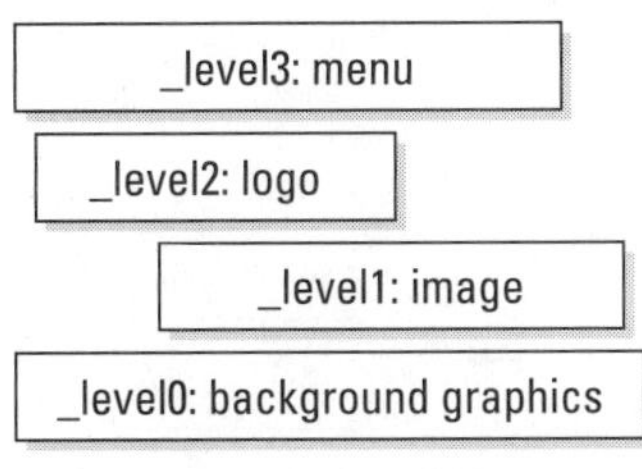

Figure 34-3: Levels stack on top of one another in the Flash Player.

Levels do not need to be accessed or loaded in a successive fashion. That means you can load a Flash movie into _level5, leaving _level1 through _level4 empty.

In past projects, we have often left gaps between Levels for content, just in case we needed to modify or add new content in later revisions. For example, if you know a loaded element should always appear on top of all content in your Flash presentation, you can load that content into _level10. That gives you eight levels to use for other content.

You can also load Flash content into MovieClip objects. MovieClip objects work within a specific Level. Therefore, the master movie in _level0 can direct the loading of a Flash movie into _level1. That movie can then direct the loading of assets into MovieClip objects within _level1. Or, if you choose not to use Levels at all, you can simply load your assets into MovieClip objects in the master movie at _level0. Figure 34-4 shows a master movie that loads three SWF files into MovieClip objects. In this figure, dashed boxes represent empty MovieClip objects that are filled with other Flash content (SWF files for this example).

Figure 34-5 shows a combined levels and MovieClip object loading strategy. The main.swf master movie is first loaded into _level0. Once loaded, the master movie directs the loading of the content on other levels. Each of those SWF files can load additional assets as well. In this example, the main.swf file preloads a Shared Library file named sharedLib.swf, which shares its assets (such as a font used in menu items and logo artwork) with the menu.swf and logo.swf files. It's not necessary to preload a Shared Library, but preloading the sharedLib.swf file ensures that the logo.swf and menu.swf files load without waiting for the sharedLib.swf to download. Dashed boxes represent empty MovieClip objects that load other Flash content (SWF files or JPEG images), whereas dashed paths represent the use of an element from the sharedLibrary.swf file.

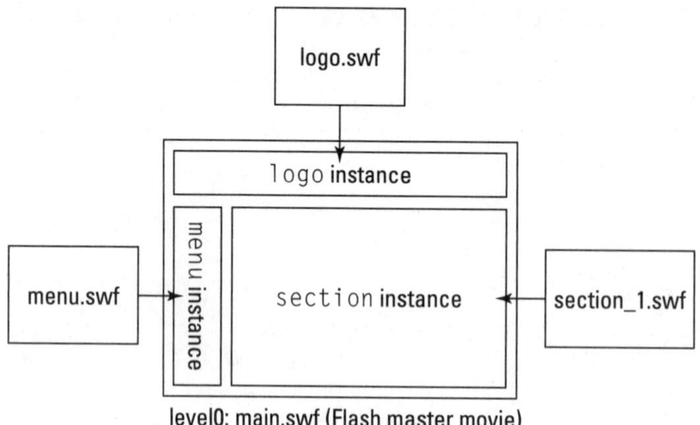

Figure 34-4: MovieClip objects can be targeted to load Flash content.

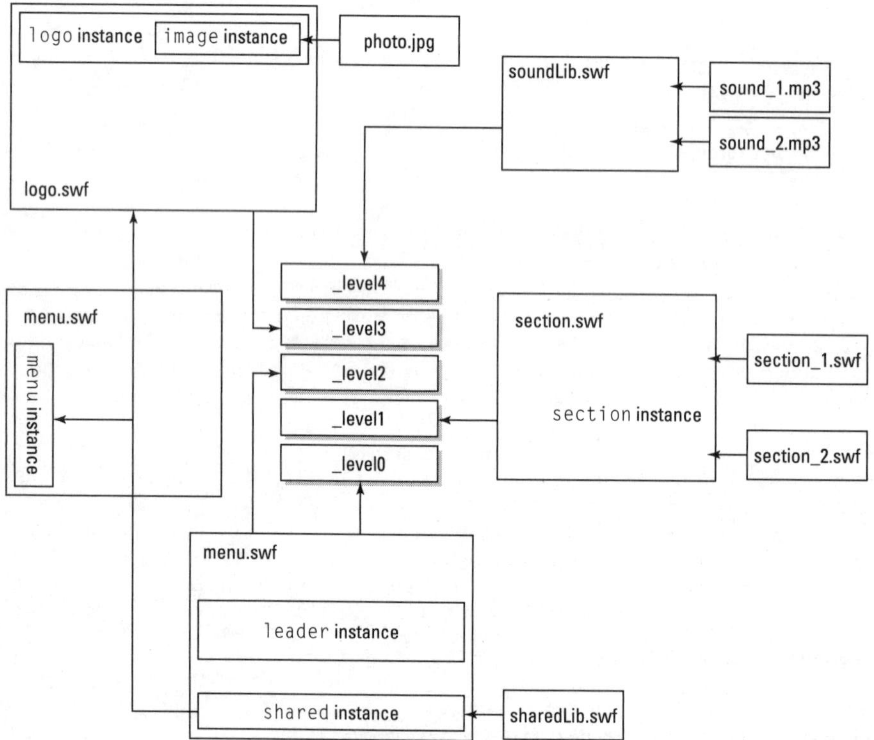

Figure 34-5: You can load movies into levels and MovieClip objects to create interdependent Flash asset structures.

Planning and devising the Flash project's loading structure should not be overlooked or done quickly. Everything from the visibility of artwork to the proper execution of ActionScript code can be affected, depending on a thorough and well-mapped project. All members of the production team should be able to provide input and suggest optimizations wherever possible. When the structure is finalized, every member of the team should receive a copy of the loading structure to reference from their work.

Be sure to test a prototype of your architecture as early in the production process as possible. Because Flash movies are timeline-based, you might find glitches or bugs with the way in which one asset's actions execute relative to another asset's actions.

As you can see, dividing a Flash project into several smaller Flash movies and individual pieces of content gives you and your team members the freedom to work on several files at once. While one person is working on `main.swf`, another person can be developing the ActionScript functionality of the menu instance in the `menu.swf` movie.

The schematics we have provided here are relatively basic and can become much more advanced with the quantity and type of data represented in the charts. You may even feel compelled to create wall-sized charts that examine every detail of your Flash project.

The remainder of this chapter explores ways you can use ActionScript to load content into a Flash movie.

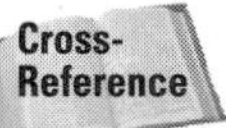

Read more about file hierarchy in Chapter 3.

Loading Content into Flash Movies

Once you have a solid understanding of the assets you will need to manage with your Flash project, you can dive into the process of producing functional prototypes and final versions of the actual Flash movies that will make everything come together. Of course, ActionScript will be the glue that keeps your master movie and supporting assets bonded to one another. This section shows you how to preload a Flash movie as well as the external assets that load into a master movie.

Much of the discussion in this section can be more fully explored with other examples and coverage described earlier in this book. If you haven't already read the `MovieClip`, `Sound`, `XML`, and `LoadVars` chapters, you might want to refer to them now before proceeding with this section.

The information in this section provides ActionScript workflows designed for Flash Player 6 and Flash Player 7. Some methods and objects are also available in Flash Player 5 and are noted as such in the text.

Overview of Objects and Methods

Two properties work uniformly with `MovieClip`, `Sound`, `LoadVars`, and `XML` objects in Flash Player 6 or later:

✦ **getBytesLoaded():** As its name implies, you can use this method to retrieve the current number of bytes that have loaded into the Flash movie. By comparing this value to the value returned by `getBytesTotal()` (discussed next), you can determine how much of the asset has downloaded into the movie. The value returned by this method is a number datatype.

✦ **getBytesTotal():** Use this method to retrieve the total number of bytes in the asset or content that is loading into the Flash movie. The value returned by this method is a number datatype.

`getBytesLoaded()` and `getBytesTotal()` are methods, not properties. Many beginners mistakenly omit the opening and closing parentheses after the method's name in their ActionScript code. Be sure *always* to use the parentheses to ensure that the methods will function properly.

Some of the V2 components in Flash MX 2004 also have `bytesLoaded` and `bytesTotal` properties.

Although each class loads content with a different method, each instance of a class accesses these properties identically:

```
var nLBytes:Number = content.getBytesLoaded();
var nTBytes:Number = content.getBytesTotal();
```

In this code, the `nLBytes` and `nTBytes` variables are set to equal the current bytes loaded and the total bytes, respectively, of an object named `content`. You'll use these variables in an actual example later, in the "Building a Basic Preloader for a Flash Movie" section. Let's review the methods that load assets or data into each class of objects in ActionScript code.

Flash Movies and JPEG Images

You can load Flash movies (SWF files) and standard JPEG images (JPG or JPEG files) into Levels or `MovieClip` objects in another Flash movie (SWF file). The `loadMovie()` method is used to load content into a `MovieClip` object, whereas the `loadMovieNum()` action is used to load these content types into Levels. The following code loads a Flash movie named `section_1.swf` into a `MovieClip` object named `mcHolder`:

```
mcHolder.loadMovie("section_1.swf");
```

You can also use `loadMovie()` with an empty `MovieClip` object created in code:

```
var mcHolder:MovieClip = this.createEmptyMovieClip("mcHolder", 1);
mcHolder.loadMovie("section_1.swf");
```

The syntax is nearly identical for JPEG images — simply change the file extension of the file's URL in the `loadMovie()` method:

```
mcHolder.loadMovie("background.jpg");
```

You cannot load progressive JPEG or GIF images directly into Flash Player 6 or 7 at runtime. If you are working with these or other bitmap image formats, you need to manually import the file(s) into a Flash document and publish a Flash movie (SWF file) containing the embedded bitmap. For dynamic applications, you can also use server-side scripts or applications to convert images to SWF files on the fly. Because Flash Player 5 does not support JPEG loading at runtime, you might need to explore a server-side solution for dynamic image delivery for older Flash Players.

To load content into Levels, use the loadMovieNum() action. The following code loads a file named soundLib.swf into Level 5 (_level5):

```
loadMovieNum("soundLib.swf", 5);
```

Do not try to use loadMovieNum() or loadMovie() as a method for a Level. The following syntax does *not* work: _level5.loadMovie("file.swf");. In addition, you cannot declare a variable to a Level that isn't occupied with an actual Flash movie (SWF file).

MP3 Sounds

The Sound class is responsible for loading MP3 sounds (MP3 files) into Flash movies. As discussed in Chapter 23, the loadSound() method of the Sound class can load an MP3 sound:

```
var snd_1:Sound = new Sound();
snd_1.loadSound("track_1.mp3", true);
```

Remember that the loadSound() method requires two arguments: the file URL and an isStreaming Boolean value. If you want the sound to begin playback as soon as enough of the sound has buffered into the Flash Player, use true as the second argument. If you want the sound to completely load into the Flash Player before playback can begin, set the second argument to false.

Even though MP3 sounds can be streamed into a Flash movie, they do not function as stream sounds that force playback of the movie to synchronize with the frame rate (fps) assigned in the Document Properties dialog box. In addition, the buffer quantity for streaming MP3 sounds varies from one MP3 encoding to another. To see how much data from the MP3 needs to download before playback begins, test the MP3 loading with a progress bar (as you'll learn later in this chapter).

Flash Video Files

The NetStream class, discussed in Chapter 24, can be used to access real-time audio/video streams for a Flash Communication Server MX server-side application using RTMP (Real Time Messaging Protocol) with Flash Player 6 or 7. The NetStream class can also be used to load an FLV file from a standard Web server using HTTP (Hypertext Transfer Protocol) with Flash Player 7. The process for accessing an FLV file over HTTP is a bit more involved than loading a SWF, JPEG, or MP3 file. The following code loads a Flash Video file (FLV file) named sample.flv with a NetStream instance named nsVideo and displays it in a Video object named vidWin:

```
var ncApp:NetConnection = new NetConnection();
ncApp.connect(null);
var nsVideo:NetStream = new NetStream(ncApp);
nsVideo.onStatus = function(oInfo:Object):Void {
   trace("nsVideo.onStatus >");
   trace("   level: " + oInfo.level);
   trace("    code: " + oInfo.code);
};
vidWin.attachVideo(nsVideo);
nsVideo.setBufferTime(5);
nsVideo.play("sample.flv");
```

Note

As you'll see later in this chapter, the NetStream class has bytesLoaded and bytesTotal properties, which can be used to monitor the download progress of an FLV file.

When you load an FLV file over HTTP with Flash Player 7, the file is treated as a progressive download. Like other HTTP-loaded assets, the FLV file, once downloaded, is stored locally in the Web browser's cache directory. When you use RTMP with Flash Player 6 or 7 and a Flash Communication Server application, the audio and video streamed from an FLV file is never cached—the audio and video is stored only with a buffer of the Flash Player.

LoadVars and XML Data

So far, we have discussed loading media types (SWF, JPEG, MP3, and FLV files) into Flash movies. You can also monitor the loading of URL-encoded text or XML data using the `LoadVars` and `XML` classes, respectively.

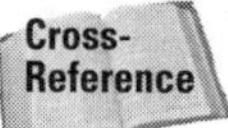

For more information on the `XML` and `LoadVars` classes, see Chapter 26.

Most text data will not be a large download that will occupy much of the user's time—you might decide that you don't need to monitor or display a progress bar for text data. However, if you are accessing files greater than 50KB, you may want to provide some indication to users on slower connections how much data they are waiting to receive. The following code loads a text file into a `LoadVars` object named `lvData`:

```
var lvData:LoadVars = new LoadVars();
lvData.load("products.txt");
```

The syntax is nearly identical for the `XML` class. The following code loads an XML document into an `XML` object named `xmlData`:

```
var xmlData:XML = new XML();
xmlData.load("products.xml");
```

You can also use the `sendAndLoad()` method to send variables from `XML` or `LoadVars` objects and receive subsequent data from a server-side script.

If you are receiving dynamic URL-encoded text or XML data from a server-side script, the `getBytesTotal()` method of the `XML` or `LoadVars` object might return an `undefined` value if the server does not transmit an HTTP content-length header. Test your specific server-side script with the `getBytesTotal()` method to see whether this header is included with the data.

Building a Basic Preloader for a Flash Movie

In this section, you learn how to preload a Flash movie whose assets are all internal. You construct a movie timeline containing a preload section. This section contains a frame with a `checkLoad()` function that will continuously execute (using `setInterval()`) until the entire movie has loaded into the Flash Player. While the movie is loading, a loader graphic updates to display the progress of the download.

We are mindful that Flash MX 2004 has added a `ProgressBar` component and a new `MovieClipLoader` class. We feel it's in your best interest to know how to build loading scripts from scratch, so that you can customize your projects for a variety of Flash Player versions.

Before you begin this exercise, let's look at a process flowchart of the procedure (see Figure 34-6).

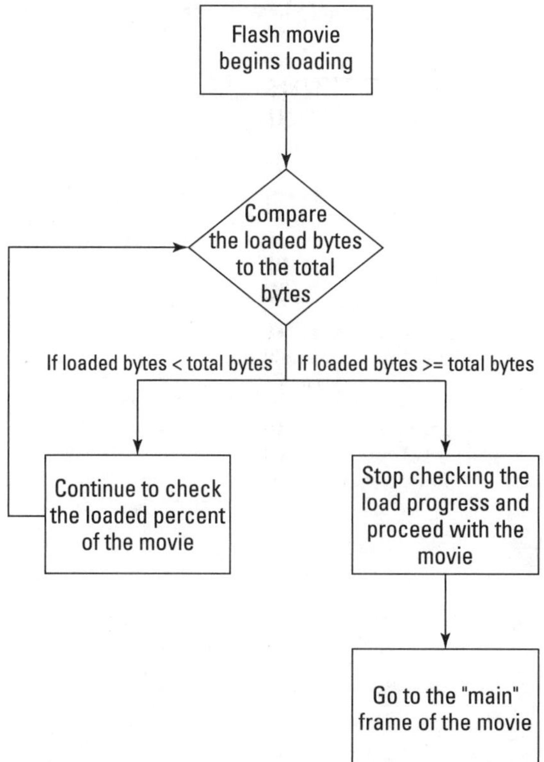

Figure 34-6: A process flowchart of the loading procedure

The decision point (that is, the diamond symbol) shown in Figure 34-6 will be handled by a function named `checkLoad()`. `checkLoad()` will calculate the `getBytesLoaded()` and `getBytesTotal()` of the main timeline, which represents the entire Flash movie (SWF file). Using these values, `checkLoad()` will control the X scale of a progress bar—increasing the size as more of the movie has downloaded. A text field will also display the current percent loaded and the total file size (in KB) of the Flash movie. The "Continue to check the loaded percent of the movie" functionality of the movie (as shown in Figure 34-6) is governed by a `setInterval()` function, which constantly invokes the `checkLoad()` function (every 50 milliseconds). Let's get started with the exercise.

Make a copy of the `checkLoad_starter.fla` file, located in the `ch34` folder of the book's CD-ROM.

1. Open the starter file in Flash MX 2004 and resave the document as `checkLoad_100.fla`.
2. Rename Layer 1 `content`.
3. Create an empty keyframe (F7) on frame 10 of the content layer. Drag an instance of the `hallwayImage` Graphic symbol to the stage on this keyframe. Center the instance on the stage, and use the Free Transform tool to resize the instance to fit the stage.

4. Select frame 20 of the content layer and press the F5 key to extend the layer to this frame.

5. Create a new layer and rename it `labels`. Place this layer at the top of the layer stack.

6. Select frame 1 of the labels layer. In the Property inspector, assign this frame a label of `preload`.

7. Add a keyframe on frame 10 of the labels layer, and label this frame `main` in the Property inspector. Your document should now resemble Figure 34-7.

Figure 34-7: The content of this movie starts on the main label.

8. Create a new layer and name it `mcLoader`. Place this layer underneath the labels layer.

9. With frame 1 of the `mcLoader` layer highlighted, select the Rectangle tool. Make sure that you specify a stroke and fill color in the toolbox. Draw a rectangle on the stage. In the Property inspector, size both the stroke and fill of the rectangle to 300 × 10. This rectangle will be the progress bar that indicates the loading of movie bytes into the Flash Player.

10. With the stroke and fill of the rectangle selected, press the F8 key. In the Convert to Symbol dialog box, choose the Movie Clip behavior. Name the symbol `loaderClip`, and click the top-left registration point, as shown in Figure 34-8. Click OK.

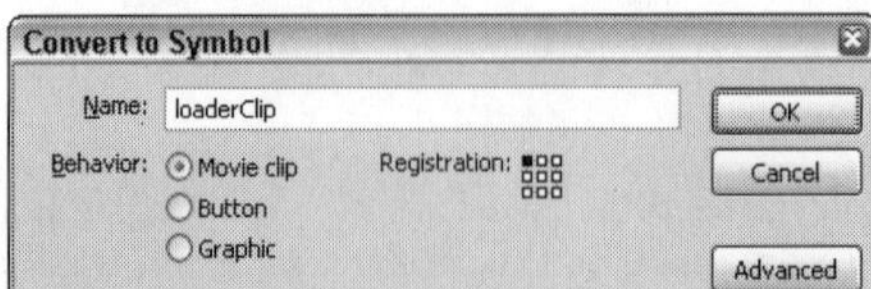

Figure 34-8: The rectangle artwork will be part of the loaderClip symbol.

11. With the new instance selected on the stage of the main timeline, name the instance mcLoader in the Property inspector.

12. Double-click the mcLoader instance on the stage. In Edit mode, rename Layer 1 of the loaderClip symbol mcBar. Create another layer and name it frame. Make sure the frame layer is above the mcBar layer.

13. Select the stroke of the rectangle and cut it (Ctrl+X or ⌘+X). Select frame 1 of the frame layer and paste the stroke in place (Edit ➪ Paste in Place, or Ctrl+Shift+V, or ⌘+Shift+V). Lock the frame layer so you won't accidentally select the border outline in the next step.

14. On the mcBar layer, select the fill of the rectangle. Convert this fill to a Movie Clip symbol named barClip. In the Convert to Symbol dialog box, choose the middle-left registration point.

15. With the new instance selected on the stage of the loaderClip symbol, name the instance mcBar in the Property inspector. In the Transform panel, scale the width of the instance to 1.0 percent, as shown in Figure 34-9. (You might need to reset the X position of the mcBar instance back to 0 in the Property inspector after you have transformed the width.) When the movie first starts to load, you do not want the mcBar instance scaled at full size (100 percent) — as the bytes of the movie load into the Flash Player, the _xscale of the mcBar instance will increase. (You will insert the code to do this later.)

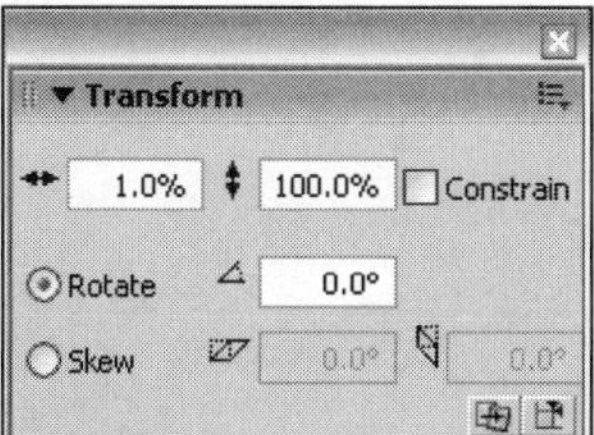

Figure 34-9: Decrease the X scale of the mcBar instance to 1.0 percent in the Transform panel.

16. Create another layer and name it textfield. Place this layer at the bottom of the layer stack in the loaderClip symbol.

17. Select the Text tool and create a Dynamic text field on frame 1 of the textfield layer. Place the text field underneath the mcBar instance, as shown in Figure 34-10. In the *<Instance Name>* field of the Property inspector, name the text field tPercent. You will use this text field to display what percentage of the Flash movie is currently loaded. You do not need to enable the Show Border (or other options) for this text field.

18. Go back to the main timeline (that is, Scene 1). Select the mcLoader instance on the stage and center it using the Align panel. Select frame 10 of the mcLoader layer and insert an empty keyframe (F7). You need only the mcLoader instance to appear as the movie is preloading.

19. Create a new layer and name it actions. Place this layer underneath the labels layer.

20. Select frame 1 of the actions layer and open the Actions panel. In the Script pane, insert the code shown in Listing 34-1. Each line of code is explained in comments within the code. If you don't want to type this code, you can copy the contents of the Listing34-1.as file (located in the ch34 folder of the CD-ROM), or you can attach the AS file to this frame with an #include directive.

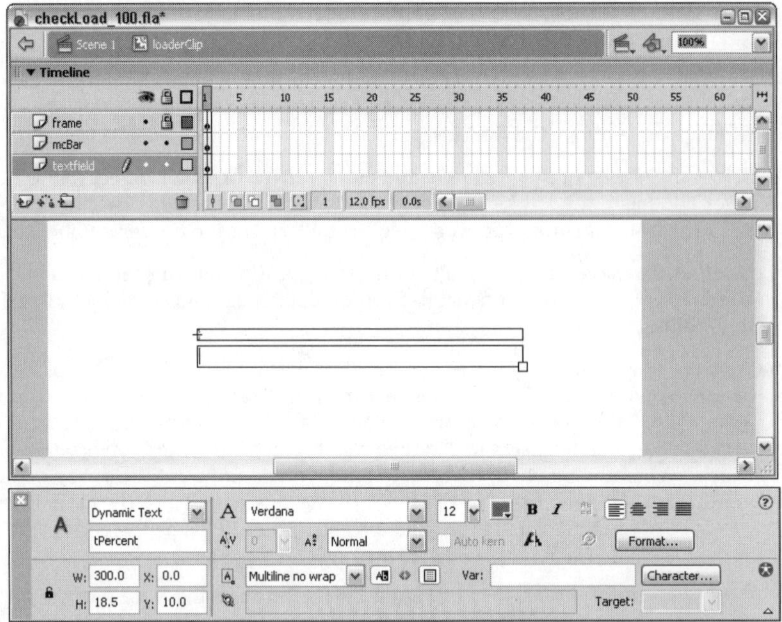

Figure 34-10: The tPercent field displays what percentage of the movie is currently loaded.

Listing 34-1: **The checkLoad() Function**

```
function checkLoad(mcTarget:MovieClip):Void{

  // nLBytes stores the current bytes that have loaded

  var nLBytes:Number = mcTarget.getBytesLoaded();

  // nTBytes stores the total bytes of the movie

  var nTBytes:Number = mcTarget.getBytesTotal();

  // nPercent calculates the percent of the movie that
  // has loaded into the Flash Player.

  var nPercent:Number = (nLBytes/nTBytes)*100;

  // Apply the nPercent value to the X scale of the
  // mcBar instance within the mcLoader instance

  mcLoader.mcBar._xscale = nPercent;
```

```
// Fill the tPercent field within the mcLoader instance
// with the nPercent value followed by the text
// "% of " and the total kilobytes of the movie. For
// example, when half of a 64K movie has loaded, the text
// field will display "50% of 64K loaded."

var sPercent:String = Math.floor(nPercent).toString();
var sKBytes:String = Math.floor(nTBytes/1024).toString();
var sMessage:String = sPercent + "% of " + sKBytes + "K loaded.";
mcLoader.tPercent.text = sMessage;

// If the loaded bytes are greater than or equal to the
// total bytes of the movie and the total bytes are
// greater than 0

if (nLBytes >= nTBytes && nTBytes > 0) {

  // Check to see if the nCount variable is greater than
  // or equal to 12. If it is, execute the nested code.
  // This if/else code pauses the movie once 100% of the
  // movie has loaded into the Flash Player.

  if (nCount >= 12) {

    // exit the loading sequence by removing the
    // setInterval ID established later in this frame

    clearInterval(nProgress);

    // jump to the "main" frame

    mcTarget.gotoAndStop("main");

  // otherwise, if the movie has completely loaded and
  // nCount is less than 12.

  } else {

    // add 1 to the count variable
    nCount++;

    // continue executing the checkLoad() function with
    // setInterval(). There is no further code to insert
    // here, as this will happen automatically if
    // clearInterval() is not executed.
  }
}

// force the stage to refresh the screen independent of
// the frame rate of the movie
```

Continued

Listing 34-1 (continued)

```
  updateAfterEvent();
}

// Initialize a count variable (to pause the loader briefly
// at 100%) with a value of 0

var nCount:Number = 0;

// As soon as this frame is played, start executing the
// the checkLoad() function continuously, passing a
// reference of the Flash movie (this) as an argument

var nProgress:Number = setInterval(checkLoad, 100, this);

// stop the movie

stop();
```

21. Save your Flash document as `checkLoad_100.fla` and test it (Ctrl+Enter or ⌘+Enter). When you enter Test Movie mode, choose View ➪ Show Streaming, or press Ctrl+Enter or ⌘+Enter again. As shown in Figure 34-11, you will see the movie's download progress reflected in the `_xscale` property of the `mcBar` instance, as well as an updated percent value and the total file size in the `tPercent` field. When the movie is fully loaded, the loader will pause for about a second and go to the `main` label.

You can find the completed file, `checkLoad_100.fla`, in the `ch34` folder of the book's CD-ROM.

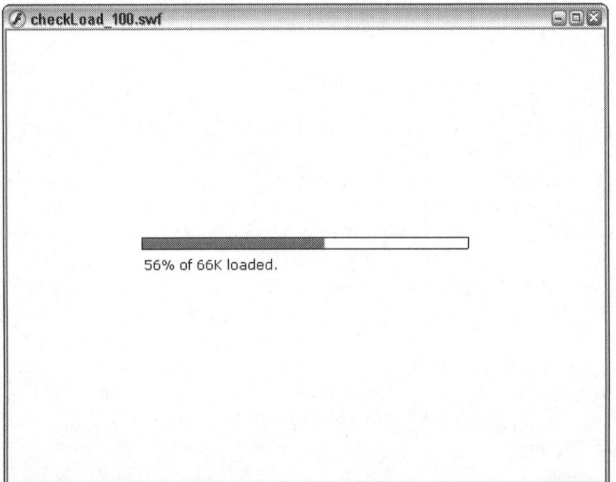

Figure 34-11: The progress bar will grow as the movie loads into the Flash Player.

Once you have this example working properly, you can copy and paste the preload frame and mcLoader instance into other Flash movies. For small Flash projects, you might simply want to build an internal preloader for every Flash movie you develop. However, if you will be loading several assets into the Flash movie, you might need some that can adapt to different file types. In the next section, you learn how to make a preloader that can be dynamically attached to the movie to monitor the loading progress of several file types.

The setInterval() and clearInterval() functions work only in Flash Player 6 or later.

Making a Multipurpose Preloader

In this section, you learn how to add a preloader that monitors the download progress of most media assets, whether it is a SWF, JPEG, or MP3 file. This preloader combines the same methodology employed by the preloader you built in the previous section:

1. Check the bytes loaded of an asset file. Update a progress bar with the currently loaded percentage of the asset.
2. If the bytes loaded match the total bytes of the file, remove the loader from the stage and proceed with the movie.
3. If the bytes loaded are fewer than the total bytes of the file, continue checking the bytes loaded.

However, in this version of the preloader, the loader does not appear on the Stage until a loadMovie() or loadSound() method has been invoked. You will make a Flash movie that has an Input text field, into which you can type a relative or absolute URL to any Flash movie, JPEG, or MP3 file. After you enter the URL, you click a Button component instance to initiate the loading of the asset. Once the loading has started, a loader is dynamically attached to the stage. This instance monitors the loading progress of the asset. When the asset has finished loading, the loader removes itself from the stage.

As you can see in Figure 34-12, the checkLoad() function is contained within the loader. One of the steps in the following exercise moves the preload code from the main timeline to the loaderClip symbol timeline. You will make some minor modifications to the checkLoad() function so that it knows which object (MovieClip or Sound instance) to target.

Before you enhance the loader, you will create a loadFile() method that checks the last three letters of the URL that is typed into the Input text field (named tURL). If the URL ends in "swf" or "jpg", the loadFile() method loads the URL into a MovieClip object named mcHolder. If the URL ends in "mp3", the method loads the URL into a Sound object named snd_1. After the load has been initiated, an oInit object is created. The oInit object contains the information that the loaderClip symbol will need to work. The X and Y position of the loaderClip instance is based on the position of the tURL text field. The mcTarget variable (which is specified in the checkLoad() function within the loaderClip symbol) is set to either mcHolder or snd_1, depending on what type of media file is being loaded. Finally, the attachMovie() method attaches the loaderClip symbol from the movie's library to the main timeline, passing it the properties of the oInit object. When the loaderClip instance appears on the stage, the checkLoad() function within the instance will start to monitor the download of the target object. Figure 34-13 demonstrates an overview of this procedure in a process flowchart.

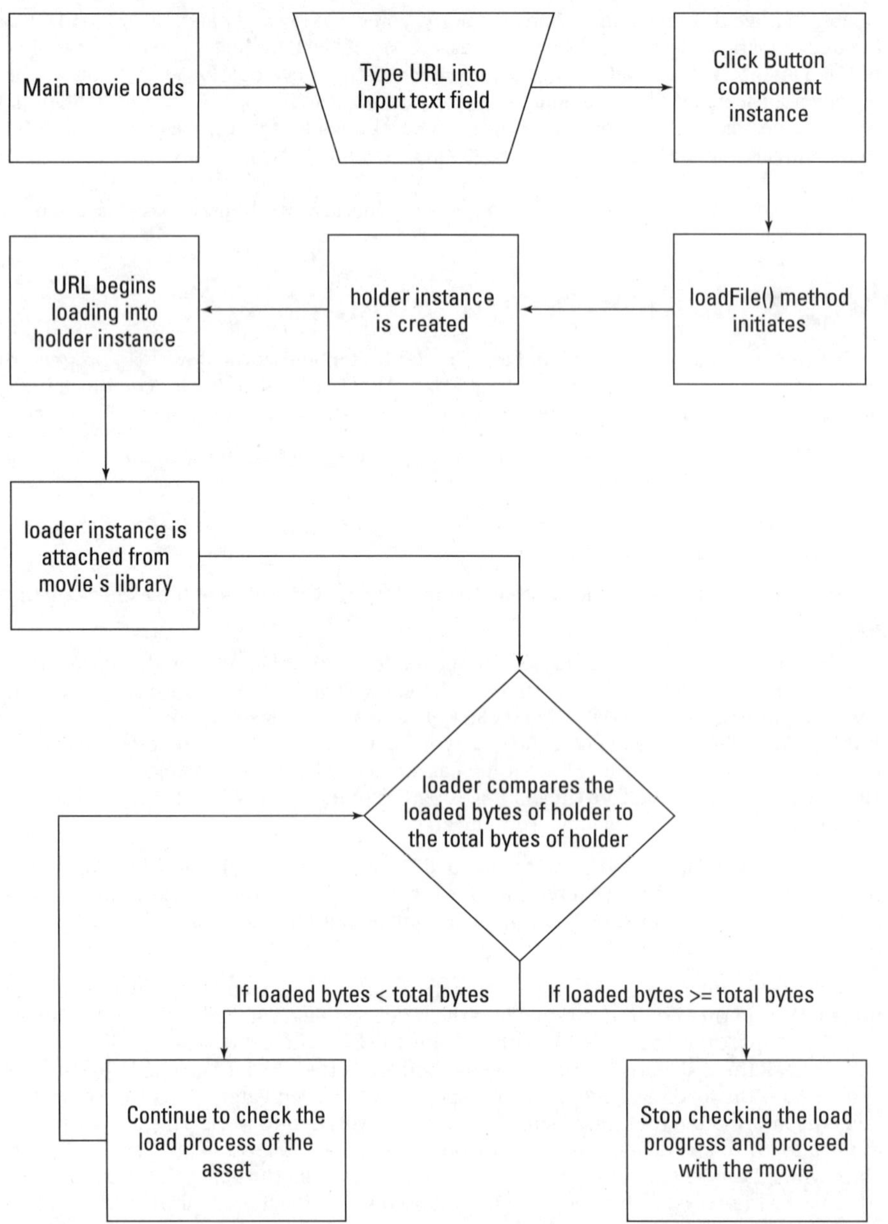

Figure 34-12: The loader instance monitors the download of the asset into the holder instance.

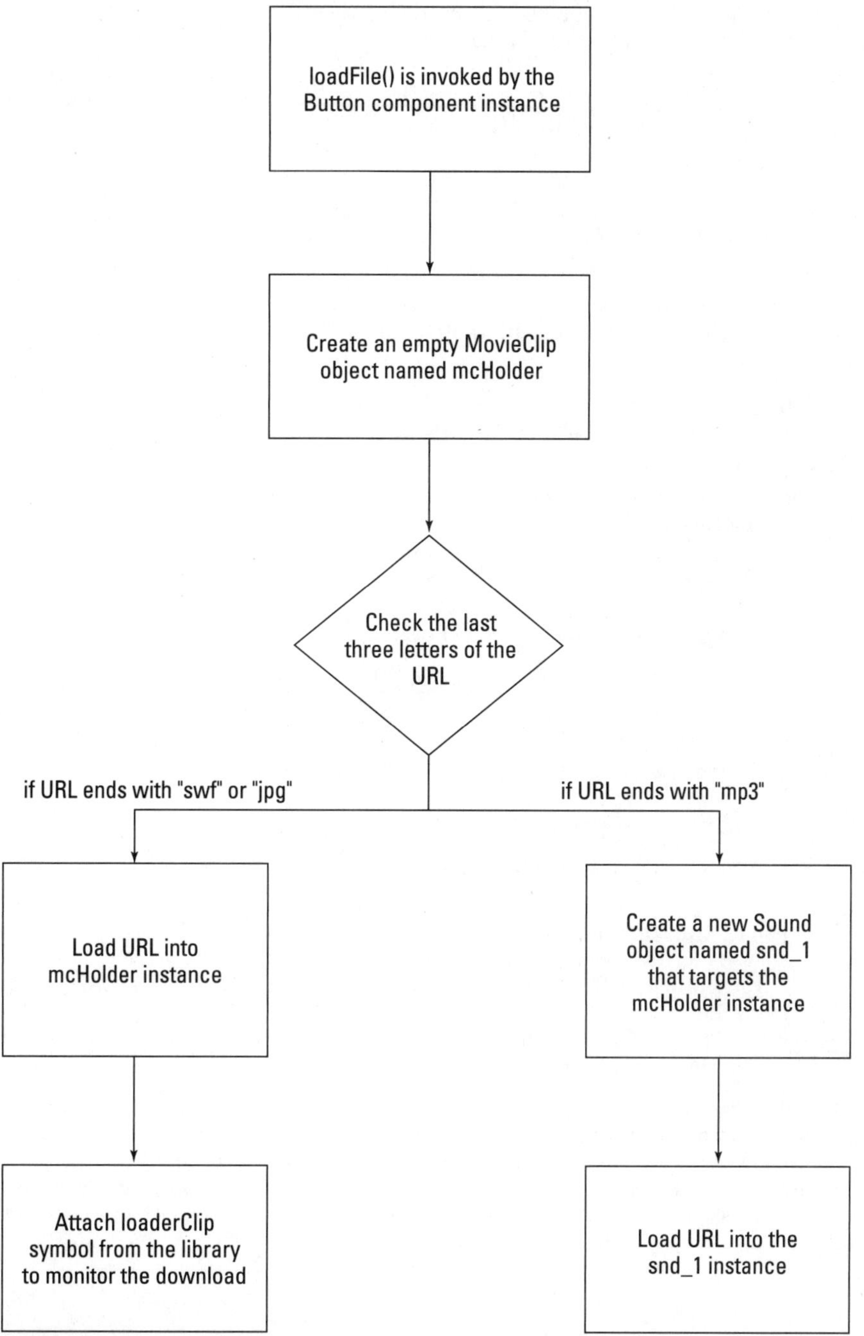

Figure 34-13: The loadFile() method uses the appropriate load method and object for the designated URL.

In the following steps, you combine the `loaderClip` symbol from the `checkLoad_100.fla` with the ActionScript functions described earlier.

Make a copy of the `Listing34-2.as` and `Listing34-3.as` files, located in the `ch34` folder of this book's CD-ROM.

1. Create a new Flash document (File ➪ New). Save this document as `checkLoad_200.fla`. Leave this document open while you open the document in the next step.
2. Open the `checkLoad_100.fla` document located in the ch34 folder of the CD-ROM. Select the `mcLoader` instance on the stage and copy it (Edit ➪ Copy). Close the `checkLoad_100.fla` document window after you have copied the instance.
3. Go to the `checkLoad_200.fla` document and paste the `mcLoader` instance onto the stage (Edit ➪ Paste). All of the content associated with the `mcLoader` instance will now appear in the Library panel for this document.
4. Delete the `mcLoader` instance from the stage. In the Library panel, right-click (or Control-click on the Mac) the `loaderClip` symbol, and choose Linkage from the context menu. In the Linkage Properties dialog box, select the Export for ActionScript check box. The `loaderClip` name will automatically appear in the Identifier field (see Figure 34-14). Click OK to accept this value.

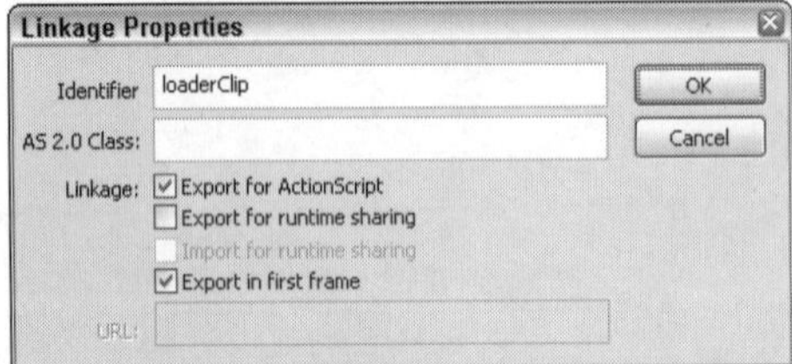

Figure 34-14: The Linkage Properties dialog box

5. Rename Layer 1 of the main timeline (that is, Scene 1) to `textfield`. On frame 1 of this layer, use the Text tool to create an Input text field named `tURL`. At runtime, the user will type a URL for a Flash movie, JPEG, or MP3 file into this field. The URL will then be used by the `loadFile()` method (defined in a later step). Position the text field in the lower-right portion of the stage. Assign the field options in the Property inspector, as shown in Figure 34-15.
6. Create a new layer and name it `cbtLoad`. On frame 1 of this layer, drag a `Button` component from the Components panel onto the stage. Place the instance below the text field, aligned to the left edge. In the Property inspector, name the instance `cbtLoad`. In the Parameters tab, assign a label value of `Load File` (see Figure 34-16). This instance will be assigned a listener that invokes the `loadFile()` method, which is defined in the next step.

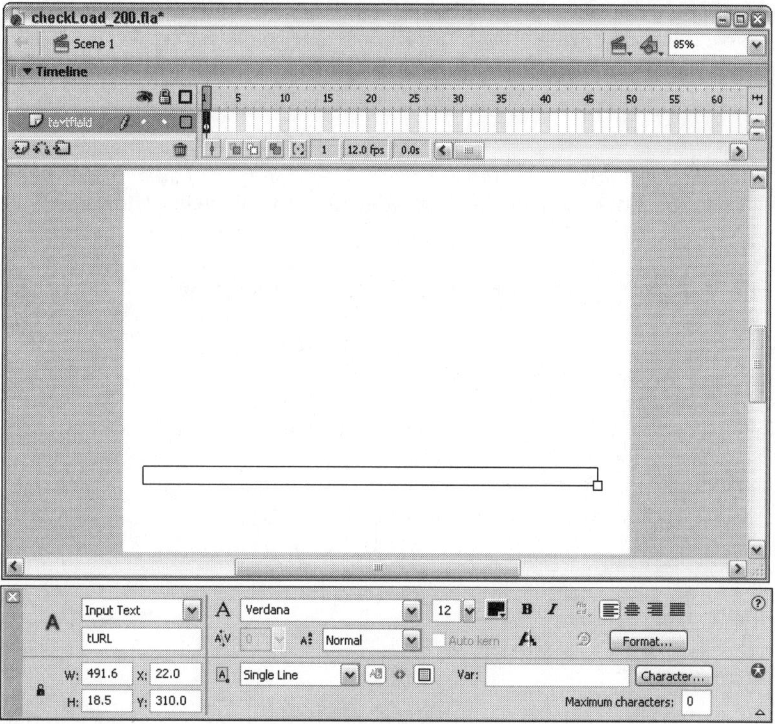

Figure 34-15: The options for the tURL text field

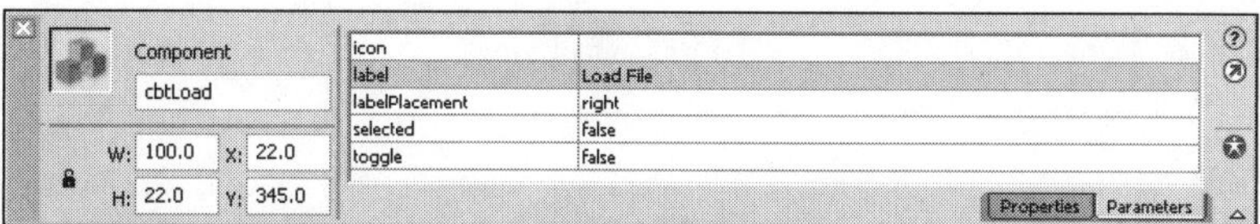

Figure 34-16: The parameters for the cbtLoad instance

7. Create a new layer and name it `Actions`. Select frame 1 of this layer and open the Actions panel. In the Script pane, define the `loadFile()` method with the code shown in Listing 34-2. (You can opt to use an `#include "Listing34-2.as"` directive in place of this code.)

8. The functionality of the main timeline is now in place. Now you need to define a modified version of the `checkLoad()` function inside of the `loaderClip` symbol. Double-click the `loaderClip` symbol in the Library panel. On the `loaderClip` symbol timeline, create a new layer named actions. Select frame 1 of this layer and open the Actions panel. In the Script pane, add the code shown in Listing 34-3. (You can opt to use the `#include "Listing34-3.as"` directive in place of this code.)

9. Exit Edit mode on the `loaderClip` symbol timeline and return to the main timeline. Save the Flash document and test it (Ctrl+Enter or ⌘+Enter). Type a URL into the Input text field. You can use the following test URL:

   ```
   http://www.flashsupport.com/images/beach.jpg
   ```

   Alternatively, you can type the name of a file in the same location as the tested movie on your hard drive. Click the Load File button, and the `mcLoader` instance will appear above the Input text field, indicating the progress of the file's download.

Listing 34-2: The loadFile() Method and Listener

```
this.loadFile = function(oEvent:Object):Void {
   var mcOwner:MovieClip = oEvent.target._parent;
   var sFileExt:String = tURL.text.substr(-3);
   var mcHolder:MovieClip = mcOwner.createEmptyMovieClip("mcHolder", 1);
   if(sFileExt == "swf" || sFileExt == "jpg"){
      mcHolder.loadMovie(tURL.text);
      var loadObj:MovieClip = mcHolder;
   } else if(sFileExt == "mp3"){
      snd_1 = new Sound(mcHolder);
      snd_1.loadSound(tURL.text, true);
      var loadObj:Sound = snd_1;
   }
   var oInit:Object = {
      _x: tURL._x,
      _y: tURL._y - 40,
      target: loadObj,
      loadExit: null
   };
   var mcLoader:MovieClip = mcOwner.attachMovie("loaderClip", "mcLoader", ⮐
      2, oInit);
};
var snd_1:Sound;
cbtLoad.addEventListener("click", this.loadFile);
```

Listing 34-3: The Modified checkLoad() Function

```
function checkLoad():Void {
  var nLBytes:Number = this.target.getBytesLoaded();
  var nTBytes:Number = this.target.getBytesTotal();
  var nPercent:Number = (nLBytes/nTBytes)*100;

  this.mcBar._xscale = nPercent;
```

```
  var sPercent:String = Math.floor(nPercent).toString();
  var sKBytes:String = Math.floor(nTBytes/1024).toString();
  var sMessage:String = sPercent + "% of " + sKBytes + "K loaded.";
  this.tPercent.text = sMessage;

  if (nLBytes >= nTBytes && nTBytes > 0) {
    if (nCount >= 12) {
      clearInterval(this.nProgress);
      this._parent[this.loadExit]();
      this.removeMovieClip();
    } else {
      nCount++;
    }
  }
  updateAfterEvent();
}
var nCount:Number = 0;
var nProgress:Number = setInterval(this, "checkLoad", 50);
stop();
```

Once the loading mechanism is working properly, try a URL for each of the media formats that Flash Player 6 or later can load dynamically. If a file fails to load, check the same URL in a Web browser.

You can find the completed document, `checkLoad_200.fla`, and sample JPEG and MP3 files in the `ch34` folder of the book's CD-ROM. You can also find a modified version, named `checkLoad_300.fla`, which includes additional code to monitor the download progress of an FLV (Flash Video) file.

Using Shared Libraries for Font Management

As we have shown in previous flowchart and schematic illustrations, Shared Library movies can provide universal project elements to several Flash movies within the presentation or application. One of the most effective Shared Library assets is a Font symbol. By creating a Font symbol, you can reuse the same font outlines for every movie in your project. Fonts are ideal shared assets because an entire font face can easily consume over 20KB. Adding 20KB to several loaded Flash movies can quickly bloat the file size of your entire project. Moreover, if you need to make global changes to a text field, you can simply change the shared font in one document — any file that references the shared font will update during runtime. In this section, you learn how to share a font with manually created text fields and text fields created on the fly with the `createTextField()` method of the `MovieClip` object.

Refer to basic Shared Library use in *Macromedia Flash MX 2004 Bible* by Robert Reinhardt and Snow Dowd (Wiley, 2004). This section explores specific font issues with Shared Libraries.

For the purposes of these examples, you will use Verdana, a readily available font, for your Shared Library font symbol. In practice, you'd likely choose to embed and share fonts that aren't commonly installed in your users' systems. Feel free to use a different font face in your actual Flash documents.

Whenever a Shared Library asset is used in another Flash movie, the entire Shared Library movie file must download into the Flash Player before the frame of the Flash movie using any shared asset(s) is allowed to play. For this reason, you might want to make sure that your Shared Library files are as small as possible. Moreover, you might want to preload the Shared Library file into a Flash Player Level or `MovieClip` object. See the "Preloading a Shared Library" section, later in this chapter, for more information.

Sharing a Font with Manually Created Text Fields

In this exercise, you learn how to create a Shared Library movie that contains a Font symbol. The Font symbol will be shared by two other Flash movies in the project.

1. Create a new Flash document. Save the document as `shared_lib.fla` in a folder named `shared` on your hard drive. The `shared` folder will be referenced in the Shared Library URL that is used for the Font symbol.

2. Open the Library panel. In the options menu (located at the top-right corner of the panel), choose New Font. In the Font Symbol Properties dialog box, choose Verdana in the Font menu, and type `Verdana_Shared` in the Name field, as shown in Figure 34-17. Click OK to accept these values.

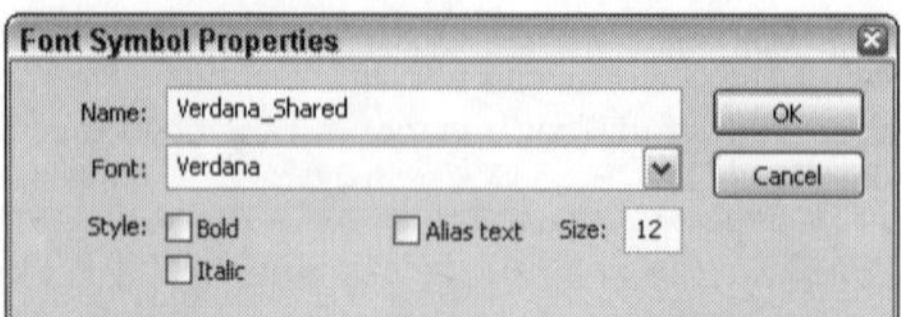

Figure 34-17: The Font Symbol Properties dialog box

3. Now you need to specify this Font symbol as a linked and shared asset. Right-click (or Control-click on the Mac) the `Verdana_Shared` symbol in the Library panel, and choose Linkage in the context menu. In the Linkage Properties dialog box, select the Export for ActionScript and the Export for runtime sharing check boxes. The Identifier field will automatically be filled with the name `Verdana_Shared`. In the URL field, type `shared/shared_lib.swf`. This is the path that other assets will use to access the shared asset. Click OK to accept these values, as shown in Figure 34-18. (The Export for ActionScript option will come into play with the next section's example.)

4. Open the Publish Settings dialog box (File ➪ Publish Settings). In the Formats tab, clear the HTML check box. Do not change the Flash movie filename. It's critical to ensure that the final Flash movie (SWF file) retains the name specified in the URL field of the Linkage Properties dialog box.

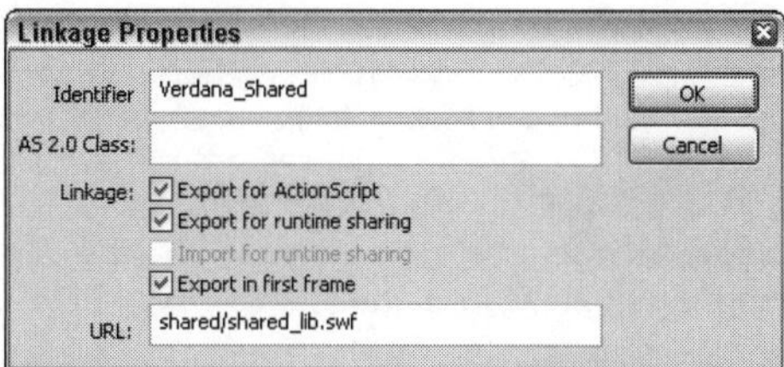

Figure 34-18: The Linkage Properties dialog box

Because the URL value in the Linkage Properties dialog box is a relative path, all Flash movies that use this asset must be located in the parent directory of the `shared` folder. If the Flash movies are located across several directories, you might need to use an absolute URL such as `http://www.myserver.com/shared/shared_lib.swf`. Alternatively, you can specify a path such as `/shared/shared_lib.swf`, which specifies a `shared` folder located at the root of the current URL used by the Flash movies. As long as there is a folder named `shared` at the root of your public Web server folder, all movies will be able to access the `shared_lib.swf` file (and its assets) inside of the `shared` folder.

5. Save your Flash document again, and publish the Flash movie (File ➪ Publish). When the file has finished publishing, go to the `shared` folder and look at the file size of the `shared_lib.swf` file. For this example, the shared Verdana font alone is nearly 17KB. By making a shared asset for this font, you can save 17KB on every Flash movie that needs to use the font. At this point, you are ready to create a Flash document (and movie) that uses the shared font.

6. Close the `shared_lib.fla` document and create a new document. Save this file as `section_shared.fla` in the folder above the `shared_lib.swf` file.

7. Choose File ➪ Import ➪ Open External Library and select the `shared_lib.fla` file inside the `shared` folder. A Library panel will open displaying the `Verdana_Shared` symbol. Drag the `Verdana_Shared` symbol from the Library panel to the stage of the `section_shared.fla` document. When you are finished, close the Library panel for `shared_lib.fla`.

8. Rename Layer 1 to `static text`. On frame 1 of this layer, use the Text tool to create a Static text block containing some text. For this example, type "`The quick brown fox jumped over the lazy dog`" into the field. Most importantly, in the Font menu of the Property inspector, choose Verdana_Shared*. All shared fonts appear with an asterisk (*) after the font name.

9. Save your Flash document and test it (Ctrl+Enter or ⌘+Enter). In Test Movie mode, open the Bandwidth Profiler (View ➪ Bandwidth Profiler). Notice that the file size of the Flash movie is fewer than 200 bytes! Because the font outlines are being loaded from the `shared_lib.swf` file, the `section_shared.swf` file needs to store only the text characters shown in the Static text field — not the actual font outlines for the Verdana font. (If you doubt this, return to the Flash document and change the Static text field to use Verdana as the font face instead of Verdana_Shared. Test the movie and note the difference in file size.)

10. Now you can add a Dynamic text field to the same Flash document. Return to the main timeline and create a new layer named `dynamic text`. Using the Text tool, create a Dynamic text field with an instance name of `tArticle`. In the Font menu of the Property inspector, choose Verdana_Shared* (if it's not selected already). With this text field selected, click the Character button in the Property inspector. In the Character Options dialog box, Shift+select the top four character ranges as shown in Figure 34-19, and click OK. Do not type any text in the text field. In the next step, you will fill the field using ActionScript.

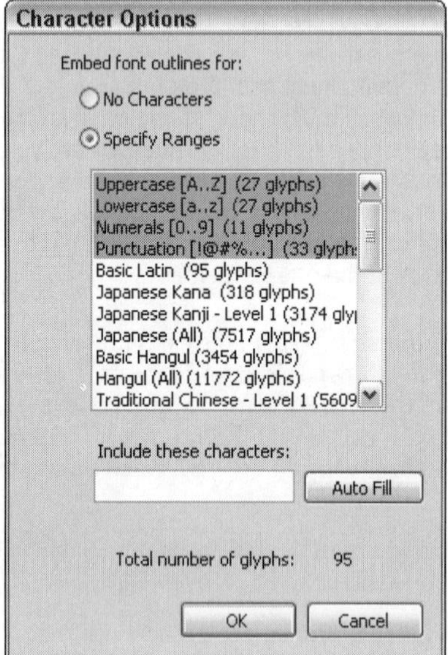

Figure 34-19: The Character Options dialog box

11. Create a new layer and name it `Actions`. Select frame 1 of the actions layer and open the Actions panel. In the Script pane, type the following code:

```
tArticle.text = "Welcome to shared libraries in Flash.";
```

12. Save your document and test it (Ctrl+Enter or ⌘+Enter). Look in the Bandwidth Profiler to see the movie's file size. In this example, the SWF file's size should be just over 300 bytes. The font outlines displayed in the Dynamic text field are loaded from the `shared_lib.swf` file. Therefore, the font outlines do not need to be included with the `section_shared.swf` file.

You can continue to make more Flash movies that use the `Verdana_Shared` font. Once a Shared Library has loaded into the Flash Player, it does not need to be downloaded for any other Flash movies that use assets from that library. In the next section, you learn how to embed a shared font into a text field created on the fly with ActionScript.

You can replace the font specified in the Font symbol of the `shared_lib.fla` file. Once you publish a new `shared_lib.swf` file, all of the Flash movies (SWF files) using the shared font will show the new font face. Effectively using this method of font management enables you to change fonts in every Flash movie of a project within seconds.

Sharing a Font with Dynamically Created Text Fields

Before you begin this exercise, some strange "rules" of shared fonts must be defined. You won't find this information in any of Macromedia's printed documentation, but our research has led us to believe the following tenets for shared fonts with ActionScript-created text fields:

✦ If you want to use a shared font in a Flash movie that uses the `createTextField()` method to create dynamic text, you have to create a Static, Dynamic, or Input text field on the stage with the Text tool first. This nonscripted field must specify the shared font's name in the Font menu of the Property inspector. If you use a Dynamic or Input text field, you don't actually have to embed the font characters into the field or type any text into the field. This "dummy" text field will force the Shared Library file to load into the Flash Player so that the Font symbol(s) are ready to be used in ActionScript. If you don't use any of the Shared Library assets in your actual artwork or symbols in the Flash movie, the Shared Library file won't load into the Flash Player. Remember that whenever a Shared Library item is used within a Flash movie, the entire Shared Library SWF file must download into the Flash Player before the frame using the shared asset can play — the movie will not display its frame containing the shared asset until the Shared Library has loaded.

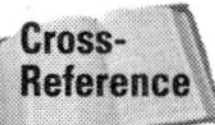

To monitor the loading of a Shared Library file, read the "Preloading a Shared Library" section, later in this chapter.

✦ A `TextFormat` object that styles a `TextField` object with a shared font should be defined and applied to the `TextField` object in ActionScript before the `text` property of the `TextField` object is invoked to fill the field with text.

✦ The `font` property of a `TextFormat` object should specify the actual name of the shared font — not the linkage identifier name. For example, if you created a Font symbol containing the Marigold font (from the Mac OS) and gave the font a symbol and linkage name of Marigold_Shared, you would not use the name Marigold_Shared for the font property value. Rather, the font's name should be specified as it shows up in the Font menu — for this example, Marigold.

This last rule is in direct contradiction with the use of embedded fonts and native (that is, non-shared) Font symbols. If you have a Font symbol that is not imported as a Shared Library element, use the linkage identifier name for the `font` property of the `TextFormat` object.

With these rules in mind, you will build a Flash document that creates a text field on the fly, and imports a shared font for that field. Now, you might already be thinking, But if I use the font's actual name for the embedded font in the new `TextField` object, isn't the Flash Player just using the installed system font? If you have the font installed, you might not know whether the movie is displaying your system font or the Shared Library font unless you deactivate or temporarily uninstall the font from your system. For the following example, we will eliminate all doubt by giving you access to a premade Shared Library file that has two Mac fonts, Marigold and Monaco; as well as another nonstandard font, Blur Medium. You will make a Flash movie that creates a text field displaying characters in any of these three fonts — even if you don't have them installed in your system.

You will need to copy the fonts.swf Shared Library file into the folder named shared on your hard drive. Refer to the previous exercise to learn how to properly set up your Shared Library folder structure. You can find a copy of the fonts.swf file in the ch34/shared folder of this book's CD-ROM.

1. Create a new Flash document and save it as dynamic_shared.fla in the folder located above the shared_lib.swf file. If the dynamic_shared.fla file is in the same folder as the shared_lib.swf file, this procedure will not work.

2. In this step, you will create new Font symbols in the document. You don't need to open a Shared Library document in the Flash MX 2004 authoring document to access shared elements—you can create "empty" symbols that will point to the URL of the Shared Library asset. Open the Library panel and choose New Font from the options menu. In the Font Properties dialog box, type BlurMedium_Shared into the Name field. Instead of selecting a font in the Font menu, type BlurMedium into the Font field (see Figure 34-20). (This Name and this Font are exactly the same ones specified in the fonts.fla file used to create the fonts.swf file. You can find the fonts.fla file in the ch34/shared folder of this book's CD-ROM.)

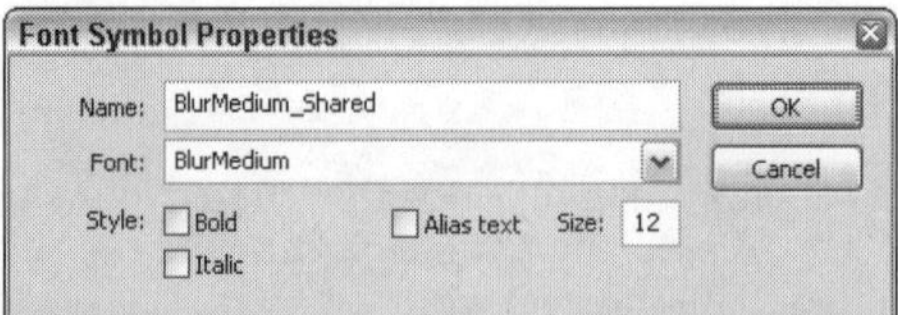

Figure 34-20: Create a new Font symbol referring to BlurMedium.

3. Once the BlurMedium_Shared symbol is defined in the Library panel, right-click (or Control-click on the Mac) the symbol, and choose Linkage. In the Linkage Properties dialog box, select the Import for runtime sharing check box. In the URL field, type shared/fonts.swf, as shown in Figure 34-21. Click OK when you are finished.

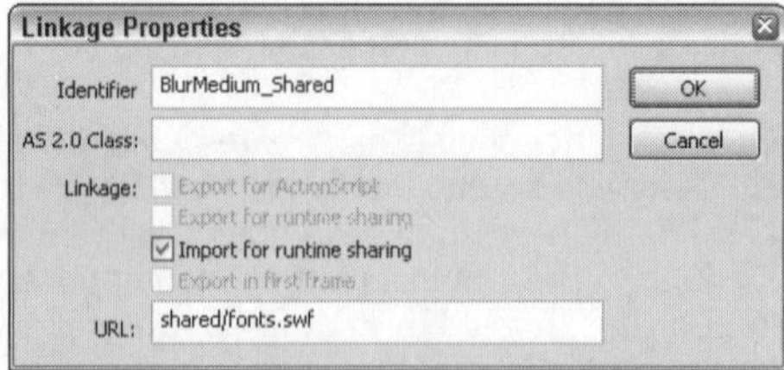

Figure 34-21: Use the Linkage Properties dialog box to define the source of the Shared Library.

4. Repeat Steps 2 through 3 with the symbol names Marigold_Shared (Marigold as the Font name) and Monaco_Shared (Monaco as the Font name). When you are finished, your Library panel should list three Font symbols, as shown in Figure 34-22.

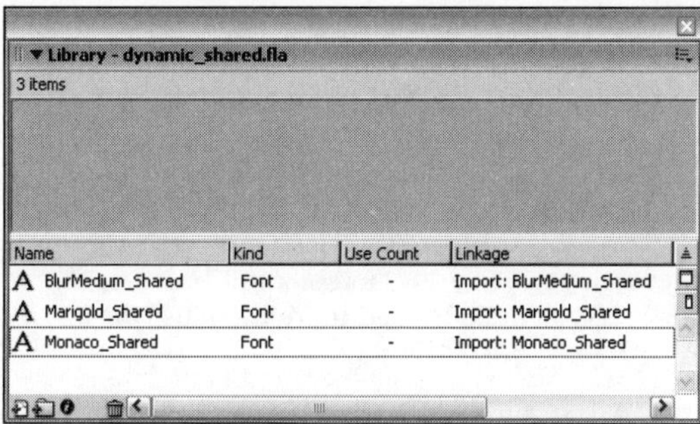

Figure 34-22: The three imported Font symbols

5. Now you're ready to create the "dummy" text field that will force the Flash movie to load the `fonts.swf` file into the Flash Player. Rename Layer 1 `tDummy`. Using the Text tool, create a small Dynamic text field with an instance name of `tDummy`. In the Property inspector, choose one of the three shared font names in the Font menu (`BlurMedium_Shared*`, `Marigold_Shared*`, or `Monaco_Shared*`). If you don't want this field to be visible, make sure the Show Border option is not enabled.

6. Create a new layer and name it `actions`. Select frame 1 of the `actions` layer, and open the Actions panel. In the Script pane, type the following code. In this code, a `TextField` object named `tTitle` is created. A `TextFormat` object named `tfSharedStyle` specifies the BlurMedium font loaded from the Shared Library movie. The `tfSharedStyle` object is applied to the `tTitle` object with the `setNewTextFormat()` method. As mentioned earlier, it's crucial that `tTitle.text` is the last action applied to the `tTitle` object—neither the font nor the text will display in the field if text is executed before the other actions.

```
this.createTextField("tTitle", 1, 10, 10, 400, 25);
tTitle.embedFonts = true;

var tfSharedStyle:TextFormat = new TextFormat();
tfSharedStyle.font = "BlurMedium";
tTitle.setNewTextFormat(tfSharedStyle);

tTitle.text = "Welcome to the world of ultimate shared text.";
```

7. Save your Flash document and test it (Ctrl+Enter or ⌘+Enter). If your Flash movie is saved in the correct location (relative to the `fonts.swf` file), you will see the text `"Welcome to the world of ultimate shared text."` appear on the stage.

Go back to the actions on frame 1 and try out the other font names (Monaco and Marigold) as the values of the `tfSaredStyle.font` property. Once you have the example working with all of the fonts, take some time to create your own Font library file(s). Once you have a collection of font libraries, you can reuse them from project to project.

You can find the completed file, `dynamic_shared.fla`, in the ch34 folder of this book's CD-ROM.

Preloading a Shared Library

When a Flash movie uses an asset from a Shared Library, the frame using the asset needs to wait for the entire SWF file containing the shared asset to download. If you are constructing substantial Shared Library file(s), you might not want your Flash presentations to suddenly pause when a shared asset is downloading. To prevent this unwanted effect, you can preload a Shared Library file into a `MovieClip` object before the Flash movie(s) requiring the assets loads into the presentation. However, if you are using ActionScript to create dynamic elements on-the-fly, such as `TextField` objects, you need to load more than just the Shared Library SWF file.

To successfully use Shared Library assets with any loaded file in your project, you should observe the following load order:

1. Load the SWF file for the Shared Library into a `MovieClip` object created within the master movie for the presentation.

2. Load a "dummy" Flash movie into another `MovieClip` object created within the master movie. This dummy movie should contain any of the shared elements from the Shared Library SWF file loaded in Step 1. If you are sharing fonts with other movies that create `TextField` objects with the `createTextField()` method, we recommend that you create an empty Dynamic text field, specifying any one of the shared fonts in the Shared Library file. You don't need to type any text into this field — just make sure you use one of the shared font names in the Font menu of the Property inspector. (See the previous section's exercise for more information on creating dummy text fields.)

3. Load the file(s) for the presentation into other `MovieClip` objects within the master movie. These are the files that create the interface, content, and user interactivity for the presentation. At this point, you can load any SWF file that uses a shared asset — when the frame requiring the asset plays, the Flash Player will not pause to download the Shared Library file.

Using these steps, you can create several Shared Library files that are loaded at the beginning of your presentation. By loading all shared assets before they are required, you can avoid jarring pauses in playback when a shared asset is used in the movie.

You can find an example of such a loading sequence in the `ch34` folder of this book's CD-ROM. The `checkLoad_shared.fla` uses a modified version of the `loadFile()` method from the `checkLoad_200.fla` example you created in this chapter. An array specifying the filenames is created on frame 1 of the shared lib actions layer, specifying the load order of three files: `shared/fonts.swf`, `empty_shared.swf`, and `menu_shared.swf`. The `initLoad()` function is called each time an asset has fully loaded. The final file, `menu_shared.swf`, is a basic menu system. The BlurMedium and Monaco fonts from the `fonts.swf` Shared Library are used in the pop-up menu of the `menu_shared.swf` file.

We'd like to know what you thought about this chapter. Visit `www.flashsupport.com/feedback` to fill out an online form with your comments.

Summary

- ✦ A master Flash movie (SWF file) controls the direction and flow of content within the Flash presentation or application.
- ✦ Everything from JPEG images to Flash movies to XML data can be considered an external asset to the master movie. Flash Players 6 and 7 support a wide variety of media and data file types.
- ✦ Be sure to consider how the goals of your project might influence the structure of assets required for the presentation.
- ✦ Organizational charts and process flowcharts can help you define the loading structure of assets within a Flash project.
- ✦ Flash movies (SWF files) can be loaded into Flash Player Levels or `MovieClip` objects within any Level. Determine how you will use Levels and/or `MovieClip` objects as load targets before you begin production on your Flash project.
- ✦ The `MovieClip`, `Sound`, `LoadVars`, and `XML` objects use the `getBytesLoaded()` and `getBytesTotal()` methods to monitor the download progress of data loaded into objects of these classes.
- ✦ You can load Flash movies (SWF files) and JPEG images (JPG files) into `MovieClip` objects with the `loadMovie()` method or into Levels with the `loadMovieNum()` action.
- ✦ MP3 files can be loaded into `Sound` objects with the `loadSound()` method.
- ✦ Using the `NetConnection`, `NetStream`, and `Video` classes, you can load FLV files into your Flash Player 7 movies. If you use Flash Communication Server MX, you gain the benefit of real-time streaming and compatibility with Flash Player 6 and later.
- ✦ `LoadVars` and `XML` objects use the `load()` method to acquire external data.
- ✦ By comparing the values returned by `getBytesLoaded()` to `getBytesTotal()` of an object that is in the middle of loading content, you can create preloaders that display progress bars to the user.
- ✦ You can use Shared Libraries to organize and share fonts, graphics, sounds, and other symbols with several Flash movies (SWF files) in your project. Shared Library workflows require careful attention to load order.

✦ ✦ ✦

Sending and Loading Data

✦ ✦ ✦ ✦

In This Chapter

Working with LoadVars

Loading raw data

Loading XML data to generate an application

Introducing Flash Remoting

✦ ✦ ✦ ✦

In previous chapters, you looked at some of the theory behind sending and loading data into your Flash applications using `LoadVars` and XML. This chapter looks at some more practical applications of loading data from external sources such as server-side scripts. It also introduces some of the basics of Flash Remoting, a technology that enables you to use the proprietary AMF messaging format to efficiently send and receive serialized data within Flash.

Using LoadVars to Send and Load Data

Of all the techniques discussed in this chapter, the `LoadVars` techniques provide the most targeted and specific kinds of functionality. Typically, `LoadVars` is most useful when you want to send simple data. When you're loading data or sending complex values, the `LoadVars` class is typically not the most appropriate choice.

In this exercise, you'll create an e-mail form in Flash similar to one you find on many Web sites. The form uses the v2 UI components, so you might want to refer back to Chapter 28 if you didn't yet read it or if you want to refresh your memory. You'll also use the `LoadVars` class to send the data to a server-side script and to receive a simple verification from the server. If you want to refresh your memory on how to use the `LoadVars` class, refer back to Chapter 26.

1. The first thing you'll want to do is set up the server-side script. On the CD-ROM, you'll find the following scripts: `sendMail.cfm`, `sendMail.cgi` (Perl), `sendMail.php`, and `sendMail.asp`.

   a. Select the correct script that corresponds to the technology available on your server and copy it to your Web server.

   b. If you are testing the script on your own Web server (a server that you administrate), make sure that the mail settings are properly configured. If you are using ColdFusion, you need to make sure that the SMTP server is assigned in the ColdFusion Administrator. If you are using PHP, you need to make sure that the SMTP variable is set in the `php.ini` file. The Perl script runs only on servers running sendmail, and you need to edit the script so that it points to the correct location for that.

2. Open a new Flash document and save it as `emailForm001.fla`.
3. Rename the default layer Form.
4. Create the following component instances on the stage:
   - One `ComboBox` instance named `ccbDepartments`
   - Two `TextInput` instances named `ctiSenderEmail` and `ctiSubject`
   - One `TextArea` instance named `ctaMessage`
   - One `Button` instance named `cbtSend`
   - Four Label instances named clblDepartments, clblSenderEmail, clblSubject, and clblMessage
5. Resize the component instances using the Property inspector as follows:
   - Set the width of the `ComboBox` and the `TextInput` instances to 150 pixels.
   - Set the width of the `TextArea` to 300 and the height to 200.
6. Arrange the component instances on the stage as shown in Figure 35-1. The `ctiSenderEmail` instance should be above the `ctiSubject` instance, and the `Label` instances should match up with the controls with corresponding names (that is, `clblDepartments` matches with `ccbDepartments`).

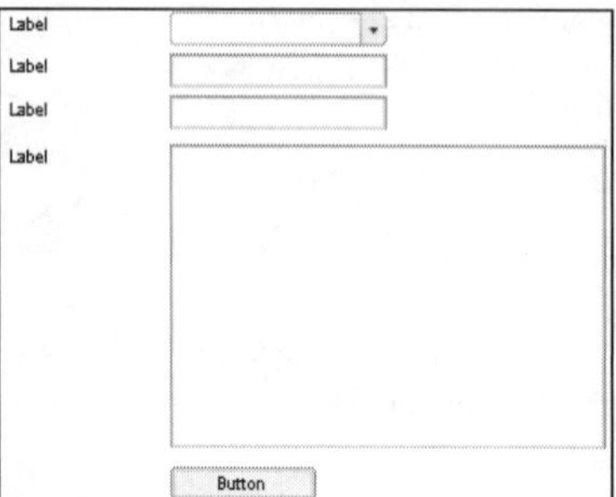

Figure 35-1: The layout of the e-mail form

7. Add a new layer named Actions.
8. Add the following code to the first frame of the `Actions` layer:

```
function initForm():Void {

  // Define the label text.
  clblDepartment.text = "Department:";
  clblSenderEmail.text = "Your Email:";
  clblSubject.text = "Subject:";
  clblMessage.text = "Your Message:";
  cbtSend.label = "Send";
```

```
  // Populate the departments. Make sure to use your
  // own valid email addresses as the data values.
  ccbDepartment.dataProvider = [{label: "Customer Service", ⮐
data: "cstmsrv@domain.com"}, {label: "Sales", data: ⮐
"sales@domain.com"}, {label: "Webmaster", data: ⮐
"webmaster@domain.com"}];

  // Set the tab indices for the components, the initial
  // focus, and the default button.
  ccbDepartment.tabIndex = 1;
  ctiSenderEmail.tabIndex = 2;
  ctiSubject.tabIndex = 3;
  ctaMessage.tabIndex = 4;
  cbtSend.tabIndex = 5;
  ccbDepartment.setFocus();
  focusManager.defaultPushButton = cbtSend;
}

// This function is called when the value is returned from
// the server indicating that the email was successfully
// sent. It sets the visible property of all the form
// elements to false.
function hideForm():Void {
  clblDepartment.visible = false;
  clblSenderEmail.visible = false;
  clblSubject.visible = false;
  clblMessage.visible = false;
  ctiSenderEmail.visible = false;
  ctiSubject.visible = false;
  ctaMessage.visible = false;
  ccbDepartment.visible = false;
  cbtSend.visible = false;
}

// Create the listener for the Button instance.
function createListener():Void {
  var oListener:Object = new Object();
  oListener.click = function(oEvent:Object) {

    // Add the properties and values to the sending
    // LoadVars object where the values are extracted
    // from the form elements.
    lvEmail.toAddress = ccbDepartment.value;
    lvEmail.fromAddress = ctiSenderEmail.text;
    lvEmail.subject = ctiSubject.text;
    lvEmail.message = ctaMessage.text;
```

```
      // Send the data to the server-side script, and tell
      // it to return any value to the lvReceiver LoadVars
      // object. Make sure that you specify the correct URL
      // as the first parameter.
      lvEmail.sendAndLoad("http://localhost/sendMail.php", ⮐
lvReceiver, "POST");
    };
    cbtSend.addEventListener("click", oListener);
}

initForm();
createLoadVars();
var lvEmail:LoadVars = new LoadVars();
var lvReceiver:LoadVars = new LoadVars();

// When the server returns a value, it returns either
// success=0 or success=1. If success is 1 then the send
// was successful. In that case, hide the form and pop up
// a new label with the value of Thank you.
lvReceiver.onLoad = function() {
  if(this.success == 1) {
    hideForm();
    mx.managers.PopUpManager.createPopUp(_root, ⮐
mx.controls.Label, true, {text: "Thank you"});
  }
};
createListener();
```

9. Test the movie. You should be able to fill out the form, click the Send button, and see the `Thank you` message. Assuming you sent the e-mail to an e-mail address you can check, check your e-mail to ensure you received the message.

Loading Plain Text and HTML

You can override the `onData()` method of either a `LoadVars` object or an `XML` object so that you can work with the raw data that is received instead of allowing the object to try and parse it. You've seen how to define an `onLoad()` method to handle the response from the server. But `onLoad()` is actually called only after `onData()` has finished processing the data. In a `LoadVars` object, the built-in `onData()` method parses the value passed to it from the server into properties on the `LoadVars` object. With an `XML` object, the `onData()` method parses the value passed to it from the server into the `XML` object's data tree. By defining your own custom `onData()` method for a `LoadVars` or `XML` object, you prevent the object from parsing the data and calling `onLoad()`. This can be particularly useful when you want to load data that is plain text or HTML-formatted text, for example.

In this exercise, you create a Flash movie that loads some text from a text file and displays the text in an HTML-enabled `TextArea` component instance. The text from the file is HTML-formatted text that contains `<a href>` tags that use the `asfunction` directive to call a function within the Flash movie. The links call a function that loads images into a `Loader` component instance.

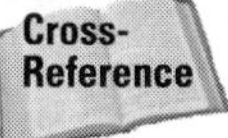

For more information about the `asfunction` directive, refer back to Chapter 17, "The TextField and Selection Classes."

1. Create a new text file and add text to it using the following as an example. The key is that the `<a href>` tags should have values using the `asfunction` directive. These values should call a function called `loadImage` and pass it a parameter that is a URL to a valid nonprogressive JPEG file.

```
Welcome to the photo gallery section of the site.
In this section there are all kinds of images you can view.
If you click on any of the links in this text then the
accompanying image will load to the right.

The first group of images are images from the most recent
board meeting. There's a picture of our
<a href="asfunction:loadImage,http://www.person13.com
/asb/image1.jpg"><font color="#FF0000"><u>CEO dancing in his
boxers</u></font></a>, and another of the
<a href="asfunction:loadImage,
http://www.person13.com/asb/image2.jpg">
<font color="#FF0000"><u>CTO photocopying
his face</u></font></a>.

Next are the images of our dedicated staff at work. Take a look
at the picture of our <a href="asfunction:loadImage,
http://www.person13.com/asb/image1.jpg">
<font color="#FF0000"><u>Web team playing video
games</u></font></a>. And be sure to check out our
<a href="asfunction:loadImage,http://www.person13.com
/asb/image2.jpg"><font color="#FF0000"><u>marketing team
taking a nap</u></font></a>.
```

2. Save the file as `display.txt`.
3. Open a new Flash document and save it as `loadImage.fla` in the same directory in which you saved `display.txt`.
4. Add a `TextArea` component instance to the upper-left side of the stage. Name the instance `ctaDisplay`.
5. Using the Property inspector, resize the `TextArea` instance to 200 pixels in width and 300 pixels in height.
6. Add a `Loader` component instance just to the right of the `TextArea` instance. Name the `Loader` instance `cldImage`.
7. Resize the `Loader` instance using the Property inspector to 300 pixels in width and 300 pixels in height.
8. Rename the default layer `Components` and add a new layer named `Actions`.

9. On the first frame of the Actions layer, add the following code:

```
// Define a global function named loadImage(). The
// function accepts a parameter that specifies the URL
// of the image to load, and it calls the cldImage.load()
// method to load that image into the Loader instance.
_global.loadImage = function(url):Void {
  cldImage.load(url);
};

// Instantiate the LoadVars instance.
var lvText:LoadVars = new LoadVars();

// Define the onData() method for the LoadVars object.
// When the data is received, display it as HTML in the
// TextArea instance.
lvText.onData = function(data):Void {
  ctaDisplay.editable = false;
  ctaDisplay.html = true;
  ctaDisplay.text = data;
};

// Load the text.
lvText.load("display.txt");
```

10. Test the movie.

When you test the movie, you should see the text loaded into the TextArea. The links should appear in red and underlined because of the <u> and <font> tags in the loaded text. If you click one of the links, it should load the image into the Loader instance. Figure 35-2 shows an example.

Figure 35-2: The LoadImage application

Loading XML

Working with XML in Flash is one of the most effective and quickest ways to handle complex data or structured data without using Flash Remoting (see the next section). Many types of applications now use XML, and XML is even the basis for many other Web-based protocols such as the SOAP protocol used by many Web services. The `XML` class is utilized by many of the Professional data components as well. But without having to rely on the data components (and this is good news if you don't have the Professional version of Flash MX 2004), you can still employ the power of XML readily in your applications.

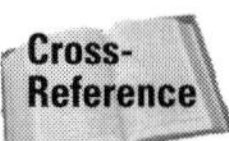

For more information about Web services and the Professional data components, refer to Chapter 36, "Using the Built-In Web Service Functionality."

In this exercise, you create a simple slide viewer that loads all the data, including image and thumbnail locations, caption text, color, and border color, from an XML file. This exercise uses the `XML` class (see Chapter 26) as well as the `ScrollPane`, `Loader`, and `TextArea` components (see Chapter 28).

1. Copy the slides directory from the CD-ROM, including all of the JPEG files it contains, to a location on your hard disk.
2. Create a new XML document using a text editor and add the following code to it. Alternatively, you can use the XML file included on the CD-ROM. However, if you use the XML file on the CD-ROM, you should still review the code to make sure you understand the XML structure and data.

```
<slides>
  <slide>
    <image full="slides/sunset1.jpg" ⮐
thumbnail="slides/sunset1_th.jpg" />
    <caption borderColor="0xEAE4AC" textColor="0x7D7620">⮐
a picture of a sunset over Los Angeles.</caption>
  </slide>
  <slide>
    <image full="slides/sunset2.jpg" ⮐
thumbnail="slides/sunset2_th.jpg" />
    <caption borderColor="0xB8C8EB" textColor="0x1D3467">⮐
another picture of a sunset.</caption>
  </slide>
  <slide>
    <image full="slides/sunsetGlow.jpg" ⮐
thumbnail="slides/sunsetGlow_th.jpg" />
    <caption borderColor="0xEAE4AC" textColor="0x7D7620">⮐
this time the sunset is kind of blurred and glowing.</caption>
  </slide>
  <slide>
    <image full="slides/plant.jpg" ⮐
```

```
thumbnail="slides/plant_th.jpg" />
    <caption borderColor="0xDADADA" textColor="0x3C9713">⮐
a plant in Malibu.</caption>
  </slide>
  <slide>
    <image full="slides/rock.jpg" ⮐
thumbnail="slides/rock_th.jpg" />
    <caption borderColor="0xEAE4AC" textColor="0x7D7620">⮐
A nice rock.</caption>
  </slide>
  <slide>
    <image full="slides/rocks.jpg" ⮐
thumbnail="slides/rocks_th.jpg" />
    <caption borderColor="0xDCC2BA" textColor="0x2F057E">⮐
a bunch of rocks </caption>
  </slide>
  <slide>
    <image full="slides/tree.jpg" ⮐
thumbnail="slides/tree_th.jpg" />
    <caption borderColor="0xC4E0B6" textColor="0x375C27">⮐
a picture of a pretty tree.</caption>
  </slide>
</slides>
```

3. Save the XML file as `slides.xml` to the same directory to which you copied the slides directory.

4. Create a new Flash document and save it as `slides001.fla` to the same directory as the XML file.

5. Rename the default layer as Components.

6. Add a `Loader` component instance to the stage and name it `cldImage`.

7. Using the Property inspector, resize `cldImage` to 500 by 250 pixels and place it at 25,16.

8. Add a `TextArea` component instance to the stage and name it `ctaCaption`.

9. Using the Property inspector, resize `ctaCaption` to 500 by 50 pixels and place it at 25,270.

10. Add a `ScrollPane` component instance to the stage and name it `cspThumbnails`.

11. Using the Property inspector, resize `cspThumbnails` to 500 by 75 pixels and place it at 25,324.

12. Create a new Movie Clip symbol named `EmptyMC`. The symbol should not contain any artwork.

13. Open the linkage properties for `EmptyMC`, check the Export for ActionScript box, and give it a linkage identifier of `EmptyMCSymbol`.

14. Add a new layer named `Actions`.

15. On the first frame of the `Actions` layer, add the following code:

```
function loadThumbnails():Void {
  // Load the EmptyMC instance into the ScrollPane so that
  // the ScrollPane's content property will be defined.
  cspThumbnails.contentPath = "EmptyMCSymbol";

  // For each slide in the array...
  for(var i:Number = 0; i < aSlides.length; i++) {

    // ...create a nested MovieClip instance to hold the
    // loaded JPEG. Then, create an instance nested within
    // that MovieClip object into which you can load the
    // JPEG itself.
    cspThumbnails.content.createEmptyMovieClip("mcHolder" + ⮐
i, cspThumbnails.content.getNextHighestDepth());
    cspThumbnails.content["mcHolder" + ⮐
i].createEmptyMovieClip("mcJPEG", 1);
    cspThumbnails.content["mcHolder" + ⮐
i].mcJPEG.loadMovie(aSlides[i].thumbnail);

    // Place the thumbnails so that they are not
    // overlapping.
    cspThumbnails.content["mcHolder" + i]._x = i * 70 + 10;

    // Set a property on the MovieClip that holds the
    // index of the array that it represents, then
    // define an onRelease() event handler method so that
    // when the user clicks on the image the
    // loadFullImage() function is called with that index.
    cspThumbnails.content["mcHolder" + i].index = i;
    cspThumbnails.content["mcHolder" + i].onRelease = ⮐
function():Void {
      loadFullImage(this.index);
    };
  }
}

function loadFullImage(index:Number):Void {

  // Load the image into the Loader instance.
  cldImage.load(aSlides[index].full);

  // Set the text within the TextArea and call
  // the setStyles() function to set the styles
  // for the TextArea.
  ctaCaption.text = aSlides[index].captionText;
  setStyles(aSlides[index].captionTextColor, ⮐
aSlides[index].captionBorderColor);
}

function setStyles(nTextColor:Number, nBorderColor:Number):Void {
```

```
  // If the nBorderColor is either not a number or 0 then
  // set the borderStyle to none. Otherwise, set it to
  // solid.
  ctaCaption.setStyle("borderStyle", (isNaN(nBorderColor) || ⮐
nBorderColor == 0) ? "none" : "solid");

  // Set the color and borderColor styles for the
  // TextArea. Turn off the border for the ScrollPane.
  ctaCaption.setStyle("color", nTextColor);
  ctaCaption.setStyle("borderColor", nBorderColor);
  cspThumbnails.setStyle("borderStyle", "none");
}

function initXML():Void {

  // Set the XML object to ignore whitespace nodes when it
  // parses the loaded XML.
  xmlSlides.ignoreWhite = true;

  xmlSlides.onLoad = function():Void {

    // Create a variable to reference the childNodes array
    // of the root node of the XML object. This makes for
    // less to type later.
    var aTemp:Array = this.firstChild.childNodes;
    var oSlide:Object;

    // Loop through all the child nodes (all the <slide>
    // tags) and extract the values, assigning them to
    // the properties of an object. Then add that object
    // to the aSlides array. This just makes it easier to
    // work with the data later on.
    for(var i:Number = 0; i < aTemp.length; i++) {
      oSlide = new Object();
      oSlide.full = aTemp[i].firstChild.attributes.full;
      oSlide.thumbnail = ⮐
aTemp[i].firstChild.attributes.thumbnail;
      oSlide.captionText = ⮐
aTemp[i].lastChild.firstChild.nodeValue;
      oSlide.captionBorderColor = ⮐
parseInt(aTemp[i].lastChild.attributes.borderColor);
      oSlide.captionTextColor = ⮐
parseInt(aTemp[i].lastChild.attributes.textColor);
      aSlides.push(oSlide);
    }

    // Once all the data has been extracted into aSlides,
    // call loadThumbnails() to display the thumbnails.
    loadThumbnails();
  };
```

```
  // Load the XML.
  xmlSlides.load("slides.xml");
}

var aSlides:Array = new Array();
var xmlSlides:XML = new XML();
initXML();
setStyles(0, 0);
```

16. Save and test the movie. Figure 35-3 shows an example of what the movie should look like.

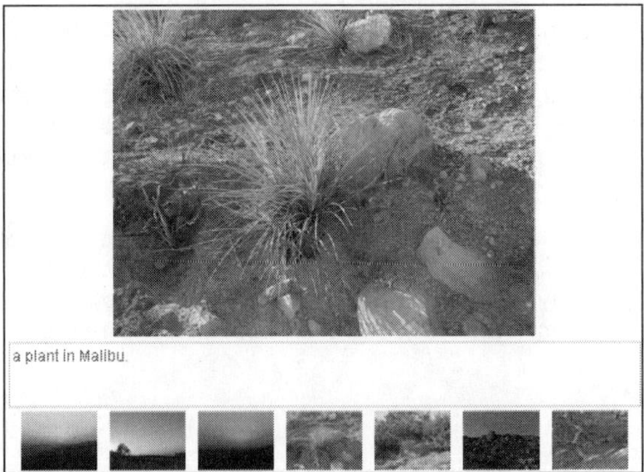

Figure 35-3: The slide application

Introducing Flash Remoting

Flash Remoting is a technology introduced by Macromedia that provides the most efficient and powerful way to send and load data using Flash. Flash Remoting sends and receives data packets through the `NetConnection` class, which is built into the Flash Player. Within Flash, the `NetConnection` class knows how to properly serialize and deserialize all the data sent and loaded. This means that you can send and load both primitive and reference datatypes using Flash Remoting without having to use third-party libraries such as WDDX to serialize and deserialize the data. The server must have the appropriate Flash Remoting gateway installed in order to be able to receive and send these data packets. Flash Remoting gateways are officially available for ColdFusion MX, J2EE application servers, and .NET. In addition, several unofficial Flash Remoting gateways have been developed for PHP, Perl, and others.

Here are some of the many benefits of Flash Remoting:

- ✦ The capability to send and load all the standard datatypes such as string, number, `Boolean`, `Array`, `Object`, `Date`, and so on, as well as custom datatypes (requires a few additional steps).
- ✦ No additional coding required to serialize and deserialize data either in Flash or on the server.

- The capability to call CFC methods, Java class methods, DLL methods, and Web services from a Flash application.
- Data is transferred in the proprietary *AMF format*—a binary messaging protocol that is 25 percent the size of the SOAP equivalent. That means significantly faster data transfer.

This section contains only a very basic overview of Flash Remoting. Many powerful aspects of Flash Remoting are beyond the scope of this book but can be found in *Complete Flash Remoting MX*, by Joey Lott (Wiley, 2003).

Getting Started with Flash Remoting

Aside from Flash, there are two additional things you need in order to get started with Flash Remoting. First, although you don't technically need any additional client-side functionality in order to use Flash Remoting, there is a set of utility classes that Macromedia provides free of charge. This download is called the *Flash Remoting Components.* Once you've downloaded the file, run it from your computer and follow any instructions it provides. It will install these extra classes on your computer so that Flash can access them. You can download the Flash Remoting Components at `www.macromedia.com/software/flashremoting/downloads/components`.

In order for Flash Remoting to work properly, you need to make sure that you have the Flash Remoting gateway installed on the server. If you are running ColdFusion MX on your server, the Flash Remoting gateway comes installed by default. If you are using a J2EE application server or the .NET framework, you need to purchase and install the appropriate gateway.

You can find more information on these gateways at `www.macromedia.com/software/flashremoting`. There is a 30-day trial available. You might also want to check out the AMFPHP project (the PHP gateway) at `www.amfphp.org`, the FLAP project (the Perl gateway) at `www.simonf.com/flap`, and the OPENAMF project at `www.openamf.org`. The three aforementioned projects are open-source Flash Remoting solutions that are alternatives to Macromedia's gateways. There are additional commercial Flash Remoting projects that go above and beyond the Macromedia Flash Remoting specification. One such example is FlashORB at `www.flashorb.com`.

Follow the instructions provided with the Flash Remoting gateway to install it. You will need to know the URL to access the gateway. The examples in this chapter use a standard ColdFusion-type gateway URL. More details on installing and configuring the gateway (this is not a required step with ColdFusion) are provided in *Complete Flash Remoting MX* by Joey Lott.

The remaining portion of this chapter provides information on how to work with Flash Remoting as it was implemented in Flash MX. The information will work in Flash MX 2004 as well, provided you are using the correct set of Flash Remoting Components. At the time of this writing, Macromedia announced that they would be updating the Flash Remoting Components to provide new ways to work with Flash Remoting in Flash MX 2004. You can check at `www.person13.com` for updated information on Flash Remoting as it becomes available.

Introducing Flash Remoting ActionScript

The client-side ActionScript for working with Flash Remoting is not particularly complex. There are essentially five steps to a Flash Remoting service method call.

1. Include the utility classes.
2. Create a gateway connection.
3. Create a service object.
4. Create a response object to handle a result or status (error) value returned from the service method request.
5. Call the service method (such as a CFC method, Java class method, or DLL method).

Including the Utility Classes

Rather than working directly with the `NetConnection` class, the Flash Remoting Components installation provides you with several utility classes. You should include the utility classes in your Flash files with the following line of code:

```
#include "NetServices.as"
```

Notice that you should *not* add a semicolon to the end of an `#include` directive.

Setting Up a Gateway Connection

Once you've included the necessary classes, the next step in Flash Remoting projects is to set up a gateway connection. This means that you tell Flash where it can find the server-side gateway and request that it create a `NetConnection` object that connects to that gateway. Here's the recommended way to accomplish this:

1. Call the static method `setDefaultGatewayUrl()` from the `NetServices` class. This defines a default gateway that Flash will use when you are testing the application within the test player. This gateway URL is *not* used, however, when you run the application in a browser.

   ```
   NetServices.setDefaultGatewayUrl("http://localhost/⮐
   flashservices/gateway");
   ```

2. If the application will run from a Web browser, edit the HTML page and pass the gateway URL to the Flash movie using `FlashVars`. (For more information on `FlashVars`, see Chapter 31.) Passing the gateway URL to the Flash movie with `FlashVars` makes it much simpler to move the application from server to server (development, testing, and production, for example) because you need only modify the gateway URL in the HTML page rather than editing and re-exporting the SWF file.

3. Call the static method `createGatewayConnection()` from the `NetServices` class. If you've completed Steps 1 and 2 (2 is necessary only if the application is going to be run from a Web browser), you don't need to pass any parameters to the `createGatewayConnection()` method. The method returns a new `NetConnection` object. However, if you use strong typing, type the return value as `Object` because at the time of this writing Flash doesn't support Flash Remoting `NetConnection` properties and methods for strongly typed variables.

   ```
   var ncGateway:Object = NetServices.createGatewayConnection();
   ```

Defining the Service Object

Define the service object by calling the `getService()` method from the `NetConnection` object. The service is the fully qualified name of the CFC, Java class, or DLL (as a few examples of services). You need to pass the name to the `getService()` method as a string, and it will then return a service object, which you should type as `Object`. For example, if you have a CFC named `UserUtils.cfc` that is in the user package, the `getService()` call would look something like:

```
var srvUserUtils:Object = ncGateway.getService("user.UserUtils");
```

Configuring the Response Object

A response object is an object that handles the response from the server after a service method has been called (which is the next step). In order to work, a response object must at least have an `onResult()` method defined. The `onResult()` method is called when the server returns a value from the service method. The value is passed to the `onResult()` method as a parameter. Here's an example of a service object with an `onResult()` method defined:

```
var resLogin:Object = new Object();
resLogin.onResult = function(oUserInfo:Object) {
  // Code here.
};
```

In the preceding example, the expected return type from the service method is an associative array. That means that the service method has a return statement that returns a server-side value that Flash Remoting will convert into an ActionScript `Object` object—a value such as a ColdFusion `Struct` or a Java `HashMap`.

A response object can also have an `onStatus()` method. The `onStatus()` method is called when there is some kind of error in calling the service method.

Calling the Service Method

A service method is a CFC method, Java method, DLL method, and so on. You can call a service method from the service object you created in Step 3 of "Setting Up a Gateway Connection." When you call the service method, you need to always pass it at least one parameter—the response object. The first parameter you pass to a service method call from ActionScript is interpreted by Flash to be the response object you want to handle the server response. Flash will not actually pass that value to the service method. Therefore, if you want to pass any parameters on to the service method, they should follow the response object. For example, if the `UserUtils` CFC has a method named `login` that expects two parameters—the username and password—your service method call might look something like this:

```
srvUserUtils.login(resLogin, ctiUsername.text, ctaPassword.text);
```

Enabling Services for Flash Remoting

Flash Remoting enables you to work with many types of services, including ColdFusion pages, CFCs, Web services, ASPX pages, DLLs, servlets, and Java classes. That is just a partial list of the types of services with which Flash Remoting can work. Some of those service types require special programming and configuration in order to work with Flash Remoting, and are therefore outside the scope of this book. The services that work most effectively with Flash Remoting are CFCs, ASP.NET DLLs, Java classes, and Web services.

Web services can be consumed from Flash without setting up server-side proxies when working with the ColdFusion and .NET gateways. The same feature is not configured for the J2EE gateway, so if you want to consume Web services using the J2EE gateway, you need to set up server-side proxy classes.

Without any additional configuration to the services, Flash Remoting enables you to call public methods from ASP.NET DLLs and Java classes. In order to call a method of a CFC, Flash Remoting requires that you set the `access` attribute for that method to `"remote"` (bold code shows the change):

```
<cffunction name="login" access="remote" ...
```

Understanding Datatypes

Flash Remoting handles conversion of datatypes automatically for all standard datatypes. This means that you don't need to worry about any kind of serialization issues in the client or on the server.

It is also possible to work with custom datatypes in Flash Remoting, but it requires some steps that are beyond the scope of this book.

For a list of the supported datatypes, see the following links on the Macromedia livedocs for Flash Remoting: `http://livedocs.macromedia.com/flashremoting/mx/Using_Flash_Remoting_MX/UseASData3.htm` and `http://livedocs.macromedia.com/flashremoting/mx/Using_Flash_Remoting_MX/UseASData4.htm`.

Working with Recordsets

When you installed the Flash Remoting Components, the `RecordSet` class was one of the many classes installed. The `RecordSet` class is automatically included when you include `NetServices` in your Flash document, and it allows you to work with recordsets returned from a service method (that is, ColdFusion `Query` objects, Java `ResetSet` objects, and C# `DataTable` objects). The `RecordSet` class also enables you to perform tasks such as reading and modifying the data, but such tasks are beyond the scope of this book.

Practicing Using Flash Remoting

The following exercise uses a ColdFusion CFC to query a database and return the results to a Flash movie. The ActionScript portion of the exercise works with any service type, but if you want to work with a language other than ColdFusion, that is left up to you.

1. Copy the `ActionScriptBible.mdb` file from the CD-ROM to the machine running ColdFusion.
2. Set up a new ColdFusion datasource in the ColdFusion administrator. The datasource name should be `ActionScriptBible`, the driver should be for Microsoft Access, and it should point to the MDB file you copied to the server.
3. Create a new CFC file named `ActionScriptBible.cfc`, and save it to the Web root.

4. Add the following code to the CFC file and save it:

```
<cfcomponent>
  <cffunction name="getTOC" access="remote" returntype="query">
    <cfquery datasource="ActionScriptBible" name="qTOC">
    SELECT CHAPTER.CHAPTER_ID,
    AUTHOR.AUTHOR_NAME,
    CHAPTER.CHAPTER_TITLE
    FROM AUTHOR, CHAPTER
    WHERE AUTHOR.AUTHOR_ID = CHAPTER.CHAPTER_AUTHOR_ID
    </cfquery>
    <cfreturn qTOC>
  </cffunction>
</cfcomponent>
```

   The CFC method getTOC queries the database to select three columns from the tables. The columns contain the chapter number, chapter title, and author name. The method then returns that Query object.

5. Open a new Flash document and save it as book001.fla.
6. Rename the default layer Components.
7. Create a new DataGrid instance on the stage. Name the instance cdgTOC, and resize it using the Property inspector so that it is 550 pixels wide and 300 pixels in height. If you are not using Flash MX Professional 2004, and therefore don't have the DataGrid component available, you can use a List component instead. Name the List instance clTOC, and make it 550 pixels by 300 pixels.
8. Add a new layer named Actions.
9. Add the following code to the first frame of the Actions layer (note differences when using the List instance in the comments):

```
#include "NetServices.as"

// If you are using the List instead of DataGrid, omit
// this function.
function formatDataGrid():Void {

  // Set the column names.
  cdgTOC.columnNames = ["Chapter", "Author", "Title"];

  // Set the widths of the columns.
  cdgTOC.getColumnAt(0).width = 75;
  cdgTOC.getColumnAt(1).width = 125;

  // Set which columns in the RecordSet match up with
  // which columns in the DataGrid.
  cdgTOC.getColumnAt(0).columnName = "CHAPTER_ID";
  cdgTOC.getColumnAt(1).columnName = "AUTHOR_NAME";
  cdgTOC.getColumnAt(2).columnName = "CHAPTER_TITLE";
}
```

```
// If you are using List then you don't need to call the
// formatDataGrid() function.
formatDataGrid();

// Define the default gateway URL. Make sure the URL you
// use matches with your gateway.
NetServices.setDefaultGatewayUrl("http://localhost/↩
flashservices/gateway");

// Create the connection.
var ncBook:Object = NetServices.createGatewayConnection();

// Create the service.
var srvBook:Object = ncBook.getService("ActionScriptBible");

// Define the response object.
var resBook:Object = new Object();
resBook.onResult = function(rsTOC:RecordSet) {

  // Set the dataProvider for the DataGrid equal to the
  // items property of the RecordSet (the items property
  // is an array of objects). If you are using a List
  // instead of a DataGrid then change the name of cdgTOC
  // to clTOC.
  cdgTOC.dataProvider = rsTOC.items;
}

// Call the service method, and tell it what response
// object to use to handle the returned data.
srvBook.getTOC(resBook);
```

10. Test the movie. You should see (perhaps after a moment or two) something like Figure 35-4.

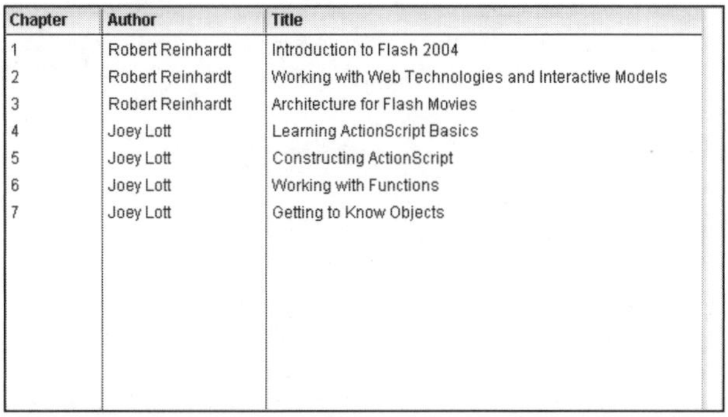

Chapter	Author	Title
1	Robert Reinhardt	Introduction to Flash 2004
2	Robert Reinhardt	Working with Web Technologies and Interactive Models
3	Robert Reinhardt	Architecture for Flash Movies
4	Joey Lott	Learning ActionScript Basics
5	Joey Lott	Constructing ActionScript
6	Joey Lott	Working with Functions
7	Joey Lott	Getting to Know Objects

Figure 35-4: The DataGrid instance populated with the data returned with Flash Remoting

Flash Remoting is one of the most impressive and important Flash-related technologies developed in the last several years. Although a full discussion is well beyond the scope of this book, you are invited to learn and read more at the Macromedia Flash Remoting DevNet center at `www.macromedia.com/devnet/mx/flashremoting`. You can also pick up a copy of *Complete Flash Remoting MX,* by Joey Lott (Wiley, 2003).

Additionally, at the time of this writing the status of Flash Remoting in relation to Flash MX 2004 is unknown. We don't know whether Macromedia will be releasing ActionScript 2.0 versions of the Flash Remoting Components. Check in at `www.person13.com/asb` for updates on the status of Flash Remoting in Flash MX 2004.

We'd like to know what you thought about this chapter. Visit `www.flashsupport.com/feedback` to fill out an online form with your comments.

Summary

In this chapter, you have learned some practical solutions to data integration and Flash. The techniques discussed include:

- ✦ Using `LoadVars` to send and load URL-encoded data. In the exercise in this chapter, you sent data from a Flash movie to a server-side script to send an e-mail.
- ✦ Overriding the `onData()` method of a `LoadVars` or `XML` object to load raw data. Use this technique when you want to load the text just as it appears in the external file or as the script returns it. This is particularly useful for loading HTML. In the relevant exercise, you loaded HTML from an external file that contained links with the `asfunction` directive.
- ✦ Using the `XML` class. This class is invaluable, considering all the XML used in application development today. In the exercise, you loaded and parsed XML data in order to create a slide show.
- ✦ Incorporating Flash Remoting. This is one of the most powerful technologies for data transfer with Flash. It enables your Flash application to seamlessly integrate with server-side services.

✦ ✦ ✦

Using the Built-In Web Service Functionality

✦ ✦ ✦ ✦

In This Chapter

Using databinding

Using components to call Web services

Working with ActionScript to call Web services

Understanding security issues with Web services in Flash

✦ ✦ ✦ ✦

Flash MX Professional 2004 provides a set of data components including a `WebServiceConnector` component that allows you to connect to Web services from your Flash applications. In this chapter, you'll learn about how to work with the `WebServiceConnector` component as well as how to consume Web services using the lower-level `WebService` class directly.

Databinding

One of the features of the data components is the capability to use databinding. Databinding means you can tell Flash you want to associate a parameter of one component with another. This is a great shortcut that enables you to set up data-rich applications at authoring time. For example, you can databind the values from a `ComboBox` and `TextInput` component to the input values for a `WebServiceConnector`. Then, you can databind the output value from a `WebServiceConnector` to a `TextArea` component so that when the server returns a result, it is automatically displayed to the user.

The simplest way to set up databinding is to use the Bindings tab in the Component Inspector panel. Based on the schema for the components, you can then databind nodes of one component to nodes of another. For example, if you are using a `WebServiceConnector` component instance, once Flash has analyzed the WSDL document, it will set up the proper schema for the `WebServiceConnector` component so it reflects the expected parameters and result. (You can read more about Web services in the next section.) You can then use databinding to associate, for example, the value of a `TextInput` with one of the parameter nodes for the Web service. That means that when the user types a value into the `TextInput` instance, that value is automatically passed over to the `WebServiceConnector` instance to be used as one of the parameters for the Web service method call.

When you click the Add binding button (the plus button) within the Bindings tab of the Component Inspector panel, Flash opens the Add Binding dialog box. The dialog box gives you a selection of all the nodes within the component. You should select one of those nodes for which you want to add databinding. Once you click OK, the dialog box closes, and the node that you selected shows up in the databound list of nodes in the Bindings tab. You can then select that item from the list; in the lower pane of the panel, the node's binding information should appear. It asks for the following information:

- ✦ The direction for the databinding — in, out, or both.
- ✦ The node to which to you want to make the association.
- ✦ The formatter, if any, that you want to apply. This allows you to apply some formatting to values without having to write extra ActionScript code.
- ✦ The formatter options. This applies only if you have applied a formatter.

This should give you a general overview of databinding. You'll look at how you can use databinding in more practical ways in following sections.

Working with Web Services

A Web service is a way of distributing functionality across the Internet. It means that an application running on one server can allow other applications on other servers to utilize some type of functionality that it provides without having to reinvent it locally. Some Web services are private and some are public.

There are many, many Web services publicly available, and the number is growing daily. You can look at Web service lists on sites such as `www.xmethods.net` and `www.salcentral.com` to find Web services that might meet your application's needs. For example, you may want to access a Web service that returns the current weather conditions given a location. Or you might want to use a Web service to perform a search on a popular site such as Amazon.com. Google provides a Web service that allows you to perform Web searches. The possibilities are far too numerous to list.

Web services must describe themselves using WSDL, or Web Service Document Language. The WSDL is typically published to the Web, and then the requesting application targets that WSDL document. The document provides the requesting application with all the information it needs such as how to access the actual service, the methods available, and the types of permissible request and response messages. The Web service then uses HTTP to transfer request and response packets over the Web. The requesting message tells the Web service what method to call and what parameters to pass to it. Then, once the operation has finished, the Web service sends a response message back that contains the return data. Web services can use several XML variations for the request and response messages, but many Web services use something known as SOAP (Simple Object Access Protocol). Most of the time you don't have to concern yourself with the details of the message format because in most languages the serialization and deserialization of the messages is handled behind the scenes. When you use the `WebService` class (either through code or via the `WebServiceConnector` component), Flash will handle all the SOAP messages for you automatically.

The `WebService` class uses the built-in `XML` class to send and load messages. Therefore, you can expect the messages to be typically about four times the size of a Flash Remoting AMF packet. That means that in terms of message size, Flash Remoting is four times as efficient as using the `WebService` class. Although the `WebService` class is a great new feature in Flash MX Professional, it is recommended for enterprise-level applications.

Using a WebServiceConnector Component

You can use a `WebServiceConnector` component to have your Flash application interact with Web services. Here are the basic steps to using a `WebServiceConnector` component by configuring the parameters through the Component Inspector panel:

1. Drag an instance of the `WebServiceConnector` component from the Components panel to the stage and name the instance.
2. Assign a value to the `WSDLURL` parameter. This should be the complete URL to the WSDL document, including the protocol (such as `http://www.xmethods.net/sd/2001/CurrencyExchangeService.wsdl`).
3. Once you've set the `WSDLURL` parameter, if you are connected to the Internet, Flash will analyze the document and populate the operation parameter value field with a list of the available operations. You can then choose the correct operation from the list. Or, if you are not connected to the Internet, you can just type the name of the operation.
4. With the operation selected, Flash then generates the schema for the Web service. You can then set up databinding with any UI components.
5. Call the `trigger()` method of the `WebServiceConnector` instance when you're ready to submit the Web service method call.

Probably the simplest way to understand the `WebServiceConnector` component is to try it for yourself. So in the following exercise you create a short application that utilizes the `WebServiceConnector` to connect to a Web service that returns the currency exchange rate between two countries.

This exercise requires that you be connected to the Internet.

1. Open `www.xmethods.net` in a Web browser.
2. Scroll to the bottom of the page, and locate and click the link to the Currency Exchange Rate Web service. Leave this page open, as you'll return to it in just a moment.
3. Open a new Flash document, and save it as `WebServiceConnector001.fla`.
4. Rename the default layer to `Components`.
5. Drag an instance of the `WebServiceConnector` component from the Components panel to the stage. The location is not particularly important; at runtime, the instance is not visible. Name the instance `cwscExchangeRate`.
6. Create three instances of the `TextInput` component on the stage, naming them `ctiCountryOne`, `ctiCountryTwo`, and `ctiRate`. Place the instances so they appear in a vertical column with `ctiCountryOne` at the top and `ctiRate` at the bottom.

7. Create a `Button` component instance. Name the instance `cbtSubmit`. At this point, your application should look similar to what you see in Figure 36-1.

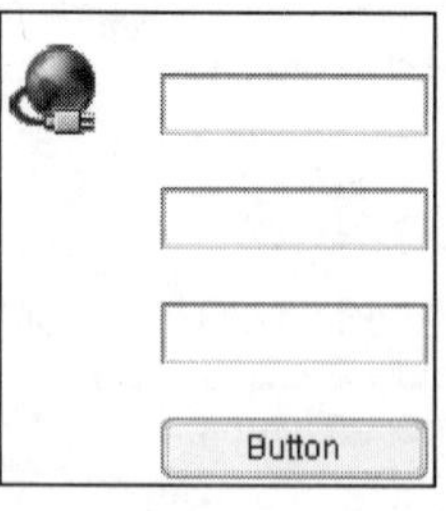

Figure 36-1: The layout of the WebServiceConnector application

8. Next, you'll want to set the properties on the `WebServiceConnector` component instance. So select the instance on the stage, and then open the Component Inspector panel.

   a. You can get the value for the `WSDLURL` parameter by copying and pasting it from the `xmethods.net` page that you still have open in the Web browser. The URL to the WSDL is `www.xmethods.net/sd/2001/CurrencyExchangeService.wsdl`. (Keep the Web page open because you're going to reference it again.)

   b. Once you've entered the value for the `WSDLURL` parameter, Flash should automatically populate the possible values for the operation parameter. The Web service has only one method named `getRate`. So select the `getRate` option for the operation parameter.

9. Next, you will set up the databinding.

   a. First, with the `WebServiceConnector` instance opened, click the Schema tab in the Component Inspector panel. You will see that Flash has created the schema based on the WSDL document and it automatically knows that the `getRate` Web method requires two string parameters and returns one number value.

   b. Click the Bindings tab in the Component Inspector panel.

   c. Click the Add binding button (the plus sign).

   d. Select the `country1` parameter from the list and click OK.

   e. In the Bindings tab, make sure you've selected the `params.country1` item in the list and in the lower pane double-click in the Value column for the bound to parameter. This opens the Bound To dialog box.

   f. From the list of component instances in the Bound To dialog box, select `ctiCountryOne`.

   g. In the right pane you'll notice that the text property appears in the list. It should be already selected because it is the only databindable property.

   h. Click the OK button.

   i. Follow the same steps to databind `params.country2` to the `ctiCountryTwo.text` property and results to the `ctiRate.text` property.

10. The remaining task is to trigger the Web service method call when the user clicks the `Button` instance.

    a. Create a new layer named Actions.

    b. On the first frame of the Actions layer, add the following code to add a listener to the `Button` instance.

```
var oListener:Object = new Object();
oListener.click = function(oEvent:Object):Void {

  // When the user clicks the Button, trigger the Web
  // service method call.
  cwscExchangeRate.trigger();
};

// Add a label.
cbtSubmit.label = "Submit";

// Add the listener.
cbtSubmit.addEventListener("click", oListener);
```

11. Test the movie. Reference the list of country names in the `xmethods.net` Web page you have open. You can try entering United States in the first `TextInput` and Canada in the second `TextInput`, for example. Then, when you click the button, the Web service method is called, and the result is displayed in the third `TextInput`.

Calling Web Services without WebServiceConnector

The `WebServiceConnector` component can provide a nice interface for working with Web services. However, if you want more programmatic control, you can work directly with the `WebService` class. The `WebService` class is utilized by the `WebServiceConnector` component, so when you work with the `WebService` class you are just working at a slightly lower level.

The `WebService` class is not included as part of the standard ActionScript library of class files. Instead, it is tucked away in an SWC that you must add to the library of your Flash document. You can locate the SWC by selecting Window ➪ Other Panels ➪ Common Libraries ➪ Classes. This opens the Classes common library, in which you can find `WebServiceClasses`. Just copy the `WebServiceClasses` SWC from the `Classes` library to the library of your Flash document.

Once you've included the `WebServiceClasses` SWC, you can work with the `WebService` class in your application. The class is in the `mx.services` package, so you might want to import the class to make your code more readable.

```
import mx.services.WebService;
```

You then create a `WebService` object by calling the constructor and passing it the URL to the WSDL as a parameter. For example:

```
var sWSDLURL:String = ⮐
"http://www.xmethods.net/sd/2001/CurrencyExchangeService.wsdl";
var wsExchangeRate:WebService = new WebService(sWSDLURL);
```

You can call the Web service method directly from the WebService object. For example:

```
var oCallback:Object = wsExchangeRate.getRate("United States", "Canada");
```

You'll notice that when you call a Web service method in this way, it returns a new object. The object is the callback object for the Web service method call. It is what can handle the responses from the server. You can define two methods for the callback object to handle the two types of responses. The onResult() method is called when a successful response is returned from the Web service method. The returned value is automatically passed to the onResult() method as a parameter. The onFault() method is called when an error occurred.

```
oCallback.onResult = function(nRate):Void {
  trace(nRate);
};
oCallback.onFault = function():Void {
  trace("an error occurred");
};
```

In the following exercise, you have the opportunity to work with the WebService class for yourself.

1. Open WebServiceConnector001.fla from the previous exercise, and save it as WebService001.fla.
2. Open the library and delete the WebServiceConnector SWC. You'll notice the instance also disappears from the stage and all the databinding that was associated with it is also removed.
3. Open the Classes common library, and copy the WebServiceClasses SWC to the library for WebService001.fla.
4. Modify the code on the first frame of the Actions layer so that it is as follows:

```
// Import the class to make your code more readable.
import mx.services.WebService;

// Create the listener for the Button.
var oListener:Object = new Object();
oListener.click = function(oEvent:Object):Void {

  // Define the URL to the WSDL you want to use.
  var sWSDLURL:String = ⮐
"http://www.xmethods.net/sd/2001/CurrencyExchangeService.wsdl";

  // Create the WebService object.
  var wsExchangeRate:WebService = new WebService(sWSDLURL);

  // Call the getRate Web service method, and pass it
  // the values from the TextInput instances.
  var oCallback:Object = ⮐
wsExchangeRate.getRate(ctiCountryOne.text, ctiCountryTwo.text);
```

```
    // Define the callback's onResult() method so that it
    // displays the returned value in the ctiRate TextArea.
    oCallback.onResult = function(nRate):Void {
      ctiRate.text = nRate;
    };
  };
  cbtSubmit.label = "Submit";
  cbtSubmit.addEventListener("click", oListener);
```

5. Test the movie. Enter country names in the first and second `TextInput` instances and click the button.

The application should work just as in the first version. The difference is that this second version uses the `WebService` class directly rather than utilizing the `WebServiceConnector` component.

Working with Recordsets

When you get a recordset value returned from a Web service, you should consider placing the data within a `DataSet` component instance. The `DataSet` component provides you with a way to manage recordset data that is not otherwise available natively within Flash.

Managing data with a `DataSet` offers several advantages, including:

- ✦ You can databind a `DataSet` to other components.
- ✦ You can perform filters and sorts on the data in a `DataSet`.
- ✦ When the data in a `DataSet` changes, the `DataSet` dispatches events to notify listeners.

One good example of how a `DataSet` can be advantageous is illustrated when you try and databind a recordset to a `DataGrid` component instance. If you have a `WebServiceConnector` that you use to retrieve a recordset returned by a Web service method, you cannot directly databind that result to the data provider of the `DataGrid`. If you do, the `DataGrid` will display the values correctly, but you will not be able to sort them or filter them correctly. Instead, you should use an intermediary `DataSet`. You can databind the recordset returned to the `WebServiceConnector` to the data provider of the `DataSet`. Then you can databind the data provider of the `DataSet` to the data provider of the `DataGrid`.

Dealing with Security Issues

Because the `WebService` class relies on the XML class to connect to Web services, it is subject to the same security restrictions. That is, if you are serving the Flash application from a Web server, the Web service must either be in the same domain as the Flash application, or the server that provides the Web service must have a `crossdomain.xml` document that permits Flash applications from other domains to access the services. Because neither of those scenarios is likely to be the case most of the time, there is another possibility: You can create a proxy script on the same server as the Flash application. The `WebService` or `WebServiceConnector` can use the local proxy script as the URL, and the proxy script can relay all the messages between the Flash application and the Web service.

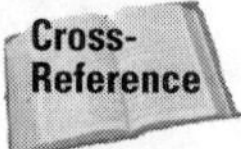

For more information regarding sandbox security and `crossdomain.xml` policy files, see Chapter 21.

We'd like to know what you thought about this chapter. Visit `www.flashsupport.com/feedback` to fill out an online form with your comments.

Summary

- You can use the databinding feature to associate properties of various components so that you can quickly set up simple applications without much ActionScript.
- You can call Web service methods using the `WebServiceConnector` component or the `WebService` class. The `WebServiceConnector` component is available only in Flash MX 2004 Professional, whereas the `WebService` class is available in both.
- Because Web service requests and responses use the `XML` class in the player, they are subject to the standard sandbox security issues as other data connections (`XML`, `LoadVars`, and so on).

✦ ✦ ✦

Making Flash Forms

✦ ✦ ✦ ✦

In This Chapter

Understanding the elements used to create a form in Flash

Putting together a basic, one-page form

Submitting form data

Checking form data

Populating form elements dynamically

Prefilling forms with saved data

✦ ✦ ✦ ✦

Flash has matured into much more than a simple vector animation platform. With `LoadVars`, XML, Flash Remoting, and the `WebServiceConnector` component or `WebService` class (Professional version only), Flash now provides many ways for a movie to serve as the user interface for a rich client-server application. One of the key features of most any application is the form. A form enables users to input data that can be sent to the server portion of the application. In this chapter, you take a look at building forms in Flash MX 2004.

Using Forms

Through the evolution of many Internet technologies, Flash included, various forms of user interaction have developed. However, there is still only one means by which users can effectively and intuitively enter information to be submitted through your Web site or application. So the first question to be answered is not so much how a form functions but why you would need a form in the first place.

There are seemingly many reasons to use forms in your applications. Here are a few examples:

- **Gathering or modifying user or statistical information:** There are plenty of examples of this type of form use. Surveys, registration/user account pages, and forms gathering usage information before downloading software are all good examples.
- **Performing searches:** Google is a perfect example of this type of use. Although it is simple (a single text field), Google's use of forms is central to its functionality when it comes to searching on keywords. But there are more complex examples, as well. Many sites allow users to search a database of information based on many different criteria. The criteria can sometimes be entered through very complex forms that include radio buttons, check boxes, and combo boxes.
- **Gathering feedback:** Gathering feedback has been one of the steadfast uses of forms. Most sites seem to implement this use of forms by providing a means for user feedback.
- **E-commerce:** E-commerce would not be possible without forms. Forms are used to allow users to keep track of items in "shopping carts," as well as making final checkout decisions. Of course, there is some overlap here with gathering and modifying user information in that a major component of e-commerce is user information.

Creating a Basic Form

In Chapter 28, you learned how to work with the v2 UI components that come predefined in Flash MX 2004. With these components you have all the elements necessary for creating a basic form in Flash. Of course, there are many types of form controls you can use (especially if you are using Flash MX Professional 2004), but there are a handful of components that form the basic types of form controls. Let's take a look at each of them briefly and how they can be used in a form.

TextInput and TextArea

The `TextInput` and `TextArea` components are used when you want to allow the user to input a textual response in a free-form manner. If you want to provide the user with a set of options, you should choose to use one of the other types of controls listed in the subsequent sections. `TextInput` and `TextArea` are well-suited for scenarios in which the user's response is likely to be something unique. For example, an e-mail address or a response to an essay question would both be types of answers for which the user should be able to enter the value in a free-form manner.

`TextInput` controls are intended for one-line responses. For example, you may want to ask a user for their username. You can also use `TextInput` controls in password mode to ensure that the value that is entered is not viewable to other nearby users. That makes the `TextInput` control a good choice for allowing a user to enter his or her password as well.

The `TextArea` control, on the other hand, is intended to enable the user to enter multiple lines of text. When a response might require that the user enter a paragraph or more, the `TextArea` is a good choice.

ComboBox and RadioButton

You should use `ComboBox` and `RadioButton` components to handle form elements that require a user to select a single choice from a group of predefined choices. Which one you choose is largely a matter of personal preference — the one you think better displays the options in the form. As a general rule, however, you probably want to use a `ComboBox` component when there are many choices from which to select for a particular form element simply because the `ComboBox` makes more efficient use of the space on the stage. On the other hand, a group of `RadioButton` component instances would be well-suited for allowing users to choose their gender (male or female) or their age range from a handful of ranges (< 21, 21–40, 41–65, 65+). But a `RadioButton` component would probably be ill-suited for allowing a user to select country of residence. In that case, it would likely be better to allow a user to choose the country from a `ComboBox`.

Remember to define a group name for each `RadioButton` component in a group.

List

`List` components are very similar to `ComboBox` components, but with one major difference. `List` components enable users to select multiple choices for each form element. This is ideal for situations in which you want to present users with a variety of options, from which several may be applicable for a single user. An example is that of hobbies. In a form that gathers user information, you may want to present users with a list of hobbies from which they can choose all that apply to them.

CheckBox

CheckBox components are appropriate for any form element that can have only two choices — yes or no (true or false). Such elements might include whether the user wants to be added to a mailing list, if the user agrees to the terms and conditions of use, or if the user wants to have his or her username and password stored to avoid having to log in for future uses. A group of CheckBox instances can also be used in the same types of situations as a List instance. Of course, the same considerations apply as when determining whether to use a group of RadioButton instances or a ComboBox instance. If there are many options, typically a List is a better choice because it makes better use of the space on stage.

Label

Of course, the Label component is an important part of any form. You can use a Label instance to display a name or simple instruction next to another form control. For example, you might use a Label instance to display Email: next to a TextInput instance so that users know to enter their e-mail address.

Button

Just about every form needs at least one Button instance. Even in the simplest of cases, you typically want to enable the user to submit the form data by clicking a Button.

Putting Together the Form Elements

In the simplest of forms, you can place the instances of each of the components on the stage within a MovieClip object (which could include _root). Sometimes, however, you may want to present the form so that the user can scroll the contents. In order to achieve this, use a ScrollPane component instance. Chapter 28 showed how to use a ScrollPane to scroll the contents of a form placed within a Movie Clip symbol.

Making a Simple Form

In this exercise, you will create a basic form using TextInput, List, Label, and Button components. You'll add a click() handler for the Button instance, but at this point you'll not yet be submitting the data to the server. Instead, you'll just use trace() to display the values in the Output panel. In a later exercise, you'll continue working on this example so that it submits to a server-side script.

1. Open a new Flash document and save it as simpleForm001.fla.
2. Rename the default layer Form and create a new layer named Actions.
3. On the Form layer add the following:
   - One TextInput component instance. Give it a name of ctiEmail. Resize the instance with the Property inspector so that it is 150 pixels wide.
   - One List component instance. Name the instance clProducts. Resize the instance with the Property inspector so that it is 150 pixels wide.

- One `Button` component instance. Name the instance `cbtSubmit`.
- Two `Label` component instances. Name them `clblEmail` and `clblProducts`, and place them to the left of the corresponding `ctiEmail` and `clProducts` instances. The layout should appear as shown in Figure 37-1.

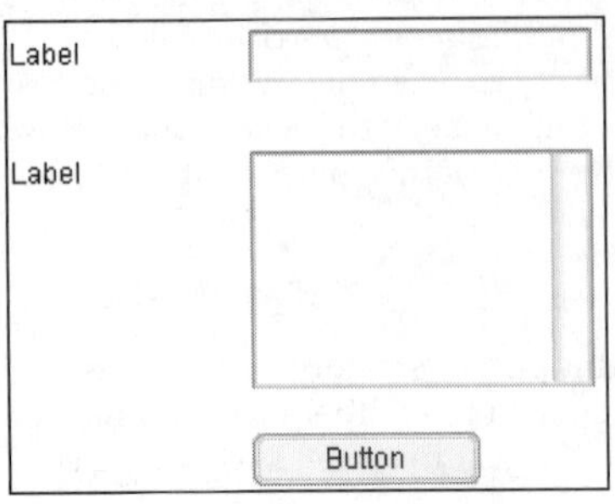

Figure 37-1: The layout of the simpleForm001.fla application

4. Add the following code to the Actions layer:

```
// Add values to the labels.
clblEmail.text = "Email:";
clblProducts.text = "Products Owned:";

// Set the data provider for the List component instance.
clProducts.dataProvider = [{label: "Flash", data: "f"}, ⮐
{label: "Dreamweaver", data: "dw"}, ⮐
{label: "Fireworks", data: "fw"}, ⮐
{label: "ColdFusion", data: "cf"}, ⮐
{label: "Freehand", data: "fh"}];

// Sort the items in the List.
clProducts.dataProvider.sortItemsBy("label");

// Allow multiple selections.
clProducts.multipleSelection = true;

// Create the listener object for the Button.
var oListener:Object = new Object();
oListener.click = function(oEvent:Object):Void {

  // Get the email and selected products.
  var sEmail:String = ctiEmail.text;
  var aProductItems:Array = clProducts.selectedItems;
  var aProductData:Array = new Array();

  // Loop through all the selected products, and append
  // the data value to the aProductData array.
  for(var i:Number = 0; i < aProductItems.length; i++) {
    aProductData.push(aProductItems[i].data);
  }
```

```
    // Display the values.
    trace(sEmail + " " + aProductData);
  };
  cbtSubmit.label = "Submit";
  cbtSubmit.addEventListener("click", oListener);
```

5. Test the movie. Add an e-mail address and select products, and then click the button.

Submitting Form Data

Once you have created a form, the next thing is to actually do something with that form data. This is usually referred to as *submitting* the form data because typically you *submit* the data for processing to a server-side script or Web application. The data may then get written to a file or to a database or any number of other types of processing.

Basic Form Data Submitting

Submitting a form usually involves clicking a button of some kind. Although this is not necessary (it could be a timed process, or it could be submitted once the user has made a selection), it is the most common way to submit a form. Therefore, you can choose to use any kind of button-like control such as a `Button`, `MovieClip`, or a `Button` component instance as used in the exercise in the previous section.

Using LoadVars to Send Data

Once a form has been filled out, the next likely step is to actually transmit that data to something, be it a CGI, PHP, or ColdFusion page, as a few examples. If you are sending the data to some such server-side script or application, you have several options. First, take a look at how to send it using a `LoadVars` object.

In this exercise you'll use a `LoadVars` object to submit the data from the form to a script.

1. On the CD-ROM you'll find PHP and ColdFusion versions of a script called either `asbSubmitFormLoadVars.php` or `asbSubmitFormLoadVars.cfm`. Copy the appropriate script from the CD-ROM to the Web root of the server.

2. Open `simpleForm001.fla` and save it as `submitFormLoadVars001.fla`.

3. Modify the code on the Actions layer as follows (changes appear in bold):

```
clblEmail.text = "Email:";
clblProducts.text = "Products Owned:";
clProducts.dataProvider = [{label: "Flash", data: "f"}, ⮐
{label: "Dreamweaver", data: "dw"}, ⮐
{label: "Fireworks", data: "fw"}, ⮐
{label: "ColdFusion", data: "cf"}, ⮐
{label: "Freehand", data: "fh"}];
clProducts.dataProvider.sortItemsBy("label");
clProducts.multipleSelection = true;
var oListener:Object = new Object();
```

```
oListener.click = function(oEvent:Object):Void {
  var sEmail:String = ctiEmail.text;
  var aProductItems:Array = clProducts.selectedItems;
  var aProductData:Array = new Array();
  for(var i:Number = 0; i < aProductItems.length; i++) {
    aProductData.push(aProductItems[i].data);
  }

  // Create the submitting LoadVars object.
  var lvSender:LoadVars = new LoadVars();

  // Create the LoadVars object for receipt.
  var lvReceipt:LoadVars = new LoadVars();

  // Define the onLoad() method.
  lvReceipt.onLoad = function():Void {
    trace("receipt");
  };

  // Assign the email and products values to properties on
  // the sending LoadVars object.
  lvSender.email = sEmail;
  lvSender.products = aProductData.toString();

  // Send the data to the script. Make sure to use the URL
  // that correctly points to the script on your server.
lvSender.sendAndLoad("http://localhost/↩
asbFormSubmitLoadVars.php", lvReceipt);
};
cbtSubmit.label = "Submit";
cbtSubmit.addEventListener("click", oListener);
```

4. Test the movie. Enter some data and then click the button to send the data to the server-side script.

5. A file called `asb.txt` is created in the same directory as the server-side script. If you view that file, you can see the entry that was just made.

Some Web servers might not allow for a file to be written in the same directory as the script file.

Using XML to Send Data

Depending on the type of data with which you're working, XML can be a good choice for sending data from Flash to a server-side script. In this exercise, you'll modify the Flash application to send XML data to the server-side script.

1. On the CD-ROM are PHP and ColdFusion scripts named `asbFormSubmitXML.php` and `asbFormSubmitXML.cfm`, respectively. Choose the appropriate script and copy it to the Web root on your server.

2. Open simpleForm001.fla and save it as submitFormXML001.fla.

3. Modify the code on the Actions layer as follows (changes shown in bold):

```
clblEmail.text = "Email:";
clblProducts.text = "Products Owned:";
clProducts.dataProvider = [{label: "Flash", data: "f"}, ⮐
{label: "Dreamweaver", data: "dw"}, ⮐
{label: "Fireworks", data: "fw"}, ⮐
{label: "ColdFusion", data: "cf"}, ⮐
{label: "Freehand", data: "fh"}];
clProducts.dataProvider.sortItemsBy("label");
clProducts.multipleSelection = true;
var oListener:Object = new Object();
oListener.click = function(oEvent:Object):Void {
  var sEmail:String = ctiEmail.text;
  var aProductItems:Array = clProducts.selectedItems;

  // Create the XML string containing the data from the
  // input form.
  var sXMLData:String = "<formdata><email>" + ⮐
sEmail + "</email><products>";
  for(var i:Number = 0; i < aProductItems.length; i++) {
    sXMLData += "<product>" + aProductItems[i].data + ⮐
"</product>";
  }
  sXMLData += "</products></formdata>";

  // Create the XML object for sending the data.
  var xmlSender:XML = new XML(sXMLData);

  // Create the XML object for receipt.
  var xmlReceipt:XML = new XML();
  xmlReceipt.onLoad = function():Void {
    trace("receipt");
  };

  // Send the XML data to the server-side script using
  // HTTP GET. xmlSender.sendAndLoad("http://localhost/⮐
asbFormSubmitXML.php", xmlReceipt, "GET");
};
cbtSubmit.label = "Submit";
cbtSubmit.addEventListener("click", oListener);
```

4. Test the movie. Enter some data into the form controls, and then press the button.

5. A file named asb.txt is created on the server in the same directory as the script. Open the file and you will see that the values from the Flash form have been written to the file.

Using the WebService Class to Submit Form Data

You can also submit form data to a Web service using the `WebService` class. In this exercise, you'll modify the simple input form application to send the data to a Web service.

The Web service code in this exercise is provided in ColdFusion format only. And the `WebService` class is available only in Flash MX Professional 2004.

1. Copy `asbFormSubmitWebService.cfc` from the CD-ROM to your ColdFusion Web root.
2. Open `simpleForm001.fla` and save it as `formSubmitWebService001.fla`.
3. Open Window ➪ Other Panels ➪ Common Libraries ➪ Classes.
4. Copy the `WebServiceClasses` compiled clip from the `Classes` library to the library for `formSubmitWebService001.fla`.
5. Modify the code on the Actions layer as follows (changes in bold):

```
// Import the WebService class.
import mx.services.WebService;

clblEmail.text = "Email:";
clblProducts.text = "Products Owned:";
clProducts.dataProvider = [{label: "Flash", data: "f"}, ➥
{label: "Dreamweaver", data: "dw"}, ➥
{label: "Fireworks", data: "fw"}, ➥
{label: "ColdFusion", data: "cf"}, ➥
{label: "Freehand", data: "fh"}];
clProducts.dataProvider.sortItemsBy("label");
clProducts.multipleSelection = true;
var oListener:Object = new Object();
oListener.click = function(oEvent:Object):Void {
  var sEmail:String = ctiEmail.text;
  var aProductItems:Array = clProducts.selectedItems;
  var aProductData:Array = new Array();
  for(var i:Number = 0; i < aProductItems.length; i++) {
    aProductData.push(aProductItems[i].data);
  }

  // Set the URL to point to your CFC. Make sure that you
  // append the ?WSDL so that ColdFusion will generate the
  // WSDL document for the Web service.
  var sWSDLURL:String = "http://localhost/➥
asbFormSubmitWebService.cfc?WSDL";

  // Create the WebService object.
  var wsSubmitter:WebService = new WebService(sWSDLURL);

  // Call the Web method called submitFormData().
  var oCallback:Object = wsSubmitter.submitFormData(➥
sEmail, aProductData);

  // Define the onResult() method for the callback.
```

```
    oCallback.onResult = function(nSuccess:Number):Void {
      trace("receipt");
    };
  };
  cbtSubmit.label = "Submit";
  cbtSubmit.addEventListener("click", oListener);
```

6. Test the movie. Enter some data and click the button to send the data to the Web service.

7. Open the `asb.txt` file in the same directory as the CFC file. You will see that data has been written to the file.

Validating Form Data

If you have filled out forms on the Internet or even just offline, you have undoubtedly encountered forms that require you to fill out certain data in the form in order to be able to submit it. In HTML forms, this is often done with a JavaScript function that gets called when the form is submitted. Almost the same process can be implemented in ActionScript.

The most common validation tasks are:

✦ **Checking to make sure that required form elements have been filled out:** For example, you may require that a user enter a name before submitting the form.

✦ **Checking to make sure that free-form elements match a pattern:** For example, you may want to confirm that e-mails and telephone numbers are in valid formats before allowing the form data to be submitted. This is best done using regular expressions.

Regardless of whether one or the other or both of the techniques is used, the basic idea is the same: When the user triggers the form to submit the data, first validate the data. If the data passes the tests, continue by submitting the data. Otherwise, do not. Typically, if the data does not pass the validation tests, you'll want to display a message to the user telling her what she needs to do to correct the information.

Checking for Defined Values

The simplest kind of validation is when you just check to ensure that the user has entered or chosen a value for a form control. For example, you can simply check to make sure that the text property of a `TextInput` instance is not undefined. This kind of validation does not verify that the data entered is actually valid, and it is typically most useful for verifying that the user has selected a value or values from a form control with predefined options such as a `List` or `ComboBox` instance. The following is an example of a `click()` method defined on a listener object, which it checks to make sure the user has selected at least three values from a `List` control:

```
oListener.click = function(oEvent:Object):Void {
  var aIndices:Array = clProducts.selectedIndices;
  if(aIndices.length < 3) {
    trace("You must select at least three products.");
  }
  else {
    // Continue with processing.
  }
};
```

Verifying Data Format

When you are validating values that a user enters free-form with a `TextInput` or `TextArea` control (or even by way of a `TextField` object), you generally need to do more than just verify that the user has entered some value. You typically want to verify that the value matches the expected type of value. For example, if you have asked the user for an e-mail address, you probably want to verify that the e-mail address is at least a valid e-mail address format.

The best way to verify freeform values entered by the user is to use regular expressions. On the CD-ROM, you will find a chapter ("The RegExp Object") on how to use the `RegExp` class (as well as the `RegExp.as` class file).

Here's an example of a `click()` method defined for a listener object in which it ensures that the user has entered a valid e-mail address.

```
oListener.click = function(oEvent:Object):Void {
  var reEmail:RegExp = new RegExp("^([\\w\\-\\.]+)@((
[\\w\\-]{2,}\\.)+[\\w\\-]{2,3})$");
  if(!reEmail.test(sEmail)) {
    trace("Please enter a valid email address.");
  }
  else {
    // Continue with processing.
  }
};
```

Alerting the User

When the user needs to correct some information in the form before submitting the data, you will want to bring that to the user's attention. If you use Flash MX Professional 2004 you can use the `Alert` component to accomplish that task. If you do not have the `Alert` component, it is up to you to create a mechanism by which to present the user with the message.

Practicing Data Validation

In this exercise, you will modify the simple form to validate the data. You will check to make sure the user has entered a valid e-mail address and that the user has selected at least one product. If either of those conditions is not met, you'll open an Alert window to tell the user what is incorrect.

1. Open `simpleForm001.fla` and save it as `simpleForm_datavalidation001.fla`.
2. Modify the code on the Actions layer as follows (changes in bold):

```
clblEmail.text = "Email:";
clblProducts.text = "Products Owned:";
clProducts.dataProvider = [{label: "Flash", data: "f"},
{label: "Dreamweaver", data: "dw"},
{label: "Fireworks", data: "fw"},
{label: "ColdFusion", data: "cf"},
{label: "Freehand", data: "fh"}];
```

```
clProducts.dataProvider.sortItemsBy("label");
clProducts.multipleSelection = true;
var oListener:Object = new Object();
oListener.click = function(oEvent:Object):Void {
  var sEmail:String = ctiEmail.text;
  var aProductItems:Array = clProducts.selectedItems;
  var aProductData:Array = new Array();
  for(var i:Number = 0; i < aProductItems.length; i++) {
    aProductData.push(aProductItems[i].data);
  }

  // Create a RegExp object to validate the email address.
  var reEmail:RegExp = new RegExp("^([\\w\\-\\.]+)@((⮐
[\\w\\-]{2,}\\.)+[\\w\\-]{2,3})$");

  // Check to make sure the email is valid. If not, then
  // open an Alert window. Next, check to see if the user
  // has selected at least one product from the List. If
  // not display an Alert window. Then, if both conditions
  // pass, continue with whatever further processing. For
  // example, you could use the code from the LoadVars,
  // XML, or WebService example to then send the data to
  // the server.
  if(!reEmail.test(sEmail)) {
    mx.controls.Alert.show("Please enter a valid ⮐
email address.");
  }
  else if(aProductData.length < 1) {
    mx.controls.Alert.show("Please select at least ⮐
one product.");
  }
  else {
    // Continue with processing.
  }
};
cbtSubmit.label = "Submit";
cbtSubmit.addEventListener("click", oListener);
```

3. Test the movie.
4. Click the button before entering a valid e-mail address.
5. Close the Alert window.
6. Enter a valid e-mail address.
7. Click the button without selecting a product.
8. Close the Alert window.
9. Select at least one product from the list.
10. Click the button. This time you should not get any Alert window.

Incorporating Advanced Form Features

So far you have learned about basic form creation and submission. However, you may encounter projects in which you want to do more complex things with forms. In this section, you look at how to populate form elements with data dynamically and how to prefill a form based on a user's previous answers.

Dynamic Form Data

Hardcoding form data into the Flash application works just fine for applications in which the data is not likely to change often. However, more often than not it is beneficial to be able to load the form data from an external source, whether that be from an XML document or from a database by way of a server-side script. In this exercise, you'll modify the simple form to load the product data from an XML file.

1. Create a new XML document.
2. Add the following code to the document:

```
<products>
  <product name="ColdFusion" value="cf" />
  <product name="Flash" value="f" />
  <product name="Dreamweaver" value="dw" />
  <product name="Fireworks" value="fw" />
  <product name="Freehand" value="fh" />
</products>
```

3. Save the document as `products.xml`, making sure to save it to the same directory as the `simpleForm001.fla` file.
4. Open `simpleForm001.fla` and save it as `dynamicForm001.fla` in the same directory.
5. Modify the code on the Actions layer as follows (changes in bold):

```
clblEmail.text = "Email:";
clblProducts.text = "Products Owned:";

var xmlProducts:XML = new XML();
xmlProducts.ignoreWhite = true;
xmlProducts.onLoad = function(bSuccess:Boolean):Void {
  var aProductNodes:Array = this.firstChild.childNodes;
  for(var i:Number = 0; i < aProductNodes.length; i++) {
    clProducts.addItem(aProductNodes[i].attributes.name,
                       aProductNodes[i].attributes.value);
  }
  clProducts.dataProvider.sortItemsBy("label");
};
xmlProducts.load("products.xml");
```

```
clProducts.multipleSelection = true;
var oListener:Object = new Object();
oListener.click = function(oEvent:Object):Void {
  var sEmail:String = ctiEmail.text;
  var aProductItems:Array = clProducts.selectedItems;
  var aProductData:Array = new Array();
  for(var i:Number = 0; i < aProductItems.length; i++) {
    aProductData.push(aProductItems[i].data);
  }
  trace(sEmail + " " + aProductData);
};
cbtSubmit.label = "Submit";
cbtSubmit.addEventListener("click", oListener);
```

6. Test the movie. The form data should appear just as when the values were hardcoded.
7. Modify the XML document by adding or removing a `<product>` tag.
8. Test the movie again. Notice how the data is updated without you having had to modify the code in the Flash document.

Prefilling a Form

With many forms, it makes sense to present the form to the user with no information selected or otherwise filled out. For example, you probably would not want to present a user with a comments form with all the information already there. That would not make a lot of sense. On the other hand, consider the case of a user information form that enables the user to modify his or her existing registration information. In this case, it would not make sense *not* to have the information already filled out. Having forms automatically filled out with some information is called prefilling a form, and it is a common practice in many applications similar to the one described previously with a user information modification form. Pretty much any form that enables a user to make some kind of modification to existing data should be filled with the existing data.

Pre-populating a form is a much simpler process than it might sound. You might load data in any of the following ways:

- ✦ From a local shared object. You might use a local shared object to store some simple preferences for a user, for instance.
- ✦ Using a `LoadVars` object.
- ✦ Using an `XML` object.
- ✦ Using a Web service.
- ✦ Using Flash Remoting.

Once the data has been loaded into your Flash movie, you can use it to set the values for each form element.

In this exercise, you'll modify the simple form so that it will store the information in a local shared object. When the user returns to the form, it will automatically prefill the form with any pre-existing data.

1. Open `simpleForm001.fla` and save it as `simpleForm_prefill001.fla`.
2. Modify the code on the Actions layer as follows (changes shown in bold):

```
clblEmail.text = "Email:";
clblProducts.text = "Products Owned:";
clProducts.dataProvider = [{label: "Flash", data: "f"}, ⮐
{label: "Dreamweaver", data: "dw"}, ⮐
{label: "Fireworks", data: "fw"}, ⮐
{label: "ColdFusion", data: "cf"}, ⮐
{label: "Freehand", data: "fh"}];
clProducts.dataProvider.sortItemsBy("label");
clProducts.multipleSelection = true;

// Create the local shared object.
var lsoData:SharedObject = SharedObject.getLocal("productInfo");

// If the email was already saved, assign that value
// to the TextArea.
if(lsoData.data.email != undefined) {
  ctiEmail.text = lsoData.data.email;
}

// If the selected indices in the List were previously
// saved then assign those indices as the selected
// indices.
if(lsoData.data.productIndices != undefined) {
  clProducts.selectedIndices = lsoData.data.productIndices;
}

var oListener:Object = new Object();
oListener.click = function(oEvent:Object):Void {
  var sEmail:String = ctiEmail.text;
  var aProductItems:Array = clProducts.selectedItems;
  var aProductData:Array = new Array();
  for(var i:Number = 0; i < aProductItems.length; i++) {
    aProductData.push(aProductItems[i].data);
  }

  // Save the email and selected indices to the local
  // shared object.
  lsoData.data.email = sEmail;
  lsoData.data.productIndices = clProducts.selectedIndices;

};
cbtSubmit.label = "Submit";
cbtSubmit.addEventListener("click", oListener);
```

3. Test the movie. Enter values in the form.
4. Close the movie.
5. Test the movie again. You should see the previously selected values are already prefilled.

We'd like to know what you thought about this chapter. Visit `www.flashsupport.com/feedback` to fill out an online form with your comments.

Summary

- Most form needs can be met by putting together elements comprised of v2 UI component instances.
- The basic, single-page form generally consists of populating the form elements and submitting form data. Additionally, you may opt to validate form data before submitting it.
- Submitting form data is generally handled by using the `LoadVars` class, XML, Web services, or Flash Remoting.
- Form elements can be dynamically populated with values stored in external sources such as local shared objects, text files, or databases.
- Prefilling a form is a good practice that saves users the confusion and frustration of having to fill out a form they have filled out in the past. This is a good way to allow a user to modify previously entered information.

✦ ✦ ✦

APPENDIX A

What's on the CD-ROM

✦ ✦ ✦ ✦

This appendix provides you with information on the contents of the CD-ROM that accompanies this book. You can also refer to the ReadMe file located at the root of the CD-ROM for last-minute changes. Here is what you will find in this appendix:

- System requirements
- What's on the CD
- Troubleshooting

System Requirements

Make sure that your computer meets the minimum system requirements listed in this section. If your computer doesn't match up to most of these requirements, you might have a problem using the contents of the CD-ROM.

For Windows 98, Windows 2000, or Windows XP:

- PC with a Pentium III processor (or equivalent) running at 600MHz or faster
- At least 128MB of total RAM installed on your computer
- CD-ROM drive

For Macintosh:

- Mac OS X, version 10.2.6 or higher
- At least 128MB of total RAM installed on your computer
- CD-ROM drive

What's on the CD-ROM

The following sections provide a summary of the software and other materials you'll find on the CD-ROM.

Using the Example FLA Files

In the chapter directories of the CD-ROM, you will find files included for each exercise in that chapter. Some exercises provide a starter Flash document (FLA file) that includes necessary artwork and other assets. When an exercise indicates that you should use a starter file, you will find it in the appropriate chapter directory on the CD-ROM. Additionally, all exercises are accompanied by a completed Flash document so that you can compare your work to the desired result. These files are also found in the appropriate chapter directories.

Some exercises use additional files (other than the FLA files). For example, some exercises rely on XML documents or AS files. You will find these files provided with the FLA files as well. If you move the FLA files, you will also need to move the accompanying files.

Using the Server-Side Files

Some exercises in the book rely on server-side scripts. When indicated in the chapter, those files have been provided. You will find these files in the same directory on the CD-ROM in which the FLA, XML, or any other files for the chapter are found. Move these files to the appropriate directories and make the necessary configurations for these files to work with your server. If you are unfamiliar with how to properly set up the server-side script on your server, you might need to consult another reference or your hosting provider.

Applications

The CD-ROM included with this book provides you with the software and other assorted files you will need to practice what you learn. On the CD-ROM, you will find the following applications.

Macromedia Flash MX 2004

A 30-day trial version for Macintosh and Windows. The trial version of Flash MX 2004 is fully functional for 30 days from when you install it. You can use this trial version to work with the exercises in this book if you do not already own Flash MX 2004.

Sapien PrimalScript 3.1

A 30-day trial version for Windows. PrimalScript is a fully featured scripting environment that fully supports ActionScript 2.0.

Macromedia ColdFusion MX 6.1

A 30-day trial version for Windows. ColdFusion MX 6.1 is an application server product from Macromedia that allows for extensive server-side application development such as database queries. ColdFusion MX 6.1 also includes Flash Remoting.

Other applications discussed in the book might be available online. If so, links to the downloads have been provided in the relevant chapters. You can also check for updated information at `www.flashsupport.com`.

Shareware programs are fully functional trial versions of copyrighted programs. If you like particular programs, register with their authors for a nominal fee to receive licenses, enhanced versions, and technical support. *Freeware programs* are copyrighted games, applications, and utilities that are free for personal use. Unlike shareware, these programs do not require a fee or provide technical support. *GNU software* is governed by its own license, which is included inside the folder of the GNU product. See the GNU license for more details.

Trial, demo, or evaluation versions are usually limited either by time or functionality (such as being unable to save projects). Some trial versions are very sensitive to system date changes. If you alter your computer's date, the programs will "time out" and will no longer be functional.

Troubleshooting the CD-ROM

If you have difficulty installing or using any of the materials on the companion CD-ROM, try the following solutions:

- **Turn off any anti-virus software that you have running.** Installers sometimes mimic virus activity, and can make your computer incorrectly believe that it is being infected by a virus. (Be sure to turn the anti-virus software back on later.)
- **Close all running programs.** The more programs you're running, the less memory is available to other programs. Installers also typically update files and programs; if you keep other programs running, installation might not work properly.
- **Reference the ReadMe file:** Please refer to the ReadMe file located at the root of the CD-ROM for the latest product information at the time of publication.

We'd like to know what you thought about this book. Visit `www.flashsupport.com/feedback` to fill out an online form with your comments.

If you still have trouble with the CD-ROM, please call the Wiley Customer Care phone number: (800) 762-2974. Outside the United States, call 1 (317) 572-3994. You can also contact Wiley Customer Service by e-mail at `techsupdum@wiley.com`. Wiley Publishing, Inc. will provide technical support only for installation and other general quality control items; for technical support on the applications themselves, consult the program's vendor or author.

✦ ✦ ✦

Index

Page numbers in **bold** refer to Chapter 38, which is on the CD-ROM.

SYMBOLS AND NUMERICS

Continued

C

Continued

Continued

D

Continued

Continued

E

Continued

F

Continued

G

L

M

N

Continued

O

P

Continued

Continued

Q

R

Continued

Continued

U

V

Continued

X

Y

Z

Wiley Publishing, Inc.
End-User License Agreement

READ THIS. You should carefully read these terms and conditions before opening the software packet(s) included with this book "Book". This is a license agreement "Agreement" between you and Wiley Publishing, Inc. "WPI". By opening the accompanying software packet(s), you acknowledge that you have read and accept the following terms and conditions. If you do not agree and do not want to be bound by such terms and conditions, promptly return the Book and the unopened software packet(s) to the place you obtained them for a full refund.

1. **License Grant.** WPI grants to you (either an individual or entity) a nonexclusive license to use one copy of the enclosed software program(s) (collectively, the "Software") solely for your own personal or business purposes on a single computer (whether a standard computer or a workstation component of a multi-user network). The Software is in use on a computer when it is loaded into temporary memory (RAM) or installed into permanent memory (hard disk, CD-ROM, or other storage device). WPI reserves all rights not expressly granted herein.
2. **Ownership.** WPI is the owner of all right, title, and interest, including copyright, in and to the compilation of the Software recorded on the disk(s) or CD-ROM "Software Media". Copyright to the individual programs recorded on the Software Media is owned by the author or other authorized copyright owner of each program. Ownership of the Software and all proprietary rights relating thereto remain with WPI and its licensers.
3. **Restrictions on Use and Transfer.**
   - **(a)** You may only (i) make one copy of the Software for backup or archival purposes, or (ii) transfer the Software to a single hard disk, provided that you keep the original for backup or archival purposes. You may not (i) rent or lease the Software, (ii) copy or reproduce the Software through a LAN or other network system or through any computer subscriber system or bulletin-board system, or (iii) modify, adapt, or create derivative works based on the Software.
   - **(b)** You may not reverse engineer, decompile, or disassemble the Software. You may transfer the Software and user documentation on a permanent basis, provided that the transferee agrees to accept the terms and conditions of this Agreement and you retain no copies. If the Software is an update or has been updated, any transfer must include the most recent update and all prior versions.
4. **Restrictions on Use of Individual Programs.** You must follow the individual requirements and restrictions detailed for each individual program in the About the CD-ROM appendix of this Book. These limitations are also contained in the individual license agreements recorded on the Software Media. These limitations may include a requirement that after using the program for a specified period of time, the user must pay a registration fee or discontinue use. By opening the Software packet(s), you will be agreeing to abide by the licenses and restrictions for these individual programs that are detailed in the About the CD-ROM appendix and on the Software Media. None of the material on this Software Media or listed in this Book may ever be redistributed, in original or modified form, for commercial purposes.

5. **Limited Warranty.**

   (a) WPI warrants that the Software and Software Media are free from defects in materials and workmanship under normal use for a period of sixty (60) days from the date of purchase of this Book. If WPI receives notification within the warranty period of defects in materials or workmanship, WPI will replace the defective Software Media.

   (b) **WPI AND THE AUTHOR(S) OF THE BOOK DISCLAIM ALL OTHER WARRANTIES, EXPRESS OR IMPLIED, INCLUDING WITHOUT LIMITATION IMPLIED WARRANTIES OF MERCHANTABILITY AND FITNESS FOR A PARTICULAR PURPOSE, WITH RESPECT TO THE SOFTWARE, THE PROGRAMS, THE SOURCE CODE CONTAINED THEREIN, AND/OR THE TECHNIQUES DESCRIBED IN THIS BOOK. WPI DOES NOT WARRANT THAT THE FUNCTIONS CONTAINED IN THE SOFTWARE WILL MEET YOUR REQUIREMENTS OR THAT THE OPERATION OF THE SOFTWARE WILL BE ERROR FREE.**

   (c) This limited warranty gives you specific legal rights, and you may have other rights that vary from jurisdiction to jurisdiction.

6. **Remedies.**

   (a) WPI's entire liability and your exclusive remedy for defects in materials and workmanship shall be limited to replacement of the Software Media, which may be returned to WPI with a copy of your receipt at the following address: Software Media Fulfillment Department, Attn.: *Flash MX 2004 ActionScript Bible,* Wiley Publishing, Inc., 10475 Crosspoint Blvd., Indianapolis, IN 46256, or call 1-800-762-2974. Please allow four to six weeks for delivery. This Limited Warranty is void if failure of the Software Media has resulted from accident, abuse, or misapplication. Any replacement Software Media will be warranted for the remainder of the original warranty period or thirty (30) days, whichever is longer.

   (b) In no event shall WPI or the author be liable for any damages whatsoever (including without limitation damages for loss of business profits, business interruption, loss of business information, or any other pecuniary loss) arising from the use of or inability to use the Book or the Software, even if WPI has been advised of the possibility of such damages.

   (c) Because some jurisdictions do not allow the exclusion or limitation of liability for consequential or incidental damages, the above limitation or exclusion may not apply to you.

7. **U.S. Government Restricted Rights.** Use, duplication, or disclosure of the Software for or on behalf of the United States of America, its agencies and/or instrumentalities "U.S. Government" is subject to restrictions as stated in paragraph (c)(1)(ii) of the Rights in Technical Data and Computer Software clause of DFARS 252.227-7013, or subparagraphs (c) (1) and (2) of the Commercial Computer Software - Restricted Rights clause at FAR 52.227-19, and in similar clauses in the NASA FAR supplement, as applicable.

8. **General.** This Agreement constitutes the entire understanding of the parties and revokes and supersedes all prior agreements, oral or written, between them and may not be modified or amended except in a writing signed by both parties hereto that specifically refers to this Agreement. This Agreement shall take precedence over any other documents that may be in conflict herewith. If any one or more provisions contained in this Agreement are held by any court or tribunal to be invalid, illegal, or otherwise unenforceable, each and every other provision shall remain in full force and effect.